Michelle dedicates this book to her students, past and present, inside and outside, who offer inspiration, a bit of frustration, and real hope for a better future.

Kristin would like to dedicate this book to Jeff, William, and Christopher, who are a constant reminder of everything that is good (and deviant) in this world.

Randy would like to dedicate this book to supportive friends and family, of which he is so lucky to have so many in his life.

DEVIANCE

AND

SOCIAL CONTROL

A SOCIOLOGICAL PERSPECTIVE

MICHELLE INDERBITZIN
Oregon State University

KRISTIN BATES
Cal State University, San Marcos

RANDY GAINEY
Old Dominion University, Norfolk

Los Angeles | London | New Delhi
Singapore | Washington DC

Los Angeles | London | New Delhi
Singapore | Washington DC

FOR INFORMATION:

SAGE Publications, Inc.
2455 Teller Road
Thousand Oaks, California 91320
E-mail: order@sagepub.com

SAGE Publications Ltd.
1 Oliver's Yard
55 City Road
London EC1Y 1SP
United Kingdom

SAGE Publications India Pvt. Ltd.
B 1/I 1 Mohan Cooperative Industrial Area
Mathura Road, New Delhi 110 044
India

SAGE Publications Asia-Pacific Pte. Ltd.
3 Church Street
#10-04 Samsung Hub
Singapore 049483

Acquisitions Editor: Jerry Westby
Production Editor: Libby Larson
Copy Editor: Gillian Dickens
Typesetter: C&M Digitals (P) Ltd.
Proofreader: Wendy Jo Dymond; Eleni Georgiou
Indexer: Enid Zafran
Cover Designer: Gail Buschman
Marketing Manager: Erica DeLuca
Permissions Editor: Karen Ehrmann

Printed in the United States of America

Library of Congress Cataloging-in-Publication Data

Inderbitzin, Michelle, 1962-

Deviance and social control : a sociological perspective / by Michelle Inderbitzin, Kristin Bates, Randy Gainey.

p. cm.
Includes bibliographical references and index.

ISBN 978-1-4129-7377-9 (pbk.)

1. Deviant behavior. 2. Social control. I. Bates, Kristin Ann.
II. Gainey, Randy R. III. Title.

HM811.D528 2013
303.3′3—dc23   2012002544

This book is printed on acid-free paper.

12 13 14 15 10 9 8 7 6 5 4 3 2 1

Brief Contents

Foreword   xv
> Howard S. Becker

Preface   xvii

PART I. INTRODUCTION TO THE STUDY OF DEVIANCE AND SOCIAL CONTROL   1

Chapter 1. Introduction to Deviance   2

Chapter 2. The Diversity of Deviance   47

Chapter 3. Researching Deviance   87

PART II. TRADITIONAL APPROACHES TO STUDYING DEVIANCE   145

Chapter 4. Anomie/Strain Theory   146

Chapter 5. Social Disorganization Theory   202

Chapter 6. Differential Association and Social Learning Theory   233

Chapter 7. Social Control Theories of Deviance   284

PART III. SOCIAL CONSTRUCTIONIST APPROACHES TO STUDYING DEVIANCE   339

Chapter 8. Labeling Theory   340

Chapter 9. Marxist/Conflict Theories of Deviance   375

Chapter 10. Critical Theories of Deviance   427

PART IV. RESPONSES TO DEVIANCE   485

Chapter 11. Social Control of Deviance   486

Chapter 12. Deviant Careers and Career Deviance   559

Glossary   600
References   604
Photo Credits   612
Index   614
About the Editors   625

Detailed Contents

Foreword   xv
Howard S. Becker

Preface   xvii

**PART I. INTRODUCTION TO THE STUDY OF DEVIANCE AND
SOCIAL CONTROL**   1

Chapter 1. Introduction to Deviance   2
    Introduction   3
    Conceptions of Deviance   4
        How Do YOU Define Deviance?   5
    The Sociological Imagination   5
        Deviance in Popular Culture   7
    The Importance of Theory   8
        Studies in Deviance   10
        Now YOU . . . Use Your Sociological Imagination   11
    Conclusion: Organization of the Book   13
    EXERCISES AND DISCUSSION QUESTIONS   13
    KEY TERMS   13

READINGS
    1. Body Ritual Among the Nacirema   14
      Horace Miner
        An examination of the unique society and rituals of the Nacirema.
    2. The Mystification of Social Deviance   18
      Stuart L. Hills
        Examines the relativist and absolutist conceptions of deviance.
    3. Criminology and the Study of Deviance   26
      James F. Short, Jr. and Robert F. Meier
        *Documents the changes in efforts to explain different aspects of crime
and deviance.*
    4. Status, Deviance, and Sanctions: A Critical Review   37
      Ralph Wahrman
        *Examines three concepts common to the student of deviance: "status," "norms,"
and "sanctions."*

Chapter 2. The Diversity of Deviance   47

Introduction   47

Deviance and Its Varied Forms   48

    THINKING LIKE A SOCIOLOGIST—STRICT CONFORMITY AS DEVIANCE   49

Physical Deviance and Appearance: Ideals of Beauty and Everyone Else   50

    DEVIANCE IN POPULAR CULTURE   51

Relationships and Deviance   52

Deviance in Cyberspace: Making Up the Norms as We Go   54

    STUDIES IN DEVIANCE   54

Subcultural Deviance   54

Elite Deviance, Corporate Deviance, and Workplace Misconduct   55

Positive Deviance   56

    NOW YOU . . . TRY AN EXPERIMENT IN POSITIVE DEVIANCE!   57

Question: So Who Are the Deviants? Answer: It Depends on Who You Ask   58

Conclusion   58

EXERCISES AND DISCUSSION QUESTIONS   59

KEY TERMS   59

READINGS

5. The "Simmie" Side of Life: Old Order Amish Youths' Affective Response to Culturally Prescribed Deviance   60

    Denise M. Reiling

      Examines the "simmie" period in which Amish youth are almost forced to explore American lifestyles before choosing to either commit to their Amish culture or leave it forever.

6. Nonsuicidal Self-Injury Among Nonclinical College Women: Lessons From Foucault   70

    Efrosini Kokaliari and Joan Berzoff

      Describes and documents self-injury, a unique form of deviance among a relatively "normal" sample of college women.

7. Corporate Transgressions Through Moral Disengagement   80

    Albert Bandura, Gian-Vittorio Caprara, ad Laszlo Zsolnai

      Explores elite deviance or "corporate transgressions" through the concept of moral disengagement; the authors outline concepts and strategies that allow for corporate deviance to occur.

Chapter 3. Researching Deviance   87

Introduction   88

Methodological Approaches to Studying Deviance   89

    Experimental Strategies in the Study of Deviance   89

    DEVIANCE IN POPULAR CULTURE   90

    Large-Scale Survey Research   92

    Field Research: Pure Observer to Full Participant   93

    STUDIES IN DEVIANCE   96

Content Analysis   97

Secondary Data Sources   99

    The Uniform Crime Report   99

Substance Abuse and Mental Health Services Administration 101
Monitoring the Future 102
Archived Data: Inter-University Consortium for Political and Social Research 103
Now YOU ... Conduct the Research 104
Ethical Considerations in Studying Deviance 105
Conclusion 106
ENDNOTE
EXERCISES AND DISCUSSION QUESTIONS 107
SUGGESTED ADDITIONAL READINGS 107
KEY TERMS 107

READINGS

8. Bullies Move Beyond the Schoolyard: A Preliminary Look at Cyberbullying 108
Justin W. Patchin and Sameer Hinduja
A very innovative approach to studying a relatively new form of violence.

9. "They Must Be Crazy": Some of the Difficulties in Researching "Cults" 122
Marybeth Ayella
Certain subcultures are especially difficult to study; this paper focuses on
a popular area of sociological research into deviance.

10. The Problems of Researching Sensitive Topics: An Overview and Introduction 132
Raymond M. Lee and Claire M. Renzetti
A more general discussion of researching sensitive issues.

PART II. TRADITIONAL APPROACHES TO STUDYING DEVIANCE 145

Chapter 4. Anomie/Strain Theory 146
Introduction 146
Emile Durkheim and Anomie 147
Robert Merton and Adaptations to Anomie/Strain 148
Merton's Adaptations to Anomie 148
Deviance in Popular Culture 150
Richard Cloward and Lloyd Ohlin, Differential Opportunity 151
Robert Agnew—General Strain Theory 153
Studies in Deviance 154
Steven Messner and Richard Rosenfeld: Crime and the American
Dream—Institutional Anomie Theory 154
Contemporary/Empirical Studies in the Anomie and Strain Tradition 155
Anomie and the Abuse at Abu Ghraib 155
The American Dream and Incarcerated Young Men 156
Institutional Anomie Theory and Student Cheating 157
Critiques of Anomie and Strain Theories 157
Conclusion 158
Now YOU ... Use the Theory 158
EXERCISES AND DISCUSSION QUESTIONS 159
KEY TERMS 159

READINGS

11. Social Structure and Anomie 160
Robert K. Merton

*Merton basically argues that deviance is built into the very fabric of our society;
deviance is a result of the collision of culturally defined goals and the social
structures that limit the modes of achieving those goals.*

12. Durkheim's Concept of Anomie and the Abuse at Abu Ghraib   168
    Stjepan G. Mestrovic and Ronald Lorenzo
      *The authors use Durkheim's ideas on anomie to help explain the abuse at Abu Ghraib,
arguing that the dysfunction and disorganization at Abu Ghraib were so great
that the breaking of norms and abuse of prisoners were inevitable.*

13. The Maximizer: Clarifying Merton's Theories of Anomie and Strain   188
    Daniel S. Murphy and Mathew B. Robinson
      *An extension of strain theory; the authors advocate for a new mode of adaptation to
supplement Merton's model, "the Maximizer," someone who simultaneously uses and
incorporates both legitimate and illegitimate means in their quest for the American Dream.*

Chapter 5. Social Disorganization Theory   202

Introduction   202
History and Early Work on Social Disorganization Theory   203
Shaw and McKay Study of Juvenile Delinquency and Urban Areas   205
    DEVIANCE IN POPULAR CULTURE   206
Rebirth of Social Disorganization Theory   207
    STUDIES IN DEVIANCE   209
More Theoretical and Empirical Advances and Divergences: Social and Physical Disorder   210
    Collective Efficacy   210
Conclusion   212
    NOW YOU . . . USE THE THEORY   213
EXERCISES AND DISCUSSION QUESTIONS   213
SUGGESTED ADDITIONAL READINGS   214
KEY TERMS   214

READINGS

14. Neighborhood Social Disorganization as a Cofactor in Violence Among People With Mental
Disorders   214
    Eric Silver
      *A short piece that moves social disorganization theory beyond juvenile delinquency
and crime to other forms of deviance.*

15. Physical Deterioration, Disorder, and Crime   217
    Timothy C. O'Shea
      *This article links social disorganization theory to theories
more focused on social disorder.*

16. Perceived Neighborhood Social Disorder and Attitudes Toward Reporting Domestic
Violence Against Women   225
    Enrique Gracia and Juan Herrero
      *Shifts the focus on social disorganization theory and issues of social disorder to crimes
within the home.*

Chapter 6. Differential Association and Social Learning Theory   233

Introduction   233
Edwin Sutherland and Differential Association   234
    DEVIANCE AND POPULAR CULTURE   236

Akers's Social Learning Theory · 237

Social Structure and Social Learning · 238

STUDIES IN DEVIANCE · 239

Research on Differential Association and Social Learning · 240

Some Limitations of Differential Association and Social Learning Theories · 242

Now YOU . . . USE THE THEORY · 243

Cultural Deviance Theory and Subcultural Explanations of Deviance · 244

Conclusion · 245

EXERCISES AND DISCUSSION QUESTIONS · 245

KEY TERMS · 245

READINGS

17. Social Learning Theory and Partner Violence: A Research Note · 246
    Christine Sellers, John K. Cochran, and Kathryn A. Branch
    How do we learn to hurt the ones we love? A brief introduction.

18. A Social Learning Theory Analysis of Computer Crime Among College Students · 253
    William F. Skinner and Anne M. Fream
    An interesting investigation into a relatively new form of deviance through social learning theory.

19. Liquor Is Quicker: Gender and Social Learning Among College Students · 270
    Lonn Lanza-Kaduce, Michael Capece, and Helena Alden
    An introduction to gender issues in relation to social learning theory with a well-suited population.

Chapter 7. Social Control Theories of Deviance · **284**

Introduction · 285

Classical Social Control Theory · 285

Nye · 286

Hirschi · 286

Techniques of Neutralization · 288

DEVIANCE IN POPULAR CULTURE · 289

Contemporary Additions to Social Control Theory · 290

Power-Control Theory · 290

Theory of Self-Control · 291

Life Course Theory · 292

STUDIES IN DEVIANCE · 295

Empirical Studies · 296

Critiques of Social Control Theory · 297

Conclusion · 297

Now YOU . . . USE THE THEORY · 298

EXERCISES AND DISCUSSION QUESTIONS · 299

KEY TERMS · 299

READINGS

20. Social Control, Delinquency, and Victimization Among Kibbutz Adolescents · 300
    Ben-Zion Cohen and Ruth Zeira
    Examines the relationship between an overall index of social control and self-reported delinquency and victimization among high school students in the kibbutzim of Northern Israel.

21. Truancy in Late Elementary and Early Secondary Education: The Influence of Social Bonds and Self-Control—The TRAILS Study 309

René Veenstra, Siegwart Lindenberg, Frank Tinga, and Johan Ormel

Examines an early initiated deviant behavior—persistent school truancy—that appears to be a predictor of later, more serious forms of deviance as well as negative consequences for the individual (e.g., school failure and dropout, unemployment).

22. Online Consumer Misbehaviour: An Application of Neutralization Theory 322

Lloyd C. Harris and Alexia Dumas

Examines the neutralization techniques used to justify illegal "peer-to-peer" downloading of CDs, DVDs, video games, or other software.

PART III. SOCIAL CONSTRUCTIONIST APPROACHES TO STUDYING DEVIANCE — 339

Chapter 8. Labeling Theory — 340

Introduction 341
Theoretical Background 342
How the Labeling Process Works 342
DEVIANCE IN POPULAR CULTURE 343
Labeling and Mental Illness 344
Labeling and Delinquency 345
Contemporary Theoretical and Empirical Studies in Labeling 347
    Braithwaite (1989): *Crime, Shame and Reintegration* 347
    Matsueda (1992): "Reflected Appraisals, Parental Labeling, and Delinquency" 347
    Rosenfield (1997): "Labeling Mental Illness" 348
    Davies and Tanner (2003): "The Long Arm of the Law: Effects of Labeling on Employment" 348
STUDIES IN DEVIANCE 349
Impact of Labeling Theory 349
Conclusion 351
NOW YOU . . . USE THE THEORY 352
EXERCISES AND DISCUSSION QUESTIONS 352
KEY TERMS 353

READINGS

23. The Saints and the Roughnecks 353

William J. Chambliss

Explores the deviance of and community reaction to two groups of boys— the upper-middle-class "Saints" and the working-class "Roughnecks"; although they start out quite similar, as adults, their lives turn out very differently.

24. On Being Sane in Insane Places 363

David L. Rosenhan

A classic study of labeling and mental illness: Eight sane adults simulated symptoms of psychosis and gained admission to 12 mental hospitals. How would they be treated, and how long would it be before they were released?

25. "Introduction." *Our Guys: The Glen Ridge Rape and the Secret Life of the Perfect Suburb* 370

Bernard Lefkowitz

Introduction to the book about the case in Glen Ridge, New Jersey, when a group of popular high school athletes gang raped a mentally impaired 17-year-old girl with a baseball bat and a broom. How did power and labels affect the community's reactions?

Chapter 9. Marxist/Conflict Theories of Deviance — 375

Introduction — 376
Marxist Theory — 377
    Conflict — 378
    Dialectical Materialism — 378
    Marxism and Revolution — 378
    Marxism and Deviance — 379
    Instrumental and Structural Marxism and the Law — 379
    A Marxian Theory of Deviance — 380
    DEVIANCE IN POPULAR CULTURE — 381
Conflict Theory — 382
    Gusfield — 382
    Kitsuse and Spector — 382
    Vold — 383
    Turk — 384
    Quinney — 385
    STUDIES IN DEVIANCE — 386
    Chambliss — 387
Critiques of Marxism and Conflict Theory — 388
    NOW YOU . . . USE THE THEORY — 389
Contemporary/Empirical Studies — 390
Conclusion — 390
EXERCISES AND DISCUSSION QUESTIONS — 391
KEY TERMS — 391

READINGS

26. *The Communist Manifesto* — 391
    Karl Marx and Friedrich Engels
        Excerpt from The Communist Manifesto *describing the Bourgeoisie*
        and the Proletarians.
27. The Spawn of Slavery: The Convict-Lease System in the South — 398
    W. E. B. Du Bois
        Documents the way blacks and whites were historically dealt with by the criminal
        justice system in the South.
28. Racial Profiling by Store Clerks and Personnel in Retail Establishments: An Exploration
    of "Shopping While Black" — 404
    Shaun L. Gabbidon
        Examines another potential source of targeting (like Driving While Black)—Shopping
        While Black.
29. Violent Police-Citizen Encounters: An Analysis of Major Newspaper Accounts — 415
    Kim Michelle Lersch and Joe R. Feagin
        Uses power-conflict theory to better understand police misconduct.

Chapter 10. Critical Theories of Deviance — 427

Introduction — 427
Peacemaking — 428
    Peacemaking and Homelessness — 429
    DEVIANCE IN POPULAR CULTURE — 430

Feminist Criminology 431
   Feminism and Homelessness 432
    STUDIES IN DEVIANCE 433
Critical Race Theory 434
   Critical Race Theory and Homelessness 435
    NOW YOU . . . USE THE THEORY 436
Critiques of Critical Theories 437
Conclusion 438
EXERCISES AND DISCUSSION QUESTIONS 438
KEY TERMS 438

READINGS

30. Reflections on Women's Crime and Mothers in Prison: A Peacemaking Approach 438
   Polly F. Radosh
    Argues that we need to move toward a peacemaking approach as opposed to a
    deterrent or retributionist approach to dealing with women in prison.
31. "But Sometimes I Think . . . They Put Themselves in the Situation": Exploring Blame and
   Responsibility in Interpersonal Violence 449
   Suruchi Thapar-Björkert and Karen J. Morgan
    Examines the perception that volunteers have about victims of abuse.
32. Racial Profiling and Immigration Law Enforcement: Rounding Up
   of Usual Suspects in the Latino Community 468
   Mary Romero
    Examines the injustices Latino Americans (legal citizens and illegal residents) faced
    during a 5-day immigration raid in the late 1990s known as the Chandler
    Roundup, which took place in Chandler, Arizona.

PART IV. RESPONSES TO DEVIANCE 485

Chapter 11. Social Control of Deviance 486
Introduction 486
Medicalization of Deviant Behavior 487
Policing, Supervision, and the Impact of Incarceration on Disadvantaged
   Populations and Communities 488
   DEVIANCE IN POPULAR CULTURE 489
Total Institutions 490
Correctional Facilities and the Purposes of Punishment 491
Gresham Sykes and the Pains of Imprisonment 491
Juvenile Correctional Facilities 492
   STUDIES IN DEVIANCE 493
Reentry—Challenges in Returning to the Community After Time in an Institution 494
   Felon Disenfranchisement 495
Public Fear and Social Control: The Case of Sex Offenders 495
Collateral Consequences—Effects on Communities and Families 496
Conclusion 497
   NOW YOU . . . THINK ABOUT SOCIAL CONTROL 498
EXERCISES AND DISCUSSION QUESTIONS 498
KEY TERMS 499

READINGS

33. On the Run: Wanted Men in a Philadelphia Ghetto   499

Alice Goffman

Paints a vivid picture of young black men who have warrants out for their arrest, often for minor infractions, and how they work to avoid the police and incarceration.

34. Lessons From a Juvenile Training School: Survival and Growth   519

Michelle Inderbitzin

Takes readers inside a cottage for violent offenders in one state's end-of-the-line juvenile correctional facility and contrasts the lessons the institution intended to impart to its "residents" with the life lessons the young men actually learned during their incarceration.

35. Walking the Talk? What Employers Say Versus What They Do   532

Devah Pager and Lincoln Quillian

An experimental study to test whether employers would be willing to hire ex-offenders and how race factored into that decision, if at all.

Chapter 12. Deviant Careers and Career Deviance   **559**

Introduction   560

Criminal Careers and Career Criminals   560

DEVIANCE IN POPULAR CULTURE   561

Getting Into Deviance: Onset of a Deviant Career   562

Risk and Protective Factors for Onset   564

Maintaining a Deviant Career: Living the Life   566

STUDIES IN DEVIANCE   567

Getting Out of the Game: Desistance From Career Deviance   568

NOW YOU ... THINK ABOUT DEVIANT CAREERS   572

Conclusion   572

EXERCISES AND DISCUSSION QUESTIONS   573

KEY TERMS   573

READINGS

36. The Fifth Element: Social Class and the Sociology of Anorexia   574

Muriel Darmon

A sociological analysis of deviance that is usually covered by psychology or the fields related to mental health.

37. The Professional Ex- Revisited: Cessation or Continuation of a Deviant Career?   586

Susan F. Sharpe and Trina L. Hope

Some people exit one deviant career (e.g., alcohol and drug use) only to find other forms of deviance related to that career.

Glossary   **600**

References   **604**

Photo Credits   **612**

Index   **614**

About the Editors   **625**

Foreword

Howard S. Becker

By the time sociology came to universities, at the beginning of the 20th century, all the "good" topics had been snatched up by earlier arrivals: Historians got to write about wars and kings and queens, economists acquired the market as their special turf, and political science took control of the state and government. Sociology was left with whatever topics were left over, especially (chief among these less desirable subjects) the "bad behavior" nice people didn't like in the increasingly urbanized society they lived in: slums, gangs, prostitution, alcoholism, and crime. No one had to worry, then, about defining this field or justifying all these disparate topics being treated under one heading. It seemed obvious to all right-thinking people that these things were problems that needed looking into. Sociologists took them over as their own, and the nature of these problems (and the solutions to them everyone hoped the new science would provide) defined the nature of the field.

Since university disciplines like to make sense of what they are doing, sociologists soon began to look for a unifying thread, for what all these things had in common that justified calling studying them a scientific field. Once you question the commonsense idea that they all simply exemplified "bad behavior" or "social problems," you commit yourself to finding a more logical and scientifically defensible description of what you're doing. Sociologists worked hard to come up with that definition. What they came up, in the end, was not a definition, but definitions, lots of them. Because to go beyond saying these were all simply differing versions of badness, to define what made bad people's behavior bad, created great difficulties because people don't agree on that kind of definition. The commonsense understanding of "badness" included a mixture of very different things: drunkenness, stealing, craziness—the definition really consisted of nothing more than a list of activities that the law banned. Because legislatures don't make laws to define the subject matter of a science but rather to satisfy constituents, the science part comes hard.

For many years, taking commonsense ideas of bad behavior at face value and accepting conventional definitions of what "bad" was, sociologists tried to make science by accepting and trying to prove and improve upon equally commonsense explanations of why people behaved badly. They mostly relied on one of two ideas. On one hand, some theories said that people did bad things because they were inherently bad—there were plenty of genetic theories in the early history of criminology, identifying potential criminals by physical markers of bad heredity, similar to the markers of feeble-mindedness, another topic that sociology and criminology had on their hands—or because they lived in bad circumstances, which turned otherwise normal children into delinquents, sane people into the mentally ill, and healthy people into alcoholics and drug addicts.

These general ideas, scarcely worth being dignified as general theories, for many years dominated the classes taught under such titles as "Social Disorganization" or "Social Problems." Textbooks and lectures proceeded along a well-marked path of problems, dominated by well-known kinds of crimes—starting with juvenile delinquency and following criminal types through more adult crimes like robbery, theft, burglary, and murder—and equally familiar kinds of personal pathologies, revolving around pleasurable forms of behavior that right-thinking people thought were wrong—sex, drugs, and alcohol, all three leading to mental illness. Teachers and books rehearsed the numerous and varied things that had been found to be correlated with bad behavior and presumably to cause them: living in a slum neighborhood, coming from a broken home (that is, a household not headed by a married heterosexual couple), low educational achievement, and a long list of other phenomena usually correlated with some measure of social class so that, in some fundamental sense, the cause of all this pathology seemed to be being poor.

Such an approach did not produce a lot of results. What one study found was often contradicted by another study, and eventually some sociologists and criminologists began to take a more neutral approach to these subject matters, seeing them not as signs of bad character or heredity but rather as signs of a mixed-up society, whose operations and organization made it likely that some sizable number of people would find it attractive and/or profitable to engage in behavior that led them into conflict with the law (as the gang members in *West Side Story* sang, "We're not depraved, we're deprived!").

Since finding the causes of bad behavior in society did not produce reliable results, any more than genetic and psychological theories had, some sociologists began to look further. They asked about a larger spectrum of things and focused on what we might call "the crime industry," the agencies and organizations that made laws that defined what things were crimes, that devoted themselves to finding people who had violated these laws, adjudicating their cases, and administering the punishments and forms of supervision the resolution of those cases dictated: the legislatures that made the laws, the police who found the guilty parties, the courts where their cases were decided, the jails and prisons where they served their sentence, and the parole offices and officers that oversaw those who came out at the other end of this process.

All this research is best summarized, as the authors of this book have done, by considering the variety of theories that sociologists and criminologists have created to make sense of this confusing mass of ideas and of the research the variety of ideas has engendered. Reading their crisp, informative summaries of so many conflicting ideas, and then the wisely chosen illustrative examples of what you get from each approach, will give students the best possible introduction to a lively and still-developing field of research.

Preface

While there are many textbooks and readers on deviant behavior currently on the market, this book is unique for two reasons. First, it is framed within and written entirely from a sociological perspective. We explain the development of major sociological theoretical perspectives and detail how those theories have been used to think about and study the causes of deviant behavior and the reactions to it. We find the theories fascinating, and we think you will, too. The second unique aspect of this book is that as a text-reader, it is a true hybrid, offering both original text and primary readings. It includes both substantial original chapters that give an overview of the field and the theories, as well as carefully selected articles on deviance and social control that have previously appeared in leading academic journals and books. In the following, we describe how *Deviance and Social Control: A Sociological Perspective* differs from existing texts on the market.

While the widely used textbooks on deviant behavior have strong points, our book provides a very different expérience for students by combining original text with existing studies. Professors will be able to assign one book (rather than a textbook and accompanying reader) and will be assured that their students are presented with both clear explanations of sociological perspectives on deviance, along with some of the best examples of research from the field. While some classic research articles are included, most of the primary readings were chosen because they are excellent, cutting-edge, contemporary examples of the use of theory to explain deviance. They offer the opportunity to explore a deviant topic more thoroughly, yet still with an eye toward the importance of theory in that exploration.

In contrast to most of the popular readers and textbooks on deviant behavior, this book is primarily organized around theories and perspectives of deviance, rather than types of deviant behavior or a singular approach to understanding deviance. While taking a broad sociological perspective, we move beyond theory by including additional sections focused on researching deviance, social control of deviance, and deviant careers.

We hope this book will serve as a guide to students delving into the fascinating world of deviance for the first time, offering clear overviews of issues and perspectives in the field as well as introductions to classic and current academic literature. *Deviance and Social Control: A Sociological Perspective* is intended to replace standard deviance textbooks or readers; it can be used in both undergraduate and graduate deviance courses.

◈ Overview of Features

Deviance and Social Control: A Sociological Perspective includes topics generally found in textbooks on deviant behavior, including the major sociological theories of deviance and discussion of rulemaking and societal reaction to deviance. As a text-reader, it is significantly different from other deviance textbooks and readers that are currently on the market. It is neither a standard textbook (a summary of current research, with very little original material) nor simply a reader (a collection of articles on different topics). This book is a true hybrid that combines original text offering clear explanations and discussion of concepts and theories and carefully selected articles on relevant topics. This book features the following:

1. An introductory section explaining the sociological perspective on deviance and social control. This section provides an overview on the organization and content of the book and also introduces relevant themes, issues, and concepts while providing a framework for the text and articles that follow, to assist students in understanding the perspectives and articles. Along with the introduction, we have full chapters on the diversity of deviance and researching deviance, and we include a brief segment offering students tips on how to read a journal article.

2. Each chapter includes three different textbox features that prompt students to engage with the material, apply the concepts, and learn more about current research. The features include the following:

   a. *Deviance in Popular Culture*—offers several examples of films and/or television shows and encourages students to apply the concepts and theories to the behavior depicted.

   b. *Studies in Deviance*—offers a brief overview of a recent published study on diverse types of deviant behavior.

   c. *Now YOU . . .*—asks students to apply the material they learned in the chapter to specific questions or examples.

3. Each of the included readings is preceded by a brief introduction in which we provide an overview of the article and its key contribution.

4. Each chapter includes discussion questions and exercises/assignments that will give students a chance to test and extend their knowledge of the material.

5. The book contains a glossary of key terms.

◈ Structure of the Book

We chose very deliberately to organize our book around sociological theories rather than around types of deviance. This is in direct opposition to most of the competing texts on the market, and it is one of the reasons you might consider using our book. We believe the theoretically based approach offers students fertile ground for learning and exploring the realm of deviant behavior and social control. Once they learn the different theoretical perspectives, students will be able to apply the different theories to virtually any type of deviant behavior and, furthermore, be able to compare and contrast the theoretical models and decide for themselves which offers the most compelling explanation for the behavior. This is the kind of understanding and flexibility we hope our students achieve—while studying types of deviance is certainly interesting, being able to consider both individual and macro-level causes and explanations seems to us the larger and more important goal.

The book is divided into 12 chapters that cover an overview of the field of deviance and social control, methods and examples of researching deviance, the major theoretical traditions used in studying deviance, and a glimpse into the social control of deviance and deviant careers. The theory chapters each provide an overview of the theoretical perspective and its development, critiques of the perspective, and examples of current developments and research in that theoretical tradition. The chapters are as follows:

Chapter 1—Introduction to Deviance: We first provide the basic building blocks for studying deviant behavior from a sociological perspective. Different conceptions of deviance are described, and students are encouraged to develop and use their sociological imagination in studying deviant behavior. We explain the organization of the book and why we believe theory is so critical to understanding and researching deviance.

Chapter 2—The Diversity of Deviance: In this chapter, we offer an overview of some of the many types of deviance and show how our conceptions of deviance vary widely and change over time. We encourage students to think broadly about deviance and to always consider the culture, context, and historical period in which the "deviant" act takes place.

Chapter 3—Researching Deviance: This chapter addresses the many ways one might go about researching deviant behavior and social control. We highlight different research methods and the strengths and weaknesses of each approach. Examples are used throughout to make abstract concepts concrete for students.

Chapter 4—Anomie/Strain Theory: This chapter looks at one of the first sociological theories of deviance and traces the development of anomie and strain theories from Durkheim, Merton, and Cloward and Ohlin's macro-level ideas on how the very structure of society contributes to deviant behavior, to Agnew's general strain theory and Messner and Rosenfeld's institutional strain theory, which offer contemporary views on individual and institutional strain and the resulting deviance.

Chapter 5—Social Disorganization Theory: We discuss another early sociological perspective on deviance in this chapter; with its roots in Chicago, social disorganization theory developed to explain patterns of deviance and crime across social locations such as neighborhoods. We offer an overview of the perspective and show how it is being used today to explain high levels of deviance and violence in particular neighborhoods.

Chapter 6—Differential Association and Social Learning Theory: How do individuals learn to become deviant? This chapter covers ideas and research that try to answer that exact question. We explain the key ideas of Sutherland's differential association and Akers's social learning theories and offer an overview of the development of a sociological perspective that argues that deviance is learned through communication with intimate others.

Chapter 7—Social Control Theories of Deviance: Social control theories begin by flipping the question; rather than asking why individuals deviate, social control theories ask, If we are born prone to deviance, what keeps us from committing deviant acts? In this chapter, we trace the development of social control and life course theories, looking at the importance of the individual's social bonds to conforming society.

Chapter 8—Labeling Theory: In this chapter, we look at the importance of being labeled deviant. We begin with a brief overview of symbolic interactionism, which then leads to a discussion of the labeling process and how it can affect individuals' self-concepts and life chances.

Chapter 9—Marxist/Conflict Theories of Deviance: Within the conflict perspective, power and inequality are key considerations in defining who and what is deviant in any given society. In this chapter, we begin with the ideas of Karl Marx and go on to show how Marxist perspectives have been used to study lawmaking and how the process of defining and creating deviant behavior is used to maintain positions of power in society.

Chapter 10—Critical Theories: In this chapter, we focus on theories that examine deviance from a perspective that questions the normative status quo. We offer brief overviews of peacemaking criminology, feminist criminology, and critical race theory as alternative perspectives for studying deviance and social control.

Chapter 11—Social Control of Deviance: In this chapter, we offer a brief look into informal and formal social control of deviance. We discuss the medicalization (and medication) of deviance, mental hospitals, prisons and juvenile correctional facilities, felon disenfranchisement, and general effects of stigma on those labeled deviant.

Chapter 12: Deviant Careers and Career Deviance: For our final chapter, we explore the concept of deviant careers. While much attention is focused on getting into deviance, we think it is important to consider the full deviant career, including desistance, or the process of exiting deviance.

Each chapter offers original material that introduces students to the issues, concepts, and theories covered in that chapter and contextualizes the selected readings. Each chapter also includes three to four primary source readings that will offer students the chance to learn about current research on deviance and social control from that perspective.

◈ Ancillaries

To enhance the use of this text and to assist those using this book, we have developed high-quality ancillaries for instructors and students.

Instructor Resource Site. A password-protected site, available at www.sagepub.com/inderbitzin, features resources that have been designed to help instructors plan and teach their course. These resources include the following:

- An extensive test bank that includes multiple-choice, true/false, short-answer, and essay questions for each chapter

- Chapter-specific PowerPoint slide presentations that highlight essential concepts and figures from the text

- Sample syllabi for semester, quarter, and online courses

- Access to recent, relevant full-text SAGE journal articles and accompanying article review questions

- Class assignments and activities that can be used in conjunction with the book throughout the semester

- Links to Web resources, which direct both instructors and students to relevant websites for further research on important chapter topics

- Audio and video resources for use in class to jump-start lectures and emphasize key topics of your discussions

- Figures and tables from the text

Student Study Site. An open-access study site is available at www.sagepub.com/inderbitzin. This site provides access to several study tools, including the following:

- eFlashcards, which reinforce students' understanding of key terms and concepts presented in the text

- Web quizzes for student self-review

- Web resources organized by chapter for more in-depth research on topics presented in each chapter

- Access to relevant full-text SAGE journal articles that were selected by the authors

- Audio and video resources for a more in-depth understanding of the material covered in class and in the text

◈ Acknowledgments

First, we thank Jerry Westby for shepherding this manuscript and its authors through the entire publication process. Jerry's faith in this book and our vision for it helped to sustain the project through difficult patches and busy schedules.

We would also like to thank our graduate school mentors and friends; our time with these people in the University of Washington sociology program contributed a great deal to our lasting understanding of deviant behavior and social control: Bob Crutchfield, George Bridges, Joe Weis, Charis Kubrin, Sara Steen, Rod Engen, Edie Simpson, Ed Day, and Tim Wadsworth—thanks to you all! We particularly want to thank Howie Becker for being a great role model, scholar, and teacher and for writing the foreword to this book.

Michelle would like to thank Kristin Bates and Randy Gainey for being wonderful, supportive coauthors and friends; she also offers particular thanks to friends and colleagues Charis Kubrin, Chris Uggen, Scott Akins, Kristin Barker, Becky Warner, and Debbie Storrs for many, many thought-provoking conversations about teaching and writing.

Randy and Kristin would like to thank Michelle for her leadership and hard work and for asking them to take this adventure with her. We had fun!

We would also like to thank the reviewers: Angela Butts, Rutgers the State University of New Jersey, New Brunswick; Philip Davis, Georgia State University; Heather Griffiths, Fayetteville State University; S. Walter DeKeseredy, University of Ontario Institute of Technology; Stephen Hagan, Southern Illinois University; Charles Hanna, Duquesne University; Angie Henderson, University of Northern Colorado Greeley; Robert J. Homant, University of Detroit Mercy; Lutz Kaelber, University of Vermont, Burlington; Chad Kimmel, Shippensburg University of Pennsylvania; Brenda Lauts, University of New Mexico; Gina Luby, Depaul University Chicago; Kate Luther, Pacific Lutheran University; Michelle Mackinem, Claflin University; Michael Massoglia, Pennsylvania State University; James D. Orcutt, Florida State University, Tallahassee; Pete A. Padilla, University of Colorado, Denver; Victor Shaw, California State University, Northridge; Melissa Thompson, Portland State University; Janelle Wilson, University of Minnesota; and Edward F. Vacha, Gonzaga University.

PART I

Introduction to the Study of Deviance and Social Control

CHAPTER 1

Introduction to Deviance

Founded in 1972, the Fremont Fair is one of Seattle's most beloved neighborhood street festivals, featuring a weekend of eclectic activities that celebrate the quirky community of Fremont, the self-proclaimed 'center of the universe.' Held annually in mid-June to coincide with the Summer Solstice, the event draws more than 100,000 people to shop, eat, drink, mingle, groove, and enjoy all manners of creative expression. Artistic highlights include craft and art booths, street performers, local bands, wacky decorated art cars, the free-spirited Solstice Parade produced by the Fremont Arts Council, and many other oddities that personify Fremont's official motto "Delibertus Quirkus"—Freedom to be Peculiar.

—Fremont Fair (2010)

The Fremont Arts Council (FAC) is a community-based celebration arts organization. We value volunteer-ism; community participation; artistic expression; and the sharing of arts skills. The Fremont Solstice Parade is the defining event of the FAC. We celebrate the longest day of the year through profound street theater, public spectacle, and a kaleidoscope of joyous human expressions. We welcome the participation of everyone regardless of who they are, or what they think or believe. However, the FAC reserves the right to control the content presented in the Fremont Solstice Parade.

The rules of the Fremont Solstice Parade, which make this event distinct from other types of parades, are:

- No written or printed words or logos
- No animals (except guide dogs and service animals)
- No motorized vehicles (except wheelchairs)
- No real weapons or fire

—Fremont Arts Council (2010)

It is true that a parade with no logos, animals, or motorized vehicles is different from most parades that we experience in the United States. But one more thing sets the Fremont Solstice Parade apart from other parades—the public displays of nudity. Every year at the parade, there is a contingent of nude, body-painted bicyclists (both men and women) who ride through the streets of Fremont as part of the parade. Rain or shine (and let's face it, in June in Seattle, there can be a lot of rain), a large group of naked adults cycle down the street as the crowds cheer and wave. The Fremont City Council estimates that more than 100,000 people visit the weekend fair, and pictures show that the streets are crowded with parade watchers, from the very young to elderly.

Contrast this event to the following story of a flasher in San Diego County. Between the summer of 2009 and the summer of 2010, there were numerous reports of an adult man flashing hikers and runners on Mission Trails near Lake Murphy in San Diego. An undercover operation was set in motion to catch this flasher, and on July 19, 2010, an adult man was apprehended while flashing an undercover officer who was posing as a jogger in the park. He was held on $50,000 bail while waiting for arraignment (KFMB-News 8, 2010).

While both these events center around public displays of nudity, one is celebrated while the other is vilified. Why?

▲ Photo 1.1 & 1.2   When is a public display of nudity considered deviant? When is it celebrated?

◈ Introduction

You might expect that a book about deviance would start with a definition of what deviance is. But, like all things worth studying, a simple definition does not exist. For example, in the stories above, the public display of nudity is not only welcomed but also celebrated by 6-year-olds and grandmothers alike in one instance, and in the other it can lead to arrest and jail time. Why? This chapter and this book explore how it can be that the Fremont Summer Solstice Parade can be celebrated in the same summer that a flasher is arrested and held on $50,000 bail until he is charged.

◈ Conceptions of Deviance

All deviance textbooks offer their "conceptions of deviance." Rubington and Weinberg (2008) argue that there are generally two conceptions of deviance as either "objectively given" or "subjectively problematic." Clinard and Meier (2010) also suggest two general conceptions of deviance, the reactionist or **relativist** conception and the **normative** conception. Thio (2009) argues that we can view deviance from a positivist perspective or a constructionist perspective.

While none of these authors are using the same language, they are defining similar conceptions of deviance. The first conception—that of an "objectively given," normative, or positivist conception of deviance—assumes that there is a general set of norms of behavior, conduct, and conditions for which we can agree. **Norms** are rules of behavior that guide people's actions. Sumner (1906) broke norms down into three categories: folkways, mores, and laws. **Folkways** are everyday norms that do not generate much uproar if they are violated. Think of them as behaviors that might be considered rude if engaged in—like standing too close to someone while speaking or picking one's nose. **Mores** are "moral" norms that may generate more outrage if broken. In a capitalist society, homelessness and unemployment can elicit outrage if the person is considered unworthy of sympathy. Similarly, drinking too much or alcoholism may be seen as a lapse in moral judgment. Finally, the third type of norm is the **law,** which is considered the strongest norm because it is backed by official sanctions (or a formal response). In this conception, then, deviance becomes a violation of a rule understood by the majority of the group. This rule may be minor, in which case the deviant is seen as "weird but harmless," or the rule may be major, in which case the deviant is seen as "criminal." The obvious problem with this conceptualization goes back to the earlier example of the reaction to public nudity, where we see that violation of the most "serious" norm (laws) receives quite different reactions, which leads to the second conception.

The second conception of deviance—the "subjectively problematic," reactionist/relativist, **social constructionist** conception—assumes that the definition of deviance is constructed based on the interactions of those in society. According to this conception of deviance, behaviors or conditions are not inherently deviant; they become so when the definition of deviance is applied to them. The study of deviance is not about why certain individuals violate norms but instead about how those norms are constructed. Social constructionists believe that our understanding of the world is in constant negotiation between actors. Those who have a relativist conception of deviance define deviance as those behaviors that illicit a definition or label of deviance:

> Social groups create deviance by making the rules whose infraction constitutes deviance, and by applying those rules to particular people and labeling them as outsiders. For this point of view, deviance is not a quality of the act the person commits but rather a consequence of the application by others of rules and sanctions to an "offender." The deviant is one to whom that label has successfully been applied; deviant behaviors is behavior that people so label. (Becker, 1973, p. 9)

This is a fruitful conceptualization, but it is also problematic. What about very serious violations of norms that are never known or reacted to? Some strict reactionists/relativists would argue that these acts (beliefs or attitudes) are not deviant. Most of us would agree that killing someone and making it look like he or she simply skipped the country is deviant; however, there may be no reaction.

A third conception of deviance that has not been advanced in many textbooks (for an exception, see DeKeserdy, Ellis, & Alvi, 2005) is a critical definition of deviance (Jensen, 2007). Those working from a critical conception of deviance argue that the normative understanding of deviance is established by those in power to maintain and enhance their power. It suggests that explorations of deviance have focused on a white, male, middle- to upper-class understanding of society that implies that people of color, women, and the working poor are by definition deviant. Instead of focusing on individual types of deviance, this conception critiques the social system that exists that creates such norms in the first place. This too is a useful approach, but frankly, there are many things that the vast majority of society agree are immoral, unethical, and deviant and should be illegal and that the system actually serves to protect our interests.

Given that each of these conceptualizations is useful but problematic, we do not adhere to a single conception of deviance in this book because the theories of deviance do not adhere to a single conception. You will see that several of our theories assume a normative conception, while several assume a social constructionist or critical conception. As you explore each of these theories, think about what the conception of deviance and theoretical perspective mean for the questions we ask and answer about deviance.

HOW DO YOU DEFINE DEVIANCE?

As Justice Stewart of the Supreme Court once famously wrote about trying to define obscene materials, "I shall not today attempt further to define the kinds of material I understand to be embraced within that shorthand description; and perhaps I could never succeed in intelligibly doing so. But I know it when I see it" (*Jacobellis v. Ohio,* 1964). Those who do not study deviance for a living probably find themselves in the same boat; it may be hard to write a definition, but how hard could it be to "know it when we see it"?

Choose some place busy to sit and observe human behavior for one hour. Write down all the behaviors that you observe during that hour. Do you consider any of these behaviors to be deviant? Which conception of deviance are you using when you define each as deviant? Might there be some instances (e.g., places or times) when that behavior you consider to be nondeviant right now might become deviant? Finally, bring your list of behaviors to class. In pairs, share your list of behaviors and your definitions of deviant behaviors with your partner. Do you agree on your categorization? Why or why not?

◈ The Sociological Imagination

Those of us who are sociologists can probably remember the first time we were introduced to the concept of the **sociological imagination.** Mills argues that the only way to truly understand the experiences of the individual is to first understand the societal, institutional, and historical conditions that individual is living under. In other words, Mills believes that no man, woman, or child is an island. Below is an excerpt from C. Wright Mills's (1959/2000) profound book, *The Sociological Imagination* (Oxford University Press):

> Men do not usually define the troubles they endure in terms of historical change and institutional contradiction. The well-being they enjoy, they do not usually impute to the big ups and downs of the societies in which they live. Seldom aware of the intricate connection between the patterns of their own lives and the course of world history, ordinary men do not usually know what this connection means for the kinds of men they are becoming and for the kinds of history-making in which they might take part. They do not possess the quality of mind essential to grasp the interplay of man and society, of biography and history, of self and world. They cannot cope with their personal troubles in such ways as to control the structural transformations that usually lie behind them.
>
> The sociological imagination enables its possessor to understand the larger historical scene in terms of its meaning for the inner life and the external career of a variety of individuals. It enables him to take into account how individuals, in the welter of their daily experience, often become falsely conscious of their social positions. With that welter, the framework of modern society is sought, and within that framework the psychologies of a variety of men and women are formulated. By such means the personal uneasiness of individuals is focused upon explicit troubles and the indifference of publics is transformed into involvement with public issues.
>
> The first fruit of this imagination—and the first lesson of the social science that embodies it—is the idea that the individual can understand his own experience and gauge his own fate only by locating himself within his period, that he can know his own chances in life only by becoming aware of those of all individuals in his circumstances. In many ways it is a terrible lesson; in many ways a magnificent one.
>
> In these terms, consider unemployment. When, in a city of 100,000, only one man is unemployed, that is his personal trouble, and for its relief we properly look to the character of the man, his skills, and his immediate opportunities. But when in a nation of 50 million employees, 15 million men are unemployed, that is an issue, and we may not hope to find its solution within the range of opportunities open to any one individual. The very structure of opportunities has collapsed. Both the correct statement of the problem and the range of possible solutions require us to consider the economic and political institutions of the society, and not merely the personal situation and character of a scatter of individuals.
>
> What we experience in various and specific milieux, I have noted, is often caused by structural changes. Accordingly, to understand the changes of many personal milieux we are required to look beyond them. And the number and variety of such structural changes increase as the institutions within connected with one another. To be aware of the idea of social structure and to use it with sensibility is to be capable of tracing such linkages among a great variety of milieu. To be able to do this is to possess the sociological imagination. (pp. 3–11)

One of our favorite examples of the sociological imagination in action is the "salad bar" example. In the United States, one of the persistent philosophies is that of individualism and personal responsibility. Under this philosophy, individuals are assumed to be solely responsible for their successes and failures. This philosophy relies heavily on the notion that individuals are rational actors who weigh the cost and benefit of their actions, can see the consequences of their behavior, and have perfect information. The salad bar example helps individuals who rely heavily on this conception of the individual to see the importance of social structure to individual behavior.

No one doubts that when you order a salad bar at a restaurant, you are responsible for building your own salad. Every person makes his or her own salad, and no two salads look exactly alike. Some make salads with lots of lettuce and vegetables, very little cheese, and fat-free dressing. Others create a salad that is piled high with cheese, croutons, and lots and lots of dressing. Those who are unhappy with their choices while making their salad only have themselves to blame, right? Not necessarily.

A salad is only as good as the salad bar it is created from. In other words, individuals making a salad can only make a salad from the ingredients supplied from the salad bar. If the restaurant is out of croutons that day or decided to put watermelon out instead of cantaloupe, the individual must build his or her salad within these constraints. Some individuals with a great sense of personal power may request additional items from the back of the restaurant, but most individuals will choose to build a salad based on the items available to them on the salad bar. In other words, the individual choice is constrained by the larger social forces of delivery schedules, food inventory, and worker decision making. The sociological imagination is especially important to understand because it is the building block for our understanding of sociological theory.

▲ **Photo 1.3** The salad bar can represent the restriction on choices that individuals have. We can only make our salad with the ingredients offered to us on the salad bar.

DEVIANCE IN POPULAR CULTURE

Many types of deviance are portrayed and investigated in popular culture. Films and television shows, for example, illustrate a wide range of deviant behavior and social control. There are often several interpretations of what acts are deviant in each film—how do you know when an act or person is deviant? One way to develop your sociological imagination is to watch films and television shows from a critical perspective and to think about how different theories would explain the deviant behavior and the reactions portrayed. To get you started, we've listed a number of films and television shows that you might watch and explore for examples of cultural norms, different types of deviant behavior, and coping with stigma.

Films

Trekkies—a documentary following the stories of individuals who are superfans of *Star Trek*. Known as Trekkies, these individuals have incorporated *Star Trek* into their everyday lives. Some wear the

(Continued)

(Continued)

uniforms or speak and teach the various languages from the show, one has considered surgery to alter the shape of his ears, and some have legally changed their names and incorporated *Star Trek* into their businesses and workplaces. The movie documents their fandom and experiences navigating these consuming obsessions while in mainstream society.

American Beauty—the story of a suburban family that, from the outside, appears to be "perfect." However, the characters are leading far from perfect lives filled with depression, lies, drug dealing, homophobia, and self-loathing.

Crumb—a movie about the cartoonist Robert Crumb, who was a pioneer of the underground comix. This movie offers a dark portrait of an artist besieged with personal and family demons.

Usual Suspects—a story of five men who are brought in for questioning for a crime they did not commit. While being held on suspicion of that crime, they agree to work together on another crime. They soon realize they are being set up by someone they had wronged in the past.

Television

Reality television and The Learning Channel (TLC), in particular, feature a number of programs offering an inside view of people perceived as deviant or different in some way and showing how they deal with stigma from various sources:

Sister Wives—inside the world of a polygamist marriage: This reality show introduces viewers to a man, his four wives, and 16 children. His motto: "Love should be multiplied, not divided."

Seinfeld—a situation comedy that is simply masterful at focusing on small behaviors or characteristics that break norms and are perceived as deviant. Episodes on the close-talker, the low-talker, the high-talker, for example, all illustrate unwritten norms on interpersonal communication.

In each of the chapters that follow, we will offer suggestions of one or more films or television shows for you to watch from the theoretical perspective outlined in the chapter. We think you'll soon agree: Deviance is all around us.

◈ The Importance of Theory

The three of us (the authors of this book) have spent many hours discussing the importance of **theory** as we wrote this book. Why did we choose to write a textbook about deviance with theory as the central theme? Many of you may also be asking this question and worrying that a book about theory may suck the life right out of a discussion about deviance. Really, who wants to be thinking about theory when we could be talking about "nuts, sluts, and preverts" (Liazos, 1972)? But, this is precisely why we must make theory central to any discussion of deviance—because theory helps us *systematically* think about deviance. If it weren't for theory, classes about deviance would be akin to watching *Jersey Shore* (MTV) or the *Real Housewives of New Jersey* (Bravo) (why is New Jersey so popular for these shows?)—it may be entertaining, but we have no clearer understanding of the "real" people of New Jersey when we are done watching.

Theory is what turns anecdotes about human behavior into a systematic understanding of societal behavior. It does this by playing an intricate part in research and the scientific method.

The **scientific method** is a systematic procedure that helps *safeguard against researcher bias* and the power of anecdotes by following several simple steps. First, a researcher starts with a research question.

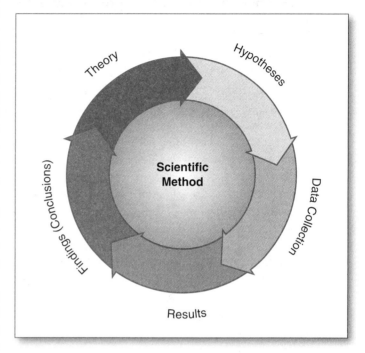

Figure 1.1 The Scientific Method Allows Us to Systematically Examine Social Phenomena Such as Deviance

If the researcher is engaging in deductive research, this question comes from a theoretical perspective. This theory and research question help the researcher create hypotheses (testable statements) about a phenomenon being studied. Once the researcher has created hypotheses, she collects her data to test these hypotheses. We discuss data and data collection methods for deviance research in detail in Chapter 3. She then analyzes these data, interprets her findings, and concludes whether or not her hypotheses have been supported. These findings then inform whether the theory she used helps with our understanding of the world or should be revised to take into consideration information that does not support its current model. If a researcher is engaging in inductive research, she also starts with a research question, but in the beginning, her theory may be what we call "grounded theory." Using qualitative methods such as participant observation or in-depth interviews, the researcher would collect data and analyze these data looking for common themes throughout. These findings would be used to create a theory "from the ground up." In other words, while deductive researchers would start with a theory that guides every step of their research, an inductive researcher might start with a broad theoretical perspective, a research question, and from the systematic collection of data and rigorous analyses would hone that broad theoretical perspective into a more specific theory. This theory would then be tested again as the researcher continued on with her work, or others, finding this new theory to be useful and interesting, might opt to use it to inform both their deductive and inductive work.

STUDIES IN DEVIANCE

The Poverty of the Sociology of Deviance: Nuts, Sluts, and Preverts

By Alexander Liazos, in *Social Problems, 20*(1), 103–120

Liazos argues that the study of deviance used to be the study of "nuts, sluts, and preverts," a sensationalistic ritual in finger pointing and moralizing. The focus was on individuals and their "aberrant" behavior. This meant that the most harmful behaviors in society, the ones that affected us most thoroughly, were ignored and, in ignoring them, normalized. Liazos referred to these forms of deviance as *covert institutional violence.*

According to Liazos, the poverty of the study of deviance was threefold: First, even when trying to point out how normal the "deviance" or "deviant" is, by pointing out the person or behavior, we are acknowledging the difference—if that difference really were invisible, how and why would we be studying it? This meant by even studying deviance, a moral choice had already been made—some differences were studied; some were not. Second, by extension, deviance research rarely studied elite deviance and structural deviance, instead focusing on "dramatic" forms of deviance such as prostitution, juvenile delinquency, and homosexuality. Liazos argues that it is important to, instead, study covert institutional violence, which leads to such things as poverty and exploitation. Instead of studying tax cheats, we should study unjust tax laws; instead of studying prostitution, we should study racism and sexism as deviance. Finally, Liazos argues that even those who profess to study the relationship between power and deviance do not really acknowledge the importance of power. These researchers still give those in positions of power a pass to engage in harmful behavior by not defining much elite deviance as deviance at all.

The implication of this is that those who study deviance have allowed the definition of deviance to be settled for them. And this definition benefits not only individuals in power but also a system that has routinely engaged in harmful acts. While Liazos wrote this important critique of the sociology of deviance in 1972, much of his analysis holds up to this day. In this book, we examine theories expressly capable of addressing this critique.

As you explore each of the theories offered to you in this book, remember Liazos's critique. Which theories are more likely to focus on "nuts, sluts, and preverts"? Which are more likely to focus on elite deviance and new conceptions of deviance?

If we go back to our example of reality shows about people from New Jersey, we may see the difference between an anecdote and a more theoretically grounded understanding of human behavior. After watching both *Jersey Shore* and the *Real Housewives of New Jersey,* we may conclude that people from New Jersey are loud, self-absorbed, and overly tan (all three of which might be considered deviant behaviors or characteristics). However, we have not systematically studied the people of New Jersey to arrive at our conclusion. Using inductive reasoning, based on our initial observation, we may start with a research question that states that because the people of New Jersey are loud, self-absorbed, and overly tan, we are interested in knowing about the emotional connections they have with friends and family (we may suspect that self-absorbed people are more likely to have relationships with conflict). However, as we continue along the scientific method, we systematically gather data from more than just the reality stars of these two shows. We interview teachers and police officers, retired lawyers and college students. What we soon learn as we analyze these interviews is that the general public in New Jersey is really not all that tan, loud, or self-absorbed, and they speak openly and warmly about strong connections to family and friends. This research leads us to reexamine our initial theory about the characteristics of people from New Jersey and offer a new theory based on systematic analysis. This new theory then informs subsequent research on the people of New Jersey. If we did not have theory and the scientific method, our understanding of deviance would be based on wild observations and anecdotes, which may be significantly misleading and unrepresentative of the social reality.

In addition to being systematic and testable (through the scientific method), theory offers *solutions to the problems* we study. One of the hardest knocks against the study of deviance and crime has been the historically carnival sideshow nature (Liazos, 1972) of much of the study of deviance. By focusing on individuals and a certain caste of deviants (those without power), with less than systematic methods, deviance researchers were just pointing at "nuts, sluts, and preverts" and not advancing their broader understanding of the interplay of power, social structure, and behavior. Theory can focus our attention on this interplay and offer solutions beyond the individual and the deficit model. Bendle (1999) also argued that the study of deviance was in a state of crisis because researchers were no longer studying relevant problems or offering useful solutions. One of Bendle's solutions is to push for new theories of deviant behavior.

Theoretical solutions to the issue of deviance are especially important because many of our current responses to deviant behavior are erroneously based on an individualistic notion of human nature that does not take into account humans as social beings or the importance of social structure, social institutions, power, and broad societal changes for deviance and deviants.

NOW YOU . . . USE YOUR SOCIOLOGICAL IMAGINATION

Liazos (1972), in his article "The Poverty of the Sociology of Deviance: Nuts, Sluts, and Preverts," argues that the sociology of deviance focuses too much attention on individual idiosyncrasies and not enough attention on structural dynamics and the deviance of the powerful. The following graph is taken from a Web page from the U.S. Energy Information Administration (part of the Department of Energy) explaining the U.S. energy consumption for 2009. Following this chart is a section taken from the Environmental Protection Agency (also a federal agency) explaining the effects of fossil fuels on climate change. Using your sociological imagination, how might you discuss the figures and text as an example of deviance? How might the relationship between the U.S. government, lobbyists, and oil companies affect the conversation around climate change? Pretend you are an oil executive: Which might be more deviant in your view, the breakdown of U.S. energy consumption or the research on climate change? Why? Now pretend that you are an oceanographer studying changes in the Gulf of Mexico or a zoologist studying polar bear migration: What might you define as deviant? Why? Would both groups define the same information as deviant? Do you consider either the breakdown of the U.S. consumption of energy or the discussion of climate change to be deviant? Why or why not?

(Continued)

(Continued)

Figure 1.2 U.S. Energy Consumption by Energy Source, 2009

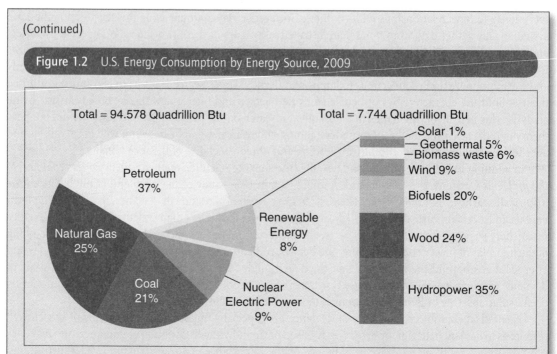

Source: U.S. Energy Information Administration, *Annual Energy Review 2009,* Table 1.3, Primary Energy Consumption by Energy Source, 1949–2009 (August 2010).

Note: Sum of components may not equal 100% due to independent rounding.

For over the past 200 years, the burning of fossil fuels, such as coal and oil, and deforestation have caused the concentrations of heat-trapping "greenhouse gases" to increase significantly in our atmosphere. These gases prevent heat from escaping to space, somewhat like the glass panels of a greenhouse.

Greenhouse gases are necessary to life as we know it, because they keep the planet's surface warmer than it otherwise would be. But, as the concentrations of these gases continue to increase in the atmosphere, the Earth's temperature is climbing above past levels. According to NOAA and NASA data, the Earth's average surface temperature has increased by about 1.2°F to 1.4°F in the last 100 years. The eight warmest years on record (since 1850) have all occurred since 1998, with the warmest year being 2005. Most of the warming in recent decades is very likely the result of human activities. Other aspects of the climate are also changing such as rainfall patterns, snow and ice cover, and sea level.

If greenhouse gases continue to increase, climate models predict that the average temperature at the Earth's surface could increase from 3.2°F to 7.2°F above 1990 levels by the end of this century. Scientists are certain that human activities are changing the composition of the atmosphere, and that increasing the concentration of greenhouse gases will change the planet's climate. But they are not sure by how much it will change, at what rate it will change, or what the exact effects will be. (Environmental Protection Agency, 2011)

◈ Conclusion: Organization of the Book

This book is organized into four sections: (1) an introduction to deviance—types of deviance and researching deviance, (2) traditional theories of deviance, (3) social constructionist theories of deviance, and (4) responses to deviance. We start your introduction to deviance by examining the diversity of deviance, how our definitions of deviance change over time, and how we research deviance. The next two sections focus on theories of deviance, starting with the traditional, positivist theories of deviance and moving to social constructionist and critical theories of deviance. We also try to present the theories in a fairly chronological manner. While all these theories are still in use in the study of deviance, some have been around longer than others. Positivist theories have been around longer than social constructionist theories, and within positivist theories, anomie has been around longer than social disorganization. We think this offers you a general road map of how thinking and theories have developed about deviance. In each of these chapters, we present the classical versions of each theory and then the contemporary version, and along the way, we explore several types of deviance that may be explained by each given theory. Finally, we offer a section that examines our individual and societal responses to deviance.

This book has been written with a heavy emphasis on theory. We think you will agree as you read the book that theory is an important organizational tool for understanding (1) why deviance occurs, (2) why some behavior may or may not be defined as deviant, and (3) why some individuals are more likely to be defined as deviant. It is important to note that you probably won't have the same level of enthusiasm for every theory offered here. Some of you will really "get" anomie theory, while others might be drawn to labeling or feminist theory. Heck, we feel the same way. But what is important to remember is that ALL of these theories have been supported by research, and all help answer certain questions about deviance.

Along the way, we present examples of specific acts that may be considered deviant in both the research and pop culture. You will be introduced at the beginning of each chapter to a vignette that discusses a social phenomenon or behavior. In addition, each chapter includes three to four original articles that offer an example of how sociologists are examining deviance. As you learn more about theory, you can decide for yourself how and why these acts and actors may be defined as deviant. One of our goals for you is to help you start to think sociologically and theoretically about our social world and the acts we do and do not call deviance.

EXERCISES AND DISCUSSION QUESTIONS

1. After reading the article on the Nacerima (Reading 1), choose your own population to observe and write about. What are the deviant behaviors and beliefs of this population?

2. Choose any half-hour sitcom. While watching the show, examine its treatment of "deviant" behavior. Is there a character whom others treat as different or deviant? Why do others treat him or her this way? Is there a character that you would describe as deviant? Is he or she treated this way by others in the show? What conception of deviance are you using to determine the deviant behavior on the show?

3. Why is theory important to our understanding of deviance?

KEY TERMS

Folkways

Laws

Mores

Normative deviance

Norms

Relativist deviance

Scientific method

Social construction

Sociological imagination

Theory

READING 1

This short anthropological essay describes a unique society with rituals and ceremonies so different from our own that the reader must immediately come to the conclusion that the relativist stance must be the only way to view different cultures. The description of the unique society and associated rituals and ceremonies of the Nacirema may be novel to those who have never seen a *National Geographic* magazine or explored other societies and cultures on the Internet. But keep an open mind—there are many commonalities to modern society that could be brought up if one thinks outside the box.

Body Ritual Among the Nacirema

Horace Miner

The anthropologist has become so familiar with the diversity of ways in which different peoples behave in similar situations that he is not apt to be surprised by even the most exotic customs. In fact, if all of the logically possible combinations of behavior have not been found somewhere in the world, he is apt to suspect that they must be present in some yet undescribed tribe. This point has, in fact, been expressed with respect to clan organization by Murdock (1949:71). In this light, the magical beliefs and practices of the Nacirema present such unusual aspects that it seems desirable to describe them as an example of the extremes to which human behavior can go.

Professor Linton first brought the ritual of the Nacirema to the attention of anthropologists twenty years ago (1936: 326), but the culture of this people is still very poorly understood. They are a North American group living in the territory between the Canadian Cree, the Yaqui and Tarahumare of Mexico, and the Carib and Arawak of the Antilles. Little is known of their origin, though tradition states that they came from the east. According to Nacirema mythology, their nation was originated by a culture hero, Notgnishaw, who is otherwise known for two great feats of strength—the throwing of a piece of wampum across a great river and the chopping down of a tree in which the Spirit of Truth resided.

Nacirema culture is characterized by a highly developed market economy which has evolved in a rich natural habitat. While much of the people's time is devoted to economic pursuits, a large part of the fruits of these labors and a considerable portion of the day are spent in ritual activity. The focus of this

Source: Miner, Horace. 1956. "Body Ritual Among the Nacirema." *American Anthropologist* 58:503–507. Published by the American Anthropological Associations (AAA). http://www.aaanet.org/publications/permissions.cfm

activity is the human body, the appearance and health of which loom as a dominant concern in the ethos of the people. While such a concern is certainly not unusual, its ceremonial aspects and associated philosophy are unique.

The fundamental belief underlying the whole system appears to be that the human body is ugly and that its natural tendency is to debility and disease. Incarcerated in such a body, man's only hope is to avert these characteristics through the use of the powerful influences of ritual and ceremony. Every household has one or more shrines devoted to this purpose. The more powerful individuals in the society have several shrines in their houses and, in fact, the opulence of a house is often referred to in terms of the number of such ritual centers it possesses. Most houses are of wattle and daub construction, but the shrine rooms of the more wealthy are walled with stone. Poorer families imitate the rich by applying pottery plaques to their shrine walls.

While each family has at least one such shrine, the rituals associated with it are not family ceremonies but are private and secret. The rites are normally only discussed with children, and then only during the period when they are being initiated into these mysteries. I was able, however, to establish sufficient rapport with the natives to examine these shrines and to have the rituals described to me.

The focal point of the shrine is a box or chest which is built into the wall. In this chest are kept the many charms and magical potions without which no native believes he could live. These preparations are secured from a variety of specialized practitioners. The most powerful of these are the medicine men, whose assistance must be rewarded with substantial gifts. However, the medicine men do not provide the curative potions for their clients, but decide what the ingredients should be and then write them down in an ancient and secret language. This writing is understood only by the medicine men and by the herbalists who, for another gift, provide the required charm.

The charm is not disposed of after it has served its purpose, but is placed in the charm-box of the household shrine. As these magical materials are specific for certain ills, and the real or imagined maladies of the people are many, the charm-box is usually full to overflowing. The magical packets are so numerous that people forget what their purposes were and fear to use them again. While the natives are very vague on this point, we can only assume that the idea in retaining all the old magical materials is that their presence in the charm-box, before which the body rituals are conducted, will in some way protect the worshipper.

Beneath the charm-box is a small font. Each day every member of the family, in succession, enters the shrine room, bows his head before the charm-box, mingles different sorts of holy water in the font, and proceeds with a brief rite of ablution. The holy waters are secured from the Water Temple of the community, where the priests conduct elaborate ceremonies to make the liquid ritually pure.

In the hierarchy of magical practitioners, and below the medicine men in prestige, are specialists whose designation is best translated "holy-mouth-men." The Nacirema have an almost pathological horror and fascination with the mouth, the condition of which is believed to have a supernatural influence on all social relationships. Were it not for the rituals of the mouth, they believe that their teeth would fall out, their gums bleed, their jaws shrink, their friends desert them, and their lovers reject them. (They also believe that a strong relationship exists between oral and moral characteristics. For example, there is a ritual ablution of the mouth for children which is supposed to improve their moral fiber.)

The daily body ritual performed by everyone includes a mouth-rite. Despite the fact that these people are so punctilious about care of the mouth, this rite involves a practice which strikes the uninitiated stranger as revolting. It was reported to me that the ritual consists of inserting a small bundle of hog hairs into the mouth, along with certain magical powders, and then moving the bundle in a highly formalized series of gestures.

In addition to the private mouth-rite, the people seek out a holy-mouth-man once or twice a year. These practitioners have an impressive set of paraphernalia, consisting of a variety of augers, awls, probes, and prods. The use of these objects in the exorcism of the evils of the mouth involves almost unbelievable ritual torture of the client. The holy-mouth-man opens the client's mouth and, using the above-mentioned tools, enlarges any holes which decay may have created in the teeth. Magical materials are put into these holes. If there are no naturally occurring holes in the teeth, large sections of one or more teeth are gouged out so that the supernatural substance can be applied. In the client's view, the purpose of these ministrations is to arrest decay and to draw friends. The extremely sacred and traditional character of the rite is evident in the fact that the natives return to the holy-mouth men year after year, despite the fact that their teeth continue to decay.

It is to be hoped that, when a thorough study of the Nacirema is made, there will be a careful inquiry into the personality structure of these people. One has but to watch the gleam in the eye of a holy-mouth-man, as he jabs an awl into an exposed nerve, to suspect that a certain amount of sadism is involved. If this can be established, a very interesting pattern emerges, for most of the population shows definite masochistic tendencies. It was to these that Professor Linton referred in discussing a distinctive part of the daily body ritual which is performed only by men. This part of the rite involves scraping and lacerating the surface of the face with a sharp instrument. Special women's rites are performed only four times during each lunar month, but what they lack in frequency is made up in barbarity. As part of this ceremony, women bake their heads in small ovens for about an hour. The theoretically interesting point is that what seems to be a preponderantly masochistic people have developed sadistic specialists.

The medicine men have an imposing temple, or *latipso,* in every community of any size. The more elaborate ceremonies required to treat very sick patients can only be performed at this temple. These ceremonies involve not only the thaumaturge but a permanent group of vestal maidens who move sedately about the temple chambers in distinctive costume and headdress.

The *latipso* ceremonies are so harsh that it is phenomenal that a fair proportion of the really sick natives who enter the temple ever recover. Small children whose indoctrination is still incomplete have been known to resist attempts to take them to the temple because "that is where you go to die." Despite this fact, sick adults are not only willing but eager to undergo the protracted ritual purification, if they can afford to do so. No matter how ill the supplicant or how grave the emergency, the guardians of many temples will not admit a client if he cannot give a rich gift to the custodian. Even after one has gained admission and survived the ceremonies, the guardians will not permit the neophyte to leave until he makes still another gift.

The supplicant entering the temple is first stripped of all his or her clothes. In every-day life the Nacirema avoids exposure of his body and its natural functions. Bathing and excretory acts are performed only in the secrecy of the household shrine, where they are ritualized as part of the body-rites. Psychological shock results from the fact that body secrecy is suddenly lost upon entry into the *latipso.* A man, whose own wife has never seen him in an excretory act, suddenly finds himself naked and assisted by a vestal maiden while he performs his natural functions into a sacred vessel. This sort of ceremonial treatment is necessitated by the fact that the excreta are used by a diviner to ascertain the course and nature of the client's sickness. Female clients, on the other hand, find their naked bodies are subjected to the scrutiny, manipulation, and prodding of the medicine men.

Few supplicants in the temple are well enough to do anything but lie on their hard beds. The daily ceremonies, like the rites of the holy-mouth-men, involve discomfort and torture. With ritual precision, the vestals awaken their miserable charges each dawn and roll them about on their beds of pain while performing ablutions, in the formal movements of which the maidens are highly trained. At other times they insert magic wands in the supplicant's mouth or force him to eat substances which are supposed to be healing. From time to time the medicine men come to their clients and jab magically treated needles into their flesh. The fact that these temple ceremonies may not cure, and may even kill the neophyte, in no way decreases the people's faith in the medicine men.

There remains one other kind of practitioner, known as a "listener." This witch-doctor has the power to exorcise the devils that lodge in the heads of people who have been bewitched. The Nacirema believe that parents bewitch their own children. Mothers are particularly suspected of putting a curse on children while teaching them the secret body rituals. The counter-magic of the witch-doctor is unusual in its lack of ritual. The patient simply tells the "listener" all his troubles and fears, beginning with the earliest difficulties he can remember. The memory displayed by the Nacirema in these exorcism sessions is truly remarkable. It is not uncommon for the patient to bemoan the rejection he felt upon being weaned as a babe, and a few individuals even see their troubles going back to the traumatic effects of their own birth.

In conclusion, mention must be made of certain practices which have their base in native esthetics but which depend upon the pervasive aversion to the natural body and its functions. There are ritual fasts to make fat people thin and ceremonial feasts to make thin people fat. Still other rites are used to make women's breasts large if they are small, and smaller if they are large. General dissatisfaction with breast shape is symbolized in the fact that the ideal form is virtually outside the range of human variation. A few women afflicted with almost inhuman hyper-mammary development are so idolized that they make a handsome living by simply going from village to village and permitting the natives to stare at them for a fee.

Reference has already been made to the fact that excretory functions are ritualized, routinized, and relegated to secrecy. Natural reproductive functions are similarly distorted. Intercourse is taboo as a topic and scheduled as an act. Efforts are made to avoid pregnancy by the use of magical materials or by limiting intercourse to certain phases of the moon. Conception is actually very infrequent. When pregnant, women dress so as to hide their condition. Parturition takes place in secret, without friends or relatives to assist, and the majority of women do not nurse their infants.

Our review of the ritual life of the Nacirema has certainly shown them to be a magic-ridden people. It is hard to understand how they have managed to exist so long under the burdens which they have imposed upon themselves. But even such exotic customs as these take on real meaning when they are viewed with the insight provided by Malinowski when he wrote (1948:70):

> Looking from far and above, from our high places of safety in the developed civilization, it is easy to see all the crudity and irrelevance of magic. But without its power and guidance early man could not have mastered his practical difficulties as he has done, nor could man have advanced to the higher stages of civilization.

READING 2

In this well-written essay, Dr. Hills put forth a very persuasive argument for the relativity of deviance. In contrast to the absolutist who views deviance as something "inherently . . . self-evidently, immoral, evil, and abnormal," the relativist looks toward the reaction to similar sorts of behaviors and asks what makes one behavior deviant and the other normal or even socially desirable. Why, for example, is a glass of wine at dinner perfectly acceptable, normal, and even "glamorous," but a slug of MD 20/20 or Thunderbird (fortified wines) taken on a sidewalk in the early morning may be viewed with contempt? Thus, the strict relativist argues that "deviance, then is simply human behavior, beliefs, or attributes that elicit social condemnation by others in particular social situations." Hill's examples may seem dated, but similar examples abound today. One might not question a tattoo or two, but is a full-body tattoo "normal and okay" to a parent or employer? What makes the act deviant to the relativist is the social reaction it creates. One of the authors of this book was in a bar recently, and the bartender had a unique haircut dyed several different shades, multiple tattoos, and piercings. In a completely unsolicited comment, she remarked that it was getting more and more difficult to get a reaction to her appearance. The goal, it would seem, was to "be deviant." Given the time in which he was writing (the 1970s), as one might expect, most of Hills's examples of absolutists' views are fairly "conservative." The eager antiestablishment relativist should question his or her own assumptions carefully: Is not the pure-vegan, fur-painting activist also an absolutist? Are there some behaviors, attitudes, and beliefs that we generally feel compelled to react to individually or as a society? The strict relativist offers much to the sociological imagination, but perhaps there is a compromise.

The Mystification of Social Deviance

Stuart L. Hills

Who in contemporary America is more deviant: a 19-year-old Boy Scout or a student at an Ivy League university who smokes pot? A 29-year-old unmarried virgin or a militant women's liberationist? A New York City legislator who tries to ban the film *Last Tango in Paris* as "evil, obscene, and pornographic" or a rural minister who condemns *The Grapes of Wrath,* assigned as reading in a high school English class, as "the work of the devil"? A Wall Street stockbroker who dabbles in the occult or a middle-class suburban housewife who worships a 15-year-old oriental guru? A Harlem janitor who plays the numbers game at the corner candy store or the Baptist who censures her atheist neighbors as sinful for their Saturday night poker games? A Mississippi man who swears he has boarded a spaceship filled with strange creatures from another planet or the members of a mystic cult in New Jersey who flee to a mountaintop to await the imminent end of the world? A General Electric vice-president who conspires with other corporate officials to fix prices or an executive who refuses to do so? A San Francisco college girl who enjoys oral-genital sex with her boyfriend or her roommate who contends that such behavior is disgusting and abnormal? A man who

Source: Hills, Stuart L. 1977. "The Mystification of Social Deviance." *Crime & Delinquency* 23:417–426. Reprinted with permission of SAGE Publications, Inc.

burglarizes a psychiatrist's office in the name of national security or a Catholic priest who spills blood over draft files to protest pilots' "roasting babies alive" by bombing Vietnamese villages?

Most readers would have difficulty in answering these questions with assurance. Nevertheless, many groups and individuals, including some scientists and psychiatrists, define deviance as departure from an absolute set of values. Only a minority of persons view deviance as man-made, shifting, and frequently ambiguous.

◈ Absolutist and Relativist Views

In both the popular and scientific histories of social deviance, two basic ways of looking at the subject stand out: the *relativist* and the *absolutist*. Each of these views pervades the vast writings on social deviance, influencing the definition of deviance, research topics, assumptions as to the causes of deviance and characteristics of deviants, interpretation of research findings and current events, and policies of social control.[1]

The *absolutist* perspective is shared by the largest and most influential segments of the public. According to this view, fundamental human behavior may be classified as *inherently* proper or, conversely, self-evidently immoral, evil, and abnormal. The absolutist believes that most persons agree on the basic goals that people should pursue; he believes in a fundamental harmony of values and a general social good that transcends the mundane interests of individuals and groups in society.

The *relativist* position, held in some manner by many contemporary sociologists, sharply challenges this view. Relativists view complex societies as dynamic, a mosaic of groups with different values and interests who sometimes agree and cooperate on some issues but frequently conflict and struggle to realize their own interests and ends. Deviance is seen as being in large measure a matter of human evaluation and differential power. Thus the nature of deviance will vary significantly among different groups and subcultures within a society as well as between societies. As J. L. Simmons observes, an astonishing variety of human actions and characteristics have been considered deviant:

> If we went back through history and assembled together all of the people who have been condemned by their contemporaries, the range [would include] the Plains Indian youth who was unable to see visions, the big-breasted Chinese girl, the early Christian skulking in the Roman catacombs, the Arab who liked alcohol instead of hashish, the Polynesian girl who didn't enjoy sex, and the medieval man who indulged himself by bathing frequently.[2]

For relativists, deviance is not inherently "unnatural" nor is it intrinsic to any particular act, belief, or human attribute. Instead, deviance is socially *created* by collective human judgments. Deviance, like beauty, lies largely in the eyes of the beholder and is relative to particular social standards and particular social settings. As Thomas Szasz points out, it is not by their behavior but by the traditional sexual double standard that men are labeled "virile" and women "nymphomaniacs." If a person appears to be talking to God while kneeling at an altar, he is thought to be praying; however, if he insists that God has been talking to him, he is described as schizophrenic and we try to "cure" him of his "mental illness."[3] Similarly, the concrete act of injecting heroin into a vein is not inherently deviant. It is obviously acceptable for a doctor to inject a narcotic drug into a patient. Only when the drug is administered in a manner publicly forbidden does this action become

---

[1]The use of the terms *relativist* and *absolutist* draws upon the fine discussion of these two perspectives in Jock Young, *The Drugtakers* (London: Paladin, 1971), ch. 3; and Erich Goode, *The Drug Phenomenon: Social Aspects of Drug Taking* (Indianapolis: Bobbs-Merrill, 1973), pp. 26–37.

[2]J. L. Simmons, *Deviants* (Berkeley, Calif.: Glendessary, 1969), p. 4.

[3]Thomas Szasz, *The Second Sin* (Garden City, N.Y.: Doubleday, 1973), pp. 101, 112–13.

deviant. The deviant nature of the act depends upon the way it is defined in the public mind. Thus, under one conception of deviance, a person may continue to live as an ordinary citizen; under another, he may be treated as a criminal.

Further, the degree of harm or danger of specific acts to the welfare of others is not, according to the relativist, necessarily a decisive factor in the application of a stigmatizing label or in the severity of punishment. Is the husband who violently rapes his resisting, estranged wife in their home less dangerous than the 26-year-old Kentucky mountaineer jailed in Chicago on statutory rape charges for having consensual sexual intercourse with a 16-year-old girl? In the former case, the police may refuse to take any action (the courts have a long-standing aversion to public interference in family disputes). In the latter, the man's justification that "she was willing" and that back home "if they're big enough they're old enough" is no legal defense. In another instance, the operators of a coal company whose evasion of the federal mine-safety laws was partly responsible for the deaths of 78 coal miners in an explosion were merely admonished by the federal mine inspectors to begin complying with the law. But a 21-year-old Massachusetts Institute of Technology senior was sentenced in a Boston courtroom to five years in prison for the sale of marijuana to his college friends. Former Vice-President Spiro Agnew, charged with extorting thousands of dollars in kickbacks from building contractors seeking preferential treatment, "copped a plea" and convicted only of income tax evasion and given a three-year informal probation. George Jackson, black and 18 years old, was sentenced to prison for from one year to life for stealing $70 from a gas station. Szasz makes the point nicely:

> Policemen receive bribes; politicians receive campaign contributions. Marijuana and heroin are sold by pushers; cigarettes and alcohol are sold by businessmen. Mental patients

who use the courts to regain their liberty are troublemakers; psychiatrists who use the courts to deprive patients of their liberty are therapists.[4]

Deviance, then, is simply human behavior, beliefs, or attributes that elicit social condemnation by others in particular social situations. Kai Erikson succinctly expresses this relativist view: "Deviance is not a property *inherent* in certain forms of behavior; it is a property *conferred upon* these forms by the audiences which directly or indirectly witness them."[5]

◈ Deviance and Power

Not all views of deviance gain an equal public hearing or have an equal social impact on those persons considered deviant. Those groups dominating the key positions in our major institutions in the community and in society as a whole—the mass media, legislatures, government agencies, schools, corporations, military, crime control agencies, and so forth—are best situated to disseminate information and make far-reaching policy decisions. These "social audiences" have effectively legitimated their versions of morality and immorality in the community or larger society and are supported by the law in their conceptions of wrongdoing. Repressive measures are potentially applicable (though selectively administered) to all those individuals and groups whose activity or existence threatens the dominant, controlling views of deviance. To challenge openly certain social norms is to risk becoming an outsider, a deviant who is "in" but not "of" the community. For example, in many small communities the outspoken atheist becomes an outsider—a heretic. The drug user or the homosexual may view others with disdain, but each risks arrest, imprisonment, public disgrace, and economic discrimination.

The sense of alienation and estrangement from the larger community that many deviants experience is

---

[4]*Id.,* p. 25.

[5]Kai Erikson, "Notes on the Sociology of Deviance," in Howard S. Becker, ed., *The Other Side* (New York: Free Press, 1964), p. 11.

caused not only by the threat of arrest and retribution from official agencies but more fundamentally by the day-to-day indignities—the insults, the stares, the frowns, the jokes, "the shushed conversations which engender the sense that you are a stranger in a strange land."[6] A young black with a white girl friend in a small midwestern town vividly describes this sense of isolation:

> When this white chick and I first started making it I felt like I'd been plunked down in the middle of Russia, like I was a spy. . . . After we were sleeping together I hated to show up for work even, and I finally quit. I had this feeling that everybody was looking. And there was no place for us to go.[7]

◈ The Pathology of Diversity and Dissent

For the absolutist, deviant activity is not merely an alternative, perhaps valuable way of functioning in society. There is no provision for multiple conceptions of social reality, no allowance that some groups might legitimately find the conventional demands for conformity oppressive, unfulfilling, often dehumanizing. The possibility that alternative life styles might be personally meaningful is almost inconceivable. Instead, the refusal by some persons to embrace the Puritan work ethic or the nuclear family, to defer gratification until the "proper occasions," or to repress bisexual or "promiscuous" sexual feelings is automatically undesirable. For many citizens, such departures from conventional expectations may trigger strong feelings of anger. One sociologist tells of his conversation with a British woman about the attempt by some hippies to occupy a deserted building in downtown London. In response to his question of why she found this rather harmless activity so disgusting and upsetting,

she replied in an angry tone: "It's shocking and shameful, wasting their lives like that. They should be taken and whipped with the rod."[8]

Clearly, in the view of the absolutist, deviancy is not something in which a healthy, well-adjusted person would engage but is, rather, a malfunction, comparable to malignant cells in an organism, to be eliminated, treated, or contained. The source of this pathological condition may be located in the individual's own make-up or in the social environment, and the condition itself may be described in genetic terms, as mental illness, maladjustment, undersocialization, social disorganization, and so on. Whatever the mode of explanation, the absolutist sees as valid only the conventional norms and values and customary ways of behavior. These become synonymous with *reality,* and forms of deviance are diseases in the body of society.

Deviancy is explained by the absolutist as a product of either *internal coercion*—enslavement to inner compulsions, a weak ego, a pathological or dependent personality, inadequate socialization, an unharnessed libido—or *external constraint,* the corruption of the innocent and immature by other disturbed persons (e.g., drug users seduced by the syndicate drug pusher). Free choice and preference thus become illusory freedoms. To depart from the norm is to exhibit some form of disturbance.

Thus, drug use may not be simply pleasurable activity but must necessarily reflect a deep-seated personality flaw. Indulgence in illegal mood-altering substances is prima facie evidence of an "abnormal" or "inadequate" personality, an "escape from reality," a "rebellion against authority," a deep-seated dread of intimacy," a "defective supergo," and so on. In 1970, Dr. Robert Baird testified at a government crime committee hearing:

> Anyone who smokes marijuana . . . already has a mental problem. They are taking it to escape reality, to get high. . . . I do not care

---

[6]Simmons, *op. cit. supra* note 2, p. 73.

[7]*Id.,* pp. 73–74.

[8]Robert A. Scott, "A Proposed Framework for Analyzing Deviance as a Property of Social Order," in Robert A. Scott and Jack D. Douglas, eds., *Theoretical Perspectives on Deviance* (New York: Basic Books, 1972), p. 16.

what euphemism you want to employ, they are mentally ill.[9]

As Erich Goode points out, in order for the absolutist to discredit the deviant activity effectively, the alleged pleasures of the condemned act must be seen as inauthentic or as dangerous and insidious. The state of euphoria experienced by some drug users becomes defined by one writer as "an artificial, exaggerated sense of pleasure and well-being." The contention that marijuana is fun is countered by the specter of a greased path to more evil kinds of pleasure.

> If . . . the main reason for smoking pot is pure fun, does it not follow that sniffing, then injecting, heroin might be the most fun of all? After experiencing the much-touted delights of marijuana, wouldn't a person, at the very least, be tempted to try the greater glories of the big H? It seems likely.[10]

In Russia, political liberals who openly criticize the ruling regime have been declared "mentally ill" and are incarcerated for their treasonous views. And the use of such pathological labels is not restricted to political dissent. Many government officials are concerned about the increasingly casual attitude toward premarital sex among Russian teen-agers, who view it as a "physical necessity" rather than an expression of "true love." One Soviet scholar comments on the pathology of passionate sex outside the sanctified context of love and marriage:

> Any fashion in love with a light-hearted attitude toward sexual intercourse, female promiscuity or a male insolence, I consider pathological. A psychologically and physically

healthy person would never let passion into this sacred sanctum of life.[11]

◈ Moral Indignation

The vehemence with which citizens have deplored deviant values, such as the hippie values of sexual expressiveness and spontaneity, may thinly disguise their own unfulfilled desires and fantasies, their own nagging doubts about the adequacy of their lives. Deviant impulses such as these—in themselves and in others—must be vigorously suppressed. As Philip Slater observes, "The peculiarly exaggerated hostility that hippies tend to arouse suggests that the life they strive for is highly seductive to middle-class Americans."[12] Thus, the basis for moral indignation is frequently the dual fascination and repulsion that often coexist in the minds of those who would fervently condemn moral transgressions from the dominant social norms.

As many observers have noted, significant segments of the conforming public are to some degree ambivalent about illicit and unconventional pleasures. Their feelings are bound up in a complex tangle of conflicting values, desires, fears, fantasies, and guilt. These ambivalent conformists who defer gratification, who at considerable psychic cost deny or inhibit impulses toward forbidden pleasures (such as escape, spontaneity, adventure, uninhibited sex, disdain for work, physical aggression, excitement, autonomy, etc.), thus often react with righteous hostility toward persons who appear to flout the officially sanctioned moral codes and rules. Deviants are frequently viewed as unjustly rewarded, irresponsible persons who have not earned their pleasures through productive, legitimate work and by compliance with social rules. Especially where the "victimless" deviant act (e.g., illicit sex, psychedelic drugs, gambling, pornography) does not appear to threaten directly the life, possessions,

---

[9]Quoted in Goode, *op. cit. supra* note 1, p. 3.

[10]Both quotations cited in Goode, *op. cit. supra* note 1, p. 34.

[11]*New York Times,* Nov. 24, 1973, p. 8.

[12]Philip Slater, *The Pursuit of Loneliness* (Boston: Beason, 1970), p. 7.

or immediate welfare of conventional citizens, the out-pouring of moral indignation may be triggered by the suspicion that the wicked are undeservedly realizing the pleasures and rewards secretly desired by the virtuous. Richard Blum nicely describes this fascination-repulsion relationship in regard to illicit drugs:

> Pharmaceutical materials do not dispense themselves and the illicit drugs are rarely given away, let alone forced on people. Consequently, the menace lies within the person, for there would be no drug threat without a drug attraction. Psychoanalytic observations on alcoholics suggest the presence of simultaneous repulsion and attraction in compulsive ingestion. The amount of public interest in stories about druggies suggests the same drug attraction and repulsion in ordinary citizens. "Fascination" is the better term since it implies witchcraft and enchantment. People are fascinated by drugs—because they are attracted to the states and conditions drugs are said to produce. That is another side to the fear of being disrupted; it is the desire for release, for escape, for magic, and for ecstatic joys. That is the derivation of the menace in drugs—their representation as keys to forbidden kingdoms inside ourselves. The dreadful in the drug is the *dreadful* in ourselves.[13]

Moreover, it is this very ambivalence that the mass media exploits, first titillating the public's sensibilities and then reassuring its prejudices and upholding the public morality by condemnation and symbolic punishment of the deviant. Television, movies, and the tabloids use these distant and misperceived deviant outsiders as a kind of lurid projection screen—as scapegoats through which the collective fears, frustrations, and forbidden impulses of the conforming public are vicariously expressed and perhaps to a degree partly neutralized. By portraying deviants as immoral persons invariably coming to a bad end, as "innocents" who have been corrupted by the wicked but who may be "saved," as "sick" persons in need of "treatment," or as persons whose actions are basically meaningless or contain their own built-in horrors (LSD leads to madness, illicit sex to venereal disease, homosexuality to neurosis), the mass media thus reinforce, legitimate, and partly create the images and myths of a basically consensual and just society.[14]

◈ The Noble Lie

From the perspective of the dominant groups, socialization is considered successful in a society when its members come to accept the "noble lie" that the limited range of options available in the dominant culture are the only real, proper, and natural ways of acting, thinking, and feeling and that they constitute the full extent of human freedom. Part of this process involves instilling in neophyte members the belief that the traditional social rules and institutionalized social practices are inevitable and binding. To depart from these culturally approved moral paths is to court danger and disaster.

Such reality-constricting propaganda and social control tend to alienate a person from the many potential selves and life styles possible, from what he might become were he more aware of the arbitrariness and narrowness inherent in the conventional social rules and behavior roles and were he accorded a wider range of options.[15] During the last decade, hippie countercultures, gay and women's liberation movements, organizations such as the Committee for a Sane Drug Policy, and other activist groups have emerged to challenge the traditional and conventional social order, offering alternative ways to be human and liberated.

---

[13]Richard H. Blum and Associates, *Society and Drugs*, Vol. 1 (San Francisco: Jossey-Bass, 1969), p. 335.

[14]Jock Young, "The Myth of the Drug Taker in the Mass Media," in Stanley Cohen and Jock Young, eds., *The Manufacture of News* (Beverly Hills, Calif,: Sage, 1973), pp. 314–22.

[15]Erich Goode, *Drugs in American Society* (New York: Knopf, 1972), p. 232.

◈ Enemy Deviants

Such challenges clearly pose an effective threat to the notions of the dominant group. These activists are neither repentant nor ill, and they defend their behavior as morally legitimate, openly contesting the dominance of the moral codes embodied in the criminal law or in the official political and economic policies of the society. The Black Panthers, the Chicago Seven, the American Indian Movement, Aleksandr Solzhenitzyn, the South African novelist who depicted the tabooed black-white racial love affairs and provoked an official ban of his books, Allen Ginsberg—all are cast in the role of *enemy deviants* threatening the legitimacy of the dominant social order.

Whether it be an attempt by hippies to smoke marijuana openly by staging a "puff-in" at the Hall of Justice in San Francisco and demanding legalization of the drug, a raid on a Maryland draft board by militant priests and nuns who spill blood on selective service files, a parade of homosexuals down Fifth Avenue chanting "gay is good," or an open defiance of local "committees for decency" by theater owners showing films such as *Deep Throat,* a direct clash in moralities is precipitated. Challenges such as these expose the precarious nature of the absolutist conception of social reality. Consequently, various strategies come into play to discredit these competing views. These strategies typically take on an aura of *mystification:* by obscuring the fact that both deviant and normal activities are basically arbitrary, the dominant group masks the underlying conflict of interests and mainsprings of power.

◈ The Cooptation of Scientists

Increasingly in modern Western societies, scientists are contributing—sometimes unwittingly—to these ideological struggles. Interest groups use scientific research and data as moral armaments to bolster their contentions; in so doing they mystify human behavior by imputing an inexorability and inevitability to man-made social creations. In effect, scientists and their ostensibly impartial research are used to make establishment rules and their enforcement appear rational, humane, and just. All other views must be seen in error. Persons who challenge the conventional rules must be discredited as individual wrongdoers (as sick, pathological, or criminal), not accepted as willful, normal participants involved in legitimate political conflict and viable social movements.

As Goode reminds us, during an earlier period this "mystification process was religious in character; views in competition with the dominant one were heretical and displeasing to the gods—hence, Galileo's 'crime.'" Today, however, "nothing has greater discrediting power . . . than the demonstration that a given assertion has been 'scientifically disproven.'"[16] Scientists, Goode notes, have become our contemporary "pawnbrokers of reality" (and, I would add, psychiatrists our arbiters of normality), operating under a value-free cloak of objectivity that Western civilization assigns to this prestigious enterprise. Dominant interest groups thus mobilize psychologists, physicians, pharmacologists, criminologists, psychiatrists, and other highly regarded "experts" operating under the scientific banner to render unconventional behavior meaningless, harmful, and unnatural. If such authorities certify behavior as pathological or dangerous, the labels become potent rhetorical weapons of social control. These controls are effectively disguised in reasonable, humanitarian garb—restriction of certain kinds of behavior is morally desirable and scientifically correct, good for both the individual and the society.

In every complex society there are what Howard Becker calls "*hierarchies of credibility,*" by which some prestigious and respectable persons have greater power than others to define what is true and false, what is proper and improper, what is normal and abnormal, what is safe and dangerous.[17] Such prestigious

---

[16]Erich Goode, *The Marijuana Smokers* (New York: Basic Books, 1970), pp. 52–53.

[17]Howard S. Becker, "Whose Side Are We On?" *Social Problems,* Winter 1967, pp. 239–47.

organizations as the American Medical Association, the Federal Bureau of Narcotics, the American Psychiatric Association, the Federal Bureau of Investigation, the National Institute of Mental Health, and the American Bar Association and their bureaucratic officials help filter out scientific findings that do not conform to official prevailing views. In 1971, Dr. Wesley Hall, newly elected president of the AMA, was quoted in a widely publicized UPI news story as saying that an AMA study left "very little doubt" that marijuana would cause a significant reduction in a person's sex drive (observing that a 35-year-old man might have his sex drive reduced to that of a 70-year-old man). He also implied that certain scientific evidence demonstrated that this illicit drug caused birth defects. In an interview several weeks later, Dr. Hall said he had been misquoted but added that he didn't mind:

> I don't mind ... if this can do some good in waking people up to the fact that, by jingo, whether we like to face it or not, our campuses are going to pot, both literally and figuratively.... If we don't wake up in this country to the fact that every college campus and high school has a problem with drug addiction, we're going down the drain not only with respect to morality, but ... the type of system we're going to have.[18]

When confronted by the comment that such misleading statements might damage the credibility of the AMA, Dr. Hall answered, "I'm tired of these phrases about the credibility gap. *We're talking about the morality of the country ... and respect for authority and decency.*"[19] Dr. Hall not only disapproves of marijuana but also exploits such drug use as a vehicle for expression of his own ideological views toward other kinds of activities and attitudes that he deplores. But in view of the AMA's prestige and power, such selective and distorted use of empirical evidence is not likely to impair its credibility significantly in future pronouncements on the dangers of illicit drug use.

Research and writing on deviance are replete with such value-laden language as "social maladjustment," "sexual promiscuity," "inadequate personality," "hedonism," "perversion," "escape from reality," "artificial euphoria," "abnormality," "social irresponsibility," and "underachievement"—terms and expressions which, used under the pretext of unbiased, scientific objectivity, serve to further mystify the nature of deviance. And such mystification is not without its powerful effects on the deviant himself. The responses of others to persons stigmatized as deviant may affect the deviant's world in such self-fulfilling ways as to substantiate the validity of popular and scientific views. Thus some deviants also may come unwittingly to embrace, internalize, and act out the stereotypical conceptions. Heroin addicts or persons diagnosed as mentally ill and incarcerated for therapeutic reasons may come to see themselves in the absolutist's terms—as dependent, inadequate, psychotic, asocial, or demoralized. Some homosexuals echo the imagery pervading their community and come to hate themselves as unworthy, dirty "queers." Some heavy drinkers may come to embrace the stigmatizing label of alcoholic, thereby excusing their own and others' failures. As Jock Young has argued, such mystifications may function to amputate a significant portion of a person's human potentiality, severely limiting his capacity to conceive of radically alternative social arrangements and forms of human consciousness—the ability to create, to choose his action rather than be propelled and imprisoned by current social structures and circumstances.[20] Perhaps herein lies the real tragedy of the mystification of deviance.

[18]Quoted in Goode, *op. cit. supra* note 15, p. 15.

[19]*Id.,* p. 16.

[20]Young, *op. cit. supra* note 1, p. 68.

READING 3

In this important article, Short and Meier document historical changes in theoretical efforts to explain quite different aspects of crime and deviance. Prior to the 1950s, they argue, traditional theorists were interested in what distinguished deviants and criminals from conventional citizens. That is, the focus was on the distribution and etiology of deviant behavior. In the 1950s, researchers and theorists were "more interested in exploring the meaning and nature of deviant acts." What structural and/or cultural factors are conducive to different forms of deviance became the dominant question in the study of deviance and crime. Continuing on, the 1960s saw another shift in focus from the causes or explanations of deviance to the study of the reactions to deviance—the study of rulemaking and rule breaking. In some ways and for a variety of reasons, the next decade brought us back, to some extent, to the traditional theories and researchers interested in what distinguished deviants from nondeviants, be it social class, race, gender, IQ, or a host of other personality and social factors. Following this historical account, the authors direct us to think about three different levels of explanation and how they might interact. The first is the micro level that emphasizes individual characteristics as identified by biological, psychological, and social psychological sciences. The second level of explanation is macrosociological, which focuses on culture and social systems (e.g., capitalism and patriarchy). And finally, the microsociological level is concerned with interaction patterns between individuals and groups and how they shape deviant behavior. The authors conclude that while efforts to reconcile and integrate these perspectives have been made, the theory of crime and deviance is still fairly remedial, but there is hope in that there is more common ground than differences among students of crime and deviant behavior.

Criminology and the Study of Deviance

James F. Short, Jr., and Robert F. Meier

 ## The Shift in Theoretical Focus

Scholars prior to 1950 concentrated their efforts on characteristics of criminals—and other deviants—to see on what bases these persons differed from noncriminals. Theories of crime were presumed to account not only for individual differences (etiology) but also the distribution of these differences at the group level in time and space (epidemiology). As such, the leading theoretical perspectives, and the accompanying empirical research designed to evaluate these theories, emphasized social characteristics on which criminals and noncriminals could be differentiated. Play group activities (Thrasher), the absence of effective community controls and the learning of "criminal traditions" (Shaw and McKay), and the acquisition of criminal norms (Sutherland) constituted the leading answers to the question "why do they do it?" From detecting such differences, it was only a short conceptual (but

Source: Short, James F., Jr., and Robert F. Meier. 1981. "Criminology and the Study of Deviance." *American Behavioral Scientist* 24:462–478. Reprinted with permission.

long logical) step to infer "causation" to answer fully etiological questions.

The theorizing in the 1950s reflects a subtle, but discernible shift from earlier concerns. Beginning with the work of Sutherland (1949), and continuing through the work of Cohen (1955), Bloch and Neiderhoffer (1958), Miller (1958), and Cloward and Ohlin (1960), there was less interest in identifying factors that would differentiate deviants from nondeviants and more interest in exploring the meaning and nature of deviant acts. Sutherland's attempt to reform criminological theory by conceptualizing and researching white-collar crime focused on violations previously ignored by social scientists, giving rise to debate which continues to this day concerning whether white-collar violations are "really crimes." Cohen's theory, the subtitle notwithstanding, is not a theory of delinquency, but of the conditions under which delinquent norms arise. As such, deviant acts came to be seen as behavior that conformed not to conventional norms but deviant norms, a theme that is evident in Sutherland's earlier work as well. Another important issue concerned the location of deviant norms in social space. (Sutherland found them in the corporate world; Cohen identifies them in the problems facing lower-class boys forcing a collective solution; Miller's analysis located them in lower-class culture generally; Bloch and Niederhoffer focused on cleavages in the age-generation structure; Matza in subterranean values of conventional society; and Cloward and Ohlin find them arising from specific neighborhood conditions.) Studies of delinquent subcultures and delinquent gangs (Cloward and Ohlin appear to confuse the two) helped affirm the importance of conventional and deviant norms by illustrating the ambiguity of distinguishing between the two in specific situations. Empirical studies exploring group dynamics within delinquent gangs found the locus of delinquency in the interaction of members of groups with one another and with others in the neighborhood and larger community. These studies indicated, contrary to suggestions in cultural deviance theories, that delinquent behavior resulted only indirectly from normative compliance. Rather, group norms guided the choice of status-rewarding behaviors, and these, in turn, involved boys in the interactions which often produced delinquent outcomes. Behavioral outcomes thus involve the micro- as well as the macrosociological level of explanation (Cohen and Short, 1976).

While the origins of, and conformity to, deviant norms continued to occupy sociologists through the 1960s, another current began to take hold. It became obvious that studies of the origins of deviant norms were only a subclass of the study of the origin of all norms. The study of rule-making and rule-enforcement was the major focus of interactionist and labelling theorists. The emphasis in this view centered around the creation of the rules which, in turn, were the necessary but not sufficient conditions for rule breaking, and the process by which an individual "becomes" deviant in interaction with social control agents.

It was within these views that the nature and meaning of research on deviance and crime changed. Since "deviance" was not a quality of persons, but of rules and their enforcement, research was needed to explicate how these rules came about and the consequences of rule enforcement. Deviant behavior was class-specific behavior (as it was interpreted during the 1950s), but this was now explained in a different way: There are not more rule breakers in the lower classes, merely more rule enforcement. Official statistics did not measure "deviants," but the actions of the police not criminals (Kitsuse and Cicourel, 1963); and, mental hospital admissions measured less the behavior of patients than that of psychiatrists (Scheff, 1966).

A common confusion in this literature equates a reactivist or labelling definition of deviance with what is commonly called the interactionist perspective. The labelling view presents a conception of deviance that defines it in terms of negative reactions; deviance is conduct that is negatively reacted to, usually via a sanction (Becker, 1973). Interactionist theory, on the other hand, is a body of literature that seeks to *explain patterns* of deviance as a consequence of social control efforts (Lemert, 1972). Some interactionist theorists define deviance as a violation of a norm (e.g., Lemert, 1951; Scheff, 1966), rejecting a labelling definition. The now frequent observation that the labelling conception is not a theory is correct, but like all definitions of this sort, the labelling conception is neither right nor wrong, only more or less useful. The interactionist perspective (particularly the "theory" of secondary deviation) has been the subject of a number of empirical tests dealing with a broad range of deviant activities (e.g., Gove, 1980). That research, in our view, seems to point to the conclusion that the consequences of sanction application—for example, through arrest, conviction, and imprisonment of criminals—are not precisely as predicted by most versions of interactionist thought; some persons may continue in deviance (to secondary deviation) at least partly as a result of applying sanctions, but others clearly do not. To date, little progress has been made in specifying the conditions under which one or the other outcome will occur.

While normativist conceptions of deviance (those that define deviance as the violation of a norm) often remark about the relativity of deviance (because norms are relative to different social groups), labelling and interactionist views made relativism a virtue; it helped explain the diversity of deviant conduct and the importance of rule-enforcement, as well as the differential occurrence of deviance in social time and space. The labelling conception made explicit the notion that deviance was relative not only to the social audience which applied negative reactions but also to those persons and groups in positions of power to make and enforce rules, such as laws. From the relativistic view comes the idea that people evaluate events, construct meanings for activities and sentiments, and generally define their social worlds differently (e.g., Douglas, 1970). Deviance as well as other "social problems" are only tenuously (Spector and Kitsuse, 1977), if at all (Mauss, 1975), tied to an objective social reality; they are reflections of alternative versions of reality. Not only are deviance and social problems relative but also they are social constructions not necessarily shared by others and without necessarily being tied to "real" conditions. As such, the predominant issue for study is how one version of social reality (e.g., what is considered a social problem) comes to be accepted.

Examples of work in this tradition include Becker's (1973) studies of the role of the Federal Bureau of Narcotics in creating a "new class of outsiders—marijuana users," and the role of more entrepreneurs generally in creating rules defining deviance; Gusfield's (1963) analysis of "Status Politics and the American Temperance Movement"; Duster's (1970) examination of "The Legislation of Morality" with respect to opiates; Chambliss's (1964) interpretation of historical records concerning the law of vagrancy in England; studies of interest groups promoting specific changes in laws relating, for example, to prostitution (Roby, 1969) and marijuana (Galliher et al., 1974); historical inquiries into "The Invention of Delinquency" (Platt, 1969); studies of the role of professional groups in defining and implementing deviance, for example, delinquency (Hagan and Lyon, 1977), and mental illness (Rothman, 1980); and, studies of the role of governments with respect to political deviance (Connor, 1972). In these works, not only solutions to social problems but also the problems themselves are constructed out of the social fabric, thereby suggesting that deviance, under certain circumstances, can be negotiated and otherwise socially "created."

In addition to giving rise to new theoretical viewpoints, the labelling conception of deviance also seemed to prompt a positivistic resurgence in the field. Critiques of labelling (Gibbs, 1966), ethnomethodology and phenomenology (Coser, 1975), and conflict perspectives (to be discussed presently) made strong demands for empirical evidence, long the cornerstone of positivistic sociology. When such tests were forthcoming, they were often equivocal. "Tests" of the conflict perspective, for example, generated renewed debates and often raised more questions than they answered (e.g., Chiricos and Waldo, 1975; Greenberg, 1977; Newman, 1976; McDonald, 1976). Critics and defenders of these perspectives disagreed as to the nature of "critical" tests, and even what might be considered relevant data. Some expressed the uneasy feeling that labelling conceptions of deviance might prove to be unfalsifiable (Gibbs and Erickson, 1975). Thus the major empirical and methodological advances of the postwar period were applied to questions posed prior to World War II, rather than to the new theoretical orientations. In principle, however, the importance of the latter was enhanced by studies that found "deviance" to be more widespread than previous indicators had suggested.

◈ Expansion of the Empirical Base

The research of Alfred Kinsey and his associates on sexual behavior documented what many had suspected all along, namely, that sexual behavior defined as deviant (e.g., premarital intercourse, intercourse with prostitutes, and homosexual behavior) were engaged in by higher proportions of the U.S. populations than simplistic notions of deviants as different-kinds-of-people could account for. That research documented the social distribution of such behavior and gave impetus to an enormous volume of studies of similar and other phenomena by sociologists (for a review of these studies, see Davis, 1976).

Sociologists had long been dissatisfied with the validity and the reliability of available data on crime, delinquency, and other forms of deviant behavior. They were active in support of efforts to secure more reliable and valid data on common crime (e.g., in an advisory capacity in establishing the FBI's Uniform Crime Reporting system) and in efforts to identify types of behavior inadequately conceptualized in law and reported to official agencies (e.g., white-collar crime). Early studies of "hidden delinquency" (Murphey ct al., 1946; Porterfield, 1946) had documented the fact that behavior for which youth might be apprehended, brought before the courts, and incarcerated was engaged in by many who never became involved with official agencies charged with juvenile and criminal justice responsibilities. It was not until the 1950s, however, that self-reported delinquency studies became common. These studies revealed both commonalities and differences with reports of official agencies. Studies conducted during the 1950s found delinquent behavior (adult crime has never been studied systematically by means of self-reports) to be virtually universal among populations studied. However,

greater frequency and serious involvement were found to characterize youngsters officially defined as delinquent, and males reported greater involvement than females, although the differences were smaller than were reflected in official statistics. Social class and racial differences were found to be smaller still. More recent research has studied more representative samples of adolescents and has employed a broader range of delinquencies than did the earlier work. Findings of this later work support some of the conclusions of the earlier work, but offer some methodological criticisms of that work as well. A study conducted by the Illinois Institute for Juvenile Research (1972) found that black boys reported more involvement in serious offenses of violence than did white boys, in some measure supporting official data in this respect. A smaller national sample in 1972 found few such differences, but some of the more serious violent offenses studied in Illinois were not included in the national sample (cf. Gold and Reimer, 1975). These kinds of findings point to the importance of recognizing the limitations of self-reports: They typically measure less serious delinquency while official statistics report more serious offenses. However, when the limitations of both official and self-reported delinquency are taken into account, it appears the each source presents consistent estimates of sex, race, and social class differentials in delinquent involvement (Hindelang et al., forthcoming). There is also evidence that many self-report studies have not been sensitive to measuring repetitive delinquency, which often consists of more serious offenses; when self-reports are designed with these problems in mind (i.e., obtaining estimates of a wide range of conduct, including serious and repetitive delinquency), both racial and class differences are detected, as in a recent national survey (Elliott and Ageton, 1980). Thus, the research that began in the 1950s concerning alternative estimates of crime than those contained in official estimates continues, in some ways challenging official estimates and in other ways supporting them.

The President's Commission on Law Enforcement and Administration of Justice (1967a, 1967b), this nation's most recent "crime commission," added still another component to the measurement of crime when it sponsored studies of criminal victimization (Ennis, 1967). These studies were continued in cooperation with the U.S. Bureau of Census (National Criminal Justice Information and Statistics Service, 1974, 1975, 1976; Hindelang, 1976). Concern over victims of crime has led to still other state and local studies. As a result, the data base for studying the extent and social distribution of crimes has been greatly extended. The fact that most common crime is committed by young males has permitted comparison of official data, self-reports, and victim reports (see Hindelang, 1978). Together with critical assessments of each methodology (e.g., Reiss, 1976), these have contributed to a greater appreciation of the complexity of even the simplest questions regarding the extent and nature of criminal and delinquent behavior.

The empirical base of sociological studies of delinquency and crime has been enhanced in recent years by a few longitudinal studies. Based chiefly on police contacts, these studies have focused primarily on descriptions of the involvement of cohorts of young people rather than on theory testing (see, e.g., Wolfgang et al., 1972; Center for Studies in Crime and Delinquency, 1974; Shannon, 1978; Elliott and Voss, 1974). Replication of these studies in a variety of places and times is necessary (at least one, in Philadelphia, is under way) if findings are to be generalized. Findings to date have been reasonably consistent and in general confirm findings on the social distribution of crime based on cross-sectional data. Large-scale studies employing self-reports and observational techniques have been employed to test a variety of hypotheses drawn from theoretical perspectives formulated prior to World War II, as well as those which have emerged since. Note, however, that self-report and victimization data are not relevant to the reactivist conception of deviance, since here deviance is defined in terms of reactions that are measured reasonably accurately by official statistics. However, such data are pertinent to some of the issues posed earlier. Combined with the concomitant development of more powerful statistical techniques, they have provided the opportunity for sociologists to "go back to the basics" of the field, reassessing and collecting again

"facts a theory must fit" (Cohen, 1955). Recently, for example, using self-reported and victimization data, there has been a revival of interest in "correlates" of crime. The relevance of such factors as race (Hindelang, 1978), IQ (Hirschi and Hindelang, 1977), gender (Steffensmeier and Steffensmeier, 1980), and social class (Tittle et al., 1978; Elliott and Ageton, 1980) have again received empirical attention.

The topic of white-collar crime received renewed attention during the 1970s, although this work, like that generated directly by Sutherland in the early 1950s, appeared hampered by inadequate conceptualization and data (Geis and Meier, 1977). The concept of "organizational crime" has been useful for purposes of theory (e.g., Ermann and Lundman, 1978; Schrager and Short, 1978) and research (e.g., Clinard, 1979), although not all instances of what is conventionally considered white-collar crime can be so regarded. Statistics on white-collar crime are virtually nonexistent, and the scope of the problem, its impact and consequences, and the "best" means of studying the topic are in dispute (see Reiss and Biderman, 1980).

 ## The Level of Explanation Problem

Calls for interdisciplinary theory and research have been frequent in recent years, but integration of knowledge continues to elude scholars within, as well as between, disciplines (see Inkeles, 1959; Cohen, 1966). The problem is exacerbated, we believe, by the failure to recognize different levels of explanation and to seek conceptual bridges between them (Finestone, 1976). In this brief review, following Cohen and Short (1976), we distinguish three levels of explanation. First, there is the individual level, which inquires as to what individual characteristics account for behavior; though most frequently addressed by psychology and the biological sciences, this level directs much of the research effort of social psychologists of sociological persuasion. Second, there is the macrosociological level which seeks explanation in the characteristics of social systems and cultural variation. Third, there is the microsociological level which examines characteristics of ongoing inter-action which shape behavior outcomes. All three levels of explanation address questions relevant to the etiol-ogy of deviant behavior. While only the macrosociologi-cal level is usually concerned with the origins of norms, all three levels may be employed to explain the manner in which norms influence individual behavior, by those who define deviance, or are involved in interaction with deviants, as well as the behavior of deviants per se.

Macrosociological Developments

Broad social structural and cultural theories of the origins of norms seem necessarily limited to the study of legal norms since there is great difficulty in identifying social norms that are shared by all diverse segments of modern, pluralistic societies (this is a main tenet of the relativistic conception of deviance; see Lemert, 1964). The "conflict" perspective is one such perspective. The conflict perspective's answer to "where do laws come from?" resides basically in the conflict between groups with differing interests and power to realize those interests. Spurred by statements advocating the sociological adoption of value stances in its research (e.g., Becker, 1967), conflict theorists have concentrated on the role of elites in defining as criminal those acts that most seriously threaten elite interests (Taylor et al., 1973).

Conflict theorists stress the fact that the state is not a disinterested party in rule creation; instead, it is a tool for the elite to be used in (1) defining nonelite conduct deemed undesirable or threatening by elites as illegal and (2) repressing, through the use of legiti-mated state force such as the police, behavior that is threatening to those elite interests. Capitalism, in effect, gets the crime it deserves if only because it cre-ates its own crime. While studies of rule enforcement had something of a tradition (if only a recently formed tradition) in the relativistic conception of deviance, this line of work took on increasing political signifi-cance in the conflict view (Quinney, 1980). The conflict perspective places high value on historical research since the origins of most laws predate the modern conflict view itself. Thus, studies of the origins of specific laws (e.g., Chambliss, 1974), as well as government bureaucracies concerned with crime control (e.g., Quinney, 1974), are appropriate research foci.

In almost direct ideological contrast with conflict theorists are some observers who argue that the legal system can and should be more instrumental in con-trolling crime (Wilson, 1975). These "new pragmatists" have sought to define retribution as the proper goal of the legal system (van der Haag, 1975). In this view, however, retribution is used quite differently than in classical or philosophical statements (see the review in Newman, 1978): Traditionally, retribution was a goal of penal philosophy that justified punishment not on the basis of some presumed social utility (e.g., crime con-trol), but solely on the basis that the offender "deserved" punishment. Stimulated by an increased sensitivity to the apparent failure of rehabilitation in correctional settings (e.g., Lipton et al., 1975), these persons have advocated a movement to a "just deserts" philosophy where punishment is justified on the basis of both its retributive *and* crime control nature. To the extent that this line of reasoning is persuasive, recent trends toward the use of, for example, determinant sentencing is more than merely a rejection of rehabilitation as a legitimate goal of the legal system; it is a conscious attempt to reorient the current system of justice.

Such interests, of course, do not preclude a contin-ued interest in the etiology of deviant behavior. A popular perspective, referred to as "control" theory, maintained that long-standing tradition. In control theory, however, there is little interest in what moti-vates a person to deviate from conventional norms; indeed, one of the assumptions of this view is that most persons would deviate given the chance. For this reason, conformity not deviance requires explanation (cf. Merton, 1938). Control theorists have examined the nature of deviant-inhibiting forces within small intimate groups, such as the family (Nye, 1958), as well as larger social structures. Perhaps the most sophisti-cated spokesman for control theory is Hirschi (1969), who asserts that conformity is largely a function of an individual's bond with conventional society. Once that bond is weakened or broken, deviance is permitted. This body of research is also compatible with the "drift" hypothesis of Matza (1964), where a person may drift into deviance once the restraining power of conventional norms is neutralized (Sykes and Matza, 1957) or made irrelevant to a particular situation. (Control theory is also compatible with Freudian psychology which views deviance as the result of inborn, constant impulses that are restrained only by internal controls and by social structure.)

Control theory asks not why people deviate from norms, but why they conform. One possible answer is that they fear punishments for deviance. The past decade has witnessed a virtual flurry of research on deterrence or conformity to legal norms that results directly from the fear of legal punishments. This body of literature is centrally concerned with the consequences of sanctions, but more accurately it has devoted more attention to the anticipation of sanctions (called general deterrence) rather than the effects of sanctions once applied (called specific deterrence). While the research as a whole clearly justifies reopening various debates concerning legal threats as deterrents (see Tittle and Logan, 1973; Gibbs, 1975), this work is largely atheoretical and divorced from a body of ideas that predicts the conditions under which legal threats inhibit criminality. While there has been some effort to link the work on deterrence with more inclusive theoretical perspectives, such as control theory (e.g., Minor, 1977), insufficient attention has thus far been devoted to the construction of a grander theory of legal impact or, better yet, of social control; short of that, research that integrates what we know about extralegal inhibition would seem a convenient starting point for such theories (e.g., Meier and Johnson, 1977). As matters stand now, the deterrence literature—while impressively large and sophisticated—is little more than a set of propositions concerning the relationship between legal threats and crime without a theory to make full sense of them.

Individual Level Developments

While interest in general etiological theories of crime and deviance declined following World War II, that tradition was not eliminated from the agenda of sociologists.

Perhaps the most influential theory, Sutherland's differential association, has received much attention during the past 20 years, both in empirical tests and in efforts to reformulate the theory to meet various objections. Two attempted reformulations are notable during this period, the work of Burgess and Akers (1966) to restate Sutherland's theory in terms of modern learning theory and DeFleur and Quinney's (1966) effort to identify the major properties of the theory in terms of set theory. The Burgess and Akers reformulation showed essentially that Sutherland's central ideas were consistent with a large body of literature concerning social learning patterns. This, however, cannot be taken as "support" for differential association since the theory merely asserts that criminal behavior is learned in accord with some rather general principles (Freese and Sell, 1980: 316–320). The theory has not been shown to be any more easily testable under such a formulation than before. The DeFleur and Quinney reformulation, while increasing the formal properties of the theory, similarly did not demonstrate its scientific validity. Continued "tests" of the theory seem doomed to failure in the absence of agreement on how the theory might be falsified.

One of the most important features of social learning theory lies in its reaffirmation that deviance is not a quality of persons, but of deviant values and norms that can be acquired in the course of social life. The "acquisition" of deviance thus parallels the acquisition of any other component of culture; thus, such seemingly disparate forms of deviance as homosexuality, crime, problem drinking, and suicide are amenable to a social learning interpretation (cf. Akers, 1977).

The influence of social learning theory, as well as the development of control theory as a major sociological perspective on deviance, perpetuated interest in other social psychological variables, particularly "self-concept." Self-concept has traditionally been used as an indicator of social (read personal) control or "inner containment" which inhibits deviance (e.g., Reckless et al., 1957). Wells (1978) has noted that while traditional research viewed self-concept as an independent variable that helped explain deviant behavior (see Glaser, 1956), subsequent conceptualizations have used self-concept as a dependent variable (usually termed "deviant identity") with deviant labels. Consistent with the interactionist theory from which this latter use of self-concept came, it was stipulated that deviant identities were the result of official stigmatization (labels) that "spoiled" self-conceptions (Goffman, 1963). Research on this point, however, has found that deviant identities are not invariably associated with stigmatization and that such conditions as reference group membership (Short and Strodtbeck, 1965) and race (Harris, 1976) may mediate "negative" effects of official labelling. Silberman (1978) has analyzed the role of verbal jousting—known variously as "playing the dozens," signifying, or "toasting"—in transforming the rage of black men "into a source of entertainment and play." He hypothesized, in explaining rising rates of violence among black males, that "the process no longer works; black adolescents and young men have begun to act out the violence and aggression that, in the past, had been contained and sublimated in fantasy and myth" (Silberman, 1978: 152). While the hypothesis is attractive, a somewhat broader interpretation seems more in accord with the data. Several studies suggest that the experience of blacks and perhaps other minorities (notably Chicanos) in the United States—especially the lower class experience of these minorities—often results in a world view that is less "polarized" between conventional and nonconventional, legitimate and illegitimate, attitudes, values, and what is considered acceptable behavior (in addition to the above, see Moore et al., 1978; Valentine, 1978). This interpretation, if it should prove correct, has profound implications for theories of deviance (and for social policy).

The Microsociology of Delinquency and Crime

The commonsense observation that what people do or say "depends on the situation" has been conceptualized in role and reference group theory terms, but rarely in terms of the properties and processes of ongoing interaction. Suggestive leads at this microsociological level of explanation as yet have had little impact on major sociological formulations, which continue to address questions of etiology at the individual and macrosociological levels.

Descriptive accounts of gang delinquency (Short and Strodtbeck, 1965), "victim-precipitated homicide" (Wolfgang, 1958) and other offenses (e.g., Pittman and Handy, 1964; Amir, 1971; Curtis, 1973), "violence in the family" (Steinmetz and Straus, 1973), the interactions of juveniles with police (Piliavin and Briar, 1966; Werthman and Piliavin, 1967), and other situations in which deviant outcomes result, provide raw materials for theory in this area. Theoretical suggestions have not been lacking in this research, but the lack of formal theory and systematic data have hampered their development and acceptance. The most promising leads are found in suggestions concerning group processes (Short and Strodtbeck, 1965; Jansyn, 1966) and the calculus of decision making in a variety of social settings (see e.g., Klein and Crawford, 1967; Berk, 1974; Goode, 1970; Steinmetz and Straus, 1973).

The hope, but not as yet the promise, of microsociological level work is in its transitive or bridging nature. The detailed probing into ongoing interaction which is the hallmark of this level of inquiry necessarily directs attention to the individual and macrosociological levels as well. Thus, the "social disabilities" of gang boys (Short and Strodtbeck, 1965; Gordon, 1966; Klein and Crawford, 1967) at the individual level, and qualities associated with the lower class settings of gang interaction, as well as the nature of gangs and local communities as social systems, at the macro-level, become salient—indeed necessary—to micro-level explanations. Thus far, however, the rich descriptive materials and theoretical suggestions at this level remain in a very elementary state, without systematic documentation or exposition.

◈ Conclusion

Theories of delinquency, crime, and deviance all contain "partial insights," as often as has been noted (e.g., Finestone, 1976). Attempts to integrate—even to reconcile—these theories have been only partially successful. Typologies of "criminal behavior systems," suggested by Sutherland, have received a good deal of attention in the post-World War II period (see, especially, Clinard and Quinney, 1973; Gibbons, 1975). While the promise of theoretical typologies has been unfulfilled, the better efforts have the distinct advantage that they describe and, at times, seek explanation in addressing etiological questions at the macrosociological level.

"Tests" of a variety of theoretical ideas, occasionally in an integrative framework, have been made possible by advances in statistical methodology and computer technology. Despite expansion of the empirical base, however, theoretical measures remain primitive and suspect, as do the results of statistical models based upon them. When properly employed, statistical models can force conceptual and theoretical clarity. Too often, however, available data are simply manipulated until an interpretable result is discovered. While empirical findings so derived may be of interest, possibly as grist for further speculation, little theoretical advance can be expected from such an approach.

Related to this is the fact that much of what is going on in the name of theory in criminology and the study of deviance are efforts to integrate existing theoretical perspectives (e.g., Elliott et al., 1979) and perspectives based on several interpretations of Marxist social and economic thought (Quinney, 1980). A recent review of criminological theory suggests that future theoretical work will concentrate largely on relatively minor puzzles left over from earlier theories or on questions that may eventually bring criminology closer to conventionally conceived sociological theory (Gibbons, 1979). To this assessment must be added the challenge to conventional sociological perspectives posed by human capital economies and adaptations of this theory and of econometric methods by sociologists (Cohen and Felson, 1979; Cohen et al., forthcoming).

Some of the theoretical and empirical problems discussed in this article relate to the immaturity of the parent disciplines upon which the study of crime, delinquency, and deviance is derived. Yet, there is reason for optimism. Schur (1980) argues that the range of "common concerns and mutually agreeable propositions" upon which sociologists of varying persuasion agree is broader than that which continues to divide.

Whether this is the case, we prefer "healthy ferment" to rigid conformity in choice of problem, as well as in theoretical or empirical approach.

◈ References

AKERS, R. L. (1977) Deviant Behavior: A Social Learning Approach. Belmont. CA: Wadsworth.

AMIR, M. (1971) Patterns in Forcible Rape. Chicago: Univ. of Chicago Press.

BECKER, H. S. (1973) Outsiders: Studies in the Sociology of Deviance. New York: Free Press.

—— (1967) "Whose side are we on?" Social Problems 14: 239–247.

BERK, R. (1974) "A gaming approach to crowd behavior." Amer. Soc. Rev. 39: 355–373.

BLOCH, A. and A. NEIDERHOFFER (1958) The Gang: A Study in Adolescent Behavior. New York: Philosophical Library.

BURGESS, R. L. and R. L. AKERS (1966) "A differential association-reinforcement theory of criminal behavior." Social Problems 14: 128–147.

Center for Studies in Crime and Delinquency (1974) Teenage delinquency in small town America. NIMH Research Report, 5. Washington, DC: Government Printing Office.

CHAMBLISS, W. J. (1974) "The state, the law, and the definition of behavior as criminal or delinquent," pp. 7–43 in D. Glaser (ed.) Handbook of Criminology. Skokie, IL: Rand McNally.

—— (1964) "A sociological analysis of the law of vagrancy." Social Problems 12:67–77.

CHIRICOS, T. G. and G. P. WALDO (1975) "Socioeconomic status and criminal sentencing: An empirical assessment of a conflict proposition." Amer. Soc. Rev. 40:753–772.

CLINARD, M. B. (1979) Illegal Corporate Behavior. Washington, DC: Government Printing Office.

—— (1973) Criminal Behavior Systems: A Typology. New York: Holt, Rinehart and Winston.

CLOWARD, R. A. and L. E. OHLIN (1960) Delinquency and Opportunity: A Theory of Delinquent Gangs. New York: Free Press.

COHEN, A. K. (1966) Deviance and Control. Englewood Cliffs, NJ: Prentice-Hall.

—— (1955) Delinquent Boys: The Culture of the Gang. New York: Free Press.

—— and J. F. SHORT, Jr. (1976) "Crime and juvenile delinquency," in R. K. Merton and R. Nisbet (eds.) Contemporary Social Problems. New York: Harcourt Brace Jovanovich.

COHEN, L. E. and M. FELSON (1979) "Social change and crime rate trends: a routine activity approach." Amer. Soc. Rev. 44: 588–608.

—— and K. LAND (forthcoming) "Property crime in the United Slates: A macro-dynamic analysis, 1947–1977, with ex ante forecasts for the mid-1980's." Amer. J. of Sociology.

CONNOR, W. D. (1972) Deviance in Soviet Society. New York: Columbia Univ. Press.

COSER, L. (1975) "Two methods in search of a substance." Amer. Soc. Rev. 40: 691–700.

CURTIS, L. A. (1973) Violence, Race, and Culture. Lexington. MA: D. C. Heath.

DAVIS, K. (1976) "Sexual behavior," in R. K. Merton and R. Nisbet (eds.) Contemporary Social Problems. New York: Harcourt Brace Jovanovich.

DeFLEUR, M. L. and R. QUINNEY (1966) "A reformulation of Sutherland's differential association theory and strategy for empirical verification." J. of Research in Crime and Delinquency 3: 1–22.

DOUGLAS, J. D. (1970) Understanding Everyday Life. Chicago: Aldine.

DUSTER, T. (1970) The Legislation of Morality. New York: Free Press.

ELLIOTT, D. S. and S. S. AGETON (1980) "Reconciling race and class differences in self-reported and official estimates of delinquency." Amer. Soc. Rev. 45: 95–110.

ELLIOTT, D. S. and H. L. VOSS (1974) Delinquency and Dropout. Lexington, MA: Lexington Books.

ELLIOTT, D. S., S. S. AGETON, and R. J. CANTER (1979) "An integrated theoretical perspective on delinquent behavior." J. of Research in Crime and Delinquency 16: 3–27.

ENNIS, P. H. (1967) Criminal Victimization in the United States: A Report of a National Survey. Chicago. National Opinion Research Center.

ERMANN, D., and R. LUNDMAN [eds.] (1978) Corporate and Government Deviance. New York, Oxford Univ. Press.

FINESTONE, H. (1976) "The delinquent and society: The Shaw and McKay tradition," pp. 23–49 in J. F. Short, Jr. (ed.) Delinquency, Crime, and Society. Chicago: Univ. of Chicago Press.

FREESE, I., and J. SELL (1980) "Constructing axiomatic theories in sociology: Part II," in I. FREESE (ed.) theoretical Methods in Sociology: Seven Essays. Pittsburgh: Univ. of Pittsburgh Press.

GALLIHER, J. F., J. L. McCARTNEY, and B. BAUM (1974) "Nebraska's marijuana law: A case of unexpected legislative innovation." Law and Society Rev. 8: 441–455.

GEIS, G. and R. F. MEIER (1977) White-Collar Crime: Offenses in Business, Politics and the Professions. New York: Free Press.

GIBBONS, D. C. (1979) The Criminological Enterprise. Englewood Cliffs, NJ: Prentice-Hall.

—— (1975) "Offender typologies two decades later." British J. of Criminology 15: 140–156.

GIBBS, J. P. (1975) Crime, Punishment and Deterrence. New York: Elsevier.

—— (1966) "Conceptions of deviant behavior: The old and the new." Pacific Soc. Rev. 9: 9–14.

—— and M. L. ERICKSON (1975) "Major developments in the sociological study of deviance." Annual Review of Sociology 1: 21–42.

GLASER, D. (1956) "Criminality theories and behavioral images." Amer. J. of Sociology 61: 433–444.

GOFFMAN, E. (1963) Stigma: Notes on the Management of Spoiled Identity. Englewood Cliffs, NJ: Prentice-Hall.

GOLD, M., and D. J. REIMER (1975) "Changing patterns of delinquent behavior among Americans 13 through 16 years old: 1967–72." Crime and Delinquency 7: 483–517.

GOODE, W. J. (1970) "Violence among intimates," in D. Mulvihill and M. Tumin with the assistance of L. C. Curtis (eds.) Violent Crime: A Task Force Report to the National Commission on the Causes and Prevention of Violence. Washington, DC: Government Printing Office.

GORDON, R. (1966) "Social level, social disability and gang interaction" Amer. J. of Sociology 73: 42–62.

GOVE, W. R. (1980) The Labelling of Deviance. Beverly Hills, CA: Sage.

GREENBERG, D. F. (1977) "Socioeconomic status and criminal sentences: Is there an association?" Amer. Soc. Rev. 42: 174–176.

GUSFIELD, J. R. (1963) Symbolic Crusade: Status Politics and the American Temperance Movement. Urbana: Univ. of Illinois Press.

HAGAN, J. and J. LYON (1977) "Rediscovering delinquency: Social history, political ideology, and the sociology of law." Amer. Soc. Rev. 42: 587–598.

HARRIS, A. M. (1976) "Race, commitment to deviance, and spoiled identity." Amer. Soc. Rev. 41: 432–442.

HINDELANG, M. J. (1978) "Race and involvement in common law personal crimes." Amer. Soc. Rev. 43: 93–109.

—— (1976) Criminal Victimization in Eight American Cities: A Descriptive Analysis of Common Theft and Assault. Cambridge, MA: Ballinger.

—— T. HIRSCHI, and J. WEIS (forthcoming) The Measurement of Delinquency by the Self-Report Method. New York: Academic Press.

HIRSCHI, T., and M. J. HINDELANG (1977) "Intelligence and delinquency: A revisionist review." Amer. Soc. Rev. 42: 571–587.

Illinois Institute tor Juvenile Research (1972) Juvenile Delinquency in Illinois. Chicago: Illinois Department of Mental Health.

INKELES, A. (1959) "Personality and social structure," pp. 293–305 in R. K. Merton et al. (eds.) Sociology Today: Problems and Prospects. New York: Basic Books.

JANSYN, L. R., Jr. (1966) "Solidarity and delinquency in a street corner group." Amer. Soc. Rev. 31: 600–614.

KITSUSE, J. I. and A. V. CICOUREL (1963) "A note on the uses of official statistics." Social Problems II: 131–139.

KLEIN, M., and L. Y. CRAWFORD (1967) "Groups, gangs, and cohesiveness." J. of Research in Crime and Delinquency 4: 63–75.

LEMER, T. F. (1972) Human Deviance, Social Problems, and Social Control. Englewood Cliffs, NJ: Prentice-Hall.

—— (1964) "Social structure, social control and deviation," pp. 57–97 in M. B. Clinard (ed.) Anomie and Deviant Behavior. New York: Free Press.

—— (1951) Social Pathology. New York: McGraw-Hill.

LIPTON, D., R. MARTINSON, and J. WILKS (1975) The Effectiveness of Correctional Treatment. New York: Praeger.

MATZA, D. (1964) Delinquency and Drift. New York: Wiley.

MAUSS, A. L. (1975) Social Problems as Social Movements. Philadelphia: J. B. Lippincott.

McDONALD, L. (1976) The Sociology of Law and Order. Boulder, CO: Westview.

MEIER, R. E., and W. T. JOHNSON (1977) "Deterrence as social control: The legal and extralegal production of conformity." Amer. Soc. Rev. 42: 292–304.

MERION, R. K. (1938) "Social structure and anomie." Amer. Soc. Rev. 1: 672–682.

MILLER, W. B. (1958) "Lower-class culture as a generating milieu of gang delinquency." J. of Social Issues 14: 5–19.

MINOR, W. W. (1977) "A deterrence-control theory of crime," pp. 117–137 in R. F. Meier (ed.) Theory in Criminology. Beverly Hills, CA: Sage.

MOORE, J. W. with R. GARCIA, C. GARCIA, L. CERDA, and F. VALENCIA (1978) Homeboys: Gangs, Drugs, and Prison in the Barrios of Los Angeles. Philadelphia: Temple Univ. Press.

MURPHEY, F. G., M. M. SHIRLEY, and H. L. WITMER (1946) "The incidence of hidden delinquency." Amer. J. of Orthopsychiatry 16: 686–696.

National Criminal Justice Information and Statistics Service (1976) Criminal Victimization in the United States: A Comparison of 1973 and 1974 Findings. Washington, DC: Government Printing Office.

—— (1975) Criminal Victimization Surveys in the Nation's Five Largest Cities. Washington, DC: Government Printing Office.

—— (1974) Crimes and Victims: A Report on the Dayton-San Jose Pilot Survey of Victimization. Washington, DC: Government Printing Office.

NEWMAN, G. (1978) The Punishment Response. Philadelphia: J. B. Lippincott.

—— (1976) Comparative Deviance. New York: Elsevier.

NYE, F. I. (1958) Family Relationships and Delinquent Behavior. New York: Wiley.

PILIAVIN, I., and S. BRIAR (1966) "Police encounters with juveniles." Amer. J. of Sociology 70: 206–214.

PIIMAN, D. J., and W. HANDY (1964) "Patterns in criminal aggravated assault." J. of Criminal Law, Criminology, and Police Sci. 55: 462–470.

PLATT, A. (1969) The Child Savers. Chicago: Univ. of Chicago Press.

PORTERFIELD, A. (1946) Youth in Trouble. Fort Worth, TX: Leo Potishman Foundation.

President's Commission of Law Enforcement and Administration of Justice (1967a) The Challenge of Crime in a Free Society. Washington, DC: Government Printing Office.

—— (1967b) Task Force Report: Crime and Its Impact—An Assessment. Washington, DC: Government Printing Office.

QUINNEY, R. (1980) Class, State and Crime. New York: David McKay.

—— (1974) Critique of Legal Order. Boston: Little, Brown.

RECKLESS, W. R., S. DINITZ, and B. KAY (1957) "The self component in potential delinquency and potential non-delinquency." Amer. Soc. Rev. 22: 566–570.

REISS, A. J., Jr. (1976) "Settling the frontiers of a pioneer in American criminology: Henry McKay," pp. 64–88 in J. F Short, Jr. (ed.) Delinquency, Crime, and Society. Chicago: Univ. of Chicago Press.

—— and A. D. BIDERMAN (1980) Data Sources on White-Collar Law Breaking. Washington, DC: Bureau of Social Science Research.

ROBY, P. (1969) "Politics and criminal law: Revision of the New York State penal law on prostitution." Social Problems 17: 83–109.

ROIHMAN, D. (1980) Conscience and Convenience. Boston: Little, Brown.

SCHEFF, I. J. (1966) Being Mentally Ill. Chicago: Aldine.

SCHRAGER, L., and J. F. SHORT, Jr. (1978) "Toward a sociology of organizational crime." Social Problems 25: 407–419.

SCHUR, E. M. (1980) "Can the 'old' and 'new' criminologies be reconciled?" pp. 277–286 in J. Inciardi (ed.) Radical Criminology: The Coming Crisis. Beverly Hills, CA: Sage.

SHANNON, L. (1978) "A longitudinal study of delinquency and crime," pp. 121–146 in C. Wellford (ed.) Quantitative Studies in Criminology. Beverly Hills, CA: Sage.

SHORT, J. F., Jr., and F. L. STRODTBECK (1965) Group Process and Gang Delinquency. Chicago: Univ. of Chicago Press.

SILBERMAN, C. E. (1978) Criminal Violence, Criminal Justice. New York: Random House.

SPECTOR, M., and J. I. KITSUSE (1977) Constructing Social Problems. Menlo Park, CA: Cummings.

SIEFFENSMEIER, D., and R. H. SIEFFENSMEIER (1980) "Trends in female delinquency: An examination of arrest, juvenile court, self-report, and field data." Criminology 18: 62–85.

STEINMETZ, S., and M. STRAUS [eds.] (1973) Violence and the family. New York: Dodd, Mead.

SUTHERLAND, E. H. (1949) White Collar Crime. New York: Dryden Press.

SYKES, G. M., and D. MATZA (1957) "Techniques of neutralization: A theory of delinquency." Amer. Soc. Rev. 22: 664–670.

TAYLOR, L., P. WALTON, and J. YOUNG (1973) The New Criminology. London: Routledge and Kegan Paul.

TITTLE, C. R., and C. H. LOGAN (1973) "Sanctions and deviance: Questions and remaining issues." Law and Society Rev. 7: 371–392.

TITTLE, C. R., W. J. VILLMEZ, and D. A. SMITH (1978) "The myth of social class and criminality: An empirical assessment of the empirical evidence." Amer. Soc. Rev. 43: 643–656.

VALENTINE, B. (1978) Hustling and Other Hard Work: Life Styles in the Ghetto. New York: Free Press.

van den HAAG, E. (1975) Punishing Criminals. New York: Basic Books.

WELLS, L. E. (1978) "Theories of deviance and the self-concept." Social Psychology 41: 189–204.

WERTHMAN, C., and I. PILIAVIN (1967) "Gang members and the police," pp. 56–98 in D. J. Bordua (ed.) The Police: Six Sociological Essays. New York: Wiley.

WILSON, J. Q. (1975) Thinking About Crime. New York: Basic Books.

WOLFGANG, M. E. (1958) Patterns in Criminal Homicide. New York: Wiley.

——, R. FIGLIO, and I. SELLIN (1972) Delinquency in a Birth Cohort. Chicago: Univ. of Chicago Press.

READING 4

In this article, Wahrman points to three concepts common to the student of deviance: "status," "norms," and "sanctions." These are common sociological concepts, but they are at best fuzzy and in need of deep contemplation if we are to advance our understanding of some basic issues in the study of deviance. The concept of status, for example, is multidimensional and may refer to "esteem," "admiration," or "prestige." In the study of deviance, we tend to think that these concepts are associated with power and the ability to "get away with stuff." Wahrman reminds us that both the conceptualization and the context may affect how status affects behavior and reaction to behavior. Similarly, one of the most common definitions of deviance is "the violation of group norms." Wahrman discourages us from oversimplifying the term and uses experimental studies to show just how complicated the concept can be. Finally, the term *sanctions,* which is so common in the study of deviance, is no more clear. Wahrman makes a strong case that experimental studies of sanctions have been far too narrow for the student of deviance to make much use of them. Two important things can be taken from this article. First, it seems to us that Wahrman makes clear the overlapping and interacting nature of these key concepts and how, taken together, we find ourselves in quite murky waters. Second, he argues against the overly simplistic notion that status is simply a measure of power that protects certain persons who violate norms; to illustrate his claim, he points to contexts where high-status persons may be particularly subject to sanctions and low-status persons may be less sanctioned than those holding power.

Status, Deviance, and Sanctions: A Critical Review

Ralph Wahrman

Groups Have Norms

Group members abide by the norms because they believe the norms are proper or because they fear that sanctions will be applied by other group members who *do* believe in the norms. High-status members apparently have less to fear. We frequently find that nonconforming high-status members of a group are not sanctioned (Wahrman, 1970a). On those rare occasions when they do receive sanctions, those who possess high status may be more severely sanctioned than lesser members (Wahrman, 1970b).

There are two schools of thought about the reasons high status so often enables people to avoid sanctions. One approach suggests that nonconformity is perceived as deviant regardless of who performs it. Because high status and high power often go together, less powerful members of the group fear retaliation and therefore do not act on their perceptions (Blau, 1964a; McGrath, 1964; Homans, 1961).

The other approach suggests that behavior is perceived differently depending on who the actor is and that nonconformity by high-status group members is not seen as deviance but as innovation, tolerable idiosyncrasy, occasion for changing the norm or broadening its limits, and so on. In other words, what strikes an outside observer as "deviance" appears to the group as an event which does not call for sanctions (Hollander, 1961).

Disentangling the circumstances under which each approach is correct and the circumstances under which

Source: Wahrman, Ralph. 2010. "Status, Deviance, and Sanctions: A Critical Review." *Small Group Research* 41:91–105. Reprinted with permission of SAGE Publications, Inc.

certain levels and types of status do or do not make it possible to violate certain types of norms is the sort of problem for which field and laboratory experiments are eminently suitable. Therefore, this review concentrates on experimental studies of status and deviance. The literature is not a large one, but the issues and their implications are not only significant for understanding abstract questions about the dynamics of social control in informal groups but are also of relevance for students of delinquency (Black & Reiss, 1970) and adult crime (Wolfgang et al., 1962), for students of social change (e.g., Putney & Putney, 1962; Fathi, 1968), students of intergroup relations (Sherif, 1962; Julian et al., 1969), and for students of leadership (Hollander, 1964).

Although the literature is not generally thought of as a large one, it is much smaller than we usually admit. I exclude from this review studies which have asked about the *willingness* of high-status people to violate norms. These are generally inaccurately cited in social psychology texts as supplying evidence for the *ability* of high-status people to get away with deviance. Willing and able are not the same things.

I exclude here also studies of credibility (Berlo et al., 1969; Griffin, 1967; Simons, et al., 1970) for several reasons. First, they tend not to study normative issues but rather issues on which subjects tend to have quite weak personal opinions (Hovland, 1959). Second, the speakers tend not to be members of groups of which subjects are members. Space limitations suggest that I focus here on situations in which subjects and deviants, if only temporarily, are members of the same group, and the deviant has some reason to be aware of the existence of the group and its norms.

Although this review examines limitations of existing research, my basic intention is to suggest research possibilities for the future. Let us first examine the basic concepts "status," "norms," and "sanctions" as utilized in studies which attempt to combine all three.

◈ Status

Groups do not value all members equally. Abstractly, we can say that some members have higher value to the group because they possess rewarding (or potentially rewarding) qualities and abilities, and their fellow members reward them in turn by according them "status" or social approval (Secord and Backman, 1964; Homans, 1961; Thibaut and Kelley, 1959).

The particular qualities for which one is accorded varying levels of status vary with the nature and purpose of the group, and depending on the circumstances, a group may have more than one status hierarchy. Researchers studying the effects of status on deviance have not been clear about whether their studies were addressed to studying "status," "prestige," "esteem," or "admiration" (compare. Ellis, 1962; Ellis & Keedy, 1960), which should be thought of as different kinds of rankings with potentially different consequences for the possessor. Although these terms tend to be used mainly by sociologists who wish to refer to responses to one's possession of formal roles separately from personal reactions to the role incumbent, students of informal groups have utilized similar distinctions and supplied an additional vocabulary related to roles and dimensions of behavior in informal groups. "Status" may have reference to a task or social-emotional activity hierarchy (Slater, 1955) or to attractiveness as a workmate or roommate (Jennings, 1943), to private or public popularity (Taylor, 1954), to integration (Blau, 1960), or to whatever shows up on some global observational measure like Sherifs "effective initiative" (Sherif & Sherif, 1969) or a global question such as "who are your most valued members?" or "who would you select to represent this group at a conference?" All of these are presumably valid measures of some of the kinds of things referred to as "status," but there is no evidence that behavior permitted to or forbidden people who score high on one measure applies to someone who scores high on another. Although most of these conceptions of status are represented in studies cited below, I am not aware of a single study which attempted to compare reactions to the deviance of people who scored high on different measures of status. Perhaps this is only another way of saying that our research on status and deviance is not systematic and tends not to represent attempts to formulate and test theories about status. Rather, the theoretical discussion sections of most of the studies cited below appear to be plausible justifications of hunches about the circumstances under which a high-status deviant will elicit a certain kind of reaction rather than strict derivations from any kind of theory.

Whether we choose to study status one dimension at a time or to use a global measure, we will ultimately have to start studying complex variables (group characteristics) such as status congruence, consensus on status, and the distances between ranks as suggested by Videbeck (1964). We must go beyond oversimplified problem formulations which ask only if high status (nature unspecified) always (or ever) protects one from sanctions.

The typical approach to status manipulation is to utilize extreme dimensions of competence or socioeconomic status or academic rank—that is, highly competent versus incompetent, professor versus department store clerk, graduate student versus freshman, and so on. Although these extreme differences may be necessary for a strong manipulation, they neglect an important consideration. People at both extremes may be treated quite differently from the way anyone in the middle ranks is treated.

Responses may follow a curvilinear pattern. Furthermore, even close to the extremes, people may be responded to differently: Leading members may not receive the same response as *the leader* who has not only high status but a role which may have to be taken into account in understanding reactions to his deviance (see Hollander, 1964). The leader, for example, is expected to innovate even if it means disregarding certain norms. A high-status nonleader's innovation may be responded to with "who asked you?"

The issue of roles and status enters into consideration in another way. We have tended to utilize a somewhat simple model of status in our research and assumed that what one high-status person will be permitted or forbidden to do will be also permitted or forbidden to every other person of equally high status. This may not be so. For example, a task leader and a social-emotional leader may be equally valued, but each may find himself with freedom or restraints on deviation in quite different realms of behavior (Wahrman, 1970b). This may appear obvious and trivial, but it

bears on an important point in interpreting research findings: Groups *may* be misperceiving or inventing excuses or good motives by which they excuse a high-status person for violating a norm which is applicable to all members *or* it may be that it was never intended or expected that a certain norm be applicable to that particular actor (see Sampson, 1963).

◆ Norms

If the nature of "status" is a something on which there is low consensus, "norms" are no less confusing (see Gibbs, 1965, 1968).

Norms may be thought of as a range of permitted behaviors (Jackson, 1965; Sherif & Sherif, 1969) or as a single permissible behavior. They may be seen as matters of high consensus, or amount of consensus may be thought of as a contingent attribute of norms rather than part of their definition (Gibbs, 1965, 1968). Research on status and deviance has tended to utilize the single-behavior model, and laboratory studies have attempted to find behaviors on which virtually all subjects could be expected to agree. As was suggested for status earlier, research should consider amounts of consensus on norms and other qualities of norms as variables. One can see in descriptions of status manipulations some understanding that there may be different types of status: The conceptions are more or less standard distinctions and dichotomies—e.g., liking versus working, respect versus affection. In the study of norms, there are no commonly accepted classifications or typologies. Procedures for scaling norms in terms of relevance or importance, such as that of Mudd (1968), or for tapping dimensions, such as those suggested by Jackson (1965), have not been introduced into the study of status and deviance in the laboratory or outside. This makes it difficult to specify the types of norms to which the study is an attempt to generalize.

Again, this may be considered a reflection of the unsystematic nature of research on status and deviance. Although, as noted, we have never had high degree of consensus on which phenomena to reserve the concept "norm" for, one difference between the way social psychologists and sociologists tend to use the work involves the issue of "sharedness." Homans (1961), Newcomb et al. (1965), and others have argued that what makes a norm different from any old garden-variety belief about appropriate behavior held by a given individual is that they would reserve the term for a belief which a certain number of members of a group share, are aware they share, and believe they have a right to demand that other people abide by. Homans (1961) further suggests that a norm effectively exists when the people who believe in it can effectively apply sanctions more or less freely; i.e., others who are not particularly committed to the norm will permit those who do care to enforce it.

Studies in which a deviant performs in the presence of more than one subject are unusual (Sampson and Brandon, 1964; Alvarez, 1968; Sabath, 1964; Harari and McDavid, 1969). This is unfortunate, not only because knowledge that other people share a belief about proper behavior gives norms their character, but also because the response to a deviant may not be a simple function of individual reactions but may be the result of a *collective* interpretation of what the act represents, and some people's opinions may carry more weight than the opinions of others. Studying individual responses has its advantages, but the question of who stands up to tell the deviant to stop doing whatever he is doing, or of what happens if the lower-status members disapprove while the high-status members back the alleged deviant, and other questions about social control as a dynamic process are ignored if we limit ourselves to considering individual responses to an esteem questionnaire as the sole dependent variable. The aforementioned studies, which have utilized group situations, have presumably produced overt responses in other subjects; i.e., the other subjects must have glared, questioned the deviant, or asked him to stop whatever it was that he was programmed to do, but with the exception of Sampson and Brandon's Interaction Process Analysis (Bales, 1950), this dialogue remains unreported and unacknowledged.

With one exception (Hollander, 1961), no study has attempted to use the same stimulus person to study more than one norm. Hollander asked each of his subjects to imagine a hypothetical person of high or low status and then to imagine that this person had performed eight behaviors and to indicate how much they disapproved of each of these eight acts. Hollander apparently formulated no hypotheses, but he reports that several of these behaviors elicited statistically significant differences in disapproval. Although, as Doob and Gross (1968) note, the sanctions one says he would hypothetically give and what he actually does may be quite different; the hypothetical situation may be the only feasible way to compare reactions in a group to violations of different norms by the same person.

The area is still in its infancy, which perhaps explains why many researchers tend to ask their confederates to violate several norms *simultaneously*. Hollander (1960), for example, asked his confederate to violate several procedural norms. Sabath (1964) had his confederate violate several procedural and courtesy norms, and so did Alvarez. As one reads the descriptions of the manipulations, it is clear that these researchers have achieved great spontaneity and realism at the cost of replicability (see Wahrman & Pugh, 1971), as well as understanding of the norms to which subjects were responding.

Only one study in this literature has attempted to work without a confederate. Videbeck (1964) set up three-man discussion groups and instructed the members privately about the best way to perform in a discussion group, always instructing one differently from the other two. He found a positive relationship between amount of nonconformity and status assigned by others at the end of the discussion. The basis for assigning status is not described. Videbeck's study appears to me to confuse the processes involved in gaining status with those involved in maintaining status (Hollander, 1960). This is the only study in this literature that has considered consensus on norms and consensus on status as variables.

Thibaut and Riecken (1955) had two confederates, one of high status and one of low status, simultaneously first refuse to share certain materials with the subject and then simultaneously agree to share these materials. Thibaut and Riecken then asked subjects for their interpretations of the sudden generosity of each confederate. They did not ask about subject interpretations of the confederates' selfishness. This is the only study that exposed subjects to high- and low-status people simultaneously violating the same norm.

◈ Sanctions

"Sanctions" are no less fuzzy a concept than "norms" and "status." Gibbs (1966) points out that we cannot seem to agree on such basic issues as whether a sanction must be a response to deviance that is intended to punish the deviant or whether it must be intended to prevent future occurrences of the behavior, whether it must be perceived by the deviant or it must merely be the sort of internal response that would distress the deviant if he were aware of it.

At least, among the researchers cited here, there seems to be consensus that some measure of loss of esteem is a minimal if not completely adequate measure of sanctioning.

Nonetheless, there is some question of what responses should be considered sanctions. For example, Sampson and Brandon (1964) had a liberal confederate take a somewhat reactionary position on the appropriate treatment for a Negro delinquent. Although, on sociometric measures, the confederate appeared not to suffer a loss of esteem, during the discussion significantly more questions and hostile comments were directed to her than to a bigot who scored low on the esteem measures. Should Sampson and Brandon have considered the questions and hostility to be sanctions, as does Israel (1956)?

Hollander (1960) found that a confederate who was highly competent but who violated procedural norms early in the course of a meeting temporarily lost influence over the group's decisions. A confederate who waited until later in the session to violate these norms did not suffer such influence loss. Shall we assume that this patient deviant did not suffer a loss of esteem (Hollander did not ask esteem questions), or shall we go along with Hollander and argue that the only relevant sanction is the one he chose to utilize—actual loss of influence? Doob and Gross (1968) had confederates in either new, expensive cars or old, inexpensive cars remain at traffic lights after the signals had changed.

People blocked by the old car honked their horns sooner and more frequently. Is it possible that the new car owner was cursed more vehemently in the privacy of the honkers' cars (male students in a classroom situation claimed they would have honked faster at the newer car than the field data indicated they probably would have)? Or does it not matter? Harari and McDavid (1969) suborned high- and low-status classroom and club members, had the children in class steal money from the teacher's desk, and had the club members break the club leader's tape recorder. When interrogated in the presence of another child (witness), peers turned in high-status children. When interrogated alone, peers did not turn them in. Low-status children were turned in whether the "fink" was interrogated alone or in the presence of another. Shall we say that if the child was not turned in he was not therefore sanctioned—e.g., peers did not lose respect for him? Or shall we say that if others did not blow the whistle on him he was unsanctioned? This is the only study of status and deviance I am aware of which utilized an actual group member as a confederate rather than using a trained confederate.

Evan and Zelditch (1961) found, in the simulated organization they set up, subjects privately disobeyed an incompetent supervisor and ignored his instructions. Shall we say that because there was no overt defiance, the supervisor is unsanctioned?

The answers to these questions depend on how one chooses to utilize the term *sanction*. In the case of sanctions, perhaps more than in the case of norms and status, the question represents more than semantic quibbling. Although the majority of studies cited here have been limited to studying individual responses on various paper-and-pencil esteem measures, in the world outside the laboratory, overt responses are important cues for letting other group members know whether the norm is still in effect for the deviant or for other members of the group.

One can possibly make equally valid arguments for the relative importance of covert or overt responses, but if the reader decides to limit his consideration only to studies of overt sanctions, he remains with a quite tiny experimental literature using quite nonequivalent sanctions. On what scale does one equate, let us say, "finking" to the teacher with horn-honking, or refusal to follow a deviant across the street against the light (Lefkowitz et al., 1955), particularly in terms of other possible overt responses within those experimental situations. Mudd (1968) is the only one I am aware of who attempts to scale overt behaviors and sanctions, but this technique has not been used in the context of status, deviance, and sanctions.

As noted earlier, some theorists have interpreted an absence of overt sanctions to mean that the group must have been intimidated by high-status people into withholding sanctions that would otherwise have been applied. The vast majority of the studies cited here appear to lend little support to this interpretation. Most of them find that the high-status person's behavior is interpreted quite generously. Certainly there are occasions when high-status people are perceived as deviant and do intimidate the group into withholding sanctions. This body of literature is not helpful in understanding such situations, not only because subjects did not appear to disapprove of the high-status confederate, but because, even if they had disapproved, the situations were not structured in such a way as to enable them to actually react overtly to the deviant.

The few studies that do provide evidence of greater disapproval of the high-status deviant also restrict the sorts of responses subjects could make.

Iverson's (1964) subjects disapproved of a high-status person who was self-punitive but who praised his audience. Subjects were aware that they were rating a tape-recorded person and could only react by means of a rating scale.

Alvarez's (1968) subjects apparently withdrew esteem (4-point scales multiplied by 100 and presented without statistical tests are not strong evidence) from a high-status deviant, but nothing is reported about subject reactions in any of the four 1-hour meetings at which the deviant insulted subjects and violated rules of procedure.

Hollander's (1961) subjects would hypothetically have disapproved of certain behavior if the actor was of high status, but he does not explore what they would hypothetically have done about it.

Harari and McDavid's students presumably disapproved of the confederate's theft or vandalism. Since the researchers were not observing the act, but only the later willingness to identify the culprit, there is not much they can say about subject responses.

Thibaut and Riecken (1955) found that some of their subjects, not the majority, disapproved more of a high-status confederate who refused to share certain materials, but the subjects were in no position to do much about it. Wahrman's (1970b) subjects were more severe in their criticism of a high-status deviant, but again were not in a position to do anything about it.

Evan and Zelditch (1961) ran subjects individually, and although subjects were apparently willing to sanction by disobedience the confederate's violation of the normative expectation that supervisors ought to be competent, subjects were alone, and perhaps the absence of social support made it less likely than otherwise that they would openly rebel.

Apparently, we have not selected sufficiently strong manipulations to produce laboratory answers to such problems as the circumstances under which high-status deviance will both be disapproved and acted upon. Keeping subjects isolated from one another makes it easier to study individual responses uncontaminated by interaction with others, but it may, where subjects disapprove of the high-status deviant, underestimate the severity of responses which subjects in interaction would have produced.

◈ Explanations of Extreme Responses to High-Status Deviants

Many studies of criminal justice, anecdotes, field studies, and experiments back up the proposition that high status frequently enables the possessor to receive minimal or no sanctions for acts that would be harshly dealt with if the perpetrator were of middle or low rank.

Much less evidence exists for the proposition that penalties for certain acts of deviance may be more severe for those of high status than for those of lesser rank—e.g., indulgence of upper-rank behavior has limits.

Little attempt has been made to explain both kinds of response in the same theory (compare Hollander & Willis, 1967; Wahrman, 1967, 1970a, 1970b). Rather, many explanations have been offered for the mild response, and the more severe response has been barely acknowledged.

Mild Response

Let us first consider explanations of why high status often gives license to misbehave. As noted earlier, there are two schools of thought on this issue. Sociologists have tended to consider the prospect that power and status often go together. They suggest that the group may well perceive the act as equally deviant regardless of whether the actor has high or low status, but because group members of lesser rank may be intimidated by those of high rank, they do not act on their perceptions.

Psychologists have tended to ignore the prospect of power-blocking sanctions and have provided a good deal of evidence that the behavior is perceived differently when an actor has high status. The actor's power is irrelevant if others see nothing wrong in his behavior. The experiments cited above have tended to provide support for this approach, although, as noted earlier, those instances where there was greater disapproval of the high-status deviant have not offered subjects much opportunity to express this to the deviant.

If one accepts for the moment the proposition that most of the time high-status nonconformity is not perceived as inappropriate and leaves for future research the question of what happens if and when it is, one still has the problem of explaining why this should be so. What *do* the subjects perceive? Why does what strikes the outside observer as deviance not strike the members this way?

The studies have offered a variety of explanations of what subjects might have perceived and why this should have been so. With very few exceptions (e.g., Iverson, 1964; Pepitone, 1958), the researchers *assumed*

that certain thoughts were occurring to their subjects but neglected to ask for confirmation. Iverson (1964) reports that some of his subjects saw, in extrapunitive behavior by an expert on retardation, missionary zeal and concern for his fellow man, whereas they saw in identical behavior exhibited by a speaker described as a high school student, "impudence."

Pepitone (1958) reports that his subjects found justifications for the rudeness of a renowned expert toward an ignorant student. Hollander (1960) reports that when his competent confederate delayed his procedural nonconformity several groups changed the norms and followed his example. Thibaut and Riecken (1955) had low- and high status deviants first simultaneously refuse and then simultaneously agree to share certain materials. They report no subject explanations for the original selfish acts. Asking subjects any kind of question about how they justified the deviance is clearly the exception rather than the rule.

There are a number of theories which can be offered to explain why an act is not perceived as deviant. The various consistency theories can be and have been offered as explanations for why it is uncomfortable to perceive "good" people as guilty of "bad" acts, though the various theories do not appear to be sufficiently developed to explain why one deviant act results in a complete change in the norm for all, another results in an excuse being made for the actor but the norm being retained, still another ends up with the norm's range being broadened for the deviant but no one else, while still another deviant act is denied to have occurred to begin with.

Berkowitz and Goranson (1964), Kelman and Eagly (1965), and Manis (1961) provide evidence that the act may be "assimilated" to fit the norm. Exchange theory can be invoked (Wahrman, 1970a) to explain why groups would prefer not to admit deviance is possible in people who have been granted status in exchange for conformity; i.e., this is to admit that they have foolishly given status to an unworthy person. Sherif and Hovland's (1961) conception of "latitudes of acceptance" may be invoked to suggest that the range of permissible behaviors can be widened to incorporate behavior previously not within the latitude of accep-tance. One can argue for a primacy effect, earlier good behavior being weighted more heavily in judgments than more recent deviant behavior (Hendrick & Constantini, 1970; Petronko & Perin, 1970).

Asch's (1946) theory can be invoked to explain why the act has a different meaning if performed by different actors. It strikes me that what I am doing here is changing vocabularies rather than explaining any-thing. Nor has anyone attempted to test the utility of one of these perceptual explanations against another. Certainly there is a difference between attributing benevolent motives to the nonconformer and retaining the norm and changing the norm for the actor or for the whole group, but we do not know how these differ-ences occur. It may help to ask subjects to explain their responses instead of inferring what they must have believed or perceived.

Hollander (1958) and Homans (1961) have both suggested "bank account" models of status from which group members draw for deviance. Homans implies that although a given act costs everyone the same number of units, those of high status have more to spare and therefore may retain their standing as the highest-ranked members even if they violate some norms.

Hollander suggests that the price of deviance is lower for those of high status; they lose fewer units per act of deviance than would lesser members and therefore suffer only mild drops in status for deviance. Hollander's idea of sanctions is unclear. He suggests that one uses up "idiosyncrasy credits" by violating norms, but that, if one does not use up his credits, there will be no sanctions. In other portions of his theory, he suggests that one *needs* these credits to innovate. Unless I seriously misunderstand Hollander, losing these cred-its is in itself a sanction if it inhibits the actors' freedom to innovate at a later date.

In any case, neither Homans nor Hollander nor anyone else can supply us with acceptable measures of what such units or credits might be. How these units get translated into various interpretations of behavior is not yet known. The question of what hap-pens when one has lost sufficient units so that the

person who had been next ranking is suddenly one's superior remains to be explored.

Severe Response

The question of why and when—despite the aforemen-tioned tendencies toward consistency, assimilation, benevolent motive attribution, and the like—groups not only decide the high-status people are deviant but are also worthy of more severe penalties than lesser deviants would have received remains unclear and unexplored. It is not clear whether the deviance is seen as *more* deviant and therefore worthy of more severe penalties or it is seen as equally deviant but, for some unclear reason, more severe penalties are applied.

Wahrman (1970b) found evidence that subjects found a psychology graduate who insisted on giving strict discipline to a delinquent (who clearly required warmth) a good deal more disturbing than they did a graduate biologist or undergraduate psychology major who espoused the same position.

Wiggins et al. (1965) found that a highly competent confederate whose violation of the experimenter's pro-cedural rules resulted in the experimenter's penalizing the group severely was sanctioned more severely than a confederate of moderate competence who provoked the experimenter into equally harsh treatment of the group.

Walster et al. (1966); Rokeach and Rothman (1965); and Wyer (1970) also supply evidence of over-reaction to those of high status.

This phenomenon may result from a calculation of what it takes to make a high-status deviant feel sanctioned—a one-dollar fine means less to a wealthy man than to a pauper—or may involve some less cal-culated process. Hollander and Willis (1967) suggest that high-status people are seen as more in control of their own behavior and therefore their deviance repre-sents greater willfulness on their part. Perhaps, as Wahrman (1970a) suggests, extreme penalties should be thought of as a response to an exchange agreement which high-status people are seen as having betrayed. The excess esteem withdrawn is the psychological equivalent of interest; i.e., a penalty for betrayal is added to the normal penalty for deviance.

It may be that, as Sampson (1963) and Turner (1962) suggest, we cannot interact with people effectively unless we know how to anticipate their behavior, and it may be more important for people in important roles to live up to their expectations than those of less value to the group. The annoyance produced by deviance would, if this approach is correct, be less disturbing than the fact of unpredictability. The confusion surrounding interpretation of how to respond to the actor in the future would be more responsible for the severe penalties than the deviance itself.

Although one could invent other explanations in addition to these, we have not yet been in a position to test the explanations we already possess.

◈ Conclusions

We have reason to believe that high status tends to protect the possessors from sanctions. On those occasions when it does not protect them, it tends to make them more vulnerable than lesser members of the group would be. It is, apparently, rare for the same sanctions to be applied to high-status people as are applied to those of moderate or low status.

Future research will have to systematically vary types of status and types of norms. The available literature has tended to rely on individual responses to rating scales and has ignored both the process by which groups reach consensus on how to interpret the behavior and consensus on what overt responses to make to deviance.

Research on status and deviance has drawn on the vocabularies of a number of theories but has not been strictly derived from theory. There is need for theories which will clearly predict not only whether sanctions will be stronger or milder for those of high status but also which of a variety of mild or strong outcomes will occur.

◈ References

Bales, R. F. (1970) Personality and Interpersonal Behavior. New York: Holt, Rinehart & Winston.

———. (1955) "How people interact in conferences." Scientific A mer. 192, 3: 31–35.

———. (1954) "In conference." Harvard Business Rev. 32: 44–50.

———. (1953) "The equilibrium problem in small groups," pp. 111–161 in T. Parsons et al., Working Papers in Theory of Action. New York: Free Press.

———. (1952) "Some uniformities of behavior in small social systems," pp. 146–159 in G. E. Swanson et al. (eds.) Readings in Social Psychology. New York: Holt.

———. (1950) Interaction Process Analysis: A Method for the Study of Small Groups. Reading, Mass.: Addison-Wesley.

Bales, F.F. and A. P. Hare (1965) "Diagnostic use of interaction profile." J. of Social Psychology 67 (December): 239–258.

Bales, R. F. and F. L. Strodtbeck (1951) "Phases in group problem solving." J. of Abnormal Social Psychology 46: 485495.

Bennis, W. G. and H. A. Shepard (1956) "A theory of group development." Human Relations 9: 415437.

Bion, W. R. (1961) Experience in Groups: and Other Papers. New York: Basic Books.

Borgatt, A. E. F. (1963) "A new systematic interaction observation system: behavior cores system (BSS system)." J. of Psych. Studies 14: 24–44.

———. (1962) "A systematic study of interaction process scores, peer and self assessments, personality, and other variables." Genetic Psychology Monographs 65: 219–291.

Borgatt, A. E. F. and R. F. Bales (1953) "Task and accumulation of experience as factors in the interaction of small groups." Sociometry 16: 239–252.

Carter, L. F. (1954) "Recording and evaluating the performance of individuals as members of small groups." Personnel Psychology 7: 477484.

Couch, A. S. (1960) "Psychological determinants of interpersonal behavior. Ph.D. dissertation. Harvard University.

Coyle, G. L. (1930) Social Process in Organized Groups. New York: Smith.

Dewey, J. (1933) How We Think. Lexington, Mass.: D. C.Heath.

Dunphy, D. C. (1964) "Social change in self-analytic groups." Ph.D. dissertation. Harvard University.

Effrat, A. (1968) "Editor's introduction." Soc. Inquiry 38 (Spring)· 97–104.

Freud, S. (1949) Group Psychology and the Analysis of the Ego. New York: Liveright.

Hare, A. P. (1969) "Four dimensions of interpersonal behavior." (unpublished)

———. (1968) "Phases in the development of the Bicol Development Planning Board," in S. Wells and A. P. Hare (eds.) Studies in Regional Development. New York: Bicol Development Planning Board.

Hare, A. P., and A. Effrat (1969) "Content and process of interaction in Lord of the Flies." (unpublished)

Hare, A. P., N. Waxler, G. Saslow and J. D. Matarazzo (1960) "Interaction process in a standardized initial psychiatric interview." J. of Consulting Psychology 24: 193.

Heinicke, C. and R. F. Bales (1953) "Developmental trends in the structure of small groups." Sociometry 16: 7–38.

Horsfall, A. B, and C. M. Arens Berg (1949) "Teamwork and productivity in a shoe factory." Human Organization 8, 1: 13–25.

Landsberger, H. A. (1955) "Interaction process analysis of the mediation of labor-management disputes." J. of Abnormal Social Psychology 51: 552–558.

Lanzetta, J. T., G. R. Wendt, P. Langham, and D. Haefner (1956) 'The effects of an 'anxiety-reducing' medication on group behavior under threat." J. of Abnormal Social Psychology 52: 103–108.

Leary, T. (1957) Interpersonal Diagnosis of Personality. New York: Ronald.

Lennard, H. and A. Bernstein with H. C. Hendln and E. B. Palmore (1967) The Anatomy of Psychotherapy: Systems of Communication and Expectation. New York: Columbia Univ. Press.

Mann, R. D. (1967) Interpersonal Styles and Group Development. New York: John Wiley.

Matarazzo, J. D., G. Saslow, R. Matarazzo, and J. S. Phillips (1957) "Stability and modifiability of personality patterns during standardized interviews," in P. A. Hoch and J. Zubin (eds.) Psychopathology of Communication. New York: Grune & Stratton.

Mills, T. M. (1964) Group Transformation: An Analysis of a Learning Group. Englewood Cliffs, N.J.: Prentice-Hall.

Parsons, T. (1961) Article, pp. 30'79 in T. Parsons et al. (eds.) Theories of Society. New York: Free Press.

Parsons, T., et al. (1953) Working Papers in the Theory of Action. New York: Free Press.

Plank, R. (1951) "An analysis of a group therapy experiment." Human Organization 10, 3: 5–21;4: 26–36.

Psathas, G. (1960) "Phase movement and equilibrium tendencies in interaction process in psychotherapy groups." Sociometry 23: 177–194.

Schutz, W. C. (1958) FIRO: A Three-Dimensional Theory of Interpersonal Behavior. New York: Holt.

———. (1955) "What makes groups productive?" Human Relations 8: 429465.

Slater, P. E. (1966) Microcosm: Structural, Psychological, and Religious Evolution in Groups. New York: John Wiley.

Stock, D. and H. A. Thelen (1958) Emotional Dynamics and Group Culture: Experimental Studies of Individual and Group Behavior. New York: New York Univ. Press.

Stone, P. J., D. C. Dunphy, M. S. Smith, and D. M. Ogilvie (l966) The General Inquirer: A Computer Approach to Content Analysis. Cambridge, Mass.: MIT Press.

Talland, G. A. (1955) "Task and interaction process: some characteristics of therapeutic group discussion." J. of Abnormal Social Psychology 50: 105–109.

Theodorson, G. A. (1953) "Elements in the progressive development of small groups." Social Forces 31: 311–320.

Tuckman, B. W. (1965) "Developmental sequence in small groups." Psych. Bull. 63 (June); 384–399.

Van Zelst, R. H. (1952) "An interpersonal relations technique for industry." Personnel 29: 68–76.

CHAPTER **2**

The Diversity of Deviance

What would you think if you were walking down the street and passed a man entirely covered in leopard spots? It would definitely make you look twice and would qualify as a deviant appearance. Would you wonder what he was thinking, how it felt to live within those spots, and why he would choose such a visible form of body modification? Tom Leppard once held the title of the most tattooed man in the world, with 99% of his body covered in tattooed leopard spots. For more than 20 years, Leppard lived as something of a hermit in a shack with no electricity or furniture on the Scottish island of Skye. Despite his solitary lifestyle, Leppard clearly enjoyed the attention of

▲ Photo 2.1 What would you think if you were at the grocery store and ran into Tom Leppard, who has tattooed leopard spots over 99% of his body?

strangers, at least to some degree. He spoke of choosing his "leopard" appearance and his visible status: "I've loved every minute and when you're covered in leopard tattoos you certainly get noticed—I became a bit of a tourist attraction on Skye" (Irvine, 2008).

◈ Introduction

Now that you've been introduced to the concept of deviance and the importance of understanding deviant behavior from a theoretical perspective, we want to spend some time exploring the various forms that deviance can take. When you think about deviance, what do you typically think about? Take a moment to quickly think of five types of deviant behavior. What immediately comes to mind? You probably came up with examples that reflect criminal behavior such as drug dealing, assault, robbery, or homicide. These are quite common responses, especially given the way the media cover crime and deviance. Yet deviance is not always criminal in nature. Nor does it always reflect an act or a behavior. There is a much broader array of what constitutes deviance in our society. In short, deviance can take many forms.

In this chapter, we discuss the diversity of deviance and explore its broad array in American society. It is our hope that by introducing you to deviance in its varied forms, you'll gain a deeper understanding of its nature before we move on to learning about how deviance is researched (Chapter 3), explained (Chapters 4–10), and responded to in society (Chapters 11–12). This chapter on the different types of deviance is a good place to begin an analysis of the sociological field of deviance and the phenomena it investigates.

A chapter on "types of deviance" is difficult to write because deviance as a field of study is very subjective. Many textbooks offer a survey or overview of different types of deviant behavior, devoting entire chapters to such topics as physical deviance, sexual deviance, drug use, mental disorders, and corporate deviance. As authors of this text, we do not necessarily agree with those categories or characterizations of different behaviors, attitudes, and physical attributes as deviant. Indeed, even between the three of us, we sometimes disagree on what is deviant and what is not. Rather than writing simply from our own points of view and trying to persuade you to adopt our perspectives, however, we offer the following as a glimpse into the field of deviance as it has been defined, studied, and treated throughout the years.

◈ Deviance and Its Varied Forms

While deviant behavior and crime certainly overlap, deviance encompasses much more than crime. Sociologists who have studied deviance have researched and written about a range of topics, including the disabled (E. Goffman, 1963), the mentally ill (Link, Phelan, Bresnahan, Stueve, & Pescosolido, 1999), the voluntarily childless (Park, 2002), the homeless (L. Anderson, Snow, & Cress, 1994), Jewish resisters during the Holocaust (Einwohner, 2003), topless dancers (Thompson, Harred, & Burks 2003), bisexuals (Weinberg, Williams, & Pryor, 2001), anorexics and bulimics (McLorg & Taub, 1987), self-injurers (P. A. Adler & Adler, 2007), and gay male Christian couples (Yip, 1996), to name just a few. This research is in addition to the many studies of criminal deviance, too numerous to list here. You can get a sense of the range of deviant behavior and how it has been studied simply by exploring the contents of the academic journal that is devoted to this very topic: *Deviant Behavior.* In addition to this introductory chapter exploring the many forms of deviance, we include short summaries of recent research on different types of deviant behavior in each chapter of this book.

The diversity of deviance and how drastically norms and attitudes may change over time is attested to in research conducted by J. L. Simmons (1965), who, several decades ago, surveyed 180 individuals, asking them to "list those things or types of persons whom you regard as deviant." More than 250 different acts and persons were listed. The range of responses not only included expected items such as prostitutes, drug addicts, and murderers but also included liars, Democrats, reckless drivers, atheists, self-pitiers, career women, divorcees, prudes, pacifists, and even know-it-all professors! The most frequent survey responses are listed in Table 2.1.

Imagine conducting a similar survey today. Which responses from this list might still occur with some frequency? Which might be less frequent? Whatever you imagined, there is little doubt that the list would look different today compared to 1965, reflecting the key point that what constitutes deviance changes depending on the historical context, something we discuss more later on in this chapter. For now, we want you to simply recognize the sheer range of deviance and its diversity.

Table 2.1 Most Frequent Responses to the Question, "What Is Deviant?"

Response	%
Homosexuals	49
Drug addicts	47
Alcoholics	46
Prostitutes	27
Murderers	22
Criminals	18
Lesbians	13
Juvenile delinquents	13
Beatniks	12
Mentally ill	12
Perverts	12
Communists	10
Atheists	10
Political extremists	10

Source: Simmons (1965).

It would be nearly impossible to describe deviance in *all* its varied forms. Rather than try to provide an exhaustive list of the different realms of deviance, we have chosen to highlight a few to illustrate the broad spectrum of behaviors, attitudes, and characteristics that have been deemed deviant by at least some segments of the larger society.

THINKING LIKE A SOCIOLOGIST—STRICT CONFORMITY AS DEVIANCE

A student film, *55: A Meditation on the Speed Limit,* which can be viewed on YouTube (www.youtube .com/watch?v=1B-Ox0ZmVIU), illustrates a potential problem with strict conformity. In the 5-minute video, college students filmed an experiment where they managed to have cars in every lane of the freeway driving exactly the speed limit. This created a wall of traffic and frustrated drivers in the cars behind them, leading to visible road rage. Do you think strict conformity can also be a form of deviance? Why or why not? Can you think of other circumstances in which strict conformity might be considered deviant?

◆ Physical Deviance and Appearance: Ideals of Beauty and Everyone Else

Physical deviance is perhaps the most visible form of deviance, and it can evoke stereotypes, stigma, and discrimination. Sociologists have described two types of physical deviance, including (1) violations of aesthetic norms (what people should look like, including height, weight, and the absence or presence of disfigurement) and (2) physical incapacity, which would include those with a physical disability (Goode, 2005).

Erving Goffman (1963) opens his book, *Stigma,* with a letter a 16-year-old girl wrote to Miss Lonely-hearts in 1962. She writes about how she is a good dancer and has a nice shape and pretty clothes, but no boy will take her out. Why? Because she was born without a nose:

> I sit and look at myself all day and cry. I have a big hole in the middle of my face that scares people even myself. . . . What did I do to deserve such a terrible bad fate? Even if I did do some bad things, I didn't do any before I was a year old and I was born this way. . . . Ought I commit suicide? (reprinted in E. Goffman, 1963, first page)

As suggested by the letter to Miss Lonelyhearts, physical deviance may be viewed as a marker of other forms of deviance. In other words, passersby may notice people with numerous tattoos, heavily muscled female bodybuilders, or those with visible physical disabilities and may attribute other characteristics to those individuals. You may notice, for example, when talking to a person who is hard of hearing that others in the conversation may slow their speech considerably and use smaller words, as well as speaking louder than usual; this suggests an implicit assumption that the individual has difficulty understanding as well as hearing.

Our ideas of what is acceptable or desirable in terms of physical appearance vary widely depending on the context. You can get a sense of this by visiting a local museum or simply flipping through an art book showing paintings and photographs of women thought to be very beautiful in their time. From the rounded curves of the women painted by Peter Paul Rubens in the 1600s (which is where the term *Rubenesque* originated to describe an hourglass figure), to the very thin flappers considered ideal in the 1920s, to Marilyn Monroe in the 1950s, Twiggy in the 1960s, Cindy Crawford in the 1980s, Kate Moss in the 1990s, and Kim Kardashian in 2010, our ideals of beauty and the most-desired body types clearly change and evolve over time.

Along with professionally styled hair and makeup and the use of meticulous lighting and angles, editors can now touch up photographs to remove wrinkles and traces of cellulite and to make beautiful models' already thin limbs and waists trimmer and more defined. This is of concern to sociologists because setting a truly unattainable standard for the ideal physical appearance can lead to deviant behavior, including harmful eating disorders, such as anorexia nervosa or bulimia, or unnecessary plastic surgeries.

Another form of physical deviance is **self-injury**—cutting, burning, branding, scratching, picking at skin or reopening wounds, biting, hair pulling, and bone breaking. P. A. Adler and Adler (2007) found that most self-injurers never seek help from mental health professionals, most of the self-incurred wounds do not need medical attention, and the majority of self-injurers thus remain hidden within society. Why would anyone purposely hurt themselves? P. A. Adler and Adler explain the reasoning like this:

> Although self-injury can be morbid and often maladaptive, our subjects overwhelmingly agree that it represents an attempt at self-help. They claim that their behaviors provide immediate but short-term release from anxiety, depersonalization, racing thoughts, and rapidly fluctuating emotions. . . . It provides a sense of control, reconfirms the presence of one's body, dulls feelings, and converts unbearable emotional pain into manageable physical pain. (p. 540)

P. A. Adler and Adler (2007) suggest that self-injury is currently being "demedicalized"—shifting out of the realm of mental illness and categorized instead as deviance, characterized by the voluntary choice of those involved.

While there are certainly other forms of physical deviance, body modification is the last example we will discuss. **Body modification** includes extreme tattooing, like Mr. Leppard from the opening story who paid to have more than 99% of his body covered in inked leopard spots. It also includes piercings, scarification, and reconstructive and cosmetic surgery. The reasons for body modification vary, but more than 3,500 people have joined the Church of Body Modification and view their physical changes as a way to spiritually strengthen the connection between body, mind, and soul.

Individuals choose to engage in body modification, but the choice may not be respected by the larger society. In September 2010, a 14-year-old freshman girl, Ariana Iocono, was suspended from school for wearing a small stud in her nose and violating the school's dress code, which forbids piercings. The girl and her mother were members of the Church of Body Modification and claimed that the nose ring was a religious symbol, but school administrators were unsympathetic, arguing that Ariana had not met the criteria for a religious exemption (Netter, 2010).

DEVIANCE IN POPULAR CULTURE

A wide variety of deviance can be examined by paying careful attention to popular culture. Below are a number of documentary films and television shows that offer concrete examples of specific cultural norms, different types of deviant behavior, and how individuals cope with **stigma**. What messages about norms and acceptable behavior are portrayed in each of these examples? What is the deviant behavior in each film/episode? What does the reaction to the deviant behavior tell you about the larger culture?

Films

Devil's Playground—a documentary following four Amish teenagers through the experience of Rumspringa, when they are given freedom to experience the outside world before deciding whether or not to commit to a lifetime in the Amish community.

Enron: The Smartest Guys in the Room—a documentary investigating white-collar crime and the greed that toppled what was once the seventh largest corporate entity in the United States and left 20,000 employees without jobs.

Deliver Us From Evil—a documentary investigating sexual abuse within the Catholic Church. The focus is on Father Oliver O'Grady, a pedophile who sexually assaulted dozens of children.

Dark Days—a documentary featuring people living in the tunnels under the subway system in New York City; filmed in black and white, it shows how one segment of the homeless population built homes and a community under the city.

(Continued)

(Continued)

Television

Reality television and The Learning Channel (TLC), particularly, feature a number of programs offering an inside view of people perceived as deviant or different in some way and showing how they deal with stigma from various sources:

Little People, Big World—offers an inside view of the life of the Roloff family. The parents, Matt and Amy, are "Little People" standing only four feet tall, and they are raising four children on a 34-acre farm.

Hoarders—an A&E series focusing on individuals whose hoarding of belongings has led them to the verge of personal disasters, including eviction, loss of their children, divorce, jail time, or demolition of their homes.

In paying attention to popular culture and how different subcultures and characteristics are portrayed, we can easily see that deviance is all around us.

◇ Relationships and Deviance

Sexually unconventional behavior is another central topic of discussion when it comes to deviance. As a society, we are generally intrigued with others' intimate relationships and sexual practices. Goode (2005, p. 230) asks, Why are there so many norms about sexual behavior? And why are the punishments for violating sexual norms so severe? Concerning the first question, Goode rightly claims the ways that we violate mainstream society's norms by engaging in variant sexual acts are almost infinite. The realm of **sexual deviance** may include exotic dancers, strippers, sex tourism, anonymous sex in public restrooms, bisexuality, online sexual predators, prostitutes, premarital chastity, and many others. As with virtually every kind of deviance, sexual deviance is largely determined by the community, culture, and context.

Even within the United States, there is considerable disagreement about what sexual activities should and should not be allowed. The issue of gay marriage is one current example where community values are being tested and defined on political ballots across the country. Another example where context matters is prostitution. While considered a crime in most of the country, prostitution is legal in many areas of Nevada. Certain counties in Nevada are allowed to regulate and license brothels, a multimillion-dollar industry based on legalized prostitution.

While societal norms shape our conceptions of appropriate sexual behavior, those boundaries are regularly tested by new fads and businesses and by many different **subcultures** making up their own rules as they go along. The Ashley Madison Agency, for example, bills itself as the world's premiere discreet dating service; it is marketed to those who are married and wish to have affairs. The agency's slogan captures the intent succinctly: "Life is short. Have an affair." The Ashley Madison Agency courts publicity, advertising widely on billboards, in magazines, and on television commercials. Interested adults can go on the website and purchase the "Affair Guarantee" package; if they do not find a suitable partner within

3 months, they can get a refund. With over seven million anonymous members, it is clear that there is widespread interest in relationships outside of marriage. The need for anonymity and discretion also suggests that there is still enough stigma attached to such relationships that it is preferable to shop for a partner before identifying oneself.

Polygamy is another frequently discredited form of relationship. In the United States, monogamy is the legal norm, yet some religions and subcultures still allow and encourage men to take multiple wives. The conflict between a subculture's values and the larger societal norms came vividly into play in 2008 when the state of Texas conducted a military-style raid on the Yearning for Zion Ranch, a polygamous religious sect of the Fundamental Church of Jesus Christ of Latter-day Saints.

Warren S. Jeffs, the leader of the Fundamental Church of Jesus Christ of Latter-day Saints, had been convicted a year earlier on felony charges as an accomplice to rape for his role in coercing the marriage of a 14-year-old girl to her 19-year-old cousin. When the raid on the Yearning for Zion Ranch took place, Jeffs was in the early phases of a 10-year-to-life sentence while awaiting trial on other sex charges in Arizona.

On the basis of an accusation of sexual abuse from an anonymous 16-year-old girl, SWAT teams raided the Yearning for Zion Ranch and forcibly removed more than 400 children from their homes and families. Texas child welfare officials believed that the children were in danger; they suspected young girls were being made into child brides among other physical and sexual abuse within the polygamous community.

This clash of cultures and values played out dramatically in the media. After being removed from their homes and the insular community in which they were raised, the children of the ranch were suddenly exposed to many strangers, different foods, varied styles of dress, and a new set of norms. When some of their mothers voluntarily left the ranch to be with the children, they were visibly out of their element in their prairie dresses and old-fashioned hairstyles, forced to move to the suburbs and shop at Walmart rather than tend to their gardens and livestock on the ranch.

In the end, the telephone calls that set the raid in motion may have been a hoax or a setup, but the damage was irreparably done. The children of the Yearning for Zion Ranch were returned to their parents approximately 2 months later, but the trauma inflicted on the families from such a forced separation could not be taken back. While this was clearly a difficult situation for all involved, it presents sociologically interesting questions about what is deviant and who gets to decide. Those living at the Yearning for Zion Ranch were nearly self-sufficient and seemed to live quietly by their own rules and norms within its bounds. At what point do you think it would be appropriate for the state of Texas to step in and take the children away from their families? Who should ultimately decide? Who are the deviants in this case—the polygamous families or the state of Texas for breaking up those families and traumatizing a whole community? These are interesting and complex questions without easy answers, which is part of what makes deviance such a fascinating—and ever-changing—field of study.

▲ **Photo 2.2** Community members from the Yearning for Zion Ranch react after the state of Texas forcibly removed more than 400 children from their homes and families.

Deviance in Cyberspace: Making Up the Norms as We Go

One way to clearly see that our ideas about deviance and deviant behavior change over time is to consider the creation of whole new categories of deviant behavior. As new technology has developed, brand-new forms of deviance have also taken shape. Cyberdeviance, for example, is a relatively new phenomenon, but it already has many different forms, including the online pedophile subculture, cyberbullying, online misbehavior of college students, "sexting," and the illegal downloading of music, movies, and readings.

If such behavior is prevalent, particularly among younger people and hidden populations, should it still be considered deviant? That question is difficult to answer; norms and laws are being created and modified all the time, even as technology improves and offers new possibilities for deviant behavior.

STUDIES IN DEVIANCE

Examining the Virtual Subculture of Johns

By Kristi R. Blevins and Thomas J. Holt (2009), in *Journal of Contemporary Ethnography, 38*, 619–648.

An example of a deviant subculture that crosses the boundaries between cyberdeviance and criminal deviance is the online subculture of "johns" or male heterosexual clients of sex workers. In their qualitative study, Blevins and Holt (2009) explored Web forums in a number of U.S. cities in an attempt to identify the norms and values in the mostly hidden world of the client side of sex work. The authors analyzed Web forums where heterosexual "johns," or male clients of prostitutes, shared questions and information while minimizing exposure to law enforcement.

Blevins and Holt (2009) particularly focus on the "argot" or specialized language of the virtual subculture of johns, and they use extensive quotes to illustrate their points. Three themes related to argot emerged from their analysis. The first theme was "experience," which, among other things, categorized the "johns" across a hierarchy of novices or "newbies" to the more experienced "mongers, trollers, or hobbyists" (note that the derogatory term *john* was not used in the argot of the subculture). The second theme was "commodification"—the notion that the prostitutes themselves and the acts they wanted were a commodity that came with a cost. This issue brought a great deal of discussion over how much different prostitutes or different sexual acts were worth or likely to cost. Finally, a related theme of "sexuality" or the various sexual acts desired or experienced was posted with a unique argot for a host of sexual activities. The language and subject matter are crude but offer a glimpse at the subcultural norms and values of these online communities or subcultures of "johns."

Subcultural Deviance

The virtual subculture of johns is just one example of many subcultures that might be considered deviant by at least some segment of the population. While the johns are generally a hidden population, as you can see from the earlier example of the Yearning for Zion Ranch, some subcultures are easily identifiable and can be singled out for holding different norms and values than the larger society. That case is particularly dramatic as children were taken from their parents and homes, but many other subcultures draw strong reactions from the outside community.

Research on subcultures has been wide-ranging. Hamm (2004) studied terrorist subcultures, examining the "complex ways in which music, literature, symbolism and style are used to construct terrorism" (p. 328). Others have written about "fat admirers," men who have a strong, erotic desire for obese women (Goode, 2008b); radical environmentalist organizations (Scarce, 2008); and the subculture of UFO contactees and abductees (Bader, 2008).

The Amish are another example of a subculture, but the question of deviance becomes quite complicated—particularly during the time when Amish youth are encouraged to go outside of the community and explore the "English" way of life. In this case, some types of deviant behavior are sanctioned for a short time before the teenagers choose their adult path and decide whether to be baptized and become an Amish adult in good standing or basically be ostracized from their parents and communities. We include with this chapter a very interesting article by Denise Reiling on this topic: Amish youths' response to culturally prescribed deviance.

◈ Elite Deviance, Corporate Deviance, and Workplace Misconduct

Elite deviance is an important topic, but one that does not generally receive as much attention as the potentially more dramatic violent acts and property crimes ("street crimes") that affect individuals on a personal level. While individuals tend to actively fear being victimized by street crimes, they probably do not realize the enormous impact elite deviance may have on their everyday lives. Mantsios (2010) offers a strong statement/indictment on how the corporate elite gain and maintain their status:

> Corporate America is a world made up of ruthless bosses, massive layoffs, favoritism and nepotism, health and safety violations, pension plan losses, union busting, tax evasions, unfair competition, and price gouging, as well as fast buck deals, financial speculation, and corporate wheeling and dealing that serve the interests of the corporate elite, but are generally wasteful and destructive to workers and the economy in general.
>
> It is no wonder Americans cannot think straight about class. The mass media is neither objective, balanced, independent, nor neutral. Those who own and direct the mass media are themselves part of the upper class. (pp. 240–241)

Elite deviance has been defined as "criminal and deviant acts by the largest corporations and the most powerful political organizations" (D. R. Simon, 2008, p. xi). In the introduction to his book on the topic, D. R. Simon (2008) explains that elite deviance refers to acts by elites or organizations that result in harm; he distinguishes between three different types of harm: physical harms, including death or physical injury; financial harms, including robbery, fraud, and various scams; and moral harms, which are harder to define but encourage distrust and alienation among members of the lower and middle classes (p. 35). Simon further breaks the topic of elite deviance down into three types of acts: economic domination, government and governmental control, and denial of basic human rights.

The reading at the end of this chapter by Bandura, Caprara, and Zsolnai (2000) discusses corporate transgressions through moral disengagement. It offers an interesting analysis of how corporations adopt institutional practices that violate laws and harm the public. The authors briefly highlight four famous cases, including an industrial disaster in Bhopal, India; the Ford Pintos that burst into flame on impact; Nestle's selling of infant formula to developing countries—a practice that led to the malnutrition of babies in Third World countries; and the Three Mile Island case, the most severe accident in U.S. commercial nuclear power plant history. Unlike most elite deviance, these cases garnered widespread public attention and brought notice—at least temporarily—to harmful corporate practices.

A much more common and smaller scale form of deviance is workplace deviance. Employee misconduct undoubtedly leads to business failures and higher consumer costs; studies estimate that as many as two thirds of workers are involved in employee theft or other forms of employee deviance. Table 2.2 documents the percentage of employees taking part in the "invisible social problem" of workplace misconduct (Huiras, Uggen, & McMorris, 2000).

Table 2.2   Employee Deviance in the Previous Year

	Percentage Reporting Act
Got to work late without a good reason	51.0
Called in sick when not sick	47.9
Gave away goods or services	32.7
Claimed to have worked more hours than really did	9.7
Took things from employer or coworker	9.1
Been drunk or high at work	7.2
Lied to get or keep job	5.8
Misused or took money	2.5
Purposely damaged property	2.1

Source: Huiras, Uggen, and McMorris (2000).

◈ Positive Deviance

Even within sociology, there is some debate as to whether such a thing as **positive deviance** exists. Goode (1991), for example, believes that positive deviance is a contradiction in terms or an oxymoron; Jones (1998) and others disagree. We encourage you to try the exercise on random acts of kindness in the box on the next page and compare your results with your classmates. In conducting your own small research project, you are addressing a research question (does positive deviance exist?), collecting data (observing your own feelings and the reactions of others), and drawing conclusions. As a social scientist, what are your thoughts on positive deviance? Which side do you land on in the debate?

While the exercise on random acts of kindness gives you a chance to think about positive deviance on an individual level, scholars have recently been studying the idea of positive deviance at the organizational or corporate level. Spreitzer and Sonenshein (2004) define positive deviance as follows: "intentional behaviors that significantly depart from the norms of a referent group in honorable ways" (p. 841). An example from Spreitzer and Sonenshein's article helps to clarify the concept:

> In 1978, Merck&Co., one of the world's largest pharmaceutical companies, inadvertently discovered a potential cure for river blindness, a disease that inflicts tremendous pain, disfigurement, and blindness on its victims. The medication was first discovered as a veterinarian antibiotic, but it quickly created a major dilemma for Merck when its scientists realized the medication could be adapted to become a cure for river blindness. Because river blindness was indigenous to the developing world, Merck knew that it would never recover its research or distribution expenses for the drug. In addition, the company risked bad publicity for any unexpected side effects of the drug that in turn could damage the drug's reputation as a veterinary antibiotic (Business Enterprise Trust, 1991). Departing from norms in the pharmaceutical industry, Merck decided to manufacture and distribute the drug for free to the developing world, costing the company millions of dollars. Consequently, Merck helped eradicate river blindness, at its own expense. (pp. 834–835)

Spreitzer and Sonenshein (2004) argue that Merck's action in this case is an excellent example of positive deviance. The organization faced great cost and risk to develop, manufacture, and distribute the drug, yet Merck chose to depart from corporate norms prioritizing profit and gains and, in doing so, prevented further suffering from river blindness.

The idea of positive deviance is growing, at the individual, organizational, and community levels, and new research continues to stretch the concept and add to our understanding of how this "oxymoron" may play out in everyday life. Tufts University even hosts its own Positive Deviance Initiative; the initiative takes as its starting point:

> Positive Deviance is based on the observation that in every community there are certain individuals or groups whose uncommon behaviors and strategies enable them to find better solutions to problems than their peers, while having access to the same resources and facing similar or worse challenges. (http://www.positivedeviance.org/)

NOW YOU . . . TRY AN EXPERIMENT IN POSITIVE DEVIANCE!

One way to explore the idea of positive deviance is to conduct your own small-scale experiment and then decide whether you think positive deviance exists. For this exercise, your task is to go out and commit random acts of kindness—arguably, a form of positive deviance.

Many introductory sociology classes ask students to conduct a breaching experiment by breaking a norm and then observing the reactions of those around them. In this case, the goal is to perform a face-to-face act of kindness for a *stranger* and to take note of the reaction to your behavior.

(Continued)

(Continued)

Think about the following questions in completing your act(s) of kindness (you may find it helpful, necessary, or interesting to repeat the act more than once):

1. Why did you choose to do this particular act of kindness?

2. How did you feel while doing the random act of kindness and why do you think you felt this way?

3. How did the recipient—and any others who witnessed the kindness—react? Speculate as to why they reacted the way they did. If the situation was reversed, do you think you would have reacted differently?

Be safe and smart in your choice of kindnesses—be careful not to inflict trauma on yourself or the recipient and be certain that you do not put yourself in a dangerous position. After conducting your experiment, reflect on how you felt and what the reactions to your act of kindness were. Did you take age or gender into consideration in choosing your "target"? Did you feel the need to explain that your act was an experiment or assignment for class? Based on this data, do you think positive deviance exists? Why or why not?

Adapted from Jones (1998) (full article available on SAGE supplemental website).

▲ **Photo 2.3**   Would you consider the "Free Hugs" movement a form of positive deviance? Why or why not?

◈ Question: So Who Are the Deviants? Answer: It Depends on Who You Ask

We cannot emphasize enough how much context matters in any discussion or explanation of deviant behavior. You simply can't discuss forms of deviance without some reference to culture, context, and historical period. What some people regard as deviant, others regard as virtuous. What some might praise, others condemn. To say that deviance exists does not specify which acts are considered deviant by which groups in what situations and at any given time.

◈ Conclusion

We hope that after reading this chapter—and delving further into this book—your ideas about deviant behavior and social control will have greatly expanded. The more commonly studied types of deviant behavior, such as criminal deviance (including street crime) and elite deviance (including corporate and white-collar crimes), are explored further throughout the book. Our goal in this chapter is simply to help broaden your understanding of what constitutes deviance and to realize the question, "What is deviance?" must be followed by the qualifier, "According to whom?" We realize that this chapter and this book will not resolve these issues for you and may very well raise more questions than it answers. Still, our goal is to broaden your understanding of deviance and its many forms.

With that goal in mind, we provide a few extra exercises and discussion questions in this chapter to help you explore boundaries, conduct your own experiments, form your own analyses, and begin to think about deviance and social control very broadly. Chapter 3 delves much more specifically into the art and science of researching deviance—you'll soon see that deviance is a very interesting topic to study and research. For now, we hope you will take a close look at the norms and behavior of your community and the larger society; we think you will soon discover an enormous amount of diversity in the deviance that is all around you.

EXERCISES AND DISCUSSION QUESTIONS

1. Look again at Table 2.1, compiled by Simmons in 1965. Ask several friends or family members the same question Simmons used: "list those things or types of persons whom you regard as deviant," and compile the responses. Do any of the categories from your small study overlap with those that Simmons found? Do any of the categories from 1965 disappear entirely? How would you explain this?

2. Pay attention over the next 24 hours and see what kinds of deviant behavior you notice. It can be behavior you witness, you commit (hopefully nothing that will get you in trouble!), or you hear about on the news or media. What did you notice? How many different types of deviance were you exposed to in one day?

3. To explore the idea of stigma and how a physical trait can deeply affect an individual's life, you might try imagining a day with a disability. This exercise will begin with a diary entry: record a typical day (e.g., what you did, the interactions you had, etc.), and then assign yourself a visible attribute typically associated with deviance (e.g., being blind, obese, missing a limb). Rewrite your diary entry to reflect what you imagine would be different that day given your stigma. What obstacles would you face? Would people treat you differently? What did you learn about deviance, social norms, stigma, and coping by completing this exercise?

4. In a recent example of a polygamous lifestyle, the reality television show *Sister Wives* portrays a polygamist family and begins at the point where the husband is courting his fourth wife. His motto is "Love should be multiplied, not divided." Do you think this kind of polygamy—where the relationships are consensual and the brides are all adults—is deviant? Why or why not?

KEY TERMS

Body modification

Elite deviance

Physical deviance

Polygamy

Positive deviance

Self-injury

Sexual deviance

Stigma

Subcultures

READING 5

This fascinating article presents a number of complex questions regarding the nature of deviance, the social contexts that determine what is and what is not deviance, and the social and emotional consequences that explorations into deviance can cause. The researcher observed and interacted with a particular settlement of the Old Order Amish, a unique Christian and collectivist subculture largely guarded from "conventional American society." Among this settlement, it is common (to some extent, expected and tolerated) for youth in American society to deviate in their teenage years from the controlled childhood from which they recently emerged and prior to becoming an adult and fulfilling the roles of an adult. In the Amish subculture, the staging of the life course is taken to an extreme. Childhood is far more guarded and controlled than is conventional American society, with very little deviance tolerated. However, beginning with their 16th birthday and ending only when they are baptized and accept the Amish religion and subcultural practices or they leave the settlement, the youth are expected to engage in deviant behaviors. In this "simmie" period, youth are almost forced to explore American lifestyles (referred to as "English" lifestyle) before choosing to either commit to their Amish culture or leave it forever. The ritualized "simmie" period is characterized by a number of deviant behaviors (especially deviant for the very conservative Amish people), including alcohol consumption, bedding (sleepovers with the opposite sex where, although intercourse is not permitted, it happens, as do other forms of sexual behavior), and other deviances actually quite common and viewed as less "deviant" in American culture. The "simmie" period is psychologically and emotionally difficult for the Amish youth because they are expected to do things they have been told are wrong and that can literally send them to hell for all of eternity. That is, they believe that the baptism that occurs when they accept the Amish way of life does not necessarily wipe away their sins, even during a time when they are expected to deviate (sin). The description of the Old Order Amish youth culture is interesting and useful; they are living between rules, and the question of what is deviant—and to whom—takes on a whole new meaning during this timeframe.

The "Simmie" Side of Life

Old Order Amish Youths' Affective Response to Culturally Prescribed Deviance

Denise M. Reiling

Until fairly recently, youth culture has not been viewed as a sufficiently important sociological phenomenon to be worthy of separate study. It can be argued that this stance is a direct reflection of the marginalized status of youth in the larger social context (Adler & Adler, 1998; Hutchby & Moran-Ellis, 1998). The prevailing understanding of youth culture within society, as well, has been that youth culture is

Source: Reiling, Denise M. 2002. "The 'Simmie' Side of Life: Old Order Amish Youths' Affective Response to Culturally Prescribed Deviance." *Youth & Society* 34(2):146–171. Reprinted with permission.

simply a phase or a stage that adolescents pass through on their way to becoming an adult.

Others, however, describe youth culture as a highly vital and dynamic process that is instrumental and productive to the formation of the adult individual, particularly as it influences the development of identity (Adler & Adler, 1998; Baumeister & Muraven, 1996; Corsaro & Eder, 1990; Danielsen, Lorem, & Kroger, 2000; Hutchby & Moran-Ellis, 1998). According to this view, children and youth are separate, autonomous social actors, capable of demonstrating fairly high levels of social competence and agency (Adler & Adler, 1998; Hutchby & Moran-Ellis, 1998).

Terror Management Theory (TMT) (Pyszczynski, Greenberg, & Solomon, 1997; Solomon, Greenberg, & Pyszczynski, 1991) provides a theoretical framework through which to examine social competence and agency during the youth period. One of the primary tenets of TMT is that youth culture develops as a "cultural-anxiety buffer" against the reality of mortality. Accordingly, one would expect that as one's own death becomes salient through conscious reminders of death, defense of one's culture would increase. As we contemplate our own mortality, we depend on our culturally constructed worldview to make life and death more rational and bearable. Therefore, if reminded of death during the youth period, allegiance to and defense of youth culture should be high (Greenberg et al., 1990; Janssen, Dechesne, & Van Knippenberg, 1999).

Janssen et al. (1999) found support for TMT, in that they discovered that youth culture did function as a specialized cultural-anxiety buffer, in that reminding youth of death caused them to more greatly identify with and defend their youth culture. As with adult culture, youth culture constructs a worldview that provides youth with an explanation for life, death, and the after-life experience. Youth culture also influences an adolescent's self-esteem, functioning as a measuring rod for their social performance (Janssen et al., 1999).

Within this article, the special case of the Old Order Amish, a predominately North American Christian subculture, has been offered through which to examine selected propositions of TMT. Several unique cultural dynamics found among the Amish make them a valuable research population. Of particular importance is that Amish youth enter a decision-making period, beginning on their 16th birthday and lasting for potentially several years, within which they are to contemplate whether they will retain or repudiate Amish identity (Hostetler, 1993). During this "simmie" period, Amish youth must respond to implicit cultural prescriptions for deviance that have been constructed by adult Amish culture. Because most Amish parents do not openly object to this deviance (Hostetler, 1993) the deviance is implicitly sanctioned.

The Amish believe that exposing their youth to deviance functions to select out those who would not be adult Amish people. The Amish articulate a Social Darwinist analysis, wherein to assure the cohesion of their group, it is necessary for those not suitable to be "weeded out early lest they infect the rest of the group." As they explain, for this selection process to be fully effective, the individual must have the opportunity to deny the profane by being exposed to temptation. This belief prevents Amish parents from acting against, and in many cases causes them to condone and even encourage, the more serious forms of deviance, such as the consumption of alcohol.

Engaging in this deviance, however, creates an extraordinary and complex dilemma for Amish youth. The Amish believe that engaging in this culturally prescribed deviance endangers the individual's salvation, making their fate after death, at best uncertain, and at worst, condemnation to Hell. As such, this decision-making period instigates a search for existential meaning. But, to not engage in the culturally prescribed deviance during the simmie period would be a deviant act that would not be culturally sanctioned. Conforming to youth culture necessitates engaging in deviance to test their suitability as adult Amish people. Thus, Amish youth must negotiate the dilemma of being damned if they do and damned if they don't. This cultural dynamic provides an excellent and rare opportunity for social competence, agency, and TMT to be explored in a natural setting.

◇ **Methods and Setting**

The setting for this research was a nonmetropolitan county, located in a north-central state within the United States. This particular Amish settlement has an approximate population size of 12,500 members, around 40% of the county's total population. The research findings emerged as part of a larger, ethnographic study of Old Order Amish culture, with the primary data collection techniques being in-depth interviews and participant observation.

Observational data were collected over a period of 10 years, during which time the Amish extended to me as "complete membership" (Alder & Adler, 1987) as possible for a non-Amish person, spending summers, many weekends, and academic recess in one particular Amish home. Entrée was facilitated by three important factors, the first of which was the investment of time. As one Bishop noted, he respected the fact that I simply observed patiently for more than a year before asking direct questions. The second factor was that my having been raised on a farm allowed me a respectable level of cultural competence within this agrarian culture.

The third factor that facilitated entrée was that I quickly assumed the role "fieldworker as resource" (Emerson & Pollner, 2001), which, as collectivists, the Amish appreciated for the reciprocal relationship that being a resource created. I was known as someone who "takes down stories," but I was also known as someone who gave two highly valued things in return: information and confidentiality. As a medical sociologist, I became a resource for information concerning health, particularly mental health. As a researcher, I became a trusted confidant because of the confidentiality that I could promise them in that role. Amish people could say things to me that their cultural prescription against the expression of negative emotion and their cultural for gossip prevented them from saying to each other.

In addition to the observational data collected through my unique position and length of time within the Amish settlement, more than 60 in-depth interviews on the particular topic of the youth decision-making period were conducted with Amish participants,

within the last year of the research endeavor. The average length of the interviews was 5 hours. Interviews were also collected from non-Amish mental health professionals and non-Amish criminal justice agents. Non-Amish public school officials were also interviewed because it had been reported that approximately 80% of the Amish children in this settlement attend public rather than parochial schools.

Twenty interviews were gathered from participants within each of the three Amish participant pools that were constructed: prebaptism Amish, postbaptism Amish, and defected coethnics. Prebaptism Amish were defined as Amish youth who were in the culturally mandated decision-making period concerning the adoption or repudiation of Amish identity, between the ages of 16 and approximately 25. Postbaptism Amish were defined as Amish adults who had passed through the decision-making period and had formally adopted Amish identity by publicly taking adult baptism. Defected coethnics were defined as adults who had been born Amish, had passed through the decision-making period, but had repudiated Amish identity by publicly refusing to take adult baptism. They had subsequently defected from the group and had adopted "English" identity (a label the Amish use to denote the non-Amish population living within the same geographic area).

Although not by design, the 40 interviews of the postbaptism Amish and the defected coethnics were actually interviews of couples, not individuals. Indicative of the interdependent relationship that develops within marriages in this context, almost every participant requested that their spouse participate in these interviews. This circumstance proved to be highly productive and did not appear to inhibit free and full disclosure.

Even though the youth period was the focus of this line of inquiry, those who had already passed through this period, the postbaptism Amish and the defected coethnics, were included as interview participants for three reasons. First, because the Amish go to extraordinary lengths to protect their children from outside influence, if I had asked to interview only the youth, this request would have been met with suspicion, and most likely, entrée to the youth would have been denied. Participants within the two adult groups were interviewed first to establish trust. The second reason was that because the Amish are a collectivist culture, it was imperative to seek what they would view as a fair and balanced voice, by allowing for representation of all group members, including those who had defected.

The third reason for the inclusion of adults was that adults had been part of the larger, ethnographic study. I had assumed prior to interviewing that the adult accounts would differ notably from those of the youth. I expected the accounts of the adults to be more introspective, as a reflection of the length of time that had passed. I also anticipated that their standpoint as an adult would make their retrospective accounts more negative than the concurrent accounts of the youth. This was not found to be true, however. The accounts of both adult groups were virtually indistinguishable from those of the youth. There was not a notable difference in perspective. The youth appeared to have given as much thought as the adults to the consequences of deviance on their lives, as well as the lives of their future children.

The problem of social desirability merits some comment. One could speculate that the Amish would have a high need to protect the construction of Amish culture as virtuous, so how much could their reports and portrayals be trusted? The ability to answer that question with a great deal of certainty is always limited, but one of the best ways to assess the impact of social desirability is to study over time. Throughout the past 10 years of knowing the Amish, I have become convinced that social desirability is not a significant concern. Among the Amish, social desirability would more likely function to prohibit participation, rather than taint the data. Chances are that if they feel they cannot be truthful they will not grant an interview. I was also not concerned that social desirability would result in respondent bias because I received nearly total compliance with my requests for an interview.

A random sampling design of all Amish households was used to pull the Amish samples, using the Amish Directory (a census that the Amish compile) as a population list. I was able to locate the defected coethnics using the Amish Directory, too, because the Amish continue to list their names and geographic locations in the Directory. Because of the shame attached to defection, the Amish believe that listing the names of those who defect will function to limit defection. The age of the resultant interview participants ranged from age 16 through age 76, although most participants were approximately age 16 to 40. The sex ratio was equal.

Assessment of the affective response to deviance was based solely on participants' qualitative self-reports and descriptions of their experiences. Qualifiers have been used in reporting the findings to illustrate the degree of the affective response and the representativeness of the reports, for example, "every subject," "most subjects," "very high anxiety," and so on. The text has been illustrated with excerpts from the interviews that were tape-recorded. Verbatim transcriptions of the tapes and my field notes were analyzed using the NUDIST program for qualitative data analysis.

It should be noted that most of the prebaptism Amish did not want their interview to be tape-recorded. These participants did not give an explanation for their refusal to be tape-recorded, and human participants constraints prohibited probing their decline. Based on observation, their wariness about having their voice tape-recorded was understood as reflective of the conflicted state that their ambiguous, interstitial identity was generating. These participants did not appear to be uncomfortable with my note-taking, however, so it is possible that having their voice tape recorded, an act that would otherwise have been culturally prohibited, extended them beyond their already overextended deviance comfort zone.

Description of Old Order Amish Youth Culture

The Old Order Amish can be defined as a Christian subculture for which "Amish" has developed as a non-racialized, ethnic identity. They are reportedly direct descendants of Anabaptists (Christians believing in adult rather than infant baptism) who emerged in

Switzerland between 1525 and 1536 (Huntington, 1988), as part of a religious-based social movement throughout Europe (Nolt, 1992). Due to religious persecution in Europe, the Old Order Amish, what was to remain the most conservative faction of the original Anabaptist group, began immigrating to the United States in the 1700s, primarily into Pennsylvania (Huntington, 1988). Migration from Pennsylvania to Ohio and Indiana occurred primarily between 1815 and 1860 (Huntington, 1988). By 1991, Old Order Amish settlements had been located in 22 states within the United States (Nolt, 1992).

Each of the following practices that were advocated by the early Anabaptists are reportedly still in place today: adult baptism; non-assimilation with the dominant culture; in-group conformity; endogamy; nonproselytization; nonparticipation in military service; high, unrestrained fertility; a disciplined lifestyle; conformity in dress and hairstyle; a prohibition against alcohol and drug use by adults; strong proscriptions against modernization and technology-based living; and strong prescriptions for reciprocity (Hostetler, 1993; Huntington, 1988; Nolt, 1992).

As with the early Anabaptist groups, the Amish settlement under study continues to represent a near ideal type of collectivist, or Gemeinschaft, society. Each of what Triandis (1990) has identified as the defining attributes of a collectivist society were evidenced within this particular settlement: in-group primacy; the maintenance of in-group harmony through consensus and face-saving; a lack of out-group memberships; an emphasis on obedience and conformity to the exclusion of creativity, competition, and individual achievement; gossip as a key mechanism of social control; and strong boundary maintenance practices, which result in an almost total exclusion of the out-group.

Among the Old Order Amish, the 16th birthday signifies that the "child" has entered a rite of passage, wherein the "youth" is to begin to deliberate his or her identity. During this time, the youth will decide whether they want to take adult baptism and become "Amish" or whether they want to defect from the Amish and become "English." The end of this period is signified by the child's announcement of his or her decision to either repudiate or adopt Amish identity (Hostetler, 1993). And indeed, approximately 20% to 25% of youths within this settlement do eventually defect from the Amish. Most youth remain in this decision-making period for only 2 to 3 years, whereas others do not make their decision for as much as 8 to 10 years. It was reported that those who remain for an extended period of time are generally those who know they will eventually defect (Reiling, 2000).

Upon defection, the youth immediately becomes excommunicated from the Amish church. In this context, excommunication also results in ostracism and, in almost every case, physical displacement from the family and from the entire Amish settlement. In essence, those who defect become outcasts for an indeterminate period of time, ranging from a few months to their entire lifetime. Varying degrees of estrangement remain, however, in those relationships where some level of communication is eventually reestablished. It was reported that defection is a permanent state, despite the fact that it was also reported that many in this particular settlement believe that defection from the Amish results in damnation to Hell (Reiling, 2000).

The Amish in this settlement have constructed a label for youth in this decision-making period. As explained, the label of "simmie" is applied to Amish youth to signify that they are "foolish in the head." Whereas a range of descriptors was given, all participants agreed that this label signifies that youth are immature and not yet ready to be adult Amish persons. As one Amish man explained, "What happens during this time is that they start joining the group, the young folks. They want to be top grade, but they're still greener than a colt. They aren't trained yet. But once they're trained and mature, then they'll act like the rest of us. But these young kids aren't broke yet. They want to try to do what the others do, and they make a lot of dumb moves. So we call them simmies."

The application of this label is not automatic, however, although most youth experience the application of this label for some period of time. It is expected that after an initial period of being particularly immature, the youth will begin to "gel" or "pull themselves together," "to get ahold on themselves a bit more." One Amish woman, who had exited the simmie period only within the last year, explained that "the young folk generally aren't simmies anymore once they turn 18. When they get to be around 18, for some reason they become a little more sensible. It's just natural. Then we don't call them simmies anymore."

The label of simmie came to be understood as a "black sheep" label (Marques, 1986) that is applied in a preemptive attempt to shame or warn the adolescent into keeping his or her culturally prescribed period of deviance within culturally prescribed boundaries. As one Amish woman explained, "You don't brag about it. It's a put-down. It means you're gullible, or you're dangerous, because you've broken loose." And indeed, it is important to note that not all forms of deviance have been positively sanctioned. It certainly is not a situation of "anything goes." As illustrated by the following quote given by a middle-aged Amish woman, it was reported by every participant that limits to deviance were well known: "I just knew that I was doing something that I wouldn't want them (parents) to know. They would not have approved of how I was. I had gone too far outside of what's allowed for even a simmie."

Reports concerning deviant behavior during the simmie period should be kept in cultural perspective, however, as it is important to understand that constructions of normative behavior are numerous and rigid among the Amish. As such, the chance of being labeled as deviant is great. Granted, more serious forms of deviance, such as excessive consumption of alcohol and sexual exploration, do occur, but many of the behaviors that constitute deviance among the Amish would be considered quite benign in most other cultural contexts.

For example, because of the high standards that have been set for Amish behavior, being irresponsible, intentionally hurting another person's feelings, telling lies, being unkind by excluding another person from a group activity, or just acting in an unwise, reckless, or impractical fashion is considered deviant in the Amish context. As one Amish man remembered, "I did things that I know I shouldn't have, so I deserved the name simmie, I'm quite sure. I remember one time I left my flashlight at her (girlfriend's) place, but I didn't want to go back and admit I'd left it there, so I just went home without my flashlight. That was a simmie thing to do."

Identity during this decision-making period was reported to be highly ambiguous. Almost every participant's description depicted this decision-making period as one of limbo, wherein the child does not identify as Amish, even though continuing to live in an Amish home and to engage in Amish cultural practices. Nor does the child identify as English, even though many will wear English clothes outside of the home, cut their hair, drive cars, and engage in "worldly culture." This interstitial state resonates with the ambiguous identities of bisexuals, Christianized Jews, and light-skinned Blacks, as analyzed by Adam (1978). One Amish male, who was approximately 20 years old and had just taken adult baptism and formally adopted Amish identity 1 month prior to the interview, expressed this ambiguity: "During that time, I wouldn't have even admitted that I was Amish. I wouldn't have claimed it. I don't have a name for what I was during that period. We really don't think about what we were, just what we weren't—we weren't Amish kids. I wouldn't have a name for it, but I wouldn't have said I was an Amish person."

Virtually every participant reported that they experienced social isolation during this time, which generated a high level of depression and anxiety. Amish youth are caught in a double bind because even though they are culturally mandated to explore their identity, they are granted very little room to do so openly. First, it is believed to be necessary to emotionally distance themselves from their parents to fully explore English identity. Second, the youth are forced to quit school when they turn 16. These conditions create the ironic consequence of Amish youth's becoming socially isolated from English youth and emotionally isolated from their Amish parents at a time when they are deliberating which of those two identities they will adopt.

Every participant reported that their decision concerning whether to join or to defect from the Amish was made in relative isolation, without much discussion or deliberation with others. The explanation for this circumstance was that to consider defection was to consider committing a very serious sin, and as such, involving others in the deliberation would exacerbate the offense. Defection was considered sinful because defection dishonors parents' desires for the child to join the church, which is thought to violate the 5th commandment of their religious text, to honor one's mother and father (Book of Exodus 20, Holy Bible). Consequently, defection could possibly result in the individual's going to Hell for all of eternity. The following quote from a 25-year-old Amish man illustrates this belief: "We're taught that if we leave, if you don't stay with what you were raised in, and honor your parents, which they say is doing exactly as I tell you to, if you're not honoring me, then you'll go to Hell."

It was further reported that they did not discuss their deliberations out of concern for the stress this discussion would cause their parents. Even though parents knew that their child was to consider defection during the simmie period, the parents reportedly acted as if their particular child was not. Because of the suppression of discussion of the matter, a sense of shame accompanied this isolation. The youth reported that they saw the paradox inherent in this situation, that they were being required to explore and consider becoming what their parents would then be ashamed of. They could also clearly articulate the function of this practice. As one simmie youth stated, "It's like we have to go through this period of feeling what it would feel like to suffer our parents' disappointment and rejection, so that we live right to avoid this pain. Even those of us who would never consider leaving the Amish have to feel what it would feel like to be turned away, 'cause when we are forced to think about it, we are much more likely to stay."

It was discovered in earlier research that, in this particular Amish settlement, approximately 80% of Amish youth attend public rather than parochial school. So until their 16th birthday, Amish children

actually have a great deal of interaction with non-Amish youth within the school setting. But, it is not generally the case that English and simmie youth develop extensive friendship networks. Informants within the public schools gave the explanation that English youth do not want to publicly associate with simmies because of the high level of stigmatization that is applied to the Amish in general and Amish youth in particular. As evidence of this circumstance, the English youth have developed the slang term "jerked-over" to signify disdain for simmies whom they believe are attempting to jerk-over to the other side (Reiling, 2000).

It was reported by public school officials that much of the hostility that the English youth feel toward the simmies stems from their perception of Amish youth and adults as unfair economic competition, due to the construction of the Amish as superior workers. As validation of this perception, the county's Chamber of Commerce reported the presence of a large Amish workforce to be the greatest incentive to industry location. More specific to the youth experience, because withdrawing from school at age 16 is a cultural practice, non-Amish employers do not view Amish "dropouts" in a negative light (Reiling & Nusbaumer, 1997). At age 16, Amish youth are expected to join, and they are fully welcomed into, the adult, non-Amish, paid-labor workforce.

Despite the stigmatizing label, the social and emotional isolation, and the identity conflict that accompanied this period, it was reported by every participant that the 16th birthday was greatly anticipated because the youth was finally freed from the highly subjugated role of the child. For example, they would no longer need to be accompanied outside the home by one of their parents, and they were free to more fully develop relationships and to explore their social world. As one prebaptism Amish male, who had been in the decision-making simmie period for about a year, reported, "When I was 10, it seemed like 20 years from 10 to 16. That's how much you look forward to turning 16." Certainly, elation over this period of emancipation from parental control resonates quite well with the experience of youth within many other cultural contexts. As such, the positive affective response the Amish youth make to this changed circumstance necessitates no further comment or articulation.

It is more important to examine the discovery that this period was also greatly dreaded because of other affective responses that were negative, namely depression and anxiety. These affective states are not unheard of responses to this period of increasing independence and identity exploration, either, for we know that other youth experience adolescence as disruptive (Erikson, 1968; Rumbaut, 1996). However, the strength of the Amish youths' negative affective response and the source of their angst are certainly noteworthy.

Almost every participant interviewed reported that engaging in the culturally prescribed deviance generated fairly high levels of depression and anxiety because the youth judged this deviance to be a "morally wrong" practice, despite the fact that it was culturally sanctioned by adults. The strong affective response of these youth caused them to internally reject youth culture as an ideology, and internally identify with adult culture, even though they felt compelled to continue to engage in this period of deviance. The conflicted state that was generated and its consequences have been examined more closely below, along with implications of the application of the case of Amish youth to TMT (Pyszczynski et al., 1997).

Findings Concerning the Affective Response to Deviance During the Simmie Period

The negative affective response made to culturally prescribed deviance during the simmie period was influenced heavily by two factors: the seriousness of the deviance that the youth engaged in and the length of time the youth spent in the simmie period. In general, the more serious the deviance and/or the greater the length of time in this period, the more intense the contemplation of their mortality, and hence, the greater the rejection of youth culture. Virtually no Amish youth exited the simmie period without having committed

numerous acts of the more innocuous deviance, such as being irresponsible, reckless, or disrespectful to their parents. But more strikingly, particularly because the interview sample was pulled in a random fashion, was the discovery that almost every participant had also engaged in the more serious forms of deviance, those they viewed as morally wrong practices, particularly drinking alcohol.

Most expressed high levels of anxiety over the presence of, or having felt forced, encouraged, or allowed to participate in, these more deviant acts. As an extension of this belief, many of the participants expressed having been afraid for their salvation during the simmie period, as they feared that they would be "caught out," meaning that because they were not yet baptized, they were afraid that they would die in a state of sin. In essence, they were concerned for their soul. The participants understood the function of this period of deviance, but even those currently in the simmie period expressed a greater belief in, and preference for, the norms of adult culture.

Anxiety did not automatically dissipate, however, upon taking adult baptism or upon defection. This is so because the Amish do not adhere to the "plan of salvation" (Book of John, verse 3:16, Holy Bible) as do most Christian churches (Hostetler, 1993; Reiling, 2000), wherein the acknowledgment of "Jesus Christ as the Son of God" and the acceptance of "Jesus Christ as Lord and Savior" through the taking of baptism guarantees acceptance into Heaven. Instead, the Amish believe that accepting "Jesus Christ as Lord and Savior" may be necessary to achieve salvation, but acceptance alone may not be sufficient. For the Amish, their God is continually judging whether they are "fit for Heaven," even after baptism.

As such, anxiety over transgressions committed during the simmie period did not diminish for most upon taking adult baptism because they believed that their God could still hold them accountable for these acts. Consequently, regret over their behavior was high. As evidence of the strength of this belief, almost every one of the defected coethnics reported still fearing for their salvation, even though they had subsequently joined a Christian church that did accept John 3:16 as the plan of salvation. New ideology did not totally supplant the old beliefs.

The following quote from a 25-year-old Amish man illustrates this belief, as well as the conviction that the risk was necessary for the survival of the group: "I'm very concerned about my children coming to the youth age and running with the crowd. I realize other youth, the English, aren't perfect and there's going to be problems, but that's different, 'cause the Amish say, you know, they sow their wild oats and they go out and do things for a while, but then they come back to the church. But then I'm thinking, but someday, somebody's children are going to be in that state and Jesus is coming. That is my greatest concern. That my children will be in that stage and caught out when Jesus comes. But that's a risk we've all had to take to get to be Amish, passing through that period."

High levels of anxiety were generated because the Amish apparently had not constructed, or had at least not been able to articulate, an explanation of what happens to an Amish youth who dies not only without having achieved adult baptism but while living in what they believed to be a morally wrong way. There was no definitive answer for them, other than a vague notion that "sinners probably go to Hell." Participating in this deviance caused youth to engage in a high level of contemplation of their mortality. More correctly, what they contemplated was not the fact that someday they would die, but the question of what would happen to them when they did.

As one simmie girl explained, "I just hope Jesus understands that I'm just doing what I'm expected to do."

To more fully illustrate the experience, each of the four types of culturally prescribed deviance, or morally wrong practices, that were identified as particularly problematic will be discussed more fully below: differential norms, alcohol use, bedding, and parental complicity in deviance.

It was reported that the amount and type of deviance that was allowed varied greatly by district. The lack of uniformity of norms was considered to be a morally wrong cultural practice because it left the youth uncertain as to their fate after death. Amish people attempt to live within their stated ideology, and as such, it is imperative to have consensus concerning that ideology. The anomic state created by differential norms generated a high level of anxiety. As one Amish woman noted, "Each district being so different about what's right and wrong sends mixed messages to kids. That was one thing that was real hard for me, 'cause is there more than one way to be right?"

◇ Discussion

The expression of angst and turmoil among the Amish youth must be put into perspective as a characteristic of most youth cultures and not necessarily Amish specific. The fact that they had identity crises, as such, was not surprising when considering that the youth period has long been theorized as disruptive, particularly in terms of identity (Erikson, 1968). Nor should the affective responses of anxiety and depression be unexpected, given that youth, in general, have been found to have higher rates of emotional distress (Rumbaut, 1996).

But what is context specific and therefore different for Amish youth is the complex nature of their deviance, and their negative affective response to that deviance, especially because the deviance is prescribed and sanctioned by adult culture. This circumstance is created by primarily four unique factors. First and foremost, on the child's 16th birthday, norms become immediately inverted. Amish youth literally wake up one morning and find themselves in an intense state of anomie. Even though the youth knows that change is coming, there is no transition period, no anticipatory socialization within which to prepare gradually.

Second, norms for the youth period are radically different from the adult norms the youth had been following. Unlike other cultural contexts, Amish youth are not engaging in anticipatory socialization when engaging in youth deviance. Learning to drink alcohol, for example, is not anticipatory socialization because drinking alcohol is not a part of adult culture. Neither are fornication (symbolic or literal), sanctioning deviant behavior, or sanctioning differential norms. The youth view these behaviors as morally wrong cultural practices because these behaviors are not part of adult cultural practice.

The third factor is that the norms that Amish adult culture prescribes for Amish youth vary so greatly from the norms that English adult culture prescribes for English youth living within their same geographic area. Because of this, Amish youth have a very difficult time dealing with the enormity of their lived contradictions, especially when comparing themselves to the English. The Amish way of life has been socially constructed as more virtuous, and yet many times Amish youth are more deviant than English youth, with the complicit permission of their "virtuous" parents. As such, self-discrepancy generates a level of depression and anxiety among Amish youth that would probably measure far higher than for youth in other cultural contexts.

The fourth and final factor that makes the youth period particularly disruptive is that, after 16 years of intense family socialization, Amish youth have very firmly internalized the more rigid adult norms. As such, having norms suddenly inverted, and to such an extraordinary degree, is experienced as tremendous culture shock. One could argue that the inversion of norms is a characteristic of most youth cultures, but a vital distinction must be made in that Amish youth are not choosing for the norms to be inverted. Adults, not youth, construct Amish youth culture.

◈ References

Adam, B. D. (1978). *The survival of domination: Inferiorization and everyday life.* New York: Elsevier.

Adler, P., & Adler, P. (1987). *Membership roles in field research.* Newbury Park, CA: Sage.

Adler, P., & Adler, P. (1998). *Peer power: Preadolescent culture and identity.* New Brunswick, NJ: Rutgers University Press.

Baumeister, R. F., & Muraven, M. (1996). Identity as adaptation to social, cultural, and historical context. *Journal of Adolescence, 19,* 405–416.

Corsaro, W., & Eder, D. (1990). *Children's peer culture. Annual Review of Sociology, 76,* 197–220.

Danielsen, L. M., Lorem, A. E., & Kroger, J. (2000). The impact of social context on the identity-formation process of Norwegian late adolescents. *Youth & Society, 31,* 332–362.

Emerson, R., & Pollner, M. (2001). Constructing participant/observation relations. In R. M. Emerson (Ed.), *Contemporary field research: Perspectives and formulations* (pp. 239–259). Prospect Heights, IL: Waveland.

Erikson, E. H. (1968). *Identity: Youth and crisis.* New York: Norton.

Greenberg, J., Pyszczynski, T., Solomon, S., Rosenblatt, A., Veeder, M., Kirkland, S., et al. (1990). Evidence for terror management theory II: The effects of mortality salience on reactions to those who threaten or bolster the cultural worldview. *Journal of Personality and Social Psychology, 58,* 308–318.

Hostetler, J. A. (1993). *Amish society.* Baltimore: Johns Hopkins Press.

Huntington, G. E. (1988). *Ethnic families in America: Patterns and variations.* New York: Elsevier.

Hutchby, I., & Moran-Ellis, J. (1998). *Children and social competence: Arenas of action.* London: Falmer.

Janssen, J., Dechesne, M., & Van Knippenberg, A. (1999). The psychological importance of youth culture: A terror management approach. *Youth & Society, 31,* 152–167.

Marques, J. M. (1986). *Toward a definition of social processing of information: An application to stereotyping.* Doctoral dissertation.

Nolt, S. M. (1992). *A history of the Amish.* Intercourse, PA: Good Books.

Pyszczynski, T., Greenberg, J., & Solomon, S. (1997). Why do we need what we need? A terror management perspective on the roots of social motivation. *Psychological Inquiry, 8,* 1–21.

Reiling, D. M. (2000). *An exploration of the relationship between Amish identity and depression among the Old Order Amish.* Dissertation. UMI9985454.

Reiling, D. M., & Nusbaumer, M. R. (1997). The Amish Drug Task Force: A natural history approach to the construction of a social problem. *Journal of Multicultural Nursing & Health, 3,* 25–37.

Rumbaut, R. G. (1996). The crucible within: Ethnic identity, self-esteem, and segmented assimilation among children of immigrants. In A. Portes (Ed.), *The new second generation* (pp. 119–170). New York: Russell Sage.

Solomon, S., Greenberg, J., & Pyszczynski, T. (1991). A terror management theory of social behavior: The psychological functions of self-esteem and cultural worldviews. *Advances in Experimental Social Psychology, 24,* 93–159.

Triandis, H. C. (1990). Theoretical concepts that are applicable to the analysis of ethnocentrism. In R. W. Brislin (Ed.), *Applied cross-cultural psychology* (pp. 34–55). Newbury Park, CA: Sage.

READING 6

In the chapter, we discussed self-injury as one form of physical deviance. P. A. Adler and Adler (2007) argued that self-injury was essentially being demedicalized, changing definitions from one of mental illness to one of individual choice. When working at a college counseling center, the authors of this article, Kokaliari and Berzoff, also noticed that self-injury appeared to be on the rise among college females. Following this observation, they reviewed the literature that supported the notion that self-injury was on the rise among nonclinical populations, especially among high school and college-age female students, with research providing estimates as high as 18% to 38%. They conducted a survey in a small liberal arts women's college and found that 91 of the 166 participants (over 50%) who turned in their surveys reported self-injury. Using several tests measuring various psychological disorders, they restricted the sample to 20 nonclinically diagnosed ("healthy") young women and then conducted in-depth interviews with 10 of them. A number of themes emerged from the interviews, including characteristics of their upbringing (e.g., taught to be self-reliant and to deny feelings), self-injury as a "Western form of personal and social control," and the idea of self-injury as a "quick fix" to alleviate difficult or painful emotions and allow them to continue being productive. The authors offer vivid quotes from these women documenting a unique form of deviance among a relatively "normal" sample of college women. The authors look at the implications for the larger society and the many challenges young women face in Western society.

Nonsuicidal Self-Injury Among Nonclinical College Women

Lessons From Foucault

Efrosini Kokaliari and Joan Berzoff

Nonsuicidal self-injury refers to purposeful, non-life-threatening self-inflicted injuries without suicidal intent that aim to alleviate emotional distress. The most common method of self-injury is cutting, followed by burning, hitting, or biting oneself; pulling one's hair; scratching to the point of

Source: Kokaliari, Efrosini, and Joan Berzoff. 2008. "Nonsuicidal Self-Injury Among Nonclinical College Women: Lessons From Foucault." *Affilia: Journal of Women and Social Work,* 23(3): 259–269.

bleeding; and interfering with one's wounds. Nonsuicidal self-injury most often involves the arms and legs but may also include the abdomen, genitals, and breasts (Andover, Pepper, & Gibb, 2007; Favazza, 1996; Walsh, 2006; Whitlock, Powers, & Eckenrode, 2006). The onset of nonsuicidal self-injury is generally found to be in early adolescence (ages 12 to 14; Muehlenkamp & Gutierrez, 2004, 2007; Ross & Heath, 2002), often reaching its peak in early adulthood (age 24), predominantly among White single or separated women (Hawton, Rodham, & Evans, 2006; Kokaliari & Lanzano, 2005; Skegg, 2005; Whitlock, Powers, et al., 2006). Most often, trauma (Allen, 2001; Connors, 2000; Van der Kolk, 1996), borderline psychopathology (Bohus & Schmahl, 2007; Gunderson, 2001; Linehan 1993), major disruptions in attachment (Farber, 2000; Levenkron, 1998), and major psychiatric disorders (Favazza, 1996) have been cited as the underlying reasons for self-injurious behaviors.

However, there has been a change in the profile of people who self-injure. A newer trend suggests an increase of self-injury in nonclinical populations (Fennig, Carlson, & Fennig, 1995; Gratz, Conrad, & Roemer, 2002; Turp, 1999; Walsh, 2006; Whitlock, Powers, & Eckenrode, 2006). These studies have revealed that self-injury is on the rise, especially among school- and college-aged students. The rate of self-injury in these populations varies from 16% to 38% (Gratz, 2003, 2006; Gratz et al., 2002; Kokaliari, 2005; Muehlenkamp & Gutierrez, 2004; Ross & Heath, 2002; Whitlock, Powers, et al., 2006). Self-injury appears to be most prevalent in advanced Western civilizations (Conterio & Lader, 1998; Kokaliari, 2005; Sargent, 2003; Shaw, 2002) and to occur disproportionately among females (Favazza, 1996; Kokaliari, 2005; Levenkron, 1998; Shaw, 2002).

The spread of the phenomenon in recent years among nonpsychiatric populations and the high prevalence of this behavior among females have challenged the view that self-injury arises out of psychopathology alone. Most explanations for self-injury have been psychological and have located the problem of self-injury within the individual. However, these explanations have not addressed why this symptom has increased in nonclinical populations or how it may reflect the society in which the individual who self-injures resides. Self-injury needs to be explored as a manifestation of a greater problem with both psychological and social meanings (Potter, 2003; Shaw, 2002). This article addresses the social dimensions of women's self-injury using Foucault's theory.

 ## Foucault's Views on Power and Objectification of the Body

Foucault, a brilliant but controversial French philosopher and historian, was highly regarded for his revolutionary ideas on discipline and power. He was interested in discourses of power and identified power as a method of social and personal control. In contrast with major theorists, such as Karl Marx (who saw power in relation to class conflict), Foucault (1980) contended that power circulates but is neither local nor static.

Foucault (1984) theorized that systems of knowledge, such as medicine, psychology, and religion, exercise particular power, which he referred to as "disciplines." Disciplines define "how the culture attempts to normalize individuals through increasingly rationalized means" (Dreyfus & Rabinow, 1982, p. xxvii). Disciplines like medicine and psychology determine what is normal and what is abnormal in each society. Thus, systems of power implicitly and invisibly exert control over the individual and the society (Foucault, 1990). Disciplines represent systems, such as governmental institutions or schools, that function as the secret police of societies (Richer, 1992).

Foucault examined how societies impose marginalization and even punishment as a way of maintaining social control. This type of social control has taken different forms at different times in history (Driver, 1994). Foucault (1979) specifically discussed the transition of the exercise of power from obvious torture to what he called "docile bodies." That is, he initially viewed power as exercised through external forms, such as torture or execution. However, over time, torture has somewhat disappeared as a form of "public spectacle" (Foucault, 1979, p. 7); instead, punishment has gradually become a more "hidden part of the penal system" (p. 9). Foucault identified four types of punishment that have been manifest at different times in Western societies, which Cooper (1981, p. 81) summarized as follows: Classical Greek and Roman citizens could suffer exile, banishment, and exclusion from certain areas; confiscation of their property, or destruction of their homes. The antique Germanic tradition practiced compensation, atonement, and fines as the chide method. In the Middle Ages, marks of power might be inscribed directly on one's body by branding, wounding, or mutilation. Finally, there was jail.

Jail belonged to what Foucault (1979, p. 293) labeled the "carceral regime," in which the focus of power and control was not only on punishing individuals but also on producing obedient individuals. Referring to the 18th century, he argued that carceral regimes "looked to disciplinary training as a means of producing docile obedient individuals . . . reformed individuals" (quoted in Driver, 1994, p. 118). Obedient individuals were produced by creating a Panopticon society that Foucault (1979) described as follows:

> Incarceration is the omnipresent armature; the delinquent is not outside the law; he is from the very outset, in the law, at the very heart of the law or at least in the midst of those mechanisms that transfer the individual imperceptibly from discipline to the law, from deviation to offence. (p. 301)

Foucault's theory of the Panopticon society was inspired by Jeremy Bentham's Panopticon (Foucault, 1979), an architectonic design of a model prison. This model prison was designed to be semicircular, with a cabin at the center used by guards for surveillance. Cells designed around the perimeter would accommodate only one person each. The building was designed to allow guards to observe prisoners at any time, but the prisoners could not observe the guards. The hope was that eventually the prisoners would start observing, controlling, and disciplining themselves. Another objective of the Panopticon was to control deviance through the isolation of the inmates by ensuring that all personal and spiritual needs could be met without prisoners leaving their cells without prisoners moving from their cells" (p. 61): Although the Panopticon was never built, it provided Foucault with a paradigm for demonstrating how discipline could be imposed and how it might operate.

The power of the Panopticon was "to induce in the inmate a state of conscious and permanent visibility that assured the automatic functioning of power" (Foucault, 1979, p. 201). It was designed "to use uncertainty as a measure of subordination" (Lyon, 1994, p. 65). Hence, external power would result in internal discipline that was exercised gradually, even without the presence of guards or observers. In other words, "the inmates should be caught up in a power situation of which they are themselves the bearers" (Foucault, 1979, p. 201) Foucault argued that the most effective form of exercised power in modern democracies is indirect and masked. In his words, "power is tolerable only on condition that it masks a substantial part of itself. . . . Its success is proportional to its ability to hide its own mechanisms" (Foucault, 1990, p. 86).

For Foucault, the body was the perfect medium on which power relations, societal structures, and politics were enacted and exercised. The body also was directly involved in a political field. "Power relations have an immediate hold upon the body; they invest it, mark it, train it, torture it, force it to carry out tasks, to perform ceremonies, to emit signs. . . . It is largely as a force of production that the body is invested with relations of power and domination" (Foucault, 1990, p. 173). The body, then, was a useful component and force in the system only "if it is both a productive body and a subjected body" (Foucault, 1979, p. 26).

Foucault saw bodies—more specifically, women's bodies—as sites in which power is exercised "in the struggle over who knows them best, who gets to say what is normal, healthy or hysterical" (quoted in

Allen, 1999, p. 71). Foucault wrote about the objectification of the female body and the subsequent "hysterisation" of women. According to him, the body is also treated like an object. Women are much more vulnerable to the objectification process because they are "ascribed a specific identity by men and relegated to the spheres of nature, emotion, desire, and the household" (Eckerman, 1997, p. 156).

 Method

Rationale

Having worked in college counseling services in a high-achieving all-women's college, we were struck by the number of women who were self-injuring but who otherwise excelled academically and socially. Hence, we decided to identify and examine a nonclinical population of college-age women who were self-injuring.

The underlying question of this study was: What psychosocial functions does self-injury serve in a nonclinical population of college women? Specifically, we were interested in the increased prevalence of nonsuicidal self-injury among college women and the psychosocial meanings of self-injurious behaviors. Our findings report on women's narratives from a social perspective.

Research Design and Procedure

Our first task was to find a relatively "healthy" sample of college women who self-injured. To locate these women, we used a mixed-method design and conducted the study in two phases. After we received approval by the college human subjects review committee, we initiated Phase 1. We administered survey to 400 random students in a small, liberal arts women's college to screen for a sample of women who engaged in self-injurious behaviors but did not meet the criteria for borderline pathology or post-traumatic stress disorder (PTSD) and who were classified as securely attached. This way, we would eliminate the usual criteria that are used to explain self-injurious behaviors. The survey consisted of the following five instruments: a demographic questionnaire, the Self-injury Behavior Questionnaire (McArdle, 2003), which assessed the prevalence and type of self-injurious behaviors that students engaged in, and the Personality Disorders Questionnaire (Hyler, Rieder, Williams, & Spitzer, 1988), which was used to rule out borderline pathology. The Purdue Post-Traumatic Stress Disorder Questionnaire-Revised (Lauterbach & Vrana, 1996) was used to rule out PTSD. Bartholomew and Horowitz's (1991) Self-Report Attachment Style Prototypes questionnaire served to assess the students' attachment styles and to rule out self-injuring women with insecure attachment styles. The results indicated alarming rates of self-injury in that 91 of the 166 participants who returned the surveys reported self-injurious behaviors. Of the 166 participants, then, 16 (9.7%) met the criteria for borderline personality disorders and 16.7% met the criteria for PTSD. In terms of attachment styles, 32.7% had secure attachment styles. By ruling out students with borderline pathology, PTSD, and insecure attachment styles, we were able to proceed to Phase 2 of the research, in which we selected a "healthier" subsample of 20 women who had self-injured.

We then contacted this subsample by mail and asked whether they were willing to participate in in-depth, semistructured interviews of up to 2 hours to explore the psychological and social functions of their self-injurious behaviors. The first 10 participants who responded were asked to be interviewed because of the limited time available to us. Each participant was paid $30 in appreciation for her time.

Demographic data were obtained from each participant that included race, ethnicity, income, sexual orientation, and grade point average (GPA). The participants were provided with informed consent forms and could withdraw at any point from the interview and from the study. The study questions included personal experiences with self-injury, the values of the families in which they had been raised, and the degree to which each family valued self-reliance, independence, and autonomy. Questions about possible contagion, objectification of the body, and how self-injury can be related to wider social issues were also included.

All the interviews were digitally recorded, transcribed in full, and analyzed using the grounded theory approach (Strauss & Corbin, 1990) using ATLAS.ti software. There has been limited research on society's contribution to the emergence of self-injury (Conterio & Lader, 1998; Shaw, 2002; Turp, 1999); thus, grounded theory provided multiple perspectives for generating hypotheses about nonsuicidal self-injury and its psychological and social functions through women's own voices.

Participants

All the respondents were in the process of obtaining their bachelor's degrees from an elite all-women's college. The 10 participants ranged in age from 18 to 23 (M = 20.6). Eight were White, 1 was Asian, and 1 was biracial (White and Native American). The sample was diverse in terms of sexual orientation in that 3 students identified as bisexual, 2 identified as lesbian, 4 identified as heterosexual, and 1 saw herself as questioning. Each participant excelled academically, with GPA's greater than 3.0. In terms of relationship status, 8 were single and 2 had partners. In addition, the participants came from diverse family backgrounds. Five came from intact families in which their parents were still married, 3 had parents who were divorced, and 2 came from single-parent families.

In terms of educational family backgrounds, the parents of 7 of the 10 participants had graduate degrees, including doctoral education, the parents of 1 participant had undergraduate degrees, and the parents of 2 participants had high school degrees or had attended some college. Two participants were from affluent environments, 3 were from upper-middle-class families, 1 was from a middle-class family, and 2 were from working-class families; 2 did not identify their class backgrounds. Six of the 8 participants from two-parent families reported that both parents worked when they were growing up, and the remaining 2 participants said that one parent was working and one stayed home; each of the 2 participants from single-parent families reported that her parent worked. Nine participants described experiencing their parents as protective.

All but 1 participant had engaged in multiple non-suicidal self-injurious behaviors. In terms of frequency, scratching to the point in bleeding was reported most often, followed by cutting, burning, self-hitting, and self-biting.

◆ Findings

Autonomy, Self-Reliance, and the Denial of Feelings

Among the 10 participants, there was a considerable consensus that self-injury could be understood as a social phenomenon. All the women spoke of the ways in which their families had shaped them to be self-sufficient and independent. Each also reported coming from environments that valued individualism as one of the desirable goals. Their own values indicated that self-reliance had been highly valued in childhood. All the participants consistently spoke of their discomfort with dependence and emotions. One participant said that emotions were considered to be a weakness in her family and that it was important that she be independent: "Well, feelings were not acknowledged. . . . You are to be strong. You are not to cry. . . . Well, it was not discouraged, but you can never feel like you need someone, to depend on someone" (Antigone, age 20). Another said that her family denied emotions so much that they even laughed about it: "We have this joke that denial is a river that runs through our family" (Ismini, age 19).

For many, feelings were discouraged. "We lead a very active life, so I do not have to feel a lot of emotions. . . . I never really acknowledged my own emotions . . . my feelings took a backseat" (Antigone, age 20). Artemis, age 21, underscored how important self-reliance had been in her family of origin, saying,

> When I was 12, I believe, my parents decided that I needed to be more economically self-reliant . . . so my parents told me they were not going to give me any sort of allowance unless I had made like a certain amount of money elsewhere. And they were not going to buy me shampoo or my face wash or whatever, and it was really difficult. You know, I was doing sports at least 3 hours a day, and I was in seventh grade.

And so it was really difficult to then, like, go baby-sit at night so [I could] make money. I had to wake up at 4:30 in the morning to go to sports, and there were so many little things. . . . I just think it was totally unreasonable.

Andromeda, age 23, said that she recalled her mother saying that "the biggest success of every parent is to see their child become self-reliant."

Needing to Be Perfect, Just Like Men

The participants also talked about how they needed to control and perfect their bodies. For example, Ismini, age 19, said, "Eating disorders are just another form of self-injury, and all these are based on control, and you know, at that point, I could control my body, and so appear perfect." Penelope, age 21, added that self-injury offered her a kind of control. She said, "Yeah. I mean, it is the way that you can determine what's going on with you and your body, and I had a friend who both self-injured and was anorexic, and she definitely needed something she could control in her life."

Many of the high-achieving women in this study spoke of the high and often unrealistic expectations for them that were then enacted on their bodies. "I think maybe because we have more of a push to be better than men, to strive to be better, to work harder, there are more expectations of us. And these expectations are climbing" (Antigone, age 20).

Ariadne, age 21, addressed a similar concern, as follows:

In women, there is just so much pressure to be like men or, you know, to be stick-thin, and to just be all these things, and being them all at once is impossible. Women have to choose who we want to be and not according to what society pressures us to be. I think there is much more external pressure on women. . . . Men, more often than women, are recognized more for what they do. I really think it is just that women . . . we still are not willfully fighting with men, and we get a lot more pressure from the society, from our parents, and from everything around us.

Arethusa, age, 19, added,

I really think in a society there is lot more pressure on women than men . . . and there is also . . . this has just occurred to me now, but there is also, you know, with like women's liberation and everything, there is also pressure for women to succeed and to have as many successes as men. And in order to do that, I think a lot of women feel like they need to put themselves through a lot in order to be that person.

Hence, each of these women described needing to control and discipline herself to be like, or even be more successful than, men.

Self-Injury as a Western Form of Personal and Social Control

Some participants saw self-injury as a particularly Western phenomenon that functioned to make them comply with socially determined expectations for high productivity. For example, Artemis, age 21, said,

I see Western society, and I do not know exactly what it is about Western society, but I do see that there is something enabling this [self-injury]. I mean, I do not think it is promoting it, but there is something that is causing it and enabling it to happen.

A number of students commented that Western societies, which value independence over interdependence, socialize their members to deal with their pain alone. As Athena, age 21, put it, I am wondering if it says something about our culture's need to deal with something on your own as opposed to deal with something with other people or with healthy means. . . . You can't rely on other people to help you, and sort of like an independent self-sufficient mentality is pretty widespread.

As in the Panopticon, in which prisoners were kept in solitude and relatedness was avoided, 9 of the 10 women reported performing self-injury in solitude (Kokaliari, 2005). Also, as in the Panopticon, these women appeared to discipline themselves and, when appropriate, alter their emotional states to comply with the need to be productive as college students. For example, Ariadne, age 21, said, "In our Western culture, the feeling of being in control and being able to . . . you know. . . . We all have issues; we all have problems, let us just suppress them and get on with it!"

Among these 10 women, then, self-injury was a private act that controlled emotions to make them productive commodities. Self-injury seemed to them to be a particularly Western construct that provided a method of self-surveillance in which power was exercised in private. On a similar note, one high-achieving student discussed how self-injury helped her keep up with expectations of productivity,

> There would be so much going on in my head that I could not focus on my homework. So like, every couple of hours . . . it was like smoking a cigarette. Every couple of hours, I would, just make, like, one little cut, and then I could, like, deal with that and then go back and focus. But then, like, it was really awful. I mean . . . it really . . . was like taking a cigarette break, and it was something that enabled me to do what I had to do . . . what I needed to do. (Artemis, age 21)

Artemis was overwhelmed, initially, by her school's, family's, and society's demands for high productivity. Her self-injury functioned as a form of social control in that it allowed her to localize her pain and control it. Although it produced more pain, it paradoxically helped her to focus on her work. What had been an external control became self-imposed.

Another participant also used nonsuicidal self-injury to block her feelings to focus on her work.

> Because if you can do that, I mean . . . coming back on a track and focus on all different things, you know, trying to block out the fact that you are upset or you are overwhelmed . . . because it's always like, "Oh, I need to focus. I need to focus on this and this and this. I need to get this done, you

know" . . . You have no time to think about your emotions . . . you need to be in control of your emotions. . . . You can focus on everything that you have to do for you to succeed. (Alkyone, age 19)

It is interesting that cutting gave her the illusion of control over her emotions.

Self-Injury as a Quick Fix

All 10 participants discussed self-injury as a "quick fix" that provided immediate alleviation of painful or difficult emotions that got in the way of their productivity. Rather than seeking relationships when stressed, these women were harming their bodies, in private, to be able to function productively in the world. As Penelope, age 22, put it, "I think to some degree it is a quick fix. . . . I think it can help you relieve that stress immediately, and it's a little faster than having to drive to someone to talk to them about the whole process." Aphrodite, age 22, added that not only was self-injury a quick fix, but it was like fast food.

She said, "It is definitely a quick fix. . . . Welcome to McDonald's society, right where we came from, fast food, anything into a sugar high and then it drops!" In this way, she was condensing the consumer society's need for quick fixes and for gratification in the service of greater productivity.

◈ Discussion

Modern Western societies have been organized to accumulate capital and power. At their core are competition, earning, and consuming. This structure has an impact on every aspect of life and shapes social relationships (Castells, 1999). In addition, modern Western societies tend to blame the individual for any kind of suffering, especially psychological. In discussing Kovel's (1980) article, Gilford (1999, p. 3) noted, "Capitalism displaces the true and social political causes of psychological suffering and locates them within individuals instead of in society." In this view, Western society has become like Foucault's Panopticon. As Foucault (1979) wrote, "Is it surprising that prisons resemble factories, schools barracks, hospitals, which all resemble prisons?" (p. 228). Indeed, Foucault (1979) called modernity the "disciplined society" "where the routines of everyday life have become transparent as never before" (quoted in Lyon, 1994, p. 37). This Panopticon-driven disciplined society has increased pressure to develop new behaviors that require new types of personalities and expressions (Lasch, 1979). Docile bodies subordinate individuals to ensure a society's survival. Masked social forces operate subtly and invite individuals to cope with all these rapid changes by crossing boundaries between normality and what is defined as madness (Kovel, 1980).

Foucault would assert that women in modern societies internalize forces of discipline and punishment. These now-internalized systems of social control become self-regulatory and extreme. "When people are treated as objects they see themselves as objects and tend to torture their bodies and desires to fit instructions and specifications" (Eckerman, 1997, p. 157). History has given us similar examples with such disorders as hysteria and eating disorders that have been predominantly seen in women. These symptoms served as vehicles to carry female distress (Farber, 2000; Pipher, 1994). Nonsuicidal self-injury, like eating disorders, then, appears to function as a form of self-surveillance. Eckerman (1997) argued that self-starvation serves women because asceticism represents an aspect of the objectification and self-surveillance of bodies. The same concept applies to self-injury. On a psychological level, nonsuicidal self-injury has been described as a mechanism that helps the body reorganize unbearable affects, but on a social level, self-injury may help the body regain its capacity to produce and be a useful subjugated body in the service of capitalism.

Self-injury, then, may be a phenomenon that has "escaped" from psychiatric settings and now functions as an internalized punishment system that quickly alleviates emotional or mental pain. It makes obsolete the more time-consuming sources of relief to which people have traditionally turned, including family, friends, colleagues, or nature. This behavior has, however, become medicalized and has been seen as a form of individual pathology. Thus, society is not considered responsible for having produced the symptoms. Instead, the individual can be "treated," sometimes in restricted settings like psychiatric hospitals. The human suffering brought about by political or societal pressures is turned into a personal and private pathology.

Nonsuicidal self-injury appears to be an insidious form of social control. As Danziger (1990, p.190) noted, it involves "the management of persons through the subjection of individual action to an imposed analytic framework and cumulative measures of performance." Self-injury, then, offers a way to regulate socially unacceptable affects, to isolate the person from her feelings, and to modify states of the ego so that the person regains the capacity to produce. The demands of productivity do not allow space for the expression of emotion. Nonsuicidal self-injury appears to serve as both a symptom and a symbol of our time. It is low in cost. It is effective in imposing control over the body, including feeling states, and it is congruent with what Conterio and Lader (1998, p. 9) referred to as "a quick fix and immediate gratification." The combination of patriarchy and of a modern disciplined society encourages individuals to seek solutions for emotional issues internally and in solitude, "which would return individuals to self-reliance while maintaining structural barriers related to economic, racial and sexual class that limit and curtail the individual" (Eisenstein, 1992, p. 191).

At a moment in history when women have achieved, after enormous effort, the right to become more active in society, they are also being seduced by society into adopting the goal of achievement at any cost, even at the cost of denying their feelings. At a time when women are finally claiming social equality, self-injury may emerge as a subtle manifestation of self-surveillance to undermine their success within capitalistic values, such as individualism and maximized profits.

Self-injury, then, can be seen as a representation of women's oppression that has become self-imposed. As Shaw (2002) argued, it is a "reflection of women's experience of trauma, silencing, and objectification within a patriarchal culture" (p. 59). Devenaux (1994, p. 225) suggested that self-injury becomes "the ultimate expression of the self-disciplinary female caught up in an insane culture," especially in Western societies with their "irrational passion for dispassionate rationality" (Rieff, cited in Harris, 2000).

Implications for Clinical Practice

Exploring self-injury within a nonclinical population has implications for practice. Nonsuicidal self-injury may reflect not simply individual pathology but societal pathology. Given that self-injury may be associated with intense social pressures, these pressures need to be analyzed and understood in groups in which women may discuss some of these issues with one another. Women may need help understanding that when a symptom, such as self-injury, manifests in such alarming rates, it is a sign not only of individual distress but also of dysfunction in the larger social context.

Clinicians need to be mindful that self-injury cannot be exclusively understood as a reflection of trauma, borderline personality, or another major pathology. It is important that women who self-injure be less pathologized and that more attention be paid to the social pressures that they encounter that lead to these behaviors. Hence, consultation with deans, faculty members, and college mental health personnel is essential to treating some of the causes of the behaviors.

Conclusion

This exploratory study has raised many important issues. Is self-injury an individual pathology, or does it reflect social pathologies? Do women self-injure as a discipline, and do they do so in serving society's needs for greater productivity? Do women self-injure as a way of internalizing society's demands for compliance and as a way to suppress emotion? Do women self-injure because of socially sanctioned expectations for independence and autonomy? Do women self-injure as a way of perfecting themselves by taking the toll on their bodies? Is self-injury a social construction? This small sample of psychologically healthy women, although limited by its size and lack of representation across class, race, and ethnicity, certainly indicated that self-injury is not just a response to trauma or major attachment disruptions nor a function of borderline pathology. Instead, it may be a response to a more invisible kind of trauma that has arisen in the context of Western societies that value high achievement, productivity, and individuality at the cost of individual emotions. Future research in this area, using a larger sample of healthy women who self-injure, will shed more light on this interesting phenomenon.

References

Allen, B. (1999). Power/knowledge. In K. Racevskis (Ed.), *Critical essays* (pp. 69–81). New York: G. K. Hall.

Allen, J. (2001). *Traumatic relationships in serious mental disorders.* Northvale, NJ: John Wiley.

Andover, M., Pepper, C., & Gibb, B. (2007). Self-mutilation and coping strategies in a college sample. *Suicide and Life-Threatening Behavior, 37,* 238–243.

Bartholomew, K., & Horowitz, L. M. (1991). Attachment styles among young adults: A test of a four-category model. *Journal of Personality & Social Psychology, 61,* 226–244.

Bohus, M., & Schmahl, C. (2007). Psychopathology and treatment of borderline personality disorder. *Nervenartz, 78,* 1069–1080.

Castells, M. (1999). The global network. In C. Lamert (Ed.), *Social theory: The multicultural and classic readings* (2nd ed., pp. 617–621). Boulder, CO: Westview.

Connors, R. (2000). Self-injury: Psychotherapy with people who engage in self-inflicted violence. Northvale, NJ: Jason Aronson.

Conterio, K., & Lader, W. (1998). Bodily harm: The breakthrough healing program for self-injurers. New York: Hyperion.

Cooper, B. (1981). Michel Foucault: An introduction to the study of his thought. New York: Edwin Mellen.

Danziger, K. (1990). *Constructing the subject.* New York: Cambridge University Press.

Devenaux, M. (1994). Feminism and empowerment. A critical reading of Foucault. *Feminist Studies, 20,* 223–237.

Dreyfus, H., & Rabinow, P. (1982). Beyond *structuralism and hermeneutics* (2nd ed.). Chicago: University of Chicago Press.

Driver, F. (1994). Bodies in space: Foucault's account of disciplinary power. In C. Jones & R. Porter (Eds.), *Reassessing Foucault: Power, medicine and the body* (pp. 113–131). New York: Routledge.

Eckerman, L. (1997). Foucault, embodiment and gendered subjectivities: The core of voluntary starvation. In A. Peterson & R. Burton (Eds.), *Foucault, health and medicine* (pp. 151–172). New York: Routledge.

Eisenstein, Z. (1992). The sexual politics of the new right: Understanding the crisis of liberalism for the 1980's. In M. Humm (Ed.), *Modern feminisms: Political, literary, cultural* (pp. 189–192). New York: Columbia University Press.

Farber, S. K. (2000). *When the body is the target: Self-harm, pain, and traumatic attachments.* Northvale, NJ: Jason Aronson.

Favazza, A. R. (1996). *Bodies under siege: Self-mutilation and body modification in culture and psychiatry (2nd ed.).* Baltimore, MD: John Hopkins University Press.

Fennig, S., Carlson, G. A., & Fennig, S. (1995). Contagious self-mutilation. *Journal of the American Academy of Child and Adolescent Psychiatry,* 34, 402–403.

Foucault, M. (1979). *Discipline and punish: The birth of the prison* (A. Sheridan, Trans.). New York: Vintage Books.

Foucault, M. (1980). Truth and power. In C. Gordon (Ed.), *Power/knowledge: Selected interviews and other writings by Michel Foucault* (pp. 109–133). New York: Random House.

Foucault, M. (1984). The ethic of care for the self as a practice of freedom: An interview translated by J. D. Gauthier, S. J. In J. Bernauer & D. Rasmussen (Eds.), *The final Foucault* (pp. 1–20). Cambridge, MA: MIT Press.

Foucault, M. (1990). *History of sexuality.* New York: Vintage Books. (Original work published 1978)

Gilford, P. (1999). The normalizing effects of managed care on psychotherapy. In K. Weisgerber (Ed.), *Traumatic bond between the psychotherapist and managed care* (pp. 199–216). Northvale, NJ: Jason Aronson.

Gratz, K. L. (2003). Risk factors and functions of deliberate self-harm: An empirical and conceptual review. *Clinical Psychology, Science and Practice,* 10, 192–205.

Gratz, K. L. (2006). Risk factors for deliberate self-harm among female college students: The role and interaction of childhood maltreatment emotional inexpressivity and affect intensity/reactivity. *American Journal of Orthopsychiatry,* 76, 238–250.

Gratz, K. L., Conrad, S. D., & Roemer, L. (2002). Risk factors for deliberate self-harm among college students. *American Journal of Orthopsychiatry,* 72, 128–140.

Gunderson, J. (2001). *Borderline personality disorder: A clinical guide.* Washington, DC: American Psychiatric Publishing.

Harris, J. (2000). Self-harm: Cutting the bad out of me. *Qualitative Health Research,* 10, 164–173.

Hawton, K., Rodham, K., & Evans, E. (2006). *By their own hands. Deliberate self-injury and suicidal ideas in adolescents.* London: Jessica Kingsley.

Hyler, S. E., Rieder, R. O., Williams, J. B. W., & Spitzer, R. I. (1988). The Personality Diagnostic Questionnaire: Development and preliminary results. *Journal of Personality Disorders,* 2, 229–237.

Kokaliari, E. D. (2005). Deliberate self-injury: An investigation of the prevalence and psychosocial meanings in a non-clinical female college population (Doctoral dissertation, Smith College, 2005). *Dissertation Abstracts International,* 65(11-A), 4348.

Kokaliari, E. D., & Lanzano, K. (2005). Deliberate self-injury. A consumer-therapist co-run group. A choice or a necessity? *Epidemiologia e Psichiatria Sociale,* 14(1), 32–38.

Kovel, J. (1980). The American mental health industry. In D. Inglesby (Ed.), *Critical psychiatry: The politics of mental health* (pp. 72–101). New York: Random House.

Lasch, C. (1979). The culture of narcissism: American life in an age of diminishing expectations. New York: Norton.

Lauterbach, D., & Vrana, S. (1996). Three studies on the reliability and validity of a self-report measure of post-traumatic stress disorder. *Assessment,* 3(1) 17–25.

Levenkron, S. (1998). *Cutting: Understanding and overcoming self-mutilation.* New York: Norton.

Linehan, M. (1993). *Cognitive-behavioral treatment of borderline personality disorder.* New York: Guilford.

Lyon, D. (1994). *The electronic eye: The rise of surveillance society.* Minneapolis: University of Minnesota Press.

McArdle, E. (2003). HPA-AXIS *reactivity to interpersonal stress in young adults who self-injure.* Unpublished doctoral dissertation, University of Massachusetts at Amherst.

Muehlenkamp, J. J., & Gutierrez, P. M. (2004). An investigation of differences between self-injurious behavior and suicide attempts in a sample of adolescents. *Suicide and Life-Threatening Behavior,* 34(1), 12–23.

Muehlenkamp, J. J., & Gutierrez, P. M. (2007). Risk for suicide attempts among adolescents who engage in non-suicidal self-injury. *Archives of Suicide Research,* 11, 69–82.

Pipher, M. (1994). *Reviving Ophelia: Saving the selves of adolescent girls.* New York: Ballantine.

Potter, N. N. (2003). Commodity/body/sign: Borderline personality disorder and the signification of self-injurious behavior. *Philosophy, Psychiatry, & Psychology,* 10(1), 1–16.

Richer, P. (1992). An introduction to deconstructionist psychology. In S. Kvale (Ed.), *Psychology and postmodernism* (pp. 110–119). Thousand Oaks, CA: Sage.

Ross, S., & Heath, N. (2002). A study of the frequency of self-mutilation in a community sample of adolescents. *Journal of Youth and Adolescence,* 31, 67–77.

Sargent, C. (2003). Gender body meaning: Anthropological perspectives on self-injury and borderline personality disorder. *Philosophy, Psychiatry, & Psychology,* 10, 25–27.

Shaw, N. (2002). The complexity and paradox of female self-injury: Historical portrayals, journeys toward stopping, and contemporary interventions (Doctoral dissertation, Harvard University, 2002). *Dissertation Abstracts International,* 63 (6–B), 3025.

Skegg, K. (2005) Self-harm. *Lancet,* 366, 1471–1483.

Strauss, A., & Corbin, J. (1990). *Basics of qualitative research: Grounded theory procedures and techniques.* Newbury Park, CA: Sage.

Turp, M. (1999). Encountering self-harm in psychotherapy and counseling practice. *British Journal of Psychotherapy,* 15, 306–321.

Van der Kolk, B. A. (1996). The complexity of adaptation to trauma: Self-regulation, stimulus discrimination, and characterological development. In B. A. van der Kolk, M. Farlane, & L. Weisaeth (Eds.), *Traumatic stress: The effects of overwhelming experience on mind, body and society* (pp. 182–213). New York: Guilford.

Walsh, B. W. (2006). *Treating self-injury: A practical guide.* New York: Guilford.

Whitlock, J., Eckenrode, J., & Silverman, D. (2006). Self-injurious behaviors in a college population. *Pediatrics,* 117, 1939–1948.

READING 7

This brief article explores elite deviance or "corporate transgressions" through the concept of moral disengagement. The authors outline concepts and strategies that allow for corporate deviance to occur and why corporate deviants' consciences are not seemingly bothered. Strategies include moral justification (justifying the rightness of their actions), euphemistic labeling (changing the deviant status of an activity by changing its label to something innocuous or even positive), advantageous comparison (making something look better by comparing it to something much worse), displacement of responsibility (placing the blame elsewhere), diffusion of responsibility (taking less blame by placing it on the group), dehumanization (ascribing less than human qualities to the victim so they appear less deserving), and the attribution of blame (placing the blame on others or on certain circumstances). They then describe four famous case studies of elite deviance: (1) an industrial disaster in Bhopal, India, in 1984, where "at least 2,500 people were killed, 10,000 seriously injured, 20,000 partially disabled, and 180,000 other affected" in other ways; (2) the Ford Pinto case where faulty designs led to hundreds of burn deaths; (3) the Nestle case where the company sold infant formula to Third World countries where environmental and social conditions interacted with the formula so that it was not good for the babies' health; and (4) the Three Mile Island case involving a devastating accident at a nuclear power plant and how it was dealt with by those in charge. The case examples show how corporations were able to disregard the consequences of their negligent and harmful behavior.

Corporate Transgressions Through Moral Disengagement

Albert Bandura, Gian-Vittorio Caprara, and Laszlo Zsolnai

In the past decades corporate transgressions have became a major socio-political problem both in developed and developing countries. The phenomenon of corporate deviance requires critical, cross-disciplinary studies that might illuminate the darker side of contemporary business practice. We have to acknowledge that one is dealing with institutional practices that are not easily examinable by conventional means. Study of corporate transgressions is highly reliant on scandals, the media, public inquiries, police investigations and whistle-blowers for glimpses of the concealed world of top management and its involvement in dirty tricks. Much research relies therefore on published secondary sources.[1]

Corporate transgression is about the exercise and abuse of power that is closely linked to the legitimate conduct of business. The essence of business is pursuit of legitimate interests of the parties involved in transactions circumscribed by rules that protect both the parties and their relationship to the interests of the public, society, state and regulatory agencies.[2]

Source: Bandura, Albert, Gian-Vittorio Caprara, and Laszlo Zsolnai. 2000. "Corporate Transgressions Through Moral Disengagement." *Journal of Human Values* 6(1): 57–64. Originally published in the *Journal of Human Values,* Indian Institute of Management, Kolkata. All rights reserved. Reproduced with the permission of the copyright holders and the publishers, SAGE Publications India Pvt. Ltd, New Delhi.

Although a great deal of corporate transgression is never classified as crime and the law plays a minor role in its regulation, the greatest discrepancy between common and white-collar violations is that corporations have the power to mobilize resources to influence the rules that cover their own conduct. In many cases corporations actively defend their interests in ways that would normally be unthinkable for common law breakers.[3]

The most striking aspect of corporate transgression is that it is committed not by dangerous criminally-oriented mavericks, but by eminent members of the business community who break rules ostensibly in the interests of their companies and their own.[4] The challenging question is why otherwise good managers engage in dirty business and why their conscience never bothers them.[5] In this article we draw on the theory and empirical findings of moral psychology to shed some light on this paradox.

◈ Social Cognitive Theory of Moral Agency

Social cognitive theory addresses the exercise of moral agency.[6] In this explanatory framework personal factors in the form of moral thought and self-evaluative reactions, moral conduct and environmental influences operate as interacting determinants of each other. Within this triadic reciprocal causation, moral agency is exercised through self-regulatory mechanisms. Transgressive conduct is regulated by two sets of sanctions, social and personal. Social sanctions are rooted in the fear of external punishment, while self-sanctions operate through self-condemning reactions to one's misconduct. After people adopt moral standards, self-sanctions serve as the main guides and deterrents that keep behaviour in line with moral standards.

The adoption of moral standards does not create a fixed control mechanism within the person. There are many psycho-social mechanisms by which moral control can be selectively engaged or disengaged from detrimental conduct.[7] The mechanisms of moral disengagement enable otherwise considerate people to commit transgressive acts without experiencing personal distress.

Moral Justification

People do not ordinarily engage in reprehensible conduct until they have justified to themselves the rightness of their actions. In this process of moral justification detrimental conduct is made personally and socially acceptable by portraying it in the service of valued social or moral purposes.

Euphemistic Labelling

Activities can take on markedly different appearances depending on what they are called. Euphemistic labelling provides a convenient tool for masking reprehensible activities or even conferring a respectable status upon them. Through sanitized and convoluted verbiage destructive conduct is made benign and those who engage in it are relieved of a sense of personal agency.

Advantageous Comparison

Behaviour can also assume very different qualities depending on what it is contrasted with. By exploiting advantageous comparison injurious conduct can be rendered benign or made to appear to be of little consequence. The more flagrant the contrasted activities, the more likely it is that one's own injurious conduct will appear trifling or even benevolent.

Displacement of Responsibility

Under displacement of responsibility people view their actions as springing from social pressures or dictates of others rather than as something for which they are personally responsible. Because they are not the actual agents of their actions, they are spared self-censuring reactions. Hence, they are willing to behave in ways they normally repudiate if a legitimate authority accepts responsibility for the effects of their actions.

Diffusion of Responsibility

The exercise of moral control is also weakened when personal agency is obscured by diffusion of responsibility for detrimental conduct. Any harm done by a group can always be attributed largely to the behaviour of others. People behave more cruelly under group responsibility than when they hold themselves personally accountable for their actions.

Disregarding or Distorting the Consequences

Additional ways of weakening self-deterring reactions operate by disregarding or distorting the consequences of action. When people pursue activities harmful to others for personal gain or because of social inducements they avoid facing the harm they cause or they minimize it. In addition to selective inattention and cognitive distortion of effects, the misrepresentation may involve active efforts to discredit evidence of the harm that is caused.

Dehumanization

Self-censure for injurious conduct can be disengaged or blunted by dehumanization that divests people of human qualities or attributes bestial qualities to them. Once dehumanized, they are no longer viewed as persons with feelings, hopes, and concerns, but as subhuman objects.

Attribution of Blame

Blaming one's adversaries or compelling circumstances is still another expedient that can serve self-exonerating purposes. In moral disengagement by attribution of blame, people view themselves as faultless victims driven to injurious conduct by forcible provocation. By fixing the blame on others or on circumstances, not only are one's own injurious actions excusable, but one can even feel self-righteous in the process.

Moral disengagement can affect detrimental behaviour both directly and indirectly. People have little reason to be troubled by guilt or to feel any need to make amends for harmful conduct if they construe it as serving worthy purposes or if they disown personal agency for it. High moral disengagement is accompanied by low guilt, thus weakening anticipatory self-restraints against engagement in detrimental behaviour. Self-exoneration for harmful conduct and self-protective dehumanization of others and treating them as blameworthy spawn a low pro-social orientation. Low pro-socialness in turn contributes to detrimental conduct in two ways: having little sympathy for others both removes the restraining influence of empathetic consideration of others and activates little anticipatory guilt over injurious conduct; and under some circumstances effective moral disengagement creates a sense of social rectitude and self-righteousness that breeds ruminative hostility and retaliatory thoughts for perceived grievances.

Moral Disengagement Strategies of Corporations

A corporation is similar to a person in some important respects. First, the reciprocal causation operates among corporate modes of thinking, corporate behaviour and the environment. Second, a corporation can be viewed both as a social construction and as an agentic system with the power to realize its intentions. Third, corporate identity is crucial for the development and functioning of a corporation. Moreover, the practices of a corporation operate through self-regulatory mechanisms. These mechanisms regulate the allocation of resources in the pursuit of the goals and objectives of the corporation in accordance with its values and standards. When corporations engage in reprehensible conduct they are likely to do so through selective disengagement of moral self-sanctions. The following brief analyses of famous business ethics cases illustrate the disengagement practices.

The Bhopal Case[8]

On 3 December 1984 the world's worst industrial disaster happened in Bhopal, India. Some 40 tonnes of methyl isocyanate (MIC) gas escaped from the Union

Carbide India Limited (UCIL) pesticide production plant. At least 2,500 people were killed, 10,000 seriously injured, 20,000 partially disabled and 180,000 others affected in one way or another.

Very early in the morning of that day a violent chemical reaction occurred in a large storage tank at the Union Carbide factory. A huge amount of MIC—a chemical so highly reactive that a trace contaminant can set off a chain reaction—escaped from the tank into the cool winter's night air. A yellow-white fog, an aerosol of uncertain chemical composition, speared over the sleeping city of some 800,000. The mist, which hung close to the ground, blanketed the slums of Bhopal. Hundreds of thousands of residents were roused from their sleep, coughing, vomiting and wheezing.

The Bhopal plant was operated by UCIL, a subsidiary of the Union Carbide Corporation headquartered in Danbury, Connecticut. Despite Indian law limiting foreign ownership of corporations to 40 per cent, the US parent company was allowed to retain majority ownership (50.9 per cent) of UCIL because it was considered a 'high-technology' enterprise.

Union Carbide officials claimed that they did not apply a 'double standard' in safety regulation. Warren Anderson, chairman of Union Carbide Corporation, insisted that there were no differences between the Bhopal plant and Union Carbide's West Virginia plant. This argument was erroneous but served as an advantageous comparison for Union Carbide. In reality, the Bhopal plant had violated the company's safety standards and operated in a way that would not have been tolerated in the United States.

Two years before the disaster a three-member safety team from Union Carbide headquarters had visited the Bhopal plant and submitted a revealing report on the dangers of the MIC section. The report had recommended various changes to reduce the risks at the plant, but the recommendations were never implemented. Union Carbide's main strategy was to displace responsibility by blaming the Indian government for its failure to effectively regulate the plant and for allowing people to live nearby.

Union Carbide was allowed to locate its factory in the middle of Bhopal, just 2 miles from the Bhopal railway station. It was convenient for shipping, but proved to be disastrous for the people living nearby. For years the plant had been ringed with shanty-towns, mostly populated by squatters. All three of the worst-affected communities in the disaster apparently existed before the Union Carbide plant opened. In court trials Union Carbide refused to pay anything to the Indian victims and their families, whose impoverished status made them easy to be dehumanized and disregarded.

The Ford Pinto Case[9]

On 10 August 1978 a tragic automobile accident occurred on US Highway 33 near Goshen, Indiana. Sisters Judy and Lynn Ulrich and their cousin Donna Ulrich were struck from the rear in their 1973 Ford Pinto by a van. The gas tank of the Pinto ruptured, the car burst into flames and the three teenagers were burnt to death.

This was not the only case when the Ford Pinto caused a serious accident by explosion. By conservative estimates Pinto crashes had caused at least 500 burn deaths. There were lawsuits against Ford because it had been proven that the top managers of the company were informed about the serious design problem of the model. Despite the warnings of their engineers, the Ford management decided to manufacture and sell the car with the dangerously defective design.

Ford used different moral disengagement strategies to defend its highly controversial decision. First, Ford continuously claimed that the 'Pinto is safe,' thus denying the risk of injurious consequences. Ford managers justified their claim by referring to the US safety regulation standards in effect till 1977. In doing so they displaced their responsibility for a car that caused hundreds of deaths to the driving practices of people who would not have been seriously injured if their Ford Pinto had not been designed in a way that made it easily inflammable in a collision.

Ford engineers concluded that the safety problem of the Pinto could be solved by a minor technological adjustment. It would have cost only $11 per car to prevent the gas tank from rupturing so easily. Ford produced an intriguing and controversial cost-benefit analysis study to prove that this modification was not cost effective to society. The study provided social justification for not making that option available to customers.

Ford convinced itself that it was better to pay millions of dollars in Pinto jury trials and out-of-court settlements than to improve the safety of the model. By placing dollar values on human life and suffering, Ford simply disregarded the consequences of its practice relating to the safety of millions of customers.

The Nestle Case[10]

Nestle has been the largest producer and seller of infant formula products in Third World countries. Its marketing practices received worldwide criticism during the seventies and eighties. Infant formula is not harmful to the consumer when used properly under appropriate conditions. However, it is a demanding product that can be harmful to users when risk conditions are present. Nestle sold its infant formula to mothers in Africa, Latin America and South Asia, many of whom lived under circumstances that made the use of such products a highly risky practice.

First, infant formula must be sold in powdered form in tropical environments, requiring that mothers mix the powder with locally available water. When water supplies are of poor quality, as they are in many developing countries, infants are exposed to disease. Second, since the product must be mixed, preparation instructions are important and mothers must be able to read them. However, the rate of female illiteracy is very high in many developing nations. Third, since infant formulas are relatively expensive to purchase there is a temptation to overdilute the powder with water. Unfortunately, overdiluted formula preparations provide very poor nutrition for infants. Having decided to bottle-feed their babies in order to increase their chances for a healthy life many mothers discovered to their horror that they had actually been infecting and starving their infants.

During the late seventies the infant formula controversy became increasingly politicized in Europe and the United States. A Swiss public action group labelled Nestle as the 'baby killer.' Others claimed that Nestle causes 'commerciogenic malnutrition' in Third World countries—malnutrition brought about because of its commercial practices. In 1978 a powerful consumer boycott of Nestle and its products was begun in the United States.

The company's representatives charged that the boycott was a conspiracy of religious organizations and an indirect attack on the free enterprise system. Nestle tried to defend and morally justify its questionable marketing practice by referring to the freedom of production and marketing. The Nestle statement was a political disaster. The company was denounced for its foolishness in the US media.

Companies may not close their eyes once their product is sold. They have a continuing responsibility to monitor the product's use, resale and consumption to determine who are actually using the product and how they are using it. Postmarketing reviews are a necessary step in this process. In 1978 Nestle confessed that like other companies in the industry it did no such research and did not know who actually used its products and the manner in which they did so. In this negligent attitude towards learning about the effects of its product, Nestle was acting on the strategy of disregarding the harmful consequences of its practice in developing countries.

In 1984 Nestle's self-discrediting experience with the controversy over its infant formula finally came to an end by adopting the policy recommendations of the WHO international marketing code. However, the company and the morale of its employees suffered a major blow. It is difficult to say how long it will take for Nestle to regain its good name and for the public to regard the company once again as a good corporate citizen.

The Three Mile Island Case[11]

The most severe accident in US commercial nuclear power plant history occurred at the Three Mile Island

Unit 2 in Harrisburg on 28 March 1979. People were told to stay indoors and pregnant mothers and small children were advised to leave the area. There were widespread rumours of a general evacuation. Indeed, some 100,000 people simply voted with their feet and got up and left the area. Although there were no direct deaths or injuries, there was talk of a possible explosion equivalent to a 1-megaton bomb. There were 4 million litres of contaminated water blown out of the system. Figures for the clean-up were initially set at somewhere between $200 and 500 million. Ten years later the cleaning was still continuing.

Babcock and Wilcox built the reactor, General Public Utilities ran Three Mile Island and Metropolitan Edison owned it. During and after the event Metropolitan Edison simply refused to face up to the seriousness of the situation. The company tried to distort consequences by continually issuing denials and minimizing the accident. In effect, the public was told there was no problem, no danger and everything was routine. They also used euphemisms and displacement of responsibility to 'operator error' in providing a public explanation that tended to play down the seriousness of the accident.[12]

Later on Metropolitan Edison made strong efforts to diffuse responsibility among the other main actors involved, namely, Babcock and Wilcox, General Public Utilities and the Nuclear Regulatory Commission. All endeavoured to avoid blame for the accident in which the United States had just narrowly escaped its Chernobyl.

Table 1 shows the moral disengagement mechanisms used in the analyzed cases. The listed ones probably underestimate the scope of the mechanisms employed because they are confined to publicly observable manifestations of moral disengagement. The enlistment of exonerate practices is often buried in corporate memos and surreptitious sanctioning practices rather than being publicly expressed.

What is informative in these cases is that the moral collusion can end in justifying actions whose outcomes continue to be disapproved. The belief system of the corporation may remain unaffected for a long time by practices that are detrimental to it as well as to the general public. Selective disengagement mechanisms are deployed to mask such a contradiction and to perpetuate harmful corporate practices.

Table 1 Disengagement Mechanisms Used in Different Business Ethics Cases

Disengagement Mechanisms	Bhopal Case	Ford Pinto Case	Nestle Case	Three Mile Island Case
Moral justification		✓	✓	
Euphemistic labeling				✓
Advantageous comparison	✓			
Displacement of responsibility		✓		
Diffusion of responsibility				✓
Disregarding or distorting the consequences		✓	✓	✓
Dehumanization	✓			
Attribution of blame	✓			

◈ Implications for Business Ethics

When the mechanisms of moral disengagement are at work in corporations, business ethics is difficult to manage, especially when the sanctioning practices are surreptitious and the responsibility for policies is diffused. Numerous exonerative strategies can be enlisted to disengage social and moral sanctions from detrimental practices with a low sense of personal accountability. A central issue is how to counteract moral disengagement strategies of corporations.

From the perspective of business ethics, there are several strategies for counteracting resort to moral disengagement. One approach is to monitor and publicize corporate practices that have detrimental human effects. The more visible the consequences are on the affected parties for the decision makers, the less likely it is that they can be disregarded, distorted or minimized for long. Another approach is to increase transparency of the discourse by which the deliberation of corporate policies and practices are born. The more public the discourse about corporate decisions and policies, the less likely are corporate managers to justify the reprehensible conduct of their organizations.

Diffused and ambiguous responsibility structures make it easy to discount personal contribution to harmful effects. Instituting clear lines of accountability curtail moral disengagement. Exposing sanitizing language that masks reprehensible practices is still another corrective. The affected parties often lack social influence and status that make it easy to dehumanize and disregard them. They need to be personalized and their concerns publicized and addressed.

◈ Notes and References

1. M. Punch, *Dirty Business: Exploring Corporate Misconduct* (London: Sage Publications, 1996).

2. M. Clarke, *Business Crime* (Cambridge: Polity Press, 1990).

3. Punch, *Dirty Business* (n. 1 above).

4. M. Levi, *Regulating Fraud: White-collar Crime and the Criminal Process* (London: Tavistock, 1987).

5. Punch, *Dirty Business* (n. 1 above).

6. A. Bandura, *Social Foundations of Thought and Action: A Social Cognitive Theory* (Englewood Cliffs, NJ: Prentice-Hall, 1986); and ibid., 'Social Cognitive Theory of Moral Thought and Action,' in W. M. Kurtines and J. L. Gewirtz, eds., *Handbook of Moral Behavior and Development* (Englewood Cliffs, NJ: Lawrence Erlbaum Associates, 1991), Vol. 1, 44–103.

7. A. Bandura, 'Mechanisms of Moral Disengagement,' in W. Reich, ed., *Origins of Terrorism: Psychology, Ideologies, States of Mind* (Cambridge: Cambridge University Press, 1990), 45–103; and ibid., 'Social Cognitive Theory of Moral Thought and Action' (n. 6 above).

8. D. Weir, *The Bhopal Syndrome* (San Francisco: Sierra Club Books, 1987).

9. M. W. Hoffman, 'The Ford Pinto,' in W. M. Hoffman and R. E. Frederick, eds., *Business Ethics: Readings and Cases in Corporate Morality* (New York: McGraw-Hill, 1984), 552–59.

10. K. E. Post, 'The Ethics of Marketing: Nestlé's Infant Formula,' in W. M. Hoffman and R. E. Frederick, eds., *Business Ethics* (n. 9 above), 416–21.

11. Punch, *Dirty Business* (n. 1 above).

12. C. Perrow, *Normal Accidents* (New York: Basic Books, 1984).

CHAPTER 3

Researching Deviance

(Continued)

by participating in a research study. While our study is not designed to ask questions about deviant or criminal behavior, given our potential sample, the IRB committee is very focused on the likelihood that our subjects might discuss their criminal behavior. What are the safeguards we have in place to protect the subjects? What are the safeguards we have in place to protect the community? What are we obligated to report should our subjects discuss deviant behavior?

Story 3

Ethnographers necessarily have a special relationship with the data—we're immersed in it and interact continually with the people and places that we study. I have chosen to do most of my research in prisons and juvenile correctional facilities; this kind of work is certainly not as dangerous as researching crack dealers or gang members on the streets, but it does present its own challenges. You have to follow all of the rules of the institution, of course, always remembering that security is the first priority for staff members and administrators. You have to build trust with inmates, which can take time, patience, and an open mind. And, you have to set clear boundaries for yourself and your research. Getting too close may compromise the research and your access to the institution. The hardest and most important lesson that I learned in doing this kind of research was to find a way to keep emotional distance between myself and the people in the institution. There are people in prisons and juvenile facilities that have worked hard for second chances that they may never get. You will get to know some very likable people who will never have the opportunity for a better life. These are difficult truths to accept, but as my wise advisor reminded me, as a researcher, I'm not where the action is in their lives, nor should I be. I can witness the process, share their stories, and analyze the system, but I probably can't make things substantially better or drastically change the life chances of any one individual. Once I was able to accept this painful reality, it got easier to take a step back and do my job as a researcher and a sociologist— giving others on the outside a chance to learn about and understand prison culture.

◈ Introduction

On one hand, studying deviant behavior is exciting, intellectually and practically rewarding, and often quite fun. On the other hand, studying deviance can be stressful, heart wrenching, and plagued with difficulties that are extremely difficult to grapple with. Serious researchers must be armed with numerous tools necessary to help deal with problems encountered in the study of behaviors that are often shielded from public purview and/or forced underground by mainstream society. Researchers must also be cognizant of the ethical issues that plague the investigation of deviance. First, researchers must be aware that their influence on individuals through, for example, an experiment can have purely unintended consequences. Second, simply studying the attitudes and beliefs of people can be problematic because holding deviant attitudes and beliefs can be costly to individuals even if they never act on them. Indeed, we all probably hold certain attitudes and beliefs we would not like other people to know. In this chapter, we discuss various issues that confront researchers of deviance as well as strategies to overcome those difficulties. Not all hurdles surrounding a full understanding of issues related to deviance can be overcome, but we argue that through persistence and the use of multiple methods, almost invariably, a better understanding of deviance can be achieved.

The stories provided above by each of the authors of this book offer insights into several problems associated with researching deviance. The first story brings up issues of measurement and how different interviewers may elicit different responses from subjects. Research has shown that when conducting interviews, good interviewers can get almost anyone to discuss their deviant behavior, attitudes, and beliefs, if they can get them to feel comfortable. However, a number of factors, mostly factors that are unknown, will affect how good the information is that is collected. For example, in the first story related earlier, we suggested that the "attractive" woman was better able to get the respondent to talk. However, it could have been that the respondent had simply recently relapsed and felt the need to talk about it. The male interviewer might have elicited the same or very similar responses. The story also relates to the utility and potential problems of paying respondents for their interview time. Although paying respondents for their time is relatively commonplace today, there are many who have advocated against the practice.

The second story introduces the existence of human subjects review boards, which are a part of virtually all universities and research organizations. These review boards are developed in an effort to protect human subjects, researchers, and the university or organization. These review boards can literally squelch research; alternatively, they can be very helpful in thinking through the research process, and their questions and recommendations can actually make a research project better. We discuss human subjects research in detail toward the end of the chapter.

The third story makes us critically aware that studying deviants—be they criminals, "street" people, or persons with severe illnesses such as AIDS—can be tremendously disturbing emotionally. Recognizing that there is often very little we can do to help deserving people is not easy. Furthermore, becoming emotionally involved with those we study, while not necessarily a bad thing, may be a slippery slope: It can lead to a loss of objectivity and potentially damage relationships with institutions or gatekeepers to the research. We return to these types of issues when we discuss field research later in this chapter, in particular, qualitative fieldwork.

◈ Methodological Approaches to Studying Deviance

Experimental Strategies in the Study of Deviance

Experiments have been called the "gold standard" for determining causal relationships in the social sciences. In a true experimental design, subjects are randomly assigned to one of two or more conditions that are thought to affect some outcome, usually a behavior. Random assignment ensures that any differences following the intervention or "experimental" stimulus must have been caused by the intervention.

For example, Maass, Cadinu, Guarnieri, and Grasselli (2003) were interested in whether men exposed to an identity threat (e.g., exposure to a fictitious feminist vs. traditional female interaction) might be more influenced to engage in sexual harassment as measured by sending pornography to a fictitious female through the computer when instigated by another fictitious male (he was supposedly sending porn and encouraging the subject to do so as well). So, in this case, participating males were randomly assigned to one of two conditions. The experimental subjects

▲ **Photo 3.1** Experiments are the gold standard for determining causal relationships, but are often difficult in the study of deviance.

were presented with an interaction shown to act as an identity threat in previous studies (interaction with a female with a strong feminist stance) and then were encouraged by a confederate to send pornography to a fictitious female. The males in the control group were presented with an innocuous stimulus (interaction with a female with "traditional" gender values) and then encouraged to send porn to the traditional female confederate. The results of the experiment were consistent with the notion that threatening males' identity can lead to a heightened risk of engaging in a particular form of deviance—sexual harassment.

Studies such as the one described earlier are praised because of the high level of internal validity. That is, the subjects are randomly assigned, and the only difference between conditions is planned, controlled, and carried out consistently by the researcher. Hence, no other factor should explain the higher levels of sexual harassment in the experimental condition. Alternatively, such studies are often criticized because of concerns with external validity, that is, to what extent the results can be applied to other contexts, particularly "the real world." So, for example, in the sexual harassment study, the experimental subjects were encouraged by a fictitious confederate who was also sexually harassing the supposed/hypothetical victim. The results suggest that identity threats may increase sexual harassment but only in conditions where the potential victim is anonymous (no face-to-face or verbal contact) and there is considerable pressure from peers to engage in the deviant activity. Given the availability of pornography on the Internet, the situation is obviously possible, but the experiment was clearly contrived and may not be likely to occur in natural settings.

DEVIANCE IN POPULAR CULTURE

The documentary, *Quiet Rage: The Stanford Prison Experiment,* depicts one of the most famous and disturbing experiments in the history of psychology, deviant behavior, and social control. In 1971, Professor Philip Zimbardo set out to answer the question, "What happens when you put good people in an evil place?"

In an elaborate setup, Zimbardo and colleagues converted part of the basement of the Stanford psychology department into a simulated jail, complete with cells, solitary confinement ("the hole"), and standardized uniforms for both the prisoners and guards.

Zimbardo and colleagues recruited psychologically healthy male college students to participate in the study; individuals were randomly assigned to be either a guard or a prisoner. The experiment was planned to run for 2 weeks but was ended after only 6 days amid grave concerns about the psychological damage incurred by both prisoners and guards.

Watch the film and consider the following questions:

1. What are the ethical considerations that emerged from the Stanford Prison Experiment? What are the potential problems with doing a study like this? The young men agreed to participate in the study and were compensated as agreed upon—what other responsibilities do researchers have to their subjects?

2. Do you think it would be possible to have learned the information garnered from the study in any other way? Why or why not?

3. Do you think the same patterns they found in the Stanford Prison Experiment exist in real prison settings? Why do you think as you do?

Problems with true experimental designs have led to a host of "not quite experimental designs" referred to as quasi-experiments (Campbell & Stanley, 1963). The breadth of these designs precludes a thorough discussion in this chapter. Suffice it to say that **quasi-experimental designs,** in general, lose points in terms of internal validity; the requirement of true random assignment is often relaxed. Alternatively, in many cases, external validity is enhanced; that is, oftentimes, quasi-experiments move to less contrived environments that may have more validity.

For example, suppose you are interested in examining the effectiveness of a school-based drug prevention program. You find two junior high schools that are interested, but you realize that you cannot randomly assign students in the schools to receive the intervention because the nature of the intervention needs to be in a particular type of class (e.g., health education), and it would be impossible to move students between the two schools. Furthermore, you suspect that even if you could move students around, they may come back to their home school and share what they had learned with control students contaminating the manipulation. So the only real way to do this is to assign one school to the intervention and let the other be the control (you may even offer the control school to have the intervention a year or so later if they will participate in the research). The problem, of course, is that the schools may be quite different in terms of faculty and resources, and the student body may be quite different in terms of demographics, exposure to risk factors for drug use, and actual proclivity to use drugs. Still, you may have a relatively large sample from each school to compare. In addition, you can do pretests in both schools to assess those differences and statistically adjust for those differences.[1] While still problematic, this may be a useful starting point and is actually a fairly common problem/solution in the prevention literature.

Another form of quasi-experiment useful in the study of crime and deviance takes advantage of "naturally occurring" events. For example, researchers might compare rates of "deviance" before and after a major event such as natural disaster (e.g., Hurricane Katrina) or some other social or legal change (e.g., the implementation of a new law or policy). These types of studies can inform both theory and policy. For example, recently Chamlin (2009) theoretically considered the impact of a 2001 race riot in Cincinnati as a potential event to examine consensus or functionalist perspectives versus conflict theory explanations (see Chapter 9). The race riot emerged following the shooting and killing of Timothy Thomas, a 19-year-old black man who was wanted for several nonserious, nonviolent crimes such as loitering and not wearing a seat belt (Chamlin, 2009, p. 545). In the prior 6 years, 15 other black males had been killed by the Cincinnati police—no whites had been killed by police during this time. Subsequently and as a direct result of the shooting, 3 days of riots ensued. Chamlin thought that, from a conflict perspective, the riots might result in a heightened crackdown on robbery, which is a crime particularly more highly interracial than most crimes. Through a sophisticated statistical analysis, he showed that the riots (a challenge to authority) resulted in significantly higher levels of arrests for robbery. Although there are numerous challenges to Chamlin's interpretation, he supplemented his analyses in a variety of ways and provides unique insights into conflict and consensus perspectives.

Although policy recommendation might be gained from Chamlin's research, his focus is primarily theoretical. In contrast, in a recent article published in *Criminology and Public Policy,* Kovandzic, Vieraitis, and Boots (2009) analyzed state-level data from 1977 to 2006 to examine the impact of changes in death penalty policy, as well as actual executions, on rates of homicide. The objective was to assess the deterrent effect of having the potential of the death penalty as well as the use of the death penalty to deter homicide. This is an expanded study design compared to that used by Chamlin, who used only one city over time. Here the researchers used data from all U.S. states, which remained stable in regard to the death penalty and those that changed their policies at different times and executed offenders at different rates at different times, making a very persuasive test for or against the deterrent effect of the death penalty. Employing advanced statistical models, the authors conclude that there is no deterrent effect of the death penalty and that while policy makers can still support the practice based on retribution or other philosophical justifications, they should not justify killing offenders on the basis of a deterrent effect. As the reader can imagine, this is controversial research, and in the same issue of the journal, responses from other highly regarded researchers in the field are provided. The point is, however, that quasi-experimental designs can be quite rigorous and useful, especially when true experimental manipulation is impossible, illegal, or unethical, as in the case of much research on deviance.

In conclusion, although experimental and quasi-experimental designs have a long history in the sociological study of deviance, they are fairly rare compared to other research designs. Alternatively, there appear to be more and more experimental and quasi-experimental designs being conducted in criminology and criminal justice—hence the new publication of the *Journal of Experimental Criminology,* which began in 2005. Certainly not all but much of this research focuses on prevention, early intervention, or treatment programs for criminals, juvenile delinquents, or at-risk youth rather than on the etiology of deviance. Research on deviance is often descriptive or correlational, focused on factors associated with how deviance is distributed across different groups or factors thought to be causes or consequences of deviance. We now turn to other research designs more common among studies of deviance.

Large-Scale Survey Research

If experimental designs are the "gold standard" for determining causality, then survey research might be considered a "gold mine" of information for the student of deviance. Ever since Kinsey and his colleagues' work in the 1930s and 1940s on human sexuality (something many believed one couldn't or shouldn't ask about), literally thousands of studies have used survey research techniques to better understand deviant behavior and its correlates—that is, how deviance is distributed across individual, social, and environmental conditions.

We assume that most readers are familiar with various forms of survey research. In fact, we are all literally bombarded with surveys, be they via phone, mail, or the Internet. We are queried by political scientists about who we will vote for; by sociologists about our family and household characteristics; by economists regarding our employment, income, and expenditures; and, of course, by businesses, which are interested in what we are attracted to buying. So we will briefly discuss a few things that scientific surveys attempt to do and how, and then we examine the role that surveys have played in a better understanding of deviance as well as some of the limitations of survey research.

In general, for students of deviance, survey research involves asking a *sample* of a *target population* questions about their behaviors, attitudes, values, and beliefs. The two italicized words in the previous sentence bear some consideration. A target population is all units in some universe. The target population could be almost anything—for example, all adult residents of the United States in 2012, all fifth-grade students in a particular school district in a particular academic year, or all homeless families staying in homeless shelters between 9 p.m. and 8 a.m. in New York City on December 25, 2012. A sample simply refers to a subset of the target population. When dealing with people, it is usually quite difficult (if not impossible), time-consuming, and expensive to survey an entire target population. Unless one wished to define the target population, for example, as students who show up on time to an Introduction to Sociology class on Wednesday at 1:30 p.m., October 5, 2012, things tend to get tricky, and generally we are more interested in generalizing to larger populations. Generally, when people survey students in courses, we refer to the outcome as a convenience sample—indicating, perhaps, that the class is composed of many different kinds of students since most students take "intro soc" and "may reflect" the population of undergraduates, or at least freshmen and sophomores. Of course, in reality, we wish that the sample reflected an even larger population, but that is not very likely. Note that this is not a problem solely of survey research. Much of the experimental studies, especially in psychology, are studies of how manipulations affect college students because they are a convenient population.

Survey researchers usually want a representative sample of the target population so that the sample provides a smaller but accurate description of the population and they can use statistical procedures to generalize to the larger population. There are many ways of obtaining a representative sample, but the simplest in some ways is a random sample. Unfortunately, garnering a random sample generally requires having data on the entire population so that a sample can be drawn from the population. That is, everyone in the population has an equal chance of being surveyed, although only a subset is actually drawn. Thus, for the social scientist, *random* has a very specific meaning that doesn't sound very "random" to the layperson who might think "randomly approaching potential respondents in a mall" to be collecting a random sample. Such an approach produces ANYTHING BUT a random sample.

Suffice it to say that there are many strategies for surveying samples of large populations, but it is still an expensive process and usually conducted by large research agencies with considerable funding. Even very well-funded projects have problems drawing adequate samples that are representative of the target population and often have to oversample certain populations that are hard to access. For example, most phone surveys of adults we have been involved in result in an older, more female sample, and sometimes samples that overreflect certain racial groups. It is likely that these groups are more likely to have adults at home, to have a home phone, and to be willing to answer a call and respond to the survey.

Hence, a major concern for social scientists is the response rate and how that might affect the results of a survey. If the response rate is low, the sample may still reflect the population, but this is highly unlikely and would occur only if the various demographic groups were equally likely to respond and those who respond versus those who do not respond were similar in all respects related to the study. Of course, this is highly unlikely, especially in the study of deviant behavior, where some may be less willing to provide information, especially to certain types of investigators (see Pruitt, 2008).

A somewhat related concern involves the appropriate sample size. To address many questions, relatively small samples (e.g., 100–200 cases and sometimes even much smaller) may be more than sufficient, and of course, much qualitative research will use only a few subjects. Garnering enough cases to obtain a nationally representative sample of registered voters' attitudes toward a presidential candidate, or even their opinion on "deviant issues" such as abortion, pornography, or fear of being a victim of crime, may take a thousand or more cases. Indeed, the General Social Survey of the United States, which has been conducted since 1972, includes about 1,500 cases at each time point; it cuts the sample in half for some questions and still provides a solid description of the demography of Americans as well as our attitudes, values, and beliefs. Using a sample like this, we would feel quite confident about describing how the American population stands on various issues as well as how these attitudes and beliefs vary across groups and with other social variables. This is because the issues that surveys address are generally fairly common, and a significant proportion of the population is willing to express their attitudes and beliefs about the subject. Alternatively, when events are very rare, much larger samples are required to garner enough respondents to accurately describe the population and describe how they vary across subgroups. For example, contrary to popular belief, serious victimization (e.g., rape, robbery, aggravated assault) is fairly rare, and so the National Crime Victimization survey requires approximately 12,000 respondents at each sampling. Similarly, studies such as the Monitor the Future project, which includes involvement in serious drug use, including cocaine, heroin, and methamphetamines among children and young adults, now includes approximately 50,000 respondents annually (see next section). It should be clear from the preceding discussion that researchers of deviance need various strategies other than national probability sampling to study many forms of deviance.

Field Research: Pure Observer to Full Participant

Field research, too, can be a gold mine for investigating various forms of deviance and especially deviant groups and subcultures. *Field research* is a term that brings to mind the anthropologist immersing himself or herself into some foreign, perhaps indigenous, society, learning the language, customs, beliefs, and behaviors of its members. Or the researcher of a religious cult who feigns to be a believer and observes others always under the dangerous possibility that his or her identity will be revealed and he or she will, at best, be alienated from the study site or, worse, physically harmed or even killed. These are of course examples of real cases of fieldwork, but in our perspective, *fieldwork* is a more generic term with several dimensions and polar extremes. True, the term clearly delineates fieldwork practices from the large-scale mail, phone, or Internet surveys that are indicative of much social survey research. Alternatively, at one polar end, we might include as field research going into a school district or a neighborhood and systematically surveying students/ residents, even with short, close-ended survey questions about deviance. On the other extreme, taking a job as a stripper to better understand—indeed, truly empathize with—what the lives of these women (and men) are like and the social structures and relations that dictate a major part of their lives is more likely to be viewed as field research. So to some extent, unless one is studying the deviance of college students actually in the classroom, field research more generally means getting outside the "ivory tower"—getting one's hands dirty, so to speak—to better understand some form of deviance, be it behavior, attitudes, or beliefs.

Excluding our more structured example of handing out surveys to students, two types of fieldwork are sometimes viewed as two points on a continuum between pure observation and participant observation. Before distinguishing the two, it is important to recognize that both strategies typically involve extensive observation and recording of those observations. Historically, this has been done primarily in written form, although audio recording in various formats has been around for a long time. However, for a variety of reasons, even these audio recordings often need to be transcribed sooner or later.

Let's start with pure observations, which would theoretically entail observing people, not only with them not knowing the researcher is observing them but also with them not observing the researcher whatsoever. Of course, this can be done; one can look through a peephole, through a one-way mirror, or down at a place of social interaction such as a park from a higher building. A study at one of the author's universities involved simply sitting at various intersections and documenting the running of red lights (Porter & England, 2000) and various characteristics of drivers and automobiles associated with the transgressions. It is very unlikely that drivers at these intersections would observe the researchers and even less likely that they would allow it to affect their behavior. Another study at one our universities studied hand-washing behavior (or lack thereof). This was about as close as it comes to pure observation, although usually it was clear that someone was in the stall doing something (presumably something other than observing). Still, knowledge that there is someone in a nearby stall may influence people's behavior (Monk-Turner et al., 2005).

A recent study by McCleary and Tewksbury (2010) used an almost pure observation strategy to study female patrons of sexually oriented book-video-novelty stores in three major counties in California over a 2-year period. Trained researchers observed 33 stores and customers who entered them with a total of 271 observation periods totaling 162 hours. The researchers were trained to remain as unobtrusive as possible. McCleary and Tewksbury write,

> Working from a common protocol, researchers observed customers from at least 250 feet away for 30 consecutive minutes. Researchers were allowed to break the 30-minute rule if necessary. Observation ended before 30 minutes in approximately 20 percent of the trials and lasted longer than 30 minutes in 60 percent of the trials. In every instance, researchers cited the need to remain unobtrusive as the rationale for breaking the 30-minute rule. (p. 212)

This was a greatly improved study focusing on a much larger sample of stores across a much wider network than had previously been studied. The authors found that women were much more likely than men to come to sexually oriented business with other females (46%) or in mixed-sex groups (22%) or as a male–female couple (15%). In contrast, men were most likely to come alone (76%) or in same-sex groups (18%). Women also preferred "safer" appearing stores with security guards, more employees, and more business traffic. They avoided stores with "viewing booths," which the authors argued are often viewed as places for male–male encounters. Interestingly, across all observations, approximately half of the employees were female, but women were significantly less likely to patronize stores with a larger numbers of women employees.

So researchers often study various forms of deviance with no or very little interaction with the persons they are observing. The benefit of this approach is that the presence of the researcher is very unlikely to affect the behavior of the research subjects. This is similar to what medical researchers do in a double-blind study, in that the medical researchers have very little potential to affect the results of the experiment because they don't know if they are administering a new drug or a placebo. Here, of course, the researcher may have biases in his or her observations, but they should not affect the actual behavior of the observed. So if there are multiple observers, this threat to validity should be minimized even further.

Let's move to the other extreme of the spectrum and examine the strategies of researchers who actively interact with and participate in the activities of the deviants they study—**participant observation.** In contrast to the "objective" pure observer, for other social scientists, active participation is the only way to truly understand the attitudes, beliefs, and behaviors of deviant actors and the factors that shape and affect deviance. People have "become" nudists (Weinberg, 1966), panhandlers (Lankenau, 1999), erotic dancers (Ronai & Ellis, 1989), and "lookouts" for men engaging in homosexual acts in public restrooms (Humphreys, 1970), among many others. A classic study of high-level drug dealing and smuggling was conducted by Patricia Adler (1993). Although Adler was not a drug dealer herself, she revealed that she used marijuana and cocaine; she serendipitously came to know a major dealer, and deals were done in her presence and even in her home. Through this contact, she met many drug dealers as well as smugglers covertly (they assumed she was in the business) and overtly when she asked to interview them. Her research with drug dealers and smugglers continued for 6 years and resulted in a classic book in the field, *Wheeling and Dealing: An Ethnography of an Upper-Level Drug Dealing and Smuggling Community.* This research was dangerous as many of the dealers obviously did not want others to know about their illegal enterprises. It also raised important ethical considerations. The author obviously knew about illegal behavior and did not report it. Of course, the research could not have been conducted if she reported the behavior, and indeed reporting it would have harmed her subjects—something as researchers we should strive very hard not to do. Indeed, it is unlikely that this research would be approved by most university human subjects committees.

Mark Fleisher (1995) also gained entry into a community of street hustlers, drug addicts, and alcoholics in the Seattle area. Over the course of 3 years (1988–1990), Fleisher completed in-depth interviews of nearly 200 ($n = 194$) deviant street people of various ages (preteens to people older than 50) and races, ethnicities, and genders. Unlike Patricia Adler, who clearly befriended her primary source as well as other dealers, Fleisher was skeptical of the responses of street hustlers, especially those based on short interviews on issues that could not be supported with other information.

> I distrust data gathered in a few interviews with informants whom I don't know well or for whom I can't verify the facts with reliable documents. Hustlers,' inmates,' and former inmates' self-reports are, until proven otherwise, just "folklore," simply informants' comments, opinions, and explanations often engineered to sound legitimate. After all, these informants have been shown to be untrustworthy, manipulative, and disingenuous. Why should they be otherwise with me? (p. 21)

Given his concerns over the self-reports of the hustlers he met, he made many attempts to confirm their responses, for example, with arrest histories from the local police. Similarly, he attempted to confirm past events and stories with family and other peers who could verify the information.

This is not to say that there were not interviewees that he came to like and even felt concern for—indeed, he tried to help several get the help they needed. However, his overall commentary on the street hustlers was not pretty or very sympathetic. Ultimately, Fleisher uses his field research to inform both theory and policy. In regard to theory, his work seems most consistent with Gottfredson and Hirschi's (1990) theory of low self-control (see Chapter 7) and the role certain parents play in not socializing their children appropriately. In fact, he argues that the hustlers' lives are largely shaped by abusive, drug- and alcohol-abusing parents. In terms of policy, his conclusions are conservative and emphasize incarceration and making offenders work. Overall, Fleisher's ethnography provides very powerful insights into the lives of "beggars and thieves" in streets of Seattle and elsewhere.

Participatory observation, be it **covert** or **overt observation,** can be dangerous, emotionally and physically draining, and—quite simply—very hard work. It can also be intellectually and emotionally rewarding. Hands-on research of this type brings one much closer to the lives of the deviant and therefore enables greater sense of empathy and a much closer sense of the experiences of those people shunned by society. Some have argued that this participant observation is the best if not the only approach to truly study deviance (Ferrell & Hamm, 1998). We would disagree and argue that yes, participant observation is a powerful methodology with many benefits, but like all methodologies, it has many limitations as you will come to see in the readings at the end of this chapter.

STUDIES IN DEVIANCE

How Close Is Too Close? Balancing Closeness and Detachment in Qualitative Research

By Shana L. Maier and Bryan A. Monahan, in *Deviant Behavior, 31,* 1–32

One of the trickiest parts of conducting research in the area of deviance is making and maintaining contact with the deviant group being studied. Especially in qualitative research, an important component of collecting data is developing rapport and establishing trust with those you are studying. How might we ever understand the experiences of heroin addicts unless we are allowed to study their daily lives? Why would heroin addicts invite us into their lives if they are worried we might betray their trust? However, while researchers need to establish a trusting bond with their interviewees, the question becomes, what are the issues that might arise as researchers establish a bond with their research participants? How might a researcher balance the relationship between an interviewee and himself or herself? While a major concern of qualitative research used to be that the researcher might get too close, this concern has really shifted to one that the researcher may not get close enough to get authentic, useful data.

Maier and Monahan interviewed 29 researchers to examine their experiences as researchers of deviance and crime. They found that "a researcher's efforts to balance closeness and detachment were often complicated by three common elements of qualitative research" (p. 23). These elements include the amount of time that researchers spend with their research participants to establish a trusting bond—given there are no clear-cut rules about what is appropriate. In addition to the amount of time researchers invest, Maier and Monahan also found they invest a significant amount of emotion into the researcher/participant bond. And finally, researchers often feel compelled to "give something back" to research participants, which makes balancing closeness and detachment difficult. These elements mean that researchers sometimes find themselves in situations that have no clear-cut boundaries or rules. From these interviews, Maier and Monahan also found that it was evident that "researchers need to find a balance between closeness and detachment that is right for them" (p. 23).

Maier and Monahan conclude that qualitative research in all of its messiness needs to be celebrated because the reality is that it is a method that does not and cannot come with a rulebook but offers a rich, important understanding of the lives of others.

◈ Content Analysis

Content analysis may be a term less familiar to undergraduate students in general or students of deviance in particular. The research strategy, however, has a long history in the study of deviance and deviant behavior. Content analysis involves reviewing records of communication and systematically searching, recording, and analyzing themes and trends in those records. Sources of communication are virtually unlimited, often free, or quite cheap, making content analysis another gold mine of opportunity, especially for the undergraduate student of deviance.

Sources of communication used for studying deviance include transcribed interviews or open-ended responses to surveys, historical documents, legal codes, newspapers, advertisements from many sources, song lyrics, movies, TV shows, books and magazines, and websites and chat rooms, among myriad others. Indeed, all of these have been the source of content analyses in the study of deviance. Keys to a successful content analysis include (1) a solid research question, (2) a reasonably good understanding of the population of the materials/sources of interest, (3) a strategy for sampling records of communication, and (4) a systematic approach to extracting and coding themes or looking for trends.

A solid research question is probably the best starting place, and it can come from many directions and levels. The most interesting questions tend to emerge from theory, previous research or an apparent lack of research on a particular subject, debates and conflicts, or suspected myths that one may want to empirically examine to support or debunk. The research question(s) may be very exploratory especially at first or when there is little or conflicting theoretical or empirical guidance. For example, Pruitt and Krull (2011) recognized that there was actually little systematic research on why males seek female prostitutes and exactly what they want; what little research was available was based on nonrepresentative samples. She argued that a content analysis of female escort Internet advertisements might provide information on what men want from prostitutes, assuming that the escorts are accurate in their perceptions of what males want and therefore choose to advertise it. Analyzing 237 female escort advertisements, she found that ads focused on "girl friend experiences, unrushed encounters, and escort-type services" were far more common than were specific sex acts.

▲ **Photo 3.2**   Measurement is critical to every scientific discipline but is especially interesting and important in the study of deviance.

Alternatively, Tuggle and Holmes (1997) were interested in the politics surrounding a smoking ban in California and especially in Shasta County, where the debate included 105 letters to the editor, which the authors of the article content analyzed. It was no surprise, and even expected, that pro-ban supporters tended to be nonsmokers and anti-ban supporters smokers. The logic of the arguments might also be expected with the former focusing on health risks (especially the risks associated with secondhand smoke) versus the latter focusing on individuals' right to smoke. What might not have been predicted was that the power, measured by personal property, held by the pro-ban moral crusaders was much greater than the smokers arguing for the status quo. Given the large disparity in power, the fact that the ban was successful was not terribly surprising.

As discussed earlier, developing a reasoned understanding of the population of interest and then strategy for sampling cases to study is not an easy task. If one is interested in the prevalence of "derogatory depictions of women" in pornography, are we talking about magazines, movies, Internet sites, and so on? Once this question has been answered and refined, the sampling process should most likely be determined by a systematic process that fits into one's time and budget constraints.

The final issue, developing a systematic approach to extracting and coding themes or looking for trends, is another important consideration in a quality content analysis. Sticking with the example above, consider how different people are in their perceptions of what is derogatory and what is innocuous or simply entertaining; they may have very different points at which they believe something becomes derogatory. Developing an operationalization of "derogatory depictions" that can be selected and categorized consistently and replicated by others can be a very difficult issue to grapple with. Developing clear and consistent guidelines is paramount in this endeavor.

Content analysis is an exciting research avenue for those interested in studying deviant behavior and reactions to deviance. As mentioned, because "records of communication" are often available for free or are accessible quite cheaply, this is an excellent research design for undergraduate students interested in conducting a class research project. Since the topic areas are largely unbounded, we simply offer a few recent examples to stir up interest and possibilities.

Between 1940 and 1950, a new term, *criminal abortion,* was found in coroners' reports in New Orleans, Louisiana. Frailing and Harper (2010) used those data along with a systematic content analysis of three newspapers to show how the practice of midwifery changed from a conventional practice to a deviant and even criminalized profession that provided the medical field with a new source of income. Historical and contemporary newspapers are available online and through university libraries and hold a very interesting wealth of information on how deviant behaviors are perceived and reacted to by the larger society.

Gauthier and Chaudoir (2004) were interested in the lives of female-to-male transsexuals (FTMs), particularly the legal, emotional, medical, and especially social challenges they face. They searched the Internet for relevant "web sites, chat rooms, message boards, web rings, and private chat groups" to garner insight from those in the process of transitioning from female-to-male status as well as those who had completed the process. Over a 2-year period, they were able to collect nearly 1,000 pages of information from FTMs. A number of themes regarding the lives of FTMs emerged from the study, including physical and social issues in the transition, medical procedures (e.g., the surgery, hormone treatment), and issues related to appearance and "passing" (hair and dress, mannerisms, and attempts at "passing"). The Internet is an excellent source for garnering information from individuals who have formed a cyber community that might be quite difficult to enter except for the easy access via the Internet.

H. Klein and Shiffman (2008) collected a random sample of cartoons stratified by decade from 1930 to 1990 to examine "what cartoons tell us about assault." They found that assaults in cartoons, as might be expected, are quite frequent, although rarely are there significant or serious physical consequences. Among other things, they found that simple assault was the most common form of violence, and this declined precipitously from 1930 to 1970, when it began to rise significantly again. They also found gender differences, with females more often the aggressor toward males and males more often the victim. Anger was the primary cause of violence (about 40%) followed by revenge and self-defense (both around 20%). Cartoons, whether they be in newspapers or magazines, on the Internet, or elsewhere, may shed light on any number of deviant social issues and how those issues are perceived in society.

Like any research strategy, content analyses are subject to numerous flaws and limitations. For example, what are we to make from the previous study of cartoon violence? It summarizes what many see in cartoons, but does it tell us much about the actual causes and consequences of violence? Probably not, but it may tell us something about how violence is viewed, tolerated, and reacted to under different circumstances, which can provide much fodder for thinking about violence within or across certain societies over time. Given the wealth of data readily available, we find content analyses an excellent strategy for the study of deviant behavior.

◈ Secondary Data Sources

Very important data have already been collected and are readily available for the study of crimes and other forms of deviance. These sources all have limitations but can still be extremely useful for conducting research. In addition, sometimes different sources can be used in conjunction with each other to better understand the causes and consequences of various deviant phenomena. Here we discuss just four general sources of **secondary data;** thus, we do not cover the entire spectrum of secondary sources but rather highlight just a few of the more useful ones for undergraduate students interested in deviant behavior.

The Uniform Crime Report

The Uniform Crime Report was developed by the Federal Bureau of Investigation in the 1930s. Data from nearly 17,000 police agencies are compiled by the bureau and presented online and in many published documents. Data on crimes known to the police include violent crimes (murder, forcible rape, robbery, and aggravated assault) and property crimes (burglary, larceny theft, and motor vehicle theft). Data are generally provided in terms of numbers and rates and can be organized by region, state, and city and for longitudinal comparisons. With very little skill, figures such as the following can be created online. Figure 3.1 shows that the rate of murder and nonnegligent manslaughter dropped precipitously between 1993 and 2000 and from there remained relatively stable through 2008 (this figure was created by the authors from data available from the FBI website at www.fbi.gov/ucr/cius2008/data/table_01.html).

Figure 3.1   Violent Crime Rate (1989–2008)

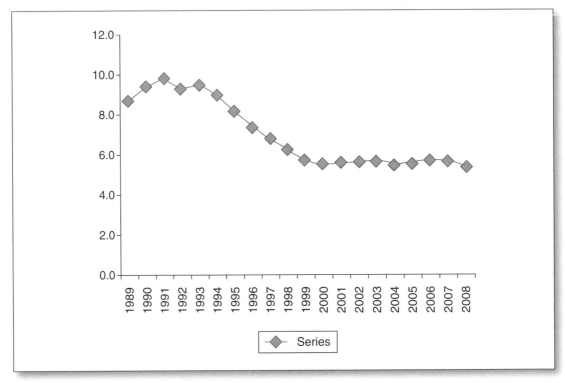

Source: Data from FBI.gov.

A number of problems are associated with these data. For example, we don't know much about crimes known to police other than the type of offense and where it was detected or reported. For example, the gender, race, and age of the offender are often not known or not provided. However, data are also provided on arrests where we do have demographic information on the accused. Limitations of these data are fairly obvious. First, although they are important crimes, only certain offenses are recorded and others are ignored, including both street crimes and white-collar offenses. Second, demographic data often used from arrest statistics may reflect not only crime but also activities of the police. That is, arrest statistics may provide a better picture of what the police do, as opposed to what criminals do. Finally, there is what has come to be referred to as the "dark figure" of crime and deviance, which reminds us that these data do not take into account all of the crimes that the police never become aware of—and that figure would appear to be huge. Consider all the rapes, assaults, burglaries, and thefts that are never reported to the police or every joint or crack pipe smoked or every shoplifted item that was just listed as missing inventory. In fact, it is common knowledge among criminologists that the best statistics are probably for murder and motor vehicle theft because there is usually a body for the former, and insurance requires a police report for stolen vehicles. Still, these statistics can be very useful and are at the heart of a great deal of criminological research.

Substance Abuse and Mental Health Services Administration

The Substance Abuse and Mental Health Services Administration (SAMHSA) is an agency of the U.S. Department of Health and Human Services. This agency provides critical information on drug use and mental health, making it an excellent source for the student of deviance. In particularly, it supports a "public health surveillance system," DAWN or the Drug Abuse Warning Network. This system provides information from emergency rooms and medical examiner reports. The former records "emergency room episodes" that involve one or more drugs, including overdoses, hallucinations, and suicide attempts, as well as people requesting help with drug addiction (e.g., detoxification or withdrawals), among others. It also collects data from medical examiners who report on drug-related causes of death through their autopsies. DAWN provides statistics on all types of drugs, including legal and illegal, prescription and nonprescription, alcohol alone, and alcohol in conjunction with other drugs. It even includes dietary supplements and nonpharmaceutical inhalants, so it taps into both criminal and noncriminal incidences. They tabulate data for a variety of comparisons, in particular, longitudinal analyses that allow us to evaluate trends in the types of drugs causing the most problems in terms of death and emergency room visits.

SAMHSA also supports and provides statistics from the National Survey on Drug Use and Health, which collects self-report data on alcohol and other drug use that better reflects general deviance not resulting in

Figure 3.2 Marijuana Use in Past Year Among Persons Aged 12 or Older, by State: Percentages, Annual Averages Based on 2006 and 2007 National Survey on Drug Use and Health

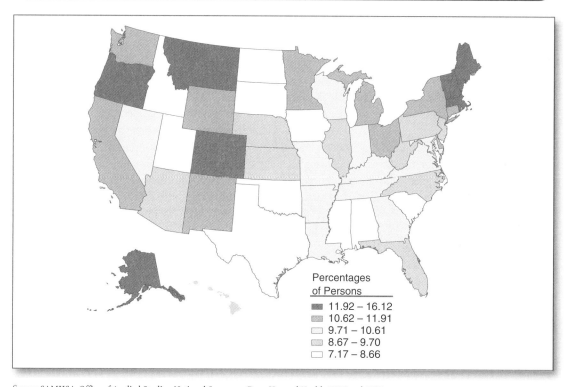

Percentages
of Persons

- 11.92 – 16.12
- 10.62 – 11.91
- 9.71 – 10.61
- 8.67 – 9.70
- 7.17 – 8.66

Source: SAMHSA, Office of Applied Studies, National Survey on Drug Use and Health, 2006 and 2007.

such serious consequences as emergency room episodes or death. The research is equally impotant, however, for many questions raised by the student of deviance. These data also can provide trend-level data that might be used to triangulate with data provided by DAWN. State-level comparisons are also possible, and maps of various indicators of drug use can be obtained. The following figure was obtained at www.oas.samhsa .gov/2k7State/Ch2.htm#Fig2–5 on May 22, 2010, and shows the past year self-reported prevalence of marijuana use among persons 12 years or older across states in the mid-2000s. With a few exceptions, it appears that marijuana use is highest in northern states—at least people are more willing to report it there.

SAMSHA also provides a wealth of data on mental health. For example, the Community Mental Health Services' (CMHS) Uniform Reporting System Output Tables provide demographic data (age, race, gender) on people receiving mental health services by state. Various comparisons can be made between states or between a particular set of states and national estimates. These data can be easily found at http:// mentalhealth.samhsa.gov/cmhs/MentalHealthStatistics/URS2002.asp.

Monitoring the Future

Although related to SAMHSA, Monitoring the Future (MTF) is such a major, large-scale, longitudinal project that we discuss it separately. Through funding from the National Institutes of Health and National Institute on Drug Abuse, the projects involve surveying students about their attitudes, behaviors, and beliefs concerning legal and illegal drug use (alcohol, tobacco, and other illegal drugs such as marijuana, cocaine, and heroin). The project began in 1975 and involved data collected from approximately 16,000 twelfth graders in 133 high schools. In 1991, the study was expanded to include approximately 18,000 eighth graders in 150 schools and 17,000 tenth graders in 140 schools. So in all, there are approximately 50,000 students in 420 schools surveyed in their classrooms annually. Prior to the survey, flyers are put up announcing the survey and letters are sent to parents so that they are aware of the study and can decline their child's participation. In addition, to these surveys, a mailed follow-up survey is sent to a subsample of the 12th-grade sample after they graduate (a young adult sample). The data collected allow researchers to examine changes over time across all four age groups. Because the sample is age graded, "age effects" can also be examined. Behaviors can also be linked to large social contexts (e.g., school characteristics) for very interesting analyses. Some of the data are easily downloaded for analysis, and there are online mechanisms to analyze the data, although much of the data containing confidential or identifying characteristics are restricted.

In addition to the tables and figures publicized every year, literally hundreds of journal articles, book chapters, research monographs, and reports have been published using these data. We will just give a few examples here. In 2007, O'Malley and Johnson (two primary investigators involved in MTF) published an interesting article examining the relationship between driving and drugs between 2001 and 2006. There were many findings, but of particular interest, they found that high school seniors were more likely to drive after smoking marijuana than after consuming five or more drinks (13% vs. 9.5%). Exposure to drug- or alcohol-using drivers in the prior month declined between 2001 and 2006 from 35% to 31%, but obviously this still is a major concern.

In another study, Yacoubian and Peters (2005) used MTF data to examine the prevalence and correlates of MDMA or "ecstasy" use among 2,258 high school seniors. In contrast to much media hype at the time suggesting that this was a major epidemic, they found that about 10% of students reported ever using ecstasy, 7% in the past year, and 3% in the past month. Given other evidence that the drug was primarily used by "rave attendees," the authors argued that prevention efforts should be targeted to those groups rather than on broad campaigns that would primarily reach those not at high risk of use or abuse.

Finally, De Li (2004) used data on 4,866 tenth-grade students from the 2000 wave of the MTF project to provide a theoretical test of Gottfredson and Hirschi's theory of self-control and Hirschi's social control or social bond theory (see Chapter 7). Consistent with each theory, they found that those with low levels of self-control had greater involvement in delinquency, while social bonds were associated with less delinquency. More important, some of the variables seemed to work in combination (interact), suggesting that some theoretical integration might be warranted.

Archived Data: Inter-University Consortium for Political and Social Science Research

People who have been gathering data for a while sometimes are willing to share the data with other researchers for further analyses. In fact, currently the National Institute of Justice (NIJ) requires that the data from research projects it funds be made available to researchers. These data as well as others are archived in the Inter-University Consortium for Political and Social Science Research or the ICPSR. While the majority of data housed by the ICPSR is not relevant to students of deviance, much data are available on crime and the criminal justice system as well as softer forms of deviance. Students working on class projects or senior theses are encouraged to see if their college or university is a member of the ICPSR; they can explore the many offerings the ICPSR provides (www.icpsr.umich.edu/icpsrweb/ICPSR/). We discuss a just a few of the data sets that might be of interest to students of deviance.

Elaine Sharpe provided a data set on how 10 city governments in the United States responded to morality issues in the 1990s. The focus was on how municipalities react to deviant issues such as "gay rights, abortion rights, abortion clinic protests, needle exchange programs for drug users, hate speech, hate groups, gambling policies and regulations, animal rights, and regulations pertaining to the sex industry, which included pornography, prostitution, and adult entertainment." Data on these issues (451 incidents) were derived from reviewing local newspapers and public government records. Social (e.g., demographic and religious), economic (e.g., females in the labor force and unemployment), and political (e.g., elected officials) information on the 10 cities is also provided. There is a wealth of information in this collection that could provide for very interesting secondary analyses.

Martin Monto was the principal investigator on a project that examined characteristics of arrested clients of street prostitutes in four western cities (Portland, Oregon; San Francisco and Santa Clara, California; and Las Vegas, Nevada) between 1996 and 1999. Men arrested for soliciting prostitutes ("johns") were court referred to client intervention workshops where they were anonymously surveyed. In addition to basic demographic information, clients were asked extensively about various sexual behaviors and encounters (with prostitutes as well as other sexual relations), attitudes regarding women in general and prostitutes in particular, and beliefs about violence against women and the legality of prostitution. Again the detailed nature of the data, as well as the fact that there were a large number of cases in each city, makes this a very useful data set to better understand the attitudes, beliefs, and behaviors of men who have been arrested for soliciting a prostitute.

In another study related to sexual deviance, Estes and Weiner provided ICPSR data on the Commercial Sexual Exploitation of Children in the United States (1997–2000). This project attempted to collect systematic data on "the nature, extent, and seriousness of child sexual exploitation (CSE) in the United States." The researchers surveyed staff in nongovernment and government organizations that were tasked with dealing with the transnational trafficking of children for sexual purposes. For example, local family agencies who dealt with runaway children and homeless youth were surveyed. In addition, local law enforcement officers, court personnel (e.g., prosecutors and public defenders), and correctional workers who dealt with sexually exploited children were interviewed. Characteristics of the agencies, including their location, are also provided. Because address data (city, state, and ZIP code) were collected, the data could be matched with other data to examine other contextual factors that might affect the agencies' ability to detect and affect the sexual exploitation of children (e.g., state laws or the number of local agencies in the city or county). The ability to match the data with other sources of data makes further analyses virtually unlimited.

NOW YOU . . . CONDUCT THE RESEARCH

The Southern Poverty Law Center documented 932 hate groups in the United States in 2010. The following is a map showing the number of hate groups in each state. As a deviance researcher, you are interested in studying *white supremacy* groups. As a researcher, you need to establish your research question, define your population, and determine your sample. Do you want to conduct macro-level research on trends and characteristics of these hate groups in the United States? Or would you prefer to engage in micro-level research that examines participants in these groups? How will you conduct this research? How will you collect your data? What may some of the challenges be with a study on this topic?

Figure 3.3   Active U.S. Hate Groups

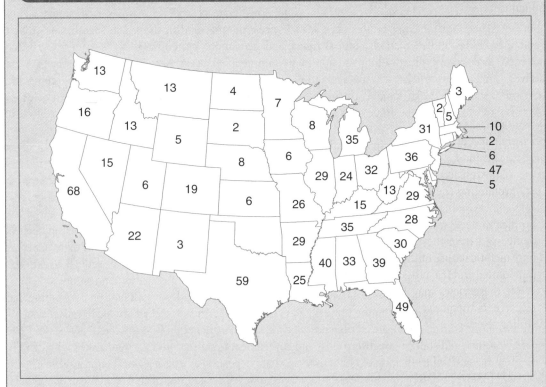

Source: Reprinted by permission of the Southern Poverty Law Center.

◈ Ethical Considerations in Studying Deviance

As has been hinted at earlier in this chapter, there are serious ethical considerations in the study of deviance. Many experiments conducted not so long ago would no longer be allowed on college campuses or elsewhere. In the 1960s, Milgram created a study where subjects were told to shock other participants when they provided an incorrect response to a question. The shocks got more intense with each wrong answer. What made this experiment potentially unethical was not causing pain to humans as no one actually received the shocks. Rather, it was that people quite often continued to shock the confederate until it resembled torture, and it was quite likely that subjects experienced guilt and remorse over what they had just done.

Experimental studies are not the only methodology where ethical concerns are raised. A classic study (Humphreys, 1970) of male homosexual encounters in public bathrooms (the Tearoom Trade) is often cited as unethical research. Laud Humphreys acted as a "lookout" in these venues. He did not disclose to the subjects that he was studying them, but more important, he collected license plate numbers and through a police officer contact obtained addresses to do "market research." He then interviewed these men under the guise that he was doing a social health survey. So, several issues of **ethics in research** are raised. Observing behavior that is public, even if attempts are made to hide the behavior, is probably relatively innocuous, although some might question the ethics of acting as a "lookout" for cops and "straights." He lied to a police officer to access addresses, which certainly fractures the call for honesty and may even be illegal. Finally, he lied to the respondents when he interviewed them, not disclosing that he was actually interested in their homosexual acts.

Today there are structured committees associated with universities and other research organizations set up to protect human subjects. These committees are referred to as **Institutional Review Boards** (IRBs) and are generally composed of persons from different fields (e.g., scientists and nonscientists), an outside person from the community, and a legal representative, among others. These boards meet and review applications to conduct research. Some research is exempt from full IRB review, particularly research involving public observations, research using surveys or interviews when the data are collected and recorded anonymously, and studies involving standard educational strategies. Interestingly, because universities have become such bureaucracies, the IRB or a subcommittee needs to review the research to decide whether the research is indeed exempt from IRB review.

Many researchers have come to hold a dim and jaded view of IRBs. They are often seen as gatekeepers prohibiting the researcher from engaging in important research that poses little to no risk to the **human subjects** involved and the researchers' own exposure to risk is there business, not that of "big brother." Indeed, some see IRBs as being "more concerned about preventing their parent institution from being sued than the rights of human subjects" (Goode, 2008a, p. 121). Furthermore, because of the bureaucratic nature of the beast, IRBs often seem more concerned that the appropriate boxes are checked ("i's" dotted and "t's" crossed) than with any possible harm the research might present to human subjects. While these views may be accurate in some institutions, many individuals on these committees are researchers themselves, and even those not directly involved in research generally have no interest in stifling the pursuit of knowledge; rather, the job requires thinking about all aspects of the research and making sure human subjects are protected, and frankly, getting the correct box checked is often not as difficult as it may appear.

There are several general concerns when considering the protection of human subjects. The first comes from the medical adage—"first do no harm." This is an especially problematic issue in experimental studies where subjects are asked to do things they wouldn't normally do. If there are risks, the subjects need to be aware of those risks and how the risks will be minimized. Even an anonymous survey that asks sensitive questions may invoke unpleasant emotions, especially among certain populations (e.g., victims of crimes or other abuses). These risks might be reduced by making the survey voluntary and letting respondents know they can stop at any time or ignore any question. If it is an especially vulnerable population, a referral might be provided to a common service provider. Research must be voluntary, which brings up how subjects are recruited, how they are asked to participate, and what sorts of incentives might be offered for their participation (which should not be coercive). Whether the research is voluntary can be tricky. A recent study from health sciences recently came to our attention where subjects in the military were going to be asked to wear very heavy backpacks and run until they basically collapsed. The health scientists were going to measure heart rates and a few other bodily measures. What concerned the committee, of course, was making the subjects run until they collapsed; however, this was not the research—they were going to do this regardless of whether or not they participated in the research, which simply involved the physiological tests. The military can make soldiers do many things, but it cannot (or should not) make them be test subjects in a university research study. In fact, the research component might have the benefit of having medical professionals on hand. So, the consent form given to soldiers basically stated that "the military is going to make you do X, Y, Z. We would like you to participate in a research aspect of this exercise by letting us take your blood pressure. . . ." While the committee could say nothing about the dangerous part of the exercise, they could make it clear that the soldiers' participation in the research had to be voluntary.

This brings up an interesting issue regarding informed consent. Providing subjects with sufficient information to make the decision to participate in various forms of research from surveys to interviews to experiments should be provided if at all possible. We think, however, that often times formal consent forms, especially signed ones, can be off-putting to potential subjects and sometimes result in increased risk. Consider a 5-minute survey; do you really need to have respondents read a two- to three-page consent form? In most cases, probably not; in fact, a long consent form may thwart otherwise interested respondents from participating. Generally, a paragraph that requests participation, stating that the research is voluntary and how the respondent's identity will be protected, is plenty. Second, consider a study of many deviant populations where others simply finding out that respondents are among a deviant population may be risky to employment, law enforcement, or social relations. If we required signed consent to study persons with AIDS, those who use drugs, or those who have been arrested for soliciting prostitution, we may find it very hard to get persons to agree to the research. More important, their signature on the form puts them at risk as it is basically a legal document with their signature saying that they have AIDS, use drugs, or have recently solicited prostitution. Thus, anonymity rather than confidentiality is often far safer for the individuals studied, and a consent form may be totally inappropriate.

◈ Conclusion

In this chapter, we have presented the reader with several strategies to investigate and answer questions regarding deviance. We have not favored any particular approach, resting on the belief that the appropriate methodology comes after the research questions have been decided and the population of interest specified, as well as the resources and skills of the researcher or research team spelled out. In fact, it would seem much more profitable to think about how different methodologies might work in concert to better understand the phenomenon at hand than immediately relegating it to a specific methodology. A few in-depth interviews might "snowball" into a larger sample or a survey might be developed based on the interviews to give to a large, more representative sample. Alternatively, results of a large-scale survey may suggest a subpopulation to where more detailed investigation is warranted. Given that these methodologies are not very conducive to tests of causal relationships, an experiment or quasi-experiment might be designed to aid in our knowledge of what factors affect some deviant attitude, belief, or behavior. In conclusion, we find that combining or triangulating research methods may be the only way to truly understand issues involving deviance.

ENDNOTE

1. While beyond the scope of this chapter, there are several ways of matching students across schools or to make statistical adjustments so that more reasonable comparisons can be made.

EXERCISES AND DISCUSSION QUESTIONS

1. Compare the similarities and differences between experimental and quasi-experimental designs. Give an example of one subject that might be best studied using each design.

2. Discuss survey research. What is the importance of sampling and response rates for a good representative sample?

3. What is the difference between being a "pure observer" versus "full participant" of social events?

4. What are official data? What are the strengths and weaknesses of official data?

5. Discuss the ethical concerns that come with studying deviance. In your opinion, how might we balance these ethical concerns with research on deviant behavior?

SUGGESTED ADDITIONAL READINGS

Adler, P. A. (1993). *Wheeling and dealing: An ethnography of an upper-level drug dealing and smuggling community* (2nd ed.). New York: Columbia University Press.

Goode, E. (1999). Sex with informants as deviant behavior: An account and commentary. *Deviant Behavior, 20,* 301–324.

Lee, R. M. (1993). *Doing research on sensitive topics.* Newbury Park, CA: Sage

Maier, S. L., & Monahan, B. A. (2007). How close is too close? Balancing closeness and detachment in qualitative research. *Deviant Behavior, 31,* 1–32.

KEY TERMS

Covert and overt observation

Ethics in research

Experiments and quasi-experimental designs

Field research

Human subjects

Institutional Review Boards

Participant observation

Secondary data

READING 8

In this article, the authors developed an online Web-based questionnaire and attached it to a popular music artist's website to attract a target youth sample who may have bullied others over the Internet, been victimized online, or witnessed cases of cyberbullying. The study brings up several issues and problems concerning the ability to obtain informed consent, surveying a youth population that cannot legally provide informed consent, and the use of incentives to improve the response rate. The study also provides some excellent insights into the prevalence of cyberbullying.

∽ ———————————— ∾

Bullies Move Beyond the Schoolyard

A Preliminary Look at Cyberbullying

Justin W. Patchin and Sameer Hinduja

The home, neighborhood, and school are all recognized as important social and physical contexts within which adolescents develop. Bullying—an all too common form of youthful violence—has historically affected children and teenagers only while at school, while traveling to or from school, or in public places such as playgrounds and bus stops. Modern technology, however, has enabled would-be bullies to extend the reach of their aggression and threats beyond this physical setting through what can be termed cyberbullying, where tech-savvy students are able to harass others day and night using technological devices such as computer systems and cellular phones. Computers occupy a significant proportion of the homes in which children reside and are frequently used for social, entertainment, academic, and productivity needs (National Telecommunications and Information Administration [NTIA], 2002). Moreover, cellular phones are gaining widespread popularity and use among the younger age groups because they are perceived as a status symbol, allow for conversations with friends in different physical spaces, and provide a virtual tether of sorts for parents, allowing for supervision from afar.

Though they are intended to positively contribute to society, negative aspects invariably surface as byproducts of the development of new technologies such as these. The negative effects inherent in cyberbullying, though, are not slight or trivial and have the potential to inflict serious psychological, emotional, or social harm. When experienced among members of this highly impressionable and often volatile adolescent population, this harm can result in violence, injury, and even death (e.g., Meadows et al., 2005; Vossekuil, Fein, Reddy, Borum, & Modzeleski, 2002) and later criminality for both the initiator and recipient of bullying (e.g., Olweus, Limber, & Mihalic, 1999; Patchin, 2002). One particularly horrendous anecdotal account deserves mention. In May of 2001, viciously offensive messages denigrating and humiliating a high school sophomore girl who suffered from obesity and multiple sclerosis were posted anonymously to an online message board associated with a local high school in Dallas, Texas (Benfer, 2001). In time, the bullying crossed over to the

Source: Patchin, J. W., and Hinduja, S. (2006). Bullies move beyond the schoolyard: A preliminary look at cyberbullying. *Youth Violence and Juvenile Justice, 4*(2), 148–169. Reprinted with permission.

physical world as the victim's car was vandalized, pro-fanities were written on the sidewalk in front of her home, and a bottle filled with acid was thrown at her front door—which incidentally burned her mother. This example vividly depicts how bullying online can lead to physical harm offline.[1]

Little research to date has been conducted on cyberbulling. However, research on the correlates of traditional bullying can assist in comprehending the reality and growth of this new phenomenon. To begin, the desire to be and remain popular takes on almost life-like proportions among kids and teenagers during certain stages of their life, and their self-esteem is largely defined by the way that others view them. Although it is unclear exactly when self-esteem increases or decreases during a child's life (Twenge & Campbell, 2001), it unquestionably shapes a child's development in profound ways. According to the social acceptance model, self-esteem stems from the perceptions that others have of the individual (Cooley, 1902). When individuals perceive themselves to be rejected or otherwise socially excluded, a number of ill effects can result (Leary, Schreindorfer, & Haupt, 1995). Much research has validated this theory (Leary & Downs, 1995; Leary, Haupt, Strausser, & Chokel, 1998; Leary, Tambor, Terdal, & Downs, 1995) and has pointed to the following potentially negative outcomes: depression (Quellet & Joshi, 1986; Smart & Walsh, 1993), substance abuse (Hull, 1981), and aggression (Coie & Dodge, 1988; French & Waas, 1987; Hymel, Rubin, Rowden, & LeMare, 1990; Paulson, Coombs, & Landsverk, 1990; Stewart, 1985). In addition, low self-esteem tends to be found among chronic victims of traditional bullying (Hoover & Hazier, 1991; Neary & Joseph, 1994; Rigby & Slee, 1993).[2] It is expected that cyberbullying can similarly cripple the self-esteem of a child or adolescent, and without a support system or prosocial outlets through which to resolve and mitigate the strain, the same dysphoric and maladaptive outcomes may result. Despite these solemn possibilities, there has been very little empirical attention to date devoted toward better understanding the electronic variant of this deviance (exceptions include Berson, Berson, & Ferron, 2002; Finn, 2004; Ybarra & Mitchell, 2004).

This research seeks to fill this gap by exploring cyberbullying and examining its potential to become as problematic as traditional bullying—particularly with society's increasing reliance on technology. Its goal is to illuminate this novel form of deviance stemming from the intersection of communications and computers and to provide a foundational backdrop on which future empirical research can be conducted. First, what is known about traditional bullying will be summarized to provide a comparative point of reference. Second, data collected from various media sources will be presented to describe the technology that facilitates electronic bullying and to portray its prevalence. Third, preliminary findings from a pilot study of adolescent Internet users will be presented, highlighting the characteristics of this group and their involvement (both as victims and offenders) in the activity. Finally, suggestions for future empirical research will be offered as guidance for additional exploration of this subject matter.

◈ Traditional Bullying

Bullying Defined

A variety of scholars in the disciplines of child psychology, family and child ecology, sociology, and criminology have articulated definitions of bullying that generally cohere with each other. To begin, the first stages of bullying can be likened to the concept of harassment, which is a form of unprovoked aggression often directed repeatedly toward another individual or group of individuals (Manning, Heron, & Marshal, 1978). Bullying tends to become more insidious as it continues over time and is arguably better equated to violence rather than harassment. Accordingly, Roland (1989) states that bullying is "longstanding violence, physical or psychological, conducted by an individual or a group directed against an individual who is not able to defend himself in the actual situation" (p. 21).[3] Stephenson and Smith (1989) contend that bullying is

> a form of social interaction in which a more dominant individual [the bully] exhibits

aggressive behavior which is intended to and does, in fact, cause distress to a less dominant individual [the victim]. The aggressive behavior may take the form of a direct physical and/or verbal attack or may be indirect as when the bully hides a possession that belongs to the victim or spreads false information about the victim. (p. 45)

Providing perhaps the most panoptic definition, Nansel et al. (2001) asserted that bullying is aggressive behavior or intentional "harm doing" by one person or a group, generally carried out repeatedly and over time and that involves a power differential. Many characteristics can imbue an offender with perceived or actual power over a victim and often provide a sophistic license to dominate and overbear. These include, but are not limited to, popularity, physical strength or stature, social competence, quick wit, extroversion, confidence, intelligence, age, sex, race, ethnicity, and socioeconomic status (Olweus, 1978, 1993, 1999; Rigby & Slee, 1993; Roland, 1980; Slee & Rigby, 1993). Nonetheless, research on the relevance of these differences between bullies and their victims has been inconclusive. For example, differences in physical appearance was not predictive of one's likelihood of being a bully or a victim (Olweus, 1978), but physical shortness (Voss & Mulligan, 2000) and weakness (Leff, 1999) were found to be relevant in other research.

Although the harassment associated with bullying can occur anywhere, the term *bullying* often denotes the behavior as it occurs among youth in school hallways and bathrooms, on the playground, or otherwise proximal or internal to the school setting. Bullies can also follow their prey to other venues such as malls, restaurants, or neighborhood hangouts to continue the harassment. In the past, interaction in a physical context was required for victimization to occur. This is no longer the case thanks to the increased prevalence of the Internet, personal computers, and cellular phones. Now, would-be bullies are afforded technology that provides additional mediums over which they can manifest their malice.

The following sections outline the scope, breadth, and consequences of traditional bullying as a reference point from which cyberbullying can subsequently be viewed and understood.

Extent and Effects of Traditional Bullying

It is unclear exactly how many youth are bullied or bully others on any given day. In 1982, 49 fifth grade teachers from Cleveland, Ohio, reported that almost one fourth (23%) of their 1,078 students were either victims or bullies (Stephenson & Smith, 1989). More recently, a nationally representative study of 15,686 students in grades 6 through 10 identified that approximately 11% of respondents were victims of bullying, 13% were bullies, and 6% were both victims and bullies during a year (Nansel et al., 2001). Additional research conducted by the Family Work Institute substantiated these findings through interviews with 1,000 youth in grades 5 through 12. Their study found that 12% of youth were bullied five or more times during the previous month (Galinsky & Salmond, 2002). Finally, the Bureau of Justice Statistics reports that 8% of youth between the ages of 12 and 18 had been victims of bullying in the previous 6 months (Devoe et al., 2002). That said, conservative estimates maintain that at least 5% of those in primary and secondary schools (ages 7–16) are victimized by bullies each day (Bjorkqvist, Ekman, & Lagerspetz, 1982; Lagerspetz, Bjorkqvist, Berts, & King, 1982; Olweus, 1978; Roland, 1980).

Many young people are able to shrug off instances of being bullied, perhaps because of peer or familial support or higher self-efficacy. Nonetheless, others are not able to cope in a prosocial or normative manner or reconcile the pain experienced through more serious episodes or actions. Suicidal ideation, eating disorders, and chronic illness have beset many of those who have been tormented by bullies, whereas other victims run away from home (Borg, 1998; Kaltiala-Heino, Rimpela, Marttunen, Rimpela, & Rantanen, 1999; Striegel-Moore, Dohm, Pike, Wilfley, & Fairburn, 2002). In addition, depression has been a frequently cited consequence of bullying (e.g., Hawker & Boulton, 2000) and seems to perpetuate into adulthood, evidencing the potentially long-term implications of mistreatment during adolescence (Olweus, 1994). Finally, in extreme cases, victims have responded with extreme violence such as physical assault, homicide, and suicide (Patchin, 2002; Vossekuil et al., 2002).

Following the fatal shootings at Columbine High School in Littleton, Colorado, in 1999, the educational system was challenged to address bullying because the two teenagers involved in the massacre were reported to have been ostracized by their classmates. Additional school violence research of 37 incidents involving 41 attackers from 1974 to 2000 found that 71% (29) of the attackers "felt bullied, persecuted, or injured by others prior to the attack" (Vossekuil et al., 2002, p. 21). It was also determined that the victimization played at least some role in their subsequent violent outburst. Other less serious but equally as negative outcomes can result from repeated bullying. For example, students who are constantly harassed may attempt to avoid the problems at school as much as possible, leading to tardiness or truancy (BBC News, 2001; Richardson, 2003; Rigby & Slee, 1999). Truancy has been identified as a significant antecedent to delinquency, dropout, and other undesirable outcomes in the juvenile justice literature (Farrington, 1980; Garry, 1996; Gavin, 1997; Nansel et al., 2001). Based on these findings, it is clear that victims of bullies are at risk to have a discontinuous developmental trajectory for many years.

The aggressors in the bullying dyad also appear to be more likely to engage in antisocial activities later in life (Tattum, 1989). For example, approximately 60% of those characterized as bullies in grades six through nine were convicted of at least one crime by the age of 24, compared to 23% who were not characterized as either bullies or victims (Olweus et al., 1999). Further underscoring the relationship between bullying and future criminality, Olweus and colleagues (1999) found that 40% of bullies had three or more convictions by the age of 24, compared to 10% of those who were neither instigators nor victims of bullying.

Based on this brief review, it is clear that both bully victims and offenders are at an increased risk for developmental problems that can continue into adulthood. As such, it is imperative that researchers seek to better understand the antecedents and consequences of bullying behavior, for practitioners to develop and implement antibullying programs in schools and for societal institutions to better understand the ways in which bullying behaviors are carried out, both in traditional and nontraditional settings.

◈ Cyberbullying

Because of the advent and continued growth of technological advances, the transmutation of bullying has occurred—from the physical to the virtual. Physical separation of the bully and the victim is no longer a limitation in the frequency, scope, and depth of harm experienced and doled out. As instances of bullying are no longer restricted to real-world settings, the problem has matured. Although a migration to the electronic realm is a seemingly logical extension for bullies, little is currently known regarding the nature and extent of the phenomenon. In short, we define *cyberbullying* as willful and repeated harm inflicted through the medium of electronic text. Based on the literature reviewed above, the constructs of malicious intent, violence, repetition, and power differential appear most salient when constructing a comprehensive definition of traditional bullying and are similarly appropriate when attempting to define this new permutation. To be sure, cyberbullies are malicious aggressors who seek implicit or explicit pleasure or profit through the mistreatment of other individuals. Violence is often associated with aggression and corresponds to actions intended to inflict injury (of any type). One instance of mistreatment, although potentially destructive, cannot accurately be equated to bullying, and so cyberbullying must also involve harmful behavior of a repetitive nature. Finally, because of the very nature of the behavior, cyberbullies have some perceived or actual power over their victims. Although power in traditional bullying might be physical (stature) or social (competency or popularity), online power may simply stem from proficiency. That is, youth who are able to navigate the electronic world and utilize technology in a way that allows them to harass others are in a position of power relative to a victim.

A brief editorial published in 2003 in *Journal of the American Academy of Child and Adolescent Psychiatry* pointed to the lack of academic references to this topic despite its anticipated proliferation (Jerome & Segal, 2003). Despite this call for research, very little scholarly attention has been devoted to the topic. In a notable exception, Ybarra and Mitchell (2004) conducted telephone surveys of 1,498 regular Internet users between the ages of 10 and 17, along with their parents, and found that 19% of youth respondents were either on the giving or receiving end of online aggression in the previous year. The vast majority of offenders (84%) knew their victim in person, whereas only 31% of victims knew their harasser in person. This fact is noteworthy; it appears that power and dominance are exerted online through the ability to keep the offender's identity unknown (Ybarra & Mitchell, 2004). When comparing those who were only aggressors to those who had no involvement in online harassment, the former were significantly more likely to be the target of offline bullying, to display problematic behavior, to have low school commitment, and to engage in alcohol and cigarette use. When comparing those who had experience being both an offender and a victim with those who had no involvement in online harassment, the significant differences were the same as above—with the exception of low school involvement. It is interesting to note that real-world variables that play a contributive role in traditional forms of delinquency and crime—such as general deviance, low commitment to prosocial institutions such as school, and substance abuse—also are significantly related to bullying on the Internet.

There are two major electronic devices that young bullies can employ to harass their victims from afar. First, using a personal computer, a bully can send harassing e-mails or instant messages, post obscene, insulting, and slanderous messages to online bulletin boards, or develop Web sites to promote and disseminate defamatory content. Second, harassing text messages can be sent to the victim via cellular phones.

Personal Computers

Research by the U.S. Department of Commerce noted that almost 90% of youth between the ages of 12 and 17 use computers, and by age 10, youth are more likely than are adults to use the Internet (NTIA, 2002). Demonstrating the broad reach of instant messaging and chat programs, 20 million kids between the ages of 2 and 17 logged onto the Internet in July 2002, and 11.5 million used instant messaging programs (NetRatings, 2002). Similarly, according to a study of 1,081 Canadian parents conducted in March 2000, 86% stated that their kids used the Internet, 38% had their own e-mail address, 28% used ICQ (an instant messaging program short for "I seek you"), and 28% regularly spent time in chat rooms (Network, 2001). Indeed, America Online (AOL, 2002, 2003)—the most popular Internet service provider with more than 35 million users—states that members join in on more than 16,000 chat sessions and send more than 2.1 billion instant messages per day across their network. As a point of reference, 1.9 billion phone calls are made each day in the United States. Finally, the Internet relay channels provide a venue for many other users on a daily basis. For example, on the morning of an average Saturday in May 2005, there were more than 1 million users online in more than 800 chat rooms (Gelhausen, 2005).

Pew Internet and American Life Project (2001) conducted an extensive research endeavor in 2001 to ascertain demographic and behavioral characteristics of teenagers who use the Internet. A telephone survey was administered to 754 children between the ages of 12 and 17 in November and December of 2000. Though not generalizable to the population of online teenagers across the United States because of many methodological limitations, the study paints an interesting picture of the user population and their activities while connected to the Internet. About 17 million youth aged 12 to 17 regularly use the Internet. This figure represents approximately three fourths (73%) of those in this age bracket.

According to the Pew Internet and American Life Project (2001), approximately 29% of youth younger than 12 regularly go online. Among teenagers, approximately 95% of girls and 89% of boys have sent or received e-mail, and 56% of girls and 55% of boys have visited a chat room. Almost three fourths of teenagers (74%; 78% of girls and 71% of boys) in the study use instant messaging to communicate with their friends, with 69% using the technology several times a week.

Almost half (46%) of respondents who report using instant messaging programs spend between 30 and 60 minutes per session doing so, whereas 21% state that they spend more than 1 hour in the activity in an average online session. Testifying to the benefits of textual communication over verbal communication, 37% used it to say something they would not have said in person. Underscoring the potential for harassment and negative treatment online, 57% have blocked messages from someone with whom they did not wish to communicate, and 64% had refused to answer messages from someone with whom they were angry.

Cellular Phones

In the United States, more than 150 million individuals, including half of the youth between 12 and 17 years of age, own cellular phones (Fattah, 2003). It is estimated that 74% of Americans between the ages of 13 and 24 will have a wireless device by 2006 (O'Leary, 2003). Cell phone usage is much higher among teenagers and young adults in Europe compared to the United States, 60% to 85% compared to 25% (O'Leary, 2003). Research estimates that by 2007 nearly 100 million individuals will use the text messaging service on their wireless device (Fattah, 2003). Statistics compiled in November 2001 by UPOC (2001)—a wireless communications firm in the United States—found that 43% of those who currently use text messaging are between the ages of 12 and 17. To note, the text messaging capabilities of cellular phones are being exploited to a greater degree in European and Asian countries. In 2002, approximately 90 billion text messages were sent through the two major telecommunication service providers in China, which equals approximately 246 million per day (CD, 2003). In Europe and Asia, more than 30 billion text messages are sent between individuals each month (Katz, 2002). It is predicted that 365 billion text messages will be sent across western Europe in 2006, up from 186 billion in 2002 (GSMBox, 2002).

Issues Specific to Cyberbullying

Gabriel Tarde's (1903) law of insertion suggests that new technologies will be applied to augment traditional activities and behaviors. Certain characteristics inherent in these technologies increase the likelihood that they will be exploited for deviant purposes. Cellular phones and personal computers offer several advantages to individuals inclined to harass others. First, electronic bullies can remain virtually anonymous. Temporary e-mail accounts and pseudonyms in chat rooms, instant messaging programs, and other Internet venues can make it very difficult for adolescents to determine the identity of aggressors. Individuals can hide behind some measure of anonymity when using their personal computer or cellular phone to bully another individual, which perhaps frees them from normative and social constraints on their behavior. Further, it seems that bullies might be emboldened when using electronic means to effectuate their antagonistic agenda because it takes less energy and fortitude to express hurtful comments using a keyboard or keypad than using one's voice.

Second, supervision is lacking in cyberspace. Although chat hosts regularly observe the dialog in some chat rooms in an effort to police conversations and evict offensive individuals, personal messages sent between users are viewable only by the sender and the recipient and are therefore outside regulatory reach. Furthermore, there are no individuals to monitor or censor offensive content in e-mail or text messages sent via computer or cellular phone. Another contributive element is the increasingly common presence of computers in the private environments of adolescent bedrooms. Indeed, teenagers often know more about computers and cellular phones than do their parents and are therefore able to operate the technologies without worry or concern that a probing parent will discover their participation in bullying (or even their victimization; NTIA, 2002).

In a similar vein, the inseparability of a cellular phone from its owner makes that person a perpetual target for victimization. Users often need to keep it turned on for legitimate uses, which provides the opportunity for those with malicious intentions to send threatening and insulting statements via the cellular phone's text messaging capabilities. There may truly be no rest for the weary as cyberbullying penetrates the walls of a home, traditionally a place where victims could seek refuge.

Finally, electronic devices allow individuals to contact others (both for prosocial and antisocial purposes) at all times and in almost all places. The fact that most adolescents (83%) connect to the Internet from home (Pew Internet and American Life Project, 2001) indicates that online bullying can be an invasive phenomenon that can hound a person even when not at or around school. Relatedly, the coordination of a bullying attack can occur with more ease because it is not constrained by the physical location of the bullies or victims. A veritable onslaught of mistreatment can quickly and effectively torment a victim through the use of these communications and connectivity tools.

Does Harm Occur?

Of course, cyberbullying is a problem only to the extent that it produces harm toward the victim. In the traditional sense, a victim is often under the immediate threat of violence and physical harm and also subject to humiliation and embarrassment in a public setting. These elements compound the already serious psychological, emotional, and social wounds inflicted through such mistreatment. One might argue that a victim of bullying in cyberspace—whether via e-mail, instant messaging, or cellular phone text messaging—can quickly escape from the harassment by deleting the e-mail, closing the instant message, and shutting off the cellular phone and is largely protected from overt acts of violence by the offender through geographic and spatial distance. Such an argument holds much truth; however, the fact remains that if social acceptance is crucially important to a youth's identity and self-esteem, cyberbullying can capably and perhaps more permanently wreak psychological, emotional, and social havoc.[4] It is not a stretch to say that physical harm—such as being beaten up—might even be preferred by some victims to the excruciating pain they experience from nonphysical harm because the former can heal quicker. Furthermore, it is yet to be determined if there is a causal pathway between cyberbullying and traditional bullying, and so physical harm might very well follow as a logical outcome of a continually increasing desire on the part of the offender to

most severely hurt the victim. To be sure, this must be explored in future studies.

With regard to public embarrassment, life in cyberspace is often intertwined with life in the real world. For example, many kids and teenagers spend days with their friends in school and nights with those same friends online through instant message programs and chat channels. That which occurs during the day at school is often discussed online at night, and that which occurs online at night is often discussed during the day at school. There is no clean separation between the two realms, and so specific instances of cyberbullying—disrespect, name calling, threats, rumors, gossip—against a person make their way around the interested social circles like wildfire.

Does the mistreatment experienced through online bullying lead to the same feelings that result from traditional bullying—such as self-denigration, loss of confidence and self-esteem, depression, anger, frustration, public humiliation, and even physical harm? This remains to be clearly depicted through empirical research but seems plausible based on the linchpin role of self-esteem among children and teenagers previously described and on anecdotal evidence specifically related to online aggression (BBC News, 2001; Benfer, 2001; Blair, 2003; Meadows et al., 2005; ÓhAnluain, 2002; Richardson, 2003).

Because of the widespread availability of electronic devices, there is no lack of participants using the technologies. Their ubiquity provides a seemingly endless pool of candidates who are susceptible to being bullied or to becoming a bully. Unfortunately, however, little is known in terms of how often these technologies are mobilized for deviant purposes. One empirical study has been conducted to date: In 2002, the National Children's Home (NCH, 2002)—a charitable organization in London—surveyed 856 youth between the ages of 11 and 19 and found that 16% received threatening text messages via their cellular phone, 7% had been bullied in online chat rooms, and 4% had been harassed via e-mail. Following the victimization, 42% told a friend, 32% told a parent or guardian, and 29% did not reveal the experience to anyone. Because more information is clearly warranted, a study was designed to explore the nature and extent of cyberbullying.

◈ Current Study

Method

The current study involved an analysis of youthful Internet users in an effort to assess their perceptions of, and experiences with, electronic bullying. It is difficult to individually observe the nature and extent of electronic bullying among adolescent Internet users because of the "private" nature of e-mails, cellular phone text messages, and instant messages and one-on-one chat messages within online chat channels. To be sure, if the instances of cyberbullying occur in a public forum such as a popular chat channel and in the view of all chat room members, then direct observation and consequent analyses may be possible. Most of the time, however, they occur through private (nonpublic), person-to-person communications. A survey methodology was therefore designed to collect data by requiring participants to recall and relate their cyberbullying practices and experiences via a questionnaire that was linked from the official Web site of a popular music artist revered by the target age group. An electronic format was selected as it allows for efficiency in collecting data from a large number of participants (Couper, 2000; McCoy & Marks, 2001; Smith, 1997). The survey was active between May 1, 2004, and May 31, 2004.

The context of the Internet must be considered when dealing with consent issues because forcing all online researchers to comply with traditional procedures in this area is unduly onerous, particularly when possible harm is little to none. Because it is impossible to personally obtain informed consent from participants in much online survey research that solicits participants from postings on Web sites, implied consent has generally been accepted (Walther, 2002). This involves the presentation of informed consent information in electronic text (e.g., on a Web page), along with specific actions that must be performed prior to initiation of the survey. These actions often include the checking of a check box (agreeing to participate) and clicking on a submit button to send the information to the server. From this, consent can be reasonably inferred (King, 1996). For the current study, researchers instructed participants who were younger than 18 to obtain permission from their parent or guardian. Permission was demonstrated by the parent entering his or her initials in a specified box. Again, because of matters of anonymity associated with Internet research, it was impossible to actually verify that adolescents obtained proper permission prior to completing the survey.

With survey research conducted over the Internet, questions also arise as to the reliability of the data (Cho & LaRose, 1990). Participants are self-selected, which introduces some bias as individuals are not randomly chosen for inclusion in the study. Often, a convenience sample, where individuals are chosen because they are available (e.g., because they visit a particular Web site and see a solicitation for research participation), is employed. As a result, the sample obtained may not necessarily be representative of all Internet users. Moreover, online demographic groups may not mirror those found in the real world (Witte, Amoroso, & Howard, 2000). Generalization to a larger population, then, becomes impossible with convenience sampling (Couper, 2000), but the technique has demonstrated utility for exploratory studies intended to probe a novel phenomenon. Researchers who seek to tap the resources of the World Wide Web will continue to face these challenging issues. Although these limitations are an unfortunate cost of conducting Internet-based research, results from this preliminary study will help to inform a more methodologically rigorous investigation in the future.

The survey went through numerous iterations to optimize its design and presentation of questions. Prior research has determined that poor design can render dubious the quality of responses and may even affect completion rate (Crawford, Couper, & Lamias, 2001; Krosnick, 1999; Preece, Rogers, & Sharp, 2002; Schwarz, 1999). Specifics to the survey design bear mentioning. Demographic data were solicited at the beginning of the survey, which has been shown to decrease rates of attrition because individuals are not surprised by more personal questions at the resolution of their participation (Frick, Bachtiger, & Reips, 2001). The survey in its entirety was presented to the respondent on one screen, which has also been shown to increase response rates (Crawford et al., 2001). Although our survey did consist of a vast number of questions, findings related to the relationship between survey length and response rate have been mixed and inconclusive (Brown, 1965; Bruvold & Comer, 1988; Eichemer & Habermehl, 1981; Jobber & Saunders, 1993; Mason, Dressel, & Bain, 1961; Sheehan, 2001; Witmer, Colman, & Katzman, 1999; Yammarino, Skinner, & Childers, 1991).

Incentives to participate in the form of cash or other prizes via a lottery has also been shown to increase response rate; human beings are motivated by the possibility of receiving something in return for their efforts, and this trait is manifested in survey participation as well (Cho & LaRose, 1999; Frick et al. 2001). As such, participants in the current study were entered into a random drawing to win one of three autographed photographs of the musical artist from whose fan Web site they reached the survey. We also specified that the institutional review board at the researchers' university had approved the project to verify its legitimacy and strengthen the trust relationship between the researchers and the potential participants (Cho & LaRose, 1999).

A final point bears mentioning. As the Internet protocol (IP) address and timestamp was recorded with each participant's responses, we were able to eliminate entries where all of the responses were completely the same. This might happen when a respondent fills out the questionnaire, clicks submit, goes back to the previous page where all of his or her responses are stored within the survey form, and then clicks submit again (and continues in this pattern). To note, there were survey entries from the same IP address but with completely different responses to the questions posed. This was because some Internet service providers route multiple users through one IP address when connecting from their internal network to the external Internet. To summarize, we browsed through all of the data and attempted to determine which entries were fraudulent and which were valid.

Findings

Because this was an Internet-based survey, anyone could participate. Even though the survey was associated with a teen-oriented Web site, individuals from all ages also frequent the site and therefore completed the survey. Out of the 571 total respondents, 384 were younger than 18 (67.3%; henceforth referred to as the youth sample). In both groups, the vast majority of respondents were female. This finding is likely attributable to the nature of the Web site on which the survey was linked (a female pop music star). Similarly, the vast majority of respondents were Caucasian. There are several potential interpretations of this finding. First, individuals from different racial and ethnic backgrounds may be less interested in this particular entertainer than are others and may therefore be unlikely to visit the Web site to see the survey solicitation. Alternatively, the overrepresentation of Caucasian respondents could be evidence of the oft-mentioned digital divide, where some populations are not privy to the access and use of technology such as computers and the Internet. As expected, most respondents were between the ages of 12 and 20, and the average age of the youth sample was 14.1. Moreover, more than 70% of respondents from the complete sample were in grades 2 through 12. High school respondents (9th through 12th grade) represented the modal category of respondents for both groups. As might be expected, the vast majority of all respondents came from English-speaking countries (the Web site and survey were written in English), and about 60% of respondents in both groups reported living in the United States. It must be mentioned that because online identity is completely malleable (Hafner, 2001; Turkle, 1995), the demographic data obtained may not be completely accurate because of a lack of trust in our research project, mischief, or purposeful obfuscation. Research performed over the Internet cannot entirely preempt this problem—at least in its current stage of technological development—and so a caveat is justified.

The remainder of the findings discussed relate only to those respondents who were younger than 18 when they completed the survey ($n = 384$). Online bullying was specifically defined on the questionnaire for respondents as behavior that can include bothering someone online, teasing in a mean way, calling someone hurtful names, intentionally leaving persons out of things, threatening someone, and saying unwanted, sexually related things to someone. Almost 11% of youth reported bullying others while online, more than 29% reported being the victim of online bullying, and more than 47% have witnessed online bullying. Cyberbullying was most prevalent in chat rooms, followed by computer text messages and e-mail. Bullying using newsgroups or cellular phones was not as prominent for members of this sample. Indeed, although it is clear that all who responded to the survey have access to a computer, it is unknown what proportion of respondents have access to a cellular phone.

As previously described, youth were asked a general question regarding their involvement in online bullying. In addition, youth were asked to relate whether they experienced a number of behaviors that may be associated with bullying. Notably, 60.0% of respondents have been ignored by others while online, 50.0% reported being disrespected by others, almost 30.0% have been called names, and 21.4% have been threatened by others. In addition, a significant proportion of youth were picked on by others (19.8%) or made fun of by others (19.3%) or had rumors spread about them by others (18.8%).

In addition to asking respondents whether they have experienced bullying online, researchers also asked youth how frequently the bullying occurred during the previous 30 days. For example, 83 youth reported being victimized in a chat room an average of 3.36 times during the previous 30 days.

[In total], 42.5% of victims were frustrated, almost 40.0% felt angry, and more than 27.0% felt sad. Almost one third (31.9%) reported that it affected them at school, whereas 26.5% reported that it affected them at home. Only 22.1% were not bothered by the bullying they experienced, and less than 44.0% stated that the bullying did not affect them.

Notably, almost 20% of victims were forced to stay offline, whereas almost 32% had to remove themselves from the environment in some capacity or way. Victims also revealed a hesitation to tell authority figures about their experiences. Even though most confided in an online friend (56.6%), fewer than 9.0% of victims informed an adult.

Additional analyses were conducted to attempt to uncover correlates of online bullying. There were no statistically significant associations among age, race, or gender and who is likely to be a victim of online bullying. The lack of relationship among race or gender and victimization may be more a function of the homogeneous nature of the data than any substantive finding and must be further tested. In accordance with intuition, youth who participate in more activities online (represented by a variety score of 13 different activities) were more likely to experience online bullying. Also not surprising, youth who bully others were more likely to be victims of online bullying. In all, 75% of youth who have bullied others online have been victims of bullying, whereas fewer than 25% of youth bullies have never been on the other end of such malicious actions. Future research should seek to better understand what additional factors are associated with online bullying.

◈ Discussion

The results of this study point to a number of key issues. First, bullying is occurring online and is impacting youth in many negative ways. Almost 30% of the adolescent respondents reported that they had been victims of online bullying—operationalized as having been ignored, disrespected, called names, threatened, picked on, or made fun of or having had rumors spread by others. Admittedly, being ignored by another person may simply reflect obnoxious behavior that warranted the outcome rather than actual and willful aggression. We were not able to parcel out the stimuli of instances when people were ignored but chose to include a measure of it in the current analyses. This is because universal social acceptance is still largely desired by children and adolescents, even if as adults we understand that it is impossible to please everyone at all times. Being ignored would introduce dissonance and instability to the already tenuous relational and social equilibria sought by youths and may accordingly be considered a passive-aggressive form of bullying. Along similar lines, although some of this harassment may be characterized as trivial (e.g., being ignored by others or being disrespected), more than 20% reported being threatened by others. Anger and frustration was a commonly reported emotional response to the harassment. Finally, almost 60% of victims were affected by the online behaviors at school, at home, or with friends.

Several policy implications stem from the aforementioned findings. It is hoped that this harmful phenomena can be curtailed by proactively addressing the potentially negative uses of technology. Parents must regularly monitor the activities in which their children are engaged while online. Teachers, too, must take care to supervise students as they use computers in the classrooms. Police officers must investigate those instances of cyberbullying that are potentially injurious and hold responsible parties accountable. Unfortunately, there are no methods to discern which harassment involves simple jest and which has the potential to escalate into serious violence. Future research must analyze case studies and anecdotal stories of cyberbullying experiences to help determine when intervention by authority figures is most appropriate. Overall, parents, teachers, police officers, and other community leaders must keep up with technological advances so that they are equipped with the tools and knowledge to identify and address any problems when they arise.

Limitations of the Current Study

The most notable limitations of this study relate to its administration because data were collected exclusively online. With regard to sampling, it is unquestionable that Internet users are dissimilar from those who do not go online. However, Walther (2002, p. 209) argues that concerns related to the generalizability of data collected from the Internet to a target population assume that random samples of Internet users are sought in any study and that a sample obtained from the Internet is able to be generalized to other populations. We would have liked to obtain a random sample of all Internet users younger than 18 to ascertain the extent and prevalence of online bullying, but such a task is impossible as

no reliable sampling frame of individuals in cyberspace exists. Thus, we carefully targeted certain Web sites presumably visited by at least some adolescents who have personal experience in the phenomenon. As it turned out, the sample was disproportionately Caucasian and female, and results therefore may be skewed toward these subgroups. As a result, any findings from the research should be very cautiously applied to the larger group of Internet-using youth.

Another issue related to online data collection concerns misrepresentation of age by participants in this research. Undoubtedly, we cannot guarantee that respondents honestly indicated their age during participation. Any qualms, though, can be overcome by considering the fallibility of traditional research methods such as phone surveys or surveys distributed in highly populated settings (e.g., large college classes) or through the mail and even individual, face-to-face administration of questionnaires. A person can lie about his or her age in any of these contexts, and it is unreasonable to assume that a person would be more likely to do so in an online research setting (Walther, 2002).

Directions for Future Research

The current study provides the framework for future empirical inquiry on electronic bullying. Indeed, the authors are currently involved in a more comprehensive study that involves both Internet-based research and traditional paper-and-pencil surveys. As with any social scientific endeavor, replication is necessary to more fully understand the phenomena under consideration. There are several questions future research in this area must address. First, data must be collected to more accurately ascertain the scope, prevalence, and nuances of cyberbullying. For example, it is important to discover whether cyberbullies are simply traditional bullies who have embraced new technologies to accomplish their intentions or if they are youth who have never participated in traditional, school-based bullying. Moreover, do personal computers enable the stereotypical victims of bullies (i.e., those who are smart, physically small, and/or socially challenged) to retaliate using means that ensure their anonymity? It would also be important to determine whether commonly accepted stimuli for traditional bullying—the need to (a) exert power and dominate, (b) compensate for victimization in another area of one's life, (c) cope with one's insecurities, and (d) attract attention and popularity—are similarly predictive in cyberspace-based instances of the deviance.

Also of interest is the extent to which electronic bullying results in harm to adolescents in their physical environments (e.g., at school or in their neighborhoods). Are threats made in cyberspace followed through on the playground? Are victims of cyberbullying the same individuals who are also victims of traditional bullying, or are they distinct groups? What about offenders? One could hypothesize that the victims of traditional bullying may turn to the Internet to exact revenge on their schoolyard aggressors. That is, the victim becomes the offender by using his or her technological knowledge to inflict harm on the original bully.

In addition, it is useful to identify whether adults also participate in electronic harassment. Although they may frequent chat rooms to a lesser degree than do children and adolescents, cellular phone use and even instant messaging programs are commonly utilized for both professional and personal purposes. Does electronic harassment occur to the same extent among adults as compared to a population of adolescents? Does it occur in a more controlled and subtle manner or with the same degree of perceivably overt cruelty? Does it occur for fundamentally similar reasons across both groups, or are there factors endemic to youth or adult life that condition and dictate bullying in an online context? These are just some of the important questions that need further examination.

Finally, future research efforts ought to more thoroughly examine the results of this preliminary investigation using more rigorous methodology that ensures a more representative sample of responses. As indicated, the intent of this research is to generate scholarly interest in this unique form of adolescent harassment and therefore should be viewed simply as a small, but we think significant, platform on which further research efforts should be built.

◈ Conclusion

The preceding review provides a description of bullying in cyberspace for the purposes of introducing it as a topic meriting academic inquiry and underscoring its often inescapable pernicious nature. Indeed, 74% of the youth in this study reported that bullying occurs online, and almost 30% of the youth reported being victimized by others while online. Some may dismiss electronic bullying as normative behavior that does not physically harm anyone. To be sure, some have this perception regarding traditional bullying, dismissing it as a rite of passage or an inevitable and even instructive element of growing up. Because of the familiarity and memorability of bullying as almost unavoidable in both the schoolyard and neighborhood milieu during one's formative years, perhaps the reader may share those sentiments.

Because no consensus exists when considering whether cyberbullying merits increased attention because of society's continued progression into a wired world, perhaps it should just be considered another contemporary cultural challenge that kids often face when transitioning into adulthood. Conceivably there is no need to panic when introduced to the concept that online bullying does and will continue to take place as children seek to carve out an identity for themselves and cope with various pressures associated with their development. Alternatively, perhaps there is a need for alarm as both those who bully and those who are bullied might yield readily to other criminogenic influences and proceed down a path of deviance online, offline, or both. Regardless, cyberbullying is very real, and it is hoped that this work has highlighted its relevance for the purposes of inspiring additional interest in its etiology and consequences.

◈ Notes

1. The interested reader is encouraged to see Blair (2003) or ÓhAnluain (2002) for more examples.

2. It should be mentioned that research has not identified a link between low self-esteem and the offenders of traditional bullying (Hoover & Hazier, 1991; Rigby & Slee, 1993).

3. To be sure, females are also bullied to a substantive degree and must not be excluded from any analyses of the phenomenon.

4. Cyberbullying repercussions have permanence because e-mails can be saved, instant messages and chat conversations can be logged, and Web pages can be archived for an offender, victim, or third party to read over in the future and thereby relive the experience.

◈ References

America Online. (2002). *AOL facts—2002.* Retrieved September 2, 2003, from http://www.corp.aol.com/whoweare/Factbook_F.pdf

America Online. (2003). *Who we are: Fast facts.* Retrieved September 2, 2003, from http://www.corp.aol.com/whoweare/fastfacts.html

BBC News. (2001). *Girl tormented by phone bullies.* Retrieved January 16, 2001, from http:// news.bbc.co.uk/l/hi/education/1120597.stm

Benfer, A. (2001). *Cyber slammed.* Retrieved July 7, 2001, from http://www.dir.salon.com/mwt/feature/2001/07/03/cyber_buJlies/index.html

Berson, I. R., Berson, M. J., & Ferron, J. M. (2002). Emerging risks of violence in the digital age: Lessons for educators from an online study of adolescent girls in the United States. *Journal of School Violence, 1*(2), 51–71.

Björkqvist, K., Ekman K., & Lagerspetz, K. (1982). Bullies and victims: Their ego picture, ideal ego picture, and normative ego picture. *Scandinavian Journal of Psychology, 23,* 307–313.

Blair, J. (2003). New breed of bullies torment their peers on the Internet. *Education Week.* Retrieved February 5, 2003, from http://www.edweek.org/ew/ewstory.cfm?slug=21cyberbully.h22

Borg, M. G. (1998). The emotional reaction of school bullies and their victims. *Educational Psychology, 18,* 433–444.

Brown, M. (1965). Use of a postcard query in mail surveys. *Public Opinion Quarterly, 29,* 635–637.

Bruvold, N. T., & Comer, J. M. (1988). A model for estimating the response rate to a mailed survey. *Journal of Business Research, 16*(2), 101–116.

CD. (2003). *Thumbs down on mobile messaging.* Retrieved July 22, 2003, from wwwl.chinadaily.com.cn/en/doc/2003-07/22/content_247257.htm

Cho, H., & LaRose, R. (1999). Privacy issues in Internet surveys. *Social Science Computer Review, 14,* 421–434.

Coie, J. D., & Dodge, K. A. (1988). Multiple sources of data on social behavior and social status in the school: A cross-age comparison. *Child Development, 59,* 815–829.

Cooley, C. H. (1902). *Human nature and the social order.* New York: Scribner.

Couper, M. P. (2000). Web-based surveys: A review of issues and approaches. *Public Opinion Quarterly, 64,* 464–494.

Crawford, S., Couper, M. P., & Lamias, M. (2001). Web surveys: Perceptions of burden. *Social Science Computer Review, 19,* 146–162.

Devoe, J. F., Ruddy, S. A., Miller, A. K., Planty, M., Peter, K., Kaufman, P., et al. (2002). *Indicators of school crime and safety.* Washington, DC: U.S. Department of Education, National Center for Education Statistics, U.S. Department of Justice, Bureau of Justice Statistics.

Eicherner, K., & Habermehl, W. (1981). Predicting the response rates to mailed questionnaires (comment on Herberlien & Baumgartner). *American Sociological Review, 46,* 1–3.

Farrington, D. (1980). Truancy, delinquency, the home, and the school. In L. Hersov & I. Berg (Eds.), *Out of school: Modern perspectives in truancy and school refusal* (pp. 49–63). New York: John Wiley.

Fattah, H. (2003). *America untethered.* Retrieved September 1, 2003, from http://www.upoc.com/corp/news/UpocAmDem.pdf

Finn, J. (2004). A survey of online harassment at a university campus. *Journal of Interpersonal Violence, 19,* 468–483.

French, D. C., & Waas, G. A. (1987). Social-cognitive and behavioral characteristics of peer-rejected boys. *Professional School Psychology, 2*(2), 103–112.

Frick, A., Bachtiger, M. T., & Reips, U.-D. (2001). Financial incentives, personal information, and drop out in online studies. In U.-D. Reips & M. Bosnjak (Eds.), *Dimensions of Internet science* (pp. 209–219). Lengerich, Germany: Pabst Science.

Galinsky, E., & Salmond, K. (2002). *Youth and violence: Students speak out for a more civil society.* New York: Families and Work Institute.

Garry, E. M. (1996). *Truancy: First step to a lifetime of problems.* Washington, DC: U.S. Department of Justice, Office of Juvenile Justice and Delinquency Prevention.

Gavin, T. (1997). *Truancy: Not just kids' stuff anymore.* Washington, DC: Federal Bureau of Investigation.

Gelhausen, A. (2005). *Summary of IRC networks.* Retrieved May 7, 2005, from http://irc.netsplit.de/ networks/

GSMBox. (2002). *Ten years of SMS messages.* Retrieved August 10, 2003, from uk.gsmbox.com/news/mobile_news/all/94480.gsmbox

Hafner, K. (2001). *The well: A story of love, death & real life in the seminal online community.* New York: Carrol and Graf.

Hawker, D, S. J., & Boulton, M. J. (2000). Twenty years' research on peer victimization and psychological maladjustment: A meta-analysis review of cross-sectional studies. *Journal of Child Psychology and Psychiatry, 41,* 441–445.

Hoover, J., & Hazier, R. (1991). Bullies and victims. *Elementary School Guidance and Counseling, 25,* 212–219.

Hull, J. G. (1981). A self-awareness model of the causes and effects of alcohol consumption. *Journal of Abnormal Psychology, 90,* 586–600.

Hymel, S., Rubin, K. H., Rowden, L., & LeMare, L. (1990). Children's peer relationships longitudinal prediction of internalizing and externalizing problems from middle to late childhood. *Child Development, 61,* 2004–2021.

Jerome, L., & Segal, A. (2003). Bullying by Internet—Editorial. *Journal of the American Academy of Child and Adolescent Psychiatry, 42,* 751.

Jobber, D., & Saunders, J. (1993). A note on the applicability of the Brurold-Comer model of mail survey response rates to commercial populations. *Journal of Business Research, 26,* 223–236.

Kaltiala-Heino, R., Rimpelä, M., Marttunen, M., Rimpetä, A., & Rantanen, P. (1999). Bullying, depression, and suicidal ideation in Finnish adolescents; school survey. *British Medical Journal, 319*(7206), 348–351.

Katz, A. R. (2002). *Text messaging moves from cell to home.* Retrieved August 15, 2003, from www.iht.com/articles/51I52.html

King, S. (1996). Researching Internet communities: Proposed ethical guidelines for the reporting of results. *The Information Society, 12,* 119–128.

Krosnick, J. A. (1999). Survey research. *Annual Review of Psychology, 50*(1), 537–567.

Lagerspetz, K. M. J., Björkqvist, K., Berts, M., & King, E. (1982). Group aggression among school-children in three schools. *Scandinavian Journal of Psychology, 23,* 45–52.

Leary, M. R., & Downs, D. L. (1995). Interpersonal functions of the self-esteem motive: The self-esteem system as a sociometer. In M. H. Kernis (Ed.), *Efficacy, agency, and self-esteem* (pp. 123–144). New York: Plenum.

Leary, M. R., Haupt, A. L. Strausser, K. S., & Chokel, J. T. (1998). Calibrating the sociometer: The relationship between interpersonal appraisals and state self-esteem. *Journal of Personality and Social Psychology, 74,* 1290–1299.

Leary, M. R., Schreindorfer, L. S., & Haupt, A. L. (1995). The role of self-esteem in emotional and behavioral problems: Why is low self-esteem dysfunctional? *Journal of Social and Clinical Psychology, 14,* 297–314.

Leary, M. R., Tambor, E. S., Terdal, S. J., & Downs, D. L. (1995). Self-esteem as an interpersonal monitor: The sociometer hypothesis. *Journal of Personality and Social Psychology, 68,* 518–530.

Leff, S. (1999). Bullied children are picked on for their vulnerability. *British Medical Journal, 318*(7190), 1076.

Manning, M., Heron, J., & Marshal, T. (1978). Style of hostility and social interactions at nursery school, and at home: An extended study of children. In A. Lionel, M. B. Hersov, & D. Shaffer (Eds.), *Aggression and antisocial behavior in childhood and adolescence* (pp. 29–58). Oxford, UK: Pergamon.

Mason, W., Dressel, R., & Bain, R. (1961). An experimental study of factors affecting response to a mail survey of beginning teachers. *Public Opinion Quarterly, 25,* 296–299.

McCoy, S., & Marks, P. V., Jr. (2001, August). *Using electronic surveys to collect data: Experiences from the field.* Paper presented at the AMCIS Annual Conference, Boston.

Meadows, B., Bergal, J., Helling, S., Odell, J., Piligian, E., Howard, C., et al. (2005, March 21). The Web: The bully's new playground. *People,* pp. 152–155.

Nansel, T. R., Overpeck, M., Pillar, R. S., Roan, W. J., Simons-Morton, B., & Schmidt, P. (2001). Bullying behaviors among US youth: Prevalence and association with psychosocial adjustment. *Journal of the American Medical Association, 285,* 2094–2100.

National Children's Home. (2002). *1 in 4 children are the victims of "on-line bullying" says children's charity.* Retrieved September 1, 2003, from http://www.nch.org.uk/news/news5.asp?auto=195

National Telecommunications and Information Administration. (2002). *A nation online: How Americans are expanding their use of the Internet.* Retrieved June 13, 2004, from www.ntia.doc.gov/ntiahome/dn/ariationonline2.pdf

Neary, A., & Joseph, S. (1994). Peer victimization and its relationship to self concept and depression among schoolgirls. *Personality and Individual Differences, 16*(1), 183–186.

NetRatings, N. (2002). *IM programs draw US kids and teens online.* Retrieved July 30, 2003, from http://www. nua.com/surveys/index. cgi?f=S&art_id=905358261&rel=true

Network, M. A. (2001). *Canada's children in a wired world: The parents' view—Final report.* Retrieved July 30, 2003, from http://www.mediayiwareness.ca/english/resources/special_initiatives/survey_resources/parents_survey/loader.cfm?url=/commonspot/security/getfile.cfm&PageID=31576

ÓhAnluain, D. (2002). *When text messaging turns ugly.* Retrieved September 4, 2002, from www.wired.com/news/school/0,1383,54771,00.html

O'Leary, N. (2003). *Cell phone marketers tap teens as the next frontier.* Retrieved February 17, 2003, from http://www.adweek.com/aw/magazine/-article_display.jsp?vnu_content_id=1818786

Olweus, D. (1978). *Aggression in the schools: Bullies and whipping boys.* Washington, DC: Hemisphere Press.

Olweus, D. (1993). *Bullying at school.* Oxford, UK: Blackwell.

Olweus, D. (Ed.). (1994). *Bullying at school: Long-term outcomes for victims and an effective school-based intervention program.* New York: Plenum.

Olweus, D. (1999). Norway. In P. K. Smith, Y. Morita, J. Junger-Tas, D. Olweus, R. Catalano, & P. Slee (Eds.), *Nature of school bullying: A cross-national perspective* (pp. 28–48). London: Routledge.

Olweus, D., Limber, S., & Mihalic, S. (1999). *Bullying prevention program.* Boulder CO: Center for the Study and Prevention of Violence.

Patchin, J. (2002). Bullied youths lash out: Strain as an explanation of extreme school violence. *Caribbean Journal of Criminology and Social Psychology,* 7(1–2), 22–43.

Paulson, M. J., Coombs, R. H., & Landsverk, J. (1990). Youth who physically assault their parents. *Journal of Family Violence,* 5(2), 121–133.

Pew Internet and American Life Project. (2001). *Teenage life online: The rise of the instant-message generation and the Internet's impact on friendships and family relationships.* Retrieved July 13, 2004, from http://www.pewintemet.org/pdfs/PIP_Teens_Report.pdf

Preece, J., Rogers, Y., & Sharp, S. (2002). *Interaction design: Beyond human-computer interaction.* New York: John Wiley.

Quellet, R., & Joshi, P. (1986). Loneliness in relation to depression and self-esteem. *Psychological Reports, 58,* 821–822.

Richardson, T. (2003). *Bullying by text message.* Retrieved February 20, 2003, from www.theadvertiser.news.com.au/common/story_page/0,5936,6012025%5E2682,00.html

Rigby, K., & Slee, P. T. (1993). Dimensions of interpersonal relating among Australian school children and their implications for psychological well-being. *The Journal of Social Psychology, 133*(1), 33–42.

Rjgby, K. & Slee, P. T. (1999). Australia. In P. Smith, Y. Morita, J. Junger-Tas, D. Olweus, R. Catalano, & P. Slee (Eds.), *The nature of school bullying: A cross-national perspective* (pp. 324–339). London: Routhedge.

Roland, E. (1980). *Terror i skolen* [Terrorism in school]. Stavanger, Norway: Rogaland Research Institute.

Roland, E. (1989). Bullying: The Scandinavian research tradition. In D. P. Tattum & D. A. Lane (Eds.), *Bullying in schools* (pp. 21–32). Stroke-on-Trent, UK: Trentham.

Schwarz, N. (1999). Self-reports: How the questions shape the answers. *American Psychologist, 54*(2), 93–105.

Sheehan, K. B. (2001). E-mail survey response rates: A review. *Journal of Computer Mediated Communication, 6*(2). Retrieved January 18, 2006, from http://jcmc.indiana.edu/vol6/issue2/sheehan.html

Slee, P. T., & Rigby, K. (1993). The relationship of Eysenck's personality factors and self-esteem to bully/victim behaviour in Australian school boys. *Personality and Individual Differences, 14,* 371–373.

Smart, R., & Walsh, G. (1993). Predictors of depression in street youth. *Adolescence, 28,* 41–53.

Smith, C. B. (1997). Casting the net: Surveying an Internet population. *Journal of Computer Mediated Communication, 3*(1). Retrieved January 18, 2006, from http://jcmc.indiana.edu/vol3/issue1/smith.html

Stephenson, P., & Smith, D. (1989). Bullying in junior school. In D. P. Tattum & D. A. Lane (Ed.), *Bullying in schools* (pp. 45–58). Stroke-on-Trent, UK: Trentham.

Stewart, M. A. (1985). Aggressive conduct disorder: A brief review. 6th Biennial Meeting of the International Society for Research on Aggression (1984, Turku, Finland). *Aggressive Behavior, 11,* 323–331.

Striegel-Moore, R. H., Dohm, F.-A., Pike, K. M., Wilfley, D. E., & Fairburn, C. G. (2002). Abuse, bullying, and discrimination as risk factors for binge eating disorder. *The American Journal of Psychiatry, 159,* 1902–1907.

Tarde, G. (Ed.). (1903). *Gabriel Tarde's laws of imitation.* New York: Henry Holt.

Tattum, D. P. (1989). Violence and aggression in schools. In D. P. Tattum & D. A. Lane (Eds.), *Bullying in schools* (pp. 7–19). Stroke-on-Trent, UK: Trentham.

Turkle, S. (1995). *Life on the screen: Identity in the age of the Internet.* New York: Simon & Schuster.

Twenge, J. M., & Campbell, W. K. (2001). Age and birth cohort differences in self-esteem: A cross-temporal meta-analysis. *Personality and Social Psychology Review, 5,* 321–344.

UPOC. (2001). *Wireless stats.* Retrieved September 1, 2003, from http://www.genwireless.com/ \stats.html

Voss, L. D., & Mulligan, J. (2000). Bullying in school: Are short pupils at risk? Questionnaire study in a cohort. *British Medical Journal, 320*(7235), 612–613.

Vossekuil, B., Fein, R. A., Reddy, M., Borum, R., & Modzeleski, W. (2002). *The final report and findings of the Safe School Initiative: Implications for the prevention of school attacks in the United States.* Retrieved August 29, 2003, from http://www.secretservice.gov/ntac/ssi_final_report.pdf

Walther, J. B. (2002). Research ethics in Internet enabled research: Human subjects issues and methodological myopia. *Ethics and Information Technology, 4,* 205.

Witmer, D. F., Colman, R. W., & Katzman, S. L. (1999). From paper-and-pencil to screen-and-key-board. In S. Jones (Ed.), *Doing Internet research: Critical issues and methods for examining the Net* (pp. 145–161). Thousand Oaks, CA: Sage.

Witte, J. C, Amoroso, L. M., & Howard, P. E. N. (2000). Research methodology—Method and representation in Internet-based survey tools—Mobility, community, and cultural identify in Survey 2000. *Social Science Computer Review, 18,* 179–195.

Yammarino, F. J., Skinner, S., & Childers, T. L. (1991). Understanding mail survey response behavior. *Public Opinion Quarterly, 55,* 613–639.

Ybarra, M. L., & Mitchell, J. K. (2004). Online aggressor/targets, aggressors and targets: A comparison of associated youth characteristics. *Journal of Child Psychology and Psychiatry, 45,* 1308–1316.

READING 9

In this provocative article, Ayella raises a number of problematic issues in the study of "cults," "new religious movements," "charismatic groups," or "world-rejecting groups." The study illustrates problems common to the study of many deviants: gaining and maintaining access and issues related to gatekeepers, including the decision of whether the researcher should let gatekeepers or followers know of the intention to conduct research or to act as a potential follower. Sampling what members to interact with (or simply realizing the potentially unique group that a gate-keeper sets the researcher up with) is complicated, especially if the timeframe is relatively short. In addition to the sampling issues raised above, cults change and evolve over time with different leaders and followers. Researchers clearly leave with a snapshot, but what things will look like in the future is really unknown. Finally, researchers must confront the limitation of what information they are walking away with and how they will use it.

Source: Ayella, M. (1990). "They must be crazy": Some of the difficulties in researching "cults." *American Behavioral Scientist, 33,* 562–577. Reprinted with permission.

"They Must Be Crazy": Some of the Difficulties in Researching "Cults"

Marybeth Ayella

This article examines some of the methodological difficulties encountered in researching "cults." The last 10 years have seen an enormous amount of research and writing on groups known variously as "cults," "new religious movements," "charismatic groups," or "world-rejecting groups," to name some of the most commonly used terms.[1]

In this article, I use the term "cult." What I am interested in exploring is how one does research on groups popularly labeled "cults." This labeling of a group as a cult makes this a sensitive topic to study, for given the public's predominantly negative assessment of cults,[2] one is researching a group considered by many to be deviant.

I will discuss some of the methodological problems which I think are particularly vexing in the study of cults, and I will point to some solutions suggested by researchers. My examination will be limited to one kind of research done by sociologists: field research.[3] I focus on this type of research because it seems to have been stimulated by cults. Robbins (1988) pointed to a virtual explosion of anthropological-like studies by sociologists of religion. Field research seems to be an attempt to get behind the strangeness and controversial aspects of cults. This method provides the closest look at cult groups, and it thus has the potential to provide in-depth understanding of the group examined, as well as the group's self-understanding. This research has as its strong point debunking overly psychiatric or psychological "brainwashing" perspectives, in showing the interactional aspect of becoming and remaining a cult member. This humanizes cult members—they are portrayed as more than crackpots, psychological basket cases, or brainwashed robots.

◈ Gaining Access

Contingencies of Research

Mitchell, Mitchell, and Ofshe (1980, chap. 9), Wallis (1977a, 1977b), Bromley and Shupe (1979, Shupe & Bromley, 1980), and Barker's (1984, chap. 1) discussions of their research on Synanon, Scientology, and the Unification Church highlight the contingencies of research, which are those aspects of research over which the researcher has little or no control. One very important contingency is the group's present social reputation.

Richard Ofshe's research on Synanon began in the summer of 1972 with a chance visit to Synanon's Tomales Bay facilities. Ofshe's neighbor, a marine biologist, was asked by Synanon for help in setting up a lab for a sewage-treatment system. Ofshe accompanied him on a visit, and was given a trail-bike tour of the ranching facility. After the visit, Ofshe asked the ranch director if he could come back to do research. During the next year, Ofshe paid over 50 visits, during which he did participant observation, to the ranch and Synanon facilities in Oakland, San Francisco, and Santa Monica. In addition, five of his students did research on Synanon over a three-month period, joining the Oakland "game club" and participating in games and in Synanon community life to varying degrees.

Ofshe's and students' professional interests and intentions to observe and analyze were made known to management and community members from the initial contact. Ofshe's entry was welcomed. Two aspects of Synanon's history seem important in explaining his welcome: (a) in 1972, Synanon considered itself a social movement and an alternative society, and it welcomed middle-class professionals, hoping to recruit them as members; and (b) Ofshe followed three researchers who had visited Synanon and written books favorable to the organization. Synanon's openness seemed based on its changing self-conception and its good reputation, which grew largely out of its claims of unprecedentedly effective drug rehabilitation.

Roy Wallis offers a contrasting example. He presented himself at an introductory "Communications Course" in Scientology as an interested newcomer.

He wanted "to learn how 'anyman' coming in off the street would be received, not how a visiting sociologist doing a thesis on Scientology would be treated" (Wallis, 1977b, p. 155). He arranged to stay in a Scientology "boarding house" during this course. Wallis left after two days because he found it too difficult to continue. He felt he would have been able to stay only if he were in agreement with what he was officially learning. Not feeling this agreement, Wallis felt it would have been dishonest to indicate agreement. When Wallis later officially requested help from the movement's leaders, this earlier abrupt exit, as well as the movement's knowledge that Wallis had surveyed (with a questionnaire) present and ex-members, needed to be explained. Scientologist David Gaiman commented in an appendix to Wallis' article that he "could not understand at that time, and still do not understand, the ethics of his failing to declare this to me in his initial approach" (Wallis, 1977b, p. 168).

Wallis had initially thought to do covert participant observation, because he anticipated a hostile reaction to an open request from a sociologist, given previous, critical investigations by the Food and Drug Administration (FDA) in the United States and by government bodies in Australia and New Zealand, and because he thought "that approaching the leaders and officials of such a public-relations-conscious social movement directly, for assistance with my research, was simply to invite public relations" (Wallis, 1977b, p. 152).

David Bromley and Anson Shupe's simultaneous participant observation of the Unification Church (UC) and the "anti-cult" movement seemingly originated in two chance events. While writing a conference paper on the enormous negative media coverage of the Unification Church, they requested information from the headquarters for the National Ad Hoc Committee— Citizens Engaged in Freeing Minds (CEFM)—and discovered that it was based in a nearby metropolitan area. At the same time, two high-ranking and 50 rank-and-file members of the Unification Church arrived in the area, seeking to recruit university students. One of the researchers was acting chair of his university's sociology department and he agreed, "on civil libertarian principles," to be faculty sponsor for a UC campus student organization. In exchange, Bromley and Shupe were permitted to conduct in-depth interviews and were allowed to observe the group.

Eileen Barker's research on the Unification Church is unique in that, after two years of negotiating with the Church to do research on her terms (e.g., receiving a list of all members, so that she might draw a random sample to interview), she seemed to have been granted relatively free access to the group. However, she did not search out the Unification Church; rather, she was in the favorable position of being sought out by the Church to do research on it. Being sought out may have put her in a more powerful position to negotiate for a favorable research "bargain."

The UC apparently sought her out as an established sociologist of religion. She participated in one conference which the UC sponsored, and in a "series of three residential weekend 'Roundtables on Science and Religion'" (Barker, 1984, p. 13) held at the UC's national headquarters in London, before she was asked if she would like to write about the Church. A Moonie she knew sought her out because he was worried about a sociologist of religion doing research on the group, based on negative reports. Barker replied that it was "hardly surprising that he had to rely on negative reports, as it was well-nigh impossible to get any other kind of information" (p. 14). She later found out that the UC agreed to let her do her research because she "had been prepared to listen to their side of the argument, and they could not believe that anyone who did that could write anything worse than what was already being published by people who had not come to find out for themselves" (p. 15). They felt she was open-minded enough to present a fair picture of them. This seeking her out, and her negotiating for certain conditions of research, allowed her free and long-term access to the group.

There are several points worth noting from these brief descriptions of extant research on cults. Most important, the researcher should be critical of access, asking the question of why the group has allowed the researcher in, looking to the recent history of the group and its present self-understanding in answering this question. One should question the kind of access one is being given, ever conscious of the possibility of saniti- zation or impression management. The researcher should not simply assume that the group he or she is studying understands and agrees with the unfettered pursuit of scientific inquiry. The researcher should learn as much as he or she can about the group— through newspaper/media accounts, public relations materials, or efforts such as open houses, and through interviews with ex-members or present members— before undertaking field research. These actions, how- ever, may have unforeseen consequences.

Researcher as Person

Downes and Rock (1982, p. 30), in discussing research on deviance, made the point that "one will not be at ease everywhere. There are always likely to be certain social groups who defy research by certain sociolo- gists. . . . Many of the barriers which divide people from one another in everyday life also keep the sociologist at bay." Field research highlights the researcher. Some researchers, like informants, are simply better able to establish rapport and to feel at ease in a new, let alone strange, setting. Wallis (1977b, p. 155) said of himself in his brief participant observation on Scientology: "Good participant observation required a particular personal- ity or discipline which I did not possess. Outside a 'mass' context I felt uncomfortable in my role. It felt like spying and a little dishonest. In general, I tried to shift the situation to an 'open' interaction context as quickly as possible."

Among the problems relating to the researcher are: culture shock, handling emotional responses to the group (the chief difficulty here is that overrapport may hinder objectivity), handling conversion attempts of the group, and the stigma of investigating a group considered by many to be deviant.

Balch (1985, p. 24) emphasized that the authoritar- ian social worlds of cults may rub against the grain of researchers' views of reality, since researchers tend to be humanists. In addition, there is the question of deal- ing with bizarre behaviors. Balch stated his first reac- tion to the UFO cult which he and Taylor studied: "My gut reaction to this message was something like:

'They look normal to me, so how can they possibly believe this nonsense?'" (p. 24). Continued interaction with the group overcame these responses, in a way similar to anthropologists' dealing with culture shock.

Whose Perspective? Sampling Members

In researching any group, the question arises imme- diately as to who and what to sample. The prob- lem of sampling interacts with that of brief field research. That is, if one is going to observe a group for a very short time, the question of who one inter- views becomes more important. With longer time in the group, one can make efforts to gain a sampling of members to represent the various viewpoints that are present in the group.

Drawing a representative, random sample of a cult or of ex-cult members (of one group or of all groups) is very difficult. If the group presents a sample of members to a researcher, how does the researcher know if these members are representative? Perhaps they are more intelligent, more likely to be "true believers," or those thought more likely to pres- ent the group in a good light than other members. How does the researcher determine how they were selected? Given the high turnover in most cults, longi- tudinal analysis of a sample of members is also difficult, and such longitudinal analyses of conversion are few (Balch, 1985).

Different understandings within a group are a fact of life. These differences of perspective are the result of one's role and status in the group, one's length of time in the group, and analytical abilities, among other things. In studying any group, the researcher needs to get a sampling of views from all factions to come up with a complete picture of the "reality" of the group. One problem in identifying these factions is that cults often are precisely those organizations which brook no public dissent, so that the only view expressed is the official view. That is, the group presents the appearance of unanimous agreement to outsiders and insiders. Factions do not emerge as organized entities with a recognized different point of view. Individuals remain in a state of pluralistic ignorance of discontent and doubt or criticism of the group. They do not know that others share doubts; they feel only they have doubts (Ayella, 1985; Bainbridge & Stark, 1980).

Yet, here too, "politics" are a fact of life, and it is important for the researcher to assume that members experience the group differently, even when confronted by apparent unanimity. As Rochford (1985, p. 41) concluded from his study of the Hare Krishnas, "First, many, if not most settings are characterized by local politics. To take on a membership role necessarily involves making choices about what sort of member the researcher wants to be." This role will then influence how other members treat the researcher. The researcher would be wise to accept Downes and Rock's (1982, p. 27) advice on researching deviant behavior: "It is only by taking a jaundiced perspective on the world that its disreputable life becomes apparent. Surfaces reveal little. They certainly do not point one at deviant populations." The deviance to be searched for here is doubt, uncertainty, and less than total commitment to the official group ideology.

An additional aspect of sampling remains. New religious movements (NRM) researchers have often described leavers of cult groups as "apostates," and they discount their accounts (of their entry, life, and exit from the group) as being valid sources of data on the group, as being biased—as being not more than "atrocity tales" cultivated in deprogramming sessions. On the other hand, they often accept accounts from current members as being acceptable sources of information on the group. Beckford (1985) is one NRM researcher who has criticized this approach to ex-members' accounts, asserting the desirability of taking ex-members' testimony as seriously as that of current members, and rejecting "the idea that ex-members' accounts can all be subsumed under the heading of 'atrocity tales'" (p. 146). Having made this statement, Beckford felt compelled to defend himself from the assumption that he is an anti-cultist (pp. 146–147).

If one sees only ex-members, one's sample is likely to be of people who were unhappy enough with the group to leave on their own, or people who were deprogrammed. The methodological question is how one interprets these ex-members' versions of the group and its effect on them. One way is to recognize the contextual construction of individual accounts of participation and leave-taking—that is, the fact that such accounts are strongly shaped by individuals' present reference groups. Thus a present member's account is shaped by other members' views, including the desirability of presenting the appearance of complete commitment.

Beckford (1978) and Rochford (1985) both emphasized how the group's ideology presents itself as a "screen" by which members can reinterpret their past and present. Balch (1985) also emphasized how retrospective reinterpretation must be taken into account in interviewing *both* members and ex-members. Recognizing that neither group, present members nor ex-members, can express the complete "truth" is a step toward resolving this problem. In addition, Wright (1987) and Solomon's (1981) research showed that individuals' modes of leaving the group shape their evaluation of the group. Solomon's questionnaire study of ex-Moonies suggested differences in adjustment between ex-cultists who have been deprogrammed and those who have not. She emphasized that we cannot generalize to all members or ex-members of cults from samples of ex-cultists who seek therapy, because we do not know how they compare to ex-cultists who do not seek therapy.

◈ Maintaining Access

Easy Access, Difficult Maintenance

Conversion-oriented groups provide a paradoxical research setting, where access may be easy, but continued presence or interaction is more difficult. This is the result of their expectation that one should accept the group's perspective—and convert—within some specified time period. This carries with it the expectation that one's behavior should change to reflect this conversion or commitment (e.g., living with the group, and giving up previous ties or jobs).

John Lofland, in his now-classic (and disguised) study of the early Unification Church, "assumed the standard seeker's posture, namely, interested and sympathetic but undecided" after he and two fellow graduate students decided in 1962 to study the group (Lofland, 1966, pp. 270–271). The group pressured the three to commit themselves to serious study of the Divine Principle (the group's theology) and to move in with the group. Lofland then expressed interest in doing a sociological study of the group and met with enthusiastic approval from the group's leader. For 11 months, he did participant observation on the group: From February through October of 1962, he spent about 15 hours a week with the group; and from November 1962 through January 1963, he lived in the center four days a week. During this time, Lofland thought there was a shared understanding of his interest in the group, that "I was personally sympathetic to, and accepting of, them and desired to understand their endeavors, but I was not likely to be a convert" (p. 274). In January 1963, the leader told Lofland "that she was tired of playing the 'studying the movement' game" (p. 274). Given his apparent unlikeliness to convert, the leader saw no further reason for his presence, and Lofland left the group. However, a sociology undergraduate student who feigned conversion and joined the group provided information to Lofland until June 1963.

Lofland's experience highlights the problem of adopting a long-term, participant-observer stance to a conversion-oriented group. What happens if one does not convert after what the group considers a reasonable time? Robbins, Anthony and Curtis (1973) also illustrated an unsuccessful resolution of this dilemma in Anthony's participant observation study of a Jesus Freaks group. When confronted by questions as to his religious beliefs, Anthony refused to discuss them, feeling that the religious beliefs he held would alienate group members and end his observation. This response brought strenuous pressure by the group on him to convert. Anthony responded to the pressure by gradual withdrawal.

Richardson, Stewart, and Simmonds (1978) suggested that this outcome of ejection from the group may be averted by the expression of honest difference of opinion, admitting (in their case, that of a fundamentalist commune) that one is aware of the necessity to be "saved," but that one rejects it. This strategy apparently was successful, for they had maintained a relationship with the group for almost seven years at the time of publication of this article. Gordon (1987), too, found this strategy to be successful in his research on two fundamentalist Jesus groups. He suggested that researchers in these groups cultivate distance in the interaction. Two methods of doing this are to be forthright about one's own, differing beliefs, and to emphasize one's research role. Doing so did not alienate members of the group he studied; paradoxically, he felt a sense of greater rapport. Gordon theorized that this open discussion and emphasized researcher role kept the group from feeling that their persuasion efforts had failed.

Shupe and Bromley's (1980; Bromley & Shupe, 1979) articles describing their research on both the Unification Church and the anticult movement also illustrated initially easy access and difficulty as interaction continued. Their role as sociologists was important in two ways in reducing the barriers between themselves and the groups: The role itself "carried a certain degree of legitimacy," and "each group was seeking some type of legitimation to which it was perceived we might contribute" (1980, p. 8). Underpinning both groups' welcome of the researchers was the understanding that "to 'really know' their respective positions was to come to believe in them" (1980, p. 12). The difficulties arose when this did not occur in each group with greater knowledge.

Each group knew that Bromley and Shupe were investigating both groups, and this presented one of the difficulties they faced. Neither group could understand why the researchers needed information from the other group, and Bromley and Shupe were continually forced to explain each dealing with the other group. When time passed and it was clear the researchers were no longer ignorant of the group, members of each group pressured them to take a public stand in support of their respective group, advocating for the group in the media and to other interest groups. Their delicate solution to this persistent dilemma was to "avoid interviews that seemed superficial, highly partisan, or exploitative" (1980, p. 13), and to present each group in its complexity when doing an interview or giving a public talk.

As their research proceeded, Bromley and Shupe sought more extensive and more sensitive information. In attempting to visit the UC's seminary, they became involved in a lengthy negotiation process. They feared this access would not be granted because "the authors' published work was perceived as not sufficiently 'objective' and sensitive to the uses to which the information might be put by others" (1980, p. 9). The UC scrutinized their written work, requested a list of the questions they wanted to ask, and a seminary faculty member visited their campus to "test fully our good will, honesty, and neutrality" (1980, p. 14). Part of the UC's concern stemmed from the fact that they were unable to locate Bromley and Shupe on a supporter/opponent continuum, and they felt they had been harmed by previous researchers to whom they had granted access.

How can researchers cope with the pressures to adopt the group's perspective, to become a committed participant instead of a researcher concerned with objectivity? Richardson et al. (1978) emphasized the importance of maintaining a base camp at the research site to daily reinforce, through conversation with co-workers, one's alternative (to the group) reality. This may facilitate the handling of culture shock and prevent researcher conversion, but it also helps the researcher in other ways. Two (or more) researchers can share the moral dilemmas encountered during the research; they can correct each other's biases (Stone, 1978); and they can alleviate the loneliness of the "professional stranger" role. Barker (1984, pp. 21–22) described her reaction to a BBC producer who

> spent some time with me doing "joint participant observation" in preparation for the filming. Each time we ended a visit I would thrust a tape recorder into her bands and beg her to pour out whatever occurred to her. The fact that her impressions largely coincided with my own did not, of course, prove that we were right and everyone else wrong, but it was enormously reassuring to learn that I was not totally idiosyncratic.

The Researcher's Role in the Group

Groups vary in the kind of access they allow; "potential convert" may be the only way they conceptualize outsiders, in spite of the researcher's identification of self as researcher. In my three-week participant observation of the Unification Church (Ayella, 1977), I identified myself as a researcher from the start. I was told I could observe the group, but I was treated throughout more as a "potential convert" than as a researcher. When attempting to get background information on members or newcomers, I was repeatedly interrupted and asked to do something else. One night, when I chose to skip a lecture (I had learned that that week's set of lectures was virtually identical to the set of lectures given the previous week) to read and take notes, I was confronted with repeated requests from other members to attend. Finally, I decided to do so, thinking that the members would simply stay with me and request until the lecture was over. When I returned to the trailer in which I was staying, the article I had been reading (on Synanon) was gone, as were some notes. No one remembered seeing the article when I questioned members; neither article nor notes ever turned up. This incident was one of the events that destroyed my trust—I doubted the group really meant for me to do research. The consequence was that I stopped taking notes to the degree that I had previously.

In contrast, Rochford (1985) mentioned that at the time of his research on the Hare Krishnas, the movement was changing from an exclusionist group to more of an inclusionist group. As an exclusionist group, one was either an insider or an outsider. At the time of Rochford's research, the movement was developing a role for less committed individuals: that of movement sympathizer. This allowed him to continue participant observation beyond the stage allowed for in the "potential convert" role. This also illustrates some of the contingencies of research. That is, Rochford was in the right place at the right time to do long-term participant observation.

Rochford's reflections (1985, chap. 2) on his research on the Hare Krishna group also highlight the difficulties of long-term participant observation. The

Hare Krishnas demanded high commitment and belief from members, so one problem was how much to participate in the group's activities. As Rochford stated, "Because of strong pressures to participate in the activities of the group, it often becomes difficult to work out a role that is acceptable both to the researcher and to those under study" (1985, p. 22). Rochford's role in the group evolved over the seven years of his research. After the first year, he became a "fringe" member of the group, and he was able to maintain this "fringe" devotee role in the group's Los Angeles community for the next several years. This status enabled him to research ISKCON (International Society for Krishna Consciousness) communities in other parts of the country: "I sent each of these communities a letter from a well-known and respected devotee, who showed his support for my research and pointed out my general sympathies toward Krishna Consciousness and ISKCON" (1985, p. 29). In his own letter of request, Rochford emphasized his five years' involvement, his interest both sociologically and spiritually, and his involvement in the community school and the "bhakta" program for newcomers. He gained stronger support for his research in the form of a higher rate of questionnaire completion from the other communities. However, in his own (Los Angeles) community, Rochford's fringe devotee status resulted in the lowest rate of questionnaire completion.

Rochford pointed out other instances in which his being a fringe member made research personally difficult; for example, at times he was shown to be an "incompetent" member of the group by his repeated ignorance of Sanskrit. Reflecting on this, he realized that learning the language was of lesser importance to him than were other research occupations. In addition, he had "little or no access to the dynamics of recruitment," and he avoided asking questions when he was not sure of something, because he was "very sensitive not to appear ignorant in the eyes of devotees" (1985, p. 31).

◈ Leaving the Field

After successfully gaining access to a group and studying it in-depth, several important questions confront the researcher: To what, if anything, can one generalize from one's research? How representative of the group are one's observations? How representative of cults is this group? While field research may substantially increase our understanding of a particular group, it certainly complicates generalization.

The longer one is with the group, the more confident one may be that one has (a) pierced the public front of the group; (b) gained the trust of members, which often precedes the researcher's entry to back regions of a group; and (c) seen the difference between attitude and behavior. Cults, as social movements, change continually in response to both internal (e.g., in response to a charismatic leader's desires) and external events (e.g., a spate of negative media publicity); thus "snapshots" of the group may soon be outdated. Knowledge of the long-term development of the group may help to establish how representative a snapshot of the group is, but the difficulty is that one does not know at times whether one is at the beginning, the middle, or the end of the group's history. Lofland's (1966) *Doomsday Cult* portrayal of the early Unification Church would not have led one to predict its evolution into a larger and more successful group.

Very few researchers are going to be able to do many in-depth studies—for example, Barker had been studying the Moonies for six years before she published *The Making of a Moonie* (1984). At the time of publication of "Researching a Fundamentalist Commune" (1978), Richardson et al. had been doing research for almost seven years on this group. Rochford had studied the Hare Krishnas for about eight years before his *Hare Krishna in America* was published in 1985. Compounding the difficulty, Balch (1985, p. 24) argued that one cannot compare groups using other people's research, for "any secondary analysis of the current research is apt to get bogged down by ambiguous terms, incomplete data, and idiosyncratic research methods."

In addition to the question of what the researcher can generalize to after doing field research, there is the difficulty of getting published. Cults may attempt to prevent critical research from being published, or may respond to published critical research by litigation.

Both Beckford (1983) and Horowitz (1981) pointed to the Unification Church's efforts to prevent their research from being published and distributed. Wallis's (1977b) account of his difficulty in getting his research on Scientology published is daunting. Synanon responded to the publication of Mitchell, et al.'s (1980) book, *The Light on Synanon*, with libel suits, necessitating countersuits by the defendants which dragged on for years.

◈ Conclusion

If politics are present at the level of the individual researcher and cult, they are also present at the level of scientific community and society. Jonestown seems to have been a watershed event in terms of public awareness and evaluation of cults. This event was widely publicized, and in its wake, greater credibility was given to those critical of cults, stimulating government investigations and legislation to regulate cult practices (Barker, 1986). As Barker (1986, p. 332) saw it:

> After Jonestown they tended to be all lumped together under the now highly derogatory label "cult." Despite pleas from the movements themselves . . . , all the new religions were contaminated by association, the worst (most "sinister" and "bizarre") features of each belonging, by implication, to them all.

Applying Schur's (1980) concept of "deviantizing," cults are engaged in "stigma contests," or battles over the right to define what shall be termed deviant. The outcome of deviantization is the loss of moral standing in the eyes of other members of society. A negative assessment of a group by a researcher may be used in this stigma contest and may change public opinion significantly, making it more difficult for the group to mobilize resources of people and money to accomplish its goals. Conversely, a positive assessment may assist the cult in countering accusations of deviance (e.g., being labeled as an "unauthentic" religion). In Schur's analysis of the politics of deviance, the more powerful group usually has the edge in stigma contests. In this

instance, the more powerful cults have the resources to use the courts to assert their rights. Robbins (1988, p. 181) described cults' reaction to the "anticult" movement: "However, the latter, buoyed by their initial 'institutionalized freedom' and insulation from routinized controls, stridently affirms their 'rights,' which are interpreted as granting to 'churches' freedom from all interference."

If the group studied is powerful, it can use its resources to hinder critical evaluations from being published. Scientology's wealth enabled it to successfully insist on changes in Wallis's manuscript, using the threat of an expensive libel suit, which neither Wallis nor his publisher wanted. Synanon is another group which used its considerable resources—the unpaid labor of its many lawyer members—to discourage journalists and other observers from making critical public comment. The group's use of lawsuits charging libel and seeking multi-million-dollar damages so deterred large newspapers and news magazines that the small newspaper, the *Point Reyes Light*, was the only one willing to publish the negative reports of Synanon (Mitchell et al., 1980).

Co-optation of the researcher can be a major problem for the unwary researcher, because he or she can become, without intent, a "counter" in the ongoing stigma contest between cult and anticult. Openness to social scientists (with their relativizing, "debunking" perspective) can be used as evidence to counter accusations of extreme authoritarianism or totalism of belief and practice. The researchers' participation in cult-sponsored conferences and publication in cult-printed publications can lend the prestige of social science to the group, fostering social respectability. Perhaps the most noteworthy example of this is the Unification Church's sponsorship of conferences and publication of the conference proceedings. The journal *Sociological Analysis* devoted a 1983 issue to discussion of a conference on the propriety of participation in such proceedings. Beckford (1983) emphasized that individual participation may have long-term "transindividual" negative consequences for social scientists specializing in the study of new religious movements. In this instance, Beckford worried that UC sponsorship of conferences and publications will restrict publication to those approved by the UC, and divide the academic specialist community.

The point here is that research has consequences: to generate favorable or unfavorable publicity; an increase or a loss of social prestige; funding or financial support or its loss; or an increase or loss of moral standing (in the case of people considered to be "cultists," they are not just regarded as less prestigious people, but as different kinds of people—as "nuts" or "crackpots"). The fact that many of the groups referred to as cults are social movements, which need an ongoing relationship with the society outside their doors to survive and to grow, means that they are particularly sensitive to public opinion. In the wake of Jonestown, however, I am arguing that "stigma contests" increased, making cults even more sensitive to public opinion.

Stigma contests over what is acceptable behavior continue to be fought by cults. It is inevitable that researchers will be caught up in these contests, because concerns with respectability and social power are ever-present concerns of cults, given the widespread perception of them as deviant. This fact of stigma contests can influence researchers' gaining and maintaining of access, their analysis of research, and their perceived credibility. The important point to emphasize here is that the researcher should not let his or her research agenda be set by the movement. Maintaining one's own agenda will undoubtedly cause various problems, not all of which can be determined in advance.

◈ Notes

1. It is impossible to explore here the range of theoretical and methodological issues involved in this research. Whichever term we use, these groups have been very controversial, and this is also true of the research done on the groups. The two predominant theoretical positions are those of the "new religious movements" and the "destructive cult" researchers. For the uniformed reader, I recommend Robbins's *Cults, Converts, and Charisma* (1988) for the most comprehensive and well-balanced analysis of the research. Beckford's *Cult Controversies* (1985) provides a compelling analysis of the controversiality of cults. Both of these are from the perspective

of "new religious movements" researchers. For a statement of the issues from "destructive cult" researchers, I suggest Clark, Langone, Schecter, and *Daly's Destructive Cult Conversion: Theory, Research, and Treatment* (1981).

2. Barker (1984, p. 2) illustrated widespread public awareness and negative assessment of these groups and events by referring to a late 1970s survey in which a thousand Americans born between 1940 and 1952 were given a list of 155 names and asked how they felt about each of them. Only 3 per cent of the respondents had not heard of the Reverend Moon. Only 1 per cent admitted to admiring him. The owner of no other name on the list elicited less admiration, and the only person whom a higher percentage of respondents did not admire was the ritual killer Charles Manson.

Elsewhere, Barker (1986, p. 330) referred to a December 1978 Gallup Poll which found that "98% of the US public had heard or read about the People's Temple and the Guyana massacre—a level of awareness matched in the pollsters' experience only by the attack on Pearl Harbor and the explosion of the atom bomb."

3. I suggest the collection of papers edited by Brock K. Kilbourne, *Scientific Research and New Religions: Divergent Perspectives* (1985), as the best source of information on this research. Both "new religious movements" and "destructive cult" researchers are represented, so that one obtains a sampling of both perspectives as they influence analyses of research.

◈ References

Ayella, M. (1977). *An analysis of current conversion practices of followers of Reverend Sun Myung Moon.* Unpublished manuscript.

Ayella, M. (1985). *Insane therapy: Case study of the social organization of a psychotherapy cult.* Unpublished doctoral dissertation, University of California at Berkeley.

Bainbridge, W. S., & Stark, R. (1980). Scientology: To be perfectly clear. *Sociological Analysis, 41,* 128–136.

Balch, R. W. (1985). What's wrong with the study of new religions and what we can do about it. In B. K. Kilbourne (Ed.), *Scientific research and new religions: Divergent perspectives* (pp. 24–39). San Francisco: American Association for the Advancement of Science.

Barker, E. (1983). Supping with the devil: How long a spoon does the sociologist need? *Sociological Analysis, 44,* 197–206.

Barker, E. (1984). *The Making of a Moonie.* New York: Blackwell.

Barker, E. (1986). Religious movements: Cult and anticult since Jonestown. *Annual Review of Sociology, 12,* 329–346.

Beckford, J. A. (1978). Accounting for conversion. *British Journal of Sociology, 29,* 249–262.

Beckford, J. A. (1983). Some questions about the relationship between scholars and the new religious movements. *Sociological Analysis, 44,* 189–196.

Beckford, J. A. (1985). *Cult controversies.* New York: Tavistock.

Bromley, D. G., & Shupe, A. D. (1979). Evolving fool in participant observation: Research as an emergent process. In W. Shaffir, A. Turowitz, & R. Stebbins (Eds.), *Fieldwork experience: Qualitative approaches to social research* (pp. 191–203). New York: St. Martin's.

Clark, J. G., Jr., Langone, M. D., Schecter, R. E., & Daly, R. C. B. (1981). *Destructive cult conversion: Theory, research, and treatment.* Weston, MA: American Family Foundation.

Downes, D., & Rock, P. (1982). *Understanding deviance.* New York: Oxford University Press.

Gordon, D. (1987, August). *Getting close by staying distant: Field work on conversion-oriented groups.* Paper presented at the annual meeting of the American Sociological Association, New York City.

Horowitz, I. (1981). The politics of new cults. In T. Robbins & D. Anthony (Eds.), *In gods we trust* (pp. 161–170). New Brunswick, NJ: Transaction Books.

Kilbourne, B. K. (Ed.). (1985). *Scientific research and new religions: Divergent perspectives.* San Francisco: American Association for the Advancement of Science, Pacific Division.

Lofland, J. (1966). *Doomsday cult.* Englewood Cliffs, NJ: Prentice-Hall.

Mitchell, D., Mitchell, C., & Ofshe, R. (1980). *The light on Synanon.* New York: Seaview Books.

Richardson, J. T., Stewart, M. W., & Simmonds, R. B. (1978). Researching a fundamentalist commune. In J. Needleman & G. Baker (Eds.), *Understanding the new religions* (pp. 235–251). New York: Seabury.

Robbins, T. (1988). *Cults, converts, and charisma.* Newbury Park, CA: Sage.

Robbins, T., Anthony, D., & Curtis, T. (1973). The limits of symbolic realism: Problems of empathetic field observation in a sectarian context. *Journal for the Scientific Study of Religion, 12,* 259–272.

Rochford, E. B. (1985). *Hare Krishna in America.* New Brunswick, NJ: Rutgers University Press.

Schur, E. M. (1980). *The politics of deviance.* Englewood Cliffs, NJ: Prentice-Hall.

Shupe, A. D., Jr., & Bromley, D. G. (1980). Walking a tightrope: Dilemmas of participant observation of groups in conflict. *Qualitative Sociology, 2,* 3–21.

Solomon, T. (1981). Integrating the "Moonie" experience: A survey of ex-members of the Unification Church. In T. Robbins & D. Anthony (Eds.), *In gods we trust* (pp. 275–294). New Brunswick, NJ: Transaction Books.

Stone, D. (1978). On knowing how we know about the new religions. In J. Needleman & G. Baker (Eds.), *Understanding the new religions* (pp. 141–152). New York: Seabury Press.

Wallis, R. (1977a). *The road to total freedom.* New York: Columbia University Press.

Wallis, R. (1977b). The moral career of a research project. In C. Bell & H. Newby (Eds.), *Doing sociological research* (pp. 149–169). London: Allen & Unwin.

Wright, S. (1987). *Leaving cults: The dynamics of defection* (Monograph No. 7). Washington, DC: Society for the Scientific Study of Religion.

READING 10

Lee and Renzetti begin by noting that a "sensitive topic" is actually a difficult and vague description that is not well defined in the literature, and they discuss various definitions to help us think through the problem. They make a very interesting point that results from studies concerning sensitive topics are likely to be accepted by the public regardless of how poorly the research was conducted. For example, Kinsey's research finding that about 10% of his sample was homosexual. We have heard that stated as fact and even exaggerated and extended to all cultures and societies. Kinsey's sample was a nonprobability sample and was not intended to represent the U.S. population (and certainly not all societies) even at the time of his publication. As other articles have emphasized, sampling is almost always a problem when dealing with sensitive topics, but the authors put a unique spin on the issue as they discuss legal issues surrounding sampling. Finally, the authors provide some especially interesting examples of ethical issues in the study of sensitive issues.

Source: Lee, Raymond M., and Claire M. Renzetti. 1990. "The Problems of Researching Sensitive Topics." *American Behavioral Scientist* 33:510–528. Reprinted with permission.

The Problems of Researching Sensitive Topics

An Overview and Introduction

Raymond M. Lee and Claire M. Renzetti

Defining "Sensitive" Topics

One difficulty with the notion of a "sensitive topic" is that the term is often used in the literature as if it were self-explanatory. In other words, the term usually is treated in a commonsensical way, with no attempt at definition. Consider the substantive topics addressed by the articles in this issue. Child abuse, AIDS, and policing in Northern Ireland, for instance, are topics that most social scientists would generally regard without much reservation as sensitive. Why? What is it about these topics that makes them "sensitive," relative to other research topics?

A starting point for answering these questions is provided by Sieber and Stanley (1988). They define "socially sensitive research" as

> studies in which there are potential consequences or implications, either directly for the participants in the research or for the class of individuals represented by the research. For example, a study that examines the relative merits of day care for infants against full-time care by the mother can have broad social implications and thus can be considered socially sensitive. Similarly, studies aimed at examining the relation between gender and mathematical ability also have significant social implications. (p. 49)

A major advantage of defining sensitive research in this way is that it is broad in scope, thereby allowing for the inclusion of topics that ordinarily might not be thought of as "sensitive." In addition, it alerts researchers to their responsibilities to the wider society. This is entirely appropriate, given the ethical and professional issues which form the primary focus of Sieber and Stanley's article. The difficulty is that Sieber and Stanley do not specify the scope or nature of the kinds of consequences or implications, that they have in mind. As a result, their definition logically encompasses research that is consequential in any way. This would include presumably almost any kind of applied research, even where it had limited scope or was wholly beneficial. Therefore, the term "sensitive," as used by Sieber and Stanley, almost seems to become synonymous with "controversial." Moreover, while the importance of ethical issues should not be diminished, one needs to remember that research on sensitive topics raises a whole range of problems, including those of a more specifically technical or methodological kind. The definition proposed by Sieber and Stanley tends to draw attention away from these problems.

An alternative approach to defining sensitive topics would be to start with the observation that those topics which social scientists generally regard as sensitive are ones that seem to be threatening in some way to those being studied. Another way to put this is to say that sensitive topics present problems because research into them involves potential costs to those participating in the research. It is true, of course, that all research involves some cost to those who participate, if only in terms of time and possible inconvenience. While there are cases in which research makes demands on participants that are quite substantial, the potential costs in the case of sensitive topics go beyond the incidental or merely onerous. Thus, for a topic to be sensitive, the threat it poses should at least be moderate, although probably more often it is severe.

At the same time, sensitive topics seem to involve particular kinds of costs. On one hand, these may take the form of psychic costs, such as guilt, shame, or embarrassment. Alternatively, sensitive topics are threatening because participation in research can have unwelcome consequences. For instance, wrongdoing uncovered by the research might bring with it the possibility of discovery and sanction. As a result, the relationship between the researcher and the researched may become hedged with mistrust, concealment, and dissimulation. This, in turn, has obvious detrimental effects on levels of reliability and validity, and raises a concomitant need for ethical awareness on the part of the researcher.

Finally, it is important to remember that research can be threatening to the *researcher* as well as to the researched. Researchers may be placed in situations in which their personal security is jeopardized, or they may find themselves stigmatized by colleagues and others for having studied particular topics (e.g., sexual deviance).

This is an important point to which we will return shortly. Now, however, we are in a position to offer at least a preliminary definition of a sensitive topic. The threatening character of the research, and its potential consequentiality for both researcher and researched, suggests that

> a sensitive topic is one which potentially poses for those involved a substantial threat, the emergence of which renders problematic for the researcher and/or the researched the collection, holding, and/or dissemination of research data.

Although one could attempt to develop a comprehensive list of sensitive topics based on this definition, it seems more fruitful to look at the conditions under which "sensitivity" arises within the research process.

◈ Sensitive Topics and the Research Process

The sensitive nature of a particular topic is emergent. In other words, the sensitive character of a piece of research seemingly inheres less in the topic itself and more in the relationship between that topic and the social context within which the research is conducted.

It is not uncommon, for example, for a researcher to approach a topic with caution on the assumption that it is a sensitive one, only to find that those initial fears had been misplaced. Nor is it unusual for the sensitive nature of an apparently innocuous topic to become apparent once research is underway. Just as Goyder (1987) hypothesized that different social groups attribute different meanings to requests for participation in research, it may well be that a study seen as threatening by one group will be thought innocuous by another.

It is probably possible for any topic, depending on context, to be a sensitive one. Experience suggests, however, that there are a number of areas in which research is more likely to be threatening than others. These include (a) where research intrudes into the private sphere or delves into some deeply personal experience; (b) where the study is concerned with deviance and social control; (c) where it impinges on the vested interests of powerful persons or the exercise of coercion or domination; and (d) where it deals with things sacred to those being studied which they do not wish profaned.

Intrusions into the private sphere need not always be threatening. Day (1985), for instance, concluded that there is no fixed private sphere. Topics and activities regarded as private vary cross-culturally and situationally. Commonly, however, areas of social life concerned with sexual or financial matters remain shielded from the eyes of nonintimates. Other areas of personal experience, such as bereavement, are not so much private as emotionally charged. Research into such areas may threaten those studied through the levels of emotional stress which they produce.

Research involving the investigation of deviant activities has frequently been regarded as having a sensitive character. Those studied are likely to fear being identified, stigmatized, or incriminated in some way. Areas of social life which are contentious or highly conflictual often produce topics for research which are sensitive. Normally, this is because in such situations research can be seen by those involved as threatening the alignments, interests, or security of those in a conflict, especially those who are in positions of relative power. Finally, the values and beliefs of some groups are threatened in an intrinsic way by research. Some religious groups—old-time fundamentalists, for example—quite literally regard research into their beliefs and activities as anathema (Homan, 1978; Homan & Bulmer, 1982).

Sensitivity, as we have used the term here, affects almost every stage of the research process from formulation through design to implementation, dissemination, and application (Brewer, this issue; Sieber & Stanley, 1988; Seigel & Bauman, 1986). Perhaps only the actual process of data analysis is likely to remain relatively untouched (although considerations relating to the confidentiality of data can add complexities even here). The problems that arise at each stage can take a variety of forms. Sensitive research raises methodological, technical, ethical, political, and legal problems, as well as having potential effects on the personal life of the researcher (Plummer, 1983), not least in some contexts at the level of personal security (Brewer, this issue).

Research on sensitive topics has tended to have two rather contradictory outcomes. First, the difficulties associated with sensitive research have tended to inhibit adequate conceptualization and measurement (Herzberger, this issue). However, the problems raised by sensitive topics have also led to technical innovation in the form of imaginative methodological advances (e.g., see Caplan, 1982). As a result, research on sensitive topics has contributed to methodological development in both the widest and the narrowest sense. Good examples here are the development of strategies for asking sensitive questions on surveys (Bradburn & Sudman, 1979) and technical means for preserving the confidentiality of research data (Boruch & Cecil, 1979).

Sensitive topics also raise wider issues related to the ethics, politics, and legal aspects of research. In recent years, the ethical and legal aspects of social research have become increasingly salient. In many countries, there has been a growing concern for individual rights, including those of research participants, and for the rights of social groups who may be affected by research. Such trends are likely to intensify as researchers move toward more complex research designs (Kimmel, 1988) and a greater involvement in applied research.

Such issues impinge on all research, whatever its character, but they may impinge most forcefully in the case of sensitive topics. In many cases, of course, neither the problems raised by sensitive research nor the issues involved can be dealt with in any simple way. However, the experiences of researchers studying sensitive topics, of the kind represented in this special issue, may serve to guide researchers embarking on sensitive research, and to sharpen debate about critical issues.

◈ Issues and Problems in Researching Sensitive Topics

Duelli-Klein (1983, p. 38) pointed out that "the 'what' to investigate must come prior to the decision of 'how' to go about doing one's research." In a number of important respects, what is studied can be constrained in significant ways by the sensitive character of the topic. For example, powerful gatekeepers can impose restrictions on researchers in ways that constrain their capacity to produce or report on findings that threaten the interests of the powerful. Funding agencies, it has been argued, tend to prefer research having a particular character: research that is relevant to the policymaking process (Abrams, 1981; Sjoberg & Nett, 1968); based on individualistic, rather than structural explanations (Galliher & McCartney, 1973; Hanmer & Leonard, 1984); and which is quantitative or positivistic in its methodology (Broadhead & Rist, 1976; Ditton & Williams, 1981). One lesson which some writers have drawn from this is that the organization of research funding tends to serve the interests of powerful groups in society by excluding support for research on topics which they might consider sensitive or detrimental to their interest. The institutional context within which researchers operate is also seen to abet this tendency since, it is argued, universities and research institutes dislike offending local elites or putting in jeopardy sources of possible funding (Broadhead & Rist, 1976; Moore, 1973; Record, 1967).

Sensitivity, as we have defined it, can also affect the "what to investigate" in other ways. According to Sieber and Stanley (1988, p. 50), the very fact that a researcher poses a particular theory or research question can have major social implications even if the research is never performed. Thus framing a specific research question about a sensitive topic presents an initial set of problems. Consider, for instance, research on domestic violence. The question that has dominated this area of inquiry for more than two decades has been, Why do battered women stay with partners who abuse them? Regardless of the answers generated, posing the question itself establishes the parameters of the problem of spouse abuse in terms of the behavior of battered women. Attention is deflected from batterers onto victims. It is battered women who are defined as deviant for remaining in abusive relationships, not their partners who are deviant for battering them (Loseke & Cahill, 1984). In short, asking "Why do battered women stay?"—rather than "What factors make it possible or even permissible for men to batter women?"—creates a scientific and popular milieu for blaming the victim. To paraphrase Sieber and Stanley (1988, p. 50), faulty ideas drawn from social science research may powerfully affect social conceptions of significant social problems and issues regardless of the adequacy of the research findings.

This is a point taken up in this issue in Sharon Herzberger's article on studying child abuse. Herzberger, a psychologist, examines the methodological difficulties that arise when studying this sensitive topic. She is especially concerned with empirical tests of the widely accepted "cyclical hypothesis," the notion that individuals who were physically abused by their parents tend to become child abusers themselves. Herzberger argues that research on child abuse has been plagued by four major problems: inconsistent operational definitions, lack of control or comparison groups, failure to utilize multivariate analysis, and the limits of retrospective studies. Although these are problems that occur in many research areas, the deficiencies which Herzberger identifies can be generalized to research on other sensitive topics. For example, Renzetti (1988) noted in her research on homosexual partner abuse that vague and inconsistent definitions of the behavior in question make comparisons of findings across studies difficult at best and also give rise to disagreements and confusions over important "facts," such as the incidence of the behavior.

In the case of child abuse, Herzberger argues, the methodological flaws which she identifies seriously undermine many of the early studies of the cyclical hypothesis. Later, better designed research has provided only modest support for the proposition. As Sieber and Stanley (1988, p. 53) pointed out, "Sensitive research topics are more likely to have applications in the 'real' world that society will enthusiastically embrace, irrespective of the validity of the application." Perhaps for this reason many social scientists and lay people continue to treat the cyclical hypothesis as fact. Herzberger contends, however, that this has serious consequences: It provides a shaky foundation on which to build future research and inhibits accurate theory building by researchers; it misguides social service personnel and policymakers as they attempt to develop effective programs; and it arouses stress and fear in many formerly abused adults who are misled into believing that they will inevitably abuse their own children.

Problems deriving from the recruitment of study participants are especially acute for researchers investigating sensitive topics. In studies of relatively innocuous behavior or issues, complete sampling frames are often available which allow for random sampling and a sound estimate of sampling bias. This is rarely the case, however, in studies of sensitive topics. Indeed, the more sensitive or threatening the topic under examination, the more difficult sampling is likely to be, since potential participants have greater need or incentive to hide their involvement.

Systematic treatments of sampling issues related to deviant populations can be found in Becker (1970) and for rare populations in Sudman and Kalton (1986), Sudman, Sirken, and Curran (1988), and Kish (1965). The major strategies that can be used, singly or in combination, for sampling "special" populations which are rare and/or deviant in some way are (a) the use of lists, (b) multipurpose surveys, (c) household screening procedures, (d) the location of locales within which sample members congregate as sites for the recruitment of respondents, (e) the use of networking or "snowballing" strategies, (f) advertising for respondents, and (g) obtaining sample participants in return for providing a service of some kind. In the study of deviant populations, probably the most common method used has been the "snowball" sample. Ironically, though, as qualitative researchers have begun to develop a more critical assessment of the limitations of this method (Biernacki & Waldorf, 1981), survey researchers have become more open to using similar network sampling methods in order to locate rare or elusive populations (Rothbart, Fine, & Sudman, 1982; Sudman & Kalton, 1986; Sudman et al., 1988).

Martin and Dean (this issue) had both ethical and technical reasons for rejecting screening procedures in order to generate a sample for their study of the impact of the AIDS epidemic on the emotional and behavioral functioning of gay men. They reasoned that the stigma attached to homosexuality, along with growing antigay harassment and violence, would likely bias the sampling frame toward gay men who were self-assured and open about their sexual preference. Neighborhood screening would also produce biases, since the logical choice—in this case, Greenwich Village—is a predominantly white, upper middle-class neighborhood of highly visible gay men. (In any case, as a number of researchers have recorded [Hope, Kennedy, & DeWinter, 1976; McRae, 1986], the costs of having to screen large populations to uncover individuals possessing relatively rare traits is a major limitation on such methods.)

Martin and Dean's choice was to use network sampling using a variety of sources to "seed" their initial sample. Sudman and Kalton (1986) recently demonstrated that lists which provide only partial coverage of some populations may still provide a useful starting point for the development of an adequate sample. Among the sources which Martin and Dean used to provide the base, or "generation zero" as they call it, for their sample was the membership list of gay organizations in New York City. Although they tried to control for many of the difficulties inherent in network or snowball sampling, they were unable to determine precisely to what extent they had been successful in generating a reliable sample. Nevertheless, cross-group comparison and comparisons with two random samples of gay men indicate that they obtained a fairly

representative sample of gay men who have not been diagnosed as having AIDS. Their article is likely to be helpful to researchers interested in developing a workable sampling strategy for a survey of a hidden population. Martin and Dean's work suggests that even in the absence of external validating criteria, it is possible to go a long way despite imperfect circumstances.

Perhaps because of its historical development, sampling has tended to be seen primarily as a technical matter. However, sampling decisions can rarely be divorced from theoretical issues, particularly those dealing with how populations are to be defined (for problems of this kind which arise in AIDS research, see Siegel & Bauman, 1986), or from ethical or political issues. Gillespie and Leffler (1987), for example, noted that controversy over the technical adequacy of samples can enter into political conflicts over the status of social science knowledge. In a similar way, as Hartley (1982) pointed out, ethical problems may arise because of the potential for invasions of privacy when lists are used for sampling purposes.

While research participants should, in general, expect their rights to privacy, anonymity, and confidentiality to be protected, maintaining confidentiality of research data is especially important where informants or respondents are being asked to reveal intimate or incriminating information. Recently, AIDS researchers have begun to be concerned about public health reporting laws and the power of courts to subpoena research data (Melton & Gray, 1988). This last is an issue which at various times has attracted considerable interest and concern among researchers involved in the study of deviant and criminal behavior. As Marybeth Ayella indicates in her article (this issue), the law also has impinged on scholars researching the plethora of "new" or "alternative" religious movements which emerged as a novel social phenomenon in the West in the 1960s and 1970s.

The legal system both regulates research and intervenes in the research process. The state, for instance, regulates the relationship which researchers have to those they study either, commonly in Europe, through data protection legislation (Akeroyd, 1988) or, to take the U.S. case, by compelling prior ethical review. There have been a number of suggestions that legal regulation can lead to research of a sensitive nature being inhibited or sanitized. Thus the Data Inspection Board in Sweden has required researchers to remove questions judged to be sensitive from questionnaires (Flaherty, 1979; Hammar, 1976; Janson, 1979), while researchers in the United States have charged that for a period in the 1970s, government regulations increased the difficulty of undertaking research on deviance or controversial topics (Ceci, Peters, & Plotkin, 1985; Hessler & Galliher, 1983; Reiss, 1979).

Although malpractice suits against researchers apparently remain only a theoretical possibility (Reiss, 1979; Useem & Marx, 1983), the law has intervened in the research process on a number of occasions. In the United States, legal intervention has been seen most commonly in attempts by prosecutors and courts to subpoena research data (Brahuja & Hallowell, 1986; Knerr, 1982). In contrast, legal threats in Britain usually have taken the form of actual or threatened libel actions (Braithwaite, 1985; Punch, 1986; Wallis, 1977). In both instances, the risks of legal intervention are felt most keenly by those researching sensitive topics. Thus attempts have been made to subpoena data relating to criminal activities, while powerful groups on occasion have been able to use the threat of libel litigation to suppress or substantially modify the accounts that social scientists give of their activities (Ayella, this issue; Braithwaite, 1985). In neither Britain nor the United States are research data legally privileged, although some limited protection does exist in the United States (Melton & Gray, 1988; Nelson & Hedrick, 1983). Again, few researchers will have the resources to fight cases or to pay the necessary penalties if they lose. This is particularly so in Britain where libel laws are stringent, and where libel damages can be substantial.[1]

Although she discusses the problems of sampling and some of the legal issues raised by research on new religious movements or "cults," the primary focus of Marybeth Ayella's article (this issue) is with the process of gaining entry to the group or setting one wants to study. (In field research, concerns over sampling traditionally have been superseded by a preoccupation with problems of access.) Although there is a general assumption that deviant groups are difficult to study, Ayella points out that gaining initial access to some groups may be relatively easy, but that once inside, access may be difficult to sustain. Some cults, for instance, may welcome the researcher at first, perceiving him or her as an interested newcomer and potential convert. However, when conversion does not appear within a given period of time, the researcher may be ejected from the group and denied further access. Ayella notes that some researchers are able to maintain access by establishing a unique role or special category of membership for themselves, such as "fringe devotee." Others apparently handle this problem successfully by honestly expressing their disagreements with the group and by stressing their role as researcher rather than as member. Still others negotiate access by establishing a reciprocal relationship with the group, for example, by lending, in effect, legitimacy or respectability to the group in exchange for access, although Ayella rightly warns of the dangers of co-optation of the researcher in such situations. In line with Johnson (1975), who argued that access is not an initial phase of entry to the setting around which a bargain can be struck, but rather a continuing process of negotiation and renegotiation, Ayella advises researchers not to allow the groups which they wish to study to set the research agenda for them.

Ayella examines a number of other problems, such as culture shock and handling one's emotional responses to stressful research situations, that are related to sustaining a research project on deviant groups. John Brewer, from Queen's University of Belfast, elaborates on many of the points raised by Ayella in his discussion of the difficulties of conducting research in a setting that is politically, psychologically, and physically threatening to both researchers and study participants. One of the most significant aspects of Brewer's article is that it highlights the contextual nature of sensitive research. Although other field studies of police officers demonstrate that the police in general are a difficult group to study (Fielding, this issue; Hunt, 1984; Klockars, 1985; Van Maanen, 1988), the politically charged and conflict-ridden atmosphere of Northern Ireland renders a study of the police force there especially sensitive.

To conduct research on the Royal Ulster Constabulary (RUC), Brewer first had to obtain permission from the Chief Constable. This had the potential for severely restricting the research, since "gatekeepers" frequently impose explicit conditions on the way in which research may be conducted as well as on how the findings may be disseminated. Although this did not happen in Brewer's case, obtaining permission from the Chief Constable created other problems, not the least of which was the suspicion it produced among ordinary police officers about the researchers' and police managers' objectives and motives.

In short, although gaining initial access to the RUC proved fairly straightforward, Brewer and his research assistant had to pass through a second set of gatekeepers, the ordinary police officers. Since, as in organizational contexts generally, the RUC is characterized by what Dingwall (1980) called a "hierarchy of consent," it was assumed that superiors have the right to permit subordinates to be studied. However, this does not insure that the subordinates will be cooperative. As Brewer and others have discovered, people in research situations may intentionally undermine the research through obfuscation and deception. In addition, researchers may be subjected to repeated "trust tests" which force them to legitimate themselves in the eyes of study participants and, like some of the researchers cited by Ayella, they may have to construct or capitalize on a special identity.

During the research, the identity of Brewer's research assistant proved to be an important factor. She was a Catholic studying mostly Protestants, an innocuous element in other contexts, but in the context of Northern Ireland, it prompted the researchers to try (unsuccessfully) to conceal her religious identity from those studied. As the research proceeded, the fieldworker found herself being "culturally contextualized" (Warren, 1988), in terms of both her religion and her sex.

As other female fieldworkers have noted, women researchers may become "encapsulated in the stereotypical [gender] role designated by subjects" and consequently have limited access to data, especially data in such male-dominated groups as the police (Hunt, 1984, p. 286). However, Warren (1988) maintained that gender itself is a negotiated rather than an ascribed status in the field. Furthermore, she pointed out that researchers may be able to capitalize on the sexism of study participants. For instance, while doing fieldwork in a drug rehabilitation center, Warren discovered that she had relatively free access to areas usually off-limits to outsiders and could even investigate the contents of file drawers because the male staff at the center often viewed themselves as too engaged in "important business" to worry about a harmless female (p. 18). Brewer's research assistant encountered a similar attitude among some RUC officers. Of course, Warren also noted that this trade-off of accepting sexism to obtain information often is both personally and politically repugnant to female researchers. In addition, she showed that while gender issues in the field have usually been most problematic for women, male researchers must deal with them at times. Johnson (1986), for example, reported that he encountered considerable resistance to his presence from the female elementary school teachers he was observing because these women typically had their professionalism and authority undercut by their male colleagues and supervisors. As Johnson interpreted it, the teachers needed to determine if he, as a man, could be trusted.

Brewer's article also raises the issue of the researcher's personal security. In the context of the kind of violent social conflict found in Northern Ireland, research can be a dangerous activity (Burton, 1978; Lee, 1981). Indeed, at various times, researchers have been forced into hiding or have had to leave Northern Ireland due to fears (apparently unfounded, it should be said) that research materials were finding their way to the security forces (Taylor, 1988). While many researchers are unlikely to face the stresses produced by research in a violent social situation, it should also be borne in mind that "researcher jeopardy" can take a number of forms. As we noted earlier, work with deviant groups also can lead to unwelcome consequences for researchers who may find themselves subject to "stigma contagion." This seems to be particularly true of research on human sexuality. Those involved in the study of sexual deviance have frequently remarked on their stigmatization by colleagues, university administrators, and students (Plummer, 1981; Troiden, 1987; Weinberg & Williams, 1972). In a similar way, research in controversial areas which produce findings unpopular among colleagues can lead to negative consequences for the researcher (Sieber & Stanley, 1988).

Brewer's research points to how research participants, at least in naturalistic settings, can be threatened and discomforted by research, as well as to some of the ways in which they may artfully deal with such threats. The threatening character of research and its implications for the relationship between researcher and researched form a focus for the articles by Bertilson and Fielding (this issue). Hal Bertilson, a social psychologist, addresses some of the ethical and methodological issues that arise in research on human aggression. As he remarks in his article, the study of human aggression is sensitive for reasons of methodology rather than of topic. This is because experimentally-based research on aggression in social psychology incorporates both aggressive behaviors in the form of electric shocks delivered to research subjects, as well as their deception about the purposes of the research. Research participants, it would seem, are therefore capable both of being harmed and of being wronged (Macintyre, 1982) by the research.

In responding affirmatively to the question, "Can aggression be [ethically] justified in order to study aggression?," Bertilson produces a number of justifications. Drawing in part on the ethical guidelines published by the American Psychological Association, he argues that research of the kind he describes can be ethically undertaken if three conditions are met: (a) if the potential benefits to society are great enough; (b) if the research is planned in a way that maximizes the yield of generalizable knowledge; and (c) if the risks to participants are controlled and minimized.

Ethical debates in the social sciences have tended to be conducted between those, on one hand, who espouse Ideological conceptions of ethics, frequently based around a utilitarian calculus of costs and benefits, and those, on the other, whose underlying ethical conceptions are deontological in character (Kimmel, 1988). Pointing to the appalling human cost of aggression

in terms of violence, Bertilson presents a robust defense of a position based on an essentially utilitarian conception. Readers will no doubt judge for themselves how compelling Bertilson's argument is in relation to aggression research. By its very nature, however, research on sensitive topics, because it sharpens ethical dilemmas, tends to reveal the limits of existing ethical theories.

Where sensitive topics are involved, utilitarianism can lead to a lessened rather than to a heightened ethical awareness, while deontological theories may be too restrictive, replacing the sin of callousness with the sin of scrupulosity. Thus Macintyre (1982) argued that one difficulty with a utilitarian approach to ethical decision making is that there is no consensus among social scientists about what counts as a benefit. Moreover, apparently disinterested assertions about risks and rewards may actually be self-serving because researchers have greater power than research participants to define costs and benefits. One can also note that to assume that there are substantial benefits to society from a particular piece of research is also to assume that the relationship between the production of knowledge and its application is linear and nonproblematic with no scope for misuse.

If this argument is accepted, it becomes necessary to be careful before concluding, as Bertilson does, that experiments on aggression that incorporate aggressive behaviors and deception are "moral imperatives." (Bertilson is perhaps too dismissive of nondeceptive research procedures, such as the use of role-plays and simulation. It should be noted, though, that their use does not automatically prevent harm to research participants, as the Stanford prison experiment graphically demonstrated [Barnes, 1979; Zimbardo, 1973]). On the other hand, if one follows the kind of line taken by Macintyre, there is the danger of excluding as legitimate research a number of areas judged earlier to be sensitive. According to Macintyre (1982, p. 188):

The study of taboos by anthropologists and of privacy by sociologists show how important it is for a culture that certain areas of personal and social life should be specially protected. Intimacy cannot exist where everything is disclosed, sanctuary cannot be sought where no place is inviolate, integrity cannot be seen to be maintained—and therefore cannot in certain cases be maintained—without protection from illegitimate pressures.

For Macintyre, to violate those sanctuaries is to do a wrong to those one studies. This is despite the fact that, as Macintyre acknowledges, research into the areas of human life which he wants to protect—he uses bereavement as an example—would lead to substantial good in terms of increasing knowledge. Whatever the benefits accruing from these gains, however, Macintyre insists that it cannot be right to do a wrong to anyone. One difficulty with Macintyre's position is that his assertion of the inviolability of the intimate sphere is justified by reference to empirical research by anthropologists and sociologists on the functions of privacy. However, if Macintyre's point of view is accepted, research of this kind would be unethical. It also would not be possible to assess Macintyre's own claims empirically. At the same time, permitting research on the private sphere might reveal that in many instances, particularly in sensitive areas, research participants desire catharsis rather than sanctuary (Lee, 1981). That is, research on sensitive topics may produce not only gains in knowledge, but also effects that are directly beneficial to research participants.

A complicating factor in all of this is that empirical studies of researchers' ethical decision making are surprisingly lacking (Stanley, Sieber & Melton, 1987). One suspects, however, that relatively few researchers actually desist from research either because the costs involved exceed the benefits or on grounds of moral principle. Paradoxically, this may be especially true where research has a sensitive character. In sociology, for example, the sensitive nature of a study has frequently been used as a justification for the use of covert methods, a practice which many regard as ethically dubious. (A range of articles debating this issue may be found in Bulmer, 1982.) The argument is made that because the topic under investigation is sensitive, research into it can be conducted only in a covert way (see, for example, Humphreys, 1970).

The issue of the ethical character of the relationship between the researcher and the researched in ethnographic studies lies at the heart of Nigel Fielding's article (this issue). Fielding, a criminologist, is critical, on one hand, of the naturalistic approach to field research. This approach advocates that the researcher should take an "appreciative" stance (Matza, 1969) toward his or her informants and their accounts of events and behavior. Naturalism stresses rapport and empathic relations with informants in the field. Fielding notes that this is easier to accomplish in studies of nonthreatening or non-threatened groups than in those of "unloved" groups, such as the police. Moreover, the naturalistic approach establishes a false dichotomy in relation to the accounts of the research given by those involved: Those of the study participants are viewed as complete and accurate, while those of the researcher are viewed as partial and flawed.

An alternative approach to research based on the appreciative stance involves "investigative research," or the use of "conflict methodologies" (Douglas, 1976; Galliher, 1973). Such approaches—involving the use of covert research, the analysis of publicly available data, the seeking out, for example, of dissatisfied former employees as informants, and so on—have the advantage in that they do not require the cooperation of powerful subjects. Fielding, however, is critical of the assertive skeptical role embodied in this kind of research, for he sees a danger that the researcher may become manipulative and deceitful with informants or that skepticism may turn into cynicism that prevents informants' accounts from being taken seriously by the researcher.

Instead, Fielding calls for field researchers to take an "intercalary role" in relation to study participants, an approach not unlike Maguire's (1987) participatory research model. Taking an intercalary role places the field researcher in a position between passive recipient of informants' accounts and skeptical investigator. In this model, fieldworker and study participants are simultaneously inquirers into the group's culture and educators of one another with respect to that culture. In this way, the researcher and the researched coproduce fieldwork. Fielding skillfully demonstrates the usefulness of the intercalary role for studying sensitive topics and groups through his discussion of an incident that occurred during his own field research on the criteria of competence in urban policing. One particularly valuable outcome of adopting the intercalary role is that it presents the opportunity to understand the issue of sensitivity from the point of view of the study participants, rather than solely from the perspective of the researcher.

The final article in this issue is by economist J. J. Thomas who focuses on the difficulties of studying the hidden or underground economy. There are many respects in which Thomas's article echoes the concerns about operationalization and measurement raised by Herzberger. He notes that disagreement over definitions of the underground economy has led to considerable confusion. More important, however, is his point that two factors have constrained research on this sensitive topic and have inhibited the development of a comprehensive understanding of it: the training of economists to analyze rather than collect data, and a lack of interest in criminal behavior among mainstream economists.

After reviewing several indirect measures of the underground economy using both macro- and micro-economic data sources, and delineating the strengths and weaknesses of each, Thomas suggests that an interdisciplinary approach to the study of the underground economy may be more fruitful. While mindful of the problems involved, he urges economists to adopt various methods used by other social scientists, such as the use of surveys and participant observation techniques, and he encourages collaborative research between economists and other social scientists. It is this interdisciplinary emphasis which led us to conclude this issue with Thomas's article. We share his optimism that interdisciplinary research endeavors may generate higher quality data, not only in studies of the underground economy, but in studies of other sensitive topics as well.

At this point, it may appear to readers that researching sensitive topics is a daunting enterprise. Brewer (this issue) notes that the many problems which arise in studying a sensitive topic may indeed defeat the researcher unless he or she brings a tough, single-minded, tenacious but pragmatic attitude to the task. Moreover, the fact that sensitive topics pose complex issues and dilemmas for researchers does not imply that such topics should not be studied. As Sieber and Stanley (1988, p. 55) convincingly argued,

> Sensitive research addresses some of society's most pressing social issues and policy questions. Although ignoring the ethical issues in sensitive research is not a responsible approach to science, shying away from controversial topics, simply because they are controversial, is also an avoidance of responsibility.

Likewise, we argue that ignoring the methodological difficulties inherent in researching sensitive topics is also socially and scientifically irresponsible since this ignorance may potentially generate flawed conclusions on which both theory and public policy subsequently may be built If social scientists are not to opt out of research on sensitive topics, they must confront seriously and thoroughly the problems and issues that these topics pose. This issue of *American Behavioral Scientist* is a step in that direction.

◈ Note

1. Of course, problems of confidentiality do not arise only in relation to raw data. What Boruch and Cecil (1979) referred to as "deductive closure" is also possible. Here, particular or distinctive combinations of attributes permit the identification of individuals by secondary analysts or the readers of published reports. For a range of strategies for preserving the confidentiality of research data, see Borneo and Cecil (1979), Boruch (1979), and Campbell, Boruch, Schwartz, and Steinberg (1977). There are some situations in which these strategies may not be useful, such as when the identity of research participants is itself sensitive information. It is also the case that it is more difficult to maintain the confidentiality of qualitative data by technical means than it is for quantitative data. Yet qualitative researchers are facing mounting pressure to protect the confidentiality of their data, both from the growth of field research in applied settings, where there, may be greater likelihood of legal intervention (Broadhead 1984), and from the increasing use of computers to analyze qualitative data (Tesch, 1988). This last advance, in particular, has come about at a time when national data protection laws are becoming increasingly common (Akeroyd, 1988).

◇ References

Abrams, P. (1981). Visionaries and virtuosi: Competence and purpose in the education of sociologists. *Sociology, 15,* 530–538.

Akeroyd, A. V. (1988). Ethnography, personal data and computers: The implications of data protection legislation for qualitative social research. In R. G. Burgess (Ed.), *Studies in qualitative methodology: Vol. I. Conducting qualitative research* (pp. 179-200). Greenwich, CT: JAI.

Barnes, J. A. (1979). *Who should know what? Social science, privacy and ethics.* Harmondsworth: Penguin.

Becker, H. S. (1970). Practitioners of vice and crime. In R. Haberstein (Ed.), *Pathways to data* (pp. 30-49). Chicago: Aldine.

Biemacki, P., & Waldorf, D. (1981). Snowball sampling: Problems and techniques of chain referral sampling. *Sociological Methods and Research, 10,* 141–163.

Boruch, R. F. (1979). Methods of assuring personal integrity in social research: An introduction. In M. Bulmer (Ed.), *Censuses, surveys and privacy* (pp. 234-248). London: Macmillan.

Boruch, R. F., & Cecil, J. S. (1979). *Assuring the confidentiality of social research data.* Philadelphia: University of Pennsylvania Press.

Bradburn, N. M., & Sudman, S. (1979). *Improving interview method and questionnaire design.* San Francisco, Jossey-Bass.

Brailhwaite, J. (1985). Corporate crime research: Why two interviewers are needed. *Sociology, 19,* 136–138.

Brajuha, M., & Hallowell, L. (1986). Legal intrusion and the politics of fieldwork: The impact of the Brajuha case. *Urban Life,* 14, 454–478.

Broadhead, R. S. (1984). Human rights and human subjects: Ethics and strategies in social science research. *Sociological Inquiry, 54,* 107–123.

Broadhead, R. S., & Rist, R. C. (1976). Gatekeepers and the social control of social research. *Social Problems, 23,* 325–336.

Bulmer, M. (1982). *Social research ethics.* London: Macmillan.

Burton, F. (1978). *The politics of legitimacy: Struggles in a Belfast community.* London: Routledge & Kegan Paul.

Campbell, D. T., Boruch, R. F., Schwartz, R. D., & Steinberg, J. (1977). Confidentiality-preserving modes of access to files and interfile exchange for useful statistical analysis. *Evaluation Quarterly, 1,* 269–300.

Caplan, A. L. (1982). On privacy and confidentiality in social science research. In T. L. Beauchamp, R. R. Faden, R. J. Wallace, Jr., & L. Waters (Eds.), *Ethical issues in social science research* (pp. 315-325). Baltimore: Johns Hopkins University Press.

Ceci, S. J., Peters, D., & Plotkin, J. (1985). Human subjects review, personal values and the regulation of social science research. *American Psychologist, 40,* 994–1002.

Day, K. J. (1985). *Perspectives on privacy: A sociological analysis.* Unpublished doctoral dissertation, University of Edinburgh.

Dingwall, R. G. (1980). Ethics and ethnography. *Sociological Review,* 28, 871–891.

Ditton, J., & Williams, R. (1981). *The fundable versus the doable* (Occasional paper). Glasgow: University of Glasgow, Department of Sociology.

Douglas, J. D. (1976). *Investigative social research.* Beverly Hills, CA: Sage.

Duelli-Klein, R. (1983). How to do what we want to do: Thoughts about feminist methodology. In G. Bowles & R. Duelli-Klein (Eds.), *Theories of women's studies.* London: Routledge & Kegan Paul.

Flaherty, D. (1979). *Privacy and government data banks: An international comparison.* London: Mansell.

Galliher, J. F. (1973). The protection of human subjects: A reexamination of the Professional Code of Ethics. *American Sociologist, 9,* 93–100.

Galliher, J. F., & McCartney, J. L. (1973). The influence of funding agencies on juvenile delinquency research. *Social Problems, 21,* 77–90.

Gillespie, D. L., & Leffler, A. (1987). The politics of research methodology in claims-making activities: Social science and sexual harassment. *Social Problems, 34,* 490–501.

Goyder, J. (1987). *The silent minority: Non-respondents on sample surveys.* Cambridge: Polity.

Hammar, T. (1976). The political resocialization of immigrants project. In T. Dalenius & A. Klevamarken (Eds.), *Personal integrity and the need for data in the social sciences* (pp. 37–42). Stockholm: Swedish Council for Social Research.

Hanmer, J., & Leonard, D. (1984). Negotiating the problem: The OHSS and research on violence in marriage. In C. Bell & H. Roberts (Eds.), *Social researching: Politics, problems and practice* (pp. 32–65). London: Routledge & Kegan Paul.

Hartley, S. F. (1982);, Sampling strategies and the threat to privacy. In J. E. Sieber (Ed.), *The ethics of social research: Surveys and experiments* (pp. 167-190). New York: Springer-Verlag

Hessler, R. M., & Galliher, J. F. (1983). Institutional Review Boards and clandestine research: An experimental test. *Human Organization, 42,* 82–87.

Homan, R. (1978). Interpersonal communication in Pentecostal meetings. *Sociological Review, 26,* 499–518.

Homan, R., & Bulmer, M. (1982). On the merits of covert methods: A dialog. In M. Bulmer (Ed.), *Social research ethics* (pp. 105–121). London: Macmillan.

Hope, E., Kennedy, M., & De Winter, A. (1976). Homeworkers in North London. In D. L. Barker & S. Allen (Eds.), *Dependence and exploitation in work and marriage* (pp. 88-109). London: Longman.

Humphreys, L. (1970). *Tearoom trade: Impersonal sex in public places.* Chicago: Aldine.

Hunt, J. (1984). The development of rapport through the negotiation of gender in field work among police. *Human Organization, 43,* 283–296.

Janson, C. (1979). Privacy legislation and social research in Sweden. In E. Mochman & P. J. Mullaer (Eds.), *Data protection and social science research: Perspectives from ten countries* (pp. 27-47). Frankfurt: Campus Verlag.

Johnson, J. M. (1975). *Doing field research.* New York: Free Press,

Johnson, N. B. (1986). Ethnographic research and rites of incorporation: A sex- and gender-based comparison. In T. L. Whitehead & M. E. Conway (Eds.), *Self, sex and gender in cross-cultural fieldwork* (pp. 164–181). Urbana: University of Illinois Press.

Kimmel, A. J. (1988). *Ethics and values in applied social research*. Newbury Park, CA: Sage.

Kish, L. (1965). *Survey sampling*. New York: Wiley.

Klockars, C. (1985). *The idea of police*. Beverly Hills, CA: Sage.

Knerr, C. R. (1982). What to do before and after a subpoena of data arrives. In J. E. Sieber (Ed.), *The ethics of social research: Surveys and experiments* (pp. 191-206). New York: Springer-Verlag.

Lee, R. M. (1981). *Interreligious courtship and marriage in Northern Ireland*. Unpublished doctoral dissertation, University of Edinburgh.

Loseke, D. R., & Cahill, S. E. (1984). The social construction of deviance: Experts on battered women. *Social Problems, 31*, 296–310.

Macintyre, A. (1982). Risk, harm and benefit assessments as instruments of moral evaluation, In T. L. Beauchamp, R. R. Faden, R. J. Wallace, Jr., & L. Waters (Eds.), *Ethical issues in social science research* (pp. 175–189). Baltimore: Johns Hopkins University Press.

Maguire, P. (1987). *Doing participatory research: A feminist approach*. Amherst: Center for International Education, University of Massachusetts.

Matza, D. (1969). *Becoming deviant*. Englewood Cliffs, NJ: Prentice-Hall.

McRae, S. (1986). *Cross-class families*. Oxford: Clarendon.

Melton, G. B., & Gray, J. N. (1988). Ethical dilemmas in AIDS research: Individual privacy and public health. *American Psychologist, 42*, 735–741.

Moore, J. (1973). Social constraints on sociological knowledge: Academics and research concerning minorities. *Social Problems, 21*, 65–77.

Nelson, R. L., & Hedrick, T. E. (1983). The statutory protection of confidential research data: Synthesis and evaluation. In R. F. Boruch & J. S. Cecil (Eds.), *Solutions to ethical and legal problems in social research* (pp. 213–236). New York: Academic Press.

Plummer, K. (1981). Researching into homosexualities. In K. Plummer (Ed.), *The making of the modern homosexual* (pp. 211–230). London: Hutchinson.

Plummer, K. (1983). *Documents of life: An introduction to the problems and literature of a humanistic method*. London: Allen & Unwin.

Punch, M. (1986). *The politics and ethics of fieldwork*. Beverly Hills, CA: Sage.

Record, J. C. (1967). The research institute and the pressure group. In G. Sjoberg (Ed.), *Ethics, politics and social research* (pp. 25–49). Cambridge, MA: Schenckman.

Reiss, A. J. (1979). Government regulation in scientific inquiry: Some paradoxical consequences. In C. B. Klockars & F. W. O'Connor (Eds.), *Deviance and decency: The ethics of research with human subjects* (pp. 61–95). Beverly Hills, CA: Sage.

Renzetti, C. M. (1988). Violence in lesbian relationships: A preliminary analysis of causal factors. *Journal of Interpersonal Violence, 3*, 381–399.

Rothbart, G. S., Fine, M., & Sudman, S. (1982). On finding and interviewing the needles in a haystack: The use of multiplicity sampling. *Public Opinion Quarterly, 45*, 408–421.

Seigel, K., & Bauman, L. J. (1986). Methodological issues in AIDS-related research. In D. A. Feldman & T. M. Johnson (Eds.), *The social dimensions of AIDS* (pp. 15–39). New York: Praeger.

Sieber, J. E., & Stanley, B. (1988). Ethical and professional dimensions of socially sensitive research. *American Psychologist, 43*, 49–55.

Sjoberg, G., & Nett, R. (1968). *A methodology for social research*. New York: Harper & Row.

Stanley, B., Sieber, J. E., & Melton, G. B. (1987). Empirical studies of ethical issues in research: A research agenda. *American Psychologist, 42*, 735–741.

Sudman, S., & Kalton, G. (1986) New developments in the sampling of special populations. *Annual Review of Sociology, 12*, 401–429.

Sudman, S., Sirken, M. G., & Curran, C. D. (1988). Sampling rare and elusive populations. *Science, 240*, 991–996.

Taylor, R. (1988). Social, scientific research on the "troubles" in Northern Ireland. *Economic and Social Review*, 19, 123–145.

Tesch, R. (1988). Computer software and qualitative analysis: A reassessment In G. Blank, J. L. McCartney, & E. Brent (Eds.), *New technology in sociology* (pp. 141–154). New Brunswick, NJ: Transaction Books.

Troiden, R. R. (1987). Walking the line: The personal and professional risks of sex education and research: *Teaching Sociology, 15*, 241–249.

Useem, M., & Mara, G. T. (1983). Ethical dilemmas and political considerations. In R. B. Smith (Ed.), *Handbook of social science methods: Vol. 1. An introduction to social research* (pp. 169–200). Cambridge: Ballinger.

Van Maanen, J. (1988). *Tales of the field*. Chicago: University of Chicago Press.

Wallis, R. (1977). The moral career of a research project In C. Bell & H. Newby (Eds.), *Doing sociological research* (pp. 149–167). London: Allen & Unwin.

Warren, C.A.B. (1988). *Gender issues in field research*. New bury Park, CA: Sage.

Weinberg, M., & Williams, C. J. (1972). Fieldwork among deviants: Social relations with subjects and others. In J. D. Douglas (Ed.), *Research on deviance* (pp. 165–186). New York: Random House.

Zimbardo, P. G. (1973). On the ethics of intervention in human psychological research: With special reference to the Stanford prison experiment. *Cognition, 2*, 243–256.

PART II

Traditional Approaches to Studying Deviance

CHAPTER 4

Anomie/Strain Theory

> In April 1992, a young man from a well-to-do East Coast family hitchhiked to Alaska and walked alone into the wilderness north of Mt. McKinley. Four months later his decomposed body was found by a party of moose hunters. . . .
>
> His name turned out to be Christopher Johnson McCandless. He'd grown up, I learned, in an affluent suburb of Washington, D.C., where he'd excelled academically and had been an elite athlete.
>
> Immediately after graduation, with honors, from Emory University in the summer of 1990, McCandless dropped out of sight. He changed his name, gave the entire balance of a twenty-four-thousand-dollar savings account to charity, abandoned his car and most of his possessions, burned all the cash in his wallet. And then he invented a new life for himself, taking up residence at the ragged margin of society, wandering across North America in search of raw, transcendent experience. His family had no idea where he was or what had become of him until his remains turned up in Alaska.
>
> Jon Krakauer (1996), *Into the Wild*, Author's Note. Copyright ©1996 by Jon Krakauer. Published by Anchor Books, a division of Random House, Inc.

◈ Introduction

Christopher McCandless grew up in a conforming, upper-middle-class family and seemed to be on the fast track to success. He graduated from Emory University with a 3.72 grade point average, and he spoke of going to law school. Instead, he turned his back on his family, adopted the new name of Alexander Supertramp, and set out to make his way alone in the wilderness. How might we explain this drastic turnaround and McCandless's blatant rejection of societal norms and expectations?

Anomie/strain theories are among the first truly sociological explanations of the causes of deviant behavior. These theories seek to understand deviance by focusing on social structures and patterns that emerge as individuals and groups react to conditions they have little control over. The question these theories address is, how exactly does the structure of society constrain behavior and cause deviance?

Strain theories are generally macro-level theories, and they share several core assumptions: first, the idea that social order is the product of a generally cohesive set of norms; second, that those norms are widely shared by community members; and third, that deviance and community reactions to deviance are essential to maintaining order.

Emile Durkheim and Anomie

Emile Durkheim's classic statement of **anomie** set the stage for one of the most important theoretical traditions in criminology. Durkheim is often considered the father of sociology. In one of his major works, he studied suicide in 19th-century Europe. While suicide is often considered a very individualistic and personal act, Durkheim effectively argued that characteristics of communities influence suicide rates, independent of the particular individuals living in those communities. He found that some countries had consistently high rates of suicide over several decades, while other countries had consistently low rates. How to explain these macro-level differences?

In brief, Durkheim argued that suicide was related to the amount of regulation in a society and the degree of group unity. For Durkheim, social integration and social change are key factors in deviant behavior. As a society undergoes rapid change, norms will be unclear and a state of anomie will result. Anomie is a state of normlessness where society fails to effectively regulate the expectations or behaviors of its members; it occurs when aspirations are allowed to develop beyond the possibility of fulfillment. In better functioning societies, ambitions are restrained and human needs and desires are regulated by the collective order.

Durkheim argued that "no living being can be happy or even exist unless his needs are sufficiently proportioned to his means" (Durkheim, 1897/1951, p. 246). In Durkheim's understanding, society alone held the moral power over the individual to moderate expectations and limit passions. Durkheim suggested that a state of anomie, or normlessness, results from a breakdown in the regulation of goals; with such lack of regulation, individuals' aspirations become unlimited and deviance may result. Durkheim argued that in a stable society, individuals are generally content with their positions or, as later scholars interpreted, they "aspire to achieve only what is realistically possible for them to achieve" (Cloward & Ohlin, 1960, p. 78).

A macro-level example may clarify the concept of anomie: Think back to what you know about the 1960s in the United States. What was happening nationally at that time? The country was undergoing enormous changes as the civil rights movement took hold, women became more liberated and fought for equal rights, and America sent its young men to war in Vietnam. There was rapid and significant social change. Imagine what it would have been like to be a college student in the 1960s—whole new worlds of opportunities and challenges were opening for women and minorities. What should young people expect? How high could they aspire to go? The answers simply were not clear; the old norms no longer applied. With norms and expectations unclear for a large segment of the society, anomie theory would lead us to expect higher rates of deviance.

Anomie might also be applied to the normative expectations for physical attractiveness. Think for a moment about the standard for female beauty in the United States. Is there one ideal type? Or are there common characteristics we can identify? One trait that has been idealized for decades is that female beauties are nearly always thin, sometimes dangerously thin. Fashion models in magazines and walking the runway are very tall and extremely thin. They spend hours being tended to by professional hair and makeup artists, being photographed by the best photographers in the world, and even so, their photos are often airbrushed and Photoshopped to make the already beautiful absolutely perfect.

This vision of ideal beauty is pervasive in the media. Young women (and increasingly young men) are exposed to unrealistic expectations of how they should aspire to look. For a time, network television shows glorified improving one's looks through plastic surgery with "reality" shows like *The Swan* and *I Want a Famous Face*. To frame this in terms of the theory, society has failed to regulate the expectations of its members when it comes to physical attractiveness, and we see deviance in the form of eating disorders and extensive elective plastic surgery resulting.

◈ Robert Merton and Adaptations to Anomie/Strain

Informed by Durkheim's writing on anomie, Robert K. Merton narrowed the focus and extended the theory to the United States in his 1938 article on "Social Structure and Anomie." Merton argued that anomie does not result simply from unregulated goals but rather from a faulty relationship between cultural goals and the legitimate means to access them. While we are all socialized to desire success, we do not all have the same opportunities to become successful; thus, Merton defined several adaptations to anomie and strain.

Merton, himself, was born Meyer Schkolnick, the son of Eastern European Jewish immigrants. He grew up in poverty in a "benign slum" in south Philadelphia. He legally changed to the "Americanized" name of Robert King Merton after he earned a scholarship to Temple University and entered college; he went to Harvard for his PhD and became a professor at Columbia University and one of the most famous sociologists in the world. His own story seems to capture a piece of the "American Dream." Growing up in the pre-Depression era, there was, according to Merton, a sense of "limitless possibilities." As Cullen and Messner (2007) suggest, this sense of limitless possibilities is illuminating. It relates to Merton's view not simply that Americans were urged to pursue some rigidly defined goal of success but rather that there also was a broad cultural message that everyone—even those in Merton's impoverished circumstances—could seek social mobility and expect to enjoy a measure of success (p. 14).

Given this biographical background, Merton's ideas begin to come to life. In "Social Structure and Anomie" (1938), Merton focused on the needs, desires, and processes of cultural socialization. He argued that in the United States, we are all socialized to believe in the sense of limitless possibilities and to desire success on a large scale. These cultural goals are widespread; the problem, however, is that the social structure "restricts or completely eliminates access to approved modes of acquiring these symbols for *a considerable part of the same population*" (p. 680). In other words, **structural impediments** or obstacles exist for whole classes of people who wish to attain wealth using legitimate means. For those in the lower classes who share the cultural goals for success but have limited means to attain them, lack of education and job opportunities create a strain toward anomie, which may translate into deviance.

Merton argued that there are five general adaptations to anomie. The key to each is whether there is an acceptance or rejection of the cultural goal of success (or to adopt a concept that is easier to measure, wealth attainment) and whether or not the choice is to strive for the goal via legitimate or conforming means.

Merton's Adaptations to Anomie

Conformity is the most common adaptation. Conformists have accepted the cultural goal of success or wealth attainment, and they are trying to achieve it via legitimate means. Most college students might be considered conformists as they work hard to earn degrees to get better jobs and have more success after graduation. For Merton, conformity was the only nondeviant adaptation to strain and anomie.

Innovation is the adaptation for those who have accepted the cultural goal of success/wealth attainment but are trying to achieve it via illegitimate means. Any crime for profit would be an example of innovation: Robbers, thieves, drug dealers, embezzlers, and high-priced call girls all would be classified as innovators in Merton's adaptations.

Ritualism is the category for those who have abandoned the cultural goal of success/wealth attainment but continue to use legitimate means to make their living. The dedicated workers who will never advance to management might be considered ritualists in Merton's typology.

Retreatism is the adaptation of those who have rejected the cultural goal of success/wealth attainment and have also rejected the legitimate means. Merton describes people who adapt in this way as "in the society but not of it. Sociologically, these constitute the true aliens" (Merton, 1957, p. 153). The chronically homeless and serious drug addicts might be considered retreatists in this model. Christopher McCandless, from this chapter's opening story, is a vivid individual example of a retreatist. He clearly rejected the conforming goals and lifestyle of his parents and the larger society; he chose instead to exist in the margins, occasionally working low-level jobs, hitching rides, and ultimately attempting to live off the land in Alaska.

Rebellion is the category for political deviants—those who don't play by the rules but work to change the system to their own liking. Rebels reject the cultural goal of success/wealth attainment and replace it with another primary goal; they may use either legitimate or illegitimate means to achieve this goal—one way to think about it is that rebels will use whatever means necessary to reach their chosen goal. Perhaps the clearest example of rebellion would be terrorist groups, who often use violence in an attempt to achieve political goals.

Figure 4.1   Robert K. Merton's Deviance Typology

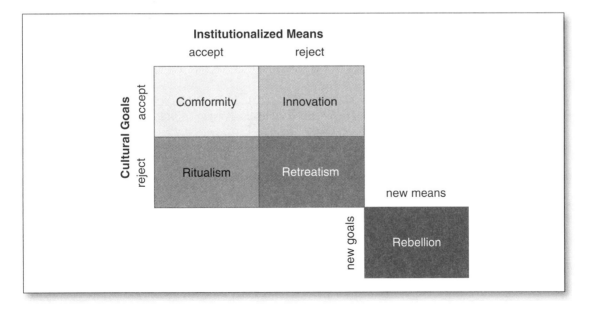

Merton's 1938 article on "Social Structure and Anomie" (SS&A) remains one of the most influential and referenced works in all of criminology and sociology. Reflecting on his seminal ideas in an interview five decades later, Merton observed that

It holds up those goals of success, especially economic, as a legitimate expectation for everybody. You do not have statements anywhere in the history of American aspirations that say: "You the poor, and you the ethnically subordinate—you can have no hopes or legitimate expectation of upward social mobility." You have never heard that said . . . call it rhetoric, call it ideology, call it myth, call it what you will, call it the American Dream. . . . Now that is not typical of other cultural structures and other historical times and places. So it is a very powerful, if you will, theoretically sensitized observation. . . . SS&A '38 was saying what is universal for all is the legitimacy of striving to better yourself, to rise upward and onward. . . . That's the universal thing and that differs from other cultures . . . in which you say: "Of course, you have no right; you are a servant class and you know your place." . . . Now that's the dynamic new component of the cultural structure, and that is what is being said—what is common to all. (Cullen & Messner, 2007, p. 24)

▲ **Photo 4.1**   This photo might represent either conformity or ritualism in Merton's adaptations. Which concept do you think it best illustrates? Why do you think so?

DEVIANCE IN POPULAR CULTURE

Robert Merton's ideas on strain theory and particularly the adaptation of innovation can be easily seen in many movies dealing with the drug trade, audacious heists, kidnappers holding victims for ransom, or virtually any other crime for profit. Many examples are available, including the following:

Blow—a movie based on the true story of George Jung, a working-class kid who built an illegal empire and attained the cultural goal of wealth attainment, making a fortune via illegitimate means first by dealing marijuana and then importing cocaine.

Set It Off—A fictional story of four young African American women struggling to survive in Los Angeles. As their personal troubles mount, they begin robbing banks to solve their money woes.

Merton's other adaptations are less common in film, as they often make for less dramatic stories, but they are represented in popular culture:

Leaving Las Vegas—the story of an alcoholic man who has lost his wife and family and goes to Las Vegas to literally drink himself to death may be viewed as an example of Merton's retreatism.

Murder in Mississippi—a film based on the true story of the murder of three civil rights workers in Mississippi in 1964. The civil rights workers might be viewed as rebels in Merton's typology: They are working and risking their lives for social change. While this was clearly considered deviant in the South, it is another good illustration of how norms and boundaries change over time, perhaps in response to positive deviance and collective action.

As you watch films over the next few weeks and months, try to keep the sociological theories of deviance in mind. It may surprise you how many can easily be applied to the stories and perspectives on the screen.

◈ Richard Cloward and Lloyd Ohlin, Differential Opportunity

Richard Cloward was a student of Merton's and undoubtedly knew his work well. Cloward added an important dimension to anomie/strain theory by extending our focus to include the idea of illegitimate means. Cloward (1959) argued that while not everyone has equal access to the legitimate means of attaining wealth, we cannot assume that everyone has access to illegitimate means either. This is a key point—imagine that you wanted to become a successful drug dealer. Where would you begin? Would you know where to purchase your product? Would you know where to access customers and how to gain their trust and their business? Would you be able to keep your illicit business going without getting caught and punished? Cloward's point makes perfect sense in this context: Just because you might wish to gain wealth and success via illegitimate means does not mean that you will have the skills and connections to do so.

Cloward teamed up with Lloyd Ohlin in 1960 to write the book *Delinquency and Opportunity.* Just as Cloward was a student of Merton's, Ohlin was a student of Donald Sutherland's, and he was well versed in the ideas of differential association (see Chapter 6 for more details on Sutherland and differential association). They found a research puzzle to be explored in Merton's work: While Merton may generally be accurate in describing pressures and motivations that lead to deviant behavior, the particular type of deviant behavior is unexplained. Cloward and Ohlin argued that we need to understand not just the motivations of individuals to commit deviant behavior but also the availability of opportunities to learn about and participate in illegal or deviant acts.

Cloward and Ohlin incorporated Sutherland's ideas into their theory and argued that criminal and deviant behavior is learned like any other behavior and, importantly, that not everyone has the same opportunities to learn criminal skills and have criminal careers. Their particular focus was on delinquent gangs and the circumstances under which different types of gangs emerged. They focused on neighborhood conditions (still a macro-level theory) and the opportunities available to learn and practice legitimate or illegitimate skills. Ultimately, Cloward and Ohlin suggested that only neighborhoods in which crime flourishes as a stable institution are fertile criminal learning environments for the young.

To further clarify their ideas, Cloward and Ohlin argued that the different kinds of illegitimate opportunities available in poor urban neighborhoods lead to three types of criminal subcultures: criminal, conflict, and retreatist. Because the focus is on disadvantaged neighborhoods, the assumption is that most young people growing up in these conditions will have poor and limited legitimate opportunities for attaining wealth and success. Thus, the availability of illegitimate opportunities becomes extremely important in shaping the deviance that takes place in these neighborhoods and the types of adolescent gangs that develop.

Criminal subcultures develop among lower-class adolescent boys in neighborhoods with open illegitimate opportunity structures. These neighborhoods are characterized by systematic, organized crime, and they provide an outlet in illegal employment for youths to attain wealth and "get paid" via illegitimate means. Successful criminals populate the neighborhood and become visible, distinctive role models for children growing up in the community. For those young people who aspire to emulate their illegitimate role models, there is generally an age-graded criminal structure in place where young males may do low-level jobs and learn from the older criminals in the neighborhood. In this way, social learning takes place, and the young acquire the skills and norms to fully take advantage of the illegitimate opportunities available to them. Compared to alternative poor neighborhoods, those with criminal subcultures are very structured and are relatively safe places to grow up and live. There is an absence of violence in these neighborhoods because violence—and the attention it draws—would be considered disruptive to both criminal and conventional activities.

Conflict subcultures develop in disorganized communities where illegitimate opportunities are largely absent and those that exist are closed to adolescents (see Chapter 5 for more information on social disorganization). Such neighborhoods are characterized by social instability, and youth growing up in these conditions are deprived of both conventional (legitimate) and criminal (illegitimate) opportunities. As Cloward and Ohlin (1960) explained it, "The disorganized slum . . . contains the outcasts of the criminal world . . . what crime there is tends to be individualistic, unorganized, petty, poorly paid, and unprotected" (pp. 173–174). With no real access to legitimate or illegitimate opportunities, adolescents growing up in disorganized neighborhoods suffer acute frustration and turn to violence to prove their personal worth. Social controls are weak in these areas, and violence for violence's sake is valued. With few role models and little chance at success, young men work to earn the toughest reputation and, through their physical prowess, to command some level of respect and deference from those around them.

Retreatist subcultures are associated with drug use and the drug culture among some lower-class adolescents. Cloward and Ohlin characterized adolescents in retreatist subcultures as "double failures" who cannot find a place for themselves in either criminal or conflict subcultures. While closely related to Merton's concept of retreatists, Cloward and Ohlin directed attention to the social environment and the conditions that help to explain the formation of each type of deviant subculture. The "double failures" in poor neighborhoods may withdraw from the larger society and retreat into drug use and relative isolation.

It is important to remember that Cloward and Ohlin are still explaining deviance at the macro level. Criminal, conflict, and retreatist subcultures develop primarily because communities are organized differently and offer varying legitimate and illegitimate opportunities.

◈ Robert Agnew—General Strain Theory

Anomie and strain theories have a long history in sociology and criminology and have surged and waned in popularity over the years. Classic strain theories dominated criminological research in the 1950s and 1960s, and their relevance was marked in public policy of the time, particularly in strain theory's impact on the War on Poverty during the 1960s (Cullen & Agnew, 2006). Strain theory came under attack in the 1970s as relativist theorists shifted the focus to conflict and labeling theories (see Chapters 8 and 9), offering a new perspective on societal influences on both crime and punishment.

Robert Agnew (1992) breathed new life into the tradition with his **general strain theory (GST).** Strain theory focuses on what circumstances lead individuals and groups within a society to engage in deviant behavior. Agnew suggests that they are "pressured into crime." Along with the failure to achieve valued goals, Agnew argues that strain may also result from negative relationships. Agnew specifies three major types of negative relations where others

1. prevent or threaten to prevent the achievement of positively valued goals (for example, preventing monetary success or popularity with peers),

2. remove or threaten to remove positive stimuli (for example, the death of a parent or the breakup of a romantic relationship),

3. present or threaten to present negative stimuli (for example, physical assaults, failing grades, public insults).

Such negative relations will likely lead to anger and frustration, which may then lead to deviant behavior, such as physical violence, running away from home, illicit drug use, or self-harming behavior.

Agnew (2006) argues that some types of strain are more likely to cause crime and deviance than others. He identifies the following characteristics as most likely to cause crime: The strain is high in magnitude, the strain is seen as unjust, the strain is associated with low self-control, and the strain creates some pressure or incentive for criminal coping. More specifically, examples of strains that are likely to cause crime include parental rejection, erratic or excessively harsh discipline, child abuse and neglect, negative school experiences, abusive peer relationships, chronic unemployment, marital problems, criminal victimization, residence in economically deprived neighborhoods, and discrimination based on characteristics such as race/ethnicity and gender.

Agnew is careful to point out that not all individuals respond to strains with crime and deviance, and, in fact, most people cope in legal and conforming ways. There are many possible coping strategies, including behavioral coping, cognitive coping, and emotional coping (Agnew, 2006). The resources and social support available to the individuals are important: Do they have conforming friends and family they can turn to for help? Do they associate with criminal others? What is their level of self-control? Is the cost of criminal coping high or low? For some individuals, there is low risk in criminal or deviant coping because they have little to lose—they may not have jobs or close relationships that would be put at risk with criminal or deviant acts. While it is difficult to tease out the exact impact of each of these factors, Agnew argues that whether by personality traits, socialization, or learned attitudes and behavior, some individuals are simply more disposed to crime than are others.

STUDIES IN DEVIANCE

Stress and Deviance in Policing

By Michael L. Arter (2008), in *Deviant Behavior, 29*, 43–69

Policing, as a whole, is one of the most stressful occupations in the United States. But even within policing, certain assignments are considered much more stressful than others. One of these assignments is undercover police work. Arter uses general strain theory to examine these stressful assignments and the reported deviant responses that many police in these assignments report engaging in.

Arter interviewed 32 police officers who were currently in an undercover position, had been in an undercover position in the past, or had never held an undercover position. In addition to discussing the types and levels of stress associated with all of their policing duties, Arter also had the interview participants discuss their perceived deviant behaviors. Arter defined deviance in a couple ways: (1) as behavior that was considered deviant by the department (the officer could be sanctioned for it) or a violation of the law and, using a phenomenological approach, (2) as a behavior that the participant defined as deviant, whether it was a departmental or a legal violation.

Arter found that individuals in exceptionally stressful policing positions were more likely to report deviant behavior than those in less stressful policing positions. In addition, he found that if stress was reduced through reassignment out of an undercover position, deviant behavior also decreased.

◈ Steven Messner and Richard Rosenfeld: Crime and American Dream—Institutional Anomie Theory

Messner and Rosenfeld (2007) turn attention to the American Dream and how it contributes to crime and deviance:

> The essence of our argument is that the distinctive patterns and levels of crime in the United States are produced by the cultural and structural organization of American society. A strong emphasis on the goal of monetary success and a weak emphasis on the importance of the legitimate means for the pursuit of success characterize American culture. This combination of strong pressures to succeed monetarily and weak restraints on the selection of means is intrinsic to the dominant cultural ethos: the American Dream. The "American Dream" refers to a cultural commitment to the goal of economic success to be pursued by everyone under conditions of open, individual competition. The American Dream contributes to crime directly by encouraging people to employ illegal means to achieve goals that are culturally approved. (p. x)

Messner and Rosenfeld argue that the American Dream fosters an "anything goes" mentality when pursuing personal goals. They go on to identify the values underlying the American Dream as follows: achievement, individualism, universalism, and materialism. Achievement is connected to personal worth; Messner and Rosenfeld argue that the cultural pressures to achieve are enormous, and failure to achieve is often perceived as a failure to make any sort of meaningful contribution to society. Individualism encourages everyone to find a way to "make it" on his or her own. Within this framework of intense competition to succeed, others in the society are viewed as competitors and rivals, and thus, general restraints on behavior are disregarded in the pursuit of personal goals. Universalism echoes Merton's ideas that virtually everyone in American society is encouraged to aspire to success and wealth attainment. Messner and Rosenfeld point out that while everyone may dream about success, "the hazards of failure are also universal" (p. 70). Materialism is the last value that underlies the American Dream. Money has special significance in American culture; it is the preeminent way in which we measure success and achievement.

At the institutional level, Messner and Rosenfeld argue that the major institutions in the United States, including the family, school, and political system, are all dominated by economic institutions. Noneconomic goals and accomplishments are valued much less than economic pursuits and gains, and economic norms have infiltrated and overpowered other important societal institutions.

Messner and Rosenfeld suggest that the American Dream leads to crime and deviance because of its exaggerated emphasis on monetary success and its resistance to restraint or limits on individual pursuit of success. Thus, they extend Merton's idea that the very fabric of American society promotes at least some level of deviance. Even as we all aspire to achieve and believe it is possible to realize our dreams, the social structure constrains pathways to success and leads to deviance as a segment of society pursues alternative success models by any means necessary.

▲ Photo 4.2   Do you agree with Messner and Rosenfeld that the American Dream fosters an "anything goes" attitude when pursuing monetary success?

◈ Contemporary/Empirical Studies in the Anomie and Strain Tradition

Today, classic strain theory has renewed support, and it is used to examine group differences in crime rates, economic inequality, and relative deprivation. Agnew continues to actively revise and refine his ideas on general strain theory. Many, many studies have tested pieces of Agnew's theory and offer limited support; there are still many hypothesizes to be discovered, tested, and explained. While research on general strain theory is quite easy to find in the sociological and criminological literature, in the following we highlight three studies that explore different aspects of anomie and strain.

Anomie and the Abuse at Abu Ghraib

A recent study analyzed the abuse at Abu Ghraib prison in Iraq in terms of Durkheim's concept of anomie (Mestrovic & Lorenzo, 2008). You may remember the vivid images of American soldiers torturing and humiliating Iraqi prisoners: Photos were published of soldiers threatening the nude men with snarling dogs, smiling over the bodies of dead Iraqis, forcing the prisoners to walk around and pose nude with hoods and blindfolds blocking their vision, and offering a "thumbs-up" to the cameras as they posed in front of literal piles of prisoners in humiliating positions.

Mestrovic and Lorenzo (2008) argue that there were high levels of social disorganization or anomie at Abu Ghraib and within the social structures of the U.S. Army, other government agencies, civilian contractors, and others who interacted with and had responsibility for the prisoners at Abu Ghraib. The authors argue that the social system at Abu Ghraib was disorganized and anomic from the outset and grew progressively worse over time; this confusion produced widespread deviance among prisoners and U.S. personnel alike.

Mestrovic and Lorenzo (2008) identify several sources of confusion that contributed to the anomie and deviance, including confusion as to who was in charge, insufficient training, lack of social integration within the military units at Abu Ghraib, rapid changes in the social milieu, intense pressure to obtain intelligence, confusion as to which norms to follow, "unhealthy mystique," failure of self-correcting mechanisms, and cultural insensitivity. The authors go on to explain,

▲ **Photo 4.3** American soldiers purposely degraded and humiliated Iraqi prisoners at Abu Ghraib. How does Durkheim's theory of anomie help to explain such abuse?

The extent of social disorganization, social chaos, dysfunction, lack of coordination, and of a general state of *anomie* was so great at Abu Ghraib that abuse and the breaking of norms that are documented was the *inevitable* outcome and should have been expected. (p. 202)

We have included a longer excerpt from Mestrovic and Lorenzo's article in the readings for this chapter so that you can read the primary source and think more deeply about their claims as they relate to anomie.

The American Dream and Incarcerated Young Men

Another recent article focused on boys in a juvenile prison who held deeply to the idea of the American Dream but had few legitimate means to achieve it (Inderbitzin, 2007). The decline of manufacturing jobs and their replacement with low-wage and unskilled work has made it difficult for young men, particularly those with poor educations, to be successful. The ongoing racism experienced by minorities in the labor market imposes an additional barrier to economic success through legitimate mean; as such, the loss of viable work for young, poorly educated, minority males seems inextricably linked to their criminal behavior. Committing crimes for profit can help such young men meet their financial needs and counter threats to their self-perception as competent men. It may be, too, that the American Dream holds particular relevance for minority males:

Money and material possessions can be terribly important to those who do not have them and lack access to conventional opportunities for obtaining them. This may be especially the case among Blacks, who are generally devalued in American society because of their race and who often are denied access to the broader criteria of prestige available to Whites. In this sort of environment, a

material/monetary yardstick becomes a critical and very tangible symbol of having "made it."
(Cernkovich, Giordano, & Rudolph, 2000, p. 150)

The young men in the study followed the lure of money and status into illegal endeavors that led to confrontations with the law and conforming society. Profit or "getting paid" (M. L. Sullivan, 1989) was frequently cited as one of the main motivating factors in their crimes. They were examples of Merton's innovators—"men who hold fast to culturally emphasized goals while abandoning culturally approved ways of seeking them" (Merton, 1964, p. 218). Thus, Merton's ideas remain both useful and relevant some eight decades after the publication of "Social Structure and Anomie."

Institutional Anomie Theory and Student Cheating

One attempt to extend and refine Messner and Rosenfeld's (2007) **institutional anomie theory** took their ideas and applied them to individual student cheating. Muftic (2006) sought to test the idea that the exaggerated emphasis on economic success in the United States has bled into other social institutions, including academia. She surveyed American and international undergraduate students and asked them about their cheating behavior and their economic goals. Results suggested that American students were more oriented to economic goals and were more likely to admit to cheating: "Students with higher adherence to the cultural values of universalism and the fetishism of money had a higher likelihood of cheating. . . . Location of birth (i.e., born in the United States) appeared to have the strongest impact on cheating" (Muftic, 2006, p. 648).

While she found some support for institutional anomie theory, Muftic also points out that adherence to the American Dream is not universal. Even in a fairly homogeneous sample, American students embraced the cultural ideal at varying levels. Muftic concludes her article by suggesting that both micro-level (neighborhood cohesiveness, levels of informal social control) and macro-level (poverty, family disruption, racial heterogeneity, and social mobility) analyses be combined in future studies of institutional anomie theory.

◈ Critiques of Anomie and Strain Theories

Messner and Rosenfeld (2007) discuss four primary critiques of Merton's argument and anomie theory. First, Merton assumes that value consensus exists in society and that the goal of monetary success is held above all. As Muftic (2006) pointed out, we should not assume those values are universal; other goals may be equally important, or more important, for many Americans. Second, Merton's theory and many versions of classical strain theory are class biased and have difficulty accounting for deviance among the privileged classes. Third, Merton seems to suggest that providing more equal opportunity offers a realistic solution to crime and deviance in the United States; Messner and Rosenfeld do not believe this to be the case. Finally, Merton never precisely defines anomie.

Messner and Rosenfeld (2007) dispense with the first two critiques as being oversimplified readings of Merton's argument, suggesting that Merton never claimed complete value consensus but that monetary success is a particularly powerful benchmark in the United States. Furthermore, Merton's basic argument can be used to explain deviance and criminal behavior in the middle and upper classes as well, as the definition of success is relative and must still be achieved despite structural constraints.

Conclusion

Anomie and strain theories have a more clearly developed history than other theoretical traditions. Nearly everyone can agree that these ideas began with Durkheim and Merton and were extended in important ways by Cloward and Ohlin and a handful of other theorists. One recent revision of the theory views strain as a function of **relative deprivation.** In this model, the reference group is a key element. Your own absolute success or wealth is less important than your position relative to those around you. Comparing yourself to those with more wealth and more material success may lead to strain and deviant behavior. Today, Messner and Rosenfeld's institutional anomie theory might be considered the leading version of anomie theory, and Agnew's general strain theory might be considered the leading version of strain theory (Cullen & Agnew, 2006).

Research continues on both anomie and strain theories. More sophisticated methods are allowing for analyses that bridge both macro-level and micro-level variables, which will offer an ever-increasing understanding of how cultural goals and the social structure affect individuals and lead to deviant behavior.

NOW YOU . . . USE THE THEORY

The following is a graph of the suicide rates in the United States between 1950 and 2003. Note that the data are broken down by age and gender. Using anomie or general strain theory, explain the following:

The overall trend (all ages, age adjusted) between 1950 and 2003. Start by describing the trend; then choose one of the two theories to explain it.

The trend, over time, for 45- to 64-year-olds between 1950 and 2003. Start by describing the trend; then choose one of the two theories to explain it.

The trend for male suicides and female suicides over time. According to one of the two theories, why might women always be less likely to engage in suicidal behavior than men?

U.S. Suicide Rates, 1950–2003 (per 100,000 population)

	1950	1960	1970	1980	1990	1995	2000	2001	2002	2003
All ages, age adjusted	13.2	13.2	13.2	13.2	12.5	11.8	10.4	10.7	10.9	10.8
5–14 years	0.2	0.3	0.3	0.4	0.8	0.9	0.7	0.7	0.6	0.6
15–24 years	4.5	5.2	8.8	12.3	13.2	13.0	10.2	9.9	9.9	9.7
15–19 years	2.7	3.6	5.9	8.5	11.1	10.3	8.0	7.9	7.4	7.3
20–24 years	6.2	7.1	12.2	16.1	15.1	15.8	12.5	12.0	12.4	12.1
25–44 years	11.6	12.2	15.4	15.6	15.2	15.1	13.4	13.8	14.0	13.8
25–34 years	9.1	10.0	14.1	16.0	15.2	15.0	12.0	12.8	12.6	12.7

	1950	1960	1970	1980	1990	1995	2000	2001	2002	2003
35–44 years	14.3	14.2	16.9	15.4	15.3	15.1	14.5	14.7	15.3	14.9
45–64 years	23.5	22.0	20.6	15.9	15.3	13.9	13.5	14.4	14.9	15.0
45–54 years	20.9	20.7	20.0	15.9	14.8	14.4	14.4	15.2	15.7	15.9
55–64 years	26.8	23.7	21.4	15.9	16.0	13.2	12.1	13.1	13.6	13.8
65 years and over	30.0	24.5	20.8	17.6	20.5	17.9	15.2	15.3	15.6	14.6
65–74 years	29.6	23.0	20.8	16.9	17.9	15.7	12.5	13.3	13.5	12.7
75–84 years	31.1	27.9	21.2	19.1	24.9	20.6	17.6	17.4	17.7	16.4
85 years and over	28.8	26.0	19.0	19.2	22.2	21.3	19.6	17.5	18.0	16.9
Male, all ages	21.2	20.0	19.8	19.9	21.5	20.3	17.7	18.2	18.4	18.0
Female, all ages	5.6	5.6	7.4	5.7	4.8	4.3	4.0	4.0	4.2	4.2

Source: Graph from World Health Organization.

EXERCISES AND DISCUSSION QUESTIONS

1. Provide another example of a state of anomie. How did it affect rates of deviance?

2. Give a specific example of each of Merton's five adaptations.

3. What are the policy recommendations you might make based on Cloward and Ohlin's ideas? In other words, using Cloward and Ohlin's ideas on delinquency and opportunity, what programs might be put into place to prevent crime and deviance?

4. Institutional anomie theory argues that our economic goals and system have permeated and overrun other social systems/institutions in the United States. Do you think this is true? Can you think of examples from politics, education, and families?

5. Do you think that Agnew is correct that individuals are pressured into crime and deviance? Can you think of an example of a time when you were faced with a negative relationship but did *not* turn to deviant behavior? How did you react instead?

KEY TERMS

Anomie

Conflict subculture

Criminal subculture

General strain theory (GST)

Institutional anomie theory

Relative deprivation

Retreatist subculture

Strain

Structural impediments

READING 11

This piece by Merton is one of the most widely read and cited articles in all of sociology and criminology. In this article, Merton basically argues that deviance is built into the very fabric of our society; deviance is a result of the collision of culturally defined goals and the social structures that limit the modes of achieving those goals. Specifically, he argues that in American society, we very much value economic success, but the structure of society is such that not everyone can be successful. This necessitates several potential modes of adaptation. The first and presumably most common is simply to accept the goals and means provided by society and conform. The vast majority of society works to get an education and then works to achieve material success—most will not become millionaires, but they may perhaps live the middle-class American Dream. This, of course, is not a deviant adaptation but conformity. Alternatively, some will hold on to the American Dream but realize that it cannot be achieved legitimately and adapt by "innovating" and pursuing the dream though illegitimate means. In direct contrast, others may simply give up on the American Dream and but stick fast to the means, working the 9–5 drudge, knowing that economic success will never happen. Perhaps the rarest form of adaptation occurs when individuals reject both the goals and the means provided by society (i.e., the mentally ill, drug and alcohol addicts). Merton does not say a great deal about a fifth mode, rebellion, where both the goals and the means of society are rejected but new goals and means are developed and implemented. We include the original article in its entirety here so that you can read the theory in Merton's own words and see how he explains each of his adaptations. For a fascinating follow-up interview with Merton some 50 years later, see the article by Cullen and Messner (2007) on the SAGE website with our supplemental readings.

Social Structure and Anomie

Robert K. Merton

There persists a notable tendency in sociological theory to attribute the malfunctioning of social structure primarily to those of man's imperious biological drives which are not adequately restrained by social control. In this view, the social order is solely a device for "impulse management" and the "social processing" of tensions. These impulses which break through social control, be it noted, are held to be biologically derived. Nonconformity is assumed to be rooted in original nature.[1] Conformity is by implication the result of an utilitarian calculus or unreasoned conditioning. This point of view, whatever its other deficiences, clearly begs one question. It provides no basis for determining the nonbiological conditions which induce deviations from prescribed patterns of conduct. In this paper, it will be suggested

Source: Merton, Robert K. 1938. "Social Structure and Anomie." *American Sociological Review* 3(5): 672–82.

[1]E.g., Ernest Jones, *Social Aspects of Psychoanalysis,* 28 London, 1924. If the Freudian notion is a variety of "original son" dogma, then the interpretation advance in this paper may be called the doctrine of "socially derived sin."

that certain phases of social structure generate the circumstances in which infringement of social codes constitutes a "normal" response.[2]

The conceptual scheme to be outlined is designed to provide a coherent, systematic approach to the study of socio-cultural sources of deviate behavior. Our primary aim lies in discovering how some social structures *exert a definite pressure* upon certain persons in the society to engage in nonconformist rather than conformist conduct. The many ramifications of the scheme cannot all be discussed; the problems mentioned outnumber those explicitly treated.

Among the elements of social and cultural structure, two are important for our purposes. These are analytically separable although they merge imperceptibly in concrete situations. The first consists of culturally defined goals, purposes, and interests. It comprises a frame of aspirational reference. These goals are more or less integrated and involve varying degrees of prestige and sentiment. They constitute a basic, but not the exclusive, component of what Linton aptly has called "designs for group living." Some of these cultural aspirations are related to the original drives of man, but they are not determined by them. The second phase of the social structure defines, regulates, and controls the acceptable modes of achieving these goals. Every social group invariably couples its scale of desired ends with moral or institutional regulation of permissible and required procedures for attaining these ends. These regulatory norms and moral imperatives do not necessarily coincide with technical or efficiency norms. Many procedures which from the standpoint of *particular individuals* would be most efficient in securing desired values, e.g., illicit oil-stock schemes, theft, fraud, are ruled out of the institutional area of permitted conduct. The choice of expedients is limited by the institutional norms.

To say that these two elements, culture goals and institutional norms, operate jointly is not to say that the ranges of alternative behaviors and aims bear some constant relation to one another. The emphasis upon certain goals may vary independently of the degree of emphasis upon institutional means. There may develop a disproportionate, at times, a virtually exclusive, stress upon the value of specific goals, involving relatively slight concern with the institutionally appropriate modes of attaining these goals. The limiting case in this direction is reached when the range of alternative procedures is limited only by technical rather than institutional considerations. Any and all devices which promise attainment of the all important goal would be permitted in this hypothetical polar case.[3] This constitutes one type of cultural malintegration. A second polar type is found in groups where activities originally conceived as instrumental are transmuted into ends in themselves. The original purposes are forgotten and ritualistic adherence to institutionally prescribed conduct becomes virtually obsessive.[4] Stability

---

[2] "Normal" in the sense of a culturally oriented, if not approved, response. This statement does not deny the relevance of biological and personality differences which may be significantly involved in the *incidence* of deviate conduct. Our focus of interest is the social and cultural matrix; hence we abstract from other factors. It is in this sense, I take it, that James S. Plant speaks of the "normal reaction of normal people to abnormal conditions." See his *Personality and the Cultural Pattern,* 248, New York, 1937.

[3] Contemporary American culture has been said to tend in this direction. See André Siegfried, *America Comes of Age,* 26–37, New York, 1927. The alleged extreme(?) emphasis on the goals of monetary success and material prosperity leads to dominant concern with technological and social instruments designed to produce the desired result, inasmuch as institutional controls become of secondary importance. In such a situation, innovation flourishes as the *range of means* employed is broadened. In a sense, then, there occurs the paradoxical emergence of "materialists" from an "idealistic" orientation. Cf. Durkheim's analysis of the cultural conditions which predispose toward crime and innovation, both of which are aimed toward efficiency, not moral norms. Durkheim was one of the first to see that "contrairement aux idées courantes le criminel n'apparait plus comme un être radicalement insociable, comme une sorte d'element parasitaire, de corps étranger et inassimilable, introduit au sein de la société; c'est un agent régulier de la vie sociale." See *Les Régles de la Méthode Sociologiqu,* 86–89, Paris, 1927.

[4] Such ritualism may be associated with a mythology which rationalizes these actions so that they appear to retain their status as mean, but the dominant pressure is in the direction of strict ritualistic conformity, irrespective of such rationalization. In this sense, ritual has proceeded farthest when such rationalizations are not even called forth.

is largely ensured while change is flouted. The range of alternative behaviors is severely limited. There develops a tradition-bound, sacred society characterized by neophobia. The occupational psychosis of the bureaucrat may be cited as a case in point. Finally, there are the intermediate types of groups where a balance between culture goals and institutional means is maintained. These are the significantly integrated and relatively stable, though changing, groups.

An effective equilibrium between the two phases of the social structure is maintained as long as satisfactions accrue to individuals who conform to both constraints, viz., satisfactions from the achievement of the goals and satisfactions emerging directly from the institutionally canalized modes of striving to attain these ends. Success, in such equilibrated cases, is twofold. Success is reckoned in terms of the product and in terms of the process, in terms of the outcome and in terms of activities. Continuing satisfactions must derive from sheer *participation* in a competitive order as well as from eclipsing one's competitors if the order itself is to be sustained. The occasional sacrifices involved in institutionalized conduct must be compensated by socialized rewards. The distribution of statuses and roles through competition must be so organized that positive incentives for conformity to roles and adherence to status obligations are provided *for every position* within the distributive order. Aberrant conduct, therefore, may be viewed as a symptom of dissociation between culturally defined aspirations and socially structured means.

Of the types of groups which result from the independent variation of the two phases of the social structure, we shall be primarily concerned with the first, namely, that involving a disproportionate accent on goals. This statement must be recast in a proper perspective. In no group is there an absence of regulatory codes governing conduct, yet groups do vary in the degree to which these folkways, mores, and institutional controls are effectively integrated with the more diffuse goals

which are part of the culture matrix. Emotional convictions may cluster about the complex of socially acclaimed ends, meanwhile shifting their support from the culturally defined implementation of these ends. As we shall see, certain aspects of the social structure may generate countermores and antisocial behavior precisely because of differential emphases on goals and regulations. In the extreme case, the latter may be so vitiated by the goal-emphasis that the range of behavior is limited only by considerations of technical expediency. The sole significant question then becomes, which available means is most efficient in netting the socially approved value?[5] The technically most feasible procedure, whether legitimate or not, is preferred to the institutionally prescribed conduct. As this process continues, the integration of the society becomes tenuous and anomie ensues.

Thus, in competitive athletics, when the aim of victory is shorn of its institutional trappings and success in contests becomes construed as "winning the game" rather than "winning through circumscribed modes of activity," a premium is implicitly set upon the use of illegitimate but technically efficient means. The star of the opposing football team is surreptitiously slugged; the wrestler furtively incapacitates his opponent through ingenious but illicit techniques; university alumni covertly subsidize "students" whose talents are largely confined to the athletic field. The emphasis on the goal has so attenuated the satisfactions deriving from sheer participation in the competitive activity that these satisfactions are virtually confined to a successful outcome. Through the same process, tension generated by the desire to win in a poker game is relieved by successfully dealing oneself four aces, or, when the cult of success has become completely dominant, by sagaciously shuffling the cards in a game of solitaire. The faint twinge of uneasiness in the last instance and the surreptious nature of public delicts indicate clearly that the institutional rules of the game *are known* to those who evade them, but that the emotional supports of these rules are largely vitiated by cultural exaggeration

---

[5] In this connection, one may see the relevance of Elton Mayo's paraphrase of the title of Tawney's well known book. "Actually the problem *is not that of the sickness of an acquisitive society' it is that of the acquisitiveness of a sick society." Human Problems of an Industrial Civilization,* 153, New York, 1933. Mayo deals with the process through which wealth comes to be a symbol of social achievement. He sees this as arising from a state of anomie. We are considering the unintegrated monetary-success goal as an element in producing anomie. A complete analysis would involve both phases of this system of interdependent variables.

of the success-goal.[6] They are microcosmic images of the social macrocosm.

Of course, this process is not restricted to the realm of sport. The process whereby exaltation of the end generates a *literal demoralization,* i.e., a deinstitutionalization, of the means is one which characterizes many[7] groups in which the two phases of the social structure are not highly integrated. The extreme emphasis upon the accumulation of wealth as a symbol of success[8] in our own society militates against the completely effective control of institutionally regulated modes of acquiring a fortune.[9] Fraud, corruption, vice, crime, in short, the entire catalogue of proscribed behavior, becomes increasingly common when the emphasis on the *culturally induced* success-goal becomes divorced from a coordinated institutional emphasis. This observation is of crucial theoretical importance in examining the doctrine that antisocial behavior most frequently derives from biological drives breaking through the restraints imposed by society. The difference is one between a strictly utilitarian interpretation which conceives man's ends as random and an analysis which finds these ends deriving from the basic values of the culture.[10]

Our analysis can scarcely stop at this juncture. We must turn to other aspects of the social structure if we are to deal with the social genesis of the varying rates and types of deviate behavior characteristic of different societies. Thus far, we have sketched three ideal types of social orders constituted by distinctive patterns of relations between culture ends and means. Turning from these types of *culture patterning,* we find five logically possible, alternative modes of adjustment or adaptation *by individuals* within the culture-bearing society or group.[11] These are schematically presented in the following table,

	Culture Goals	Institutionalized Means
I. Conformity	+	+
II. Innovation	+	−
III. Ritualism	−	+
IV. Retreatism	−	−
V. Rebellion[12]	±	±

---

[6] It is unlikely that interiorized norms are completely eliminated. Whatever residuum persists will induce personality tensions and conflict. The process involves a certain degree of ambivalence. A manifest rejection of the institutional norms is coupled with some latent retention of their emotional correlates. "Guilt feelings," "sense of sin," "pangs of conscience" are obvious manifestations of this unrelieved tension; symbolic adherence to the nominally repudiated values or rationalizations constitute a more subtle variety of tensional release.

[7] "Many," and not all, unintegrated groups, for the reason already mentioned. In groups where the primary emphasis shifts to institutional means, i.e., when the range of alternatives is very limited, the outcome is a type of ritualism rather than anomie.

[8] Money has several peculiarities which render it particularly apt to become a symbol of prestige divorced from institutional controls. As Simmel emphasized, money is highly abstract and impersonal. However acquired, through fraud or institutionally, it can be used to purchase the same goods and services. The anonymity of metropolitan culture, in conjunction with this peculiarity of money, permits wealth, the sources of which may be unknown to the community in which the plutocrat lives, to serve as a symbol of status.

[9] The emphasis upon wealth as a success-symbol is possibly reflected in the use of the term "fortune" to refer to a stock of accumulated wealth. This meaning becomes common in the late sixteenth century (Spenser and Shakespeare). A similar usage of the Latin *fortuna* comes into prominence during the first century B.C. Both these periods were marked by the rise to prestige and power of the "bourgeoisie."

[10] See Kingsley Davis, "Mental Hygiene and the Class Structure," *Psychiatry,* 1928, I, esp. 62–63; Talcott Parsons, *The Structure of Social Action,* 59–60, New York, 1937.

[11] This is a level intermediate between the two planes distinguished by Edward Sapir; namely, culture patterns and personal habit systems. See his "Contribution of Psychiatry to an Understanding of Behavior in Society," *Amer. J. Sociol.,* 1937, 42:862–70.

[12] This fifth alternative is on a plane clearly different from that of the others. It represents a *transitional* response which seeks to institutionalize new procedures oriented toward revamped cultural goals shared by the members of the society. It thus involves efforts to *change* the existing structure rather than to perform accommodative actions *within* this structure, and introduces additional problems with which we are not at the moment concerned.

where (+) signifies "acceptance," (−) signifies "elimination" and (±) signifies "rejection and substitution of new goals and standards."

Our discussion of the relation between these alternative responses and other phases of the social structure must be prefaced by the observation that persons may shift from one alternative to another as they engage in different social activities. These categories refer to role adjustments in specific situations, not to personality *in toto*. To treat the development of this process in various spheres of conduct would introduce a complexity unmanageable within the confines of this paper. For this reason, we shall be concerned primarily with economic activity in the broad sense, "the production, exchange, distribution and consumption of goods and services" in our competitive society, wherein wealth has taken on a highly symbolic cast. Our task is to search out some of the factors which exert pressure upon individuals to engage in certain of these logically possible alternative responses. This choice, as we shall see, is far from random.

In every society, Adaptation I (conformity to both culture goals and means) is the most common and widely diffused. Were this not so, the stability and continuity of the society could not be maintained. The mesh of expectancies which constitutes every social order is sustained by the modal behavior of its members falling within the first category. Conventional role behavior oriented toward the basic values of the group is the rule rather than the exception. It is this fact alone which permits us to speak of a human aggregate as comprising a group or society.

Conversely, Adaptation IV (rejection of goals and means) is the least common. Persons who "adjust" (or maladjust) in this fashion are, strictly speaking, *in the* society but not of it. Sociologically, these constitute the true "aliens." Not sharing the common frame of orientation, they can be included within the societal population merely in a fictional sense. In this category are *some* of the activities of psychotics, psychoneurotics, chronic autists, pariahs, outcasts, vagrants, vagabonds, tramps, chronic drunkards and drug addicts.[13] These have relinquished, in certain spheres of activity, the culturally defined goals, involving complete aim-inhibition in the polar case, and their adjustments are not in accord with institutional norms. This is not to say that in some cases the source of their behavioral adjustments is not in part the very social structure which they have in effect repudiated nor that their very existence within a social area does not constitute a problem for the socialized population.

This mode of "adjustment" occurs, as far as structural sources are concerned, when both the culture goals and institutionalized procedures have been assimilated thoroughly by the individual and imbued with affect and high positive value, but where those institutionalized procedures which promise a measure of successful attainment of the goals are not available to the individual. In such instances, there results a twofold mental conflict insofar as the moral obligation for adopting institutional means conflicts with the pressure to resort to illegitimate means (which may attain the goal) and inasmuch as the individual is shut off from means which are both legitimate *and* effective. The competitive order is maintained, but the frustrated and handicapped individual who cannot cope with this order drops out.

Defeatism, quietism and resignation are manifested in escape mechanisms which ultimately lead the individual to "escape" from the requirements of the society. It is an expedient which arises from continued failure to attain the goal by legitimate measures and from an inability to adopt the illegitimate route because of internalized prohibitions and institutionalized compulsives, *during which process the supreme value of the success-goal has as yet not been renounced.* The conflict is resolved by eliminating *both* precipitating elements, the goals and means. The escape is complete, the conflict is eliminated and the individual is a socialized.

---

[13] Obviously, this is an elliptical statement. These individuals may maintain some orientation to the values of their particular differentiated groupings within the larger society or, in part, of the conventional society itself. Insofar as they do so, their conduct cannot be classified in the "passive rejection" category (IV). Nels Anderson's description of the behavior and attitudes of the bum, for example, can readily be recast in terms of our analytical scheme. See *The Hobo*, 93–98, *et passim*, Chicago, 1923.

Be it noted that where frustration derives from the inaccessibility of effective institutional means for attaining economic or any other type of highly valued "success," that Adaptations II, III and V (innovation, ritualism and rebellion) are also possible. The result will be determined by the particular personality, and thus, the *particular* cultural background, involved. Inadequate socialization will result in the innovation response whereby the conflict and frustration are eliminated by relinquishing the institutional means and retaining the success-aspiration; an extreme assimilation of institutional demands will lead to ritualism wherein the goal is dropped as beyond one's reach but conformity to the mores persists; and rebellion occurs when emancipation from the reigning standards, due to frustration or to marginalist perspectives, leads to the attempt to introduce a "new social order."

Our major concern is with the illegitimacy adjustment. This involves the use of conventionally proscribed but frequently effective means of attaining at least the simulacrum of culturally defined success,—wealth, power, and the like. As we have seen, this adjustment occurs when the individual has assimilated the cultural emphasis on success without equally internalizing the morally prescribed norms governing means for its attainment. The question arises, Which phases of our social structure predispose toward this mode of adjustment? We may examine a concrete instance, effectively analyzed by Lohman,[14] which provides a clue to the answer. Lohman has shown that specialized areas of vice in the near north side of Chicago constitute a "normal" response to a situation where the cultural emphasis upon pecuniary success has been absorbed, but where there is little access to conventional and legitimate means for attaining such success. The conventional occupational opportunities of persons in this area are almost completely limited to manual labor. Given

our cultural stigmatization of manual labor, and its correlate, the prestige of white collar work, it is clear that the result is a strain toward innovational practices. The limitation of opportunity to unskilled labor and the resultant low income can not compete in terms of conventional standards of achievement with the high income from organized vice.

For our purposes, this situation involves two important features. First, such antisocial behavior is in a sense "called forth" by certain conventional values of the culture *and* by the class structure involving differential access to the approved opportunities for legitimate, prestige-bearing pursuit of the culture goals. The lack of high integration between the means-and-end elements of the cultural pattern and the particular class structure combine to favor a heightened frequency of antisocial conduct in such groups. The second consideration is of equal significance. Recourse to the first of the alternative responses, legitimate effort, is limited by the fact that actual advance toward desired success-symbols through conventional channels is, despite our persisting open-class ideology,[15] relatively rare and difficult for those handicapped by little formal education and few economic resources. The dominant pressure of group standards of success is, therefore, on the gradual attenuation of legitimate, but by and large ineffective, strivings and the increasing use of illegitimate, but more or less effective, expedients of vice and crime. The cultural demands made on persons in this situation are incompatible. On the one hand, they are asked to orient their conduct toward the prospect of accumulating wealth and on the other, they are largely denied effective opportunities to do so institutionally. The consequences of such structural inconsistency are psycho-pathological personality, and/or antisocial conduct, and/or revolutionary activities. The equilibrium between culturally designated means and ends becomes highly unstable

---

[14] Joseph D. Lohman, "The Participant Observer in Community Studies," *Amer. Sociol. Rev.,* 1937, 2:890–98.

[15] The shifting historical role of this ideology is a profitable subject for exploration. The "office-boy-to-president" stereotype was once in approximate accord with the facts. Such vertical mobility was probably more common then than now, when the class structure is more rigid. (See the following note.) The ideology largely persists, however, possibly because it still performs a useful function for maintaining the *status quo*. For insofar as it is accepted by the "masses," it constitutes a useful sop for those who might rebel against the entire structure, were this consoling hope removed. This ideology now serves to lessen the probability of Adaptation V. In short, the role of this notion has changed from that of an approximately valid empirical theorem to that of an ideology, in Mannheim's sense.

with the progressive emphasis on attaining the prestige-laden ends by any means whatsoever. Within this context, Capone represents the triumph of amoral intelligence over morally prescribed "failure," when the channels of vertical mobility are closed or narrowed[16] *in a society which places a high premium on economic affluence and social ascent for all its members.*[17]

This last qualification is of primary importance. It suggests that other phases of the social structure besides the extreme emphasis on pecuniary success, must be considered if we are to understand the social sources of antisocial behavior. A high frequency of deviate behavior is not generated simply by "lack of opportunity" or by this exaggerated pecuniary emphasis. A comparatively rigidified class structure, a feudalistic or caste order, may limit such opportunities far beyond the point which obtains in our society today. It is only when a system of cultural values extols, virtually above all else, certain *common* symbols of success *for the population at large* while its social structure rigorously restricts or completely eliminates access to approved modes of acquiring these symbols *for a considerable part of the same population,* that antisocial behavior ensues on a considerable scale. In other words, our egalitarian

ideology denies by implication the existence of non-competing groups and individuals in the pursuit of pecuniary success. The same body of success-symbols is held to be desirable for all. These goals are held to *transcend class lines,* not to be bounded by them, yet the actual social organization is such that there exist class differentials in the accessibility of these *common* success-symbols. Frustration and thwarted aspiration lead to the search for avenues of escape from a culturally induced intolerable situation; or unrelieved ambition may eventuate in illicit attempts to acquire the dominant values.[18] The American stress on pecuniary success and ambitiousness for all thus invites exaggerated anxieties, hostilities, neuroses and antisocial behavior.

This theoretical analysis may go far toward explaining the varying correlations between crime and poverty.[19] Poverty is not an isolated variable. It is one in a complex of interdependent social and cultural variables. When viewed in such a context, it represents quite different states of affairs. Poverty as such, and consequent limitation of opportunity, are not sufficient to induce a conspicuously high rate of criminal behavior. Even the often mentioned "poverty in the midst of plenty" will not necessarily lead to this result. Only insofar as poverty and

---

[16] There is a growing body of evidence, though none of it is clearly conclusive, to the effect that our class structure is becoming rigidified and that vertical mobility is declining. Taussig and Joslyn found that American business leaders are being *increasingly* recruited from the upper ranks of our society. The Lynds have also found a "diminished chance to get ahead" for the working classes in Middletown. Manifestly, these objective changes are not alone significant; the individual's subjective evaluation of the situation is a major determinant of the response. The extent to which this change in opportunity for social mobility has been recognized by the least advantaged classes is still conjectural, although the Lynds present some suggestive materials. The writer suggests that a case in point is the increasing frequency of cartoons which observe in a tragi-comic vein that "my old man says everybody can't be President. He says if ya can get three days a week steady on W.P.A. work ya ain't doin' so bad either." See F. W. Taussig and C. S. Joslyn, *American Business Leaders,* New York, 1932; R. S. and H. M. Lynd, *Middletown in Transition,* 67 ff., chap. 12, New York, 1937.

[17] The role of the Negro in this respect is of considerable theoretical interest. Certain elements of the Negro population have assimilated the dominant caste's values of pecuniary success and social advancement, but they also recognize that social ascent is at present restricted to their own caste almost exclusively. The pressures upon the Negro which would otherwise derive from the structural inconsistencies we have noticed are hence not identical with those upon lower class whites. See Kingsley Davis, *op. cit.,* 63; John Dollard, *Caste and Class in a Southern Town,* 66 ff., New Haven, 1936; Donald Young, *American Minority Peoples,* 581, New York, 1932.

[18] The psychical coordinates of these processes have been partly established by the experimental evidence concerning *Anspruchsniveaus* and levels of performance. See Kurt Lewin, *Vorsatz, Wille und Bedurfnis,* Berlin, 1926; N. F. Hoppe, "Erfolg und Misserfolg," *Psychol. Forschung,* 1930, 14:1–63; Jerome D. Frank, "Individual Differences in Certain Aspects of the Level of Aspiration," *Amer. J. Psychol.,* 1935, 47: 119–28.

[19] Standard criminology texts summarize the data in this field. Our scheme of analysis may serve to resolve some of the theoretical contradictions which P. A. Sorokin indicates. For example, "not everywhere nor always do the poor show a greater proportion of crime ... many poorer countries have had less crime than the richer countries ... The [economic] improvement in the second half of the nineteenth century, and the beginning of the twentieth, has not been followed by a decrease of crime." See his *Contemporary Sociological Theories,* 560–61, New York, 1928. The crucial point is, however, that poverty has varying social significance in different social structures, as we shall see. Hence, one would not expect a linear correlation between crime and poverty.

associated disadvantages in competition for the culture values approved for *all* members of the society is linked with the assimilation of a cultural emphasis on monetary accumulation as a symbol of success is antisocial conduct a "normal" outcome. Thus, poverty is less highly correlated with crime in southeastern Europe than in the United States. The possibilities of vertical mobility in these European areas would seem to be fewer than in this country, so that neither poverty *per se* nor its association with limited opportunity is sufficient to account for the varying correlations. It is only when the full configuration is considered, poverty, limited opportunity and a commonly shared system of success symbols, that we can explain the higher association between poverty and crime in our society than in others where rigidified class structure is coupled with *differential class symbols of achievement.*

In societies such as our own, then, the pressure of prestige-bearing success tends to eliminate the effective social constraint over means employed to this end. "The-end-justifies-the-means" doctrine becomes a guiding tenet for action when the cultural structure unduly exalts the end and the social organization unduly limits possible recourse to approved means. Otherwise put, this notion and associated behavior reflect a lack of cultural coordination. In international relations, the effects of this lack of integration are notoriously apparent. An emphasis upon national power is not readily coordinated with an inept organization of legitimate, i.e., internationally defined and accepted, means for attaining this goal. The result is a tendency toward the abrogation of international law, treaties become scraps of paper, "undeclared warfare" serves as a technical evasion, the bombing of civilian populations is rationalized,[20] just as the same societal situation induces the same sway of illegitimacy among individuals.

The social order we have described necessarily produces this "strain toward dissolution." The pressure of such an order is upon outdoing one's competitors.

The choice of means within the ambit of institutional control will persist as long as the sentiments supporting a competitive system, i.e., deriving from the possibility of outranking competitors and hence enjoying the favorable response of others, are distributed throughout the entire system of activities and are not confined merely to the final result. A stable social structure demands a balanced distribution of affect among its various segments. When there occurs a shift of emphasis from the satisfactions deriving from competition itself to almost exclusive concern with successful competition, the resultant stress leads to the breakdown of the regulatory structure.[21] With the resulting attenuation of the institutional imperatives, there occurs an approximation of the situation erroneously held by utilitarians to be typical of society generally wherein calculations of advantage and fear of punishment are the sole regulating agencies. In such situations, as Hobbes observed, force and fraud come to constitute the sole virtues in view of their relative efficiency in attaining goals,—which were for him, of course, not culturally derived.

It should be apparent that the foregoing discussion is not pitched on a moralistic plane. Whatever the sentiments of the writer or reader concerning the ethical desirability of coordinating the means-and-goals phases of the social structure, one must agree that lack of such coordination leads to anomie. Insofar as one of the most general functions of social organization is to provide a basis for calculability and regularity of behavior, it is increasingly limited in effectiveness as these elements of the structure become dissociated. At the extreme, predictability virtually disappears and what may be properly termed cultural chaos or anomie intervenes.

This statement, being brief, is also incomplete. It has not included an exhaustive treatment of the various structural elements which predispose toward one rather than another of the alternative responses open to individuals; it has neglected, but not denied the relevance

---

[20] See M. W. Royse, *Aerial Bombardment and the International Regulation of War,* New York, 1928.

[21] Since our primary concern is with the socio-cultural aspects of this problem, the psychological correlates have been only implicitly considered. See Karen Horney, *The Neurotic Personality of Our Time,* New York, 1937, for a psychological discussion of this process.

of, the factors determining the specific incidence of these responses; it has not enumerated the various concrete responses which are constituted by combinations of specific values of the analytical variables; it has omitted, or included only by implication, any consideration of the social functions performed by illicit responses; it has not tested the full explanatory power of the analytical scheme by examining a large number of group variations in the frequency of deviate and conformist behavior; it has not adequately dealt with rebellious conduct which seeks to refashion the social framework radically; it has not examined the relevance of cultural conflict for an analysis of culture-goal and institutional-means malintegration. It is suggested that these and related problems may be profitably analyzed by this scheme.

READING 12

As highlighted in the text, Mestrovic and Lorenzo used Durkheim's ideas on anomie to help explain the abuse at Abu Ghraib. They argue that the dysfunction and disorganization at Abu Ghraib was so great that the breaking of norms and abuse of prisoners was inevitable. The authors reframe from a sociological perspective an important government report documenting the abuse at Abu Ghraib. They highlight the following conditions leading to anomie and abuse: confusion as to who was in charge, insufficient training, lack of social integration within the military units at Abu Ghraib, rapid changes in the social milieu, intense pressure to obtain intelligence, cultural insensitivity, and confusion as to which norms to follow. The conclusion is especially interesting as the authors argue that the courts-martial at Fort Hood, Texas, were meant to bring justice to the abuses and restore the collective conscience. They further argue that this did not happen; rather, a few "bad apples" were punished, which may not be nearly enough to "make things right" for those directly involved or for the worldwide audience. We think this piece is both useful and interesting for students, teachers, and researchers. It offers a vivid example of how "classic" sociological theories and ideas can still be used today to gain new insight into current examples of deviant behavior.

Durkheim's Concept of Anomie and the Abuse at Abu Ghraib

Stjepan G. Mestrovic and Ronald Lorenzo

The overall conclusion reached by the various US government reports on the abuse committed at Abu Ghraib prison in Iraq is that abuse did in fact occur; that no direct orders to commit the abuse were issued by officials high in the chain of command; and that some personnel low in the chain

Source: Mestrovic, Stjepan G. and Ronald Lorenzo. 2008. "Durkheim's Concept of Anomie and the Abuse at Abu Ghraib." *Journal of Classical Sociology* 8(2): 179–207. Reprinted with permission.

of command should be prosecuted for some of the abuse (Mestrovic, 2007, Strasser, 2004). These same reports also expose evidence of high levels of social disorganization and what sociologists call *anomie* at Abu Ghraib and within the social structure of the US Army and of other government agencies (OGA), among civilian contractors, and among others who were involved with policing, interrogating, and incarcerating prisoners at Abu Ghraib as well as in Afghanistan, Guantánamo, and elsewhere in Iraq. The occurrence of social disorganization and *anomie* ranges from the most microscopic level of analysis (such as the unauthorized merging of the roles of Military Intelligence and Military Police at Abu Ghraib, which led to the policy that MPs 'softened up' prisoners for MI) through mid-levels of analysis (such as the question of who was the executive officer in charge at Abu Ghraib) to macro-levels of analysis (such as which interrogation procedures were approved by the US Army and the Department of Defense at which period of time and in which theater of action, as well as the question whether the Geneva Conventions apply in whole or in part or in what specific aspect, and also what is the significance of the denial of findings contained in International Committee of the Red Cross reports).

Sociological theory and research holds that social disorganization and *anomie* inevitably cause what sociologists call deviance or the breaking of social norms. However, the government reports use metaphors such as 'poisoned climate,' rather than the word *anomie,* to describe the social setting at Abu Ghraib. The authors of these reports prefer the word 'abuse' to the sociological concept of 'deviance.' The military judge allowed an expert witness in sociology to use and explain the concept '*anomie*' in open court during testimony at three of the courts-martial pertaining to Abu Ghraib that were held at Fort Hood, Texas, in 2005.[1] However, what appears to be a straightforward sociological representation of the chaotic social setting leading to abuse at Abu Ghraib as an anomic one actually involves intricate and complex interpretation. It raises questions for sociological theory that have been dormant for

decades, including but not limited to the following: Is *anomie* a condition of *dérèglement,* as Durkheim taught, or is it a condition of 'normlessness,' as conceptualized by structural functionalists and repeated in hundreds of textbooks? Is anomie primarily a 'deranged' state of disorganization involving lack of coordination and other variations of social chaos that sets the stage for violence and abuse, as taught by Durkheim, or is it a 'normless' condition, as taught by the functionalists? One's assumptions in replying to these and related questions will have a profound impact on how one understands what caused the abuse and how one approaches the task of repairing the damage to social structure caused by abuse at Abu Ghraib and elsewhere. If Durkheim is correct, then the US Army needs to be put into a collective therapy of sorts, along the lines of the remedies that he proposed for healing the evil consequences of *anomie* (Durkheim, 1933 [1893], 1951 [1897], 1983b [1950]). These remedies include establishing fixed normative referents, promoting social integration, and ensuring that existing norms are coordinated, incorporated into policies, and function properly. If the functionalists are correct, then any working 'normative' solution is adequate to the task of restoring social order, even if the norms in question are out of sync with, say, the norms of the international community, such as the Geneva Conventions. In fact, functionalists assume that social systems self-correct automatically when it comes to fixing anomie: 'social life has a tendency to be and to remain a functionally integrated phenomenon' (Theodorson and Theodorson, 1969: 133).

These issues are important and have long-lasting consequences. As of this writing, strict adherence to the Geneva Conventions is *not* part of the discourse for fixing the damage to social relations caused by the abuse at Abu Ghraib. Instead, the US government has chosen to rely on the Army Field Manual as its standard, with the caveat that it can be changed at any time (and has been changed several times in the past six years). According to the Bush Administration, the Geneva Conventions did not and do not apply against Al-Qaida, but did and do apply in the war in Iraq (Danner, 2004). Yet policies from Guantánamo—where the Geneva Conventions were ruled to be irrelevant—were transferred to Abu Ghraib—where the Geneva Conventions were supposed to apply (see Falk et al., 2006). A Durkheimian sociological analysis would apprehend this 'migration' of unlawful policies and contexts as itself a confusing, chaotic, and *anomie*-producing process. Moroever, as the war in Iraq continues to be re-conceptualized as part of a global war against terror, the importance of the Geneva Conventions as an example of firm moral boundaries in the Durkheimian sense is diminishing. New 'norms' relating to torture and warfare are being created, causing moral confusion among lawyers, officers, soldiers, and everyone else involved in this discourse.

For many decades, sociological theory pertaining to anomie and its relationship to deviance has been used by criminologists to study ordinary crime, but not war crimes, torture, and abuse. This vacuum in sociological theorizing has been filled by Philip Zimbardo, who draws upon the obedience-to-authority paradigm in social psychology. Zimbardo (2007) claims that his famous Stanford Prison Experiment explains the abuse at Abu Ghraib on the basis of 'good' people turning 'evil' as the result of 'situational' factors. Space does not permit a full analysis of *anomie* theory (further distinguishable into Durkheimian and functionalist versions) versus the obedience-to-authority paradigm in Zimbardo's book. Suffice it to say that facts and reports concerning Abu Ghraib suggest the opposite of what Zimbardo intends: an egregious lack of authority and leadership at Abu Ghraib seems to have been responsible for the abuse that ensued. Against Zimbardo's position, Durkheim's assumption seems to be that ordinary people (who exhibit a mixture of 'good' and 'bad' traits depending in part upon society's definitions) at Abu Ghraib behaved in ways that some—but not all—aspects of society label as 'evil.' Our purpose here is to clarify, deepen, and apply a genuinely sociological theory of anomie to the issue at hand.

◈ Conceptualizing the Problem

The factual evidence for the presence of extreme social disorganization and *anomie* comes from the US government reports pertaining to Abu Ghraib as well as testimony from the courts-martial—described meticulously by Mestrovic (2007) based upon eyewitness accounts of the trials as well as participation in three of them as an expert witness in sociology—and includes, but is not limited to, the following:

- a systemic lack of accountability;

- a disorganized filing system;

- the fact that other government agencies (OGA), including the CIA, operated outside established rules and procedures established by the Army Field Manual as well as the Geneva Conventions;

- the fact that nobody was certain who was in charge of Abu Ghraib;

- overcrowding; a dysfunctional system for releasing prisoners;

- failure to screen detainees at the point that they were arrested as well as the point that they were brought to Abu Ghraib;

- the lack of screening for civilian contractors;

- the introduction of new elements (but not entire units) into the personnel structure (a process that the Army calls cross-leveling);

- failure to adequately train MPs and MIs in policing as well as in interrogation procedures;

- the fact that MPs did not know what they or MIs were not allowed to do;

- lack of military discipline;

- intense pressure to obtain information from a population of prisoners that was not capable of providing the desired information;

- lack of training; lack of familiarity with the Geneva Conventions; the fact that the US military upheld the Geneva Conventions while various attorneys for the White House opined that the Geneva Conventions did not wholly apply to the treatment of prisoners;

- poor paperwork procedures; and

- poor reporting procedures.

These facts, along with a host of others, suggest extreme social chaos. For example, the supply officer at Abu Ghraib, Major David DiNenna, testified that he begged the Army for adequate water, food, toilets, light bulbs, and generators, and that his pleas fell on deaf ears. He testified in open court that he felt 'abandoned' by the Army at Abu Ghraib (Mestrovic, 2007: 107).

The above findings of fact constitute evidence of egregious social disorganization, dysfunction, and anomie, which sets the stage for deviance. The term 'anomie' was coined by Émile Durkheim in *The Division of Labor in Society* (1933 [1893]) and in *Suicide* (1951 [1897]). Durkheim refers specifically to *dérèglement* as the synonym for *anomie*: 'l'état de dérèglement ou *d'anomie*' (1983a [1897]: 287). *Anomie* is depicted by Durkheim as a general societal condition of *dérèglement* or derangement—literally, 'a rule that is a lack of rule' (1951 [1897]: 257), or in the original French: 'consciences déréglées et qui erigent en règle le dérèglement dont elles souffrent' (1983a [1897]: 287). Jean-Marie Guyau preceded Durkheim in using this concept in 1885: 'C'est l'absence de loi fixe, qu'on peut désigner sous le terme *d'anomie*' (1907 [1885]: 165). Note that Guyau referred to the lack of 'fixed' moral boundaries, but not a lack of laws or norms per se. French dictionaries such as the *Littré* refer to *dérèglement* as a state of corruption, evil, agitation, torment, impiety, and intemperance which leads to general suffering and torment.[2] All these terms can be applied to the social conditions at Abu Ghraib as revealed in testimony and reports, and are in line with Durkheim's general assumptions about anomie: that

it is a disorganized social condition that leads to suffering and distress (see Mestrovic, 1988; Mestrovic and Brown, 1985; Orru, 1987). Durkheim treats *anomie* as acute and temporary as well as chronic and long-lasting. In *Suicide*, he also addresses several varieties of anomie, among them conjugal, marital, religious, political, military, and intellectual, pertaining to various social institutions. Durkheim's scaffolding for understanding *anomie* includes: Arthur Schopenhauer's philosophy, in which the imperious 'will' is unrestrained by rational categories or 'representations'; theological understandings of *anomia* as sin (Lyonnet and Sabourin, 1970); and the ideas of various other European philosophers (Mestrovic, 1985).

Durkheim's perspective was modified and changed considerably in its interpretation by the most influential American sociologist of the twentieth century, Talcott Parsons (1937). Parsons established what has come to be known as the Harvard School of Sociology, and elaborated anomie in relation to the Hobbesian meaning of 'the war of all against all' (Parsons, 1937: 407). His most famous disciple was Robert K. Merton, whose 'Social Structure and *Anomie*' (1957) became the most cited article in sociology. According to Merton: 'as initially developed by Durkheim, the concept of *anomie* referred to a condition of relative normlessness in a society or group' (1957: 161). Merton established that *anomie* will lead to crime and other forms of deviance when society—at any level of analysis, from the macrosociological to the microsociological—establishes agreed-upon *goals* but fails to provide for agreed-upon *means* for achieving those goals. Merton's theory has been applied in numerous studies of crime and deviance— but not to the phenomena of war crimes, torture, and abuse. At first glance, it seems to fit some aspects of the social state of affairs at Abu Ghraib that emerges from the US government reports: intense pressure was put on the military personnel at Abu Ghraib to reach the *goal* of obtaining information from prisoners, but the *means* for obtaining this information were unlawful, or, in Merton's words, 'innovative.' According to Merton's paradigm, this systemic discrepancy between socially approved goals and means is, by itself, sufficient to cause many sorts of deviance (the breaking of social norms), including, but not limited to, the type of abuse that has been documented at Abu Ghraib.

But is a Parsonian, or a Mertonian, conceptualization of the problem adequate? The government reports, as well as testimony at the courts-martial pertaining to Abu Ghraib at Fort Hood, Texas, show that abuse was not limited to seemingly rational interrogation techniques that involved goals and means. Some abuse occurred *ad hoc* in showers, hallways, stairwells, and other places not used for interrogation; some abuse was committed for sport and amusement, not for any official purpose at all; and most prisoners did not have the information the Army sought. Thus, the rationality of the goals in the goals-means equation can be called into question. The prosecutor at the courts-martial revealed in open court that 100 percent of the abused prisoners were not a threat to Americans and had no information to give them (Mestrovic, 2007: 11). In fact, it is highly irrational, chaotic, and 'deranged' to use torture for the sake of obtaining information on prisoners who had no information to give. Even if the soldiers who abused the prisoners did not always know that their victims did not have information to give them, the more important Durkheimian point is that there were no established social mechanisms in place for ascertaining this important fact (for example, no screening, no judicial review boards, no assumption that prisoners were innocent until proven guilty, no implementation of the Geneva Conventions on processing and treating prisoners, and so on). As for the means, the reports, as well as testimony, suggest that nobody could discern whether the rational-legal authority for the approved techniques is to be found in the Army Field Manual, various memorandums, or the Geneva Conventions, none of which are consistent with each other.

From a Durkheimian point of view, the state of anomie and social chaos documented at Abu Ghraib was all-pervasive and fundamentally irrational in that it clouded soldiers' judgments concerning what constituted acceptable versus unacceptable thought, emotion, and behavior. Evidence for such a point of view is to be found in the numerous references to 'confusion' found in the reports and disclosed in testimony at the courts-martial (Danner, 2004; Mestrovic, 2007; Strasser, 2004). Soldiers could not discern the difference between normative versus abusive situations. For example, the Company Commander, Captain (CPT) Donald Reese, testified that when he inquired as to why prisoners were forced to wear women's panties on their heads, he was told by his superiors that it was 'a supply issue' or 'an MI thing.' There was no established social system in place to validate his concerns, and the same was true for scores of other whistleblowers at Abu Ghraib, who were routinely invalidated and in some cases threatened (Mestrovic, 2007). The new issues that are raised by this Durkheimian reading include, but are not limited to, the following: Who was responsible for causing, allowing, and failing to ameliorate the state of *anomie* or dysfunctional social organization at Abu Ghraib? What are the different levels of responsibility—sociologically speaking—for the abuse that occurred vis-à-vis the chain of command? Doctors, medics, lawyers, supply officers, and other professionals at Abu Ghraib were all responsible for limited and specific aspects of the division of labor, which was dysfunctional overall. In *Professional Ethics and Civic Morals,* Durkheim (1983b [1950]) suggests that the professional groups who govern the conduct of such individual professionals are ultimately responsible for the outcome. In the present case, this would mean that the American Medical Association, the American Bar Association, and other professional groups share some of the responsibility for the abuse. Even if orders for the abuse were not given from positions high in the chain of command, why were the social conditions that led to the abuse not corrected? A Parsonian-inspired reply to the effect that officers could wait for or could trust in the system to self-correct seems inadequate.

The US government reports thus document not only abuse but also high levels of social disorganization and anomie at Abu Ghraib—but these reports lay the primary blame for specifically sexual and violent abuse on a 'few bad apples' (morally corrupt individuals) and neglect the question of blame for the state of social chaos that led to the abuse. Furthermore, these same reports document a systemic state of chaos in command, procedure, organization, and societal structure *vis-à-vis* the detainment and interrogation of prisoners at Guanátnamo, in Afghanistan, and in Iraq. Logically, one is forced to draw the conclusion that a large segment of the 'apple orchard' was contaminated. It is important to determine the different levels of responsibility (international, national, local), sociologically speaking, not only for the abuse but also for the chaotic state of affairs that led to the abuse. A functionalist perspective might assume that social systems are self-correcting—but the dysfunctional military society at Abu Ghraib did not self-correct. In the words of CPT Jonathan Crisp, defense counsel for Lynndie England, the dysfunctional social system not only failed to self-correct, 'but was self-perpetuating' (Mestrovic, 2007: 175). Durkheim, however, assumes that *anomie* becomes chronic until self-conscious and deliberate remedies are sought from outside the dysfunctional system.

In general, functionalists who follow in the footsteps of Parsons and Merton tend to assume that society is a stable, self-maintaining, and self-correcting system made up of norms, values, beliefs, and sanctions.[3] All of these assumptions can be questioned with regard to the reality of abuse at Abu Ghraib. The functionalists typically do not address problems in synchronizing international with local dimensions of such units of analysis. In other words, there exist several layers of norms (international, national, local, and other finer distinctions), and the same holds true for the other system components (values, beliefs, and sanctions). But in the case of Abu Ghraib, the international norms (exemplified by the Geneva Conventions) were sometimes out of sync with national norms (based upon the US Constitution as well as US Army field manuals) as well as local norms (memorandums and competing interpretations of permissible interrogation methods). US values concerning the importance of democracy, due process, and human rights were out of sync with the dehumanizing atmosphere established at Abu Ghraib. The collective belief that Americans were liberators was out of sync with the belief that Americans acted like tormentors at Abu Ghraib. The sanctions exemplified by courts-martial of low-ranking soldiers are out of sync with sanctions for 'grave breaches' of the Geneva Conventions which call for the prosecution of high-ranking leaders, or what is referred to as the doctrine of command responsibility (see Human Rights Watch, 2006).

The important point is that even though the doctrine of command responsibility exists as an international norm, and has been incorporated into the Uniform Code of Military Justice (UCMJ), it was dysfunctional at Abu Ghraib. It has been and continues to be applied at the tribunals at the Hague to punish high-ranking civilian as well as military officials, but has not been applied at the courts-martial at Fort Hood, where most of the blame for the abuse has been heaped onto low-ranking soldiers. Again, the problem seems to lie not in a lack of norms and moral boundaries, but in a lack of coordination, in confusion, and in dysfunction in implementing such norms and boundaries. From a Durkheimian perspective, all these factors and more constitute a widespread collective condition of *dérèglement*.

◈ Cultural Frames of Reference

An important development in social theory since Durkheim and Parsons has been the introduction of a variety of cultural perspectives. Every culture relies upon a frame of reference that is used to apprehend events ranging from natural disasters to wars and acceptable modes of leisure (see Cushman and Mestrovic, 1995; Goffman, 1986). Like a picture frame, a cultural frame excludes elements from discourse at the same time that it includes other elements. And some of these elements are contradictory. In part because of publicity given to the Abu Ghraib abuses, the image of the United States, too, has been framed by some members of the international community as the country that 'liberated' Iraq *and* as the country that became Iraq's brutal 'occupier.' The notorious prison that Saddam Hussein used to inflict torture, Abu Ghraib, served as a symbol of Arab oppression for Americans who framed themselves as liberators, but later became a symbol of American abuse and torture. One could multiply these and similar examples of how the popular consciousness changes the focus and frame of reference for perceiving events and their significance.

Sociological theory itself is not immune to the effects of cultural framing. There is no doubt that Durkheim's discussions of anomie are framed in a European context while Parsonian approaches are framed in an American context. Durkheim assumes a pessimism concerning human nature that is found in European cultural traditions. Parsons assumes a sunny-side-up American optimism. Perhaps it is significant that Durkheim comes from a cultural background including descent from several generations of German rabbis, and was a French Jew living in a deeply anti-Semitic France at the time. On the other hand, Parsons was the son of a Congregationalist minister whose writings bespeak the Puritan 'habits of the heart' described by Alexis de Tocqueville (2004 [1848])—specifically, Parsons seems to imply the doctrine of American exceptionalism (see Lipset, 1997). Durkheim was personally involved in the defense of Captain Alfred Dreyfus, a French Jewish officer from the German Alsace region (where Durkheim was also born) wrongly convicted of treason (see Lukes, 1985). Given these and other cultural and contextual differences between the USA and Europe, Parsons and Durkheim, it would not be surprising that Durkheim's and Parsons's understandings of *anomie* would differ despite overall similarities (Mestrovic, 1988). Writings such as Seymour Martin Lipset's *Continental Divide* (1990), which point to cultural differences that persist even between the United States and Canada, for example, serve to demystify some of the assumptions in functionalism which seem to reflect Protestant, American values from the 1930s. Perhaps because of these cultural differences, the European scholar André Lalande defines anomie as 'absence d'organisation, de coordination' (1980 [1926]: 61) and refers to Durkheim,

while the American writers Theodorson and Theodorson define it as 'a condition characterized by the relative absence or confusion of values in a society or group' (1969: 12) and refer to Parsons and Merton.

James Loewen's book *Lies My Teacher Told Me: Everything Your American History Textbook Got Wrong* (2007) exposes how facts about American history change in meaning when one questions one's assumptions and frames of reference in approaching these facts. We are approaching the meanings of *anomie* in a similar way, with the implied subtext: 'Lies My Social Theory Teacher Told Me: What Your Social Theory Textbooks Got Wrong Regarding *Anomie*.' While it is beyond the scope of this essay to review the many criticisms of Parsons and structural functionalism extant in the literature, the most important point, for this discussion, is that the Parsonian-Mertonian misinterpretation of *anomie* as 'normlessness' remains unseen and unchallenged.[4]

The conceptualization of cultural frames of reference also becomes significant when the sociologist addresses issues pertaining to law, crime, and justice. How and why do societies frame some acts as crimes in general and crimes of war in particular, yet exclude other similar acts from such frames of reference? How do societies distinguish between just laws and punishments versus inhumane punishment? How does the collective consciousness frame international war crimes tribunals as just versus 'victor's justice,' or as scapegoating? The concept of 'war crime' was not formally and legally conceptualized until the twentieth century and especially the end of World War II (Solis, 1998). Although massacres and mass killings are to be found throughout history, it is only in the post-Nuremberg era that genocide, persecution, and other war crimes came to be defined and distinguished from other crimes per se (Gutman and Rieff, 1999). The central focus of the relatively new conceptual frame regarding war crimes is that these sorts of crimes are typically depicted as being intentional, rational, planned from the top of a hierarchical organization, and widespread (Bauman, 1990). War crimes imply the existence of an organized bureaucracy and well-developed, modernist, state functions. This collective, cognitive shift—the ability to conceive of war crimes in a frame of reference that goes beyond the old adage that all wars are brutal—involves a fundamental ambiguity or ambivalence from the outset in conceptualizing war crimes as well as crimes committed during wars. It involves the forced conjunction of radically 'split' categories: that which is regarded highly (the many manifestations of modernism embodied in bureaucracy and the idea of the chain of command) and what is despicable (the passion and chaos of crime). The idea of a war crime conjoins numerous cultural refractions of highly idealized 'grand narratives of the Enlightenment' (Lyotard, 1984) with numerous cultural refractions of passionately devalued notions of crime. The inherent contradiction in depicting war crimes as intentional, rational, planned, and widespread is that modern, Western societies value highly the notions of agency, rationality, planning, and organization. Part of the shock of the Holocaust remains the fact that genocide was carried out in a cold, calculated, organized and almost business-like manner. It is as if the West's most esteemed virtues came to be twisted into the most hated vices. Additionally, contemporary Western societies seem to insist that international war crimes must be distinguished, conceptually, from crimes that are spontaneous and limited in scope, which is to say, distinguished from ordinary crimes of passion committed by a few corrupt individuals.

Nevertheless, it seems to be the case that regardless of how logically academics and jurists conceptualize war crimes in theory, an event or set of events comes to be regarded as criminal only when these events offend what Durkheim (1933 [1893]) called the collective consciousness. The so-called 'world community' responded in widely divergent ways to war crimes in the former Yugoslavia, Rwanda, Cambodia, Sierra Leone, and Abu Ghraib, among other sites. Reactions of the collective consciousness are emotional, unplanned, unscripted, and even disorganized—in Durkheim's (1995 [1912]) view, this is because they are based upon a spontaneous 'collective effervescence.' To be offended is to give in to passion. When one is discussing international war crimes, one needs to analyze which collective consciousness is offended, by which aspects of a given situation, at what time, and why. One also needs to ascertain whether a true, global, international collective consciousness exists or can exist. Can the international community maintain a consistent frame of reference with respect to war crimes?

Durkheim pronounced in 1893 that an act—no matter how heinous—that is not punished by the collective consciousness is not a crime. Conversely, a punitive reaction by a collective consciousness transforms an event into a crime. Durkheim's counter-intuitive assessment has withstood the test of time and of rigorous research pertaining to crimes committed by individuals. A crime is that which offends the collective conscience in a strong and consistent manner, but not all acts that some people might deem criminal or immoral will necessarily offend a particular collective conscience in a specific cultural setting. In Durkheim's words, 'an act is criminal when it offends strong and defined states of the collective consciousness' (1933 [1893]: 80). And he elaborates:

> In other words, we must not say that an action shocks the common conscience because it is criminal, but rather that it is criminal because it shocks the common conscience. We do not reprove it because it is a crime, but it is a crime because we reprove it. (1933 [1893]: 81)

It seems that one could extend Durkheim's understanding of crime *vis-à-vis* a particular collective conscience to instances of *anomie vis-à-vis* an international collective conscience. We must not say that collective abuse shocks the international community because it is criminal, but rather that it is an international war crime because it shocks the international collective conscience. We do not reprove it because it is anomic, but it is anomic because the world reproves it. To put it another way, cultures vary greatly in their responses to collective abuse, ranging from the acts of the Pol Pot regime and various forces in the Balkans to the perpetrators of the Holocaust. The fact that the international community will respond to certain events and thereby transform them into crime is universal, but the acts which provoke this strong reaction are not universal. Yet the very concept of international war crimes seems to presuppose a universal standard for what is deemed criminal. In fact, as already noted, the world community responds in a politicized and inconsistent manner to war crimes—as defined by the Geneva Conventions—depending upon various factors and cultural frames of reference. For various reasons, a critical mass of the international community responded with passionate revulsion to the war crimes in Yugoslavia and Rwanda sufficient to establish international tribunals. Yet other sites of apparent international war crime failed to offend the international community's collective conscience strongly enough for it to react punitively, including the abuses at Abu Ghraib, in Afghanistan, and at Guant ánamo. In general, Durkheim's insight regarding crime and its relationship to a collective conscience has not been extended into the domain of crimes committed upon an international stage, which range from acts labeled as war crimes to terrorism. But without the scaffolding of his sociological theory, the conceptualization of international war crimes can be reduced easily to explanations of vengeance, 'victor's justice,' scapegoating, and particularized politics (coercing some nation-states to hand over alleged war criminals to an international tribunal, while looking the other way for other nation-states).

The new millennium has raised the concept of international war crime to a much higher level of public consciousness than at any other time since World War II. However, the cultural frame of reference pertaining to the law that is being applied at Abu Ghraib constitutes a significant departure from the ways that crimes of war have been conceptualized since the Nuremberg era. If Zygmunt Bauman (1990) and others are correct that war crimes in general and genocide in particular are modernist phenomena (in that they necessarily involve rational planning, systematic procedures, and a chain of command with top-down hierarchy), then how can one conceptualize or prosecute crimes of war that are conceptualized primarily as irrational, chaotic, unsystematic, and as perpetrated by individuals who operate outside the chain of command? In other words, how does society understand a war crime as being anomic or disorganized and chaotic? This seems to constitute a gaping conceptual hole in sociological theory as well as in international law pertaining to war crimes.

In general, the law does not assume, as some other cultural institutions—for example, some religions—do, that everyone is a sinner, and that everyone deserves forgiveness. The law, as depicted by Durkheim, condemns the criminal and punishes him or her in the name of upholding social order and in the name of the 'sacred' and highly idealized symbolic status of the rest of society. Durkheim asserted that modern societies put more emphasis on restitution and less emphasis on extreme punishment (mutilation, torture, the death penalty, and so on) than do traditional societies, but in all human societies at every phase of development, the function of the law is to preserve the integrity of the group at the expense of the criminal, namely, he or she who dares to put him- or herself above the law. Foucault (1977) argued against Durkheim that in the punitive exercise of sovereignty, criminals were punished not because they had offended the collective conscience but because they had offended a particular 'sovereign' or symbolically charged political figure.[5] This divergence between Durkheim and Foucault on the role of society in punishment needs to be extended to the international stage and the concept of war crimes. How should the international community respond when a nation-state behaves as if it were above international law? Who or what is 'the sovereign' when it comes to 'the sovereignty of nations'?

In practice, at the Hague, contemporary international law has found culpable leaders in the chain of command who may not have pulled the trigger, who may not have known that crimes were committed low in the chain of command and who did not order crimes and abuse, but who laid out a policy that led to abuse and crime or who failed to prevent criminal and abusive acts (Hazan, 2004). Moreover, in all of the cases where the defendant was found guilty by the Tribunals for Yugoslavia and Rwanda, the Tribunal's judgments asserted that none of the guilty parties necessarily had to be 'an architect or the prime mover' of the established persecution in order to be deemed guilty of war crimes. Instead, the precedent established by the Tribunals is that the guilty war criminal could have known or *should* have known, and therefore prevented, the criminal actions of subordinates. The Tribunal's precedents have been reversed at the courts-martial pertaining to Abu Ghraib: the United States military chose to prosecute primarily low-ranking soldiers and not to prosecute officers high in the chain of command, in addition to accepting the excuse offered by many officers that they did not know about the abuse, without raising the issue that they should have known (see Karpinski, 2005).

In general, jurists and lawyers do not display what C. Wright Mills (1959) called the 'sociological imagination,' by which he meant grasping the interplay between a particular 'biography' and 'history.' For the most part, they act out their social roles without reflecting on the meaning of those roles and its attendant vocabulary. The commonly used legal terms 'widespread,' 'systematic,' 'planned,' 'command responsibility,' 'chain of command,' 'rational,' and other elements of judicial vocabulary are essential to lawyers who engage each other in verbal battle in various courtrooms that involve crimes of war, because without these concepts, given acts could not rise to the level of being framed as war crimes. Yet the 'biographies' of seven particular soldiers whom the government labeled as 'rotten apples' has been imperfectly linked to the sociological 'history' of the abuse at Abu Ghraib, which is connected to abuse at Guantánamo and elsewhere. Thus, opinion-makers, journalists, and some organizations such as the International Committee of the Red Cross (ICRC) and Amnesty International have noted that some acts committed by American soldiers and political leaders in both Gulf Wars qualify as war crimes, especially with regard to the abuse and torture inflicted upon prisoners in Abu Ghraib, Guantánamo Bay, and other American-run prisons around the world (Danner, 2004). But no one engaged in these discussions of alleged war crimes committed by Americans, or other Westerners such as Britons, seriously believes that an American or a Briton will be put on trial for war crimes at the Hague in the near future. Instead, the United States has put forth the argument that it will monitor and try American military lawbreakers under its Uniform Code of Military Justice (UCMJ). More significantly, some journalists as well as human rights groups claim to have uncovered evidence that leaders high in the 'chain of command' either knew or should have known and should have

taken steps to prevent alleged abuses and war crimes committed by US troops in Iraq (Danner, 2004; Hersh, 2004). The ICRC, in particular, has labeled the abuses at Abu Ghraib as 'routine,' hence systematic, not as isolated incidents. A plethora of US government reports on abuses committed by American soldiers arrived at the general conclusion that abuse occurred, but offered competing and contradictory interpretations regarding who knew or ordered what sort of abuse or torture in the chain of command (Strasser, 2004). The discourse on this explosive subject avoids completely the subject of putting on trial Americans who are high in the chain of command and who should have known and should have taken steps to prevent the abuse even if they did not order it.

Thus, the sociologist must take seriously the general criticism leveled by postmodernists such as Baudrillard (1986) and other cultural theorists that Western institutions are self-privileging and regard themselves as exceptional in the world community; that: (1) the West in general and the United States in particular derive their cultural frame of reference from a specific cultural base, namely, Western Europe; (2) this Western European and American cultural base is depicted in terms of the grand narratives of the Enlightenment, which is considered unique to the West; and (3) the West is reluctant to apply this frame of reference to itself with regard to war crimes yet does sometimes apply it to cultural sites and actors which are labeled as non-Western. Put together, these assumptions seem to be part of what Lipset (1997) and others call American exceptionalism. Specifically, officials high in the chain of command in Yugoslavia and Rwanda were prosecuted and many were found guilty of war crimes even though several may not have known of and did not order crimes or abuse or other breaches of the Geneva Conventions. On the other hand, the Abu Ghraib torture scandal has been framed by the US government as a set of events that involved a small group of disorganized and unprofessional soldiers who were labeled as morally corrupt. The dominant frame of reference in the United States, namely, American exceptionalism, cannot tolerate the cognitive dissonance that an American (as the idealized representative of highly superior values) could engage in seemingly Balkan acts unless he or she was acting outside the American frame of reference. At the same time, some journalists in the information media and some organizations such as Human Rights Watch (2006) frame the abuses at Abu Ghraib as a set of events that flowed from a general 'climate' of disregard for the Geneva Conventions that was established at the highest levels of the United States military and political chain of command and that trickled down to the soldiers on the ground. The perspective taken in the present study supposes that it is a matter not of choosing between top-down versus bottom-up explanations, but of integrating both perspectives and finding a middle ground between them. Specifically, soldiers low in the chain of command clearly committed abuses, but officers high in the chain of command should have known and should have taken steps to prevent the abuse.

It is likely that the abuse at Abu Ghraib was not the result of direct orders that came top-down from high in the chain of command. But it is also unlikely that the abuse at Abu Ghraib was solely the result of a handful of unprofessional soldiers at the bottom of the chain of command. The most complete explanation must involve some middle-level explanation that includes elements of both the top-down and bottom-up explanations. In Major General (MG) Fay's words, an 'unhealthy mystique' developed at Abu Ghraib (Strasser, 2004: 53). Who is responsible for creating the unhealthy mystique? What effect did it have on the soldiers at Abu Ghraib? One can rephrase these questions in a sociological vocabulary: How did *anomie* develop at Abu Ghraib? What were its consequences for the soldiers as well as the relationship between the United States and the rest of the world? And how can it be remedied?

◈ A Socio-cultural Analysis of MG George R. Fay's Report

The most comprehensive US government report on the abuse at Abu Ghraib was written by MG Fay and is referred to as the Fay report.[6] In the remainder of this paper, we shall re-read portions of his report in a sociological and specifically Durkheimian context, with a particular focus on the relationship between 'confusion' and what Durkheim calls *anomie*. MG Fay writes:

> This investigation found that certain individuals committed offenses in violation of international and US law to include the Geneva Conventions and the UCMJ and violated Army Values. Leaders in key positions *failed properly to supervise the interrogation operations at Abu Ghraib* and failed to understand *the dynamics created at Abu Ghraib.* (p. 7, emphasis added)

Note that several layers of normative structure are invoked (international, national, and local), and that MG Fay is treating Abu Ghraib as a social system, although he does not use this sociological term explicitly. MG Fay continues:

> The *environment* created at Abu Ghraib contributed to the occurrence of such abuse and the fact that it remained undiscovered by higher authority for a long period of time. What started as nakedness and humiliation . . . carried over into sexual and physical assaults by a *small group of morally corrupt and unsupervised Soldiers and civilians.* (pp. 9–10, emphasis added)

Throughout his report, MG Fay makes the quasi-sociological and basically correct connection between the social 'environment' and abuse. Although he does not say it explicitly, he is clearly not writing about the environment and atmosphere as phenomena pertaining to meteorology. He is using these terms to refer to 'social environment' as a system of norms, values, sanctions, and beliefs, although he does not use this sociological vocabulary explicitly. First, he makes it clear that the sexual and physical abuse was part of the overall 'poisoned' or anomic atmosphere at Abu Ghraib. Second, he makes it clear that the sexual and physical abuse was part of an overall pattern of normative breakdown that includes other forms of abuse, including unauthorized use of dogs, the improper use of isolation, and humiliating and degrading forms of treatment. Third, he fails to explain how and why the social system at Abu Ghraib would have permitted morally corrupt individuals to perform acts of deviance or failed to properly sanction them after the initial acts of deviance. As stated at the outset, Parsons assumed that a healthy social system would correct itself, while Durkheim would have claimed that an unhealthy or anomic social system becomes increasingly anomic unless it is self-consciously corrected. Fourth, and finally, morally corrupt individuals (for example, persons who can be identified as sadists, perverts, or otherwise severely disturbed through psychological testing) exist in all social settings, but this does not mean that they are able to easily impose their deviant fantasies and behavior onto others. Under normal conditions, a healthy social system will keep morally corrupt individuals under control through a system of norms, values, sanctions, and beliefs (as postulated by Parsons) that regulates everyone, from the healthiest individuals to the most corrupt.

Before launching into an extended discussion of MG Fay's report, it is worth examining the sequence of logical steps he uses to arrive at his conclusion. On p. 71, he writes, regarding physical and sexual abuse at Abu Ghraib: 'They were perpetrated or witnessed by individuals or small groups.' Acts can only be perpetrated by individuals, acting alone or in small groups, but such individuals are always acting in the context of some social system. He continues: 'Such abuse can not be directly tied to a systemic US approach to torture or approved treatment of detainees' (p. 71). In this sentence, MG Fay leaps to the national level of normative discourse (the norms of the United States) and leaves open the possibility that the abuse might be *indirectly* tied to such a national level of norms. However, one should also note that MG Fay leaves out other logical possibilities, which he, in fact, supports with evidence in his report, namely that such abuse can be directly linked to a systemic approach at Abu Ghraib; that such abuse can be indirectly linked to a systemic approach at Abu Ghraib; that such direct as well as indirect links at Abu Ghraib are themselves linked in some fashion, through the chain of command, to national systems of norms, and to international systems of norms *vis-à-vis* the

ICRC and information media coverage. By implication, MG Fay seems to take the position that there was a social environment or climate at Abu Ghraib for the very types of abuse (sexual and physical) that he attributes to morally corrupt individuals, as when he writes elsewhere in this same passage: 'The *climate* created at Abu Ghraib provided the opportunity for such abuse to occur and to continue undiscovered by higher authority for a *long period of time*' (p. 71, emphasis added). This claim begs the question: What was the state of dialogue between US Army and other US national organizations and the local 'climate' at Abu Ghraib? MG Fay leaves this question unanswered. He then makes the critical logical leap: 'What started as undressing and humiliation, stress and physical training (PT), *carried over* into sexual and physical assaults by a small group of morally corrupt and unsupervised Soldiers and civilians' (p. 71, emphasis added). Again, the sociologist must ask the question: How and why did the unauthorized undressing and humiliation begin in the first place? What defect in the social system led to the initial breach of norms (primary deviance), and how did these breaches 'carry over' into systemic breaches of norms (secondary deviance)? This is the crux of the issue that needs to be explained. Based upon the facts that MG Fay reports, it seems that the social system at Abu Ghraib was disorganized and anomic from the outset; that this state of social disorganization and *anomie* grew progressively worse over time; and that these defects in the social system produced widespread forms of deviance among prisoners and US personnel alike. Abu Ghraib was a dangerous, stress-inducing, deviance-producing social setting for everyone who was forced to be there. There existed several specific sources of 'confusion' which contributed to this anomic state of affairs. We shall now consider these in more detail.

◈ Confusion as to Who Was in Charge

MG Fay notes that at Abu Ghraib, 'people made up their own titles as things went along' (p. 43). He adds that 'some people thought COL Pappas was the Director; some thought LTC Jordan was the Director' (p. 43). Can one imagine a sociology department or medical office or any other institutional setting in which people made up their own titles and did not know who was in charge? This fundamental confusion concerning roles and authority bespeaks extreme anomie.

◈ Confusion Between Approved and Abusive Activities

MG Fay writes: 'Theater Interrogation and Counter-Resistance Policies (ICRP) were found to be *poorly defined,* and *changed several times.* As a result, interrogation activities *sometimes crossed into abusive activity*' (p. 7, emphasis added). This state of affairs, alone, is sufficient to create the state of 'derangement' that is discussed by Durkheim. It is less a case of 'normlessness,' in that norms did exist, than it is a case of chaos and confusion regarding norms.

MG Fay notes that non-doctrinal approaches that were approved for use in Afghanistan and Guantánamo Bay ('GTMO') 'became *confused* at Abu Ghraib and were implemented without proper authorities or safeguards' and that 'soldiers were not trained on non-doctrinal interrogation techniques' (p. 8, emphasis added). One of these approaches involved the use of dogs, based on 'several documents that spoke of exploiting the Arab fear of dogs' (p. 10). MG Fay concludes that '[t]he use of dogs in interrogations to "fear up" detainees was utilized without proper authorization' (p. 10).

MG Fay returns to the improper use of dogs later in his report. He reports that as of 20 November 2003, 'abuse of detainees was already occurring and the addition of dogs was just one more abuse device' (p. 83). There arose controversy over who 'owned' the dogs and how they would be used. The presence of the dogs is mysteriously 'associated with MG G. Miller's visit,' but this link is not explored by MG Fay. MG Fay concludes this section: 'COL Pappas did not recall how he got the authority to employ dogs; *just that he had it* (p. 83, emphasis added). In any bureaucracy based upon a hierarchical rational-legal authority, including the US Army, it is an indicator of *anomie* that a commanding

officer would claim that he 'just had' authority without rational-legal justification.

Elsewhere MG Fay writes that '[e]ven with all the apparent *confusion over roles, responsibilities and authorities,* there were early indications that MP and MI personnel knew the use of dog teams in interrogations was abusive' (p. 84). If personnel knew that their use was abusive, at the same time that they engaged in abuse made possible and even encouraged by social disorganization, they were placed in what sociologists and psychologists call a 'double-bind' situation: one is damned if one does and damned if one does not engage in abuse. The double-bind situation has been researched thoroughly and found to be a causal factor in a plethora of forms of deviance, and mental breakdowns of various sorts.

◈ Insufficient Training

MG Fay writes: 'As pointed out clearly in the MG Taguba report, MP units and individuals at Abu Ghraib *lacked sufficient training on operating a detainment/interrogation facility*' and that 'MI units and individuals also *lacked sufficient, appropriate, training to cope with the situation encountered at Abu Ghraib*' (p. 46, emphasis added). In sociological terms, the MP and MI units were not able to internalize the proper and required norms, values, sanctions, and beliefs appropriate to their mission. This was, sociologically speaking, an invitation for abuse to occur.

The state of confusion was so great that MG Fay asserts that soldiers did not know what they were permitted to do or not do:

> Guard and interrogation personnel at Abu Ghraib were *not adequately trained or experienced and were certainly not well versed in the cultural understanding off the detainees.* MI personnel were *totally ignorant* of MP lanes in the road or rules of engagement. A common observation was that MI knew what MI could do and what MI couldn't do; but MI did *not know* what the MPs could or could *not* do in their activities. (p. 46, emphasis added)

In this passage MG Fay seems to imply that role confusion occurred such that MI did not know the role expectations for MPs. However, in another passage, MG Fay suggests that this role confusion was pervasive, and extended to the role expectations for MIs, MPs, and their perceptions of each other's role expectations: 'Again, who was allowed to do what and how exactly they were to do it was *totally unclear. Neither of the communities (MI and MP) knew what the other could and could not do*' (p. 70, emphasis added). The phrase 'totally unclear' refers to all of the personnel at Abu Ghraib, and constitutes a very powerful description of the drastic extent of anomie at Abu Ghraib. According to MG Fay: 'Most of the MPs were *never trained* in prison operations' (p. 46, emphasis added). From a sociological perspective, one could not expect even the minimal semblance of 'social order' and consensus in a social milieu which relied upon actors who were not trained in the normative expectations for their roles. This aspect of the social milieu at Abu Ghraib might be likened to a university whose professors were not trained in the subject areas they were teaching, or a clinic run by personnel untrained in medicine. Again, norms exist—but they are not coordinated or implemented properly.

Furthermore, according to MG Fay, 'approximately 35% of the contract interrogators lacked formal military training as interrogators' (p. 50). In addition: 'Proper oversight did not occur at Abu Ghraib due to a *lack of training and inadequate contract management and monitoring*' (p. 52, emphasis added).

◆ Lack of Social Integration Within the Military Units at Abu Ghraib

MG Fay writes: 'The JIDC [Joint Interrogation Detention Center] was created in a very short time period with *parts and pieces of various units. It lacked unit integrity, and this lack was a fatal flaw*' (p. 9, emphasis added). Elsewhere, MG Fay elaborates that 'cross-leveling' occurred with the 'disadvantage of inserting Soldiers into units shortly before deployment who had never trained with those units' (p. 32). In summary,

'The Soldiers did not know the unit' and 'the unit and the unit leadership did not know the Soldiers' (p. 32). COL Pappas had at his disposal 'disparate elements of units and individuals, including civilians, that had never trained together, but now were going to have to fight together' (p. 32). Later in the report, MG Fay emphasizes this point:

It is important to understand that the MI units at Abu Ghraib were far from complete units. They were small elements from those units. Most of the elements that came to Abu Ghraib came *without their normal command structure.* The unit Commanders and Senior NCOs did *not* go to Abu Ghraib but stayed with the bulk of their respective units. (p. 41, emphasis added)

'JIDC interrogators, analysts, and leaders were unprepared for the arrival of contract interrogators and had no training to fall back on in the management, control, and discipline of these personnel' (p. 19). Moreover, the contract interrogators were supposed to be screened yet '[s]uch screening was not occurring' (p. 40).

In his conclusions, MG Fay explains:

The JIDC was established in an ad hoc manner without proper planning, personnel, and logistical support for the missions it was intended to perform. Interrogation and analyst personnel were quickly klu[d]ged together from a half dozen units in an effort to meet personnel requirements. Even at its peak strength, interrogation and analyst manpower at the JIDC was too shorthanded to deal with the large number of detainees at hand. (p. 113)

Lack of social integration among the individuals who make up a social system is one of the keystones of Durkheim's entire system of thought in the analysis of modern forms of social pathology. Lack of social integration has been found by sociologists to be consistently related to the breaking of norms. In his landmark study *The American Soldier,* Samuel Stouffer (1949) found that strongly integrated military units performed better than less cohesive units. It would be important to investigate in future theoretical and empirical work whether social integration is better understood in Durkheim's terms of a coordinated division of labor versus that functionalist view which tends to quantify integration in terms of instances of social interaction and bonding (Gibbs, 1982).

◈ Rapid Changes in the Social Milieu

MG Fay writes: 'By mid-October, interrogation policy in Iraq had changed three times in less than 30 days' (p. 28). Elsewhere he writes: 'There is no formal advanced interrogation training in the US Army' (p. 17). Furthermore, 'Most interrogator training that occurred at Abu Ghraib was on-the-job training' (p. 18). Rapid social and normative change is in itself a promoter of stress and contributes to social disorganization.

◈ Intense Pressure to Obtain Intelligence

MG Fay writes that 'as the *need for actionable intelligence rose,* the realization dawned that pre-war planning had not included planning for detainee operations' (p. 24, emphasis added). Later in the report, he elaborates: 'LTG Sanchez did not believe significant pressure was coming from outside of CJTF-7 [Combined Joint Task Force Seven], but *does confirm that there was great pressure placed upon the intelligence system to produce actionable intelligence*' (p. 42, emphasis added). Elsewhere MG Fay writes: 'COL Pappas perceived *intense pressure for intelligence* from interrogations,' and that this pressure was passed 'to the rest of the JIDC leadership' (p. 45). MG Fay elaborates that '[p]ressure consisted in deviation from doctrinal reporting standards' and other ways (p. 45). Philip Zimbardo and others have found that intense pressure upon a police unit is one of the key components that lead to abuse, though without explaining the social structural reasons for this

connection (see Huggins et al., 2002). Note that Fay volunteers the Durkheimian-sounding explanation that intense pressure may have led to a breaking of moral boundaries, which in turn led to abuse.

◈ Confusion as to Which Norms to Follow

MG Fay writes: 'Soldiers on the ground are confused about how they apply the Geneva Conventions and whether they have a duty to report violations of the conventions' (p. 19). Further confusion is documented on p. 28 of the Fay report, wherein the General discusses CPT Wood's chart on 'Interrogation Rules of Engagement.' MG Fay writes:

> The chart was confusing, however. It was not completely accurate and could be *subject to various interpretations.* . . . What was particularly confusing was that nowhere on the chart did it mention a number of techniques that were in use at the time: removal of clothing, forced grooming, hooding, and yelling, loud music and light control. Given the detail otherwise noted on the aid, the failure to list some techniques *left a question of whether they were authorized for use without approval.* (p. 28, emphasis added)

From a sociological point of view, the soldiers would have had a very difficult time making out the difference between what is normative versus what is not if the commanding officer present could not. The commanding officer represents, in a Durkheimian sense, the values, norms, sanctions, and beliefs of the US Army and other, related organizations.

◈ 'Unhealthy Mystique'

MG Fay claims that the 'acronym "Other Government Agency" (OGA) referred almost exclusively to the CIA' and that 'CIA detention and interrogation practices *led to a loss of accountability, abuse, reduced interagency cooperation, and an unhealthy mystique* that further *poisoned the atmosphere* at Abu Ghraib' (pp. 52–3, emphasis added). MG Fay adds that 'the *systemic lack of accountability* for interrogator actions and detainees *plagued* detainee operations in Abu Ghraib' (p. 54, emphasis added). A 'systemic' lack of accountability suggests a social milieu that approximates social chaos much more than any semblance of social order. It is intriguing that MG Fay uses words such as 'unhealthy,' 'poisoned,' and 'plagued' when referring to the social milieu at Abu Ghraib. He repeatedly and explicitly describes a toxic social environment in terms similar to the vocabulary that Durkheim uses to describe an anomic social environment.

According to MG Fay, several abusive incidents 'were *widely known within the US community* (MI and MP alike) at Abu Ghraib' (p. 54, emphasis added). He adds: 'Speculation and *resentment* grew over the lack of personal responsibility, *of some people being above the laws and regulations.* The resentment contributed to the *unhealthy environment* that existed at Abu Ghraib' (p. 54, emphasis added). MG Fay refers again to a social 'atmosphere' at Abu Ghraib when he writes: 'According to COL Pappas, MG G. Miller said they, GTMO, used military working dogs, and that they were effective in *setting the atmosphere for interrogations*' (p. 58, emphasis added). Clearly, the 'social atmosphere' at Abu Ghraib was out of sync with Army Doctrine, the Geneva Conventions, and other systems of agreed upon social norms.

MG Fay implies that humiliating nudity was part of the social atmosphere at Abu Ghraib: 'Many of the Soldiers who witnessed the nakedness were told that this was an *accepted practice*' (p. 68, emphasis added). Because MG Fay lists nakedness as a form of abuse in his summary, he is implying that nudity was part of the deviant subculture that was created at Abu Ghraib. He does not address who told whom and with what regularity that this form of abuse was 'accepted practice.' Elsewhere he adds: 'MI interrogators started directing nakedness at Abu Ghraib as early as 16 September 2003 to humiliate and break down detainees'

(p. 69). This observation gives one some indication of the long time-frame in which this form of abuse was practiced.

 ## Failure of Self-Correcting Mechanisms

MG Fay's report is replete with instances of soldiers objecting to or reporting abuse, and supervisors ignoring them, failing to take corrective action, or invalidating their morally correct observations. Consider incident #1 as an illustration: '1LT Sutton, 320th MP BN IRF intervened to stop the abuse and was told by the MI soldiers, "we are the professionals; we know what we are doing." They refused 1LT Sutton's lawful order to identify themselves' (p. 71). 1LT Sutton reported the incident 'to the CID [Criminal Investigation Command] who determined the allegation lacked sufficient basis for prosecution' (p. 71). Clearly, options other than prosecution were available, but were not pursued. In fact, '[t]his incident was not further pursued based on limited data and the absence of additional investigative leads' (p. 72). Incident #19 quotes an unnamed Colonel as responding as follows to a sergeant who cited the Geneva Conventions as objection to the abuse he witnessed: 'fine Sergeant, you do what you have to do, I am going back to bed' (p. 80). There is no need to go over the forty-plus other documented 'incidents' in detail here: taken as a whole, they suggest that a climate of abuse was prevalent at Abu Ghraib; that soldiers were not in a position to have their objections validated by superiors; and that officers high in the chain of command did not follow their role expectations to correct the abuse within the social system that was Abu Ghraib. The significance of this conclusion is that it contradicts MG Fay's interpretation that the abuse in question was the result of a few corrupt individuals. Clearly, using the facts in his own report, one may arrive at the conclusion that the abuse was widespread, systematic, and that normative mechanisms which existed did not function as intended, so that soldiers were not validated by their superiors or the dysfunctional social system in objecting to the abuse.

In summary, the language used by MG Fay to describe the social environment at Abu Ghraib is remarkably similar to Durkheim's (1951 [1897]) descriptions of *anomie* as a social condition that is *déréglée*. MG Fay stops short of making the connection that an unhealthy environment of this sort inevitably leads to deviance, but this is precisely Durkheim's conclusion.

◈ Cultural Insensitivity

MG Fay writes that US soldiers at Abu Ghraib were 'certainly not well versed in the cultural understandings of the detainees' (p. 46). There is ample evidence to support this claim, but the problem goes far deeper than not being 'well versed.' A sociological reading of the US government reports on the abuse at Abu Ghraib suggests that the US Army failed to understand and predict the impact of forced nudity upon a specifically Muslim population. Moreover, this form of abuse seems to transcend the normative chaos at Abu Ghraib, to appear in other facilities. MG Fay writes: 'Removal of clothing was not a technique developed at Abu Ghraib, but rather a technique which was *imported and can be traced though Afghanistan and GTMO*' (p. 87, emphasis added).

'Removal of clothing is *not* a doctrinal or authorized interrogation technique but appears to have been directed and employed at various levels within MI as an "ego down" technique' (p. 88, emphasis added). Furthermore: 'It is apparent from this investigation that removal of clothing was *employed routinely* and *with the belief it was not abuse*' (p. 88, emphasis added). After an ICRC visit, CPT Reese is quoted as saying: 'We could not determine what happened to the detainee's original clothing' (p. 88). MG Fay makes the interpretation that '[t]he use of clothing as an incentive (nudity) is *significant* in that it likely *contributed to an escalating "de-humanization"* of the detainees and *set the stage for additional and more severe abuses to occur*' (p. 88, emphasis added). Note that this observation by MG Fay, and other ones like it, supports the sociological interpretation that an unhealthy, anomic social atmosphere was established at Abu Ghraib, which led to abuse. According to the anthropologist Akbar S. Ahmed (1992), nudity is a cardinal normative violation in Islamic culture because this culture puts a high premium on modesty.[7] Based on Ahmed's and other sociological and anthropological research into Islamic culture, one may conclude that forced nudity was a form of psychic abuse for most of the prisoners, due to its significance as an extreme form of humiliation in Islamic culture.

MG Fay writes:

> The interrogators believed they had the authority to use clothing as an incentive, as well as stress positions, and were not attempting to hide their use.... It is probable that use of nudity was sanctioned at some level within the chain-of-command. If not, lack of leadership and oversight permitted the nudity to occur. (p. 90)

In general, MG Fay lists the following as organizational and sociological problems at Abu Ghraib:

- There was a lack of clear Command and Control of Detainee Operations at the CJTF-7 level.

- The JIDC was manned with personnel from numerous organizations and consequently lacked unit cohesion.

- Leaders failed to take steps to effectively manage pressure placed upon JIDC personnel.

- Some capturing units failed to follow procedures, training, and directives in the capture, screening, and exploitation of prisoners.

- The JIDC was established in an *ad hoc* manner without proper planning, personnel, and logistical support for the missions it was intended to perform.

- Interrogation training in the Laws of Land Warfare and the Geneva Conventions was ineffective.

- MI leaders did not receive adequate training in the conduct and management of interrogation operations.

- Critical records on detainees were not created or maintained properly, thereby hampering effective operations.

- OGA interrogation practices led to a loss of accountability at Abu Ghraib.

- ICRC recommendations were ignored by MI, MP, and CJTF-7 personnel.

But each and every one of these shortcomings also produced a cultural impact upon a primarily Islamic population of prisoners that was interpreted—by their cultural standards—as offensive, disrespectful, dehumanizing, uninterested in their cultural backgrounds, and hostile to their culture. In other words, the social disorganization among the American soldiers at Abu Ghraib promoted cultural suspicion and still more anomie from the point of view of Muslim culture. The results included riots by prisoners, which in turn led to vengeance by some American guards, which in turn escalated to more riots, and so on. Cultural insensitivity contributed to an initial state of *anomie,* which, left unchecked, contributed to a clash of cultures and still more anomie, which, in turn, set the stage for further abuse.

◈ Conclusions

The extent of social disorganization, social chaos, dysfunction, lack of coordination, and of a general state of *anomie* was so great at Abu Ghraib that abuse and the breaking of norms that are documented was the *inevitable* outcome and should have been expected. Moreover, because the social system at Abu Ghraib could not self-correct, as functionalists might claim to predict, its disintegration increased and it could not respond to corrective measures outside the system, including but not limited to the ICRC. Recent reports by journalists and human rights groups point to an increase in incidents of abuse at other military posts throughout Iraq,

suggesting that the toxic or anomic state of affairs at Abu Ghraib has spread. All of this poses a challenge both to sociological theory and, practically, to the US Army.

Regarding social theory, sociologists need to re-examine the largely dormant understandings of anomie by Durkheim and by functionalists, compare and contrast them critically, and apply them appropriately to contemporary contexts, including but not limited to Abu Ghraib. Mountains of theory and research on the relationship of ordinary crime to *anomie* do not seem to be helpful in understanding international war crimes, abuse, and torture, which have become important global issues since World War II. Moreover, criticisms as well as applications of Parsonian or Mertonian functionalism have failed to settle the question whether anomie is a condition of normlessness that will correct itself. Durkheim seems more convincing in arguing that *anomie* is a grievous social evil characterized by genuine social 'derangement' that produces equally grievous and long-lasting negative consequences. In this case, the abuse at Abu Ghraib has stained American intentions of liberating Iraq, has contributed to a clash of civilizations between the West and Islamic cultures, and may have contributed to the insurgency movement. The Parsonian assumption that social systems can automatically self-correct thus seems to be off the mark. If Durkheim's classical perspective is the more correct one, then one should take seriously his proposed program for repairing anomic social systems.

This last point holds immediate consequences for the US Army and government. The Abu Ghraib courts-martial at Fort Hood, Texas, were supposed to repair the damage caused by the abuse, and restore justice. But if Durkheim is correct, the fact that the Army chose to shift all the blame onto a handful of low-ranking soldiers may not appease the collective conscience in the long run. In fact, Durkheim (1995 [1912]) introduced the concept of scapegoating to account for such instances of anomic miscarriage of justice, in which the 'sins' of a larger social group are displaced onto a few individuals, animals, or even objects.[8] In the case at hand, the Government's own reports, as well as the outcomes of the courts-martial, suggest a Durkheimian interpretation that the responsibility of American society as a whole and many of its institutions for the abuses at Abu Ghraib was displaced onto a handful of so-called 'rotten apples.' Durkheim's own public defense of Captain Alfred Dreyfus, also a target of collective scapegoating, lends further support to such a conclusion. In addition, Durkheim's concept of scape-goating suggests that the prisoners at Abu Ghraib were themselves the scapegoats for American society's pain and rage in response to the terrorist event that has come to be known as 9/11. Durkheim writes:

> When society undergoes suffering, it feels the need to find someone whom it can hold responsible for its sickness, on whom it can avenge its misfortunes: and those against whom opinion already discriminates are naturally designated for this role. These are the pariahs who serve as expiatory victims. (in Lukes, 1985, p. 345)

No credible evidence has linked Iraq to 9/11, and MG Fay's as well as other reports and testimony make it clear that the prisoners at Abu Ghraib had no connection to 9/11 or any other sort of terrorist activity. In the final analysis, the abuse committed against the inmates at Abu Ghraib prison comes cross as an exercise in irrationality and scapegoating, or what Durkheim called *dérèglement.*

◈ Notes

1. Matt Taibbi writes: 'Mestrovic described Abu Ghraib as a "state of *anomie.*" "A what?" [Colonel] Pohl snapped, frowning. "A state of *anomie,*" the doctor repeated. Pohl shuddered and sipped his coffee, seeming to wonder whether such a word was even legal in Texas' (2005: 48).

2. According the Littré *Dictionnaire de la langue française* ([1863], 1963 vol. 2, p. 1672), the principal meaning of *dérèglement* is derangement: '*Dérèglement, dérangement* are words expressing two nuances of moral disorder: What is *dérangé* is disarranged [*hors de son rang*] or is without place. What is *déréglé* is out of rule [*hors de la régle*]. The state of *déréglement* is more serious than that of derangement.' One of the many sources that Litté cites is Jacques Bossuet, who describes dérèglement in the following

terms, among others: *mal, égarement, péché, tourments, infini de miséres, maladie, désordre, dangereux, souffrir, impiété, intemperance, desséchement, miserable captivité* (Bossuet, [1731] 1836 pp. 43–79). It is interesting that many English equivalents of these words are used by soldiers and investigators to describe the social climate at Abu Ghraib.

3. These assumptions are ubiquitous and mostly unquestioned in literally hundreds of articles, treatises, and textbooks. However, one is at a loss to find any of these secondary interpreters quoting Durkheim in these regards.

4. The reader is free to consult any contemporary sociology textbook as evidence for this persistent misunderstanding. Thoughtful alternatives to functionalist misrepresentations of Durkheim's concept of *anomie* are also sidelined in sociological theory and textbooks. For example, in *The Lonely Crowd,* David Riesman writes: 'Anomic is English coinage from *Durkheim's anomique* (adjective of *anomie*) meaning ruleless, ungoverned' ([1950] 1977 p. 242). But in his discussion, Riesman seems to imply that different types of *anomie* correspond to tradition-, inner-, and other-directed forms of social character. However, despite being acknowledged as one of sociology's most important writers, Riesman's analysis of *anomie* in the context of his overall theory has been largely ignored.

5. Foucault writes: 'The ceremony of punishment, then, is an exercise of "terror" . . . to make everyone aware, through the body of the criminal, of the unrestrained presence of the sovereign' (1977, p. 49).

6. It is also sometimes referred to as the Jones-Fay report, for internal, bureaucratic reasons within the structure of the US Army that need not be explored here. Reports by MG Antonio Taguba and James Schlesinger also exist (Strasser, 2004), along with other reports, but the Fay report is chosen here in the interest of conserving space. For a fuller discussion of the government reports on Abu Ghraib, see Danner (2004) and Mestrovic (2007).

7. It would be important to devote a separate study to Ahmed's observation about the relative meaning of nudity in American, Muslim, and other social contexts. Moreover, there are hints in the government reports, which cannot be pursued here, that American interrogators deliberately used this knowledge concerning nudity in Islamic culture to establish policies at Abu Ghraib. If true, such deliberate strategies are out of sync with the policies on interrogation that existed at the time of the abuse, and constitute yet another instance of *anomie,* specifically, lack of coordination with lawful Army policies on interrogation.

8. Durkheim writes: When the pain reaches such a pitch, it becomes suffused with a kind of anger and exasperation. One feels the need to break or destroy something. One attacks oneself or others. One strikes, wounds, or burns oneself, or one attacks someone else, in order to strike, wound, or burn him. Thus was established the mourning custom of giving oneself over to veritable

orgies of torture. It seems to be probable that the vendetta and head hunting have no other origin. If every death is imputed to some magical spell and if, for that reason, it is believed that the dead person must be avenged, the reason is a felt need to find a victim at all costs on whom the collective sorrow and anger can be discharged. This victim will naturally be sought outside, for an outsider is a subject *minoris* resistentiae; since he is not protected by the fellow-feeling that attaches to a relative or a neighbor, nothing about him blocks and neutralizes the bad and destructive feelings aroused by the death. Probably for the same reason, a woman serves more often than a man as the passive object of the most cruel mourning rites. Because she has lower social significance, she is more readily singled out to fill the function of scapegoat. ([1912] 1995 p. 404)

◈ **References**

Ahmed, Akbar S. (1992) *Postmodernism and Islam.* London: Routledge.

Baillot, Alexandre (1927) *Influence de la philosophie de Schopenhauer en France (1860—1900).* Paris: J. Vrin.

Baudrillard, Jean (1986) *America,* trans. Chris Turner. London: Verso.

Bauman, Zygmunt (1990) *Modernity and the Holocaust.* Ithaca, NY: Cornell University Press.

Bossuet, Jacques (1836) *Traité de la concupiscence.* Paris: Éditeurs des Portes de France. (Orig. pub. 1731.)

Cushman, Thomas and Stjepan G. Mestrovic (eds) (1995) *This Time We Knew: Western Responses to Genocide in Bosnia.* New York: New York University Press.

Danner, Mark (2004) *Torture and Truth: America, Abu Ghraib and the War on Terror.* New York: New York Review of Books.

Durkheim, Émile (1933) *The Division of Labor in Society,* trans. Simpson. New York: Free Press. (Orig. pub. 1893.)

Durkheim, Emile (1951) *Suicide: A Study in Sociology,* trans. John A. Spaulding and George Simpson. New York: Free Press. (Orig. pub. 1897.)

Durkheim, Emile (1983a) *Le Suicide: Etude de sociologie.* Paris: Presses Universitaries de France. (Orig. pub. 1897.)

Durkheim, Emile (1983b) *Professional Ethics and Civic Morals,* trans. Cornelia Brookfield. Westport, CT: Greenwood Press. (Orig. pub. 1950.)

Durkheim, Émile (1995) *The Elementary Forms of Religious Life,* trans. Karen E. Fields. New York: Free Press. (Orig. pub. 1912.)

Falk, Richard, Irene Gendzier and Robert Jay Lifton (eds) (2006) *Crimes of War: Iraq.* New York: Nation Books.

Foucault, Michel (1977) *Discipline and Punish: The Birth of the Prison,* trans. Alan Sheridan. New York: Vintage. (Orig. pub. 1975.)

Gibbs, Jack P. (1982) 'Testing the Theory of Status Integration and Suicide Rates,' *American Sociological Review* 47: 227—37.

Goffman, Erving (1986) *Frame Analysis: An Essay on the Organization of Experience.* Boston: Northeastern University Press.

Gutman, Roy and David Rieff (1999) *Crimes of War.* New York: Norton.

Guyau, Jean-Marie (1907) *Ésquisse d'une morale sans obligation ni sanction.* Paris: Alcan. (Orig. pub. 1885.)

Hazan, Pierre (2004) *Justice in a Time of War: The True Storybehind the International Criminal Tribunal for the Former Yugoslavia.* College Station, TX: Texas A&M University Press.

Hersh, Seymour M. (2004) *Chain of Command: The Road From 9/11 to Abu Ghraib.* New York: HarperCollins.

Huggins, Martha K., Mika Haritos-Fatouros and Philip G. Zimbardo (2002) *Violence Workers: Police Torturers and Murderers Reconstruct Brazilian Atrocities.* Berkeley: University of California Press.

Human Rights Watch (2006) 'By the Numbers: Findings of the Detainee Abuse and Accountability Project,' 18: 1–28.

Karpinski, Janis (2005) *One Woman's Army: The Commanding General of Abu Ghraib Tells Her Story.* New York: Hyperion.

Lalande, André (1980) *Vocabulaire technique et critique de la philosophie.* Paris: Presses Universitaires de France. (Orig. pub. 1926.)

Lipset, Seymour M. (1990) *Continental Divide: The Values and Institutions of the United States and Canada.* London: Routledge.

Lipset, Seymour M. (1997) *American Exceptionalism: A Double-Edged Sword.* New York: Norton.

Littré, Émile (1963) *Dictionnaire de la langue frangaise.* Vols. 1–9. Paris: Gallimard. (Orig. pub. 1863.)

Loewen, James (2007) *Lies My Teacher Told Me: Everything Your American History Textbooks Got Wrong.* New York: Touchstone Books.

Lukes, Steven (1985) *Émile Durkheim: His Life and Work.* Stanford: Stanford University Press. (Orig. pub. 1973.)

Lyonnet, Stanislas and Leopold Sabourin (1970) *Sin, Redemption and Sacrifice: A Biblical and Patristic Study.* Rome: Biblical Institute Press.

Lyotard, Jean-François (1984) *The Postmodern Condition.* Minneapolis: University of Minnesota Press.

Merton, Robert K. (1957) *Social Theory and Social Structure.* New York: Free Press.

Mestrovic, Stjepan G. (1985) 'Anomia and Sin in Durkheim's Thought,' *Journal for the Social Scientific Study of Religion* 24: 119–36.

Mestrovic, Stjepan G. (1988) *Emile Durkheim and the Reformation of Sociology.* Tottowa, NJ: Rowman & Littlefield.

Mestrovic, Stjepan G. (2007) *The Trials of Abu Ghraib: An Expert Witness Account of Shame and Honor.* Boulder, CO: Paradigm Publishers.

Mestrovic, Stjepan G. and Hélène M. Brown (1985) 'Durkheim's Concept of *Anomie as Dérèglemenf,* Social Problems 33: 81–99.

Mills, C. Wright (1959) *The Sociological Imagination.* New York: Oxford University Press.

Orru, Marco (1987) *Anomie: History and Meanings.* London: Allen & Unwin.

Parsons, Talcott (1937) *The Structure of Social Action.* Glencoe, IL: Free Press.

Riesman, David (1977) *The Lonely Crowd.* New Haven, CT: Yale University Press. (Orig. pub. 1950.)

Solis, Gary (1998) *Son Thang: An American War Crime.* New York: Bantam. Stouffer,

Samuel (1949) *The American Soldier: Adjustment during Army Life.* Princeton, NJ: Princeton University Press.

Strasser, Steven (2004) *The Abu Ghraib Investigations: The Official Reports of the Independent Panel and the Pentagon on the Shocking Prisoner Abuse in Iraq.* New York: Public Affairs.

Taibbi, Matt (2005) 'Ms. America,' *Rolling Stone,* 20 October, pp. 47–8.

Theodorson, George A. and Achilles G. Theodorson (1969) *A Modern Dictionary of Sociology.* New York: Thomas Y. Crowell.

Tocqueville, Alexis de (2004) *Democracy in America,* trans. George Lawrence. New York: Library of America. (Orig. pub. 1848.)

Zimbardo, Philip G. (2007) *The Lucifer Effect: Understanding How Good People Turn Evil.* New York: Random House.

READING 13

Murphy and Robinson frame their article as an extension of strain theory, tracing its heritage through the work of Merton, Cloward and Ohlin, and Messner and Rosenfeld. The authors offer a useful, additional overview of key ideas from these theorists but suggest there is a gap in the theory. They argue that Merton's categories of conformist and innovator are not mutually exclusive, as some individuals use a combination of legitimate and illegitimate means in pursuing the goal of wealth attainment. Murphy and Robinson then advocate for a new mode of adaptation to supplement Merton's model, "the Maximizer," someone who simultaneously uses and incorporates both legitimate and illegitimate means in the quest for the American Dream. Most research focusing on Merton's theory would likely emphasize differentials in deviant behavior based on economic standing or social class (i.e., "innovators" and "retreatists" would be primarily composed of those who do not live the American Dream through legitimate means). Alternatively, one of the more interesting distinctions this variant of the theory brings to the table is a focus on white-collar and corporate offenders who use both legitimate and illegitimate practices to achieve the economic success and beyond.

The Maximizer

Clarifying Merton's Theories of Anomie and Strain

Daniel S. Murphy and Mathew B. Robinson

◇ Introduction

This paper builds on, but attempts to add to, anomie and strain theories as the latter have been conceived by Robert Merton (1938), Steven Messner and Richard Rosenfeld (1994), and Richard Cloward and Lloyd Ohlin (1961). We provide an additional mode of adaptation to anomie and strain—*maximization*—which

Source: Murphy, Daniel S., and Mathew B. Robinson. 2008. "The Maximizer: Clarifying Merton's Theories of Anomie and Strain." *Theoretical Criminology* 12(4):501–521. Reprinted with permission.

refers to the simultaneous utilization of legitimate or institutionalized means and illegitimate means in pursuit of the so-called American Dream.

The *Maximizer,* an extension of Merton's typology and the focus of the present paper, is the inductive product of research which has explored perceived stringency in punishment compared to actual punishment as delineated in the United States Sentencing Commission Guideline Manual. The original research presented respondents with a set of vignettes and queried what the appropriate punishment should be for each criminal act described. These data were then compared to actual punishments as prescribed in the Guideline Manual.

In doing this research, we noted an anomaly in prescribed sentencing as compared to Guideline dictates for a vignette in which a contractor built a bridge—illegally breaking code in pursuit of profit—while simultaneously operating a legitimate business. The outcome of the illegal behavior perpetrated by the contractor was the collapse of the bridge and the death of five motorists. Consistently respondents indicated 'the contractor should have a fine imposed,' 'the contractor should have their license revoked,' 'perhaps it was the workers' fault and not that of the contractor,' and other similar reactions. The researchers were struck by respondents' tendency to justify the illegal activities of the contractor; acts that led to the death of five human beings. This led us to suspect that one reason for this rationalization was that people perceived the contractor as working toward the socially inculcated goal of the American Dream (legitimate means of opportunity), a goal so overweening that it was taken to justify the illegal actions of cutting corners in construction and breaking code (illegitimate means of opportunity). Moreover, the common finding of justification for such actions suggested that varied people in US society are perceived as willing to, or actually engaged in, such combined legal and illegal activities. Thus, we developed the concept of the *Maximizer,* someone who simultaneously uses and incorporates legitimate and illegitimate means of opportunity in the pursuit of profit and/or monetary gain (the American Dream).

In introducing this concept, the present paper also suggests that Merton's categories of conformist and innovator are not mutually exclusive. Rather, the pursuit of the American Dream leads social actors to combine both legitimate and illegitimate means in an effort to 'succeed' within corporate culture. While Merton's theories of anomie and strain have been well supported over the decades, Merton did not explicitly consider utilization of both legitimate and illegitimate means of opportunity in pursuit of the American Dream. On the contrary, though, we suggest that it is possible to utilize both legitimate and illegitimate means in pursuit of goals, as vaguely suggested yet not delineated by Cloward and Ohlin (1961) in their theory of differential opportunity. The goal of the present paper is to advance Merton's ideas regarding anomie and strain by exploring an additional adaptation—*maximization*—which refers to implementing both legitimate and illegitimate means of opportunity in pursuit of the socially inculcated American Dream.

◆ Literature Review

Merton's anomie and strain theories sought to explain why certain cultures, groups, and individuals were more prone to engage in antisocial and/or illegal behaviors. Merton asserted that members of society receive messages of what is *normal*—including acceptable behaviors—from societal institutions. Normal, according to Merton (1957: 132), is that which is the 'psychologically expectable, if not culturally approved, response to determinate social conditions.' Most people, most of the time, abide by society's rules of behavior, thereby remaining 'normal.' Yet pressures from social institutions, and specifically from expectations associated with the American Dream, can lead some 'to engage in nonconforming rather than conforming conduct.' These pressures should explain not only higher deviance by individuals who experience them, but also higher group deviance by members of the classes that most experience such pressures (Merton, 1957: 132).

Merton's central hypotheses regarding deviance and criminality assert that criminality is a function of an overemphasis on the goals associated with the American Dream (e.g. wealth), as well as a disjuncture between the goals valued by society and the means available to people to achieve them (Merton, 1957: 162). Thus, the primary mechanism through which deviance and criminality is fostered has its origin in *goals-means discrepancies* (whether because of an overemphasis on cultural goals or goal blockage). However, Merton did not explicitly consider utilization of both *legitimate* and *illegitimate means* of opportunity in pursuit of the American Dream.

Anomie and strain theories posit that criminality is due to an array of social causes. One explanation is that criminality results from personal states of egoism and selfishness caused by a lack of integration into, and regulation by, society, as in anomie theory and microanomie theory (Durkheim, 1893, 1897; Konty, 2005). Another is that it results from pressures to achieve at any cost imposed by the American Dream and the relative importance of the economy in our lives, as in *anomie theory and institutional anomie theory* (Merton, 1957; Messner and Rosenfeld, 1994). Some relevant theories deal with frustration that arises from increased wants and desires in the context of globalization and neoliberalism, as in global anomie and dysnomie theory (Passas, 2000). Others focus on discrepancies in cultural goals and the legitimate means to achieve them, as in *strain theory* (Merton, 1957) and on goal blockage, the loss of valued items, negative emotion, and noxious stimuli, as in *general strain theory* (Agnew, 1992, 1999, 2002; Agnew et al., 2002; Baron, 2004; Brezina, 1996; Brezina et al., 2001; Capowich et al., 2001; Eitle, 2002; Gibson et al., 2001; Jang et al., 2003; Mazerolle et al., 2000; Simons et al., 2003; Wright et al., 2001). Finally, some criminologists have emphasized a shared sense of relative deprivation, as in *macrolevel general strain theory* (Pratt and Godsey, 2003), as well as unlimited desires for wealth in the context of limited means, leading to a problem of adjustment, as in *differential opportunity theory* (Cloward and Ohlin, 1961).

All of these theories, to one degree or another, blame crime on the overpowering influence of the economy on our lives. The theories most relevant for economic sources of anomie and strain, as analyzed here, include Merton's separate but related anomie and strain theories, Messner and Rosenfeld's institutional anomie theory, and Cloward and Ohlin's theory of differential opportunity. Each is reviewed below. We first review Merton's anomie and Messner and Rosenfeld's institutional anomie theories, and then move on to Merton's strain and Cloward and Ohlin's differential opportunity theories. We believe this is the most logical order in which to discuss these theories, given that Messner and Rosenfeld (1994) adapted Merton's theory of anomie, and Cloward and Ohlin adapted Merton's theory of strain.

Anomie and Strain Perspectives

Before offering a brief review it is important to note that, although most criminological attention has been placed on Robert Merton's theory of strain, his seminal work—*Social Structure and Anomie*—contains within it two related but independent lines of theoretical argument (Bernard, 1987; Featherstone and Deflem, 2003; Messner, 1988). Bernard (1987: 267) refers to one as a 'cultural argument' (dealing with the value of monetary success and the importance of using legitimate means in pursuit of this goal), and the other as a 'structural argument' (dealing with the distribution of legitimate opportunities in society). The former explains criminality as a function of pressures placed on individuals living in a capitalistic American society, the latter as a function of differential opportunities.

Similarly, Messner (1988: 31) asserts that Merton's work relates to both a 'cultural structure' (pertaining to the normative values governing behaviors that are common to society, and which can be broken down into culturally defined goals and culturally defined means to achieve those goals), as well as to the 'social structure' (pertaining to a set of social relationships). Thus, Messner attributes to Merton a theory of social organization (relevant to the components of social systems) and a theory of deviant motivation (relevant to sources of pressure on individuals to violate social norms). Messner lays out the two theories this way: the first attributes criminality to a 'disjuncture within the cultural structure itself ... [due to] an exaggerated emphasis on goals in comparison with the emphasis on means'; the second attributes criminality to 'disjuncture between social structural arrangements and cultural prescriptions [when the] cultural structure extols the common success goals, while the social structure restricts access to the normative means' (Messner, 1988: 37).

Additionally, Featherstone and Deflem (2003: 472) point out that Merton's work developed two separate but related theories. These include a theory of anomie (positing that there exists in American society a disjuncture in emphasis on culture goals and the means to achieve them), as well as a strain theory (positing that goal blockage leads to pursuing illegitimate means). According to these authors, criminality emerges due to anomie caused by an overemphasis on the goals associated with the American Dream, and due to strain caused by blocked opportunities for those seeking the American Dream.

Anomie and Institutional Anomie

Beginning with Merton's first theory—anomie theory—one of Merton's main points is that the so-called 'American Dream' is both criminogenic and the over-riding institutionalized goal in our country. Stated simply, the American Dream means 'making it,' 'winning the game,' or achieving independence and wealth. When these goals are so emphasized that they get far more attention that the institutionalized means to achieve them, the result is anomie and criminality. When discussing a hypothetical poorly integrated culture, Merton explained that it is possible for culturally prescribed goals to overcome and completely dominate consideration of culturally prescribed means. In his words, 'there may develop a very heavy, at times virtually exclusive, stress upon the value of particular goals, involving comparatively little concern with the

institutionally prescribed means of striving toward these goals' (Merton, 1957: 132). According to Merton, American institutions of the 1950s placed greater emphasis on culture goals than upon institutional or legitimate means to achieve them. This resulted in an overwhelming focus on the cultural goals of American institutions with relatively little emphasis on the institutionalized means. When emphasis on institutionalized means relax and goals are overemphasized, criminality is permissible.

As Merton asserted, 'an extreme cultural emphasis on the goal of success attenuates conformity to institutionally prescribed methods of moving toward this goal' (Merton, 1957: 169). Thus, the American Dream itself may be viewed as criminogenic.

Essentially, Merton was asserting that our focus on the American Dream is too strong because emphasis on the goal has so attenuated the satisfactions deriving from sheer participation in the competitive activity that only a successful outcome provides gratification' (Merton, 1957: 135). In other words, 'winning' or 'making it' according to the rules becomes secondary to 'winning' or 'making it' by *any means necessary.*

Merton's analysis meant that he recognized crime as to be expected, given the prevalence of messages related to pursuing wealth in the US. Relatedly, Bernard (1987: 266) called this a 'uniform cultural value on monetary success.' In Merton's words again:

> In some large measure, money has been consecrated as a value in itself, over and above its expenditure for articles of consumption or its use for the enhancement of powers. Money is particularly well adapted to become a symbol of prestige ... However acquired, fraudulently or institutionally, it can be used to purchase the same goods and services. (Merton, 1957: 136)

Perhaps this is one reason why even the rich seek more. According to Merton:

> in the American Dream there is no final stopping point. The measure of 'monetary success'

is conveniently indefinite and relative. At each income level ... Americans want just about twenty-five percent more (but of course this 'just a bit more' continues to operate once it is obtained). (Merton, 1957: 136)

Passas underscores the never-ending pressure inherent in the motives of capitalism toward consumerism and an insatiable drive for *more:*

Regardless of whether people strive for more; due to natural drives or because of cultural encouragement, the point is that market economies cannot perform without lofty aspirations, consumerism, emphasis on material/ monetary goals, and competition. All this leads to the pursuit of constantly moving targets and systematic sources of frustration. (2000: 19)

Such frustration is one form of what Merton (1957: 139) referred to as *strain.* Hence, Merton's conclusion that the American Dream is criminogenic.

An important part of the mantra of the American Dream is the ethos that success and monetary achievement result from 'personal' strengths, that is, from hard work and determination of people with strong wills. Thus, failure in the United States is generally perceived as a 'personal' failure rather than a systemic flaw (Merton, 1957: 138). Assuming all failures are personal/ moral failures rather than system failures, the threat or fear of defeat may serve to motivate people to succeed, to attain the American Dream, by any and all means necessary. According to Merton, 'The moral mandate to achieve success ... exerts pressure to succeed, by fair means if possible and by foul means if necessary' (Merton, 1957: 169). This is precisely what the Maximizer tries to accomplish.

Thus, Merton understood that quitting is the only option that is not acceptable in America:

Americans are admonished not to be a quitter or in the dictionary of American culture, as in the lexicon of youth, 'there is no such word as fail.' The cultural manifesto is clear; one must not quit, must not cease striving, must not lessen his goals, for not failure but low aim is crime. (1957: 139)

Merton also stated that the American Dream emphasizes 'penalizing' those who draw in their ambitions' (Merton, 1957: 138), as does the ritualist.

Nearly 40 years later, Steven Messner and Richard Rosenfeld (1994) put forth their institutional anomie theory which expanded on Merton's theory of anomie. Institutional anomie theory also attributes high crime rates in the US to our allegiance to the American Dream. For Messner and Rosenfeld, this dream' is defined as the broad cultural ethos that entails a commitment to *the goal of material success,* to be pursued by everyone in society, under conditions of open, individual competition' (Messner and Rosenfeld, 1994: 6, emphasis added).

Similar to the claims of Merton, these authors asserted that the American Dream 'encourages an exaggerated emphasis on monetary achievement while devaluing alternative criteria of success, it promotes a preoccupation with the realization of goals while de-emphasizing the importance of the ways in which these goals are pursued' (Messner and Rosenfeld, 1994: 10). The American Dream thus creates pressure to achieve, but minimizes the pressure to play by the rules. Under these circumstances, people become more likely to use the most technically efficient means necessary in reaching their goals. The result is a higher rate of predatory crime' (Bernburg, 2002: 732).

Messner and Rosenfeld asserted that the needs and health of the economy in modern America take precedence over other important social institutions like the family, schools, and even places of worship. This is due to the fact that the primary task for non-economic institutions such as the family and schools is to inculcate beliefs, values, and commitments other than those of the marketplace' (Vold et al., 1998: 176). Thus, we should not expect these types of institutions to control antisocial and criminal behaviors when they are weakened. Instead, when other institutions such as polity, religion, education, and the family are unable to regulate human impulses generated by the economy, criminality and deviance are more likely' (Robinson, 2004: 227; citing Chamlin and Cochran, 1995).

According to Messner and Rosenfeld (1994), the economy takes precedence in capitalism when: (1) non-economic institutions are devalued; (2) norms and values of non-economic institutions give way to norms and values of economic institutions; and (3) non-economic institutions make accommodations to economic institutions (also see Chamlin and Cochran, 1995; Maume and Lee, 2003; Piquero and Piquero, 1998; Savolainen, 2000). Criminal behavior is most likely when 'the value-orientation of the market economy, that is, the pursuit of self-interest, attraction to monetary rewards, and competition, become exaggerated relative to the value-orientations of institutions such as the family, education, and the polity' (Bernburg, 2002: 732). There are at least two reasons criminality results from this arrangement: The emphasis on the American Dream leads to both intense cultural pressures for monetary success and an increase in anomie [and the] dominance of the economy in the social structure . . . weakens the regulatory efficacy of noneconomic institutions' (Maume and Lee, 2003: 1140).

The phenomenon of cultural pressures pushing toward monetary success is explained by Savolainen, who writes:

> An institutional balance of power in which the economy dominates other institutions is assumed to be the most conducive to high rates of serious crime because such an arrangement is the least capable of restraining criminal motivations stimulated by the logic of egalitarian market capitalism. At the level of culture, institutional imbalance of this description generates value orientations that emphasize efficiency norms at the expense of moral considerations . . . the 'mood' of the society becomes more predatory. At the level of social structure, weak noneconomic institutions are less capable of providing stakes in conformity in the form of meaningful social roles. (2000: 1022)

Thus, the theory 'sees crime rates as a function of the American Dream's cultural emphasis on economic success in combination with an institutional structure dominated by the economy' (Pratt and Godsey, 2003: 615).

Strain and Differential Opportunity

Robert Merton's second theoretical idea—strain theory—holds that a disjuncture between goals and *means is* responsible for criminality. According to Merton (1957: 132), 'culturally defined goals, purposes and interests' are comprised of 'a frame of aspirational reference. They are the things "worth striving for."' These goals are institutional in that they arise from, and are reinforced by, social institutions including informal sources of culture goals such as families and schools (Merton, 1957: 137). The 'acceptable modes of reaching out for these goals' are the institutionalized or legitimate means. They are' regulations, rooted in the mores or institutions, of allowable procedures for moving toward [cultural objectives]' (Merton, 1957: 132). Certain means are required, some are allowed, others are preferred, while illegitimate means are prohibited. Merton's terms for these, respectively, are *prescriptions, permissions, preferences, and proscriptions* (Merton, 1957: 132).

Living in a 'culture-bearing society' (especially under the pressures produced by the American Dream) causes great difficulty for individuals including strain (Merton, 1957: 139). Merton developed five modes of adaptation to cultural strain: Conformity, Innovation, Ritualism, Retreatism, and Rebellion. These adaptations to strain are depicted in Table 1. Each of the five categories refers to 'role behavior in specific types of

Table 1   Merton's Modes of Adaptation to Anomic Strain

Modes of adaptation	Cultural goals	institutional means
Conformity	Accept	Accept
Innovation	Accept	Reject
Ritualism	Reject	Accept
Retreatism	Reject	Reject
Rebellion	Reject/Replace	Reject/Replace

situations, not to personality types of more or less enduring response, not types of personality organization' (Merton, 1957: 140).

Conformity, 'the most common and widely diffused' adaptation refers to acceptance of both cultural goals, and institutional means to achieve them (Merton, 1957: 141). *Innovation* describes 'the individual [who] has assimilated the cultural emphasis upon the goal without equally internalizing the institutional norms governing ways and means for its attainment' (Merton, 1957: 141). Merton (1957: 144–145) thus asserted that not only do the poor accept the American Dream but also that the avenues available for moving toward this goal are largely limited by the class structure to those of deviant behavior.' *Ritualism* 'involves the abandoning or scaling down of the lofty cultural goals of great pecuniary success and rapid social mobility to the point where one's aspirations can be satisfied.' *Retreatism,* the least common adaptation according to Merton, involves a rejection of both the goals of the culture, and the institutionalized means to achieve them; the Marxist construct of the lumpen proletariat would fit under the aegis of this adaptation. Merton's final adaptation to strain, *Rebellion,* also involves rejection of both the culture goals and institutionalized means. But those who pursue rebellion develop their own substitute goals and means that often conflict with those endorsed by societal institutions such as the family and schools.

Richard Cloward and Lloyd Ohlin (1961: 85) concurred with Merton's central thesis concerning strain. They discussed how people's desires for wealth are virtually unlimited. As they asserted, There is every reason to think that persons variously located in the social hierarchy have rather different chances of reaching common success-goals despite the prevailing ideology of equal opportunity.' The variants of success in pursuit of the American Dream lead to feelings of strain in individuals, or what Cloward and Ohlin called a major problem of adjustment.' Strain not only can lead to criminality among individuals, but can also lead to shared feelings of oppression and thus a subculture:

> The disparity between what lower-class youth are led to want and what is actually available to them is the source of a major problem of adjustment. Adolescents who form delinquent subcultures . . . have internalized an emphasis upon conventional goals. Faced with limitations on legitimate avenues of access to these goals, and unable to revise their aspirations downward, they experience intense frustrations; the exploration of nonconformist alternatives may be the result.

Some barriers to success discussed by Cloward and Ohlin include educational, cultural, and economic obstacles that lead to incorporation of illegitimate means of opportunity.

Cloward and Ohlin were among the first to explicitly state that both legitimate and illegitimate opportunities can vary among people and places. Other anomie and strain theories were incomplete, Cloward and Ohlin (1961: 145) argued, because they ignored 'the *relative availability* of illegal alternatives to various potential criminals.' Just as there is a differential distribution of legitimate means, there also is a differential distribution of illegitimate means.

In sum, Cloward and Ohlin delineated the reality that an *Innovator* needs to learn the skills of, and have opportunities for, illegitimate behavior, just as the *Conformist* needs to learn the skills requisite in, and have opportunities for, the socially acceptable pursuit of the American Dream. It seems logical that, for many individuals, groups, types of occupational roles, and subcultures, opportunities will exist for simultaneously engaging in legitimate and illegitimate behaviors, or both Conformity and Innovation, and that in some circumstances, regularly engaging in conforming and innovative behaviors is actually expected of people.

◈ A Gap in the Literature

Although Merton's theories posit modes of adaptation as ideal types rather than types of personality—meaning that the modes of adaptation are not mutually exclusive since individuals can behave in ways consistent with more than one mode of adaptation—to date no anomie or strain theory has explicitly recognized the possibility that individuals simultaneously and regularly hold norms consistent with more than one mode of adaptation.

In this paper, we present a new mode of adaptation—Maximization—referring to simultaneously and regularly accepting the norms of Conformity and Innovation (i.e. law-abiding and law-breaking behaviors). We assert that the American Dream contains within it situations that encourage and even sometimes mandate violating the criminal law as a component or codicil of legitimate activity in pursuit of the American Dream.

It is clear from the work of Cloward and Ohlin (1961: 150) that 'each individual occupies a position in both legitimate and illegitimate opportunity structures.' This means, of course, that it is possible to simultaneously implement legitimate and illegitimate means in pursuit of goals. Yet, neither Merton nor Cloward and Ohlin explicitly explored this adaptation to strain, nor has any anomie or strain theorist since.

Our assertion, to be developed in the remainder of this paper, is that some individuals, groups, occupational roles, and subcultures regularly accept (and engage in) both legitimate and illegitimate means of opportunity in pursuit of the American Dream. These people abide by the law and the rules of the game as well as break them, often simultaneously, in order to achieve the consecrated value of money, to overcome goals-means discrepancies, and/or to win the game.

We are not saying that Maximization is a unique personality type, any more so than Conformity or Innovation (or other modes of adaptation). As noted earlier, Merton explained that a mode of adaptation also refers to role behavior in specific types of situations, not to personality . . . types of more or less enduring response, not types of personality organization' (Merton, 1957: 140). We assert that since people regularly and simultaneously pursue legitimate and illegitimate means of opportunity in pursuit of their goals, Merton's characterization of the Conformist and Innovator is incomplete.

◈ An Expanded Typology

When one explicitly considers illegitimate means in pursuit of the American Dream, a new adaptation to strain emerges. Our Table 2 depicts this new mode of adaptation. Table 2 illustrates that Merton's five modes of adaptation are left intact. Since we have already defined those modes of adaptation, we will only focus here on the one we have added: the Maximizer. Note that we have added a third column to Merton's typology. The new column represents acceptance or rejection of utilization of illegitimate means (i.e. criminality) in pursuit of one's goals.

Table 2 Merton's Modes of Adaptation to Anomic Strain, Expanded to Include Non-Institutionalized Means

Modes of adaptation	Cultural goals	Institutional means	Criminality
Conformity	Accept	Accept	Reject
Innovation	Accept	Reject	Accept
Ritualism	Reject	Accept	Reject
Retreatism	Reject	Reject	Accept
Rebellion	Reject/Replace	Reject/Replace	Accept
Maximization	Accept	Accept	Accept

The Maximizer

Those involved in *Maximization,* like those involved in *Conformity,* accept culture goals and therefore are in pursuit of the American Dream. The difference is that those who utilize strategies of Conformity pursue legitimate or institutionalized means to achieve their goals of making it' or winning' the game, whereas those who utilize strategies of *Maximization* pursue legitimate or institutionalized means as well as illegitimate or non-institutionalized means in pursuit of culture goals. Thus, *Maximization* involves a combination of Conformity and Innovation. Maximization, we believe, refers to a role behavior that emerges in specific types of situations and that it is a form of enduring response to strain found in those specific types of situations.

An example of Maximization might better illustrate our intended meaning. A building contractor involved in legitimate business is, by definition, using legitimate or institutionalized means in pursuit of the American Dream. This is Conformity. Those contractors who also regularly accept norms that allow criminal behavior as part of the job and thus commit deviant acts and/or break the law to achieve even greater profit/wealth would be characterized as *Maximizers.* The Maximizer is one who utilizes both legitimate and illegitimate means in pursuit of the American Dream. He or she must have the knowledge, skills, and opportunities

necessary to engage in a legal trade, as well the knowledge, skills, and opportunities necessary to successfully commit criminal behavior aimed at maximizing the American Dream.

In America, it appears that chief executive officers (CEOs) and chief financial officers (CFOs) of large and small businesses are often willing to commit deviant acts and/or break the law to achieve even greater wealth (Huffington, 2003; Reiman and Leighton, 2003). These too are Maximizers. In fact, it appears that to no small degree, in the business world, Maximization is *the* preferred strategy used to increase profits and wealth. Because of this, criminality within corporations appears quite normal within many corporate subcultures.

The Maximizer: Contemporary Examples

Research shows Maximization to be a mode of adaptation regularly used in the business world to adapt to strain in the workplace. For example, in his study of heavy electrical equipment antitrust cases, Geis (1996) illustrated how high-ranking business figures in two major corporations charged with antitrust violations justified their violations. To some, their crimes were justified by the altruistic purpose of economic improvement. Others rationalized their illegal behaviors as law-abiding since their behaviors led to reward. Still others acknowledged their actions as illegal but asserted they were not harmful and thus were acceptable. Some saw the behavior as so normal that it could not be seen as illegal.

Most important to the concept of Maximization is that many corporate executives asserted that their behaviors were *normal* in the context of big business. Geis suggested that, for some individuals, the illegal behaviors were just part of a way of life entered into like other parts of the job. For example, antitrust violations were not only acceptable but also an expected way of doing business, especially for those who were team players and who wanted to advance to higher positions within the corporation. Many illegal acts committed in this context can be seen as a form of Conformity, one that might not be generally appropriate for free society' but that is actually expected in the realm of big business. Consider again Merton's point that failure to succeed in America is perceived as a personal failure. This is strong motivation to succeed by any means, including illegal ones if necessary. Given that high-level corporate executives made it clear that price fixing was normal' and to be expected, and since quitting is not an option, it is not surprising that some executives engaged in these illegal activities.

Executives in the Geis study said that their illegal acts were an inevitable part of business, caused by the nature and extent of competition within and between businesses. Thus, some executives justified their acts with the belief that if they did not do it, someone else would. Here, executives were likely offering some after-the-fact excuses—or techniques of neutralization'—for their criminal behaviors (Sykes and Matza, 1958).

But our main interest here is not the excuses offered by offenders after they are apprehended and are likely trying to avoid serious consequences for their acts of wrongdoing. Rather, we assert that maximizing strategies correspond to many situation in US society (especially within the business world) where groups and individuals are expected to pursue illegal acts in the context of legal acts in order to 'get ahead', to 'win the game'.

More recent cases of corporate crime support this notion. For example, studies of both defective products and the tobacco industry illustrate the concept of Maximization. Many of the most well-known cases deal

with automobiles. Automobiles are typically found to be defective in one of two ways. First, there are design defects that are discovered by corporations and not fixed. Secondly, corporations routinely resist safety devices until forced to adopt them by public demand (Robinson, 2006). Examples of the latter include resisting putting in safety windshields and air bags.

The most well known case of a defective product involved a car that was known by its manufacturer to be defective—the Ford Pinto—but was not recalled for the purpose of saving the company money (Henry, 1982). This automobile was manufactured in the 1970s despite the findings of pre-crash tests showing that fuel lines regularly ruptured as a result of rear-end collisions. Ford learned that it would cost only $11 per car to fix the automobiles. Yet, in a cost-benefits analysis, Ford calculated that it would still save $87.5 million by not fixing the cars (Robinson, 2006). This was based on the assumption that hundreds of people would be killed and injured and thousands of cars burned, at minimal costs to the company. Unfortunately for Ford and the driving public, Ford underestimated the prevalence of the crashes and the size of the civil judgments against it. In actuality, it would have been cheaper to fix the cars before they rolled out onto the nation's streets (Becker et al., 2002).

Examination of the Ford Pinto case supports the construct of maximization. Ford Engineer Dennis Gioia says that engineers knew the

> hazard existed in the Pinto [and that] managers made a cost-benefit decision that the cost of fixing the problem outweighed the human cost of accidents it might cause. Bad moral choices were made because [I] was following schematized scripts prevalent in the decision environment of the company. In this case, ethical [and] moral considerations were not part of the preferred scripts ... so [they] did not influence the decision-making process to any great extent. (1996: 139)

In other words, Maximization took precedence over morality.

More recently, the 'Ford/Firestone fiasco' led to dozens of deaths as consumers died when their Ford Explorers rolled over after their Firestone tires exploded (Karr, 2001, 2002). Ford Explorers, like other SUVs with a high center of gravity, are prone to rollovers. Further, Firestone tires, when under-inflated, are prone to tread separation. Apparently, the combination leads to deadly results. CEOs of both Ford and Firestone denied any wrongdoing or fault, and each pointed the finger at the other. Firestone tires on Ford Explorers were replaced in more than 10 other countries almost two years earlier than in the United States, and the Ford Explorer was subsequently redesigned for a smoother ride' (Robinson, 2006).

Documents internal to the companies show that they were aware of the problems and kept them secret. This is typical in defective products cases, including other automobiles such as General Motors (GM) approved conversion vans, defective seat belts and seat belt buckles in some GM and Ford cars, faulty back-door latches in Chrysler minivans (that open when struck from the rear or side and cause passengers to be thrown out on to the street), and GM sidebag and side-saddle gas tanks located on the side of trucks outside of the protective frame that easily rupture when struck from the side. In 1992, NHTSA asked GM to voluntarily recall pickup trucks with such gas tanks but GM refused. The Department of Transportation Secretary found in 1994 that GM had known about the defect since the 1970s. General Motors entered into a deal with the Department of Justice to avoid a recall and paid hundreds of millions in settlements to victims instead.

In at least some companies of the automobile industry, Maximization thus appears to be the norm. The companies make a legal product in pursuit of the American Dream (Conformity) while simultaneously and regularly cutting corners and failing to follow required safety regulations (Innovation) in order to save money and be more successful than the competition. The fact that people are injured and die as a result—including their own customers!—appears to be irrelevant. Clearly, some major American car companies accept and promote norms in favor of Conformity as well as Innovation, simultaneously. And they regularly use both in producing, advertising, and selling their products.

Another example of Maximization can be found in the tobacco industry. Tobacco use is the leading cause of preventable death in the United States, making cigarettes the most commonly recognized defective product in the United States. Simply stated, cigarettes—a delivery device for the addictive drug of nicotine—contain thousands of chemicals and more than 60 known and suspected carcinogens (Centers for Disease Control and Prevention, 2006). Studies of tobacco activities and internal documents of tobacco companies show that major tobacco corporations purposely misled the public and Congress for more than 40 years with regard to the dangers of smoking cigarettes. Research has also documented: intentional marketing to children and adolescents through misleading product advertisements in magazines, movies, and popular hang-outs; making products increasingly addictive by adding nicotine and chemicals that heightened the effects of nicotine; attacking and attempting to discredit anti-smoking advocates and whistle-blowers; and lying under oath to Congress when asked about the addictiveness of their products. As if this were not bad enough, companies have also been shown to financially coerce other companies which make smoking-cessation products and to intentionally fund and produce faulty science through a 'Tobacco Institute' that clouds over significant issues (Glantz et al., 1998; Lovell, 2002; Mollenkamp et al., 1998; Orey, 1999; Wolfson, 2001). Civil juries in some states have found tobacco companies liable for reckless disregard for human life, outrageous conduct, negligence, misrepresentation of the facts, fraud, and even selling a defective product.

Probably more than any other industry, actions by executives at large tobacco companies best represent the concept of Maximization. The culture of big tobacco—referring to the beliefs, values, and norms that dictate its corporate practices and the behaviors of its employees—is crimino-genic. Although the companies make a legal product in pursuit of the American Dream (Conformity), they simultaneously and regularly engage in reckless, negligent, and knowing behaviors that lead to the deaths of hundreds of thousands of Americans every year (Innovation). That 430,000 Americans die every year from tobacco-related illness, millions more are 'injured' by smoking, and that $75 billion is spent on direct-health care costs treating tobacco-related illnesses is irrelevant to the behaviors of the 'Maximizers' in the tobacco industry. Instead, like car companies, tobacco companies accept and promote norms in favor of Conformity and Innovation simultaneously. And they regularly use both in producing, advertising, and selling their products.

Some of the most recent research on corporate and white-collar crimes also finds evidence consistent with Maximization as a mode of adaptation to strain associated with the business world. For example, research on occupational fraud (Holtfreter, 2005), corporate accounting fraud (Pontell, 2004), environmental crimes (Wolf, 2006), so-called 'accidents' of the chemical industry (Pearce and Tombs, 1998), the manipulation of the natural environment which exacerbates natural disasters (Green, 2005), creating global hunger through monopolization of bio-technology (Walters, 2006), and even the awarding of post-war construction contracts in Afghanistan and Iraq (Hogan et al., 2006) finds that such acts are normal and expected parts of the business world. That some of these acts are not criminal' is irrelevant (Passas, 2005). Given the harms they cause and the intentional, reckless, negligent, and knowing character of the acts, they can easily be considered 'criminal' in the sense of involving actions that are fundamentally wrong (Robinson, 2005).

◈ Conclusion

There are at least two reasons to expect that those who have money and power—those who have already made it—will continue to experience anomie and strain. First, as Merton, Messner and Rosenfeld, Cloward and Ohlin, and other anomie and strain theorists have pointed out, one can never have enough in the US. Someone always has more, giving us all something to strive for so that keeping up with the Joneses has escalated to keeping up with Warren Buffet and ultimately Bill Gates. Secondly, to some degree, deviance and criminality are widespread among powerful elites, especially corporate CEOs and CFOs (Reiman and Leighton, 2003; Robinson, 2005). This means wealthy individuals

often debate whether to abide by the law (because it is the right thing to do for society) or to abide by the expectations imposed on them to abide by the rules of the game which sometimes call for violating the law (because it is the right thing to do for the company). We assert that it is very likely that within the American corporation (legitimate means), deviance (illegitimate means) is no longer deviant but rather normal among corporate leaders (Clinard and Yeager, 2005; Friedrichs, 2008; Geis and Pontell, 2006; Mokhiber and Weissman, 1999; Rosoff et al., 2002; Simon, 2006; Simon and Hagan, 1999). That is, Maximization is widespread in the corporate world.

In the contemporary US, the reluctance to see white-collar and corporate offenders as criminals (Friedrichs, 2003) may be due to the fact that they are viewed as important men and women (mostly men) who are in pursuit of the American Dream—often at any and all costs. Rather than labeling such actors as criminals, we accept them as shrewd, smart, and successful men' harking back to the robber barons of times past (Merton, 1957: 142).

Anomie and strain theories blame crime on the overpowering influence of the economy on our lives. In particular, Merton's theories of anomie and strain, Messner and Rosenfeld's theory of institutional anomie, and Cloward and Ohlin's theory of differential opportunity assert that criminality is a function of factors such as: goals-means discrepancies; the consecration of money itself as a value; internalizing the goals of the American Dream while failing to internalize legitimate means of opportunity; an overemphasis on the goal of the American Dream; an exaggerated emphasis on monetary gain and pursuit of self-interest; and impulses unregulated by non-economic institutions.

Merton created five modes of adaptation to such sources of anomie and strain, but failed to consider utilization of legitimate and illegitimate means of opportunity in pursuit of one's goals. Cloward and Ohlin suggested that, as means of legitimate opportunity vary, so too do means of illegitimate opportunity. Yet, in their work on subcultural responses to strain, they also did not consider utilization of legitimate and illegitimate means of opportunity in pursuit of one's goals.

Thus, in this paper, we expanded Merton's typology by adding explicit consideration of the utilization of illegitimate means simultaneously with legitimate or institutionalized means in pursuit of goals subsumed within the American Dream. The result is a new mode of adaptation to strain. We focused on the adaptation to strain implemented by the *Maximizer,* who merges both legitimate and illegitimate means in pursuit of the socially inculcated American Dream. Maximization is an adaptation whereby individuals simultaneously and regularly accept and utilize legitimate and illegitimate means of opportunity in pursuit of the American Dream. As argued here, we believe the manufacture of defective products, as well as the actions of big tobacco companies, represent the adaptation of Maximization. If so, pressures to achieve at any cost imposed by the American Dream are a significant reason why much corporate crime occurs in the United States.

◈ References

Agnew, Robert (1992) 'Foundation for a General Strain Theory of Crime and Delinquency,' *Criminology* 30: 47–87.

Agnew, Robert (1999) 'A General Strain Theory of Community Differences in Crime Rates,' *The Journal of Research in Crime and Delinquency* 36: 123–55.

Agnew, Robert (2002) 'Experienced, Vicarious, and Anticipated Strain: An Exploratory Study on Physical Victimization and Delinquency,' *Justice Quarterly* 19: 603–32.

Agnew, Robert, Timothy Brezina, John Wright and Francis Cullen (2002) Strain, Personality Traits, and Delinquency: Extending General Strain Theory,' *Criminology* 40: 43–71.

Baron, Stephen (2004) 'General Strain, Street Youth and Crime: A Test of Agnew's Revised Theory,' *Criminology* 42: 457–83.

Becker, Paul, Arthur Jipson and Alan Bruce (2002) 'State of Indiana v. Ford Motor Company Revisited,' *American Journal of Criminal Justice* 26(2): 181–204.

Bernard, Thomas (1987) 'Testing Structural Strain Theories,' *Journal of Research in Crime and Delinquency* 24(4): 262–80.

Bernburg, Jon (2002) 'Anomie, Social Change and Crime,' *The British Journal of Criminology* 42: 729–42.

Brezina, Timothy (1996) 'Adapting to Strain: An Examination of Delinquent Coping Responses,' *Criminology* 34: 39–60.

Brezina, Timothy, Alex Piquero and Paul Mazerolle (2001) 'Student Anger and Aggressive Behavior in School: An Initial Test of Agnew's Macro- level Strain Theory,' *The Journal of Research in Crime and Delinquency* 38: 362–86.

Capowich, George, Paul Mazerolle and Alex Piquero (2001) 'General Strain Theory, Situational Anger, and Social Networks: An Assessment of Conditioning Influences,' *Journal of Criminal Justice* 29: 445–61.

Centers for Disease Control and Prevention (2006) 'Toxic Chemicals in Tobacco Products,' URL: http://www.cdc.gov.tobacco/research_data/ product/objective21–20.htm

Chamlin, Mitchell and John Cochran (1995) 'Assessing Messner and Rosenfeld's Institutional Anomie Theory: A Partial Test,' *Criminology* 33: 411–29.

Clinard, Marshall and Peter Yeager (2005) *Corporate Crime.* New York: Transaction.

Cloward, Richard and Lloyd Ohlin (1961) *Delinquency and Opportunity: A Theory of Delinquent Gangs.* New York: The Free Press. Durkheim, Emile (1893) *De la Division du Travail Social. Paris:* F. Alcan.

Durkheim, Emile (1897) *Le Suicide. Paris:* F. Alcan.

Eitle, David (2002) 'Exploring a Source of Devian'ce-producing Strain for Females: Perceived Discrimination and General Strain Theory,' Journal of *Criminal Justice* 30: 429–42.

Featherstone, Richard and Mathieu Deflem (2003) 'Anomie and Strain: Context and Consequences of Merton's Two Theories,' *Sociological Inquiry* 73(4): 471–89.

Friedrichs, David (2003) *Trusted Criminals: White-collar Crime in Contemporary Society.* Belmont, CA: Wadsworth.

Geis, Gilbert (1996) 'The Heavy Electrical Equipment Antitrust Cases: Price-Fixing Techniques and Rationalizations,' in David Ermann and Richard Ludman (eds) *Corporate and Government Deviance: Problems of Organizational Behavior in Contemporary Society.* New York: Oxford University Press.

Geis, Gilbert and Henry Pontell (2006) *White Collar Crime.* Upper Saddle River, NJ: Prentice Hall.

Gibson, Chris, Marc Swatt and Jason Jolicoeur (2001) 'Assessing the Generality of General Strain Theory: The Relationship Among Occupational Stress Experienced by Male Police Officers and Domestic Forms of Violence,' *Journal of Crime & Justice* 24: 29–57.

Gioia, Dennis (1996) 'Why I Didn't Recognize Pinto Fire Hazards: How Organizational Scripts Channel Managers' Thoughts and Actions,' in David Ermann and Richard Ludman (eds) *Corporate and Government Deviance: Problems of Organizational Behavior in Contemporary Society.* New York: Oxford University Press.

Glantz, Stanton, John Slade, Lisa Bero, Peter Hanauer and Deborah Barnes (1998) *The Cigarette Papers.* Berkeley: University of California Press.

Green, Penny (2005) Disaster by Design: Corruption, Construction, and Catastrophe,' *British Journal of Criminology* 45(4): 528–46.

Henry, Frank (1982) Capitalism, Capital Accumulation, and Crime,' *Crime and Social Justice* 18: 79–87.

Hoffmann, John and Timothy Ireland (2004) Strain and Opportunity Structures,' *Journal of Quantitative Criminology* 20: 263–92.

Hogan, Michael, Michael Long, Paul Stretesky and Michael Lynch (2006) Campaign Contributions, Post-War Construction Contracts, and State Crime,' *Deviant Behavior* 27(3): 269–97.

Holtfreter, Kristy (2005) 'Is Occupational Fraud 'Typical' White-collar Crime? A Comparison of Individual and Organizational Characteristics,' *Journal of Criminal Justice* 33(4): 353–65.

Huffington, Arianna (2003) *Pigs at the Trough: How Corporate Greed and Political Corruption are Undermining America.* New York: Crown.

Jang, Sung Joon and Byron Johnson (2003) 'Strain, Negative Emotions, and Deviant Coping Among African Americans: A Test of General Strain Theory,' *Journal of Quantitative Criminology* 19: 79–105.

Karr, Al. (2001) 'Ford/Firestone Update,' *Traffic Safety* 1(4): 7.

Karr, Al. (2002) NHTSA Rebuffs Firestone: Decides Not to Probe Ford Explorer Safety,' *Traffic Safety* 2(3): 6.

Konty, Mark (2005) 'Microanomie: The Cognitive Foundations of the Relationship Between Anomie and Deviance,' *Criminology* 43: 107–31.

Lovell, Georgina (2002) *You are the Target: Big Tobacco: Lies, Scams–Now the Truth.* British Columbia, Canada: Chryan Communications.

Maume, Michael and Matthew Lee (2003) 'Social Institutions and Violence: A Sub-National Test of Institutional Anomie Theory,' *Criminology* 41: 1137–72.

Mazerolle, Paul and Alex Piquero (1998) 'Linking Exposure to Strain with Anger: An Investigation of Deviant Adaptations,' *Journal of Criminal Justice* 26: 195–211.

Mazerolle, Paul, Velmer Burton Jr, Francis Cullen, David Evans and Gary Payne (2000) 'Strain, Anger, and Delinquent Adaptations Specifying General Strain Theory,' *Journal of Criminal Justice* 28: 89–101.

Merton, Robert (1938) 'Social Structure and Anomie,' *American Sociological Review* 3: 672–82.

Merton, Robert (1957) *Social Theory and Social Structure.* Glencoe, IL: The Free Press.

Messner, Steven (1988) 'Merton's "Social Structure and Anomie": The Road Not Taken,' *Deviant Behavior* 9(1): 33–53.

Messner, Steven F. and Richard Rosenfeld (1994) *Crime and the American Dream.* New York: Wadsworth Publishing Company.

Mokhiber, Russell and Robert Weissman (1999) *Corporate Predators: The Hunt for Mega-Profits and the Attack on Democracy.* Monroe, ME: Common Courage Press.

Mollenkamp, Carrik, Joseph Menn and Adam Levy (1998) *The People vs. Big Tobacco: How the States Took on the Cigarette Giants.* New York: Bloomberg Press.

Orey, Michael (1999) *Assuming the Risk: The Mavericks, the Lawyers, and the Whistle-blowers who Beat Big Tobacco.* New York: Little, Brown and Company.

Passas, Nikos (2000) Global Anomie, Dysnomie, and Economic Crime: Hidden Consequences of Neoliberalism and Globalization in Russia and Around the World,' *Social Justice* 27: 16–44.

Passas, Nikos (2005) 'Lawful but Awful: "Legal Corporate Crimes",' *The Journal of Socio-economics* 34(6): 771–86.

Pearce, Frank and Steve Tombs (1998) Toxic Capitalism: Corporate Crime and the Chemical Industry. Aldershot: Ashgate.

Pontell, Henry (2004) 'White-collar Crime or Just Risky Business? The Role of Fraud in Major Financial Debacles,' *Crime, Law and Social Change.* 42(4–5): 309–24.

Pratt, Travis and Timothy Godsey (2003)'Social Support, Inequality, and Homicide: A Cross-national Test of an Integrated Theoretical Model,' *Criminology* 41: 611–43.

Reiman, Jeffrey and Paul Leighton (2003) 'Getting Tough on Corporate Crime? Enron and a Year of Corporate Financial Scandals,' URL: *http://www.pauls* justicepage.com/RichGetRicher/fraud.htm

Robinson, Matthew (2004) *Why Crime? An Integrated Systems Theory of Antisocial Behavior.* Upper Saddle River, NJ: Prentice Hall.

Robinson, Matthew (2005) *Justice Blind? Ideals and Realities of American Criminal Justice.* Upper Saddle River, NJ: Prentice Hall.

Robinson, Matthew (2006)'Defective Products,' *Encyclopedia of Corporate and White-collar Crime.* Croton-on-Hudson, NY: Golson Books.

Rosoff, Stephen, Henry Pontell and Robert Tillman (2002) *Profit Without Honor: White-collar Crime and the Looting of America.* Upper Saddle River, NJ: Prentice Hall.

Savolainen, Jukka (2000) Inequality, Welfare State, and Homicide: Further Support for the Institutional Anomie Theory,' *Criminology* 38: 1021–42.

Simon, David (2006) *Elite Deviance.* Boston, MA: Allyn and Bacon.

Simon, David and Frank Hagan (1999) *White-collar Deviance.* Boston: MA: Allyn and Bacon.

Simons, Ronald, Yi-Fu Chen, Eric Stewart and Gene Brody (2003) 'Incidents of Discrimination and Risk for Delinquency: A Longitudinal Test of Strain Theory with an African American Sample,' *Justice Quarterly* 20: 827–38.

Sykes, Gresham and David Matza (1958) 'Techniques of Neutralization,' *American Sociological Review* 22: 664–70.

Vold, George, Thomas Bernard and Jeffrey Snipes (1998) *Theoretical Criminology,* 4th edn. New York: Oxford University Press.

Walters, Reece (2006) 'Crime, Bio-Agriculture and the Exploitation of Hunger,' The British Journal of *Criminology* 46(1): 26.

Wolf, Brian (2006)'Environmental Crime and Justice: The Organizational Composition of Corporate Noncompliance,' *Dissertation Abstracts International* 66(7).

Wolfson, Mark (2001) *The Fight Against Big Tobacco: The Movement, the State, and the Public's Health.* New York: Aldine Transaction.

Wright, John, Francis Cullen, Robert Agnew and Timothy Brezina (2001) '"The Root of All Evil"? An Exploratory Study of Money and Delinquent Involvement,' *Justice Quarterly* 18: 239–68.

CHAPTER 5

Social Disorganization Theory

GROUNDING STORY

To LaJoe, the neighborhood had become a black hole. She could more easily recite what wasn't there than what was there. There were no banks, only currency exchanges, which charged up to $8.00 for every welfare check cashed. There were no public libraries, skating rinks, movie theaters, or bowling alleys to entertain the neighborhood's children. For the infirm there were two neighborhood clinics... both of which teetered on bankruptcy and would close by the end of 1989. Yet the death rate of new born babies exceeded the infant mortality rates in a number of third world countries, including Chili, Costa Rica, Cuba, and Turkey. And there was no rehabilitation center, though drug abuse was rampant.

According to a 1980 profile of Twenty-seventh ward—a political configuration drawn, ironically, in the shape of a gun and including Henry Horner and Rockwell Gardens, a smaller but no less forbidding housing complex—60,110 people lived here, 88 percent of them black, 46 percent of them lived below the poverty level. It was so impoverished that when Mother Teresa visited in 1982, she assigned nuns from her Missionaries of Charity to work at Henry Horner.

Source: Kotlowitz (1988, p. 12).

◈ Introduction

Kotlowitz's (1988) description of these Chicago neighborhoods provides an interesting introduction to social disorganization theory, a theory developed to explain patterns of deviance and crime across social locations such as neighborhoods. Unlike many of the micro-level theories discussed in this book, which attempt to explain variation in deviant behavior across individuals, social disorganization theory is a macro-level theory that focuses on larger units of analysis such as neighborhoods, schools, and cities and even states or countries. This is a unique contribution because it is so clear that some places are safer than others and that all sorts of deviances flourish in other places. Rodney Stark (1987) accurately described a major problem in criminology stemming from the advent of self-report surveys:

> This transformation soon led repeatedly to the "discovery" that poverty is unrelated to delinquency. . . . Yet, through it all, social scientists somehow knew better than to stroll the street at night in certain parts of town or even to park there. And despite the fact that countless surveys showed that kids from upper and lower income families scored the same on delinquency batteries, even social scientists know that the parts of town that scared them were not upper-income neighborhoods. (p. 894)

Indeed, violence, drug use, prostitution, mental illness, and other forms of deviance are commonplace in neighborhoods like Henry Horner and Rockwell Gardens. Other places seem to be able to control crime and deviance (or at least the deviance that does exist is far less visible in some areas than others). Social disorganization theory attempts to explain this variation. Why are certain neighborhoods able to control levels of deviance while others are unable to minimize it or eliminate it entirely?

In this chapter, we begin with some history behind the theory of **social disorganization,** including the creation of a major program in sociology at the University of Chicago toward the end of the 19th century and the social milieu of Chicago at this point in time. We then discuss the development of social disorganization theory and early empirical tests of the theory, focused primarily on juvenile delinquency. Historically, the theory was put on the backburner for many years, only to come back strong in the 1980s. We discuss this revitalization as well as new advances of the theory. Today, social disorganization theory and variants of it are quite popular and are used quite often when investigating deviance at the aggregate level: neighborhoods, schools, cities, even internationally.

History and Early Work on Social Disorganization Theory

To provide context for an understanding of the theory of social disorganization, we need to go back to end of the 19th and turn of the century. With a background in history and economics, Albion Woodbury Small joined the faculty at the University of Chicago (1892) with the task of developing the first department of sociology in the United States. Consider this task—with no PhD-granting university in sociology in the United States, who do you hire to teach sociology? Well, you hire people from outside of the country with degrees in sociology (very expensive and not very practical) or you hire those with other degrees obtainable in America who have an interest in social issues and who think and do research like sociologists. So, Albion Small hired economists, historians, and even journalists who were interested in the scientific study of society.

For additional context, consider Chicago at the turn of the century (perhaps not so different in terms of deviance than it is today—plenty to go around!). Many of the new faculty members at the University of Chicago were from rural and religious backgrounds. They were coming to Chicago, where crime and deviance were not hard to find—indeed, they were right in your face. Gambling, prostitution, alcohol consumption, violence, police abuse of power, and many other forms of deviance were common and well known to the citizens of Chicago. The question for these researchers was why these forms of deviance existed and seemed to flourish in certain areas of the city while other areas seemed to be able to control these social problems.

Alternatively, how did people in general explain deviance at the turn of the century? That is, what were the popular explanations of crime and deviance? Much like today, the explanations focused on individuals and groups—that is, "types of people" explanations. The criminals and deviants were the "new immigrants." Immigrants who brought their old traditions and had not been appropriately socialized into the new world were seen as the causes of the social problems of the day. The popular advertisement shown in Photo 5.1 glorifies the prejudice of the day. Irish immigrants need not apply; we do not have work for you. Of course, at different times, different groups felt the brunt of ethnic prejudice and were seen as the cause of various social ills. Italians certainly faced ethnic discrimination and were seen as a source of trouble. Indeed, in 1918, when labor was in high demand and employers were scrounging for workers, advertisements read "Italians and Coloreds" may apply, suggesting an ethnic stratification ranking of Italians as close to African Americans (Luhman, 2002). German Jews immigrating to the United States during the early to mid-1800s because of the repression and discrimination in Germany faced fewer legal restrictions here, but there were still some, including restrictions from "holding public office, becoming lawyers, and serving as officers in state militia" in certain regions (Luhman, 2002, p. 149). Immigration from China beginning around 1850 also brought political and social reaction, leading to Chinese immigrants being viewed as deviant. Hispanics, too, have faced ethnic stereotyping and discrimination. Finally, coming to America as slaves, African Americans have always faced prejudice and discrimination, but as they moved from the South to northern cities, they too became the scapegoat and the "cause" of social problems.

▲ **Photo 5.1** Immigrants faced many problems when they arrived in the United States at the turn of the century—including discrimination.

Fortunately, science was also making important discoveries and influencing how we thought about deviance and other social problems. The Chicago school was very familiar with scientific strides being made in plant and animal biology. For example, Darwin's *Origin of Species,* published in 1859, was well known to Chicago sociologists and influenced how they approached the study of human behavior. In contrast to the classical school of criminology, which focused on free will and the role of the government in controlling free will, the Chicago perspective did not ask whether plants "willed" themselves to do better in certain environments than others or whether animals "willed" themselves to reproduce and thrive in certain areas versus others. Rather, they believed that environmental factors affected whether certain plants would grow in certain areas and certain animals would flourish in others. The early Chicago researchers believed that they could find the causes of crime in the structure of the environment. Much like today, with the explosion of information and analysis provided by geographic information systems such as Mapquest or Google Earth, the principle of the Chicago school was that if you want to understand something—Map It! Through this process of mapping social deviance, researchers were able to demonstrate that types-of-people explanations were often limited if not downright wrong. Indeed, certain types of deviance seemed to flourish in some areas over time, even though the "types of people" (racial and ethnic groups) who lived there changed dramatically.

◈ Shaw and McKay Study of Juvenile Delinquency and Urban Areas

The origin of social disorganization theory is generally attributed to Clifford Shaw and Henry McKay's (1942/1969) seminal work, *Juvenile Delinquency and Urban Areas* (originally published 1942), where they plotted on maps the home addresses of (1) boys brought to the court for an alleged delinquent activity, (2) boys committed by the court to a correctional facility, and (3) "boys dealt with by the police probation officers with or without court appearance" (p. 44). Data on court cases and commitments were available for 1900, 1920, and 1930, while police contacts centered around 1930. As the authors noted, "The distribution of delinquents at different periods of time afford the basis for comparison and for analysis of long-term trends and processes that could not be made for a single period" (Shaw & McKay, 1942/1969, p. 45). Their maps clearly show three things. First, delinquency does not appear to be distributed randomly across the neighborhoods of Chicago. Second, rates of delinquency appear to cluster in certain neighborhoods and appear highest close to the **central business district** (CBD). Shaw and McKay noted that in addition to the high rates of delinquency near the CBD, delinquency was highest in neighborhoods in or around "areas zoned for industry and commerce." Third, delinquency, by and large, tends to decline as you move away from the

▲ **Photo 5.2** Which color is to be tabooed next?

CBD. Indeed, their analyses clearly show that rates of delinquency as measured by juvenile commitments across five **concentric zones** around 1900, 1920, and 1930, fall precipitously as you move away from the central business district.

Shaw and McKay (1942/1969) examined these zones and characterized Zone II, the one closest to the CBD, as a **zone in transition.** Here resided the most recent immigrants to the city, the poorest and least educated citizens, and those who needed to live close to the CBD for work, that is, when they could find it. Shaw and McKay found that as you moved away from the zones in transition, you would find residents from earlier waves of immigrants. These were people who had learned English, had received more education, had better jobs, and could afford to get out of the impoverished inner city where only those who had no other choice lived. What was most interesting is that the people who lived in the zone in transition changed—indeed, no one really wanted to live there, and immigrants quickly left the high crime rate areas for safer neighborhoods as soon as they could afford to, only to be replaced by another group of immigrants who were forced to live in the zone in transition.

To better understand why crime rates declined as one moved out from the inner city, Shaw and McKay (1942/1969) looked to other social factors that characterized these areas. So, other than high rates of delinquency, what characterized the neighborhood? Shaw and McKay highlighted three factors that characterized neighborhoods with high rates of delinquency: **poverty,** population turnover, and **racial/ethnic heterogeneity.** Shaw and McKay did not emphasize a direct link between poverty and delinquency (Bursik, 1988); rather, they found that poor neighborhoods are characterized by population turnover and racial and ethnic heterogeneity.

Bursik argues that, "in its purest formulation, social disorganization refers to the inability of local communities to realize the common values of their residents or solve commonly experienced problems" (p. 521). When the primary goal of the residents is to move out of the neighborhood, there is little incentive to try to make it a better place. These people are poor and do not own their own residences, and the landlords ("slum lords") have little interest in making these places better. In fact, it is in their best interest to invest as little as possible in their buildings because, as the city expands, they will be bought out, only to be torn down and replaced with industrial structures. Similarly, because the populations are changing and composed of people with different ethnic and/ or racial backgrounds, there are further barriers such as limited motivation to work together to reduce the crime and other deviance that characterizes the area. These structural factors (poverty, population turnover, and racial/ ethnic heterogeneity) consistently characterized high delinquency areas even though the specific "types of people" changed over the decades studied.

Shaw and McKay's (1942/1969) pioneering work in social disorganization theory was sharply criticized on a number of grounds and then waned in popularity and importance for several reasons as described in a review by Bursik (1988). First, the field of criminology shifted and became far more focused on individuals as opposed to groups, and macro theories such as social disorganization rarely have anything to say about individuals, only groups and places. Second, longitudinal data (data collected over time) are expensive and sometimes impossible to collect, and later studies typically were restricted to cross-sectional designs (data collected at only one point in time). Cross-sectional designs are problematic in the study of deviance, especially studies of a theory based on longitudinal data, because they typically assume a static view of urban life that seems inconsistent with history. Finally, there was considerable confusion about what social disorganization actually was and how it should be measured. In particular, there seemed to be some confusion in distinguishing social disorganization from delinquency itself, resulting in criticisms that the theory was tautological, that is, true by definition, circular, and therefore not testable. However, a number of important works in the late 1970s and 1980s gave social disorganization theory a rebirth.

DEVIANCE IN POPULAR CULTURE

When people are asked what causes crime, they tend to think in terms of individualistic causes of deviance. That is, they are looking to answer why certain individuals engage in crime and deviant behavior and others do not. The social disorganization perspective asks a different question: Why is there more crime in certain areas than in others? *What community-level characteristics influence the rate of crime/ deviance in any given area?*

The documentary film, *Hoop Dreams,* follows two young boys from inner-city Chicago as they are recruited into a private high school and different colleges in pursuit of their goal of basketball stardom. Watch the first 45 minutes of *Hoop Dreams* (freshman and sophomore years of high school), paying careful attention to the different environments that are captured on tape.

- What did you notice about the neighborhood(s) that Arthur and William grew up and lived in? What did the neighborhoods look like? What kinds of things went on there? What did people say about these areas?

- Now think about the neighborhood in which the school, St. Joe's, is located. What did it look like? What did people say about it?

- Which neighborhood do you think had higher crime rates? Why do you think so? What are the important characteristics to consider?

- Think about the neighborhood that you grew up in. What was it like? What factors do you think contributed to the crime rates (high or low) in your neighborhood?

- If you were trying to lower crime/deviance rates in a given neighborhood, where would you start? What specifically would you target and try to improve?

Documentary films can sometimes tell us a great deal about deviance and social control, even if that is not the expressed intent of the story. The Chicago neighborhoods shown in *Hoop Dreams* have very different levels of social organization, which affect level of crime and deviance and the life chances of individuals such as Arthur and William and their family members. Considering the neighborhood you grew up in as an additional case study can help to illustrate how social disorganization affects communities— and how it may have affected you and your friends, even though you may not have realized it at the time. Applying the theories to real examples helps to remind us that these are more than big ideas—deviance is all around us, and sociological theories can help us make sense of our own social worlds.

◈ Rebirth of Social Disorganization Theory

In her classic work, *Social Sources of Delinquency,* Ruth Kornhauser (1978) divided the classic theories of juvenile delinquency into three basic types: cultural deviance (e.g., differential association and social learning), strain, and social disorganization. She clearly puts social disorganization as a macro-level control theory whereby residents of certain neighborhoods are able to control and minimize unwanted deviance, while residents in some neighborhoods, characterized by poverty, population turnover, and racial/ethnic heterogeneity, cannot control their environments and achieve common goals. Although Shaw and McKay (1942/1969) discussed the subculture found in socially disorganized neighborhoods, Kornhauser and others who followed tended to focus solely on the structural aspects of the theory. Following this important work, a number of scholars began reflecting on and promoting the potential of the theory. Stark (1987), for example, used social disorganization theory along with 100 years' worth of theorizing and empirical research on social ecology to develop 30 propositions linking neighborhood characteristics to high rates of deviance, including "(1) density; (2) poverty; (3) mixed [land] use; (4) transience; and (5) dilapidation" (p. 895).

In turn, Bursik (1988) documented the reasons for the decline in the popularity of the theory and suggested several lines for pursuing the theory, including (1) thinking about the neighborhood as a social context for individual behavior, (2) focusing on measures of deviance that are not the result of official responses by law enforcement such as self-reported behavior and victimization surveys, and (3) considering the possible feedback effects of crime and delinquency on social disorganization (the ability to control the environment). Finally, several studies were conducted that empirically tested the validity of the theory.

One of the first innovations and empirical tests of the theory involved consideration of the mediating factors hypothesized between the social structural variables identified by Shaw and McKay (1942/1969) and crime and delinquency. Sampson and Groves (1989) argued that sparse friendship networks, unsupervised teen peer groups, and low organizational participation should largely explain the relationship between poverty, ethnic heterogeneity, population turnover, family disruption, and urbanization. That is, neighborhoods characterized by these factors would be less able to control certain forms of deviance because residents were not communicating with one another and allowed teens to roam the streets unsupervised. The model is described in Figure 5.1.

Figure 5.1   Sampson and Groves's Model of Social Disorganization

Low Socioeconomic Status

Ethnic Heterogeneity   Sparse Networks

Residential Mobility $\longrightarrow$ Unsupervised Youth $\longrightarrow$ Crime and

Family Disruptions   Organizational Participation   Delinquency

Urbanization

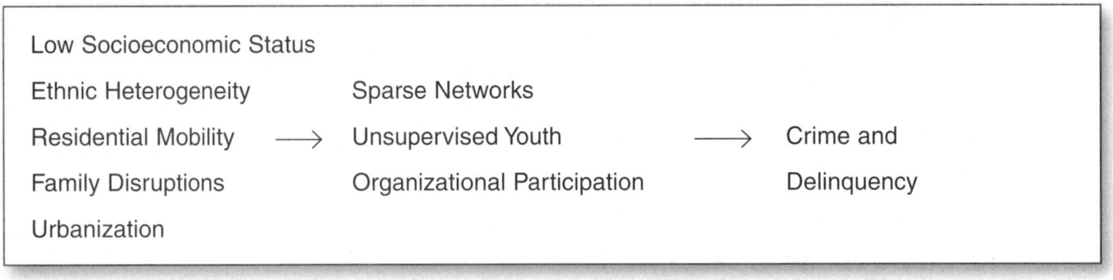

Sampson and Groves (1989) analyzed data from the 1982 British Crime Survey (BCS), which included data on more than 10,000 respondents across 238 localities in England and Wales and then replicated the analyses using data from a slightly larger number of individuals residing in 300 British communities. They found that neighborhoods with sparse friendship networks, unsupervised teenage peer groups, and low organizational participation were associated with higher rates of victimization and self-reported offending (violence and property crimes) and that these variables explained much of the effect of the standard structural variables generally used to test social disorganization theory.

A year later, Veysey and Messner (1999) replicated these analyses using slightly more sophisticated statistical modeling techniques. They were more cautious in their interpretation of the results of their analyses in terms of the theory. They found that the mediating social disorganization variables (sparse friendships, unsupervised teens, and organizational participation) only partially explained the effects of the structural variables and argued that the results were partially consistent with social disorganization theory but were also consistent with theories focused on peer affiliation such as differential association theory (see Chapter 6). Again using the British Crime Survey, but this time with data from 1994 (more than a decade later), Lowenkamp, Cullen, and Pratt (2003) replicated Sampson and Groves's (1989) model using similar measures. The results were largely consistent, and the authors argued that the consistency of the findings suggests that Sampson and Groves's model was not an idiosyncratic result of the timing of the original study but that the theoretical model is generalizable across time.

Classic social disorganization theory has continued to be tested in other environments. For example, given that Shaw and McKay and many others have focused on urban environments, some have questioned whether the theory is applicable to nonurban areas. Osgood and Chambers (2000) examined the structural correlates of homicide, rape, weapon offenses, and simple assault arrest rates across 264 nonmetropolitan counties in Florida, Georgia, South Carolina, and Nebraska. They found that population turnover, family disruption, and ethnic heterogeneity are all related to these arrest statistics. Jobes, Barclay, and Weinand (2004) found support for social disorganization in 123 rural government areas in rural New South Wales, Australia.

A criticism raised against Shaw and McKay's (1942/1969) original analyses and many other analyses is the focus on official measures of crime. However, Sampson and Groves's (1989) classic analysis, as well as replications (Lowencamp et al., 2003; Veysey & Messner, 1999) with self-reported offending and victimization with the British Crime Survey, clearly shows the generalizability of the theory. In an interesting approach, Warner and Pierce (1993) used calls to police rather than reactions by the police (e.g., arrests) across 60 Boston neighborhoods in 1980 and found support for social disorganization theory. Finally, while most studies have focused on juvenile delinquency and street crimes, Benson, Wooldredge, and Thistlethwaite (2004) found that neighborhood factors associated with social disorganization theory affect both black and white rates of domestic violence.

As the reader might surmise, the theory of social disorganization has largely focused on delinquency and street crimes, especially violent street crimes, rather than on other forms of deviance, especially what might be seen as "soft deviance." This is not entirely the case, however, as even early researchers were interested in how social disorganization theory might help us understand the geographic concentration of mental illness, prostitution, gambling, alcoholism, and drug use. Some of these are discussed in the readings at the end of the chapter and also in the following "Studies in Deviance."

STUDIES IN DEVIANCE

Gender, Social Disorganization Theory, and the Location of Sexually Oriented Business

By Michelle Edwards (2010), in *Deviant Behavior, 31*(2), 135–158

Edwards examines the neighborhood characteristics of three types of sexually oriented businesses: adult sexuality boutiques, adult entertainment clubs, and adult bookstores. Using social disorganization theory, she critiques the placement of these different businesses and the impact of race, class, and gender on their placement.

Examining four urban counties in Texas, Edwards determined the existence of the three types of sexually oriented businesses using a generally agreed-upon definition of each type of business. Adult sexuality boutiques are usually stores in which sexually explicit materials such as lingerie, sex toys, fetish paraphernalia, and bachelorette party supplies are sold. These businesses are more likely to be run by women and often emphasize female sexual health. Adult entertainment clubs are usually clubs that specialize in nude or topless dancing by females. These clubs usually cater to men. Finally, adult bookstores also sell sexual paraphernalia like adult sexuality boutiques, but these stores usually specialize in the sale or rental of pornographic videos and magazines and cater to male clientele.

Edwards finds that adult sexuality boutiques (which are predominately visited by women) are more likely to be in socially organized and cohesive neighborhoods, while adult entertainment clubs and bookstores (which are predominately visited by men) are more likely to be in socially disorganized neighborhoods. While white men are the predominant clientele of both adult entertainment clubs and adult bookstores, the disorganized neighborhoods the businesses are in are more likely to be lower income and higher minority resident neighborhoods. This suggests that "certain groups are able to keep their neighborhoods separated from [certain] sexually oriented businesses, while also maintaining anonymity if they choose to visit these businesses" (p. 155).

◈ More Theoretical and Empirical Advances and Divergences: Social and Physical Disorder

Concern over minor misbehavior (e.g., prostitution, public rowdiness or drunkenness) and signs of **physical disorder** (e.g., litter, graffiti, broken windows) and their relationship to crime has been a concern at least since the 1800s. About 30 years ago, Wilson and Kelling (1982) published an essay titled "Broken Windows: The Police and Neighborhood Safety" in the *Atlantic Monthly* that brought the issues back into the public limelight as well as to the attention of scholars interested in crime and deviance. Basically, the authors argued that disorder leads to greater disorder, as well as attracts and promotes more serious forms of deviance. The notion is simple to the young man living in an area characterized by graffiti and broken windows: Why not break another window—it is fun and what's the harm? Signs of disorder lead to further disorder. This led to the policy implication that police (and other agents of social control) attack crime at its roots and target minor forms of **social disorder** deviance that seem to be critical causes of the escalation of crime and further deviance. In other words, focus on less serious forms of deviance, and you may deter more serious forms of crime.

Although the theories are clearly unique, the parallels with social disorganization theory are fairly obvious. The key to social disorganization theory is the ability of residents to control delinquency and crime, things that most everyone would like to minimize. Similarly, there are areas where residents able to do this and other areas where residents have difficulty minimizing social disorder—also things that most people would like to avoid if they had the ability to control them or could afford to live in "better" neighborhoods.

Considerable research links physical and social disorder with more serious street crimes. Skogan's (1990) *Disorder and Decline: Crime and the Spiral of Decay in American Neighborhoods,* for example, provides a compelling argument and data that disorder is a major root cause of urban crime. Alternatively, Harcourt (2001) is critical and argues that not enough empirical attention has been given to the causal link between disorder and crime, and the policies (e.g., zero-tolerance policies) drawn from the "theory" are often inappropriate and/or ineffective. Furthermore, Sampson and Raudenbush (2004) provide a very unique test of the relationship between disorder and crime and find that while the two are correlated, factors including poverty and the concentration of minority groups are even stronger predictors. The readings following this chapter include a more recent empirical test of the relationship that provides some unique policy implications. Because it is simple and appealing to the public and public officials, Wilson and Kelling's (1982) **broken windows theory** will likely remain active and persuasive in terms of policies and practices. Why not focus on problems residents are concerned with, even if they don't have a causal link to more serious crime? In fact, social disorder may really simply be "less serious" crime and deviance.

▲ **Photo 5.3**   Can broken windows actually encourage crime and other forms of deviance?

Collective Efficacy

Another advance in social disorganization theory comes from Robert Sampson and his colleagues (Sampson, Raudenbush, & Earls, 1997), who drew an analogy between individual efficacy (i.e., an individual's ability to accomplish a task) and neighborhood or **collective efficacy** (i.e., a neighborhood's ability to recognize common goals of a safe environment, largely free from crime and deviance). They defined collective efficacy "as social cohesion among neighbors combined with their willingness to intervene on the behalf of the common good" (p. 918). **Social cohesion** and trust between neighbors are seen as necessary conditions for residents to be willing to intervene for the common good. Basically, the authors made the argument that collective efficacy is an important mediating effect between structural factors associated with social disorganization and deviant behavior, particularly violent behavior.

Sampson et al. (1997) examined data from the Project on Human Development in Chicago Neighborhoods. Census tracts are often used as the unit of analysis to characterize neighborhoods. This is a reasonable strategy but nowhere near perfect as they often have arbitrary borders that do not reflect what residents perceive to be as "their neighborhood." To get a better measure of neighborhoods, the researchers combined 847 Chicago census tracts into 343 neighborhood clusters in an attempt to a create unit of analysis that made meaningful sense in terms of composition and geographic boundaries (e.g., roads, water ways). They interviewed 8,782 residents across all neighborhood clusters in the residents' homes. They measured "informal social control" by asking respondents how likely their neighbors could be counted on to intervene in various ways if

- children were skipping school and hanging out on a street corner,
- children were spray-painting a building,
- children were showing disrespect to an adult,
- a fight broke out in front of their house, or
- the fire station closest to the house was threatened with budget cuts.

Cohesion and trust were measured by asking respondents how strongly they agree with the following:

- People around here are willing to help their neighbors.
- This is a close-knit neighborhood.
- People in this neighborhood can be trusted.
- People in this neighborhood generally don't get along with each other.
- People in this neighborhood do not share the same values.

The two scales were so highly correlated at the neighborhood level that they were combined into a single composite scale termed *collective efficacy*.

Structural variables related to social disorganization theory included concentrated disadvantage, immigrant concentration, and a lack of residential stability. The dependent measures of violence included perceived violence in the neighborhood and violent victimization from the neighborhood survey and the homicide rate from official records. Sampson et al. (1997) were able to assess the influence of structural variables on collective efficacy and the mediating effect of collective efficacy on violence. The results were consistent and robust. The structural variables were clearly related to collective efficacy, and collective efficacy in turn affected each measure of violence. The results strongly supported this modified version of social disorganization theory.

Subsequent to this publication, numerous studies have examined the role that collective efficacy plays on violence and other forms of deviance as well as reactions to deviance (e.g., residents' fear of crime). For example, Bernasco and Block (2009) found that collective efficacy keeps robbers out of certain census tracts in Chicago, while D. Martin (2002) found that social capital (politically active citizens) and collective efficacy (active community organizations) were negatively related to burglary across Detroit neighborhoods in the mid-1990s. Browning (2002) showed that the effects of collective efficacy extend beyond violence and street crime to affect intimate partner violence, and Cancino (2005) showed that collective efficacy not only is important in inner cities but applies to nonmetropolitan areas as well.

J. Wright and Cullen (2001) developed the analogous concept of "parental efficacy," focused on parents' ability to control their children's behavior through parent–child attachment, rules, and supervision but also social support. Rankin and Quane (2002) linked these ideas directly to the community and examined how collective efficacy leads to greater parent efficacy, which leads to greater social competency and lower levels of problems behavior among children. More recently, Simons and his colleagues (Simons, Simons, Burt, Brody, & Cutrona, 2005) showed that collective efficacy promoted positive parenting strategies and showed that both were related to lower levels of deviant peer association and delinquency involvement. More interestingly, they found that authoritative parenting had pronounced effects in communities with higher levels of collective efficacy, suggesting that both factors are important in themselves but that in conjunction, the effects are even stronger.

Clearly, collective efficacy has proven to be an important concept that has extended and promoted thought on social disorganization theory and on factors that affect neighborhood deviance. For the most part, research in this area has been largely restricted to violence and other forms of crime, and little attention has been given to its potential implication for other forms of deviance. More research in this direction is clearly warranted.

◈ Conclusion

The original work of Shaw and McKay (1942/1969) was clearly groundbreaking in its day and continues to influence the study of deviance to this day. The major contribution of the original work was showing how crime, deviance, and other social problems cannot be understood, at least at the aggregate level, with "types of people" explanations. They found that crime and deviance were consistently located in particular parts of Chicago, even though the types of people who resided there had changed across several decades. New versions of the theory continue to help us understand the factors that limit social control in certain neighborhoods.

Places such as Henry Horner in Alex Kotlowitz's (1988) *There Are No Children Here* continue to have high rates of crime and deviance (1) because the residents there do not have the resources (political or economic) to control crime and deviance; (2) there is high residential instability or population turnover, resulting in limited social networking that might lend itself to decreased social control; and (3) there is very little collective efficacy in that residents lack the willingness and ability to intervene when problems confront them. Most people residing in truly disadvantaged neighborhoods do not engage in a great deal of crime and deviance, and most would love to live in less dangerous places where they could raise their children safely without the opportunities and pressures to deviate. They stay because their opportunities are strictly limited.

NOW YOU . . . USE THE THEORY

The map below is of Norfolk, Virginia. The dots represent prostitution arrests, and the shaded areas represent different levels of social disorganization as measured by a social disorganization scale based on the level of racial heterogeneity, level of female-headed households, level of unemployment, and level of poverty in a certain area. The top of the map represents the section of the city next to the bay. This section of the city was very popular many years ago but fell into disrepute. Since it is on the water, there has been some gentrification recently, as wealthier individuals and business owners have moved back and reclaimed the space as a desirable area. The southern end of the map is where the central business district is located.

Using social disorganization theory, explain the location of prostitution arrests in Norfolk, Virginia. Can you use the theory to help explain how prostitution arrests cluster in Norfolk? Why might the prostitution arrests be clustered on the edge of the most disorganized areas of the city?

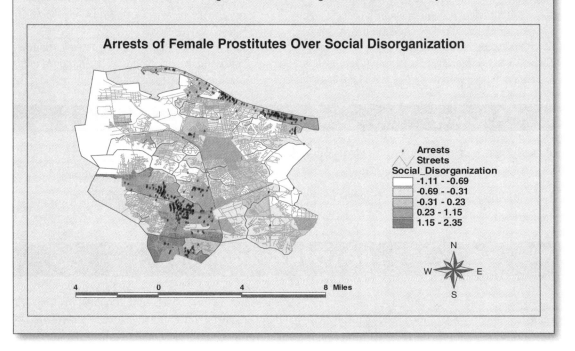

Arrests of Female Prostitutes Over Social Disorganization

• Arrests
／ Streets
Social_Disorganization
☐ -1.11 - -0.69
☐ -0.69 - -0.31
☐ -0.31 - 0.23
☐ 0.23 - 1.15
☐ 1.15 - 2.35

EXERCISES AND DISCUSSION QUESTIONS

1. Explain how Shaw and McKay's theory moved us away from "types of person explanations."

2. Why do you think we are so focused on individual-level explanations rather than on characteristics of social contexts?

3. How does the work of Sampson and his colleagues expand our understanding of social disorganization theory?

4. How does Wilson and Kelling's "broken windows theory" relate to social disorganization?

5. Consider the city you live in and where the safe areas are, as well as where one might likely go to buy drugs or find a prostitute. What other factors characterize these areas of the city?

6. Go to www.youtube.com/watch?v=niJ3IiURCnE for a presentation of Chicago's deadliest neighborhoods and write a personal reaction to the video.

SUGGESTED ADDITIONAL READINGS

Bursik, R. J., Jr., & Grasmick, H. G. (1993). *Neighborhoods & crime: The dimensions of effective community control.* New York: Lexington Books.

Harcourt, B. (2001). *The illusion of order.* Cambridge, MA: Harvard University Press.

Morenoff, J. D., Sampson, R. J., & Raudenbush, S. W. (2001). Neighborhood inequality, collective efficacy and the special dynamics of urban violence. *Criminology, 39,* 517–559.

Shaw, C. A., & McKay, H. (1969). *Juvenile delinquency in urban areas.* Chicago: University of Chicago Press. (Original work published 1942)

Silver, E. (2001). Neighborhood social disorganization as a cofactor in violence among people with mental disorders. *International Journal of Offender Therapy and Comparative Criminology, 45,* 403–406.

Skogan, W. (1990). *Disorder and decline: Crime and the spiral of urban decay in American neighborhoods.* New York: Free Press.

Wilson, J. Q., & Kelling, G. (1982). Broken windows: Police and neighborhood safety. *Atlantic Monthly, 249,* 29–38.

KEY TERMS

Broken windows theory	Physical disorder	Social disorder
Central business district	Poverty	Social disorganization
Collective efficacy	Racial/ethnic heterogeneity	Zone in transition
Concentric zones	Social cohesion	

READING 14

As early as the work of Faris and Dunham (1939), at least some researchers have observed that mental disorders do not appear to be randomly distributed geographically and that they seem to be concentrated in areas characterized by social disorganization. However, the majority of work on mental disorders has focused on individual characteristics. In this review, Silver reviews a series of studies that look at individual and contextual factors associated with violence among those diagnosed with severe mental health disorders—"schizophrenia, affective disorders, delusional disorders, brief reactive psychosis, substance abuse disorder, or a personality disorder." Findings of the review are fairly straightforward—context matters! Controlling for a host of individual characteristics, those with mental disorders were far more likely than the rest of the community to reside in socially disorganized neighborhoods and that those who did were far more likely than those who lived in more affluent neighborhoods to engage in violent behaviors.

Source: Silver, Eric. 2001. "Neighborhood Social Disorganization as a Cofactor in Violence Among People With Mental Disorders." *International Journal of Offender Therapy and Comparative Criminology* 45:403–406. Reprinted with permission.

Neighborhood Social Disorganization as a Cofactor in Violence Among People With Mental Disorders

Eric Silver

An important, although often ignored, cofactor in the violent behavior of people with mental disorders (MDO) is the neighborhood context in which they live. This editorial summarizes the results of a series of recent studies that examined the effects of neighborhood social disorganization on violence among a sample of discharged psychiatric patients (Silver, 2000a, 2000b, 2001; Silver, Mulvey, & Monahan, 1999). The basic premise of these studies is that neighborhood characteristics account for variation in the violent behavior of people with MDO that is not explained by their individual-level characteristics.

In recent years, substantial effort has been devoted to the development of actuarial tools for predicting violence among people with MDO (for a review, see Monahan et al., 2001). The risk factors identified in the risk assessment literature focus primarily on individual-level characteristics, such as previous violence, substance abuse, psychopathy, employment status, impulsiveness, anger, and lack of social support. Notably absent from this literature are measures reflecting the neighborhood contexts in which people with MDO live. The emphasis on individual, as opposed to social-contextual, risk factors is due largely to the difficulty of collecting relevant social-contextual measures and to the belief that violence risk is individually determined. However, from the standpoint of understanding why people with MDO engage in violence, an exclusive focus on individual-level risk factors is not justifiable.

The notion that neighborhood characteristics are important determinants of outcomes related to MDO has a long history in sociology. As early as 1939, Chicago School researchers, Faris and Dunham (1939) observed that "high rates of insanity appear to cluster in the deteriorated regions in and surrounding the center of the city" (p. 35). Faris and Dunham offered a "social stress" explanation of this finding, arguing that the "confused, frustrated, and chaotic" behaviors of people with MDO resulted, in part, from their location in socially disorganized neighborhoods. Subsequent debates over the relative merits of a social stress versus a social drift explanation for the association between mental illness and socioeconomic status remain unresolved to this day (see Dohrenwend, 1990, 2000).

Although Faris and Dunham (1939) did not study violence, the social disorganization perspective they helped develop is highly relevant for understanding the violent behavior of people with MDO, particularly in the postdeinstitutionalization era. Prior to the 1960s, individuals with MDO had access to and were likely to be treated for long periods of time in the back wards of psychiatric "total institutions." Since that time, however, deinstitutionalization policies implemented in the United States reduced significantly the number of people who could be admitted long term to state and county psychiatric hospitals. As a result, people with MDO currently reside in communities where psychiatric care is provided, when available, by acute care, community-based, mental health facilities. This sociohistoric change in the treatment of people with MDO has increased their susceptibility to influences from the neighborhood context.

Thus, my colleagues and I undertook a series of studies to measure the influence of neighborhood characteristics on people with MDO. The studies examined data on 270 psychiatric patients treated and discharged from the Western Psychiatric Institute and Clinic between 1992 and 1995. The data were drawn from the Pittsburgh site of the MacArthur Foundation's Violence Risk Assessment Study. Methods of the study have been reported in detail elsewhere (see Steadman et al., 1998). Briefly, the participants included in the study were civil admissions, between the ages of 18 and 40, English speaking, White or African American, who also were diagnosed with a major MDO (schizophrenia, affective disorder, brief reactive psychosis, delusional disorder, substance abuse disorder, or a personality disorder).

Hospital data collection was conducted in two parts: an interview by a trained lay interviewer to obtain a wide array of background data and an interview by a trained research clinician (Ph.D., M.A., or M.S.W.) to obtain a *Diagnostic and Statistical Manual of Mental Disorders Third Edition, Revised* diagnosis (using the *DSM-III-R* Checklist). Two attempts were made during the 20-week period following hospital discharge to recontact and interview enrolled patients in the community (approximately every 10 weeks). A collateral informant also was interviewed using the same interview schedule. Official records provided additional information about the patients' behavior in the community.

Census tract measures were used to describe the neighborhood contexts of the patients. Census tract boundaries are drawn to encapsulate relatively homogeneous populations in terms of demographic and economic characteristics and reasonably approximate the usual conception of a neighborhood. The following aspects of the neighborhood context were examined: neighborhood poverty (i.e., percentage of all persons in households with income below the federal poverty level and percentage of households that had public assistance incomes), neighborhood wealth (i.e., mean household wages and percentage of families with income greater than $50,000 per year), neighborhood family structure (i.e., percentage of families headed by a female), neighborhood employment (i.e., adult unemployment rate and percentage of employed persons with executive or managerial positions), neighborhood residential stability (i.e., percentage of residents who lived in the same housing unit 5 years earlier), neighborhood ethnic composition (i.e., percentage of neighborhood residents who are foreign born), and neighborhood housing stock (i.e., percentage of housing units that are vacant).

Using factor analysis, these measures were reduced to two underlying dimensions: neighborhood socioeconomic disadvantage and neighborhood residential mobility. Factor scores for these dimensions were linked to the patient data set using census tract identifiers corresponding to the addresses at which patients resided following discharge from Western Psychiatric Institute and Clinic. Overall, the 270 patients in this study were discharged to 145 neighborhoods in the Allegheny County, Pennsylvania region.

Violence was measured using questions from the Conflict Tactics Scale, as expanded by Lidz, Mulvey, and Gardner (1993). Participants and collateral informants were asked whether the subject had committed each of eight categories of violent behavior in the past 10 weeks. In addition, official arrest and rehospitalization records were examined for evidence of violent behavior during the follow-up period. Acts were categorized as violent if they included acts of battery that resulted in physical injury, sexual assaults, assaultive acts that involved the use of a weapon, or threats made with a weapon in hand. The studies focused on violence that occurred during the first 20 weeks following hospital discharge, coded as a dichotomous (0 and 1) variable.

The main findings were as follows: First, discharged patients were far more likely than members of the general population to reside in disadvantaged neighborhoods. Second, patients discharged into disadvantaged neighborhoods were significantly more likely to commit violent acts than were patients discharged into less disadvantaged neighborhoods. This result held after controlling for a wide range of individual-level risk factors for violence, including age, race, marital status, socioeconomic status, drug abuse, anger, impulsiveness, degree of symptomatology, psychopathy, and prior violence. Residential mobility was not significantly related to patient violence. Second, the significant association between African American racial status and violence was completely eliminated when neighborhood disadvantage was controlled. In other words, although African Americans were significantly more likely to live in disadvantaged neighborhoods, African American and White patients who lived in comparably disadvantaged neighborhoods exhibited the same rates of violence.

These findings highlight the importance of assessing contextual conditions as well as individual-level characteristics when predicting and managing the risk for violence posed by discharged psychiatric patients. Furthermore, the finding regarding race suggests that erroneous conclusions can be drawn about the effects of individual-level attributes when the social context is not also taken into account. However, these results do not imply that mental illness is unimportant as a cause of violence nor do they seek to contradict the neurobiological foundations on which many MDOs are believed to rest. Rather, this study follows Hiday (1997) in taking the position that "neurobiological factors may be the origin of severe mental illness; but social factors affect its course, manifestations, and connections to violence" (p. 412).

Clearly, it was not possible for me to discuss all of the implications of these findings in this limited space. Nor was it possible for me to describe in adequate detail all of the substantive and statistical nuances of the original work. For that, the reader must consult the studies themselves (Silver, 2000a, 2000b, 2001; Silver, Mulvey, & Monahan, 1999). My purpose in writing this editorial was to help direct attention toward an important, although often ignored, cofactor in the violent behavior of people with MDO: the neighborhood contexts in which they live.

 References

Dohrenwend, B. P. (1990). Socioeconomic status (SES) and psychiatric disorders. *Social Psychiatry and Psychiatric Epidemiology, 25,* 41–47.

Dohrenwend, B. P. (2000). The role of adversity and stress in psychopathology: Some evidence and its implications for theory and research. *Health and Social Behavior, 41,* 1–19.

Faris, R.E.L., & Dunham, H. W. (1939). Mental disorders in urban areas: An ecological study of schizophrenia and other psychoses. Chicago: University of Chicago Press.

Hiday, V. A. (1997). Understanding the connection between mental illness and violence. *International Journal of Law and Psychiatry, 20,* 399–417.

Lidz, C. W., Mulvey, E. P., & Gardner, W. (1993). The accuracy of predictions of violence to others. *Journal of the American Medical Association, 24,* 1007–1011.

Monahan, J., Steadman, H. J., Silver, E., Appelbaum, P. S., Robbins, P. C., Mulvey, E. P., Roth, L. H., Grisso, T., & Banks, S. (2001). Rethinking risk assessment: The MacArthur study of mental disorder and violence. Oxford, UK: Oxford University Press.

Silver, E. (2000a). Extending social disorganization theory: A multilevel approach to the study of violence among persons with mental illnesses. *Criminology, 38,* 1043–1074.

Silver, E. (2000b). Race, neighborhood disadvantage, and violence among persons with mental disorders: The importance of contextual measurement. *Law and Human Behavior, 24,* 449–456.

Silver, E. (2001). Mental illness and violence: The importance of neighborhood context. New York: LFB.

Silver, E., Mulvey, E. P., & Monahan, J. (1999). Assessing violence risk among discharged psychiatric patients: Toward an ecological approach. *Law and Human Behavior, 23,* 235–253.

Steadman, H., Mulvey, E., Monahan, J., Robbins, P., Appelbaum, P., Grisso, T., Roth, L., & Silver, E. (1998). Violence by people discharged from acute psychiatric inpatient facilities and by others in the same neighborhoods. *Archives of General Psychiatry, 55,* 393–401.

READING 15

In this article, O'Shea provides an empirical test of the "broken windows theory" of crime proposed by Wilson and Kelling (1982) in Mobile, Alabama. Measures of physical deterioration and social disorder were collected by trained observers of a random sample of 349 blocks. Violent and property crime data were collected from the police based on calls for service; other demographic information (e.g., population, percent renters) came from the census. O'Shea

Source: O'Shea, Timothy C. 2006. "Physical Deterioration, Disorder, and Crime." *Criminal Justice Policy Review* 17:173–187. Reprinted with permission.

raises a unique and important analysis issue in interpreting Wilson and Kelling's argument: The relationships between physical deterioration, disorder, and crime are not straightforward or additive. Rather, physical deterioration interacts with social disorder to affect levels of crime. Another way of thinking about this is that the effect of disorder on crime is dependent on levels of physical disorder (or vice versa). O'Shea finds statistical support for this hypothesis that leads him to be skeptical of simple zero-tolerance policies that some have argued are supported by the theory. He argues that "simple arrests of the disorderly (however broadly defined) and citation of negligent property owners . . . may not be the most efficient use of those scarce law enforcement resources."

Physical Deterioration, Disorder, and Crime

Timothy C. O'Shea

Crime and disorder are not randomly distributed. As anyone who has ever found himself or herself in an unfamiliar city knows, one must be careful where one goes. In the 1983 film *National Lampoon's Summer Vacation* (Simmons & Ramis, 1983), Chevy Chase's character gets off the interstate highway in a big city at the wrong exit. He and his family, in short order, are stripped of their belongings by an assortment of offenders. The scene is entertaining because it makes light of the fear that we all have of suddenly finding ourselves in that "wrong" place. The home purchasing decision calculus, when one lives in a large urban area, almost always includes consideration of the crime and disorder conditions. Location, location, location. Few, if anyone, would argue that the safety (or conversely, the dangerousness) of geographical spaces varies and that clusters of safe and dangerous spaces remain relatively stable across time.

The idea that crime and place are related dates back, in an academic sense, to the mid-19th century. Guerry (1833/2002) and Quetelet (1842) looked at the distribution of crime in French departments and found clear spatial variance. Studies around the same time in Britain found that crime and disorder clustered within particular geographical spaces (Glyde, 1856; Mayhew, 1862/1968; Plint, 1851).

Throughout most of the 20th century, American sociologists constructed an elaborate theory of crime in which its spatial distribution played a role. The Chicago school built on the early works of Burgess (1916), who drew linkages between social conditions and the incidence of crime. Burgess found that these conditions formed within certain geographical spaces. He is best known for his observation that cities formed concentric circles around a central business district. Each concentric circle provided an invisible boundary that separated particular forms of land use and types of socioeconomic groups. Crime and disorder clustered within the zones immediately adjacent to the downtown district (the so-called inner city). Shaw (1929) and Shaw and McKay (1931) pursued this idea and found the same pattern that Burgess described in other American cities (e.g., Seattle, Denver, Richmond, and Philadelphia). Other studies in the United States found that crime patterns extended to larger geographical spaces. Harries (1971) and Lottier (1938) found that the distribution of crime varied by state. Others noted that boundaries as large as regions (Hackney, 1969) form patterns in the distribution of crime.

Although American sociologists found that crime clustered around certain discernable geographical spaces, those physical locations were not considered independent predictors of criminal behavior. The causes of crime, they insisted, were the product of various social conditions (e.g., single-parent family, low education, unemployment, class conflict, etc.). There may have been reasons for certain socioeconomic groups to cluster around particular geographical spaces, and crime may have been greater in those spaces, but the space itself had nothing to do with criminal behavior. It was not until the early 1960s that the physical space independently was posited as an explanatory variable.

Jacobs (1961), Jeffrey (1971), and Newman (1972) all insist that the physical space is a variable that is capable of being manipulated in a fashion that could affect the nature and extent of crime in a city. The overall goal of this approach was to control crime rather than to control the criminal. The researcher's eye was focused on the physical space; its relationship to crime became the central question.

Some researchers have directed their attention to the link between disorder and crime. Biderman, Johnson, McIntyre, and Weir (1967) show a relationship between neighborhood disorderly conditions and residents' fear of crime. Killing's (1981) examination of police foot patrol seems to show that although the extent of crime might not change with foot patrol, the fear of crime did decrease. Skogan's (1990) research Finds compelling evidence that "crime and disorder go together in a substantial way" (p. 74). Several studies (Green, 1995; Koper, 1995; Sherman & Weisburd, 1995; Weisburd & Green, 1995) show that police activities aimed at reducing disorderly conditions within targeted "hot" crime areas reduced overall crime.

Wilson and Kelling's (1982) "Broken Windows" article in *Atlantic Monthly* is arguably the most policy-influencing work in the crime and place literature. Wilson and Kelling, however, did not limit their explanation of crime to physical space, although it did play an important role in their discourse. They, rather, lumped together the deterioration of physical space with resident behavior—disorderly behavior, specifically. According to Wilson and Kelling, the physical deterioration of a neighborhood in combination with the increase in disorderly behaviors produces places that are attractive to the pool of individuals predisposed to various predatory-like criminal behaviors. The idea that the physical condition of a neighborhood and certain disorderly behaviors of individuals in that neighborhood could attract or, conversely, repel individuals with a propensity toward crime rang true to many policy makers.

In many respects, the crime and place relationship provided both an answer to the crime problem and some hope to citizens, elected officials, and criminal justice practitioners. Policy implications that flowed from the sociological model were expensive and had not proven to be effective in reducing crime, disorder, and the fear of crime. It is not cheap to attack substandard housing and schools, unemployment, racism, and the like. Equally as important, the public was left out of the solution; they had to rely on the "experts" to solve these complex sociological, economic, and political problems.

Those, on the other hand, who argued that crime and place were related suggested policies that were relatively inexpensive, had a common-sense appeal, fit a more conservative, pragmatic mind-set, and effectively empowered the masses. Citizens, elected officials, and criminal justice workers could "do something." Elected officials could support policies that appeared to be more directly connected to criminal activity (e.g., "zero tolerance" police operations). Citizens could install safety lights and burglar alarms, hire private security to guard their property, put secure deadbolt locks on their homes, erect signs of proprietorship (e.g., fences, shrubs, nameplates) that told predators that the resident was watching and cared about his or her property, and so on. The police could engage in various tactical operations in high crime areas and thereby dissuade predators from targeting a neighborhood (arrest the disorderly, conduct drug sweeps, stop and question suspicious people, etc.). Many in the academic community, elected officials, and the general public were understandably attracted to this idea.

This new approach to the crime and disorder problem is not without its critics. Harcourt (2001) maintains that "broken windows policing has not received enough critical attention" (p. 6). He examines the empirical evidence that supports a connection between disorder and crime and finds it flawed. He also claims that the order-maintenance approach is not theoretically sound. Order, Harcourt insists, as defined by the broken-windows proponents "leads to an uncritical dichotomy between disorderly people and law abiders" (p. 7). Ultimately, these definitions of disorder simply mask or, more probably, rationalize repressive police tactical policies (e.g., zero-tolerance policing). Finally, Harcourt argues that authorities (e.g., Bratton, 1998) who attribute reductions in crime rates to broken-windows police tactics are simply misleading the public.

Sampson and Raudenbush (1999) argue that the relationship between public disorder and crime is spurious. They, rather, present "a theory combining structural constraints with local collective efficacy as an alternative to the 'broken windows' interpretation of the disorder-crime link" (p. 605). A particularly damning criticism of earlier research into the link between crime and disorder is Sampson and Raudenbush's contention that disorder is merely a less serious form of crime. "Public disorder and predatory crime are manifestations of the same explanatory process, albeit at different ends of the 'seriousness' continuum" (p. 607).

The literature points clearly to an area that deserves greater attention. In a democratic state, we grudgingly accept the cost of relinquishing individual liberties only when we are reasonably convinced that the benefit obtained will create a substantial increase in personal safety. Law enforcement officials implicitly and explicitly make just this promise in exchange for aggressive tactical operations. In this article, I examine the link between disorder, physical deterioration of neighborhoods, and crime. In so doing, I also propose to contribute to the academic controversy that surrounds the broken-windows philosophy.

 # Method

Hypotheses

I am concerned with the relationship between disorder, physical deterioration, and crime. Skogan (1990) empirically verified the linkage between crime and disorder. Harcourt has challenged both the empirical evidence and the logic of the argument. Here, I propose that as disorder increases, so does the extent of criminal activity in a neighborhood. In keeping with the general crime and place literature, I also propose that as a neighborhood's physical space deteriorates, crime will likewise increase. I distinguish between disorder and physical deterioration. I define disorder as certain definable behaviors that individuals engage in. I define physical deterioration as certain observable physical characteristics of a geographical space.

The Chicago school and its derivatives would argue that although place and crime are related, the true causal factors are various social dynamics playing out in the neighborhood. The physical condition of the neighborhood and disorder independently should not explain the variance in crime. Thus, several theoretically relevant variables are included in the model to control for this argument.

In addition, I am also interested in the possible interaction between disorder and physical deterioration. The literature to this point, in my view, has failed to adequately explore the linkage between the two variables. Wilson and Kelling (1982), in "Broken Windows," imply that the variance in crime is explained by an interaction between physical deterioration of a neighborhood and disorder. Any investigation that examines the contribution of physical deterioration and disorder to crime should consider the interaction possibility.

Location of Study

Mobile is located in southwest Alabama, approximately 30 miles from the Gulf of Mexico and from the borders of Florida and Mississippi. Population has grown steadily during the past 15 years to its current size of approximately 200,000, making it the third-largest city in Alabama. Mobile's crime rate, according to the Uniform Crime Report (UCR) figures, is somewhat higher than the national averages. Current strength of the Mobile Police Department is just fewer than 500 sworn members. The city is divided into four police precincts. The high-crime, low-income precincts (the first and third) surround the downtown area and occupy the northeastern and southeastern quadrants of the city. During the past 20 years, the city has expanded to the west; these quadrants of the city, the northwestern and southwestern (the second and fourth precincts), report the least crime.

The Environmental Data

The environmental survey instrument was designed to provide a measure, as objectively as possible, of the physical condition of the targeted residential blocks. The procedure involved in-person observations by trained raters of several types of physical cues that have been associated with residents' fear of crime and actual crime rates. Three hundred forty-nine blocks were randomly selected in the first and third police precincts in Mobile, Alabama. The survey was conducted throughout the month of November 2001.

Cues measured by the instrument included symbolic signs of physical deterioration (such as abandoned or unkempt housing and such "incivilities" as litter and vandalism) and real signs of vulnerability (such as dark and empty streets).

A second set of cues concerned territorial signs, represented by homes in which residents clean up and beautify their property. Territorial indicators may be manifest in a variety of ways, such as personalization of the physical environment (e.g., decorating one's yard or putting one's name on a door), that convey ownership, protection, and a separation between one's self or family and "outsiders."

Finally, there are certain nonpermanent characteristics of the environment that are even more directly related to a criminal's propensity to strike. A residential area with adequate lighting, surveillance opportunities, and barriers to entry, for example, is said to have defensible space. Survey items were intended to measure these various cues in the targeted area.

Three measures were constructed. One measure summed the positive aspects of the block (physical characteristics that would likely repel would-be predators). The second scale summed the negative aspects of the block (physical characteristics that would attract would-be predators). A third measure subtracted the negative score from the positive score, producing an overall measure of the block's physical state (deterioration). The measure was constructed so that the higher the number, the more deteriorated the block face.

Crime and Disorder Data

Crime data were obtained from the Mobile Police Department's COMPASS database. All field case reports data are entered into the COMPASS system. Crime data were collected for the period from January 1, 2001, through December 31, 2002. Crime-against-person data consisted of homicide, sex offenses (all), robbery (all), and assault (first and second degree). Property crime incidents consisted of theft (from yard and residence), burglary, vehicle burglary, and vehicle theft.

Disorder incidents were obtained from Mobile Police Department's calls-for-service data. The disorder incidents consisted of shots fired, disorder, fight, harassment, loud noise, and suspicious person or activity. This approximates Kelling and Coles's (1996) definition of disorder. Counting the incidents from police calls, in my view, provides a more comprehensive picture of disorder than field observations. Putting sufficient observers in sufficient locations for sufficient time to reasonably capture the extent of disorder behaviors is cost prohibitive.[1] Although calls-for-service data admittedly have their limitations, the problems associated with observer staff size, location diffusion, and time on-site are substantially reduced. Even with the noise of calls for service, we get a more comprehensive picture of disorderly behavior than what we could expect from trained observers.

Recall also that Sampson and Raudenbush (1999) maintain that crime and disorder are neither conceptually nor empirically independent. Kelling and Cole (1996) insist that although the behaviors that they refer to as disorder (aggressive panhandling, street prostitution, drunkenness and public drinking, menacing, harassment, vandalism, public urination, etc.) "may be designated as criminal, they are usually classified as misdemeanors or petty offenses under state laws and city ordinances, and are most often punishable by fines or community service" (p. 15).

Why, then, do we regulate disorderly behavior if it does not rise to the level of seriousness that felonies or even some other forms of misdemeanors (e.g., simple assault) do? According to Kelling and Cole (1996), "the answer lies in the immediate fear that such disorderly behavior engenders in the local community when it reaches a critical mass, and the potential for more serious crime, urban decline, and decay that ultimately follow on the heels of unconstrained disorder." (p. 16). Thus, although the UCR may designate disorderly behaviors as Part II crimes, policy makers and citizens draw a distinction between crime and disorder.

Police officers, I would argue, draw a similar conceptual distinction. Officers who are assigned calls for service that we use here to define disorder generally do not consider the assignment to be of a criminal nature. Unless the nature of the call is different from what was assigned, the car returns to service with a code; a report is completed only if the call is actually a reportable incident. For example, on arrival to a shots-fired call, the responding officer finds a person shot. The assigned officer will then advise the dispatcher of the status of the call and will ask for a report number for aggravated battery. The calls-for-service data will then override the shots-fired call with an aggravated battery. The computer-assisted dispatch database will record one aggravated battery.

The calls-for-service incidents that we use here to measure disorder, then, in nearly every case result in police action limited to restoring order. In my own experience as a police officer, these types of calls-for-service nearly always resulted in a 5F (five frank) return-to-service code. The translation of 5F is "order restored, no further service required." It was by far the most frequent back-in-service code used by beat cars.

Skogan (1990) argues that defining disorder is not straightforward. It varies according to community norms. Behaviors that may be tolerated in one community may not be tolerated in another. Nevertheless, the police are required to act on certain forms.

◈ Discussion

Police departments across the nation have enthusiastically adopted tactical operations that they claim conform to a broken-windows theoretical framework. Police policy makers in many jurisdictions have adopted aggressive field operations, the legitimacy of which is based on the assumption that crime and disorder are related. Officials of New York City (Bratton, 1998) have made claims that the dramatic reductions in street crime there, most notably the impressive drops in murder, are a direct result of zero-tolerance operations that attempt to attack disorderly behaviors of various sorts.

Efforts by law enforcement agencies to identify hot crime and disorder areas in which to apply zero-tolerance operations have been greatly enhanced by advances in hardware and software technologies (O'Shea & Nicholls, 2003). In particular, crime and disorder data in nearly all large police departments (i.e., departments with more than 100 sworn personnel) are in digital format. Most large departments also now use some form of geographical information systems (GIS) to graphically represent concentrated disorder calls for service and reported crimes. In many cities where a formal crime analysis unit exists (which, according to O'Shea and Nicholls, 2003, is most large departments), GIS density mapping is the primary tool used to identify concentrations of hot crime and disorder. A good deal of research effort has examined processes and outcomes of tactical police operations to address hot spot locations (Block & Block, 1995; Green, 1995; Koper, 1995; O'Shea & Nicholls, 2003; Sherman & Rogan, 1995; Sherman & Weisburd, 1995; Weisburd & Green, 1995).

Harcourt (2001) raises interesting and, at times, troubling questions about the connection between crime and disorder and, in particular, about the types of police activities that derive from the assumed link between the two. He maintains that we have no convincing empirical evidence of a connection between disorder and crime. Harcourt goes on to caution against a zero-tolerance (in its various forms) approach; he argues, as many do, that the police power should be limited and exercised only when there is compelling evidence that the benefits of security outweigh the inherently oppressive costs associated with enforcement tactics (e.g., disorder-related arrests). Furthermore, he offers, the selection of hot, concentrated enforcement activities raise troublesome issues of discrimination.

Sampson and Raudenbush (1999) offer a compelling argument that they claim casts serious doubt on the broken-windows theory generally and on the broken windows-grounded police operations specifically. Like Harcourt (2001), Sampson and Raudenbush insist that disorder cannot explain crime because disorder is merely a variation of crime; thus, the explanation for one (crime) is the explanation for the other (disorder).

The evidence we present here adds an additional layer to our understanding of the complex, dynamic nature of the criminal incident. Disorder and neighborhood physical condition, according to these findings, are related to criminal incidents. The evidence presented here thus support police operations designed to suppress disorder. The findings should, however, alert police managers to the need for a more careful analysis of both the potential consequences and the efficiencies of concentrating zero-tolerance-type operations in hot areas, in many cases to the exclusion of potentially more sensitive and vulnerable geographical spaces.

Findings here suggest that police field operational decisions should be sensitive to the linkage between disorder and physical deterioration. Moreover, police managers should consider that increases in disorder may have different effects on the extent of escalation of criminal incidents, depending on the physical condition of the block. Blocks with low physical deterioration may be more susceptible to the effects of disorder on violent and property crime than are more deteriorated blocks. Blocks defined by their physical condition may reach a deterioration saturation point after which

additional units of disorder will have little effect on the extent of violent and property crime. If this is so, then police analysts must be more sensitive to the emergence of disorder in areas that may currently be ignored (i.e., the relatively "cool" neighborhoods depicted in digital density maps), thus requiring a substantially different understanding of hot.

These findings raise questions about the calculus that police managers use to arrive at operational policies that result in the allocation of police resources. I make no claims at having the answer. What I can say with some degree of confidence is that simple arrest of the disorderly (however broadly defined) and citation of negligent property owners in currently defined hot deteriorated neighborhoods (the hallmark of zero tolerance) may not be the most efficient and effective use of those scarce law enforcement resources. Law enforcement data analysts must gain a better sense of the dynamics between disorder, physical deterioration, and crime. They must establish a better understanding of the threshold at which any additional units of police service dramatically decline in serving the end goal of controlling crime.

Finally, the evidence presented here, albeit exploratory and tentative, lend some measure of support to those who criticize zero tolerance. Law enforcement agencies must justify aggressive zero-tolerance policies; the benefits of law enforcement control practices must exceed the costs of additional units of aggressive police practices. These practices should draw even more careful scrutiny because they are currently directed at low-income, primarily minority sections of our cities. The findings here make no claim at the appropriateness of aggressive police practices; they simply raise questions about the assumptions from which law enforcement managers currently form the policies that determine the places in which these practices are directed. These findings also point to an example of the type of questions that police crime analysts and, ultimately, managers should be asking of the available police data and of the additional data that they must seek to collect (e.g., environmental data) before forming recommendations for police operational policies.

◈ Notes

1. Consider, for example, Sampson and Raudenbush's (1999) effort at measuring disorder in Chicago. No one can criticize the effort. They were clearly successful in producing a rigorous, systematic, reliable observation of activity on Chicago streets from 7 a.m. to 7 p.m.; however, one can take issue with the validity of the measurement. As anyone who has ever worked in a police car can attest to, the real disorder does not begin until the late evening and early morning hours.

2. There is a vast array of structural dimensions that sociologists have examined in the study of crime. The variable selection criteria that I adopted was simple. I selected a set of variables that were not highly correlated and at the same time provided a picture of sociological conditions that have been associated with crime.

3. In models that include the interaction term (Models 2 and 4), the contributing variables (deterioration and disorder) have been centered. The centered values were then used to produce the product terms. This avoids multicollinearity problems associated with a product term, and it has no effect on simple slopes, standard errors, and t tests (Aiken & West, 1991). Collinearity diagnostics for each model confirmed the absence of multicollinearity.

◈ References

Aiken, L., & West, S. (1991). *Multiple regression: Testing and interpreting interaction.* Newbury Park, CA: Sage.

Biderman, A., Johnson, L., McIntyre, J., & Weir, A. (1967). *Report on a pilot study in the District of Columbia on victimization and attitudes about law enforcement.* Washington, DC: Government Printing Office.

Block, R., & Block, R. (1995). Space, place, and crime: Hot spot areas and hot places of liquor-related crime. In J. Eck & D. Weisburd (Eds.), *Crime and place* (pp. 145–184). Monsey, NY: Willow Tree.

Bratton, W. (with P. Knobler). (1998). *Turnaround: How America's top cop reversed the crime epidemic.* New York: Random House.

Burgess, E. (1916). Juvenile delinquency in a small city. *Journal of the American Institute of Criminal Law and Criminology, 6,* 724–728.

Friedrich, R. (1982). In defense of multiplicative terms in multiple regression equations. *American Journal of Political Science, 26*(4), 797–833.

Glyde, J. (1856). Localities of crime in Suffolk. *Journal of the Statistical Society of London, 19,* 102–106.

Green, L. (1995). Cleaning up drug hot spots in Oakland, California: The displacement and diffusion effects. *Justice Quarterly, 12*(4), 737–754.

Guerry, A. M. (2002). *A translation of Andre-Michel Guerry's essay on the moral statistics of France.* Lewiston, NY: Edwin Mellen. (Original work published 1833)

Hackney, S. (1969). Southern violence. *American Historical Review, 74,* 906–925.

Harcourt, B. (2001). *The illusion of order.* Cambridge, MA: Harvard University Press.

Harries, K. (1971). The geography of American crime. *Journal of Geography, 70,* 204–213.

Jacobs, J. (1961). *The death of great American cities.* New York: Random House.

Jeffrey, C. (1971). *Crime prevention through environmental design.* Beverly Hills, CA: Sage.

Kelling, G. (1981). *The Newark foot patrol experiment.* Washington, DC: The Police Foundation

Kelling, G., & Coles, C. (1996). *Fixing broken windows: Restoring order and reducing crime in our communities.* New York: Free Press.

Koper, C. (1995). Just enough police presence: Reducing crime and disorderly behavior by optimizing patrol time in crime hot spots. *Justice Quarterly, 12*(4), 649–672.

Lottier, S. (1938). Distribution of criminal offenses in sectional regions. *Journal of Criminal Law, Criminology, and Political Science, 29*(3), 329–344.

Mayhew, H. (1968). *London labour and the London poor.* New York: Dover. (Original work published 1862)

Newman, O. (1972). *Defensible space.* New York: MacMillan.

O'Shea, T., & Nicholls, K. (2003). Police crime analysis: A survey of U.S. police departments with 100 or more sworn personnel. *Police Practice and Research, 4*(3), 233–250.

Plint, T. (1851). *Crime in England.* London: Charles Gilpin.

Quetelet, M.A. (1842). *Treatise on man.* Edinburgh, Scotland: William and Robert Chambers.

Sampson, R., & Raudenbush, S. (1999). Systematic social observation of public spaces: A new look at disorder in urban neighborhoods. *American Journal of Sociology, 105*(3), 603–651.

Shaw, C. (1929). *Delinquency areas.* Chicago: University of Chicago Press.

Shaw, C., & McKay, H. (1931). *Social factors in juvenile delinquency.* Washington, DC: Government Printing Office.

Sherman, L., & Rogan, D. (1995). Effects of gun seizures on gun violence: "Hot spots" patrol in Kansas City. *Justice quarterly, 12*(4), 673–694.

Sherman, L., & Weisburd, D. (1995). General deterrent effects of police patrol in crime "hot spots": A randomized, controlled trial. *Justice Quarterly, 12*(4), 625–648.

Simmons, M. (Producer), & Ramis, H. (Director). (1983). *National Lampoon's Summer Vacation* [Motion picture]. United States: Warner Bros.

Skogan, W. (1990). *Disorder and decline: Crime and the spiral of urban decay in American neighborhoods.* New York: Free Press.

Weisburd, D., & Green, L. (1995). Policing drug hot spots: The Jersey City drug market analysis experiment. *Justice Quarterly, 72*(4), 711–736.

Wilson, J. & Kelling, G. (1982, March). Broken windows: Police and neighborhood safety. *Atlantic Monthly, 249,* 29–38.

READING 16

Domestic violence is clearly a form of deviance in our society as well as others and is a relatively common event. In this article, Gracia and Herrero cite statistics from population-based studies showing that between 10% and 69% of women report physical abuse. If violence against women is a form of deviance, then it stands to reason that condoning the crime by not reporting it may also be deviant. Gracia and Herrero are particularly interested in the individual and contextual factors associated with the willingness to report violence against women. Specifically, how do neighborhood characteristics such as social disorder affect willingness to report domestic violence? On the basis of a nationally representative survey of adults ($n = 14{,}994$) in Spain, the researchers find that at the individual level, males were less likely than females to report physical abuse; age was also related to willingness to report domestic violence, with the youngest and the oldest individuals least likely to report abuse. Socioeconomic status was positively associated with willingness to report. Most important, however, those living in areas characterized or perceived as low or only moderate (as opposed to high) were significantly more likely to be willing to report domestic violence. The authors conclude that their results are consistent with newer versions of social disorganization theory, specifically those emphasizing the importance of collective efficacy. Social disorder lessens trust between people; their willingness to intervene is also weakened.

Perceived Neighborhood Social Disorder and Attitudes Toward Reporting Domestic Violence Against Women

Enrique Gracia and Juan Herrero

Domestic violence against women (DVAW) is a social and public health problem as well as a human rights abuse with a high prevalence worldwide. The World Health Organization's (WHO, 2002) *World Report on Violence and Health* offers a summary of 48 population-based surveys from around the world in which 10% to 69% of women reported being physically assaulted by an intimate partner at some point in their lives. Results from prevalence surveys carried out in Western countries suggest that around one in four women suffers some form of violence at the hands of a male partner or ex-partner (American Medical Association, 1994; Bachman &

Saltzman, 1992; Browne, 1993; Council of Europe, 2002; WHO, 2002). For example, an analysis of 10 prevalence studies of DVAW in European countries showed a high degree of consistency between the results, as all studies concluded that about 25% of women suffered domestic violence, and 6% to 10% of women suffered violence in a given year (Council of Europe, 2002). Prevalence data in Spain, where this study was conducted, are similar to other Western countries, with estimates ranging from 4.0% to 12.4% (Instituto de la Mujer, 2000, 2003; Medina-Ariza & Barberet, 2003). However, despite these shocking statistics, research worldwide indicates that many, perhaps most, instances of DVAW are never

Source: Gracia, Enrique, and Juan Herrero. 2007. "Perceived Neighborhood Social Disorder and Attitudes Toward Reporting Domestic Violence Against Women." *Journal of Interpersonal Violence* 22:737–752. Reprinted with permission.

reported to legal authorities (American Psychological Association, 1996; Bachman & Saltzman, 1992; Heise, Ellsberg, & Gotte-moeller, 1999; Straus & Gelles, 1986). For example, only between 3% and 8% of the total estimated cases of DVAW in Spain are reported to the authorities (Instituto de la Mujer, 2004).

Although research has paid some attention to the reasons that female victims of intimate partner violence do not report their victimization to authorities (Rhodes, 1998; Shrader & Sagot, 2000), almost no attention has been paid to factors influencing public attitudes toward reporting known cases of DVAW. DVAW in Western countries is increasingly considered as counternormative behavior but is not usually reported by those who are aware of incidents of DVAW. Silence remains a prevalent community response to DVAW, and not only do the victims contribute to this silence but also those who know about the violence and choose to be silent and passive (Jenkins, 1996). This is an important issue because public attitudes of indifference or passivity can help to maintain a climate of social tolerance (Biden, 1993). For example, in Europe, there are still widespread attitudes, such as victim blaming, that condone domestic violence against women, contributing to a climate of social acceptability (European Commission, 1999; Gracia & Herrero, 2006). This social tolerance not only reduces inhibitions for perpetrators but also probably makes it more difficult for women to make domestic violence visible, choosing not to report or abandon the relationship. Alternatively, a social climate of intolerance toward DVAW may act as an inhibiting force for perpetrators, reducing at the same time inhibitions toward reporting, for those in the community who may know who the perpetrators are as well as for the victims (Gracia, 2004). Positive attitudes toward reporting DVAW would help to strengthen a climate of social intolerance toward domestic violence, thus increasing the social costs for perpetrators (e.g., the loss of respect from significant others and neighbors in the community, the threat of the violence being reported by someone other than the victim, the violence as a "private matter" becoming public), and might act as an important deterrent (Fagan, 1989; Gelles, 1983; Williams, 1992). This social

climate of intolerance toward DVAW would also contribute to the social control of domestic violence.

Although personal and social norms—cost/benefit analysis of helping and nonhelping (Batson, 1998), stereotypes and prejudices toward women (Dobash & Dobash, 1997), victim blaming (Weiner, 1980), subculture of violence (Wolfgang & Ferracuti, 1982), privacy of the family and intimate relationships (Jenkins, 1996)—may affect attitudes toward reporting DVAW, community-related variables in which victims are embedded may also influence attitudes toward reporting DVAW. From an ecological framework of analysis, the links between community characteristics (poverty, social isolation, lack of social cohesion, social disorganization, community violence) and domestic violence, in particular child maltreatment, have long been pointed out (Coulton, Korbin, & Su, 1999; Garbarino & Sherman, 1980; Gelles, 1992; Gracia & Musitu, 2003; Korbin, 2003). However, the possible influence of these factors on public attitudes toward reporting domestic violence has been neglected in the literature. Our research interest draws from this ecological framework of analysis and from theoretical ideas and research on the link between community characteristics and violence, and the capacity of communities in preventing domestic violence (Sabol, Coulton, & Korbin, 2004).

Neighborhood Social Disorder and Attitudes Toward Reporting DVAW

Concentrated disadvantage and disorder in neighborhoods has been linked to the lack of social control in the community (Perkings, Meeks, & Taylor, 1992; Ross & Jang, 2000; Sampson & Raudenbush, 1999; Taylor & Shumaker, 1990). Social disorder refers to people and can be exemplified by the presence of people taking drugs on the streets, drug dealing, fighting on street corners, prostitution, crime, or other activities (both criminal and noncriminal) that create a sense of danger and that are perceived by residents as signs of the breakdown of social control (Ross & Jang, 2000; Ross & Mirowsky, 2001; Skogan & Maxfield, 1981; Taylor & Shumaker, 1990;

Wilson & Kelling, 1982). Social disorder also encompasses the physical environment and local demography (e.g., distribution of housing tenure and density). According to the broken window metaphor (Wilson & Kelling, 1982), disorder indicates to residents that their neighborhoods are dangerous places, making them afraid to take an active role in promoting social order in their communities and leading them to withdraw from community life. For Sampson and colleagues (Sampson & Raudenbush, 1999; Sampson, Raudenbush, & Earls, 1997), the broken window metaphor is apt insofar as it asserts that disorder signals neighbors' unwillingness to intervene when a crime is being committed or to ask the police to respond. Furthermore, neighborhoods with a higher incidence of social problems can create a sense of danger and insecurity. In deprived neighborhoods, where social problems tend to be compounded and intensified, conditions not only deteriorate residents' lives but they also may increase the feeling of powerlessness about their communities (Ross, Mirowsky, & Pribesh, 2001). As Ross et al. (2001) found, perceived neighborhood disorder, common in disadvantaged neighborhoods, influences mistrust by increasing residents' perceptions of powerlessness. Therefore, the willingness to get involved in other residents' lives or to intervene in neighborhood problems may be affected by the levels of mistrust. Residents may also fear retaliation if they intervene in neighborhood problems (Bursik & Grasmick, 1993). This fear of reprisal may inhibit the residents' willingness to intervene, probably even more when it is a "private matter" or "family business" (Anderson, 1999). As research from the social disorganization theory suggests, crime and disorder lead to fear, which weakens neighborhood cohesion and facilitates more crime and disorder (Markowitz, Bellair, Liska, & Liu, 2001).

Neighborhood disadvantage and disorder, and associated feelings of mistrust and powerlessness, can also diminish the collective efficacy of residents in achieving neighborhood social control (Markowitz, 2003; Ross et al., 2001; Sampson & Raudenbush, 1999; Sampson et al., 1997). In their conceptualization of collective efficacy, Sampson and colleagues link residents' perceptions of their communities with their tendency to intervene in problems and supervise residents to maintain public order. These neighborhood conditions may negatively influence attitudes to intervene and, as a consequence, attitudes toward reporting crime. As Sampson and colleagues (Sampson & Raudenbush, 1999; Sampson et al., 1997) suggest, one is unlikely to take action in a neighborhood context where people mistrust one another, and where neighborhood residents share a sense of powerlessness, it is difficult to bring about collective action. From this perspective, attitudes toward reporting DVAW would also be affected by community-level factors such as neighborhood social disorder, diminished collective efficacy, and low social control in the community. As Block and Skogan (2002) noted, the few studies that exist suggest that, when a neighborhood enjoys greater collective efficacy, the violence-reduction benefits may accrue not only to those who are victimized on the street or in public places but also to those who are victimized behind close doors (see also Browning, 2002). Reporting incidents of DVAW in the neighborhood is a way of exerting social control, but levels of social control are hypothesized to be lower among people who perceived their neighborhoods as characterized by social disorder resulting from a diminished sense of trust and collective efficacy.

This study is conducted in the context of the European culture, specifically in Spain, where research examining levels of neighborhood social disorder is virtually nonexistent. In our analysis of the potential links between perceived neighborhood social disorder and attitudes toward reporting DVAW, we therefore rely heavily on the existing research literature in the United States. Drawing from this research tradition, we expect, therefore, that perceived social disorder in the neighborhood will negatively influence residents' attitudes toward reporting DVAW to the police.

◈ Method

We used data from a national representative sample of 14,994 Spaniards 18 years old and older (Centro de Investigaciones Sociológicas, 1995). Multistage clustered sampling with selection of sampling primary units (provinces) and random proportional sampling of secondary units (census tracks) was used. Cities of smaller provinces were overrepresented in this study so that the number of interviews in these cities was enough to guarantee statistical inference. We applied regression weights to correct for the fact that most provinces had very similar sample sizes, no matter how large or small their population. These weights make an adjustment to ensure that each city is represented in proportion to its population size. Sampling of secondary units (census tracks) is randomly proportional to its population size. Data were collected through face-to-face home interviews after selecting individuals by quotas of sex and age.

Perceived neighborhood social disorder was operationalized upon responses to the following questions: In your opinion, what is the frequency of the following situations in your neighborhood? (a) prostitution, (b) overt behavior of racism and xenophobia, (c) children being exploited for mendicity, and (d) scandals and fighting in the streets. Replies were coded (1) *practically never,* (2) *a little,* (3) *often,* and (4) *a lot.* Variables selected to define perceived neighborhood social disorder (prostitution, child abuse and neglect, social problems, and delinquency) were based on criteria used by Spanish Local Government Departments to define "high risk neighborhoods" and "priority social action areas" (see Gracia, García, & Musitu, 1995, for a similar approach).

Overt behavior of racism and xenophobia was also included because in Spain, immigration is still a recent phenomenon, and ethnically defined residential areas are not common. Immigrants, especially those illegally residing in the country, tend to seek out housing in low-rent neighborhoods, which are often deprived residential areas. Native and immigrant populations tend to share these same residential areas, and conflict usually arises in the form of hostility and violence toward the minority group. According to research in Europe, reasons for this hostility among those more socially disadvantaged are competition with minorities for scarce resources, blaming the minorities for issues such as crime and job insecurity, feelings of personal insecurity, fear of crime, and distrust in others (European

Commission, 1997; European Monitoring Centre on Racism and Xenophobia, 2005).

Exploratory factor analysis was used to ascertain if the four items clustered into a theoretically meaningful factor. A one-factor solution was obtained with all four loadings greater than .64. Explained variance for this factor was 48%. Factor scores were summed to create the variable perceived neighborhood social disorder (Cronbach's alpha = .80). Three groups were created through cluster analysis: low social disorder, medium social disorder, and high social disorder. To further test for the predictive validity of the variable perceived neighborhood social disorder, we conducted analyses of variance to test if participants perceiving different levels of neighborhood social disorder had been victims of any of the following misdemeanors and offenses in their neighborhood within the past year: theft of personal belongings in the street or at home and personal aggressions. Mean differences were statistically significant with participants perceiving high neighborhood social disorder also informing of more misdemeanors and offenses in their neighborhood within the past year, as compared with participants perceiving medium and low neighborhood social disorder.

Attitudes toward reporting DVAW were measured by the following question: "Here, I would like to show you a list of situations that could occur at any time. I would like you to tell me whether or not you would report them to the police in case you had knowledge of them or you were present while they were occurring. While in your home, you hear that a neighbor is abusing his wife." Possible replies were (0) "No, I would not report it"; (1) "Yes, I would report it"; (2) "I don't know"; and (3) no response. We retained participants in the (0) and (1) categories.

To evaluate the influence of perceived neighborhood social disorder on attitudes toward reporting DVAW net of other possible confounding correlates, we controlled for sociodemographic variables (gender, age, socioeconomic status) and for other potentially relevant information also available in the survey (perceived frequency of DVAW in Spain, and size of city). Sociodemographtc variables have been identified as relevant external correlates of bystander intervention (e.g.,

Borofsky, Stollak, & Messé, 1971; Eagly & Crowley, 1986). Hence, we expect that women, the younger, and the more educated will have more positive attitudes toward reporting DVAW.

Gender was coded (0) male and (1) female. Age of participants was coded 1 to 6 if they belonged to any of the following six groups: (1) 18 to 24 years old, (2) 25 to 34 years old, (3) 35 to 44 years old, (4) 45 to 54 years old, (5) 55 to 64 years old, and (6) 65 years old and older. Socioeconomic status was measured with a composite measure of educational level—from (1) no formal education to (4) university education—and social class, based on the Spanish National Classification of Occupations—(1) low, (2) middle, and (3) high. To combine these two measures, we used the one-factor solution factor score of education and social class (explained variance = 76%, factor loadings = .87). Size of the city was computed from (1) 50,000 to 100,000 to (4) more than 1 million inhabitants.

As for the distribution of sociodemographic data of this study, gender, age, and education were compared to Spanish Census Data (Instituto Nacional de Estadística, 2001). In Spain, males represent about 48.9% of the adult population 18 years and older (49% in our study), about 13% of adult Spaniards have university studies (10.5% in our study), and 40.2% of the Spanish population live in cities larger than 100,000 inhabitants (52.4% in our study). The larger proportion of inhabitants of larger cities in our study is explained by the fact that the sample covers the Spanish population living in cities larger than 50,000 inhabitants. Except for size of city, participants in this study were representative of the Spanish population.

We also specifically controlled for participants' perceived frequency of DVAW within Spanish families, as they may also help shape public attitudes toward reporting DVAW. The rationale for this is that people who perceive higher neighborhood social disorder may be more aware of the pervasiveness of DVAW. Also, perceived frequency of DVAW may be related to the outcome variable of this study (Herrero & Gracia, 2005). As Klein, Campbell, Soler, and Ghez (1997) have suggested, the belief that a problem is widespread and

represents a threat for the community may be related to people's greater sense of responsibility, thus affecting attitudes to intervene. Controlling for the association between perceived neighborhood social disorder and perceived frequency of DVAW allows for exploring the specific relationship between perceived neighborhood social disorder and attitudes toward reporting DVAW. Perceived frequency of DVAW was measured by the following question: As far as you know, what is the frequency of DVAW within Spanish families? Replies were coded (0) low frequency or (1) high frequency.

◈ Discussion

Our results showed that participants perceiving low or moderate neighborhood social disorder showed a positive attitude toward reporting DVAW as compared with participants perceiving high neighborhood social disorder, once other significant correlates are taken into account (age, socioeconomic status, and size of city). These results support the idea that perceived neighborhood social disorder is negatively associated with residents' attitudes toward reporting DVAW, probably as a result of a diminished sense of trust and collective efficacy. Sampson and colleagues (1997) suggested that concentrated disadvantage and disorder leads to mistrust between people and reduced social control. This study has observed, in line with these ideas, that perceived neighborhood social disorder may reduce the willingness of residents to exert social control in cases of DVAW. In this respect, our study also illustrates the value of extending research on social disorganization and collective efficacy to the field of domestic violence (Browning, 2002).

Negative attitudes toward reporting DVAW can help to strengthen a climate of tolerance and, as our data suggest, these negative attitudes appear to be reinforced in participants who perceived high social neighborhood disorder. This is not only important in terms of the informal social control of DVAW but is also important for the victims because, as Browning (2002) noted, the social environment may be perceived by women as more or less supportive or effective in managing partner violence. A climate of tolerance of DVAW would make it easier for perpetrators to persist in their violent behavior and makes it more difficult for women to disclose domestic violence (Gracia, 2004). In terms of DVAW, there is a need for a social environment characterized by low tolerance and an increased sense of social and personal responsibility toward DVAW (Gracia & Herrero, 2006). This, in turn, would contribute to a social environment more effective in terms of social control of DVAW (Sabol et al., 2004).

In the European Union, as in other Western countries, many advances (legal and criminal justice reforms, law enforcement changes, prevention and treatment programs, educational campaigns, and social advocacy groups) have been made in the past decades aiming to reduce DVAW and to change public attitudes that nurture this violence. In Spain, although DVAW has only recently reached centrality in the political and social agenda (Medina-Ariza & Barberet, 2003), a new series of laws to combat violence against women have been introduced in the past years with a particular emphasis on prevention and public education. In this context, new initiatives to improve training for doctors, psychologists, and judges and to fund new shelters have been put in place (Loewenberg, 2005). Despite these initiatives, the current rates of female victims of domestic violence in our societies are still disturbingly high. Public awareness and education campaigns aiming to lower social tolerance and to increase the sense of social and personal responsibility toward DVAW are needed but, as our data suggest, in order to reduce and prevent DVAW, it is also important to address those conditions leading to mistrust between people and diminished social control such as concentrated disadvantage and disorder.

Limitations of the Study

The study has some limitations. First, the study relies on individuals' perceptions (perceived neighborhood social disorder) that may not match the realities of the ecological context in which participants live. However, in our study, perceived neighborhood social disorder was positively associated with the number of offenses experienced in the neighborhood during the past year (see Method section), suggesting that those perceiving

high social disorder were actually living in more socially disordered neighborhoods. Despite these associations, we cannot extend our findings to a contextual argument because information concerning the neighborhoods was absent from the survey. In this respect, it is also important to note the problem of selection bias. It is possible that the "perceived neighborhood social disorder" coefficient represents both contextual and selection effects (i.e., the tendency of persons who are less likely to report domestic violence to move into disordered neighborhoods), which cannot be accounted for with our data set. Further research taking into account neighborhood-level characteristics would help to better understand the processes outlined in this study. Second, because participants' responses are based on an in-home interview, the tendency to offer socially approved responses and the role of gender differences and compatibilities between the interviewer and participant may partially bias participants' responses. Third, the survey does not provide information about real cases of witnessing DVAW and the subsequent response of the witness (reporting or inhibition). Although our results indicate that perceiving neighborhood social disorder is negatively associated with a positive attitude toward reporting, further research should be directed to better explore whether these attitudes translate into real inhibition toward reporting. Fourth, other possible predictors of attitudes toward reporting DVAW such as attitudes toward family privacy, victim blaming, attitudes that condone and legitimize men's violence, trust in the authorities' effectiveness, the support available to victims, or the effects of public educational policies also deserve attention and should be the focus of more research efforts. Despite these limitations, due to the lack of attention that research has paid to this important issue, we believe that this article should stimulate further research on the factors that may influence attitudes toward reporting DVAW.

References

American Medical Association. (1994). *Diagnostic and treatment guidelines on domestic violence.* Chicago: Author.

American Psychological Association. (1996). *Violence and the family: Report of the American Psychological Association Presidential Task Force on Violence and the Family.* Washington, DC: Author.

Anderson, E. (1999). *Code of the street: Decency, violence, and the moral life of the inner city.* New York: W. W. Norton.

Bachman, R., & Saltzman, L. (1992). *Bureau of Justice Statistics special report: Violence against women: Estimates from the redesigned survey* (NCJ-154348). Washington, DC: U.S. Department of Justice, Bureau of Justice Statistics.

Batson, C. D. (1998). Altruism and prosocial behavior. In D. T. Gilbert, S. Fiske, & G. Lindzey (Eds.), *The handbook of social psychology* (Vol. 2, pp. 282–316). New York: McGraw-Hill.

Biden, J. R., Jr. (1993). Violence against women: The congressional response. *American Psychologist, 48,* 1059–1061.

Block, C. B., & Skogan, W. G. (2002). *Community crime prevention and intimate violence in Chicago, 1985–1998* (ICPSR version) |Computer file|. Chicago: Illinois Criminal Justice Information Authority.

Borofsky, G. Stollak, F., & Messé, L. (1971). Bystander reactions to physical assault: Sex differences in reactions to physical assault. *Journal of Experimental Psychology, 7,* 313–318.

Browne, A. (1993). Violence against women by male partners: Prevalence, outcomes, and policy implications. *American Psychologist, 48,* 1077–1087.

Browning, C. R. (2002). The span of collective efficacy: Extending social disorganization theory to partner violence. *Journal of Marriage and Family, 64,* 833–850.

Bursik, R. J., & Grasmick, H.G. (1993). *Neighborhood and crime.* New York: Lexington Books.

Centro de Investigaciones Sociológicas. (1995). *Demanda de seguridad y victimización* (Estudio No. 2.220) [Demand of Security and Victimization Survey|. Madrid, Spain: Author.

Coulton, C. J., Korbin, J. E., & Su, M. (1999). Neighborhoods and child maltreatment: A multilevel study. *Child Abuse & Neglect, 23,* 1019–1040.

Council of Europe. (2002). *Recommendation Rec(2002)5 of the Committee of Ministers to member states on the protection of women against violence adopted on 30 April 2002 and explanatory memorandum.* Strasbourg, France: Author.

Dobash, R. E., & Dobash, R. (1997). *Violence against wives.* New York: Free Press.

Eagly, A. H., & Crowley, M. (1986). Gender and helping behavior: A meta-analytic review of the social psychological literature. *Psychological Bulletin, 100,* 283–308.

European Commission. (1997). *Racism and xenophobia in Europe* (Eurobarometer 47.1). Brussels, Belgium: Author.

European Commission. (1999). *Europeans and their views on domestic violence against women* (Eurobarometer 51.0). Brussels, Belgium: Author.

European Monitoring Centre on Racism and Xenophobia. (2005). *Racist violence in 15 EU member states. A comparative overview of findings from the RAXEN National Focal Points Reports 2001–2004.* Brussels, Belgium: Author.

Fagan, J. A. (1989). Cessation of family violence: Deterrence and dissuasion. In M. Tony & L. Ohlin (Eds.), *Crime and justice: An annual review of research* (pp. 377–425). Chicago: University of Chicago Press.

Garbarino, J., & Sherman, D. (1980). High-risk neighbourhoods and high-risk families: The human ecology of child maltreatment. *Child Development, 51,* 188–198.

Gelles, R. J. (1983). An exchange/social control theory. In D. Finkehor, R. J. Gelles, M. Straus, G. Hotaling, et al. (Eds.), *The dark side of families* (pp. 151–l65). Beverly Hills, CA: Sage.

Gelles, R. J. (1992). Poverty and violence towards children. *American Behavioral Scientist, 35,* 258–274.

Gracia, E. (2004). Unreported cases of domestic violence against women: Towards an epidemiology of social silence, tolerance, and inhibition. *Journal of Epidemiology and Community Health, 58,* 536–537.

Gracia, E., García, F., & Musitu, G. (1995). Macrosocial determinants of social integration: Social class and area effect. *Journal of Community and Applied Social Psychology, 5,* 105–119.

Gracia, E., & Herrero, J. (2006). Acceptability of domestic violence against woman in the European Union: A multilevel analysis. *Journal of Epidemiology and Community Health, 60*(2), 123–129.

Gracia, E., & Musitu, G. (2003). Social isolation from communities and child maltreatment: A cross-cultural comparison. *Child Abuse & Neglect, 27,* 153–168.

Heise, L., Ellsberg, M., & Gottemoeller, M. (1999). *Ending violence against women* (Population Reports, Series L, No. 11). Baltimore, MD: Johns Hopkins University School of Public Health. Retrieved from http://www.infoforhealth.org/pr/ll ledsum.shtml

Herrero, J., & Gracia, E. (2005). Perceived frequency of domestic violence against women and neighbourhood social disorder. *Psychological Reports, 97,* 712–716.

lnstituto de la Mujer. (2000). *La violencia contra las mujeres. Resultados de la macroencuesta. II Parte* [Violence against women. Results from the macrosurvey, Part I]. Madrid, Spain: Author.

lnstituto de la Mujer. (2003). *La violencia contra las mujeres. Resultados de la macroencuesta. II Parte* [Violence against women. Results from the macrosurvey, Part II]. Madrid, Spain: Author.

lnstituto de la Mujer. (2004). *Denunciaspor malos tratas fsproducidas por el cónyuge o análogo. Año 2003* [Reported maltreatment by spouses or partners. Year 2003|. Madrid, Spain: Author.

lnstituto Nacional de Estadfstica. (2001). *Censo de población y viviendas* [Population and housing census|. Madrid, Spain: Author.

Jenkins, P. (1996). Threads that link community and family violence: Issues for prevention. In R. L. Hampton, P. Jenkins, & T. P. Gullotta (Eds.), *Preventing violence in America* (pp. 33–52). London: Sage.

Klein, E., Campbell, J., Soler, E., & Ghez, M. (1997). *Ending domestic violence: Changing public perceptions/halting the epidemic.* London: Sage.

Korbin, J. E. (2003). Neighborhood and community connectedness in child maltreatment research. *Child Abuse & Neglect, 27,* 137–140.

Loewenberg, S. (2005). Domestic violence in Spain. *Lancet, 365,* 464.

Markowitz, F. E. (2003). Socioeconomic disadvantage and violence. Recent research on culture and neighborhood as explanatory mechanisms. *Aggression and Violent Behavior, 8,* 145–154.

Markowitz, F. E., Bellair, P. E., Liska, A. E., & Liu, J. (2001). Extending social disorganization theory: Modeling the relationships between cohesion, fear, and disorder. *Criminology, 38,* 205–218.

Medina-Ariza, J., & Barberet, R.(2003). Intimate partner violence in Spain. *Violence Against Women, 9,* 302–322.

Menard, S. (1995). *Applied logistic regression analysis* (Sage University Papers Series on Quantitative Applications in the Social Sciences). Thousand Oaks, CA: Sage.

Pample, F. (2000). *Logistic regression. A primer* (Sage University Papers Series on Quantitative Applications in the Social Sciences). Thousand Oaks, CA: Sage.

Perkings, D. D., Meeks, J. W., & Taylor, R. B. (1992). The physical environment of street blocks and resident perceptions of crime and disorder: Implications for theory and measurement. *Journal of Environmental Psychology, 12,* 21–34.

Raferty, A. (1995). Bayesian model selection in social research. In P. Marsden (Ed.), *Social methodology* (pp. 11–163). London: Tavistock.

Rhodes, N. R. (1998). Why do battered women stay?: Three decades of research. *Aggression and Violent Behavior, 3,* 391–406.

Ross, C. E., & Jang, S. J. (2000). Neighborhood disorder, fear, and mistrust: The buffering role of social ties with neighbors. *American Journal of Community Psychology, 28,* 401–420. Ross, C. E., & Mirowsky, J. (2001). Neighborhood disadvantage, disorder, and health. *Journal of Health and Social Behavior, 42,* 258–276.

Ross, C. E., Mirowsky, J., & Pribesh, S. (2001). Powerlessness and the amplification of threat: Neighborhood disadvantage, disorder, and mistrust. *American Sociological Review, 66,* 568–591.

Sabol, W. J., Coulton, C. J., & Korbin, J. (2004). Building community capacity for violence prevention. *Journal of Interpersonal Violence, 19,* 322–340.

Sampson, R. J., & Raudenbush, S. W. (1999). Systematic social observation of public spaces: A new look at disorder in urban neighborhoods. *American Journal of Sociology, 105,* 603–651.

Sampson, R. J., Raudenbush, S. W., & Earls, F. (1997, August 15). Neighborhoods and violent crime: A multilevel study of collective efficacy. *Science, 277,* 918–924.

Shrader, E., & Sagot, M. (2000). *Domestic violence: Women's way out.* Washington, DC: Pan American Health Organization.

Skogan, W. G., & Maxfield, M. G. (1981). *Coping with crime: Individual and neighborhood reactions.* Beverly Hills, CA: Sage.

Straus, M., & Gelles, R. (1986). Societal change and change in family violence from 1974 to 1985 as revealed by two national surveys. *Journal of Marriage and Family, 48,* 465–479.

Taylor, R. B., & Shumaker, S. A. (1990). Local crime as a natural hazard: Implications for understanding the relationship between disorder and fear of crime. *American Journal of Community Psychology, 18,* 619–641.

Weiner, B. (1980). A cognitive (attribution)-emotion-action model of motivated behavior: An analysis of judgments of help giving. *Journal of Personality and Social Psychology, 39,* 186–200.

Williams, K. R. (1992). Social sources of marital violence and deterrence: Testing an integrated theory of assaults between partners. *Journal of Marriage and Family, 54,* 620–629.

Wilson, J. Q., & Kelling, G. (1982, March). Broken windows: The police and neighborhood safety. *Atlantic Monthly,* pp. 29–38.

Wolfgang, M., & Ferracuti, F. (1982). *The subculture of violence* (2nd ed.). London: Tavistock.

World Health Organization. (2002). *World report on violence and health.* Geneva: Author.

CHAPTER 6

Differential Association and Social Learning Theory

The Internet is a hotbed of deviant information. Indeed, within a couple of minutes, we found various sites that encouraged a wide variety of deviant behavior and others that provided step-by-step guides offering the basic techniques to learn how to engage in deviance. You can learn how to grow the best marijuana indoors and out, or you can learn how to convert cocaine into crack. Of course, crack is readily available in some neighborhoods, but the knowledge of how the product can be made from regular cocaine is important for some—perhaps middle-class kids with access to powder cocaine but not crack. For the person considering bulimia, there are "Pro Bulimia Tips and Tricks." There are tips on building a bomb with typical household items. The would-be burglar can get instructions on how to pick locks. And amid all of the porn, there are now websites helping married men and women to have affairs. The World Wide Web is clearly a source for virtually any form of deviance.

◈ Introduction

The discussion of websites above suggests something that many sociologists of deviance believe today and study—the notion that much deviance, if not all deviant behavior, needs to be learned and that instruction is often required. All of these websites offer encouragement to engage in deviance as well as information to help people learn the techniques necessary to engage in deviance. It might not take much to learn to smoke pot or crack, but the drug needs to be made available and—given its illegal status and the "war on drugs"—for many it would require a certain amount of encouragement.

Of course, the Web is not the only way we learn about deviance. We learn it from family, friends, other media sources, and so on. In this chapter, we discuss two prominent sociological theories that emphasize the importance of learning in the development of deviance. The first, developed by Edwin Sutherland in the 1930s and still prominent today, is differential association theory. The second modifies and builds on differential association theory; it is widely known as social learning theory and is primarily associated with Ronald Akers. We also provide a brief description of a related theory focused on culture and subcultures—cultural deviance theory. Following a general overview and evaluation of the theories, we discuss how the theories have been useful in understanding a wide range of deviant behaviors from a sociological perspective.

◈ Edwin Sutherland and Differential Association

Edwin Sutherland (1883–1950) was a pioneer in sociological criminology responding and attacking many of the mainstream criminological ideas of his time and providing a solid sociological approach to understanding crime. While his focus was clearly on "crime," his work has obvious implications for other noncriminal forms of deviant behavior. He was a prolific scholar producing numerous scientific publications, was the president of the American Sociological Association, and mentored many students who continued to advance the field of criminology and the study of deviance. Two of his books are of particular importance for this chapter: *White Collar Crime* (1949b) and a textbook in 1924 later to be titled *Principles of Criminology* (1934).

Sutherland titled his presidential address to the American Sociological Association, "Is White Collar Crime, Crime?" challenging mainstream criminologists who focused almost exclusively (and to some extent still overly focus) on street crime. Here Sutherland set the stage for his classic work *White Collar Crime,* published 4 years later. Although white-collar crime has become an important area of inquiry and students today are generally familiar with highly exposed cases of white-collar crime, what is important here is what Sutherland brought to the proverbial table: that "conventional generalizations about crime and criminality are invalid because they explain only the crime of the lower classes" (Sutherland, 1949, p. 217). He viewed crime as ubiquitous, happening across dimensions of social class, race, gender, and other social conditions. This important work drew attention to crimes of the middle and upper class whose perpetrators were obviously not suffering from poverty or biological predispositions.

Across editions, Sutherland modified and advanced *Principles of Criminology* to finally include in 1947 his full-fledged theory of **differential association,** including his nine propositions. Sutherland's text continued to be updated even after his death in 1950, with Donald Cressey and later David Luckenbill as coauthors. But neither Sutherland nor his collaborators changed the wording or modified in any way the nine propositions. Given the history of the propositions, we list the propositions as originally written in Table 6.1, but in our summary and examples, we use the term *deviance* and use noncriminological examples to better fit this text.

We will focus on the first seven propositions as the latter two are not terribly relevant for our discussion and were later discounted in later formulations (see Akers, 1985; Burgess & Akers, 1966). The first proposition suggests that deviant behavior is learned and not inherited or the result of some biological trait. Today, even those interested in biological predictors of crime and deviance do not argue that *behavior* is inherited, but rather that there may be predispositions that make some folks more likely to engage in behavior (see, e.g., Rowe, 2002; Walsh, 2000). The fact remains that the behavioral repertoire of babies is pretty limited. They hold few if any deviant (or nondeviant) thoughts; they don't know how to light a joint or know why they would want to; they may have a predisposition for alcoholism, but they don't know why they would want to drink or where to find a bar. This may seem obvious to many, but Sutherland was responding to the early biological and psychological traditions that were fairly deterministic in nature. Even today we speak of "crack babies" as if they are destined to a life of drug use. Furthermore, other schools of thought—in

Table 6.1   Sutherland's (1947) Nine Propositions of Differential Association Theory

1. Criminal behavior is learned.

2. Criminal behavior is learned in interaction with other persons in a process of communication.

3. The principal part of the learning of criminal behavior occurs within intimate personal groups.

4. When criminal behavior is learned, the learning includes (a) techniques of committing the crime, which are sometimes very complicated, sometimes very simple, and (b) the specific direction of motives, drives, rationalizations, and attitudes.

5. The specific direction of motives and drives is learned from definitions of the legal code as favorable or unfavorable.

6. A person becomes delinquent because of an excess of definitions favorable to violation of law over definitions unfavorable to violation of the law.

7. Differential associations may vary in frequency, duration, priority, and intensity.

8. The process of learning criminal behavior by association with criminal and anticriminal patterns involves all of the mechanisms that are involved in any other learning.

9. Although criminal behavior is an expression of general needs and values, it is not explained by those general needs and values because noncriminal behavior is an expression of the same needs and values.

particular, certain social control theorists—still argue that for the most part, the learning necessary for most deviance is trivial and of little theoretical importance (Gottfredson & Hirschi, 1990).

From the second and third propositions, we can conclude that deviance is learned from other people, particularly intimate others—one's family and friends. Remember that Sutherland was writing during a time when people were not bombarded with mass media; current researchers have moved beyond intimate others in examining sources of deviance. However, even today much learning takes place between parents and children and between friends and acquaintances. Much research suggests that early deviant behaviors are group activities. Underage drinking, smoking pot or using other drugs, vandalism, bullying, and so on are more often done in groups than in isolation (Warr, 2002).

The fourth proposition suggests that two things need to be learned. First, one must know how to engage in the deviant behavior, and this may be simple or complex. Little technique is needed to vandalize a building by breaking a window. Alternatively, picking locks, hotwiring cars, and recognizing a drug buying opportunity versus a police sting are more complex. Second, we need to know why people would want to engage in the behavior in the first place. Sutherland believed that people need to learn the motivations, drives, rationalizations, and appropriate attitudes for engaging in deviant behavior. For example, given that smoking is illegal for minors, the massive ad campaigns on the hazards of smoking, and that fact that parents and teachers (even if they are smokers themselves) admonish smoking, why do thousands of youngsters start smoking each year? There must be other sources of "information" that motivate youngsters to start smoking. Hence, the fifth proposition suggests that direction of the motives and drives varies and is learned from exposure to **definitions** (statements, attitudes, beliefs) that are favorable or unfavorable to engaging in particular behaviors.

The sixth proposition is the most important proposition to differential association theory and states that an excess of definitions favorable to deviant behavior over definitions unfavorable to deviant behavior increases the likelihood of committing deviant acts. Going back to the adolescent smoking example, with all of the definitions (laws, warnings of parents and teachers, ad campaigns) unfavorable to smoking, why would one smoke? For Sutherland, the likely answer is that many definitions favorable to smoking (via parents, peers, famous actors and actresses, and other influential people) make smoking appear "cool." Some young people come to hold more definitions favorable to smoking than not smoking and begin the process of becoming a smoker.

The seventh proposition specifies this further and states that differential associations vary in terms of frequency (how often exposed), duration (how often exposed), priority (how early in life one is exposed), and intensity (the respect or admiration one holds for the person providing the definitions). Again, one can see that even in a society that rebukes smoking (at least symbolically via law, rules, and campaigns), some people are exposed to definitions favorable to smoking: frequently, for a long durations of time, from an early age where youth are impressionable, and from people they are expected to respect (e.g., parents, an older sibling, or media figures), making them more likely to engage in the behavior themselves. It is important to note that Sutherland did not emphasize differential association with persons but rather differential exposure to definitions. Although the two variables may be related, they are clearly not the same thing. Smokers (and other deviants) can provide definitions that are favorable ("smoking makes you look cool; try one") or unfavorable ("hock, hock, wheeze, wheeze, I wish I could quit these!").

Sutherland's theory of differential association is perhaps the most longstanding and most popular theory of deviance in terms of empirical evaluation, and it has made important inroads to policy and programs. It has been instrumental in studying a wide array of criminal and noncriminal deviant behaviors and has found much support. The theory has also been sharply criticized and challenged on a number of grounds (see Kubrin, Stucky, & Krohn, 2009, for a recent overview of the issues). However, it is still cited widely in the social sciences and has been modified and expanded by Ronald Akers and his colleagues.

DEVIANCE AND POPULAR CULTURE

Differential association holds that deviant behavior is learned behavior. Try to think of examples of behaviors that you have learned—deviant or not, the more specific, the better—and the specific processes that you went through to learn those behaviors. Did you learn them from people close to you? Did you learn both attitudes about the behavior and techniques to commit the behavior?

If you are having a hard time thinking of examples, popular culture offers many films and television shows that illustrate the process of learning deviant attitudes and behaviors:

American History X—a disturbing film that explores the topic of learning hatred and racism; it chronicles the relationship of a neo-Nazi skinhead and his hero-worshipping younger brother.

GoodFellas—Based on a true story, this film shows the rise to power of gangster Henry Hill. The narration by Henry and his wife offers a perspective on life as part of the mob and how it all came to seem very normal to them.

The television series, *Weeds,* tells the fictional story of Nancy, a recently widowed white mother living in an affluent suburb in California. After the death of her husband, Nancy begins a career selling marijuana. As the seasons progress, she builds her customer base, expands her business, and deals with increasing risk to herself and her family.

◈ Akers's Social Learning Theory

An early attempt at a serious reformulation of Sutherland's differential association theory came from Robert Burgess and Ronald Aker's (1966) "A Differential Association Reinforcement Theory of Criminal Behavior," which attempted to introduce the psychological concepts of operant conditioning to the theory. The notion behind operant conditioning is that learning is enhanced by both social and nonsocial reinforcement. Their collaboration led to a seven-proposition integration of differential association and operant conditioning concepts. We need not list all seven propositions for the reader to get the gist; therefore, we list the first three (note that Burgess and Akers used the term *criminal behavior* as did Sutherland, but in later work, Akers modified the propositions referencing *deviant behavior,* recognizing the generality of theory—see Akers, 1985):

1. Deviant behavior is learned according to the principles of operant conditioning.

2. Deviant behavior is learned both in nonsocial situations that are reinforcing or discriminating and through that social interaction in which the behavior of other persons is reinforcing or discriminating for such behavior.

3. The principal part of the learning of deviant behavior occurs in those groups that comprise or control the individual's major source of reinforcements.

The attempt at integration was notable and important but never terribly popularized, except that Akers has continued to modify and advance his version of social learning theory (see Akers, 1998). His more recent work focuses on four specific concepts rather than on a larger number of propositions, but he still argues that his is not a new theory but an integration of ideas built around the important contributions of Sutherland. The four concepts are differential association, definitions, differential reinforcement, and imitation. Note that two of the four concepts come directly from Sutherland.

According to Akers (1998), *definitions* are attitudes, beliefs, and rationalizations that define a behavior as good or bad, right or wrong, appropriate or inappropriate. Definitions can be general or specific. For example, a general definition that might endorse skipping school is the belief that "school rules are arbitrary and discriminatory." Alternately, a more specific definition might be the statement "If I can get good grades and miss a few classes, why shouldn't I skip a few classes?" Definitions can also be favorable to a behavior, neutralizing, or reproachful of a behavior. For example,

- Favorable—School is a waste of time and skipping school is cool.

- Neutralizing—Skipping school doesn't hurt anyone.

- Reproachful—Skipping school not only hurts the offender but other members of the class.

So definitions—these beliefs, orientations, and rationalizations people hold—encourage deviance or neutralize restraints that conventional society might impose. The stronger these definitions favoring or encouraging deviance, the more likely a person is to engage in such behavior.

Definitions are important, but where do they come from? Like Sutherland, Akers argues that definitions are learned from *differential association* with the persons one interacts with. Early on, these contacts are primarily with the family—parents, siblings, and perhaps children of parental friends. Later, children meet other peers on their own in the neighborhood and later in school. Later, people get jobs, find romantic relationships, and join new social networks, where new and different sorts of definitions and behaviors are modeled and encouraged (see Capaldi, Kim, & Owen, 2008; Warr, 1993).

▲ **Photo 6.1**   "It is all in the learning"...
Practicing smoking with candy cigarettes!

Differential reinforcement is clearly a concept that Akers adds to Sutherland's original theory. The concept "refers to the balance of anticipated and actual rewards and punishments that follow or are the consequences of behavior" (Akers, 1998, pp. 66–67). Sutherland wrote a great deal about exposure to definitions but did not say much about how behavioral patterns are actually learned. Akers argues that to the extent that the likelihood of behaviors will be rewarded or punished (frequently and in terms of quantity), they will reinforce or diminish the behavior. Therefore, we see differential reinforcement as a factor that should largely predict the continuation or escalation of a behavior rather than initiation.

The final concept discussed by Akers (1998) is **imitation**, which is simply observing modeled behavior. Perhaps you may have seen children imitating cigarette smoking with a stick or straw (at least one of us remembers doing that as a child). Candy cigarettes, too, were once popular with children, allowing them to imitate adult smokers. Whether candy cigarettes promote smoking or whether modeling is a strong predictor of anything is still debated, but the evidence is fairly clear that the tobacco industry hoped they would (J. D. Klein & St. Clair, 2000).

◈ Social Structure and Social Learning

The vast majority of Akers's theorizing and research, as well as other scholars interested in furthering and evaluating his theory, has focused on the four variables discussed above (definitions, differential association, differential reinforcement, and imitation)—that is, individual-level factors affecting various forms of deviant behavior. More recently, Akers (1998) has expanded his theory to incorporate characteristics of the **social structure** where the "learning" takes place, and he refers to this modified theory as social structure and social learning theory (SSSL). He argues that characteristics of the social structure provide a context for social learning. Figure 6.1 depicts the causal sequence outlined by Akers and Sellers (2004, p. 97). Note that there are no direct links between the social structural variables and deviant and conforming behavior. This suggests that the social learning processes can fully explain the relationship between social structure and deviant and conforming behaviors.

Figure 6.1   A Depiction of Akers's View of the Causal Effects of Social Structural Variables on Social Learning

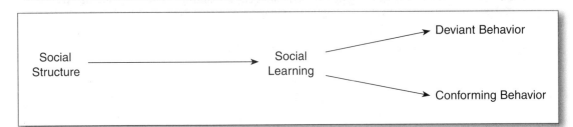

He proposes four key characteristics of the social structure that might affect social learning: (1) differential social organization, (2) differential location in the social structure, (3) theoretically defined structural variables, and (4) differential social location in groups. **Differential social organization** refers to structural correlates of crime—in our case, deviance. These are "ecological, community, or geographic differences across social systems" (Akers, 1998, p. 332). They might include age/gender composition of the community, urban as opposed to rural or suburban communities, or the unemployment rate. **Differential location in the social structure** refers to social and demographic characteristics of individuals that define or influence one's position or role in the larger social structure. Social class, gender, race/ethnicity, and age are key variables that may influence who one is exposed to as well as the rewards and punishment for behaviors individuals may anticipate or receive. For example, young boys from poor neighborhoods may be differentially exposed to deviant definitions promoting various forms of deviance (gambling, alcohol/drug use, vandalism, graffiti art). **Theoretically defined structural variables** might include "anomie, class oppression, social disorganization, group conflict, patriarchy," among others (Akers, 1998, p. 333). Socially disorganized communities, for example, because of scarce resources, racial/ethnic heterogeneity, and rapid population turnover, are said to be less able to control crime, delinquency, and other forms of deviance (see Chapter 5). These theoretical variables may also influence the types of people one is exposed to as well as the reinforcing patterns associated with various activities, including deviance. Finally, **differential social location in groups** refers to membership in various groups such as the family, peer groups in the neighborhood, school or work, and sports or other recreational groups. An obvious example of group membership that might influence social learning is a gang in which various forms of crime and deviant behavior are learned. Alternatively, being the oldest sibling in a family with responsibility for taking care of younger siblings may be a membership that promotes conforming behavior.

The SSSL version of Akers's theory would appear to be a ripe area for sociological theorizing as it clearly attempts to incorporate social variables, both at the macro and micro levels. At the macro level, there is room to think about community characteristics such as social disorganization or the prevalence of prosocial institutions and organizations such as good schools and churches. At the societal level, we might consider linking patriarchy or class oppression to social learning. At a more micro level, we can think about how gender, race, or social class may affect association with deviant or conforming peers, which may affect the learning process. To date, there have been only limited theoretical or empirical advances in this direction, and in a symposium following the publication of *Social Learning and Social Structure* (Akers, 1998), all three reviewers of the book seemed to think the theory was underdeveloped (Krohn, 1999; Morash, 1999; Sampson, 1999). Still, the theory offers fertile ground for thinking about the social structural variables that may affect the social learning of deviant behavior.

STUDIES IN DEVIANCE

Are You Kynd? Conformity and Deviance Within the Jamband Subculture

By Pamela M. Hunt (2010), in *Deviant Behavior, 31*, 521–551

One of the many areas of deviance is the study of subcultures. This article, by Pamela Hunt (2010), is the study of the jamband subculture. The jamband subculture is an extension of the Deadhead subculture that used to follow the Grateful Dead from venue to venue around the country, listening to their

(Continued)

(Continued)

concerts. Jambands follow such bands as Phish and the Dave Matthews Band, much the way the Deadheads followed the Grateful Dead. Jambands promote a counterculture philosophy of "kynd" behavior—involving the sharing of resources; transitory, communal living; and an aversion to status and authority.

Hunt uses differential association theory to examine whether these counterculture behaviors (albeit, considered prosocial) are learned the way other deviant behaviors are learned. In this manner, she is extending the use of differential association theory by examining within-group differences in prosocial and antisocial behavior. In other words, many might want to compare the jamband subculture to larger society—asking why members might opt to follow a particular band across country, but Hunt, instead, examines why some jamband members espouse a stronger "kynd" philosophy than others in the subculture.

Hunt administered 379 surveys to participants in jamband concerts in the Midwest, Southeast, and Northeast. Her participants reported participating in between 1 and 150 jamband-related events per year—with an average of 18 events. Hunt found that those who attend more jamband events and are more emotionally connected to others in the subculture and are more likely to believe in and promote "kynd" behaviors. In addition, those who became part of the jamband subculture at a younger age were also more likely to have a strong, positive belief in its philosophy. Those who might follow the subculture, but not as closely, or came later in life to the subculture did not have a strong, positive belief in the philosophy.

◈ Research on Differential Association and Social Learning

Differential association and social learning theories have been among the most thoroughly investigated theories in the study of crime and deviance, and a wide variety of forms of crime and deviance have been investigated. Some have criticized this research because a great deal of the research has come from Akers himself as well as his colleagues and students. For a variety of reasons, smoking has been a theme of this chapter, so we will start there. Smoking is clearly a deviant behavior as defined by at least three criteria: (1) It is illegal for certain segments of our society (those younger than age 18 in most, if not all, states) and in certain places (restaurants and bars in certain states and/or cities), (2) it is clearly a social/health harm in itself and is related to other forms of substance use, and (3) it is likely to bring negative reactions by at least certain segments of society. Akers himself was involved in a longitudinal study of teenage smoking in Iowa (see Akers, 1998). Each of the four key measures of Akers's standard social learning theory was included, and each of the learning variables was shown to be related to smoking behavior. Others have also tested the ability of social learning theory to explain smoking behavior among youth. For example, in a large nationwide study of 3,460 youth ages 11 to 19, Monroe (2004) found unique independent effects of measures of differential association, differential reinforcement, definitions, and imitation on having ever been a smoker.

Other types of substance use have also been studied via social learning theory. Akers and several of his colleagues (see Akers, 1998) were also involved in a large-scale study of drug and alcohol use. A novel aspect of this project was that it not only focused on use versus abstinence but also examined separately the effects of social learning variables on the onset, persistence/escalation, and desistence/cessation of the use of drugs and alcohol. The study involved a self-report study of just over 3,000 students in Grades 7 to 12 in the Midwest. The results showed that social learning variables were predictive of alcohol and marijuana use as well as problems associated with drug and alcohol use (Akers, 1998). In addition, Akers and Cochran (1985) were able to show that social learning variables were more powerful predictors of marijuana use than either social control theory or strain theory.

Other researchers have shown that differential association and social learning variables are predictive of substance use. In a study of more than 4,846 male and 576 female juveniles committed to the department of juvenile justice in Virginia (1998–2003), peer substance use was one of the strongest factors affecting substance use for both males and females (Neff & Waite, 2007). In a study at four universities in Florida, Kentucky, Tennessee, and Virginia, Higgins and his colleagues (Higgins, Tewksbury, & Mustaine, 2007) found that peer associations were among the strongest factors affecting binge drinking at college sporting events. Finally, Reed and Rountree (1997) found that direct peer pressure exerted little influence on substance use but that differential association and definitions favorable to substance use were important factors affecting substance use. Social learning would appear to be an important theory predictive of both substance use and abuse.

A very large number of studies have focused on general or overall delinquency, so our review here focuses focus on some interesting and more recent findings. For example, Hochstetler, Copes, and DeLisi (2002) analyzed data from the National Survey of Youth (NYS), a longitudinal data set, and showed that variables derived from differential association theory (e.g., friends' attitudes and beliefs) were moderately to strongly related to delinquent behavior and, more important, that these effects were not contingent on the presence of co-offenders. This provides support for both differential association and social learning theories and suggests that it is not just peer pressure but the socialization of deviant definitions and differential social reinforcement that leads to delinquent behavior. In another analysis of the NYS, Ploeger (1997) explored the often unanticipated positive correlation between employment and delinquent behavior among youth. He found that the positive correlation between employment and delinquency was largely explained by the deviant peers one encountered in the workplace.

In perhaps the most direct test of Sutherland's differential association theory, Dana Haynie (2002) provided as detailed examination of adolescent peer networks ($n = 2,606$) via the National Longitudinal Adolescent Health Survey (1995–1996). She found that peer networks were very heterogeneous, with a majority of youth having networks with both deviant and conforming associations. She found that "delinquent behavior is influenced by the ratio of definitions favorable to those unfavorable to law violation" and that the percentage of delinquent friends was that strongest factor affecting delinquent behavior (Haynie, 2002, p. 99).

Differential association and social learning theories have been criticized in that they have largely focused on juvenile delinquency and other relatively minor forms of deviance (smoking, drinking, and relatively minor forms of drug use). However, the theories do have relevance for other, more serious forms of deviance. Akers himself, for example, has given a great deal of thought to the applicability of social learning theory on rape and sexual aggression (Akers, 1985). Boeringer, Shehan, and Akers (1991) asked a sample of male undergraduates about proclivities to engage in rape and sexual aggression (e.g., "If you could be assured that you could in no way be punished for engaging in the following acts, how likely, if at all would you be to force a female to do something sexual she didn't want to do?"). Social learning variables were important factors affecting self-reported proclivity to use force or commit rape. A second study of male undergraduate students was conducted with basically the same dependent variables, but there was the addition of another form of nonphysical technique of sexual aggression, "plying a woman with alcohol or drugs with the intent of making her so intoxicated that she will be physically or mentally unable to refuse sexual intercourse" (Akers, 1998, p. 270). Again, social learning variables were important predictors of these forms of sexual deviance.

We have reviewed several empirical studies focusing on or at least including measures derived from differential association and social learning theories—often studies conducted by Akers and his colleagues. There are many studies not included, but this review should provide the reader with evidence that the theories are quite versatile and large in terms of scope and that the theories are able to explain a wide variety of deviant behaviors. In addition, the theory is likely to explain what Goode (2008a, p. 270) has come to refer to as "cognitive or intellectual deviance." He argues, for example, that in U.S. culture, being an atheist and not believing in God is a cognitive deviance. Indeed, a large number of political, religious, and social beliefs are considered deviant by mainstream society, and as the websites in the introductory story would indicate, there are thousands of websites where one can learn about various deviant beliefs. Our review of differential association and social learning theories has been quite favorable, but we do recognize that there are limitations to the theory. The next section provides a short critique of the theories.

◆ Some Limitations of Differential Association and Social Learning Theories

We have argued that differential association and social learning theories are general theories that can explain a wide variety of deviant behaviors. In this regard, the theories can be described as wide in scope. There are, however, various forms of deviance that social learning theory would have a hard time explaining. Although today we are bombarded by images of serial killers in the popular media, historically it would be difficult to argue that serial killers learn the techniques and motivations to kill through communication with intimate others (but see Castle & Hensley, 2002). Similarly, while there is good evidence to suggest that social factors have a great deal to do with how mentally ill patients are treated (see Krohn & Akers, 1977), the best evidence seems to suggest that the mentally ill are indeed mentally ill (Gove, 1975). All in all, however, differential association and social learning theories would appear to be robust in terms of the scope.

Perhaps one of the greatest debates over differential association concerns the theoretical and empirical role of differential association, often measured as deviant behavior of one's peers. Some have argued that this measure is really a measure of one's own behavior, especially given that much criminal and delinquent behavior is done with peers. Control theorists in particular have charged that birds of a feather flock together and that there is no feathering necessary to understanding deviant behavior (Glueck & Glueck, 1950; Hirschi, 1969). There is probably something to this line of argument, and the correlations found between certain measures of differential association and deviance, especially in cross-sectional studies, are likely somewhat inflated. Alternatively, some good evidence from studies with careful measurement and with longitudinal designs seem to indicate that some of the learning (both motivation and techniques) does come from differential association with deviant others where behavioral patterns are reinforced with rewards and punishments (see Capaldi et al., 2008; Haynie, 2002; Heimer & Matsueda, 1994) and that differential association affects not only group behavior but solo offending as well (Hochstetler et al., 2002).

For example, in a longitudinal study of youth, Elliot and Menard (1996) found delinquent peer associations, more often than not, temporally preceded—or came before—delinquent behavior. Furthermore, Thornberry and his colleagues (Thornberry, Lizotte, Krohn, Farnworth, & Sung Joon, 1994) hypothesized and found that association with delinquent peers leads to delinquency, which leads to exposure to other delinquent peers, which again encourages more delinquency. Warr (2002) has argued persuasively that criminologists have been misguided by a black/white or dichotomous conception of the role of peer influence versus selection (i.e., birds of a feather flock to together)—there is no reason why both can't be true (see also Akers, 1998).

NOW YOU . . . USE THE THEORY

Texting has been declared one of the most dangerous activities to do while driving because it involves all three types of distraction—visual, manual, and cognitive.

According to Madden and Lenhart (2009),

75% of all American teens ages 12–17 own a cell phone, and 66% use their phones to send or receive text messages. Older teens are more likely than younger teens to have cell phones and use text messaging; 82% of teens ages 16–17 have a cell phone and 76% of that cohort are cell texters. One in three (34%) texting teens ages 16–17 say they have texted while driving. That translates into 26% of all American teens ages 16–17. Half (52%) of cell-owning teens ages 16–17 say they have talked on a cell phone while driving. That translates into 43% of all American teens ages 16–17. 48% of all teens ages 12–17 say they have been in a car when the driver was texting. And, 40% say they have been in a car when the driver used a cell phone in a way that put themselves or others in danger. (p. 2)

When asked about their experiences with texting while driving, teens reported,

"I don't really get worried because everyone does it," one middle school-aged girl wrote. "And when my mother is texting and driving I don't really make a big deal because we joke around with her about it." (Madden & Lenhart, 2009, p. 7)

And

"[My dad] drives like he's drunk. His phone is just like sitting right in front of his face, and he puts his knees on the bottom of the steering wheel and tries to text." (Madden & Lenhart, 2009, p. 7)

Using social learning theory, explain the above statistics and quotes concerning texting while driving. Even though it has been declared one of the most dangerous behavior to engage in while driving, why might teens continue to engage in this behavior in such alarmingly large numbers?

Excerpt is reprinted with permission from Madden, Mary, and Amanda Lenhart. 2009. *Teens and Distracted Driving: Texting, Talking and Other Uses of the Cell Phone Behind the Wheel.* Pew Internet and American Life Project, Washington, D.C. Reprinted with permission of Pew Internet & American Life Project.

**Cultural Deviance Theory and
Subcultural Explanations of Deviance**

Cultural deviance theories, in general, emphasize the values, beliefs, rituals, and practices of societies that promote certain deviant behaviors. Subcultural explanations then emphasize the values, beliefs, rituals, and practices of subgroups in society that distinguish them from the larger society. To answer the question, "Why do some groups appear to behave in ways so different from mainstream society?" the cultural deviance theorist looks to the unique aspects of the culture or subculture to assess how people learn to tolerate, justify, and approve of deviant activities, at least in certain situations.

Cultural deviance, particularly subcultural explanations, has been very influential in the study of all kinds of deviance, and there is an interesting yet somewhat intractable debate over the relationship between cultural deviance theories and differential association/social learning theories. Thumbing through numerous databases, articles, and abstracts, you will often see cultural deviance theory linked to differential association or social learning theories as if they were one and the same. Similarly, numerous theorists (especially control theorists) link differential association and social learning theories under a cultural deviance label (see Hirschi, 1969; Kornhauser, 1978). Alternatively, Akers (1996) rejects the subcultural label for both Sutherland's differential association and his own social learning theory. He does, however, recognize that culture plays an important role in differential association theory and can play a role in social learning theory. The commonality, of course, is socialization and what one is exposed to and has reinforced in a given culture or subculture.

The linkages between cultural deviance theory and differential association/social learning theory are quite apparent, and this would appear to be an appropriate place for a brief discussion of the important role that theory has played in the study of deviance. The southern subculture of violence thesis (Gastil, 1971; Hackney, 1969) was an early subcultural explanation of deviance focused on the high rates of violence (especially lethal violence) in the South. The authors characterize the history and cultural tolerance of violence along with the acceptance and availability of firearms as contributing factors to the high rates of violence in the South. Wolfgang and Ferrcuti (1967) also focus on subcultures of violence but shift the focus to the high rates of homicide among young, minority males in inner cities. They formulate a subcultural theory that clearly links their subcultural theory to differential association and social learning theory, as can be seen in their sixth proposition, which states that "the development of favorable attitudes toward, and the use of violence in a subculture usually involve learned behavior and the process of differential learning, association, or identification" (Wolfgang and Ferrcuti, 1967, p. 161).

Extending this line most recently, E. Anderson (1999) contrasts "decent" and "street" families, terms recognized and used by the residents he studied in a poor, inner-city, largely African American community. He argues that the child-rearing practices vary tremendously between the two groups—the former are strict and focused on the values of mainstream society, and the latter socialize their children to deal with problems aggressively and with violence that fits the environment of the "code of the streets." However, Anderson argues that the "code of the streets" subculture exists and promotes violent responses to signs of disrespect among inner-city African American youth regardless of whether they come from a "decent" or "street" family.

Subcultural explanations have been useful far outside the study of violence. Indeed, such explanations have historically been used to understand virtually any form of deviance. Recently, subcultural explanations have been used to understand, for example, computer hacking (Holt & Copes, 2010); online gaming (Downing, 2009); ecstasy use in a drug-using subculture (Gourley, 2004); corporate crime (Robinson & Murphy, 2009); excessive thinness and starvation among athletes (Atkinson, 2011; Atkinson & Young, 2008); bondage, discipline, and sadomasochism (Stiles & Clark, 2011), and Internet "johns" seeking prostitutes (Blevins & Holt, 2009), among many others.

◈ Conclusion

In our reviews of differential association and social learning theories, we have emphasized studies that examine social learning through communication with intimate others, or at least persons known to the deviant. We have shied away from other sources of learning such as music, movies, TV, video games, and the Internet. We did this for two reasons. First, both differential association and social learning theories have historically focused on learning from intimate others. Second, the research on the effects of the media on various behaviors is complex and far from conclusive. Alternatively, we began this chapter with a list of websites from which people could learn both the techniques necessary to engage in a variety of deviances as well as the motivations and definitions favorable to engaging in a variety of deviant behaviors. It is clear that the Internet has changed our world and has become a viable source for those wishing to know more about almost any form of deviance and as a source of support for those involved in various forms of deviant behavior. Indeed, the Internet is a place where one can be involved in a vast array of deviant activities from online gambling, to cyber porn and cyber sex, to political protests, to hate crimes. Many technologies provide us with mechanisms to learn deviant techniques, attitudes, and beliefs and to explore deviant (and nondeviant) relationships. Warr (2002) writes, "There is no evidence as yet that such virtual peer groups have replaced or supplanted real ones, but no one who visits the United States can fail to be struck by the remarkable similarity among adolescents who live thousands of miles apart in highly disparate communities and climates, or by teenagers who seem to include fictional characters in their real-life reference groups" (p. 87). Clearly, physically present intimate others is not a necessary component of deviant learning anymore.

EXERCISES AND DISCUSSION QUESTIONS

1. Explain the process of differential association. How might one learn to dump toxic waste according to this theory?

2. Explain the difference between favorable, neutralizing, and reproachful definitions of behavior.

3. What are the four key characteristics of the social structure that might affect social learning?

4. Discuss how prosocial behavior can be explained using social learning theory.

5. What are the similarities and differences between differential association and social learning theory?

6. As you continue on to read about social control theory (Chapter 7), think about the differences between how social control theory and differential association theory explain deviant behavior. Which explanation are you most convinced by?

KEY TERMS

Cultural deviance theory

Definitions

Differential association

Differential location in the social structure

Differential reinforcement

Differential social location in groups

Differential social organization

Imitation

Social structure

Theoretically defined structural variables

READING 17

Our chapter on social learning theory did not say a great deal about how the experience of abuse or witnessing violence as a child might affect the propensity to engage in violent behavior later in the life course, although one can imagine how such experiences may relate to imitation (the behavior was modeled), how one may acquire definitions favorable to such behavior through differential association (behavior may be accompanied by statements positively related to the behavior), and how the behavior is reinforced to the extent violence works and the offender is rewarded. Indeed, the cycle of violence often described in research on domestic violence has clear affiliations with a social learning approach. In this article, Christine Sellers and her colleagues describe how social learning theory can subsume two theories of partner violence—the intergenerational transmission of violence theory and the male peer support theory. They argue that social learning theory provides a more systematic and logical framework for understanding partner violence. They then assess the empirical validity of the theory by analyzing data on individuals in dating relationships ($n = 945$) and marital relations ($n = 255$). Their results suggest that both differential association and differential reinforcement are important factors affecting partner violence but that imitation and definitions were not significantly related to partner violence.

Social Learning Theory and Partner Violence

A Research Note

Christine S. Sellers, John K. Cochran, and Kathryn A. Branch

The study of violence and aggression against partners in intimate relationships began in the 1970s with studies of spouse abuse, particularly physical aggression. This area of inquiry rapidly expanded to include non-physical forms of aggression, child abuse and neglect, elder abuse, abuse of parents, abuse among siblings, aggression within same-sex couples, and dating/courtship violence. Research in partner violence now enjoys several academic journals devoted to this area of inquiry, has produced hundreds, if not thousands, of scholarly works, receives considerable extramural support, has prominence at professional meetings for a variety of disciplines, and has played a very influential role informing public opinion and affecting legislation and public policy. In short, the study of violence among intimates is no longer a new and emergent field of study; it has arrived.

Yet this area of research reasonably can be criticized for the paucity of theoretical scholarship into the etiology of partner violence. Two efforts have made significant progress toward this end: intergenerational transmission theory (Straus, Gelles, and Steinmetz 1980) and male peer support theory (DeKeseredy and Schwartz 1993). Intergenerational transmission theory argues that witnessing or experiencing household violence during childhood is likely to lead to future violence or victimization in adulthood as children learn to imitate such aggression in their later intimate relationships. Though an attractive theory due to its policy implications, empirical tests of intergenerational transmission theory have been mixed and inconclusive (Sugarman and Hotaling 1989).

Alternatively, male peer support theory stresses the influence of patriarchy within intimate male-female relationships, especially when the male partner perceives that his authority has been challenged. A challenge to the male's authority (i.e., when his partner refuses him, argues with him, nags or berates him, threatens to end the relationship, etc.) leads him to experience stress and to seek support from his male peers, often from within all-male social groups such as fraternities, athletic teams, or gangs. Within these groups, patriarchal values and norms are promulgated that legitimate, justify, and even encourage physical aggression against the female partner. While male peer support theory has received a small amount of empirical support, its theoretical scope is quite limited. That is, male peer support theory is specifically designed to explain male-to-female partner violence; it cannot account for female-to-male or same-sex partner violence.

Despite their limitations, each of these theories of partner violence shares common theoretical elements consistent with those of social learning processes. Intergenerational transmission theory stresses imitation within the family across generations while male peer support theory stresses the transmission of group values. While both theories share these elements of learning, both lack a systematic and logically consistent theoretical framework that delineates the specific mechanisms by which partner violence is learned. Moreover, each lacks a general level of scope to account for all forms of partner/intimate violence. It is our contention that Akers' (1973, 1977, 1985) social learning theory accommodates and integrates the key theoretical elements of both intergenerational transmission theory and male peer support theory into a general theoretical framework that effectively addresses these limitations. It is the purpose of this study to develop a social learning model of intimate partner violence and to test its efficacy with self-report data specifically designed for this purpose.

 ## A Social Learning Model of Intimate Partner Violence

Social learning theory (SLT) is comprised of four key elements: imitation, definitions, differential associations, and differential reinforcement. Imitation refers to the extent to which one emulates the behavior of role models. These role models are significant others whom one admires, whom one has a perceived personal relationship, and whom one has directly observed behaving. In the present context the theory, consistent with the tenets of intergenerational transmission theory, predicts a greater probability of the use of physical aggression against one's partner for those individuals who have personally observed admired others engaging in acts of violence against their partners.

Definitions, the second element of social learning theory, refers to the attitudes and values individuals hold regarding the morality of the law in general and the wrongfulness of specific deviant/criminal behaviors. These attitudes may approve, disapprove, or be morally neutral toward a specific deviant behavior. Moreover, attitudes may vary in strength or salience and they may be rendered situationally inoperative. That is, while deviant behavior is likely among those who approve of it, such approval is not required for deviant behavior to occur. Instead, weakly held conventional morals and values or situationally neutralized morals and values are sufficient to generate deviant behavior. Conversely, the more individuals that endorse norms and values against deviant behavior, the less likely they are to engage in it. Thus, partner violence is predicted to be most likely among those who accept it, weakly oppose it, or have their opposition situationally neutralized. All of these attitudinal contexts are consistent with the patriarchal norms and values that are the foundation of male-to-female partner violence asserted by male peer support theory. However, social learning theory allows for a greater range of definitions that, in turn, broadens its scope into a more general theory of crime and deviant behavior.

Differential association is the third element of social learning theory. Because it refers to the influence of the definitions (attitudes) and behaviors of significant others on individuals' conduct, it too is logically consistent with similar influences implied by both intergenerational transmission theory and male peer support theory. According to social learning theory, exposure to the definitions and behaviors of others with whom one interacts has a powerful effect on one's own definitions and behaviors. The impact of this exposure varies according to the frequency, duration, intensity, and priority of the different associations individuals have with others. In terms of partner violence, social learning theory predicts that the probability of physical aggression against one's partner is greater among those whose close associates (family, friends, and significant others) endorse or engage in such conduct themselves.

Lastly, differential reinforcement refers to the net balance of anticipated costs and rewards associated with a given behavior. While not an element of either intergenerational transmission theory or male peer support theory, the concept of differential reinforcement is not inconsistent with their theoretical argumentation. According to social learning theory, an act that is expected to yield a greater balance of rewards than costs is more likely to be engaged. Persons in intimate relationships most inclined to employ physical aggression against their partner are those who view partner violence as more rewarding than costly. Such rewards may derive from the act of partner violence itself, such as the domination, power, and control one has over another. The rewards of partner violence also may derive from the support and encouragement one receives from others (such as the all-male peer groups identified by male peer support theory). Conversely, partner violence is less likely to occur among those for whom the anticipated costs exceed the anticipated rewards. These costs are the various social and non-social losses a person suffers—or could suffer—as a direct result of engaging in partner violence. These could include the fear of arrest, the loss of the relationship, guilt/remorse, shame and embarrassment, social approbation, physical injury, and so forth.

As applied to partner aggression, social learning theory predicts that the prevalence of such violence is greater among those who have witnessed others they admire using aggression against a partner; who hold definitions that approve, only weakly disapprove, or are situationally neutralized with regard to the use of partner violence; who associate with significant others who hold definitions consistent with the use of partner violence and/or engage in partner violence themselves; and who anticipate a greater balance of social and non-social rewards from partner violence than costs.

Akers' social learning theory easily integrates and accommodates the key theoretical elements of the leading theories of intimate partner violence while also addressing the various limitations associated with these other theories. However, it has not, to date, been extensively tested as an explanation of intimate partner violence. Our review of the available research literature yields only two sets of direct tests of social learning theory against data on partner violence. The first of these, Boeringer and Akers (see Boeringer, Shehan, and Akers 1991 and Akers 1998) found support for a social learning model of sexual aggression and rape in dating and acquaintance relationships in two studies of university males. In the second study, Sellers and her associates (Sellers, Cochran, and Winfree 2003) examined the efficacy of a social learning model to explain dating/courtship violence among a sample of college students; they also tested its ability to mediate the effects of gender. While their social learning model accounted for a significant amount of the variation in courtship violence and substantially reduced the effects of gender, it did not completely mediate these gender effects. Beyond these two sets of studies, we are unaware of any additional tests of social learning theory as a more general explanation of intimate partner aggression. The current study provides a further test of the scope of the social learning model by testing each of its four key elements against self-report data on the prevalence of physical aggression against an intimate partner among a sample of currently married or currently dating college students.

◈ Methods

The data for this study were gathered through a self-administered survey of students attending a large urban university in Florida. The students were surveyed in graduate and undergraduate classes randomly selected from the course offerings of five colleges (Arts and Sciences, Business Administration, Education, Engineering, and Fine Arts) during the first four weeks of the Spring 1995 semester. Courses were sampled from each college in proportion to the enrollments each college contributed to the university's total enrollment. This sampling strategy targeted a total of 2,500 students; however, absenteeism on the day of the survey and enrollments of students in more than one sampled course produced an overall response rate of 73%. The current study is based on two subsets of 1,641 students who completed the questionnaire and who report having had at least one serious relationship: (1) for analyses examining the use of violence in current dating relationships we use 945 students who indicated that they were currently dating, going steady, engaged, and/ or cohabiting with an intimate partner, and (2) for analyses examining violence in marital relationships we use 255 students who indicated that they were currently married. Married students were on average older than the total sample and the dating subsample (30.4 years of age vs. 24.2 and 22.5, respectively). Married students also were more likely to be graduate students, seniors, and juniors and less likely to be freshmen or sophomores. Other than these two differences, the socio-demographic profiles of both subsamples were nearly identical to that for the sample as a whole. Moreover, the socio-demographic profile of the overall sample was very similar to that of the total enrollment at the university.

The dependent variable consists of a measure of self-reported violence against a current partner. The measure is drawn from the physical aggression items in Straus' (1979) Conflict Tactics Scale. Specifically, respondents were asked how many times they had done any of the following during their current marital or dating relationship: (1) threw something at a partner, (2) pushed, grabbed, or shoved a partner, (3) slapped a partner, (4) kicked, bit, or hit a partner with a fist, (5) hit their partner with something, (6) beat up their partner, (7) threatened their partner with a knife or gun, and (8) used a knife or gun against their partner. Responses to these items were never, once or twice, 3 to

5 times, 6 to 10 times, 11 to 20 times, and 21 or more times, coded from 0 to 6.

A principal components factor analysis of these items produced two factors with eigenvalues greater than 1.00; however, the scree discontinuity test revealed that a single factor solution best fits these data. Five of the eight items produced factor loadings on this factor greater than .70; the remaining three items yielded loadings of .28 to .52. Despite weaker loadings, these three items were retained to maintain consistency with the Conflict Tactics Scale. Responses to these eight items were summed to create a physical aggression scale with possible values ranging from 0 to 48 (Cronbach's alpha = .79). Because the distribution on this variable is so strongly skewed, we have dichotomized it into a "prevalence of physical aggression" indicator, where 0 = never used any form of physical aggression against a partner and 1 = used some form of physical aggression at least once against a partner.

The independent variables in this study are drawn from Akers' four social learning constructs: imitation, differential reinforcement, definitions, and differential associations. Imitation was measured as an additive index of the total number of admired models which the respondent had actually seen using physical actions, such as hitting, slapping, kicking, or punching a partner during a disagreement. Admired models included actors on television or in movies, parents, siblings, other relatives, friends, and other people. Scores on the imitation index range from 0, for no models observed, to 7, for all models observed (Cronbach's alpha = .53).

Several items were used to measure differential reinforcement. First, respondents were asked to report the actual or anticipated reaction of four different sets of significant others (i.e., friends, parents, partners, and other significant persons) to respondent's use of violence against a partner. Respondents indicated that these significant others would either 1 = approve and encourage it, 2 = neither approve nor disapprove, 3 = disapprove but do nothing, 4 = disapprove and try to stop it, or 5 = disapprove and report to the authorities. Second, a single three-point, ordinal measure of overall balance of reinforcement for partner violence was included. This item ascertained the respondent's perception of the usual or anticipated net outcome of using violence against a partner (1 = mostly bad, 2 = about as much good as bad, or 3 = mostly good). Third, the net rewards-to-costs of using violence against a partner was measured by asking respondents to indicate which, if any, of eight rewards and eight costs they associated with using aggression against a partner. The eight rewards were: "It gave me a satisfying and rewarding feeling," "It made me feel more masculine and tough," "It ended the argument," "It got my partner off my back," "I felt powerful," "My friends respected me more," "My partner respected me more," and "I felt more in control." The eight costs were: "It made my relationship more stressful," "My friends criticized me," "I got arrested," "It made me feel out of control," "I felt ashamed," "It made the argument worse," "My family criticized me," and " I felt guilty." To compute the net rewards-to-costs, the sum of identified costs was subtracted from the sum of identified rewards; this produced a measure with values ranging from –8 (all costs with no rewards) to +8 (all rewards with no costs). Finally, two items were combined to assess respondent's perceived certainty and severity of formal criminal justice responses to intimacy violence.

Definitions is measured by three additive scales: a two-item additive scale of respondent's attitudes toward the law in general, a three-item additive scale of approving definitions of partner violence, and a three-item additive scale of partner violence neutralizing definitions. For each item comprising these scales, respondents were asked to indicate the extent to which they agreed/disagreed with the following Likert-type statements (1 = strongly agree to 5 = strongly disagree): "We all have a moral duty to abide by the law (reverse coded)," "It is okay to break the law if we do not agree with it," "It is against the law for a man to use violence against a woman even if they are in an intimate relationship" (reverse coded), "It is against the law for a woman to use violence against a man even if they are in an intimate relationship" (reverse coded), "Laws against the use of physical violence, even in intimate relationships, should be obeyed" (reverse coded), "Physical violence is a part of a normal dating/marital relationship," "I believe victims provoke physical violence," and "In dating/marital relationships, physical abuse is never justified" (reverse coded).

Lastly, several items were employed to create our three measures of differential association. First, a three-item additive scale of mother's, father's, and respondent's best friend's attitudes toward partner violence were measured by asking respondents to indicate to what degree each of these significant others would approve/disapprove of the use of physical violence against a partner (1 = strongly disapprove; 4 = strongly approve). Respondents also were asked to indicate the proportion of their best friends who had used violence against a partner (1 = none or almost none, 2 = less than half, 3 = more than half, and 4 = all or almost all). Lastly, respondents were asked to report how often their mother, father, and best friend had used physical actions against a partner (1 = never, 2 = seldom, 3 = usually, and 4 = always); these items comprise the third composite measure of differential association.

◈ Discussion

Despite being a fairly well-established field of inquiry, intimate partner violence still suffers from its rather atheoretical nature. To date, very few theoretical accounts of intimate partner violence have been generated. Of these, two of the more prominent approaches are especially noteworthy. These are the intergenerational transmission theory originally developed by Straus and his associates (1980) and DeKesseredy and Schwartz' (1993) male peer support theory. Intergenerational transmission theory has enjoyed great popularity despite the rather inconclusive nature of empirical tests of its validity. Conversely, male peer support theory is severely limited in its theoretical scope even though it has received a small but consistent amount of empirical support.

It is our contention that the study of intimate partner violence will best advance through the development and testing of systematic and logically consistent general theories of its cause (Sellers 1999). Toward this end we have introduced Akers' social learning theory. We have established that social learning theory can easily and logically subsume (integrate) the key theoretical elements of both intergenerational transmission theory and male peer support theory and can do so within a parsimonious, logically consistent, systematic, and general theoretical framework. Furthermore, we have shown with self-report data on marital and courtship violence that this social learning model is viable. Those who anticipate a greater net balance of rewards to costs from intimate partner violence or who associate with others who use violence against their partners, who hold attitudes supportive of such violence, and who do not react negatively to others' use of intimacy violence are significantly more likely to use violence against their partners.

Moreover, our models further establish the generality of Akers' social learning theory. That is, while Akers' theory has successfully withstood more than 100 attempts at falsification (Sellers et al. 2000) it has been criticized as a theory of minor and/or youthful misbehavior (Curran and Renzetti 1994; Rojek and Jensen 1996; Morash 1999) because most tests of its empirical validity have been limited to adolescent substance use (Akers et al. 1979; Akers and Cochran 1983; Sellers and Winfree 1990; Winfree and Bernat 1998; Winfree and Griffiths 1983; Winfree, Griffiths, and Sellers 1989) and other minor forms of youthful deviance such as academic dishonesty (Lanza-Kaduce and Klug 1986), computer crimes (Skinner and Fream 1997), or premarital sex (DiBlasio and Benda 1990). This study shows that social learning theory also can explain a significant amount of variation in serious violent and adult crime/deviance (see also Boeringer et al. 1991; Akers 1998; Sellers et al. 2000; Akers et al. 1989).

We note, however, that not each of the four social learning constructs were significant predictors of intimate partner violence; in fact, only two of the four produced measures that attained statistically significant effects: differential association and differential reinforcement. Measures of both definitions and

imitation consistently failed to attain statistically significant associations with intimate partner violence in these data. The absence of significant effects for the three measures of definitions is quite unusual when compared to the findings of most tests of Akers' social learning theory; in fact a recent meta-analysis of such studies revealed that measures of definitions are typically among the strongest social learning elements, second only to measures of differential association (Sellers et al. 2000).

While early research established a relationship between attitudinal acceptance of violence and its usage (Cate et al. 1982; Stets and Priog-Good 1987), we believe that university students have subsequently become heavily indoctrinated against the endorsement of violence. Thus, responses to the items that comprise our definitions scales may reflect a social desirability bias.

The failure of the imitation index to significantly predict intimate partner violence also is understandable. The role models from which imitation effects derive are often the same persons with whom one is in differential association. As such our measures of imitation and differential association may tend to covary such that the effects of one (imitation) are subsumed by those for the other (differential association).

As uniquely predicted by social learning theory, the influence of the social and non-social rewards relative to costs associated with partner violence is a powerful and important correlate that is rarely included in studies of intimacy violence. This is unfortunate because such neglect may have stunted the development of this field of research. Moreover, because differential reinforcement integrates the idea of "rational actors" into the social learning process, the absence of inquiry into the rewards and costs associated with partner violence has denied policy-makers key insights into potentially effective forms for intervention.

Finally, social learning theory's ability to "explain" intimate partner violence varies across the different forms of intimate partners sampled. That is, the amount of variation in the prevalence of intimate partner violence among married students accounted for by social learning theory (29%) was twice that accounted for among dating students (16.2%). While we are not able to fully address why this is the case, we suspect that the reason may be due, at least in part, to the more enduring and embedded context of marriage, on average, compared to that of dating relationships, especially among college students. Clearly additional work is badly needed both in the development and testing of alternative theories of intimate partner violence and in the continued development and testing of Akers' social learning theory.

◇ References

Akers, Ronald L. 1973. *Deviant Behavior: A Social Learning Approach.* Belmont, CA: Wadsworth.

——. 1977. *Deviant Behavior: A Social Learning Approach.* Second ed. Belmont, CA: Wadsworth.

——. 1985. *Deviant Behavior: A Social Learning Approach.* Third ed. Belmont, CA: Wadsworth.

——. 1998. *Social Learning and Social Structure: A General Theory of Crime and Deviance.* Boston, MA: Northeastern University Press.

Akers, Ronald L. and John K. Cochran. 1983. "Adolescent Marijuana Use: A Test of Three Theories of Deviant Behavior." *Deviant Behavior* 6:323–346.

Akers, Ronald L., Marvin D. Krohn, Lonn Lanza-Kaduce, and Marcia Radosevich. 1979. "Social Learning and Deviant Behavior: A Specific Test of a General Theory." *American Sociological Review* 44:635–55.

Akers, Ronald L., Anthony J. LaGreca, John K. Cochran, and Christine S. Sellers. 1989. "Social Learning Theory and Alcohol Behavior among the Elderly." *Sociological Quarterly* 30:625–38.

Boeringer, Scot, Constance L. Shehan, and Ronald L. Akers. 1991. "Social Context and Social Learning in Sexual Coercion and Aggression: Assessing the Contribution of Fraternity Membership." *Family Relations* 40:558–64.

Cate, R. M., J. M. Heston, J. Koval, F. S. Christopher, and S. Lloyd. 1982. "Premarital Abuse: A Social Psychological Perspective." *Journal of Family Issues* 3:79–90.

Curran, Daniel and Claire M. Renzetti. 1994. *Theories of Crime.* Boston, MA: Allyn and Bacon.

DeKeseredy, Walter S. and Martin D. Schwartz. 1993. "Male Peer Support and Woman Abuse: An Expansion of DeKeseredy's Model." *Sociological Spectrum* 13:393–413.

DiBlasio, F. and Bruce B. Benda. 1990. "Adolescent Sexual Behavior: A Multivariate Analysis of a Social Learning Model." *Journal of Youth and Adolescence* 5:449–466.

Lanza-Kaduce, Lonn and Mary Klug. 1986. "Learning to Cheat: The Interaction of Moral Development and Social Learning Theories." *Deviant Behavior* 7:243–59.

Morash, Mary. 1999. "A Consideration of Gender in Relation to Social Learning and Social Structure: A General Theory of Crime and Deviance." *Theoretical Criminology* 3:451–62.

Rojek, Dean G. and Gary F. Jensen. 1996. *Exploring Delinquency: Causes and Control.* Los Angeles, CA: Roxbury.

Sellers, Christine S. 1999. "Self-Control and Intimate Violence: An Examination of the Scope and Specification of the General Theory of Crime." *Criminology* 37:375–404.

Sellers, Christine S., John K. Cochran, and L. Thomas Winfree, Jr. 2003. "Social Learning Theory and Courtship Violence: An Empirical Test." Pp. 109—127. In *Social Learning Theory and the Explanation of Crime, Advances in Criminological Theory,* vol. 11, edited by Ronald L. Akers and Gary F. Jensen. New Brunswick, NJ: Transaction.

Sellers, Christine S., Travis C. Pratt, L. Thomas Winfree, Jr., and Francis T. Cullen. 2000. "The Empirical Status of Social Learning Theory: A Meta-Analysis." Paper presented at the annual meetings of the American Society of Criminology, November, San Francisco, CA.

Sellers, Christine S. and L. Thomas Winfree, Jr. 1990. "Differential Associations and Definitions: A Panel Study of Youthful Drinking Behavior." *International Journal of the Addictions* 25:755–71.

Skinner, William F. and A. M. Fream. 1997. "A Social Learning Theory Analysis of Computer Crime among College Students." *Journal of Research in Crime and Delinquency* 34:495–518.

Stets, Jan E. and Maureen A. Priog-Good. 1987. "Violence in Dating Relationships." *Social Psychology Quarterly* 50:237–46.

Straus, Murray A. 1979. "Measuring Intrafamily Conflict and Violence: The Conflict Tactics (CT) Scales." *Journal of Marriage and the Family* 41:75–88.

Straus, Murray A., Richard J. Gelles, and Suzanne Steinmetz. 1980. *Behind Closed Doors: Violence in the American Family.* New York: Anchor/Doubleday.

Sugarman, David B. and Gerald T. Hotaling. 1989. "Dating Violence: Prevalence, Context, and Risk Markers." Pp. 3–32. In *Violence in Dating Relationships: Emerging Social Issues,* edited by Maureen A. Pirog-Good and Jan E. Stets. New York: Praeger.

Winfree, L. Thomas, Jr. and Frances P. Bernat. 1998. "Social Learning, Self Control and Substance Abuse by Eighth Grade Students: A Tale of Two Cities." *Journal of Drug Issues* 28:539–58.

Winfree, L. Thomas, Jr. and Curt Taylor Griffiths. 1983. "Social Learning and Adolescent Marijuana Use: A Trend Study of Deviant Behavior in a Rural Middle School." *Rural Sociology* 48:219–39.

Winfree, L. Thomas, Jr., Curt T. Griffiths, and Christine S. Sellers. 1989. "Social Learning Theory, Drug Use, and American Indian Youths: A Cross-Cultural Test." *Justice Quarterly* 6:395–417.

READING 18

Computer crime has the potential to affect virtually everyone in society and has become a major concern of policy makers, actors in the criminal justice system, and the general public. It has also become a hot area of legal and social science research. Historically, much of the work has focused on small samples of offenders, financial costs, and legal implications and repercussions of computer crime. Unfortunately, much of the work has lacked a theoretical context. In this article, Skinner and Fream test the ability of social learning theory to better understand computer crime among college students. Specifically, they focus on pirating software, attempts to get other people's passwords without their permission, accessing others' computers without permission, changing information in others' computers, and using viruses to destroy computerized data. Skinner and Fream use self-report measures of (1) definitions (e.g., positive and negative beliefs and attitudes about computer crime), (2) differential association (e.g., how many of your friends engage in various computer crimes), (3) differential reinforcement/punishment (e.g., focus on the perceived certainty and severity of punishments rather than rewards), and (4) imitation (e.g., how much they have learned about different computer crimes from various sources such as books, magazines, or TV).

There is tremendous variation in the prevalence of different types of computer crimes, as well as variation in computer crimes across demographics (gender and race) and other measures relevant to college students (college, year in school). More important, they found at least some support for each component of social learning theory and overall strong support for the theory. One of the most interesting findings of the study concerns the law. On one hand, perceptions concerning the likelihood or severity of legal consequences had little effect on computer crime commission. On the other hand, the computer crime laws may be important in that they define certain activities as criminal, and at least some people will refrain from computer crime simply because it is against the law.

A Social Learning Theory Analysis of Computer Crime Among College Students

William F. Skinner and Anne M. Fream

Computer crime is a fairly new area of research in the field of criminology and deviance. Awareness of computer crime emerged in the early 1960s (Parker 1976), and since then, estimates of damage done by computer hackers or thieves have ranged between $145 million to $5 billion annually in the United States alone (American Bar Association 1984; McEwen, Fester, and Nugent 1989; Parker 1987).

Source: Skinner, William F., and Anne M. Fream. 1997. "A Social Learning Theory Analysis of Computer Crime Among College Students." *Journal of Research in Crime and Delinquency* 34(4):495–518. Reprinted with permission.

And there are estimates that "the average computer crime costs about $630,000" (Gottleber 1988:47). Of the few studies conducted on computer crime, most have been directed toward identifying individual and corporate victims of computer crime, consequences of the crime, profiles of the perpetrators, and the criminalization of computer crime (American Bar Association 1984; Gottleber 1988; Parker 1976; Schwartz, Rothfeder, and Lewyn 1990; Wong and Farquhar 1986).

These studies tend to represent the most extreme (costly) instances of computer crime that were detected. To date, little is known about the majority who have managed to escape detection. Hollinger (1988, 1991, 1992) was one of the first criminologists to examine computer crime among college students. He found that during a 15-week semester, 10 percent of his college-based sample reported being involved in software piracy and 3.3 percent had gained unauthorized access to another computer account. Although his study is highly informative and provides the groundwork for the current analysis, Hollinger examined only two types of illegal computer activity and did not provide an organized theoretical analysis of why college students commit computer crime.

There are two main objectives to this study. First, using a multistage sample of students at a southern university, we examine the lifetime, past year, and past month occurrence of five illegal computer activities— software piracy, guessing passwords to gain unauthorized access, gaining unauthorized access solely for the purpose of browsing, gaining unauthorized access for the purpose of changing information, and writing or using a program like a virus that destroys computerized data.[1] Second, because virtually no research has examined the etiology of computer crime, we examine the ability of social learning theory to explain these behaviors (Akers 1985). On the basis of multiple regression procedures, we demonstrate that measures of differential association, differential reinforcement and punishment, definitions, and sources of imitation are significantly related to computer crime.

 Previous Literature

Most studies on computer crime have been done on the victims of computer crime rather than the perpetrator. This literature has centered on documenting which businesses were being targeted as victims of computer crime and how much it cost them (O'Donoghue 1986; Schwartz et al. 1990; Wong and Farquhar 1986). For instance, the American Bar Association (1984) found in its survey of 283 businesses and organizations (banks, accounting or financial services, computer and electronic firms, and major federal government departments and agencies) that 25 percent had been victims of computer crime and that individually, average losses were between $2 to $10 million. And although 39 percent of the companies could not identify the perpetrators of specific crimes, in 77 percent of the cases where the companies actually caught a computer criminal, the offender was a company employee.

One of the first statistical studies on unknown perpetrators of computer crime was done by Hollinger (1992) at the University of Florida. The computer-related crimes that 1,766 students responded to dealt with (1) giving or receiving "pirated" computer software and (2) accessing another person's computer account or files without the owner's knowledge or permission. The findings showed that during a 15-week semester, 10 percent of the respondents had broken copyright laws on computer software and 3.3 percent had unauthorized access to someone else's computer account or files. Although these figures may not seem to pose a real threat to computer security, Hollinger extrapolated this information to the rest of the student body to show that there would be more than 3,500 instances of felony piracy on campus and over 1,000 instances of illegal intrusions per semester.

Hollinger's examination of correlates of computer crime indicated that those students most likely to be involved in piracy were male, 22 years of age and older, seniors and graduate students, Asian or Hispanic, cohabiting with someone of the opposite sex, and enrolled in majors dealing with forestry, engineering, business, liberal arts, and science. For involvement in unauthorized computer accounts access, the only significant difference occurred for gender, with male students significantly more likely than female students to engage in this type of computer crime. All other variables, although showing some trends, were not significantly correlated with unauthorized access.

Hollinger did find two variables that were strongly correlated with computer crime—friends' involvement and perceived certainty of being caught. When students in Hollinger's study reported that none of their best friends had been occasionally involved in piracy, less than 2 percent had committed the act. On the other hand, when more than half of the students' best friends had occasionally committed piracy, almost 40 percent had committed the act themselves. Similarly, about one-third of the students who had more than half their best friends involved in illegal computer account access had engaged in the same activity. Hollinger also found that when the source of social control was university officials, there was a moderately strong negative relationship between perceived certainty of being caught and frequency of piracy. A similar negative relationship was found between perceived certainty of being caught by fellow students and self-reported piracy. These two deterrence variables did not, however, significantly relate to unauthorized access to computer accounts.

We are in the very beginning stages of understanding and explaining computer crime. Most information to date has been anecdotal, based on face-to-face interviews with a few known computer criminals, or gleaned from victim surveys that were more interested in whether the perpetrators were employees. Although Hollinger's (1992) study was highly informative and lays the groundwork for future research, it was limited: (1) Only two acts of computer crime were included in the questionnaire, (2) the prevalence and incidence of computer crime were restricted to the previous four months, (3) the analysis did not examine a theoretical model explaining computer crime, and (4) no multivariate analysis was done.

This study attempts to overcome these limitations by first providing additional epidemiological information about computer crime. This includes the lifetime, past month, and past year prevalence of five types of illegal computer activity (see note 1). Second, we test hypotheses that relate social learning theory variables (Akers 1985) to the past year frequency of three types of computer crime and a computer crime index using multivariate procedures.

◇ Social Learning Theory and Computer Crime

As one of the major theories of deviance and crime, social learning theory provides an ideal context in which to understand computer crime. First, it has been empirically verified across numerous studies. Furthermore, it claims to be a general theory that applies to all types of deviant behavior (see Akers 1985 for a discussion). Thus, it should be applicable to illegal computer activities. Second, the very nature of computer crime requires that individuals learn not only how to operate a highly technical piece of equipment but also specific procedures, programming, and techniques for using the computer illegally. And third, as Sutherland and Cressey (1974) state, "An individual learns not only the techniques of committing the crime, no matter how complex or simple, but he/she learns specific motives, drives, rationalizations, and attitudes" (p. 75). Akers's (1985) theoretical synthesis of differential association and operant behavioral principles (Bandura 1986; Skinner 1953) elaborates on this theme.

Social learning theory is organized around four major concepts: differential association, differential reinforcement/punishment, definitions, and imitation. Differential association refers to the process by which individuals, operating in different social contexts, become exposed to, and ultimately learn, normative definitions favorable and unfavorable to criminal and legal behavior (Akers 1994). Although the family and peer groups tend to be the most important social groups in which differential association occurs, other contexts such as schools can be equally important to learning normative definitions. Research has clearly demonstrated a moderate to strong relationship between association with conforming and deviant others and deviant behavior (Burkett and Jensen 1975; Kandel et al. 1976, Krohn et al. 1985).

Definitions are attitudes about certain behavior learned through the process of differential association, imitation, and general interaction or exposure to various sources of learning located in one's social environment. In essence, they are "orientations, rationalizations, definitions of situations, and other evaluative and moral attitudes that define the commission of an act as right or wrong, good or bad, desirable or undesirable, justified or unjustified" (Akers 1994:97). Definitions can be of a general nature (e.g., moral or religious norms that guide general behavior) or specific to particular conforming and nonconforming behavior. Moreover, social learning distinguishes between positive, negative, and neutralizing definitions. Positive definitions define illegal behavior as desirable, acceptable, and permissible. Negative definitions define illegal behavior as undesirable, unacceptable, and wrong. And neutralizing definitions define illegal behavior as excusable, justifiable, and tolerable.

Differential reinforcement/punishment is a concept that captures the diversity of anticipated and actual consequences of engaging in certain behavior. It refers to the balance of social and nonsocial (i.e., physical) rewards and punishments associated with behavior. As Akers (1997) contends, positive reinforcers (e.g., approval from friends, family, teachers) and negative rein-forcers (e.g., the avoidance of unpleasant experiences) tend to increase the likelihood that a certain act will occur. On the other hand, positive punishers such as reprimands or more punitive reactions to behavior and negative punishers such as the removal or retraction of rewards, praise, or affection tend to decrease the likelihood that a certain act will occur. Both reinforcers and punishers can, and most of the time do, exist for any behavior. Therefore, it is the balance between these two exigencies that predicts behavior: "Whether individuals will refrain from or commit a crime at any given time (and whether they will continue or desist from doing it in the future) depends on

the past, present, and anticipated future rewards and punishment for their actions" (Akers 1994:98).

Finally, imitation refers to the modeling of certain behavior through the observation of others. Sources of imitation or modeling come primarily from salient social groups (parents, peers, teachers) and other sources such as the media. Imitation tends to be more important in the initial stages of learning deviant behavior and less important, although still having some effect, in the maintenance and cessation of behavior.

Because of its complexity, any full test of social learning theory requires operationalizing and measuring numerous variables (Akers et al. 1979; Akers and La Greca 1991; Krohn et al. 1985). We do not claim in this study to completely test social learning theory and, in some instances, do not operationalize the concepts as directly as more extensive studies. However, learning theory does provide a theoretical basis for hypothesizing relationships among selected learning variables and computer crime. Therefore, findings of hypothesized relationships provide support for the theory, and findings counter to the hypothesized relationships detract from the theory.

Because peer groups are undoubtedly the major social context in which college students interact, they will undoubtedly have a great impact on learning computer crime. Friends can be a source for learning the "technical" component of computer crime (e.g., how to bypass a security system or program a virus). They also can provide access to software for the purposes of pirating. Most important, it is in the peer group where an individual is exposed to the various norms and values relating to legal and illegal computer activities. This interaction can be face-to-face or through a "virtual" peer group, where interaction occurs electronically. Thus, we would expect that the more college students associate with peers who are engaging in illegal computer activity, the greater the frequency of the behavior.

Legal statutes provide a source for negative definitions of computer crime. Virtually every state has enacted legislation making a variety of computer activities illegal (Hollinger and Lanza-Kaduce 1988; Soma, Smith, and Sprague 1985). And in our sample, close to

90 percent of college students know that pirating software, guessing passwords, and unauthorized accessing of computer accounts are illegal (Fream 1993). Thus, we would expect that greater endorsement of the laws against computer crime would reduce the frequency of the behavior. Although students may approach the computer world with their moral and ethical beliefs intact, social groups such as friends or older students can influence illegal computer activity under the guise that "everybody does it." That is, students begin to adopt attitudes or neutralizing definitions that rationalize these unethical and illegal computer practices. These rationalizations, learned from friends, movies, printed media, and other sources temper the illegality of the act. In this study, we operationalize a number of neutralizing definitions and hypothesize them to be positively related to computer crime.

Hollinger (1992) found a fairly strong negative relationship between perceived certainty of apprehension and software piracy. On one hand, this could be a surprising finding because judicial leniency has been a problem that the federal war on computer crime has recently experienced. The biggest computer crime cases in history have resulted in dismissals or relatively light punishments (Hafner and Markoff 1991; Hanson 1991; Lewyn and Schwartz 1991). Consequently, young computer criminals may realize from reading articles and from experiences they or their friends have had that they are very unlikely to get caught and if they do, very little will be done to punish them.

On the other hand, with the increase in computer literacy, a heightened awareness primarily ascribable to the media of how computer crime affects individuals, and slightly stiffer penalties given to perpetrators, the perceived threat of legal apprehension and punishment may, as Hollinger's data suggest, serve as a source of differential reinforcement/punishment that deters individuals from committing computer crime. Two aspects of deterrence—perceived certainty of apprehension and severity of punishment—are used in this study to test the hypothesis that the greater the perceived deterrent effect of being caught and severely punished, the less likely college students will engage in illegal computer activities.

Finally, certain role models can serve as a source of imitation for computer crime. Besides family and friends, one of the major sources of imitation for college students is college teachers. Teachers' behavior can impart moral and legal standards. However, if a teacher advocates or engages in any form of computer crime, it can have the damaging effect of condoning and reinforcing (either directly or vicariously) illegal computer activities. For example, a university faculty member, in his letter to the editor of the New York Times, recommended that "bright youngsters who breach computer security should receive commendation, not condemnation" (Pfuhl, 1987:121). And Parker (1987) notes that at the California Institute of Technology, students reportedly received course credit for taking control of the computerized scoreboard during the 1984 Rose Bowl game. Thus, we hypothesize that the more students learn about computer crime from family and teachers, the more they will engage in the behavior. In addition, to the extent that college students hear about or observe teachers engaging in or encouraging students to become involved in computer crime, they may begin to imitate this behavior.

Another very influential area where role models abound is the media. As Hollinger and Lanza-Kaduce (1988) convincingly demonstrate in their study of the criminalization process of computer laws, "there are several ways in which the media influence perceptions about crime and criminal enactment" (pp. 114–15). They argue that the media provide the public with a "sense of frequency" about computer crime and help to symbolically "influence the social definition of the phenomenon," both of which fuel the criminalization process. Paradoxically, the media cannot only be viewed as a mechanism for communicating the social threat of computer crime but also contain numerous examples of negative role models that are imitated by would-be computer criminals. Such images serve as teaching roles by giving their audience new or creative methods of hacking into systems or writing sophisticated programs. Because computer-literate people with an affinity toward improving and challenging their technical abilities are always looking for new information, one can expect that the frequency of computer crime will increase as individuals are exposed to various media sources—books/magazines, TV/movies, and computer bulletin boards—where they can learn about computer crime and where the illegal activity is portrayed in a favorable, glamorous, and appealing light.

◈ Methodology

Sample and Procedures

A multistage sampling procedure was used to administer a confidential, self-administered questionnaire to a sample of 581 undergraduate students at a major university in a southern state. The aim was to survey students enrolled in three colleges within the university that have academic departments with the highest levels of computer usage and students who have a broad knowledge of computer applications and are more likely to know how to commit a computer crime. As such, we do not have a representative sample of all students attending the university. Rather, we purposively sample students to maximize variation on our dependent variable—computer crime.

The first stage involved a selection of colleges from among the 17 within the university that had the highest levels of computer usage by students. The three colleges chosen were Arts and Sciences, Business and Economics, and Engineering. These particular colleges were specifically selected on the basis of the findings from Hollinger's (1992) study, which indicated that the highest rates of computer crime would come from the departments that belonged to those three colleges. Also, the university's computer security and contingency planning officer suggested that illegal computer activity, if it has occurred, would most likely be committed by students within those three colleges more so than any of the other 14 colleges.

In the second stage, departments were selected from the three colleges. The 13 departments chosen within the College of Arts and Sciences were limited to the social sciences and natural sciences.[2] These departments have typically required some degree of computer expertise other than basic word processing skills to be applied to course work and assignments.

All five departments within the College of Business and Economics and all eight departments from the College of Engineering were incorporated into the sampling frame.[3]

In the third stage, undergraduate classes were randomly selected from those departments. The list of undergraduate classes offered in the spring of 1993 was reduced to include only those classes that were required or considered as departmental electives by the university for degree status. This excludes internships, independent studies, fieldwork, or self-directed reading courses. A random selection of 45 classes was taken from the edited sampling frame until about 950 students had been chosen, based on the maximum enrollment figures given for each class.[4] Of those 45 classes, 30 were scheduled to be surveyed.[5] A total of 581 students participated in the study, which represented a 60.2 percent response rate of the 965 students enrolled in the classes.

Table 1 shows the demographics of the sample as compared to the university's 1992 fall enrollment figures. Most participants are male (60.8 percent). However, it should be noted that the college with the largest number of participants, Engineering, is 84 percent male and has the lowest number of female students (276) enrolled than any other college within the university (Kentucky Council on Higher Education 1992). There was also a larger percentage of White students completing surveys (87.6 percent) than any other race or ethnic group, but that number is equivalent to the university's enrollment figures. Because the principle sampling unit was undergraduate classes, it was not unexpected that close to 90 percent of the sample contains 18- to 25-year-olds.

Measurement of Variables

To estimate the prevalence and frequency of computer crime, five types of activities were measured: (1) knowingly used, made, or gave to another person a "pirated" copy of commercially sold computer software; (2) tried to guess another's password to get into his or her computer account or files; (3) accessed another's computer account or files without his or her knowledge

Table 1   Demographics of Sample

Demographics	Sample	1992 Enrollment
Gender		
Female	37.9 (220)	50.4 (12,190)
Male	60.8 (353)	49.6 (12,007)
Race		
White	87.6 (509)	88.1 (21,315)
African American	4.3 (25)	4.1 (998)
Asian	5.9 (34)	1.4 (327)
Other	1.5 (9)	6.4 (1,557)
Age		
18–19	22.4 (130)	19.5 (4,715)
20–21	35.3 (205)	23.0 (5,564)
22–25	29.6 (172)	26.7 (6,463)
26 and over	11.3 (66)	30.6 (7,407)
College		
Agriculture	4.1 (24)	4.5 (1,078)
Arts and Sciences, Natural Sciences	9.5 (55)	6.8 (1,646)
Arts and Sciences, Social Sciences	16.7 (97)	8.0 (1,944)
Arts and Sciences, other	6.4 (37)	17.4 (4,220)
Arts and Sciences, total	32.5 (189)	32.3 (7,810)
Business & Economics	23.1 (143)	11.3 (2,746)
Engineering	29.4 (171)	8.7 (2,107)
Other	10.5 (61)	43.2 (10,456)
Year[3]		
Freshman	10.7 (62)	16.6 (4,027)
Sophomore	19.8 (115)	14.7 (3,550)
Junior	29.3 (170)	15.2 (3,685)
Senior	33.2 (193)	21.5 (5,200)
Graduate	5.0 (29)	20.6 (4,980)
Total	100.0 (581)	100.0 (24,197)

or permission just to look at the information or files; (4) added, deleted, changed, or printed any information in another's computer files without the owner's knowledge or permission; and (5) wrote or used a program that would destroy someone's computerized data (e.g., a virus, logic bomb, or trojan horse). Prevalence rates were computed from responses (never, within the past month, within the past year, one to four years ago, and five or more years ago) to questions on the lifetime, past year, and past month occurrence of each type of offense. Frequency was measured by asking students how often in the past year they had committed each of the five types of computer crimes. The response categories were the following: never, 1 to 2 times, 3 to 5 times, 6 to 9 times, and 10 times or more. Finally, a computer crime index was created that summed the responses to the frequency measure (Cronbach's alpha = .60).

Differential association was measured using the following question: "How many of your best friends have done one or more of the five computer acts?" The possible responses were (1) none, (2) just a few, (3) about half, (4) more than half, and (5) all or almost all. To measure negative definitions, respondents were asked to indicate their agreement or disagreement with the statement, "Because it is against the law, I would never do anything illegal using a computer." The responses range from (1) strongly disagree to (4) strongly agree. Neutralizing definitions were assessed on the same 4-point scale using the following statements: (1) If people do not want me to get access to their computer or computer systems, they should have better computer security; (2) I should be able to look at any computer information that the government, a school, a business, or an individual has on me even if they do not give me access; (3) I would never turn in a friend who used, made, or gave to another person a "pirated" copy of software; (4) I would never turn in a friend who accessed another's computer account or files without the owner's knowledge or permission; and (5) it is OK for me to pirate commercial software because it costs too much for me to buy.

We asked respondents to respond to a series of deterrence questions as our measure of differential reinforcement/punishment.[6] In earlier work, Akers (1973, 1977) has shown how deterrence variables can be subsumed under social learning theory. The certainty of apprehension dimension of deterrence was measured using the following questions: (1) How likely is it that you would be caught using, making, or giving to another person a "pirated" copy of software? and (2) How likely is it that you would be caught accessing or trying to access another's computer account or files without his or her knowledge or permission? Possible answers ranged from (1) never to (5) very likely. The severity of punishment aspect to deterrence was measured by the following questions: (1) How severe do you think the punishment would be if you got caught using, making, or giving to another person a "pirated" copy of software? and (2) How severe do you think the punishment would be if you got caught accessing or trying to access another's computer account or files without his or her knowledge or permission? Possible answers ranged from (1) not severe at all to (4) very severe.

To assess the sources of imitation, students were asked the following question: How much have you learned about . . . [the five computer crimes listed for the dependent variables] from each of the following: (1) family, (2) teachers, (3) books or magazines, (4) television and movies, and (5) computer bulletin boards. These variables do not directly measure observation of the behavior as Akers conceptualized imitation but rather assume that by observing the behavior or reading about it, students imitate and learn computer crime from different sources. For each source of imitation, the students had a 5-point measure ranging from (1) learned nothing to (5) learned everything. Two additional measures of imitation from teachers were how many times the student had seen or heard any of their college or high school teachers (1) offer students the chance to "pirate" a copy of commercially sold computer software and (2) praise or encourage students who have done computer activities you thought they should not be doing. The possible responses ranged from (1) never to (5) 10 times or more. The former measure referencing teachers could be seen as tapping opportunity and the latter tapping vicarious reinforcement, but both still reflect the extent to which teachers are sources of imitation for students.

 ## Results

Extent of Computer Crime

The percentage of college students engaging in computer crime is reported in Table 2. In general, the lifetime, past year, and past month rates tend to decrease as the seriousness of the activity increases. For instance, the most common form of illegal activity reported was pirating software. At least once in their lives, 41.3 percent of the students surveyed had knowingly used, copied, or given to another person a copy of pirated software; 33.9 percent had pirated software in the past year; 12.4 percent had done so within the past month. On the other end of the seriousness continuum, 2.1 percent had written or used a program like a virus or logic bomb to destroy someone's computerized data at least once in their life; 1.7 percent had done so in the past year; only 0.3 percent (less than five cases) had done so in the past month. In total, 49.7 percent of the students surveyed had at some point during their lives committed at least one of the five computer crimes examined in this study.

In general, there is a 3:1 to 2:1 ratio of male students to female students among those who admitted committing the activities. And as the far right columns in Table 2 indicate, writing or using a virus is strictly the province of male college students. With the exception of lifetime and past year prevalence of guessing passwords, White and Asian students are more likely to engage in illegal computer acts than other racial groups (Swinyard, Heikki, and Ah 1990). There does not seem to be a consistent relationship between the prevalence of illegal computer activity and the student's college. For instance, engineering students report the highest involvement in pirating software, whereas agricultural students tend to have the highest prevalence for guessing passwords, gaining access to accounts to change files, and writing or using a virus. Finally, except for the unusually high

percentage of graduate students who pirate software, there does not appear to be any substantial relationship of computer crime to age and year in school. Indeed, subsequent correlational analysis indicated that age had a small, negative relationship with only frequency of guessing a password ($r = -.07$).

Table 3 shows both how often those involved in computer crime committed the act and an estimated minimum and maximum incidence figure. Most of the students who had admitted to committing a computer crime had done so fairly infrequently. For instance, most password guessers (73.4 percent), browsers (63.1 percent), and virus writers/users (85.7 percent) had done this act one to two times in the past year. However, it is interesting to note that whereas about 44 percent of students who pirate software did so only 1 to 2 times in the past year, about one-third (31.8 percent) had committed this crime 10 times or more. By taking the minimum number for each of the following categories (1–2 times, 3–5 times, 6–9 times, and 10 times or more), we calculated the minimum and maximum number of occurrences for each of the five crimes in the past year. These figures indicate that 198 students pirated software at least 906 times and possibly more than 1,167 times. Assuming that the pirated software was priced between $100 and $500, these students cost software companies and distributors between about $90,600 and $453,000 in lost revenues. Also, in the past year, there were between 223 and 335 occurrences of students who tried to guess passwords to gain unauthorized access to computer accounts or files. Illegally gained access, whether the purpose was to just browse the files or to change information, occurred between 312 and 451 times in the past year. And although an extremely small number of students were involved in writing or using viruses, they did so at the very least 9 times and possibly more than 17 times in the past year.

These findings add to a small store of knowledge on the extent and seriousness of computer-related violations. They do not help, however, in explaining individual differences in committing computer crimes. We have argued that the explanation lies at least, in part, in differences in exposure to models of association with other offenders, taking on definitions favorable to

Table 2 Prevalence of Software Piracy, Guessing Passwords to Gain Unauthorized Access, Unauthorized Access Just to Browse, Unauthorized Access to Change Files, and Writing or Using a Virus by Demographics[a]

	Piracy			Guessing Passwords			Browse			Change Files			Virus		
	Lifetime	Past Year	Past Month	Lifetime	Past Year	Past Month	Lifetime	Past Year	Past Month	Lifetime	Past Year	Past Month	Lifetime	Past Year	Past Month
Gender															
Female (220)	19.5	15.0	3.2	13.6	10.5	3.2	9.5	5.9	1.8	2.3	2.3	0.9	0.0	0.0	0.0
Male (353)	55.5	46.5	18.4	25.2	20.1	6.2	22.7	17.8	4.2	10.5	6.8	2.0	3.4	2.8	0.6
Race															
White (509)	43.4	35.6	13.6	20.6	16.3	4.9	18.5	13.9	5.5	7.8	5.1	1.6	2.2	1.8	0.4
African American (25)	4.0	4.0	0.0	24.0	16.0	4.0	12.0	8.0	0.0	0.0	0.0	0.0	0.0	0.0	0.0
Asian (34)	38.2	29.4	5.9	14.7	14.7	8.8	8.8	8.8	0.0	8.8	8.8	2.9	2.9	2.9	0.0
Other (9)	33.3	33.3	0.0	22.2	11.1	0.0	11.1	0.0	0.0	0.0	0.0	0.0	0.0	0.0	0.0
Age															
18–19 (130)	33.1	25.4	6.2	23.1	22.3	8.5	16.2	13.8	4.6	5.4	4.6	1.5	1.5	1.5	1.5
20–21 (205)	40.5	36.1	13.12	23.9	18.5	6.3	18.0	13.7	4.9	7.8	4.4	0.5	2.4	2.0	0.0
22–25 (172)	47.1	37.2	16.3	16.3	12.8	1.7	16.3	11.6	3.5	6.4	4.1	1.2	1.7	1.2	0.0
26 and over (66)	47.8	37.3	13.4	16.4	6.0	3.0	22.4	14.9	9.0	11.9	9.0	4.5	1.5	1.5	0.0
College															
Agriculture (24) Arts and Sciences	45.8	37.5	8.3	33.3	20.8	12.5	20.8	8.3	8.3	12.5	8.3	4.2	4.2	4.2	0.0

	Piracy			Guessing Passwords			Browse			Change Files			Virus		
	Lifetime	Past Year	Past Month	Lifetime	Past Year	Past Month	Lifetime	Past Year	Past Month	Lifetime	Past Year	Past Month	Lifetime	Past Year	Past Month
Natural Sciences (55) Arts and Sciences	29.1	21.8	9.1	16.4	20.9	3.6	18.2	12.7	5.5	3.6	3.6	1.8	1.8	1.8	0.0
Arts and Sciences (97)	43.3	35.1	14.4	20.6	14.4	2.1	18.6	12.4	3.1	7.2	6.2	1.0	3.1	3.1	1.0
Arts and Sciences, other (37)	21.6	18.9	2.7	16.2	16.2	2.7	24.3	24.3	5.4	8.1	5.4	0.0	0.0	0.0	0.0
Business and Economics (134)	32.8	29.1	9.7	20.1	17.2	6.0	14.2	11.2	3.7	6.0	4.5	30	0.7	0.7	0.0
Engineering (171)	57.3	47.4	19.9	23.4	18.7	6.4	16.4	12.9	4.7	10.5	5.8	1.2	3.5	2.3	0.6
Other (61)	32.8	3.3	14.8	13.1	3.3	19.7	13.1	8.2	1.6	0.0	0.0	0.0	0.0	0.0	0.0
Year															
Freshman (62)	32.3	24.2	8.1	22.6	22.6	4.8	14.5	12.9	3.2	6.5	4.8	1.6	0.0	0.0	0.0
Sophomore (115)	35.7	29.6	7.8	22.6	20.9	10.4	13.9	12.2	7.0	7.8	7.8	1.7	2.6	2.6	1.7
Junior (170)	41.2	35.9	13.5	22.4	15.3	5.3	20.6	14.1	4.1	8.8	4.7	0.6	2.4	2.4	0.0
Senior (193)	43.5	33.7	14.0	18.1	13.0	2.1	19.2	14.0	5.2	6.7	3.6	2.1	2.1	1.0	0.0
Graduate (29)	72.4	65.5	24.1	17.2	13.8	3.4	13.8	10.3	3.4	3.4	3.4	0.0	0.0	0.0	0.0
Total (581)	41.3	33.9	12.4	20.7	16.4	5.0	17.6	13.1	4.8	7.4	5.0	1.5	2.1	1.7	0.3

a. Number of cases in parentheses.

Table 3   Frequency and Incidence of Computer Crime in the Past Year

Frequency	Pirated Software	Guessed Passwords	Unauthorized Access Just to Browse	Unauthorized Access to Change Files	Wrote or Used a Virus
1–2 times	43.9 (87)	73.4 (69)	63.1 (48)	40.0 (10)	85.7 (6)
3–5 times	16.7 (33)	12.8 (12)	13.2 (10)	40.0 (10)	14.3 (<5)
6–9 times	7.6 (15)	3.2 (<5)	9.2 (7)	8.0 (<5)	—
10 times or more	31.8 (63)	10.6 (10)	14.5 (11)	12.0 (<5)	—
Minimum incidents	906	223	230	82	9
Maximum incidents[a]	1,167+	335+	330+	121+	17+

a. The maximum number of incidents is based on the highest number of each of the given ranges. For the category of "10 times or more," estimates were based on 11 occurrences, so the actual maximum number may be higher.

engaging in unlawful computer uses, and failing to be deterred by fear of being caught and punished for such acts. We turn now to examining these social learning hypotheses.

Social Learning Theory Analysis

The regression analysis for determining the predictive value of the social learning variables included in this study appears in Table 4. The responses on two of the illegal computer acts examined in this study—gaining access to change files and writing/using a virus—were so limited that the acts were not included in this analysis. An index including all individual acts was used in the regression analysis as a global measure of computer crime.[7]

The results of the regression analysis show significant support for the application of social learning theory to illegal computer behavior by college students. When all the relevant variables were incorporated into the full regression model for each of the four dependent variables, 37 percent of the variance was explained in software piracy, 20 percent for guessing passwords to gain unauthorized access, 16 percent for unauthorized access for the purpose of browsing, and 40 percent for the computer crime index. If gender is

entered first into the regression equation and all the learning variables second, the learning variables by themselves account for about 75 percent of the reported explained variance when gender does have a significant effect and 90 percent when gender does not have a significant effect.

Table 4 shows that the sources of imitation variables operate differently depending on the type of computer crime. Learning about illegal computer activities from family members has a significant positive relationship with piracy. A similar positive effect is evident when students frequently observe or hear about teachers pirating software. Teachers also significantly affect guessing passwords if students frequently observe or hear them encourage students to engage in illegal computer activity. It is also interesting to note that the more students learn about illegal computer activity from computer bulletin boards, the more likely they are to guess passwords and be frequently involved in all types of computer crime examined in this study. This points to the viability of the "virtual" peer group as a source of learning computer crime.

The two main social learning variables in this study, differential association and definitions, consistently influence all types of reported computer offenses.

Table 4   Standardized (Unstandardized) Regression Coefficients for Social Learning Predictor Variables (*N* = 545)

	Piracy	Guess Password	Illegal Access to Browse	Computer Crime Index
Sources of imitation				
Family	.12 (.18)*	−.06 (−.05)	−.02 (−.01)	.04 (.10)
Teachers	−.05 (−.07)	.05 (.04)	.03 (.02)	.01 (.01)
Books/magazines	.03 (.04)	−.07 (−.05)	.03 (.02)	.02 (.05)
TV/movies	−.07 (−.11)	.01 (.01)	−.07 (−.06)	.08 (−.20)
Bulletin boards	.04 (.08)	.12 (.13)*	.07 (.08)	.10 (.37)*
Teacher pirated	.12 (.20)*			.14 (.45)*
Teacher encouraged	−.01 (−.03)	.10 (.13)*	−.01 (−.01)	.02 (.09)
Differential association				
Friends	28 (.38)*	.18 (.13)*		.26 (.62)*
Reinforce-punish				
Certainty-piracy	.03 (.05)			.03 (.10)
Severity-piracy	−.01 (−.02)			.06 (.04)
Certainty-access		.07 (.05)	.02 (.01)	.02 (.04)
Severity-access		−.07 (−.05)	−.13 (−.10)*	−.08 (−.22)*
Definitions				
Against the law	−.15 (−.22)*	−.18 (−.14)*	−.18 (−.15)*	−.23 (−62)*
Better security		.17 (.13)*	.12 (.09)*	.06 (.15)
Any access		.01 (.01)	.00 (.00)	−.04 (−.09)
Never report friend				
Piracy	.12 (.21)*			.13 (.40)*
Never report friends				
Access		.04 (.04)	.07 (.07)	−.04 (−.11)
Software too costly	.11 (.17)*			.07 (.20)
Control variable Gender	−.12 (−.33)*	.01 (.02)	−.04 (−.07)	−.08 (−.39)*
R²	.37*	.20*	.16*	.40*
M	1.78	1.24	1.23	6.35
SD	1.32	0.68	0.72	2.35

* *p* < .05.

Differentially associating with friends who participate in computer crime is the strongest predictor of piracy and the computer crime index. Definitions associated with adherence to the laws against these acts are significantly and negatively related to all types of computer crime and are the most important predictor of illegal access to browse.

Whereas our findings on friends' effects concur with those reported by Hollinger (1992), the findings on certainty of apprehension are at odds with his findings. That is, we did not find that the certainty of apprehension was negatively related to piracy. Also, the severity of punishment for piracy did not predict this type of behavior. However, our findings do concur with Hollinger's in that certainty of apprehension for illegal access to computer accounts does not deter college students from committing the act. Indeed, the only deterrence variable that significantly predicted computer crime (e.g, illegal access to browse) was the severity of punishment associated with illegal access. The hypothesis that differences in perceived punishment account for differences in violative behavior, therefore, was not supported. As we noted earlier, this variable did not incorporate perceived differences in social and nonsocial reinforcement for committing the acts. By leaving out that side of the balance, we have most likely underestimated the effects of the differential reinforcement process.

Our analysis of neutralizing definitions showed modest support for our hypotheses. College students who feel that companies and institutions should provide better security were more likely to guess passwords and browse accounts illegally than students not feeling this way. Also, when students felt that (1) software companies overpriced their product and (2) they would not report a friend who pirated software, they were more likely to pirate software and commit different types of computer crime than those not holding these attitudes. The other neutralizing definitions had no effect on any of the illegal acts.

Finally, gender plays an important role in explaining at least one type of illegal computer activity and computer crime in general. Controlling for the social learning variables in the equations, female students were significantly less likely to pirate software and be involved, overall, in computer crime than were male students.

◆ Discussion and Conclusion

We looked at a segment of the population who are in an educational environment that not only offers access to the tools and techniques necessary to compete in a computer-literate society but also may provide conditions favorable to learning and committing computer crime. The prevalence analysis indicated that these activities may be higher and more widespread than was previously indicated by other studies. Hollinger (1992) found that during a 15-week semester, 10 percent of his sample had pirated software and 3.3 percent had gained illegal access to computer accounts without the owner's knowledge or permission. This study found that 34 percent of the sample had pirated software in the past year (12.4 percent in the past month) and 16 percent had gained illegal access, whether to browse or to change information (5 percent in the past month). Just by comparing the past month's rates of this study to Hollinger's 15-week rate, it is obvious that there is a higher prevalence of computer crime in our sample. However, this could be due to the fact that our sample was purposively selected from students in academic disciplines where computer crime was thought to be more concentrated, whereas Hollinger's sample was a random selection of the entire study body at his university. Also, this study was conducted one year later than the Hollinger study. Consequently, students in 1993 may be more exposed to, and involved with, computers than students in 1992. In essence, taken together, these two studies could be viewed as establishing high and low estimates of computer crime among college students. And although slightly higher levels of computer crime were reported by males, Whites, Asians, and engineering students, computer crime reaches across gender, race, age, year, and college categories.

The multivariate analysis showed strong support for social learning theory as a conceptual framework for understanding computer crime in general. It showed modest support for the theory as an explanation of some particular forms of computer crime such as gaining illegal access to browse other accounts and files. As with other types of deviance, one of the major predictors of computer crime is associating with friends who engage in the activity. Friends who are successful at certain activities or in scholastic areas are generally the ones whom other students seek out for help and advice. Also, friends are usually more willing to share such information or challenge others to best them at their new found games, programs, or techniques. Thus, it comes as no surprise that learning computer crime is primarily peer driven.

Our analysis of other sources of imitation indicated that computer crime is learned from a variety of conventional sources. Students learn about pirating from family members undoubtedly because they are the sources of pirated software. Siblings and even parents may have copies of new programs and games they illegally acquired from other sources and make them available to others in the family. Similarly, our analysis indicated that teachers who not only condoned piracy but who strongly advocated it by words and actions increased the frequency of piracy and commission of any type of computer crime among students.

However, one of the most interesting findings regarding sources of imitation concerns computer bulletin boards. Our analysis indicated that using computer bulletin boards increased the frequency of trying to guess passwords to gain illegal access and the number of illegal acts as measured by the computer crime index. This could be explained by the fact that computer bulletin boards are notorious for underground networks that post passwords to various corporate, governmental, and institutional computer systems. Because many government bulletin boards and various other systems use the generic password "anonymous," some students may have tried to gain access with this method only to find out that the system is open only to specific authorized users. Also, with electronic bulletin boards and the Internet, students can now see what computer systems throughout the world have to offer in the way of interesting applications, games, or information.

However, because some of these offerings are view-only or have noninteractive access, students may try to find illegal ways of accessing this information.

Although most students were aware that computer crime is illegal, the possibility of suffering penalties seemed to have little effect on their behavior. Contrary to the Hollinger study, we did not find that the perceived certainty of apprehension and severity of punishment decreased the frequency of piracy. In fact, the only significant deterrent effect was associated with severity of punishment for illegally accessing accounts. One possible reason for this difference is that Hollinger specified the agents of social control—other students and administrative officials—and we did not. A more substantive interpretation is that there is neither a general nor specific deterrent effect that serves as a differential reinforcement/punishment for computer crime. Subsequent analysis of our data indicated that of the total number of students who participated in the survey, only 42 students (7.3 percent) have been caught and only 75 (13.3 percent) of those who responded had friends who were caught during or after illegal computer activity. If this is coupled with the more general recognition that "notorious" computer criminals are rarely apprehended or punished, there appears to be little incentive from a deterrence perspective for students to quit engaging in illegal computer activity. Also, as we have noted, the general concept of differential reinforcement that includes both rewards and punishment was underspecified in this study.

Where the law does affect the frequency of computer crime is in its educative effect. Our analysis indicated that in addition to differential association, the other most consistent predictor of computer crime was the negative definition that "because it is against the law, I would never do anything illegal using a computer." As Hollinger and Lanza-Kaduce (1988) indicate, "Computer crime laws are symbolic in that they 'educate,' 'moralize,' and 'socialize' computer users" (p. 114). They point out, as we do above, 'that "if the primary function of the new computer statutes was to deter rampant abuse, one would expect the new laws to result in vigorous prosecution" (p. 117). However, vigorous prosecution has not been forthcoming. Indeed, Kevin Mitnick, the most recent hacker to receive nationwide publicity, was charged with 23 counts of breaking into a San Francisco area computer network. He plea-bargained and admitted to illegally possessing 15 telephone numbers to gain access to computer systems. For that crime, he received eight months in jail and had the other 22 counts dropped ("Hacker Is Said" 1995). If harsher punishments were levied against computer criminals, we would have expected a stronger effect from the deterrent variables. Thus, our data support Hollinger and Lanza-Kaduce's contention that computer laws serve more of a symbolic than a deterrent function.

We have not conducted a full test of social learning, and one could argue that if we had conducted such an analysis, we would have explained even more variance in computer crime. However, this study has demonstrated the utility of social learning in understanding a variety of illegal computer activities among college students. Future research should expand on these measures and test more complete social learning models. Moreover, because gender was found to influence some types of computer crime, additional research could focus on possible interaction effects between gender and the learning variables. Other types of samples should also be used to further investigate computer crime. Systematic studies of business employees, Internet companies, and Internet users could offer some valuable insights for understanding the breadth and depth of computer crime, its threat to the security of private information, and its monetary cost to society. Clearly, widespread illegal computer acts are being committed every day. Because educational institutions are teaching students how to use computers and provide access to computer technology, the best place to start teaching them computer ethics and laws should be in the classrooms.

◆ Notes

1. The Penal Code of the Kentucky Revised Statutes Sections 434.845, 434.850, and 434.855 relating to unlawful access to a computer and misuse of computer information became effective on July 13, 1984. Section 434.845 entitled "Unlawful Access to a Computer in the First Degree" states the following:

(1) A person is guilty of unlawful access to a computer in the first degree when he knowingly and willfully, directly or indirectly accesses, causes to be accessed, or attempts to access any computer software, computer program, data, computer, computer system, computer network, or any part thereof, for the purpose of: (a) Devising or executing any scheme or artifice to defraud; or (b) Obtaining money, property, or services for themselves or another by means of false or fraudulent pretenses, representations, or promises; or (c) Altering, damaging, destroying or attempting to alter, damage, destroy any computer, computer system, or computer network, or any computer software, program, or data; (2) Accessing, attempting to access, or causing to be accessed any computer software, computer program, data, computer, computer system, computer network, or any part thereof, even though fraud, false or fraudulent pretenses, representations, or promises may have been involved in the access or attempt to access shall not constitute a violation of this section, if the sole purpose of the access was to obtain information and not to commit any other act proscribed by this section; and (3) Unlawful access to a computer in the first degree is a Class C felony.

Section 434.850 entitled "Unlawful Access to a Computer in the Second Degree" states the following:

(1) A person is guilty of unlawful access in the second degree when he without authorization knowingly and willfully, directly or indirectly accesses, causes to be accessed, or attempts to access any computer software, computer program, data, computer, computer system, computer network, or any part thereof and (2) Unlawful access to a computer in the second degree is a Class A misdemeanor.

Section 434.855 entitled "Misuse of Computer Information" states the following:

(1) A person is guilty of misuse of information when he: (a) Receives, conceals, or uses, or aids another in doing so, any proceeds of a violation of KRS 434.845; or (b) Receives, conceals, or uses or aids another in doing so, any books, records, documents, property, financial instrument, computer software, computer program, or other material, property, or objects, knowing the same to have been used in or obtained from a violation of KRS 434.845 and (2) Misuse of computer information is a Class C felony.

According to Section 532.020 of the Penal Code of the Kentucky Revised Statues, a class C felony has a prison term of at least 5 years but not more than 10 years. A person convicted of a class A misdemeanor can be sentenced to prison at least 90 days but not more than 12 months and could be fined up to a maximum of $500.

2. The social science departments chosen from the College of Arts and Science were composed of Anthropology, History, Economics, Geography, Political Science, Psychology, and Sociology. The natural sciences contained the following departments from the College of Arts and Sciences: Biology, Chemistry, Computer Science,

Mathematics, Physics and Astronomy, and Statistics. This excludes a total of 12 departments in the College of Arts and Sciences: Classical Languages, English, Studies, and Spanish and Italian. The following Interdisciplinary Minors were also excluded: African American Studies, French, German, Latin American Studies, Linguistics, Military Science, Philosophy, Russian and Eastern Appalachian Studies, Religious Studies, and Women's Studies.

3. For the College of Business and Economics, these included Accounting, Decision Sciences, Economics, Finance, Management, and Marketing. For the College of Engineering, these included Agricultural Engineering, Chemical Engineering, Civil Engineering, Electrical Engineering, Engineering Mechanics, Geological Sciences, Material Science Engineering, Mechanical Engineering, and Mining Engineering.

4. Additional classes whose combined enrollments were in excess of the needed 500 to 600 students were chosen for several reasons. It was reasonable to assume that some faculty members would prefer that their classes not be surveyed or that the time period of data collection may conflict with class curriculums that would not be able to be adjusted to include the administration of the survey. Also, the number given on the database was the maximum number of available openings for each class. However, fewer students may actually have enrolled in any of the classes that were chosen or they may have dropped the class during the drop/add process at the beginning of the semester. The reverse was also a possibility if the faculty member allowed more than the stated number of students in his or her classroom. In addition, those students who attended more than one class where the survey was conducted were asked not to complete the survey for a second time. Also, students who were enrolled in one of the randomly selected classes and were minors (under the age of 18) were asked not to complete a questionnaire because of the necessity and difficulty associated with acquiring written parental consent and any breaches to confidentiality that could occur.

5. A total of 15 classes in the sample were not surveyed because a faculty member did not want his or her class included in the study, the timing of the data collection could not be scheduled into his or her curriculum, the students had been oversurveyed in a particular class, or the class chosen was a lab where the students would have been conducting experiments that would be difficult to interrupt.

6. We recognize that these measures do not capture important sources of rewards and punishments from family and friends that may be attached to successful pirating or other acts. The measures used in this study include only the punishment component of differential reinforcement emanating from formal social control. As such, these measures offer an incomplete test of the differential reinforcement/punishment process.

7. Multicollinearity is a concern in any multivariate analysis. In checking for this problem in the regression analysis, we found no variance inflation factor (VIF) over 2.00. Also, the threat of multicollinearity is reduced because we have not operationalized all the dimensions of the core concepts of social learning theory, in particular, differential reinforcement/punishment for family and friends and other moral or normative definitions.

 # References

Akers, Ronald L. 1973. Deviant Behavior: A Social Learning Approach. Belmont, CA: Wadsworth.

——. 1977. Deviant Behavior: A Social Learning Approach. 2d ed. Belmont, CA: Wadsworth.

——. 1985. Deviant Behavior: A Social Learning Approach. 3d ed. Belmont, CA: Wadsworth.

——. 1994. Criminological Theories: Introduction and Evaluation. Los Angeles: Roxbury.

——. 1997. Criminological Theories: Introduction and Evaluation. 2d ed. Los Angeles: Roxbury.

Akers, Ronald L., Marvin D. Krohn, Lonn Lanza-Kaduce, and Marcia Radosevich. 1979. "Social Learning and Deviant Behavior: A Specific Test of a General Theory." American Sociological Review 44 (4): 636–55.

Akers, Ronald L. and Anthony LaGreca. 1991. "Alcohol Use among the Elderly: Social Learning, Community Context, and Life Events." Pp. 242–62 in Society, Culture, and Drinking Patterns Re-Examined, edited by David Pittman and Helene Reskin White. New Brunswick, NJ: Rutgers Center of Alcohol Studies.

American Bar Association. 1984. Report on Computer Crime: June 1984. Chicago: Task Force on Computer Crime, Section on Criminal Justice.

Bandura, Albert. 1986. Social Foundations of Thought and Action: A Social Cognitive Theory. Englewood Cliffs, NJ: Prentice Hall.

Burkett, Stephen and Eric Jensen. 1975. "Conventional Ties, Peer Influence, and Fear of Apprehension: A Study of Adolescent Marijuana Use." Sociological Quarterly 16:522–33.

Fream, Anne. 1993. The Prevalence and Social Learning Predictors of Computer Crime among College Students. Unpublished master's thesis, University of Kentucky, Lexington.

Gottleber, T. T. 1988. "Teaching Ethics in the Community College Data Processing Curriculum." Community/Junior College Quarterly 12:47–54.

Hacker is said to agree to a plea bargain. 1995. New York Times, July 2, pp. VI44, 22.

Hafner, Katie and John Markoff. 1991. Cyberpunk. New York: Simon & Schuster.

Hanson, Gayle. 1991. "Computer Users Pack a Keypunch in a High-Tech World of Crime." Insight, April 15, pp. 8–17.

Hollinger, Richard C. 1988. "Computer Hackers Follow a Guttman-Like Progression." Sociology and Social Research 72 (3): 199–200.

——. 1991. "Hackers: Computer Heros or Electronic Highwaymen?" Computers & Society 21 (1): 6–17.

——. 1992. "Crime by Computer: Correlates of Software Piracy and Unauthorized Account Access." Security Journal 2 (1): 2–12.

Hollinger, Richard C. and Lonn Lanza-Kaduce. 1988. "The Process of Criminalization: The Case of Computer Crime Laws." Criminology 26:101–26.

Kandel, Denise, Donald Treiman, Richard Faust, and Eric Single. 1976. "Adolescent Involvement in Legal and Illegal Drug Use: A Multiple Classification Analysis." Social Forces 55:438–58.

Kentucky Council on Higher Education. 1992. University of Kentucky fall 1992 enrollment figures.

Kentucky Revised Statutes. 1984. Sections 434.845, 434.850 and 434.855.

Krohn, Marvin L., William F. Skinner, James L. Massey, and Ronald Akers. 1985. "Social Learning Theory and Adolescent Cigarette Smoking: A Longitudinal Study." Social Problems 32 (5): 455–73.

Lewyn, Mark and Evan Schwartz. 1991. "Why the Legion of Doom Has Little Fear of the Feds." Business Week, August 6, p. 31.

McEwen, J. Thomas, Dennis Fester, and Hugh Nugent. 1989. Dedicated Computer Crime Units. Contract no. OJP-85-C-006. Washington, DC: National Institute of Justice.

O'Donoghue, Joseph. 1986. Mercy College Report on Computer Crime in Forbes 500 Companies: The Strategies of Containment. Dobbs Ferry, NY: Mercy College.

Parker, Donn B. 1976. Crime by Computer. New York: Scribner.

———. 1987. "Information Crime and Security." Computer Fraud & Security Bulletin 9 (5): 1–4.

Pfuhl, Edwin H., Jr. 1987. "Computer Abuse: Problems of Instrumental Control." Deviant Behavior 8 (2): 113–30.

Schwartz, Evan I., Jeffrey Rothfeder, and Mark Lewyn. 1990. "Viruses? Who You Gonna Call 'Hackbusters.'" Business Week, August 6, pp. 71–72.

Skinner, B. F. 1953. Science and Human Behavior. New York: Macmillan.

Soma, John T., P. Smith, and R. Sprague. 1985. "Legal Analysis of Electronic Bulletin Board Activities." Western New England Law Review 7:571–626.

Sutherland, Edwin H. and Donald R. Cressey. 1974. Criminology. New York: J. B. Lippincott.

Swinyard, William R., Rinne Heikki, and Keng Kau Ah. 1990. "Morality of Software Piracy." Journal of Business Ethics 9:655–64.

Wong, Ken and Bill Farquhar. 1986. "Computer Fraud in the UK–The 1986 Picture." Computer Fraud & Security Bulletin 9 (1): 3–11.

READING 19

As we mentioned in previously, there have been few attempts to empirically test Akers's social structure social learning theory. The following article does this and more. Granted, given data limitations, it is a somewhat weak test (as the authors themselves note), but it goes beyond including a single variable (gender) to explore differential location in the social structure. The authors use feminist theory (i.e., theoretically defined structural variables) to derive three hypotheses relating structural variables to their dependent variable—the use of alcohol prior to sexual activity among male and female college students, some in sororities and fraternities and other independents. They use secondary data, which leads to the relatively weak test of the theory as they could not design the questionnaire and thus relied on two measures of Akers's concepts. Student were asked about positive (e.g., alcohol makes me sexier) and negative (e.g., risks associated with drinking and sexual activity) aspects of combining alcohol and sex. These can be seen as definitions favorable and unfavorable to combining alcohol and sex.

Basically, Akers argues that social learning variables subsume other structural variables—that is, they work through social learning theory. Alternatively, feminist theories would disagree, suggesting that some measure should not work entirely through the socialization process. The authors' basic goal, then, is to compare and contrast a feminist perspective with social learning theory. Some support for Akers's theory is found; for example, the effect of gender was mediated by the risk and rewards measures. Alternatively, the limited number of social

Source: Lanza-Kaduce, Lonn, Michael Capece, and Helena Alden. 2006. "Liquor Is Quicker: Gender and Social Learning Among College Students." *Criminal Justice Policy Review* 17(2):127–143. Reprinted with permission.

learning variables did not mediate the "Greek effect" supporting the feminist perspective. In this regard, we are left with a quandary where we can either stick with a feminist perspective or argue that we simply need more and better measures of social learning theory. As usual, we are left hoping for future research to help resolve these issues.

Liquor Is Quicker

Gender and Social Learning Among College Students

Lonn Lanza-Kaduce, Michael Capece, and Helena Alden

Candy

Is dandy

But liquor

Is quicker

—Ogden Nash (1931/1992)

 ## Social Structure-Social Learning Theory and Feminism

Social Structure-Social Learning Theory (SS-SL) represents Akers's (1998) recent effort to integrate social structural elements with the social learning process that he has specified during the past three decades (Akers, 1973, 1977, 1985, 1994; Akers, Krohn, Lanza-Kaduce, & Radosevich, 1979; Burgess & Akers, 1966). His new general theory of crime and deviance was the subject of a symposium in which several critics raised questions about the integration. Krohn (1999), for example, argued that Akers seemed "content to add social structural dimensions as exogenous variables" (p. 473) rather than provide propositions relating social structure to the social learning process. Morash (1999) more specifically

faulted SS-SL for failing to give adequate attention to gender and for ignoring theories and research on gender and crime or deviance.

Akers (1999) responded to Morash's criticism by explicitly including gender in his position that "the social learning process ... mediate[s] a substantial portion of the relationship between most structural variables" and behavior (Akers, 1998, p. 340; also cited in Akers, 1999, p. 485). His position is that variables representing the social learning process (differential association, personal definitions, differential reinforcement and punishment contingencies, and imitation and modeling) will mediate rather than moderate or modulate the effects of social structure. Evidence of a moderating or modulating effect could be discerned by statistical interactions between structural variables, such as gender, and social learning variables (Baron & Kenny, 1986). The expectation of mediation rather than statistical interaction is one he and his colleagues have long held (Krohn, Lanza-Kaduce, & Akers, 1984).

Akers's response, however, is unlikely to silence those who insist that researchers "must begin to do more than consider gender as a variable.... We must theorize gender" (Chesney-Lind & Faith, 2001, p. 290). One of the specific foci of Chesney-Lind and Faith's (2001) argument is how sexual expression is sanctioned to regulate sexuality. Part of the challenge includes taking "feminist insights about gender and applying them to male behavior" (p. 294).

◈ Gender and Alcohol Use and Sex

This research examines Akers's mediation hypothesis in a context that incorporates structural variables that are suggested by feminist theory. The dependent variable—drinking before sexual intercourse among unmarried White heterosexual college students—is unusual in that it is neither clearly criminal nor deviant. It does, however, intersect two behaviors that implicate how people "do gender" or behave in gendered ways (Miller, 2000, p. 28). Inasmuch as Akers's general theory, in the tradition of Sutherland's (1947) exposition of differential association, purports to explain all behaviors (i.e., conforming and nonconforming ones), the choice of the dependent variable does not detract from scrutinizing the theoretical linkages between social structure and social learning.

Although Akers (1997, 1998, chap. 4) has insisted that social learning theory is not a theory of cultural deviance (which can only explain group differences), he readily accepts that culture is important to the learning process.

> Since the general conventional culture in modern society is not uniform and there are conflicts and variations among subgroups . . . , the individual is likely to be exposed to different and perhaps conflicting cultural definitions of specific acts as good or bad. The theory

does not assume that one's own attitudes are a perfect replication of those cultural patterns. (Akers, 1998, p. 102)

In other words, the structural patterns that exist in society are incorporated into SS-SL—they are expected to provide the contexts within which the learning processes operate. However, SS-SL does not provide a priori information about those larger structural arrangements.

Both alcohol, especially more frequent and heavier consumption, and its use in courtship and seduction are gendered (Boswell & Spade, 1996; Martin & Hummer, 1989). The adage "candy is dandy but liquor is quicker" may be dated but probably is not outdated. The subjective reasons for combining sex with alcohol are not the immediate concerns of behaviorist theories or of efforts to integrate behavior processes with structural patterns. What is important is that the intersection between alcohol and sex offers a strategic site for studying masculinist patterns within a given context or situation. In this sense, gender has import that transcends Akers's (1998) characterization of it as a "sociodemographic correlate" that represents "differential location in social structure" (p. 333).

Patterned use of alcohol in courtship reflects the kind of masculinity that is a common concern across feminist theories (Daly & Chesney-Lind, 1988). A feminist focus on structured masculinity leads to an expectation (one that would not surprise Akers but one that SS-SL does not generate): Males will report more use of alcohol before sex than females will even if only some of their efforts to seduce through alcohol are successful and even if some females employ a similar method. Because most students are assumed to be heterosexual, the difference probably will not be large. Akers (1999) anticipated this possibility; he insists that the

> question is the same whether there is a greater (as in the case of most crime and deviance) or smaller (as in the case of smoking, some other drug use, and some minor offenses) gender difference in the dependent variable. (p. 484)

His position, however, is clear: Gender differences will be mediated by social learning processes.

SS-SL is helpful in sensitizing scholars to the various levels of social structure through which factors such as gender can operate. It urges a consideration of institutional and other macrolevel social organizations as well as mesolevel primary, secondary, and reference groups (as distinguished from intimate family and friendship groups with which individuals are in differential association). The immediate challenge is to identify additional structured factors related to gender that would help explain male-female differences in alcohol use before sex.

One such structural variable in college contexts that comes immediately to mind is an affiliation with fraternities. Whether in popular renditions such as *Animal House* (Reitman, Simmons, & Landis, 1978) or in systematic research (Boswell & Spade, 1996; Martin & Hummer, 1989; Sanday, 1990), fraternity involvement is linked to alcohol consumption often in combination with sexual pursuit. The "brothers" use the fraternity at least as a reference group if not as a substitute primary group. The prediction that male campus Greeks will be more likely to drink alcohol before sex than will others can be more easily derived from feminist theorizing than from SS-SL.

The theorizing, however, may be double edged. Although fraternities are gender-linked social contexts that order the social life of their members, they are also linked to sororities in ways that help order gender relations for both fraternity men and sorority women. Fraternity men may be using alcohol in courtship, but they are probably drinking with and courting sorority women—a prediction that is easily derived from the differential association construct in social learning theory. Feminist theorists may be correct when they argue that gender ordering is a more important variable than gender, but the structural gender-ordered patterns that emerge may also be mediated by social learning processes, much as Akers posits.

Another school condition which may differentiate males from females is success or, perhaps more specifically, how the genders define success and deal with the lack of success. Feminist theorists have weighed in on this issue in a way that counters the position of SS-SL. "For White males (privileged by gender and race), the accomplishment of gender in school means either doing well . . . or if unsuccessful in the classroom, achievement elsewhere" (Simpson & Elis, 1995, p. 71). Simpson and Elis (1995) hypothesized that "adverse educational experiences . . . will increase delinquency among all youth, but effects will be more pronounced among females than among males" (p. 55). Although their focus was on students in secondary school and on violent and property crime, their hypothesis may extend to college students and sex and alcohol behavior. They found some gendered differences (the relationships were also affected by race and class). This interaction between gender and school success is not predicted by Akers.

◈ Research Hypotheses

To this juncture, the Krohn (1999) and Morash (1999) criticisms of SS-SL have been used to go beyond Akers's integrative theory—beyond a mere absorption of structural variables by social learning processes. Feminist theory can be used to advance more precise predictions about differences between males and females in drinking before sex and to consider how gender orders the college context to explain that difference. Feminist theory's focus on masculinist patterns suggests the following hypotheses (Akers's arguments are used to present positions on the respective hypotheses):

1. Male students will be more likely than female students to drink before sex. (Akers would entertain the hypothesis to the extent that it reflects dominant cultural patterns but would argue that the impact of gender on conforming or deviant behaviors would be mediated by social learning processes.)

2. Male campus Greeks will be more likely to drink before sex than will male independents or female campus Greeks and independents. (Akers would entertain the hypothesis because it reflects general cultural patterns but would

issue an important caveat: Fraternity men are likely to differentially associate with sorority women, so drinking before sex will also be high for sorority women.)

3. Adverse educational experiences, as indicated by low grades, will affect drinking and sex for both males and females but will affect females more. (Akers predicts no interaction by gender because the impact of school success should be mediated by social learning processes similarly for males and females.)

SS-SL theory does not generate or challenge any of these hypotheses. Akers does not provide a propositional integration between social learning and structural theories. Rather, he posits that the hypothesized relationships will be mediated to a large extent by social learning variables such as personal definitions and anticipated rewards or punishments. His assertion contains several implications that are amenable to empirical examination. First, the statistical significance and magnitude of relationships between the social structural variables (gender, Greek-system involvement, and academic success) and drinking before sex will be reduced substantially when social learning variables are entered with the structural ones in a multivariate analysis. That is, if the effects of the structural variables are mediated, then their relationships with the dependent variable should be attenuated when the social learning variables are entered into the analysis. Second, the social learning variables will relate to drinking before sex similarly for males and females, for Greek-system participants and independents and for those who earn high grades and those who earn low grades. If the effects of the structural variables are largely mediated by social learning variables, the structural variables should not interact statistically with the learning variables to explain the dependent variable.

A caveat is in order before proceeding. These issues are explored via secondary analysis. Consequently, the operationalizations for both the social structural and social learning variables are neither as extensive nor as exacting as would be desired. In particular, neither the definitions nor the differential association construct in social learning theory can be operationalized adequately. As such, this research represents a weak test of the hypotheses, especially Akers's mediation hypothesis. If this research has merit, it lies in the effort to show how other theories can be integrated via propositions into the SS-SL framework and to show how gender helps structure the learning process.

Method

Sample, Data, and the Dependent Variable

The data used in this analysis were obtained from eight colleges where the long form of the Core Alcohol and Drug Survey was administered to students in the mid-1990s. Each of the colleges gave permission for the researchers to obtain its data from the Core Institute at Southern Illinois University, provided they did not identify any of the colleges. The Core survey consists of four pages of self-report questions that focus primarily on alcohol and drug use on campus. Unfortunately, many of the items contain double-barreled wording in that they ask about both alcohol and drugs in the same question. This practice limited the items that could be used.

The colleges varied markedly. They were spread throughout the United States from the Northeast to the Southeast to the Midwest and West. They included public and private institutions that varied in size. The majority of the student body in one school was African American, the plurality in another school was Asian American, and a third school had a mix of Hispanic, White, and Asian American students. Although no claims can be made that either the students in the study were representative of their respective colleges or the Core samples were representative of U.S. college students generally, the schools and the students were diverse enough to permit examining the theoretical linkages between social structural variables and social learning ones.

Because of the focus on gender, alcohol, and sex, additional sources of diversity could have complicated the effort to examine theoretical linkages. For example, feminist theorists note that gender plays out differently by race (Christian, 1985; Collins, 2000). Alcohol use (Goode, 2001) and sex patterns (Laumann, Gagnon, Michael, & Michaels, 1994) vary by race as well. Rather than trying to examine everything at once (including whether race interacts with gender; with other structural variables, such as Greek-system involvement; with social learning variables; and in various combinations), we simplified the research by using the subsample of White students. Subsequent analysis can be performed to see how different the findings are for students from other ethnic or racial backgrounds. Subsample selection was also used to control for other potential confounding effects, including marital status, age, prior alcohol use, and sexual activity. This analysis focused on White, single adult (18 years of age or older) students who reported both alcohol use and sexual activity in the preceding year. The important issue of how race and gender intersect (see Chesney-Lind & Faith, 2001) warrants separate treatment and can be joined later.

The dependent variable was whether students reported having drunk alcohol the last time they had sexual intercourse. This "alcsex" variable was coded 1 for yes and 0 for no. More than 75% of those in the original subsample indicated that they had not drunk before their last sexual encounter. The dichotomous dependent variable suggested the use of logistic regression, including its classification of cases, as the appropriate statistical analysis for such data. Unfortunately, classification analysis is altered by skewed distributions. If one predicted every case involved no alcohol use before sex, one would be right more than 75% of the time, leaving little room for the structural and learning variables to improve the accuracy of classifications. To obtain a more even split between students who recently had drunk before sex and those who had not, a 33% subsample, taken at random, of the cases in which drinking had not occurred before sex was pulled. These cases ($n = 349$) were joined with the total population of cases in which drinking

had preceded sex ($n = 339$) to form the subsample used in the analyses.

Operationalization of Independent Variables

The integration of SS-SL and feminist theory identified three structural variables that were hypothesized to relate to whether drinking occurred before sex: gender, campus Greek-system involvement, and grades. Gender was dummy coded (0 for female and 1 for male). According to Akers, these variables locate individuals in social environments. Thus, they serve as rough indicators of social structural contexts.

Greek-system involvement (Greek) was also dummy coded. Students who reported being actively involved with or in a leadership position in social fraternities or sororities were coded as 1. All other students were coded as 0. Nearly as many female respondents in the subsamples were actively involved in campus Greek activities as were male respondents.

The survey also asked respondents to report their approximate cumulative grade average (ranging from A+ to F). A and B grades were coded together to indicate academic success (coded 1); lower grades were collapsed (coded 0) to indicate less success. Academic success locates students in the educational structure.

The Core survey contained only a few items that operationalized social learning constructs. One survey item asked students to anticipate the risk of harm (risk) involved when individuals "consume alcohol prior to being sexually active." The responses were categorized into *great risk (4), moderate risk (3), slight risk (2), and no risk (1)*. Males were less likely to anticipate as much harm as females.

Several items asked students to consider the anticipated positive consequences (rewards) of mixing alcohol and sex. Again, an index was constructed. One item asked whether (coded 1 or 0) alcohol "facilitates sexual opportunities." Another item asked whether (coded 1 or 0) alcohol "makes me sexier." A third item used in the index was whether alcohol made the opposite sex sexier. The survey did not distinguish heterosexuals from homosexuals or bisexuals, so for males, the response to whether alcohol makes females sexier was used, and for females, the response to whether alcohol makes males sexier was used. The rewards index ranged from 0 (*no anticipated positive consequences*) to 3 (*yes to all indexed items*).

Data Analysis Strategy

The data analyses are driven by the respective hypotheses. For the first hypothesis, cross-tabular analysis is used to examine whether gender is related to using alcohol before sex (alcsex). Logistic regression is used to examine whether any gender effect (gender as a structural location) is mediated by social learning variables (risk and rewards).

The second hypothesis is examined via cross-tabular analysis. To see whether fraternity men are most likely to have drunk alcohol before having sex, we elaborate the cross-tabular relationship between Greek and alcsex by including gender. The differential association feature of SS-SL suggests that sorority women will also frequently use alcohol before sex. Unfortunately, no differential association measure is available in this data set to examine whether gender differences are mediated by differential association.

The third hypothesis looks for an interaction between gender and academic success. Feminist theorizing predicts that grades will relate to other behaviors more for females than for males; Akers does not expect an interaction. The analysis begins with elaborating the cross-tabulation between grades and alcsex by gender. If an interaction is found, a new variable will be constructed (with coding reversed so that females are

coded 1) and incorporated into a logistic regression model to see whether its impact is mediated by social learning variables (risk and reward).

Finally, the relationships that emerged in the previous steps are incorporated into an overall model and logistic regression analysis is performed. This permits us to examine which variables (or interactions) relate to and help account for drinking before having sex.

Results

Hypothesis 1

The beverage relationship between gender and drinking before sex (alcsex) is presented in Table 1. As feminist theory suggests, a masculinist pattern emerges. Males are somewhat more likely to report drinking before having sex (55.3%) than are females (42.6 %). The percentage difference is statistically significant (corrected $\chi^2 = 9.97$, $df = 1$, $p < .01$). The relationship is not strong ($F = .13$).

Next, gender is entered into the first block of a logistic regression analysis. The social learning variables (risk and rewards) are then entered on the second block. Gender is significantly related to having sex after drinking in Block 1 ($B = 0.50$, $SE = 0.16$, Wald = 9.83; $df = 1$, $p < .01$). The odds ratio is 1.65 (i.e., males are more than 1.5 times more likely to use alcohol before having sex). When the social learning variables are entered in the second block, the gender relationship is no longer statistically significant ($B = 0.15$, $SE = 0.18$, Wald=0.36, $df = 1$, $p < .56$). Its odds ratio is reduced to 1.11. The masculinist pattern is mediated by social

Table 1 Cross Tabulation of Gender With Drinking Before Sex

Drank Before Sex?	Female		Male		Total		χ^2	p	
	n	%	*n*	%	*n*	%			
No	182	57.4	147	44.7	329	50.9			
Yes	135	42.6	182	55.3	317	49.1			
Total	317		329		646		9.97	.001	.13

learning variables consistent with Akers's position. If gender is considered to be a mere locator in the larger social structure, its effects may operate almost entirely through social learning processes.

Hypothesis 2

The second hypothesis reflects feminist theorizing that gender is more than a variable—it comes into play in how social settings are structured or ordered. One structured context within which gender orders interactions and behaviors is the social Greek system on college campuses. The masculinist pattern that is expected is that fraternity men will be most likely to engage in drinking before having sex. The countervailing consideration derived from social learning theory's differential association construct is that fraternity men will be associating with sorority women, so sorority women will also be likely to drink before engaging in sex. Table 2 presents the relevant results from a cross-tabulation between Greek participation and alcsex, controlling for gender.

Table 2 presents the results. Consistent with masculinist patterns, fraternity men are most likely to report using alcohol before having sex (67.3%). But consistent with the differential association expectation,

sorority women are next most likely to use alcohol before having sex (57.8%). Half of the independent males report drinking before sex, but only 37.2% of independent females do. The relationship between Greek and alcsex is significant for both females (corrected $\chi^2 = 9.86$, $df = 1$, $p < .01$) and males (corrected $\chi^2 = 7.82$, $df = 1$, $p < .01$).[1]

Hypothesis 3

The third hypothesis is derived from feminist research that expected and found that academic success related to crime differently by gender. Less academic success among females had a bigger impact than for males. This interaction is not predicted by Akers. Table 3 presents the cross-tabulation between grades and alcsex, controlling for gender. The results show that females with low grades (61.5%) are most likely to use alcohol before having sex. Females with high grades are least likely (38.5%). Males fall in between (about 55% of men drink before sex regardless of their grades). The chi-square tests of independence confirm the interaction. For females, grades are related to alcsex (corrected $\chi^2 = 9.62$, $df = 1$, $p < .01$); for males, they are not (corrected $\chi^2 = 0$, $df = 1$, $p = 1$).

Table 2   Cross-Tabulation of Greek Involvement With Drinking Before Sex, Controlling for Gender

Drank Before Sex?	Non-Greek		Greek		Total		χ^2	p	
	n	%	n	%	n	%			
Female									
No	147	62.8	35	42.2	182	57.4			
Yes	87	37.2	48	57.8	135	42.6			
Total	234		83		317		9.86	.001	.18
Male									
No	114	50	33	32.7	147	44.7			
Yes	114	50	68	67.3	182	55.3			
Total	228		101		329		7.82	.004	.16

Table 3   Cross-Tabulation of Grades With Drinking Before Sex, Controlling for Gender

Drank Before Sex?	C, D, and F		A and B		Total		χ^2	p	$>$
	n	%	n	%	n	%			
Female									
No	20	38.5	153	63.0	173	58.6			
Yes	32	61.5	90	37.0	122	41.4			
Total	52		243		295		9.62	.001	−.19
Male									
No	52	44.8	89	44.5	141	44.6			
Yes	64	55.2	111	55.5	175	55.4			
Total	116		200		316		.000	1.00	.003

An interaction term is computed (females with low grades and all males are coded 0, and females with high grades are coded 1). This interaction between two structural variables is entered in the first block of a logistic regression analysis. It is significant ($B = -0.77$, $SE = 0.17$, Wald = 20.44, $df = 1$, $p < .01$); the odds ratio is 0.46. When the social learning variables are entered in the second block of the logistic regression analysis, the interaction term remains significant at the .01 level ($B = -0.46$, $SE = 0.18$, Wald = 6.35, $df = 1$). The odds ratio changes a little (to a 0.63). Clearly, this gendered interaction is not mediated by the social learning variables that are available in this data set.

An Overall Model

To this point, the respective hypotheses have been dealt with individually. The variables that are implicated, however, can be used to advance a multivariate model that allows us to see what helps account for having sex after drinking. The complete model is examined via logistic regression with the significant structural variables that were identified previously entered in the first block (Greek and Grade × Gender interaction). The two social learning variables (risk and rewards) are entered in the second block. The relevant results are reported in Table 4.

In Block 1, both Greek involvement and the Grade × Gender interaction (females with high grades = 1 and all others = 0) are significantly related to alcsex. The unstandardized coefficient for Greek is 0.87 with a standard error of 0.19 (Wald = 21, $df = 1$, $p < .01$). Its odds ratio is 2.40. In other words, fraternity men and sorority women drink before engaging in sex 2.5 times more often than do independent students. The unstandardized coefficient for the Grade × Gender interaction is -0.75 with a standard error of 0.17 (Wald = 18.64, $df = 1$, $p < .01$). Its odds ratio is 0.47. In other words, females with high grades are less likely to report using alcohol before having sex. These two structural variables correctly predict 58.9% of the cases—an improvement over the 50–50 split between those who had reported drinking before sex and those who did not report drinking before sex.

Table 4 Having Sex After Drinking (Alcsex) Regressed on the Block of Social Structural (SS) Variables and the Block of Social Learning (SL) Variables

	Block 1					Block 2				
	B	*SE*	*p*	Wald	Exp(*B*)	*B*	*SE*	*p*	Wald	Exp(*B*)
SS variables										
Greek	.87	.19	.00	21.00	2.40	.86	.19	.00	19.77	2.40
Grade × Gender	−.75	.17	.00	18.64	0.47	.44	.19	.02	5.59	0.64
SL variables										
Rewards						.26	.09	.00	8.73	1.30
Risk						−.31	.08	.00	13.38	.074
Correct classifications										
No alcsex (%)			38.5					65.1		
Yes alcsex (%)			80.0					62.7		
Overall (%)			58.9					63.9		

The results for Block 2 show little change in the structural variables when the social learning variables are entered into the logistic regression analysis. The Greek variable continues to account for drinking before sex; students with Greek-system involvement use alcohol before sex more often than other students. Greek showed virtually no change (it remained statistically significant and its odds ratio remained high at 2.40). The Grade × Gender interaction changed slightly. It is no longer significant at the .01 level but is significant at a .05 level. Its odds ratio moved to 0.64 (from 0.47). Block 2 shows that both learning variables also relate to drinking before sex. The unstandardized coefficient for risk (which had four ordinal categories) is -0.31 with a standard error of 0.08 (Wald = 13.38, $df = 1$, $p < .01$). The odds ratio is 0.74. The unstandardized coefficient for rewards (which had four interval categories) is 2.60 with a standard error of 0.09 (Wald = 8.73, $df = 1$, $p < .01$). The odds ratio is 1.30. The percentage of correctly classified cases increased to 63.9% (from 58.9%).

 Discussion and Conclusion

This research used feminist theory to advance three hypotheses relating structural variables to individual behaviors regarding the combination of alcohol and sex by unmarried White college students. These variables were used to determine if there are structural variables that work independently of Akers's social learning process. The feminist perspective would not expect all group dynamics to be mediated by social psychological processes. Akers and his associates argue that such relationships will be substantially mediated by social learning variables, and they do not expect to find significant interactions. In this research, the Akers position and feminist theory both received partial support.

A masculinist effect was found for the structural variable gender. When gender was entered into a logistic regression with the social learning variables risk and reward, its effect was mediated by those social learning variables, as Akers predicts.

Greek-system males were most likely to use alcohol before having sex—a finding that would not surprise feminist theorists. We used Akers's arguments about differential association to predict that Greek-system females would also frequently drink before having sex. Greek-system males and females were more likely to drink before having sex than were independents, male or female. Unfortunately, there were no adequate measures of differential association in these data to examine whether differential association would mediate the Greek effect. The logistic regression that was performed included two other social learning variables (risk and reward). Their inclusion did not reduce the effect of Greek-system involvement. Given that Akers et al. (1979) expect differential association to be correlated with the other leading variables, some mediation would have been expected. Without a differential association measure, conclusions about mediation need to remain tentative.

The analysis of the interactions produced the most interesting conclusions. Akers would predict no interactions because the effects of the structural variables would be mediated by the social learning process. Gender reemerged as an important theoretical consideration because it interacted with academic success as measured by grades. The logistic regression, which included Greek-system involvement, the Gender × Grade interaction, and the social learning variables risk and reward, indicate that Greek-system involvement and the Gender × Grade interaction were not mediated by the social learning variables. The inclusion of the social learning variables, however, did improve the percentage of cases correctly classified. The results indicate that structural variables can act independently of the mediating effects of the social learning process and that interactions may complicate our efforts to understand outcomes. Gender in particular may interact with other variables in ways that social learning processes do not mediate.

Finding structural effects that are not mediated by learning processes raises a basic philosophy of science issue: To what extent are group phenomena reducible? SS-SL assumes that group dynamics translate into social psychological processes to account for individual

behavior. Durkheim (1893/1964) would have us believe that there are social facts—entities "out there"—that control and shape human behavior; these social facts would not be reduced or mediated by a social psychological process. The discontinuity between the group and the individual will not be completely bridged, and the search for additional processes or better measurements will be futile. Some groups may have higher rates of behavior, and we may not be able to predict which members engage in the behavior or why they do so using social psychological principles.

Akers deserves credit for staking out a clear position that is applicable to a broad array of structural arrangements and individual behaviors. His mediation hypothesis is one that can be empirically examined. His position was confirmed when gender was considered to be nothing more than a structural location; its effects were mediated. Hypotheses were advanced regarding how gender orders social relations (e.g., campus Greek life) and how it interacts with other social conditions (e.g., academic performance). The effects of Greek-system involvement and grades on drinking before having sex were not mediated by learning processes. Akers's theory can help us understand why sorority women also frequently engage in drinking before sex; they differentially associate with fraternity men, who are doing the same thing. The effect of Greek-system involvement may have been mediated had there been adequate measures of this theoretical construct. The interaction between gender and academic success (as measured by grades) is not anticipated by SS-SL. The finding points to the need to explicate ways in which we need to theorize gender. Why does academic performance operate differently for females than it does for males? Suffice it to say that this research among unmarried, White college students found that there could be structural variables that are not mediated by the social learning process. Additional research is needed to identify which structural relationships are substantially mediated, which are not mediated, which interact, and which are population specific.

The conclusions in this research are to be viewed as tentative, given the limited measures of the social learning variables in this data set. The structural indicators are also not precise gauges of social contexts. Our findings need to be corroborated. To do that, data need to be collected that have adequate measures of both structural and social learning variables. The research also needs to go beyond the White college student sample we used. Future research should include race as a structural variable. Race has been shown to be a significant predictor of drinking behavior among college students (Capece, Schantz, & Wakeman, 2002) and has been linked to other problem behaviors of students (Simpson & Elis, 1995).

◈ Policy Implications

The problem with alcohol use, abuse, and associated problems on college campuses is well documented (Baer, Kiviahan, & Marlatt, 1995; Berkowitz & Perkins, 1986; Engs & Hanson, 1985). In the 1980s and 1990s, alcohol use increased among college women (Engs & Hanson, 1985, 1990; Harrington, Brigham, & Clayton, 1997), although college men generally still drink more frequently and more heavily than college women (Berkowitz & Perkins, 1987; Engs & Hanson, 1990; Perkins, 1999).

Racial patterns of alcohol use are less clear. Some earlier investigations reported that Black students drink more than (or at least as much as) White students (Blane & Hewitt, 1977; Maddox & Williams, 1968). In contrast, the recent studies report that Whites have higher rates of consumption than Blacks (Engs & Hanson, 1985; Haworth-Hoeppner, Globetti, Stern, & Morasco, 1989; Wechsler, 1996). Haworth-Hoeppner et al. (1989) account for lower consumption among Blacks because Black students, for the most part, do not participate in the White campus culture that encourages drinking.

Fraternity and sorority members, especially house residents, are more prone to heavy alcohol use. Wechsler, Kuh, and Davenport (1996) report from a national study that virtually all resident fraternity and sorority members drink: Ninety-nine percent of men and 98% of women, and 86% of fraternity house residents and 71% of fraternity nonresident members, engaged in binge drinking. This compares to 45% of nonfraternity men. In this same study, 80% of resident sorority members engaged in binge drinking at least once in the previous 2 weeks, compared to 35% of nonsorority members. Furthermore, nonmembers are most likely to abstain from alcohol: 16% of nonmember men and 17% of nonmember women. Additionally, even those without a history of binge drinking or heavy alcohol use became more likely to engage in it after joining a fraternity or sorority. Sorority members were the most likely to acquire heavy drinking behaviors when entering college and were more likely to experience alcohol-related problems. Lack of prior experience with drinking tends to place sorority members at greater risk to develop alcohol-related problems (Wechsler et al., 1996; Wechsler & Wuethrich, 2002).

Studies also examine problems related to drinking, including negative physical effects such as hangovers, vomiting, and injuries to self or others. Nonphysical effects include delinquent and/or criminal behavior (e.g., date rape, damage to property, fighting, drinking and driving), relationship troubles, and academic difficulties (Baer et al, 1995; Harrington et al., 1997).

Akers's (1998) SS-SL and the results of our research provide insight into how to change drinking behavior and related problems on college campuses; the drinking culture needs to be changed by altering the drinking climate, addressing drinking practices among both male and female Greek-system members, changing interaction and associational patterns, and encouraging administration, faculty, and staff to model appropriate drinking behavior. The expression *change the drinking culture* is now part of the college administrator's language when discussing the problem of alcohol use, abuse, and related problems on college campuses. The emphasis on changing the culture has prompted meetings between campus administration and political leaders, bar owners, and others in the community to discuss ways to work together to deal with student alcohol use and abuse ("Local Officials Discuss Alcohol Abuse," 2005). Consistent with Akers, there seems to be agreement that to change the drinking culture, change needs to take place on the structural and associational and interactional levels.

On the structural level, advertising of alcohol could be reduced significantly or eliminated from college campuses and college sporting events. This could also include advertising of drink specials by local bars on campus. We understand that there are significant economic considerations involved in this type of change. This effort would be an ongoing effort that would take place across a period of time. Additionally, the university could deemphasize the use of alcohol at official university events.

On the associational and interactional level, alcohol use and abuse among those in Greek-system organizations needs to be addressed. As past research seems to indicate, and as our research further substantiates, heavy drinking in Greek-system organizations may no longer be a male thing. Our results show that Greek-system women and men are both using alcohol before sex. It may no longer be an issue of men preying on women as much as it is a mutually reinforcing interaction between fraternity men and sorority women.

Changing the Greek-system drinking culture can also be addressed by the national Greek-system offices directly responsible for their respective members across the country. Responsibility could be shared between the national and regional Greek-system offices to implement drinking guidelines and consequences for underage drinking and/or drinking violations by their membership. Additionally, Greek-system members and the general student population might include group responsibility for drinking in addition to individual responsibility. Social controls could come from those around the drinker, much like "friends don't let friends drink and drive" has spread the responsibility for drinking and driving among bartenders, those hosting parties, and the friends of the drinker. Bartenders and those who own and operate package stores could also help with the social controls by doing what they can to combat underage purchasing of alcohol.

The drinking problem on college campuses would not be eliminated if we just address the Greek-system issue. Our research found that there was a relationship between females with low grades and drinking before sex. We assume that there are other subgroups of college students who are prone to inappropriate drinking. As these student subgroups are identified, interventions can be designed to address their particular needs.

The problem of excessive drinking on college campuses can be addressed by looking at the cultural context in which alcohol is used. Akers's theory and our research provide some valuable insight into how the problem can be viewed and confronted. The difficulty, of course, is that the college campus operates in a larger cultural context. If the larger cultural context is not willing to address this issue, it will be more difficult to affect change on campus.

◈ Note

1. Social learning theory led us to expect that many sorority women would report drinking before sex because of their differential association with fraternity men. A measure of differential association is not available in these data. Consequently, we can only begin to examine whether the impact of Greek would be mediated by social learning processes. A logistic regression was performed to see whether other social learning variables (risk and rewards) mediated the impact of Greek. They did not.

◈ References

Akers, R. L. (1973). *Deviant behavior: A social learning approach.* Belmont, CA: Wadsworth.

Akers, R. L. (1977). *Deviant behavior: A social learning approach (2nd ed.).* Belmont, CA: Wadsworth.

Akers, R. L. (1985). *Deviant behavior: A social learning approach (3rd ed.).* Belmont, CA: Wadsworth.

Akers, R. L. (1994). *Criminological theories: Introduction and evaluation.* Los Angeles: Roxbury.

Akers, R. L. (1997). *Criminological theories: Introduction and evaluation (2nd ed.).* Los Angeles: Roxbury.

Akers, R. L. (1998). *Social learning and social structure: A general theory of crime and deviance.* Boston: Northeastern University Press.

Akers, R. L. (1999). Reply to Sampson, Morash, and Krohn. *Theoretical Criminology, 3,* 477–493.

Akers, R. L., Krohn, M. D., Lanza-Kaduce, L., &Radosevich, M. (1979). Social learning and deviant behavior: A specific test of a general theory. *American Sociological Review, 44,* 635–655.

Baer, J. S., Kiviahan, D. R., & Marlatt, G. A. (1995). High-risk drinking across the transition from high school to college. *Alcoholism: Clinical and Experimental Research, 19,* 54–61.

Baron, R. M., & Kenny, D. A. (1986). The moderator-mediator variable distinction in social psychological research: Conceptual, strategic, and statistical considerations. *Journal of Personality and Social Psychology, 51,* 1173–1182.

Berkowitz, A. D., & Perkins, H. W. (1987). Recent research on gender differences in collegiate alcohol use. *Journal of American College of Heath, 36,* 123–129.

Berkowitz, A. D., & Perkins, H. W. (1986). Problem drinking among college students: A review of recent research. *Journal of American College of Health, 35,* 1–28.

Blane, H. T., & Hewitt, L. E. (1977). *Alcohol and youth: An analysis of the literature, 1960–1975.* Springfield, VA: National Institute on Alcohol Abuse and Alcoholism.

Boswell, A. A., & Spade, J. Z. (1996). Fraternities and collegiate rape culture. Why are some fraternities more dangerous places for women? *Gender and Society, 10,* 133–147.

Burgess, R. L., & Akers, R. L. (1966). A differential association-reinforcement theory of criminal behavior *Social Problems, 14,* 128–147.

Capece, M., Schantz, D., & Wakeman, R. (2002). Fraternity and sorority alcohol use: Does race matter? *Journal of Applied Sociology, 19,* 9–21.

Chesney-Lind, M., & Faith, K. (2001). What about feminism? Engendering theory-making in criminology. In R. Paternoster & R. Bachman (Eds.), *Explaining criminals and crime* (pp. 287–302). Los Angeles: Roxbury.

Christian, B. (1985). *Black feminist criticism, perspectives on Black women writers.* New York: Pergamon.

Collins, P. H. (2000). *Black feminist thought.* New York: Routledge.

Daly, K., & Chesney-Lind, M. (1988). Feminism and criminology. *Justice Quarterly, 5,* 497–538.

Durkheim, E. (1964). *The division of labor in society* (G. Simpson, Trans.). New York: Free Press. (Original work published 1893)

Engs, R. C., & Hanson, D. J. (1985). The drinking-patterns and problems of college students: 1983. *Journal of Alcohol and Drug Education, 31,* 65–82.

Engs, R. C. & Hanson, D. J. (1990). Gender differences in drinking patterns and problems among college students: A review of the literature. *Journal of Alcohol and Drug Education, 35,* 36–47.

Goode, E. (2001). *Deviant behavior (6th ed.).* Englewood Cliffs, NJ: Prentice Hall.

Harrington, N. G., Brigham, N. L., & Clayton, R. R. (1997). Differences in alcohol use and alcohol-related problems among fraternity and sorority members. *Drug and Alcohol Dependence, 47,* 237–246.

Haworth-Hoeppner, S., Globetti, G., Stern, J., & Morasco, F. (1989). The quantity and frequency of drinking among undergraduates at a Southern university. *The International Journal of the Addictions, 24,* 829–857.

Krohn, M. (1999). Social learning theory: The continuing development of a perspective. *Theoretical Criminology, 3,* 462–476.

Krohn, M. D., Lanza-Kaduce, L., & Akers, R. L. (1984). Community context and theories of criminal behavior: An examination of social learning and social bonding theories. *Sociological Quarterly, 25,* 353–371.

Laumann, E. O., Gagnon, J. H., Michael, R. T., & Michaels, S. (1994). *The social organization of sexuality: Sexual practices in the United States.* Chicago: University of Chicago Press.

Local officials discuss alcohol abuse. (2005, January 20). *Gainesville Sun,* p. 1.

Maddox, G. L., & Williams, J. R. (1968). Drinking behavior of Negro collegians. *Quarterly Journal of Studies of Alcohol, 29,* 117–129.

Martin, P. Y., & Hummer, R. A. (1989). Fraternities and rape on campus. *Gender and Society, 3,* 457–473.

Miller, J. (2000). Feminist theories of women's crimes: Robbery as a case study. In S. S. Simpson (Ed.), *Of crime and criminality* (pp. 25–46). Thousand Oaks, CA: Pine Forge.

Morash, M. (1999). A consideration of gender in relation to social learning and social structure: A general theory of crime and deviance. *Theoretical Criminology, 3,* 452–461.

Nash, O. (1992). Reflections on ice breaking. In J. Kaplan (Ed.), *Bartlett's Familiar Quotations* (16th ed., p. 709). Boston: Little, Brown. (Original work published 1931)

Perkins, H. W. (1999). Stress-motivated drinking in collegiate and post-collegiate young adulthood: Life course and gender patterns. *Journal of Studies on Alcohol, 60,* 219–227.

Reitman, I., Simmons, M. (Producers), & Landis, J. (Director). (1978). *Animal house* [Motion picture]. United States: Universal Pictures.

Sanday, P. R. (1990). *Fraternity gang rape: Sex brotherhood and privilege on campus.* New York: New York University Press.

Simpson, S. S., & Elis, L. (1995). Doing gender: Sorting out the caste and crime conundrum. *Criminology, 33,* 47–81.

Sutherland, E. H. (1947). *Principles of criminology.* Philadelphia: J. B. Lippincott.

Wechsler, H. (1996). Alcohol and the American college campus: A report from the Harvard School of Public Health. *Change, 28,* 20–25, 60.

Wechsler, H., & Wuethrich, B. (2002). *Dying to drink: Binge drinking on college campuses.* Emmaus, PA: Rodale.

Wechsler, H., Kuh, G., & Davenport, A. E. (1996). Fraternities, sororities, and binge drinking: Results from a national study of American colleges. *National Association of Student Personnel Administrators Journal, 33,* 260–279.

CHAPTER 7

Social Control Theories of Deviance

Nick and David are twins born 23 years ago.

They grew up with an older sister in a suburb in Ohio and had a fairly middle-class upbringing. They went to schools in a well-funded school district, had the opportunity to learn music, and participate in school plays or various sports teams. Their high school had advanced placement courses, up-to-date schoolbooks, and an active PTA.

Both boys earned fairly good grades all throughout school. Nick seemed to enjoy science a bit more than David; David seemed to be better at literature and the arts. They got along very well with their teachers, never really earning trips to the principal's office or getting suspended for bad behavior. After high school, they went to college—the state university in a nearby state. While both boys were at the same university, they hung out with different friends, although they saw each other on a regular basis.

Nick and David took yearly family vacations with their parents—even their first summer in college. They didn't always agree on the destination for the vacation (what teenager is 100% happy to see Mt. Rushmore with his or her parents?), but they usually ended up having a good time. In addition to the family vacation, the family always participated in "family fun night," which meant that once a week, the family went out to dinner together, saw a movie, or went to a baseball game or to the park to rollerblade.

Both boys had summer jobs in high school and part-time jobs in college. Nick waited tables for a local restaurant chain; David worked retail jobs, usually at big-box stores.

Nick and David graduated from college last year. Nick got an entry-level job with a company he really liked; the money wasn't great, but he saw a lot of room for advancement. David also got an entry-level position with a company after college; the money was a bit better than what Nick made, but David did not feel the job would become a career for him. He was still looking for the "perfect job."

Throughout their high school and college days, both boys engaged in minor forms of deviance at one time or another. Most notably, when both started high school, they started going to parties and drinking beer, and when they got to college, David started smoking pot. David had a series of girlfriends in high school and college but was never very serious about any of them. Nick did not date in high school.

After they graduated from college, David began to gamble in online gaming sites. In addition, he organizes two yearly trips (for example, to Las Vegas or Atlantic City, or the Del Mar racetrack in Del Mar, California) to gamble with several friends of his. His gambling does not get in the way of him successfully doing his job, but he gambles quite a bit of money at one time.

Nick, on the other hand, does not gamble and has not engaged in even minor forms of deviance since college. He has dated the same partner since his sophomore year in college and recently has started to think he might make a lifetime commitment.

◈ Introduction

Nick and David are pretty normal siblings. They have engaged in deviance, worked, gone to school, and socialized with their family and friends. At any one time, one or both of them have engaged in deviant behavior. This chapter presents the perspective of social control theory and will explain the behavior of Nick and David using the theories examined here.

Social control theories of deviance got their start from the early classical theories usually associated with Beccaria. Both the classical school and the neoclassical school have, as a basis, a belief in the free will and rationalistic hedonism of the individual (Bernard, Snipes, & Gerould, 2009). Beccaria, writing in the 18th century, viewed the individual as a rational actor (the popular belief of the time) and sought under this belief system to reform the system of punishment (Bernard et al., 2009). Most important for modern control theories is Beccaria's overall support for the notion that being free actors, individuals need controls in their lives to keep them from hedonistic action (if that action was harmful to society).

Control theorists assert that human beings are basically antisocial, assuming that deviance is part of the natural order in society; individuals are attracted to the idea of norm violation and thus motivated to deviate. This leads control theorists to assert that concern for deviant motivation alone does not account for the forces leading people to deviate—all people are capable of feeling a certain motivation to deviate. "The important question is not 'why do men not obey the rules of society,' but rather 'why do men obey the rules of society'" (Traub & Little, 1985, p. 241).

◈ Classical Social Control Theory

Our first theorist is important for two reasons. The first is that he is one of the first theorists to formulate the assumptions of the classical school into a sociological theory of deviance and social control. But more important, he is one of the first to articulate a distinction between *internal* and *external* social control. While later theorists do not always explicate their theories in the same dichotomy of internal and external, most accept the notion of internal social control (or a conversation with oneself—in other words, through thoughtful introspection, one decides not to engage in deviance) and **external control** (society places formal controls on the individual to keep him or her from engaging in crime).

Nye

Nye's (1958) position is that most deviant behavior is the result of insufficient social control. He offered four clusters of social control.

The first cluster is internalized control exercised from within through our conscience. Nye argues that every society tries to instill its rules and norms in the conscience of its children. This cluster is the most powerful; in fact, Nye states that if internal controls were entirely effective, then there would be no need for the other three clusters of social control. Unfortunately, internal controls, for a variety of reasons, are never completely effective. He argues that one reason for a variance in effectiveness is that the rules and norms of society are not always agreed upon at a level that allows for perfect socialization. Nye also argues that strong **internal control** can only be accomplished when the child completely accepts the parent—to the extent that the parent–child relationship is not a perfect one, internal control may not be as effective as necessary.

The second cluster Nye refers to as parents and indirect control. Nye argues that while parents are important to the internalizing of controls, they can also place indirect controls on juveniles. Nye sees these indirect controls as the disapproval the parent might show should the juvenile engage in deviant behavior. To the extent that the juvenile cares about the parent's disapproval, he or she will not engage in deviant behavior, thus being indirectly controlled through the parent's opinion of his or her behavior.

The third cluster is direct control imposed from without by means of restriction and punishment. Nye argues that no society relies solely on the individual to regulate his or her own behavior. Additional controls in the form of punishment, disapproval, ridicule, ostracism, or banishment are used by informal groups or society as a whole to control deviant behavior. These controls are often imposed by the police or other officials.

The final cluster is needed to give individuals reason not to engage in deviant behavior. Nye believes that alternative means to need satisfaction (goals and values) are needed so that individuals do not have to engage in deviant behavior to get what they want. A readily available set of alternatives will mean that the above three clusters of social control will have a stronger influence on the likelihood of deviant behavior.

Since all variations of social control theory assume that individuals *want* to engage in deviance and therefore the abnormal (or not expected) outcome is those *not* engaging in deviance, we use social control theory to explain those instances when Nick and David are not engaging in deviance.

Given that Nick and David never engaged in much deviance of a serious nature (most of their acts would be considered victimless deviance), Nye might argue that while not perfect, their internalized controls are fairly strong, but their indirect or direct controls have been weakened at various stages. For example, after leaving for college, David began to smoke pot. Given that leaving for college meant he was no longer under the direct supervision of his parents, he may have felt freer to deviate than he had when he had lived in his parents' house.

Hirschi

The person most associated with control theories is Travis Hirschi. Hirschi's (1969) version of social control theory is often referred to as social bonding theory. This theory concentrates on indirect controls of behavior. Hirschi's social control theory suggests that deviance is not a response to learned behavior or stimuli or the strains surrounding an individual (like differential association theory or strain theory suggests)—instead, social control theory assumes that deviant activity is a given, and it is the absence of deviance that needs to be explained. In fact, not only are we capable, but we are also willing creators and participants in deviance. The reason we do not engage in deviance or crime is because we have social bonds to conformity that keep us from engaging in socially unacceptable activities. This **social bond** comprises four parts—attachment, commitment, involvement, and belief.

Attachment is the "emotional" component of the bond. This component suggests that we do not engage in deviance because we care about what conforming others think about us. Hirschi argued that if we are strongly attached to others, we will contemplate what their reaction to our behavior will be before we engage in it. In other words, we will not engage in deviance if we think those we are attached to will be disappointed in us. This is the element of the social bond that may have us saying, "What would Mom think?" or "Mom would be mad if she found out." Hirschi believed that our most important attachment is probably to our parents (and, by extension, other family members), but he also thought that attachments to friends (even if they were not always conforming themselves) and teachers would also keep us from deviating.

Commitment is the "rational" component of the bond. This component suggests that individuals will be less likely to engage in deviance when they have a strong commitment to conventional society. This strong commitment to conventional society will cause them to weigh the costs and benefits of deviant behavior. Those who have more to lose will not misbehave. Hirschi believed that conventional activities were most likely one's education and other school activities for juveniles and, for those who had successfully completed high school, work and occupational attainment. Hirschi actually believed that juveniles who entered adulthood too soon (for example, became young parents or worked while in high school) were more likely to become deviant, not less likely (Kubrin et al., 2009).

Involvement is the component of the bond that suggests the more time spent engaged in conforming activities, the less time available to deviate. Hirschi (1969) characterized this bond as "idle hands are the devil's workshop" (p. 187). In other words, Hirschi argued that juveniles who spend their time in conventional activities, such as sports, homework, or band practice, have, literally, less time for deviant activities. The difference between commitment and involvement (since we have mentioned school and after-school activities in both) is that commitment is the bond that focuses on not wanting to lose the benefits of the conventional activity one is engaging in (you don't want to be benched on the football team because you were caught drinking). Involvement, however, refers specifically to the time you engage in a conventional activity (if you are at football practice, you cannot also be shoplifting at the same time).

Finally, **belief** is the component of the bond that suggests the stronger the awareness, understanding, and agreement with the rules and norms of society, the less likely one will be to deviate. Given that social control is a normative theory (it assumes that there is societal agreement and understanding about the norms and rules of society), an individual with weakened norms is not thought to be completely unaware of the norms and rules—however, he or she is less accepting of the "moral validity of the law" (Kubrin et al., 2009, p. 172).

Hirschi would argue that both Nick and David experienced a weakening of the social bonds in high school, which led to their partying. This may have come in the form of decreased attachment to parents or school, or it may have come in a lessening of the belief that drinking alcohol was a deviant or rule-breaking activity.

▲ **Photo 7.1** In Hirschi's theory of Social Control, finding alternative activities for kids, such as music programs, may keep them from engaging in deviant behavior.

◈ Techniques of Neutralization

Sykes and Matza (1957) offer an explanation for why individuals might engage in deviance even though they understand it is wrong. Asking, "Why would we violate the norms and laws in which we believe?" they suggest that we employ techniques of neutralization to rationalize away our understanding of the rules. They argue that society is organized for these sorts of rationalizations because much of our understanding of the rules comes with a certain flexibility already. In other words, they point out, while we understand the normative system, we also understand that under certain circumstances, those norms do not apply. For example, while killing someone is generally wrong, we know that during times of war or in self-defense, it is not. Under criminal law, an individual can avoid being guilty because of "non-age, necessity, insanity, drunkenness, compulsion, self-defense, and so on" (p. 666). In other words, if the individual can prove she or he did not *intend* to do harm.

> It is our argument that much of delinquency is based on what is essentially an unrecognized extension of defenses to crimes, in the form of justifications for deviance that are seen as valid by the delinquent but not by the legal system or society at large. (p. 666)

Sykes and Matza (1957) argue that we can silence our internalized norms (what Nye refers to as our internalized controls) and external norms by using these techniques of neutralization. They suggest there are five of them:

1. The Denial of Responsibility

The first technique is used by individuals to argue that they are not responsible for their behavior. While some of this might be an argument that their behavior was a mistake or accident, Sykes and Matza (1957) argue that denial of responsibility goes well beyond just the claim that "it was an accident." This technique essentially is used to suggest that the individual is somehow compelled by forces beyond his or her control. The individual is "helplessly propelled" into bad behavior by unloving parents, a bad teacher, a boss, or a neighborhood.

2. The Denial of Injury

This technique focuses on whether the deviance is perceived to cause injury or harm to anyone. It might be symbolized by the statement "but no one was hurt by it." It is probable that this technique is used frequently in the justification for deviant behavior since much behavior defined as deviant is not defined as harmful enough to be against the law. In these instances when the behavior may go against understood societal norms but not be very harmful to others, it is easy for individuals to argue that their behavior should be allowed and is not really all that bad because it isn't hurting anyone.

3. The Denial of Victim

An extension of the denial of injury is the rationalization that while a victim might exist, that person deserved the harm or "brought it on themselves." This technique of neutralization focuses on the fact that the victim deserves to be harmed because it is retaliation or punishment for some slight the victim has perpetrated on the deviant. The behavior becomes justified just as Robin Hood's behavior of stealing from the rich to give to the poor is justified. It may be against the rules to steal, but the rich brought it upon themselves by stealing from the poor first.

4. The Condemnation of the Condemners

This technique shifts the focus or blame to the individuals who are pointing the finger at the deviant's behavior. It is a diversionary tactic used to point out that others' behavior is also deviant, and therefore, those "condemners" have no right to call into question the behavior of the deviant individual. As with all diversionary tactics, the goal of this one is not to have a meaningful conversation about anyone's deviance but to deflect attention from the original assertion and help the deviant slip from view.

5. The Appeal to Higher Loyalties

The final technique of neutralization is one in which the wishes of the larger group (society) lose out to the wishes of a smaller, more intimate group. In other words, when an individual sees himself or herself as loyal to a group that demands behavior that violates the rules of society, he or she may argue that that loyalty requires breaking the rules for the good of the smaller group. In this instance, the individual may see himself or herself caught between the two groups. For example, a young man may know he should not fight another boy but may do it to protect his younger brother or because his friends demand he show loyalty to their group.

Sykes and Matza (1957) offer five phrases to sum up the five techniques of neutralization: "I didn't mean it, I didn't really hurt anybody, they had it coming to them, everybody's picking on me, and I didn't do it for myself" (p. 669). With these phrases come the ability to rationalize away an individual's understanding of the normative behavior expected of him or her and allows for deviant behavior.

While our example of Nick and David does not actively include techniques of neutralization, they might use these neutralizations in the following ways: Both Nick and David might use the denial of responsibility to argue it is not their fault that they occasionally drink beer or smoke pot. They might argue that all their friends are doing it, that they will be thought of as uncool or will not invited back to parties if they don't also drink or smoke. Because most of their behavior is victimless deviance (alcohol use, drug use, and online gambling), both young men could easily use the technique of denying injury—for example, Nick might argue that because it is just beer, he isn't really doing anything wrong—there is no harm being committed (as one of our sisters used to say, "At least I am not doing drugs. You should be happy I am not doing drugs.") Finally, David may use the condemnation of the condemners when he is confronted by his parents about his behavior. David might argue that his parents also drink (and get drunk in front of their kids) and that while in college also smoked pot (thus giving us another good reason to not share all our past behaviors with our kids).

DEVIANCE IN POPULAR CULTURE

The ideas of social control theory can easily be applied to novels and films in popular culture. We offer two examples here but encourage you to think about the storylines of other books and films and see if you can apply the ideas of the theory to the different characters to explain their deviance and/or conformity.

The Outsiders is a book written by a 16-year-old girl, S. E. Hinton, in the 1967 and made into a film in 1983 by Francis Ford Coppola. Hinton examines the experiences of two groups of juvenile delinquents divided by social class: She calls them the Greasers and the Socs. *The Outsiders* is narrated by

(Continued)

(Continued)

14-year-old, Ponyboy Curtis, a greaser, who lives with his two brothers, Darry and Sodapop, and considers the rest of the "gang"—Johnny, Dally, and Two-bit—his family.

The Outsiders depicts a world without significant adults; the boys are accountable to each other more than anyone else. Johnny's parents are abusive, the Curtis brothers' parents were killed in a car accident, and the other boys' parents are rarely mentioned. Ponyboy is the only boy in his gang who is interested in school; Soda and Darry work full-time and try to stay out of trouble, attempting to hold their small family together after the death of their parents.

Social control theory can help to explain the relative conformity and deviance of each character. As an example, compare the social bonds of Ponyboy and Dally and see if the theory fits the outcome at the end of the novel/film.

For another example from a quite different era and setting, you might apply the ideas of social control theory to the film *Boyz n the Hood*. Set in South Central Los Angeles, the film focuses on the challenges of growing up in an extremely violent setting. The three main characters—Tre, Ricky, and Doughboy—are African American teenage boys with different backgrounds and opportunities.

Using Hirschi's theory, compare and contrast the social bonds of Tre, Ricky, and Doughboy. Do you think the relative strength of attachment, commitment, involvement, and belief explains their different levels of deviant behavior? Why or why not?

◈ Contemporary Additions to Social Control Theory

Power-Control Theory

Developed by Hagan, Gillis, and Simpson (Hagan, 1989; Hagan, Gillis, & Simpson, 1985, 1990; Hagan, Simpson, & Gillis, 1987), power-control theory combines class and control theories of deviance to explain the effects of familial control on gender differences in crime. Hagan et al. (1987) argue that parental positions in the workforce affect patriarchal attitudes in the household. Patriarchal attitudes, in turn, result in different levels of control placed on boys and girls in these households. Finally, differing levels of control affect the likelihood of the children taking risks and ultimately engaging in deviance. In other words, because of the greater levels of control placed on girls in patriarchal households, there are greater gender differences in delinquency in such households with boys being more delinquent than girls.

Power-control theory begins with the assumption that mothers constitute the primary agents of socialization in the family. In households in which the mother and father have relatively similar levels of power at work, "balanced households," mothers will be less likely to differentially exert control upon their daughters. Thus, in balanced households, both sons and daughters will have similar levels of control placed upon them, leading them to develop similar attitudes regarding the risks and benefits of engaging in deviant behavior. This line of reasoning suggests that balanced households will experience fewer gender differences in deviant behavior. Power-control theorists further assume that households in which mothers and fathers have dissimilar levels of power in the workplace, so-called unbalanced households, are more "patriarchal" in their attitudes regarding gender roles. In such households, parents will place greater levels of control upon daughters than sons. Therefore, daughters will develop attitudes unfavorable toward deviance—higher levels of perceived risk and fewer perceived benefits for engaging in deviant acts. Thus, in unbalanced households, the theory predicts significant gender differences in deviant behavior, with male children being more likely than females to engage in deviant acts.

Initial tests of power-control theory suggested that these gender differences in crime come about because girls are differentially controlled in the household. In other words, female delinquency increases or decreases depending on the level of patriarchy and, thus, control in the household. Later tests of the theory (McCarthy, Hagan, & Woodward, 1999) suggest that gender differences in deviance and crime probably decrease because *both* male and female deviants are affected. Most important, McCarthy et al. (1999) demonstrate that in less patriarchal households, sons have more controls placed on them, decreasing their level of deviance.

Theory of Self-Control

Gottfredson and Hirschi introduced their general theory of crime in 1990, situating the theory in the classical school of criminology. Of all the theories discussed in this chapter (and, perhaps, in this book), this theory may be, arguably, the one best positioned to predict deviant behavior. This is because this theory was designed to be able to predict *all* behavior, not just criminal or delinquent behavior.

According to Gottfredson and Hirschi, crime and deviance are just like any other behaviors and should not be set apart as somehow different than, say, brushing one's teeth or listening to music. Using concepts from the classical school (Bentham, 1789/1970), they argue that people engage in all behavior to maximize pleasure and minimize pain. As rational creatures, humans will make choices in their lives that help them increase pleasure and avoid pain whenever they can. In this conception, deviance, then, is just like any other behavior—individuals freely choose to engage in that behavior when it is pleasurable to them.

Gottfredson and Hirschi (1990) define crime (and deviance) as "acts of force or fraud undertaken in pursuit of self-interest" (p. 15). Using the Uniform Crime Reports to illustrate the nature of crime, they argue that there is no difference between trivial and serious crime, between expressive and instrumental crime, between status offense and delinquency, between victim and victimless crimes—the difference lies not in the behaviors but, to some extent, in the individual. While a strict classical theory would argue that all individuals are likely to make the decision to engage in deviance if it brings with it a reward for the individual and that the likelihood to not engage in deviance is based on that individual's social bond to society, Gottfredson and Hirschi argue that there may be a difference in individuals and their behavior that cannot be explained by the social bond: "What classical theory lacks is an explicit idea of self-control, the idea that people also differ in the extent to which they are vulnerable in the temptations of the moment" (p. 87).

Gottfredson and Hirschi (1990) argue that self-control is a stable construct that develops early in the socialization process (or lack thereof) of an individual. Most likely, it develops from an "absence of nurturance, discipline, or training" (p. 95). In other words, the major cause of low self-control is bad parenting or ineffective childrearing. But Gottfredson and Hirschi are emphatic in their assertion that low self-control is not actively created; it is what happens in the absence of socialization, not in the presence of socialization. In other words, Gottfredson and Hirschi believe that since deviant behavior "undermines harmonious group relations and the ability to achieve collective ends" (p. 96), no one would actively teach, learn, or promote deviant behavior.

Six elements make up the construct of low self-control, according to Gottfredson and Hirschi (1990):

1. Criminal acts provide **immediate gratification** of desires. A major characteristic of people with low self-control is therefore a tendency to respond to tangible stimuli in the immediate environment, to have concrete "here and now" orientation. People with high self-control, in contrast, tend to defer gratification.

2. Criminal acts provide **easy or simple** gratification of desires. They provide money without work, sex without courtship, revenge without court delays. People lacking self-control also tend to lack diligence, tenacity, or persistence in a course of action.

3. Criminal acts are **exciting, risky, or thrilling.** They involve stealth, danger, speed, agility, deception, or power. People lacking self-control therefore tend to be adventuresome, active, and physical. Those with high levels of self-control tend to be cautious, cognitive, and verbal.

4. Crimes provide **few or meager long-term benefits.** They are not equivalent to a job or a career. On the contrary, crimes interfere with long-term commitments to jobs, marriages, family, or friends. People with low self-control thus tend to have unstable marriages, friendships, and job profiles. They tend to be little interested in and unprepared for long-term occupational pursuits.

5. Crimes require **little skill or planning.** The cognitive requirements for most crimes are minimal. It follows that people lacking self-control need not possess or value cognitive or academic skills. The manual skills required for most crimes are minimal. It follows that people lacking self-control need not possess manual skills that require training or apprenticeship.

6. Crimes often result in **pain or discomfort for the victim.** Property is lost, bodies are injured, privacy is violated, trust is broken. It follows that people with low self-control tend to be self-centered, indifferent, or insensitive to the suffering and needs of others. It does not follow, however, that people with low self-control are routinely unkind or antisocial. On the contrary, they may discover the immediate and easy rewards of charm and generosity. (pp. 89–90)

Gottfredson and Hirschi argue that these traits are stable in individuals. In other words, they do not vary over time—once a person with low self-control, always a person with low self-control. What Gottfredson and Hirschi say may vary is the ability or opportunity for individuals to engage in deviance. So while individuals with low self-control might always be inclined to make an easy score, that easy score has to come along first.

Gottfredson and Hirschi would argue that both Nick and David have fairly low levels of self-control, although David's appears to be lower. Because our level of self-control is set by about age 8, all behaviors after this age can be explained by our level of self-control and our opportunity to deviate at any given time. Both Nick and David have engaged in deviant acts over an extended period of time, but David has found more opportunities for deviance than Nick. These differing levels of deviance may signify differing levels of self-control—in other words, Nick has a small taste for an exciting life with immediate gratification, but David's taste for the quick, easy, gratifying life is greater. Therefore, while we see Nick drink beer in high school, he does not engage in more serious deviance that may also be considered criminal (drug use) or more disruptive to his life (online gambling and long gambling trips). He doesn't have a taste for these more "thrilling" activities.

Life Course Theory

While traditional social control or social bonding theory focuses attention on the social bonds that juveniles and young adults maintain—attachment to parents and teachers, commitment to school, involvement in activities such as sports or band—life course theory extends this examination of social bonds from adolescents to adulthood (Sampson & Laub, 1993, 1995). Hirschi (1969) argued that bonds may be weak or broken (or may vary over time), but he never really explored the nature of that variance, while Gottfredson and

Hirschi (1990) argue that life events (as they are related to social bonding) do not have an effect on deviant behavior because levels of self-control are set at an early age. Sampson and Laub (1993) argue that over the course of one's life, individuals are likely to go through stages that present them with social bonding opportunities and that while we may be able to see trajectories toward crime throughout the life course, these trajectories can change with changes in life events.

According to Sampson and Laub (1993), a **trajectory** is a "pathway or line of development over a life span . . . [that] refer[s] to long-term patterns of behavior and [is] marked by a sequence of transitions" (p. 8). A **transition,** then, is a shorter or specific life event that is embedded in a trajectory. For example, your life could be said to be on a working-class trajectory—born in a working-poor neighborhood to parents who had stable but low-paying employment, you receive no schooling past high school and end up working in the service sector. Then you marry and get an entry-level position in your in-laws' furniture business (same pay as your other job but significant room for advancement). You could have been said to have been on a trajectory for a working-poor lifestyle, barely making ends meet, most likely always working in the service sector, always worrying about the likelihood you might lose your job; your marriage (the transition) offers a sudden change from that earlier trajectory.

Sampson and Laub focus on an age-graded theory of informal social control. They argue that there are social bonds between (1) members of society and (2) wider social institutions, such as family, school, and work. As an age-graded theory, they argue that life events may have an effect on the likelihood to persist or desist with deviance (although it is the quality of these life events, not just the existence of them that is important). They offer three components to their theory. The first is that during childhood and adolescence, social bonds to family and school are important for explaining the likelihood to engage in deviance. Those who hold strong bonds to family and school are less likely to engage in deviance than those with weak or broken bonds. The second component is the argument that there is a certain level of stability to the likelihood to engage in deviance. In other words, those who don't engage in deviance as adolescents are more likely to not engage in deviance as adults, and those who do engage in deviance as adolescents are more likely to engage in deviance as adults. Sampson and Laub argue this is for two reasons: First, there are stable individual differences in the likelihood to engage in deviance (some people are just more likely to engage in deviance), but, second, there is also a dynamic process by which the adolescent deviant behavior has an effect on later adolescent and adult social bonds (for example, an individual who has been incarcerated or labeled a deviant may have less prosperous job prospects).

Finally, the third component, which is where they spend a significant amount of explanatory time, is that important life events in adulthood have the likelihood of changing a trajectory. "In other words, we contend that trajectories of crime are subject to modification by key institutions of social control in the transition to adulthood" (Sampson & Laub, 1995, p. 146). These are likely to be such transitions as attachment to labor force participation or a particularly cohesive marriage. Sampson and Laub argue that it is not enough for these transitions to just happen; they must be quality transitions (in other words, just getting married or committing to a partner is not enough; it must be a cohesive commitment).

Moffitt (1993, 2003, 2006) makes an extended life course argument saying that there are two offender groups. The first is considered a life course persistent group whose deviance stems from neurodevelopmental processes—these individuals are predicted to be fairly consistent in their deviant behavior. In other words, over their life, they are more likely to engage in crime. Moffitt considers this to be a fairly small group. The second is called adolescence limited. This group is much larger—their deviance stems from social processes, and over time, it is likely that most will stop engaging in deviant behavior (Piquero, Daigle, Gibson, Leeper Piquero, & Tibbetts, 2007).

These variations on the life course theory are often used to explain the **age-crime curve.** The relationship between age and crime is so strong at the aggregate level that many believe it is invariant (meaning that it does not change over era or type of crime, for example), and while this is probably not the case (for two discussions, see Farrington, 1986; Piquero et al., 2007), it is a very strong relationship—we see, in general, that the likelihood for crime rises sharply as one ages into the teenage and late teenage/early adult years and then not quite as swiftly drops off (see Figure 7.1). Steffensmeier, Allan, Harer, and Streifel (1989) found that the age-crime relationship was extremely strong but varied for type of crime (for example, while the relationship between age and property crimes might peak at about 17, the relationship between age and violent crime peaks a bit later).

Theorists who use the life course theory argue that this age-crime relationship exists because as people age, they go through stages that allow them to be more or less deviant. For example, as adolescents become teenagers, they are more likely to pull away from their parents' control, perhaps becoming less attached to their parents and more attached to their peers. Then as individuals become even older, they enter new stages of their life in which deviant behavior may be less rewarding or available, and thus they begin to engage in less and less deviance and more and more conformity—we call this "aging out of crime and deviance."

Life course theorists, such as Sampson and Laub, would note that both Nick and David had engaged in deviance as adolescents. Again, while it was victimless, it would suggest a trajectory of deviant behavior in the future. To explain Nick's movement off of this trajectory, Sampson and Laub would be interested in two events in the example. The first would be the difference between Nick and David's job prospects after college. While

Figure 7.1   Age-Specific Arrest Rates: Robbery and Burglary in 1985

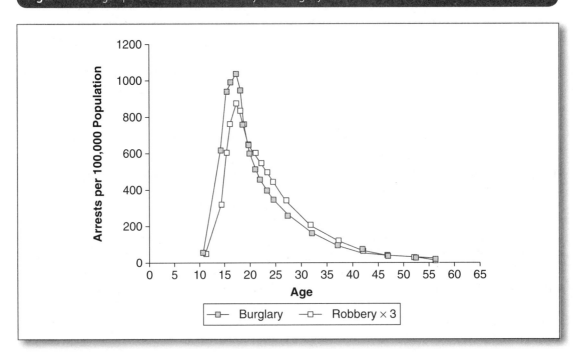

Source: Blumstein (1995).

both jobs are described as entry level, and David earns a bit more money than Nick at his job, what is important for the life course theory is the quality of the job for Nick. He sees his job as offering him a future (he sees a lot of room for advancement), while David does not see his job as something he wants to do in the future (therefore he is not as bonded to the job). In addition, while David has dated more throughout high school and college, Nick sees his partner as someone he wants to make a lifetime commitment to. This commitment (or Nick's definition that this is a quality relationship) means that he is bonded to his partner and worries about what his partner will think of him—thus making it less likely he will continue with deviant behavior.

STUDIES IN DEVIANCE

Relationships With Children and AIDS-Risk Behaviors Among Female IDUs

By Susan F. Sharp (1998), in *Deviant Behavior, 19*, 3–28

Sharp (1998) examined the effect of social bonds on the likelihood of female intravenous drug users (IDUs) to engage in AIDS-risk behaviors (specifically, sharing drug needles and engaging in unprotected sex). What makes this research especially important is (1) it was conducted on individuals who were already engaged in risky behavior (IDU) and was examining the likelihood that individuals varied in their likelihood to engage in secondary risky behavior, and (2) most research of this nature has been conducted on men, finding that careers and marriage are important predictors of risk behaviors—men who are married and have careers that are important to them are less likely to engage in risky behavior. However, research has already found that women are less likely to have meaningful careers than are men, and marriage is less likely to keep them from risky behavior.

Sharp conducted in-depth interviews with 18 female IDUs and 2 former IDUs. The interviewees were recruited using a snowball sample (interviewees were asked to refer other IDUs to be interviewed). Each participant received $15 for her time. The participants were between the ages of 20 and 53.

This research found that weakening or rupturing of existing bonds with children—most important, if a child had been removed from the custody of the mother (formally or informally)—led to an increase in risky behaviors in the form of unprotected sex and needle sharing. Women who had not lost custody/contact with their children were less likely to report sharing needles or engaging in unprotected sex (even though they were already intravenous drug users).

As Casey, an interviewee, sums up,

Casey: yeah, they convinced DHS that I was putting them in danger and all so they took them and gave them to him and his mom.

S: How did that affect you?

Casey: How the hell do you think? My kids were everything and they were all I had left. I went crazy. I threatened to kill James and his mother. That's when they got the injunction where I couldn't see my kids. I was sick—and I just quit caring anymore. I stayed totally loaded all the time and did whatever it took to get high so I didn't have to think or go home to an empty house. I turned tricks at truck stops for dope money—whatever. (p. 13)

◆ Empirical Studies

As you can tell, most versions of social control theory, both the classical and contemporary additions, have explanations for deviance that rely heavily on the socializing capacity of the family. In other words, social control theory, in all of its forms, points to the family as the primary controlling agent of deviance. While the family can be found as a component of many theories of deviance, it plays a central role in empirical works examining the predictive abilities of social control theory. Below is an example of the research examining the socializing abilities of the family.

Instead of an intricate look at the structural characteristics of the single-parent family, some researchers have suggested that family process or family quality should also be a serious focus of the examination (Patterson & Dishion, 1985; Rutter & Giller, 1984; Vazsonyi & Klanjsek, 2008) because structure may mask other processes or events in the juvenile's life (Haas, Farrington, Killias, & Sattar, 2004). Studies that have simultaneously examined family structure and family process have generally found that family structure is not a significant predictor of delinquency once family process has been added (Cernkovich & Giordano, 1987; Van Voorhis, Cullen, Mathers, & Garner 1988) and that family structure at most had an indirect effect on delinquency through measures of family process (Laub & Sampson, 1988; Petts, 2009; Sampson & Laub, 1993).

▲ **Photo 7.2**   All the theories connected to Social Control suggest that family relationships are an important factor in stopping deviant behavior.

Family process and/or family quality studies have been less systematic. Many of the studies examine the relationship between attachment and juvenile delinquency. However, the concept, attachment, has been measured in a variety of ways—love or affection, interest or concern, support and help, caring and trust, encouragement, lack of rejection, parental conflict, and control and supervision (J. H. Rankin & Kern, 1994; see also J. H. Rankin & Wells, 1990). These measures of attachment could also be measures of other theoretical components.

Other family quality measures, in addition to attachment, are overall home quality, discipline, supervision, and level of conflict. For the most part, family process variables, no matter what they are called or how they are operationalized, are significant predictors of juvenile delinquency. Researchers have found that overall home quality (Van Voorhis et al., 1988), level of supervision (Cernkovich & Giordano, 1987; Laub & Sampson, 1988; Sampson & Laub, 1993), attachment to parents (Hirschi, 1969; Johnson, 1986; Krohn & Massey, 1980; Laub & Sampson, 1988; J. H. Rankin & Kern, 1994; J. H. Rankin & Wells, 1990; Sampson & Laub, 1993; Warr 1993), and type of discipline (Laub & Sampson, 1988; Sampson & Laub, 1993) are strong predictors of juvenile delinquency.

Levels of attachment in the family have long been linked to juvenile delinquency (Hirschi, 1969; Nye, 1958; J. H. Rankin & Kern, 1994; Sampson & Laub, 1993, 1994; Sokal-Katz, Dunham, & Zimmerman, 1997; Warr, 1993). While much of this research has examined the direct effect of attachment on delinquency, some have taken a more extensive look at family processes, including such variables as family involvement, family conflict, or supervision (Sampson & Laub, 1993, 1994; Smith & Krohn, 1995), and some have examined the effect that racial and ethnic diversity might have on the effect of attachment (Smith & Krohn,

1995; Weber et al., 1995), finding that there does seem to be a relationship between ethnicity and the effect of attachment. Levels of attachment in conjunction with structure have also been examined with various findings. Some studies have shown that attachment is a better predictor of delinquency than structure (Sokol-Katz et al., 1997), while others have found a relationship between attachment and structure (J. H. Rankin & Kern, 1994).

Supervision is a second extensively researched process within the family that is said to affect the likelihood of delinquency (Broidy, 1995; Greenwood, 1992; Jang & Smith, 1997; Junger & Marshall, 1997; Wells & Rankin, 1988). Most of these studies show a relationship between levels of supervision and delinquency (Greenwood, 1992; Jang & Smith, 1997; Junger & Marshall, 1997), although this relationship does depend on how family supervision is measured (Broidy, 1995; Wells & Rankin, 1988).

◈ Critiques of Social Control Theory

The earliest versions of social control theory were criticized for having underdeveloped constructs that could not be easily tested. This changed with Hirschi's version of social control theory. Not only did Hirschi present a test of his theory with his initial book (1969), but the theory may be one of the most tested theories in criminology today (Kubrin et al., 2009). Numerous researchers have found support for the theory using cross-sectional studies, although longitudinal studies show less support (Kubrin et al., 2009).

However, some theorists and researchers argue that traditional social control theory (specifically Hirschi's form of social bonding theory) is better at predicting minor forms of deviance and crime than more serious forms of deviance and crime (Krohn & Massey, 1980) and that the four bonds do not really predict future deviance with any success at all (Agnew, 1985).

Contemporary versions of control theory have actually been critiqued by other control theorists—most notably, there is a robust exchange between Hirschi and Gottfredson (1995) and Sampson and Laub (1995) on the merits of the theory of self-control and life course theory. One of their central critiques is whether control varies throughout a person's life or whether that control is set by a certain (young) age. Specifically, critics of self-control argue that self-control may be something that changes over time in one's life (as opposed to being set in someone by the time they are 7 or 8).

Perhaps one of the most common and general critiques about all the theories that fall under the general heading of social control theory is that there is a background assumption that individuals are both rational and have the capacity to perceive the consequences of their behavior. These theories assume that people will weigh the costs and benefits of their behavior and in instances where they do not want to give up the connections they have made to society (attachment to their parents, benefits in school, a good job, a good marriage, the esteem of their friends and colleagues), they will be less likely to deviate. However, as we know, when we engage in deviant behavior, often we do not take those things into consideration. For example, we know when we sit down with a pint of ice cream in the middle of the night to watch Spike TV's *The Ultimate Fighter* that the pint of ice cream is not good for us, but the consequences of those actions are far off (if perceived at all), while the benefits (a mindless night of chocolate chip mint ice cream and violent TV) are immediate.

◈ Conclusion

After discussing the theories above that traditionally fall under the heading of social control theory, it might be easy to suggest that they do not have much in common. The commonality between these theories is their reliance on background assumptions that are based in the classical tradition of criminology—that is, the belief in a rational mind, an ability to make choices, and a belief that individuals want to maximize their pleasure and minimize their pain and must be restrained from engaging in deviance—because deviance is a natural and normal tendency. And while many of these theorists might have robust disagreements about parts of their theories, this is what makes this particular theory such a dynamic and central explanatory mechanism for deviance.

NOW YOU . . . USE THE THEORY

Below are the copyright infringement statistics for the University of Delaware for academic year 2009–2010. These statistics and their violation policy are reprinted from the University of Delaware security webpage (www.udel.edu/security/copyrightstats.html). Using social control theory and its variations, answer the following questions:

1. How might social control theory explain copyright infringement on a college campus?

2. How might social control theory explain the decrease in copyright infringement on the University of Delaware college campus?

3. In addition to the policies below, what might a social control theorist suggest as a policy to decrease copyright infringement on campuses?

Copyright Infringement Statistics Academic Year 2009–2010

This page shows the number of student computers that have been cited for copyright infringement and removed from the university's network in the current academic year. If you are a student, and you violate copyright laws, you

1. receive a *Copyright Violation Notice* with infringement specifics in your university e-mail account;

2. have your network access disabled;

3. must complete the Copyright Education course in Sakai;

4. must schedule an appointment to have your computer examined by IT-Client Support & Services. You will be charged a fee for this service; and

5. will have your network access restored upon your completion of the Sakai course and examination of your system by IT-Client Support & Services.

Future incidents of alleged copyright infringement will be referred to the Office of Student Conduct.

Copyright Violations by Month

September '09	October '09	November '09	December '09	January '10	February '10	March '10	April '10	May '10	June '10	July '10	August '10
63	60	66	59	23	27	35	40	33	11	9	2

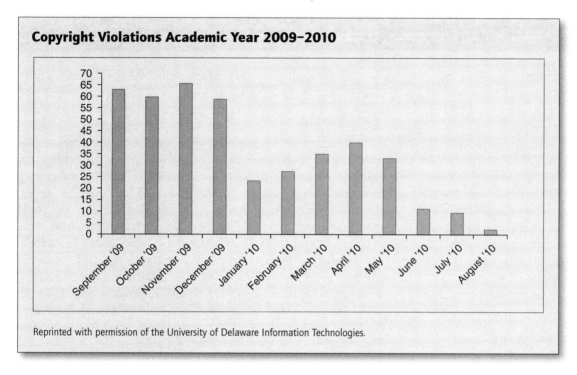

Copyright Violations Academic Year 2009–2010

Reprinted with permission of the University of Delaware Information Technologies.

EXERCISES AND DISCUSSION QUESTIONS

1. Explain Sykes and Matza's techniques of neutralization. For each technique, give a real-world example of how that technique is in use today.

2. Watch a political exchange on CNN, MSNBC, or Fox News (preferably one in which two political parties are debating) or follow an exchange from an Internet news source. Can you identify techniques of neutralization in place to justify the behavior of either of the political parties?

3. Compare and contrast the theory of self-control (from *A General Theory of Crime* by Gottfredson and Hirschi, 1990) and the life course theory (from *Crime in the Making* by Sampson and Laub, 1993).

4. Explain the general difference between internal and external social controls. Choose one version of social control theory to illustrate the differences.

5. Explain Hirschi's four components of the social bond.

KEY TERMS

Age-crime curve

Attachment

Belief

Commitment

External control

Internal control

Involvement

Low self-control

Social bond

Supervision

Trajectory

Transition

READING 20

Hirschi originally tested his theory with a sample of male high school students in Richmond, California, a community close to the University of California, Berkeley, where he attended graduate school. Subsequently, there have been numerous empirical tests of social control theory, primarily focusing on juvenile delinquency, with more representative samples of the U.S. population that also include females. However, most of the research has focused on adolescents in the United States, and few studies have attempted to assess the generalizability of the theory outside the United States. Furthermore, while there are both theoretical and empirical reasons to believe that delinquency and victimization might be linked, few studies have examined the relationship between Hirschi's four bonds to society (attachment, commitment, involvement, and belief) and deviance. Here, Cohen and Zeira examine the relationship between an overall index of social control, including indicators of each of the four dimensions of social control developed by Hirschi and self-reported delinquency and victimization among high school students in the Kibbutzim of northern Israel. The Kibbutzim is a collective society originally based on an agricultural economy with socialist and Zionist ideals. The economy has expanded beyond agriculture and is much more capitalistic in nature. Still, the society is unique and provides a rare test of social control theory outside of mainstream American culture. The authors find that their measure of social control is negatively associated with unlicensed driving offenses and shoplifting as well as an index of victimization. Further multivariate analyses show that their measure of social control is not related to delinquency or victimization once gender and other measures are included. It is too bad that the analyses were not extended to examine the effects of social control separately for males and females as gender seemed to be the only variable associated with delinquency in the multivariate models. Still, this article does provide limited support that Hirschi's social control theory may be generalized outside the United States and to quite different societies and cultures.

Social Control, Delinquency, and Victimization Among Kibbutz Adolescents

Ben-Zion Cohen and Ruth Zeira

The kibbutz is one of the proudest accomplishments of Israeli society. For some six decades after the first kibbutz was founded at Degania in 1909, these collective settlements, although they rarely encompassed more than about 5% of the Israeli population, symbolized the pioneering spirit of the

Source: Cohen, Ben-Zion, and Ruth Zeira. 1999. "Social Control, Delinquency, and Victimization Among Kibbutz Adolescents." *International Journal of Offender Therapy and Comparative Criminology* 43:503–513. Reprinted with permission.

young Jewish state. The men and women of the kibbutz toiled long and hard to build and maintain their
idealistic way of life, engaging in a wide range of
physical labors and governing themselves with a
unique system of members' committees and rotating
executive assignments. The dominant branch of the
kibbutz economy was agriculture and the workers
were the members of the collective, although some
kibbutzim even in the 1950s had developed industrial
enterprises and many were employing limited numbers of salaried workers from the nearby towns in
agriculture, industry, and services. The kibbutz raised
and educated its children in the collective spirit and
children lived with their peers in the children's houses
until age 18 or 19 when they joined the army and were
usually granted independent housing units. The kibbutzim, in most cases, maintained their own educational institutions with schools belonging jointly to
several kibbutzim in the same area. During this
period, with rare exceptions, the image of the kibbutz
in Israeli society was untainted by images of corruption, delinquency, or deviance.

The kibbutzim entered into a series of radical
changes in the 1960s. Industry and commerce
became more important as agriculture became less
labor intensive. Virtually all the kibbutzim conducted grand debates on child rearing and then
moved the children into the parents' quarters for
sleeping. Capitalist economics began to compete
with socialist ideals in the workplace, and the Israeli
media began to be more critical of kibbutz society,
even reporting on such previously unheard-of topics
such as alcohol, drugs, and delinquency in the kibbutz. Characteristically, social commentators tended
to blame the first manifestations of deviant behavior
in the kibbutzim on the young European and American volunteers who came to the kibbutzim after the
1967 Six Day War. Eventually, both the kibbutzim
and their many urban supporters began to acknowledge the existence of such social problems as substance abuse and delinquent behavior in the indigenous kibbutz population.

The kibbutzim have a long-standing tradition of
handling their problems internally and in many cases
still prefer to cope with their own resources. Many
kibbutz members considered calling on such outside
agencies as the police or welfare authorities embar-
rassing, disloyal, and an admission of helplessness. In
recent times, the kibbutzim have been more forthcoming about the presence of social problems, including delinquency, in their society. Kibbutz supporters
have regarded the acknowledging of imperfections as
a sign of resilience and as a cause for optimism about
the survival of the kibbutz way of life. Today, there is
enough openness in the system to allow studies such
as the present research even if they do not guarantee
complimentary results (Shoham, 1996).

The kibbutz is a self-contained, well-defined
social system that has fought against economic
inequality and promoted mutual responsibility
among its members; even as the kibbutz economy has
become more capitalistic in recent years, great effort
has been invested in preserving these ideals (Oz,
1997). Similar to any complex social system, however,
stratification proceeds along several dimensions, one
of which is age. The norms of the older generation are
quite different from those of the younger members,
and the norms of the kibbutz adolescents are, as
expected, considerably different from those of their
parents. The adolescents are subject to a wide range of
efforts by the adult establishment to reduce nonconformity and to induce the younger people to focus on
becoming productive members of the kibbutz. Clearly,
these efforts are not wholly successful. Some of the
sons and daughters will not become members of the
kibbutz at all; they will leave and go to the city. Others
will become productive members; still others may
become members but with imperfect motivation for
productivity. The pressures to conform provide the
backdrop for the study of kibbutz delinquency in the
present study, which employs a theoretical framework
derived from Hirschi's theory of social control (Hirschi, 1969). More than any other theory in criminology,
social control theory seeks to understand delinquency
as the failure of the social system to generate conformist behavior.

The roots of social control theory, according to
Kornhauser (1978), can be found in Thrasher's (1927)

classic *The Gang.* Thrasher viewed both delinquent behavior and gang membership as results of ineffective social control. Shaw and McKay (1942) stressed the cultural transmission of delinquent norms but they too included the notion of controls in their theoretical formulations.

Additional early proponents of social control theories of delinquency include Reiss (1951), Toby (1957), Nye (1958), and Matza (1964). Reiss (1951) distinguished between personal and social controls and explained delinquency as the result of the failure of both types to direct behavior according to conventional norms. Toby (1957) regarded crime rates as reflecting social disorganization but his explanation of why certain persons in high-crime areas commit crimes (and others do not) referred to the individual's stake in conformity. Nye (1958) identified four different control factors: internalized control, or self-regulation; indirect control, which results from identification with noncriminals; needs satisfaction, which refers to the capacity to cope with the demands of school, work, friends, and so on; and direct control, which is the external system of rewards and punishments. Matza (1964) viewed delinquents as "drifting" between conventional commitments and criminal behavior patterns, with the drift into delinquency usually taking place when the naturally occurring bond between the individual and the moral order is temporarily weakened by the neutralization of conscience in the presence of temptation.

Building on the work of his predecessors, Hirschi (1969) articulated the most comprehensive social control explanation of delinquent behavior. His theory began with the assumption, found also in Nye (1958), that conformist behavior not delinquent behavior was the phenomenon requiring explanation. Hirschi explained conformist behavior as a consequence of the bond between society and individual. He also specified the elements of the social bond: attachment, commitment, involvement, and belief. *Attachment* has to do with sensitivity to the feelings and opinions of relevant others. *Commitment* refers to a person's investment of time and energy in a way of life. *Involvement* results from commitment; the choice of a way of life determines how

an individual becomes involved in a delimited range of actions and relationships. *Belief,* according to Hirschi's theory, is the acceptance of the moral validity of conventional norms. Liska and Reed (1985) developed a nonrecursive version of social control theory, building on the assumption that the social bond not only affects delinquent behavior but is also affected by it. Their findings were consistent with their model of reciprocal influence.

Hirschi's (1969) study of 4,000 urban male junior and senior high school students in California confirmed the hypotheses derived from his theory of social control. Similar findings for rural male and female students in Grades 6 through 12 were presented by Hindelang (1973).

Krohn and Massey (1980) tested the elements of control theory on the self-report data of approximately 3,000 Grade 7 through 12 male and female students in the midwestern United States and found the components of social control theory differentially useful for explaining the delinquent behavior of subsamples of the participants in their study. Wiatrowski, Griswold, and Roberts (1981) constructed a more complex version of Hirschi's (1969) model and tested it on a large sample of 10th-grade boys from across the United States. Their findings supported control theory, as did those of Wiatrowski and Anderson (1987), who also studied a large national sample of adolescent males. Robbins (1984, 1985) explored the association of social control with delinquent behavior among American Indian youth living on reservations. The findings were somewhat ambiguous, but social control theory proved useful in explaining most of them. Social control variables were associated with all types of delinquent behavior in 12 of 13 countries (the single exception: vandalism in Holland) included in a collection of studies of self-report delinquency (Junger-Tas, Terlouw, & Klein, 1994).

Hirschi's more recent theoretical approach, developed with Gottfredson (Gottfredson& Hirschi, 1990), represents a shift of emphasis from social explanation of delinquent behavior to explanations based on individual differences. The theory of delinquency underlying the present research is Hirschi's earlier (1969) theory.

A classic tenet in the study of victimology (Hindelang, Gottfredson, & Garofalo, 1978; Lauritsen, Sampson, & Laub, 1991; Schafer, 1968) is the similarity of victim and offender in social status. From this proposition, it follows that if degree of social control predicts delinquent behavior within a given population, it should also be associated with delinquency victimizations within that population. Individuals with weaker ties to the social order should be more vulnerable. Moreover, previous research has found that in juvenile populations, involvement in delinquency is a predictor of victimization (Esbensen & Huizinga, 1991; Jensen & Brownfield, 1986; Thornberry & Figlio, 1974).

The present research is designed to test the utility of Hirschi's theory for understanding delinquent behavior and victimization in a sample of kibbutz adolescents. The hypothesis of this study is that the likelihood of both delinquency and victimization will be greater for those youth for whom the bonds of social control are weaker.

Method

Sample

The participants in the research were 440 10th-, 11th-, and 12th-grade students drawn by a simple random sampling procedure from the 22 high schools belonging to the secular kibbutz movements and located in Northern Israel (north of Tel-Aviv). The students in these three grades totaled approximately 2,500. The description of the sample is presented in Table 1.

As can be seen from Table 1, boys and girls are represented about equally, most of the participants are in the 16 to 17 age group, and a large majority (81.1%) are pursuing their studies on the academic (college preparatory) track.

Table 1   Description of the Sample (*N* = 440)

Characteristic	Percentage	*n*
Gender		
Males	49.8	221
Females	50.2	219
Age		
19	1.4	6
18	17.7	78
17	35.7	157
16	30.7	135
15	14.5	64
Grade		
12	31.6	139
11	35.5	156
10	33.0	145

(Continued)

Table 1 (Continued)

Characteristic	Percentage	n
Track		
Academic	81.1	357
Vocational	13.2	58
Other	5.7	25
Kibbutz movement		
United Kibbutz	38.0	167
Kibbutz Artzi	61.1	269
Not identified	0.9	4

Instrument

The data were collected by means of an anonymous questionnaire containing 58 closed self-report items. These items were designed to cover the four aspects of social control (attachment, commitment, involvement, and belief) as they apply to kibbutz life, two behavioral indicators for delinquency, and six types of victimization. The social control index conforms to the requirements of content validity in that it includes measures of the four basic ingredients of control theory (Hirschi, 1969).

The 24 items measuring social control were tested for inter-item reliability and yielded a Cronbach's alpha of .72.

The measure of delinquency was a pair of Likert-type items asking whether the respondent had (*never, once, or several times*) driven a vehicle without a license or stolen goods from the kibbutz mini-market. As the problems involved in self-report studies of delinquency have been well-documented over the years (Binder& Geis, 1983; Brown, Esbensen, & Geis, 1991; Gold, 1966; Hood & Sparks, 1970; Sutton, 1978), the authors wished to avoid the pitfalls inherent in the familiar technique of presenting a long checklist of offenses to the respondent. Consequently, the authors

chose the two focal offenses (Sutton, 1978) noted earlier and asked only about them. These two focal offenses each possess two important attributes: They are acts forbidden both by the law and by the informal kibbutz code of behavior but they are prevalent enough to allow for statistical analysis in a small sample (i.e., they are not rare events).

Data Collection

Once permission was granted by the kibbutz movement authorities, the respondents were selected by means of a table of random numbers from the total population of the participating schools. A member of the research team, who is a kibbutz member, contacted the schools and arranged for the students to complete the questionnaire. All the students cooperated and returned useable questionnaires.

Results

The first item of interest in the analysis is the prevalence of delinquent behavior in the sample. Table 2 displays the percentage of respondents reporting having committed each of the two focal offenses and the percentage reporting having committed either.

Thirty percent (132) of the respondents report never having committed either focal offense. Thus, a great majority (70%, 308) admit to having committed at least one of these offenses at least once. The offense of driving without a license is the more common of the two focal offenses, with 58.6% (258) reporting having done this at least once. Theft from the kibbutz mini-market was admitted by 34.4% (151) of the youth in the study.

The frequency of reported offenses, by gender, is presented in Table 3.

The distribution of offending among the male participants is very different from that of the females. Within the three-category breakdown of Table 3, the largest number of males (81.3%, 178) report having committed more than one offense, whereas the largest group of females (46.6%, 103) are those reporting no offenses. In the single-offense category, there are many more females (23.5%, 52) than males (5.5%, 12).

The first part of the hypothesis of this study predicted an association between social control and delinquency. The Pearson correlation coefficients for the associations between the 24-item index of social control and the number of reported offenses, by offense, and for all offenses, are presented in Table 4.

As seen in Table 4, the correlations of social control with unlicensed driving offenses ($r = -.18$), with mini-market thefts ($r = -.17$), and for total offenses ($r = -.16$), are weak but in the expected direction and statistically significant.

The second part of the study hypothesis predicted an association between social control and victimization. Table 5 displays the six types of victimizations investigated, the number of respondents reporting *never, once, or more than once* having been victimized in the past year, and the mean number of victimizations by type.

As seen in Table 5, the most common type of victimization is property damage ($M = 2.6$, $SD = 2.6$) and the least common is violent sexual abuse ($M = 0.02$, $SD = 0.3$). With the exception of property offenses, the majority of respondents reported no victimizations having occurred in the past year.

Table 2   Offenses Reported By Repondent ($N = 440$)

Number of Offenses	Driving Without a License	Theft From Mini-Market	Either Offense
0	41.4%	65.6% (289)	30.0% (132)
1	12.7% (56)	13.9% (61)	14.5% (64)
2+	45.9% (202)	20.5% (90)	35.5% (244)

Table 3   Offenses Reported By Gender ($N = 440$)

Number of Offenses	Males	Females
0	13.2% (29)	46.6% (103)
1	5.5% (12)	23.5% (52)
2+	81.3% (178)	29.9% (66)
Totals	100.0% (219)	100.0% (221)

Table 4 Correlations of Social Control With Delinquency

Correlation	R	P
Social control index with unlicensed driving offenses	−.18	<.001
Social control index with mini-market theft offenses	−.17	<.001
All offenses	−.16	<.001

Table 5 Type and Number of Reported Victimizations

Type of Victimization	Number of Victimizations				
	0	1	2+	M	SD
Taking of property	133	45	247	2.6	2.6
Damage to property	200	54	173	1.4	1.7
Violent threats	323	40	70	0.7	1.6
Nonviolent sexual harassment/abuse	411	10	10	0.1	0.8
Violent sexual abuse	427	1	3	0.02	0.3

The Pearson correlation coefficient for the association between the 24-item index of social control and the number of reported victimizations is in the expected direction, of moderate strength ($r = -.18$), and statistically significant ($p < .001$).

To examine the influence of social control on delinquency with other relevant variables controlled, a multiple regression was performed. A series of independent variables likely to reflect social status of adolescents in the kibbutz were entered into the analysis. In addition to age, gender, and grade, these included whether the respondent and each of his or her parents were born in the kibbutz, how many hours per week are spent with friends, and whether the young person acts as a youth leader with younger children. The results of the multiple regression analysis appear in Table 6.

As indicated in Table 6, gender (beta = .50) is the strongest predictor of delinquent behavior; the delinquent acts are more likely to be committed by youth who are male. The contribution of the other independent variables, including social control, to the regression equation did not reach statistical significance. The variance in delinquent behavior explained by the independent variables in Table 6 reached 30%.

An additional multiple regression analysis, with the same independent variables and with number of victimizations as the dependent variable, explained only 7% of the variance and is not presented here.

◈ Discussion

The hypothesis of this study predicted that delinquent behavior and victimization among kibbutz youth would prove to be associated with social control as measured by the index developed here. The bivariate tests of the hypothesis yielded results that are, at best, ambiguous. The correlations of social control with each type of delinquency and with both in combination are in the

Table 6 Multiple Regression on Total Offenses

Independent Variable	B	SE of B	Beta
Gender	−2.57	.22	−.50*
Age	0.24	.17	.09
Time spent with friends	0.08	.05	.06
Social control	−0.34	.22	−.06
Works as youth leader (0 = no, 1 = yes)	−0.27	.24	−.05
Born in kibbutz (0 = no, 1 = yes)	−0.02	.03	.02
Age moved into children's house	−0.05	.07	−.03
Mother born in kibbutz (0 = no, 1 = yes)	−0.12	.22	−.02
Father born in kibbutz (0 = no, 1 = yes)	0.13	.22	.03
Grade	−0.02	.21	−.10

Note: R^2(adj.) = .30.

*$p < .001$.

expected direction and are statistically significant but they are too weak (< .20) to regard as confirmation of the hypothesis even at the bivariate level. The results of the multiple regression analyses lend no support to the hypothesis; only gender makes a statistically significant contribution to predicting delinquent behavior, social control does not. The association with gender is expected and virtually universal; boys reported more offenses than girls in all 13 countries included in a group of studies of self-reported delinquency (Junger-Tas et al., 1994). According to Heimer (1996), much research on the relationship of gender to delinquency attributes males' higher rates of offending to the weaker social controls usually exercised on boys. The present study, too, found the familiar pattern of higher delinquency rates for boys and also found a slightly higher degree of social control for girls ($M = 4.4$, $SD = 0.5$) than for boys ($M = 4.1$, $SD = 0.5$) in the kibbutz.

If social control was measured in a manner both valid and relevant to the social setting, and the authors believe it was, the results of this research indicate that the distribution of delinquent behaviors among kibbutz

adolescents is consistent with but not strongly supportive of social control theory. One possible reason for this may be that with the influence of the peer group in the kibbutz so powerful, the social bonds to adult society have less direct impact on adolescent behavior.

The experience of adolescence in the kibbutz, even with the extensive changes the kibbutzim are undergoing in recent years (Oz, 1997), is quite different from adolescent experience in the urban settings of North America that have served as the test sites for the dominant theories of delinquency over the years. The patterns of relationships between different age groups in the kibbutz also differ significantly from those of urban families in Israel, as do the development of gender identities, and the residents of Israel are aware of the differences. A recent study, for example, found that urban Israeli adolescents perceived their male kibbutz counterparts as more masculine (Lobel & Bar, 1997). For kibbutz adolescents, the vast majority of whom grow to maturity in the very same communities where they were born, their daily routine and physical environment are safe, structured, and familiar. Within the community structure, they usually enjoy greater access to opportunities for academic, vocational, recreational, social, and sexual experimentation than their urban cousins. The disjointedness of contemporary adolescent lifestyles in the United States, as described by Felson (1998), and the delinquent career trajectories of the rural adolescents who participated in the recent study by Myner, Santman, Cappelletty, and Perlmutter (1998) are far removed from kibbutz life. Thus, these findings should be seen as evidence from a different culture as to the relevance of control theory. Multicultural evidence can enhance criminological understanding, but generalizing across cultures requires great caution.

If opportunities can be created for additional studies in the future, the authors would suggest building multiple theoretical models whose explanatory powers can be evaluated comparatively, and adding a sample of urban youth to explore the ways in which kibbutz youth differ from their urban counterparts.

◈ References

Binder, A., & Geis, G. (1983). *Methods of research in criminal justice and criminology.* New York: McGraw-Hill.

Brown, S. E., Esbensen, F-A., & Geis, G. (1991). Criminology: *Explaining crime and its context.* Cincinnati, OH: Anderson.

Esbensen, F-A., & Huizinga, D. (1991). Juvenile victimization and delinquency. *Youth and Society, 23,* 202–228.

Felson, M. (1998). *Crime and everyday life* (2nd ed.). Thousand Oaks, CA: Pine Forge Press.

Gold, M. (1966). Undetected delinquent behavior. *Journal of Research in Crime and Delinquency, 3,* 27–46.

Gottfredson, M. R., & Hirschi, T. (1990). *A general theory of crime.* Stanford, CA: Stanford University Press.

Heimer, K. (1996). Gender, interaction, and delinquency: Testing a theory of differential social control. Social Psychology Quarterly, 59, 39–61.

Hindelang, M. J. (1973). Causes of delinquency: A partial replication and extension. *Social Problems, 20,* 471–487.

Hindelang, M. J., Gottfredson, M. R., & Garofalo, J. (1978). *Victims of personal crime: An empirical foundation for a theory of personal victimization.* Cambridge, MA: Ballinger.

Hirschi, T. (1969). *Causes of delinquency.* Berkeley, CA: University of California Press.

Hood, R., & Sparks, R. (1970). *Key issues in criminology.* New York: McGraw-Hill.

Jensen, G., & Brownfield, D. (1986). Gender, lifestyles and victimization: Beyond routine activity. *Violence and Victims, 1,* 85–99.

Junger-Tas, J., Terlouw, G., & Klein, M.W. (Eds.). (1994). *Delinquent behavior among young people in the Western world: First results of the international self-report delinquency study.* Amsterdam: Kugler.

Kornhauser, R. R. (1978). *Social sources of delinquency: An appraisal of analytic models.* Chicago: University of Chicago Press.

Krohn, M. D., & Massey, J. L. (1980). Social control and delinquent behavior: An examination of the elements of the social bond. *Sociological Quarterly, 21,* 529–543.

Lauritsen, J. L., Sampson, R. J., & Laub, J. H. (1991). The link between victimization and offending among adolescents. *Criminology, 29,* 265–291.

Liska, A. E., & Reed, M. D. (1985). Ties to conventional institutions and delinquency: Estimating reciprocal effects. *American Sociological Review, 50,* 547–560.

Lobel, T. E., & Bar, E. (1997). Perception of masculinity and femininity of kibbutz and urban adolescents. *Sex Roles, 37,* 283–293.

Matza, D. (1964). *Delinquency and drift.* New York: John Wiley.

Myner, J., Santman, J., Cappelletty, G. G., & Perlmutter, B. F. (1998). Variables related to recidivism among juvenile offenders. *International Journal of Offender Therapy and Comparative Criminology, 42,* 65–80.

Nye, F. I. (1958). *Family relationships and delinquent behavior.* New York: John Wiley.

Oz, A. (1997). On social democracy and the kibbutz. *Dissent, 44,* 39–46.

Reiss, A. J., Jr. (1951). Delinquency as the failure of personal and social controls. *American Sociological Review, 16,* 196–207.

Robbins, S. P. (1984). Anglo concepts and Indian reality: A study of juvenile delinquency. *Social Casework, 65,* 235–241.

Robbins, S. P. (1985). Commitment, belief, and Native American delinquency. *Human Organization, 44,* 57–62.

Schafer, S. (1968). *The victim and his criminal.* New York: Random House.

Shaw, C. R., & McKay, H. D. (1942). *Juvenile delinquency and urban areas.* Chicago: University of Chicago Press.

Shoham, E. (1996). The attitude of kibbutz youth to rape: Myth versus reality. *International Journal of Offender Therapy and Comparative Criminology, 40,* 212–223.

Sutton, L. P. (1978). *Federal criminal sentencing: Perspectives of analysis and a design for research.* Washington, DC: Department of Justice.

Thornberry, T. P., & Figlio, R. M. (1974). Victimization and criminal behavior in a birth cohort. In T. P. Thornberry & E. Sagarin (Eds.), *Images of crime: Offenders and victims* (pp. 102–112). New York: Praeger.

Thrasher, F. M. (1927). *The gang.* Chicago: University of Chicago Press.

Toby, J. (1957). Social disorganization and stake in conformity: Complementary factors in the predatory behavior of hoodlums. *Journal of Criminal Law, Criminology, and Police Science, 48,* 12–17.

Wiatrowski, M., & Anderson, K. L. (1987). The dimensionality of the social bond. *Journal of Quantitative Criminology, 3,* 65–81.

Wiatrowski, M. D., Griswold, D. B., & Roberts, M. K. (1981). Social control theory and delinquency. *American Sociological Review, 46,* 525–541.

READING 21

Most studies of social and self-control have focused on adolescents and young adults. Veenstra et al. turn their attention to a younger sample of preadolescents and focus on an early initiated deviant behavior, persistent school truancy, that appears to be a predictor of later, more serious forms of deviance as well as negative consequences for the individual (e.g., school failure and dropout, unemployment). In contrast to most empirical studies of social and self-control that are conducted in the United States, the study takes place in urban and rural schools in five municipalities in the north of the Netherlands. The study is also unique in that multiple indicators of truancy are measured from self-reports as well as reports of parents and teachers. Interestingly, although the different reports are significantly related, the amount of agreement between children, their parents, and their teachers was quite low. Consistent with both theories, the data show that both self-control and most measures of social control (a prosocial orientation as well as attachment to parent and teachers, but not attachment to classmates) were negatively associated with persistent truancy. The authors suggest that measures of social control may mediate the relationship between self-control and truancy—that is, that low self-control leads to lower levels of attachment, which, in turn, leads to more truancy. Their data also support this hypothesis as once measures of attachment are statistically controlled, the effect of self-control is reduced and no longer significant. However, one might question the logic of their analyses as it is just as likely (in fact perhaps more likely) that early attachment to parents is a precursor to self-control if, as Gottfredson and Hirschi argue, effective parenting and socialization lead to self-control.

Truancy in Late Elementary and Early Secondary Education

The Influence of Social Bonds and Self-Control—The TRAILS Study

René Veenstra, Siegwart Lindenberg, Frank Tinga, and Johan Ormel

◈ Introduction

Staying away from school without a valid reason, tends to be increasingly more common in the final years of secondary education (Wagner, Dunkake, & Weiss, 2004). However, some pupils already show unexcused, illegal, surreptitious absences (Kearney, 2008) in elementary education or the first years of secondary education. If pupils start at such an early age with truancy, the likelihood of their involvement in other deviant behavior increases highly (Farrington, 1980; Henry, Caspi, Moffitt, Harrington, & Silva, 1999). To prevent pupils from dropping out of school and persisting in antisocial behavior, attention must be focused on the process that leads to dropout and criminal involvement. This process seems to begin to take place at an early age (Sweeten, Bushway, & Paternoster, 2009). Early truancy might be an important aspect of that process.

Several researchers have looked at predictors of truancy. These studies are mostly exploratory rather

Source: Veenstra, René, Siegwart Lindenberg, Frank Tinga, and Johan Ormel. 2010. "Truancy in late elementary and early secondary education: The influence of social bonds and self-control—the TRAILS study." *International Journal of Behavioral Development* 34:302–310.

than theory-based (see for an exception Wagner et al., 2004). Apart from a few exceptions (Farrington, 1980; Fergusson, Lynskey, & Horwood, 1995; Fogelman, Tibbenham, & Lambert, 1980; McNeal, 1999), most previous publications on truancy are based on cross-sectional research. Besides the work of Farrington (1980) no other studies have examined truancy in elementary education. Farrington (1980) monitored truancy development in boys from a working-class neighborhood in London. Almost 6 per cent of the boys, aged 8 to 10, were considered to be truants in the last year. In secondary education, this share tripled. Farrington found strong indications that for some children truancy in elementary education persists in secondary education.

In line with Farrington (1980), we examined truancy at an early age. By truancy we refer to unexcused, illegal, surreptitious absences (Kearney, 2008). We formulated the following research question: What is the role of social control and self-control on truancy? Are weak social control (Hirschi, 1969) and a lack of self-control (Gottfredson & Hirschi, 1990) indicative of truancy? The point of departure of social control theory and self-control theory is not the question why people violate social rules, but rather why they obey them. The social control theory holds that when people are attached to others, the emotional bond to these others makes them want to conform to their expectations. The self-control theory holds that people's stable ability to restrain their impulses makes them conform to norms they themselves share.

Though the control approaches were used initially to explain juvenile delinquency, they can be applied to other kinds of deviant behavior (compare Matsueda & Heimer, 1987). These approaches seem appropriate for research on truancy. Truancy is after all unlawful behavior. From the perspective of self-control theory, it can be maintained that truancy yields many easy rewards in the short term, such as leisure time, excitement, and dodging obligations. The rewards of non-truancy are primarily paid out in the long term (involvement in the school, good achievements, and other people's trust).

There has been much written about the contradictions and compatibilities between the two control theories which we will not repeat here (see Taylor, 2001). The consensus seems to be that it would be more fruitful to integrate the two rather than to pit them against each other (Sampson & Laub, 1993). Recent developments in cognitive psychology have given rise to a synthesis between the two that is based on the role of goals and significant others for self-regulation (Lindenberg, 2008, forthcoming). Particularly relevant for this 'goal-framing' approach are the studies by Baldwin and Holmes (1987), Baldwin, Carrel, and Lopez (1990), and Shah (2003a, 2003b) which have shown that significant others (e.g., parents) can activate expectations and that thinking of significant others can influence a person's goals. Goals that significant others approve of are activated and goals they disapprove of are inhibited in the attached person. This lowers the accessibility of goals associated with 'temptations' and strengthens the goal pursuit endorsed by the significant other. Thus, for dealing with temptations, self-control (trait) can be seen as facilitator of self-regulation (state) that works through the psychological presence of significant others and the influence of their goals on cognitions, expectations, and evaluations of the person exercising self-control. Self-regulation is aided by the psychological presence of significant others not only because of their approval or disapproval but also because thinking of them reduces the attractiveness and accessibility of the deviant goal and increases the accessibility of the endorsed goal. This effect will be strengthened by a stronger prosocial orientation (paying attention to others, being attuned to their expectations, see Seeley & Gardner, 2003).

The interesting implication of this approach is that without the aid of significant others, self-control should only be a help for highly internalized norms and not for social norms for which self-regulatory capacity is relevant (Schwartz, 1977). Conversely, being attached to a person makes that person a significant other, but, contrary to the social control theory, just being attached to that person should not help against deviant behavior if the significant other is not identified with the specific norm against this behavior. In fact, it might be that the major contribution of self-control to self-regulatory capacity lies in its facilitating attachment to significant others. This view is supported by a recent finding by Eisenberg et al. (2007) that self-control (also named effortful control) correlates with sympathy (referring to caring for others and for what they want). If true, this would mean that trait self-control is a vehicle for acquiring the instruments (attachment to significant others) for state self-regulatory capacity. Hirschi himself has also moved in this direction by seeing social bonds more as means of state self-regulation than as emotional attachment that elicits a 'conventional' response (see Hirschi, 2004).

In order to examine early truancy, we derived hypotheses from the goal-framing approach just presented. From this approach it follows for self-regulation that there must be both attachment and a clear normative position of the significant others to whom a child is attached. It follows that in order to be a significant other that helps self-regulation with regard to truancy, there has to be attachment to this other and he or she has to disapprove of truancy. Parents and teachers can be assumed to disapprove of truancy at elementary school age (Croninger & Lee, 2001; Crosnoe, Kirkpatrick Johnson, & Elder, 2004; Jenkins, 1995; Lee & Burkam, 2003; McNeal, 1999). When children form a stable attachment to these adults, these adults become significant others with regard to truancy and the likelihood of truancy should be low. By contrast, classmates are likely to show no clear disapproval of truancy (some disapprove, some do not). Thus, when children form a stable attachment to their classmates, these classmates do not become significant others with regard to truancy. We can now hypothesize that:

Hypothesis 1: The likelihood of truancy decreases as attachment to parents and teachers is stronger.

Hypothesis 2: The likelihood of truancy is unrelated to the degree of attachment to classmates.

As discussed earlier, children's prosocial orientation should also diminish the likelihood of truancy because the more they care about people, the better they will be aware of what is expected of them, which renders self-regulation easier. The hypothesis then is the following:

Hypothesis 3: The likelihood of truancy decreases as young people have a stronger prosocial orientation.

Because we suggested that self-control as a temperament trait contributes to state self-regulation mainly by aiding the attachment to significant others, it would follow from this that:

Hypothesis 4: The effect of self-control on truancy is mediated by attachment to parents and teachers.

When we test these hypotheses we will also take other predictors of truancy into account because prior research indicates that they are correlated with truancy (Fergusson, Horwood, & Shannon, 1986; Henry, 2007); predictors such as sex (boys more truant than girls), socio-economic status (SES, negatively correlated with truancy), pubertal development, familial vulnerability to externalizing deviant behavior, and family breakup (all positively correlated with truancy).

Method

Sample

The present study involved the first two assessment waves of TRAILS, which started in 2001. TRAILS is designed to chart and explain the development of mental health and social development from pre-adolescence into adulthood. The TRAILS target sample involved pre-adolescents living in five municipalities in the north of the Netherlands, including both urban and rural areas (De Winter et al., 2005).

Of all children approached for enrollment in the study (selected by the municipalities and attending a school that was willing to participate, $N = 3,145$ children from 122 schools, response of schools 90.4%), 6.7% were excluded because of incapability or language problems. Of the remaining 2,935 children, 76.0% were enrolled in the study, yielding $N = 2,230$ (consent to participate: both child and parent agreed; mean age of child: 11.09, $SD = 0.55$; gender: 50.8% girls; ethnicity: 10.3% children who had at least one parent born in a non-western country; parent education: 32.6% of children had parents with a low educational level, at maximum a certificate of a lower track of secondary education). No non-response bias was found in our study for the estimation of the prevalence rates of truancy in elementary education (De Winter et al., 2005). Of the 2230 baseline participants, 96.4% ($N = 2,149$, 51.0% girls) participated in the second measurement wave, which was held two and a half years after T1. Mean age at the second wave was 13.56 ($SD = 0.53$).

Well-trained interviewers visited one of the parents (preferably the mother, 95.6%) at their homes to administer an interview covering a wide range of topics, including the child's developmental history and somatic health, parental psychopathology, and care utilization. The parent was also asked to fill out a questionnaire (the participation rate of parents was 98.1% for the interview and 92.2% for the questionnaire). Children filled out questionnaires at school, in the class, under the supervision of one or more TRAILS assistants. Absent children completed the questionnaires as soon as possible afterwards. Teachers were asked to fill out a brief questionnaire for all TRAILS children in their class (the participation rate of teachers was 86.7%). The measures used in the present study are described more extensively later in this article.

Variables

Truancy (T1 and T2). Truancy was the dependent variable in this study. By truancy we mean that a child was absent one day or more from school without a valid reason and this was reflected in the questions about truancy. To assess information about truancy, children (2 items), parents (1 item), and teachers (1 item) were asked whether, in their view, the child was currently (last six months) playing truant (in Dutch 'spijbelen'). In both waves, children reported truancy most often (T1: 9.2%; T2: 14.6%). The number of teachers who did so was smaller (T1: 4.7%; T2: 9.3%), and the number of parents was the smallest (T1: 1.2%; T2: 2.0%). The answers of teachers and children were associated at T1,

$\chi^2 (1, N = 1903) = 26.87, p < .001$, as well as T2, $\chi^2 (1, N = 1436) = 75.39, p < .001$: 12.4% of the children who said that they played truant were also categorized as such by teachers at T1. This percentage increased to 25.2% at T2. For parents and children, the answers were also associated at T1, $\chi^2 (1, N = 2031) = 12.15, p < .001$, as well as T2, $\chi^2 (1, N = 1889) = 110.60, p < .001$. For parents and teachers the association was at T1, $\chi^2 (1, N = 1770) = 33.91, p < .001$, and at T2, $\chi^2 (1, N = 1306) = 73.20, p < .001$. The range of Cohen's kappa was from .05 to .22. As in many other studies involving different groups of informants, there proved to be little agreement between children, parents, and teachers. Fogelman, Tibbenham, and Lambert (1980) found also low agreement between informants.

We decided to combine the answers of the three informants into single truancy measure. In view of the small number of truants, it seemed inadvisable to us to work with several groups. Moreover, to create a robust outcome measure we decided to focus our analyses on two groups: the children who played truant at T1 and T2 (persistent truants) and children who were non-truants at both waves. This means that the children who played truant only in either elementary or secondary education were excluded from the analyses.

Family background (T1). The TRAILS database contains various variables for socio-economic status: income level, educational level of both the father and the mother, and occupational level of each parent, using the International Standard Classification for Occupations (Ganzeboom & Treiman, 1996). Socio-economic status was measured as the average of the five items (standardized).

The scale captured 61.2% of the variance in the five items, and had an internal consistency of .84. Missing values (e.g., when there was only one parent in the family) did not affect the association of this scale with other variables. The percentage of children who had lived with the same parents from birth to pre-adolescence was 76.6. The 23.4% for whom this was not the case were divided into children who had always lived with a single parent (4.6%), who had experienced a divorce and lived with a single parent since then (10.4%), and who had experienced a divorce and lived with a step-parent (8.6%). We combined these three categories and labeled it 'family breakup.'

Familial vulnerability to externalizing behavior was measured using the Brief TRAILS Family History Interview, administered at the parent interview (Ormel et al., 2005). The parents' self-report scores for substance abuse and antisocial behavior were used to construct the index. For substance abuse and antisocial behavior, parents were assigned to any of the categories 0 = (probably) not, 1 = (probably) yes, and 2 = yes and treatment/medication (substance abuse) or picked up by police (antisocial behavior). The Brief TRAILS Family History Interview yielded lifetime rates that were by and large comparable to those found in studies in which CIDI interviews were employed, with the exception of fathers' rates for substance abuse, which were relatively low (Ormel et al., 2005).

Pubertal development (T1). Stage of pubertal development was assessed in the parent interview using schematic drawings of secondary sex characteristics associated with the five standard Tanner stages of pubertal development (Marshall & Tanner, 1969, 1970). Tanner stages are a widely accepted standard for assessment of pubertal development, and have demonstrated good reliability, validity, and parent–child agreement (Dorn, Susman, Nottelmann, Inoff-Germain, & Chrousos, 1990). A parent (usually the mother) was provided with gender-appropriate sketches, and asked to select which of the sketches 'looked most like the child.' Based on the parent ratings, children were classified into five stages of puberty, in which stage 1 corresponded to infantile and stage 5 to complete puberty (Tanner & Whitehouse, 1982). Boys and girls differed in pubertal stage, $t(2112) = 9.18$, $p < .01$. On average, girls were in a more advanced stage than boys.

Attachment (T1). To measure children's attachment to parents, we used two self-report scales based on Social Production Function (SPF) Theory (Nieboer, Lindenberg, Boomsma, & Van Bruggen, 2005). A five-point scale is used in the SPF list, with answer categories ranging from 1 (never) to 5 (always). Children's attachment to parents was measured using four items per parent, including 'he/ she likes being with me' and 'I can really trust him/her.' As the scores they gave for both parents correlated strongly ($r = .68$), we combined them ($\alpha = .76$). We also used the SPF list to measure children's attachment to teachers ($\alpha = .78$) and classmates ($\alpha = .84$). No test-retest data of the SPF list are available.

Prosocial orientation (T1). As a proxy for children's prosocial orientation we used two items in questions to teachers. These were the items 'takes the interests of other children into account' and 'apologizes when something goes wrong' ($r = .68$).

Self-control (T1). Self-control was assessed using the parent version of the Early Adolescent Temperament Questionnaire-Revised (Ellis, 2002; Putnam, Ellis, & Rothbart, 2001). Self-control as a temperamental trait is the capacity to voluntarily regulate behavior and attention (11 items, $\alpha = .86$). Sample items are 'usually gets started right away on difficult assignments' and 'finds it easy to really concentrate on a problem.' Previous research by Rothbart, Ahadi, Hershey, and Fisher (2001) has indicated that parent reports of these temperament traits in younger children (as indexed with the Children's Behavior Questionnaire) remain fairly stable over a two-year period (with test-retest rs between 0.50 and 0.79), and this seems to indicate that they reflect enduring characteristics in youths (see also Muris & Meesters, 2009).

Analyses

First, differences in individual and family characteristics between persistent and non-truants were investigated using *t*-tests. Second, we tested our hypotheses using multivariate analyses. We used logistic regression to examine the effects of independent variables on persistent truancy, a dichotomous outcome. To interpret the outcomes of the logistic regression we used marginal effects (Borooah, 2001; Liao, 1994). The marginal effect for a dummy variable is the difference between being in category 1 and being in category 0.

Figure 1 Graphical Presentation of the Effects of Self-Control on Social Bonds (path *a*), Social Bonds on Truancy (path *b*), and the Direct Effect (path *c'*) of Self-Control on Truancy. The Total Effect (*c*) of Self-Control on Truancy Is the Sum of the Direct and Indirect Effects: $c = c' + ab$.

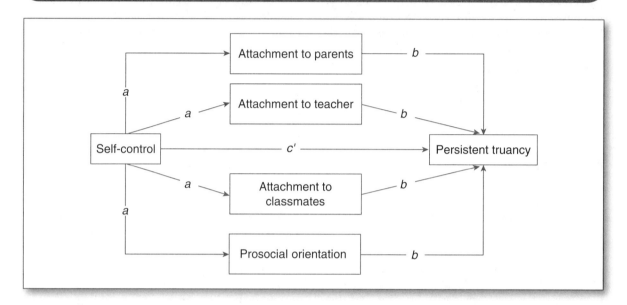

The marginal effect for a continuous variable is the effect of a variable on an outcome with one point of increase in the score of the variable. We started the analyses with a model with background characteristics and self-control. Then, we added the social bonds to the model. The idea behind this order was that on the basis of the theory, we expect self-control to influence a person's ability to form attachments.

To test multiple mediation (Baron & Kenny, 1986), we tested first whether there was a direct effect of self-control on truancy (path *c'* in Figure 1). Furthermore, we tested the effects of self-control on social bonds (path *a* in Figure 1) and social bonds on truancy (path *b* in Figure 1). Finally, we tested whether the effect of self-control was mediated. Mediation occurs if the indirect effect of self-control on truancy through social bonds is significant. To test whether the indirect effect was significant we applied a bootstrap approach (Preacher & Hayes, 2008), which enabled us to calculate the 95% confidence intervals of the indirect effect.

A macro for this procedure was downloaded from the internet (see Hayes, n.d.).

We employed corrected-item-mean (CIM) imputation to handle missing data at the item level (Huisman, 2000). At the scale level we performed multiple imputation using the MICE method of multivariate imputation (Allison, 2002; Royston, 2004). It is assumed in these procedures that the data are missing at random. As a result of the imputations, we were able to use all cases in our analyses.

Results

Prevalence and Development of Truancy

Truancy is more common in early adolescence (T2, average age of 13.5) than in childhood (T1, average age of 11). The combined children's, parents', and teachers' reports put the percentage of truants in the first wave (T1) at 12.8%. The second wave (T2) was after the transition to secondary education, and the prevalence of truancy was then 19.4%. There is a significant increase in prevalence between the waves, $t(2146) = 6.60, p < .001$.

Truancy at T1 and T2 are not independent of each other, $\chi^2 (1, N = 2147) = 83.71, p < .001$: 72.9% never played truant (non-truants) up to the start of secondary education. The group that played truant at both times (persistent truants) was 5.1%. The remaining 22% of the children played truant at T1 (7.7%), or T2 (14.3%). We excluded these children from further analyses, because we wanted to focus on differences between non-truants and persistent truants.

Descriptives of the Predictors

Table 1 contains means and standard deviation of all predictors. Because SES was based on a standardized

score, the mean is close to 0. Familial vulnerability to externalizing deviant behavior was highly skewed to the right, with a mean of 0.14 and a maximum of 4.32. All other means represent mean item scores with a range of 1 to 5. Correlations between the predictors are weak or moderate (available upon request). The highest correlations are between attachment to parents, teachers, and classmates. These correlations range from .35 to .39.

Univariate Differences Between Persistent and Non-truants

We examined the extent to which persistent truants and non-truants differed in individual and family background. The variables found in the literature to affect truancy also did so in this study. Table 1 shows that boys are overrepresented among persistent truants and

Table 1 Individual and Family Background of Persistent and Nontruants: Means (and standard deviation) or Percentages

Variable	Persistent truants (*N* = 109)	Non-truants (*N* = 1566)	Differences between categories
Sex (1 = boy)	60.6%	46.7%	$\chi^2 (1, N = 1675) = 7.79**$
SES	−0.36 (1.04)	0.09 (0.96)	$t(1653) = -4.64**$
Family vulnerability to externalizing behavior	0.29 (0.58)	0.12 (0.38)	$t(1639) = 4.34**$
Family breakup	51.4%	19.2%	$\chi^2 (1, N = 1675) = 62.83**$
Pubertal development	2.10 (0.87)	1.84 (0.74)	$t(1603) = 3.35**$
Self-control	2.95 (0.68)	3.26 (0.68)	$t(1515) = -4.30**$
Attachment to parents	4.06 (0.75)	4.34 (0.61)	$t(1642) = -4.38**$
Attachment to teacher	3.45 (0.95)	3.89 (0.75)	$t(1639) = -5.66**$
Attachment to classmates	3.39 (0.91)	3.50 (0.80)	$t(1637) = -1.34$
Prosocial orientation	3.15 (0.84)	3.56 (0.77)	$t(1447) = -4.82**$

Note. All independent variables were measured at T1.

$**p < 0.01$.

underrepresented among non-truants. It can also be seen that the parents of non-truants on average had a significantly higher SES than the parents of persistent truants. The parents of non-truants were significantly less vulnerable to externalizing behavior than the parents of persistent truants. A family breakup had occurred in the families of more than half of the persistent truants. For non-truants, the level of family breakup was 19.2%. Compared to non-truants, persistent truants were more advanced in their pubertal development.

As hypothesized, the non-truants scored higher on self-control than the persistent truants. The hypotheses about the relation of attachment to truancy are also borne out in the univariate analyses. The non-truants were more attached to their parents and teachers than the persistent truants. As expected, we found no group differences for attachment to classmates. Our results about prosocial orientation were also in line with our hypothesis. The nontruants had a higher prosocial orientation than the persistent truants.

Multinomial Logistic Regression Analysis

We wanted to know whether the hypothesized effects would remain in a multivariate analysis and whether the effect of self-control is indeed mediated by social bonds. Using logistic regression on persistent truancy, we first estimated a model, using sex, SES, familial vulnerability to externalizing behavior, family breakup, pubertal development, and self-control. Table 2 represents the marginal effects of the logistic regression. The standard error is indicated between brackets in each case. Only familial vulnerability to externalizing deviant behavior was not significantly related to persistent truancy in the multivariate analysis. The baseline level of persistent truancy was 4.8% (calculated for girls with average scores on the four continuous variables and coming from intact families). Boys scored 3.2 per cent higher on persistent truancy. Thus, their prediction of truancy was 8.0%. Children who scored one standard deviation above the mean on SES were 1.2% less likely to be a persistent truant. Children from broken families scored 7.8% higher on persistent truancy.

Children with high self-control (+1 SD) were 1.2% less likely to be a persistent truant, whereas children with high pubertal development (+1 SD) were 1.4% more likely to be a persistent truant.

In the second model we added the four social bonds characteristics. Table 2 shows that attachment to parents as well as to teachers is related to persistent truancy, in line with hypotheses 1 and 2. Again, attachment to classmates had no effect on truancy. Children with a lower prosocial orientation were more likely to be persistent truants.

With regard to the mediation hypothesis, see Figure 2, it is important to note that self-control was directly related to truancy ($b = -.25, t = -2.33, p = .02$). There are also direct associations between self-control and social bonds: self-control was positively associated with attachment to parents ($b = .08, t = 3.26, p < .01$), attachment to teachers ($b = .07, t = 2.40, p = .02$), and prosocial orientation ($b = .15, t = 5.32, p < .01$). Attachment to classmates was excluded from the mediation analysis, because it was unrelated to truancy. As can be seen in the second model and consistent with hypothesis 4, self-control was no longer related to persistent truancy when social bonds were taken into account ($b = -.17, t = -1.46, p = .14$). The reduction of the association between self-control and truancy after including attachment was statistically significant. Bootstrapping showed that the indirect effect of self-control through social bonds was significant ($ab = -.08$; CI 95% between -0.04 and -0.14). In summary, our multivariate findings are in line with the attachment hypotheses, the prosocial orientation hypothesis and the mediation hypothesis concerning the effect of self-control on truancy.

Extra Analyses

To determine how sensitive our outcomes were to the categorization of truancy, we performed analyses with a categorization of truancy based on the self-reports of children only: 79.1% of the children were non-truant and 3.7% were persistent truants. Most of our findings were the same, but there was a difference. Attachment to classmates had a significantly positive effect on persistent truancy in these extra analyses.

Table 2 Logistic Regression on Truancy (N = 1675)

Variable	Model 1 Marginal effect (SE)		Model 2 Marginal effect (SE)	
Baseline level	4.8%		4.2%	
Sex (1 = boy)	3.2%	(1.0)**	2.1%	(0.9)*
SES	−1.2%	(0.5)*	−0.9%	(0.5)
Family vulnerability to externalizing behavior	0.1%	(0.4)	0.2%	(0.3)
Family breakup	7.8%	(2.0)**	6.9%	(1.8)**
Pubertal development	1.4%	(0.5)**	1.2%	(0.4)**
Self-control	−1.2%	(0.5)*	−0.7%	(0.5)
Attachment to parents			−1.0%	(0.4)**
Attachment to teacher			−1.6%	(0.4)**
Attachment to classmates			0.7%	(0.5)
Prosocial orientation			−1.0%	(0.5)*

$N = 1675$; **$p < .01$; *$p < .05$.

Figure 2 Graphical Presentation of the Unstandardized Effects of Self-Control on Social Bonds (path a), Social Bonds on Truancy (path b), Effect (path c') of Self-Control on Truancy. The Total Effect of Self-Control on Truancy Is −.25.

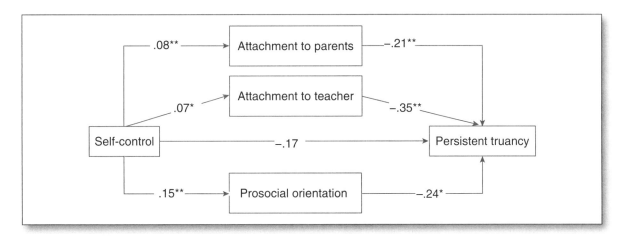

◈ Discussion

Our aim was to gain a better understanding of truancy at a relatively early age, and to investigate to what extent such risk behavior can be predicted by a goal-framing theory that combines social control (Hirschi, 1969) and self-control (Gottfredson & Hirschi, 1990) theories in the light of insights from cognitive psychology. Goal-framing theory takes self-regulation as the central mechanism of self-control and it emphasizes the important role of attachment to significant others for self-regulation. Indeed, the expectations generated by this theory were strongly supported by the data, but first, we turn to the prevalence of truancy.

At the end of elementary education, 13% of children were reported to be occasional truants by at least one informant. Two and a half years later, 19% of the participants were reported to be truants. These percentages are comparable to those for 8th and 10th graders in the USA (Henry, 2007). On the basis of numerous studies, we expect that truancy at the next TRAILS measurement wave (which will take place when the participants have reached the age of 16) will be prevalent among a considerably greater share of pupils (Farrington, 1980; Fergusson et al., 1995). Fergusson, Lynskey, and Horwood (1995) observe that the percentage of truants grows exponentially in the course of the secondary school period, and they draw a parallel with drug use, juvenile delinquency, and mental health issues.

Reports of truancy by children were supported by parents and teachers only to a small degree. This finding is in agreement with the findings of other studies involving different groups of informants (Farrington, 1980; Fergusson et al., 1995; Fogelman et al., 1980). Furthermore, Farrington (1980) found a strong indication that truancy in elementary education in a London low-SES neighborhood is followed by truancy in secondary education to an above-average degree. This supposition is consistent with our Dutch data with virtually the same percentages. Two-fifths of children who were reported to be truants in elementary education were again reported to be truants at a more advanced age. Of those children who did not engage in truancy initially, only one-sixth commenced to do so subsequently (see for similar percentages

Robins & Ratcliff, 1980). Five per cent of our sample were persistent truants.

Boys were more often persistent truants than girls. From this we may deduce that early truancy, like early antisocial behavior (Veenstra et al., 2008), is especially prevalent among boys. Children whose onset of physical puberty had commenced to a lesser degree, who came from intact families, and who had high-SES parents would more likely be non-truants. Relatively more children with disadvantaged family backgrounds were found among truants (see also Henry, 2007). Thus, background characteristics such as sex and family composition remained important predictors of whether children were persistent or non-truants. In their study of absenteeism in elementary education, Fergusson, Horwood, and Shannon (1986) arrived at a similar finding. Independent of several health indicators, children with disadvantaged social backgrounds proved to fall into the high-absence group to an above-average degree.

The explanation of truancy by a goal-framing approach led to quite specific hypotheses. The most important expectations were that attachment to people per se would not have an influence on truancy and that the effect of self-control would be mediated by attachment to significant others regarding truancy. Both expectations help to integrate the social control theory and the self-control theory. In order to aid in self-regulating school attendance, children would only be helped by attachment to those significant others whose goals support school attendance and disavow truancy. This can be said of parents and teachers but not of classmates (Croninger & Lee, 2001; Crosnoe et al., 2004; Jenkins, 1995; Lee & Burkam, 2003; McNeal, 1999). The latter are likely to have various opinions on truancy, for or against or neutral. The results clearly supported our expectation on attachment.

Our expectation on mediation was based on the idea that self-control would help to establish attachments to significant others rather than aid in self-regulation for conforming to social norms. This implies that the influence of self-control on truancy would be mediated by attachment to parents and teachers. The findings of this study were in line with this expectation. The results also supported the auxiliary hypothesis about prosocial orientation. Being socially oriented means that children take the interest of others into account and thus would be better aware of what is expected of them, which, in turn, increases their self-regulatory capacity.

We argue that self-control affects social bonds, which then impact upon truancy behavior. Although this is a reasonable sequence of events, it is also possible that social bonds affect self-control, which then has an impact on truancy. This alternative sequence is suggested by Finkenauer, Engels, and Baumeister (2005). Future research using longitudinal data on self-control and social control may want to contrast these two possible models. Of course, both sequences may operate simultaneously.

In general, the impact of social bonds with significant others representing the goal to go to school suggests that early truancy can partly be prevented or combated by focusing on children's relations with parents at home or with teachers at school. The development of prosocial orientation also appears to play a role. This leads to the question of how social bonds can be reinforced or restored. The results suggest that parents and teachers should be supportive of children (including high-risk children: Veenstra, Lindenberg, Verhulst, & Ormel, 2009) in order to gain their attachment. At the same time, parents and teachers should send out clear signals of their norms against truancy and their goals concerning school attendance (compare McCluskey, Bynum, & Patchin, 2004; Stamm, 2006). In order to do this, they should know about children's attendance and discuss their absences from school (see also Sentse, Dijkstra, Lindenberg, Ormel, & Veenstra, 2010). The teachers would thereby also send out signals that they care about absenteeism (compare Fallis & Opotow, 2003). In the American 'Check & Connect' program (Anderson, Christenson, Sinclair, & Lehr, 2004), high-frequency truants in elementary schools were supervised once a week over a period of two years by so-called monitors: professionals who closely monitored the pupils' behavior and focused on establishing positive relations between pupil, family, and school. The aim of the program was to re-instill in these pupils an awareness of the overriding importance of education. Anderson and her colleagues particularly investigated the possible effects of good relations between the monitor and the child on the child's involvement in school (attendance, achievements, and well-being). In

line with our theory about attachment and self-regulation, they found that, having taken into account a variety of factors, the perception of the relation's quality appeared to be associated with reduced school absenteeism and more positive teacher assessments of the pupil's involvement. In addition, a recent study on truancy of 14-year-olds showed that schools can have an impact on truancy levels by imposing clear demands on their pupils in combination with a caring and warm school environment (Claes, Hooghe, & Reeskens, 2009).

This study was based on a major survey involving over 2000 boys and girls and combined information from pre-adolescence and early adolescence (the transition from elementary to secondary education). Truancy is relatively hard to measure, like other rule-violating behavior that may evoke sanctions once it has been admitted. For this reason, it is an advantage that in both waves children, parents, and teachers were asked to indicate whether truancy occurred. Virtually all previous studies were based on a single informant (self-reports) or school registrations. Furthermore, we used a stringent criterion for categorizing participants as truants (we regarded a child as truant when a child was seen as truant in late elementary and in early secondary education). A limitation is that we have no information on the construct validity of our truancy measure. Future studies may want to link a truancy measure to outside criteria, such as archival school records and children's daily diaries. However, we could demonstrate that our truancy measure is related to other constructs, such as social bonds, in a meaningful and predicted way, thus bolstering its concurrent validity. Furthermore, our findings only generalize to persistent truants and not to occasional truants. Children who played truant in only elementary or secondary education were excluded from our analyses. Future research that also uses school records and children's daily diaries may be able to look at these occasional truants as well. Finally, the present findings are based on a Dutch sample and further cross-validation using samples from other countries is warranted.

In addition, it is of course wasteful to throw out all pupils who played truant at only one time point. An alternative idea to retain all the available data would be to model truancy on two different levels using multilevel modeling, with six observations, referring to two time points with three raters nested within individuals. The intercept on the individual level would then be modeled as a probability that a given rater at a given time point describes the target person as truant. An advantage of this method is that multilevel modeling would give a direct estimate of the reliability of this intercept. On Level 1, it would then be possible to include time (a dummy variable with a value of zero for T1 and one for T2 would make it possible to test whether truancy increases across time) and raters (e.g., using the teacher estimates as a reference group) as covariates. On Level 2, it would be possible to conduct the analyses that were the focus of the present study. It would be interesting to see the results of such a multilevel model in future research.

Despite these limitations, TRAILS holds unique opportunities for long-term monitoring of the behavior and the position of children involved in truancy. At the next measurement wave, our respondents will be in the final stages of their secondary education careers, and they will be questioned in detail on their truancy (including counts of absences). It will then also be possible to examine the long-term outcomes of early truancy.

Finally, our findings show that children from disadvantaged social backgrounds (in particular family breakup) and with inadequate social bonds (lack of attachment to parents and teachers) and a low prosocial orientation are at greater risk of early truancy. Bearing in mind that such pupils also often show weak achievements and many kinds of deviant behavior, we conclude that those pupils who are in need of most attention are also the ones with the lowest attendance rates at school, which makes attention to truancy an important challenge for research and a central instrument of social intervention.

◈ References

Allison, P. D. (2002). *Missing data.* Thousand Oaks, CA: Sage.

Anderson, A. R., Christenson, S. L., Sinclair, M. F., & Lehr, C. A. (2004). Check & Connect: The importance of relationships for promoting engagement with school. *Journal of School Psychology, 42,* 95–113.

Baldwin, M. W., Carrell, S. E., & Lopez, D. F. (1990). Priming relationship schemas: My advisor and the pope are watching me from the back of my mind. *Journal of Experimental Social Psychology, 26,* 435–454.

Baldwin, M. W., & Holmes, J. G. (1987). Salient private audiences and awareness of the self. *Journal of Personality and Social Psychology, 52,* 1087–1098.

Baron, R. M., & Kenny, D. A. (1986). The moderator-mediator variable distinction in social psychological research: Conceptual, strategic, and statistical considerations. *Journal of Personality and Social Psychology, 51,* 1173–1182.

Borooah, V. K. (2001). *Logit and probit. Ordered and multinomial models.* Thousand Oaks, CA: Sage.

Claes, E., Hooghe, M., & Reeskens, T. (2009). Truancy as a contextual and school-related problem: A comparative multilevel analysis of country and school characteristics on civic knowledge among 14 year olds. *Educational Studies, 35,* 123–142.

Croninger, R. G., & Lee, V. E. (2001). Social capital and dropping out of high school: Benefits to at-risk students of teachers' support and guidance. *Teachers College Record, 103,* 548–581.

Crosnoe, R., Kirkpatrick Johnson, M., & Elder, G. (2004). Intergenerational bonding in school: The behavioral and contextual correlates of student–teacher relationships. *Sociology of Education, 77,* 60–81.

De Winter, A. F., Oldehinkel, A. J., Veenstra, R., Brunnekreef, J. A., Verhulst, F. C., & Ormel, J. (2005). Evaluation of non-response bias in mental health determinants and outcomes in a large sample of pre-adolescents. *European Journal of Epidemiology, 20,* 173–181.

Dorn, L. D., Susman, E. J., Nottelmann, E. D., Inoff-Germain, G., & Chrousos, G. P. (1990). Perceptions of puberty: Adolescent, parent, and health care personnel. *Developmental Psychology, 26,* 322–329.

Eisenberg, N., Michalik, N., Spinrad, T. L., Hofer, C., Kupfer, A., Valiente, C., et al. (2007). The relations of effortful control and impulsivity to children's sympathy: A longitudinal study. *Cognitive Development, 22,* 544–567.

Ellis, L. K. (2002). *Individual differences and adolescent psychosocial development.* PhD dissertation, Department of Psychology, University of Oregon, Eugene.

Fallis, R. K., & Opotow, S. (2003). Are students failing school or are schools failing students? Class cutting in high school. *Journal of Social Issues, 59,* 103–119.

Farrington, D. P. (1980). Truancy, delinquency, the home, and the school. In L. Hersov & I. Berg (Eds.), *Out of school: Modern perspectives in truancy and school refusal* (pp. 49–63). Chichester: Wiley.

Fergusson, D. M., Horwood, L. J., & Shannon, F. T. (1986). Absenteeism among primary school children. *New Zealand Journal of Educational Studies, 21,* 3–12.

Fergusson, D. M., Lynskey, M. T., & Horwood, L. J. (1995). Truancy in adolescence. *New Zealand Journal of Educational Studies, 30,* 25–38.

Finkenauer, C., Engels, R. C. M. E., & Baumeister, R. F. (2005). Parenting behaviour and adolescent behavioural and emotional problems: The role of self-control. *International Journal of Behavioral Development, 29,* 58–69.

Fogelman, K., Tibbenham, A., & Lambert, L. (1980). Absence from school: Findings from the National Child Development Study. In L. Hersov & I. Berg (Eds.), *Out of school: Modern perspectives in truancy and school refusal* (pp. 25–48). Chichester: Wiley.

Ganzeboom, H. B. G., & Treiman, D. J. (1996). Internationally comparable measures of occupational status for the 1988 International Standard Classification of Occupations. *Social Science Research, 25,* 201–239.

Gottfredson, M. R., & Hirschi, T. (1990). *A general theory of crime.* Stanford, CA: Stanford University Press.

Hayes, A. F. (n.d.) Personal website, macros, URL (accessed 1 June 2009): http://www.comm.ohio-state.edu/ahayes

Henry, B., Caspi, A., Moffitt, T. E., Harrington, H., & Silva, P. A. (1999). Staying in school protects boys with poor self-regulation in childhood from later crime: A longitudinal study. *International Journal of Behavioral Development, 23,* 1049–1073.

Henry, K. L. (2007). Who's skipping school: Characteristics of truants in 8th and 10th grade. *Journal of School Health, 77,* 29–35.

Hirschi, T. (1969). *Causes of delinquency.* Berkeley: University of California Press.

Hirschi, T. (2004). Self-control and crime. In R. F. Baumeister & K. D. Vohs (Eds.), *Handbook of self-regulation: Research, theory, and applications* (pp. 537–552). New York: Guilford.

Huisman, M. (2000). Imputation of missing item responses: Some simple techniques. *Quality and Quantity, 34,* 331–351.

Jenkins, P. H. (1995). School delinquency and school commitment. *Sociology of Education, 68,* 221–239.

Kearney, C. A. (2008). School absenteeism and school refusal behavior in youth: A contemporary review. *Clinical Psychology Review, 28,* 451–471.

Lee, V. E., & Burkam, D. T. (2003). Dropping out of high school: The role of school organization and structure. *American Educational Research Journal, 40,* 353–393.

Liao, T. F. (1994). *Interpreting probability models: Logit, probit, and other generalized linear models.* Thousand Oaks, CA: Sage.

Lindenberg, S. (2008). Social rationality, semi-modularity and goal-framing: What is it all about? *Analyse & Kritik, 30,* 229–247.

Lindenberg, S. (forthcoming). Social rationality and well-being. In R. Wittek, T. A. B. Snijders, & V. Nee (Eds.), *Handbook of rational choice social research.* New York: Russell Sage Foundation.

Marshall, W. A., & Tanner, J. M. (1969). Variations in pattern of pubertal changes in girls. *Archives of Disease in Childhood, 44,* 291–303.

Marshall, W. A., & Tanner, J. M. (1970). Variations in pattern of pubertal changes in boys. *Archives of Disease in Childhood, 45,* 13–23.

Matsueda, R. L., & Heimer, K. (1987). Race, family structure, and delinquency: A test of differential association and social control theories. *American Sociological Review, 52,* 826–849.

McCluskey, C. P., Bynum, T. S., & Patchin, J. W. (2004). Reducing chronic absenteeism: An assessment of an early truancy initiative. *Crime & Delinquency, 50,* 214–234.

McNeal, R. B. (1999). Parental involvement as social capital: Differential effectiveness on science achievement, truancy, and dropping out. *Social Forces, 78,* 117–144.

Muris, P., & Meesters, C. (2009). Reactive and regulative temperament in youths: Psychometric evaluation of the Early Adolescent Temperament Questionnaire–Revised. *Journal of Psychopathology and Behavioral Assessment, 31,* 7–19.

Nieboer, A., Lindenberg, S., Boomsma, A., & Van Bruggen, A. C. (2005). Dimensions of well-being and their measurement: the SPF-IL scale. *Social Indicators Research, 73,* 1–45.

Ormel, J., Oldehinkel, A. J., Ferdinand, R. F., Hartman, C. A., De Winter, A. F., Veenstra, R., et al. (2005). Internalizing and externalizing problems in adolescence: General and dimension-specific effects of familial loadings and preadolescent temperament traits. *Psychological Medicine, 35,* 1825–1835.

Preacher, K. J., & Hayes, A. F. (2008). Asymptotic and resampling strategies for assessing and comparing indirect effects in multiple mediator models. *Behavior Research Methods, 40,* 879–891.

Putnam, S. P., Ellis, L. K., & Rothbart, M. K. (2001). The structure of temperament from infancy through adolescence. In A. Eliasz & A. Angleitner (Eds.), *Advances/proceedings in research on temperament* (pp. 165–182). Germany: Pabst Scientist Publisher.

Robins, L. N., & Ratcliff, K. S. (1980). The long-term outcome of truancy. In L. Hersov & I. Berg (Eds.), *Out of school: Modern perspectives in truancy and school refusal* (pp. 65–83). Chichester: Wiley.

Rothbart, M. K., Ahadi, S. A., Hershey, K. L., & Fisher, P. (2001). Investigations of temperament at three to seven years: The Children's Behavior Questionnaire. *Child Development, 72,* 1394–1408.

Royston, P. (2004). Multiple imputation of missing values. *Stata Journal, 4,* 227–241.

Sampson, R. J., & Laub, J. H. (1993). *Crime in the making. Pathways and turning points through life.* Cambridge, MA: Harvard University Press.

Schwartz, S. H. (1977). Normative influences on altruism. In L. Berkowitz (Ed.), *Advances in experimental social psychology, 10* (pp. 221–279). New York: Academic.

Seeley, E. A., & Gardner, W. L. (2003). The 'selfless' and self-regulation: The role of chronic other-orientation in averting self-regulatory depletion. *Self and Identity, 2,* 103–117.

Sentse, M., Dijkstra, J. K., Lindenberg, S., Ormel, J., & Veenstra, R. (2010). The delicate balance between parental protection, unsupervised wandering, and adolescents' autonomy and its relation with antisocial behavior. The TRAILS study. *International Journal of Behavioral Development, 34*(2), 159–167.

Shah, J. (2003a). Automatic for the people: How representations of significant others implicitly affect goal pursuit. *Journal of Personality and Social Psychology, 84,* 661–681.

Shah, J. (2003b). The motivational looking glass: How significant others implicitly affect goal appraisals. *Journal of Personality and Social Psychology, 85,* 424–439.

Stamm, M. (2006). Schulabstentismus: Anmerkungen zu Theorie und Empirie einer vermeintlichen Randerscheinung schulischer Bildung [School absenteeism: Remarks on the theory and empirical study of a supposedly marginal phenomenon of schooling]. *Zeitschrift fur Padagogik, 52,* 285–302.

Sweeten, G., Bushway, S. D., & Paternoster, R. (2009). Does dropping out of school mean dropping into delinquency? *Criminology, 47,* 47–92.

Tanner, J. M., & Whitehouse, R. H. (1982). *Atlas of children's growth: Normal variation and growth disorders.* London and New York: Academic.

Taylor, C. (2001). The relationship between social and self-control: Tracing Hirschi's criminological career. *Theoretical Criminology, 5,* 369–388.

Veenstra, R., Lindenberg, S., Oldehinkel, A. J., De Winter, A. F., Verhulst, F. C., & Ormel, J. (2008). Prosocial and antisocial behavior in preadolescence: Teachers' and parents' perceptions of the behavior

of girls and boys. *International Journal of Behavioral Development, 32,* 243–251.

Veenstra, R., Lindenberg, S., Verhulst, F. C., & Ormel, J. (2009). Childhood-limited versus persistent antisocial behavior: Why do some recover and others do not? *Journal of Early Adolescence, 29,* 718–742.

Wagner, M., Dunkake, I., & Weiss, B. (2004). Schulverweigerung. Empirische Analysen zum abweichenden Verhalten von Schülern [Truancy. An empirical analysis of the deviant behavior of pupils]. *Kölner Zeitschrift für Soziologie und Sozialpsychologie, 56,* 457–489.

READING 22

It is rare that theories of deviance make their way into marketing journals, but researchers from the Warwick Business School did exactly that in this article focused on illegal Internet "misbehavior" and the techniques of neutralization that enable primarily conventional individuals to engage in this type of deviant behavior. Sykes and Matza began with five neutralizations: denial of responsibility, denial of injury, denial of the victim, condemnation of the condemners, and an appeal to higher loyalties. Others have unearthed such neutralization techniques as defense of necessity, claim to normalcy, and denial of negative intent, among others. These researchers interviewed a convenience sample of 54 informants who had engaged in illegal "peer-to-peer" downloading of CDs, DVDs, video games, or other software in the 2 weeks prior to the interview. The researchers found that these criminals used at least one and often several neutralizations, including denial of injury, claim of normalcy, claim of relative acceptability, appeal to higher loyalties, and denial of responsibility. We are sure the reader can imagine the types of neutralizations these offenders use; you may have used some yourself and will enjoy reading about them. Perhaps more interesting, the researchers find that some techniques are typically established prior to the act (perhaps indicative of a causal relationship) as well as after the fact (e.g., to neutralize guilt). Also interesting was that more than half (61%) were against legal and free downloading, which they believed would crush the entertainment industry as creators would not be compensated. Further and consistent with Sykes and Matza, these deviants appear to understand that many consider their activities deviant, immoral, and illegal, but they believe the drift from conventional society can be justified in their cases.

Source: Harris, Lloyd C., and Alexia Dumas. 2009. "Online Consumer Misbehaviour: An Application of Neutralization Theory." *Marketing Theory* 9:379–402. Reprinted with permission.

Online Consumer Misbehaviour: An Application of Neutralization Theory

Lloyd C. Harris and Alexia Dumas

Introduction

In recent years researchers have uncovered a range of diverse behaviors by consumers which disrupt otherwise functional exchange (see for example Withiam, 1998; Fullerton and Punj, 2004; Harris and Reynolds, 2004; Harris and Reynolds, 2006; Harris 2008a). However, at the end of the 1990s, concordant with rapidly growing consumer internet use, a new type of consumer misbehaviour emerged. In 1999, Napster, the pioneer network of illegal downloading, was created and online digital piracy was popularized. Despite its closure two years later, peer-to-peer networks did not disappear; on the contrary they flourished. Neither a reinforcement of copyright, nor strengthened laws, nor the launch of online purchasing of digital media appeared able to prevent these illegal activities from becoming common practice. Indeed, the internet has become ever more convenient and user-friendly, making digital piracy easily available to consumers. Whether peer-to-peer activities involve copying music, movies, software or video games, the phenomenon affects the entertainment sector as a whole and costs the industry billions of pounds each year.

While a number of studies have explored online customer misbehaviour, typically focusing on a particular type of activity (see Hinduja, 2007), to date, broader theories regarding deviant human behaviour, such as neutralization theory (Sykes and Matza, 1957) have been neglected (see Cohn and Vaccaro, 2006; Hinduja, 2007). Sykes and Matza (1957) uncover five 'techniques of neutralization' which individuals employ to justify or rationalize their deviant behaviours. The application of the theory within criminology and broader sociology has subsequently extended these techniques and found strong support for cognitive deviance-neutralization as a justification or rationalization mechanism (e.g. Cromwell and Thurman, 2003; Fritsche, 2005). In customer-focused studies, neutralization theory has been somewhat neglected, with the notable exceptions of a small number of insightful treatises into neutralization techniques and shoplifting (Strutton et al., 1994), consumer fraud (Rosenbaum and Kuntze, 2003), and generational differences (Strutton et al., 1997), all within offline retailing. This leads both Cohn and Vaccaro (2006) and Hinduja (2007) to argue that neutralization theory provides an insightful but neglected perspective from which to explore online consumer deviance and peerto- peer deviance in particular.

The aim of this paper is to explore the extent to which peer-to-peer users employ techniques of neutralization to justify prior-to behaviour or rationalize their activities post behaviour. A particular emphasis is placed on the need to generate insights into the timing of neutralizations (that is, pre- or post-event) and in this way respond to the many studies that have called for more research into the sequencing of neutralization processes (e.g. Cromwell and Thurman, 2003; Maruna and Copes, 2005). This study is also intended to provide a better understanding of a phenomenon which increasingly troubles the entertainment industry, and can be viewed as a response to the calls by a number of researchers for more research into online consumers' neutralization practices (see Cohn and Vaccaro, 2006; Hinduja, 2007). Indeed, digital piracy, more than any other dysfunctional consumer behaviour, has significantly impacted on companies' business models.

This paper is structured in the following way. First, a review of online customer misbehaviour is provided, followed by an overview of existing research into the techniques of neutralization. Following a discussion of the research methods employed, findings regarding the peer-to-peer online misbehaviours and neutralization techniques are presented. The paper concludes with a series of implications for both theory and practice.

◈ Online Consumer Misbehaviour

Freestone and Mitchell (2004: 126) claim that the internet is the 'new environment for unethical behaviour'. Similarly to offline customers, who misbehave in a wide variety of ways (see Harris and Reynolds, 2003), online misbehaviours vary from digital piracy to fraud. These and other behaviours cost some industries billions of dollars in lost sales every year. For instance, in the music industry, the Recording Industry Association of America (RIAA) states 'global music piracy causes $12.5 billion of economic losses every year', while the Motion Picture Association of America (MPAA) declares: 'the worldwide motion picture industry [...] lost $18.2 billion in 2005 as a result of piracy'.

There are various types of online customer misbehaviour. Chatzidakis and Mitussis (2007: 306) state: 'Internet enables the proliferation of various ethically questionable consumer activities.' With the development of the internet, new kinds of dysfunctional consumer behaviour appear, taking advantage of this new technology: 'Love bug', a virus sent in May 2000 via an e-mail entitled 'I love you' and which infected tens of millions of computers (Foremski and Kehoe, 2000), software piracy, fraud (including Nigerian email fraud, cheque fraud, investment fraud, confidence fraud, auction fraud, non-delivery and credit/debit card fraud– see Mazur, 2007); piracy, illegal forms of pornography, cyber stalking, online pharmacies, organ sales and identity theft (Freestone and Mitchell, 2004). Indeed, in 2006, there were 207,492 internet crimes (or e-crimes) reported (Mazur, 2007).Simpson (2006: 14) defines 'e-crimes' as covering

many different areas, including phasing, hacking, extortion, denial of service attacks, advanced fee fraud, money laundering; virus writing, distributing malicious code, boot-herding, grooming, distributing pedophile material, internet abuse in the work place, intellectual property theft, online piracy of copyright material, and spamming.

Freestone and Mitchell (2004) suggest a complete typology of deviant internet behaviour regarding five main activities. First are *illegal activities* such as using credit card numbers discovered on the internet or a stolen credit card; downloading child pornography; spreading viruses; selling counterfeit goods over the internet; or sending malicious e-mail, to name but a few (Freestone and Mitchell, 2004). Second are *questionable activities* which are not necessarily illegal and are usually victimless (for example purchasing potentially offensive products over the internet; online gambling; or accessing distasteful websites). Third are illegal hacking related activities such as changing hardware or software products. Fourth are *human internet trading activities* such as purchasing human organs. Finally is the issue of downloading material. This is related to the downloading of movies, music, games or software from the internet for free. These activities are found to be extremely common among young internet users and not necessarily perceived as being unethical.

It is the final category of online customer misbehaviour that is the focus of the current paper. Whether it is software piracy, also named 'softlifting' (for example Logsdon et al., 1994; Simpson et al., 1994; Gupta et al., 2004; Goles et al., 2008); peer-to-peer (P2P) file-sharing or music piracy (Gopal et al., 2004; Levin et al., 2004; Chiou et al., 2005; Chen et al., 2008); or digital piracy in general (Al-Rafee and Cronan, 2006; Hill, 2007; Cronan and Al-Rafee, 2008), this type of crime has been found to be widespread and, arguably, endemic to the internet.

In an effort to explore the reasons for the prevalence of these activities, researchers have generated some insights into the drivers of illegal downloading. Ingram and Hinduja (2008) determine that illegal downloaders are likely to be males, under 21 and white. Group influence, especially through online communities, is also significant (see for example Chiou et al., 2005; Sandulli, 2007). Such studies argue that peer groups may affect consumer behaviour on the internet even more than any other consumer behaviours, since the internet enables individuals easily to contact each other and renders the creation of communities easier.

Chatzidakis and Mitussis (2007) highlight the importance of the internet's scope on unethical internet behaviour. Not only does the internet permit the accomplishment of deviant consumer behaviour anonymously but it also makes it more difficult to identify unethical activities. First, individuals can remain 'faceless'. This makes the choice to engage in aberrant internet behaviour easier (Freestone and Mitchell, 2004; Rombel, 2004), while the impersonal side of the internet alleviates the guilt created by misconduct (Logsdon et al., 1994). This theory is also supported by the work of Reynolds and Harris (2005: 328), in which one of the informants declares: 'there is no face-to-face contact so you don't feel guilty ... it definitely gives me more nerve'. Second, since individuals remain anonymous, deviant internet behaviours are difficult to detect and are more likely to go unpunished (Freestone and Mitchell, 2004; Chiou et al., 2005; Al-Rafee and Cronan, 2006). As Albers-Miller (1999: 275) highlights, 'when there is a lack of fear of punishment, people do engage in inappropriate behaviour'.

The ability to use virtual persona influences unethical internet behaviour all the more (Freestone and Mitchell, 2004). The internet's reproducibility makes deviant internet activities even more attractive. It is convenient (Sandulli, 2007) and permits the reproduction of CDs, software or DVDs very cheaply. In the case of music piracy for instance, illegally downloading enables individuals both to save money (Gopal et al., 2004; Cronan and Al-Rafee, 2008) and to end up with a 'burned' CD of virtually the same quality as a copyrighted CD (Sherman, 2000; Bhattacharjee et al., 2003).

In some regards, the internet offers an unprecedented opportunity to engage in aberrant behaviour. Ease of

engaging (Gupta et al., 2004), ease of use (Sherman, 2000), access (Levin et al., 2004), flexibility (Sandulli, 2007), situational events (Simpson et al., 1994), internet speed and proficiency (Bhattacharjee et al., 2003; Levin et al., 2004; Rombel, 2004; Cronan and Al-Rafee, 2008; Ingram and Hinduja, 2008), the possibility to customize CDs or discover new talents (Gopal et al., 2004; Sandulli, 2007) are some of the reasons affecting internet users' behaviour.

Numerous studies suggest that some consumers believe that illegal downloading is ethically acceptable. Vitell and Muncy's (1992) study reveals that 46% of the 569 US heads of households interviewed believe that it is not wrong to record an album instead of buying it. Among the 71 informants of Fukukawa's (2002) research, 58% think that copying computer software or using unauthorized software is acceptable and 32% actively softlift; furthermore, 71% claim that recording a tape or CD instead of buying a new copy in a shop is acceptable, with 52% already engaging in this deviant behaviour. Vitell and Muncy' s (2005) survey discloses that 26% of informants strongly believe that downloading music from the internet instead of and Hinduja (2008) unveil that 90% of their sample believes that downloading music illegally was an *appropriate* behaviour.

These results illustrate the problem intellectual property faces. Individuals do not give the same value to music, words or ideas that they confer to physical objects. This theory is significantly supported within the literature (Vitell and Muncy, 1992; Logsdon et al., 1994; Cheng et al., 1997; Kearns, 2001). Vitell and Muncy's (1992: 303) findings highlight that whereas 99% of informants (71% strongly) consider 'drinking a can of soda in a supermarket without paying for it' as wrong, only 34% (12% strongly) believe that 'recording an album instead of buying it' is unethical. These results are confirmed by Cheng et al. (1997: 56), who state: 'stealing a candy bar would not be tolerated while pirating software worth hundreds of dollars is generally condoned'.

In summary, illegal downloading by consumers is widespread and the nature of the internet greatly facilitates these behaviours. Moreover, many consumers appear tolerant and accepting of this misbehaviour and seem to rationalize or justify their illegal activities in some way. Given these insights, neutralization theory appears to provide an interesting perspective from which to analyse how online consumers reduce guilt or justify their actions (Cohn and Vaccaro, 2006; Hinduja, 2007).

◆ Techniques of Neutralization

The term 'techniques of neutralization' was first used in 1957 by Sykes and Matza in their article 'Techniques of neutralization: A theory of delinquency'. At that time, one of the main interests in criminology was the analysis of delinquency in order to understand such a deviant behaviour, especially among adolescents (Cromwell and Thurman, 2003). An investigation of juvenile delinquency led Sykes and Matza (1957) to propose five techniques of neutralization as an explanation of this misbehaviour (denial of responsibility, denial of injury, denial of victim, condemning the condemners and appealing to higher loyalties). Subsequently, Cohn and Vaccaro (2006: 71) note that techniques of neutralization have been employed to explain activities as diverse and numerous as shoplifting (Strutton et al., 1994; Cromwell and Thurman, 2003); marketing (Vitell and Grove, 1987); deer poaching (Elias on and Dodder, 2000); abortion (Brennan, 1974); genocide (Alvarez, 1997); religious dissonance (Dun ford and Kunz, 1973); cheating in exams (Smith et al., 2004, Atmen and Al-Hadassah, 2008); hired killing (Levi, 1981); white-collar criminality (Pique et al., 2005); and finally, music piracy (Cohn and Vaccaro, 2006; Ingram and Hinduja, 2008).

According to Sykes and Matza (1957: 666), techniques of neutralization are used in order to 'protect [...] the individual from self-blame and the blame of others after the act'. They can be linked to what Mills (1940) names 'vocabularies of motive'. They enable individuals engaging in dysfunctional consumer behaviour to diminish the impact of their misconduct in their own eyes and those of others. As Chatzidakis et al. (2004: 528) state, the techniques of neutralization are 'ways in which consumers rationalize their behaviour in order to deal with the consequences of acting in ways that are not consistent with their core ethical values and beliefs'. Individuals use techniques of

neutralization as 'guilt-reducing mechanisms' (Mitchell and Dodder, 1980: 241) in order to explain their misbehaviour and reduce both the consequences of their acts and their feelings of guilt. In the context of digital piracy, studies suggest that many (but far from all) illegal downloaders self-report their belief that their actions are ethically acceptable. This suggests five possible scenarios. First, such downloaders have rationalized or neutralized their actions to the extent that the ethical issues that were (presumably) initially encountered have been resolved (that is, neutralization has occurred and/or is occurring). Second, the psychological costs of norm violation in the form of social or legal chastisement are viewed as so improbably low as to be worth the cost/risk (a risk/cost which requires some neutralization). Third, self-reports of a belief that such actions are ethically acceptable may be reinforcing rationalizations in themselves (that is, denial of ethical issue as a neutralization technique); or fourth, the public espousal of an ethical norm does not equate to cognitive acceptance (leading to the need for neutralization/justification); or fifth, such behaviours are (and always have been) genuinely viewed as unethically unproblematic and that no neutralization or rationalization is required. Given the findings of Cohn and Vaccaro (2006) and Hinduja (2007), the first four scenarios seem eminently more probable than the fifth.

Originally, Sykes and Matza (1957) proposed five techniques of neutralization that can explain juvenile delinquency: denial of responsibility, denial of injury, denial of victim, condemning the condemners and appealing to higher loyalties.

1. *'Denial of responsibility'* enables individuals to cast the responsibility of their aberrant behaviour on someone else or on the circumstances. They are not really guilty since 'factors beyond their control' (Vitell and Grove, 1987: 434) cause their misbehaviour.

2. *'Denial of injury'* lessens the consequences of misconducts, emphasizing the lack of direct harm and therefore making the behaviour more acceptable.

3. *'Denial of victim'* is not used to refute the unethical side of the behaviour. It helps individuals to

explain their motives by claiming that 'the violated party deserved whatever happened' (Vitell and Grove, 1987: 434).

4. *'Condemning the condemners'* enables individuals to shift the attention towards those who criticize them 'by pointing out that they engage in similar disapproved behaviour' (Vitell and Grove, 1987: 434).

5. *'Appealing to higher loyalties'* is used by individuals to explain that their aberrant behaviour is 'the by-product of their attempt to actualize a higher order ideal or value' (Vitell and Grove, 1987: 434).

Subsequently, researchers have identified other techniques, including: defence of necessity and metaphor of the ledger (Klockars, 1974; Minor, 1981); claim of normalcy, denial of negative intent and claim of relative acceptability (Henry, 1990); denial of the necessity of the law and the claim that everybody else is doing it (Coleman, 1994); and justification by comparison and postponement (Cromwell and Thurman, 2003).

1. *'Defence of necessity'* is argued by Minor (1981: 298) to mean that 'if an act is perceived as necessary, then one need not feel guilty about its commission, even if it is considered morally wrong in the abstract'. This technique corresponds to Coleman's (1994) denial of the *necessity of the law*.

2. *'Metaphor of the ledger'* implicates counterbalancing all the good and bad behaviours, thereby tolerating the aberrant behaviour in question.

3. *'Claim of normalcy'* insists that everybody engages in such activities, and thereby being commonplace, such behaviour cannot really be perceived as wrong (Coleman, 1994).

4. *'Denial of negative intent'* diminishes responsibility, since the behaviour was not supposed to cause any harm.

5. *'Claims of relative acceptability'* or 'justification by comparison' intend to minimize the consequences of the aberrant behaviour by drawing a comparison with other perpetrators or with more questionable forms of behaviour.

6. *'Postponement'* enables individuals to 'simply put the incident out of their mind' (Cromwell and Thurman, 2003: 547). Cromwell and Thurman (2003) observed that during the interviews, participants often use this technique in order to explain why they engage in shoplifting.

In summary, neutralization theory provides an insightful perspective from which to elucidate how aberrant human behaviours are justified or rationalized by participants. In the case of online customer misbehaviour and illegal downloading in particular, both Cohn and Vaccaro (2006) and Hinduja (2007) argue that focusing on online consumers' use of such techniques generates useful insights into how such consumers justify their illegal activities.

◇ Research Methodology

The aim of this paper is to explore the extent to which peer-to-peer users employ techniques of neutralization to justify prior-to behaviour or rationalize their activities post behaviour. While previous studies have generated insights into online misbehaviour the nature and dynamics of online consumers' application of neutralization techniques remains understudied (Cohn and Vaccaro, 2006; Hinduja, 2007). In particular, empirical insights into the sequencing of neutralizations are limited. While experimental or longitudinal studies are needed definitely to establish causality between cognitions and acts, in the current study an exploratory research design was deemed appropriate to generate insights into the sequencing of online consumer misbehaviour.

In order to develop a greater understanding of the core concepts within this area a qualitative interview-based approach was adopted, as in-depth interviews are particularly useful in generating 'rich' and 'deep' insights into complex phenomena (see Miller, 1991; Bryman, 2004). An advantage of in-depth interviews is the capture of the informant's perspective on key issues, using their own jargon and language; characteristics which are of particular value when the issues under research are sensitive or ethically questionable (Stainback and Stainback, 1988; Iacobucci and Churchill, 2006).

In order to achieve these goals, a central issue was identifying and gaining access to suitable informants (Crimp and White, 2000). As a result, this study adopted a 'discovery-oriented' design akin to that of Mahrer (1988). To produce a knowledgeable sample, a purposive sampling plan was utilized comparable to that used and recommended by Harris and Reynolds (2003) in their study of dysfunctional downloading and their knowledge of online service dynamics. All informants had participated in peer-to-peer downloading within the last two weeks. In total, 54 informants were interviewed, of which 34 were male. The ages of informants ranged from 18 to 48 years (the average age being 26.3). Males are more represented than females in the sample, since they download more through peer-to-peer networks, and informants are all relatively young since peer-to-peer file-sharers are composed mainly of young people (Gopal et al., 2004; Sandulli, 2007; Ingram and Hinduja, 2008). All 54 informants have at least once illegally downloaded music or movies; 34 of them have also pirated software and 17 of them have illegally copied video games. The informants engaged in illegal downloading activities twice a week on average (varying from once a month to several times each day).

All the interviews were conducted individually and typically lasted 50 minutes (although some lasted for as long as 90 minutes). Given the potentially illegal nature of the activities studied, and to reduce potential social desirability bias, informant confidentiality and anonymity were guaranteed. To ensure the accuracy of data collection, all interviews were audio-recorded and subsequently transcribed by the interviewer and annotated with notes taken during the interview. As recommended by Lindolf (1995), wherever appropriate, the interviewer took the opportunity to pursue potentially interesting lines of inquiry and to encourage elaboration of particular events or episodes. Interviews began with explicit confidentiality assurances in order to aid open discussion on the part of the informant. Particular emphasis was placed on noting informants' comments regarding the timing of neutralizations (pre-, during or post behaviour) and on critically exploring timing claims.

Data collection was terminated at the point which Strauss and Corbin (1998) abel 'theoretical saturation' (the point at which no new insights are divulged). Subsequent data analysis followed a systematic process of transcript-based analysis following a form of the iterative stage process summarized by Turner (1981) and advocated by Reynolds and Harris (2005) as especially beneficial in the study of customer misbehaviour. The approach of Turner (1981) entails seven separate phases of analysis (generating categories, category saturation, abstract definition development, use of definitions, category explanation, category linkage and linkage evaluation) complemented by the iterative evaluation of the analysis after each phase. The analytical approach adopted is consistent with the suggestion of Dey (1993), in that the context of action and the social actors are described in such a way that facilitated the task of classifying and assessing the interconnectedness of themes. This approach has also been described as 'abductive reasoning' (Coffey and Atkinson, 1996). Nevertheless, it should be acknowledged that the method employed (in part) evaluates an existing theoretical framework and therefore has a deductive element.

To improve the reliability and validity of the data collection, a systematic approach to data collection and analysis was adopted (Yin, 2003). Further, internal and external veracity checks of analyses were undertaken (see Price et al., 2000). Internally, coding procedures were reviewed by an experienced researcher, while externally, preliminary and final analyses were reviewed by five consumers during ex-post interviews. To maintain the anonymity of individuals and organizations, details encompassing informants' names and locations have been changed.

◈ Findings

Data analysis reveals that peer-to-peer file-sharers employ up to seven different techniques of neutralization in order to rationalize or justify their activities: denial of victim, denial of injury, denial of responsibility, claim of normality, claim of relative acceptability, justification by comparison and appeal to higher loyalties. The remainder of this section is devoted to the discussion of each of these neutralization techniques.

Denial of Victim

This technique of neutralization is one of the most exploited by peer-to-peer file-sharers to pre-justify their illegal activities. Informants often blame entertainment companies for their misbehaviour. It is mainly the case for record labels, in particular the Big Four (Warner Music, Universal Music Group, EMI Recorded Music, Sony/BMG Entertainment), since informants mostly illegally download music from the internet, but was also used against major software companies. Interestingly, this technique of neutralization appeared to be used mainly prior to the behaviour. Throughout the interviews, participants raised two main arguments to insist on denial of victim: unjustifiably high prices; and perceived exploitation by multinational firms.

None of the interviews were conducted without the informant reproaching the excessive prices set by the software, video game, DVD and music industries. For instance, one informant confesses:

> I recently wanted to buy an album in a shop. The album is quite old so I expected it to be at a reduced price but it was actually more expensive than some brand new albums! If it had been in the shop for around 10 dollars, I would have bought it there but they set such a high price that they just encourage people to download. (Male, 26)

These findings confirm what has been previously highlighted in the literature review section: price can lead people to misbehave (see Levin et al., 2004; Al-Rafee and Cronan, 2006; Sandulli, 2007). All the participants believe that in setting high prices, companies deserve what happens with the development of peer-to-peer networks. One informant claims:

> Prices are exorbitant. Companies just try to take advantage of us. If a lot of people are downloading today, they've only got themselves to blame. (Male, 27)

Microsoft Office costs $499.95, Photoshop costs $649; how can they really believe that people won't try to obtain them freely if possible.

> I don't use Photoshop very often, but sometimes I enjoy using it to change or customize some pictures. There's no way I will spend so much on a software. I can't afford it. They should give it for free for individual use since they make so much profit with businesses. (Male, 28)

This opinion seems to be widely shared among peer-to-peer users, especially among the informants who download. According to them, the price of software is excessive, especially for individual use. Indeed, 30% of those interviewed believe that software should be free for personal use, since software companies can make their profits through their sales to businesses.

Some of the peer-to-peer file-sharers expressed feelings of being deceived by entertainment companies in order to justify their misconduct. This echoes the comments of both Levin et al. (2004) and Chen et al. (2008). Informants argue:

> The music companies think that we're dumb. I mean, 99 cents per song but twelve bucks a CD? They're just trying to bleed us dry. They deserve all they get! (Male, 47)

In this regard, informants hold profitable multinationals responsible for their deviant behaviour. It is interesting to notice that all participants at one point during the interviews differentiated big labels from new and small ones, big and lucrative multinationals from small and medium companies, or famous and rich artists from new and unknown ones. These results confirm Fullerton and Pun's (2004) observation where they highlight 'pathological socialization' as a cause of dysfunctional behaviour. Indeed, informants engage in illegal activities when they consider companies deserving of it (see Wilkes, 1978).

Denial of injury

Denial of injury is the second most common technique of neutralization used by informants to rationalize their deviant behaviour. However, in contrast to neutralization of guilt via denial of victim prior to acting, the denial of injury rationalization appeared most frequently to occur post behaviour. Of the 54 informants,

43 claim that their peer-to-peer activities do not harm anybody and that there is no direct financial impact on businesses involved. In order to illustrate their point of view, informants underline the wealth of multinationals. Moreover, they stress the non-lucrative side of their actions; they equate their downloadings with a complementary product and not a substitute one, and finally, they highlight the positive impact peer-to-peer networks may have on businesses.

The major argument used in such cases revolves around the idea that multinationals already make such a huge profit that several dollars fewer do not really matter or make a difference. These findings correspond to the 'attitude toward big businesses' cause observed by Fullerton and Punj (1993). One of the informants declares:

> I'm sure the development of peer-to-peer networks doesn't have any impact on entertainment industries. They make a lot of money anyway. I also think artists could do without their huge profits. (Male, 19)

These views support Sykes and Matza's (1957) findings, where the latter noticed that delinquents distinguish between acceptable and unacceptable victims. This observation seems to apply to peer-to-peer users too. File-sharers mainly use peer-to-peer networks to download music from famous and wealthy artists and Hollywood movies, and in that case, they did not believe that their behaviour had negative consequences. Some of the informants even highlight the fact that businesses seem to cope extremely well with the situation:

> Some big CEOs from multinationals are complaining about peer-to-peer files sharing but I don't think they have really anything to worry about. Considering share prices of Universal, Fox, Lionsgate, Infogramme and Ubisoft, and their gigantic advertising they don't seem very miserable. (Male, 26)

It is interesting to notice that in the course of the interviews, participants often use denial of victim to reinforce their denial of injury. This finding supports Cromwell and Thurman (2003), who argue that customers may use more than one technique of neutralization to justify their deviant behaviour.

To justify their illegal behaviour, 85% of informants insist that they would not have bought the product (CD, DVD, software, or video game) anyway. Downloading through peer-to-peer networks does not represent a menace for companies since the latter cannot lose money on something they cannot sell in the first place, irrespective of peer-to-peer platforms. Some of the file-sharers thus rationalize their activities:

> I wouldn't have bought them [CDs and DVDs] anyway. [. . .] If I never intended to buy something in the first place there is no real loss to anyone. (Female, 22)

> I tend to download stuff that I would buy. If it is that good, I'd buy a copy but mostly I get programmes that I'll use every now and again. (Male, 34)

Some of the informants also insist that their downloading activities do not affect their consumption habits. Even if they do use peer-to-peer platforms to download some music or films, that does not diminish their purchasing. These findings corroborate those of Azeez (2002), who claims that downloading does not impact on purchasing behaviour.

Claim of Normalcy

Data analysis reveals that three-quarters of informants seem to lessen their guilt post behaviour through the claim of normality. 'Everybody is doing it' seems to be a logical justification for peer-to-peer file-sharers to engage in their illegal behaviour. This technique pivots on claims that such actions are common to many other consumers and is distinct from the 'condemning the condemners' approach, wherein individuals accuse the other party in the conservation of undertaking similar or greater acts of deviance. Claims of normality appeared to be described by informants as occurring after the misbehaviour, enabling peer-to-peer users to rationalize the consequences of their activities.

Piracy, whether of music, films, software or more commonly video games, is often argued to be becoming commonplace. The significant number of people engaging in illegal downloading makes it easier for others to follow suit, confirming previous results (Cohn and Vaccaro, 2006; Hinduja, 2007; Bhal and Leekha, 2008). Since so many people use peer-to-peer networks in order to obtain the files they want, piracy does not seem so wrong, thereby assuaging the guilt of those using these platforms and offering them an excuse for their misbehaviour. Two informants state:

> Everybody is downloading. I mean if it was so wrong many people I know would never dare doing it. I would be an idiot not to do the same. (Female, 23)

> The world and their wife get free stuff from the Internet! I really doubt that anybody doesn't do it every now and again! (Male, 39)

These answers highlight the influence others can have on their close circle of acquaintances. Peer groups, as often observed within the literature (see Logsdon et al., 1994; Ingram and Hinduja, 2008), can influence their members, leading them to misbehave.

Claim of Relative Acceptability and Justification by Comparison

Individuals who engage in deviant behaviour may rationalize their misconduct by drawing a comparison with a more ethically questionable act (justification by comparison) or with other perpetrators whose behaviours are viewed as less acceptable (claiming relative acceptability). In this study, informants most commonly described incidents of these techniques after the online act of misbehaviour. Analysis of interviews revealed that nearly half of informants employed these techniques of neutralization in order to justify their illegal activities, each claiming that using peer-to-peer networks is nothing compared to crimes such as homicide, rape, or marital violence.

Consistent with Hinduja (2007), comparing a crime against one much more serious, even if there is no connection between them, seems a sufficient excuse for many informants to justify their illegal downloading. Indeed, when compared to homicide,

downloading becomes a rather insignificant crime. A serial softlifter argues:

> Peer-to-peer networks have become one of the main sensitive issues today. Even governments get involved. Downloading won't kill anyone. Maybe they should concentrate their effort on something more important. I mean, violence is everywhere; why lose time with irrelevant stuff. (Male, 32)

Justification by comparison enables peer-to-peer file-sharers to make their activities almost acceptable to others, since they believe they do not really harm anyone.

It is interesting to notice that a small (but significant) minority of informants draw a comparison between online piracy and shoplifting in order to rationalize their deviant behaviour. Those against online piracy often associate it with shoplifting. However, peer-to-peer file-sharers claim that they are completely different. This last justification reinforces what has been previously highlighted in the literature review: intellectual property is not regarded as a physical good, thereby diminishing the guilt of illegally obtaining a copy of files (Vitell and Muncy, 1992; Logsdon et al., 1994; Cheng et al., 1997; Kearns, 2001). An informant explains:

> That gets on my nerves when people say that downloading and shoplifting is the same thing. There is a huge difference. For example, to make a laptop you need raw material and man-hours to make it. While two laptops need twice as much material and twice as many man-hours, two copies of software don't. The cost could be covered by purchases made by companies and professionals, and there are lots of them, while clubs, radio stations, television etc. could cover the cost for music. Everybody downloads; maybe it's time now for companies to adapt themselves. (Male, 30)

The finding that peer-to-peer users do not believe that downloading is unethical is concurrent with a number of earlier studies (see Ingram and Hinduja, 2008).

Other participants use justification by comparison by claiming that they download much less than many other peer-to-peer users. They claimed they only download files occasionally, whereas some individuals pirate every day. This appears to be sufficient reason for them to continue downloading occasionally without feeling guilty about it. Those who engage in this behaviour much more than they do are the ones to blame for the possible harmful consequences. Informants declare:

> I'm not one of the big downloaders. I just download two or three items a month. It's not a big deal and compared to others, it's nothing. (Female, 27)

> I don't download night and day with several computers as some people do. (Female, 23)

> As long as others are engaged in these activities much more than they themselves are, informants believe their behaviour can be forgiven

Appeal to Higher Loyalties

The appeal to higher loyalties technique was most often described by informants as something they considered to occur before the downloading activity. Throughout the coding process, two main values stood out: discovery, and individual's rights and freedom (partly supporting similar findings in Cohn and Vaccaro, 2006).

In order to explain one of the reasons behind their illicit activities, 25 informants refer to the value of discovery. Peer-to-peer networks enable them to discover new songs, new artists, or new movies. For instance:

> When I use peer-to-peer networks I often discover new bands that I had no idea existed. (Male, 18)

> You can find some great new stuff online that you'd never hear about otherwise. (Female, 35)

The 'discovery' factor is especially important where music is concerned, confirming observations made in the literature (Gopal et al., 2004; Cohn and Vaccaro, 2006; Sandulli, 2007). Peer-to-peer networks allow informants

to listen to new songs they would never have had the chance to do otherwise. When they have to pay for a CD, they are more cautious about their choice and usually go for the band or artist they know and are sure to enjoy. The safer way is then not to try anything new, thereby not discovering anything new. Even if the radio plays a significant role in the uncovering of novel bands, not every artist or song is broadcast. Moreover, sometimes one or two good songs do not justify the purchase of a CD:

> When I really like an album I would rather buy it instead of downloading it. However when I want only one or two songs on the CD I don't want to spend my money for nothing so I just download the tracks. (Female, 22)

The importance attached to the discovery value strengthens the last argument used by informants in order to deny injury as highlighted earlier. Peer-to-peer networks allow people to discover new things but they also help artists and companies to promote their products. File-sharing in this way is a novel way of sampling before buying the product. Peer-to-peer network advocates have mainly used this argument in order to justify their activities; however, some researches have questioned its accuracy (Blackburn, 2004; Michel, 2004; Liebowitz, 2005). These results echo those of Jupiter Research's survey evoked in Azeez (2002: 14), who notes that peerto- peer networks are just another way to 'try-before-you-buy'.

Concordant with Cohn and Vaccaro (2006), consumer rights and freedom is the second value which a minority (20%) of informants mentioned in order to defend their actions, especially in the cases of music and film downloading. Informants associated music and film with culture and believe culture should be free and available to everybody:

> Music and movies are some kind of arts and should be free whoever the spectator. (Female, 23)

Peer-to-peer networks enable individuals to criticize and fight against the system. Thus, those employing this technique of neutralization argue that their engagement in such illegal behaviour is in order to defend their rights and those of others:

> It's the first time that culture and entertainment is available to everybody. Every civilisation has dreamt about it. It has happened and now everybody is outraged. Thanks to peer-to-peer networks, every individual, rich, and more importantly poor, have the ability to access liberally and free everything related to culture and entertainment. Why would someone, who is for equality between humans, want to prohibit it? (Male, 26)

Moreover, informants point out that usually they download files they were able to obtain freely. This is particularly the case for movies and television shows. When a film or programme is on television, it is easy to record it with a video tape and video player. Informants observed that they paid for the television, the tape and the video-tape recorder and that furthermore, multinational companies sell all the products necessary for this, thus facilitating consumers in recording what is transmitted on television. Thus, many informants argued that as long as a television show or movie has been broadcast on television, they believe they are entitled to use peer-to-peer networks to acquire them:

> If a television show or a movie has been broadcast, I don't know why I can't download it since I was able to record it on television. If not, just explain to me why we can buy blank tapes and a video player? (Female, 30)

> I like downloading series and even films already broadcast on television. I then consider that I don't have to pay for them since they have been already televized and I could have made a copy of them. (Female, 23)

Peer-to-peer networks are also a way to criticize the system as a whole and fight against an entertainment industry which is attracted more by profit than the will to promote the Arts. An informant contends:

> The system for distributing artist's work to consumers is so backwards that I actually resent

putting any money at all into it. Paying £35 for a television series that was just on television, when I know that most of that goes straight to the fat cat at the top, who uses it to fund things like Big Brother; I just can't believe it. (Male, 26)

Consumer rights and freedom are hence a value which peer-to-peer users endorse to neutralize guilt and rationalize their behaviour.

Denial of Responsibility

Denial of responsibility was depicted as a post-action process and was expressed by only 30% of informants, echoing Cohn and Vaccaro's (2006) findings. However, the informants who did use this technique of neutralization often brought up the argument of availability of peer-to-peer networks and their accessibility and ease of use.

Seven informants highlight the availability of peer-to-peer networks and the facility in engaging in illegal downloading due to the internet, its access and its ease of use, and thus neutralize their online misbehaviour by claiming that the conditions for illegal peer-to-peer are so favourable that their actions are justifiable. Interestingly, numerous informants argued that they do not create, develop or maintain these networks. Indeed, many informants did not share their own files with other peer-to-peer downloaders. However, since peer-to-peer file trading is available to them, they argue there is no reason for them not to use it and they cannot be held responsible for their behaviour since they have nothing to do with the creation and development of these networks. An informant declares:

> Peer-to-peer networks exist and they're free. What should I do? Not use them because some people think it's wrong? I didn't create them. I don't even make my own files available for others. I just use peer-to-peer platforms, which are easily available to me. It's not as if I was the one at the origin of these networks. (Male, 18)

These answers are consistent with previous findings which contend that opportunity can cause aberrant behaviour (see Fukukawa, 2002; Levin et al., 2004).

Accessibility and ease of use are interlinked justifications employed by other informants to deny the responsibility of their behaviour. As highlighted earlier (see Cronan and Al-Rafee, 2008; Ingram and Hinduja, 2008), the internet has made deviant behaviour easier. People have ready access to the internet and it has become increasingly less difficult to use, therefore peer-to-peer file-sharers do not understand why they should not take advantage of peer-to-peer networks. An informant stresses:

> With my broadband connection I can have access to the Internet whenever I want. In a few clicks, I can download music, films, software, and even video games. There is nothing difficult to do for that, it's available and free. It's the age of the Internet, you can't fight against it. (Male, 24)

This echoes Sherman's (2000) proposition concerning the ease of use of the internet facilitating dysfunctional behaviour.

◈ Implications

This paper attempts to explore the extent to which peer-to-peer users employ techniques of neutralization to justify their actions of prior-to behaviour or rationalize their activities post behaviour. Relatively few studies have taken an interest in both piracy and the justifications given by downloaders for engaging in such actions, at the same time (see Cohn and Vaccaro, 2006; Hinduja, 2007; Ingram and Hinduja, 2008; Bhal and Leekha, 2008). However, piracy has become a sensitive issue. Every day, billions of files are illegally downloaded throughout the world and despite the actions taken by entertainment companies and governments the movement does not seem to be slowing down.

The main contribution of this study lies not in the finding of neutralization during online consumer misbehaviour. While marketers may be surprised by such a statement (neutralization theory having received little attention by the marketing academy – see Harris, 2008b), other academies (such as criminologists) have long accepted neutralization of deviant actions to the extent that Maruna and Copes (2005) in their (already) seminal review note that such findings are not interesting in themselves. In contrast, the main contribution of the current study lies in the insights gained into the sequencing of neutralizations. This contentious aspect of neutralization theory finds many theorists divided into those that believe that neutralization occurs either pre- or post event (see Sykes and Matza, 1957; Hindelang, 1970); although Maruna and Copes (2005) extend Hirschi's (1969) 'hardening' conception into a theory of desistance. The current study contributes insights into these issues through finding evidence to support the view that both pre-event neutralizing justifications, as well as post-event ones, occur. Moreover, in this context, particular techniques appear linked to either pre- or post-event neutralization. Specifically, the denial of victims and appeal to higher loyalties techniques were found to be predominately used to justify actions prior to an event. In contrast, the denial of injury, claims of normalcy, claims of relative acceptability, justification by comparison and denial of responsibility techniques were found to be rationalizations of behaviour post-event. While the research design and methodology of this study prohibits definitive causal claims and precludes empirical generalizability, theoretical generalizability is possible and certainly the insights gained provide a good starting point for future studies (see below).

It is also worth noting here the differences between the techniques found in the current study and those found in similar studies. Hinduja (2007) observed that students engaging in softlifting particularly use denial of injury, appeal to higher loyalties, claim of relative acceptability and denial of negative intent to justify their behaviour; Bhal and Leekha (2008) state that their informants mainly employed appeal to higher loyalties and claim of normalcy. In contrast, the current study reveals that none of the participants use denial of negative intent to justify their activities, while only 30% employ claims of relative acceptability.

As Cromwell and Thurman (2003) observed, individuals engaging in misconduct tend to use more than one technique of neutralization to justify their behaviour; participants' answers confirm peer-to-peer users do the same. Moreover, in a similar way that delinquents differentiate acceptable from unacceptable victims (Sykes and Matza, 1957), peer-to-peer users distinguish multinationals from small and independent companies. Informants in the current study believe that multinational companies such as Universal, Fox and Microsoft cope perfectly with peer-to-peer networks and thus deserve the development and popularity of these platforms. However, as soon as downloading affects an entity other than a big corporate, piracy becomes not-so-acceptable behaviour. This last point has never really been mentioned in previous literature on digital piracy and it may be interesting to investigate further in future research. Furthermore, contrary to Hinduja's (2007) findings, the 54 participants often use techniques of neutralization during the interviews. All of them used at least three of the techniques.

The fact that piracy becomes unacceptable behaviour when dealing with small and independent companies deserves particular attention. Many studies have found that piracy was not necessarily regarded as illegal or unethical (Vitell and Muncy, 1992; Logsdon et al., 1994; Simpson et al., 1994; Glass and Wood, 1996; Cheng et al., 1997; Kearns, 2001; Fukukawa, 2002; Cronan and Al-Rafee, 2008). However, the problem appears to be deeper than that. During the 54 interviews, peer-to-peer users claim that their downloading is acceptable and justified. Yet 61% of them are against legal and free downloading. They claim that if peer-to-peer networks are legalized, the entertainment industry will disappear, since artists and creators will not be compensated for their work. This is in total contradiction to the 'culture should be available and free to everybody' dogma. Informants, therefore, do not seem truly to question the illegal and unethical side of peer-to-peer networks, thereby acknowledging the social and conventional norms. However, they feel that these norms should not apply to their cases, echoing Sykes and Matza's (1957) findings. Even if participants, at least this 61%, do not consider piracy to be as unethical as shoplifting for instance, they do not deny the fact that some people can perceive peer-to-peer activities as morally wrong.

It may be particularly interesting and useful for the entertainment industry to further explore this last observation. Piracy is a real phenomenon, which will not disappear easily. On the contrary, the next generation

is born with the internet and all the opportunities related to it. Some teenagers download on a daily basis but they have never bought a CD or a DVD in their life. As Sandulli (2007: 325) declares

> in the words of John Kennedy, the Chairman and CEO of the [IFPI], the main problem of the recording industry is to 'persuade a young generation of music fans to pay for music that they have become used to acquiring for free'. (IFPI, 2006)

The movie, software and video games industries, one after the other, face the same crisis. New technologies will become ever more efficient; the next generation will become even more at ease with the internet; peer-to-peer systems will be increasingly expanded and difficult to control. There is no doubt multinationals will have to come up with a new business model (as suggested by some of the informants) if they want to face up to the situation. New strategies have already been adopted. Free game samples seem to reduce, if not eliminate, illegal downloading of video games. Free software such as Open Office seems to offer an alternative to expensive ones such as Microsoft Office. However, as long as no solution is recommended, the price of some software will continue to drive some individuals into softlifting. Online purchasing of digital media is getting closer to how it should be, and eventually will become the norm. More and more individuals consider CD and DVD support as obsolete and prefer mp3 files, since they take up less space and are more convenient both to download and to keep. Laptops, mp3 players or bipods, to name but a few, have become commonplace in many people's lives, especially those of the next generation. However, before then, companies need to be realistic. The price they propose is too excessive for many people. Peer-to-peer users do not want to pay for extra 'hosting costs' because they buy a digital as opposed to a physical product. Companies will have to be very careful regarding the new business model and strategy they will adopt. Companies need to rethink their strategy and find new ways to make profits. Instead of considering peer-to-peer networks as opponents, multinationals should maybe try to use these networks to their advantage.

The fact that so many people are willing to download illegally may suggest an ignorance of the law by some consumers; or that legal loopholes may need tightening. Reinforced copyright of the products affected could be one solution. However, this may have unforeseen consequences. Consumers who actually buy the product (CD, DVD, software or videogame) may complain that they cannot make a copy of the product that they legally own. Moreover, there will always be hackers skilled enough to succeed in cracking the copyright. The legalization of such activities is likely to be infeasible. Thus, as noted by Fullerton and Punj (1997), potential solutions are likely to pivot on deterrence to reduce (but not eliminate) such behaviours.

Consequently, a prospective solution for policymakers could be to reinforce the law and implement tougher and stricter penalties. However, this does not ensure the problem will stop, as stricter laws will not convince people that engaging in digital piracy is truly wrong. This may only deter those individuals having the least impact on the problem. Staggering penalties and prison terms could really impact on digital piracy; however, these kinds of sentences would be quite improper for this type of crime. Furthermore, peer-to-peer users would create other sharing networks, which are less easily identified and devoid of proxies and data encoding.

This study highlights that the issue of software and music piracy is rooted deeper than was thought, whether digital piracy is illegal or not. The root causes of downloading should be analyzed in depth by the policymakers rather than their just hoping that increasing legal restrictions will solve the problem. Digital piracy is a sensitive issue which necessitates the generation of new ideas to tackle it. Policymakers have to rethink their strategy. However, peer-to-peer networks will not be easy to prevent or properly to legalize.

As with all studies of this nature, the findings and contributions of this study are constrained by the research design and methodology adopted; limitations which, in turn, suggest potentially fruitful avenues for future research. In particular, three issues appear especially important. First, this study explores an illegal activity. As such, interviews involve discussions of issues which could result in hefty fines or even imprisonment. These issues could constrain informant responses and interpretations. A virtual ethnography on forums related to file-sharing may allow researchers to gain more insights on the situation. Unlike face-to-face interviews, this method could anon Mize responses and may generate interesting insights. Second, while the exploratory design and qualitative methods employed facilitate rich insights, the nature of the research design and methods limit the empirical (but not the theoretical) generalizability of the findings and contributions. In this regard, while the method adopted provides insights into the ordering of neutralization techniques (pre- or post actions), only experimental or longitudinal studies can definitively address the causal ordering question. Third, additional research could generate interesting insights through focusing on the conditions in which neutralizations are employed and on interpersonal differences during technique application.

◆ References

Al-Rafee, S. and Cronan, T.P. (2006) 'Digital Piracy: Factors that Influence Attitude toward Behavior', *Journal of Business Ethics* 63(3): 237–59.

Albers-Miller, N.D. (1999) 'Consumer Misbehavior: Why People Buy Illicit Goods', *Journal of Consumer Marketing* 16(3): 273–85.

Alvarez, A. (1997) 'Adjusting to Genocide: The Techniques of Neutralization and the Holocaust', *Social Science History* 21(2): 139–78.

Atmen, M. and Al-Hadassah, H. (2008) 'Factors Affecting Cheating Behavior among Accounting Students (Using the Theory of Planned Behavior)', *Journal of Accounting, Business & Management* 15: 109–25.

Azeez, W. (2002) 'Music Downloads Used as Trial ahead of CD Purchase', *New Media* Age, 7 November, p. 14.

Bhal, K.T. and Leekha, N.D. (2008) 'Exploring Cognitive Moral Logics Using Grounded Theory: The Case of Software Piracy', *Journal of Business Ethics* 81(3): 635–46.

Bhattacharjee, S., Gopal, R.D. and Sanders, G.L. (2003) 'Digital Music and Online Sharing: Software Piracy 2.0?', *Communication of the ACM* 46(7): 107–11.

Blackburn, D. (2004) 'On-line piracy and recorded music sales', *Harvard Business School*, working paper, 1–60.

Brennan, W.C. (1974) 'Abortion and the Techniques of Neutralization', *Journal of Health and Social Behavior* 15(4): 538–65.

Bryman, A. (2004) *Social Science Research Methods*. Oxford: Oxford University Press.

Chatzidakis, A. and Mitussis, D. (2007) 'Computer Ethics and Consumer Ethics: The Impact of the Internet on Consumers' Ethical Decision-making Process', *Journal of Consumer Behaviour* 6(5): 305–20.

Chatzidakis, A., Hebert, S., Mitussis, D. and Smith, A. (2004) 'Virtue in Consumption?', *Journal of Marketing Management* 20(5): 526–43.

Chen, Y.C., Shan, R.A. and Lin, A.K. (2008) 'The Intention to Download Music Files in a P2P Environment: Consumption Value, Fashion, and Ethical Decision Perspectives', *Electronic Commerce Research and Applications* 1–12.

Cheng, H.K., Sims, R.R. and Teeter, H. (1997) 'To Purchase or to Pirate Software: An Empirical Study', Journal of *Management Information Systems* 13(4): 49–60.

Chiou, J.S., Huang, C.Y. and Lee, H.H. (2005) 'The Antecedents of Music Piracy Attitudes and Intentions', *Journal of Business Ethics* 57(2): 161–74.

Coffey, A.J. and Atkinson, P.A. (1996) *Making Sense of Qualitative Data: Complementary Research Strategies*. Thousand Oaks, CA: Sage.

Cohn, D.Y. and Vaccaro, V.L. (2006) 'A Study of Neutralization Theory's Application to Global Consumer Ethics: P2P File-trading of Musical Intellectual Property on the Internet', *Internet Marketing and Advertising* 3(1): 68–88.

Coleman, *J.W. Neutralization theory: An empirical application and assessment.* Stillwater, OK, PhD thesis, Oklahoma State University, Department of Sociology, 1994.

Crimp, M. and White, L.T. (2000) *The Market Research Process*. London, Prentice Hall.

Cromwell, P. and Thurman, Q. (2003) 'The Devil Made Me Do it: Use of Neutralizations by Shoplifters', *Deviant Behaviour* 24(6): 535–50.

Cronan, T.P. and Al-Rafee, S. (2008) 'Factors that Influence the Intention to Pirate Software and Media', *Journal of Business Ethics* 78(4): 527–45.

Dey, I. (1993) *Qualitative Data Analysis: A User-friendly Guide for Social Scientists*. London: Rutledge.

Dun ford, F.W. and Kunz, P.R. (1973) 'The Neutralization of Religious Dissonance', *Review of Religious Research* 15(1): 2–9.

Elias on, S.L. and Dodder, R.A. (2000) 'Neutralization among Deer Poachers', *Journal of Social Psychology* 140(4): 536–8.

Foremski, T. and Kehoe, L. (2000) 'Love Bites: The Ease with which a Disruptive Computer Virus Sidestepped Elaborate Safety Systems this Week has Damaged Faith in the Internet', *Financial Times*, 6 May, p. 14.

Freestone, O. and Mitchell, V.W. (2004) 'Generation Y Attitudes towards e-ethics and Internet-related Misbehaviours', *Journal of Business Ethics* 54(2): 121–8.

Fritsche, I. (2005) 'Predicting Deviant Behaviour by Neutralization: Myths and Findings', *Deviant Behaviour* 26(5): 483–510.

Fukukawa, K. (2002) 'Developing a Framework for Ethically Questionable Behavior in Consumption', *Journal of Business Ethics* 41(1): 99–119.

Fullerton, R.A. and Punj, G. (1993) 'Choosing to Misbehave: A Structural Model of Aberrant Consumer Behaviour', *Advances in Consumer Research* 20: 570– 4.

Fullerton, R.A. and Punj, G. (1997) 'Can Consumer Misbehavior be Controlled? A Critical Analysis of Two Major Control Techniques', *Advances in Consumer Research* 24: 340– 4.

Fullerton, R.A. and Punj, G. (2004) 'Repercussions of Promoting an Ideology of Consumption: Consumer Misbehaviour', *Journal of Business Research* 57(11): 1239 49.

Glass, R.S. and Wood, W.A. (1996) 'Situational Determinants of Software Piracy: An Equity Theory Perspective', *Journal of Business Ethics* 15(11): 1189–98.

Goles, T., Jayatilaka, B., George, B., Parsons, L., Chambers, V., Taylor, D. et al. (2008) 'Softlifting: Exploring Determinants of Attitude', *Journal of Business Ethics* 77(4): 481–99.

Gopal, R.D., Sanders, G.L., Bhattacharjee, S., Agrawal, M. and Wagner, S.C. (2004) 'A Behavioral Model of Digital Music Piracy', *Journal of Organizational Computing and Electronic Commerce* 14(2): 89–105.

Gupta, P.B., Gould, S.J. and Pola, B. (2004) 'To Pirate or not to Pirate: A Comparative Study of the Ethical versus other Influences on the Consumer's Software Acquisitionmode Decision', *Journal of Business Ethics* 55(3): 255–74.

Harris, L.C. (2008a) 'Fraudulent Return Proclivity: An Empirical Analysis', *Journal of Retailing* 84(4): 461–76.

Harris, L.C. (2008b) 'Introduction to the Special Session: Customers Behaving Badly: A Tribute to Christopher Lovelock', paper presented at the American Marketing Association SERVSIG International Research Conference, University of Liverpool, June. Harris, L.C. and Reynolds K.L. (2003) 'The Consequences of Dysfunctional Customer Behavior', *Journal of Service Research* 6(2): 144–61.

Harris, L.C. and Reynolds K.L. (2004) 'Jaycustomer Behavior: An Exploration of Types and Motives in the Hospitality Industry', *Journal of Services Marketing* 18(5): 339–57.

Harris, L.C. and Reynolds K.L. (2006) 'Deviant Customer Behavior: An Exploration of Frontline Employee Tactics', *Journal of Marketing Theory and Practice* 14(2): 95–111.

Henry, S. (1990) *Degrees of Deviance, Student Accounts of their Deviant Behavior*. Salem, WI: Sheffield Publishing.

Hill, C.W.L. (2007) Digital Piracy: Causes, Consequences, and Strategic Responses', Asia *Pacific Journal of Management* 24(1): 9–25.

Hindelang, M.J. (1970) 'The Commitment of Delinquents to their Misdeeds: Do Delinquents Drift?', *Social Problems* 17: 502–9.

Hinduja, S. (2007) 'Neutralization Theory and Online Software Piracy: An Empirical Analysis', *Ethics and Information Technology* 9(3): 187–204.

Hirschi, T. (1969) *Causes of Delinquency*. Berkeley, CA: University of California Press. Iacobucci, D. and Churchill G. (2006) *Marketing Research: Methodological Foundations*. Cincinnati, OH: South Western Educational Publishing.

Ingram, J.R. and Hinduja, S. (2008) 'Neutralizing Music Piracy: An Empirical Examination', *Deviant Behavior* 29(4): 334–66.

International Federation of the Phonographic Industry (IFPI) (2006) *Digital Music Report*. London: IFPI

Kearns, D. (2001) 'Intellectual Property: Napster and Ethics', *Network World* 18(15): 18.

Klockars, C.B. (1974) *The Professional Fence*. New York: Free Press.

Levi, K. (1981) 'Becoming a Hit Man: Neutralization in a Very Deviant Career', *Urban Life* 10(1): 47–63.

Levin, A.M., Dato-on, M.C. and Rhee, K. (2004) 'Money for Nothing and Hits for Free: The Ethics of Downloading Music from Peer-to-Peer Web Sites', *Journal of Marketing Theory and Practice* 12(1): 48–60.

Liebowitz, S.J. (2005) 'Pitfalls in Measuring the Impact of File-sharing on the Sound Recording Market', CESifo *Economic Studies*, 51: 439–77.

Lindolf, T.R. (1995) *Qualitative Communication Research Methods.* Thousand Oaks, CA: Sage.

Logsdon, J.M., Thompson, J.K. and Reid, R.A. (1994) 'Software Piracy: Is it Related to Level of Moral Judgment', *Journal of Business Ethics* 13(11): 849–57.

Mahrer, A.R. (1988) 'Discovery-oriented Psychotherapy Research', *American Psychologist* 43(September): 694–702.

Maruna, S. and Copes, H. (2005) 'Excuses, Excuses: What Have we Learned from Five Decades of Neutralization Research?', *Crime and Justice: A Review of Research* 32: 221–320.

Mazur, M. (2007) 'Online Fraud Continues to Be a Concern', *Community Banker* 16(6):70.

Michel, N.J. (2004) 'Internet file sharing: The evidence so far and what it means for the future', *The Heritage Foundation*, working paper, 1790, 1–6.

Miller, D.C. (1991) *Handbook of Research Design and Social Measurement* (5th ed.). Newbury Park, CA: Sage.

Mills, C.W. (1940) 'Situated Actions and Vocabularies of Motive', *American Sociological Review* 5(6): 904–13.

Minor, W.W. (1981) 'Techniques of Neutralization: A Reconceptualization and Empirical Examination', *Journal of Research in Crime and Delinquency* 18(2): 295–318.

Mitchell, J. and Dodder, R.A. (1980) 'An Examination of Types of Delinquency through Path Analysis', *Journal of Youth and Adolescence* 9(3): 239–48.

Motion Picture Association of America (MPAA) (2008) *Who Piracy Hurts*, URL (consulted August 2009): http://www.mpaa.org/piracy_WhoPiracyHurts.asp

Piquero, N.L., Tibbetts, S.G. and Blankenship, M.B. (2005) 'Examining the Role of Differential Association and Techniques of Neutralization in Explaining Corporate Crime', *Deviant Behavior* 26(2): 159–88.

Price, L.L., Arnould, E.J. and Curasi, C.F. (2000) 'Older Consumers' Disposition of Special Possessions', *Journal of Consumer Research* 27(September): 179–201.

Recording Industry Association of America (RIAA) (2008) *Report Physical Piracy*, URL (consulted August 2009): http://www.riaa.com/physicalpiracy.php

Reynolds, K.L. and Harris, L.C. (2005) 'When Service Failure is not Service Failure: An Exploration of the Forms and Motives of "Illegitimate" Customer Complaining', *Journal of Services Marketing* 19(5): 321–35.

Rombel, A. (2004) 'Security and Fraud Become Top Tech Issue', *Global Finance* 18(4): 40–2.

Rosenbaum, M.S. and Kuntze, R. (2003) 'The Relationship between Anomie and Unethical Retail Disposition', *Psychology and Marketing* 20(12): 1067–93.

Sandulli, F.D. (2007) 'CD Music Purchase Behaviour of P2P Users', *Technovation* 27: 325–34.

Sherman, C. (2000) 'Napster: Copyright Killer or Distribution Hero?', Online 24(6): 16–28.

Simpson, C. (2006) 'Review of Computer Misuse Laws Essential to Keep up with Rapidly Developing Market', *Computer Weekly*, 14 February, p. 14.

Simpson, P.M., Banerjee, D. and Simpson, C.L., Jr. (1994) 'Softlifting: A Model of Motivation Factors', *Journal of Business Ethics* 13(6): 431–8.

Smith, K.J., Davy, J.A. and Easterling, D. (2004) 'An Examination of Cheating and its Antecedents among Marketing and Management Majors', *Journal of Business Ethics* 50(1): 63–80.

Stainback, S. and Stainback, W. (1988) *Understanding and Conducting Qualitative Research*. Dubuque, IA: Kendall/Hunt.

Strauss, A. and Corbin, J. (1998) *Basic of Qualitative Research: Techniques and Procedures for Developing Grounded Theory* (2nd ed.). London: Sage.

Strutton, D., Pelton, L.E. and Ferrell, O.C. (1997) 'Ethical Behavior in Retail Settings: Is there a Generation Gap?', *Journal of Business Ethics* 16: 87–105.

Strutton, D., Vitell, S.J. and Pelton, L.E. (1994) 'How Consumers May Justify Inappropriate Behaviour in Market Settings: An Application on the Techniques of Neutralization', *Journal of Business Research* 30(3): 253–60.

Sykes, G.M. and Matza, D. (1957) 'Techniques of Neutralization: A Theory of Delinquency', *American Sociological Review* 22(6): 664–70.

Turner, B.A. (1981) 'Some Practical Aspects of Qualitative Data Analysis: One Way of Organizing the Cognitive Processes Associated with the Generation of Grounded Theory', *Quality and Quantity* 15: 225–47.

Vitell, S.J. and Grove, S.J. (1987) 'Marketing Ethics and the Techniques of Neutralization', *Journal of Business Ethics* 6(6): 433–8.

Vitell, S.J. and Muncy, J. (1992) 'Consumer Ethics: An Empirical Investigation of Factors Influencing Ethical Judgments of the Final Consumer', *Journal of Business Ethics* 11(8): 585–97.

Vitell, S.J. and Muncy, J. (2005) 'The Muncy-Vitell Consumer Ethics Scale: A Modification and Application', *Journal of Business Ethics* 62(3): 267–75.

Wilkes, R.E. (1978) 'Fraudulent Behavior by Consumers', *Journal of Marketing* 42(4): 67–75.

Withiam, G. (1998) 'Customers from Hell', Cornell Hotel and Restaurant Administration *Quarterly* 39(5): 11.

Yin, R.K. (2003) *Case Study Research: Design and Methods*. London: Sage.

PART III

Social Constructionist Approaches to Studying Deviance

CHAPTER 8

Labeling Theory

Saturday, March 24, 1984. Shermer High School, Shermer, Illinois. 60062.

    Dear Mr. Vernon, we accept the fact that we had to sacrifice a whole Saturday in detention for whatever it was that we did wrong...what we did was wrong, but we think you're crazy to make us write this essay telling you who we think we are. What do you care? You see us as you want to see us...in the simplest terms and the most convenient definitions. You see us as a brain, an athlete, a basket case, a princess and a criminal. Correct? That's the way we saw each other at seven o'clock this morning. We were brainwashed.

From *The Breakfast Club*

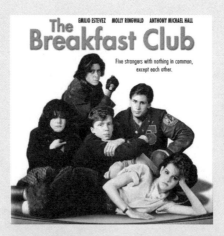

▲ Photo 8.1   The film, *The Breakfast Club*, offers a great example of labeling, with each of the main characters representing different high school cliques. Can you recall five distinct student groups from your own high school experience?

◈ Introduction

The movie *The Breakfast Club* is a classic coming-of-age film that deals squarely with the issue of labeling and how labels can affect the quality of an individual's life. In *The Breakfast Club,* the group of students represent the popular kids, the "jocks," the smart kids, the delinquents, and the outcasts. Think back to your own days in high school . . . can you identify several categories of students and a few specific traits associated with each of those groups? Were those groups treated differently by the school's staff members and the rest of the students? How so? Did that treatment then affect the way the individuals behaved and what was expected of them?

The impact of labeling has been a key idea in literature—from Hawthorne's Hester Prynne being branded with a *Scarlett Letter* for adultery in Puritan Boston to S. E. Hinton's story of the struggles of the teenage Greasers and Socs in 1960s Oklahoma in *The Outsiders,* the way individuals are perceived and labeled can have important and long-lasting consequences for how they are treated by others and the opportunities that are available to them.

The labeling perspective is situated in the larger framework of social psychology and **symbolic interactionism** in sociology. This is a micro-level, relativist perspective that is focused on individuals and the meanings they attach to objects, people, and interactions around them. Symbolic interactionists advocate direct observation of the social world as it is experienced and understood by the individuals acting in it. Labeling theorists examine the social meaning of deviant labels, how those labels are understood, and how they affect the individuals to which they are applied.

Labeling theorists argue that, to some extent, deviance is in the eye of the beholder. The reaction to the behavior or the person is the key element in defining deviance. Can you think of an act that is inherently deviant? An act that everyone would agree is and has always been deviant across cultures and across time? Chances are that any act you might initially think of has been accepted behavior in some cultures under some circumstances. For example, we generally consider taking the life of another to be a very serious criminal act; however, in times of war or acts of self-defense, taking a life can be viewed as acceptable and perhaps laudable behavior. The relativist perspective reminds us that audience reaction is key in defining deviance—no act is thought to be inherently deviant; acts are judged depending on the context and the power of the individuals and groups involved.

As Becker (1963/1973) makes clear,

> A major element in every aspect of the drama of deviance is the imposition of definitions—of situations, acts, and people—by those powerful enough or sufficiently legitimated to be able to do so. A full understanding requires the thorough study of those definitions and the processes by which they develop and attain legitimacy and taken-for-grantedness. (p. 207)

According to the labeling perspective, deviance is a status imposed on an individual or a group that may or may not be related to actual rule breaking. The focus is on reactions rather than norm violations; you could be falsely accused but still be labeled deviant and face the repercussions. When there are disagreements over when and whether an actor should be considered deviant, power is a key element through which the status of deviance is imposed. Individuals with power will be better able to both reject a label or to impose a deviant label on another; as Matsueda (1992) makes the connection clear,

> A hallmark of labeling theory is the proposition that deviant labels are not randomly distributed across the social structure, but are instead more likely to apply to the powerless, the disadvantaged, and the poor. . . . Moreover, the powerless, having fewer cultural and material resources at their disposal, may be more likely to accept deviant labels. Again, the result is a self-fulfilling prophesy:

members of disadvantaged groups are labeled delinquent, which alters their self-conceptions and causes them to deviate, thus fulfilling the prophesy of their initial label. (p. 1558)

◈ Theoretical Background

One of the earliest building blocks for the labeling perspective was developed in the work of Franklin Tannenbaum (1938). Tannenbaum suggested that police contact may turn relatively common acts of juvenile delinquency into a "dramatization of evil" that labels the individuals involved in a negative light. This societal reaction may lead to further deviant acts.

In his book *Social Pathology,* Edwin Lemert (1951) made the important distinction between primary and secondary deviation. **Primary deviance** refers to common instances where individuals violate norms without viewing themselves as being involved in a deviant social role. Primary deviance consists of incidental deviant acts—instances in which an individual breaks or violates norms but does not do so chronically. For example, teens may occasionally shoplift while with their friends, but they would not consider themselves delinquent. You can see examples of primary deviance in the readings that follow this chapter (particularly Chambliss's "The Saints and the Roughnecks"); as you read the articles, ask yourself which groups are committing deviant acts without embracing deviant social roles. How much power do they have in their situation?

With primary deviation, there is no engulfment in a deviant social role, but primary deviance can serve to trigger the labeling process. Individuals can be caught as they engage in deviant acts and they may then be labeled delinquent, criminal, or mentally ill. Once labeled, they may move into secondary deviation. **Secondary deviance** occurs when a person begins to engage in deviant behavior as a means of defense, attack, or adjustment to the problems created by reactions to him or her. In some cases when rules are broken, it elicits a reaction. In defense to the reaction, the individual may commit subsequent deviant acts and begin a more serious deviant career. Labeling someone deviant and treating that person as if he or she is "generally rather than specifically deviant produces a **self-fulfilling prophesy.** It sets in motion several mechanisms which conspire to shape the person in the image people have of him" (Becker, 1963/1973, p. 34).

For Lemert and other labeling theorists, the cause of the initial deviance is left unexplained. Rather than asking why someone commits a deviant act, the question is, who decides what is deviant, who is to be labeled deviant, and under what circumstances? Howard S. Becker's (1963/1973) explanation of this view in his book *Outsiders* has become the classic interactionist or relativist statement of labeling and deviance:

> *Social groups create deviance by making the rules whose infraction constitutes deviance,* and by applying those rules to particular people and labeling them as outsiders. From this point of view, deviance is *not* a quality of the act the person commits, but rather a consequence of the application by others of rules and sanctions to an "offender." The deviant is one to whom that label has successfully been applied; deviant behavior is behavior people so label. (Becker, 1963/1973, p. 9)

◈ How the Labeling Process Works

If diagrammed in its simplest form, the labeling process would look something like this:

Deviance → reaction → role engulfment → secondary deviance

It's not that simple, of course, and the lines would not be so direct. In fact, there would be reciprocal or circular relationships, as well, with lines going back and forth between deviance, reactions, secondary deviance, and role engulfment. Imagine that when you were a teenager, you were caught cheating on an exam. If it's your first offense (or the first time you were caught), there may be an informal reaction—a conference with your teacher and parents, a failing grade, and a strict warning. After this event, your teachers and parents may monitor your behavior more closely. You may commit more deviant or criminal acts to push the boundaries or because you are bored or your friends are involved and it looks fun. If you are caught stealing from a store, the case begins to build that you are generally a troublemaker and a "bad kid" likely to cause further trouble. When treated this way and closely monitored, you may start to *feel* like a bad kid. If the reaction is severe enough (for example, being adjudicated delinquent in juvenile court), other parents may not want their children to spend time with you. You may start hanging out with the other "bad" kids (role engulfment) and committing more serious crimes (secondary deviance).

Labeling theory is an interactionist theory and does not suggest that once on the path to deviance, one must continue in that direction. As Becker (1963/1973) explains, "Obviously, everyone caught in one deviant act and labeled a deviant does not move inevitably toward greater deviance . . . he may decide that he does not want to take the deviant road and turn back. If he makes the right choice, he will be welcomed back into the conventional community; but if he makes the wrong move, he will be rejected and start a cycle of increasing deviance" (pp. 36–37).

Labeling can lead to secondary deviance in three general and overlapping ways: altering an individual's self-concept, limiting conforming opportunities, and encouraging involvement in a deviant subculture (Kubrin et al., 2009, p. 203). Being labeled deviant may also lead to a deviant **master status,** a status that proves to be more important than most others. A deviant master status elicits strong reactions and shapes the perception and behavior of those around you. For example, being labeled a sex offender is often a master status; sex offenders may also be parents, spouses, employees, and friends, but once labeled a sex offender, that identity takes priority in the minds of others.

DEVIANCE IN POPULAR CULTURE

The process of labeling is a powerful theoretical concept and tool in studying deviant behavior. Can the way that others view you and react to you influence how you think of yourself and behave? If you cannot think of examples from your own life or family or friends, popular culture films and television shows portray a wide variety of types of deviance and examples of labeling.

One Flew Over the Cuckoo's Nest is a classic film about life in a mental hospital. When R. P. McMurphy is sent to the state mental institution, he is not crazy; he has run afoul of the law and simply believes it will be easier to serve his time in a mental hospital rather than in a corrections facility or work camp. He does not, however, understand the power of the label as it relates to mental illness. Watch this film and pay attention to how McMurphy and the other patients are treated by the hospital staff. How does it make the patients think about themselves? Why is McMurphy's presence so disruptive to the routine of the ward? How is he punished for not playing the expected role?

Girl, Interrupted, focusing on the experiences of young women, is an alternative look inside a mental institution. Based on Susanna Kaysen's memoir of more than a year of voluntary institutionalization, the film is another strong example of labeling and mental illness.

(Continued)

(Continued)

The MTV television show *Made* is all about teenagers working to change their labels—the shy boy who wants to become a ladies man, the tomboy who aspires to be a beauty queen, or the artsy drama girl who wants to make the cheerleading squad.

It's difficult to even describe the show without using labels as part of the description. What were some of your labels in high school? How do you think your life would have been different if you had a more positive or a more negative label? Do you think it's possible to re-create yourself—and the way others view you—in a relatively short amount of time as they do on *Made?* Why or why not?

◈ Labeling and Mental Illness

Scheff (1966) laid out a theory of labeling and mental illness that suggested that most mental illness begins with a form of primary deviance he calls **residual rule breaking.** Residual rule breaking is essentially deviance for which there exists no clear category—it is not a crime, but it may be behavior that draws attention and makes the societal audience uncomfortable. Inappropriate dress, conversation, or interactions may be perceived as residual rule breaking. Consistent with other labeling theorists' ideas on primary deviance, Scheff is not particularly concerned with why people commit these acts in the first place; he argues that residual rule -breaking comes from diverse sources. The acts may stem from biological, psychological, or situational conditions; most residual rule breaking is denied and deemed insignificant, and the individuals get past it and move on with their lives.

Importantly, however, residual rule breaking can activate the labeling process. Say, for example, a college student breaks up with her boyfriend and stays in bed in her pajamas for a week. If left alone, this behavior might be written off as painful but temporary heartache and the incident might pass. If, however, her concerned parents take her to a doctor or a hospital, she may be given a diagnosis of clinical depression and labeled as mentally ill. If she is hospitalized for any time at all, her roommates and friends may start treating her as if she is fragile and cannot cope with difficult circumstances.

Scheff (1966) suggests that the symptoms and stereotypes of mental illness are inadvertently reaffirmed in ordinary social interactions. Friends and family may reward those labeled mentally ill for going along with their expectations and playing the stereotyped role. At the same time, labeled deviants may be punished or blocked when attempting to resume their regular activities and return to conventional lives.

While most residual rule breaking can be explained away and deemed insignificant, it can be the starting point for the labeling process. Once labeled, many individuals will have a difficult time continuing or resuming their conventional roles. Thus, Scheff (1966) argues that among residual rule breakers, labeling is a key factor leading to more serious and lengthy deviant careers.

David Rosenhan (1973) conducted a fascinating study of labeling and mental illness when he worked with eight sane "pseudo-patients" who simulated symptoms of psychosis and were admitted to 12 mental hospitals over the course of the study. Once hospitalized, the pseudo-patients immediately stopped simulating symptoms, yet they had a difficult time proving themselves to be sane. Rosenhan begins his article with a provocative question: "If sanity and insanity exist, how shall we know them?" and he goes on to detail the treatment and medications received by the pseudo-patients during their time in the mental hospitals. Ironically, when the pseudo-patients were finally released from the hospital, each was discharged with a diagnosis of schizophrenia "in remission"; none were thought to be sane. You can read Rosenhan's full study in the articles following this chapter.

A more recent longitudinal study added depth to our understanding of the impact of being labeled mentally ill by exploring the **stigma** and social rejection experienced by mental patients once they return to the community (E. Wright, Gronfein, & Owens, 2000). The authors found that both institutionalization and community reactions affected the self-concept of former mental patients:

> Stigma is a powerful and persistent force in the lives of long-term mental patients . . . even for patients who have had extensive experience in the mental patient role, subsequent experiences of rejection increase and crystallize patients' self-deprecating feelings. . . . Our results demonstrate convincingly that exposure to stigmatizing experiences represents a potentially serious source of chronic or recurrent stress for mental patients who established identities as "mental patients." The fact that these effects persist over time and diminish feelings of mastery provides additional empirical support for modified labeling theory's claims that the impact of stigma on the self has long-term implications for a person's ability to function in society. (E. Wright et al., 2000, pp. 80–82)

◈ Labeling and Delinquency

▲ **Photo 8.2** From a labeling perspective, being hospitalized in a mental institution can be very damaging to the individual. If you were one of the pseudo-patients in Rosenhan's study, how do you think institutionalization would have affected your self-image?

Juvenile delinquency is another area where the labeling theory has been widely applied and used to create or change policies that affect the lives of young offenders. Although it predates any formal explication of the theory, the juvenile justice system, itself, was created in part because of a concern over the negative impact being labeled and treated as a criminal would have on a young person. The terminology used in juvenile court shows this concern: Offenders in the juvenile system are "adjudicated delinquent" rather than convicted of a crime. One result of this gentler language is that delinquents processed through the juvenile system do not need to check the box on job applications that asks if they have been convicted of a felony. Another example that shows concern over labeling juveniles is that in many states, an offender's juvenile record may be sealed or expunged once he or she completes the sentence and stays out of trouble for a specified period of time. In effect, this offers juvenile offenders who pass through troubled times the possibility of a clean slate as adults.

William Chambliss (1973) offered a vivid example of delinquency, social power, and labeling in his article "The Saints and the Roughnecks." Chambliss began this research project by simply spending time "hanging out" with two different groups of high school boys—the working-class "Roughnecks" and the upper-middle class "Saints"—from the same community. While both groups of boys were involved in similar levels and amounts of delinquency, the community reactions were quite different. The Saints were treated as good boys "sowing their wild oats" and were given the benefit of the doubt by teachers, police officers, and other community members. The Saints were never officially arrested for their behavior, and most went on to college and successful, conforming lives. The Roughnecks, on the other hand, were viewed as bad boys and delinquents, and they were often in trouble with the police. As adults, the Roughnecks had quite different outcomes than the Saints. You can read this study, in its entirety, in the articles that follow this chapter. Thinking about your own high school and adolescent experiences, you might be surprised at how familiar the story still sounds, decades after it was written.

Chambliss was asked recently what surprised him in studying the Saints and Roughnecks; his response speaks to the impact of labels and how difficult it can be for those with less power to resist them:

(1) How serious were the crimes of the Saints and how inconsequential were the crimes of the Roughnecks. (2) How readily the boys in each group accepted the labels attached to them even though the labels were incompatible with their actual behavior. (Inderbitzin & Boyd, 2010, p. 205)

The book, *Our Guys,* by Bernard Lefkowitz (1997), chronicles a case in Glen Ridge, New Jersey, where a group of well-to-do, popular athletes raped a 17-year-old mentally challenged girl with a baseball bat and a broomstick. When members of the community finally heard about this crime, their reaction was generally sympathy for the boys and concern for their reputations—"They'll just be ruined by this." The boys had the power in this setting, and the girl, by virtue of her gender and her mental impairment, was easily labeled as the deviant. Our guys are similar in some way to the Saints from Chambliss's study in that the community members did not see or chose to ignore their deviant behavior. The young men from Glen Ridge were obviously much more delinquent and destructive toward females in their community, but they were able to get away with their bad behavior for a surprisingly long time in part due to their positive labels as the town's golden boys. You can read the introduction to the book, *Our Guys,* in the articles that follow this chapter.

A relatively recent study on labeling and delinquency (Adams, Robertson, Gray-Ray, & Ray, 2003) examined incarcerated youths' perceived negative labels. Their perceived negative labels, particularly those imposed by teachers, parents, and peers, were related to increased involvement in self-reported delinquency. The authors viewed this as supporting labeling theory and the idea of secondary deviance. The perceived negative labels were a better predictor of serious delinquency than they were for drug-related offenses, perhaps because juveniles are rarely caught and incarcerated for drug use and drug offenses other than trafficking. Finally, this study suggests that informal labeling by teachers, peers, and parents is perhaps more important than formal processing through the system. The relationships with people in one's social circle seem to carry more weight than judgments by legal actors. It also may be the case that formal labeling may simply reinforce or legitimize already acquired deviant or criminal reputations. The authors explain, "It appears that contact with social control agents is secondary to the reaction of significant others in explaining involvement in delinquent behavior" (Adams et al., 2003, p. 183).

▲ **Photo 8.3**   Being officially labeled delinquent may decrease the life-chances of juvenile offenders; such labeling may lead to secondary deviance and more serious criminal careers.

Context also matters when considering the impact of formal sanctioning and official labels of delinquency. After conducting interviews with 20 minority youth from high-poverty urban neighborhoods, Hirschfield (2008) concluded that in the macro-level context of severely disadvantaged neighborhoods, being arrested carries little stigma. Delinquent youth in his sample were quite concerned with being informally labeled by their family and friends, but arrest and processing by the justice system were viewed as relatively normal parts of adolescence in their neighborhood and their experience. Thus, labeling still matters and affects juvenile offenders in important ways, but researchers can work to better specify how macro-level conditions affect perceptions of the label and community reaction.

Contemporary Theoretical and Empirical Studies in Labeling

Braithwaite (1989): *Crime, Shame and Reintegration*

In *Crime, Shame and Reintegration,* John Braithwaite (1989) argued that societies will generally have lower crime rates if they can effectively communicate shame about crime. Importantly, however, Braithwaite makes a critical distinction between **reintegrative shaming** and stigmatization. With reintegrative shaming, the offender can be viewed as a good person who has done a bad deed; stigmatization, on the other hand, labels the offender a bad person. Put differently, "Stigmatization is unforgiving—the offender is left with the stigma permanently, whereas reintegrative shaming is forgiving" (Braithwaite, 2000, p. 282).

In Braithwaite's conceptualization of reintegrative shaming, an accused individual is expected to admit his or her offense, essentially accepting responsibility for the act and labeling the act as deviant, but then he or she is provided with an opportunity for reintegration back into society. With reintegration ceremonies, Braithwaite and Mugford argue (1994) that "disapproval of a bad act is communicated while sustaining the identity of the actor as good. Shame is transmitted within a continuum of respect for the wrongdoer. Repair work is directed at ensuring that a deviant identity (one of the actor's multiple identities) does not become a master status trait that overwhelms other identities" (p. 142).

Braithwaite's work offers an alternative to simply labeling offenders deviant and creating new and harmful master statuses. The idea of reintegrative shaming has not been tested on a large scale in the United States as of yet, but it offers one promising alternative to punitive criminal justice policies that may engender serious deviant careers. According to Braithwaite's theory, while labeling makes things worse when it is stigmatizing, when done respectfully and focused on the act rather than the individual, labeling may actually reduce crime (Braithwaite, 2000, p. 288).

Matsueda (1992): "Reflected Appraisals, Parental Labeling, and Delinquency"

Building on the work of George Herbert Mead, Ross Matsueda (1992) developed an interactionist theory of the self and delinquency. In his study, Matsueda focused on informal labels made by an adolescent's parents and whether those parental appraisals affected delinquency by affecting the adolescent's own reflected appraisals (Matsueda, 1992, p. 1590). In essence, the idea is that labeling and the reflected appraisals of others can create a delinquent "self" that may lead the adolescent further into deviant behavior. Matsueda found that youths' reflected appraisals of themselves were strongly influenced by their parents' appraisals of them. As an example, if a youth perceives that his parents view him as a troublemaker, he may start to perceive himself that way, too, and may be more likely to act the part.

In a later study, Heimer and Matsueda (1994) explain secondary deviance as a "chain of events operating through labeling":

> Youth who are older, nonblack, urban residents, and from nonintact homes commit more initial delinquent acts than others, which increases the chances that their parents will see them as rule-violators. In turn, labeling by parents increases the likelihood that these youth will affiliate with delinquent peers and see themselves as rule-violators from the standpoint of others, which ultimately increases the likelihood of future delinquent behavior. (pp. 381–382)

Rosenfield (1997): "Labeling Mental Illness"

A prominent study on labeling and mental illness centered on the concept and meaning of *stigma* (Rosenfield, 1997). Rosenfield (1997) suggests that stigma is an important point of disagreement for labeling theorists and their critics. For labeling theorists, the stigma attached to mental illness is a serious problem; in Goffman's words, "By definition, of course, we believe the person with a stigma is not quite human. On this assumption, we exercise varieties of discrimination, through which we effectively, if often unthinkingly, reduce his life chances" (E. Goffman, 1963, p. 5). Critics of labeling theory, on the other hand, suggest that stigma may be of little consequence to the mentally ill. Rosenfield designed a research project to compare the receipt of treatment and services versus the perception of stigma on the quality of life for people with chronic mental illness.

Rosenfield's (1997) research was conducted at a clubhouse model program for people with chronic mental illness residing in the community. The club took an "empowerment approach" and offered a range of services, including psychiatric treatment, supervision, life skills, and vocational rehabilitation. Rosenfield found that "stigma is a problem for most people with chronic mental illness, and perceptions of stigma have a significant negative relationship with patients' quality of life. By contrast, services have a strong positive association with quality of life" (p. 669). As might be expected, then, Rosenfield concludes, "Life satisfaction is highest for those who experience little stigma and gain access to high quality services. Life satisfaction is lowest among those perceiving high levels of stigma and lacking such services" (p. 670).

Davies and Tanner (2003): "The Long Arm of the Law: Effects of Labeling on Employment"

A recent study on formal labeling by schools and the justice system suggests that labeling has long-term impacts on opportunities and employment. Davies and Tanner (2003) used a large, nationally representative sample to examine the effect that formal sanctions ranging from school suspension to incarceration during ages 15 to 23 had on subjects' occupational status, income, and employment 14 years later. While controlling for variables such as social background, prior deviant behavior, and family status, Davies and Tanner found that severe forms of labeling did have strong negative effects: "The indirect effects of early encounters with teachers, police officers, courts, and prison systems upon the transition from adolescence to adult work roles are significant and cumulatively damaging" (p. 399). School-based sanctioning, such as being suspended or expelled, had a negative impact on later job outcomes for females but not for males. This finding reminds us of the complexity of the social world and how difficult it can be to tease out all of the relevant factors. While the Davies and Tanner study generally supports labeling theory, there is much work still to be done to fully understand all of the variables and interactions that affect the labeling process.

Labeling and the Adoption of a Deviant Status

By Terrell A. Hayes (2010), in *Deviant Behavior, 31*, 274–302

Hayes interviewed 46 individuals who attended Debtors Anonymous meetings to examine the process by which these individuals assumed the deviant status of "debtor." He examined both the process of social labeling and self-labeling and found that most individuals went through several stages in which they slowly came to see themselves as a person with a problem.

Hayes found that social labeling involved "active cues" and "passive cues" in which the individual was confronted with the problem. The active cues involved informal interactions with close others (friends, spouses, relatives) who identified the individual's behavior as problematic.

(My husband) was saying that I was sick, sick, sick. I stayed in denial for a while saying (to him) you indulge yourself, I'm certainly entitled to indulge myself. . . . But then I began examining that finally agreeing with my husband (and others) that I overspend. (p. 281)

Passive cues, in the form of literature and other materials, can also be part of the self-labeling process.

When things got really tight I would find myself buying groceries on my Amoco gas card. . . . No one came to me and said, "You know? You are out of control. Here you need to get some help." Even my wife didn't. She never confronted me and said, "I think you need to go get some help." One day I was downtown at the library and I was just browsing through the shelves. I caught the title on the spine of the book, *How to Get Out of Debt, Stay Out of Debt, and Live Prosperously.* It seemed to describe me perfectly. (p. 286)

Finally, Hayes found that self-help groups contributed to the labeling process and likelihood that individuals would label themselves as debtors. Interestingly enough, these self-help groups were not limited to Debtors Anonymous (the group that Hayes initially found his participants through). Several of his participants actually identified their time in other self-help groups as being a catalyst for their self-identification as debtors in need of help.

◈ Impact of Labeling Theory

The labeling perspective caught hold in the United States during the 1970s and had a clear impact on public policy in two distinct areas: juvenile justice and the care of mental patients. As research showed the potential negative impact of being labeled delinquent (Chambliss, 1973) and being labeled mentally ill (Rosenhan, 1973), policy makers took notice and began to rethink how to best serve those populations.

Some change happened organically as individuals working in these systems strove for better and more humane results. Jerome Miller, the commissioner of the Department of Youth Services in Massachusetts, frustrated with the conditions in the juvenile correctional facilities in his agency, closed all of the state's training schools between 1970 and 1972 (Miller, 1998). Miller's original goal was to make the Massachusetts's reform schools more humane with more therapy and individualized treatment for incarcerated youth. But, as he tells it, "Whenever I thought we'd made progress, something happened, a beating, a kid in an isolation cell, an offhand remark by a superintendent or cottage supervisor that told me what I envisioned would never be allowed.... The decision to close the institutions grew from my frustration at not being able to keep them caring and decent" (p. 18). Over a 2-year span, Massachusetts closed its secure reform schools and moved to a system of alternative community treatment and placements for youth considered the most dangerous in the state.

Miller's closing of Massachusetts's reform schools can be viewed in the larger context of **deinstitutionalization** that was occurring in the early 1970s. As Miller (1998) explained, "While we were moving a few hundred delinquents back to the community, state departments of mental health across the United States were deinstitutionalizing thousands of mental patients" (p. 20).

Edwin Schur (1973) suggested that a better way for our juvenile justice system to operate was to not institutionalize young offenders in the first place. Schur argued strongly for a policy of radical **nonintervention**— in other words, in dealing with delinquent youth, we should choose to "leave the kids alone wherever possible." Schur advocated a "hands-off" approach to juvenile misbehavior, which would purposely take moral judgment away from juvenile courts.

In 1974, the United States passed the Juvenile Justice Delinquency Prevention (JJDP) Act, which significantly altered the juvenile corrections system. Concerns over the labeling of minor offenders as delinquents and the potential for criminal learning in juvenile institutions led to widespread attempts to deinstitutionalize youth, tolerate minor misbehavior, and use community alternatives for youth who needed intervention. The JJDP Act offered states funding as an incentive to decriminalize status offenses (behavior such as truancy, disobedience, or running away that would not be crimes if committed by adults) and to deinstitutionalize status offenders. Reform schools and secure juvenile institutions became the agency of last resort, reserved for the most serious juvenile offenders.

Times have certainly changed since then, and while the juvenile justice system still exists and attempts to resocialize delinquent youth, the United States now incarcerates more people than in any other time in history. Punitive laws have largely replaced the goal of rehabilitation as serious juvenile offenders are routinely tried and convicted as adults.

In recent years, scholars such as Braithwaite (2002) have endorsed a move to **restorative justice.** In a system of restorative justice, "the state functions as an arbiter or partner who works with the victim and the offender to reduce the harm associated with the criminal act that has been committed" (Cullen & Agnew, 2006, p. 270). Typically, restorative justice involves bringing the victims, offenders, and community members together in a mediated conference. The goal of these conferences is for the offenders to take responsibility for their actions and to reach consensus on a plan for the offenders to restore the harm they have caused, often through restitution to the victim and service to the community.

Labeling theory has been widely critiqued as an explanation for why people commit deviant acts or crime. Rather than asking why individuals commit acts against the norms or society, this perspective focuses on how and under what circumstances the individual is judged as deviant and what impact that judgment may have on his or her self-concept, relationships, opportunities, and life chances. Becker (1963/1973) suggests that labeling was never intended to be a full-blown theory of deviance, but instead it offered a perspective that shifted the focus to the process of constructing deviance. Early proponents of the labeling perspective wanted to enlarge the area taken into consideration in the study of deviant phenomena by including in it activities of others than the allegedly deviant actor ... one of the most important contributions of this approach has been to focus attention on the way labeling places the actor in circumstances which make it harder for him to continue the normal routines of everyday life and thus provoke him to "abnormal" actions (as when a prison record make it harder to earn a living at a conventional occupation and so disposes its possessor to move into an illegal one). (Becker, 1963/1973, p. 179)

◈ Conclusion

Returning for a moment to the film *The Breakfast Club,* the letter that opened this chapter also opened the film. By the end of the students' day in detention—and the end of the film—they have started to know each other and have learned to look beyond the labels of their high school cliques. They view and treat each other much differently at the end of the day than they did in the beginning. Each student contributes his or her voice to the final letter left for the principal when they are freed from detention:

Brian Johnson: Dear Mr. Vernon, we accept the fact that we had to sacrifice a whole Saturday in detention for whatever it was we did wrong ... but we think you're crazy to make us write an essay telling you who we think we are. You see us as you want to see us ... In the simplest terms and the most convenient definitions. But what we found out is that each one of us is a brain ...

Andrew Clark: ... and an athlete ...

Allison Reynolds: ... and a basket case ...

Claire Standish: ... a princess ...

John Bender: ... and a criminal ...

Brian Johnson: Does that answer your question? Sincerely yours, the Breakfast Club.

If you pay attention to the world around you, you will see labels everywhere. They offer a convenient shorthand and can be helpful in categorizing complex relationships and interactions. But, as the labeling perspective points out, being labeled deviant can have long-lasting harmful impacts on an individual's self-concept and life chances. These issues will be further discussed in Chapters 11 (Social Control of Deviance) and 12 (Deviant Careers and Career Deviance), where we will explore the role of prisons, juvenile facilities, and mental hospitals as agents of social control and examine how they can affect the individual long after the original act and deviant label.

In pointing to the larger ideas of the labeling perspective and to Howard Becker's work, particularly, as offering important sensitizing concepts for sociologists studying deviant behavior, Orcutt (1983) suggests that

the impact of labeling theory on the field of deviance cannot be measured in strictly scientific terms alone. The work of the labeling theorists not only portrayed the definition and control of deviance as analytically problematic but also as morally and politically problematic. ... This relativistic conception of labeling as a power game provides the basic ingredient for a political critique of the uses and abuses of social control by certain dominant groups in modern, complex societies. (pp. 241–242)

Certainly the relativist perspective broadened the way we think about deviant behavior and social control. Studies from labeling and conflict theories have highlighted the importance of power and inequality in defining deviance and in the differential enforcement of norms and laws. Chapter 9 will build on these ideas by introducing you to conflict theory, and Chapter 10 will provide an overview of critical theories of deviance.

NOW YOU . . . USE THE THEORY

The Power of Words: In 1983, Edwin Schur published a book on labeling and women called *Labeling Women Deviant: Gender, Stigma and Social Control*. One of Schur's arguments in the book is that women are more quickly and strongly labeled for their behavior if it steps out of normative boundaries than men are. To highlight this gender imbalance in labeling, an often used class exercise is one in which students are asked to think up all the derogatory labels that they can for men and women. Inevitably, that list is much longer for women than for men.

What are the normative expectations for women and men in society? Make a list of expected behaviors for each group. After making this list, make a list of positive labels associated with each group. Now make a list of negative labels associated with each group. How are these labels used in society? What is the relationship between power, both the use of power and the loss of power associated with these labels? According to the labels, which normative behaviors are most likely to produce a reaction if violated?

Was Schur right? Are women more likely labeled for stepping outside the normative boundaries than men are?

EXERCISES AND DISCUSSION QUESTIONS

1. Imagine you were officially labeled deviant in junior high school. How do you think this would have affected your life and your opportunities? Would your parents, teachers, and peers have treated you differently? Where do you think you would be now if you had been labeled delinquent?

2. Another surprising finding Chambliss mentioned in studying the Saints and the Roughnecks was "how easily some of them [the two football players] changed their self image, their behavior and their lives" (Inderbitzin & Boyd, 2010). What do you think made the difference for those young men? What does that suggest for how we treat delinquents?

3. What types of primary deviance do the Saints and the Roughnecks commit? Who goes on to commit

secondary deviance? What are examples from the article of secondary deviance?

4. Why do you think the athletes from Glen Ridge (in *Our Guys*) were so difficult to label deviant? What affected the process? How did the victim's gender and mental challenges contribute to the situation?

5. Can you imagine volunteering as a pseudo-patient if we were going to replicate Rosenhan's study? Why or why not? As a (presumably) sane person, how do you think being labeled as mentally ill and hospitalized would affect your self-concept?

6. Sex offenders have been particularly demonized and feared in the United States. While ostensibly set up to provide important information to the community members, sex offender registries have

taken public labeling to a whole new level. There is real reason for fear when one's vital statistics, address, and photo are posted online on sex offender registries: Vigilantes killed two sex offenders in Washington state in 2005, and two more were shot to death in Maine in 2006 (Daniel, 2006; J. Martin & O'Hagan, 2005; O'Hagan & Brooks, 2005).

7. An important issue is that the label "sex offender" is a broad one, encompassing both predatory crimes and statutory ones. Take, for example, the case of Ricky Blackman, convicted as a sex offender for having intercourse with a 13-year-old girl when he was 16. The label and his place on a sex offender registry affected Blackman's life in many ways: He couldn't go to high school, couldn't attend sporting events, and couldn't even go into the public library (Grinberg, 2010).

8. What do you think of sex offender registries? What are the strengths and weaknesses? How do you think society should deal with cases like Ricky Blackman?

KEY TERMS

Deinstitutionalization	Reintegrative shaming	Self-fulfilling prophesy
Master status	Residual rule breaking	Stigma
Nonintervention	Restorative justice	Symbolic interactionism
Primary deviance	Secondary deviance	

READING 23

For this piece, William Chambliss spent 2 years "hanging out" with two different groups of high school boys—the working-class "Roughnecks" and the upper-middle-class "Saints." While both groups were involved in similar levels and amounts of delinquency, the community reactions were quite different. The Saints were never officially arrested for their behavior, while the Roughnecks were often in trouble with the police. Chambliss poses two questions, the first dealing with why the community, school, and the police reacted so differently to the two groups and the second dealing with why the two groups had such different outcomes following high school. Concerning the first question, Chambliss cites differential visibility of the deviant behaviors, differences in demeanor toward authority figures, and bias among community residents, school officials, and the police. With regard to the second question, Chambliss kept in touch with these young men through early adulthood and was thus able to document the actual long-term outcomes of the boys. Because of the small sample size and other limitations of the data, Chambliss is cautious in answering the second question, but he clearly hints at the long-term effects of labels and community expectations on the life chances and adult careers of these two distinct groups of boys.

Source: Chambliss, William J. 1973. "The Saints and the Roughnecks." *Society,* November/December, 24–31. With kind permission from Springer Science + Business Media.

The Saints and the Roughnecks

William J. Chambliss

Eight promising young men-children of good, stable, white upper-middle-class families, active in school affairs, good pre-college students-were some of the most delinquent boys at Hanibal High School. While community residents knew that these boys occasionally sowed a few wild oats, they were totally unaware that sowing wild oats completely occupied the daily routine of these young men. The Saints were constantly occupied with truancy, drinking, wild driving, petty theft, and vandalism. Yet no one was officially arrested for any misdeed during the two years I observed them.

This record was particularly surprising in light of my observations during the same two years of another gang of Hanibal High School students, six lower class white boys known as the Roughnecks. The Roughnecks were constantly in trouble with police and community even though their rate of delinquency was about equal with that of the Saints. What was the cause of this disparity? The result? The following consideration of the activities, social class, and community perceptions of both gangs may provide some answers.

◇ The Saints From Monday to Friday

The Saints' principal daily concern was with getting out of school as early as possible. The boys managed to get out of school with minimum danger that they would be accused of playing hooky through an elaborate procedure for obtaining "legitimate" release from class. The most common procedure was for one boy to obtain the release of another by fabricating a meeting of some committee, program, or recognized club. Charles might raise his hand in his 9:00 chemistry class and ask to be excused—a euphemism for going to the bathroom. Charles would go to Ed's math class and inform the teacher that Ed was needed for a 9:30 rehearsal of the drama club play. The math teacher would recognize Ed and Charles as "good students" involved in numerous school activities and would permit Ed to leave at 9:30. Charles would return to his class, and Ed would go to Tom's English class to obtain his release. Tom would engineer Charles's escape. The strategy would continue until as many of the Saints as possible were freed. After a stealthy trip to the car (which had been parked in a strategic spot), the boys were off for a day of fun.

Over the two years I observed the Saints, this pattern was repeated nearly every day. There were variations on the theme, but in one form or another, the boys used this procedure for getting out of class and then off the school grounds. Rarely did all eight of the Saints manage to leave school at the same time. The average number avoiding school on the days I observed them was five.

Having escaped from the concrete corridors the boys usually went either to a pool hall on the other (lower class) side of town or to a café in the suburbs. Both places were out of the way of people the boys were likely to know (family or school officials), and both provided a source of entertainment. The pool hall entertainment was the generally rough atmosphere, the occasional hustler, the sometimes drunk proprietor and, of course, the game of pool. The café's entertainment was provided by the owner. The boys would "accidentally" knock a glass on the floor or spill cola on the counter—not all the time, but enough to be sporting. They would also bend spoons, put salt in sugar bowls and generally tease whoever was working in the café. The owner had opened the café recently and was dependent on the boys' business, which was, in fact, substantial since between the horsing around and the teasing they bought food and drinks.

◇ The Saints on Weekends

On weekends the automobile was even more critical than during the week, for on weekends the Saints went to Big Town—a large city with a population of over a million 25 miles from Hanibal. Every Friday and Saturday night most of the Saints would meet between 8:00 and 8:30 and would go into Big Town. Big Town activities included drinking heavily in taverns or nightclubs, driving drunkenly through the streets, and committing acts of vandalism and playing pranks.

By midnight on Fridays and Saturdays the Saints were usually thoroughly high, and one or two of them were often so drunk they had to be carried to the cars. Then the boys drove around town, calling obscenities to women and girls; occasionally trying (unsuccessfully so far as I could tell) to pick girls up; and driving recklessly through red lights and at high speeds with their lights out. Occasionally they played "chicken." One boy would climb out the back window of the car and across the roof to the driver's side of the car while the car was moving at high speed (between 40 and 50 miles an hour); then the driver would move over and the boy who had just crawled across the car roof would take the driver's seat.

Searching for "fair game" for a prank was the boys' principal activity after they left the tavern. The boys would drive alongside a foot patrolman and ask directions to some street. If the policeman leaned on the car in the course of answering the question, the driver would speed away, causing him to lose his balance. The Saints were careful to play this prank only in an area where they were not going to spend much time and where they could quickly disappear around a corner to avoid having their license plate number taken.

Construction sites and road repair areas were the special province of the Saints' mischief. A soon-to-be-repaired hole in the road inevitably invited the Saints to remove lanterns and wooden barricades and put them in the car, leaving the hole unprotected. The boys would find a safe vantage point and wait for an unsuspecting motorist to drive into the hole. Often, though not always, the boys would go up to the motorist and commiserate with him about the dreadful way the city protected its citizenry.

Leaving the scene of the open hole and the motorist, the boys would then go searching for an appropriate place to erect the stolen barricade. An "appropriate place" was often a spot on a highway near a curve in the road where the barricade would not be seen by an oncoming motorist. The boys would wait to watch an unsuspecting motorist attempt to stop and (usually) crash into the wooden barricade. With saintly bearing the boys might offer help and understanding.

A stolen lantern might well find its way onto the back of a police car or hang from a street lamp. Once a lantern served as a prop for a reenactment of the "midnight ride of Paul Revere" until the "play," which was taking place at 2:00 A.M. in the center of a main street of Big Town, was interrupted by a police car several blocks away. The boys ran, leaving the lanterns on the street, and managed to avoid being apprehended.

Abandoned houses, especially if they were located in out-of-the-way places, were fair game for destruction and spontaneous vandalism. The boys would break windows, remove furniture to the yard and tear it apart, urinate on the walls, and scrawl obscenities inside.

Through all the pranks, drinking, and reckless driving the boys managed miraculously to avoid being stopped by police. Only twice in two years was I aware that they had been stopped by a Big Town policeman. Once was for speeding (which they did every time they drove whether they were drunk or sober), and the driver managed to convince the policeman that it was simply an error. The second time they were stopped they had just left a nightclub and were walking through an alley. Aaron stopped to urinate and the boys began making obscene remarks. A foot patrolman came into the alley, lectured the boys and sent them home. Before the boys got to the car one began talking in a loud voice again. The policeman, who had followed them down the alley, arrested this boy for disturbing the peace and took him to the police station where the other Saints gathered. After paving a $5.00 fine, and with the assurance that there would be no permanent record of the arrest, the boy was released.

The boys had a spirit of frivolity and fun about their escapades. They did not view what they were engaged in as "delinquency," though it surely was by any reasonable definition of that word. They simply viewed themselves as having a little fun and who, they would ask, was really hurt by it? The answer had to be no one, although this fact remains one of the most difficult things to explain about the gang's behavior. Unlikely though it seems, in two years of drinking, driving, carousing, and vandalism no one was seriously injured as a result of the Saints' activities.

◈ The Saints in School

The Saints were highly successful in school. The average grade for the group was "B," with two of the boys having close to a straight "A" average. Almost all of the boys were popular and many of them held offices in the school. One of the boys was vice president of the student body one year. Six of the boys played on athletic teams.

At the end of their senior year, the student body selected ten seniors for special recognition as the "school wheels"; four of the ten were Saints. Teachers and school officials saw no problem with any of these boys and anticipated that they would all "make something of themselves."

How the boys managed to maintain this impression is surprising in view of their actual behavior in school. Their technique for covering truancy was so successful that teachers did not even realize that the boys were absent from school much of the time. Occasionally, of course, the system would backfire and then the boy was on his own. A boy who was caught would be most contrite, would plead guilty and ask for mercy. He inevitably got the mercy he sought.

Cheating on examinations was rampant, even to the point of orally communicating answers to exams as well as looking at one another's papers. Since none of the group studied, and since they were primarily dependent on one another for help, it is surprising that grades were so high. Teachers contributed to the deception in their admitted inclination to give these boys (and presumably others like them) the benefit of the doubt. When asked how the boys did in school, and when pressed on specific examinations, teachers might admit that they were disappointed in John's performance, but would quickly add that they "knew that he was capable of doing better," so John was given a higher grade than he had actually earned. How often this happened is impossible to know. During the time that I observed the group, I never saw any of the boys take homework home. Teachers may have been "understanding" very regularly.

One exception to the gang's generally good performance was Jerry, who had a "C" average in his junior year, experienced disaster the next year, and failed to graduate. Jerry had always been a little more nonchalant than the others about the liberties he took in school. Rather than wait for someone to come get him from class, he would offer his own excuse and leave. Although he probably did not miss any more class than most of the others in the group, he did not take the requisite pains to cover his absences. Jerry was the only Saint whom I ever heard talk back to a teacher. Although teachers often called him a "cut up" or a "smart kid," they never referred to him as a troublemaker or as a kid headed for trouble. It seems likely, then, that Jerry's failure his senior year and his mediocre performance his junior year were consequences of his not playing the game the proper way (possibly because he was disturbed by his parents' divorce). His teachers regarded him as "immature" and not quite ready to get out of high school.

◈ The Police and the Saints

The local police saw the Saints as good boys who were among the leaders of the youth in the community. Rarely, the boys might be stopped in town for speeding or for running a stop sign. When this happened the boys were always polite, contrite and pled for mercy. As in school, they received the mercy they asked for. None ever received a ticket or was taken into the precinct by the local police.

The situation in Big Town, where the boys engaged in most of their delinquency, was only slightly different. The police there did not know the boys at all, although occasionally the boys were stopped by a patrolman. Once they were caught taking a lantern from a construction site. Another time they were stopped for running a stop sign, and on several occasions they were stopped for speeding. Their behavior was as before: contrite, polite and penitent. The urban police, like the local police, accepted their demeanor as sincere. More important, the urban police were convinced that these were good boys just out for a lark. The Roughnecks

Hanibal townspeople never perceived the Saints' high level of delinquency. The Saints were good boys who just went in for an occasional prank. After all, they were well dressed, well mannered and had nice cars. The Roughnecks were a different story. Although the two gangs of boys were the same age, and both groups engaged in an equal amount of wild-oat sowing, everyone agreed that the not-so-well-dressed, not-so-well-mannered, not-so-rich boys were heading for trouble. Townspeople would say, "You can see the gang members at the drugstore, night after night, leaning against the storefront (sometimes drunk) or slouching around inside buying cokes, reading magazines, and probably stealing old Mr. Wall blind. When they are outside and girls walk by, even respectable girls, these boys make suggestive remarks. Sometimes their remarks are downright lewd."

From the community's viewpoint, the real indication that these kids were in trouble was that they were constantly involved with the police. Some of them had been picked up for stealing, mostly small stuff, of course, "but still it's stealing small stuff that leads to big time crimes." "Too bad," people said. "Too bad that these boys couldn't behave like the other kids in town; stay out of trouble, be polite to adults, and look to their future."

The community's impression of the degrees to which this group of six boys (ranging in age from 16 to 19) engaged in delinquency was somewhat distorted. In some ways the gang was more delinquent than the community thought; in other ways they were less.

The fighting activities of the group were fairly readily and accurately perceived by almost everyone. At least once a month, the boys would get into some sort of fight, although most fights were scraps between members of the group or involved only one member of the group and some peripheral hanger-on. Only three times in the period of observation did the group fight together: once against a gang from across town, once against two blacks, and once against a group of boys from another school. For the first two fights the group went out "looking for trouble"—and they found it both times. The third fight followed a football game and began spontaneously with an argument on the football field between one of the Roughnecks and a member of the opposition's football team. Jack has a particular propensity for fighting and was involved in most of the brawls. He was a prime mover of the escalation of arguments into fights.

More serious than fighting, had the community been aware of it, was theft. Although almost everyone was aware that the boys occasionally stole things, they did not realize the extent of the activity. Petty stealing was a frequent event for the Roughnecks. Sometimes they stole as a group and coordinated their efforts; other things they stole in pairs. Rarely did they steal alone.

The thefts ranged from very small things like paperback books, comics, and ball-point pens to expensive items like watches. The nature of the thefts varied from time to time. The gang would go through a period of systematically lifting items from automobiles or school lockers. Types of thievery varied with the whim of the gang. Some forms of thievery were more profitable than others, but all thefts were for profit, not just thrills.

Roughnecks siphoned gasoline from cars as often as they had access to an automobile, which was not very often. Unlike the Saints, who owned their own cars, the Roughnecks would have to borrow their parents' cars, an event that occurred only eight or nine times a year. The boys claimed to have stolen cars for joy rides from time to time.

Ron committed the most serious of the group's offenses. With an unidentified associate the boy attempted to burglarize a gasoline station. Although this station had been robbed twice previously in the same month, Ron denied any involvement in either of the other thefts. When Ron and his accomplice approached the station, the owner was hiding in the bushes beside the station. He fired both barrels of a double-barreled shotgun at the boys. Ron was severely injured; the other boy ran away and was never caught. Though he remained in critical condition for several months, Ron finally recovered and served six months of the following year in reform school. Upon release from reform school, Ron was put back a grade in school, and began running around with a different gang of boys. The Roughnecks considered the new gang less delinquent than themselves, and during the following year Ron had no more trouble with the police.

The Roughnecks, then, engaged mainly in three types of delinquency: theft, drinking, and fighting. Although community members perceived that this gang of kids was delinquent, they mistakenly believed that their illegal activities were primarily drinking, fighting, and being a nuisance to passersby. Drinking was limited among the gang members, although it did occur, and theft was much more prevalent than anyone realized.

Drinking would doubtless have been more prevalent had the boys had ready access to liquor. Since they rarely had automobiles at their disposal, they could not travel very far, and the bars in town would not serve them.

Most of the boys had little money, and this, too, inhibited their purchase of alcohol. Their major source of liquor was a local drunk who would buy them a fifth if they would give him enough extra to buy himself a pint of whiskey or a bottle of wine.

The community's perception of drinking as prevalent stemmed from the fact that it was the most obvious delinquency the boys engaged in. When one of the boys had been drinking, even a casual observer seeing him on the corner would suspect that he was high.

There was a high level of mutual distrust and dislike between the Roughnecks and the police. The boys felt very strongly that the police were unfair and corrupt. Some evidence existed that the boys were correct in their perception.

The main source of the boys' dislike for the police undoubtedly stemmed from the fact that the police would sporadically harass the group. From the standpoint of the boys, these acts of occasional enforcement of the law were whimsical and uncalled for. It made no sense to them, for example, that the police would come to the corner occasionally and threaten them with arrest for loitering when the night before the boys had been out siphoning gasoline from cars and the police bad been nowhere in sight. To the boys, the police were stupid on the one hand, for not being where they should have been and catching the boys in a serious offense, and unfair on the other hand, for trumping up "loitering" charges against them.

From the viewpoint of the police, the situation was quite different. They knew, with all the confidence necessary to be a policeman, that these boys were engaged in criminal activities. They knew this partly from occasionally catching them, mostly from circumstantial evidence ("the boys were around when those tires were slashed"),

and partly because the police shared the view of the community in general that this was a bad bunch of boys. The best the police could hope to do was to be sensitive to the fact that these boys were engaged in illegal acts and arrest them whenever there was some evidence that they bad been involved. Whether or not the boys had in fact committed a particular act in a particular way was not especially important. The police bad a broader view: their job was to stamp out these kids' crimes; the tactics were not as important as the end result.

Over the period that the group was under observation, each member was arrested at least once. Several of the boys were arrested a number of times and spent at least one night in jail. While most were never taken to court, two of the boys were sentenced to six months' incarceration in boys' schools.

◈ The Roughnecks in School

The Roughnecks' behavior in school was not particularly disruptive. During school hours they did not all hang around together, but tended instead to spend most of their time with one or two other members of the gang who were their special buddies. Although every member of the gang attempted to avoid school as much as possible, they were not particularly successful and most of them attended school with surprising regularity. They considered school a burden—something to be gotten through with a minimum of conflict. If they were "bugged" by a particular teacher, it could lead to trouble. One of the boys, Al, once threatened to beat up a teacher and, according to the other boys, the teacher hid under a desk to escape him.

Teachers saw the boys the way the general community did, as heading for trouble, as being uninterested in making something of themselves. Some were also seen as being incapable of meeting the academic standards of the school. Most of the teachers expressed concern for this group of boys and were willing to pass them despite poor performance, in the belief' that failing them would only aggravate the problem.

The group of boys had a grade point average just slightly above "C." No one in the group failed either grade, and no one had better than a "C" average. They were very consistent in their achievement or, at least, the teachers were consistent in their perception of the boys' achievement.

Two of the boys were good football players. Herb was acknowledged to be the best player in the school and Jack was almost as good. Both boys were criticized for their failure to abide by training rules, for refusing to come to practice as often as they should, and for not playing their best during practice. What they lacked in sportsmanship they made up for in skill, apparently, and played every game no matter how poorly they had performed in practice or how many practice sessions they had missed.

◈ Two Questions

Why did the community, the school, and the police react to the Saints as though they were good, upstanding, non delinquent youths with bright futures but to the Roughnecks as though they were tough, young criminals who were headed for trouble? Why did the Roughnecks and the Saints in fact have quite different careers after high school—careers which, by and large, lived up to the expectations of the community?

The most obvious explanation for the differences in the community's and law enforcement agencies' reactions to the two gangs is that one group of boys was "more delinquent" than the other. Which group was more delinquent? The answer to this question will determine in part how we explain the differential responses to these groups by the members of the community and, particularly, by law enforcement and school officials.

In sheer number of illegal acts, the Saints were the more delinquent. They were truant from school for at least part of the day almost every day of the week. In addition, their drinking and vandalism occurred with surprising regularity. The Roughnecks, in contrast, engaged sporadically in delinquent episodes. While these episodes were frequent, they certainly did not occur on a daily or even a weekly basis.

The difference in frequency of offenses was probably caused by the Roughnecks' inability to obtain liquor and to manipulate legitimate excuses from school. Since the Roughnecks had less money than the Saints, and teachers carefully supervised their school activities, the

Roughnecks' hearts may have been as black as the Saints', but their misdeeds were not nearly as frequent.

There are really no clear-cut criteria by which to measure qualitative differences in antisocial behavior. The most important dimension is generally referred to as the "seriousness" of the offenses.

If seriousness encompasses the relative economic costs of delinquent acts, then some assessment can be made. The Roughnecks probably stole an average of about $5.00 worth of goods a week. Some weeks the figure was considerably higher, but these times must be balanced against long periods when almost nothing was stolen.

The Saints were more continuously engaged in delinquency but their acts were not for the most part costly to property. Only their vandalism and occasional theft of gasoline would so qualify. Perhaps once or twice a month they would siphon a tankful of gas. The other costly items were street signs, construction lanterns, and the like. All of these acts combined probably did not quite average $5.00 a week, partly because much of the stolen equipment was abandoned and presumably could be recovered. The difference in cost of stolen property between the two groups was trivial, but the Roughnecks probably had a slightly more expensive set of activities than did the Saints.

Another meaning of seriousness is the potential threat of physical harm to members of the community and to the boys themselves. The Roughnecks were more prone to physical violence; they not only welcomed an opportunity to fight; they went seeking it. In addition, they fought among themselves frequently. Although the fighting never included deadly weapons, it was still a menace, however minor, to the physical safety of those involved.

The Saints never fought. They avoided physical conflict both inside and outside the group. At the same time, though, the Saints frequently endangered their own and other people's lives. They did so almost every time they drove a car, especially if they had been drinking. Sober, their driving was risky; under the influence of alcohol it was horrendous. In addition, the Saints endangered the lives of others with their pranks. Street excavations left unmarked were a very serious hazard.

Evaluating the relative seriousness of the two gangs' activities is difficult. The community reacted as though the behavior of the Roughnecks was a problem, and they reacted as though the behavior of the Saints was not. But the members of the community were ignorant of the array of delinquent acts that characterized the Saints' behavior. Although concerned citizens were unaware of much of the Roughnecks' behavior as well, they were much better informed about the Roughnecks' involvement in delinquency than they were about the Saints.'

 ## Visibility

Differential treatment of the two gangs resulted in part because one gang was infinitely more visible than the other. This differential visibility was a direct function of the economic standing of the families. The Saints had access to automobiles and were able to remove themselves from the sight of the community. In as routine a decision as to where to go to have a milkshake after school, the Saints stayed away from the mainstream of community life. Lacking transportation, the Roughnecks could not make it to the edge of town. The center of town was the only practical place for them to meet since their homes were scattered throughout the town and any non central meeting place put an undue hardship on some members. Through necessity the Roughnecks congregated in a crowded area where everyone in the community passed frequently, including teachers and law enforcement officers. They could easily see the Roughnecks hanging around the drugstore.

The Roughnecks, of course, made themselves even more visible by making remarks to passersby and by occasionally getting into fights on the corner. Meanwhile, just as regularly, the Saints were either at the café on one edge of town or in the pool hall at the other edge of town. Without any particular realization that they were making themselves inconspicuous, the Saints were able to hide their time wasting. Not only were they removed from the mainstream of traffic, but they were almost always inside a building.

On their escapades the Saints were also relatively invisible, since they left Hanibal and traveled to Big Town. Here, too, they were mobile, roaming the city, rarely going to the same area twice.

 ## Demeanor

To the notion of visibility must be added the difference in the responses of group members to outside intervention with their activities. If one of the Saints was confronted with an accusing policeman, even if he felt lie was truly innocent of a wrongdoing, his demeanor was apologetic and penitent. A Roughneck's attitude was almost the polar opposite. When confronted with a threatening adult authority, even one who tried to be pleasant, the Roughneck's hostility and disdain were clearly observable. Sometimes he might attempt to put up a veneer of respect, but it was thin and was not accepted as sincere by the authority. School was no different from the community at large. The Saints could manipulate the system by feigning compliance with the school norms. The availability of cars at school meant that once free from the immediate sight of the teacher, the boys could disappear rapidly. And this escape was well enough planned that no administrator or teacher was nearby when the boys left. A Roughneck who wished to escape for a few hours was in a bind. If it were possible to get free from class, downtown was still a mile away, and even if he arrived there, he was still very visible. Truancy for the Roughnecks meant almost certain detection, while the Saints enjoyed almost complete immunity from sanctions.

Bias

Community members were not aware of the transgressions of the Saints, Even if the Saints had been less discreet, their favorite delinquencies would have been perceived as less serious than those of the Roughnecks.

In the eyes of the police and school officials, a boy who drinks in an alley and stands intoxicated on the street corner is committing a more serious offense than is a boy who drinks to inebriation in a nightclub or a tavern and drives around afterwards in a car. Similarly, a boy who steals a wallet from a store will be viewed as having committed a more serious offense than a boy who steals a lantern from a construction site.

Perceptual bias also operates with respect to the demeanor of the boys in the two groups when they are confronted by adults. It is not simply that adults dislike the posture affected by boys of the Roughneck ilk; more important is the conviction that the posture adopted by the Roughnecks is an indication of their devotion and commitment to deviance as a way of life. The posture becomes a cue, just as the type of the offense is a cue, to the degree to which the known transgressions are indicators of the youths' potential for other problems.

Visibility, demeanor, and bias are surface variables which explain the day-to-day operations of the police. Why do these surface variables operate as they do? Why did the police choose to disregard the Saints' delinquencies while breathing down the backs of the Roughnecks?

The answer lies in the class structure of American society and the control of legal institutions by those at the top of the class structure. Obviously, no representative of the upper class drew up the operational chart for the police which led them to look in the ghettos and on street corners—which led them to see the demeanor of lower class youth as troublesome and that of upper-middle-class youth as tolerable. Rather, the procedures simply developed from experience—experience with irate and influential upper-middle-class parents insisting that their son's vandalism was simply a prank and his drunkenness only a momentary "sowing of wild oats" experience with cooperative or indifferent, powerless, lower class parents who acquiesced to the law's definition of their son's behavior.

◈ Adult Careers of the Saints and the Roughnecks

The community's confidence in the potential of the Saints and the Roughnecks apparently was justified. If anything, the community members underestimated the degree to which these youngsters would turn out "good" or "bad."

Seven of the eight members of the Saints went on to college immediately after high school. Five of the boys graduated from college in four years. The sixth one finished college after two years in the army, and the seventh spent four years in the air force before returning to college and receiving a B.A. degree. Of these seven college graduates, three went on for advanced degrees. One finished law school and is now active in state politics, one finished medical school and is practicing near Hanibal, and one boy is now working for a Ph. D. The other four college graduates entered submanagerial, managerial, or executive training positions with larger firms.

The only Saint who did not complete college was Jerry. Jerry had failed to graduate from high school with the other Saints. During his second senior year, after the other Saints had gone on to college, Jerry began to hang around with what several teachers described as a "rough crowd"—the gang that was heir apparent to the Roughnecks. At the end of his second senior year, when he did graduate from high school, Jerry took a job as a used car salesman, got married, and quickly had a child. Although he made several abortive attempts to go to college by attending night school, when I last saw him (ten years after high school) Jerry was unemployed and had been living on unemployment for almost a year. His wife worked as a waitress. Some of the Roughnecks have lived up to community expectations. A number of them were headed for trouble. A few were not.

Jack and Herb were the athletes among the Roughnecks and their athletic prowess paid off handsomely. Both boys received unsolicited athletic scholarships to college. After Herb received his scholarship (near the end of his senior year), he apparently did an about-face. His demeanor became very similar to that of the Saints. Although he remained a member in good standing of the Roughnecks, he stopped participating in most activities and did not hang out on the corner as often.

Jack did not change. If anything, he became more prone to fighting. He even made excuses for accepting the scholarship. He told the other gang members that the school had guaranteed him a "C" average if he would come to play football—an idea that seems far-fetched, even in this day of highly competitive recruiting.

During the summer after graduation from high school, Jack attempted suicide by jumping from a tall building. The jump would certainly have killed most people trying it, but Jack survived. He entered college in the fall and played four years of football. He and Herb graduated in four years, and both are teaching and coaching in high schools. They are married and have stable families. If anything, Jack appears to have a more prestigious position in the community than does Herb, though both are well respected and secure in their positions.

Two of the boys never finished high school. Tommy left at the end of his junior year and went to another state. That summer he was arrested and placed on probation on a manslaughter charge. Three years later he was arrested for murder; he pleaded guilty to second degree murder and is serving a 30 year sentence in the state penitentiary.

Al, the other boy who did not finish high school, also left the state in his senior year. He is serving a life sentence in a state penitentiary for first degree murder.

Wes is a small-time gambler. He finished high school and "bummed around." After several years he made contact with a bookmaker who employed him as a runner. Later he acquired his own area and has been working it ever since. His position among the bookmakers is almost identical to the position he had in the gang; he is always around but no one is really aware of him. He makes no trouble and he does not get into any. Steady, reliable, capable of keeping his mouth closed, he plays the game by the rules, even though the game is an illegal one.

That leaves only Ron. Some of his former friends reported that they had heard he was "driving a truck up north," but no one could provide any concrete information.

◈ Reinforcement

The community responded to the Roughnecks as boys in trouble, and the boys agreed with that perception. Their pattern of deviancy was reinforced, and breaking away from it became increasingly unlikely. Once the boys acquired an image of' themselves as deviants, they selected new friends who affirmed that self-image. As that self conception became more firmly entrenched, they also became willing to try new and more extreme deviances. With their growing alienation came freer expression of disrespect and hostility for representatives of the legitimate society. This disrespect increased the community's negativism, perpetuating the entire process of commitment to deviance. Lack of a commitment to deviance works the same way. In either case, the process will perpetuate itself unless some event (like a scholarship to college or a sudden failure) external to the established relationship intervenes. For two of the Roughnecks (Herb and Jack), receiving college athletic scholarships created new relations and culminated in a break with the established pattern of deviance. In the case of one of the Saints (Jerry), his parents' divorce and his failing to graduate from high school changed some of his other relations. Being held back in school for a year and losing his place among the Saints had sufficient impact on Jerry to alter his self-image and virtually to assure that he would not go on to college as his peers did. Although the experiments of life can rarely be reversed, it seems likely in view of the behavior of the other boys who did not enjoy this special treatment by the school that Jerry, too, would have "become something" had he graduated as anticipated. For Herb and Jack outside intervention worked to their advantage; for Jerry it was his undoing.

Selective perception and labeling finding, processing, and punishing some kinds of criminality and not others—means that visible, poor, nonmobile, outspoken, undiplomatic "tough" kids will be noticed, whether their actions are seriously delinquent or not. Other kids, who have established a reputation for being bright (even though underachieving), disciplined, and involved in respectable activities, who are mobile and moneyed, will be invisible when they deviate from sanctioned activities. They'll sow their wild oats—perhaps even wider and thicker than their lower class cohorts—but they won't be noticed. When it's time to leave adolescence most will follow the expected path, settling into the ways of the middle class, remembering fondly the delinquent but unnoticed fling of their youth. Tile Roughnecks and others like them may turn around, too. It is more likely that their noticeable deviance will have been so reinforced by police and community that their lives will be effectively channeled into careers consistent with their adolescent background.

READING 24

Rosenhan's is a classic study of labeling and mental illness. Eight sane adults simulated symptoms of psychosis and gained admission to 12 mental hospitals. Once admitted, they immediately stopped simulating symptoms and waited to be judged sane and discharged. Their hospitalization averaged 19 days but ranged from a low of 7 days to a high of 52 days. In that time, staff treated the "pseudo-patients" like nonpersons or like children and handed out more than 2,000 pills. At release, each of the pseudo-patients was diagnosed with schizophrenia "in remission"; none was judged to be sane. The article is quite powerful and persuasive, but it is not without critiques. Robert Spitzer (1976) published two reaction pieces following "On Being Sane in Insane Places," and he too is quite persuasive, arguing, among other things, that (1) *sane* and *insane* are legal, not psychiatric, terms, and therefore it is unreasonable to expect psychiatrists to find someone "sane." In fact, the term used, *schizophrenia in remission,* is a rarely used term and actually fits the facts as they were brought to the hospitals. (2) The patients (although faking it) gave the doctors all the signs of schizophrenia, which, in general, simply does not "just go away." Spritzer argues that the responses by hospital staff were actually remarkably good, given that they were deceived in the first place. Still, Rosenhan's study is a classic and provides the reader with a great deal to think about. As you read this study, think about the power of labels and how hard they can be to overcome. Would you volunteer to be a pseudo-patient in a study like this? Why or why not? How would it affect how others view you? How do you think it might affect your self-image?

On Being Sane in Insane Places

D. L. Rosenhan

If sanity and insanity exist, how shall we know them?

The question is neither capricious nor itself insane. However much we may be personally convinced that we can tell the normal from the abnormal, the evidence is simply not compelling. It is commonplace, for example, to read about murder trials wherein eminent psychiatrists for the defense are contradicted by equally eminent psychiatrists for the prosecution on the matter of the defendant's sanity. More generally, there are a great deal of conflicting data on the reliability, utility, and meaning of such terms as "sanity," "insanity," "mental illness," and "schizophrenia" [1].

Finally, as early as 1934, Benedict suggested that normality and abnormality are not universal [2]. What is viewed as normal in one culture may be seen as quite aberrant in another. Thus, notions of normality and abnormality may not be quite as accurate as people believe they are.

To raise questions regarding normality and abnormality is in no way to question the fact that some behaviors are deviant or odd. Murder is deviant. So, too, are hallucinations. Nor does raising such questions deny the existence of the personal anguish that is often associated with "mental illness." Anxiety and depression exist. Psychological suffering exists. But normality and abnormality, sanity and insanity, and the

Source: Reprinted from Rosenhan, D. L. 1973. "On Being Sane in Insane Places." *Science* 179:250–258, by permission of the publisher and author. Copyright 1973 by the American Association for the Advancement of Science.

diagnoses that flow from them may be less substantive than many believe them to be.

At its heart, the question of whether the sane can be distinguished from the insane (and whether degrees of insanity can be distinguished from each other) is a simple matter: do the salient characteristics that lead to diagnoses reside in the patients themselves or in the environments and contexts in which observers find them? . . . [T]he belief has been strong that patients present symptoms, that those symptoms can be categorized, and, that the sane are distinguishable from the insane. More recently, however, this belief has been questioned. . . . [T]he view has grown that psychological categorization of mental illness is useless at best and downright harmful, misleading, and pejorative at worst. Psychiatric diagnoses, in this view, are in the minds of the observers and are not valid summaries of characteristics displayed by the observed [3–5].

Gains can be made in deciding which of these is more nearly accurate by getting normal people (that is, people who do not have, and have never suffered, symptoms of serious psychiatric disorders) admitted to psychiatric hospitals and then determining whether they were discovered to be sane and, if so, how. If the sanity of such pseudopatients were always detected, there would be prima facie evidence that a sane individual can be distinguished from the insane context in which he is found. . . . If, on the other hand, the sanity of the pseudopatients were never discovered, serious difficulties would arise for those who support traditional modes of psychiatric diagnosis. Given that the hospital staff was not incompetent, that the pseudopatient had been behaving as sanely as he had been outside of the hospital, and that it had never been previously suggested that he belonged in a psychiatric hospital, such an unlikely outcome would support the view that psychiatric diagnosis betrays little about the patient but much about the environment in which an observer finds him.

This article describes such an experiment. Eight sane people gained secret admission to 12 different hospitals [6]. Their diagnostic experiences constitute the data of the first part of this article; the remainder is devoted to a description of their experiences in psychiatric institutions. . . .

Pseudopatients and Their Settings

The eight pseudopatients were a varied group. One was a psychology graduate student in his 20s. The remaining seven were older and "established." Among them were three psychologists, a pediatrician, a psychiatrist, a painter, and a housewife. Three pseudopatients were women, five were men. All of them employed pseudonyms, lest their alleged diagnoses embarrass them later. Those who were in mental health professions alleged another occupation in order to avoid the special attentions that might be accorded by staff, as a matter of courtesy or caution, to ailing colleagues [7]. With the exception of myself (I was the first pseudopatient and my presence was known to the hospital administrator and chief psychologist and, so far as I can tell, them alone), the presence of pseudopatients and the nature of the research program was not known to the hospital staffs [8].

The settings were similarly varied. In order to generalize the findings, admission into a variety of hospitals was sought. The 12 hospitals in the sample were located in five different states on the East and West coasts. Some were old and shabby, some were quite new. Some were research-oriented, others not. Some had good staff-patient ratios, others were quite understaffed. Only one was a strictly private hospital. All of the others were supported by state or federal funds or, in one instance, by university funds.

After calling the hospital for an appointment, the pseudopatient arrived at the admissions office complaining that he had been hearing voices. Asked what the voices said, he replied that they were often unclear, but as far as he could tell they said "empty," "hollow," and "thud." The voices were unfamiliar and were of the same sex as the pseudopatient. . . .

Beyond alleging the symptoms and falsifying name, vocation, and employment, no further alterations of person, history, or circumstances were made. The significant events of the pseudopatient's life history were presented as they had actually occurred. Relationships with parents and with spouse and children, with people at work and in school, consistent with the aforementioned exceptions, were described as they were or had been. Frustrations and upsets were described along with joys and satisfactions. These facts are important to remember. If anything, they strongly biased the subsequent results in favor of detecting sanity, since none of their histories or current behaviors were seriously pathological in any way.

Immediately upon admission to the psychiatric ward, the pseudopatient ceased simulating any symptoms of abnormality. In some cases, there was a brief period of mild nervousness and anxiety, since none of the pseudopatients really believed that they would be admitted so easily. Indeed, their shared fear was that they would be immediately exposed as frauds and greatly embarrassed. Moreover, many of them had never visited a psychiatric ward; even those who had, nevertheless had some genuine fears about what might happen to them. Their nervousness, then, was quite appropriate to the novelty of the hospital setting, and it abated rapidly.

Apart from that short-lived nervousness, the pseudopatient behaved on the ward as he "normally" behaved. The pseudopatient spoke to patients and staff as he might ordinarily. Because there is uncommonly little to do on a psychiatric ward, he attempted to engage others in conversation. When asked by staff how he was feeling, he indicated that he was fine, that he no longer experienced symptoms. He responded to instructions from attendants, to calls for medication (which was not swallowed), and to dining-hall instructions. Beyond such activities as were available to him on the admissions ward, he spent his time writing down his observations about the ward, its patients, and the staff. Initially these notes were written "secretly," but as it soon became clear that no one much cared, they were subsequently written on standard tablets of paper in such public places as the dayroom. No secret was made of these activities.

The pseudopatient, very much as a true psychiatric patient, entered a hospital with no foreknowledge of when he would be discharged. Each was told that he would have to get out by his own devices, essentially by convincing the staff that he was sane. The psychological stresses associated with hospitalization were considerable, and all but one of the pseudopatients desired to be discharged almost immediately after being admitted. They were, therefore, motivated not only to behave sanely, but to be paragons of cooperation. That their behavior was in no way disruptive is confirmed by nursing reports, which have been obtained on most of the patients. These reports uniformly indicate that the patients were "friendly," "cooperative," and "exhibited no abnormal indications."

◈ The Normal Are Not Detectably Sane

Despite their public "show" of sanity, the pseudopatients were never detected. Admitted, except in one case, with a diagnosis of schizophrenia [9], each was discharged with a diagnosis of schizophrenia "in remission." The label "in remission" should in no way be dismissed as a formality, for at no time during any hospitalization had any question been raised about any pseudopatient's simulation. Nor are there any indications in the hospital records that the pseudopatient's status was suspect. Rather, the evidence is strong that, once labeled schizophrenic, the pseudopatient was stuck with that label. If the pseudopatient was to be discharged, he must naturally be "in remission"; but he was not sane, nor, in the institution's view, had he ever been sane.

The uniform failure to recognize sanity cannot be attributed to the quality of the hospitals.... Nor can it be alleged that there was simply not enough time to observe the pseudopatients. Length of hospitalization ranged from 7 to 52 days with an average of 19 days. The pseudopatients were not, in fact, carefully observed, but this failure clearly speaks more to traditions within psychiatric hospitals than to lack of opportunity.

Finally, it cannot be said that the failure to recognize the pseudopatients' sanity was due to the fact that they were not behaving sanely. While there was clearly some tension present in all of them, their daily visitors could detect no serious behavioral consequences—nor, indeed, could other patients. It was quite common for the patients to "detect" the pseudopatients' sanity.... "You're not crazy. You're a journalist, or a professor [referring to the continual note-taking]. You're checking up on the hospital." While most of the patients were reassured by the pseudopatient's insistence that he had been sick before he came in but was fine now, some continued to believe that the pseudopatient was sane throughout his hospitalization [10]. The fact that the patients often recognized normality when staff did not raises important questions.

Failure to detect sanity during the course of hospitalization may be due to the fact that . . . physicians are more inclined to call a healthy person sick . . . than a sick person healthy. . . . The reasons for this are not hard to find: it is clearly more dangerous to misdiagnose illness than health. Better to err on the side of caution, to suspect illness even among the healthy.

But what holds for medicine does not hold equally well for psychiatry. Medical illnesses, while unfortunate, are not commonly pejorative. Psychiatric diagnoses, on the contrary, carry with them personal, legal, and social stigmas [11]. It was therefore important to see whether the tendency toward diagnosing the sane insane could be reversed. The following experiment was arranged at a research and teaching hospital whose staff had heard these findings but doubted that such an error could occur in their hospital. The staff was informed that at some time during the following 3 months, one or more pseudopatients would attempt to be admitted into the psychiatric hospital. Each staff member was asked to rate each patient who presented himself at admissions or on the ward according to the likelihood that the patient was a pseudopatient. . . .

Judgments were obtained on 193 patients who were admitted for psychiatric treatment. All staff who had had sustained contact with or primary responsibility for the patient—attendants, nurses, psychiatrists, physicians, and psychologists—were asked to make judgments. Forty-one patients were alleged, with high confidence, to be pseudopatients by at least one member of the staff. Twenty-three were considered suspect by at least one psychiatrist. Nineteen were suspected by one psychiatrist and one other staff member. Actually, no genuine pseudopatient (at least from my group) presented himself during this period.

The experiment is instructive. It indicates that the tendency to designate sane people as insane can be reversed when the stakes (in this case, prestige and diagnostic acumen) are high. But what can be said of the 19 people who were suspected of being "sane" by one psychiatrist and another staff member? Were these people truly "sane?" . . . There is no way of knowing. But one thing is certain: any diagnostic process that lends itself so readily to massive errors of this sort cannot be a very reliable one.

◈ The Stickiness of Psychodiagnostic Labels

Beyond the tendency to call the healthy sick—a tendency that accounts better for diagnostic behavior on admission than it does for such behavior after a lengthy period of exposure—the data speak to the massive role of labeling in psychiatric assessment. Having once been labeled schizophrenic, there is nothing the pseudopatient can do to overcome the tag. The tag profoundly colors others' perceptions of him and his behavior.

From one viewpoint, these data are hardly surprising, for it has long been known that elements are given meaning by the context in which they occur. . . . Once a person is designated abnormal, all of his other behaviors and characteristics are colored by that label. Indeed, that label is so powerful that many of the pseudopatients' normal behaviors were overlooked entirely or profoundly misinterpreted. Some examples may clarify this issue.

Earlier I indicated that there were no changes in the pseudopatient's personal history and current status beyond those of name, employment, and, where necessary, vocation. Otherwise, a veridical description of personal history and circumstances was offered. Those circumstances were not psychotic. How were they made consonant with the diagnosis of psychosis? Or were those diagnoses modified in such a way as to bring them into accord with the circumstances of the pseudopatient's life, as described by him?

As far as I can determine, diagnoses were in no way affected by the relative health of the circumstances of a pseudopatient's life. Rather, the reverse occurred: the perception of his circumstances was shaped entirely by the diagnosis. A clear example of such translation is found in the case of a pseudopatient who had had a close relationship with his mother but was rather remote from his father during his early childhood. During adolescence and beyond, however, his father became a close friend, while his relationship with his mother cooled. His present relationship with his wife was characteristically close and warm. Apart from occasional angry exchanges, friction was minimal. The children had rarely been spanked. Surely there is nothing especially pathological about such a history.... Observe, however, how such a history was translated in the psychopathological context, this from the case summary prepared after the patient was discharged.

> This white 39-year-old male ... manifests a long history of considerable ambivalence in close relationships, which began in early childhood. A warm relationship with his mother cools during his adolescence. A distant relationship to his father is described as becoming very intense. Affective stability is absent. His attempts to control emotionality with his wife and children are punctuated by angry outbursts and, in the case of the children, spankings. And while he says that he has several good friends, one senses considerable ambivalence embedded in those relationships also....

The facts of the case were unintentionally distorted by the staff to achieve consistency with a popular theory of the dynamics of a schizophrenic reaction [12]. Nothing of an ambivalent nature had been described in relations with parents, spouse, or friends.... Clearly, the meaning ascribed to his verbalizations (that is, ambivalence, affective instability) was determined by the diagnosis: schizophrenia. An entirely different meaning would have been ascribed if it were known that the man was "normal."

All pseudopatients took extensive notes publicly. Under ordinary circumstances, such behavior would have raised questions in the minds of observers, as, in fact, it did among patients. Indeed, it seemed so certain that the notes would elicit suspicion that elaborate precautions were taken to remove them from the ward each day. But the precautions proved needless. The closest any staff member came to questioning these notes occurred when one pseudopatient asked his physician what kind of medication he was receiving and began to write down the response. "You needn't write it," he was told gently. "If you have trouble remembering, just ask me again."

If no questions were asked of the pseudopatients, how was their writing interpreted? Nursing records for three patients indicate that the writing was seen as an aspect of their pathological behavior.... Given that the patient is in the hospital, he must be psychologically disturbed. And given that he is disturbed, continuous writing must be a behavioral manifestation of that disturbance, perhaps a subset of the compulsive behaviors that are sometimes correlated with schizophrenia.

One tacit characteristic of psychiatric diagnosis is that it locates the sources of aberration within the individual and only rarely within the complex of stimuli that surrounds him. Consequently, behaviors that are stimulated by the environment are commonly misattributed to the patient's disorder. For example, one kindly nurse found a pseudopatient pacing the long hospital corridors. "Nervous, Mr. X?" she asked. "No, bored," he said.

The notes kept by pseudopatients are full of patient behaviors that were misinterpreted by well-intentioned staff. Often enough, a patient would go "berserk" because he had, wittingly or unwittingly, been mistreated by, say, an attendant. A nurse coming upon the scene would rarely inquire even cursorily into the environmental stimuli of the patient's behavior. Rather, she assumed that his upset derived from his pathology, not from his present interactions with other staff members.... [N]ever were the staff found to assume that one of themselves or the structure of the hospital had anything to do with a patient's behavior. One psychiatrist pointed to a group of patients who were sitting outside the cafeteria entrance half an hour before lunchtime. To a group of young residents he indicated that such behavior was characteristic of the oral-acquisitive nature of the syndrome. It seemed not to

occur to him that there were very few things to anticipate in a psychiatric hospital besides eating.

A psychiatric label has a life and an influence of
its own. Once the impression has been formed that the
patient is schizophrenic, the expectation is that he will
continue to be schizophrenic. When a sufficient
amount of time has passed, during which the patient
has done nothing bizarre, he is considered to be in
remission and available for discharge. But the label
endures beyond discharge, with the unconfirmed
expectation that he will behave as a schizophrenic
again. Such labels, conferred by mental health professionals, are as influential on the patient as they are on
his relatives and friends, and it should not surprise
anyone that the diagnosis acts on all of them as a self-
fulfilling prophecy. Eventually, the patient himself
accepts the diagnosis, with all of its surplus meanings
and expectations, and behaves accordingly [5]. . . .

◈ Powerlessness and Depersonalization

Eye contact and verbal contact reflect concern and indi-
viduation; their absence, avoidance and depersonalization. The data I have presented do not do justice to the rich
daily encounters that grew up around matters of depersonalization and avoidance. I have records of patients
who were beaten by staff for the sin of having initiated
verbal contact. During my own experience, for example,
one patient was beaten in the presence of other patients
for having approached an attendant and told him, "I like
you." Occasionally, punishment meted out to patients for
misdemeanors seemed so excessive that it could not be
justified by the most radical interpretations of psychiatric
canon. Nevertheless, they appeared to go unquestioned.
Tempers were often short. A patient who had not heard
a call for medication would be roundly excoriated, and
the morning attendants would often wake patients with,
"Come on, you m———f———-s, out of bed!"

Neither anecdotal nor "hard" data can convey the
overwhelming sense of powerlessness which invades
the individual as he is continually exposed to the
depersonalization of the psychiatric hospital. . . .

Powerlessness was evident everywhere. The
patient is deprived of many of his legal rights by dint of
his psychiatric commitment [13]. He is shorn of credibility by virtue of his psychiatric label. His freedom of
movement is restricted. He cannot initiate contact with
the staff, but may only respond to such overtures as
they make. Personal privacy is minimal. Patient quarters and possessions can be entered and examined by
any staff member, for whatever reason. His personal
history and anguish is available to any staff member
(often including the "grey lady" and "candy striper"
volunteer) who chooses to read his folder, regardless of
their therapeutic relationship to him. His personal
hygiene and waste evacuation are often monitored. The
[toilets] may have no doors.

At times, depersonalization reached such proportions that pseudopatients had the sense that they were
invisible, or at least unworthy of account. Upon being
admitted, I and other pseudopatients took the initial
physical examinations in a semipublic room, where
staff members went about their own business as if we
were not there.

On the ward, attendants delivered verbal and occasionally serious physical abuse to patients in the presence of other observing patients, some of whom (the
pseudopatients) were writing it all down. Abusive
behavior, on the other hand, terminated quite abruptly
when other staff members were known to be coming.
Staff are credible witnesses. Patients are not.

A unbuttoned her uniform to adjust her brassiere
in the presence of an entire ward of viewing men. One
did not have the sense that she was being seductive.
Rather, she didn't notice us. A group of staff persons
might point to a patient in the dayroom and discuss
him animatedly, as if he were not there.

One illuminating instance of depersonalization and
invisibility occurred with regard to medications. All
told, the pseudopatients were administered nearly 2100
pills. . . . Only two were swallowed. The rest were either
pocketed or deposited in the toilet. The pseudopatients
were not alone in this. Although I have no precise
records on how many patients rejected their medications, the pseudopatients frequently found the medications
of other patients in the toilet before they deposited their

own. As long as they were cooperative, their behavior and the pseudopatients' own in this matter, as in other important matters, went unnoticed throughout.

Reactions to such depersonalization among pseudopatients were intense. Although they had come to the hospital as participant observers and were fully aware that they did not "belong," they nevertheless found themselves caught up in and fighting the process of depersonalization. . . .

◈ The Consequences of Labeling and Depersonalization

Whenever the ratio of what is known to what needs to be known approaches zero, we tend to invent "knowledge" and assume that we understand more than we actually do. We seem unable to acknowledge that we simply don't know. The needs for diagnosis and remediation of behavioral and emotional problems are enormous. But rather than acknowledge that we are just embarking on understanding, we continue to label patients "schizophrenic," "manic-depressive," and "insane," as if in those words we had captured the essence of understanding. The facts of the matter are that we have known for a long time that diagnoses are often not useful or reliable, but we have nevertheless continued to use them. We now know that we cannot distinguish insanity from sanity. It is depressing to consider how that information will be used.

Not merely depressing, but frightening. How many people, one wonders, are sane but not recognized as such in our psychiatric institutions? How many have been needlessly stripped of their privileges of citizenship, from the right to vote and drive to that of handling their own accounts? How many have feigned insanity in order to avoid the criminal consequences of their behavior, and, conversely, how many would rather stand trial than live interminably in a psychiatric hospital—but are wrongly thought to be mentally ill? How many have been stigmatized by well-intentioned, but nevertheless erroneous, diagnoses? . . . [P]sychiatric diagnoses are rarely found to be in error. The label sticks, a mark of inadequacy forever.

Finally, how many patients might be "sane" outside the psychiatric hospital but seem insane in it—not because craziness resides in them, as it were, but because they are responding to a bizarre setting, one that may be unique to institutions which harbor nether people? Goffman [4] calls the process of socialization to such institutions "mortification"—an apt metaphor that includes the processes of depersonalization that have been described here. And while it is impossible to know whether the pseudopatients' responses to these processes are characteristic of all inmates—they were, after all, not real patients—it is difficult to believe that these processes of socialization to a psychiatric hospital provide useful attitudes or habits of response for living in the "real world."

◈ References and Notes

1. P. Ash, J. Abnorm. Soc. Psychol. 44, 272 (1949); A. T. Beck, Amer. J. Psychiat. 119, 210 (1962); A. T. Boisen, Psychiatry 2, 233 (1938); N. Kreitman, J. Ment. Sci. 107, 876 (1961); N. Kreitman, P. Sainsbury, J. Morrisey, J. Towers, J. Scrivener, ibid., p. 887; H. O. Schmitt and C. P. Fonda, J. Abnorm. Soc. Psychol. 52, 262 (1956); W. Seeman, J. Nerv. Ment. Dis. 118, 541 (1953). For an analysis of these artifacts and summaries of the disputes, see J. Zubin, Annu. Rev. Psychol. 18, 373 (1967); L. Phillips and J. G. Draguns, ibid., 22, 447 (1971).

2. R. Benedict, J. Gen. Psychol. 10, 59 (1934).

3. See in this regard H. Becker, Outsiders: Studies in the Sociology of Deviance (Free Press, New York, 1963); B. M. Braginsky, D. D. Braginsky, K. Ring, Methods of Madness: The Mental Hospital as a Last Resort (Holt, Rinehart & Winston, New York, 1969); G. M. Crocetti and P. V. Lemkau, Amer. Sociol. Rev. 30, 577 (1965); E. Goffman, Behavior in Public Places (Free Press, New York, 1964); R. D. Laing, The Divided Self: A Study of Sanity and Madness (Quadrangle, Chicago, 1960); D. L. Phillips, Amer. Sociol. Rev. 28, 963 (1963); T. R. Sarbin, Psychol. Today 6, 18 (1972); E. Schur, Amer. J. Sociol. 75, 309 (1969); T. Szasz, Law, Liberty and Psychiatry (Macmillan, New York; 1963); The Myth of Mental Illness: Foundations of a Theory of Mental Illness (Hoeber Harper, New York, 1963). For a critique of some of these views, see W. R. Gove, Amer. Sociol. Rev. 35, 873 (1970).

4. E. Goffman, Asylums (Doubleday, Garden City, N.Y., 1961).

5. T. J. Scheff, Being Mentally Ill: A Sociological Theory (Aldine, Chicago, 1966).

6. Data from a ninth pseudopatient are not incorporated in this report because, although his sanity went undetected, he

falsified aspects of his personal history, including his marital status and parental relationships. His experimental behaviors therefore were not identical to those of the other pseudopatients.

7. Beyond the personal difficulties that the pseudopatient is likely to experience in the hospital, there are legal and social ones that, combined, require considerable attention before entry. For example, once admitted to a psychiatric institution, it is difficult, if not impossible, to be discharged on short notice, state law to the contrary notwithstanding. I was not sensitive to these difficulties at the outset of the project, nor to the personal and situational emergencies that can arise, but later a writ of habeas corpus was prepared for each of the entering pseudopatients and an attorney was kept "on call" during every hospitalization. I am grateful to John Kaplan and Robert Bartels for legal advice and assistance in these matters.

8. However distasteful such concealment is, it was a necessary first step to examining these questions. Without concealment, there would have been no way to know how valid these experiences were; nor was there any way of knowing whether whatever detections occurred were a tribute to the diagnostic acumen of the staff or to the hospital's rumor network. Obviously, since my concerns are general ones that cut across individual hospitals and staffs, I have respected their anonymity and have eliminated clues that might lead to their identification.

9. Interestingly, of the 12 admissions, 11 were diagnosed as schizophrenic and one, with the identical symptomatology, as manic-depressive psychosis. This diagnosis has a more favorable prognosis, and it was given by the only private hospital in our sample. On the relations between social class and psychiatric diagnosis, see A. B. Hollingshead and F. C. Redlich, Social Class and Mental Illness: A Community Study (Wiley, New York, 1958).

10. It is possible, of course, that patients have quite broad latitudes in diagnosis and therefore are inclined to call many people sane, even those whose behavior is patently aberrant. However, although we have no hard data on this matter, it was our distinct impression that this was not the case. In many instances, patients not only singled us out for attention, but came to imitate our behaviors and styles.

11. J. Cumming and E. Cumming, Community Ment. Health 1, 135 (1965); A. Farina and K. Ring, J. Abnorm. Psychol. 70, 47 (1965); H. E. Freeman and O. G. Simmons, The Mental Patient Comes Home (Wiley, New York, 1963): W. J. Johannsen, Ment. Hygiene 53, 218 (1969); A. S. Linsky, Soc. Psychiat. 5, 166 (1970).

12. For an example of a similar self-fulfilling prophecy, in this instance dealing with the "central" trait of intelligence, see R. Rosenthal and L. Jacobson, Pygmalion in the Classroom (Holt, Rinehart & Winston, New York, 1968).

13. D. B. Wexler and S. E. Scoville, Ariz. Law Rev. 13, 1 (1971).

READING 25

In *Our Guys*, Lefkowitz tells of a crime that shook a community and brings to light the power of labels. In 1989, in Glen Ridge, New Jersey, a group of popular high school athletes gang raped a mentally impaired 17-year-old girl with a baseball bat and a broom. When the crime became public, many community members showed more concern for the reputation of the town and its golden boys than for its powerless victim. The power dynamic in this story is an important one from the labeling perspective. In some ways, "our guys" are similar to the "Saints" in Chambliss's article. The boys had caused plenty of trouble in the past, but they (with their parents' help and the community's cooperation) were always able to reject the label of deviant. The victim of the rape, however, was easily labeled not only as "retarded" but also as a "slut" who "wanted it." The introduction to the book and to Lefkowitz's extensive investigation into the case is provided here. The entire book is recommended for anyone interested in issues of power, crime, and labeling. For an interesting review of the book in the *New York Times,* see http://www.nytimes.com/books/97/08/03/reviews/970803.03bankst.html.

Source: Lefkowitz, Bernard. 1997. "Introduction." *Our Guys: The Glen Ridge Rape and the Secret Life of the Perfect Suburb.* New York: Vintage Books, pp. 3–10. Reprinted with permission of University of California Press.

Our Guys

The Glen Ridge Rape and the Secret Life of the Perfect Suburb

Bernard Lefkowitz

◈ Introduction

I spent much of the 1980s writing about the lives of poor children and adolescents. During that time I interviewed hundreds of youngsters and visited dozens of schools and neighborhoods throughout the country. One place I returned to often was the ravaged housing projects in the Lower Broadway section of Newark, where a courageous youth worker struggled to bring a semblance of stability to the disordered lives of the children and adults in the community. During the days and nights I followed him around, I never knew that just fifteen minutes down the road was a beautiful little suburb named Glen Ridge, which, to any of the kids I was meeting, would have seemed like paradise.

I heard about Glen Ridge as most Americans did. On the night of May 23, 1986, a New York television station reported that authorities were investigating "rumors" that a group of Glen Ridge adolescent males had raped a seventeen-year-old retarded girl. Two days later, newspapers throughout the United States carried stories about the arrests of five popular high school athletes, who, police said, had penetrated the young woman's body with a baseball bat and a broomstick.

The stories conveyed a sense of shock that these atrocious acts could have happened in such a prosperous and tranquil town. If the charges were true, this was certainly an appalling crime. After thirty years as a journalist, I wasn't naive enough to believe that perfect towns produced only perfect kids. Still, I was curious about what had gone wrong in this perfect town—the antithesis of Newark—where children grew up with every advantage.

The follow-up stories added new information. First, this wasn't about just a couple of oddballs with sadistic streak. A number of young men seemed to be involved. The papers reported that on March 1, 1989, thirteen males were present in the basement where the alleged rape occurred. There also were reports that a number of other boys had tried to entice the young woman into the basement a second time to repeat the experience. This was puzzling. Glen Ridge is a small place, and there were only a hundred or so students in the senior class. What were we talking about here—20 or 30 percent of the senior males? The growing number of actual participants, would-be participants, and observers made me wonder about the environment in which they grew up. I wanted to know more about how this privileged American community raised its children, especially its sons.

I was also curious about the silence of the other kids—the Glen Ridge adolescents who had not been in the basement and would never have thought of going down there. The newspapers were saying that accounts of what had happened had circulated among the students in the high school for almost three months before the arrests, but that the kids had kept it to themselves. They hadn't gone to the police and they hadn't told their parents or teachers. Why was it so important to protect a bunch of classmates who enjoyed sticking a bat and a broom into a retarded woman? Weren't they worried about what had been done to her and what might happen to her in the future if the truth were suppressed?

Maybe the silence of Glen Ridge students was a symptom of grief and shame, colored by self-interest. Maybe they were thinking: Keep quiet for a couple of months and this will all blow over and we'll graduate and slip off to college. It was more difficult to understand the comments attributed to adolescents *after* the arrests. Some teenagers told reporters: "She teased them into it." "She asked for it." "She was promiscuous." Adults in the community were slightly more guarded in their comments: "She was always flirting." "This is Leslie just getting into more trouble." People in Glen Ridge were saying: The girl is to blame for all that happened to her. And it wasn't only a few people. The stories suggested that such views were widespread in the town.

Without doubt, a grave moral transgression had taken place in the community on March 1. Didn't the adults there see it the same way? Weren't parents worried about how their sons were growing up? Weren't they concerned about what might happen to *their* daughters? What kind of place was Glen Ridge anyway?

A large group of charismatic athletes. A retarded young woman. The silence of the students and adults. The inclination to blame the woman and exonerate the men. These elements seemed to be linked by a familiar theme in my life in journalism. I began to frame Glen Ridge as a story of power and powerlessness: the power of young males and the community that venerated them, and the powerlessness of one marginalized young woman—one woman whom I knew about from the media coverage. Maybe there were other young women with stories to tell.

The sense of social nihilism expressed by many youngsters in Newark was attributable, at least partially, to their economic condition and the social devastation it created. The immutable condition they all shared was poverty. Being poor was the ongoing trauma of their childhoods. You could draw a line from the rubble of the streets to the rubble of their lives.

Of course, Glen Ridge was different. It was a town where almost everybody was pretty well off. If I decided to write about this place, I would have to readjust my perspective. The prosperity of Glen Ridge didn't negate the impact of economics on the values of young people in this suburb. But instead of writing about the sense of impotency arising from generations of poverty, I might be writing about how affluence and privilege could inflate the self-importance of otherwise unremarkable young men, not always with good results.

This was all surmise from a distance. Before I decided to write about Glen Ridge, I wanted to take a closer look at the boys involved in the alleged rape, at the residents, and at the town. In the late afternoon of June 23, 1989, I boarded a number 33 DeCamp line bus from the Port Authority bus terminal in New York City. Forty minutes later, I got off at the intersection of Bloomfield and Ridgewood Avenues in Glen Ridge. I followed the crowd that was walking toward the field

behind the high school, where the graduation ceremonies for the Class of '89 were about to begin.

My first mental snapshot: Glen Ridge was a squeaky-clean, manicured town that liked to display its affluence by dressing its high school graduates in dinner jackets and gowns. What impressed me most was the orderliness of the place. The streets, the lawns, the houses—everything seemed in proportion. There were no excesses of bad taste, no evidence of neglect or disrepair.

Although graduation was an emotional ritual, made more intense by the recent arrest of four seniors on rape charges, there were no outbursts of feeling, no overt expression of anger, grief, or remotes. The adults and their progeny exercised near-perfect restraint.

It was as if these graduates had fulfilled the first requirements of a master plan for their lives. Their parents' success had secured them a place in this charming town. Now they would follow their parents down the same road, passing all the trailmarks that led to achievement, security, and fulfillment. The contrast with Newark was overwhelming. The youngsters I met there had no idea what they would be doing tomorrow, let alone five years from now. The teenagers in Glen Ridge seemed to exude confidence in the future. It was a future that included more years of higher education, then entrance into an occupation or career. After that, marriage, children, and perhaps, residence in Glen Ridge or a place very much like it.

They were secure in the knowledge that they would be protected as the made their passage into adulthood. Most of them would have their college board and tuition paid by their parents. If they needed to buy new clothes or a car or to pay a doctor's bill, they could depend on a check from home. Most of them had the luxury of easing into independence.

That's what I thought on the first night I visited Glen Ridge. But I also recognized that, even with all these advantages, kids don't always fulfill their parents' expectations. Some people have the benefit of wealth and nurturing parents and a good education, and still wind up morally and financially bankrupt. There are no foolproof master plans for success. I knew that because of what had happened three months before in this town, only a few blocks away from where I was sitting on this warm, humid night in June. What I didn't know was why it happened. If I found that out, I might have an interesting theme for a book.

Later that night I got my first glimpse of some of the boys who had been in the basement. They showed up for one of several parties that the town was holding for the graduates. As these thick-necked, broad-shouldered young men circulated in the crowd of students and chaperones, I felt a surge of recognition. I knew these kids! I had seen them all my life. They were the kids on my block who had developed faster than all the other boys of their age. They were out driving cars and dating and having sex while I was still fussing with my stamp collection. They were the guys in the jock clique of my high school, louder and tanner than the students who never saw sunlight because they were always home studying so they could win the Nobel Prize in chemistry before they turned fifty.

The kids in Newark, black and brown, speaking Spanglish, hoods over their heads, wheeling their stolen cars over to the local chop shop—they were aliens in America. Strange, forever separate and separated from the American ideal. But these Glen Ridge kids, they were pure gold, every mother's dream, every father's pride. They were not only Glen Ridge's finest, but in their perfection they belonged to all of us. They were Our Guys.

And that was the way they were being treated that night at the graduation party. Parents and kids collected around them, slapping them on the back and giving them big, wet, smacky kisses. Who would have guessed from this reception that some of them had been charged with rape and more of their pals would soon be arrested? In the bosom of their hometown, they were greeted like returning warriors who had prevailed in a noble crusade. Or, if you prefer, martyred heroes.

It may have all been a bravura show of scared people who saw their world crashing down on them. But it looked real to me. The accused looked like a bunch of carefree kids who had just wrapped up high school and were heading off to the shore for some sun and fun before they started college. Then I heard a voice next to me saying, "It's such a tragedy. They're such beautiful boys and this will scar them forever." The man who said that drifted away before I could ask him a question, but others I spoke to repeated this sentiment:

"It's such a tragedy." Often, they identified the victims of the tragedy. It was a short list: the young men who had been arrested, their families, and the good name of Glen Ridge. The list, more often than not, omitted the young woman in the basement and her family.

Tragedy was a curious word to describe what these young men had done. It was so carefully neutral. It made the experience in the basement sound like an act of God—a bolt of lightning or an earthquake. Even when they attached the word to the actions of individual boys—"It's a tragedy for Chris," "It's such a tragedy for Bryant"—it seemed to absolve the young men of moral responsibility. These Glen Ridge folks sounded as if they were talking about an inherited disease, a flawed gene, not a deliberate act that reflected patterns of socialization, years of social and cultural experiences.

The next morning, I woke up thinking that something was missing from the conversations I had in Glen Ridge. What was missing was a word I had heard often in Newark: character. When a teenager went out and mugged an old lady for her food stamps, the law-abiding, respectable residents of the Newark neighborhood would say: "He has a bad character." By that they meant he was responding to his defective environment: an irresponsible mother, an absent father, the gang culture on the streets, an indifferent police force. They weren't excusing his crime. They were only listing the risk factors that undermine the healthy human development of many youngsters living in poverty. They were only pointing out the obvious: Kids raised in squalor often make very harmful decisions.

But a few miles down the highway in Glen Ridge, people seemed to disconnect youngsters living in affluence form their environment. When they discussed the "incident," they substituted temperament for character. One of the guys in the basement was a "nasty" kid. Another was "hyper." And still another was always "upbeat." They seemed to be talking about inherited traits, a biological code they had no control over. But they didn't mention the life experiences that sensitize, magnify, and aggravate the predispositions of temperament; they didn't speak of the boys' characters.

That's what interested me: their characters. I wanted to know what they had acquired from the world around them and how their formative experiences found expression in a dimly lighted basement in Glen Ridge. What was it in their upbringing as children and adolescents—so seemingly comfortable and secure—that inclined them to take pleasure in the conscious degradation of a helpless woman? More particularly, I wanted to understand how their status as young athlete celebrities in Glen Ridge influenced their treatment of girls and women, particularly those of their age. I wanted to learn how the institutions of the community responded to them. What they did in the basement on March 1 was clearly a group enterprise, so I was especially curious about what license they were permitted as a clique of admired athletes and how that magnified the sense of superiority they felt as individuals.

But there were two parties to this story—victimizer and victim. This was also the victim's story. Although she was disabled, she was as responsive as the young men were to the culture of Glen Ridge. She, too, learned who was admired and who was despised; who counted and who didn't; what got you attention and what got you ignored. If she was as vulnerable as the boys were powerful, it wasn't only because she was intellectually impaired. It was because she received and accepted the message sent out by the kids and adults who lived in the "normal" world. And that message was that she was born inferior and would always remain inferior. She learned early that to be "accepted" by the popular kids in town, she would have to submit to their ever more elaborate demands. Other girls got the same messages, but they knew they had alternatives. Sooner or later, in Glen Ridge or elsewhere, they would find people who would reward them for their independence and individuality. The victim's experience in Glen Ridge left her with only two choices: submit or be cast out of the only world she knew.

In the summer of 1989, I began the effort that the adults I had met on my first visit to Glen Ridge seemed unwilling to undertake: an examination of the character of their community and the young people who grew up in it. During the six years it took to complete this work, I interviewed more than 150 people who lived or worked in the town. I am not talking about a single conversation with an individual or a family. I returned repeatedly to some people to broaden my understanding and clarify my thinking.

The "incident" became a fiercely emotional matter for them. Longtime friends and neighbors, even husbands and wives and parents and children, clashed over the ethical, legal, and moral issues raised by this experience. When attention shifted from the town to the response of the criminal justice system, I conducted more than one hundred interviews with law enforcement officials, cops, prosecutors, reporters, defense lawyers, psychologists, social workers, and psychiatrists. In these discussions I found that the issues generating such discord in Glen Ridge had now become part of a national conversation about morality, integrity, and justice.

When I started, I knew that much of my work would be concentrated in Glen Ridge. But I also recognized that the themes shaping character in this suburban town in northern New Jersey were representative of the social and psychological currents that form mainstream American culture. Every town has distinctive qualities, but there was nothing in Glen Ridge that set it apart from thousands of other upper-middle-class suburban communities throughout the country. What happened there could have happened in many other places—and probably has.

I know that now, because the natural course of the story carried it beyond the borders of Glen Ridge to the larger society. As the case slowly wound its way through the criminal justice system toward trial and judgment, the boundaries between the town and the outside world eroded. Millions of Americans discovered that Glen Ridge was not a foreign and alien culture, but all too closely resembled their own communities. Glen Ridge's test of character became America's test of character. Glen Ridge ultimately found that it could not insulate itself against the turbulence created by an outrage that in the past would have been hidden and buried. Like Glen Ridge, America has been forced in recent years to define what are fair, just, and principle relations between men and women. That has not been easy for Glen Ridge to do. And it hasn't been easy for America either.

CHAPTER 9

Marxist/Conflict Theories of Deviance

Sandy was born in 1941. She realized she was a lesbian in her late teens but did not tell anyone of her feelings for many years. It wasn't easy being gay in the late 1950s or the 1960s. Gays and lesbians were discriminated against legally and socially. Men and women were driven from their schools and their towns for being suspected of being gay. Government hearings (the McCarthy hearings) persecuted individuals who were suspected of being gay. Police harassed and arrested individuals who were suspected of being gay.

On June 28, 1969, in Greenwich Village, New York, a riot broke out in response to a police raid on an inn suspected of catering to gays and lesbians. Sandy was 28 at the time and could hardly believe that there were people in New York rioting over these raids. She had lived with the fear that someone might suspect she was a lesbian for a long time and was amazed that other individuals were so open with their feelings. These riots, called the Stonewall riots, became known as the start of the gay rights movement.

Over the years, Sandy slowly came out to her friends and family; some did not understand her feelings and were cruel and judgmental, but many were supportive, and she surrounded herself with a close group of friends and family and built a satisfying life for herself. She met an amazing woman when she was 34. She became more active in the gay rights movement, attending protests and advocating for social acceptance and legal equality.

As the years passed, she saw that for many individuals, homosexuality became an accepted lifestyle. She saw pop culture embrace gays and lesbians in many ways. In many cities, she felt accepted enough to openly acknowledge her relationship with her partner, but this was not the case everywhere in the United States. In addition, while in some circles there was a cultural acceptance of her lifestyle, legally

(Continued)

(Continued)

she was still not protected equally. Only recently had her state acknowledged domestic partnership enough that she and her partner could share health care, and while they had celebrated in a union ceremony 20 years ago, they were still struggling for the right to marry and see that marriage accepted in all 50 states in the United States.

Several states have signed bills that make same-sex marriage legal, but those laws have been challenged in court. The right to marry in California was allowed and then overturned and then spent several years in the court system. In addition, the federal government enacted the Defense of Marriage Act in 1996, which declared that marriage is a union between one man and one woman and that the states do not have to acknowledge a same-sex union (up until this act, states were required to acknowledge a marriage legally obtained in any state and offer the rights and privileges of marriage to that couple, even if they had not been married in that state).

Now in her 70s, Sandy wants more than anything to marry her longtime partner. She remembers the challenges she has faced throughout her lifetime, the social and legal discrimination against her. She knows in many ways that her lifestyle is becoming more accepted, but she also sees many ways that she is still made to feel deviant. She wonders what the next challenges will be and if she will ever get the opportunity to officially marry her partner and have that union recognized in all 50 states.

◈ Introduction

Perhaps one of the most striking ways that deviance textbooks have changed over the past 30 years is that many early textbooks on deviance had a chapter discussing homosexuality as a deviant act. Many groups in society still argue that homosexuality is a deviant lifestyle (for the most part, these groups are conservative religious groups), but the days in which the idea that gays and lesbians are deviant are waning. Advocacy groups are increasing, and the gay rights movement has been very successful in the fight for social acceptance and equal rights. A discussion of deviance in a textbook today that focused on gays and lesbians would not focus on the lifestyle as deviant but may instead focus on the discourse, the changing attitudes, and the constantly changing legal rights and the implication of these changes. This study of deviance might ask the following questions: What arguments do opponents of homosexuality make? What arguments do advocates of gays and lesbians make? How do these groups use the law to support their arguments? Under what conditions do these arguments "win" or "lose"? These questions help illustrate the **social construction** of deviance

▲ **Photo 9.1** Marxist and Conflict theories examine why laws, such as marriage laws, are written and who may benefit or not benefit from such laws.

and the social construction of gays and lesbians from a group uniformly accepted as deviant to a group growing in social acceptance, with strong, vocal advocates.

This chapter presents the perspectives of the Marxist and conflict theories. While the theorists discussed in this chapter do not always agree on all the tenets of their theories, they come from the same social constructionist or **relativist** perspective and so are often discussed together. There are two general ways in which these theories differ from each other. The first is their definition of power. Marxists focus on the political economy and the capitalist system in their analyses of power and conflict (Moyer, 2001), while conflict theorists have traditionally expanded their definitions of power beyond a singular focus on the capitalist system. The second difference between the two is the policy implications that stem from the theories. Marxists tend to advocate for a revolutionary overthrow of the capitalist system as the only way to solve power differentials and conflict, while conflict theorists are more open to reforms that do not advocate revolution (Bohm, 1982). Both theories are from the macro perspective, meaning that they focus on structural issues, institutions, and group behaviors, not on individual behavior or experiences. Much of the focus of these theories is on the creation and maintenance of laws that benefit one group over another (Liska & Messner, 1999). For a book on deviance, we might then say that Marxist and conflict theorists are interested in why and how some groups are defined as deviant and how their behavior, now defined as deviant, gets translated into illegal behavior through application of the law.

At the center of this perspective is the acknowledgment that conflict exists (especially in a capitalist society), and this conflict arises from power differentials in society. These theories focus on two questions: "Why are certain groups more likely to be considered deviant?" and "Why are some actions, which many might consider harmful, not considered deviant or criminal?" These questions have implications for what is often studied from the various theories that make up this perspective—as you see from the readings in this chapter, a variety of social phenomena, from a shift from the effects of the abolition of slavery on prison populations to police misconduct and "Shopping While Black," can be evaluated from a Marxist/conflict perspective. The rest of this chapter explores the theories that make up the Marxist/conflict perspective.

◈ Marxist Theory

The best place to start any discussion of Marxist/conflict theories is with Karl Marx (and his colleague Frederick Engels) (Marx, 1867/1992, 1885/1993; Marx & Engels, 1848/1961). Marx was not a criminologist, and he did not study crime or deviance to any extent. In fact, while criminologists claim him as a key theorist in the field, communication studies, economics, political science, and sociology all make formal claims, too. At the core of Marxist theory is a focus on the capitalist system as one that creates conflict, inequality, and power differentials. Some argue that because the capitalist system is central to Marxist thought, such phenomena as the conflict surrounding same-sex marriage cannot be adequately explained by this theory. However, Turk (2002) argues that much capitalist conflict is diversionary in nature, designed to keep the "workers" focused on issues that keep them divided, thus not uniting to fight for their rights against capitalists. "To leftists, particularly those inspired by Marxism, class, racial and other forms of discrimination, are promoted by the 'ruling class' to keep the workforce divided, thus more easily controlled" (Turk, 2002, p. 312). In other words, an emotional and heated conflict over same-sex marriage could benefit capitalism by diverting attention away from issues those in power do not want to discuss and by dividing the working class on a social issue that makes it harder for them to come together to fight the powerful when the need arises. As we examine Marxist and conflict theory, think about how this conflict may benefit the capitalist system and/or the ruling class.

Conflict

Marx, writing during the Industrial Revolution in Europe, argued that society could best be understood by its *social relationships* (Meyer, 1963), and given the era he was writing in, Marx argued that the fundamental basis of society was *class conflict*. In other words, he saw capitalism as creating a conflict between the social relationships of the owners of the means of production (bourgeoisie) and the laborers (proletariat). This conflict would arise because to maximize profits, the owners of the means of production needed to keep costs down. Since labor is one of the most significant costs in business, owners must maximize their profits by paying the laborer as little as possible. Marx argued that since the laborer was the actual creator of a given product, that laborer was the true owner of the profits from its creation. Therefore, laborers should earn the full price of the product (maximize their earnings). Laborers' maximization of their wage comes in direct conflict with the owners of the means of production maximization of profit.

Marx went on to argue that a struggle for power—in other words, **conflict**—arises as both groups try to maximize their advantage. In the short run, according to Marx, the bourgeoisie would win because they have the control over the means of production and communication. But in the long run, Marx believed, the proletariat would win. He believed that capitalism had sown the seeds of its own destruction and as soon as proletariats understood the exploitive nature of capitalism, they would rise up and overthrow the system.

Dialectical Materialism

Marx based much of his philosophy about social relationships, conflict, and the working of society on the concept of **dialectical materialism.** In many respects, this concept is the reason that Marxist and conflict theories fall under the heading of relativist theories. Marx believed that reality existed in the *material* world. In other words, the material world had a meaning or reality separate from the meaning that individuals gave it (Mayo, 1960)—or, more specifically, the material world is important, separate from ideas, and for our ideas to have importance, we must put them into action. He also believed in the *dialectic,* which in its simplest form means a negotiation of contradictions. He believed that nature (the material world) was full of contradictions (conflict) and that through a process of negotiating those contradictions, we can arrive at a new reality. Mayo (1960) explains this process as the thesis, antithesis, and synthesis of an idea (or reality). Using our legal definitions of the right to marry as an example, we can say that there has been heated debate in this country about the right for gays and lesbians to marry. The thesis of this idea may be "gays and lesbians have the right to marry," the antithesis of this reality may be "gays and lesbians do not have the right to marry," and from these contradictions may come the synthesis "gays and lesbians may have civil unions but may not marry." This synthesis becomes the new thesis, and the process starts all over again.

Marxism and Revolution

Two phenomena needed to occur before revolution could take place: The first was that the number of laborers needed to grow until the capitalist system could not support the masses. Marx believed this would certainly happen as failed entrepreneurs ended up in the laborer class and as the capitalist system became more "efficient" and less laborers were needed to produce the same level of product. The second, and most important, was that the laborer must throw off her or his **false consciousness** (Lukács, 1920/1971; Mannheim, 1936/1959) and become aware of the exploitation she or he was experiencing at the hands of the owners of the means of production and capitalism. While Marx did not use the term *false consciousness* himself, he believed that the capitalist system created in the laborer class a false sense of upward mobility, meaning that they could not see the exploitation and oppression they were experiencing because of the belief they could "move up" in the capitalist system.

Marx believed the only reason that the revolutionary end to capitalism had not already happened was that the laborer was still experiencing a false consciousness about her or his exploitation. In other words, capitalism and the owners of the means of production had convinced laborers that they were *not* being used to maximize the profits of the owners of the means of production and that, instead, capitalism benefitted them. Marx believed that as soon as laborers understood their exploitation, they would throw off the shackles of capitalism and would ultimately create a system in which capital did not accumulate unequally to one group.

Marxism and Deviance

We might argue, then, that one of the ways in which Marxist theory can help explain deviance is in the use of deviance to control certain groups for the benefit of the capitalist system. As Marx said, the power of the capitalists comes from their ability to control both the means of production and *communication.* If laborers live under a false consciousness that does not allow them to understand or acknowledge their oppression and exploitation, then the owners of the means of production can manipulate this group by labeling behaviors or groups that are dangerous to capitalism as deviant. Much of this labeling can be communicated through the media. In this instance, if same-sex marriage can be labeled as deviant and harmful, then the capitalist system and ruling class may benefit in two ways: (1) The focus is taken off of harmful/deviant behaviors that the ruling class may be engaged in, and (2) the workers will be divided over their opinion of same-sex marriage, thus weakening their own connection to other workers. In this example, while same-sex marriage may not be harmful to capitalism, by promoting it as a deviant behavior, it benefits capitalism by diverting attention away from harms (deviance) produced by capitalism and keeping individuals or groups who would benefit from banding together to fight the harms of capitalism divided over a diversionary issue (same-sex marriage).

Instrumental and Structural Marxism and the Law

While Marx was not a criminologist, he spent a fair amount of time writing about the importance of the law. He never gave a specific definition of the law (Cain, 1974), but he did discuss how law was used to maintain the status quo (keep the bourgeoisie in power). Marx saw the law as the instrument used to support the ideology of capitalism. In other words, he believed that the function of the law, in a capitalist society, was to maintain capitalism. For Marx, this meant that the law might be used to control the proletariat, but it was also used to settle disputes that might arise among the bourgeoisie because disputes weakened the power of the bourgeoisie and ultimately the power of capitalist system (Cain, 1974).

The function of the law, according to Marx and Engels, was to obscure real power, by offering power, on paper, to everyone equally (Cain, 1974; Marx & Engels, 1957). In other words, Marx believed that by emphasizing the rationality of the law and the recourse for everyone to use the law equally, the fact that in practice everyone does not have the power to use the law equally can be overlooked. In fact, not only overlooked but also actively ignored—if everyone has the right to use the law, then it becomes the *individual's responsibility* to use the law. Equality on paper means we can ignore inequality in practice.

Marxism was expanded by Piers Beirne (1979) to more specifically explain the creation of law. **Instrumental Marxism** sees the state (for example, politicians or the police) as an *instrument* of the capitalists. The bourgeoisie use the creation of laws to try to overcome conflict and benefit the ruling class. This is systematically and actively done by creating civil laws that focus on benefits for the ruling class (i.e., laws limiting workers' rights) and criminal laws that focus on street crime and the underclass, thus shifting attention from the crimes of the ruling class. In this iteration of Marxism, much agency is attributed to the ruling class as they manipulate the state to benefit themselves. **Structural Marxism,** on the other hand, does not assume that the law is controlled solely by the ruling class; instead, this theory assumes that law is less about maintaining power and benefits for the ruling class and more about maintaining the interests of the *capitalist system.* For this reason, laws that may benefit the system (such as laws against monopolies) but that do not benefit those in the ruling class are still seen as beneficial. Where instrumental Marxism sees the law as existing to benefit people, structural Marxism sees the law as existing to benefit the system.

A Marxian Theory of Deviance

▲ **Photo 9.2** Spitzer argues that as monopoly capitalism grows "problem populations" will develop. One of those problem populations is "social dynamite"– a group willing to protest those in power.

While Marx did not focus on crime or deviance, Steven Spitzer (1975, 1983) did expand on traditional Marxist thought to develop a theory of deviance. Spitzer (1975) argued that capitalism was changing to advanced (or monopoly) capitalism. This change increased the likelihood of "problem populations."

Monopoly capitalism was likely to promote two realities. The first was that as capitalism advanced, it would become more efficient. This efficiency would make it more likely that some capitalists would fail (as monopolies became stronger); these failed capitalists would fall into the laborer class, and this ever growing laborer class would become less and less useful as fewer laborers were needed to do the same work. The second was that advanced capitalism would promote increased levels of education needed to do the more advanced work of the economy. This education would create a more thoughtful population, likely to criticize the system. Spitzer called these two populations "problem populations" and argued that capitalists (those in power) would see these two groups as "social junk" (the unneeded laborers) and "social dynamite" (those critical of the system).

These problem populations would need to be controlled (most likely through criminalization—creating laws focused on their status or behaviors) when the populations got too big, too organized, or no longer responded to informal social control (for example, family or school) (Liska & Messner, 1999).

▲ **Photo 9.3** The Occupy Wall Street protests that started in the fall of 2011 are an excellent example of what many might call "the social dynamite," individuals who are protesting the current status quo and perceived sources of power in the United States (and the world).

Using Spitzer to critique same-sex marriage legislation, we may argue that same-sex marriage legislation fits in with Spitzer's notions of advanced capitalism, which are grounded in the need for conspicuous consumption (in other words, advanced capitalism only survives if individuals in the capitalist society consume as much as possible). In this scenario, the nuclear family provides many small units of consumption that work against efforts of communal arrangements. For example, if you have small families, living as separate units in separate houses with separate computers, cars, washers and dryers, refrigerators, and so on, it promotes more consumption than if you had communities or even extended families that shared these items. According to Marxist theory, anything that begins to change the traditional forms of everyday living can be understood as a threat to the macro structures that exist (even if we might argue that that "change" may not bring down capitalism—certainly the arguments opposing same-sex marriage use language suggesting that same-sex marriage will hurt the traditional family). The ideology of the traditional nuclear family also has women either at home reproducing children or as an "extra" flexible labor force that is able to work part-time or for low wages that "supplement" the household income (although given the economics today, "supplement" is often not the case—instead, two wages are needed). This provides the opportunity for men to hold higher paying jobs, thus having economic power over women. If same-sex marriage is perceived as a threat to our cultural understanding of heterosexual marriage (for example, making heterosexual marriage less important), then same-sex marriage becomes a threat to capitalism in general. By emphasizing the importance of heterosexual marriage as important and in need of defending, a patriarchal society is also emphasized, and perhaps one in which capitalism is more likely to flourish.

DEVIANCE IN POPULAR CULTURE

With its focus on power, examples of conflict theory abound in popular culture. Here we offer recommendations for a few films and television segments that you might watch; we think you will find it quite easy to apply general ideas from the conflict perspective to these specific cases.

Documentary films such as Michael Moore's *Capitalism: A Love Story* or *The Corporation* give an inside—and often critical—look at big business in the United States. Moore, in particular, juxtaposes the greed of corporations against the human suffering their actions may cause. Moore's ideas are compatible with a Marxist perspective; for a broader view of issues of power in the United States, you might watch one or more of the following:

Murder on a Sunday Morning—a documentary following the case of a 15-year-old African American male who is arrested for the murder of an elderly woman after an eyewitness places him near the scene of the crime. This film gives you a chance to question whether race still matters in our criminal justice system and how it might play out.

North Country—a woman goes to work in a Minnesota steel mine and is harassed, verbally abused, and assaulted by her male coworkers. When she decides to file a lawsuit for sexual harassment, she faces resistance from both men and women in the community.

The series *What Would You Do* from ABC News offers a number of experimental vignettes where actors stage scenes about hate crimes or "Shopping While Black" and cameras watch to see how the people witnessing the interaction will react. Many of the scenarios deal with race and ethnicity, and the reactions of the public can be directly related to the readings in this chapter. In one vivid example, a group of white boys vandalized a car in a neighborhood park as many people passed them by; few reacted or called the police. The producers then switched it up and had a group of black boys vandalize the car in the same park; in this case, there were more calls to the police and more suspicion. Most telling of all, while the white boys vandalized the car, a stranger called 911 not about the vandals but about two African American young men who were sleeping in their car in the parking lot. You can watch these vignettes online at abcnews.go.com; most run less than 15 minutes, and several provide concrete examples of conflict and labeling theories in action.

◈ Conflict Theory

While Marx did not spend much time focusing on crime or deviance, his work has been expanded by a series of criminologists who focused specifically on the law and thus definitions of crime and deviance. We have already discussed Spitzer, who remained fairly true to the Marxian fundamentals of economic structure and the social class; the following theorists focused on what some have called culture conflict. At its most basic, this expansion allows that there may be more groups in conflict than just the bourgeoisie and proletariat.

Gusfield

Gusfield (1967, 1968) examined the legislation of morality—in other words, the use of law to control behaviors that did not necessarily create victims (prostitution, drug use, gambling, and homosexuality). Gusfield argued that law had two functions: instrumental and symbolic. The instrumental function of law is one in which the behavior of individuals is proscribed; the law tells individuals what actions they can and cannot engage in, and agents of the law enforce those rules by arresting individuals who break those laws. This is important but not nearly as important as the symbolic function of the law for our understanding of culture conflict, power differentials, and the imposition of deviance in society.

The symbolic function of law does not rely on enforcement or action but instead "invites consideration" (Gusfield, 1967, 1968) of what is considered moral by a society. "In a pluralistic society these defining and designating acts can become political issues because they support or reject one or another of the competing and conflicting cultural groups in the society" (Gusfield, 1968, p. 57). In other words, a law that supports the cultural beliefs of one group over another suggests that those beliefs are the moral, normative beliefs of society as a whole. The process of creating that law becomes the political process of supporting that group. More so than even the enforcement of that law, the ability of the cultural group to claim that their beliefs are supported by law is what is important.

Applying the symbolic function of law to the continued struggles for and against same-sex marriage shows the importance of these laws in justifying the beliefs of both proponents and opponents of this legislation. Opponents of same-sex marriage are most often socially and religiously conservative. Laws that ban same-sex marriage are seen to support a socially and religiously conservative agenda. Beyond the specific prohibition that two people of the same sex may marry, these bans give strength to general cultural beliefs in social conservatism, making the whole movement stronger in areas well beyond the issue of same-sex marriage. In contrast, proponents of same-sex marriage are generally more socially and religiously progressive. Laws that support same-sex marriage are evidence of a progressive agenda that advocates for equality under the law for all groups. Laws that support same-sex marriage, then, also further other legal arguments for equality and thus strengthen the cultural beliefs of socially and religiously progressive groups.

Kitsuse and Spector

Kitsuse and Spector (1975) focused on the importance of value judgments in defining deviance and social problems. According to these theorists, value-conflict was the most important predictor of how something became defined as deviant. In other words, value judgments are what lead to definitions of deviance; when values are in conflict, those with the power to define conflicting values as deviant do so, thus "defining" or "creating" a social problem.

For Kitsuse and Spector (1973), then, the definitional process is most in need of study—what is defined as deviance is of little importance compared to *how* it is defined as deviant. Kitsuse and Spector suggest that deviance arises when groups make assertions that some act or issue is deviant. The success of these claims is based on how organized the group is and how strongly they make their claims. Many assertions of deviance and social problems do not take hold. A group is successful in its claim only if it can successfully maintain its claim. According to Kitsuse and Spector, an act or group is only continually defined as deviant as long as the group making the claim continues to exist.

This value-conflict and definitional process can be applied to the issue of same-sex marriage. First, there is a clear conflict in values between those who are opponents and those who are proponents of same-sex marriage. Same-sex marriage became an "issue" as gays and lesbians earned more social acceptance. As this occurred, the issue of allowing gays and lesbians to marry became more prominent and at this stage was focused on and defined as a deviance by those whose values conflicted (social and religious conservatives). Those opposed to same-sex marriage have presented an organized, strong argument that was accepted by the federal government through the passage of the Defense of Marriage Act. However, proponents of same-sex marriage have also become organized and stronger over time. These groups attempt to define those against same-sex marriage as the true deviants, and the definitional process of deviance continues with both sides arguing that their values should be the ones used to define deviance.

Vold

George Vold expanded on Marxist/conflict theory by developing a theory of group conflict in his 1958 book *Theoretical Criminology*. Vold describes the process by which individuals become a part of a particular group and how the relationships between various groups develop as they compete for space, resources, and power.

The Creation and Maintenance of "the Group"

Vold (1958) argues that individuals are "group-involved beings" (p. 203) who both influence and are influenced by the groups of which they are a part. Individuals become a part of their groups because of similar interest with other group-mates. The more similarity between the interests and loyalties, the stronger the group. Groups are created because of the needs of group members; groups that cannot fulfill these needs are disbanded, while groups that can fulfill the needs of individuals flourish and become stronger. Old groups are disbanded when they can no longer further their cause, and new groups form with the onslaught of new interests or needs.

Society, then, is made up of constant interaction between these various groups. Groups jockey for position and power in relation to the other groups and, through the "social process," gain and/or lose status relative to their counterparts. What is most important about this part of Vold's theory is that groups are in a constant state of action, while they fight for the interests of their constituents.

Conflict arises between groups when their interests and needs overlap. Groups that do not have overlapping interests and needs are less likely to develop a conflicted relationship with one another. When interests and needs overlap, there is the danger of one group replacing the other (or groups can perceive this danger as their worlds encroach on each other). The goal of all groups, then, becomes to not be replaced, disbanded, or abandoned. In other words, the goal of all groups is to maintain the interests and serve the needs of the group and to flourish in the face of other groups.

Vold argues that when conflicts between groups arise, and groups are threatened by the competing interest of other groups, individuals increase loyalty to their group. And the harder one must fight for her or his respective group, the more loyal that person becomes. "Nothing promotes harmony and self-sacrifice within the group quite as effectively as a serious struggle with another group for survival" (Vold, 1958, p. 206).

Vold's ideas about the creation and maintenance of a group can be applied to our example of same-sex marriage. We can argue that both same-sex and lesbian groups and religious groups are struggling for control of the definition of marriage (in other words, the interests and needs of both groups overlap on the issue of marriage). It could easily be argued that both groups have increased their solidarity and group member loyalty as the fight over same-sex marriage has intensified and that this power struggle or conflict has increased the membership of both groups. For example, many people who are not same sex or lesbian themselves now identify with the cause of marriage equality and support same-sex and lesbian groups, counting themselves as members even though, as heterosexuals, they already have the right to marry.

The Use of the Law to Maintain Interests

According to Vold, the law becomes a way for groups to maintain their interests and protect themselves. Sometimes this process is a negotiation between two competing groups, in which the political process develops a compromise that both sides can live with. Vold used the example of liquor laws to illustrate this compromise. If we see two groups—those who believe in prohibition as one group and the liquor industry as the other— we can see that the prohibition group would like to see liquor outlawed, while we can imagine that the liquor industry would prefer to have no restrictions on the selling and use of alcohol. Liquor laws, rules about where, when, and how alcohol can be sold, can then be seen as a way to compromise between these groups. (We can also see this as an example of Marx's dialectical materialism, where prohibition may be the thesis, the selling of liquor under no restriction may be the antithesis, and liquor laws may be the synthesis of the competing ideas.)

However, law can also be understood as the tool that more powerful groups can use to maintain their interests and service their needs. Vold argued that those groups that were powerful enough to control the law were also powerful enough to codify their values into law. It is this control of the law that means that certain groups who are in conflict with the values of the most powerful group(s) are more likely to be deemed criminal because they are more likely to have values and engage in behavior that is in conflict with the power group. Vold argued that this is how crime and deviance come about. While our next three theorists have written for decades—from the 1960s to the publication of this book—their most prolific work with conflict theory was in the 1960s and 1970s.

Turk

Turk (1969, 1976), like Vold, focused on the use of law as a social controlling agent. He saw law as a resource for which groups struggled for control. Groups who had the power to control the law had the power to criminalize (or make deviant) groups who did not have that power. He argued that laws were more likely to be enforced when they represented cultural values or were being enforced on subjects who had very little power (Liska & Messner, 1999).

The Use of the Law as a Socially Controlling Agent

In discussing his belief of "law as power" (p. 279), Turk (1976) argued that the resources that groups marshal go beyond just the economic resources that are often focused on in Marxist and conflict theory. Turk conceptualized five types of resource control (or power):

These are (1) control of the means of direct physical violence, i.e., war or police power; (2) control of the production, allocation, and/or use of material resources, i.e., economic power; (3) control of decision-making processes, i.e., political power; (4) control of definitions of and access to knowledge, beliefs, values, i.e., ideological power; and (5) control of human attention and living-time, i.e., diversionary power. (p. 280)

Police power means that if a group controls the law, they are often justified in using force or violence (i.e., the police) when other groups are not. For example, the police may forcefully carry protestors away from a rally or protest, but the individuals protesting may not in any way use force against the police or counter-protestors. For Turk, economic power was examining how much "economic power was enhanced or eroded by the law" (p. 280). For example, he saw the use of tax laws to protect the economic gains of the wealthy as an example of the law protecting and enhancing the resource of economic power for a certain group. Political power means that the law serves the purpose of organizing and supporting the political system. For example, the law supports the two-party system in the United States that benefits the Democrats and Republicans at the expense of those not associated with either party. Ideological power is supported by the law in two important ways. First, given that the law is the central tenet of political order, it legitimates itself (creates an ideological understanding of the importance and rightness of itself) by its very existence. Second, the law is used to both deny the rightness of certain ideas or to legitimate others who justify the overall ideology of groups in power. Finally, diversionary power means that the law can be used to divert the attention of groups and individuals from more pressing concerns. For example, our preoccupation with street crime is an excellent tactic to divert attention away from other harms that might be more far-reaching. Turk argued that the law is less likely to be used as a consensus-building negotiator of problems and is more likely to be the ultimate purveyor of power and manipulator of resources.

Quinney

While Quinney has written over many decades, spanning many theories, his work with Marxist/conflict theory was written during a similar time as Turk (1960s and 1970s). Quinney's (1963, 1970, 1991) work has ranged from positivist to relativist (Einstadter & Henry, 1995), with important works theorizing Marxist, conflict, and finally peacemaking criminologies (which you will read about in the next chapter). In his work, *The Social Reality of Crime,* Quinney (1970) puts forth a theory of the law that offers an explanation for the social construction of crime.

Process

While Quinney does not mention dialectical materialism in his discussion of process, it is easy to see the Marxian philosophy in his work. Quinney argues that most work on crime to this stage has been static (instead of dynamic). This static worldview has a strong impact on how we view deviance and crime. Quinney believes that this static view means that deviance and crime rest in the realm of the pathological (Quinney, 1970). In other words, our definition of deviance and crime is **normative**—it cannot and does not change with our understanding of the world. Quinney argues that our social relationships and thus our understanding of the world is a *process*. Because it is a process, our understanding of the world changes as the process evolves.

Conflict and Power

Quinney (1970) believes that conflict is inevitable in society and that "society is held together by force and constraint and is characterized by ubiquitous conflicts that result in continuous change" (pp. 9–10). This view of society links conflict and power very closely because it assumes that coercion is needed to keep society functioning. In other words, coercion is needed for one group to impose its beliefs or values on the society as a whole. Only those groups with sufficient power to coerce the whole will be able to impose their will.

Theory: The Social Reality of Crime

In Quinney's (1970) book, he outlined six propositions describing what he called the "social reality of crime" (p. 3). These propositions are as follows:

> **Proposition 1 (definition of crime):** Crime is a definition of human conduct that is created by authorized agents in a politically organized society. In other words . . . crime is a definition of behavior that is conferred on some persons by others.

> **Proposition 2 (formulation of criminal definition):** Criminal definitions describe behaviors that conflict with the interests of the segments of society that have the power to shape public policy.

> **Proposition 3 (application of criminal definition):** Criminal definitions are applied by the segments of society that have the power to shape the enforcement and administration of criminal law.

> **Proposition 4 (development of behavior patterns in relation to criminal definitions):** Behavior patterns are structured in segmentally organized society in relation to criminal definitions, and within this context persons engage in actions that have relative probabilities of being defined as criminal.

> **Proposition 5 (construction of criminal conceptions):** Conceptions of crime are constructed and diffused in the segments of society by various means of communication.

> **Proposition 6 (the social reality of crime):** The social reality of crime is constructed by formulation and application of criminal definitions, the development of behavior patterns related to criminal definitions, and the construction of criminal conceptions. (pp. 15–23)

Our example of same-sex marriage legislation can be evaluated using several of Quinney's propositions. The same-sex marriage debate has been played out in a very political manner in California (Proposition 1) with the right to marry or not marry being decided in several ballot measures over an extended period of time. While various state polls have suggested that a majority of Californians are not opposed to same-sex marriage, a constitutional ban on same-sex marriage was enacted with the passage of Prop 8 on November 4, 2008. The passage of this constitutional amendment then, effectively, defined same-sex marriage as deviant (or not legally allowed, like heterosexual marriage), thus illustrating the abilities of one group to define another group's actions as deviant and not sanctioned by the law.

STUDIES IN DEVIANCE

Threat to Whom? Conflict, Consensus, and Social Control

By Mitchell B. Chamlin (2009), in *Deviant Behavior, 30,* 539–559

Conflict theory is often juxtaposed against consensus theories of deviance—the basic question being, do police crackdowns in neighborhoods stem from a perceived threat to elites or a perceived threat to society as a whole? Conflict theory argues that these crackdowns happen when there is a perceived threat to the elites (for example, racial threat theory argues that when a community of color is perceived as a threat to white society, there will be an increase in social control of that group). Consensus theories, on the other hand, argue that crime is a threat to society in general; therefore, any crackdown is for the protection of society as a whole.

Chamlin (2009) studied the Cincinnati race riots of 2001 and also supported conflict theory through a racial-threat hypothesis. What made this study especially important was that Chamlin made the link between perceived threat and social control clearer by going one step further than using minority population size as a proxy for threat. Instead, Chamlin examined robbery arrests before and after the 2001 Cincinnati race riots, arguing that race riots carry much more threatening overtones to the ruling elite than just population size. He found that controlling for level of robbery, "the April 2001 riot in Cincinnati produced an appreciable and lasting increase in robbery arrests" (p. 555).

Chambliss

In his article, "Toward a Political Economy of Crime," Chambliss (1975) argues that the question, "Why do some individuals become involved with criminal behavior, while others do not?" (p. 165) is meaningless because, as he puts it, "everyone commits crime" (p. 165). In fact, much of Chambliss's (1964, 1975, 1978, 1999; Chambliss & Seidman, 1971) work focuses on the corrupt behavior and policies of "the state" (police, bureaucrats, politicians). Given that he focuses on the state, many might put his work under Marxist theory (indeed, the following excerpt detailing his paradigm of crime and criminal law is Marxian), and Chambliss does focus significantly on the corruption of the capitalist system. However, his works go beyond an analysis of the owners of the means of production and laborers, and for this reason, we have chosen to discuss him under conflict theory.

The following propositions highlight the most important implications of a Marxian paradigm of crime and criminal law.

A. On the content and operation of criminal law

1. Acts are defined as criminal because it is in the interests of the ruling class to so define them.

2. Members of the ruling class will be able to violate the laws with impunity while members of the subject classes will be punished.

3. As capitalist societies industrialize and the gap between the bourgeoisie and the proletariat widens, penal law will expand in an effort to coerce the proletariat into submission.

B. On the consequences of crime for society

1. Crime reduces surplus labor by creating employment not only for the criminals but for law enforcers, locksmiths, welfare workers, professors of criminology and a horde of people who live off of the fact that crime exists.

2. Crime diverts the lower classes' attention from the exploitation they experience, and directs it toward other members of their own class rather than towards the capitalist class or the economic system.

3. Crime is a reality which exists only as it is created by those in the society whose interests are served by its presence.

C. On the etiology of criminal behavior

1. Criminal and non-criminal behavior stem from people acting rationally in ways that are compatible with their class position. Crime is a reaction to the life conditions of a person's social class.

2. Crime varies from society to society depending on the political and economic structures of society.

3. Socialist societies should have much lower rates of crime because the less intense class struggle should reduce the forces leading to and the functions of crime. (Chambliss, 1975, pp. 152–153)

While our example of same-sex marriage is not about criminalization per se, it does illustrate several of Chambliss's propositions. Opponents to same-sex marriage spent significant amounts of time and money diverting the attention of the general public (*San Diego Union Tribune,* September 18, 2008). Opponents argued that children should only be raised in households where a father and mother (as opposed to father/father or mother/mother) are present and that society in general was threatened by same-sex marriage because if same-sex marriage remained legalized, "our children" would be exposed to its existence in the public schools. To the extent that the earlier argument that same-sex marriage threatens the hegemonic control of a patriarchal society, then it serves interests of capitalists in general to oppose same-sex marriage. Same-sex marriage was presented as a deviant idea or lifestyle that would harm groups everyone should want to keep safe—families and children.

◈ Critiques of Marxism and Conflict Theory

There are numerous critiques of both Marxist and conflict theory (for thorough and surprisingly different critiques, see Bohm, 1997; Kubrin et al., 2009; and Liska & Messner, 1999). In general, it has been argued that in dismissing **social consensus,** Marxist and conflict theorists ignore that some laws seem to protect the interests of everyone (for example, homicide laws or rape laws) (Liska & Messner, 1999). We might argue, however, that this critique is something of a straw person since so many laws (1) do not seem to protect the interests of everyone or (2) are differentially enforced on certain groups. It has also been argued that both perspectives are just that, perspectives, more than they are theories. In other words, they are hard to test, and theorists have been more focused on the theorizing than the "empirical inquiry" (Kubrin et al., 2009, p. 239). Those who argue this see the empirical inquiry as necessary to move the theory forward—without it, theory cannot be refined. There are those who go further with this critique and argue that these theories not only lack empirical evidence but, in many ways, are not theories but political statements about how the world works and how it should work (Akers & Sellers, 2004; Kubrin et al., 2009; Liska & Messner, 1999).

A critique specific to conflict theory (in which Marxist theory is held up as a "better" theory) is that conflict theory has not identified how power is established (Bohm, 1997). In other words, Marxist theory has very strictly and specifically linked the construction of power and conflict to the capitalist system, the mode of production, exploitation in general, and the creation of a ruling class that exploits a laborer class, specifically. Conflict theory, on the other hand, while it has expanded the discussion of power, has not explained where that power comes from. Why do some groups control more power than others? And how is that power conferred? A critique specific to Marxist theory is that the theory has not specified how laborers will lose their false consciousness (in other words, while there is general discussion, there are no testable propositions about how laborers come to be aware of their exploitation and then act on this awareness).

What do these and the many other critiques mean for the theories? Well, in many ways, they mean that the theories are robust and still stimulate discussion and use. They also mean that there is much room for continued work, work that focuses attention on the creation and maintenance of deviance, that is empirically testable, and that sharpens the direction of the theories as more data are analyzed. Next we will examine a sample of contemporary studies that spring from Marxist or conflict theory.

NOW YOU . . . USE THE THEORY

In April 2010, Arizona enacted SB 1070, the toughest immigration bill in existence, into law. This law requires police officers to detain people they "reasonably suspect" are undocumented and verify their status. It also makes it a misdemeanor to not carry papers proving one's immigration status. Finally, it allows individuals to sue public agencies that they think are not enforcing the law. The law was so controversial that its enactment was postponed while the courts determined its constitutionality.

In October 2010, NPR uncovered a direct link between SB 1070 and the largest private prison corporation in the nation. The law was written by Russell Pearce, a congressman for Arizona, but it was written with considerable help from a group called ALEC (American Legislative Exchange Council). ALEC comprises legislators and members of major corporations such as Reynolds Tobacco, ExxonMobil, the NRA, and Corrections Corporation of America. Pearce and Corrections Corporation of America both sit on the board of ALEC.

The Corrections Corporation of America, according to company documents, anticipates a significant portion of their future profits will come from ICE (Immigration and Customs Enforcement).

When asked if both the congressman and Corrections Corporation of America were at the same meeting in which the legislation was crafted, Michael Hough, staff director of ALEC, is quoted as saying, "Yeah. That's the way it's set up. It's a, you know, it's a public-private partnership. And that's how it's set up, so that—we believe both sides, businesses and lawmakers should be at the same table, together" (L. Sullivan, 2010).

There is nothing illegal about what Pearce or Corrections Corporation of America did in co-crafting the legislation. However, the partnership was not made public.

Use Marxist and/or conflict theory to comment on ALEC, the partnership between Pearce and Corrections Corporation of America, SB 1070, and the impact on legal immigrants, undocumented workers, and the state of immigration policy in the United States.

Source: Facts of this case were taken from NPR.org (L. Sullivan, 2010).

◈ Contemporary/Empirical Studies

A significant number of studies have used conflict theory to examine racial discrimination in the law and/ or justice system (Blalock, 1967; Bridges & Crutchfield, 1988; Chamlin, 2009; Leiber & Stairs, 1999; Percival, 2010). One of the ways these studies have used this theory is by arguing that the perceived threat of minority individuals (in many cases, racial minorities) will increase the likelihood of social control on that group. In other words, as a given minority population increases in size, the perceived threat to the ruling population also increases. Blalock (1967), in his power-threat hypothesis, argued that the relationship between minority threat and social control would be curvilinear (in other words, as the minority size increases, so would social control *to a certain point,* and then at a tipping point—in his argument, as the minority group reaches 50% of the population—the increase in minority size would actually likely lead to a decrease in formal social control). This curvilinear relationship has been partially supported in more than one study (Greenberg, Kessler, & Loftin, 1985; Jackson & Carroll, 1981), although support depends on both geography and historical time period.

Payne and Welch (2010) studied the discipline practices of 294 public schools and also supported conflict theory through a racial-threat hypothesis. Payne and Welch argued that schools are mirroring the get-tough policies of the criminal justice system even though delinquency is decreasing. They found that while most schools have a range of responses to bad behavior (from punitive to restorative), schools set in disadvantaged, urban locations with a disproportionate student population of color (black and Latino) are more likely to use punitive forms of discipline and less likely to use restorative forms of discipline.

Another contemporary study has used the ideas of conflict theory to predict perceptions of injustice of people of color—in this instance, black and Latino youth (Hagan, Shedd, & Payne, 2005). Many have argued that one of the detrimental effects of increased conflict, and thus increased social control on any minority group (people of color, women, gays, and lesbians), is that this leads to perceptions of injustice and a delegitimization of the justice system (see Cole, 1998). Hagan et al. (2005) argue that there is a comparative nature to exploitation and social control, in that disadvantaged social groups can compare their disadvantage with other groups. They find that it is indeed the case that both black and Latino youth compare their disadvantage to one another and white youth and that this comparative disadvantage does lead to increased perceptions of injustice at the hands of the criminal justice system. Hagan et al. conclude that "it is a possible further irony . . . that efforts to make city schools safer through increased deployment of the police may have the unintended consequence of alienating the students who are ostensibly being protected" (p. 400).

◈ Conclusion

The importance of Marxist/conflict theories in the study of deviance cannot be denied. As some of the first theories to take a relativist (or social constructionist) perspective on deviance, they allow us to question how deviance is defined and used to maintain positions of power in society. While the earliest tenets of these theories focus solely on the impact of the capitalist system on power, group structure, and group conflict, later iterations of the theory have shifted focus from a sole focus on capitalism to one that examines other power differentials—most notably, power differentials among racial groups and the ways in which legislation and agents of social control (the police) are used to control these groups. While these critical analyses may make some people (and groups) uncomfortable, they are necessary for a better understanding of deviance and society.

EXERCISES AND DISCUSSION QUESTIONS

1. As Reiman and Leighton (2009) wrote, "The Rich Get Richer and the Poor Get Prison." How might a Marxist or conflict theorist explain this sentence? Discuss a specific theorist.

2. Given the global recession that began in 2008, using Marxist/conflict theories, predict the trends we may see in legislation and incarceration in the United States.

3. Using the concept of dialectical materialism, trace the history of marijuana legislation in the United States.

4. Give an example of controlling "problem populations" through the creation and maintenance of deviance. How is deviance used to control this population?

5. This chapter used same-sex marriage legislation as an example of the struggle for competing groups to control the law and avoid deviant labels. Give another example of a group, its interests, and struggle for power and how legislation is used to negate this power.

6. Find a specific law in your town, city, or state. Critique its creation using Marxist or conflict theory. In other words, why was it created, and who does it benefit?

KEY TERMS

Conflict

Dialectical materialism

False consciousness

Instrumental Marxism

Normative

Relativist

Social consensus

Social construction

Structural Marxism

READING 26

This short piece from *The Communist Manifesto* may be unsettling to students—certainly the term *communism* has not held a very positive connotation in American culture, and a reading touting its virtue may come across as inconsistent (at the very least) with core American values. But it is important to recognize the background and context behind the writings of Marx and Engels. Take the introductory lines "The history or all hitherto existing society is the history of class struggles. Freeman and slave, patrician and plebeian, lord and serf, guild-master and journeyman, in a word, oppressor and oppressed." Hence, historically, conflict was endemic to society, and within capitalism, they saw horrific problems based on class that needed to be changed for a better outcome for all—long working hours in dangerous and unhealthy conditions, machinery taking over the jobs of many, and lower wages to make more wealth for the powerful. In a very different way than most theories of deviance that view the vast majority of deviance stemming from a small minority of persons who don't follow conventions, these conflict theorists see the deviance coming from the top down—the master (bourgeois) suppressing the suppressed (proletariat). Historically, they argue that the powerful control and alienate the less powerful, and it is only through class struggle and revolution that major changes in society are made. In this way, Marx has been labeled a "functionalist" recognizing the need for social change for the better. Indeed, Marx is seen by many as an optimist, with eyes open to a better society with more equalitarian social relations.

Source: Marx, Karl, and Friedrich Engels. 1848. *The Communist Manifesto.* Many editions. Many publishers.

The Communist Manifesto

Karl Marx and Friedrich Engels

A specter is haunting Europe—the specter of communism. All the powers of old Europe have entered into a holy alliance to exorcise this specter: Pope and Czar, Metternich and Guizot, French Radicals and German police-spies.

Where is the party in opposition that has not been decried as communistic by its opponents in power? Where the opposition that has not hurled the branding reproach of communism, against the more advanced opposition parties, as well as against its reactionary adversaries?

Two things result from this fact.

I. Communism is already acknowledged by all European powers to be itself a power.

II. It is high time that Communists should openly, in the face of the whole world, publish their views, their aims, their tendencies, and meet this nursery tale of the specter of communism with a Manifesto of the party itself.

To this end, Communists of various nationalities have assembled in London, and sketched the following Manifesto, to be published in the English, French, German, Italian, Flemish, and Danish languages.

◈ I. Bourgeoisie and Proletarians

The history of all hitherto existing society is the history of class struggles.

Freeman and slave, patrician and plebeian, lord and serf, guild-master and journeyman, in a word, oppressor and oppressed, stood in constant opposition to one another, carried on an uninterrupted, now hidden, now open fight, a fight that each time ended, either in a revolutionary reconstitution of society at large, or in the common ruin of the contending classes.

In the earlier epochs of history, we find almost everywhere a complicated arrangement of society into various orders, a manifold gradation of social rank. In ancient Rome we have patricians, knights, plebeians, slaves; in the Middle Ages, feudal lords, vassals, guild-masters, journeymen, apprentices, serfs; in almost all of these classes, again, subordinate gradations.

The modern bourgeois society that has sprouted from the ruins of feudal society has not done away with class antagonisms. It has but established new classes, new conditions of oppression, new forms of struggle in place of the old ones.

Our epoch, the epoch of the bourgeoisie, possesses, however, this distinctive feature: it has simplified the class antagonisms. Society as a whole is more and more splitting up into two great hostile camps, into two great classes directly facing each other: bourgeoisie and proletariat.

From the serfs of the Middle Ages sprang the chartered burghers of the earliest towns. From these burgesses the first elements of the bourgeoisie were developed.

The discovery of America, the rounding of the Cape, opened up fresh ground for the rising bourgeoisie. The East-Indian and Chinese markets, the colonization of America, trade with colonies, the increase in the means of exchange and in commodities generally, gave to commerce, to navigation, to industry, an impulse never before known, and, thereby, a rapid development to the revolutionary element in the tottering feudal society.

The feudal system of industry, under which industrial production was monopolized by closed guilds, now no longer sufficed for the growing wants of the new markets. The manufacturing system took its place. The guild-masters were pushed to one side by the manufacturing middle class; division of labor between the different corporate guilds vanished in the face of division of labor in each single workshop.

Meantime the markets kept ever growing, the demand ever rising. Even manufacture no longer sufficed. Thereupon, steam and machinery revolutionized industrial production. The place of manufacture was taken by the giant, modern industry, the place of the industrial middle class, by industrial millionaires, the leaders of whole industrial armies, the modern bourgeois.

Modern industry has established the world market, for which the discovery of America paved the way. This market has given an immense development to commerce, to navigation, to communication by land. This development has, in its turn, reacted on the extension of industry; and in proportion as industry, commerce, navigation, railways extended, in the same proportion the bourgeoisie developed, increased its capital, and pushed into the background every class handed down from the Middle Ages.

We see, therefore, how the modern bourgeoisie is itself the product of a long development, of a series of revolutions in the modes of production and exchange.

Each step in the development of the bourgeoisie was accompanied by a corresponding political advance of that class. An oppressed class under the sway of the feudal nobility, an armed and self-governing association in the medieval commune. At first, an independent urban republic (as in Italy and Germany) or a taxable "third estate" of the monarchy (as in France), afterwards, in the period of manufacture proper, serving either the semi-feudal or the absolute monarchy as a counterpoise against the nobility, and, in fact, cornerstone of the great monarchies in general, the bourgeoisie has at last, since the establishment of modern industry and of the world market, conquered for itself, in the modern representative State, exclusive political sway. The executive of the modern State is but a committee for managing the common affairs of the whole bourgeoisie.

The bourgeoisie, historically, has played a most revolutionary part.

The bourgeoisie, wherever it has got the upper hand, has put an end to all feudal, patriarchal, idyllic relations. It has pitilessly torn asunder the motley feudal ties that bound man to his "natural superiors," and

has left remaining no other nexus between man and man than naked self-interest, than callous "cash payment." It has drowned the most heavenly ecstasies of religious fervor, of chivalrous enthusiasm, of philistine sentimentalism, in the icy water of egotistical calculation. It has resolved personal worth into exchange value, and in place of the numberless indefeasible chartered freedoms, has set up that single, unconscionable freedom—Free Trade. In a word, for exploitation, veiled by religious and political illusions, it has substituted naked, shameless, direct, brutal exploitation.

The bourgeoisie has stripped of its halo every occupation hitherto honored and looked up to with reverent awe. It had converted the physician, the lawyer, the priest, the poet, and the man of science into its paid wage-laborers.

The bourgeoisie has torn away from the family its sentimental veil and has reduced the family relation to a mere money relation.

The bourgeoisie has disclosed how it came to pass that the brutal display of vigor in the Middle Ages, which reactionaries so much admire, found its fitting complement in the most slothful indolence. It has been the first to show what man's activity can bring about. It has accomplished wonders far surpassing Egyptian pyramids, Roman aqueducts, and Gothic cathedrals. It has conducted expeditions that put in the shade all former Exoduses of nations and crusades.

The bourgeoisie cannot exist without constantly revolutionizing the instruments of production, and thereby the relations of production, and with them all social relations. Conservation of the old modes of production in unaltered form, was, on the contrary, the first condition of existence for all earlier industrial classes. Constant revolutionizing of production, uninterrupted disturbance of all social conditions, everlasting uncertainty and agitation distinguish the bourgeois epoch from all earlier ones. All fixed fast-frozen relations, with their train of ancient and venerable prejudices and opinions are swept away, all newly formed ones become antiquated before they can ossify. All that is solid melts into air, all that is holy is profaned, and man is at last compelled to face with sober senses, his real conditions of life, and his relations with his kind.

The need of a constantly expanding market for its products chases the bourgeoisie over the whole face of the globe. It must nestle everywhere, settle everywhere, establish connections everywhere.

The bourgeoisie has through its exploitation of the world market given a cosmopolitan character to production and consumption in every country. To the great chagrin of reactionaries, it has drawn from under the feet of industry the national ground on which it stood. All old, established national industries have been destroyed or are daily being destroyed. They are dislodged by new industries, whose introduction becomes a life and death question for all civilized nations, industries that no longer work with indigenous raw material, but raw material drawn from the remotest regions, industries whose products are consumed, not only at home, but in every quarter of the globe. In place of the old wants, satisfied by the productions of the country, we find new wants, requiring for their satisfaction the products of distant lands and climes. In place of the old local and national seclusion and self-sufficiency, we have intercourse in every direction, a universal interdependence of nations. And as in material, so also in intellectual production. The intellectual creations of individual nations become common property. National one-sidedness and narrow-mindedness become more and more impossible, and from the numerous national and local literatures, there arises a world literature.

The bourgeoisie, by the rapid improvement of all instruments of production, by the immensely facilitated means of communication, draws all, even the most barbarian, nations into civilization. The cheap prices of its commodities are the heavy artillery with which it batters down all Chinese walls, with which if forces the barbarians' intensely obstinate hatred of foreigners to capitulate. It compels all nations, on pain of extinction, to adopt the bourgeois mode of production; it compels them to introduce what it calls civilization into their midst, *i.e.,* to become bourgeois themselves. In one word, it creates a world after its own image.

The bourgeoisie has subjected the country to the rule of the towns. It has created enormous cities, greatly increased the urban population as compared with the rural, and thus rescued a considerable part of the population from the idiocy of rural life. Just as it has made the country dependent on the towns, so it has made barbarian and semi-barbarian countries dependent on the civilized ones, nations of peasants on nations of bourgeoisie, the East on the West. More and more the bourgeoisie continues to do away with the scattered state of population, means of production, and property. It has agglomerated population, centralized means of production, and concentrated property in a few hands. The necessary consequence of this was political centralization. Independent, or but loosely connected, provinces with separate interest, laws, government and systems of taxation, became lumped together into one nation, with one government, one code of laws, one national class-interest, one frontier and one customs-tariff.

The bourgeoisie, during its rule of scarcely one hundred years, has created more massive and more colossal productive forces than have all preceding generations together. The subjection of nature's forces to man and machinery; the application of chemistry to industry and agriculture; [the development of] steam-navigation, railways and electric telegraphs; the clearing of whole continents for cultivation; the canalization of rivers and the conjuring of whole populations out of the ground—what earlier century had even a presentiment that such productive forces slumbered in the lap of social labor?

We see then: the means of production and exchange, on whose foundation the bourgeoisie built itself up, were generated in feudal society. At a certain stage in the development of these means of production and exchange, the conditions under which feudal society produced and exchanged, the feudal organization of agriculture and manufacturing industry, in one word, the feudal relations of property became no longer compatible with the already developed productive forces; they became so many fetters. They had to be burst asunder. They were burst asunder.

Into their place stepped free competition, accompanied by a social and political constitution adapted to it and by the economical and political sway of the bourgeois class.

A similar movement is going on before our own eyes. Modern bourgeois society with its relations of production, exchange and property, a society that has conjured up such gigantic means of production and exchange, is like the sorcerer, who is no longer able to control the powers of the nether world whom he has called up by his spells. For many decades the history of industry and commerce has been but the history of the revolt of modern productive forces against modern conditions of production, against the property relations that are the conditions for the existence of the bourgeoisie and of its rule. It is enough to mention the commercial crises that by their periodic return put on its trial each time more threateningly, the existence of the entire bourgeois society. In these crises a great part not only of the existing products, but also of the previously created productive forces are periodically destroyed. In these crises there breaks out an epidemic that in all earlier epochs would have seemed an absurdity—the epidemic of overproduction. Society suddenly finds itself put back into a state of momentary barbarism. It appears as if a famine or a universal war of devastation had cut off the supply of every means of subsistence. Industry and commerce seem to be destroyed. And why? Because there is too much civilization, too much means of subsistence, too much industry, too much commerce. The productive forces at the disposal of society no longer tend to further the development of the conditions of bourgeois property. On the contrary, they have become too powerful for these conditions, by which they are fettered, and so soon as they overcome these fetters, they bring disorder into the whole of bourgeois society, endanger the existence of bourgeois property. The conditions of bourgeois society are too narrow to encompass the wealth created by them. And how does the bourgeoisie get over these crises? On the one hand by enforced destruction of a mass of productive forces; on the other, by the conquest of new markets, and by the more thorough exploitation of the old ones. That is to say, by paving the way for more extensive and more destructive crises, and by diminishing the means whereby crises are prevented.

The weapons with which the bourgeoisie brought feudalism to the ground are now turned against the bourgeoisie itself.

But not only has the bourgeoisie forged the weapons that bring death to itself; it has also called into existence the men who are to wield those weapons—the modern working class—the proletariat.

In proportion as the bourgeoisie, *i.e.,* capital, develops, in the same proportion the proletariat, the modern working class, develops—a class of laborers, who live only so long as they find work, and who find work only so long as their labor increases capital. These laborers, who must sell them selves piecemeal, are a commodity, like every other article of commerce, and are consequently exposed to all the vicissitudes of competition, to all the fluctuations of the market.

Owing to the extensive use of machinery and to the division of labor, work for the proletarians has lost all individual character, and, consequently, all charm for the workman. He becomes an appendage of the machine, and it is only the simplest, most monotonous, and most easily acquired knack that is required of him. Hence, the cost of production of a workman is restricted, almost entirely, to the means of subsistence that he requires for his maintenance and for the propagation of his race. But the price of a commodity, and therefore also of labor, is equal to its cost of production. In proportion, therefore, as the repulsiveness of the work increases, the wage decreases. Nay more, to the extent that the use of machinery and the division of labor increases, to the same extent the burden of toil also increases, whether by the prolongation of working hours, the increase of the work exacted in a given time or the increased speed of the machinery, etc.

Modern industry has converted the little workshop of the patriarchal master into the great factory of the industrial capitalist. Masses of laborers crowded into the factory are organized like soldiers. As privates of the industrial army they are placed under the command of a perfect hierarchy of officers and sergeants. Not only are they slaves of the bourgeois class and the bourgeois state; they are daily and hourly enslaved by the machine, by the supervisor, and, above all, by the individual bourgeois manufacturer himself. The more openly this despotism proclaims gain to be its end and aim, the more petty, the more hateful and the more embittering it is.

The less the skill and exertion of strength involved in manual labor (in other words, the more modern industry becomes developed), the more the labor of men is replaced by that of women. Differences of age and sex have no longer any distinctive social validity for the working class. All are instruments of labor, more or less expensive to use, according to their age and sex.

No sooner is the exploitation of the laborer by the manufacturer, so far, at an end, that he receives his wages in cash, than he is set upon by the other portions of the bourgeoisie, the landlord, the shopkeeper, the pawnbroker, etc.

The lower strata of the middle class—small tradespeople, shopkeepers, retired tradesmen, handicraftsmen and peasants—all these sink gradually into the proletariat, partly because their diminutive capital does not suffice for the scale on which modern industry is carried on and is swamped in the competition with the large capitalists, partly because their specialized skill is rendered worthless by new methods of production. Thus, the proletariat is recruited from all classes of the population.

The proletariat goes through various stages of development. With its birth begins its struggle with the bourgeoisie. At first the contest is carried on by individual laborers, then by the workers of a factory, then by the laborers of one trade in one locality, against the individual bourgeois who directly exploits them. They direct their attacks not against the bourgeois conditions of production, but against the instrument of production themselves; they destroy imported wares that compete with their labor, they smash to pieces machinery, they set factories ablaze, they seek to restore by force the vanished status of the workman of the Middle Ages.

At this stage the laborers still form an incoherent mass scattered over the whole country, and divided by their mutual competition. If they unite anywhere to form more compact bodies, this is not yet the consequence of their own active union, but of the union of the bourgeoisie, which, in order to attain its own political ends, is compelled to set the whole proletariat in motion, and is moreover yet, for a time, able to do so. At this stage, therefore, the proletarians do not fight their enemies, but the enemies of their enemies, the remnants of absolute monarchy, the landowners, the non-industrial bourgeois, the petty bourgeoisie. Thus the whole historical movement is concentrated in the hands of the bourgeoisie; every victory so obtained is a victory for the bourgeoisie.

But with the development of industry the proletariat not only increases in number; it becomes concentrated in greater masses, its strength grows, and it becomes more aware of that strength. The various interests and conditions of life within the ranks of the proletariat are more and more equalized, in proportion as machinery obliterates all distinctions of labor, and nearly everywhere reduces wages to the same low level. The growing competition among the bourgeoisie and the resulting commercial crises, make the wages of the workers ever more fluctuating. The unceasing improvement of machinery, ever more rapidly developing, makes their livelihood more and more precarious. The collisions between individual workmen and individual bourgeois take more and more the character of collisions between two classes. Thereupon the workers begin to form combinations (trade unions) against the bourgeois; they join together in order to keep up the rate of wages; they from permanent associations in order to make provision beforehand for these occasional revolts. Here and there the contest breaks out into riots.

Now and then the workers are victorious, but only for a time. The real fruit of their battles lies, not in the immediate result, but in the ever-expanding union of the workers. This union is helped on by the improved means of communication that are created by modern industry and that place the workers of different localities in contact with one another. It was just this contact that was needed to centralize the numerous local struggles, all of the same character, into one national struggle between classes. But every class struggle is a political struggle. And that union, which took the burghers of the Middle Ages, with their miserable highways centuries to acquire, the modern proletarians, thanks to railways, achieve in a few years.

This organization of the proletarians into a class, and consequently into a political party, is continually being upset again by the competition between the workers themselves. But it continually re-emerges, stronger, firmer, mightier. It compels legislative recognition of particular interests of the workers, by taking advantage of the divisions among the bourgeoisie itself. Thus the ten-hours' bill in England was carried.

The sum of these collisions between the classes of the old society further, in many ways, the development of the proletariat. The bourgeoisie finds itself involved in a constant battle. At first with the aristocracy; later, with those portions of the bourgeoisie itself, whose interests have become antagonistic to the progress of industry; at all times, with the bourgeoisie of foreign countries. In all these battles it sees itself compelled to appeal to the proletariat, to ask for its help, and thus, to drag it into the political arena. The bourgeoisie itself, therefore, supplies the proletariat with its own elements of political and general education, in other words, it furnishes the proletariat with weapons for fighting the bourgeoisie.

Further, as we have already seen, entire sections of the ruling classes are, by the advance of industry, precipitated into the proletariat, or are at least threatened in their conditions of existence. These also supply the proletariat with fresh elements of enlightenment and progress.

Finally, in times when the class struggle nears the decisive hour, the process of dissolution going on within the ruling class (in fact, within the whole range of old society) assumes such a violent, glaring character, that a small section of the ruling class cuts itself adrift, and joins the revolutionary class, the class that holds the future in its hands. Just as, therefore, at an earlier period, a section of the nobility went over to the bourgeoisie, so now a portion of the bourgeoisie goes over to the proletariat, and in particular, a portion of the bourgeois ideologists, who have raised themselves to the level of comprehending theoretically the historical movement as a whole.

Of all the classes that stand face to face with the bourgeoisie today, the proletariat alone is a really revolutionary class. The other classes decay and finally disappear in the face of modern industry; the proletariat is its special and essential product.

The lower middle class, the small manufacturer, the shopkeeper, the artisan, the peasant—all these fight against the bourgeoisie, to save from extinction their existence as fractions of the middle class. They are therefore not revolutionary, but conservative. Nay more, they are reactionary, for they try to roll back the wheel of history. It by chance they are revolutionary, they are so only in view of their impending transfer into the proletariat, they thus defend not their present, but their future interests, they desert their own standpoint to place themselves at that of the proletariat.

The "dangerous class," the social scum, that passively rotting mass thrown off by the lowest layers of the old society, may, here and there, be swept into the movement by a proletarian revolution; its conditions of life, however, prepare it far more for the part of a bribed tool of reactionary intrigue.

For the proletariat, the conditions of the old society are already virtually swamped. The proletarian is without property; his relation to his wife and children has no longer anything in common with the bourgeois family relations; modern industrial labor, modern subjection to capital, the same in England as in France, in America as in Germany, has stripped him of every trace of national character. Law, morality, religion, are to him so many bourgeois prejudices, behind which lurk in ambush just as many bourgeois interests.

All the preceding classes that got the upper hand sought to fortify their already acquired status by subjecting society at large to their conditions of appropriation. The proletarians cannot become masters of the productive forces of society, except by abolishing their own previous mode of appropriation, and thereby also every other previous mode of appropriation. They have nothing of their own to secure and to fortify; their mission is to destroy all previous securities for, and insurances of, individual property.

All previous historical movements were movements of minorities, or in the interest of minorities. The proletarian movement is the self-conscious, independent movement of the immense majority, in the interest of the immense majority. The proletariat, the lowest stratum of our present society, cannot stir, cannot raise itself, without the whole overlying strata of official society being sprung into the air.

Though not in substance, yet in form, the struggle of the proletariat with the bourgeoisie is at first a national struggle. The proletariat of each country must, of course, first of all settle matters with its own bourgeoisie.

In depiction the most general phases of the development of the proletariat, we traced the more or less veiled civil war raging within existing society, up to the point where that war breaks out into open revolution, and where the violent overthrow of the bourgeoisie lays the foundation for the sway of the proletariat.

Hitherto, every form of society has been based, as we have already seen, on the antagonism between oppressing and oppressed classes. But in order to oppress a class, certain conditions must be assured to it under which it can, at least, continue its slavish existence. The serf, in the period of serfdom, raised himself to membership in the commune, just as the petty bourgeois, under the yoke of feudal absolutism, managed to develop into a bourgeois. The modern laborer, on the contrary, instead of rising with the progress of industry, sinks deeper and deeper below the conditions of existence of his own class. He becomes a pauper, and pauperism develops more rapidly than population and wealth. And here it becomes evident that the bourgeoisie is unfit any longer to be the ruling class in society and to impose on society its own conditions of existence as an overriding law. It is unfit to rule because it is incompetent to assure an existence to its slave within his slavery, because it cannot help letting him sink into such a state that it has to feed him, instead of being fed by him. Society can no longer live under this bourgeoisie. In other words, its existence is no longer compatible with society.

The essential condition for the existence, and for the sway of the bourgeois class is the formation and augmentation of capital; the condition for capital is wage labor. Wage labor rests exclusively on competition between the laborers. The advance of industry, that the bourgeoisie involuntarily promotes, replaces the isolation of the laborers, due to competition, by their revolutionary combination, due to association. The development of modern industry, therefore, cuts from under its feet the very foundation on which the bourgeoisie produces and appropriates products. What the bourgeoisie, therefore, produces, above all, is its own gravediggers. Its fall and the victory of the proletariat are equally inevitable.

READING 27

Writing in 1901, African American scholar W. E. B. Du Bois vividly documents the way blacks and whites were historically dealt with by the criminal justice system in the South. Because slaves were literally property owned by whites prior to the Civil War, they had little to do with the criminal justice system. Misbehavior was generally dealt with by their owners and informal groups of whites who worked to keeps blacks from associating, and the criminal justice system focused primarily on whites. As Du Bois puts it, the system was "lenient in theory and lax in execution." Following the war, owners lost power, but a more formal illegal group, the Klu Klux Klan, emerged. More important, however, because whites so believed in the slave system and were so convinced that freed slaves would not work as they had before, a new criminal justice system emerged "to restore slavery in everything but in name." New laws were passed, and the courts now became focused on African Americans, with the convict-lease system emerging where the labor of blacks was sold to "the highest bidder." The conditions were abysmal. The unintended consequences of the changes were to make the criminal justice system appear less legitimate and therefore ineffective. Du Bois concludes with some statistics documenting the poor governmental support for the criminal justice system in the South—there was little need as the convict-lease system was a "money maker" but a deplorable system that remains problematic.

Source: Du Bois, W. E. B. 1901. "The Spawn of Slavery: The Convict-Lease System in the South." *The Missionary Review of the World* 14:737–745.

The Spawn of Slavery

The Convict-Lease System in the South

W.E.B. Du Bois

A modified form of slavery survives wherever prison labor is sold to private persons for their pecuniary profit.

—Wines.

Two systems of controlling human labor which still flourish in the South are the direct children of slavery, and to all intents and purposes are slavery itself. These are the crop-lien system and the convict-lease system. The crop-lien system is an arrangement of chattel mortgages so fixed that the housing, labor, kind of agriculture and, to some extent, the personal liberty of the free black laborer is put into the hands of the landowner and merchant. It is absentee landlordism and the "company-store" systems united and carried out to the furthest possible degree. The convict-lease system is the slavery in private hands of persons convicted of crimes and misdemeanors in the courts. The objects of the present paper is to study the rise and development of the convict-least system, and the efforts to modify and abolish it.

Before the Civil War the system of punishment for criminals was practically the same as in the North. Except in a few cities, however, crime was less prevalent than in the North, and the system of slavery could become criminals in the eyes of the law only in exceptional cases. The punishment and trial of nearly all ordinary misdemeanors and crimes lay in the hands of the masters. Consequently, so far as the state was concerned, there was no crime of any consequence among Negroes. The system of criminal jurisprudence had to do, therefore, with whites almost exclusively, and as is usual in a land of scattered population and aristocratic tendencies the law was lenient in theory and lax in execution.

On the other hand, the private well-ordering and control of slaves called for careful cooperation among masters. The fear of insurrection was ever before the South, and the ominous uprising of Cato, Gabriel, Vesey, Turner, and Toussaint made this fear an ever-present nightmare. The result was a system of rural police, mounted and on duty chiefly at night, whose work it was to stop the nocturnal wandering and meeting of slaves. It was usually an effective organization, which terrorized the slaves, and to which all white men belonged, and were liable to active detailed duty at regular intervals.

Upon this system war and emancipation struck like a thunderbolt. Law and order among the whites, already loosely enforced, became still weaker through the inevitable influence of conflict and social revolution. The freedman was especially in an anomalous situation. The power of the slave police supplemented and depended upon that of the private masters. When the masters' power was broken the patrol was easily transmuted into a lawless and illegal mob known to history as the Ku Klux Klan. Then came the first, and probably the most disastrous, of that succession of political expedients by which the South sought to evade the consequences of emancipation. It will always be a nice question of ethics as to how far a conquered people can be expected to submit to the dictates of a victorious foe. Certainly the world must to a degree sympathize with resistance under such circumstances. The mistake of the South, however, was to adopt a kind of resistance which in the long run weakened her moral fiber, destroyed respect for law and order, and enabled gradually her worst elements to secure an unfortunate ascendancy. The South believed in slave labor, and was thoroughly convinced that free Negroes would not work steadily or effectively. The whites were determined after the war, therefore, to restore slavery in everything but in name. Elaborate and ingenious apprentice and vagrancy laws were passed, designed to make the freedmen and their children work for their former masters at practically no wages. Some justification for these laws was found in the inevitable tendency of many of the ex-slaves to loaf when the fear of the lash was taken away. The new laws, however, went far beyond such justification, totally ignoring that large class of freedmen eager to work and earn property of their own, stopping all competition between employers, and confiscating the labor and liberty of children. In fact, the new laws of this period recognized the Emancipation Proclamation and the Thirteenth Amendment simply as abolishing the slavetrade.

The interference of Congress in the plans for reconstruction stopped the full carrying out of these schemes, and the Freedmen's Bureau consolidated and sought to develop the various plans for employing and guiding the freedmen already adopted in different places under the protection of the Union army. This government guardianship established a free wage system of labor by the help of the army, the striving of the best of the blacks, and the cooperation of some of the whites. In the matter of adjusting legal relationships, however, the Bureau failed. It had, to be sure, Bureau courts, with one representative of the ex-master, one of the freedman, and one of the Bureau itself, but they never gained the confidence of the community. As the regular state courts gradually regained power, it was necessary for them to fix by their decisions the new status of the freedmen. It was perhaps as natural as it was unfortunate that amid this chaos the courts sought to do by judicial decisions what the legislatures had formerly sought to do by specific law—namely, reduce the freedmen to serfdom. As a result, the small peccadillos of a careless, untrained class were made the excuse for severe sentences. The courts and jails became filled with the careless and ignorant, with those who sought to emphasize their new-found freedom, and too often with innocent victims of oppression. The testimony of a Negro counted for little or nothing in court, while the accusation of white witnesses was usually decisive. The result of this was a sudden large increase in the apparent criminal population of the Southern states—an increase so large that there was no way for the state to house it or watch it even had she state wished to. And the state did not wish

to. Throughout the South laws were immediately passed authorizing public officials to lease the labor of convicts to the highest bidder. The lessee then took charge of the convicts—worked them as he wished under the nominal control of the state. Thus a new slavery and slave-trade was established.

◈ The Evil Influences

The abuses of this system have often been dwelt upon. It had the worst aspects of slavery without any of its redeeming features. The innocent, the guilty, and the depraved were herded together, children and adults, men and women, given into the complete control of practically irresponsible men, whose sole object was to make the most money possible. The innocent were made bad, the bad worse; women were outraged and children tainted; whipping and torture were in vogue, and the death-rate from cruelty, exposure, and overwork rose to large percentages. The actual bosses over such leased prisoners were usually selected from the lowest classes of whites, and the camps were often far from settlements or public roads. The prisoners often had scarcely any clothing, they were fed on a scanty diet of corn bread and fat meat, and worked twelve or more hours a day. After was insufficient shelter; in one Georgia camp, as late as 1895, sixty-one men slept in one room, seventeen by nineteen feet, and seven feet high. Sanitary conditions were wretched, there was little or no medical attendance, and almost no care of the sick. Women were mingled indiscriminately with the men, both in working and sleeping, and dressed often in men's clothes. A young girl at Camp Hardmont, Georgia, in 1985, was repeatedly outraged by several of her guards, and finally died in childbirth while in camp.

Such facts illustrate the system at its worst—as it used to exist in nearly every Southern state, and as it still exists in parts of Georgia, Mississippi, Louisiana, and other states. It is difficult to say whether the effect of such a system is worse on the whites or on the Negroes. So far as the whites are concerned, the convict-lease system lowered the respect for courts, increased lawlessness, and put the states into the clutches of penitentiary "rings." The courts were brought into politics, judgeships became elective for shorter and shorter terms, and there grew up a public sentiment which would not consent to considering the desert of a criminal apart from his color. If the criminal were white, public opinion refused to permit him to enter the chain-gang save in the most extreme cases. The result is that even today it is very difficult to enforce the laws in the South against whites, and red-handed criminals go scot-free. On the other hand, so customary had it become to convict any Negro upon a mere accusation, that public opinion was loathe to allow a fair trial to black suspects, and was too often tempted to take the law into their own hands. Finally the state became a dealer in crime, profited by it so as to derive a new annual income for her prisoners. The lessees of the convicts made large profits also. Under such circumstances, it was almost impossible to remove the clutches of this vicious system from the state. Even as late as 1890 the Southern states were the only section of the Union where the income from prisons and reformatories exceeded the expense.[1] Moreover, these figures do not include the county gangs where the lease system is today most prevalent and the net income largest.

The effect of the convict-lease system on the Negroes was deplorable. First it linked crime and slavery indissolubly in their minds as simply forms of the white man's oppression. Punishment, consequently, lost the most effective of its deterrent effects, and the criminal gained pity instead of disdain. The Negroes lost faith in the integrity of courts and the fairness of juries. Worse than all, the chain-gangs became schools of crime which hastened the appearance of the confirmed Negro criminal upon the scene. That some crime and vagrancy should follow emancipation was inevitable. A nation can not systematically degrade labor without in some degree debauching the laborer. But there can be no doubt but that the indiscriminate careless and unjust method by which Southern courts dealt with the freedmen after the war increased crime and vagabondage to an enormous extent. There are no reliable statistics to which one can safely appeal to measure exactly the growth of crime among the emancipated slaves. About seventy per cent of all prisoners in the South are black; this, however, is in part explained by the fact that accused Negroes are still easily convicted and get long sentences, while whites still continue to escape the penalty of many crimes even among themselves. And yet allowing for all this, there can be no reasonable doubt but that there has arisen in the South since the war a class of black criminals, loafers, and ne'er-do-wells who are a menace to their fellows, both black and white.

The appearance of the real Negro criminal stirred the South deeply. The whites, despite their long use of the criminal court for putting Negroes to work, were used to little more than petty thieving and loafing on their part, and not to crimes of boldness, violence, or cunning. When, after periods of stress of financial depression, as in 1892, such crimes increased in frequency, the wrath of a people unschooled in the modern methods of dealing with crime broke all bounds and reached strange depths of barbaric vengeance and torture. Such acts, instead of

Table 1   Income and Expense of State Prisons and Reformatories, 1890

	Earnings	Expense	Profit
New England	$299,735	$1,204,029	—
Middle States	71,252	1,850,452	—
Border States	597,898	962,422	—
Southern States[2]	938,406	890,452	$47,974
Central States	624,161	1,971,795	—
Western States	378,036	1,572,316	—

drawing the best opinion of these states and of the nation toward a consideration of Negro crime and criminals, discouraged and alienated the best classes of Negroes, horrified the civilized world, and made the best white Southerners ashamed of their land.

◈ What Has Been Done

Nevertheless, in the midst of all this a leaven of better things had been working and the bad effects of the epidemic of lynching quickened it. The great difficulty to be overcome in the South was the false theory of work and of punishment of wrong-doers inherited from slavery. The inevitable result of a slave system in for a master class to consider that the slave exists for his benefit alone—that the slave has no rights which the master is bound to respect. Inevitably this idea persisted after emancipation. The black workman existed for the comfort and profit of white people, and the interests of white people were the only ones to be seriously considered. Consequently, for a lessee to work convicts for his profit was a most natural thing. Then, too, these convicts were to be punished, and the slave theory of punishment was pain and intimidation. Given these ideas, and the convict-lease system was inevitable. But other ideas were also prevalent in the South; there were in slave times plantations where the well-being of the slaves was considered, and where punishment meant the correction of the fault rather than brute discomfort. After the chaos of war and reconstruction passed, there came from the better conscience of the South a growing demand for reform in the treatment of crime. The worst horrors of the convict-lease system were attacked persistently in nearly every Southern state. Back in the eighties George W. Cable, a Southern man, published a strong attack on the system. The following decade Governor Atkinson, of Georgia, instituted a searching investigation, which startled the state by its revelation of existing conditions. Still more recently Florida, Arkansas, and other states have had reports and agitation for reform. The result has been marked improvement in conditions during the last decade. This is shown in part by the statistics of 1895; in that year the prisons and reformatories of the far South cost the states $204,483 more than they earned, while before this they had nearly always yielded an income.

This is still the smallest expenditure of any section, and looks strangely small beside New England's $1,190,564. At the same time, a movement in the right direction is clear. The laws are being framed more and more so as to prevent the placing of convicts altogether in private control. They are not, to be sure, always enforced, Georgia having several hundreds of convicts so controlled in 1895 despite the law. In nearly all the Gulf states the convict-lease system still has a strong hold, still debauches public sentiment and breeds criminals.

The next step after the lease system was to keep the prisoners under state control, or, at least, regular state inspection, but to lease their labor to contractors, or to employ it in some remunerative labor for the state. It is this stage that the South is slowly reaching today so far as the criminals are concerned who are dealt with directly by the states. Those whom the state still unfortunately leaves in the hands of county officials are usually leased to irresponsible parties. Without doubt, work, and work worth the doing—*i.e.*, profitable work—is best for prisoners. Yet there lurks in this system a dangerous temptation. The correct theory is that the work is for the benefit of the criminal—for his correction, if possible. At the same time, his work should not be allowed to come into unfair competition with that of honest laborers, and it should never be an object of traffic for pure financial gain. Whenever the profit derived from the work becomes the object of employing prisoners, then evil must result. In the South today it is natural that in the slow turning from the totally indefensible private lease system, some of its wrong ideas should persist. Prominent among these persisting ideas is this: that the most successful dealing with criminals is that which costs the state least in actual outlay. This idea still dominates most of the Southern states. Georgia spent $2.38 per capita on her 2,938 prisoners in 1890, while Massachusetts spent $62.96 per capita on her 5,227 prisoners. Moreover, by selling the labor of her prisoners of the highest bidders, Georgia not only got all her money back, but made a total clear profit of $6.12 on each prisoner. Massachusetts spent about $100,000 more than was returned to her by prisoners' labor. Now it is extremely difficult, under such circumstances, to prove to a state that Georgia is making a worse business investment than Massachusetts. It will take another generation to prove to the South that an apparently profitable traffic in crime is very dangerous business for a state; that prevention of crime and the reformation of criminals is the one legitimate object of all dealing with depraved natures, and that apparent profit arising from other methods is in the end worse than dead loss. Bad public schools and profit from crime explain much of the Southern social problem. Georgia, Florida, and Louisiana, as late as 1895, were spending annually only $20,799 on their state prisoners, and receiving $80,493 from the hire of their labor.

Moreover, in the desire to make the labor of criminals pay, little heed is taken of the competition of convict and free laborers, unless the free laborers are white and have a vote. Black laborers are continually displaced in such industries as brick-making, mining, road-building, grading, quarrying, and the like, by convicts hired at $3, or thereabouts, a month.

The second mischievous idea that survives from slavery and the convict-lease system is the lack of all intelligent discrimination in dealing with prisoners. The most conspicuous and fatal example of this is the indiscriminate herding of juvenile and adult criminals. It need hardly be said the such methods manufacture criminals more quickly than all other methods can reform them. In 1890, of all the Southern states, only Texas, Tennessee, Kentucky, Maryland, and West Virginia made any state appropriations for juvenile reformatories. In 1895 Delaware was added to these, but Kentucky was missing. We have, therefore:

	1890	1895
New England	$632,634	$854,581
Border States	233,020	174,781
Southern States	10,498	33,910

And this in face of the fact that the South had in 1890 over four thousand prisoners under twenty years of age. In some of the Southern states—notably, Virginia—there are private associations for juvenile reform, acting in cooperation with the state. These have,

in some cases, recently received state aid, I believe. In other states, like Georgia, there is permissive legislation for the establishment of local reformatories. Little has resulted as yet from this legislation, but it is promising.

I have sought in this paper to trace roughly the attitude of the South toward crime. There is in that attitude much to condemn, but also something to praise. The tendencies are today certainly in the right direction, but there is a long battle to be fought with prejudice and inertia before the South will realize that a black criminal is a human being, to be punished firmly but humanely, with the sole object of making him a safe member of society, and that a white criminal at large is a menace and a danger. The greatest difficulty today in the way of reform is this race question. The movement for juvenile reformatories in Georgia would have succeeded some years ago, in all probability, had not the argument been used; it is chiefly for the benefit of Negroes. Until the public opinion of the ruling masses of the South can see that the prevention of crime among Negroes is just as necessary, just as profitable, for the whites themselves, as prevention among whites, all true betterment in courts and prisons will be hindered. Above all, we must remember that crime is not normal; that the appearance of crime among Southern Negroes is a symptom of wrong social conditions—of a stress of life greater than a large part of the community can bear. The Negro is not naturally criminal; he is usually patient and law-abiding. If slavery, the convict-lease system, the traffic in criminal labor, the lack of juvenile reformatories, together with the unfortunate discrimination and prejudice in other walks of life, have led to that sort of social protest and revolt which we call crime, then we must look for remedy in the sane reform of these wrong social conditions, and not in intimidation, savagery, or the legalized slavery of men.

◇ Notes

1. Bulletin No. 8, Library of State of New York. All figures in this article are from this source.

2. South Carolina, Georgia, Alabama, Mississippi, Louisiana, Texas, and Arkansas.

READING 28

Since the events of 9/11, considerable concern and debate has been raised about racial profiling, especially of people from the Middle East in airports. In the 1990s, concern arose and continues to be discussed over racial profiling by the police, who seem to be more willing or even targeting persons of color in traffic stops, referred to as Driving While Black (DWB). In this unique article, Shaun Gabbidon points us toward another potential source of targeting—Shopping While Black or SWB. The concern is with store employees and private security officers who may racially profile black shoppers. Borrowing from conflict theory, he argues that the power differential in class and race leads to racial profiling. Using key terms such as *false arrest, shoplifting,* and *racial profiling* in the LexisNexis Legal research database, he focused on 29 clear-cut cases of racial profiling from 1967 to 2002 in retail settings. Although he found only a relatively small number of cases, they are very interesting cases, and it is likely that the practice is much larger as the vast majority of unpleasant encounters between employees and shoppers probably do not make it to court or even to the attention of the police. This is an excellent example of the transitory nature of the definition of deviance. In most of these cases, these individuals were engaged in the same behaviors as the white shoppers, examining and/or paying for merchandise, yet the organizational policies of the stores, perceptions of store clerks, and color of the shopper's skin meant they were treated as deviants instead of customers. He offers several directions for future research in this regard.

Racial Profiling by Store Clerks and Security Personnel in Retail Establishments

An Exploration of "Shopping While Black"

Shaun L. Gabbidon

In the 1990s, racial profiling, often referred to as DWB, or Driving While Black, became an indelible concept in American life (Harris, 2002; Russell, 1999). According to the federal government (Ramirez, McDevitt, & Farrell, 2000),

Racial profiling is defined as any police-initiated action that relies on the race, ethnicity, or national origin rather than the behavior of an individual or information that leads the police to a particular

Source: Gabbidon, Shaun L. 2003. "Racial Profiling by Store Clerks and Personnel in Retail Establishments: An Exploration of 'Shopping While Black.'" *Journal of Contemporary Criminal Justice* 19(3):345–364. Reprinted by permission.

individual who has been identified as being, or having been, engaged in criminal activity. (p. 3)

Although the practice, the singling out of people of color (particularly Black Americans) for increased scrutiny by criminal justice officials was not new (Higginbottham, 1978, 1996; McIntyre, 1992), the increasing concerns regarding drug trafficking led some to believe that the answer to the problem could be resolved by singling out the perceived major transporters of these drugs, Black Americans. This led to states such as Maryland targeting Black drivers on Interstate 95 for frivolous pretextual stops in hopes of making a big bust. During the 1990s, 77% of the drivers stopped by Maryland state troopers for traffic violations were African Americans; however, only 17% of the drivers on the Maryland portion of Interstate 95 were African American (Russell, 1998, pp. 40–43). So although some of those stopped were in fact caught with drugs, most were not and were improperly targeted for these intrusive stops. Since the Maryland case became public, other jurisdictions have also come under scrutiny by courts for their use of racial profiling (couched within the "drug-courier profile") in the so-called "war against drugs" (Harris, 2002).

Once these controversial practices were brought to the national spotlight, public opinion polls began to consider how Americans viewed the issue. A December 1999 Gallup Poll found that most Americans believed that such activity was regularly engaged in by police (Ramirez et al., 2000). In addition, 81% of those surveyed felt the practice was wrong. There was more than a 2-point difference between Whites (56%) and Blacks (77%) when they were queried about the pervasiveness of profiling. Although only 6% of White respondents indicated they believe they had been previously stopped because of their race, 42% of Blacks believed they had been racially profiled (Ramirez et al., 2000). Moreover, "72% of Black men between the ages of 18 and 34 believed they had been stopped because of their race" (Ramirez et al. 2000, p. 4).

Because there are more than 3 times a s many private security officers as there are public law enforcement officers (approximately 2 million vs. 600,000), it seems natural to explore the extent to which similar practices exist in retail settings, where private security officers predominate. Relatedly, because on average African Americans spend more of their annual incomes on apparel and services than Whites (6% vs. 4.8% even though Whites annually make $14, 000 more a year), one would anticipate that they would visit retail establishments quite frequently (Bureau of Labor Statistics, 2002).

First, this study reviews the recent literature on Shopping While Black (SWB), while also examining legal cases where retailers have been accused of engaging in racial profiling in retail establishments. Thus, this study is guided by the following research questions: (a) What criminological theories are best suited to explain racial profiling? (b) What literature exists regarding racial profiling in the private sector? (c) What types of racial profiling incidents are currently occurring in retail settings? (d) What have been the outcomes of these incidents? And (e) What potential remedies are there for reducing SW B?

◈ Theoretical Framework

The practice of racial profiling touches on a number of criminological theories that can possibly explain the use of the practice. I briefly discuss three, beginning with the labeling perspective. Although explaining racial profiling has recently been considered by criminologists, the labeling of people of color as criminals is not new. The practice is an outgrowth of the continuing historical criminalization of Blacks (Higginbottham, 1978, 1996; McIntyre, 1992). Scholarship over the past 10 years has discussed the labeling of Blacks as criminal. Gabbidon (1994), for example, called the fear resulting from the labeling of Blacks as criminal "Blackaphobia," whereas Armour (1997) called it "Negrophobia," and Russell (1998) referred to it as the myth of the criminal Black man. Irrespective of what you call it, for centuries, Blacks have had to deal with the effects of labeling perspective was first being conceptualized in the classic work of Tannenbaum, Blacks were being profiled. Nevertheless, in his classic statement from *Crime and the Community,* Tannenbaum (1938), wrote, "The process of making a criminal . . . is a process of tagging, defining, identifying, segregating, describing, emphasizing" (p . 20). Because of this labeling process, society reacts to people differently. In the case of racial profiling, law enforcement, with the help of the media, have tagged African Americans as criminals who require additional scrutiny because of their criminal label. In line with the theory, although some African Americans conceivably take on this label and act it out (producing what some refer to as the self-fulfilling prophecy), most do not. Nevertheless, African Americans (particularly males) are all labeled by the police (or in this instance, by private security officers and retail clerks) as potential suspects—not law-abiding citizens—and are subsequently scrutinized more closely, suspected more often, and stopped more frequently for less cause than their White counterparts (Harris, 2002).

Conflict theory represents another potential perspective that can possibly explain the practice of racial profiling. Scholars have begun in earnest to examine racial profiling in police stops (Smith & Alpert, 2002; Weitzer & Tuch, 2002), with recent scholarship looking to conflict theory as one possible explanatory model (see Shepard, Calnon, & Bernard, 2002). Conflict theory centers on power differentials based on class (Quinney, 1980) and race (Hawkins, 1987). Therefore, even though there have been a number of African American celebrities who have had negative encounters with police because of racial profiling (see Russell, 1998), a considerable number of the victims have come from middle and lower socioeconomic strata (Harris, 2002). Combining the work of Quinney (1980) and Hawkins (1987), the ruling class (Whites) would only institute policies such as racial profiling (which would conceivably fall under what Quinney refers to as "crimes of control") that would principally affect the working class and minority groups (African Americans and increasingly Hispanic Americans). Such is the history of racial profiling in America.

Never has there been any such practice employed against the ruling class or majority group members; only the working class and African American and other ethnic minority groups have been subject to such scrutiny by law enforcement (Hawkins, 1994).

Finally, the colonial model (primarily internal colonialism), which was brought to the fore in the 1960s and 1970s (see Blauner, 1969; Fanon, 1963; Staples, 1975), and more recently by Tatum (1994), views racial stratification and class stratification under U.S. capitalism as separate but related systems of oppression (Feagin & Feagin, 2003). In its most recent criminological incarnation (see Tatum, 1994), it serves as an additional theoretical perspective that can, at least partially, explain racial profiling.

Based largely on the revolutionary writings of Frantz Fanon, the theory, as it relates to criminology, is a sociopsychological perspective (Tatum, 1994). Internal colonialism best speaks to racial profiling. This approach sees African Americans as being colonized in America (Tatum, 1994, p. 41). The colonization process has resulted in the following three forms of subordination: economic, political, and social (Tatum, 1994, pp. 42–48). Social subordination best explains racial profiling. Here, the colonizer creates a system that seeks to relegate the colonized (African Americans) to the lowest caste. By doing so, they ensure that "the social system reserves certain statuses and privileges for Whites" (Tatum, 1994, p. 47). This ideology results in agents of the state internalizing such thinking, which results in their inability to conceptualize that African Americans could legitimately have expensive cars or other items reserved for elite Whites. As a result, African American motorists driving expensive cars seem out of place and are indiscriminately subjected to police stops. Likewise, in the private sector, retail clerks and security officials might make similar assumptions, which results in African Americans and other minorities being indiscriminately singled out as potential shoplifters even though Whites represent 66% of the adult and 70% of the juvenile arrests for larceny-theft (Federal Bureau of Investigation, 2001). The remainder of this article provides a review of the literature, methods, and legal case studies pertaining to racial profiling in retail settings.

◈ Shopping While Black in the Literature

It is unclear where and when the term Shopping While Black came into usage, but what is clear is that, although the practice has existed for some time, very few researchers have broached the subject. Thus, as anticipated, a search of several social science and criminal justice databases revealed few articles that address the subject. Most of the articles that were found only sparsely cover the subject. Russell (1999), for example, in an enlarged article on Driving While Black, makes mention of SWB by pointing to a highly publicized case involving Eddie Bauer (which is discussed more below). Besides the one paragraph devoted to that case, there is no other mention of SWB in the 14-page article. The few scholarly articles that devote considerable attention to the subject are reviewed below.

Scholarly Articles on Shopping While Black

Based primarily on in-depth, semistructured interviews, Lee (2000) investigated the shopping experiences of Black customers in five predominantly Black neighborhoods in New York and Philadelphia. The research examined their experiences with Korean, Jewish, and Black merchants. In general, most of the 75 participants reported positive interactions with all types of merchants. Lee (2000), however, noted that the 16% of the shoppers indicated receiving negative treatment from Korean store owners, 8% from Jewish store owners, and 7% from Black store owners. The age of the customer was a critical factor in how Black customers were initially treated (p.6). As Lee noted, "Both young Black males and females, but most especially males, complain that merchants uniformly follow them as they browse in stores to ensure against customer theft" (p. 6). Interestingly,

Black merchants were found to treat Black customer just like their ethnic counterparts. Lee also found that class does matter in the treatment of Black shoppers. In most instances, middle-class Blacks are treated better than their lower class counterparts. However, this does not guarantee favorable treatment. In fact, in some instances, White customers receive preferential treatment. This comes in the form of them being attended to more quickly than Black shoppers. These types of encounters leave Blacks with a range of emotions from disbelief to paranoia (Lee, 2000, p. 12)—feelings that result in several response including lashing out at clerks, wearing clothes that speak to your income level (referred to as "wearing your class"), or avoiding establishments where Blacks are treated with undue suspicion.

Asquith and Bristow (2000) attempted to determine if students had ethnic biases in their views of the typical shoplifter and whether these views could be changed through the use of a classroom exercise. To investigate this question, they utilized a one-group pretest-posttest nonexperimental design. The study involved three stages whereby the subjects were first given a survey that inquired about their perception of the typical shoplifter. This stage was followed by a stage in which the students were shown a videotape on retail shoplifting statistics that showed that Whites were the majority of thee shoplifters in Minnesota and how some security personnel utilized racial profiling (p. 272). After exposing students to these revelations, the authors retested them on several of the original questions pertaining to their perceptions of the typical shoplifter. The authors found "that a significant gap existed between participant perceptions and a statistically based profile of retail shoplifters. Participants seemed predisposed to profile shoplifters on demographic variables" (p. 273). Following the posttest, the authors concluded that there were no significant changes in the views of the students. They further suggested that a classroom exercise was not enough to change the students' views.

Fifield (2001) centered much of his review of SWB with an examination of how it affects Black women, some of whom include journalist Gwen Fill, Houston Comets basketball star Sheryl Swoopes, Congresswoman Maxine Waters, and even Oprah Winfrey. Using illustrative examples of these figures, he showed how this insidious practice has even touched the lives of these elite African Americans. As stated earlier, this is not new, especially to African American women. In the article, Michelle Alexander of the American Civil Liberties Union is quoted as saying retail racism "[is] where women of color have their most regular experience with racial profiling" (as quoted in Fifield, 2001, p. 4).

Fifield (2001) also discussed Dillard's department stores, which have been the subject of numerous claims of racial profiling. In fact, during one such instance, it was revealed that six police officers who worked at one of the stores testified that African Americans were monitored more closely than Whites. One security guard testified, "particular people at Dillard's security would . . . prey on African Americans" (as quoted in Fifield, 2001, p. 12). Fifield also presented data that surfaced in one suit against Dillard's that showed that during 1991 to 1992, over half of the false arrest claims involved African American customers. This figure is shocking considering Dillard's own record show that African Americans represent only 16% of their customers (p. 12). No other extended scholarly articles on SWB were found in the literature; however, newspaper articles and editorials from national newspapers serve as some indicator of how far-reaching the practice of SWB has become.

Newspaper Accounts of Shopping While Black

In the 1990s, several high-profile SWB incidents brought the practice of racial profiling in retail incidents into the national spotlight. Most notable was the Eddie Bauer retail store incident in which three Black youth were falsely accused of stealing clothing that actually had been purchased at the same store a day earlier. One of the youth was forced to take off the shirt before exiting the store. When the case went to trial, they charge "consumer racism" and were

awarded a million-dollar settlement (Russell, 1999, p. 723).

Evan prominent African American officials have been subject to SWB. In 1993, an African American municipal judge, Claude Colemen, sued Bloomingdale's department store because they had falsely accused him of credit-card fraud while shopping at a mall in his jurisdiction (Bleemer, 1994). During the incident, they followed him from their store into another store within the Short Hills Mall and eventually handcuffed him and escorted him through the mall in front of numerous shoppers; the security personnel also lied to him by indicating that they had a video of him engaging in fraud. Moreover, Judge Coleman, who was also "a former Newark policeman, police director, and fire director," claimed he was subjected to "humiliating racist remarks and treatment" (p. 8). Following the incident, Coleman was "besieged by calls from people who [claimed to] have been in similar situations" (p. 8). A lawsuit was eventually settled, with one security person being fired and another being suspended.

A more recent and considerably publicized case involved The Children's Place retail store. This case involved an employee, Amanda Berube, who charged that her employer instructed her that to prevent theft, she should pay additional attention to Black shoppers. In addition, she was instructed to not give out shopping bags to them, not to invite them to open credit cards, and refrain from discussing any sales with them (Goldberg, 2000). According to the attorney general, Thomas F. Reilly, the strategy uncovered "a pattern of conduct of targeting people based on the color of their skin" (Goldberg, 2000, p. a16). The settlement in this case resulted in the company agreeing to antidiscrimination training, spending $100,000 on consultants to examine and weed out any institutionalized discrimination, and donating $50,000 to a Boston charity (p. A16).

Another account of SWB was found on the editorial page of the *Capital Time*. Writing about SWB in Madison, Wisconsin, Billups (2000) presented the following scenario of how one retailer practices SWB: "The practice is applied to both employees and customers of color. Presumably random, but suspiciously targeted and frequent searches of the packages of employees and customers of color occur regularly" (p. 9A). Drawing on the observation of a colleague who works in the retail industry, Billups further noted,

> customers are monitored closely, and without even the pretense of subtlety as they pass from area to area in the store. Employees of color, who develop personal clientele to target for sales and other customer promotions, are held in suspicion, and questioned about the amount of time spent with customers, but only those who happen to be of color. Customers of color are regularly asked to provide more proof of identification than is asked of other customers. (p. 9A)

The problem got so bed in Madison that Recommendation 15 of the city's Task Force on Race Relations was devoted to addressing the SWB problem. It called for the city's Equal Opportunities Commission to "conduct a study to determine the extent and nature of the problem" and "form a team to examine the survey results and assist in the design of a training program for retail establishments to prevent racial profiling" (Billups, 2000, p. 9A).

An unfortunate tragedy some have linked to SWB was the 2000 killing of Frederick Finley, who was suspected of shoplifting, by Lord & Taylor security officers outside a Detroit mall. Immediately following this incident, there were a flood of editorials and protests. Most of them were couched under the veil of SWB. To further explore the topic, an analysis of legal case studies was undertaken. The next section reviews that methodology used to locate the cases.

◈ Method

Locating instances of SWB is a difficult undertaking. Most retailers are likely unwilling to release information on specific instances in which racial profiling has been alleged. Furthermore, when these instances do arise, fearing profit losses from the fallout

of bed publicity, they likely settle these sorts of allegations out of court. Therefore, no current legal database will provide a complete representation of these incidents.

The Lexis-Nexis legal research database were used to locate cases within the database (going back as far as the database revealed) that were potentially SWB-related. Using a combination of the search terms "false arrest," "shoplifting," and "racial profiling," I searched individual state cases (all appeals courts) and federal (U.S. District Courts and U.S. Court of Appeals) cases to find instances in which SWB was alleged. The cases found were all decided by September 2002. Once the cases were found, several characteristics were noted.

Some basic characteristics were first recorded, such as the year the cases was decided, age of the plaintiff (adult or youth), race of the plaintiff, and the gender of the plaintiff. Other characteristics noted included more specifics of the case such as whether a racial slur or brutality was alleged in the incident.

The methods that resulted in the defendants falsely accusing the plaintiffs was also noted. The first was unsubstantiated hunches. This refers to those instances in which the defendants had a hunch—but no direct evidence—that the plaintiffs had stolen something. Another method that was potentially used was mistaken identity. This refers to the instances in which the defendants thought the plaintiffs were the ones who stole an item; however, on further investigation, it was revealed that another person had actually stolen the missing item. The final category used related to those companies that have histories of racial profiling. Within this category, somewhere in the case it was alleged race was regularly used as a key factor by the defendant to determine which customers were intensely scrutinized by sales clerks and security personnel.

Two final characteristics were recorded. First, that the defendant was a major (national) retailer. Second, the person who initiated the action or was the one accused of profiling. The categories here reflect the nature of those typically entrusted with the security function at retail chains. Typically, the sales clerks deter theft. Most retailers also have either a proprietary security force or they hire contracted security officers.

Some retailers hire off-duty police officers to perform their security function. Yet other retailers utilize their local police departments to assist them with theft-related incidents. Here, for each case, I recorded one of the following three possible outcomes: first, the plaintiff was victorious; second, the plaintiff scored a partial victory (victorious only on some points); and third, the plaintiff lost. The results of my analysis are presented in the next section.

◈ Results

The research revealed numerous false arrest cases pertaining to shoplifting in state courts dating to the early 1900s ($N = 256$). However, only within the past 30 years has there been any mention of race in state court cases related to the topic. For example, the first recorded allegation of SWB occurred in the late 1960s but was not decided until 1973. The second case occurred in the mid-1980s. Because SWB became more public in the 1990s, I examined the past 10 years (1992 to 2001) of cases to see what percentage were SWB related. During this period, there were 54 cases related to false arrest and shoplifting. Only 7% ($N = 4$) of them could be classified as instances in which SWB was alleged. My view of cases at the U.S. District Courts and U.S. Court of Appeals levels also found instances of alleged racial profiling in retail settings.

At the U.S. District Court level, there were 113 cases found (dating from 1966 to 2002) using the specified search terms of which 16 (14%) included allegations of SWB. At the U. S. Court of Appeals level, there were 44 cases (dating from 1967 to 2002) related to false arrests and shoplifting; 7 (16%) of them included allegations of SWB. In sum, there were 29 cases that were classified as instances of racial profiling in retail settings. These 29 cases serve as the basis of my analysis. As such, they provide us with some of the characteristics of the cases involving these types of allegations. An analysis of the cases can also provide us with answers to two of my research questions: (a) What type of SWB cases have come before the court? And (b) What have been the outcome of these cases?

◈ Discussion

Only in rare instances did my analysis reveal other minority groups being the victims of racial profiling. This rarity might provide the linkage between SWB and labeling theory. Because it is primarily Black who have been tagged as the criminals in America, they, therefore, are considered the ones most likely to steal. Again, following the most basic premise of the perspective, unsubstantiated hunches would be acted on in the cases of Blacks because they have been labeled as criminals. Typical of such instances is when security personnel or retail clerks relay descriptions to someone responsible for either following-up on a lead or making an arrest; however, in SWB cases, the person saw a Black person and assumed them to be the criminal. Here, particularly in the case of security personnel, there might be a sense of power over this minority population and, subsequently, they are not as concerned about errors. This is also tied to the issue of brutality in SWB cases.

In *Yvonne A. Alexis, et al. v. McDonald's Restaurants of Massachusetts, Inc.* (1995), the issue of power and lack of concern regarding the ramifications of one's actions came together in one case. The case stemmed from a visit by an African American family to a Massachusetts McDonald's restaurant on a July morning in 1990. At some point during the visit with her family, Yvonne Alexis got into a disagreement with workers at the restaurant, all of which stemmed from confusion over her order. When a manager became involved, the incident turned ugly, with the manager summoning a moonlighting off-duty police officer to come inside the restaurant and eject Ms. Alexis. The officer then approached the Alexis family, informing them that they had to leave. After further verbal exchanges, the officer demanded Alexis leave or face the possibility of arrest. When another officer arrived on the scene, the initial officer "suddenly and violently" grabbed her. The officers then tightly handcuffed her and injured her while dragging her from the booth. At several points during the incident, the officers were asked by Mr. Alexis why they were treating his spouse in such a manner, eventually crying out, "We have rights." To this, one of the officers bluntly responded, "Your people have no rights. You better shut up your [expletive] mouth before I arrest you too." Alexis was partially victorious in the courts, which the court agreeing that such action would not have taken place "were it not for the color of her skin." There was a clear sense that the officers must have felt a sense of unbridled power to carry on in such a manner over such a trivial offense.

The instances in which the monetary status of minority shoppers were questioned fall in the line with colonial theory. There were two such cases. In the case of *Billy J. Mitchell v. Dillard's* (2000), a clerk testified that when someone went to get change for a $100 bill tendered by Mr. Mitchell, he "began to act nervous and appeared anxious to leave the store." Eventually, officers stopped Mitchell and arrested him. After checking for a criminal record, Mitchell was released and later sued, winning more then $450,000 in compensatory and punitive damages. Could it be that the clerk had a belief that it was unlikely that a $100 bill tendered by a Black male was real? Such thinking was certainly a possibility in the case of *Nevin v. Citibank* (2000). Although Citibank was the defendant in the case, it was a Lore & Taylor security guard who alerted Citibank because, as he told it to a Citibank official, "a Black female was making large purchases with a Citibank Visa car" and that "she makes the purchases, she puts merchandise in her vehicle, and returns to the store." Even though the card was not reported lost or stolen, on the basis of this information, a Citibank official—suspecting the card might have been stolen—authorized Lord & Taylor to detain her. Although Nevin lost her appeal, given the facts of the case, one wonders if the perception that a Black person would not be able to make such considerable purchases contributed in part to this incident. Following the premise of social subordination within the colonial model, Blacks seem out of place making such large purchases; thus, it would only be normal to see Whites make such purchases.

When one examines the cases in which the minority plaintiff claimed there was a history of racial profiling in the company in question, this speaks to all three perspectives. In these instances, Blacks are not only labeled but there are also power structures within these establishments that see nothing wrong with treating minority groups in such a discriminatory manner. And, these same groups likely fell that African Americans are out of place shopping in their establishments. Two paradigmatic cases are *Rojas v. Alexander's* (1986) and *Jane Doe v. Barbara Dendrinos et al.* (1997). In the first case, the plaintiffs (Fernando Rojas and his wife Petruia Rojas) claimed that, on November 9, 1984, while shopping for an answering machine at an Alexander's Department Store in New York, Fernando was stopped and detained by when he did not show up, she went looking for him and later found him handcuffed in the security office. He was later acquitted of the charges of petit larceny and possession of stolen property. After his acquittal, he filed suit alleging false arrest and, among other things, that Alexander's had "[an] unstated policy to arrest more readily on suspicion of shoplifting those customers who were Black or Hispanic." Although little more is said about this allegation, there was enough evidence for the U.S. district judge to refuse to dismiss Rojas's allegation of racial profiling.

In the second, and even more troubling case, the plaintiff, Jane Doe, was accused of stealing some automotive products from a Pep Boys store in Pennsylvania. A manager in the store called the police, at which time the responding police officer arrested Jane Doe. Once the officer arrived at the police station, they received a call from the manager who informed them that he had decided not to prosecute. Although the manager declined to prosecutes, Jane Doe was held at the police station where the officer

allegedly slung racial slurs and obscenities at her. In addition, the plaintiff maintains that Officer Lewis also requested that she perform fellatio on him, and he told her that other women he had arrested "just did it and were let go." She claims that although she refused to comply with his request, Officer Lewis sexually assaulted here.

Before the latter allegations could be fully investigated, the officer committed suicide. In his absence, the matter went to trial. During the trial, Jane Doe alleged that Pep Boys had a policy of targeting minorities. To support this claim, she pointed out that between January 1992 and June 1994, the majority of those arrested for shoplifting at Pep Boys were African American. She also alleged that there was a conspiracy to cover up this practice by showing that the local police "[had destroyed] arrest reports, such as hers, which were found in a dumpster behind the police station several days after she went public with her allegations of rape and false arrest." Although Jane Doe won a partial victory on some counts, it was striking how the court used two sentences to indicate that one of the aforementioned events constituted a conspiracy in any way, which speaks volumes to how the power structure, at times, minimizes the experiences of minorities. This case is also illustrative of one of the numerous unacceptable "collateral consequences" of racial profiling (Russell, 1999). In this case, the false arrest, allegedly a product of SWB, was what brought Jane Doe into the system in which, by the allegations presented, she was sexually assaulted.

Based on the analysis of case outcomes, it appears that minority plaintiffs have a hard time securing clear victories in SWB-related cases. This again speaks to conflict theory. The courts are unwilling to give minority groups the benefit of the doubt in such cases. There seems to be a level of skepticism among judges. Even when a case reeks of SWB, the standard is so difficult to meet that only partial victories are reached. In a few cases, however, there have been some strong dissenting opinions that might change the tide. An illustration of a powerful dissent can be found in *Carl Youngblood v. Hy-Vee Food Stores, inc.* (2001). In the case, Youngblood entered the Hy-Vee Food Store and walked to the back of the store where there were cans of beef jerky. After purchasing a can of beef jerky, Youngblood was stopped at the doors by employees and accused of taking some beef jerky from another can add stuffing some in the can that he eventually bought. The police were called and he was arrested. The charges were later dismissed. Youngblood then sued claiming that he was targeted because of his race. He lost his appeal. Judge Richard Arnold, however, dissented from the majority opinion declaring that Youngblood was a victim of discrimination from the moment he walked into the store. As he put it,

> Youngblood was singled out for surveillance by the store clerk before he made his purchase, singled out for suspicion as he walked to the register to make his purchase (when the store clerk alerted the manager), and singled out for detention by three store employees as he tried to leave the store with his purchase.

Making use of the district court transcripts, he reviewed Youngblood's statements and those from former employees who claimed "that Hy-Vee had a discriminatory pattern and practice of targeting, surveillance, stopping, and prosecuting Black customers disproportionately to White customers." As a result, Judge Arnold, unlike many of his judicial colleagues in numerous other cases, saw that there was too much evidence to conclude anything other than this was a case of SWB. Some limitations of the current research are provided in the following section.

◈ Limitations of the Research

Given the limited number of cases found, one does not have a true sense of the representativeness of these SWB incidents. In addition, it is hard to speak to the prevalence of SWB with the current data. Twenty-nine cases out of a few hundred does not project that SWB is a serious problem. There still remains an uncertainty as to the extent to which retailers systematically profile minority shoppers. However, there are data that could tell us more but are not readily available to researchers. In the case of SWB, who knows how many minority shoppers fail to report such encounters? Many who do report them and follow up with representatives from the retailer in question are probably all too happy to settle of court so they can move on with their lives. But again, in these instances, we do not have a record of the number of such settlements. Until we get data on these instances, much like with crime data, there will remain a so-called dark figure of racial profiling in retail settings.

◈ Conclusion

Given the literature and the cases reviewed, three things are clear. First SWB is real. "Shopping While Black" is not a catchy phrase with no substance behind it. Yet, although it is real, it has not yet garnered the scholarly attention it deserves. Current studies of racial profiling almost exclusively focus on one facet of African American lives, driving, Considering that most people, including minorities, spend substantial amounts of time in retail establishments, it seems that a rich area of potential research has gone unnoticed or has received less interest due undoubtedly to its connection to private security, which is probably the least studied area of criminal justice. Subsequently, there are a few likely directions for future SWB research. Researchers might want to do more surveys of minorities to see if they feel they have been victims of SWB. Moreover, current and former security personnel might be also be a resource for securing information on SWB. This approach could also provide more insights into the utility of the three aforementioned criminological perspectives for explaining SWB. There is also the opportunity for covert ethnographic studies that might also yield some insights into the prevalence and use of racial profiling in retail settings. A final related area of future inquiry is the treatment of minority employees by retail security departments. Research in area would determine if racial profiling in retail settings is only reserved for minority shoppers.

Second, clearly there are standard forms of racial profiling in retail establishments. These include the following:

- mistaken identity,
- extra scrutiny while shopping,
- the requiring of additional identification for credit or check purchases,
- undue use of force, and
- the enactment of blanket policies of how to handle minorities.

Third, the best way to combat racial profiling in retail establishments is through education, legal remedies, and boycotts. A practice called the demographic test might be a useful litmus test for whether some additional education or retraining is required for specific retail security departments. Used by former Montgomery Ward district security and safety manager Mike Magill, it seeks to detect and prevent racial profiling in retail settings (Fifield, 2001). Making use of census data, he matched up the demographics of every community in which a store was located and, every 3 months, he checked to see if the arrest and detention record in every store matched the community demographics. Wherever large discrepancies were found, he instituted additional racial sensitivity training (Fifiled, 2001). Given that many of the SWB cases found in this study were initiated by sales clerks, it seems that such an approach has considerable appeal. As evidenced by the results of the Asquith and Bristow (2000) study discussed earlier, training or education is no panacea, however.

As for legal remedies, practically every major advancement regarding the civil rights of African Americans has come through the court system. Eliminating SWB will be no different. Such cases must be pursued to the fullest extent if retailers are to really get the message. In addition to legal suits, organized boycotts in conjunction with national civil rights organizations represent another avenue that has historically served African Americans well. Both strategies speak to the corporate bottom line, which in the past has gotten the attention of CEOs.

In recent years, the ire over racial profiling in the form of DWB has led to serious debate in the public, as well as in legislative chambers. This has produced legislation such as the Traffic Stop Statistics Act and other remedies. On the national level, however, no such actions have been undertaken to reduce SWB. At the federal level, the National Institute of Justice, the research section of the Department of Justice, has been given the thrust of collecting national data on traffic stops (Bureau of Justice Statistics, 2001). As such, requests for proposals relating to racial profiling have become more readily available (this has also happened at the state level in response to the federal actions). Missing, however, from the current rust to get on the racial profiling bandwagon is any serious focus on SWB. Researchers have not yet caught the same enthusiasm for profiling in retail settings. This must happen. As evidenced by the approach taken by state and federal officials regarding DWB, you must know the extent of a problem before you take informed actions to reasonably ameliorate it.

In closing, although most racial profiling in retail settings likely goes unnoticed, it is apparent from the literature that when it does surface, it comes in the form of what one can only see as a combination of race discrimination and harassment. This treatment, which is reminiscent of the Jim Crow era, does nothing to enhance race relations or catch suspected shoplifters; it only works to sour relations that have taken centuries to begin to mend.

◈ References

Armour, J.D. (1997). *Negrophobia and reasonable racism: The hidden costs of being Black in America.* New York: New York University Press.

Asquith, J.L., & Bristow, D.N. (2000). To catch a thief: A pedagogical study of retail shoplifting. *Journal of Education for Business, 75,* 271–276.

Billups, L. (2000). "Shopping While Black" still a problem here in Madison. *Capital Times,* P. 9A.

Billy J. Mitchell v. Dillard Department Stores et al., 197 Ariz. 209 (2000).

Blauner, R. (1969). *Racal oppression in America.* New York: Harper & Row.

Bleemer, R. (1994, February 7). Newark judge sues over false arrest. *New Jersey Law journal,* p. 8.

Bureau of Justice Statistics. (2001). *Traffic stop data collection policies for state police, 2001.* Washington, DC: Department of Justice.

Bureau of Labor Statistics. (2002). *Consumer expenditures in 2000.* Washington, DC: Department of Labor.

Carl Youngblood v. Hy-Vee Food Stores, Inc., 266 F.3d 851 (2001).

Fanon, F. (1963). *The wretched of the Earth.* New York: Grove-Weidenfeld.

Feagin, J.R., & Feagin, C. (2003). *Race and ethnic relations* (7th ed.). Upper Saddle River, NJ: Prentice Hall.

Federal Bureau of Investigation. (2001). *Uniform crime reports: Crime in the United States, 2001.* Washington, DC: Department of Justice.

Fifield, A. (2001). Shopping while Black. *Good Housekeeping, 233,* pp. 128–138. Retrieved November 4, 2001, from proquestumi.com/pqdweb

Gabbidon, S. L. (1994). Blackaphobia: What is it? And who are its victims? In P.R. Kedia (Ed.), *Black on Black crime: Facing Facts-challenging fictions* (pp. 232–244). Bristol, IN: Wyndham Hall.

Goldberg, C. (2000, December 22). Accused of discrimination, clothing chain settles case. *New York Times,* p. A16.

Harris, D.A. (2002). *Profiles in injustice: Why racial profiling cannot work.* New York: New Press.

Hawkins, D. F. (1987). Beyond anomalies: Rethinking the conflict perspective on race and punishment. *Social Forces, 65,* 719–745.

Hawkins, D. F. (1994). Ethnicity: The forgotten dimension of American social control. In G. S. Bridges & M. A, Myers (Eds.), *Inequality, crime, and social control* (pp. 99–116). Boulder, CO: Westview.

Higginbottom, A L. (1978). *In the matter of color: Race & the American legal Process: The colonial period.* Oxford, UK: Oxford University Press.

Higginbottom, A. L. (1996). *Shades of freedom: Racial politics and presumptions of the American legal process.* Oxford, UK: Oxford University Press.

Jane Doe v. Barbara Dendrinos et al., U.S. Dist. Lexis 2052 (1997).

Lee, J. (2000). The salience of race in everyday life: Black customers' shopping experiences in Black and White neighborhoods. *Work and Occupations, 27,* 353–376. Retrieved January 2, 2001, from proquestumi.com/pqdweb

McIntyre, C. L. (1992). *Criminalizing a race: free Blacks during slavery.* Queens, NY: Kayode.

Nevin v. Citibank. N.A., 107 f. Supp. nd, 333 (2000).

Quinney, R. (1980). *Class, state, and crime* (2nd ed.). New York: Longman.

Ramirez, O., McDevitt, J., & Farrell, A. (2000). *A resource guide on racial profiling data collection systems: Promising practices and lessons learned.* Washington, DC: Department of Justice.

Rojas v. Alexander's, 654 F. Supp. 856 (1986).

Russell, K. K. (1998). *The color of crime: Racial hoaxes, White fear, Black protectionism, police harassment, and other macroaggressions.* New York: New York University Press.

Russell, K. K. (1999). "Driving while Black": Corollary phenomena and collateral consequences. *Boston College Law Review, 40,* 717–731.

Shepard, R. E., Calnon, J. M., & Bernard, T. J. (2002). Theory and racial profiling: Shortcomings and future directions in research. *Justice Quarterly, 19,* 249.

Smith, M. R., & Alpert, G. P. (2002). Searching for direction: Courts, social science, and the adjudication of racial profiling claims. *Justice Quarterly, 19,* 673–703.

Staples, R. (1975). White racism, Black crime, and American justice: An application of the colonial model to explain crime and race. *Phylon, 36,* 14–22.

Tannenbaum, F. (1938). *Crime and the community.* New York: Columbia University Press.

Tatum, B. L. (1994). The colonial model as a theoretical explanation of crime and delinquency. In A. T. Sulton (Ed.), *African American perspectives on crime causation, criminal justice administration and prevention* (pp. 33–52). Colorado: Sulton Books.

Weitzer, R., & Tuch, S. A. (2002). Perceptions of racial profiling: Race, class, and personal experience. *Criminology, 40,* 435–456.

Yvonne A. Alexis et al. v. McDonald's Restaurants of Massachusetts, Inc., 67F. 3d 341 (1995).

READING 29

This is another article that uses the LexisNexis Legal research database to obtain data, but in this case, the focus is on police brutality. Focusing on 15 major newspapers, the authors retrieved 4,770 articles in their search and identified 130 unique incidents (often several articles focused on the same event) of police brutality in a year and a half period between 1990 and 1992. They use what they refer to as the power-conflict theory to better understand police misconduct. Their findings are largely consistent with the theory. The vast majority of cases involved minority victims: 87% black, 10% Latino, and only 4% white non-Hispanic. Furthermore, the vast majority of the officers involved in the incidents were white (93%), and only a few cases involved black officers (3 or 2.7%) or Latino offenders (5 or 4.4%). While racially and ethnically, blacks and Latinos are underrepresented among police officers, the disparity is still striking. It important to recognize that there was not a single case that suggested a black or Hispanic brutally targeted a white citizen. Penalties (e.g., loss of job, suspension, a charge filed) for the use of excessive force were found for only a minority of the cases (17 or 13%). As the authors argue, it well may be that "police departments were developed to control the poor and 'dangerous classes' of urban society," and in American society, where race and class are so highly correlated, racial minorities may be targeted as the "dangerous class."

Violent Police-Citizen Encounters

An Analysis of Major Newspaper Accounts

Kim Michelle Lersch and Joe R. Feagin

The reality of police violence was forced back into the public consciousness as a result of the national media attention given to the graphic beating of Rodney King at the hands of several white police officers in the early 1990s. While the Los Angeles Police Department (LAPD) became the focus of investigations of allegations concerning police misconduct, many police departments across the country came under greater public scrutiny. Was this incident an anomaly, or does police brutality against people of color continue to be a common occurrence across the nation?

While research concerning police brutality increased after the riots of the late 1960s, in the last decade few articles have been published focusing on contemporary police-citizen incidents and brutality trends, especially in regard to the non-lethal use of force (McLaughlin, 1992). Significantly, several well-publicized governmental studies of police malpractice have not been released for public and academic scrutiny. Official national statistics on the phenomenon of police malpractice or brutality currently do not exist.

This article investigates key issues concerning violent police misconduct against citizens across the nation using the only public data currently accessible: major newspaper accounts. To shed some light on the character of police malpractice incidents in the 1990s,

Source: Lersch, Kim Michelle, and Joe R. Feagin. 1996. "Violent Police-Citizen Encounters: An Analysis of Major Newspaper Accounts." *Critical Sociology* 22:29–49. Reprinted with permission.

we examine the racial group of the officer and the citizen involved in the altercation, the situational characteristics of the violent assault, and the penalties assessed against the officers involved.

◈ Power-Conflict Theory as Applied to Police Deviance

The power-conflict perspective will be used to better understand the phenomenon of police brutality. Power-conflict theorists focus on the great disparity in the distribution of power and resources in United States society. These inequalities may exist along lines of race, class, or gender. According to critical power-conflict theorists, the structure of capitalism in the United States in which a great proportion of the wealth is held by white corporate capitalists leads to a social system marked by exploitation and domination. Theoretical elaboration within the power-conflict perspective began historically with the works of Karl Marx and has continued to develop through the works of C. Wright Mills and others.

Feagin and Feagin (1990) developed a series of propositions to describe the power-conflict perspective: in society certain groups of people dominate over others due to their control of various important societal resources, such as wealth and income, private property that may serve to generate further wealth, and greater control over the police and military forces. As a group, white Americans are in a better position to use and mobilize both economic and political resources in times of conflict than do black Americans or other minority groups.

As applied to the problem of police deviance, power-conflict theory develops from the history of policing and the growth of capitalism within the United States. Focusing on the competition for power by various groups within society, power-conflict theorists view police brutality as a tool of subordination used by the dominant white group to protect its stronghold on limited resources. Minorities and others without political and economic power are more likely to be processed by law enforcement agents (Vold and Bernard, 1986) and experience differential enforcement of the law (Leinen, 1984; Smith and Visher, 1981).

◈ Differential Experiences of Black and White Citizens With Police Agencies: A Brief History

Organized police forces as we know them have been around for about 150 years. Prior to that time, cities were patrolled by a few men who roamed the streets in the evening hours, calling out the time or weather conditions. In 1838 Boston became the first to employ men to patrol during daylight hours. Six years later New York City combined day and night watchmen into a single organized force. Over a thirty years period after 1845, nearly every major city in the United States developed an organized police department (Platt et al., 1982).

The sharp increase in the demand for organized social control in the mid-1800s may be attributed to several factors: increased population density, growing ethnic diversity, the development of industrial capitalism, and the emergence of a hierarchical class structure. Several social theorists contend that a primary purpose of the police was, and continues to be, to protect the property, wealth, and position of the higher classes (Platt et al., 1982; Feagin and Hahn, 1973; Fielding, 1991). Historically, police relations with poor racial and ethnic groups often have been marked by aggressive domination and violence. Many times in their efforts to control the "dangerous classes," as defined by powerful white leaders and groups, the police relied on brute force. For instance, in the Draft Riot of New York City in 1863, the local police were estimated to have killed more than a thousand people, many of whom were poor and working class Irish immigrants (Platt et al., 1982).

In the South, the emergence of an organized police force was somewhat different. The history of the southern watchmen dates back to the year 1690 with the legislation of the slave codes. In order for the slave population to be adequately subordinated and controlled, all white males were given the right to stop, question, and apprehend any black person. These methods of control reflected and perpetuated the negative, often criminalized, portrayal of the black man in the white mind (Owens, 1977).

Police violence against African Americans continued throughout the history of the United States. From

1920 through 1932 white police officers killed 54 percent of the 749 blacks killed by white persons in the South and 68 percent of those killed outside of the southern region (Myrdal, 1944). Further, in an analysis of 76 race riots between 1913–1963, the immediate precipitating event in 20 percent of the uprisings was the killing of or interference with black men by white police officers. This percentage dramatically increased in the years 1964–1967, when seven of the fourteen major riots that occurred over the three-year period could be directly traced to the misconduct of white policemen against black citizens. In addition, most of the smaller riots were triggered by the larger riots and were thus indirectly linked to police-citizen encounters (Feagin and Hahn, 1973).

According to a number of analysts (see Fielding, 1991), the modern police forces, as major control agents of the state, are not only concerned with crime and its prevention but also with the surveillance and coercion of subordinate racial groups in society. Groups of individuals who are viewed as a threat to the dominant white society must be adequately controlled. There is much close patrolling of black and other minority communities. From the 1960s to the 1990s the common practice of preventive police patrolling in ghetto areas, with its "stop and frisk" and "arrest on suspicion" tactics, has led to unfavorable police contacts for black and Latino males. Harassment of this type in turn intensifies negative attitudes toward the police. In minority communities there is often a strong mistrust and even hatred of the police officers, who are frequently viewed as serving the interests of the dominant white group. The relationship between black and other minority citizens with white police officers has been, and continues to be, different from the relationship these officers typically have with white citizens (Alpert, 1989; Bogomolny, 1976; Feagin, 1991; Walker, 1992).

◈ Continuing Racial Tensions

Surveys conducted in the 1960s and early 1970s indicated that black citizens expressed great dissatisfaction with local authorities. According to a 1970 Harris poll, only a fifth of the black respondents thought that local police officers applied the law equally; 62 percent believed cops were against blacks; 73 percent considered their local law enforcement agents were dishonest; and 67 percent thought police officers were more concerned with injuring African Americans than in preventing criminal acts (Feagin and Hahn, 1973). More recently, in a 1989 Gallup poll more than 50 percent of the blacks interviewed believed most police officers view blacks as suspects and would be likely to arrest the wrong person, and 25 percent of the black men stated that they had been harassed while driving through predominantly white neighborhoods (Bessent and Tayler, 1991). In a poll conducted by The *New York Times,* 28 percent of the blacks thought that police officers would give them a harder time when stopped for a minor traffic offense, which was nearly five times the percentage for white citizens. Further, one quarter of the black citizens interviewed stated that they knew someone who was a victim of police misconduct. This percentage was two and one-half times that for white respondents (Holmes, 1991).

In addition, in a poll of 1,901 residents of Los Angeles and Orange counties in 1990, half of the black respondents believed there was a "fair amount" of police brutality, which was twice the proportion found among white citizens (Decker, 1990). A 1991 poll found that two-thirds of Latinos in Los Angeles reported that incidents of police brutality were very common in their city; 35 percent of this group said that racist attitudes were very common among law enforcement officers. At public hearings in 1991 an independent citizens' commission investigating the Los Angeles Police Department heard testimony from Mexican Americans that the department "acted like an army of occupation" (Ford and Stolberg, 1991).

Most racial relations researchers agree that selective enforcement of the law by police officers is institutionalized and routine and that officers apply a greater number of formal sanctions against minority Americans (Lienen, 1984; Smith and Visher, 1981). The relationship between minority groups and the dominant white society is marked, among other things, by competition for limited resources. Whites have a vested interest in the conservation and protection of the economic and residential resources they currently hold. The police, through differential enforcement practices and violence against blacks and other minorities, play an important role in maintaining the statues quo as whites see it (Feagin and Hahn, 1973; Fielding, 1991). The police instruments that serve to protect the dominant position of white society also serve to keep blacks and other minorities in a subservient state (Oberschall, 1973).

◈ Situational Aspects of Police-Citizen Encounters

Several research analyses have focused on the situational aspects surrounding the lethal use of force by police officers (Fridell, 1989; Fyfe, 1989). Research concerning the non-lethal use of force and the situations leading up to the encounter is rare, perhaps for a number of different reasons: the police-citizen incidents are often transitory and occur out of the public eye (McLaughlin, 1992); violent altercations with citizens are a relatively rare occurrence (Bayley and Garofalo, 1989; Fyfe, 1989); and many violent incidents go unreported by both the officer and the citizen involved.

McLaughlin (1992), in a review of several recent studies that examined use-of-force incidents, reported that many violent encounters in Orlando resulted during attempted arrests of unarmed misdemeanor suspects or of a "non-infamous felony suspect." While McLaughlin did not indicate whether or not these were minority citizens, he did state that blacks were more likely to resist arrest and that white officers were disproportionately involved in the overall number of use-of-force incidents. The Croft Report (Croft, 1985) examined 2,397 reported use of force incidents in Rochester, New York, from 1973 to 1979. This study reported that 80 percent of the incidents occurred in the course of an attempted misdemeanor crime or during a non-criminal situation. Furthermore, 30 percent of the arrests and the force necessary to subdue the citizen could have been avoided if the citizen "had ceased fighting, arguing, being verbally abusive to the officer or had obeyed orders of the officers" (Croft, 1985: 4). This finding was consistent with the findings of Reiss (1968) and Friedrich (1980), who found that suspects who were disrespectful or uncooperative were more likely to be arrested. Disrespect, however minor, for police officers is considered a major issue by many officers. Westley (1970) found that 37 percent of the responding officers indicated that illegal violence was justified if the suspect was disrespectful.

One purpose of our research is to explore the various situational aspects that lead up to violent police-citizen encounters.

◈ Penalties and Substantiation Rates: An Effective Deterrent?

According to a national advisory commission report (U.S. Commission on Civil Rights, 1973: 72, 93), "Once a finding sustains the allegations of wrongdoing, disciplinary sanctions commensurate with the seriousness of the offense that are imposed fairly, swiftly, and consistently will most clearly reflect the commitment of the department to oppose police misconduct." The report presented various penalties that could be assessed against officers based on the nature of the charge. Verbal reprimands, suspensions, demotions, reassignment, and permanent removal of duty were suggested. The article closed with the statement that "departments that are serious about preventing police misconduct can do something about it."

The commission also stressed the importance of effective controls from within, as opposed to various modes of external controls. In its view officers must be able to effectively control and monitor their own behavior, especially since there is so little criminal and civil prosecution of police malpractice. In addition, Skolnick and Fyfe (1993: 36) have argued that the attitude of police administrators is an important influence on the thinking of the individual officers: "Most excessive force cases that reach the courts show that the questionable conduct either has happened because superiors are so indifferent to the misconduct as to be grossly negligent in the performance of the duties, or occurs in fulfillment of administrative policy." If police officers do not perceive any risk of punishment for engaging in deviant behavior, then the likelihood that they will engage in this type of behavior increases.

◈ The Problem of Data

The very few recent studies of serious police malpractice by major governmental agencies have been wrapped in a cloak of secrecy. In the wake of the Rodney Kind incident, a distinguished citizen panel was appointed by the mayor of Los Angeles. The resulting Christopher Commission, a panel of seven people headed by Deputy Secretary of State Warren Christopher, was designed to provide Los Angeles with an independent study of the practices of the LAPD. This was the first comprehensive and impartial review of a major police department to be made available to the public since the 1973 Knapp Commission Report that studied the New York City.

The Christopher Commission found that officers often used excessive force, especially with minority citizens (Independent Commission on the Los Angeles Police Department, 1991). Further, the officers who employed violent techniques were rarely disciplined and were often honored or promoted. The Commission concluded that black citizens were the dominant targets of abuse in contacts with police officers, but that Latinos, Asians, and homosexuals were also victims (Kelling, 1991). The Christopher Commission Report concluded that local policing was not applied in a fair and non-discriminatory way for all citizens of Los Angeles. However, some of its important conclusions and subject matter were judged to be too sensitive to be revealed. According to Gil Ray, a spokesperson for commission, "The commission just felt it was material that needed a gestation period before it became public" ("College to be given," 1991). Interestingly, given that this was a public commission, the archives of the commission's study were given to the private University of Southern California, with some of the more critical material to be sealed for 20 years.

Further, in the wake of the Rodney King incident, the United States Justice Department conducted a review of nation-wide allegations of police brutality to investigate regional patterns of abuse and to determine if certain departments had high rates of complaints. Over a six-year period, the Justice department received 48,000 complaints against officers, of which 15,000 were formally investigated. Only 2 percent of the cases judged to merit further investigation resulted in criminal charges against the officers (Bishop, 1991; Campbell and Lopez, 1991; Lewis, 1991). This document, while it was completed in 1991, is not available to researchers or the public despite pressure from the black members of Congress for its release. According to John Conyers (DMI), the intentional withholding of the findings of the report has increased black suspicions about the insensitivity of the governmental response to police brutality at the national level (Bishop, 1991).

◈ The Research Project

Our research mainly addresses three major policing issues. First, are African Americans and other minority citizens more likely to find themselves victims of police brutality than white citizens? Second, are there certain situations that seem to have a greater likelihood of a violent police-citizen encounter? Third, are police departments taking allegations of violent police misconduct seriously?

Since there are no national statistics concerning police brutality available from any governmental source, we have used data derived from accounts of police misconduct in major newspapers for the period January 1, 1990 to May 31, 1992. We made use of one major Nexis database prepared by Mead Data Central. This database includes fifteen major newspapers updated on a daily basis and made available for computerized searches. These leading newspapers were selected by the Nexis service because of the size of their circulation and their major regional or national importance.

Using the keywords "police brutality," the following major national and regional newspapers were systematically searched for accounts of police malpractice in our time period: *The Atlanta Journal and Constitution, The Boston Globe, The Chicago Tribune, The Christian Science Monitor, The Hartford Courant, The Los Angeles Times, The Minneapolis Star and Tribune, The New York Times, Newsday, The San Francisco Chronicle,*

The Seattle Times, The Wall Street Journal, USA Today, The Washington Post, and *The Washington Times.*

Out of the database of tens of thousands of articles, a total of 4,770 newspaper stories were retrieved that had at least a brief mention of "police brutality" in them. Due to the general nature of the phrase, not all of these stories dealt with a specific account of police brutality. Some of the articles dealt with "rap" songs that discussed the phenomenon, while others were based on political platforms of reform for candidates running for office. Many of the articles dealt specifically with the Rodney King incident and its aftermath. The King incident prompted many papers to broadly analyze and discuss their own local departments' practices, while not discussing any specific case of alleged police brutality in any detail. Some of the retrieved articles dealt with the same incident, analyzing the encounter in greater depth or, in some cases, multiple newspapers reported on the same event. Combing through these 4,770 stories we found 130 distinct cases of police violence against civilians with enough detail for analysis.

We must note a few things about these data. For the purposes of this research we have accepted the designation of these incidents reported in these major newspaper accounts as cases of excessive police force, or "police brutality." It should be noted that newspapers use court, police and community sources and there is a skew in the data toward the larger cities. Incidents of excessive police force were reported for cities in fifteen different states, with the greatest number in the largest states, New York and California. Five newspapers are located in the Midwest, and two are two national digest papers that gave modest coverage to the problem of police violence. At the time of the data search, these fifteen media sources were the only newspapers available through the Lexis/Nexis service and no screening or selection process was used by the authors. The accounts of the acts of brutality varied in richness and depth. The more serious cases in which the officers were charged and tried were greatly detailed, while some other accounts of single police-citizen incidents presented only some basic details, thereby limiting the number of dimensions we can analyze in this paper.

The possibility of media bias in the major newspaper coverage of police brutality should be noted. In essence, the data is representative of the prevalence of news coverage of claims of police brutality and the level of media interest in these allegations. Why have these incidents found their way into the mass media, while many others have been ignored? In today's racially charged climate, are violent police-citizen encounters with racial overtones more likely to garner the attention of the media than those with all white participants? Given the nature of the data source, these questions are impossible to answer. Conclusions based on this data should be evaluated with these limitations in mind.

Some white readers of our work have suggested that it is only the black and other minority cases that get into the mass media. However, it seems unlikely that an incident where white citizens were beaten up badly by police officers would not make its way into newspapers, especially if the victims were middle or upper class, as is sometimes the case for minority Americans. The opposite problem seems more likely. Martindale (1986: 133), in a discussion of the media and black Americans, has offered the following:

> A vivid illustration of the black community's concern with this problem was provided in the University of Washington seminar report, which noted that although the meeting was set up to consider media-black relations, a considerable amount of time was spent discussing police-black relations. While the black participants were willing to discuss the media, the report stated, they felt such a strong animosity toward the police that the presence of newsmen was sufficient to unleash a flood of criticism against the police. The participants apparently were eager to inform reporters about their grievances concerning police behavior in the black community because they felt that if journalists became aware of this situation and exposed it to the reading public, some corrective measures might be taken. . . . The media, however, continue to ignore this problem. They also seem prone to

present the police only as upholders of law and order, black victims as possibly deserving of their fate, and black witnesses as probably unreliable.

White newspaper editors may feel pressure to affirm the integrity of the local police department and the desirability of the current societal organization. As phrased by Martindale (1986: 134), "Perhaps the media have failed to inquire deeply into this area because the truths that would emerge might prove uncomfortable to white middle-class society."

 Findings

The Racial Characteristics of Officers and Citizens

Examining the 130 relatively detailed cases of encounters reported as police brutality in these major newspapers, we found that the overwhelming majority of the civilian victims (86.9 percent) were African American, 13 (10.0 percent) were Latino, and only 5 (3.5 percent) of the victims were non-Latino whites. Additionally, three of the five white victims were in the company of a black person at the time of the police encounter.

In contrast to the citizen data, the data on the officers involved showed a different racial background: 92.8 percent (N=104) were white, 2.7 percent (N=3) were of Latino origin, and 4.4 percent (N=5) of the officers were black. The racial makeup of the officers involved in violent assaults is whiter than the racial composition of larger city police departments. For example, in the city of Chicago, blacks represent 23 percent of the force (Jackson et al., 1991), while in New York City only 8 percent of the officers are black (Mydans et al., 1991). Overall, the Justice Department reports that whites constitute 85 percent of police officers, while blacks and Latino account for 9 percent and 5 percent, respectively.

As we have noted, police departments were developed to control the poor and "dangerous classes" of urban society (Jacobs, 1979), and selective enforcement of the law by white police officers has been found to be common, with blacks and other minorities bearing a greater number of formal sanctions than whites. The cases reviewed in this analysis lend support to this contention. Almost 97 percent of the victims of police misconduct were minorities, and the vast majority (86.9 percent) of the victims were African American. Furthermore, in three of the five cases in which the victims were white, a black individual was also present. All but one of the altercations that resulted in death involved minority citizens, with black males accounting for the majority of the deaths.

It is significant that there is not a single case of white citizens being targeted for excessive force by black or Latino officers. In the cases involving Latino victims, the officers involved were either white or Latino. There were no cases of brutality involving a Latino victim and a black officer. In the two cases involving allegations of misconduct against Latino officers, the victims were either black or Latino. And in the cases in which the actions of a black police officer came under scrutiny, the victims were in all cases black citizens.

The data seem to suggest the existence of a hierarchy of racial or ethnic groups, what Feagin (1989) calls the "ladder of racial dominance." Some groups are positioned higher than others on the ladder, which results in greater power and privileges than lower groups. White citizens were rarely victims of abuse, and if they were, it was at the hands of white officers. Minority officers did not cross the line and assault those of a higher social position. In addition, white officers targeted minority group members for harsh treatment. Latinos seemed to be positioned below whites, but above blacks, in this hierarchy of force. While the low number of cases involving Latino officers suggests caution here, they show that Latino officers seemed to target members of their own group or blacks. These findings are consistent with Carter (1986) who found that Latino officers were more likely to discriminate against Latino citizens than white citizens. In the cases reviewed for this analysis, whites were not targeted by the Latino officers. Black officers were involved in brutality cases only with members of their racial group. There were no cases in which a black officer was involved in an altercation involving a white or Latino victim. Blacks seemed to occupy the lowest position on the ladder of dominance.

Situational Characteristics

The circumstances leading up to the final violent assault between the police officer(s) and the civilian victims could be analyzed in 113 of the altercations. For these 113 cases, the preceding events can be grouped into nine main categories, listed here in order of greatest occurrence: lack of respect or compliance on the part of the victim; perceived threat; traffic dispute or stop (included malfunctioning equipment or allegations of erratic driving); mistaken identity (the civilian appeared to match a description of an armed and dangerous individual); riot or protest-related incident (citizen was perceived or actually involved in a riot or protest); drug-related arrest (six of the eight reported incidents involved the forcible entry into homes of civilians in a search for drugs that did not exist); police chase or attempted escape; accidental shooting; and questioning or confession. The basis for classification was the circumstance that seemed to contribute the most to the assault. For example, if a motorist was stopped by police officers and proceeded to act in a threatening manner towards the officers, the incident was classified as a perceived threat, not a traffic stop. Only a few of the cases required this type of judgement call.

The largest proportion (29.2 percent) of the cases involving a violent police-citizen encounter stemmed from a lack of respect or compliance on the part of the citizen toward the police officer. This finding is consistent with previous findings (see, for example, Croft, 1985; Westley, 1970). The actual circumstances surrounding the inadequate display of deference toward the officer were varied: The victim may have refused to provide his or her identification to the questioning officer, the victim may not have followed orders from the officers as quickly or as well as the officers may have liked, the victim may have had a "bad attitude" or failed to give the officer the amount of deference they expected, or, in a few cases, the victim may not have been able to communicate with the officers due to a handicap or lack of fluency in the English language.

Twenty-nine cases (25.7 percent) were the result of a perceived threat—either the officer felt that his (rarely her) own life or the life of another citizen was in jeopardy. Complaints of brutality that resulted from the circumstances included within this category may be rationalized by many individuals. The police officer(s) involved felt that he or she was in a life or death situation: a gun may have been pointed at the officer or another citizen, or there may have been an escalating physical struggle. According to the findings of this study, more of the victims of police brutality had been disrespectful to officers than had posed a serious physical threat to the officers or other citizens.

In police/minority situations the use of racial slurs can be important. The use of racial slurs or epithets by officers in reference to citizens was noted by the media source in 25 of the 130 cases, with most of the targets of this form of abuse being African Americans. Only two slurs against Latino citizens were reported. Racial slurs and epithets, derogatory statements directed toward a minority group member, have been reported to be common in a number of police departments. For example, the Christopher Commission, in its review of the Los Angeles Police Department, found numerous racist comments in computer transmissions between the cars of the patrol officers, including some from sergeants who were on street patrol. Further, citizens are not the only recipients of racist treatment by the police officers. Janine Bouey, a light skinned black female officer with the Los Angeles Police Department, complained to the department about the use of racial slurs that were made against suspects while in her presence (Serrano and Soble, 1991). Gregory Thomas, also of the Los Angeles Police Department, complained to a supervisor on several occasions that a fellow officer continually referred to him as "boy" and make racist jokes on Martin Luther King Day (Hudson, 1991).

Penalties

Of the 130 cases we analyzed, only 17 (13.1 percent) had a penalty reported against the officer involved. A total of five officers lost their jobs, six were either reassigned to desk duty or suspended with pay, four were suspended from duty without pay for 10 to 60 days, and only two officers were charged with criminal offenses.

The percentage of these cases with officers being punished is a bit higher than the comparable percentages reported by several departments cited in the newspaper accounts. This may be because incidents reported in the newspapers [are] probably of a more serious nature. For example, in Long Island, New York, out of 600 complaints of excessive force over a four year period (1987–1990), only nine of the complaints (1.5 percent) resulted in any punishment. In these cases the most severe penalties involved officers losing a few days pay or some accrued time. In 31 years, only one officer has been fired for the use of excessive force on Long Island (Tayler and Bessent, 1991). Similarly, the *Chicago Tribune* reported that in 1989–1990, there were 15,596 citizen complaints filed against the city of Chicago Police Department, with only 329 (2.1 percent) upheld. Many of these cases resulted in a suspension of less than 30 days. Additionally, the Justice Department reported that of 48,000 complaints against officers over the past six years, only 2 percent resulted in charges against the officer involved (Jackson, 1991). In complaints where black citizens are involved, there seems to be an even greater likelihood that the officers will not be punished. In a study of 4,400 complaints from 1987 through mid 1990, the *Los Angeles Times* reported that only 8.4 percent of the complaints were substantiated. The study indicated that black citizens who filed complaints against white officers had the worst chance of substantiation, with only 4 percent of these complaints found to be valid by Internal Affairs investigations. Black citizens in the city of Los Angeles comprise only 13 percent of the city population, but account for 41 percent of the official complaints against officers (Rohrlich and Merina, 1991).

Several reasons have been proposed for the few penalties given to police officers because of malpractice: the lack of credible witnesses and victims; the tendency for jurors not to convict officers; and the need to maintain a working relationship between the District Attorney's office and the police department. In a trial, the defense attorneys for the accused officers have access to school, work, medical, and arrest records of complainants

and victims. However, personal information concerning the officers is not obtainable (Tayler, 1991). If the victim has a long criminal history, the jury may not find the testimony credible. Jurors are reluctant to convict officers who are charged in brutality cases. In one of the cases analyzed in this study two officers admitted on the stand that they had beaten a car theft suspect, and that something inside of them had "just snapped." The officers were found not guilty (Freed, 1991).

Before a complaint can ever be considered for prosecution, the complaint must first be filed with an agency. While some departments have outside agencies that also take complaints, in most cases the complaint must be filed directly with the police department the victim is complaining against. According to the *Hartford Courant*, when a complainant first enters the station to file a complaint against the Hartford Police Department, he or she is first told that they could be arrested for filing a false police report (Barger and Thibault, 1991). Further, in a sworn testimony given by Robert Sobel, a former Los Angeles County Sheriff Sergeant, Sobel stated that he had "shortstopped" citizen complaints against those under his command to protect them. Sobel called the complainants and gave them the impression that their complaint was being thoroughly investigated (Merina, 1991).

In a review of practices within the Oakland, California, police department, Skolnick and Bayley (1986) have discussed problems associated with departmental investigation of officers. James Chanin, an attorney who advises citizens on the filing of brutality complaints, says that he never advises clients to seek redress through Internal Affairs: "If someone comes in with black and blue marks and says this officer beat me, they will not seriously entertain the notion that the officer could have done it—or even if they do, there's no set of circumstances where they'll find the complaint substantiated" (quoted in Skolnick and Bayley: 157).

◆ Discussion and Conclusions

Our data suggest that police brutality is a national problem. The major newspapers we examined from January 1, 1990 to May 31, 1992 reported 130 detailed and important cases in 15 different states. Significantly, the nation's leaders do not seem to be willing to face these facts. The early 1990s report prepared by the Justice Department, the only nationwide review of police brutality, has not been released in any detail. While our data have some flaws, they are among the best available at this time.

The Kerner Commission report, which was prepared more than two decades ago, stated that to earn respect, police officers and the courts must administer justice in a way that is free from discrimination or prejudice. Unfortunately, the findings of our study suggest that street-level justice still is not administered in a color-blind fashion. Minority citizens accounted for the vast majority of those who were abused in a serious manner by (mostly white) police officers. These findings suggest that some serious racial discrimination exists in the application of U.S. law enforcement in the 1990s.

Our analysis uncovered several interesting findings. One was the possible existence of a "ladder of dominance" among the racial groups. In terms of who gets targeted, whites were found to be the least likely, then the Latinos, and finally the blacks. In addition, there is a similar pattern for the officers. In the few cases involving allegations against black officers, the citizens were all black. For the few cases of Latino officers, the complainants were either black or Latino, not white. Only in the case of white officers were the complainants from all three groups. This finding held true for both male and (the few) female officers. This pattern suggests that officers may only assault those whom they view as members of an equal or inferior racial group. However, before a definite conclusion can be drawn, more cases involving minority police officers would need to be analyzed. Our finding here is only suggestive.

Another interesting finding is the relative lack of penalties given to the officers involved in violent altercations with citizens. Even though the percentage of officers who were penalized in this analysis was somewhat higher than other reported statistics, in this analysis only 13 percent of the officers received some sort of penalty for their alleged involvement in assaults against citizens. Further, in only 3 percent of the cases

was the officer ultimately relieved of duty. If harsher penalties were applied, perhaps the rate of police brutality against citizens would decline. We can also recall that the *Los Angeles Times* study found that black officers were twice as likely as their white peers to be found guilty of misconduct. If the complainant was white, the substantiation rate for black officers was twice that for white officers, while Latino officers were penalized three times more often. It would be interesting to see if this finding could be replicated on a national scale, perhaps controlling for offense of the officer and other important considerations.

Some might suggest that the higher violent crime rates of black Americans might be one reason for the higher rate of police violence against black Americans, especially black men. The idea is that violent criminals are more threatening and thus more likely to provoke police violence. Thus, according to 1992 Federal Bureau of Investigation statistics, black citizens accounted for 45 percent of the total number of arrests for violent offenses (Federal Bureau of Investigation, 1993). Mutalia (1982) found that black citizens accounted for 60 percent of those who died in 1,428 justifiable shootings by police officers from 1975 to 1979. According to Mutalia, the disproportionate rate of black victims who were fatally shot by the police was in direct proportion to the level of crime committed by black citizens. However, the data suggest that this proportion is much higher than the arrest-for-violent-crime rate.

Our data suggest some serious problems with this argument. The proportion of black citizens who are victims of police brutality is higher (86.9 percent) than the rate reported for their involvement in violent criminal activity that resulted in arrest (45 percent). Furthermore, as the examination of situational characteristics demonstrates, African American citizens do not have to be involved in the commission of a crime to be victimized: having a disrespectful attitude towards the officer, being involved in a routine traffic stop, or just resembling a violent criminal could very well make an otherwise law-abiding citizen become a target for abuse. In nearly 75 percent of the cases, the victim was not recognized by the officer at the scene as being a direct threat to the officer or other citizens.

In our data more minority citizens were assaulted for lack of compliance/respect to an officer than for posing a serious threat to the officer or another civilian. It is significant that all the victims of abuse in these circumstances of "disrespect" were black or Latino. According to the earlier Kerner Commission report (1968), a criminal justice system cannot function effectively unless it receives the respect of the people it serves. However, by the same token, the criminal justice system must prove itself deserving of respect before the people will defer to it or its agents. Acts of brutality do not instill respect, only resentment and fear.

In the categories in which the officers' behavior was more pro-active in nature, the social class of the victim seemed to have some relation with the assault. Pro-active cases included the traffic stop and mistaken identity categories. In these incidents, the officer stopped the victim on his or her own accord; the civilian did not come to the officer's attention as a result of answering an assigned call. In the mistaken identity incidents, the officer stopped the citizen because he or she resembled a bank robber, mugger, or drug dealer that was reportedly loose in the neighborhood. According to the descriptions given in the media, the victims whose assault stemmed from a case of mistaken identity were of middle or upper class status. Further, half of those assaulted as a result of an incident related to traffic were of middle or upper class: college students, a former Los Angeles Lakers star, a former police liaison officer, and a successful entrepreneur. In situations where the civilians were indeed of middle or upper status and victims of pro-active enforcement by police officers, the victims were all black. These data suggest that these African Americans may have come to the attention of the police because of their "violation" of the white image of their racial group, that is, they were not lower-class blacks. The middle and upper class status of these black individuals may have indicated to the officers that the victims possessed wealth and resources that rightfully belonged to whites like themselves.

James Q. Wilson (1968) has argued that the class of the victim is more important than race as a determinant of police mistreatment. In his view race only accentuates the brutality. However, our data seem to contradict this argument. If Wilson were correct, more lower-class whites should be the victims of police brutality, and reports of police abuse against higher-class blacks should not be so common.

Finally, in our view the cost to the taxpayer of the misconduct of police officers needs to be addressed at the level of public policy. In reviewing cases for this analysis, we found that since 1989 taxpayers have paid out at least $134 million in awards to citizens alleging police brutality, with another $116 million in lawsuit awards pending. These costs did not include legal fees, which in many cases can be substantial. In the County of Los Angeles alone, $20 million had been paid to citizens alleging police brutality since 1989; this figure does not include $34 million in litigations fees in the same time period. Since only 22 different cities were found to report costs associated with lawsuits alleging police misconduct, the actual nationwide figure is certainly much higher. The costs of police brutality are not simply the scars on the minority victims, which are the most serious, but also the high costs for local governments in the United States.

 References

Alpert, Geoffrey. 1989. "Police Use of Deadly Force: The Miami Experience." Pp. 480–495 in R. Dunham and G. Alpert (eds.), *Critical Issues in Policing*. Prospect Heights: Waveland.

Barger, Theresa S. and Andy Thibault. 1991. "Violent Officers Take Toll on Public Trust, Pocketbook." *Hartford Courant* (September 29): A1.

Bayley, David, and James Garofalo. 1989. "The Management of Violence by Police Patrol Officers." *Criminology* 27: 1–23.

Bessent, Alvin E. and Letta Tayler. 1991. "Police Brutality: Is it No Problem?" *Newsday* (June 2): 5.

Bishop, Katherine. 1991. "Police Attacks: Hard Crimes to Uncover, Let alone Stop." *New York Times* (March 24): 1.

Bogomolny, R. 1976. "Street Patrol: The Decision to Stop a Citizen." *Criminal Law Bulletin* 12: 544–582.

Campbell, Linda P. and Ruth Lopez. 1991. "Police Brutality Triggers Many Complaints, Little Data." *Chicago Tribune* (March 24): 16.

Carter, David L. 1986. "Hispanic Police Officers' Perception of Discrimination." *Police Studies* 11: 204–210.

"College to be Given Archives of a Study on Police Brutality." 1991. *New York Times* (August 27): 19.

Croft, Elizabeth B. 1985. *Police Use of Force: An Empirical Analysis*. Ph.D. Dissertation. Albany: State University of New York.

Decker, Cathleen, 1990. "Most Rank Police High in L.A. and Orange Counties." *Los Angeles Times* (February 13): 1.

Feagin, Joe R. 1989. *Racial and Ethnic Relations.* Englewood Hills: Prentice Hall.

————.1991. "The Continuing Significance of Race: Antiblack Discrimination in Public Places." *American Sociological Review* 56: 101–116.

Feagin, Joe R. and Clarice B. Feagin. 1990. *Social Problems: A Critical Power-Conflict Perspective.* Englewood Cliffs, NJ: Prentice-Hall.

Feagin, Joe R. and Harlan Hahn. 1973. *Ghetto Revolts: The Politics of Violence in American Cities.* New York: MacMillan Company.

Federal Bureau of Investigation. 1993. *Uniform Crime Reports for the United States 1992.* Washington DC: U.S. Department of Justice.

Fielding, Nigel. 1991. *The Police and Social Conflict.* London and Atlantic Highlands: Althone Press.

Ford, Andrea and Sheryl Stolberg. 1991. "Latinos Tell Panel of Anger at Police Conduct." *Los Angeles Times* (May 21): A1.

Freed, David. 1991. "Police Brutality Claims are Rarely Prosecuted." *Los Angeles Times* (July 7): 1.

Fridell, Lorie. 1989. "Justifiable Use of Measures in Research on Deadly Force." *Journal of Criminal Justice* 17: 157–165.

Friedrich, Robert J. 1980. "Police Use of Force: Individuals, Situations and Organizations." *Annals of the American Academy of Political and Social Science* 452: 82–97.

Fyfe, James. 1989. "Police/Citizen Violence Reduction Project." *FBI Law Enforcement Bulletin* (May 18–23): 23–29.

Holmes, Steven A. 1991. "Poll Finds Most Satisfied with Police." *New York Times* (April 5): 5.

Hudson, Berkley. 1991. "Vemon's Role in Promotion of Officer Probed." *Los Angeles Times* (October 10): 3.

Independent Commission on the Los Angeles Police Department. 1991. *Report of the Independent Commission on the Los Angeles Police Department.* Los Angeles: International Creative Management.

Jackson, David, John O'Brien, and Art Barnum. 1991. "Police Brutality: How Widespread is It?" *Chicago Tribune* (March 24): 1.

Jacobs, David. 1979. "Inequality and Police Strength: Conflict Theory and Coercive Control in Metropolitan Area." *American Sociological Review* 44: 913–925.

Kelling, George. 1991. "The Blue-Uniformed Feat of 'Social Work.'" [Letter to the editor]. *Los Angeles Times* (July 11): 7B.

Leinen, Stephen, 1984. *Black Police, White Society.* New York: New York University Press.

Lewis, Neil A. 1991. "Police Brutality under Wide Review by Justice Department." *New York Times* (March 15): 1.

Martindale, Carolyn. 1986. *The White Press and Black America.* New York: Greenwood Press.

McLaughlin, Vance. 1992. *Police and the Use of Force: The Savannah Study.* Westport: Praeger.

Mutalia, Kenneth J. 1982 *A Balance of Forces: National Survey of Police Deadly Force.* Gaithersburg, MD: International Association of Chiefs of Police.

Mydans, Seth, Richard W. Stevenson, and Timothy Egan. 1991. "Seven Minutes in Los Angeles: A Special Report." *New York Times* (March 18): 1.

Myrdal, Gunnar. 1944. *An American Dilemma.* New York: Harper.

Oberschall, Anthony. 1973. *Social Conflict and Social Movements.* Englewood Cliffs: Prentice-Hall.

Owens, Charles. 1977. *Blacks and Criminal Justice.* Lexington: Lexington books.

Platt, Tony, J. Frappier, G. Ray, R. Schauffler, L. Trujillo, L. Cooper, E Currie, and S. Harring. 1982. *The Iron Fist and the Velvet Glove.* San Francisco: Synthesis Publications.

Reiss, Albert J., Jr. 1968. "Police Brutality: Answers to Key Questions." *Trans-Action* (July-August): 10–19.

Rohrlich, Ted and Victor Merina. 1991. "Racial Disparities Seen in Complaints to LAPD." *Los Angeles Times* (May 19): 1.

Serrano, Richard A. and Ronald L. Soble. 1991. "Grand Jury Widens Probe of King Beating." *Los Angeles Times* (March 29): 1.

Skolnick, Jerome H. and David H. Bailey. 1988. "Theme and Variation in Community Policing." Pp. 138–159 in M. Tonry and M. Morris (eds.), *Crime and Justice, 10.* Chicago: University of Chicago Press.

Skolnick, Jerome H. and James J. Fyfe. 1993. *Above the Law: Police and the Excessive Use of Force.* New York: Free Press.

Smith, Douglas A. and C.A. Visher. 1981. "Situational Determinants of Police Arrest Decisions." *Social Problems* 29: 167–177.

Tayler, Letta. 1991. "With their Lives on the Line, Cope Deny any Abuse of Power." *Newsday* (June 2): 4.

Tayler, Letta and Alvin E. Bessent. 1991. "Filing a Police Complaint often Means Fighting Red Tape and Bluecoats." *Newsday* (June 3): 7.

U.S. Commission on Civil Rights. 1973. *Internal Regulation of Police Departments.* Washington, DC: U.S. Government Printing Office.

Vold, George B. and Thomas J. Bernard. 1986. *Theoretical Criminology.* New York: Oxford University Press.

Walker, Samuel. 1992. *The Police in America: An Introduction.* 2nd ed. New York: McGraw-Hill.

Westley, William A. 1970. *Violence and the Police: A Sociological Study of Law, Custom, and Morality.* Cambridge: MIT Press.

Wilson, James Q. 1968. *Varieties of Police Behavior: The Management of Law and Order in Eight Communities.* Cambridge: Harvard University Press.

CHAPTER 10

Critical Theories of Deviance

In 2004, Little Rock, Arkansas, was voted the meanest city in United States by the National Coalition for the Homeless. What made Little Rock the meanest city toward the homeless? The city at the time "managed" the homeless population by ordering the police to engage in ongoing police raids of the 27 homeless encampments found in the area. Police came into these encampments during the day, while the inhabitants were not there, and demolished the sites, often destroying the few belongings that inhabitants owned. While the mayor of Little Rock at the time (Jim Dailey) admitted that he did not know where the homeless were supposed to go, the police continued the raids, often without warning to the residents. The city justified the raids by calling the homeless panhandlers and petty thieves. While the homeless have been cast as common criminals by the city, there is no evidence this is the case. In fact, the fastest growing homeless population in this area were single women with children. At the time, only 75 shelter beds were available for homeless women. (Adapted from Rampona, 2004)

◈ Introduction

The story above highlights an all too common problem for the homeless in the United States—the criminalization or stigmatization of their homeless plight. While many organizations—national and local, religious and secular—focus on helping the homeless, for example, through soup kitchens, shelters, and "10-year plans" to eradicate homelessness, a major governmental response to homelessness in many cities is one of social control and banishment (Beckett & Herbert, 2010).

The deviance theories examined in this chapter are considered critical theories. In other words, they examine issues of deviance and crime from a perspective that questions the normative and status quo. While earlier theories in this book might look at the plight of homelessness and ask, "How does someone become homeless?" or "Why are the homeless, homeless?" oftentimes focusing specifically on what many might consider individual flaws or propensities to engage in this "deviance"—these critical theories, instead, examine societal responses to homelessness often from the perspective of those with less societal

427

▲ **Photo 10.1**   How do we address homelessness? The answer depends on the theory we are using to understand it.

power (people of color or women) or those with nontraditional philosophies (peacemaking). In other words, just like Marxist/conflict theory in Chapter 9, the theories in this chapter will ask, what role does society play in the creation and maintenance of homelessness?

◈ Peacemaking

It is fitting to include peacemaking criminology as one of the theories in this chapter because one of its strongest proponents is Richard Quinney, the critical criminologist whose early work we read about in Chapter 9 under conflict theories. One might say that peacemaking theory (Pepinsky & Quinney, 1991; Quinney, 1995) is the contemporary extension of Quinney's work in conflict theory. Writing and theorizing with Hal Pepinsky, they continue with this theory to critically examine not only our understanding of crime and deviance but also our understanding of how we come to know what we know. In other words, they critically examine criminology *and* criminologists as well.

According to the peacemaking philosophy, most criminology today is "war-like" because at its foundation, it advocates making war on crime. This war on crime is evidenced in two ways in traditional criminology: (1) through the us versus them philosophy that suggests that those who engage in crime are somehow different from the rest of society and (2) through the advocating of punishment as the primary means to stop crime (Pepinsky & Quinney, 1991). Pepinsky and Quinney (1991) argue that neither of these viewpoints has reduced criminal activity; in fact, both have increased the suffering of not only victims but offenders alike. According to Pepinsky and Quinney,

> There are basically two kinds of criminologists, those who think criminals are different from themselves and those who don't. You cannot separate a criminal's self-understanding from our understanding of the criminal. More than empathy, understanding requires our sympathy— allowing ourselves to feel the offender's pain and committing ourselves to trying to alleviate the pain for us both. (p. 303)

Peacemaking criminology, on the other hand, is focused on a different way of seeing and organizing the world around compassion, sympathy, and understanding. Quinney (1991) defines this way of thinking:

> In other words, without inner peace in each of us, without peace of mind and heart, there can be no social peace between people and no peace in societies, nations, and in the world. To be explicitly engaged in this process, of bringing about peace on all levels, of joining ends and means, is to be engaged in peacemaking. (p. 10)

The peacemaking tradition has no single tenet or assumption, and it has many followers in both the academic world and the world of praxis (Pepinsky, 1991). In 1991, Pepinsky and Quinney published the first book on the peacemaking perspective. Pepinsky and Quinney outline three substantive areas that flourish in the peacemaking tradition: religious, feminist, and critical. Peacemakers coming from a religious perspective focus on a variety of religious traditions, including Christianity, Buddhism, Hinduism, Islam,

Judaism, and Native American (Braswell, Fuller, & Lozoff, 2001). They look to these traditions to advocate a way of meeting those who might engage in harm not as enemies but as members of the community who need understanding. "It is rather that when violence happens, they [the Mennonites] choose to try to restore peace rather than to respond in kind. And once again, the method is the way" (Pepinsky, 1991, p. 305). The feminist peacemaking tradition is broad and varied and hard to summarize in a short space. However, at its core, those working in this tradition are focused on a humane system of justice that acknowledges that women are placed at a disadvantage in a patriarchal society (Fuller & Wozniak, 2006). This patriarchy and, by definition, gendered power differences create an oppressive war-like experience for women both within and beyond the criminal justice system. Finally, the critical tradition of peacemaking also includes a robust examination of societal power differences, including, but not limited to, gender, race, and class.

All three of these traditions have in common a belief that a different paradigm must be established for criminal justice—one that focuses on restoration and not retribution. **Restorative justice** as a practical method advocates for the use of restorative practices or mediation between victims and offenders, offering victims a real opportunity to work through their victimization often by playing a central role in the offender's justice experience. The majority of the scholarly literature related to restorative justice addresses the particulars of restorative methods and/or the philosophical and theoretical bases of restorative principles (e.g., Cragg, 1992; Messmer & Otto, 1992; Strang & Braithwaite, 2001; Umbreit, 1994; M. Wright, 1996; Zehr, 1990). Also evident in the literature are the attendant critiques of statements of restorative theory and practice and discussions of the challenges facing restorative justice (e.g., Andersen, 1999; Ashworth, 1993; Hudson, 1998; LaPrairie, 1998; Minor & Morrison, 1996). These critiques echo longstanding concerns about informal justice expressed in the sociolegal literature (Abel, 1982; Merry, 1989)—namely, that the lack of formal authority involved in mediation and community dispute resolution practices may result in greater injustices than the very system it seeks to remedy.

▲ **Photo 10.2** Peacemaking theory suggests that we should help those with a "deviant" status, such as the homeless, instead of criminalizing them.

Peacemaking and Homelessness

Gregg Barak (1991) offered a peacemaking analysis of homelessness as a deviant status in the United States. At the core of his analysis was an argument that we must approach homelessness from a place of kindness and regard for those who have found themselves homeless. Most debates about homelessness have at their core an individualistic deficits model that suggests that those who are homeless are so because of individual problems or deficits of their character (they are lazy, like being homeless, are drug addicts, etc.). This characterization allows for treatment of the homeless that is war-like and inhumane.

▲ **Photo 10.3** Peacemaking theory argues that we often "make war" on deviant behavior by criminalizing it.

For example, if we assume that individuals are homeless because of personal "problems" such as laziness or drug use, it is easy to also characterize the homeless as immoral and more likely to be dangerous. These characterizations lead to public policies that focus on (1) making the homeless invisible and (2) criminalizing the homeless and homelessness.

Public policies that focus on making homelessness invisible use tactics such as banishment (Beckett & Herbert, 2010) and loitering laws that make standing or sitting on public sidewalks against the law. While these policies in the short run may move the homeless to different parts of the city or to different cities altogether, they do nothing to alleviate the problem of homelessness and offer individuals who are homeless any hope of finding permanent affordable housing.

The example at the beginning of this chapter offers an even more "war-like" law enforcement practice of using sweeps to destroy the encampments of the homeless. In most instances, this means that these individuals lose the few possessions they have saved and can mean arrest if the individuals are caught in the encampments during the sweep, although often sweeps are conducted during the day when the homeless are less likely to be onsite. This practice does nothing to help those who are homeless find affordable housing. It does exacerbate the feelings of alienation and helplessness that the homeless are likely to feel (Barak, 1991).

Peacemaking practices designed to help homelessness would not focus on an individual deficit model of homelessness but instead would focus on structural conditions that may lead to homelessness (Barak, 1991). For example, young women often run away from home because of physical, emotional, or sexual abuse they are experiencing in the home. Individuals and families often find themselves homeless because of market forces such as the tightening of the low-income housing market, an increasing unemployment rate due to market fluctuations, or the globalization of the economy. Public policies that focus on offering services and places of refuge for young women who are abused or services for workers and families who have been affected by the structural conditions of the economy are more peace-like in nature. However, even these policies can be conducted in a war-like manner if the homeless are not treated as complete human beings and are made to "prove their worth" in order to receive these services.

For example, many social service agencies require that individuals take special classes to earn the "right" to receive their help. Individualized hoops that assume that the homeless are in need of extra education are still within a deficit model that places most of the blame for homelessness on the individual. A true peacemaking approach to homelessness would offer services and empathy without assuming that the homeless are different from those who enjoy stable housing. In other words, the homeless would not need to prove their worth while getting help.

DEVIANCE IN POPULAR CULTURE

This chapter introduces you to critical theories and peacemaking criminology. As with many theoretical perspectives, the ideas may become more clear and accessible to you if you can apply them to specific examples. Popular culture and films, once again, offer compelling real-life and fictional cases for you to watch and practice using these perspectives:

The Accused is a fictional account of a young woman who is gang raped in a bar. Similar to the sentiments expressed in the reading by Thapar-Björkert and Morgan, the victim's judgment and character are questioned when she decides to take the case to court. How would feminist theory view this case? From a peacemaking perspective, how might it have been better handled?

The popular film, *Crash*, offers examples of racial prejudice and profiling from several different perspectives. Each character reveals his or her own biases throughout the film; some learn significant lessons as they interact in surprising ways, but every character feels the powerful effect of fear and racial discrimination. Each character eventually questions his or her belief system and the larger society we live in.

On an entirely different note, *The Dhamma Brothers* is a documentary film exploring the power of meditation in a maximum-security prison. The film takes you inside the Donaldson Correctional Facility in Alabama as inmates embark upon an emotionally and physically demanding program of silent meditation lasting 10 days and requiring 100 hours of meditation. Can such a program change these men, and can it change the larger culture of the prison? Is this a desirable outcome?

Finally, *Redemption* is a made-for-television movie about the life of Stan "Tookie" Williams, founder of the Crips, who was nominated for the Nobel Peace Prize while on death row. Can a man who was convicted of terrible crimes turn his life around and be a role model for youth in the larger community? From his prison cell, Tookie Williams wrote a number of children's books speaking out against gang violence; you can check out his website (www.tookie.com) to get an idea of the work he was trying to do and the population he hoped to reach. Williams was executed by the state of California in 2005; whether redemption was possible in his case is now an academic question, but it is one we would like you to consider.

◈ Feminist Criminology

Like peacemaking criminology, **feminist criminology** questions the status quo, most specifically the male-centered view that much of criminology takes. While feminist thought has a long, rich history in the United States, feminist criminology emerged in the 1970s with the influential works of F. Adler (1975), R. J. Simon (1975), and Smart (1977). As with many of these critical perspectives, there is no single ideology but rather a diversity of feminist thought with ranging, often competing, viewpoints: liberal feminism, radical feminism, Marxist feminism, socialist feminism, postmodern feminism (Burgess-Proctor, 2006; Daly & Chesney-Lind, 1988; Tong, 1998), black feminism and critical race feminism (Burgess-Proctor, 2006), psychoanalytic feminism, gender feminism, existentialist feminism, global and multicultural feminism, and ecofeminism (Tong, 1998).

While a diverse set of theories fall under the feminist perspective, these theories all stem from the critique that criminological theories and theories of deviance prior to the introduction of feminist thought treated women in one of two ways: either as subsumed under the heading of "men," assuming that general theories of deviance could explain female deviance, or in a sexist manner, assuming that women were somehow "different" or "pathological" in their makeup and their deviance stemmed from this pathology. Until the feminist perspective, none of the theories acknowledged the position of women in a patriarchal society and the structural oppression that women experienced in this society (Smart, 1977). Once these early feminists began to question the usefulness of these "general" theories, the feminist perspective offered a diverse set of theories.

For the purposes of this overview, this chapter will highlight five branches of feminism that have produced research on deviance and crime. **Liberal feminism** focuses on gender role socialization. The roles that women are socialized into are not valued as much as the roles men are socialized for—in other words, nurturing roles such as teacher are not valued as much as competitive roles such as CEO. For this reason, liberal feminists focus on equal rights and opportunities, especially in education and the workplace, that would allow women to compete fairly with men. Liberal feminist scholars argue that women engage in deviance less because they are socialized in a manner that provides them fewer opportunities to deviate (Burgess-Proctor, 2006).

Radical feminism focuses on the sexual control of women, seeing their oppression emerging from a social order dominated by men. Because of their emphasis on sexual control, radical feminists focus much of their theoretical insights on sex, gender, and reproduction (Tong, 1998), as well as in the areas of crime and deviance on domestic violence, rape, sexual harassment, and pornography (Burgess-Proctor, 2006).

Socialist feminism focuses on structural differences, especially those we find in the capitalist modes of production. Social feminists argue that both patriarchy and capitalism are oppressive forces for women, and that until the patriarchal system and the class-based system are eradicated, there can be no equality for women (Tong, 1998).

Finally, **postmodern feminism** may be closest to peacemaking criminology, in that it questions the idea of a single "truth" or way of knowing and understanding. Postmodern feminists examine the social construction of such "accepted" ideas as crime and deviance (Burgess-Proctor, 2006). Even with their rich diversity, at the center of all of these strands of feminist thought is an emphasis on the oppression of women.

Certainly for a book on deviance and social control, one of the most central forms of oppression to be examined would be the criminal justice system and prison-industrial complex. Many feminist scholars have examined the effect of increasing social controls on the experiences of women. Between 1970 and 2001, the female prison population increased from 5,600 to 161,200 women (a 2,800% increase), even though for much of this time, crime rates were actually decreasing in the United States (Sudbury, 2005). Many have looked at this increase and tried to explain it with individual-level theories that focus on increasing female criminality, but feminist scholars argue that to really understand both the reasons behind such an exponential increase and the effect such an increase has on women and society, we must examine the business of criminalization that has made more behaviors deviant and made more punishments harsh over the past 30 years.

Feminist theories examine the label of deviant from the perspective of the outsider. Like conflict theory in Chapter 9 and critical race theory later in this chapter, feminist theory argues that the label of deviant is used to control women, especially poor women and women of color (Neve & Pate, 2005; Ogden, 2005). Instead of acknowledging a structural system of oppression that pays women less than men, does not adequately support childcare, and offers far fewer opportunities for women than men, the system criminalizes sexuality, makes the rules for welfare almost impossible to follow and then considers welfare fraud a crime punishable with 5 years in prison (Ogden, 2005), and considers women deviant for many behaviors they engage in as a means of survival (for example, running away and prostitution). Feminist theorists argue that the system itself must be changed instead of a narrow focus on women's behavior.

Feminism and Homelessness

Feminist theorists have devoted themselves to the study of women and their experiences in the social world (Burgess-Proctor, 2006). Much of this research—on domestic violence, the physical and sexual abuse of teenagers, and the position of women in the economic system—can have a significant impact on our understanding of women and homelessness. Feminist theory would ask what is it about women's position in society that might affect their likelihood of becoming homeless and their experience once they are homeless.

For example, patriarchal society normalizes the abuse of women. The fact that victimization of women is considered normal or acceptable means that many women are not helped in any systematic fashion. Women who want to escape abusive situations can quickly find themselves homeless. In addition, women who have no choice but to become homeless when they want to leave an abusive relationship are likely to delay or completely cancel their escape because homelessness presents its own hardships. These women are left with few alternatives.

Extensive research has documented the experience of teenage girls who run away from home (see Chesney-Lind & Shelden, 2003). These girls are often escaping very abusive families and running away becomes a preservation technique, but our public policies for running away do not take into consideration the reasons why girls may be running away. These policies criminalize this behavior and treat the girls as deviants who need to be punished or "reformed" for leaving their families. Feminists have long argued that good public policy would acknowledge the oppressive social structure that exists and not hold young girls accountable for the systems of oppression they are subject to. In other words, public policy should not focus on the girls as deviant for running away and becoming homeless but should instead focus on services and policies that stop physical and sexual abuse in the home and services that offer girls who have been abused a safe haven—resources, affordable housing, educational and work opportunities, and counseling to make sense of their experiences.

STUDIES IN DEVIANCE

Restorative Justice, Navajo Peacemaking and Domestic Violence

By Donna Coker (2006), in *Theoretical Criminology, 10,* 67–85

This article offers an example of the intersections of three critical theories by showing how feminist, peacemaking, and critical race theories may come together to better inform our understanding of the experiences of battered women. Coker (2006) examines the use of peacemaking practices in offering alternatives to how battered women receive just outcomes for their abuse. She situates this peacemaking philosophy in a feminist and critical race understanding of both battered women's and abusers' experiences.

Coker (2006) argues that the feminist tradition advocates for safety and empowerment for abused individuals, as well as changes in both cultural and political conditions that support violence toward women. In addition, the critical race perspective advocates for an understanding of oppressive, racist environments that demand a separation-focus when addressing abuse that oftentimes leaves the victim worse off than if she had stayed with her abuser.

The peacemaking philosophy allows battered women to experience "horizontal" justice, focused on the "process" of solving the problem—including allowing women (and family members) to confront her abuser, validate her feelings, and facilitate a solution that best fits her circumstances, rather than a "vertical" justice that focuses on coercion, power, and punishment and most often does not take the wishes of the woman into account.

Coker (2006) found that the peacemaking process was a fruitful avenue for seeking justice for battered women as long as the process made safety of the women a priority and did not make forgiveness of the abuser a condition of the process.

◈ **Critical Race Theory**

Critical race theory is an extension of critical legal studies that came to prominence through the writings of legal scholars in the 1970s. Scholars of critical race theory were interested in explaining why the civil rights movement of the 1960s had stalled and why the advances in the 1960s and 1970s had come under attack (Crenshaw, Gotanda, Peller, & Thomas, 1995). These scholars offered a counterstory to the dominant, mainstream accounts of the events of the civil rights movement and the use of law as a tool of equality. According to Cornell West (1995), "Critical Race theory . . . compels us to confront critically the most explosive issue in American civilization: the historical centrality and complicity of law in upholding white supremacy" (p. xi).

While the theory first began to coalesce among legal scholars, today it is used in the areas of communication, education, and sociology by an array of race scholars who are unified by two goals:

> The first is to understand how a of regime of white supremacy and its subordination of people of color have been created and maintained in America, and, in particular, to examine the relationship between that social structure and professed ideals such as "the rule of law" and "equal protection." The second is a desire not merely to understand the vexed bond between law and racial power but to change it. (Crenshaw et al., 1995, p. xiii)

Challenging this idea of white supremacy and thus the belief that the white experience is the normative standard by which all other experiences are measured, critical race theorists argue that to understand law and racial exclusion, we must understand the experiences of people of color under this legal system. These scholars insist "that the social and experiential context of racial oppression is crucial for understanding racial dynamics, particularly the way that current inequalities are connected to earlier, more overt, practices of racial exclusion" (Taylor, 1998, p. 122). Critical race theory, then, can be used to examine the use of law to negate the experiences of discrimination and victimization of people of color, while heightening the focus on deviance that may or may not exist in communities of color.

The law, scholars argue, is not "neutral" or "objective" in its creation or application and, instead, has been used, overtly, when possible, and covertly, when necessary, to subordinate people of color (Crenshaw et al., 1995). Even in such arenas as affirmative action, a policy from the civil rights era designed to help people of color, the law has been used, in the end, to mute this goal (Aguirre, 2000; Crenshaw et al., 1995).

At its very foundation, critical race theory offers a unique position in the forum of legal critique by proposing that racism is an intricate and enduring pattern in the fabric of American life, woven into the social structure and social institutions of modern day (Crenshaw et al., 1995). This is in direct contrast to even most liberal legal and social scholars who argue that racism and discrimination, in general, are sociopathic, anomalous acts that not only can be explained by individual, evil behavior but also can be fixed through accepted legal practices (Fan, 1997). As Crenshaw et al. (1995) note,

> From its inception mainstream legal thinking in the U.S. has been characterized by a curiously constricted understanding of race and power. Within this cramped conception of racial domination, the evil of racism exists when—and only when—one can point to specific, discrete acts of racial discrimination, which is in turn narrowly defined as decision-making based on the irrational and irrelevant attribute of race. (p. xx)

One of the most important tenets of critical race theory may be its supposition that racial domination is at the center of much of today's legal and social decision making—and that this domination is so routine, it is accepted as both legally and morally legitimate. Critical race scholars in essence argue that the "white" experience is so established as the "proper" experience that this viewpoint has been institutionalized as normative, and experiences or viewpoints that deviate from this are seen as harmful and therefore deviant.

Critical Race Theory and Homelessness

Critical race theory, then, is used to analyze the use of law and legal processes to maintain the status quo or "protect" a white, middle-class interpretation of the world, in the face of poor communities and communities of color. This perspective can be used to examine the experiences of the homeless in general, focusing on how laws are used to socially control the homeless, instead of helping them. However, an excellent, specific example of this can be the experiences of the homeless, migrant populations, and Latino populations in the San Diego fire evacuations of 2007 (see American Civil Liberties Union [ACLU], 2007). According to a report published November 1, 2007, the evacuation process for many San Diegans was subject to extra scrutiny and social control for what appeared to be racially and class-motivated reasons.

On October 21, 2007, fires broke out in San Diego County that required the evacuation of thousands of residents. One of the main evacuation centers was Qualcomm Stadium in the city of San Diego. While the ACLU reports that volunteers at the evacuation center were meticulous in their help of those in need, in more than a few instances, law enforcement seemed to be working at cross-purposes with these volunteers. Two such examples were that on more than one occasion (and with only evacuees of color), law enforcement detained individuals after they had been given their supplies from volunteers and accused these individuals of looting the supplies or "taking too many supplies" for their needs. In a second example, law enforcement entered the evacuation center during the late evening and woke up evacuees, requesting that they show identification proving they were from official evacuation areas. This was especially harmful for evacuees who were homeless (but living on the streets in evacuated areas) because they had no documentation with an official address given that they were homeless. These evacuees were ordered to leave the evacuation shelters because it was assumed they were not "in need" of the services and were taking advantage of the situation by staying at the shelter. While volunteers repeatedly emphasized that the services were available for anyone who came to the facility, many of the evacuees were assumed to be there under false pretenses. The ACLU (2007) report suggests that most, if not all, of those who were accused of unlawful behavior were the homeless or evacuees of color. In other words, white, middle-class evacuees were seen as deserving of help, while the homeless or evacuees of color were not (by law enforcement, not volunteers).

Critical race theory as a theory that emphasizes the importance of capturing individuals' stories and highlighting the experiences of everyone, not just those most visible or "deserving" of storytelling, allows for a more thorough examination of many experiences that usually go unnoticed or unrecorded. Certainly during the firestorms of 2007 in San Diego County, the experiences of the homeless and evacuees of color were overlooked by most who focused on more visible evacuees. Critical race theory gives voice to individuals and experiences that may not have their story told in more traditional settings.

▲ **Photo 10.4**   When the firestorm hit San Diego County, some individuals were treated as victims while others were treated as deviants. This treatment was often based on the individual's race/ethnicity.

NOW YOU . . . USE THE THEORY

I am a middle-aged white woman from the East Coast and a town that was 99% white, who now lives in a barrio, an original neighborhood settled by Latino families residing in California for generations. The town incorporated in the early 1960s with a population of 19,000 and grew rapidly to over 80,000 by 2000. As an inland town built around agriculture, it lacks the same degree of good vibrations and laid-back atmosphere of stereotypical Southern California beach communities.

More than 75% of the households in this working-class town make less than $100,000. The Latino population is 47%, up from 38% in 2000. While the particulars of this increase are not clear, what is clear is that a large portion of that 47% live in the barrio area and have brought much to this town in terms of culture, economics, and opportunity.

Life in the barrio is richly textured. Mexican restaurants and corner stores flourish; families and friends gather in parks and yards to grill carne asada accompanied by salsa fresco. Pedestrians abound with mothers walking their children to school, youth walking to high school, and people going to stores. There are always men and women waiting for the bus and commuter train. Many people work more than one job to make ends meet in the expensive living environment of California. Being part of this vibrant community and knowing my neighbors has made it clear that their hopes, dreams, and determination include working hard to prosper and to realize the American Dream for themselves and their families. Their hopes and dreams surely mirror immigrants who have come before.

In 2005, things began to erupt between the sheriffs and the community as three young Latino men met their death through the use of lethal force by the police. Shortly after that, in early 2006, the Minute Men descended upon the town to address what they saw as a problem with "illegals." The Minute Men continued their vigilance over the "illegal" problem, shoving cameras in people's faces, waving signs that dehumanized and criminalized immigrants, and winning over the politicians of the city and effectively diminishing the numbers of day laborers in the city.

Since that time period, law enforcement in the barrio has continued. Various strategies are used to enhance routine community patrols. These strategies include directed patrols, saturation patrols, Immigration Control and Enforcement (ICE) raids, speed traps, and sweeps of buses and transit stations. These are conducted primarily in the barrio area with two checkpoints conducted in the parking lot of the county courthouse. In general, a checkpoint consists of pulling over about 1,000 cars, arresting several people, handing out numerous citations, and towing an average of 30 cars. In the entire year of 2008, for example, checkpoints garnered over 200 citations, 155 cars were impounded, and 15 were arrested for DUI. Unlicensed drivers, including immigrants without documents and cars that are not registered or insured, are impounded for 30 days. This results in approximately $1,500 fees for towing and storage. Unable to pay the impound fees, many people lose their cars.

When there are heavy patrols and checkpoints, the usually active sidewalks and stores of the city are empty. It does not take much to recognize when these are happening as there are always several black and whites in a very small area, about a square mile for hours. I have had comments from visitors who witness this and ask about it. When I tell them about these activities, they always look in disbelief.

While these activities have become routine, their impact remains disturbing. It is never routine to see people walking away from cars that will be towed, carrying their belongings, groceries, children, and car seats. It is disheartening to see people who are simply living their lives—coming home from work, going to work, going to the doctors, delivering children to school and picking them up. It is difficult to know that parents are deported and their children left with family, friends, or to fend for themselves.

There is a weariness that comes with this much law enforcement and a great sadness to see people criminalized and treated in this manner. It has also created in me a distrust of law enforcement, in those who should be trusted to protect the community. Ultimately, given the increase in the size of the prison-industrial complex of this country, it begs the question of how things will be in the future if law enforcement strategies continue in this trajectory, meaning to target large groups and populations instead of individuals. Living in the barrio has created the realization of the mutuality of freedom—that individual freedom is dependent on and relative to the freedom of all people.

By Mary Jo Poole, January 16, 2011

Using feminist, peacemaking, and critical race theories, analyze the account above. According to the theories, what would be considered deviant in the story above? Why?

◈ Critiques of Critical Theories

It may be unfair to lump the critiques of three such different critical theories as peacemaking, feminist theory, and critical race theory into one discussion, but it seems that one of the main critiques of all three theories is that "they do not see the world the way other theories see the world." In other words, the very features that set these theories apart as unique or special are used to dismiss them. For example, Akers (1998) argued that peacemaking criminology was

> a utopian vision of society that calls for reforming and restructuring to get away from war, crime, and violence. . . . This is a highly laudable philosophy of criminal justice, but it does not offer an explanation of why the system operates as it does or why offenders commit crime. It can be evaluated on other grounds but not on empirical validity. (p. 183)

Moyer (2001) argued that the peacemaking perspective was more likely in its infancy (compared to other crime and deviance theories) and pointed out that Akers offered no empirical evidence himself for his claims. Feminist criminology has often been criticized as reductionist (in other words, reducing the discussion of crime to a single variable)—a critique that is ironic given that one of the main reasons for the emergence of feminist criminology in the first place was the androcentric nature of both theory and research in the field of crime and deviance. Similarly, critical race theory is often criticized for "playing the race card" or essentially making race a singularly important predictor of experience in U.S. society (for a discussion of this critique, see Levit, 1999). In all of these criticisms, the common denominator is that the theories are denounced for critically analyzing the status quo.

Conclusion

Much of the deviance research that exists makes fairly traditional assumptions about how we define deviance. From a traditional perspective, these definitions tend to favor whites, men, and the middle and upper classes. In other words, these groups end up defining what is considered acceptable behavior and deviant behavior. The theories presented in this chapter question the status quo and offer a nontraditional definition of acceptable behavior. What this means is that our taken-for-granted assumptions about deviance are questioned and expanded, allowing for more diversity in our understanding of deviant behavior. Not only do these perspectives give voice to individuals who may more likely be considered deviant, but they also question the very makeup of society as we know it, suggesting that "war-like," patriarchal, racist systems of oppression are what are truly deviant.

EXERCISES AND DISCUSSION QUESTIONS

1. Compare the experience of Muslim Americans after 9/11 with the experience of whites in America after Timothy McVeigh was captured for the Oklahoma City bombing (1995). How would peacemaking criminology and critical race theory explain these different experiences?

2. Choose another structural deviance (like homelessness) and evaluate it using peacemaking, feminist, and critical race theories. What would each theory offer as a public policy to address this deviance?

KEY TERMS

Critical race theory

Feminist criminology

Liberal feminism

Peacemaking criminology

Postmodern feminism

Radical feminism

Restorative justice

Socialist feminism

READING 30

In this article, Radosh uses Richard Quinney's peacemaking approach to think about women, especially mothers in prison. Radosh argues quite persuasively that we need to move toward a peacemaking approach as opposed to a deterrent or retributionist approach to dealing with a social problem as opposed to a social evil. She points to the fact that the vast majority of women and mothers in prison are there for nonviolent, low-level drug dealing (often as a secondary dealer for their boyfriends or husbands) and even simple possession of drugs. Their

Source: Radosh, Polly F. 2002. "Reflections on Women's Crime and Mothers in Prison: A Peacemaking Approach." *Crime & Delinquency* 48:300–316. Reprinted by permission.

fate is due to their lack of education, resources, and support. Furthermore, women's involvement in crime is often due to past experiences and injustices (e.g., domestic violence, child physical and sexual abuse). The fact that some of these experiences were at the hands of males whose punishments were often fairly lenient adds to the injustices in the way females and mothers are dealt with by the criminal justice system. A key feature to think about here is how seriously punishing women for relatively nonserious crimes affects their children—clearly, it harms them. Finally, Radosh argues in line with peacemaking criminology that we need to provide support for the children of women convicted of crimes, not cause undue hardships on them by incarcerating nonviolent women offenders.

Reflections on Women's Crime and Mothers in Prison

A Peacemaking Approach

Polly F. Radosh

What is important in the study of crime is everything that happens before crime occurs. The question of what precedes crime is far more significant to our understanding than the act of crime itself. Crime is a reflection of something larger and deeper.

—Quinney (2000, p. 21)

Among my earliest memories of my childhood in upstate New York is learning to cut with scissors in the Irish Catholic school I attended for the first 9 years of my education. In this school, the nuns were very strict and required absolute attention and adherence to the rules and protocol of the classroom. All of the desks were in neat rows, students stood next to their desks with hands at their sides when called on the answer a question, and when the nun looked down each row of desks she wanted to see all papers aligned at the same angle on the desk and each student holding pencils, scissors, or other implements in exactly the same way. For most students the requirements were not too difficult to master, although there were always a few stray papers that shifted or children who held their pencils in defiance to the required norm, especially in the younger grades. Eventually, everyone adhered to the protocol and there was little correction needed by about the third grade. I had a problem for most of my early education, however, because I am left-handed. It was difficult to get my paper aligned at the appropriate angle on the desk, but eventually I did master this requirement. The biggest problem for me was learning to cut with scissors. The nuns could tolerate my writing with my left hand, but they would not provide left-handed scissors and I was not permitted to use my left hand to cut.

I learned to cut with my right hand because I was not permitted to use my left hand. I eventually mastered the skill completely and today I am perfectly competent in the use of right-handed scissors. I have so completely shifted away from my natural inclination that I am actually no longer able to maneuver my left hand to cut at all. I have transformed my innate preference for my left hand into an adaptation that is so complete that I am no longer able to revert back to my natural inclination, and now I must use right-handed scissors. I have many questions about my adaptation, however: What might I have been able to accomplish if I had been able to develop my natural talents? How has my adaptation shaped my thinking or my personality? What artistic masterpiece of cutting might I have produced if I had not been forced to shift to a more difficult means of achieving my cutting goals? Why was it so important that I conform? and What social, organizational, or human goal was accomplished by my conformity or punishment for nonconformity?

When I think of Richard Quinney's work, I think of my educational experience. There are several parallels to my experience and the effect that Quinney has had on my thinking about crime. First, I believe that his work helps to equip those of us who are metaphorically left-handed in a world of right-handed people with a pair of left-handed scissors. That is, he helps us to see the world as we are naturally inclined to see it, rather than as we are shaped by cultural convention or criminal justice protocol to see it.

This is especially true with his work on peacemaking criminology. From this perspective, crime is produced by factors that are out of the control of the individual, such as political, economic, or social structures that limit human potential. To address crime with violence or punishment will never solve the problem of crime because violence and punishment address only the outcome, not the source of crime. From Quinney's (1991) view, only "understanding, service, justice . . . [which] flow naturally from love and compassion, from mindful attention to the reality of all that is" (p. 4) will solve the problem of crime. To focus on individual failings as the source of crime is myopic. To solve crime by punishing individual failings is unjust and will only create more suffering. What useful purpose is served by punishing, especially for those who violate laws that serve no useful social purpose? Punishing because a violator has broken the law, without attention to the social utility of the law or the good that could be accomplished by compliance, is to attend to the letter of the law and ignore the spirit of support and communal connection that law should engender. To enforce compliance without utilitarian goals is much like forcing left-handed people to cut with right-handed scissors. We can mold most people to conform to the norms, but some people have different backgrounds, experiences, or societal impairments that make conformity differentially more difficult.

Second, he helps us to understand that adherence to laws and protocol merely for the requirement of adherence does nothing to solve social problems, address crime, or eliminate suffering. The requirement in my school that I learn to adapt to a pair of right-handed scissors was a temporary handicap for me. I eventually adapted but the requirement did no lasting good and probably some harm to my developing skills. Quinney's insights into the criminal justice system show us that we often pay such strict attention to the requirements of control and punishment that we miss the meaning of crime. We address the expression of crime, but we ignore the causes of crime. Quinney's work teaches us that humane, nonjudgmental approaches to crime will help us to achieve a more humane society. Just as the goal of using scissors should be cutting, the goal of law should be social good. Intermediary, cumbersome, or painful obstacles to attaining the goal should be eliminated.

Third, rules, law, protocol, ordinances, and all of the other mechanisms we use to "keep peace" in our society are a means of preserving order, but we often become so focused on the rules that we have forgotten why the rules were important in the first place. Often the requirement of adherence to law is much more important that the harm that would be done by law violation. Learning to cut with my right hand was important only because it was a rule, not because it would improve my skills, make me a better person, or cause chaos in the classroom if I did not adhere to the rule. Such is the case with enforcement of many laws. With women's crime, in particular, adherence to the law is required because it is the law, not because it promotes social justice, public order, or a better quality of life.

From his 1970swork that articulated the effect of capitalistic structures on individual action to Quinney's current work on peacemaking, love, and existentialism, the underlying structures that shape social action have been a thematic concern in his explanations of crime. Actions are shaped by forces that go beyond free will or opportunity. Events, structures, systems of oppression, and power affect human choices and predicate personal interests. Events that precede crime are as important to understanding crime as are the actual criminal events. Quinney's work is like the use of the metaphorical "left-handed scissors"—it helps us to see that law has layers of meaning that are obscured when we focus merely on the act of law violation. The true meanings of law, the life experiences of the law violator, and underlying social inequities that produce crime are not addressed. Instead, the illegal act is addressed through punishment.

From my first reading of Quinney's work when I was a student in the 1970s, I have returned innumerable times to his writings as a touchstone for my own understanding of women's crime. In no other field of inquiry do his theories make more sense. Structure, oppression, economic exploitation, and marginalized social opportunity explain almost all of women's crime. Minor drug crimes committed by women, for example, draw sentences as long as, and sometimes longer than, serious male crime. Women's crime is defined as symbolically equivalent to serious men's crime, even when it is not. For many years I have returned to Quinney to help in my own understanding of this apparent injustice. It is not only patriarchy that explains this but also the defining structures of capitalism that allocate authority for criminal definitions in the hands of the powerful. Women, who lack significant social power, are defined as criminal through definitions created to verify the existing social order. Prevailing popular views about crime and criminals, as well as public criminal justice policies, legitimate the existing system as a reflection of justice. If we use the metaphorical "left-handed scissors," Quinney's work helps us to see that women's crime is a reflection

of social injustice. When we see the world as it is rather than as we are conditioned to see it, women's crime has new meaning.

Women's crime is grounded in exploitation. Without exploitation there would not be crime. Nearly all of women's crime is related to sexual exploitation, abuse, poverty, and structural inequality. Quinney's most recent work, which explores the relationship between mature love and a world without crime, provides an especially clear lens with which to focus women's crime. A world without crime is one in which crime would not be possible because inner individual peace is reflected in peaceful coexistence (Quinney, 2000, p. 21). Crime is produced by human suffering. The connection between suffering and women's crime is widely acknowledged by academics as well as administrators of women's prisons. There is little dispute about the connections, but there is considerable disagreement about the most appropriate response to women's crime. A mature response would mean that we should move beyond the act of law violation and address the means by which the human needs of the law violator may be met. To focus on punishment of the offender ignores the fact that the crime reflects events that happened prior to the criminal action. The crime cannot be understood without attention to the prior experience, and punishment will do nothing to address the prior experience or to help the offender move beyond the pain that is reflected in crime.

Contemporary Thinking About Crime

Quinney's summary of the criminal justice system in the United States, organized around the belief that those who commit crimes deserve their punishments, is as true today as it was when he published *Class, State ,and Crime* in 1977 (p. 21). Modern thinking about crime says that it results from personal failures, lack of self-control, weakness, laziness, moral lapse, or other character flaws that inhibit self-restraint. Those who commit crimes should be willing to pay the penalties for their mistakes, given the widely know "hard on crime" political ideology characterized by punitive sentencing strategies that have been well-known and highly publicized for more than 20 years. According to the predominant paradigm, one of the most important goals of criminal justice policy should be deterrence produced through sure, swift, and severe punishment. A second important goal is to restore "balance" through retribution or to ensure that the offender "pays" his or her debt to society by suffering the pains of imprisonment.[1]

◈ Women Offenders

Criminologists are in general agreement that across time and in all cultures, women's crime is less serious and less frequent than men's. Even with significant changes in sentencing and a rapid increase in the prison population in the United States in recent years, women's incarceration remains a small fraction of men's.

Both arrest patterns and incarceration trends indicated that almost all of women's crime in the 20th century has been concentrated in the area of low-level property or public order (prostitution) crime.[2] In the 1980s, an additional "feminine" crime surfaced, with changes in U.S. drug laws. In 1997, for example, 74% of women in federal and 35% in state prisons had been sentenced to prison for a drug crime (Mumola, 2000, p. 6). This compares with 67% of men in federal and 23% in state prisons who were incarcerated for drug crimes. About 72% of women under correctional supervision in jail, on probation, or in prison during the 1990s had committed a property, drug, or public order offense (Greenfield & Snell, 1999).

Women's involvement in drug crime is usually low-level dealing or delivery activities, although about 10% of federal and 15% of state female inmates have been incarcerated for possession (Mumola, 2000, p. 6). Limited economic circumstances motivate some nonusers of drugs to sell. Of those women incarcerated during the 1990s, only 40% indicated that they had been employed during the months prior to their arrest (compared to 60% of men) and 30% were on welfare. Nearly 40% of those who were employed earned less than $600 per month (Greenfield & Snell, 1999, p. 8). Women with few economic alternatives, limited life skills, and great economic need often participate in the drug trade as a means of supplementing their income. Risk of detection is exacerbated by their low-level, high-visibility positions in the drug distribution network.

In addition to difficult economic circumstances, 60% of incarcerated women in state prisons indicated in surveys between 1995 and 1997 that they had been physically or sexually abused in the past (Greenfield & Snell, 1999, p. 1). Women who had spent some of their childhood in foster care or institutions indicated that they had been victims of sexual or physical abuse in 87% of cases. Of those who grew up in homes where parents abused alcohol or drugs, 76% reported prior abuse; and among those who lived in homes where a family member had been incarcerated, prior abuse was reported among 64% of female inmates. In about 95% of cases among all abused women in jail, on probation, or incarcerated in a federal or state prison, the perpetrator of the abuse was someone they knew, such as a relative, their mother's boyfriend, or a family friend (Greenfield & Snell, 1999, p. 3). Not surprisingly, 80% of those with a history of abuse were regular users of drugs at the time of their arrest (Greenfield & Snell, 1999, p. 3).

The life circumstances of incarcerated women help to explain much of their criminal behavior. Whereas many people who have lived in poverty or who have been victims of abuse do not commit crimes, the common thread of continuity that runs through the history of women's incarceration is that most women in prison share common life experiences. They are very likely to have been living in poverty, have experienced prior abuse by male friends and relatives, have had childhood experiences that included substance abuse by parents, have been sexually abused as children, and suffer with personal stress, trauma, and fear in many stages of their lives. According to the National Institute of Justice, the needs of women in prison are different from men and thus require different programming:

> Women in prison have some needs that are quite different from men's resulting in part from women's disproportionate victimization from sexual or physical abuse and in part from their responsibility for children. Women offenders are also more likely than men to

have become addicted to drugs, to have mental illnesses, and to have been unemployed before incarceration. (Morash, Bynum, & Koons, 1998, p. 1)

Each of the special problems of female inmates may seem to be a separate issue, but they actually weave together into a complex set of problems that have been rarely addressed by the correctional system. Women whose life experiences have presented many overwhelming personal problems often seek relief in substances that ease their pain. Common backgrounds of poverty, physical and sexual abuse, and accompanying feelings of loss, betrayal, depression, and desperation spawn ongoing personal problems that are highly likely to result in recidivism if they are not addressed.

◆ Incarceration Patterns

The number of people incarcerated in U.S. prisons and jails has increased to unprecedented levels in the past two decades. In 1980 the national rate of incarceration was 139, but this had risen to 682 by mid-year 1999 (Beck, 2000, p. 2; Gilliard, 1993, p. 2). Table 1 illustrates some of the growth in incarceration rates since 1980.

Women represent a small overall proportion of the prison population, even though the percentage of women in prison is increasing faster than the percentage of men (Beck, 2000, p. 1). Regardless of the rapid increase in women's incarceration, men are still 16 times more likely to serve time in a state or federal prison (Beck, 2000, p. 4). The overall greater likelihood of men to serve time in prison has meant that for most of the 20th century, women's corrections received little attention. It was not until the number of women incarcerated began to rise in the early 1980s that researchers began to address either the patterns of women's incarceration or programming in women's prisons.

As research has articulated some of the unique characteristics of female inmates, patterns that differentiate women from men have become apparent. Female inmates, for example, are more likely to have been convicted of a nonviolent crime, have a prior history of physical or sexual abuse, be incarcerated for a drug offense, and have been the primary caretaker for their children prior to their incarceration.

Traditionally, women received longer sentences than men for the same offenses because female offenders often deviated significantly from expected gender role restrictions that required a higher degree of self-control and lifestyle restrictions than would be typical expectations for men. Studies of sentencing, for example, have indicated that women were sentenced longer than men for the same offense because it often appeared

Table 1   Incarceration Trends, 1980–1999: Number and Rate[a] of Incarceration

| Year | Total | Rate | Men | | Women | |
			Number	Rate	Number	Rate
1980	315,974	139	303,643	275	12,331	11
1985	480,568	202	458,972	397	21,296	17
1990	739,980	297	699,416	575	40,564	32
1995	1,085,363	411	1,021,463	796	63,900	48
1999[b]	1,860,520	682	1,246,362	897	87,199	57

Source: Adapted from Maguire and Pastore (1999, p. 490) and Gilliard (1993, p. 4).

a. The rate of incarceration is the number of people incarcerated for every 100,000 population.

b. Mid-year estimates.

to judges that female offenders were "worse" than male offenders. Only a few women, by comparison to men, engaged in crime, which implied that such behavior by women was an especially abhorrent anomaly to typical "female behavior" (Lanagan & Dawson, 1993, p. 2; Parisi, 1982). Patriarchal definitions of women's "proper" nurturing roles affected judicial decision making in such a way that judges often believed that women's crime was not only law violation but also "unnatural." The subtle but widely dispersed belief that female criminals were "worse" than men translated into longer average sentences for women. Whereas all prisoners are serving longer sentences under new mandatory sentencing laws, much of the gender disparity in sentencing that had resulted in lengthy prison terms for women prior to the mid-1980s has been significantly reduced.

Sentencing reform in the mid-1980s highlighted rational criteria in sentencing, which reduced the disparity between men's and women's sentences. Factors such as prior offense history, use of a weapon in commission of the crime, whether the offense was violent, and other criteria related to the characteristics of both the offense and the offender are now used to set the length of sentences under minimum mandatory guidelines. Women rarely commit violent crimes, and they have much lower rates of recidivism than men. As a result, women's sentences for index crimes are comparable to equally charged and convicted men.

Although objective criteria in sentencing are much more consistent than they were prior to sentencing reform, other gender differences in offending patterns, as well as gender-specific patterns related to sentencing, do work against women in drug cases. Women's involvement in the drug trade is usually at the lowest level of participation. Under federal drug conspiracy laws, participants with minor roles are sentenced as long, and often longer, than those with key roles in the distribution network. A woman who drives her boyfriend to make drug deals and waits in the car until after the deal is completed may end up serving a longer sentence than her boyfriend, who is the actual dealer. Drug convictions and sentencing rely very heavily on informant deals. The driver in the car would not have knowledge that would be beneficial to authorities and thus could not "deal" with prosecutors on her own

behalf. Also, loyalty to boyfriends or husbands prevents many women from making deals, even when they have such knowledge. A review of more than 60,000 federal drug cases indicates that men are much more willing to sell out women to get a shorter sentence than women are likely to sell out men (Szalavitz, 1999, p. 43). Women are frequently convicted of drug crimes when they have had no involvement or very little knowledge of their boyfriend's involvement. Women, for example, have been convicted of "improper use of the telephone" or answering the phone for what later turned out to be a drug sale (Szalavitz, 1999, p. 43).

◈ Inmate Mothers

In 1999, there were about 87,000 women incarcerated in prisons and jails in the United States. This represents 6.5% of the prison population (Beck, 2000, p. 4). Although the exact percentage of female inmates with children is not known, most estimates indicate that about 80% have dependent children at the time that they are incarcerated (Watterson, 1996, p. 210; Williams, 1996, p. 80). In 1999, there were at least 126,100 children with mothers in prison, and the mean age for all children with parents in prison was 8 years (Mumola, 2000, p. 2).

There are many more children with fathers in prison than mothers, but incarcerated mothers are more likely to have been living with their children prior to incarceration (Mumola, 2000, p. 2).[3] Undoubtedly, the social and emotional trauma inherent in incarceration of a parent produces significant strain on all children with imprisoned parents, but the pain is especially significant for those whose families were broken by the incarceration of a parent. More than 60% of fathers in state prisons and more than half of those in federal prisons did not live with their children in the months before arrest. But about 60% of mothers in state prisons and 73% of those in federal prisons did live with their children before arrest (Mumola, 2000, p. 2).

In addition to the obvious stress created by separation, there are other concerns associated with incarceration of mothers. About 25% of incarcerated women are pregnant or have recently given birth at the time of their incarceration. Separation from a newborn infant creates additional stress, worry, and anxiety for an incarcerated mother. Their unique concerns are different from the typical worries of other parents who are separated from their children while in prison.

Most research on the effects of incarceration on parenting or on children have focused on the immediate issues related to stress, anxiety, maintaining strong family ties, and other programmatic concerns. The issue is much wider than the immediate needs of inmates or families, however. Factors related to the life histories and crimes of inmate mothers both explain incarceration patterns and influence post release family unity.

Although incarcerated women are not a monolithic group, their background characteristics are much more similar than those of incarcerated men. The overriding experience of abuse and very common pattern of substance abuse by female offenders are linked. Most incarcerated women enter prison with these problems. The fact that most also have dependent children means that many of the problems of female inmates also present problems for their children. To be effective, programming in women's prisons must address the unique characteristics of incarcerated women, as well as promote family growth and unity. Despite widespread recognition of the unique needs of female inmates, 39 states use the same classification instrument for men and women, in 7 states the male instrument is adapted for women, and only 3 states use a special instrument for female inmates (Mumola, 2000, p. 3). By most accounts, the special needs of female inmates are met with sporadic, inconsistent, inappropriate, or inadequate programming.

Women are very likely to return to their children after release from prison. Among the many differences between male and female inmates is an overriding concern among women for the welfare of their children while they are in prison and high anxiety about how they will provide for their children when they are released. Programming in women's prisons only sporadically addresses these concerns.

But by most accounts, programming for female inmates fails to address the issues that are most important for humanistic reasons and are most likely to reduce recidivism. As one administrator in the National Institute of Justice's survey of approaches to women's programming indicated, "Women who are victims of abuse tend to continue on as victims of abuse. Men on the other hand, tend to react to their own history of victimization by becoming abusers themselves" (Mumola, 2000, p. 10). And, as another prison administrator indicated in a private conversation, the most consistent pattern among all incarcerated women is that they "have been battered beyond belief."[4]

Female inmates have generally used more drugs and used them more frequently than men prior to their incarceration (Morash et al., 1998, p. 1). Drugs have provided a means of escape for most female inmates. Incarceration frequently provides their first opportunity to evaluate their own lives and the effects of their decisions on their children. Female inmates' needs are different from male inmates' and interrelated to both their prior history and their future parenting skills.

◈ Punishment, Women's Crime, and Parenting

Current punishment strategies that focus on instilling future goals of self-restraint, personal control, and moral strength through retribution for wrongful behavior are inadequate, illogical, and futile as a response to women's crime. The prior life experiences of incarcerated women dictate more humane and constructive approaches than characterize contemporary strategies. To use contemporary retribution models as a response to women's crime fails to recognize the prior precipitating experiences of women. Their crime does not fit the justice model for several reasons.

First, women's crime is generally nonviolent and low-level. It is often punished with serious prison time, not because of the inherent harmfulness of their criminal acts but because of their lack of power or knowledge with which to negotiate prosecutorial deals, especially in drug cases. The punishment does not fit either the crime or the offender.

Second, women's crime commonly reflects prior life experiences with men who clearly perpetrated serious criminal acts, such as childhood sexual molestation, rape, incest, and domestic violence. The fact that such offenders frequently were not prosecuted or punished cannot frame the defense of women in their current offense. Yet the underlying injustice inherent in societal tolerance of suffering on one level, while overreacting to less serious crime on another level, frames a basic violation of human rights. If the justice model, which applies a hard-on-crime strategy to combat women's drug crime, were applied evenly, the issues that frame women's incarceration would be different. The dismissal or trivial reactions to the more serious actions of prior male offenders who have abused and mistreated female offenders at earlier stages of their life, however, contributes to the profound feelings of inevitable loss and hopelessness that are graphic in the stories of female offenders. Women's crime does not fit the hard-on-crime justice model because the penalties are often especially hard-on-women's-crime. Whereas many men have been unduly sentenced to very long prison terms on the basis of this philosophy, the pattern among women is rather overwhelming.

Third, the punishment of women's relatively non-serious crime with the same vehemence with which serious male crime is addressed hurts children. Among the most consistent themes that run through the literature about inmate mothers is the intense sense of loss, betrayal, desperation, and hopelessness that accompanies their incarceration. Their children suffer the loss of their mother while the hard-on-crime political strategy publicizes justice and deterrence. Children and society would be better served by more reasonable, proportionate sentences or no punishment at all. To perpetuate injustice into the lives of children whose mothers have been incarcerated for their boyfriends' crimes, as is frequently the case with drug crime, is inhumane, counterproductive, and futile. Women who have been victimized through multiple stages of patriarchy, exploitation, and marginalized social opportunities need understanding, support, and many therapeutic services. Punishment is the least effective way to address their crime. Among women, crime is often an obvious symptom of their suffering at another level.

Fourth, in keeping with Quinney's basic principles of peacemaking, societal response to women's crime should accommodate the unique features of their offending patterns. Women's prior experiences of exploitation should be addressed in treatment. Children of women who have committed crimes should be supported with reasonable, positive opportunities for growth and development. Punishment does not serve this end.

Prison Programs for Mothers

Mothers in prison have the same worries and concerns that all parents have about their children, but their inability to fulfill parental responsibilities for their children creates fear for their emotional and physical well-being, as well as great grief and anxiety over loss of involvement in their children's lives. Common backgrounds of abuse, high likelihood of drug involvement, and probable poverty also indicate that parenting and life-skill programs are essential for post release success. Drug addiction treatment and therapy that helps offenders deal with problems of past sexual abuse and family violence are especially critical because these factors are linked to women's criminal behavior, as well as to their parenting skills.

The most common programming options available for inmate mothers are those that allow for special visitation. The "Girls Scouts Beyond Bars" program, for example, has initiated girl scout troops in five states: Ohio, New Jersey, Missouri, Maryland, and Florida (Moses 1995, p. 1). Girl scouts with incarcerated mothers may belong to special girl scout troops that meet in prison. The purpose of the program is to enhance parenting skills for the mother and maintain involvement of mothers in their daughters' lives.

Most states provide either regular or occasional special visitation for families of inmates. Ohio and Illinois, for example, allow children of inmates to camp on the grounds of the prison with their mothers on some weekends during the summer. Ohio runs a 3-day day camp where inmates interact with their children in the camp. Pennsylvania gives children a book that helps them understand the pain of separation from their mothers, and they provide in-home social work to caregivers of incarcerated mothers' children. The New York Department of Corrections provides for extended overnight visits with families at 18 prisons. They also provide transportation to the prisons and operate play areas and hospitality centers for families. Texas allows for weekly contact visits between mothers and their children.[5]

The most innovative and comprehensive programs are in New York, Nebraska, Illinois, and California. Each of these states has some variation of the prison nursery program that was started in the women's prison at Bedford Hills, New York, in 1901. Nebraska's program is patterned after the Bedford Hills program. In both of these programs, mothers who have been convicted of an offense that did not involve their children and who have less than 2 years of their sentence left to serve may keep their babies with them in prison. Counseling, support groups, parenting classes, substance abuse treatment, and employment preparation are integral components of both programs. California offers prisoner mother/infant programs, which are operated by private agencies under contract with the state, at six locations. Illinois contracts with a nonprofit agency to run the Women's Treatment Center, where inmates keep their children with them in a converted hospital (Christian, 2000; Ervin, 1998, p. 14; Lays, 1992, pp. 44–51).[6] Both the California programs and the Illinois treatment center include substance abuse treatment, occupational counseling, and support groups in their treatment strategies. Two additional states, Ohio and Vermont, are exploring the possibility of inmate nursery programs.

◈ Effectiveness of Mother-Infant Programs

Although comprehensive statistical analysis of four programs would not provide meaningful data, the success of mother-infant programs is accepted as definitive in those states that have funded these programs. The most common measures of success may give only vague insight into the utility of these programs, however. Recidivism, which measures the likelihood of reoffense among released inmates, is decidedly lower for women who participate in mother-infant programs. Women's recidivism is generally much lower than men's, but mother-infant programs claim a further reduction of 20% to 50% in recidivism. In other words, mothers who participate are not likely to return to prison (Christian, 2000; Ervin, 1998, p. 14; Lays, 1992, pp. 44–51).[7] Whether the recidivism results from the success of the programs or the selection of inmates who participate in the programs is less clear. Supporters of mother-infant programs claim that both the opportunity to interact with their infants in a controlled, supportive environment

and the comprehensive counseling that accompanies these programs are what lead to their success.

The success of children whose lives are enhanced by their mothers' opportunity to participate in a mother-infant program are less easily studied. Researchers and advocates for more humane treatment of female prisoners have pointed out for many years that children of inmate mothers suffer tremendous loss and experience profound alteration of their lives. Critics may contend that mothers should have thought of these issues prior to committing the crime for which they were incarcerated. But the pervasive patterns of physical and sexual abuse, drug addiction, and emotional pain characteristic of female inmates prohibits the sort of reflective thinking that would have prevented their crime, regardless of how much they love their children. And wider structures of patriarchy and capitalism are not even imagined as sources of women's crime, by this reasoning. The result of more compassionate response to women's crime is that children who are connected in meaningful ways with their incarcerated mothers are less likely to feel abandoned, isolated, and lonely.

Prisoner programs that address the complex nature of women's confinement, which include treatment for emotional and substance abuse problems and help them to achieve purposeful child rearing, offer the most promise for post release success and successful parenting. Models available in Nebraska, New York, Illinois, and California may provide insight into the importance of strengthening family bonds for inmate mothers and their children.

◈ Conclusions

The horrifying, heartbreaking experiences that incarcerated mothers live with, or relive in prison, often overwhelm intentions for good parenting. Thus, prison programming that addresses only parenting skills or which narrowly focuses on specific occupational skills will fail to address the needs of incarcerated women. Comprehensive approaches that treat addiction, depression, occupational skills, and parenting offer the most affective options. Women's incarceration stems not only from a conviction for a specific crime but also from an array of social problems that affect women as a group and which permeate many facets of American culture. As Quinney told us, what has gone on before the crime tells us more than the act itself. The life patterns of incarcerated women poignantly illustrate Quinney's point. Humane, supportive, and therapeutic responses to female offenders would also address what has gone on before the criminal act.

Cultural devaluation of women results in exploitation, abuse, and mistreatment. The specific illustrations of the suffering of female victims are visible in the faces of incarcerated women. To ignore the cultural problems that give rise to women's crime is to blame the victims of abuse for their own abuse. In the short term, women who are empowered to control their own lives and avoid men who abuse and exploit them will be the most successful after release from prison. They will also be better mothers who may be able to break the cycles of abuse that are very commonly characteristic of their own lives and the lives of their mothers. In the long term, ending patriarchal exploitation and economic inequality and fostering humane, compassionate respect for human potential are essential to a peaceful society, and they are what will end women's crime.

Crime will continue until we end suffering. If we robotically adhere to laws and models of justice without understanding the sources of crime, we will not be able to end suffering. With Quinney's poignant explanations of what it takes to end suffering in mind, we must abandon the philosophy of punishment and find a means of supporting female offenders by responding to the sources of their suffering. In other words, we must find a means of cutting through the arbitrary rules to find the true meaning of the actions.

◈ Notes

1. Alternative perspectives are sometimes discussed, although they have found little representation in contemporary criminal justice policies. Liberal critics of contemporary trends suggest that education, investment in neighborhoods, community building, and jobs training could counter crime with positive alternatives. Those who offer solutions to crime in this venue stress the importance of investment in programs to improve the quality of life among those most vulnerable to crime. Poor neighborhoods, inadequately funded schools, hopelessness fostered by urban decay, and insufficient investment in those with the fewest social opportunities produce crime, from this perspective. Solutions require investment and commitment to improve. For discussion of the underlying philosophy of criminal justice policy, see Walker (2001, chap. 1).

2. See, for example, Steffensmeier and Allan (1996, pp. 459—487) and Messerschmidt (1986).

3. There are estimated to be 1.3 million children with fathers in prison.

4. Conversation with Jane Higgins in 1989, when she was warden of Dwight Correctional Facility in Dwight, Illinois.

5. See the Directory of Programs for Families of Inmates at http://www.fenetwork.org/ Dir98/dir98f-n.html.

6. See the Directory of Programs for Families of Inmates at http://www.cdc.state.ca.us/program/ mother.htm.

7. See the Directory of Programs for Families of Inmates at http://www.cdc.state.ca.us/program/ mother.htm.

◈ References

Beck, A. J. (2000). Prison and jail inmates at midyear 1999. In *Bureau of Justice Statistics* Bulletin. Washington, DC: U.S. Government Printing Office.

Christian, S. E. (2000, January 25). Pregnant inmates get county help with MOM. *Chicago Tribune,* p. 1.

Ervin, M. (1998). A center for jailed mothers. *Progressive,* 62, 10.

Gilliard, D. K. (1993). Prisoners in 1992. In *Bureau of Justice Statistics Bulletin.* Washington, DC: U.S. Government Printing Office.

Greenfield, L. A.,& Snell, T. L. (1999).Women offenders. In *Bureau of Justice Statistics Special Report.* Washington, DC: U.S. Government Printing Office.

Lanagan, P., & Dawson, J. (1993). Felony sentences in state courts, 1990. In *Bureau of Justice Statistics Bulletin.* Washington, DC: U.S. Government Printing Office.

Lays, J. (1992). Babies behind bars. *State Legislatures,* 18(5), 44–51.

Maguire, K.,& Pastore, A. L. (Eds.). (1999). *Sourcebook of criminal justice statistics* 1998 (U.S. Department of Justice Statistics, Bureau of Justice Statistics). Washington, DC: U.S. Government Printing Office.

Messerschmidt, J. (1986). *Capitalism, patriarchy, and crime: Toward a social feminist criminology.* Totowa, NJ: Rowman and Littlefield.

Morash, M., Bynum, T. S., & Koons, B. A. (1998).Women offenders: Programming needs and promising approaches. In *National Institute of Justice Research in Brief* (U.S. Department of Justice Office of Justice Programs). Washington, DC: U.S. Government Printing Office.

Moses, M. C. (1995). Keeping incarcerated mothers and their daughters together: Girl scouts beyond bars. In *National Institute of Justice Program Focus.* Washington, DC: U.S. Department of Justice.

Mumola, C. (2000). Incarcerated parents and their children. In *Bureau of Justice Statistics Special Report.* Washington, DC: U.S. Government Printing Office.

Parisi, N. (1982). Are females treated differently? In N. H. Rafter & E. A. Stanko (Eds.), *Judge, lawyer, victim, thief* (pp. 205–220). Boston: Northeastern University Press.

Quinney, R. (1977). *Class, state and crime: On the theory and practice of criminal justice.* New York: David McKay.

Quinney, R. (1991). The way of peace: On crime, suffering, and service. In H. E. Pepinsky & R. Quinney (Eds.), *Criminology as peacemaking* (pp. 3–13). Bloomington: Indiana University Press.

Quinney, R. (2000). Socialist humanism and the problem of crime: Thinking about Erich Fromm in the development of critical/peacemaking criminology. In K. Anderson & R. Quinney (Eds.), *Erich Fromm and critical criminology: Beyond the punitive society* (p. 21). Urbana: University of Illinois.

Steffensmeier, D., & Allan, E. (1996). Gender and crime: Toward a gendered theory of female offending. *Annual Review of Sociology, 22,* 459–487.

Szalavitz, M. (1999, Winter). War on drugs, war on women. *On the Issues,* 8(1), 42–45.

Walker, S. (2001). *Sense and nonsense about crime and drugs: A policy guide* (5th ed.). Belmont, CA: Wadsworth.

Watterson, K. (1996). *Women in prison: Inside the concrete womb.* Boston: Northeastern University Press.

Williams, E. F. (1996, October). Fostering the mother-child bond in a correctional setting. *Corrections Today,* pp. 80–81.

❖   ❖   ❖

READING 31

Myths about violence against women abound, but those employed or who volunteer to help those violently or sexually victimized are generally educated about those myths. In particular, those who provide support for victims of violence are taught to avoid "blaming the victim." In this study, the researchers interviewed 15 victim support volunteers (13 women and 2 men) who clearly have been trained that violent victimization is not the fault of the victim. They clearly know the "correct answer" to questions regarding victim blame is that "No, I don't think the victim's to blame. Only the aggressor" (p. 41). However, on more in-depth questioning, it becomes clear that these volunteers do, at least to some extent, perceive the victim to be responsible for the victimization. The authors clearly state that they do not "blame the volunteers" but recognize the need for further training.

"But Sometimes I Think . . . They Put Themselves in the Situation"

Exploring Blame and Responsibility in Interpersonal Violence

Suruchi Thapar-Björkert and Karen J. Morgan

 Introduction

In this article, we examine some of the processes and mechanisms through which prevalent ideological and social discourses of violence provide legitimacy to the imminent nature of domestic and sexual violence in the United Kingdom. Our article draws attention to the importance of understanding the social contexts and social worlds in which violence and victimization are understood and conceptualized. We argue that these

Source: Thapar-Björkert, Suruchi, and Karen J. Morgan. 2010. "'But Sometimes I Think . . . They Put Themselves in the Situation': Exploring Blame and Responsibility in Interpersonal Violence." *Violence Against Women* 16(1): 32–59. Reprinted with permission.

social contexts inform understandings of those supporting victims of violence and thereby contribute to an ideologically dilemmatic situation between a culture of blame, on one hand, and a culture of responsibility, on the other. Drawing on empirical data, we highlight three key themes contributing to this culture of blame and responsibility: First, the burden of responsibility is placed on women for their victimization, and in doing so it absolves the perpetrators from accepting accountability for their own actions. Second, victims of violence are often placed under surveillance and expected to conform to regulated behavior by perpetrators, by those from whom they seek help, and by society at large. Third, we suggest that certain unintentional institutional attitudes may not sufficiently challenge the prevalent discourses toward victims of violence.

The article is structured in the following way: First, we highlight the qualitative methodological approaches that inform the analyses of this article. Second, we provide a background to some of the key feminist debates on domestic and sexual violence. Given the vast amount of literature already available on the topic, in this article, we emphasize those issues that are most relevant to our analysis. Third, we examine some of the discursive frameworks that facilitate a culture of blame and responsibility in relation to women experiencing violence. We believe that there is a dialectical relationship between society and discourse, with society (and culture) both being shaped by and simultaneously constituting discourse (Wodak, 1996, cited in Titscher, Meyer, Wodak, & Vetter, 2000, p. 146). This we will mainly analyze through the narratives of volunteers working for the U.K. charity, Victim Support (VS). Finally, we conclude by suggesting that a more thorough engagement with feminist research, traditions, and philosophy could lead to a reassessment of some institutional attitudes toward women experiencing violence.

◈ Method

Our focus for this article is the United Kingdom, and we will draw on discourses deployed by those with particular expertise of working with women victims of violence. We will specifically engage with the narratives of VS

volunteers who operate through a network of local charities that provide support to crime victims throughout the United Kingdom.[1] For the research on which this article is based, a total 15 VS volunteers, aged between 22 and 65, were interviewed, 13 of whom were women and 2 were men—a reflection of the gender split among outreach support volunteers in the organization as a whole (VS, 2005). According to the 2001 Census, the geographical area in which most of the research was conducted has a population that is 97.6% White, 1.4% Asian or British Asian, 0.8% mixed race, 0.7% Black or Black British, and 0.5% Chinese or Other (National Statistics Online, 2001). During 2003/2004, the ethnic breakdown of VS volunteers in the area scheme in which the research was conducted was 92.9% White and 7.1% from Black and minority ethnic groups (VS, 2005). In the specific branch from which the volunteers who participated in the research were recruited, at the time of the research, the breakdown of volunteers was 100% White. Not surprisingly therefore, all the volunteers who participated in the research were White British. Suffice it to say, however, that those interviewed for the research are not intended to be seen as a representative sample of the United Kingdom as a whole but are rather intended to illustrate the type of attitudes prevalent within certain communities.

With the agreement of the relevant VS branch coordinator, the volunteers were approached by the second author who had herself worked as a VS volunteer for several years. All those approached had previously been met by the second author at various meeting and training events, although none of them was known well and the relationship with all of them was little more than that of casual acquaintance. At a volunteers' meeting, the second author talked a little about the research and made a general request for participants. However, to avoid the possibility that any of the volunteers may have felt compelled to agree to take part by the fact that the scheme coordinator was present at the meeting (see Tisdall, 2003), they were subsequently approached individually and in private. Of the 20 volunteers asked, all agreed to be interviewed. In practice, however, it was not possible to interview all those who agreed for a variety of reasons, such as illness, personal problems, and leaving VS.

All but two of the interviews were conducted in the volunteers' own homes (the remaining two were conducted in the second author's home). All volunteer-participants readily agreed that the interviews could be recorded with none expressing any concerns about confidentiality (although two did request that the recorder be switched off for a few minutes during their interview as they gossiped about colleagues). At the beginning of each interview, informed consent was obtained, with the nature of the research being explained and confidentiality issues discussed. It was reiterated that the participant was free to refuse to answer any questions, request that the recorder be turned off, and/or terminate the interview at any time.[2] None of the participants expressed concerns about any of these issues. However, it is not clear whether their particularly relaxed attitudes were due to the fact that they knew the second author was also a volunteer with VS and thus used to dealing with sensitive and confidential matters or because they felt that they were talking about others rather than anything particularly personal.

Furthermore, although the interviews with the volunteer-participants were intended to be comparatively loosely structured, it is problematic to refer unreflexively to unstructured interviews.[3] Nevertheless, these interviews, to a large extent, were driven by the participants and provided the freedom to explore any unexpected areas that arose throughout the discussion. The interview data were analyzed bearing in mind Ruthellen Josselson's (2004) reworking of Ricoeur's (1981) hermeneutics of faith, in which the central process involves understanding the research participants' narratives from his or her point of view rather than regarding them with suspicion.[4]

VS

Although VS operates as an independent organization, at the time of the research, it received the majority of its funds from the U.K. government's Home Office and the rest from private fund-raising, local council grants, or sources such as the European Commission or Lottery funding (VS, 2006). The issue of funding is an important one, not least from a feminist perspective.

As Radford and Stanko (1996) note, "despite the commitment of some feminist volunteers within victim support, the philosophy of the national organization, Victim Support, is actively non-feminist" (p. 74). This has to be located with in the wider political climate of support, whereby "respectable" groups such as VS are supported, often at the expense of "more radical, anti-racist and pro-feminist groups" such as Women's Aid and Rape Crisis (Williams, 1999, p. 388).[5] In fact, arguably, the Victim's Charter[6] maintains the government's policy of marginalizing "pro-feminist, anti-racist and single issue, self-help victims organisations by the simple expedient of ignoring their existence" (Williams, 1999, p. 394).

Victim Support's remit at the time the research was conducted involved offering a range of services to victims of crime:

- providing free and confidential, emotional, and practical help and advice;
- liaising with criminal justice agencies on behalf of victims;
- coordinating support from other agencies and community organizations;
- carrying out research and public education into issues affecting crime victims;
- lobbying government on behalf of crime victims and witnesses;
- providing support via the Witness Service (sister organization) to witnesses attending court (Crown or Magistrates' Courts) to give evidence;
- liaising with the Witness Service to provide a continuation of service and support for victims giving evidence (National Audit Office, 2002; VS, 2006).[7]

The majority of volunteers with the organization provide support to victims of a variety of incidents, ranging from burglary to the most serious violent crimes including domestic and sexual abuse. At the time the research on which this article draws was conducted, most of the work carried out by volunteers was outreach support—going out to see victims in their homes. More recently, however, there has been a shift toward providing helpline support with only victims of more serious crimes tending to receive personal visits.

The strength of the VS role and of particular relevance for this article, we suggest, is the fact that the volunteers may be seen as expert-amateurs. Although they lack professional involvement with victims, though some volunteers may of course have a relevant professional capacity in addition to their voluntary role (in their paid employment, for example, as social workers), they are provided with specialist training that is intended to highlight the problems and issues faced by victims of crime. Accordingly, the volunteers must be seen as somewhere between those who have little or no awareness of issues relating to victims of violence (other than the commonsense understandings acquired through routine social interactions) and those who have acquired knowledge through their own victimization. It should be pointed out, of course, that the motivation for some of the volunteers working with VS is the fact that they have themselves experienced some form of victimization. The rationale for the provision of support through volunteers is that they help to restore faith in the local community. The fact that their work is unpaid is seen as going some way toward redressing the balance as regards the harm the victim has had caused to them (Personal communication, VS trainer, March, 2003).

It is worth nothing that as compared to VS, victim advocacy (as it is called in the United States)[8] seems a more formal, proactive system of support. Dunn and Powell-Williams (2007) suggest that victim advocacy in the United States has "recently become a profession in addition to a calling" (p. 978). It has therefore become increasingly professionalized, using paid staff rather than volunteers, unlike the explicitly volunteer-driven focus of VS. However, recent changes within VS in the United Kingdom have meant a greater emphasis on "advocacy," which is described as being "about taking action to help people say what they want, claim their rights, represent their interests and obtain the services they need" (VS, 2007, p. 60). Still, at present, the provision of an explicit advocacy service is not widespread within the organization.

McDermott and Garofola (2004) discuss "follow-up advocacy" and "victim safety checks," which they say "involves intrusion into the lives of battered women who did not seek services" (p. 1255). This would not happen in the United Kingdom's VS system because support is never imposed on a victim who does not request it. VS volunteers may work with a victim of domestic violence irrespective of the fact that the police or other agencies are involved and would not seek to involve the wider criminal justice system without the victim's explicit agreement.[9]

◈ Contexts of Violence

The issues that inform the work of VS in the United Kingdom (and victim advocacy in the United States) have to be located within the broad interventions made by feminist research, which has increasingly questioned the gaps in the conceptualization and in the experience of violence.[10] Feminist interventions, we would argue, have pushed the debates forward in several key areas. First, while foregrounding familiarity as a central feature of domestic and sexual violence (Boateng, 1999; Maynard, 1993; Mezey & Stanko, 1996; Smart, 1989), the debates have broadened definitions of violence to incorporate a range of behaviors including emotional and psychological as well as physical abuse, thus shifting the focus away from the "battered woman" to look at "lesser" physical forms of abuse that damage women and children psychologically and which if not checked can set the stage for more extreme incidents (hooks, 1997, p. 282; also see Lamb, 1999; Loseke, 1999). For example, hooks (1997) argues that an overfocus on forms of extreme physical violence leads to an acceptance of everyday physical abuse such as occasional hitting (also see Morgan & Thapar-Björkert, 2006). Second, they have highlighted not only the invisible and often insidious workings of male power and control within public and private spaces (cf. Corrin, 1996; Dobash & Dobash, 1997; Hester, Kelly, & Radford, 1996; Kelly, 1988, 1996; Maynard, 1993; Radford & Russell, 1992) but also the endemic and routine nature of violence (Stanko, 1985,

2003, 2006). Thus, it is not necessarily the tangible act of violence, which imposes a form of social control over women, but the "internalization through continual socialization" of the possibility of violence (Smart & Smart, 1978, p. 100). Third, many writers suggest that violence against women should be located in a broad sociostructural context. Pahl (1985) points out that violence against women can be legitimized by society at large to the extent that it becomes possible to deny that domestic violence takes place at all, or to claim that if it does happen, it is only applicable to "unusual or deviant couples" (p. 11). As Stanko (2006) argues, context governs how seriously we as a society respond to incidents of violence as (un) "acceptable" (p. 545). In fact, one of the pivotal premises of the Zero Tolerance Campaign against gendered violence in the United Kingdom was the need to "change societal attitudes towards . . . violence by making it socially unacceptable, and by challenging the norms . . . which . . . sustain it" (Cosgrove, 1996, p. 189). Fourth, debates suggest that mere theorizing is insufficient, and ideas and strategies produced as a result of investigations of women's experiences should inform as well as be informed through feminist activism (McLaughlin, 2003). This, it was argued, would also enable women who have been abused to say what they want and need (Hague & Mullender, 2006; Kelly, 1996). As Hague and Mullender (2006) note, "if services addressing domestic violence are to . . . effectively meet abused women's needs, then the views of those using them need to be heeded" (p. 568).

A part of the process of exposure has involved the explicit naming of violence and abuse by men to ensure that women's experiences of violation should not be left literally unspeakable (see Kelly, 1996). Thus, the necessity of a feminist approach that was characterized by consciousness raising and activism was emphasized. This tradition of consciousness raising coupled with the need for a sympathetic societal response led to the creation of the battered woman syndrome in the 1980s and 1990s in America (Loseke, 1992). This syndrome was viewed by many as a form of cultural compromise (Rothenberg, 2003) because although it enabled advocates to achieve their goals of public sympathy, it also created a homogenous construct

of the battered woman. The "battered woman," a "long-suffering victim," and a "mainstay client of therapists" was absorbed by the "consuming public" (Lamb, 1999, p. 116). For example, Loseke (2001) argues that support groups in the United States, through their organizational practices, promulgate the identity of a battered woman even though women victims' lived realities are often at odds with the template of the formula stories (also see Kendrick, 1998).[11] She suggests that "women's talk about their lived realities often complicates, even subverts, the straightforward narratives of the formula story of wife abuse" (Loseke, 2001, p. 110). Institutionally preferred narratives, as Holstein and Gubrium (2000) claim, lead to an "institutionalization of the selves" (p. 16).

Building on these arguments our article focuses on the tension between institutional discourses and individual perception and how these can contribute to an understanding that sometimes violence is natural, normal, to be expected, and/or understandable. For example, specific discourses that imply that women are responsible for their victimhood are reflected in statements such as "she asked for it." Separating attitudes encapsulated in statements such as this from more professional attitudes of nonblame may not always be a straightforward or easy matter. We question, therefore, whether unintentionally judgmental attitudes to women victims of violence may not be inherent in the understandings of some of those engaged in combating the effects of violence, despite their genuine desire to provide support.

Culture of Blame and Responsibility

In this article, our intention is not to deny the enabling and autonomy enhancing potential of institutional practices within statutory and voluntary organizations toward women who have experienced violence. However, we also want to acknowledge analyses that suggest that these institutions may fail some women (Westlund, 1999; see also Hague, 1998; Hague & Mullender, 2006; Malos, 2000).

Shouldering the Burden of Responsibility

Interventionist strategies for dealing with domestic abuse (such as the Duluth model in Minnesota in the United States) have alerted practitioners and activists dealing with all forms of interpersonal violence to the need for a coherent philosophical approach, which focuses on victim safety, holds offenders accountable, and eliminates victim blaming (Pence & MacMahon, 1999).

In relation to sexual violence particularly, it is argued that women are often blamed or seen as complicit in the sexual offenses against them (Berns, 2001; Corrin, 1996; Hague, 1998; Lamb, 1996; Lea, 2007; Maynard, 1993; Morgan, 2006). The attention and questioning therefore shifts toward the women rather than to men's violence. Thus an environment of victim blaming and normalization of violence is created in which women feel unable to report crimes of violence against them. As Bunch and Carrillo (1992) suggest, "women are socialized to associate their self-worth with the satisfaction of the needs and desires of others and thus are encouraged to blame themselves as inadequate or bad if men beat them" (p. 18). Women who are victims of male violence find "breaking the silence" stigmatizing because they are often perceived by others as "fallen women who have failed in the 'feminine' role" (hooks, 1997, p. 283).

Nancy Berns (2001) argues that political discourses on violence often shift the focus from abusers to the victims. She argues that the popular representation in, for example, newspapers, magazines, or television reports is responsible for constructing and reproducing images of domestic violence, which in turn influence the way individuals "construct their own conceptions of what is normal and acceptable" (p. 263; see also Berns & Schweingruber, 2007, p. 247). She refers to this perspective as patriarchal resistance and usefully highlights three implications in this resistance discourse: the normalization of intimate violence, the diversion of attention from men's responsibility in violence, and the distortion of women's violence.

Although we agree with Berns that the argument that men and women are equally violent is often used in "de-gender(ing)" the problem of domestic violence, it is still important to understand how both men and women are complicit in "gendering the blame" through the "reframe[ing]" of discourses in such a way as to "obscure[e] men's violence while placing the responsibility on women" (Berns, 2001, p. 262). To illustrate our point, we will look at some of the ideas articulated by VS volunteers who, we suggest, are potentially uniquely placed to resist and challenge some of the perceptions and stereotypes relating to women victims of violence. The increased level of understanding acquired by the volunteers that places them in such a position was appreciated by at least some of the volunteers interviewed, as expressed here by Sally:

> I think training and talking to people have opened my eyes to what goes on [in relation to victim blaming]. I mean I think perhaps people *that are on the outside* and don't have more information maybe don't see it quite that clearly. (Sally, VS volunteer; our emphasis)

As a result of their training, these volunteers see themselves as being in a position to help the victim come to them and thus to empower the victim, enabling him/her to continue with their lives. For example,

> She gradually didn't need me. Which I was really pleased about. I mean I was glad when she said she didn't need me because I thought that was good. She's—she's moving forward, isn't she? She's coping for herself. (Sally, VS volunteer)

And a little later into the same interview,

> All their self-esteem is on the floor. So I put quite a lot of effort into telling them that they're not useless and that they really are perfectly good human beings, and you know when they tell me anything that was really good that they've done, I do sort of say "that was really good what you did. That was brilliant wasn't it?" . . . Because it's horrendous the things they've come through. (Sally, VS volunteer)

Whereas in an interview with another volunteer,

Researcher: When you're with a victim, how do you know or when do you feel that—that it's been successful? That you've done a good job?

Yvonne: At the end, I feel. When you're saying "bye-bye." And then they've suddenly turned round and said "thanks, that's really helped me." And they're smiling and . . . I think if they've smiled . . . they're thinking about what I'm saying and that might just give them enough confidence to maybe to do something. . . . And then that . . . would make me feel better. If I walked out and that lady was still—or that man—was still sat there with a solemn face, then I would think I haven't done it. I haven't got them to think the other way. They're still thinking that they're still in a bottomless pit. If I walked out and they looked happy, then I think they're thinking about this. It's just enough to give somebody that little bit of confidence to think they can step over it. And find their own way out. Somehow. (Yvonne, VS volunteer)

The VS volunteers aimed to make their clients feel "not useless" and help them out of a "bottomless pit." Similarly, Dunn and Powell-Williams (2007), in their interviews with domestic violence victim advocates in a midwestern state in the United States, also state that a central aspect of the advocates' work is to make clients realize they have choices because many come in feeling defeated.

In many respects, the relationship between the VS volunteer and the victim (or client) involves much the same forms of social interactions as those that may develop in research interviews that involve "differing

aspects of social interaction such as power, friendship, reciprocity and shared understandings" (Birch & Miller, 2000, p. 190). The exact form of the volunteer/victim relationship is somewhat confused therefore, with a blurring of roles between counselor, friend, and various other positions in between. Most volunteers seemed clear that their role was to listen rather than to push for information. For example, Sally commented, "She didn't want to talk details and I wasn't probing. Because it's not what we do, is it?"

However, this blurring of boundaries has raised concerns in the past, with some VS volunteers feeing that they were being expected to take on too much of a counseling role, despite the fact that the majority are not trained counselors (Morgan, 2005). One of the workshops at the 1998 National Conference discussed whether VS is moving to a counseling role and whether it is appropriate. Key point to come out of the discussion were that VS volunteers

provide an immediate, vital response and have a specific role to fulfil, which is not counseling. VS visitors provide a good listening ear, a non-judgemental lasting relationship, empowerment and confidentiality, and they help victims to make informed choices as well as practical information, liaison [sic] with other agencies, as well as possible referrals to counseling. (Victim Support Magazine, 1998, p. 7)[12]

Most of the volunteers recognized that to restore the victim's sense of self-worth, they should be encouraged and supported in avoiding the feelings of self-blame that affect many such victims. In other words, in keeping with the VS "non-blame" rhetoric, and as pointed out by one of the interviewees quoted below, the intention is to empower the victim to acknowledge that "the only person to blame for a crime is the perpetrator" (Spackman, 2000, p. 66):

First of all you just have to let them talk. And then sort of suggest that perhaps it's not their fault and you know, if you really think about it, did you do anything wrong? So get their train of though actually working another way rather than let them sort of think that they're to blame all the time because that is very often what's been taken away from them—is the way to think for themselves . . . you're trying to help them get back upon that ladder and think for themselves. (Olive, VS volunteer)

Nevertheless, despite their training and their evident sincerity in supporting and encouraging women victims of violence, it could also be suggested that the volunteers struggle with the idea that perpetrators of violence are solely to blame for their actions. Statements of those interviewed indicated that some believe that there are occasions when women victims, to some extent, are accountable for what has happened to them. For example, women who transgress acceptable boundaries of dress, behavior, or femininity may be seen as complicit in what has happened to them—as individually responsible for their fate. Weaver (1998) notes that it has become apparent that "women are taught to believe it is their individual responsibility to restrict and censure their activities so as to avoid becoming the victim of [sexual violence]" (p. 262). As Emma (VS volunteer) stated, to avoid violence, "you've got to be careful now wherever you go and . . . like work your route out and know where you're going to go and all that sort of thing."

Although the VS volunteers are certainly not concerned with blaming the victims, they do seem to have taken on board the wider societal discourses of, to use Berns' (2001) term again, "patriarchal resistance" or "gendering" the blame. So, when directly asked about blame, the responses were as follows:

No, I don't think the victim's to blame. Only the aggressor. (Olive, VS volunteer)

No, I can't think of any reason [the victim is to blame]. No. (Ivy, VS volunteer)

[The victim is] not to blame, no, no. (Emma, Vs volunteer)

Umm. Not really. No. Umm . . . (Sam, VS volunteer)

I don't—no, I don't think there is any justifiable reason for a man to attack a woman physically or sexually. No, I couldn't justify that. Ever. (Sally, VS volunteer)

However, there were also statements that directly contradicted those quoted above:

But sometimes I think . . . they put themselves in the situation. (Edna, VS volunteer)

No I don't think you can be blamed no. But I think you—you need to look after ourselves [sic] more. (Emma, VS volunteer)

So I—you know—I'm not a subscriber to the view that women do bring it on themselves, although sometimes I think people don't know when to stop and they don't know when to shut up! (Sally, VS volunteer)

These conflicting statements do not mean that the volunteers are attempting to be misleading about their attitudes, and it is certainly not our intention to suggest that there was any element of subterfuge in the volunteers' discourses. However, statements such as this do reveal that it is possible to share different, mutually incompatible ideologies, which have to be negotiated and managed (Van Dijk, 1997). We also believe that training that fails to take into account feminist perspectives may also fail to challenge traditional gender-role beliefs that "are more likely to attribute responsibility to the victim, whilst those holding less traditional [gender]-role beliefs are less likely to attribute responsibility to the victim" (Lea, 2007, p. 497). The training provided to VS volunteers and the resource pack made available to those supporting victims of domestic violence state that the volunteers should "make sure that the responsibility for the perpetrators' behaviour rests with them and is not made the responsibility of the service user [victim]." In other words, "if patterns of abuse arise, some people will assume that they are to blame . . . don't collude with these thoughts . . . [and] instead explain that no one is ever to blame for abuse" (VS, 2003, p. 23). However, there is no real attempt to address the roots of a victim-blaming culture and the way in which it may be sustained by patriarchy. Thus, although the volunteers may well see themselves as becoming more enlightened as illustrated by Sally's quote earlier in the article, it is apparent that this is insufficient to overcome entrenched beliefs.

These internal arguments or ideological dilemmas (Billig et al., 1988) may be revealed through discourse and discursive practices and arise from the contrary themes within common sense (Billig et al., 1988). Ideology, Billig et al. suggest, takes two forms, intellectual and lived. The former consists of a "system of political, religious or philosophical thinking," whereas lived ideology is described as "society's way of life" (p. 27): in other words, the everyday aspects of life, including commonsense, that govern everyday life. Intellectual ideological processes tend to be coherent formalize forms of thought, "an internally consistent pattern" that enables thoughts and values together to construct "total mental structure" (Billig et al., 1988, p. 29). So, in terms of the initial response of many of the volunteers interviewed, the conscious acceptance of the VS philosophy that "the victim is not to blame" forms part of the volunteer's intellectual ideology. However, a dilemma arises in respect to a commonsense understanding of the world. It makes sense, for example, for women to avoid walking alone at night in certain areas or that women should try not to wind up their partners when they know them to be potentially violent, particularly when the men have been drinking. Consequently, for VS volunteers, the tensions between the intellectual ideology (the nonblame rhetoric) and the lived ideology (the commonsense knowledge, reinforced by public discourse, that it is women's responsibility to avoid violence, rather than men's responsibility to avoid committing violence) results in the simultaneous possession of opposing views. Emma, as quoted above, for example, notes that women victims of violence are not to blame for their own victimization, but she continues,

> But I think she's opening herself up to—you've got to be careful now wherever you go and umm you know they say like work your route out and know where you're going to go and all that sort of thing. (Emma, VS volunteer)

Women, therefore, have to plan where they go, consider possible dangers, and select the safest routes (see also Gardner, 1990; Morgan & Thapar-Björkert, 2006; Stanko, 1990). The volunteers' understanding that women should not be blamed and should be able to go where they want is therefore at odds with their commonsense knowledge of the world and its dangers for women.

Billig et al. (1988) see that ideological dilemmas as revealed through discursive practices illustrate that individuals do think about what they know. Indeed, it is through the possession of "opposing themes" that "ordinary people [are able] to find the familiar puzzling and therefore worthy of thought" (p. 143). Fairclough (1995) also points out that

> it is quite possible for a social subject to occupy institutional subject positions which are ideologically incompatible, or to occupy a subject position incompatible with his or her overt political or social beliefs and affiliations, without being aware of any contradiction. (p. 42)

So examining the volunteers' narratives in relation to the central question of whether they challenge or support discourses of blame and how far they are able to accept or refute the notion reveals, as noted above, a tension between the nonblaming rhetoric and commonsense understandings of the causes and consequences of violence against women.[13] Two themes that constituted these discourses were the role of alcohol in violence and the choice available to women victims to leave an abusive relationship.

Blame, alcohol, and lack of control. It is widely acknowledge among health and policy-related researchers that alcohol consumption can be a major contributor to intimate partner violence (Finney, 2004). However, it is also recognized that individual and societal beliefs that alcohol causes aggression can encourage violent behavior after drinking and the use of alcohol as an excuse for violent behavior (Field, Caetano, & Nelson, 2004). Often intoxication is invoked as a postoffense excuse (Ollett, 1994). Several of the volunteers referred to alcohol as a contributory feature in the escalation of violence.

Volunteers referred to the way in which it apparently causes the drinker (apart from one reference, they all referred to the drinker being the perpetrator, rather than the victim) to somehow lose control, to become another type of person. Almost all of those who mentioned alcohol remarked on the fact that the drinkers were actually likeable people and that the alcohol seems to have changed some essential part of their nature. So, for example, Ray, who was particularly adamant that drink causes violence said,

> I personally know people who—meet them when they're sober and they're completely different people to when they're drunk, you know? Or when they've got some alcohol in them. (Ray, VS volunteer)

Others, although perhaps not quite as adamant as Ray that alcohol is a major factor in violence, were still fairly forceful and yet still blamed the alcohol itself rather than the drinker.

> They're lovely when they're sober. I think drink's got lot to answer for. (Edna, VS volunteer)

> But that is often the result of drinks—or drugs and they're out of control. But they're not totally out of control because they still know what they're doing. But . . . they're not the same person that they are when they're sober or not on whatever it is they're on. And it alters their behavior and their character. (Sally, VS volunteer)

Consequently, it becomes possible to blame the alcohol rather than the individual for any loss of control. Finney (2004) suggests that "societal and individual beliefs about the links between alcohol and violence may encourage a person to drink to find courage to commit violent behaviour" (p. 5). It is possible, however, that men with a tendency to be violent may drink so as to provide themselves with a ready-made excuse for their behavior (Ollett, 1994, cited in Finney, 2004). This latter point seems also to be borne out by some of Jeff Hearn's (1998) research in which one of his interviewees claimed, "I did use alcohol as an excuse, like a vehicle, so that I could do it. To give me an excuse in my own head, saying 'Oh I've had a drink.' But it were an excuse for me to do it, that's all" (p. 141). Nancy Hirschmann (1997) supports these ideas and suggests that men's violence is not viewed as a choice:

> Men routinely blame their violence on alcohol, on women's nagging or deficiencies as wife and mother. And of course such men rarely see that they have chosen to subscribe to rigid sex roles that legitimize violence, but rather consider such values to be a factual account of the natural order of things. (p. 203)

As suggested from the volunteer discourses, these excuses seem to have become an integral part of the way society views violent behavior in general and men's violent behavior in particular. However, alongside the volunteers suggesting that men experience decreased self-control as a result of alcohol comes the idea that women need to adapt or modify their own behavior, whether or not they are the ones doing the drinking. In a potentially violent domestic situation, for example, this might mean that women need to avoid any from of nagging behavior. Thus,

> [It] was his drink thing you see? And she would just go on and on niggling him, until eventually he would umm I don't say he actually hit her but he sort of would throw [her] against the wall. (Edna, VS volunteer)

Whereas Yvonne, who had herself experienced a violent relationship, said,

> Well—the girl across the road, I mean she knew what was going on, and . . . she used to say to me "well don't speak to him when he's drunk, you know, and then he won't go back at you." And I said well, "yeah, probably I am winding him up then." But then I should have a right to say to him, "you're a drunken bastard" [laughter]. You know? . . . but at the start,

he was drunk and of course I used to get on my high horse with him, and of course that would make it worse and then bop! But then you—I think you get to listen to the signs and you think, "well when he's drunk, you don't say nothing." (Yvonne, VS volunteer)

Despite learning to say nothing, however, the violence continued for 4 or 5 years until eventually Yvonne left him.

So, as Radford and Stanko (1996) suggest, domestic violence tends to be resented as "either a reflection of bad marital relations, personality disputes, or intoxication substances, not the manifestation of unequal power and a need to control" (p. 77). Also, the theme of gaining and losing self-control, as Eisikovits and Buchbinder (1999) argue, become a "central motif in the metaphoric world of battered women . . . (where) her sense of survival is based on her sense of self-control over her and his violence" (p. 860). The woman shoulders the burden of controlling her partner's violence, by first controlling her own speech, actions, or demeanor.

"She went back." Whether women choose to stay, leave, or return has to be understood in terms of contextual factors and specific life circumstances that influence their decisions (see Baker, 1997; Barnett, 2000; Eisikovits & Buchbinder, 1999; Lempert, 1997). Often women are expected to adhere to a dominant cultural script that directs them to get away and stay away from their abusers (Baker, 1997). Although the volunteers appeared to try to understand and support women's choices, it was also apparent that they experienced dilemmas in relation to this. On one hand, they denied any attribution of blame (and actively sought to support the victim in avoiding this), yet they also revealed that they expected women to avoid any situation that could possibly be violent. This is amply illustrated by the following:

Researcher: Do you find it frustrating when they go back? Like this woman (client) who went back the first time?

Olive: No, no. Because I think, at the end of the day . . . you cannot tell people how to live their lives. You cannot do

that. You've just got to be there for them. That is what you are there for. Just to help them and put them in the right direction for help. It has to be their decision at the end of the day. And I always said to her you know "whatever happens, you know, if, *if* you go back to [him], that is your decision" and umm that's what she did, as I said, she went back. But then she realized that it wasn't gonna work out and left again. [But at least then] it was her *final* decision. (Olive, VS volunteer; our emphasis)

However, as the interview proceeded, the same volunteer made the following comment regarding the well-publicized violence between the English ex-footballer, Paul Gascoigne, and his then wife, Sheryl:

And I think she had a pretty raw deal . . . but on the other hand, so did he, because you [*sic*] knew he was violent, but again she kept going back for more, didn't she? And she married him *knowing how violent he was.* (Olive, VS volunteer; our emphasis)

It was evident from this narrative that to Olive, at least, Sheryl Gascoigne had to accept some responsibility for what happened to her. To make a women shoulder responsibility for abuse because she "went back for more," for not leaving the domestic situation, or for marrying the man (with a known history of violence) is problematic. It also suggests that there was a degree of consent in her abuse because the victim has the option of leaving the situation but chooses not to. In their research with domestic violence victim advocates in the United States, Dunn and Powell-Williams (2007) explore the tensions inherent in reconciling victim ideology with victim behavior. They argue that victim advocates help battered women to recognize their options and choose to leave. However, they argue that

the language the advocates use inevitably places decision-making in the hands of the clients. It is the women, not their abusers, whom they expect...to make the changes and...the only choice the advocates see as appropriate, the only acceptable agency, is leaving the violent relationship. (Dunn & Powell-Williams, 2007, p. 993)

Looking at a similar issue but from the perspective of the victim, Phyllis Baker (1997) argues that the often the dominant cultural script directs women to get away and stay away from their abusers, but in her own research she found that women victims felt that the script was too narrow and did not sufficiently reflect the complexities of their decision to stay with the abuser (Baker, 1997; also see Peled, Eisikovits, Enosh, & Winstok, 2000). In her article, "Feminism and Power," Ann Yeatman (1997) argues that it is not so much a case of consent "but a complex psycho-dynamic process whereby battered women do not possess any sense of efficacious independent agency in the face of continuing presence of their abusive male partner," their agency being continuously eroded through physical force, unequal power relations, and "a need to control" (p. 150).

Despite the training received by these volunteers, there seemed on the part of some to be a failure to recognize the myriad and complex reasons for a woman remaining with, or returning to, a violent partner. For example, women may find it difficult to leave an abusive relationship because the perpetrators often isolate and undermine women, thus rendering them dependent. "Some women attempting to survive and cope in such circumstances may feel that staying with their violent partner will appease him and thus lessen the violence" (Hester, Pearson, & Harwin, 1998, p. 22). Often, of course, the victim may continue to have positive feelings for the abuser. Westlund (1999) points out that

in between periods of high tension...life may take on a semblance of normality, giving the battered woman hope that future bouts of violence can be avoided and that the peace will hold. Women living in such conditions may even come to see their batterers as the bearers of mercy, the source of their happiness as well as their misery. (p. 1047)

Furthermore, as Dobash and Dobash (1992) note, women's reluctance to take action and to report the abusive men

is often exacerbated by social, medical and legal institutions whose actions reveal a powerful legacy of policies and practices that explicitly or implicitly accept or ignore male violence and/or blame the victim and make her responsible for its solution and elimination. (p. 4)

So women victims are expected to "remove themselves from the situation":

I mean nothing is excusable. But I think there are some women that really sort of, you know, irritate. Well it—it's just tension, isn't it? You know tension will grow umm and women won't remove themselves from the situation.... Well I think some women goad men into turning violent. You know when they belittle them and...but this is people that are not *normally* violent. (Edna, VS volunteer; our emphasis)

This means that the victims are considered to be the ones who have to change their lives and adapt themselves to the domestic situation, the ones who have to look for a solution to their problem (e.g., of being irritating). In extreme circumstances, the woman is often obliged to move away from her home to live away from the aggressor, who normally continues to stay at home, at least in the beginning. An NCH Action for Children Survey in the United Kingdom pointed out that 58% of women did not want to leave home as opposed to 49% who said that they had no place to go to (Hester et al., 1998).

These attitudes enable male perpetrators to project their violence as rational and justified. In an in-depth study conducted with 33 domestically violent heterosexual men in the United States, Anderson and Umberson (2001) suggest that some men often depict their partner's acts as "irrational and hysterical" to "justify their own violence and present themselves as calm, cool and rational men" (p. 365). Men described actions such as "[I] grabbed her and threw her down" or "sat on her" as "nonviolence" and "controlled" as opposed to the "outrageous" behavior of their female partners. In addition, Anderson and Umberson argue that "respondents also shifted blame onto female partners by detailing faults in their partner's behaviors and personalities" (p. 367). Similarly, VS volunteers seemed to imply that if women exercised greater restraint over their own behavior, then situations where violence occurs could be avoided. Moreover, it gives legitimacy to men to exercise their "controlled" power to maintain the gendered patterns of behavior. An uncomfortable idea is that it appears as if the VS volunteers interviewed here assume the power that men exercise (or expect to have) is natural and if the status quo is disturbed (through nagging, for example), then women should feel responsible for the exercise of that power.

The narratives of these volunteers raise an important issue in relation to who blames whom. How volunteers position themselves within discourses of violence is important as they also feed back to interagency policy forums. An ethos of blame/responsibility can be seen as contributing to a culture in which violence is normalized, sustained, and ultimately accepted by default. Also, an understanding of the analytically rigorous literature on sexual violence is right in suggesting that a patriarchal framework is useful to understand the persistence/existence of interpersonal violence and the ways in which men are implicated in sustaining patriarchal discourses.

Surveillance and Normalizing Judgments

This leads us to our next point that attitudes held by abusers as well as by some statutory and voluntary organizations can place women victims of violence through a regime of regulated behavior and gendered norms.[14] Andrea Westlund (1999), using Foucault's analysis of power in *Discipline and Punish: The Birth of the Prison* (1991),[15] argues that the techniques used to maintain power and control over women (experiencing sexual and domestic violence) are both premodern and modern forms of power. She illustrates her argument by looking at domestic violence within households

and battered women's interaction and treatment with modern institutions (police, domestic violence shelters, courts, medical and psychiatric professions).[16] In cases of domestic violence, the power exercised over women by the "batterer/sovereign" is, Westlund (1999) claims, often "pre-modern" in that the techniques used are "intensely corporal and brutal and . . . are wielded in a personal and sporadic rather than an impersonal and meticulous manner" (p. 1045). Corporal punishment, sometimes particularly horrific, is exercised to redress perceived contempt for authority, as illustrated by one of the volunteers talking about a victim of domestic violence, to whom she had provided support:

> He didn't treat her very well. Kept her short of money and she had to basically—to get the money it was sexual favors to him . . . and she retaliated one day rather than take the beating, and so he poured petrol over her and set her alight. (Olive, VS volunteer)

Another research participant, Yvonne, the volunteer who had also been a victim, described an incident with her ex-husband, who was annoyed at his son using the telephone without his permission:

> He just [went up] to Ian [17-year-old son] and punched him in the face. Of course, I jumped up then, in front of Ian, as I had done so many times before. . . . And, of course, Ian then pushed me out the way . . . cos [my husband] went for me—and Ian said, "you're never gonna hit her again" and I thought, "this is father and son now fighting" and I thought, "this has got to stop, this has got to stop. I'm not having him hit his son over me." And that's all it was; he hit Ian so that he knew I was going to jump up so he could have a go at me then. (Yvonne, VS volunteer)

This narrative illustrates that corporal punishment can occur directly or indirectly against a loved one. In addition to this premodern form of corporal power, however, there is a degree of close surveillance, which is more akin to the power to be found in some modern institutions such as prisons (Westlund, 1999). This surveillance is not only imposed on battered women by their abusers but requires that they learn to "nicely comport themselves exactly as their oppressors would want," seeking to regain some control over their own lives by "concentrating on the micro-practices of everyday life" (MacCannell & MacCannell, 1993, p. 211). Furthermore, if she takes the help of professional services outside the household, she is often placed within "new and different sets of power relations" by these institutions and may be pathologized as mentally unstable and incapable of appraising her own situation (Westlund, 1999, p. 1046–1049). Women are advised to "commit to" and work on their relationships, making it difficult for some women to recognize which behaviors they should or should not accept (Fraser, 2005, p. 15). This advice, although well meaning, may serve to reflect the more damaging aspects of societal opinion relation to gendered violence in reiterating the responsibility of the victim. For example, discussing sexual abuse, one of the volunteers commented on the advisability of women wearing certain clothing:

> If a woman was walking down the road, if she was dressed in a miniskirt and a tight top, is she to blame? And you know if she was sort of raped or attacked or something I wouldn't say she was to blame. . . . Her wearing that wasn't the causal factor in her getting attacked . . . But had I sort of known her and was talking to her before she did that, I'd advise her not to do it, just because I'm aware even if she's not the causal factor, the causal factors are in place, they're out there. . . . So I think there's a certain sense of . . . perhaps *you have to take responsibility for your own safety.* (Sam, VS volunteer; our emphasis)

In relation to research and experience in both Britain and the United States, Dobash and Dobash (1992) argue that when women experiencing violence have sought professional help "they have often been blamed for the violence, asked to change their behaviour in order to meet their husband's demands, and had

their own concerns and requests deflected or ignored" (p. 231). The police and refuge services are two agencies that are often involved in domestic cases (Malos, 2000). However, the growing acceptance of the police as a service provider, rather than a *force*—a term that more accurately connotes police monopoly of coercive powers—shows the tendencies of agencies to deny issues of structural power and inequality (Patel, 1999).

Even the very terms applied to women who have experienced such violence may be seen as an indication of the imposition of normalizing judgments. The rejection of the *victim* label by many of the organizations offering help and support to women and its replacement with *survivor* may impose unwanted subjectivities on those who are already feeling vulnerable and unsure of themselves. On one level, the replacement of victim with survivor is perfectly understandable as the former has become synonymous with blame, largely as a result of the work of the early victimologists (e.g., Von Hentig, 1948; Wolfgang, 1958). By using survivor, therefore, feminists and activists are seeking not only to challenge victim blaming but at the same time are stressing the resistance and coping strategies used by women and children and the extent to which they ensure their own survival (Kelly & Radford, 1996; Walklate, 2003). Furthermore, as Stanko (1985) points our, "in applying the term 'victim' . . . one implicitly separates victim from non-victim," and it is this separation that enables theorists to examine victims as a cohesive group to find defining characteristics (p. 13). As this culture of victim blaming has entered public consciousness, women who have been abused have become increasingly reluctant to identify themselves as victims. However, the alternative construction of survivor is also far from ideal for many women. Given the many difficulties faced by those forced to cope with sexual and/or domestic violence, and the high numbers killed through such acts, many feminists contend that women cannot and should not be portrayed either as "inevitable victims or as strong survivors for whom abuse has minimal consequences" (Kelly, Burton, & Regan, 1996, p. 82).

The position of many support agencies in referring to victim/survivor either as dichotomous positions or as different stages of the same situation tends to be unhelpful for those struggling to deal with their experiences. For those women who believe that they could be or should have been more proactive in dealing with what has happened to them achieving survivor status may seem unattainable, leaving them feeling that they have failed somehow to respond in the way they feel society would expect them to respond. Kelly et al. (1996) make similar points, suggesting that the victim/survivor dichotomy places individuals in an either/or position that "misrepresents both material and emotional reality" (p. 91; also see Lamb, 1996, 1999). Walkate (2003) points out that although victim and survivor tend to be presented as opposed, they are not necessarily so, as it is, of course, as "possible to think in terms of an active or passive victim, as it is to identify an active or passive survivor" (p. 36). In addition, though, not only is it possible to criticize the dichotomous construction of victim/survivor but also that used most often by feminists and agencies working with women who have experienced domestic violence, the notion of the victim-to-survivor healing journey. This alternative chronological construction of victim to survivor, in its tendency to presume passivity during the victim stage, ignores the resistance and coping strategies that many women adopt during their abuse (see Kelly et al., 1996). We would like to suggest that the meanings of survivor-victim are ambiguous and context specific, and our intent here is not to resolve these dichotomous constructions (as each category can carry elements of both strength and vulnerability) but to foreground women victims' own definitions of their situation.

Institutional Attitudes

Increasing structural pressures of state funding have led to a steady professionalization of services and an institutionalization of therapeutic vocabularies (Dunn & Powell-Williams, 2007; Eisikovits & Buchbinder, 1999; Kendrick, 1998; Lempert, 1997; Loseke, 2001). As a consequence, not only has there been a steady homogenization of women victims' diverse experiences but also increasingly institutional functioning has come to be privileged over individual needs (Loseke, 2001). Institutional files stand in for real people, which

process women victims as data points (Pence, 2005; Pence & McMahon, 1999).

Often dissimilar events and situations are lumped together in a way that fits a "discursive environment (that) privileges stories featuring the centrality of dangerous violence" (Loseke, 2001, p. 114). This means that women victims are expected to include a theme of violence in their narratives, even though women might want to talk about marital infidelity, a nonappreciative husband and family, or problems related with alcohol abuse.

In our specific research with VS volunteers, we argue that institutional discourses can nurture embedded social norms that enable society to absolve itself of any collective responsibility for tackling interpersonal violence. This is highlighted in institutional texts such as safety advice literature, aimed specifically at women, which embodies institutional thinking.

Although there is unambiguous reference in literature provided by VS to the fact that "[r]ape and sexual assault, whether by a stranger or friend, is never the woman's fault" (VS, n.d.), at the same time the personal-safety information they distribute places emphasis on the need for women to "take care." In a participant observation (2003) of domestic violence training, a male trainee (in his late 50s) who was supported in his views by a female trainee (of a similar age) suggested that young girls and women wearing "revealing clothing" were problematic because culture is making sexuality another commodity—"something you can take."

The literature exacerbates women's fear of crime, not only subjecting women to a form of social control but also under the guise of common sense creates an implicit division between women who follow the advice and those who do not. Gardner (1990) notes that it is "women's alleged responsibility for their own victimization" that results in them having to become "streetwise" and to take a variety of precautions (p. 312). This, we would suggest, maintains the status quo by reiteration of the dominant position—that it is incumbent on women to take precautions rather than on men to take control (Morgan & Thapar-Björkert, 2006). Thus we would argue that any real change would also entail making a change in the institutional texts.

The purpose of writing this is not to suggest that professional services should be removed (in fact, rather the opposite), and we recognize the invaluable work conducted by the vast majority of professional organizations and individuals offering support to women who have experienced all forms of violence. We are suggesting, however, that some professional services are in danger of imposing a set of regulatory norms on women and children who have already been subjected to an external and internalized gaze.

◈ Conclusion

The persistence of interpersonal violence in the experiences of ordinary lives is one of the main reasons for reexploring some of the mechanisms through which women (and men) experience violence. Violence is not the responsibility of women or the result of an individual pathology but a problem of the entire society, particularly the norms and attitudes that harbor prejudices relating to women victims of violence. In reviewing some of the dominant discourses that create, nurture, and sustain violence, we argue that the culture of blame and responsibility disempowers women who experience domestic and sexual violence.

In this article, we have focused on VS in the United Kingdom and suggested that the volunteers are in a unique position to have a greater understanding of the range of harms encompassed by the term violence. However, we argue that some volunteers, through no fault of their own, fail adequately to challenge discourses of blame in relation to women victims of violence because the dominant discourses of victim blame outweigh the new, less popular discourses of nonblame. Often in speech, counter theories are implicit rather than explicit, and the person expressing the discourse may not be aware of these counter-meanings in the way that a hypocrite would be (Billig et al., 1988). Thus although the organizational rhetoric, policies, and measures may provide immediate (and necessary) assistance to the victim, they fall short in addressing or changing wider social attitudes and thus providing permanent safety or genuine empowerment. The tensions between nonblame and responsibility as revealed by the volunteers appear to be part of a wider understanding of how women and men interact. Although there are problems in attributing certain discourses to patriarchal power alone, there does appear to be evidence of dominant discourses and prevalent ideologies, which are a potential source of ambiguity particularly when considering women's experiences of violence. The volunteers, explicitly faced with two opposing ideologies, are perhaps more likely to experience conflicting attitudes than most people and are therefore more likely to articulate their ideological dilemmas. The volunteers who participated in this research were attempting to reconcile the opposing discourses to which they were exposed and create a coherent schema. Perhaps, this reconciliation could have become easier if the volunteers had access to feminist discourse, which has historically encouraged a reflexive practice of the limits of our own approaches in dealing with victims of violence.

There is thus, we suggest, an urgent need for a steady and continuous change in the civic-political culture (broadly understood as a set of institutional, representational, and discursive values held by citizen and among citizens)—a change from the prevalent culture of resignation (Morgan, 2005, 2006). A culture of resignation only reiterates disempowering constructions of blame/responsibility, which do not completely map the complexity or plurality of violence toward women. Our focus should move away from a produced victim to social attitudes that may generate a victim.

◈ Notes

1. The network of affiliated charities known collectively as the National Association of Victim Support Schemes originated in Britain in 1973–1974 following the development of the Bristol Victims Support Scheme. Within 4 years, some 30 similar schemes had been set up, and by the late 1990s there were approximately 450 schemes operating throughout England and Wales (National Audit Office, 2002) with the National Office based in London.

2. The issue of obtaining informed consent is an ambiguous one. In conducting "feminist research," which was the intention here, we recognize that "knowledge production [is] . . . grounded in individual and collective experiences," and consequently at the outset of the research it is not always completely apparent where it will lead us (Miller & Bell, 2002, p. 54). So although it is extremely

important to explain the research aims to the participants, the findings may not always correspond to the original research aims. Such was the case in the research, which was intended to examine attitudes to women victims of violence and yet which surprised us in revealing the extent to which these VS volunteers possessed simultaneous yet conflicting notions of who was deserving or undeserving of violence.

3. Collins (1998) points out that using a structured/unstructured dichotomy is ultimately unhelpful when talking about interviews, as the interview situation is always structured to some extent. Mason (2002) also noted that it is not possible to conduct a "structure-free interview not least because the agendas and assumptions of both interviewer and interviewee will inevitably impose frameworks for meaningful interaction" (p. 231).

4. Ricoeur's (1981) science of hermeneutics suggests that there are two types of interpretation, the hermeneutics of faith and the hermeneutics of suspicion. The former can be "construed as the restoration of a meaning addressed to the interpreter in the form of a message. This type of hermeneutics is animated by faith, by a willingness to listen," whereas the latter is "regarded as the demystification of a meaning presented to the interpretation in the form of a disguise. This type of hermeneutics is animated by suspicion, by a skepticism towards the given" (Thompson, 1981, p. 6).

5. At the time the empirical research was conducted (2003–2004) by the second author, VS was a network of affiliated charities, operating under an umbrella organization of Victim Support National Office. In 2003, the government announced plans to direct funding via local Criminal Justice Boards rather than directly to Victim Support (VS). And in May 2007, an extraordinary General Meeting of VS voted overwhelmingly (90%) in favor of creating a single charity, a process that is now underway (VS, 2007).

6. The Victim's Charter is a statement of service standards for victims of crime (Home Office, 2004) and is available on demand from the Home Office, VS, and police stations. Interestingly, the charter mentions only VS and its Witness Service but ignores organizations such as Women's Aid and Rape Crisis (see Williams, 1999).

7. The Home Office is currently reviewing the service provided to victims of crime in a series of moves that will impact the way in which VS and other organizations operate (see Criminal Justice System, 2005).

8. Victim advocates in the United States work in shelters and criminal justice settings such as the prosecutor's office, police department, and sheriff's office (see McDermott & Garofalo, 2004).

9. Unless the volunteer has reason to believe that children may be at risk, in which case a decision may be taken to involve social services.

10. We recognize that this experience is shaped by gender, race/ethnicity, religion, class, and sexuality, which are not separate systems of domination or axes of power but are mutually constitutive (Hill Collins, 1998; Mama, 1989). These social divisions can render women of color's experiences as qualitatively different from those of White women (Crenshaw, 1994).

11. Donileen Loseke (2001) argues that "formula stories are narratives about types of experience (such as wife abuse), involving distinctive types of characters (such as battered women and the abusive man)" (p. 107).

12. Both Victim Support National Office and the Home Office consider that "the involvement of members of the community, offering their time free of charge, was vital to the work. Victims did not necessarily want full-time paid professional counselors supporting them but local people" (House of Commons, 2003, p. 8). This means, however, that the quality and extent of service available can vary significantly from area to area, although there are significant moves underway to ensure that all areas reach the same high standards.

13. It is difficult to say how these views of VS workers were reflected in their practices with victims, but the second author observed several training sessions between volunteers, VS training staff, and trainers from external professional training organizations. In these situations, all of them upheld the principles of non-blame, active listening, and nonjudgmental support. All volunteers interviewed indicated a willingness to comply with these rules in practice.

14. Other research has recognized that institutions can be as "violent and intimidating as individuals" (Hanmer & Maynard, 1987, p. 5). For example, Amina Mama (1989) argues that multi-agency responses in the United Kingdom to battered Black women (Asian, African and Caribbean), in particular, aggravate their suffering and isolation. Many Black women are often coerced into a relationship with social services, which adds "to their oppressions of violence, homelessness and racism by further disempowering rather than supporting the women" (Mama, 1989, p. 96). Also, in the British context, many women of African, Asian, and Caribbean descent would not access the "palliative" measures because of the stereotypes and preconceptions associated with their ethnicity (Mama, 1989, p. 24).

15. Michel Foucault in *Discipline and Punish* (1991) suggests that premodern power is characterized by using violence that is intensely corporal and brutal and wielded in a personal manner. Modern power is defined by using violence in a more anonymous, invisible, and lighter way. Disciplinary institutions and practices would follow this pattern, which is less violent and more invisible and diffuse but extremely invasive.

16. Different disciplines studying the problems associated with violence, such as medicine, psychology, psychiatry, and legal studies, have been redescribing women's abnormalities, pathologizing women who are victims of male dominance, created and supported at the same time by patriarchal cultures that allow female domination (Caplan, 1991).

◈ References

Anderson, K., & Umberson, D. (2001). Gendering violence: Masculinity and power in men's account of domestic violence. *Gender & Society, 15,* 358–380.

Baker, L. P. (1997). "And I went back": Battered women's negotiation of choice. *Journal of Contemporary Ethnography, 26,* 55–74.

Barnett, O. W. (2000). Why battered women do not leave, Part 1: External exhibiting factors within society. *Trauma, Violence and Abuse, 1,* 343–372.

Berns, N. (2001). Degendering the problem and gendering the blame: Political discourse on women and violence. *Gender & Society, 15,* 262–281.

Berns, N., & Schweingruber, D. (2007). "When you, re involved it's just different": Marking sense of domestic violence. *Violence Against Women, 13,* 240–261.

Billig, M., Condor, S., Edwards, D., Gane, M., Milldleton, D., & Radley, A. (1988). *Ideological dilemmas: A Social psychology of everyday thinking.* London: Sage.

Birch, M., & Miller, T. (2002). Inviting intimacy: The interview as therapeutic opportunity. *International Journal of Social Research Methodology, 3,* 189–202.

Boateng, P. (1999, November 24–25). *Living without fear: An agenda for action.* Speech made at the Home Office Special Conference on Violence Against Women. Retrieved March 1, 2007, from http://www.homeoffice.gov.uk/dometsicviolence/pbspeech.htm

Bunch, C., & Carrillo, R. (1992). *Gender violence: A development and human rights issue.* Dublin, Ireland: Attic Press.

Caplan, P. (1991). How do they decide who is normal? The bizarre but true tale of the DSM process. *Canadian Psychology, 32,* 162–170.

Collins, P. (1998). Negotiation selves: Reflections on "unstructured" interviewing. *Sociological Research Online, 3.* Retrieved from November 2, 2009, http://www.socresonline.org.uk/3/3/2.html

Corrin, C. (Ed.). (1996). *Women in a violent world: Feminist analyses and resistance across Europe.* Edinburgh, UK: Edinburgh University Press.

Cosgrove, K. (1996). No man has the right. In C. Corrin (Ed.), *Women in a violent world: Feminist analyses and resistance across Europe* (pp. 186–203). Edinburgh, UK: Edinburgh University Press.

Crenshaw, K. W. (1994). Mapping the margins: Intersectionality, identity politics and violence against women of color. In M. Fineman & R. Mykitiuk (Eds.), *The public nature of private violence* (pp. 93–121). New York: Routledge.

Criminal Justice System. (2005). *Rebuilding lives: Supporting victims of crime.* London: HMSO.

Dobash, R. E., & Dobash, R. P. (1992). *Women, violence and social change.* London: Routledge.

Dobash, R. E., & Dobash, R. P. (1997). Violence against women. In L. O'Toole & J. R. Schiffman (Eds.), *Gender violence: Interdisciplinary perspectives* (pp. 266–279). New York: New York University Press.

Dunn, L. J., & Powell-Williams, M. (2007). "Everybody makes choices": Victim advocates and the social construction of battered women's victimization and agency. *Violence Against Women, 13,* 977–1001.

Eisikovits, Z., & Buchbinder, E. (1999). Talking control: Metaphors used by battered women. *Violence Against Women, 5,* 845–868.

Fairclough, N. (1995). *Critical discourse analysis: The critical study of language.* London: Longman.

Field, C. A., Caetano R., & Nelson, S. (2004). Alcohol and violence related cognitive risk factors associated with the perpetration of intimate partner violence. *Journal of Family Violence, 19,* 249–253.

Finney, A. (2004). *Alcohol and intimate partner violence: Key findings from the research.* London: Home Office, Communication Development Unit.

Foucault, M. (1991). *Discipline and punish: The birth of the prison.* London: Penguin.

Fraser, H. (2005). Women, love, and intimacy "gone wrong": fire, wind and ice. *Affiliate, 20*(1), 10–20.

Gardner, C. B. (1990). Safe conduct: Women, crime and self in public places. *Social Problems, 37,* 311–327.

Hague, G. (1998). Interagency work and domestic violence in the UK. *Women's Studies International Forum, 21,* 441–449.

Hague, G., & Mullender, A. (2006). Who listens? The voices of domestic violence survivors in service provision in the United Kingdom. *Violence Against Women, 12,* 568–587.

Hanmer, J., & Maynard, M. (Ed.). (1987). *Women, violence and social control.* London: Macmillan.

Hearn, J. (1998). *The violences of men: How men talk about and how agencies respond to men's violence to women.* London: Sage.

Hester, M., Kelly, L., & Radford, J. (Eds.). (1996). *Women, violence and male power.* Buckingham, UK: Open University Press.

Hester, M., Pearson, C., & Harwin, N. (1998). *Making an impact: Children and domestic violence. A reader.* Essex, UK: Barnardo's.

Hill Collins, P. (1998). It's all in the family: Intersections of gender, race and nation. *Hypatia, 13,* 62–82.

Hirschmann, N. J. (1997). Toward a feminist theory of freedom. In M. L. Shanley & U. Narayan (Eds.), *Reconstructing political theory: Feminist perspectives* (pp. 195–210). Cambridge, UK: Polity.

Holstein, J. A., & Gubrium, J. F. (2000). *The self we live by: Narrative identity in a post-modern world.* New York: Oxford University Press.

Home Office. (2004). *The Victim's Charter: A statement of service standards for victims of crime.* London: Criminal Justice System.

hooks, b. (1997). Violence in intimate relationships: A feminist perspective. In L. O'Toole & J. Schiffman (Eds.), *Gender violence: Interdisciplinary perspectives* (pp. 279–285). New York: New York University Press.

House of Commons, Committee of Public Accounts. (2003). *Helping victims and witnesses: The work of victim support* (Seventeenth Report of Session 2002–2003). London: Stationery Office Limited.

Josselson, R. (2004). The hermeneutics of faith and the hermeneutics of suspicion. *Narrative Inquiry, 14,* 1–28.

Kelly, L. (1988). *Surviving sexual violence.* Cambridge, UK: Polity.

Kelly, L. (1996). When does the speaking profit us? Reflections on the challenges of developing feminist perspective on abuse and violence by women. In M. Hester, L. Kelly, & J. Radford (Eds.), *Women, violence and male power: Feminist activism, research and practice* (pp. 34–49). Buckingham, UK: Open University Press.

Kelly, L., Burton, S., & Regan, L. (1996). Beyond victim or survivor: Sexual violence, identity, and feminist theory and practice. In L Adkins & V. Merchant (Eds.), *Sexualizing the social: Power and the organization of sexuality* (pp. 77–101). Basingstoke, UK: Macmillan Press.

Kelly, L., & Radford, J. (1996). "Nothing really happened." The invalidation of women's experiences. In M Hester, L. Kelly, & J. Radford (Eds.), *Women, violence and male power* (pp. 19–33). Buckingham, UK: Open University Press.

Kendrick, K. (1998). Producing the battered woman: Shelter politics and the power of feminist voice. In N. Naples (Ed.), *Community activism and feminist politics: Organizing across race, class and gender* (pp. 151–173). New York: Routledge.

Lamb, S. (1996). *The trouble with blame: Victims, perpetrators and responsibility.* Cambridge, MA: Harvard University Press.

Lamb, S. (1999). Construction the victim: Popular images and lasting labels. In S. Lamb (Ed.), *New versions of victims: Feminists struggle with the concept* (pp. 108–139). New York: New York University Press.

Lea, J. S. (2007). A discursive investigation into victim responsibility in rape. *Feminism and Psychology, 17,* 495–514.

Lempert, L. B. (1997). The other side of help: Negative effects in the help-seeking processes of abused women. *Qualitative Sociology, 20,* 289–308.

Loseke, D. R. (1992). *The battered woman and shelters: The social construction of wife abuse.* Albany: State University of New York Press.

Loseke, D. R. (1999). *Thinking about social problems: An introduction to constructionist perspectives.* New York: Aldine de Gruyter.

Loseke, D. R. (2001). Lived realities and formula stories of "battered women." In J. F. Gubrium & J. A. Holstein (Eds.), *Institutional selves: Troubled identities in a post-modern world* (pp. 107–126). New York: Oxford University Press.

MacCannell, D., & MacCannell, J. F. (1993). Violence, power and pleasure: A revisionist reading of Foucault from the victim perspective. In C. Ramazanoğlu (Ed.), *Up against Foucault: Explorations of some tensions between Foucault and feminism* (pp. 203–238). London: Routledge.

Malos, E. (2000). Supping with the devil?: Multi-agency initiatives on domestic violence. In J. Radford, L. Harne, & M. Friedberg (Eds.), *Women, violence and strategies for action: Feminist research, policy and practice* (pp. 120–136). Buckingham, UK: Open University Press.

Mama, A. (1989). *The hidden struggle: Statutory and voluntary sector responses to violence against Black women in the home.* London: London Race and Housing Research Unit.

Mason, J. (2002). Qualitative interviewing: Asking, listening and interpreting. In T. May (Ed.), *Qualitative research in action* (pp. 225–241). London: Sage.

Maynard, M. (1993). Violence towards women. In D. Richardson & V. Robinson (Eds.), *Introducing women's studies: Feminist theory and practice* (pp. 99–122). London: Macmillan.

McDermott, J. M., & Garofalo, J. (2004). When advocacy for domestic violence victims backfires: Types and sources of victim disempowerment. *Violence Against Women, 10,* 1245–1266.

McLaughlin, J. (2003). *Feminist social and political theory: Contemporary debates and dialogues.* New York: Palgrave Macmillan.

Mezey, G., & Stanko, E. (1996). Women and violence. In K. Abel, M. Buszewicz, & E. Staples (Eds.), *Planning community mental health service for women: A multiprofessional handbook* (pp. 166–175). Routledge: London.

Miller, T., & Bell, L. (2002). Consenting to what? Issues of access, gatekeeping and "informed" consent. In M. Mauthner, M. Birch, & T. Miller (Eds.), *Ethics in qualitative research* (pp. 53–69). London: Sage.

Morgan, K. (2005). *Violence against women: The discursive construction of a culture of resignation.* Unpublished doctoral thesis, University of Bristol, UK.

Morgan, K. (2006). Cheating wives and vice girls: The construction of a culture of resignation. *Women's Studies International Forum, 29,* 489–498.

Morgan, K., & Thapar-Björkert, S. (2006). "I'd rather you'd lay me on the floor and start kicking me": Understanding symbolic violence in everyday life. *Women's Studies International Forum, 29,* 441–452.

National Audit Office. (2002, 23 October). *Helping victims and witnesses: The work of Victim Support (2001–2002)* (Report by the Comptroller and Auditor-General HC1212. Session 2001–2002). London: The Stationery Office.

National Statistics Online. (2001). *Neighbourhood statistics: Neighbourhood profile.* Retrieved 30 March, 2005, from http://www.neighbourhood.statistics.gov.uk/dissemination/AreaProfile2.do?tab=2

Ollett, B. (1994, April). *Alcohol and crime: A Women's Aid perspective: Causes of domestic violence.* Paper presented at the conference From Problems to Solutions: Alcohol and Crime, Carmarthen, UK.

Pahl, J. (Ed.). (1985). *Private violence and public policy: The needs of battered women and the response of the public services.* London: Routledge.

Patel, P. (1999). The multi-agency approach to domestic violence: A panacea or obstacle to women's struggles fro freedom from violence. In N. Harwin, G. Hague, & E. Malos (Eds.), *The multi-agency approach to domestic violence: New opportunities, old challenges?* (pp. 172–190). London: Whiting and Birch.

Peled, E., Eisikovits, Z., Enosh, G., & Winstok, Z. (2002). Choice and empowerment for battered women who stay: Towards a constructivist model. *Social Work, 45,* 9–25.

Pence, E. (2005, March). *Violence against women: Coordinating activism, research and service provision conference.* Plenary at the ESRC seminar, University of Bristol, UK.

Pence, E., & McMahon, M. (1999). Duluth: A coordinated community response to domestic violence. In N. Harwin, G. Hague, & E. Malos (Eds.), *The multi-agency approach to domestic violence: New opportunities, old challenges?* (pp. 180–194). London: Whiting and Birch.

Radford, J., & Russell, D. E. H. (Eds.). (1992). *Femicide: The politics of woman killing.* Buckingham, UK: Open University Press.

Radford, J., & Stanko, E. A. (1996). Violence against women and children: The contradictions of crime control under patriarchy. In M. Hester, L. Kelly, & J. Radford (Eds.), *Women, violence and male power* (pp. 142–157). Buckingham, UK: Open University Press.

Ricoeur, P. (1981). *Hermeneutics and the human sciences.* Cambridge, UK: Cambridge University Press.

Rothenberg, B. (2003). "We don't have time for social change": Cultural compromise and the battered woman syndrome. *Gender & Society, 17,* 771–786.

Smart, C. (1989). *Feminism and the power of law.* London: Routledge.

Smart, C., & Smart, B. (1978). Accounting for rape: Reality and myth in press reporting. In C. Smart & B. Smart (Eds.), W*omen, sexuality and social control* (pp. 10–23). London: Routledge.

Spackman, P. (2000). *Victim support handbook: Helping people cope with crime.* London: Hodder and Stoughton.

Stanko, E. A. (1985). *Intimate intrusions: Women's experience of male violence.* London: Routledge.

Stanko, E. A (1990). When precaution is normal: A feminist critique of crime prevention. In L. Gelsthorp & A. Morris (Eds.), *Feminist perspectives in criminology* (pp. 171–183). Milton Keynes, UK: Open University Press.

Stanko, E. A. (Ed.). (2003). *The meanings of violence.* London: Routledge.

Stanko, E. A. (2006). Theorizing about violence: Observations from the Economic and Social Research Council's Violence Research Programme. *Violence Against Women, 12,* 543–555.

Thompson, J. B. (1981). Critical hermeneutics: *A study in the thought of Paul Ricoeur and Jürgen Habermas.* Cambridge, UK: Cambridge University Press.

Tisdall, E. K. M. (2003). The rising tide of female violence? Researching girls' own understanding and experiences of violent behavior. In R. M. Lee & E. A. Stanko (Eds.), *Researching violence: Essays on methodology and measurement* (pp. 137–153). London: Routledge.

Titscher, S., Meyer, M., Wodak, R., & Vetter, E. (2000). *Methods of text and discourse analysis.* London: Sage.

Van Dijk, T. A. (1997). Discourse as interaction in society. In T. A. van Dijk (Ed.), *Discourses as social interaction* (pp. 1–37). London: Sage.

Victim Support. (n.d.). *Rape and sexual assault: Information for women.* London: Author.

Victim Support. (2003). *Resource pack for supporting victims of domestic violence.* London: Victim Support National Office.

Victim Support. (2005). *Service Personnel and Equal Opportunities Survey report 2004.* London: Victim Support National Office, Research and Development Department.

Victim Support. (2006). *Victim and witness review: Annual report and accounts.* London: Author.

Victim Support. (2007). *Handbook on delivering Victim Support's enhanced services* (Interim version). London: Victim Support National Office.

Victim Support Magazine. (1998, autumn). London: Author.

Von Hentig, H. (1948). *The criminal and his victim.* New Haven, CT: Yale University Press.

Walklate, S. (2003). Can there be a feminist victimology? In P. Davies, P. Francis, & V. Jupp (Eds.), *Victimisation: Theory, research and policy* (pp. 28–45). Basingstoke, UK: Palgrave Macmillan.

Weaver, C. K. (1998). Crimewatch UK: Keeping women off the streets. In C. Carter, G. Branston, & S. Allan (Eds.), *New, gender and power* (pp. 248–262). London: Routledge.

Westlund, A. (1999). Pre-modern and modern power: Foucault and the case of domestic violence. *Signs, 24,* 1046–1066.

Williams, B. (1999). The Victim's Charter: Citizens as consumers of criminal justice services. *Howard Journal, 38,* 384–396.

Wodak, R. (1996). *Disorders of discourse.* London: Longman.

Wolfgang, M. E. (1958). *Patterns in criminal homicide.* Philadelphia: University of Pennsylvania Press.

Yeatman, A. (1997). Feminism and power. In M. L. Shanley & U. Narayan (Eds.), *Reconstructing political theory: Feminist perspectives* (pp. 144–157). Cambridge, UK: Polity.

READING 32

A 1975 Supreme Court decision makes stopping persons with a "Mexican appearance" for no other reason legal under the 4th Amendment. However, because the Immigration and Naturalization Service (INS) does not keep statistics on incidents of stopping and interrogating legal residents (false positives), there is little information on the extent to which Latino Americans are differentially treated and discriminated against by the agency of the criminal justice system. In an effort to describe the injustices Latino Americans (legal citizens and illegal residents) face, Mary Romero uses a case study approach and describes a 5-day immigration raid in the late 1990s known as the Chandler Roundup, which took place in Chandler, Arizona. More than 400 stops were documented, and she examined data on 91 complaints filed during the 5 days. All of the complainants were Latino or of Mexican descent. Several (14)

Source: Romero, Mary. 2006. "Racial Profiling and Immigration Law Enforcement: Rounding Up of Usual Suspects in the Latino Community." *Critical Sociology* 32:447–473. Reprinted with permission.

were stopped more than once during the 5-day period. Nearly half of the complainants (42) were clearly not illegal immigrants. Only 33 outcomes for the 91 incidences were documented; 23 were detained, and only 3 of those were clear cases of illegal residence. Equally disconcerting is the way the "suspects" were treated, some handcuffed, while others were interrogated in a manner inconsistent with the way "white" people are typically stopped and questioned.

Racial Profiling and Immigration Law Enforcement

Rounding Up of Usual Suspects in the Latino Community

Mary Romero

"**W**here are you from?"

I didn't answer. I wasn't sure who the agent, a woman, was addressing. She repeated the question in Spanish, "*¿De dónde eres?*"

Without thinking, I almost answered her question— in Spanish. A reflex. I caught myself in midsentence and stuttered in a nonlanguage.

"*¿Dónde naciste?*" she asked again . . .

She was browner than I was. I might have asked her the same question . . .

"Are you sure you were born in Las Cruces?" she asked again.

I turned around and smiled, "Yes, I'm sure." She didn't smile back. She and her driver sat there for a while and watched me as I continued walking . . .

"Sons of bitches," I whispered, "pretty soon I'll have to carry a passport in my own neighborhood." . . . It was like a video I played over and over—memorizing the images . . . *Are you sure you were born in Las Cruces?* ringing in my ears. (Sáenz 1992: xii)

The personal and community cost of racial profiling to Mexican Americans who are treated as outside the law does not appear in official criminal justice statistics. Benjamin Alire Sáenz captured the racial-affront experience when Immigration and Naturalization Service (INS) agents use racial profiling; he emphasized the irony when Mexican-American INS agents interrogate other Mexican Americans about their citizenship. Citizenship appears embodied in skin color (that is, brown skin absent a police or border patrol uniform) serving as an indicator of illegal status. Carrying a bodily "figurative border" (Chang 1999), "Mexicanness" becomes the basis for suspecting criminality under immigration law. Mexican Americans and other racialized Latino citizens[1] and legal residents are subjected to insults, questions, unnecessary stops, and searches. Surveillance of citizenship, relentless in low-income and racialized neighborhoods along the border and in urban barrios, increases the likelihood of discrimination in employment, housing, and education. Latinos (particularly dark complected, poor, and working class) are at risk before the law. The following article uses a case study approach to identify the use of racial profiling in immigration law enforcement; and to document the impact on US citizens and legal residents.

◆ Domestic Function of Immigration Policy

Conquest of the Southwest subliminally grafted Mexicans to "the American psyche as a 'foreigner,' even though the land had once belonged to Mexico" (Romero 2001:1091). Following the Mexican-American War, special law-enforcement agencies were established to patrol the newly formed border and to police Mexicans who remained in occupied territory, as well as later migrants across the border. The most distinct form of social control and domination used by the US in this occupation was the creation of the Texas and Arizona Rangers. Maintaining the interests of cattle barons in Texas, the Texas Rangers treated Mexicans living along the border as cattle thieves and bandits when they attempted to reclaim stolen property from cattle barons. Similarly, the Arizona Rangers protected capitalist interests by protecting strikebreakers against Mexican miners. Following a parallel pattern, the INS rarely raided the fields during harvest time and scheduled massive immigration roundups during periods of economic recession and union activity (Acuña 2000). Remembering the policing functions of the Texas and Arizona Rangers and the Border Patrol (including the current militarization at the border) is crucial in recognizing the social functions accomplished by racialized immigrant raids, sweeps, and citizenship inspections (Acuña 2000; Andreas 2000; Dunn 1996; Nevins 2002). Under Operation Wetback, for example, only persons of Mexican descent were included in the campaign and thus were the only group to bear the burden of proving citizenship (Garcia 1980). Militarized sweeps of Mexicans maintained the community in "a state of permanent insecurity" in the 1950s; in response a petition was submitted to the United Nations charging the USA with violating the Universal Declaration of Human Rights (Acuña 2000:306).

A number of recent studies unveil the hypocrisy of US border policies that manage to allow enough undocumented immigrant labor in to meet employers' demands while at the same time increasing INS and Border Patrol budgets (Andreas 2000; Massey et al. 2002; Nevins 2002). Longitudinal studies comparing INS efficiency and increased budget prior to the 1986 Immigration Reform and Control Act (IRCA) to late-1990s immigration law reforms suggest that the cost of detaining unauthorized border crossers has increased (Massey et al. 2002). Immigration researchers (Chavez 2001; Massey et al. 2002) claim that we are paying for the illusion of controlled borders while politicians make a political spectacle, pandering to alarmist public discourse about a Mexican immigrant invasion, the breakdown of the US-Mexico border, and increased crime resulting from immigration (Chavez 2001).

Operation Blockade and Operation Gatekeeper failed to deter extralegal immigration from Mexico. US employers continue to have access to a vulnerable, cheap labor force created by assigning workers an "illegal" status. The worst cost of these failed policies are the increasing loss of human lives as migrants are forced to cross the border in the most desolate areas of the desert (Cornelius 2001; Eschbach et al. 1999).

In what follows I demonstrate that more than "illusion" or "political capital' is gained. Meeting employers' demand for cheap labor while appearing to deter immigration includes a cost borne by Mexican Americans and other racialized Latinos. Immigration research tends to ignore the political, social, and economic costs paid by Mexican Americans and other Latinos who are implicated by immigration policies. Racialized citizens and legal residents become subjects of immigration stops and searches, and pay the cost of increased racism—sometimes in the form of hate crimes or the decrease of government funding and services to their communities (Chang and Aoki 1997; Johnson 1993; Mehan 1997). Both Operation Blockade and Operation Gatekeeper provided impetus to anti-immigration policies that not only decreased public funding assisting low-income Latino communities in general (regardless of citizenship status) but also fueled racism and anti-affirmative action policies (Chavez 2001; Lee et al. 2001). This article explores the ways that immigration raids function as a policing practice to maintain and reinforce subordinated status among working-class US citizens and legal residents of Mexican ancestry.

Critical Race Theory and Immigration Law Enforcement

Using a critical race theory framework, I examine racial- and class-based micro- and macro-aggressions that result from the use of racial profiling in immigration law enforcement. Citizens sharing racial and cultural similarities with "aliens" targeted by immigration law enforcement agents have been, and continue to be, treated as "foreigners" and denied equal protection under the law. Racialized immigration law enforcement not only places darker Mexican Americans at risk, but threatens members of the community who are bilingual speakers, have friends or family members who are immigrants, or who engage in certain cultural practices. Critical race theory "challenges ahistoricism and insists on a contextual/historical analysis of the law" (Matsuda et al. 1993:6). It aims to illuminate structures that create and perpetuate domination and subordination in their "everyday operation" (Valdez et al. 2002:3). Applying a critical race theory perspective to immigration, legal scholar Kevin Johnson (2002:187) argues that, "exclusions found in the immigration laws effectuate and reinforce racial subordination in the United States." A history of immigration laws based on racial exclusions reinforces stereotypes the Mexicans and other third-world immigrants are inferior and "alien" (Hing 1997; Johnson 1997). Conceptualizing racial profiling practices in immigration law enforcement as micro- and macro-aggressions—a petit apartheid—helps recognize the discriminatory functions that policing and inspections have on citizenship participation and the rights of Mexican Americans, Mexican immigrants, and other racialized Latinos, particularly the poor and working class.

Building on the work of psychologist Chester Pierce, critical race theorists have found the concept of micro-aggressions useful in describing the form of policing common in communities of color: "subtle, stunning, often automatic, and non-verbal exchanges which are 'put downs' of blacks by offenders" (Pierce et al. 1978:66).[2] In her research on race and crime, Katheryn Russell distinguished between racial assaults on a personal level or micro-aggressions, and "face group affronts" or macro-aggressions. The latter type of affront is "not directed toward a particular Black person, but at Blackness in general" and may be made "by a private individual or official authority" (Russell 1998:139). Macro-aggressions reinforce stereotypes of racialized groups "either criminals, illiterates, or intellectual inferiors" (Russell 1998:140).[3] Dragan Milovanovic and Katheryn K. Russell (2001: vii) argued that both micro- and macro-aggressions work as "a cycle which

sustains hierarchy and harms of reductions and repression." "Harms of reduction occur when offended parties experience a loss in their standing . . . or restriction, preventing them from achieving a desired position or standing" (Henry and Milovanovic 1999:7–8). Harms of reduction and repression are detrimental because "they belittle, demean, ridicule or subordinate on the one hand, and on the other, they limit access to equal opportunities and fair dealings before the law" (Milovanovic and Russell 2001:xvi).

Daniel Georges-Abeyie's (2001:x) theoretical paradigm of grand and petit apartheid links current practices of racial profiling with other "negative social factors and discretional decision-making by both criminal justice agents and criminal justice agencies." Georges-Abeyie's theoretical work outlines a continuum of petit apartheid discriminatory practices ranging from the covert and informal to the overt and formal. Petit apartheid has been used to explain racial profiling in the war against drugs (Campbell 2001; Covington 2001), regulating and policing public space (Bass 2001; Ferrell 2001b), under-representation of persons of color interested in law enforcement (Ross 2001) and the use of racial derogation in prosecutors' closing arguments (Johnson 2001).

Petit apartheid relates to concerns about struggles over access to urban public space, freedom of movement, the processes of capital investment, political decision-making, and policing first theorized by Henri Lefebvre (1996 [1968]) and others (see Caldeira 2000; Ferrell 2001a; Harvey 1973, 1996; Holston 1999; Mitchell 2003). Images and perceptions of public space are used to encourage, discourage, or prohibit use and movement. Exclusionary models of public life are most noted for privileging middle-class consumers. Surveillance, stops, and searches maintain a landscape of suspicion and reinforce white, middle-class citizens' suspicions of racial minorities and protect their access to public space. When citizenship is racially embodied though law-enforcement practices that target Mexican-American neighborhoods and business areas, then Henri Lefebvre's (1996 [1968]: 174) statement about urban space is actualized: "The right of the city manifests itself as a superior form of rights: right to freedom, to individualization in socialization, to habitat and to inhabit."

Immigration law enforcement assists such exclusionary use of urban public spaces and limits freedom of movement. However, the INS is in the position of having to negotiate an adequate flow of undocumented labor to meet urban capitalist needs while maintaining the appearance of controlling immigration. Consequently, immigration law enforcement in US cities is not structured around systematic or random checking of identification but rather a pattern of citizenship inspection that maintains the landscape of suspicion. Given the class and racial segregation perpetuated by exclusive residential zoning, the INS targets ethnic cultural spaces marked by Mexican-owned businesses, agencies offering bilingual services, and neighborhoods with the highest concentration of poor and working-class Latinos. Within these areas, INS agents engage in "typing" suspected aliens (Heyman 1995; Weissinger 1996) that embodies a "figurative border" (Chang 1999). In the process of typing Mexicans as suspects, Americans are "whitened."

The 1975 Supreme Court decision that "Mexican appearance" "constitutes a legitimate consideration under the Fourth Amendment for making an immigration stop" (Johnson 2000:676) legalized micro- and macro-aggressions inflicted upon Mexican Americans. Micro- and macro-aggressions, as well as petit apartheid, are experienced by Mexican Americans when they are caught within a racially profiled dragnet in which INS agents operate with unchecked discretion. Harms of reduction and repression occur when Latinos are subjected to racially motivated (and frequently class-based) stops and searches and race-related INS abuse (Arriola 1996–97; Benitez 1994; Lazos 2002; Vargas 2001). Micro-aggressions are racial affronts on a personal level, experienced when an individual Mexican American is stopped and asked to prove citizenship status; macro-aggressions are group affronts because they are directed towards "Mexicanness" in general. Macro-aggressions target dark complexions and physical characteristics characterized as "Mexican" or "Latino;" speaking Spanish, listening to Spanish music, shopping at Mexican-owned businesses, or any other cultural practices bring on racially motivated stops.

 ## The Case of the Chandler Roundup

INS data provide statistics on the number of individuals apprehended but the agency does not collect data on the number of individuals stopped and searched who were citizens or legal residents. Consequently, the impact of racialized immigration law enforcement on communities of color is rarely visible in legal reporting procedures. However, every once in awhile, community protests against raids gain sufficient media attention to require public officials to respond by conducting investigations into allegations of law-enforcement wrongdoings. In these rare instances it becomes possible to uncover "more covert, hidden forms of discrimination" (Georges-Abeyie 2001:xiv) in the documentation of civil-rights or human-rights violations. Formal investigations reveal the group and communities targeted and the ways that public and private space is regulated under the auspices of immigration law enforcement. These institutional practices are "relations of ruling" and unravel the everyday management of social control and domination (Smith 1990, 1999).

In order to identify micro- and macro-aggressions and petit apartheid accomplished by immigration raids, I analyzed data from two official investigations into a five-day immigration raid in Chandler, Arizona. The raid was the third of its kind conducted by the Chandler Police during the summer of 1997 (Fletcher 1997). The immigration sweep came to be known as the "Chandler Roundup," reinforcing both the cowboy legacy of law enforcement in Mexican-American communities and the notion that Mexicans are "strays." On July 27, 1997, the Chandler Police Department and Border Patrol agents from Casa Grande Station and the Tucson area began a five-day immigration raid as a joint operation in the most highly populated Latino section of the city. Over the five days, 432 suspected undocumented Mexicans were arrested. The Chief Patrol Agent's *Summary Report of the Border Patrol*

Operations in Chandler, AZ cited in the Arizona Attorney General's report (Office of the Attorney General Grant Wood 1997:15–7) outlined the daily activities as follows:

Day 1—July 27, 1997: "Within three hours . . . more than 75 arrests out of approximately 100 contacts" were made through "casual contacts . . . along the streets in and around public areas." A total of 83 arrests were made that day (82 Mexicans and 1 Guatemalan).

Day 2—July 28, 1997: The target area was "expanded to one square mile of the downtown Chandler area" and "nearly all contacts occurred outside dwellings" and "the exceptions were the result of specific information or probable cause." On this day, they arrested 102 Mexicans.

Day 3—July 29, 1997: Working with Chandler Police between 4:00 AM and 8.00 AM, they arrested 69 (ethnicity not noted). Bicycle patrols working public areas and trailer parks arrested an additional 49.

Day 4—July 30, 1997: A total of 77 illegal aliens were arrested.

Day 5—July 31, 1997: 52 arrests were made.

Immigrant advocates and Mexican-American residents in Chandler began organizing and held several community meetings with the police chief, Chandler City Council members, and the State Attorney General's staff. As a consequence of the public outcry, the investigations and lawsuits that followed produced government documentation of law-enforcement practices that detail the use of micro- and macro-aggressions towards Mexican Americans and other Latinos racially profiled as criminal, unauthorized, or extralegal. The primary focus of the investigations was police misconduct and violation of civil rights. A secondary issue concerned the role of local police departments participating in joint operations with the INS.

The State Attorney General's office immediately responded to complaints and began collecting eyewitness accounts from individuals willing to be interviewed.

The Office to the Attorney General Grant Woods issued a report, *Results of the Chandler Survey,* in December 1997. Data collected and analyzed in the report included: minutes of meetings with the Latino community in Chandler, interviews with citizens and legal residents stopped during the five-day operation, minutes of City Council Meetings with community members, newspaper articles, memoranda between city officials, review of Chandler Police radio dispatch audio tapes, police field notes, and witness testimonies. The Attorney General's report is organized into the following sections: background information,[4] summary of the survey,[5] summary of the Commission on Civil Rights Reports, and an evaluation of claims of civil-rights violation and recommendations.

The following summer, the City of Chandler paid for an independent investigation (Breen et al. 1998). The final product was the three-volume report. Volume I, *Report of Independent Investigation Into July 1997 Joint Operation Between Border Patrol and Chandler Police Department,* includes a mission statement, narrative[6] and summaries of interviews conducted with public officials.[7] Volume II, *Complainants,* is the independent investigators' direct response to the descriptive accounts of civil-rights violations documented in the Office of the Attorney General's *Survey.* Incidents reported in Volume II include only complaints formally filed with the Chandler Police, the Office of the Attorney General, or the Mexican Consultant's office. Volume III, *Appendices to Report of Independent Investigation,* includes four maps (the Tucson sector of the Border Patrol, Chandler and Vicinity, Area of Operation Restoration, and areas covered in the joint operation), excerpts from policy and procedure handbooks,[8] a survey of policies regarding illegal aliens in 14 cities in border states, a survey of how media learned of the 1997 joint operation, the Chandler Police Department's Community-Oriented Policing Programs; and 89 records of Border Patrol Forms I-213 (Deportable Alien) produced during the Joint Operation.

The summary section of each report differs in the perspective taken. In the State Attorney General's report, *Results of the Chandler Survey,* the construction of immigration as a problem in Chandler is presented from the community's perspective and supported by official documents whereas the *Report of Independent Investigation Into July 1997 Joint Operation Between Border Patrol and Chandler Police Department* privileges the INS and police's documentation of a growing immigration problem and presents the "roundup" as the official response. Witness accounts cited in the *Survey* were collected immediately following the five-day immigration sweep. Each of the civil-rights violations from witness accounts noted in the Attorney General's report was investigated a year later by the independent investigators; however, only those violations corroborated by police officers' interviews, field notes, or arrest records were deemed legitimate in the *Report of Independent Investigation*. Defining validity with criteria that privileged police interviews and records (as well as INS official documentation) assured that the independent investigators' report minimized the violation of civil rights and was more favorable to the Chandler Police Department than was the Attorney General's report.

This study is an analysis of the official reports. While these data were obtained from legal documents constructed within a specific political, social, and economic context, the variety of documents produced presents diverse perspectives, including interested community members, citizens and legal residents stopped and searched, police officers participating in the raid, and City Council members. Clearly, the data analyzed do not include a complete profile of all the stops that were made during the five-day operation. However, the two reports provide a rare insight into strategically planned immigration law enforcement targeting low-income areas highly populated by Mexican Americans.

Complainants (Volume II of the *Report of Independent Investigation*) contained the following data: a profile of the type of individuals stopped and searched, activities by these individuals that warranted "reasonable suspicion," the type of documents these individuals are expected to carry, and the outcomes of stops. A few of the complaints include a brief summary of the incident in question. Not all complaints recorded by the government officials are complete, but as documentary practices

of agencies of control, the data reveal everyday processes of ruling apparatus in low-income Latino communities (Smith 1990, 1999). Although only 71 individuals made formal complaints, 91 complaints were filed because each incident was documented as a separate complaint—a number of individuals were stopped more than once. I coded each of the 91 complaints, looking for patterns of immigration enforcement, including ethnicity of complainant, age, citizenship status, sex, activity engaged in at the time of the stop, request for identification, and outcomes of the stop.

Narratives are also an important source of data for identifying micro- and macro-aggressions and petit apartheid restricting citizenship rights, freedom of movement, and use of public and private urban space. Two types of narratives were coded. First, the narrative of the reports itself. This included setting up the story of the Chandler Roundup (what is the context selected as background information to the raid?), an explanation of Mexican immigration requiring a joint operation between Chandler Police Department and INS (how is the problem defined?), and, the justification for using racial profiling (why were low-income Mexican Americans stopped and searched?). The second type of narrative appears in the Attorney General's Report. These are summaries of witness accounts and detailed descriptions of incidents documented by the police in their radio-dispatch reports. Witness accounts were coded for verbal and non-verbal racial affronts against individuals and against "Mexicanness" in general. Radio-dispatch reports were coded for incidents of racial profiling and regulation of movement and activity. In order to explore micro- and micro-aggressions and the existence of processes and structures of petit apartheid in immigration raids, witness accounts and police records were coded for discriminatory practices ranging from the covert and informal to the overt and formal.

My analysis focuses first on identifying the distinct differences in each report for explaining the occurrence of a Joint Operation between the Chandler Police and the INS. I begin with the *Report of Independent Investigation*'s narration of Mexican immigration as a problem requiring the immediate attention of the Chandler Police. Next, I contrast this with the community's depiction of Mexican immigration as a problem constructed by the Chandler City Council's urban-renewal project, Operation Restoration. I then turn to a quantitative analysis of data from the complaints complied in Volume II of the *Report of Independent Investigation*. A qualitative analysis of witness accounts from the Attorney General's Report follows. Here, I analyze the ways that citizenship is policed and the impact this form of policing has on freedom of movement and use of urban space.

◈ Narrating Mexican Immigration as a Problem

Considering that the USA acquired Arizona as a result of the Mexican-American War, and that the Chandler area is the homeland of the Tohono O'Odham Nation, the version of history narrated in the *Report of Independent Investigation*'s (Breen et al. 1998:1) is clearly biased and self serving: "Chandler, Arizona is a city of about 160,000 that has blossomed in slightly more than a century from a seed planted by Alexander Chandler, who came to Arizona in 1887 as territorial veterinary surgeon." The first mention of Mexicans in the narrative describes their presence as workers and Anglos as employers:

In the first years after the town's founding, cotton became the crop of choice for central Arizona farmers. These were the years of the Mexican Revolution, and thousands of Mexicans streamed northward to escape the violence spawned by it. Labor-intensive cotton farming provided a way for those fleeing the revolution to earn a living. Thus began a marriage between Chandler and those of Hispanic heritage that has lasted till the present day. (Breen et al. 1998:1)

This seeming "marriage" involved Mexicans providing the labor and Americans (read whites) providing the land from which the cotton was to be harvested. Mexican presence is also noted during WWII in reference to the Bracero Program: "the Arizona Farm Bureau approved the importation of Mexican workers, who found themselves harvesting cotton alongside German prisoners of war in the labor-starved market" (Breen et al. 1998:2).

The narrative continues by describing the "streams" that turn into the present "hordes" of Mexican immigrants entering the area. "Ron Sanders, chief patrol agent for the Border Patrol's Tucson sector, calls Chandler 'the most notorious hub for alien smuggling in the United States of America'" . . . until "literally thousands" of illegal aliens were in Chandler (Breen et al. 1998:2). INS intelligence in Dallas is the source for citing Chandler "as a major smuggling area as far south as Honduras and El Salvador" (Breen et al. 1998:2). The narrative continues with a litany from a handful of growers who complained about garbage, use of water, stolen fruit, and violence. To reinforce immigration as a social problem, the report lists six "homicides allegedly committed by illegal aliens" dating back to 1982 (Breen et al. 1998:10). In 1997, the Casa Grande Border Patrol station began targeting operations in groves. According to the Chandler Police, complaints about harassment of citizens and an increase in crime led to a series of joint actions in the summer of 1997. No doubt the federal government's Operations Gatekeeper, Hold-the-Line, and other steps in militarizing the USA-Mexico border, gave local authorities in Chandler tacit approval to engage in the Joint Operation.

However, the Attorney General's *Survey* argues that another chain of events led up to the Joint Operation. Based on community protests voiced at meetings and interviews given to the media, the beginning of the "immigration problem" is not dated to the founding of the city but rather to the City of Chandler's 1995 urban-renewal project, Operation Restoration. City Council members began Operation Restoration by creating a task force to study issues affecting residents. The Neighborhood Empowerment Team conducted several mail-in surveys and held neighborhood meetings. Their final report found that residents were concerned about broken streetlights, uncollected garbage, trash in the streets, and unkempt alleys. From its inception, Operation Restoration targeted four older neighborhoods in the city located next to the newly developed downtown area. The targeted areas had the highest percentage of Latinos and low-income residents in the City. Claiming the Joint Operation was about redevelopment, City Council member Martin Sepulveda argued that the Mayor's dream of transforming Chandler into "'The jewel of the East Valley' would push out poor Hispanics" (Office of the Attorney General 1997:5). Operation Restoration was perceived by the Mexican-American community as urban renewal to create high-income real estate ad zoning for strip malls, which would dislocate residents and raise land value beyond the reaches of local businesses.

In response to the community's accusation that the immigration sweep was a Mexican-American removal program, the *Report* stated that the Chandler Police involvement was merely "to undertake intensive zoning code enforcement and . . . step up patrol of the area" (Breen et al. 1998:14). Although the independent investigators' acknowledged that the Neighborhood Empowerment Team's report was limited to repairing and cleaning the surrounding area, they accepted the police department's claim that the Joint Operation with INS was conducted as their part in implementing Operation Restoration. Since Operation Restoration had already targeted "the downtown redevelopment zone, ranging from an eight-block to a four square mile area," using similar parameters for the roundup was justified and did not discriminate against Latinos.

The Attorney General's Office refuted this claim and argued that the Task Force's final report did not include reference to, or recommendations about undocumented immigrants. Importantly, the Office of the Attorney General (1997:14) found that the area targeted for the raid was "without specific articulated criminal activity." Drawing from community meetings, the Attorney General's *Survey* includes the community standpoint primarily from Latinos. They perceived the redevelopment of the downtown area as the major incentive behind the raid. Operation Restoration became a defining moment in their memory of Chandler's history when "Mexicanness" was perceived as undesirable, even as cheap labor.

The careful selection of terms used in the documents evokes associations, meanings, and images supporting political spectacle (Edelman 2001). In order to establish undocumented Mexican immigration as an increasingly dangerous problem, the independent investigators' erased Mexican Americans (and the Tohono O'Odham people) from local history. Restricting Mexican presence to discussions of "immigrants," "laborers," and "criminals" made American citizens of Mexican ancestry invisible. The terms "steams" and "hordes" found in the *Independent Investigation Report* in reference to the movement of people crossing the USA-Mexico border is consistent with the alarmist terminology noted by a number of immigration scholars (Chavez 2001; Santa Ana 2002). Mexican Americans are not mentioned in the *Report* as citizens or as long-term residents in the area but rather in the non-human category of "alien" (Johnson 1997). In the *Report,* Mexican Americans are always referred to in the present tense and only as "Hispanic." Mexican is always used as a term for the unauthorized, extralegal, or undocumented.

◈ Policing Citizenship, Movement and the Use of Urban Space

The policing of citizenship by the Chandler Roundup exemplified procedures used to determine status and urban spaces that require regulation. The focus on policing was the redevelopment area targeted under Operation Restoration; that is, the cultural space inhabited by the large Latino population, low-income residents, and a commercial area serving a Spanish-speaking clientele. However, the image of citizenship visible in the discretionary stops suggests that beyond geography, the landscape of suspicion was embodied in particular behavior and appearance. Complaints made against the Chandler Police make visible the type of persons suspected as unauthorized and thus requiring surveillance. Requests for various types of identification reveal surveillance and restraint of movement in public areas. Embedded in witness account are the aesthetics of authority that enforce exclusionary use of public urban space, remaking the Mexican cultural space into white space. The material consequences of policing reinforce the vulnerability of undocumented workers in the local economy; place low-income, racialized citizens at risk before the law; and legitimate discriminatory behavior towards persons under surveillance.

◈ Complainants Analysis

Analysis of the data in the 91 complaints indicates specific patterns of racial and ethnic typing used in the Joint Operation. Data show that cultural and class behavior or activity was only monitored in targeted locations. The dominant feature of identifiable complainants was their racial ethnic background; all were of Mexican ancestry or Latino.[9] Fourteen of the complainants were stopped more than once during the five-day raid. Complainants ranged in age from 16 to 75; 49 were male and 22 were female. The majority of males were between 18 and 39 years old and the majority of females were between the ages of 30 and 49. Complaints for 42 complainants contained the following information: 11 were US citizens of Mexican ancestry, 15 were Latino legal residents, 1 was a permanent resident, 3 had work permits, 1 had a green card, and 11 were undocumented. There is no documentation in the reports or in the newspaper coverage of a white person stopped during the raid. Ironically, one newspaper quoted a blond, blue-eyed, undocumented Irish immigrant employed at a local law firm as stating that she had never been asked to show proof of her citizenship status: "I don't have to worry. I blend in very well" (Amparano 1997:A1).

The phrase "driving while black" became familiar in debates over racial profiling, similarly the experience of "walking/driving/biking/standing while brown" is common for Mexican Americans in the vicinity of an immigration raid or during national sweeps, such as Operation Wetback in 1954 (Calavita 1992) or Operation Jobs in 1995 (US Attorney General Report 1995). The activities recorded in the complaints are accurately captured in the media's initial reporting of Mexican Americans' experience during the five-day immigration raid: "As they walked down sidewalks, drove cars or walked outside their homes" they were stopped by the police (Amparano 1997).

Based primarily on interviews with police officers assigned to the target area during the operation (few Border Patrol agents agreed to be arrested in residential areas, in front of stores (especially the local Circle K), in trailer courts, and driving between 4:00 and 6:00 AM (the time many workers are traveling to construction sites during the summer)).

The wide net that was cast made in inevitable that citizens and legal residents would be stopped by the police. The complaints indicate that, when proof of citizenship status was requested by law-enforcement agents, 33 of the 91 were driving, 24 were walking in their neighborhood or to a nearby store, 17 were at home, 10 were shopping (most were approached in the parking lot or in front of stores), 3 were riding bikes, and 2 were using public telephones. Significantly, only 2 were approached at their place of employment, suggesting the tacit desire to protect employers from possible sanctions. Specific activities are significant when class-based racial profiling is occurring. As in most urban areas, being a pedestrian is a sign of poverty. Middle and upper classes rarely walk or bike in Arizona heat unless they are engaged in exercise and dressed in special "work-out" clothes. They might be observed walking if a leashed dog is attached to their bodies. Using a public telephone is a similar sign of poverty when most homes in the Us have several phones as well as cell phones.

After the stops were made, investigators documented only 33 outcomes for the 91 incidents. Of the 33 outcomes documented in the complaints, 23 were detained. Three of the people detained were illegal and twenty were legal. Four of those detained were handcuffed, including one US citizen. The period that the 23 were detained ranged from five minutes to four hours. Some of those detained for long periods of time reported that they stood in the 100+ degree weather common in July. After they showed proof of legal status, three complainants were issued citations for minor traffic violations (e.g., a rolling stop at a stop sign, a broken windshield, a missing headlamp, or a turn into the wrong lane).

Eighty-six claims involved law enforcement agents requesting proof of citizenship status. However, the kinds of documents requested were inconsistent, at times vague, and confusing to US citizens who had never been stopped before—51 incidents involved officers requesting to see the person's "papers" or "*papeles,*" 2 incidents involved requests for immigration papers, 13 incidents requested drivers license, 9 were asked to show "an identification," 10 were asked specifically for their green cards, and 1 officer requested to see "a card." Birth certificates, Social Security cards, green cards, or driver licenses were produced by the claimants before the police allowed them to leave. In some cases, particularly for children and adolescents, family members assisted in obtaining documents.

◆ Witness Accounts Analysis

Based on the writings of immigration-critical race legal scholars (i.e., Benitiez 1994; Chang and Aoki 1997; Johnson 2000, 2004; Vargas 2001), I identified five patterns of immigration law enforcement that placed Mexican Americans at risk: (1) discretionary stops based on ethnicity and class; (2) use of intimidation to demean and subordinate persons stopped; (3) restricting the freedom of movement of Mexicans but not others in the same vicinity; (4) reinforced stereotypes of Mexican as "alien," "foreign," inferior and criminal; and (5) limited access to fair and impartial treatment before the law. Recurring expressions that witnesses used to describe stops and searches were pain and humiliation, frightened, fearful, nervous, scared, embarrassed, violated, and mortified. Witness accounts offer descriptive narratives of the micro- and macro-aggressions occurring in immigration law enforcement.

Embedded in all the accounts is the recognition that they were stopped, questioned, and inspected by the police because their physical appearance was classified by law enforcement agents as "Mexican" and, thus, they were assumed to be unauthorized to be in the US. Skin color is used in the everyday immigration law-enforcement practice of operationalizing "reasonable suspicion":

> T was stopped and questioned by Chandler police and INS/Border Patrol when he stopped at a Circle K ... The Chandler Police were stopping every "Mexican-looking" person as they entered or exited the store. "Non Mexican-looking" people entered and exited without being stopped. (Office of Attorney General Wood 1997:22)

An except from witness account "D" demonstrates community members' recognition of INS and police officers' "discretion," as well as their power to violate civil rights.

> All the people shopping at this shopping center appeared to be Hispanic and many were being stopped and questioned by the officers. D and his uncle were conversing in Spanish and leaving the store with a package when they were approached by a Chandler police officer and an INS/Border Patrol agent on bicycles. The INS/Border Patrol agent asked them in Spanish for their papers. The uncle, who had just become a United States citizen, had his citizenship papers with him and showed those to the officer. D had only a social security card and a driver's license ... D took his wallet from his pocket to get his identification; the INS/Border Patrol officer then asked him for the wallet and examined everything in it. D feared that if he did not give the officer his wallet he would be arrested. Neither officer wrote any information down or kept anything from the wallet. No explanation was given for the stop (Office of Attorney General Wood 1997:21).

Although "D" is a US citizen, he understood that he does not have the same rights as whites and has limited access to fair dealings before the law. He was intimidated by the INS officer extending the citizenship inspection beyond his driver's license and Social Security card and into his personal belongings without a search warrant or a basis for probable cause.

"U" provided a description of an incident involving a person who questioned stops without probable cause and police discretion.

U has a permit to work in the United States and is here legally ... he and his cousin stopped at a Circle K ... While they were parking their car, they were approached by a Chandler police officer on a bicycle who asked, in Spanish, for their papers. The cousin said that the police had no right to ask for papers and the Chandler police officer asked if they wanted him to call Immigration. They said yes and INS/Border patrol agents soon appeared. The cousin showed the agents his papers but U did not have his on him and when he showed them his social security card, there was a discrepancy in the computer and they were told the number had been canceled. The INS/Border Patrol agent said "I'm tired of this, everybody lies and says they have papers when they don't." The officers put U in handcuffs, searched him and took him to the Chandler Police Station where he was detained. He asked them to give him a chance to call his home and have his wife bring his papers but they refused. He was held until about 11:30 (from 7 p.m.) until his cousin and his wife brought his papers to the police station. U was afraid that the Chandler police were going to take his green card away, or that he was going to be separated from his family (Office of Attorney General Wood 1997:23).

"U" assumed protection and rights that his work permit grants and distinguished between city police officers and the INS. However, his attempt to assert his rights resulted in the use of excessive force and he was treated like a violent criminal requiring physical restraint. His account points to extensive discretionary power given to immigration law enforcement; the incident exemplified intimidation, excessive force, and the lack of probable cause in the police stop.

Since the downtown redevelopment zone targeted in the roundup was not completely racially segregated, discretionary stops of persons of Mexican ancestry who appear to be poor or working class became visible.

Public areas like stores, phone booths, and gas stations produced a spectacle for white gaze and allowed the immigration inspectors to employ stereotypes of Mexicans as foreign, alien, and criminal. However, appearances of class and citizenship can be deceiving as the following witness testimony reveals.

C is the highest ranked left handed golfer in Arizona. C is a large, dark completed, Hispanic, and native born Arizonan ... Returning from a golf match in July, he stopped ... for a cold drink and saw Chandler police officers talking to different people of apparent Mexican descent. At the time he was wearing an old tee shirt and a baseball cap. As he tried to exit the market, he was barred exit by a Chandler Police officer who asked if he was a local, if he had papers, and whether he was a citizen. C told the officer that he was a citizen and was leaving and the officer told him "No, you are not." C then walked around the officer and went over to his car which was a 1997 Acura. The officer followed him but when he saw what car he was driving, permitted him to drive off.... (Office of Attorney General Wood 1997:21)

Clearly "C" assumed "class privilege," challenging the officer's attempt to stop and search without probable cause. This account demonstrates the significance of class in immigration law enforcement. Once middle- and upper-middle-class status is identified by officers, police are less likely to violate civil rights.

In response to the extraordinary policing, community members avoided public areas. Witnesses reported that elderly neighbors feared the police, asking for assistance in obtaining food and medication so they could remain home, behind closed doors. Law enforcement agents' treatment of Mexicans thus deterred civic participation and shaped the field of action that Latinos perceived as available to them (Davis et al. 2001; Nelson 2001). By the fifth day of the operation, the community avoided local grocery stores and gas stations that had been heavily patrolled by the police and INS. Mexican shop owners complained that they lost revenue during the raid because their customers feared shopping in the area. In the absence of people in the streets and shopping areas, the police developed alternative strategies that included homes and construction sites.

Alongside stores with the largest number of Latino customers, the second major target areas were apartment complexes and trailer courts occupied by low-income Mexican Americans and Mexican immigrants. In a newspaper interview with a Chandler police officer, the claim was made that they did not bust "down doors in search of illegal immigrants." Witness accounts provide a counter narrative. Not only were neighborhoods in the targeted area searched house by house but apartment and trailer court managers assisted Chandler Police by identifying residents of Mexican descent. The following testimony describes the intimidation and demeaning actions used by law enforcement agents.

> On July 28, 1997, at approximately 11 P.M., B and his family were sound asleep in a trailer owned by his brother-in-law ... The family was wakened by a loud banging on the front door and bright lights shining through the windows. When B looked around, he saw two Chandler police officers, with an INS/Border patrol agent behind them. All officers were bicycle officers. The officers demanded to be allowed into the trailer and when B asked if they had the right to come in, he was told "We can do whatever we want, we are the Chandler Police Department. You have people who are here illegally." Although B denied that there were any undocumented aliens there, the officers insisted on entering the trailer, rousing everyone from bed. The family members were all in their sleep clothes, but the officers refused to allow them to dress. None of the children were United States citizens, and except for the brother-in-law, all the rest were legal aliens; the brother-in-law had entered the country legally but his visa had expired and he was in the process of getting it renewed.

> When the officers discovered that the brother-in-law did not have proper papers, they called a Chandler Police Department back up vehicle and took him away in a patrol car. B attempted to give his brother-in-law street clothes when the officers were taking him away, but the officers would not allow this and took him away in his sleep clothes. He was later readmitted to the United States with the renewed visa he had been awaiting. The others were detained in the trailer for approximately ninety minutes; they were not searched but they were questioned even after they showed the papers demonstrating that they were legally in United States. The police told B that they had spoken with the park manager and he had given them permission to search the trailers, had given them a map, and had marked on the map where Hispanic residents lived. The four children involved in this incident are still fearful when someone knocks at the door of the trailer, and continue to be nervous when they see police officers on the street ... Most of the police visits occurred between 10 p.m. and 11 p.m. and were precipitated by police banging on doors and windows and shining lights through the windows ... Every night someone else was taken away. (Office of Attorney General Wood 1997:19–20)

Home searches conducted in the presence of children serve as powerful socialization, teaching them about their lack of rights, inferior status, and unequal access to protection under the law. For many children, the house searches were probably their first encounter with a police officer, and they witnessed their parents, grandparents, and other family elders humiliated and treated as criminals. Witnessing stops and searches serves as an important lesson for children that the law distinguishes between family and neighbors on the basis of immigration status rather than criminal activity that harms others. Unlike stops made at shopping centers, house-to-house searches conducted on private property concealed civil and human rights violations from public view.

In addition to the house-to-house searches conducted, apartment complexes and trailer courts were also targeted for traffic enforcement. Several officers' interview summaries acknowledged that, outside of special D.U.I. enforcement, the Chandler Roundup was the first time they used traffic enforcement with a spotter. Vehicles leaving specific housing units that appeared to contain "migrant workers" were followed. Several officers reported that they "were to follow them and if probable cause was established" the vehicle was stopped. Officers were "instructed to issue a citation for the probable cause in case there was a question in reference to the stop." A summary of radio-dispatch transcripts for July 29, 1997, demonstrated that laborers driving to work were targeted as vehicles left apartment complexes housing low-income Mexican Americans and Mexican immigrants:

> The vehicles were described by make, model and/or color, as well as direction of travel. A total of forty-three (43) vehicles were specially singled out in a two hour period of time from 4:00 to 6:00 A.M. The officers identified seven (7) vehicles because of known violations of law warranting a stop. However, of the remaining thirty-six (36) vehicles called in, seven (7) calls describing vehicles were made despite the officers stating that there was no probable cause to believe that violations of the law had occurred. The other twenty-nine (29) vehicles were singled out without articulation of what, if any, violation of law may have been observed by the reporting officer. (Office of Attorney General Wood 1997:10)

Both the *Survey* and *Report* note that the Chandler Roundup extended to construction sites and permission from supervisors at the construction sites was obtained before entering the area to question employees. Even though the police arrested undocumented workers at construction sites, neither report cited employers' violation of the law. IRCA includes employer

sanctions designating penalties for employers who hire immigrants not authorized to work in the United States. While citizenship and movement of laborers were clearly documented in both reports, there is a glaring absence of enforcement of employers' compliance with IRCA. Although questioning workers at a construction site resulted in 52 arrests, no employer suffered legal sanctions for IRCA violations. Nowhere in the Attorney General's *Survey*, or in the independent investigator's *Report*, is there a mention of employers at construction sites being investigated.

 Conclusion

While legal scholars, civil rights advocates, and the general public denounced federal law enforcement practices towards Muslims and persons of Middle-Eastern descent under the Patriot Act, racialized immigration stops and searches, abuse, and harassment are ongoing processes honed over a century of citizenship inspections of Mexicans. Immigration policing is based on determining that citizenship is visibly inscribed on bodies in specific urban spaces rather than "probable cause." In the Chandler Roundup, official investigations found no evidence that stops and searches were based on probable cause of criminal activity. The conclusion drawn by the Attorney General's investigation underscores the harms of micro- and macro-aggressions and the use of petit apartheid:

> ... there were no other warrants, charges, or holds for these individuals that in any way indicated other criminal activity or that required extraordinary security or physical force. The issue raised by this type of treatment is not whether the arrest and deportation is legal, but whether human beings are entitled to some measure of dignity and safety even when they are suspected of being in the United States illegally. (1997:28–9)

The Chandler Roundup fits into a larger pattern of immigration law-enforcement practices that produce harms of reduction and repression and place Mexican

Americans at risk before the law and designate them as second-class citizens with inferior rights. Latino residents in Chandler experienced racial affronts targeted at their "Mexicanness" indicated by skin color, bilingual speaking abilities, or shopping in neighborhoods highly populated by Latinos. During immigration inspections, individuals stopped were demeaned, humiliated, and embarrassed. Stops and searches conducted without cause were intimidating and frightening, particularly when conducted with discretionary use of power and force by law enforcement agents.

Like other metropolitan areas surrounding Phoenix, Chandler depends heavily upon low-wage, non-union, undocumented Mexican workers for their tourism and construction industries. These powerful business interests are influential at the state level, and cooperative efforts are made to assure seasonal labor needs are met. Both official investigations into the Chandler Roundup demonstrate complete disregard for enforcing sanctions of employers under IRCA. Yet the ability to clearly identify the everyday work patterns of immigrants and to use these circumstances to arrest immigrants as undocumented workers indicate that employers operate with complete immunity to IRCA provisions. The case of the Chandler Roundup demonstrates how INS enforcement practices not only favor and protect employers' access to an exploitable labor force, but remove or relocate workers as specific industries' needs warrant. Enforcement is structured specifically at eliminating and relocating undocumented workers from areas no longer relevant to the local economy or redevelopment plans. The Chandler Roundup was intended to remove a low-income population to allow for urban renewal, by creating a hostile environment for citizens, violating their civil rights through immigration law enforcement employing micro- and macro-aggressions. Racialized immigration stops establish, maintain, and reinforce second-class citizenship and limit civil, political, economic, and cultural rights and opportunities. In urban barrios, the costly enterprise of selected stops and searches, race-related police abuse, and harassment results in deterring political participation, in identifying urban space racially, in classifying immigrants as deserving and

undeserving by nationalities, and serves to drive a wedge dividing Latino neighborhoods on the basis of citizenship status.

 Notes

1. Unlike the census categories, which make a distinction between race and ethnicity for the category "Hispanic," and restricting race to black and white, law enforcement clearly uses the ethnic descriptors of Mexican and Hispanic to identify an individual's physical characteristics. Therefore, this study makes a distinction between Latinos who can racially pass as white and those who are socially constructed (but nevertheless have real consequences) as racially distinct from whites or blacks (Romero 2001).

2. An example is assuming that a Mexican American cannot speak English or that she is the secretary, rather than a faculty member in the department.

3. Richard J. Herrnstein and Charles Murray's (1994) claims of Blacks' mental inferiority espoused in their book, *The Bell Curve,* is a prime example of a macro-aggressions that has received an extensive news coverage.

4. Background information is based on media coverage from local newspapers, community meetings, and the minutes from Chandler City Council Meeting.

5. The summary of the survey includes a detailed description of the Chandler Redevelopment Initiative developed by the City Council. The survey describes the Initiative's efforts and its connection to the joint operation carried out in areas with the highest concentration of Latino residents; INS protocols for joint operation; description of day-to-day activities based on Border Patrol documents; summary of witness accounts regarding children and schools, home contacts, and contacts around businesses, because these were areas that the police and public officials claimed were not included in the raid; and descriptions of the types of request made for the proof of citizenship.

6. The narrative offers a history of the City of Chandler and describes the development of immigration issues as a social problem that led to the joint operation. A description of the operation and the aftermath of community meetings, complaints, and lawsuits is also included.

7. Interviews were conducted with the police who participated in the joint operation, supervisors and officers involved with processing illegal aliens, Border Patrol agents, City Council members, and Chandler city officials.

8. Excerpts describe the duties of city officials and the Chandler Police Department, a summary of line of authority in the city, and a description of the structure and duties of the US Border Patrol.

9. Citizenship status in not recorded for 29 complainants (involved in 41 stops).

◈ References

ACUÑA, RODOLFO

200 *Occupied America*. New York, NY: Longman.

AMPARANO, JULIE

1997 "Brown Skin: No Civil rights? July Sweep on Chandler Draws Fire." *Arizona Republic* August 15:B1.

ANDREAS, PETER

2000 *Border Games, Policing the U.S.-Mexico Divide*. Ithaca, NY: Cornell University Press.

ARRIOLA, ELVIA R.

1996–97 "LatCrit Theory, International Human Rights, Popular Culture, and the Faces of Despair in INS Raids." *University of Miami Inter-American Law Review* 28:245–62.

BASS, SANDRA

2001 "Out of Place: Petit Apartheid and the Police." Pp. 43–54 in *Petit Apartheid in the U.S. Criminal Justice System, The Dark Figure of Racism*, edited by Dragan Milovanovic and Katheryn Russell. Durham, NC: Carolina Academic Press.

BENITEZ, HUMBERTO

1994 "Flawed Strategies: The INS Shift from Border Interdiction to Internal Enforcement Actions." *La Raza Law Journal* 7:154–79.

BREEN, THOMAS, SERGIO MURETA, AND JOHN WINTERS

1998 *Report of Independent Investigation Into July 1997 Joint Operation Between Patrol and Chandler Police Department*. Vol. I, II, and III, Chandler, Arizona: The City of Chandler.

CALAVITA, KITTY

1992 *Inside the State, The Bracero Program, Immigration, and the I.N.S.* New York, NY: Routledge.

CALDEIRA, TERESA P. R.

2000 *City of Walls: Crime, Segregation, and Citizenship in São Paulo*. Berkeley, CA: University of California Press.

CAMPBELL, JACKIE

2001 "Walking the Beat Alone: An African American Police Officer's Perspective on Petit Apartheid." Pp. 15–20 in *Petit Apartheid in the U.S. Criminal Justice System, The Dark Figure of Racism*, edited by Dragan Milovanovic and Katheryn Russell. Durham, NC: Carolina Academic Press.

CHANG, ROBERT S.

1999 *Disoriented: Asian Americans, Law, and the Nation-State*. New York, NY: New York University Press.

CHANG, ROEBRT S. AND KETIH AOKI

1997 "Centering the Immigrant in the Inter/National Imagination." *California Law Review* 85:1395–1447.

CHAVEZ, LEO R.

2001 *Covering Immigration, Popular Images and the Politics of the Nation*. Berkeley, CA: University of California Press.

CORNELIUS, WAYNE A.

2001 "Death at the Border: Efficacy and Unintended Consequences of US Immigration Control Policy." *Population and Development Review* 27(4):661–85.

COVINGTON, JEANETTE

2001 "Round Up the Usual suspects: Racial Profiling and the War on Drugs." Pp. 27–42 in *Petit Apartheid in the U.S. Criminal Justice System, The Dark Figure of Racism*, edited by Dragan Milovanovic and Katheryn Russell. Durham, NC: Carolina Academic Press.

DAVIS, ROBERT C., EDNA EREZ, AND NANCY AVITABILE

2001 "Access to Justice for Immigrants who are Victimized: The Perspectives of Police and Prosecutors." *Criminal Justice Policy Review* 12(3):183–96.

DUNN, TIMOTHY J.

1996 *The Militarization of the U.S.-Mexico Border*. Austin, TX: CMAS Books, University of Texas at Austin.

EDELMAN, MURRAY

2001 *The Politics of Misinformation*. New York, NY: Cambridge University Press.

ESCHABCH, KARL, JACQUELINE HAGEN, NESTOR RODRIGUES, RÚBEN HERNÁNDEZ-LEÓN, and STANLEY BARILEY

1999 "Death and the Border." *International Migration Review* 33(2):430–54.

FERRELL, JEFF

2001a *Tearing Down the Streets: Adventures in Urban Anarchy*. New York, NY: Palgrave Macmillan.

2001b "Trying to Make Us a Parking Lot: Petit Apartheid, Culture Space, and the Public Negotiation of Ethnicity." Pp. 55–68 in *Petit Apartheid in the U.S. Criminal Justice System, The Dark Figure of Racism*, edited by Dragan Milovanovic and Katheryn Russell. Durham, NC: Carolina Academic Press.

FLETCHER, MICHAEL A.

1997 "Police in Arizona Accused of Civil Rights Violations; Lawsuit Cites Sweep Aimed at Illegal Immigrants." *Washington Post* August 20:A14.

GARCIA, JUAN RAMON

1980 *Operation Wetback: The Mass Deportation of Mexican Undocumented Workers in 1954*. Westport, CT: Greenwood Press.

GEORGES-ABEYIE, DANIEL E.

1990 "Criminal Justice Processing of Non-White Minorities." Pp. 25–34 in *Racism, Empiricism and Criminal Justice*, edited by Brian D. MacLean and Dragan Milovanovic. Vancouver, BC: The Collective Press.

HARVEY, DAVID

1973 *Social Justice and the City*. Baltimore, MD: John Hopkins University Press.

1996 *Justice, Nature, and the Geography of Difference*. Oxford, UK: Blackwell.

HENRY, STUART AND DRAGAN MILOVANOVIC

1999 *Constitutive Criminology*. London: Sage Publications.

HERRNSTEIN, RICHARD J. AND CHARLES MURRAY

1994 *The Ball Curve: Intelligence and Class Structure in American Life*. New York, NY: Free Press.

JEYMAN, JOSIAH McC.

1995 "Putting Power in the Anthropology of Bureaucracy: The Immigration and Naturalization Service and the Mexico-United States Border." *Current Anthropology* 36(2):261–87.

HING, BILL ONG

1997 *To Be An American*. New York, NY: New York University Press.

HOLSTON, JAMES (ED.)

1999 *Citizens and Citizenship*. Durham, NC: Duke University Press.

JOHNSON, KEVIN

1993 "Los Olvidados: Images of the Immigrant, Political Power of Non-citizens, and Immigrant Law and Enforcement." *Binghamton Young University Law Review* 1993:1139–1241.

1997 "Racial Hierarchy, Asian Americans and Latinos as 'Foreigners,' and Social Change: Is Law the Way to Go?" *Oregon Law Review* 76(2):347–67.

2000 "The Case Against Race Profiling in Immigration Enforcement." *Washington University Law Quarterly* 78(3):676–736.

2002 "Race and the Immigration Laws: The Need for Critical Inquiry." Pp. 187–98 in *Crossroads, Directions, and a New Critical Race Theory,* edited by Francisco Valdez, Jerome McCristal Culp, and Angela P. Harris. Philadelphia, PA: Temple University Press.

JOHNSON, SHERI LYNN

2001 "Racial Derogation in Prosecutors' Closing Arguments." Pp. 79–102 in *Petit Apartheid in the U.S. Criminal Justice System, The Dark Figure of Racism,* edited by Dragan Milovanovic and Katheryn Russell. Durham, NC: Carolina Academic Press.

LAZOS VARGAS, SYLVIA R.

2002 "'Latina/o-ization' of the Midwest: *Cambio de Colores* (Change of Colors) as *Agromaquilas* Expand into the Heartland." *Berkeley la Raza Law Journal* 13(113):343–68.

LEE, YUEH-TING, VICTOR OTTATI, AND IMTIAZ HUSSAIN

2001 "Attitudes Towards "Illegal Immigration into the United States: California Proposition 187." *Hispanic Journal of Behavioral Sciences* 23(4):430–43.

LEFEBVRE, HENRI

1996 "The Right to the City." Pp. 63–181, in *Writings on Cities,* edited and translated by E. Kofman and E. Lebas. Oxford, UK: Blackwell.

MASSEY, DOUGLAS S., JORGE DURAND, AND NOLAN J. MALONE

2002 *Beyond Smoke and Mirrors: Mexican Immigration in an Era of Economic Integration.* New York, NY: Russell Sage Foundation.

MATSUDA, MARI J., CHARLES R. LAWRENCE III, RICHARD DELGADO, AND KIMBERLÈ W. CRENSHAW

1993 *Words That Wound: Critical Race Theory, Assaultive Speech, and the First Amendment.* Boulder, CO: Westview Press.

MEHAN, HUGH

1997 "The Discourse of the Illegal Immigration Debate: A Case Study in the Politics of Representation," *Discourse & Society* 8(2):249–70.

MILOVANOVIC, DRAGAN AND KATHERYN RUSSELL (EDS.)

2001 *Petit Apartheid in the U.S. Criminal Justice System, The Dark Figure of Racism.* Durham, NC: Carolina Academic Press.

MITCHELL, DON

2003 *The Right to the City: Social Justice and the Fight for Public Space.* New York, NY: The Guilford Press.

NELSON, HILDE LINDEMANN

2001 *Damaged Identities, Narrative Repair.* Ithaca, NY: Cornell University Press.

NEVINS, JOSEPH

2002 *Operation Gatekeeper, The Rise of the "Illegal Alien" and the Making of the U.S.-Mexico Boundary.* New York, NY: Routledge.

Office of the ATTORNEY GENERAL GRANT WOOD

1997 *Results of the Chandler Survey.* Phoenix, State of Arizona.

PIERCE, CHESTER M., JEAN V. CAREW, DOAMA PIERCE-GONZALEZ, AND DEBORAH WILLIS

1978 "An Experiment in Racism: TV Commercials," Pp. 62–88 in *Television and Education,* edited by Chester Pierce. Beverly Hills, CA: Sage Publications.

ROMERO, MARY

2001 "State Violence, and the Social and Legal Construction of Latino Criminality: From Bandido to Gang Member." *Denver University Law Review* 78(4):1081–1118.

ROSS, LEE E.

2001 "African-American Interest in Law Enforcement: A Consequence of Petit Apartheid?" Pp. 69–78 in *Petit Apartheid in the U.S. Criminal Justice System, The Dark Figure of Racism,* edited by Dragan Milovanovic and Katheryn Russell. Durham, NC: Carolina Academic Press.

RUSSELL, KATHERYN K.

1998 *The Color of Crime: Racial Hoaxes, White Fear, Black Protectionism, Police Harassment and Other Macroaggressions.* New York, NY: New York University Press.

SÁENZ BENJAMIN ALIRE

1992 *Flowers for the Broken: Stories.* Seattle, WA: Broken Moon Press.

SANTA ANA, OTTO

2002 *Brown Tide Rising, Metaphors of Latinos in Contemporary American Public Discourse.* Austin, TX: University of Texas Press.

SMITH, DOROTHY E.

1990 *Texts, Facts, and Femininity: Exploring the Relations of Ruling.* New York, NY: Routledge.

1999 *Writing the Social: Critique, Theory, and Investigations.* Toronto, ON: The University of Toronto Press.

U.S. ATTORNEY GENERAL OFFICE

1995 "Securing America's Borders," in 1995 annual Report of the Attorney General of the United States. Retrieved January 4, 2004 (http://www.usdoj.gov/ag/annualreports/ar95/chapter3.htm).

VALDEZ, FRANCISCO, JEROME McCRISTAL CULP, AND ANGELA P. HARRIS (EDS.)

2002 *Crossroads, Directions, and a New Critical Race Theory.* Philadelphia, PA: Temple University Press.

VARGAS, JORGE A.

2001 "U.S. Border Patrol Abuses, Undocumented Mexican Workers, and International Human Rights." *San Diego International Law Review* 2(1):1–92.

WEISSINGER, GEORGE

1996 *Law Enforcement and the INS, A Participant Observation Study of Control Agents.* New York, NY: University Press of America.

PART IV

Responses to Deviance

CHAPTER 11

Social Control of Deviance

> I will always be a felon . . . a felon is a term here, obviously it's not a bad term . . . for me to leave here, it will affect my job, it will affect my education . . . custody, it can affect child support, it can affect everywhere—family, friends, housing. . . . People that are convicted of drug crimes can't even get housing anymore. . . . Yes, I did my prison time. How long are you going to punish me as a result of it? And not only on paper, I'm only on paper for ten months when I leave here, that's all the parole I have. But that parole isn't going to be anything. It's the housing, it's the credit re-establishing . . . I mean even to go into the school to work with my child's class—and I'm not even a sex offender—but all I need is one parent who says, "Isn't she a felon? I don't want her with my child." Bingo. And you know that there are people out there like that.
>
> —"Karen," discussing how being labeled a felon will affect virtually every area
> of her life, from Manza and Uggen, *Locked Out* (2006, p. 152).
> Copyright ©2006 by Oxford University Press, Inc.

◈ Introduction

The comments above illustrate some of the long-term effects that involvement in deviance can have on individuals, families, and communities. While much of this book so far has focused on different *causes* of deviant behavior, this chapter focuses on societal reactions to deviance and will look in more detail at a few of the varied forms that social control may take.

Philosophers have suggested that human societies are possible because of the **social contract;** the idea is that individuals give up some personal freedoms and abide by general rules of conduct to live in a community and enjoy the protection and companionship of the group. If most in the group live by the social contract, what is to be done when individuals break the contract? How should the community or larger society react to the breach? Should the individual be punished? Once punished, should members of the community be responsible to help the offender reintegrate back into the community?

There are many different forms of social control. One basic distinction is between formal and informal controls. Formal social controls would include hospitalization in a mental ward or rehabilitation facility, expulsion from school, and all types of processing by the criminal justice system, including probation, parole, imprisonment, and fines. Informal controls are often just as powerful, but they are implemented by those around you—your family members, your church, or your peers. If you have ever been given the silent treatment or felt your parents' disappointment, you have experienced informal social control.

As suggested by the critical theorists in Chapter 10, social control and sanctions for deviant behavior are not meted out equally. Recent studies have made clear that the U.S. criminal justice system and particularly our reliance on mass incarceration disproportionately affect minorities and the poor and have long-lasting impact on the life chances and opportunities available to individuals, families, and whole communities (Beckett & Herbert, 2010; Haney, 2010; Pager, 2007; Tonry, 2011; Waquant, 2000; Western, 2006).

◈ Medicalization of Deviant Behavior

We don't always think of medicine as an institution of social control, but just as legal definitions turn some acts into crimes, medical definitions are important in societal conceptions of what is deemed deviant and how such behavior should be managed. Medicalization is "a process by which nonmedical problems become defined and treated as medical problems, usually in terms of illnesses or disorders" (Conrad, 1992: 209). There are many examples of medicalized deviant behavior, including mental illness, hyperactivity in children, alcoholism, homosexuality, eating disorders, compulsive gambling, and addiction. It is important to remember that these are social constructions of deviance, and our definitions can and do change over time and vary across cultures.

Medical diagnoses of deviant behavior can have an enormous impact on individuals and communities. Daphne Scholinski's (1997) memoir, *The Last Time I Wore a Dress,* offers an individual perspective on what it is like to spend one's adolescent years in a series of mental hospitals. As a troubled teenage girl, Scholinski was diagnosed with gender identity disorder, which her doctor believed she had developed around the third grade: "He said what this means is you are not an appropriate female, you don't act the way a female is supposed to act" (p. 16).

Scholinski was 14 years old when she was admitted to her first mental hospital; she was released just after her 18th birthday, when her insurance and ability to pay for the treatment ran out. Looking back on the experience, she writes, "One million dollars my treatment cost. Insurance money, but still. Three years in three mental hospitals for girly lessons" (Scholinski, 1997, p. xi). While she was generally happy to be released from her last institution, she occasionally had doubts about her ability to survive and succeed in the community: "Sometimes I wish I could return to the hospital. It's ridiculous, I know. But it's hard to figure out everything on my own. In the hospitals, I lost my ability to trust myself" (p. 196). The medicalized diagnosis and treatment of her behavior had undermined her sense of self-efficacy.

Medicalization can take many forms; on the extreme end, individuals can be institutionalized in mental hospitals and/or heavily medicated. They can also be compelled to enter counseling or to join self-help groups; once they admit they have a problem, they can begin working toward a "cure."

A recent article in a Florida newspaper (Laforgia, 2011) investigated the heavy doses of powerful drugs administered to children in state-operated jails and residential programs; they were given a lot of antipsychotic medications, which temporarily control behavior but do little to provide meaningful treatment for incarcerated youth. These drugs can also cause suicidal thoughts and harmful side effects. The reporter writes,

Overall, in 24 months, the department (Florida's Department of Juvenile Justice) bought 326,081 tablets of Seroquel, Abilify, Risperdal and other antipsychotic drugs for use in state-operated jails and homes for children. . . . That's enough to hand out 446 pills a day, seven days a week, for two years in a row, to kids in jails and programs that can hold no more than 2,300 boys and girls on a given day.

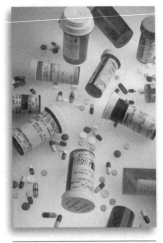

▲ **Photo 11.1** The medicalization of social control can include compelling individuals to take heavy doses of prescription drugs.

The changing definitions of deviance can clearly be seen in the field of medicalization. As Conrad (1992) explains, "A key aspect of medicalization refers to the emergence of medical definitions for previously nonmedical problems" (p. 223). While new categories of deviance emerge through medicalization, the process can also work in the opposite direction: Behaviors previously thought to be deviant can be *demedicalized*. **Demedicalization** refers to the process where problems or behaviors no longer retain medical definitions. A vivid example of demedicalization is homosexuality; if you read early textbooks on deviant behavior, you will often see homosexuality included as deviant behavior in need of treatment. Our conceptions of homosexuality changed in American society in the 1970s to the point that it is no longer defined as an illness (Conrad, 1992).

We hope that you can see that while it is often less blatant than the social control practiced by criminal justice agencies, the **medicalization of deviance** has a profound effect on individuals and communities. We now turn to a discussion of social control and surveillance by the criminal justice system.

◈ Policing, Supervision, and the Impact of Incarceration on Disadvantaged Populations and Communities

Two recent studies offer compelling insight into the way that poor and disadvantaged populations and communities are supervised and controlled. In their book, *Banished*, Beckett and Herbert (2010) discuss the way that city laws and ordinances are used to control where and how populations can congregate. Using Seattle as a case study, they describe how individuals—often poor or homeless—may be arrested and then subsequently prohibited from entering or occupying areas associated with drug dealing or prostitution. Beckett and Herbert view banishment as "an emerging and consequential social control practice . . . banishment is consequential, even more so than the civility codes that they increasingly supplant. Not only do these new tools enable banishment, they provide the police greater license to question and to arrest those who occupy public space" (p. 16).

In an ethnographic study of young African American men in Philadelphia, Alice Goffman (2009) shows how police surveillance, outstanding arrest warrants, and the status of being on probation can affect every part of "wanted" young men's lives. Among the vivid descriptions of the impact of such surveillance is the story of a young man who went to the hospital for the birth of his baby and was arrested there on an outstanding warrant. The risk of being captured makes these young men afraid to go to hospitals or other social service agencies; it compels them to keep moving and to stay "on the run" rather than find stable housing.

Goffman (2009) explains the different ways these young men find to resist the formal social control of the state, but even in their resistance, the constant threat and surveillance deeply affect their lives. Their partners are often frustrated by the lack of stability but at times also find they can control a particular young man by threatening to call the police on him. Goffman's attention to detail and careful analysis, framing the surveillance and resistance of "wanted men" in Philadelphia, is a very useful addition to research on social control. Her full article is included in the readings for this chapter so that you can explore the ideas of formal social control at the community level and the resistance of targeted individuals in further depth.

Todd Clear (2007) focuses on communities burdened by high incarceration rates, describing certain disadvantaged neighborhoods as "prison places." He explains the impact of unstable, imprisoned populations as they contribute to social disorganization (the theory described in Chapter 5) in the larger communities: "Incarceration can operate as a kind of 'coercive mobility,' destabilizing neighborhoods by increasing levels of disorganization, first when a person is removed to go to prison, then later when that person reenters the community. In high-incarceration neighborhoods, the process of incarceration and reentry create an environment where a significant portion of residents are constantly in flux" (p. 73).

Clear (2007) argues that these prison places suffer distinct disadvantages, and the effect of incarceration is felt far beyond the lives of the individual inmates: "The concentration of imprisonment of young men from disadvantaged places has grown to such a point that it is now a bedrock experience, a force that affects families and children, institutions and businesses, social groups and interpersonal relations" (p. 3).

▲ **Photo 11.2** Alice Goffman's research offers a look into the lives of "wanted" young men — those who are on probation or have warrants out for their arrest. Resisting the formal social control of the state often keeps them on the run.

DEVIANCE IN POPULAR CULTURE

There are many representations of institutions of social control in popular culture. In the chapter on labeling theory, we recommended the films *One Flew Over the Cuckoo's Nest* and *Girl, Interrupted.* While those films are good examples for labeling, they also show the role of mental hospitals as formal institutions for social control. Prisons are another popular setting for films and television documentaries; watch one or more of the following to get an inside glimpse at social control of deviance:

The Shawshank Redemption is a classic prison film that tells the fictional story of how an innocent man survives decades in prison. In the character of Brooks, we see a clear example of how a man can be "institutionalized" after living the majority of his adult life in prison—when he is finally paroled, how will he adapt? If you have not seen *The Shawshank Redemption,* it is definitely worth your time.

Girlhood is a documentary featuring Shanae and Megan, two teenage girls with troubled histories who have committed violent crimes. The filmmaker met them while they were incarcerated in the Waxter Juvenile Facility in Baltimore and follows them both in the facility and when they are

(Continued)

> (Continued)
>
> released and reunited with their mothers. By focusing on these two young women, this documentary gives human faces to larger issues of abuse, neglect, and social control.
>
> MSNBC's series, *Lockup,* travels the country to take viewers inside a wide range of prisons, jails, and juvenile facilities. By watching several episodes, you can begin to get a sense of the similarities these total institutions share, as well as the differences in how inmates are treated.
>
> The fictional film, *Little Children,* is about life in the suburbs and includes a plotline about a convicted (and registered) sex offender who has just returned from prison to live with his mother. The community's nearly hysterical reaction to his presence living among them provides a memorable example of both informal and formal social control.

◈ Total Institutions

Perhaps the most severe form of social control (other than the death penalty) is institutionalization in prisons, jails, juvenile correctional facilities, and mental hospitals. Sociologist Erving Goffman (1961) characterized such facilities as **total institutions;** he explained the defining characteristics of total institutions as follows:

> A basic social arrangement in modern society is that the individual tends to sleep, play, and work in different places, with different co-participants, under different authorities, and without an overall rational plan. The central feature of total institutions can be described as a breakdown of the barriers ordinarily separating these three spheres of life. First, all aspects of life are conducted in the same place and under the same single authority. Second, each phase of the member's daily activity is carried on in the immediate company of a large batch of others, all of whom are treated alike and required to do the same thing together. Third, all phases of the day's activities are tightly scheduled, with one activity leading at a prearranged time into the next, the whole system of activities being imposed from above by a system of explicit formal rulings and a body of officials. Finally, the various enforced activities are brought together into a single, rational plan purportedly designed to fulfill the official aims of the institution. (pp. 5–6)

As described, total institutions include prisons, jails, juvenile correctional facilities, mental hospital, rehabilitation facilities, nursing homes, boarding schools, army barracks, monasteries, and convents. While some total institutions are entered into voluntarily, others—including prisons and secure hospitals—are among society's strongest reaction or sanction to deviant behavior. If you reread the article by Rosenhan in Chapter 9 (labeling theory), you will see characteristics of total institutions in the descriptions of the mental hospitals the pseudopatients spent time in. If you also take the time to watch films such as *One Flew Over the Cuckoo's Nest* or *Girl, Interrupted,* you can get a small sense of what it might feel like to be deemed mentally ill and a threat to yourself and/or the larger society.

Once confined in a total institution, it can be extremely difficult to make the transition back out into the community. After spending months and years in the relative isolation of a prison, mental hospital, or other total institution, individuals may become institutionalized (or "prisonized" as Clemmer [1940/1958] so aptly phrased it) to at least some extent. They may become so used to the structure and routine of the facility that they may lose the confidence and capability to exist independently in the outside world.

◈ Correctional Facilities and the Purposes of Punishment

While this is not a book about the criminal justice system, it is useful to briefly examine the different rationales for formal social control and punishment. Criminologists generally differentiate between several philosophies or purposes of punishment; by understanding the purpose, we can often make better sense of why the particular sanctions are used. Hagan (1985, pp. 288–289) offers seven purposes of criminal sanctions: (1) restraint or incapacitation, (2) individual or specific deterrence, (3) general deterrence, (4) reform or rehabilitation, (5) moral affirmation or symbolism, (6) retribution, and (7) restitution or compensation.

Correctional facilities reside near the deep end of social control and are used primarily for incapacitation—to hold offenders in a contained space away from the rest of society. Punishing those individuals who act outside of the accepted range of behavior also serves the function of moral affirmation or symbolism; when an offender is caught and sanctioned, the boundaries of the community are clearly tested, set, and reaffirmed (Erikson, 1966). If individuals find the reality of incapacitation unpleasant enough, they may be prevented from committing further deviant acts; this is the idea behind specific deterrence. If punishing one individual harshly enough keeps others from committing similar crimes, general deterrence has been achieved. Retribution is punishment as a form of payment for the harm done; this view is best represented in the expressions "an eye for an eye" or "a life for a life." Restitution is repayment for damage or harm, and rehabilitation generally involves effort to treat the offender in order to make him or her more capable of living as a conforming citizen.

▲ **Photo 11.3**   Incarceration in prisons and correctional facilities is one of the most severe forms of social control. How do you think years of living in cells such as these affects the individuals?

◈ Gresham Sykes and the Pains of Imprisonment

In *Society of Captives*, a classic work on life inside a maximum-security prison, Gresham Sykes (1958) offered a sociological view of prison culture and how time spent in prison affects both inmates and staff. He outlined five central **pains of imprisonment,** highlighting the fact that the costs of confinement are both physical and psychological. The pains of imprisonment are described as follows:

Deprivation of liberty—confined to the claustrophobic world of the prison, the isolation cuts deep: "The mere fact that the individual's movements are restricted, however, is far less serious than the fact that imprisonment means that the inmate is cut off from family, relatives, and friends, not in the self-isolation of the hermit or the misanthrope, but in the involuntary seclusion of the outlaw . . . what

makes this pain of imprisonment bite most deeply is the fact that the confinement of the criminal represents a deliberate, moral rejection of the criminal by the free community" (p. 65).

Deprivation of goods and services—inmates are without most of their personal possessions; "the inmate population defines its present material impoverishment as a painful loss" (p. 68).

Deprivation of heterosexual relationships—in male prisons, the inmate is "figuratively castrated by his involuntary celibacy" (p. 70). Sykes makes clear that living with only members of your own sex can be damaging to inmates' self-image and identity.

Deprivation of autonomy—every significant movement an inmate makes is controlled by others; inmates must abide by others' decisions and submit with enforced respect and deference. Treating adult offenders in this way may make the inmates feel like helpless children.

Deprivation of security—Sykes quotes an inmate: "The worst thing about prison is you have to live with other prisoners" (p. 77). Individual inmates are likely to be tested by other inmates and may have to engage in physical fights for their own safety, sanity, and possessions.

▲ **Photo 11.4** Gresham Sykes writes about the pains of imprisonment; which do you think would be hardest to adapt to?

◈ Juvenile Correctional Facilities

Juvenile correctional facilities—often called "training schools" or "reform schools"—are quite similar to "adult" prisons. After committing a crime and being adjudicated delinquent or convicted of the offense, the youth are sentenced to confinement. Incarcerated youth experience the same pains of imprisonment as their adult counterparts, but juvenile institutions generally have more of a focus on rehabilitation so there is more emphasis on education and programming (such as therapy groups for anger management, victim empathy, or drug and alcohol issues).

Juvenile correctional facilities are the last stop and are often the last chance in the juvenile justice system for delinquent youth. If the youth commit another offense after being released from a juvenile facility, they often face adult prisons, punishments, and permanent criminal records.

Historically, juvenile facilities were used as a sort of catch-all for troubled youth, housing serious delinquents alongside status offenders (whose acts would not be crimes if they were committed by adults) and dependent and neglected children who needed help in meeting their basic needs. While grouping these children and adolescents all in one place made basic supervision and care possible, it also caused many problems as younger and weaker children were victimized by peers and staff members (Bartollas, Miller, & Dinitz, 1976; Feld, 1977), and all were branded with a delinquent label once they returned to the community.

In the 1970s, the ideas of labeling theory were taken seriously, and states were encouraged to deinstitutionalize status offenders and noncriminal youth. Juvenile correctional facilities now generally house the most serious delinquents in the state. While this once seemed like a harsh placement—particularly when compared to community options such as group homes or foster care—the comparison has now shifted. Youth incarcerated in juvenile facilities may be the lucky ones, especially when compared to youth tried and convicted as adults who will spend a significant portion of their lives in adult prisons.

The push and pull between punishment and treatment can be clearly viewed in juvenile correctional facilities as states struggle with trying to balance public fear and possibilities for rehabilitating wayward youth. The lessons juvenile correctional facilities intend to teach and those that young men and women in confinement actually learn while serving their sentences can be quite different (Inderbitzin, 2006). Knowing that nearly all juvenile offenders will return to the community within months and years, it is worth exploring what they are actually learning while they are incarcerated and thinking about what skills and coping mechanisms we would like them to learn before emerging from the institution.

STUDIES IN DEVIANCE

Values, Rules, and Keeping the Peace: How Men Describe Order and the Inmate Code in California Prisons

By Rebecca Trammell (2009), in *Deviant Behavior, 30,* 746–771

Trammell (2009) interviews former male inmates of California prisons to examine how and why some inmates follow the inmate code. There is some controversy about the existence of an inmate code, with some arguing it doesn't exist (instead inmates bring their code of the street to their experiences in prison), while others argue the code is no more than the norms in a prison. However, some argue that a clear-cut code in prison helps to organize the structure and relations of prison life.

To address these various definition of an inmate code, Trammell (2009) examines how inmates describe the informal rules of the prison and how the inmate code may or may not fit these rules. She interviewed 40 former inmates of California prisons and six correctional officers. Focusing specifically on the connections between the informal rules, underground economy of the prison, and the inmate code, Trammell found that the inmate code may have changed since it was first examined in the 1950s (Trammell was not comparing the two eras but instead notes that early research on the inmate code suggested that inmates used the code to defy the goals of prison staff). She argues that today the code is used to keep the peace, which benefits the underground economies that have emerged over time in the prison system.

Trammell (2009) found that both those within and outside gangs knew of and followed a code while in prison—if the code was followed, inmates reported having an easier time than if they did not follow the code.

> I didn't know shit going into prison. I was totally clueless. I was strung out on drugs, sick and dumb and the brothers tell me right off the bat where to go, what to do. I thought they were joking at first. I knew prison was hard but I never thought I would have to know the rules about who uses a whoer first and who sits with who and who the leasers are. I think that's why there are fights, the dumb guys don't know the code going in and they screw up (Mac). (p. 756)

Finally, according to Trammell, the code seems to have changed with the recent mass incarceration—the code is used less to defy prison authority and more to keep peace and the underground economy (mostly the sale of drugs) operating.

◈ Reentry—Challenges in Returning to the Community After Time in an Institution

Reentering society after time spent in any total institution is a shock to the system and requires adjustment by the individual, his or her family, and the larger community. As the statement that opened this chapter clearly shows, individuals with a felony record face an especially difficult time in coping with the **stigma** of their conviction and trying to overcome the numerous obstacles felons must overcome in building new lives.

These problems are shared by an ever-increasing segment of the population. Figure 11.1 shows the growth of adult correctional populations over three decades; the numbers of people in prison and on probation are striking. If state laws and community practices close doors and opportunities for the millions of individuals involved with the criminal justice system, what message of social control are we sending? How should we expect these individuals to respond?

Prisoner reentry is a delicate process. While the many challenges faced by former inmates in rebuilding their lives are relatively clear, Maruna (2011) takes a wider view and describes the challenge to the larger society: "Like the commission of a crime, the reintegration of the former outcast back into society represents a challenge to the moral order, a delicate transition fraught with danger and possibility" (p. 3).

For those who have been formally convicted of a crime, the repercussions can last a lifetime. The stigma of a felony conviction may lead to "closing of doors" (Sampson & Laub, 1993, p. 124), negatively affecting employment opportunities, educational funding, housing, and the ability to vote alongside your fellow community members. Marc Mauer (2005) provides a clear illustration of the potential **collateral consequences of imprisonment** for a felony conviction:

> An 18-year-old with a first-time felony conviction for drug possession now may be barred from receiving welfare for life, prohibited from living in public housing, denied student loans to attend college, permanently excluded from voting, and if not a citizen, be deported. (p. 610)

Figure 11.1   Adult Correctional Populations, 1980–2009

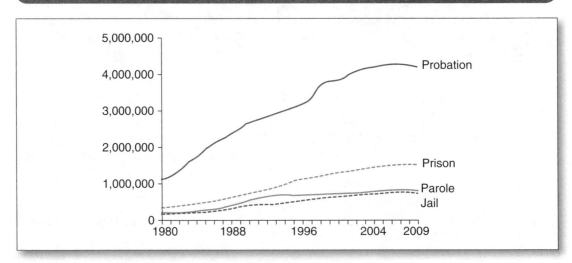

Source: Bureau of Justice Statistics Correctional Surveys (http://bjs.ojp.usdoj.gov/content/glance/corr2.cfm).

To better understand how felony convictions interact with race and affect the search for employment, Devah Pager (2007) designed an experimental study in which she sent out young men with matched credentials and fictional criminal records to apply for various entry-level jobs. While employers were generally reluctant to hire any ex-offenders, Pager and Quillian (2005) found that black ex-offenders were much less likely to be offered a job and a second chance than their white counterparts. Pager and Quillian's study is a strong example of using experimental methods to learn more about the obstacles convicted offenders face; the fact that African American males were given significantly fewer opportunities clearly shows how race and a criminal label interact to close doors and diminish individuals' life chances. You can learn more about Pager and Quillian's work in the reading that follows this chapter.

Felon Disenfranchisement

As we have illustrated, felony convictions and the stigma of incarceration limit individuals' opportunities for employment and housing. A more formal consequence of a felony conviction is "civil death" or the loss of the right to vote in local and national elections. **Felon disenfranchisement** varies by state, but most states have at least some limits in place whereby those who have committed felony offenses lose the right to participate in democratic elections. In most states, currently incarcerated felons are not allowed to vote from prison or jail. States are split as to whether parolees and probationers living in the community are allowed to vote, and some states ban ex-felons from ever voting again. For the most updated and comprehensive overview of felon voting rights, check out the website of The Sentencing Project (www.sentencingproject.org), which includes an interactive map with information available for every state.

Christopher Uggen and Jeff Manza have spent the past decade studying felon disenfranchisement, estimating the scope and number of individuals affected, as well as the impact on communities and elections. Uggen, Manza, and Thompson (2006, p. 283) estimate that there now exists a "felon class" of more than 16 million felons and ex-felons in the United States; these individuals represent 7.5% of the adult population, 22.3% of the black adult population, and 33.4% of the black adult male population. In other words, a full one third of African American men in the United States have serious criminal records.

In interviews with incarcerated felons and ex-felons, Manza and Uggen (2006) found that the right to vote did indeed matter to the individuals affected; their interviewees felt the sting of being classified as "less than the average citizen" (p. 155) even as they were still expected to pay taxes and work in the communities that denied them a voice.

◈ Public Fear and Social Control: The Case of Sex Offenders

The social control of sex offenders offers an extreme example of public fear and widespread panic over a particular offense and group. Despite relatively low recidivism rates, sex offenders are arguably the most feared and demonized of all criminals. All 50 states have adopted sex offender registration and notification laws, and more than 20 states allow involuntary **civil commitment** of sexual predators, whereby sex offenders can be held indefinitely, even after completing their criminal justice sentences (Harris & Lurigio, 2010).

Online registries and mandatory registration make it easy for community members to learn about convicted sex offenders living—or attempting to find housing—in their midst. It opens the possibility for harassment of the offenders and, in extreme cases, murder by overzealous vigilantes. Local residency laws severely restrict where sex offenders may live, stipulating, for example, that they must stay 2,500 feet away from schools, parks, and playgrounds. A story in *Newsweek* highlights the desperate circumstances sex offenders may face under such restrictions:

> The impact on the offenders was severe. Entire cities were suddenly off limits to them. They became pariahs, confined to remote and shrinking slivers of land. The most egregious example is a colony of predators camped out under the Julia Tuttle Causeway, which spans Miami's Biscayne Bay—a place so surreal and outlandish that it has become a lightning rod in the debate over America's treatment of sex offenders. . . .
>
> At the Julia Tuttle camp, the sex offenders begin trickling in around dusk. It is a squalid and dreary place. The air is thick and stifling, reeking of human feces and of cat urine from all the strays that live there. Overhead, the bridge drones and trembles with six lanes of traffic. Makeshift dwellings sprawl out in every direction—tents clinging to concrete pylons, rickety shacks fashioned out of plywood, a camper shell infested with cockroaches. There is no running water or sewage system; inhabitants relieve themselves in shopping bags and toss the sacks into a pile of refuse that they burn periodically. Some men fish along the shoreline, then gut and fry up the catch for anyone who's hungry. For diversion, there's a nightly dominoes game, or perhaps a bottle of booze sipped in solitude.
>
> The three-year-old settlement now numbers more than 70 people, including an 83-year-old deaf man, a wheelchair-bound fellow, and one woman. Some have lived there so long that their driver's licenses list their addresses as "Julia Tuttle Causeway Bridge." (Skipp, 2009)[*]

Clearly, as a society, we must learn to balance public fear and public safety with individual rights. Have individuals forfeited their rights forever once they are convicted of a crime? Or should those rights (and opportunities) be restored once they have served their mandated sentences? Are redemption and reintegration possible? These are complicated questions that we must continue to grapple with and explore. As Maruna (2011) explains,

> Criminal sanctions, for the most part, end very badly. Indeed, by most accounts, they do not end at all. Except for a very fortunate few who have their offenses formally forgiven through pardons or other legal means, individuals with felony records can remain permanently stigmatized, excluded from employment, educational and social opportunities, on the grounds of something they did many years or decades earlier. (p. 5)

◈ Collateral Consequences—Effects on Communities and Families

> If prisons affected no one except the criminals on the inside, they would matter less. But, after thirty years of penal population growth, the impact of America's prisons extends far beyond their walls. By zealously punishing lawbreakers—including a large new class of nonviolent drug offenders—the criminal justice system at the end of the 1990s drew into its orbit families and whole communities. These most fragile families and neighborhoods were the least equipped to counter any shocks or additional deprivations. (Western, 2006, p. 11)

Just as police surveillance and supervision is concentrated among poor and dominantly minority neighborhoods, incarceration is concentrated among poor, often minority men and women from disorganized

---

[*]Excerpt from "A Bridge Too Far," by Catharine Skipp, *Newsweek,* July 25, 2009. Copyright ©2009 The Newsweek/Daily Beast Company LLC. All rights reserved. Used by permission.

areas. This affects not only the imprisoned individuals but also their family members and the larger community. Todd Clear (2007) explains the impact like this:

> The way these young people cycle through our system of prisons and jails, then back into the community, leaves considerable collateral damage in its wake. Families are disrupted, social networks and other forms of social support are weakened, health is endangered, labor markets are thinned, and—more important than anything else—children are put at risk of the depleted human and social capital that promotes delinquency. After a certain point, the collateral effects of these high rates of incarceration seem to contribute to *more* crime in these places. (p. 175)

On any given day, approximately 1.5 million children have a parent serving time in a state or federal prison (Mumola, 2000). Even as they deal with depleted resources and troubled surroundings, mass incarceration in the United States affects literally millions of family members who come into prisons to visit their loved ones.

Meagan Comfort (2003, 2008) describes the "secondary prisonization" women experience in "the tube" or in the visitor waiting area at San Quentin. She calculated that approximately 95% of the visitors to the men's prison were women, and even though they were legally innocent of any crimes, they were subject to marginalization and their own pains of imprisonment due to their extended contact with the correctional facility. Comfort offers a detailed description of the rules and dress code of the prison, the women who arrive hours in advance and then wait patiently or resentfully to be allowed into the visiting room to see their loved ones, and the humiliating treatment they often receive at the hands of correctional officers processing them into and out of the institution. While inmates experience the pains of imprisonment, Comfort makes clear that their visitors also suffer from the contaminative contact of the prison.

In a second article, Comfort (2002) explores how these women work to prevent the institutionalization of their loved ones while they are in the prison. Comfort explains that the visitors move important life and family events into the prison's visiting room so that the fathers/boyfriends/husbands can maintain involvement and strengthen family ties. San Quentin allows family visits where inmates and their guests can spend nearly 2 days together in bungalows on the prison grounds. The women dip into their savings and plan carefully to purchase the approved ingredients to make memorable meals for their partners, who can in that moment escape prison food if not prison supervision.

In addition to intimate visits and special meals and celebrations in the prison visiting room, Comfort also describes weddings held within the prison (2002, 2008), happy days for the brides despite the bleak setting. She suggests that the women involved with inmates essentially fight for the sanity and souls of their men by reminding them of their families and their humanity: "Wives, fiancées, and girlfriends of inmates strive to bridge the distance between the outside world and their loved one: unable to bring him home, they bring home to him through the relocation of intimate activities inside the penitentiary walls" (Comfort, 2002, p. 492).

◈ Conclusion

In this chapter, we have given you a quick glimpse into some specific forms of social control of deviant behavior. Much more could and has been written on the topic, but we chose to keep it simple and highlight some current practices that show the challenges of effectively controlling deviant behavior without creating widespread damage to individuals, families, and communities.

We would like to point out, too, that reactions to deviant behavior and efforts at social control are constantly evolving. For example, after prison populations soared over the past several decades, states are now looking for more creative—and less expensive—responses to criminal behavior. "Ban the Box" campaigns have sprung up around the country, encouraging states and counties to eliminate the box on employment and housing forms that asks whether the applicant has a criminal conviction or criminal record. In addition, some progress has been made in efforts to restore voting rights to felons, with current research suggesting that the benefits of civic reintegration of ex-offenders far outweigh the potential risks (Uggen & Inderbitzin, 2010). What changes will be next?

In the next chapter, you will read about deviant careers and career deviance. While most theories and books on deviant behavior focus on how individuals enter deviance, we think it is just as interesting and important to examine how the majority of individuals change their life trajectories and sooner or later find a way to exit deviance.

NOW YOU . . . THINK ABOUT SOCIAL CONTROL

We have explored myriad forms of deviance in this book: police misconduct, drug use, corporate misconduct, prostitution, and making "war" on various behaviors, to name a few. What we can probably conclude by the disparate behaviors, issues, and perspectives is that deviance is often in the eye of the beholder. While one person might define the homeless person as deviant, many others might define a society that does not have enough safety nets for those in need—thus allowing homelessness—to be deviant.

In the same vein, social control of "deviants" takes on many faces. Some of this social control is "informal," while much of it has been formalized, leading to an explosion in both regulations and prison populations.

Given what you have learned about deviants, deviance, and theory in this book, what should be the relationship between deviance and social control? If we asked you to build a better vision of social control, what would your philosophy be? What behaviors would you focus on? What behaviors would you allow? Would you focus on: informal or formal social control? On individuals or groups? On making peace or war? Why?

EXERCISES AND DISCUSSION QUESTIONS

1. Do you think deviance and social control are necessary to society? What functions do they serve? Which of the purposes of punishment do you think best fit our current criminal justice system? Why do you think so?

2. Should we be concerned about the institutionalization of inmates? Why or why not? What might be done to prevent **institutionalization/ prisonization?**

3. Felony records disqualify individuals from a number of different types of jobs, not necessarily related to the type of crime committed. Do you think this is a fair practice? Why or why not? What do you think would be appropriate guidelines in terms of felony convictions and employment?

4. Check out the interactive map on The Sentencing Project's website (http://www.sentencingproject .org/map/map.cfm). How does your state compare to others and the national average in terms of corrections populations, corrections expenditures, and felon disenfranchisement? Are you surprised by any of this information?

5. Do you think persons convicted of felony offenses should be able to vote in local and national elections? What restrictions, if any, do you think would be appropriate? What are the laws in your state?

6. Should sex offenders be treated differently than other violent offenders? Does the community have a right to know and perhaps even dictate where they live and work? Do you think civil commitment of sex offenders is appropriate?

KEY TERMS

Civil commitment

Collateral consequences
of imprisonment

Demedicalization

Felon disenfranchisement

Institutionalization/
prisonization

Medicalization of deviance

Pains of imprisonment

Social contract

Stigma

Total institutions

READING 33

A fair amount of research has focused on the lives of people living in poor inner-city ghettos, but most of that research occurred before the dramatic rise in incarceration rates seen over the past few decades—what some refer to as a period of "mass incarceration." This article paints a vivid picture of young black men who have warrants out for their arrest, often for minor infractions, and how they work to avoid the police and incarceration. Goffman draws on 6 years of fieldwork in Philadelphia to show how their wanted status (and sometimes just perceptions that there "may" be a warrant out for them) affects the daily lives of these young men and their relationships to family, friends, and work. Families are often threatened by police for information. Friends, especially romantic partners, can use the wanted status to extort expected behaviors. Finally, work is hard enough for the ex-con to find, and for those wanted by law enforcement, a place of employment is one of the first places the police will look. Many of the warrants appear relatively trivial in nature (parole violations like alcohol use, failure to pay fines, or missed court appearances), but the "wanted," his family, and his romantic partners all know that the warrants can get him back in jail or prison and often for long periods of time. Goffman discusses many problems facing those on parole but also recognizes how parolees often use their wanted status for their own special interests. This piece is both a very interesting read and a thoughtful extension of the ideas of punishment and surveillance and how these forms of social control are being applied to individuals in poor black neighborhoods.

On the Run

Wanted Men in a Philadelphia Ghetto

Alice Goffman

The number of people incarcerated in the United States has grown seven times over the past 40 years, and this growth has been concentrated among Black men with little education (Garland 2001: Western 2006). For Black men in recent birth cohorts, the experience of incarceration is now typical:

Source: Goffman, Alice. 2009. "On the Run: Wanted Men in a Philadelphia Ghetto." *American Sociological Review* 74:339–357. Reprinted by permission.

30 percent of those with only high school diplomas have been to prison, and 60 percent of those who did not finish high school have prison records by their mid-30s (Pettit and Western 2004). Once in four Black children born in 1990 had a father imprisoned (Wildeman 2009). Such "mass imprisonment" (Garland 2001) transmits social and economic disadvantage, to be sure. African American former felons face significant discriminatin in the labot market, as well as health costs, obstacles to housing, and large-scale disenfranchisement (Hammett, Harmon, and Rhodes 2002; Pager 2007; Rubenstein and Mukamal 2002; Uggen and Manze 2002; Western 2006). Moreover, imprisoned and formerly imprisoned men have difficulties participating in sustained ways in the lives of their families (see Nurse 2002; Western, Lopoo, and McLanahan 2004). Their partners and children consequently become socially and economically disadvantaged in the process (for reviews, see Comfort 2007; Hagan and Dinovitzer 1999).[1]

Expansions in incarceration have been accompanied by increases in policing and supervision in poor communities. While the police were scarcely present in the ghetto decades ago, today, police helicopters can regularly be heard overhead, cameras now monitor people on the streets, and large numbers of young men—including many who have never been convicted of felonies—have pending cases in the criminal courts, are on probation, released on bail, issued low-level warrants, and are routinely chased, searched, questioned, and arrested by the police. How does this affect daily life in poor Black communities? Unfortunately, we know little in this regard. Indeed, much of the research literature, which relies on statistical data, field experiments, or interviews, most often centers on the consequences of going to prison. Although ethnographic accounts should arguably capture what enhanced policing and supervision has meant for the dynamics of daily life in poor minority communities, most ethnographies were written before the criminal justice system became such a prevalent institution in the lives of the poor (see, e.g., Anderson 1978; Liebow 1967; Stack 1974).[2]

This article, building on prior work pertaining to the urban poor, as well as broader conceptions of power in the modern era (e.g., Foucault 1979), draws on six years of fieldwork with a group of poor African American young men in Philadelphia. In doing so, it offers an extended ethnographic look at life in the policed and surveilled ghetto that has taken shape in the era of mass imprisonment. As the findings reveal, the dealings these young men have with the police, the courts, and the probation and parole board grant them an illegal or semilegal status and instill an overriding fear of capture. Suspicious even of those closest to them, young men cultivate unpredictability or altogether avoid institutions, places, and relations on which they formerly relied. Yet because being wanted is understood to be deeply constraining, it can, within the context of limited opportunity, serve as an excuse for obligations that may have gone unfulfilled anyway. The result is a complex interactive system in which ghetto residents become caught in constraining legal entanglements while simultaneously calling on the criminal justice system to achieve a measure of power over one another in their daily lives.

◈ The Urban Poor and Policing

Ethnographic accounts of poor urban communities have long included descriptions of people who commit serious crimes, stand trial, go to jail, or find themselves on the run from the police (see, e.g., Anderson 1978; Liebow 1967). Until recently, these people comprised only a small group of criminals in a neighborhood: most residents of poor Black communities did not interact much with the authorities. Before the 1990s, in fact, the ghetto was frequently described as nearly abandoned by law enforcement.

Anderson (1978:2), writing about street-corner men in Chicago in the early 1970s (he devotes a whole chapter to hoodlums), reports that "the police glance over and slow down, but they seldom stop and do anything. Ordinarily they casually move on, leaving the street-corner men to settle their own differences." Venkatesh's (2008) description of the Chicago projects some 20 years later depicts a similar scene, noting that police simply do not come when called. Instead, gang leaders step in and maintain an informal, de facto system of justice with the help of project leaders and a few neighborhood cops. In *Crack House,* Williams (1992:84) likewise describes how, in New York during the late 1980s and early 1990s at the peak of the crack boom, police typically did not disturb open air crack sales:

> The police have firm knowledge about selling spots, but they usually ignore the spots until community pressure builds to a level that forces them to take action. . . . For the most part, the police stay away. . . . One night I watched a police car, with lights flashing, move down this street past hundreds of buyers, runners, touts, and dealers marching by continually making exchanges. Over the car's loudspeaker an officer kept saying, "Move on off the block everybody. This is the police." The buyers and sellers paid no attention.

Times, however, have changed. The past few decades have seen the war on crime, the war on drugs, a blossoming of federal and state police agencies and bureaus, steeper sentencing laws, and a near unified endorsement of "zero-tolerance" policies from police and civic leaders (Beckett 1997; Simon 2007). The number of police officers per capita increased dramatically in the second half of the twentieth century in cities across the United States (Reiss 1992). In 2006, more than 14 million people were arrested and charged with a criminal offense in the United States, and more than five million people were under probation or parole supervision (Glaze and Bonzcar 2006; U.S. Department of Justice 2007).

In Philadelphia—my field site—the number of police officers increased by 69 percent between 1960 and 2000, from 2.76 officers for every 1,000 citizens to 4.66 officers.[3] The Philadelphia Adult Probation and Parole Department supervised more than 60,000

people in 2006. These people paid the city more than 10 million dollars in restitution, fines, court costs, and supervisory fees that year. In Philadelphia, 12,000 people violated the terms of their probation or parole and were issued warrants for their arrest (Philadelphia Adult Probation and Parole Department 2007). Even more people were issued bench warrants for missing court or for unpaid court fees, or arrest warrants for failure to turn themselves in for a crime. Such surveillance, policing, and supervision raise important sociological questions about the role of the state in managing poverty and maintaining racial inequality (Wacquant 2001). They also raise questions about the nature and consequences of modern surveillance and power.

Foucault (1979) suggested that the modern era would increasingly be characterized by surveillance and that state monitoring of citizens would become increasingly complete. Building on ethnographic insights, my conclusions highlight ways in which contemporary surveillance may indeed be taking the forms Foucault described in his analysis of panoptic power. Yet my conclusions also suggest that the consequences of such surveillance for everyday life may differ from those envisioned by Foucault. Rather than encouraging self-monitoring, the forms of supervision and policing found in the neighborhood I observed foster a climate of fear and suspicion in which people are pressured to inform on one another. Young men do not live as well-disciplined subjects, but as suspects and fugitives, with the daily fear of confinement.

◈ Fieldwork, the 6th Street Boys, and Neighborhood Context

When I was an undergraduate at the University of Pennsylvania, I tutored a high school student, Aisha (names of people and streets are fictitious). I began to get to know some of her friends and neighbors, and in the fall of 2002 I moved into an apartment in the poor to working-class Black neighborhood in which she lived. At this point, Aisha's mother had begun referring to me as her "other daughter" and Aisha and I became "sisters" (Anderson 1978; Stack 1974). When Aisha's cousin Ronny, age 15, came home from a juvenile detention center, Aisha and I started hanging out with him in a neighborhood about 10 minutes away called 6th Street. Ronny introduced me to Mike, who was 21, a year older than I was. When Mike's best friend Chuck, age 18, came home from county jail, we began hanging out with him too.

When I first started spending time with Ronny and Mike on 6th Street, their neighbors and relatives remarked on my whiteness and asked me to account for my presence. Ronny introduced me as Aisha's "sister," and I mentioned that I lived nearby. After a few months, Mike decided to "take me under his wing" and began referring to me as "sis." Bit by bit, other young men in the group started introducing me to others as their cousin or as a "homie" who "goes way back."

The five blocks known as 6th Street are 93 percent Black, according to a survey of residents that Chuck and I conducted in 2007. At the busiest intersection, men and boys stand outside offering bootleg CDs and DVDs, stolen goods, and food to drivers and passersby. The main commercial street includes a bullet-proofed Chinese food store selling fried chicken wings, "loosie" cigarettes, condoms, baby food, and glassines for smoking crack. The street also includes a check-cashing store, hair dresser, payday loan store, Crown Fried Chicken restaurant, and a pawnshop. On the next block, a Puerto Rican family runs a corner grocery.

Of the 217 households surveyed, roughly one fourth received housing vouchers. In all but two households, members reported receiving some type of government assistance in the past three years. The neighborhood also contains many people who make their living as teachers, bus drivers, parole officers, health care workers, and so on. Aisha's neighbors commonly referred to the area of 6th Street as "nice and

quiet," and a place they would move if they had enough money.

Chuck, Mike, and Ronny were part of a loose group of about 15 young men who grew up around 6th Street and were joined by the fact that they were, for the most part, unemployed and trying to make it outside of the formal economy. They occasionally referred to their group as "the 6th Street Boys" when distinguishing themselves from other street-corner groups, and five of them had "6th Street" tattooed on their arms. Among the 15 young men, eight were 18 or 19 years old when I met them, four were in their early 20s, and one was age 23. Ronny was 14 and Reggie was 15. Six years later, Mike was the only one to have graduated from high school. Alex worked steadily in his father's heating and air-conditioning repair shop, and four others occasionally found seasonal construction jobs or low-skilled jobs at places like Taco Bell and McDonald's. By 2002, the crack trade was in decline, as it was in other parts of the country (Jacobs 1999). Seven of the young men worked intermittently as low-level crack dealers; others sold marijuana, Wet (PCP and/or embalming fluid), or pills like Xanax. Some of the men occasionally made money by robbing other drug dealers. One earned his keep by exotic dancing and offering sex to women.

All but two of the young men lived with female relatives, although about half got evicted and slept on other people's couches or on the streets for months or years at a time. Anthony slept in an abandoned truck on 6th Street for most of the time I knew him, although Chuck later let him sleep in his basement or got the women he was seeing to let Anthony sleep on the floor when Chuck spent the night.

Between January 2002 and August 2003, I conducted intensive observation "on the block," spending most of my waking hours hanging out on Chuck's back porch steps, or along the alley way between his block and Mike's block, or on the corner across from the convenience store. In the colder months, we were usually indoors at Chuck's and a few other houses in the area. I also went along to lawyers' offices, court, the probation and parole office, the hospital, and local bars and parties. By 2004, some of the young men were in county jails and state prisons; for the next four years I spent between two and six days a week on 6th street and roughly one day a week visiting members of the group in jail and prison. I also kept in touch by phone and through letters.

The young men agreed to let me take field notes for the purpose of one day publishing the material, but I generally did not ask direct questions and most of what is contained here comes from observations I made or conversations I heard.[4] Over the course of this research I also interviewed two lawyers, a district attorney, three probation officers, two police officers, and a federal district court judge.

On Being Wanted

By 2002, curfews were established around 6th Street for those under age 18 and video cameras had been placed on major streets. During the first year and a half of fieldwork, I watched the police stop pedestrians or people in cars, search them, run their names to see if any warrants came up, ask them to come in for questioning, or make an arrest at least once a day, with five exceptions. I watched the police break down doors, search houses, and question, arrest, or chase suspects through houses 52 times. Police helicopters circled overhead and beamed search lights onto local streets nine times. I noted blocks taped off and traffic redirected as police searched for evidence or "secured a crime scene" 17 times. I watched the police punch, choke, kick, stomp on, or beat young men with night sticks 14 times during this first year and a half.

Children learn at an early age to watch out for the police and to prepare to run. The first week I spent on 6th Street, I saw two boys, 5 and 7 years old, play a game of chase in which one assumed the role of the cop who must run after the other. When the "cop" caught up to the other child, he pushed him down and cuffed him with imaginary handcuffs. He patted the other child down and felt in his pockets, asking if he had warrants or was carrying a gun or any drugs. The child then took

a quarter out of the other child's pocket, laughing and yelling, "I'm seizing that!" In the following months, I saw children give up running and simply stick their hands behind their backs, as if in handcuffs, or push their bodies up against a car, or lie flat on the ground and put their hands over their head. The children yelled, "I'm going to lock you up! I'm going to lock you up, and you ain't never coming home." I once saw a 6-year-old child pull another child's pants down and try to do a "cavity search."

When Chuck, Mike, and Steve assembled outside, the first topic of the day was frequently who had been taken into custody the night before and who had outrun the cops and gotten away. They discussed how the police identified and located the person, what the charges were likely to be, what physical harm had been done to the man as he was caught and arrested, and what property the police had taken and what had been wrecked or lost during the chase.

People with warrants out for their arrest for failure to turn themselves in when accused of a crime understand that the police may employ a number of strategies in attempting to locate them. In an interview, two police officers explained that when they are looking for a suspect, they access Social Security records, court records, hospital admission records, electric and gas bills, and employment records. They visit a suspect's "usual haunts" (e.g., his home, his workplace, and his street corner) at the times he is likely to be there, threatening his family or friends with arrest, particularly when they have their own lower-level warrants or are on probation or have a pending court case. The police also use a sophisticated computer mapping program that tracks people who have warrants or are on probation, parole, or released on bail. The police round up these potential informants and threaten them with jail time if they do not provide information about the suspect they are looking for.

In the 6th Street neighborhood, a person was occasionally "on the run" because he was a suspect in a shooting or robbery, but most people around 6th Street had warrants out for far more minor infractions. In the survey that Chuck and I conducted in 2007, of the 217 households that make up the 6th Street neighborhood, we found 308 men between the ages of 18 and 30 in residence. [5] Of these men, 144 reported that they had a warrant issued for their arrest because of either delinquencies with court fines and fees or for failure to appear for a court date within the past three years. Also within the past three years, warrants had been issued to 119 men for technical violations of their probation or parole (e.g., drinking or breaking curfew).[6]

Young men worried that they would be picked up by the police and taken into custody even when they did not have a warrant out for their arrest. Those on probation or parole, on house arrest, and who were going through a trial expressed concern that they would soon be picked up and taken into custody for some violation that would "come up in the system." Even those with no pending legal action expressed concern that the police might "find some reason to hold them" because of what they had done, who or what they knew, or what they carried on their person. In this sense, being "on the run" covers a range of circumstances. I use the term to mean anyone whose claim to a life outside of confinement is not secure or legitimate and who may be taken into custody if they encounter the authorities. People "on the run" make a concerted effort to thwart their discovery and apprehension, as Chuck, age 19, concisely put it in speaking to his 12-year-old brother:

> You hear the law coming, you merk on [run away from] them niggas. You don't be having time to think okay, what do I got on me, what they going to want from me. No, you hear them coming, that's it, you gone, period. Because whoever they looking for, even if it's not you, nine times out of ten they'll probably book you.

Police, jail, and court language permeates general conversation. Young men refer to their girlfriends as "Co-Ds" (codefendants) and speak of "catching a case"

(to be arrested and charged with a crime) when accused of some wrong by their friends and family. "Call List," the term for the phone numbers of family and friends one is allowed to call from prison or jail, becomes the term for one's close friends.

One way to understand the quantity and quality of young men's legal entanglements is to look at nine members of the group during one month. In December 2003, Anthony, who was 22 years old and homeless, had a bench warrant out for his arrest because he had not paid $173 in court fees for a case that had ended the year before. He had spent nine of the previous 12 months in jail awaiting the decision. Later in the month, two neighbors who knew that Anthony had this bench warrant called the police and got him arrested because they said he had stolen three pairs of shoes from them. Shawn, a 21-year-old exotic dancer, was in county jail awaiting trial for selling crack, a charge that would ultimately be dismissed. Chuck, age 18, had a warrant because he had not paid $225 in court fees that were due a few weeks after his case for assault was dismissed. He spent almost his entire senior year of high school in county jail awaiting trial on this case.

Reggie, then age 16, and his neighbor Randy, age 19, had detainers out for violating the terms of their probation, Randy for drinking and Reggie for testing positive for marijuana (called "hot piss"). Alex, age 22, was serving a probation sentence, and Steve, age 19, was under house arrest awaiting the completion of a trial for possession of drugs. Ronny, age 16, was in a juvenile detention facility, and Mike, age 21, was in county jail awaiting trial.

Between 2002 and 2007, Mike spent about three and a half years in jail or prison. Out of the 139 weeks that he was not incarcerated, he spent 87 weeks on probation or parole for five overlapping sentences. He spent 35 weeks with a warrant out for his arrest, and in total had 10 warrants issued on him. Mike had at least 51 court appearances over this five-year period, 47 of which I attended.

The fact that some young men may be taken into custody if they encounter the authorities is a background expectation of everyday interaction in this community. It is a starting principle, central to understanding young men's relations to family and friends, as well as the reciprocal lines of action between them.

◈ Paths to Prison and Strategies of Evasion

Once a man finds that he may be stopped by the police and taken into custody, he discovers that people, places, and relations he formerly relied on, and that are integral to maintaining a respectable identity, get redefined as paths to confinement. I am concerned here with the kinds of relations, localities, and activities that threaten a wanted man's freedom, with the techniques he commonly employs to reduce these risks, and with some of the contingencies associated with these techniques.

Hospitals and Jobs

Alex and his girlfriend, Donna, both age 22, drove to the hospital for the birth of their son. I got there a few hours after the baby was born, in time to see two police officers come into the room and arrest Alex. He had violated his parole a few months before by drinking alcohol and had a warrant out for his arrest. As an officer handcuffed him, Donna screamed and cried, and as they walked Alex away she got out of the bed and grabbed hold of him, moaning, "Please don't take him away. Please I'll take him down there myself tomorrow I swear, just let him stay with me tonight." The officers told me they had come to the hospital with a shooting victim who was in custody and, as was their custom, ran the names of the men on the visitors list.

Alex came up as having a warrant out for a parole violation, so they arrested him along with two other men on the delivery room floor. After Alex was arrested, other young men expressed hesitation to go to the hospital when their babies were born. Soon after Chuck turned 21, his girlfriend, age 22, was due with their second child. Chuck told her that he would

go to the hospital, even though he had a detainer out for a probation violation for breaking curfew. Chuck stayed with her until she was driven to the hospital, but at the final moment he said she should go ahead without him and that he would come soon. He sat with me later and discussed the situation. As we spoke, his girlfriend called his cell phone repeatedly, and he would mute the sound after a ring and stare at her picture as it came up on the screen each time. He said:

> I told her I was on my way. She mad as shit I ain't there. I can hear her right now. She going to be like, "You broke your promise." I'm not trying to go out like Alex [get arrested], though. You feel me?

Alex spent a year back upstate on the parole violation. Just after his son's first birthday he was re-released on parole, with another year left to complete it. He resumed work at his father's heating and air-conditioning repair shop, stopped smoking marijuana, and typically came home before his curfew. Three weeks before Alex was due to complete his parole sentence, he was on his way home from 6th Street when a man with a hooded sweatshirt covering his face stepped quickly out from behind the side of a store and walked Alex, with a gun in his back, into the alley. Alex said the man took his money and pistol-whipped him three times, then grabbed the back of his head and smashed his face into a concrete wall.

Alex called Mike and me to come pick him up. When we arrived, Alex was searching on the ground for the three teeth that had fallen out, and the blood from his face and mouth was streaming down his white T-shirt and onto his pants and boots. His jaw and nose were swollen and looked as if they might be broken. I pleaded with him to go to the hospital. He refused, saying that his parole officer might hear of it and serve him a violation for being out past curfew, for fighting, for drinking, or any other number of infractions.

That night, Alex called his cousin who was studying to be a nurse's assistant to come stitch up his face. In the morning, he repeated his refusal to avail himself of medical care:

> All the bullshit I done been through [to finish his parole sentence], it's like, I'm not just going to check into emergency and there come the cops asking me all types of questions and writing my information down and before you know it I'm back in there [in prison]. Even if they not there for me some of them probably going to recognize me then they going to come over, run my shit [run a check on his name]. . . . I ain't supposed to be up there [his parole terms forbade him to be near 6th Street, where he was injured]; I can't be out at no two o'clock [his curfew was ten]. Plus they might still got that little jawn [warrant] on me in Bucks County [for court fees he did not pay at the end of a trial two years earlier]. I don't want them running my name, and then I got to go to court or I get locked back up.

Alex later found out that the man who beat him had mistaken him for his brother, who had apparently robbed him the week before. Alex's jaw still bothers him and he now speaks with a kind of muffled lisp, but he did not go back to prison. Alex was the only member of the group to successfully complete a probation or parole sentence during the six years I spent there.

Like hospitals, places of employment become dangerous for people with a warrant. Soon after Mike, age 24, was released on parole to a halfway house, he got a job through an old friend who managed a Taco Bell. Mike refused to return to the halfway house in time for curfew one night, saying he could not spend another night cooped up with a bunch of men like he was still in jail. He slept at his girlfriend's house, and in the morning found that he had been issued a violation and would likely be sent back to prison, pending the judge's decision. Mike said he wasn't coming back and they were going to have to catch him. Two parole officers arrested him

the next day as he was leaving the Taco Bell. He spent a year back upstate for this violation.

A man with a warrant can get arrested on the job even if the police are not specifically searching for him. Chuck, who started working at the local McDonald's when he was 19, was issued a probation violation for driving a car (his driving privileges had been revoked as part of his probation sentence). Although he had a warrant, Chuck kept working, saying that if the police came he would simply run out the back door.

A couple of weeks later, an old employee got into a fight with three other employees, and the police shut down the McDonald's while they questioned witnesses and looked for the women who had been fighting. When the fight began, Chuck was in the storeroom talking on the phone with his girlfriend. He came out, he said, and saw six police officers staring at him. At this point he called and asked me to come and pick up his house keys, fairly certain he would be taken into custody. When I got there he was driving away in the back of the police car.

The Police and the Courts

Like going to work or to hospitals, using the police and the courts was risky. After Mike completed a year in prison he was released on parole to a halfway house. When his mother went on vacation, he invited a man he met in prison to her house to play video games. The next day Mike, Chuck, and I went back and found his mother's stereo, DVD player, and two televisions were gone. A neighbor told us he had seen the man taking these things out of the house in the early morning.

Mike called the police and gave them a description of the man. When we returned to the block, Reggie and Steve admonished Mike about the risks he had taken:

> *Reggie:* And you on parole! You done got home like a day ago! Why the fuck you calling the law for? You lucky they ain't just grab [arrest] both of you. *Steve:* Put it this way: They ain't come grab you like you ain't violate shit, they ain't find no other jawns [warrants] in the computer. Dude ain't pop no fly

shit [accused Mike of some crime in an attempt to reduce his own charges], but simple fact is you filed a statement, you know what I'm saying, gave them niggas your government [real name]. Now they got your mom's address in the file as your last known [address], so the next time they come looking for you they not just going to your uncle's, they definitely going to be through there [his mother's house].

Mike returned to the halfway house a few days later and discovered that the guards were conducting alcohol tests. He left before they could test him, assuming he would test positive and spend another year upstate for the violation. Three days later the police found him at his mother's house and took him into custody. He mentioned that he thought their knowledge of his new address must have come from the time he reported the robbery.

Using the courts was no less dangerous. Chuck, age 22, was working in construction. He had been arguing with his children's mother for some months, and she stopped allowing him to see their two daughters, ages one-and-a-half and six months. Chuck decided to take her to court to file for partial custody. At the time, Chuck was also sending $35 a month to the city toward payment on tickets he had received for driving without a license or registration; he hoped to get into good standing and become qualified to apply for a driver's license. The judge said that if he did not meet his payments on time every month, he would issue a bench warrant for his arrest,[7] and Chuck could work off the traffic tickets he owed in county jail (fines and fees can be deducted for every day spent in custody).

Five months into his case for partial custody in family court, Chuck lost his job working construction and stopped making the $35 payments to the city for the traffic tickets. He was unable to discover whether he had been issued a warrant. Chuck went to court for the child custody case anyway the next month, and when the children's mother said he was a drug dealer and not fit to get partial custody of their children, the judge ran his name in the database to see if any warrants came

up. They did not. Walking out of the courthouse, Chuck said to me and his mother:

> I wanted to run, but it was no way I was getting out of there—it was too many cops and guards. But my shit came back clean, so I guess if they is going to give me a warrant for the tickets they ain't get around to it yet.

The judge ruled in Chuck's favor, and he was granted visitation on Sundays at a court-supervised daycare site. These visits, Chuck said, made him anxious: "Every time I walk in the door I wonder, like, is it today? Are they going to come grab me, like, right out of the daycare? I can just see [my daughter's] face, like, 'Daddy, where you going?'" After a month, Chuck was allowed to go to the mother's house on the weekends and pick up his daughters. Chuck appeared thrilled with these visits because he could see his children without having to interact with the courts and risk being taken into custody for any warrant that might come up.

While people on probation or parole may make tentative use of the police and the courts, men with warrants typically stay away. During the first year and a half I spent on 6th Street, I noted 24 instances in which members of the group contacted the police when they were injured, robbed, or threatened. These men were either in good standing with the courts or had no pending legal constraints. I did not observe any person with a warrant call the police or voluntarily make use of the courts during the six years I spent there. Indeed, young men with warrants seemed to see the authorities only as a threat to their safety. This has two important implications.

First, steering clear of the police means that wanted men tend not to use the ordinary resources of the law to protect themselves from crimes perpetrated against them. This can lead a person to become the target of those who are looking for someone to rob.

Ned, age 43, and his long-time girlfriend Jean, age 46, lived on Mike's block. Jean was a heavy crack user, although Chuck noted, "she can handle her drugs," meaning she was able to maintain both a household and her addiction. Ned was unemployed and occasionally hosted "dollar parties" (house parties with a dollar entrance fee and with drinks, food, and games that all cost a dollar) for extra money and engaged in petty fraud, such as stealing checks out of the mail and stealing credit cards. Their primary income came from taking in foster children.

Jason lived on Chuck's block and sold marijuana with his younger brother. In January of 2003, the police stopped Jason on a dirt bike and arrested him for receiving stolen property (they said the bike came up stolen in California four years earlier). Jason did not appear for court and was issued a bench warrant.

Around this time, Ned and Jean discovered they might be kicked out of their house because they owed property taxes to the city. Jean called Jason, telling him to come to the house because she had some gossip concerning his longtime love interest. According to Jason, when he arrived on the porch steps, Jean's nephew robbed him at gunpoint. That night, Jean acknowledged to me that she would take this money and pay some of their bills owed to the city. Reggie later remarked that Jason should have known not to go to Ned and Jean's house: as the only man on the block with a warrant out for his arrest at the time, he was vulnerable to violence or robbery because he could not call the police.

Second, wanted people's inability to turn to the police when harmed can lead young men to use violence to protect themselves or to get back at others. Black (1983) argues that some crimes can be understood as people taking matters into their own hands, that is, punishing people whom they consider to have committed a crime. This kind of self-help crime is typically carried out when the police and the courts are unavailable (in this case, because people have warrants out for their arrest and may be held in custody if they contact the authorities).

One winter morning, Chuck, Mike, and I were at a diner having breakfast to celebrate the fact that Mike had not been taken into custody after his court appearance earlier that morning. Chuck's mother called to tell him that his car had been firebombed outside her house and that fire trucks were putting it out. According to Chuck, the man who set fire to his car was someone

who had given him drugs to sell on credit, under the arrangement that Chuck would pay him once he had sold the drugs. Chuck had not been able to pay because the police had taken the money out of his pockets when they searched him earlier that week. This was the first car that Chuck had ever purchased legally, a '94 Bonneville he had bought the week before for $400 from a used-car lot in northeast Philadelphia. Chuck was silent for the rest of the meal, and as we walked to Mike's car, he said:

> This shit is nutty, man. What the fuck I'm supposed to do, go to the cops? "Um, excuse me officer, I think boy done blown up my whip [car]." He going to run my name and shit, now he see I got a warrant on me; next thing you know my Black ass locked the fuck up, you feel me? *I'm* locked up because a nigga firebombed my whip. What the fuck, I'm supposed to let niggas take advantage?

Chuck and Mike discussed whether it was better for Chuck to take matters into his own hands or to do nothing (referred to as "letting it ride" or "taking an L" [loss]). Doing nothing had the benefit of not placing him in more legal trouble, but, as they both noted, "letting it ride" set them up to be taken advantage of by people who understood them to be "sweet."

A few days later, Chuck drove over to 8th Street with Mike and Steve and shot at the young man whom he believed was responsible for blowing up his car. Although no one was injured, a neighbor reported the incident and the police put out a body warrant for Chuck's arrest for attempted murder.

Labeling theory suggests that those accorded a deviant status come to engage in deviance because of being labeled as such (Becker 1963; Lemert 1951). This phenomenon is known as "secondary deviance" (Lemert 1951:75). Declining to engage authorities when there may be concrete reasons for doing so should be considered in this context. Young men's hesitation to go to the police or to make use of the courts when they are wronged, because of concern they will be arrested, means they became the targets of theft and violence because it is assumed they will not press charges. With the police out of reach, men then resort to more violence as a strategy to settle disputes.

Family and Friends

Like going to the hospital or using the police and the courts, even more intimate relations—friends, family, and romantic partners—may pose a threat and thus have to be avoided or at least carefully navigated. My observations of Alex made this all too clear. When I met Alex, age 21, he was on parole and living with his girlfriend Donna. Alex had recently gotten a job at his father's heating and air-conditioning repair shop. After work, he usually went to see his friends from 6th street, and occasionally he would stay on the block drinking and talking until late at night.

Donna and Alex frequently argued over what time he came home and his drunken condition. In these fights, I observed that Donna would threaten to call his parole officer and say that Alex was in violation if Alex did not return home at a reasonable hour. Donna also threatened to call the parole officer and tell him that Alex was out past curfew or associating with known criminals if he cheated on her, or if he did not contribute enough of his money to the household. Because Alex was paroled to Donna's apartment, she could also threaten to call the parole office and say that she no longer wanted Alex to live with her. If this were to happen, she explained to me, Alex would be placed in a halfway house.

In the early morning after a party, Mike and I drove Alex back to Donna's apartment. She was waiting on the step for him:

Donna: Where the fuck you been at?

Alex: Don't worry about it.

Donna: You must don't want to live here no more.

Alex: Come on, Don. Stop playing.

Donna: Matter of fact I'll give you the choice [between prison or a halfway house].

Alex: Come on, Don.

Donna: Uhn-uhn, you not staying here no more. I'm about to call your P.O. now, so you better make up your mind where you going to go.

Alex: I'm tired, man, come on, open the door. Donna: Nigga, the next time I'm laying in the bed by myself that's a wrap [that's the end].

Later that day, Donna called me and listed a number of reasons why she needed to threaten Alex:

I can't let that nigga get locked up for some dumb shit like he gets caught for a DUI or he gets stopped in a Johnny [a stolen car] or some shit. What the fuck I'm supposed to do? Let that nigga roam free? And then next thing you know he locked up and I'm stuck here by myself with Omar talking about "Where Daddy at?"

Donna stopped short of calling the police on Alex and seemed to see her threats as necessary efforts at social control. This use of the criminal justice system as threat can be seen as parallel to the way in which single mothers threaten to turn fathers over to child-support authorities if they do not contribute money informally (Edin and Lein 1997). I also witnessed women go a step further and call the police on their boyfriends or kin to punish them or get back at them.

Mike and Marie's relationship witnessed just such a tension. They had a son when they were seniors in high school and a daughter two years later. When Mike and Marie were 22, and their children were 1 and 3 years old, Mike began openly seeing another woman, Tara. Mike claimed that he and Marie had broken up and he could do as he wished, but Marie did not agree to this split and maintained they were still together and that he was in fact cheating. ("He don't be telling me we not together when he laying in the bed with me!") Mike provoked expressions of jealousy (called "stunting") as he began riding past Marie's block with Tara on the back of his ATV motorbike. Marie seemed infuriated at the insult of her children's father riding through her block with another woman for all of her family and neighbors to see, and she told him that he could no longer visit their two children. Mike and Marie spent many hours on the phone arguing over this. Mike would plead with her to let him see the children and she would explain that he would have to end things with Tara first.

Tara said she wanted to fight Marie and almost did so one afternoon. Marie stood outside her house, with six relatives in back of her, waving a baseball bat and shouting, "Get your kids, bitch. I got mine!" (Meaning that she had more claim to Mike than Tara did because they shared two children.) One of Tara's girlfriends and I held her back while she took off her earrings and screamed, "I got your bitch, bitch!" and "I'm going to beat the shit out this fat bitch."

One afternoon when Mike was sitting on a neighbor's steps, a squad car pulled up and two police officers arrested him. He had a bench warrant out for missing a court date. He said later that he never even thought to run, assuming the police were there to pick up the men standing next to him who had recently robbed a convenience store. As Mike sat in the police car, Marie talked at him through the window in a loud voice:

> You not just going to dog [publicly cheat on or humiliate] me! Who the fuck he think he dealing with? Let that nigga sit for a minute [stay in jail for a while]. Don't let me catch that bitch up there either [coming to visit him in jail].

Although Marie did call the cops and get Mike taken into custody that day, she was the first person to visit him in county jail after he got out of quarantine and she continued to visit (sometimes wearing a "Free Mike" T-shirt) throughout his year-long trial. On the day of his sentencing, she appeared in the courtroom in a low-cut top with a large new tattoo of his name on her chest.

I also observed women use the police and the courts as a form of direct retaliation. Michelle, age 16, lived with her aunt on 6th Street. When Michelle started

showing, she claimed that Reggie (who was 17 at the time) was the father. Reggie denied he had gotten her pregnant, and when Michelle said she wanted an abortion, he refused to help pay for it. Michelle's aunt declared that she and her niece were cutting off their relationship with Reggie and that he was no longer welcome in their house. Michelle threatened to have Reggie beaten up by various young men she was involved with. Reggie typically stood on the corner only two houses away from where they lived, and this became a frequent verbal conflict.

Around the same time, a newcomer to the block and to the group shot and killed a man from 4th Street during a dice game. The slain man's associates ("his boys") began driving up and down 6th Street and shooting at Reggie, Chuck, and Steve. On one of these occasions, Reggie fired two shots back as their car sped away; these bullets hit Michelle's house, breaking the glass in the front windows and lodging in the living room walls. Although the bullets did not hit anyone, Michelle was home, and called her aunt, who called the police. She told them that Reggie had shot at her niece, and the police put out a body warrant for his arrest for attempted murder.

After five weeks, the police found Reggie hiding in a shed and took him into custody. Reggie's mother and his brother Chuck tried to talk Michelle and her aunt out of showing up in court so that the charges would be dropped and Reggie could come home.[8] From jail, Reggie called his mother and me repeatedly to discuss the situation. Once when we were both on the line he said:

Reggie: The bitch [Michelle's aunt] know I wasn't shooting at them. She know we going through it right now [are in the middle of a series of shootouts with men from another block]. Why I'm going to shoot at two females that live on my block? She know I wasn't shooting at them.

Mother: What you need to do is call her up and apologize [for not taking responsibility for her niece's pregnancy].

Reggie: True, true.

Reggie did apologize and spread the word that he was responsible for making Michelle pregnant. Michelle and her aunt did not show up at three consecutive court dates, and after six months the case for attempted murder was dropped and Reggie came home. Michelle's aunt seemed pleased with this result:

> You not just going to get my niece pregnant, then you talking about it's not yours, you know what I'm saying? Fuck out of here, no. ... I mean, I wasn't trying to see that nigga sit for an attempt [get convicted of attempted murder], but he needed to sit for a little while. He got what he needed to get. He had some time to sit and think about his actions, you dig me? He done got what he needed to get.

While family members, partners, or friends of a wanted man occasionally call the police on him to control his behavior or to punish him for a perceived wrong, close kin or girlfriends also link young men to the police because the police compel them to do so. It is common practice for the police to put pressure on friends, girlfriends, and family members to provide information, particularly when these people have their own warrants, are serving probation or parole, or have a pending trial. Family members and friends who are not themselves caught up in the justice system may be threatened with eviction or with having their children taken away if they do not provide information about the young men in their lives.

Reggie, age 17, was stopped by the police for "loitering" on the corner and allowed the police to search him. When the police officer discovered three small bags of crack in the lining of his jeans, Reggie started running. The cops lost him in the chase, and an arrest warrant was issued for possession of drugs with intent to distribute.

Reggie told me that the police raided his house the next night at 3:00 a.m. He left through the back door and ran through the alley before they could catch him. The officers came back the next night, breaking open the front door (which remains broken and unlocked to this day), and ordered Reggie's younger brother and his grandfather to lie facedown on the floor with their hands on their heads while they searched the house. An officer promised Reggie's mother that if she gave up her son, they would not tell Reggie she had betrayed him. If she did not give Reggie up, he said he would call child protective services and have her younger son taken away because the house was infested with roaches, covered in cat shit, and unfit to live in.

I was present two nights later when the police raided the house for the third time. An officer mentioned they were lucky the family owned the house: if it was a Section 8 building they could be immediately evicted for endangering their neighbors and harboring a fugitive. (Indeed, I had seen this happen recently to two other families.) The police found a gun upstairs that Reggie's mother could not produce a permit for; they cuffed her and took her to the police station. When her youngest son and I picked her up that afternoon, she said they told her she would be charged for the gun unless she told them where to find Reggie.

Reggie's mother begged him to turn himself in, but Reggie refused. His grandfather, who owned the house, told Reggie's mother that he would no longer allow her to live there with her kids if she continued to hide her son from the police:

> This ain't no damn carnival. I don't care who he is, I'm not letting nobody run through this house with the cops chasing him, breaking shit, spilling shit, waking me up out of my sleep. I'm not with the late night screaming and running. I open my eyes and I see a nigga hopping over my bed trying to crawl out the window. Hell no! Like I told Reggie, if the law run up in here one more time I be done had a stroke. Reggie is a grown-ass man [he was 17]. He ain't hiding out in my damn house. We going to fuck around and wind up in jail with this shit. They keep coming they going to find some reason to book my Black ass.

Reggie's grandfather began calling the police when he saw Reggie in the house, and Reggie's mother told him that he could no longer stay there. For two months,

Reggie lived in an abandoned Buick LeSabre parked in a nearby alleyway. Reggie's mother said she missed her son and felt she had betrayed him by abandoning him, even though she had not turned him in to the police. When the police finally took Reggie into custody, she expressed relief:

> Well, at least he don't have to look over his shoulder anymore, always worried that the law was going to come to the house. He was getting real sick of sleeping in the car. It was getting cold outside, you know, and plus Reggie is a big boy and his neck was all cramped up [from sleeping in the car]....And he used to come to the back like: "Ma, make me a plate," and then he'd come back in 20 minutes and I'd pass him the food from out the window.

Whether a man's friends, relatives, or girlfriend link him to the authorities because the police pressure them to do so or because they leverage his wanted status to get back at him or punish him, he comes to see those closest to him as potential informants. Mike and Chuck once discussed how they stood the highest chance of "getting booked" because of their friends and relatives' attempts to "set them up." Mike noted:

> Nine times out of ten, you getting locked up because somebody called the cops, somebody snitching. That's why, like, if you get a call from your girl like, "Yo, where you at, can you come through the block at a certain time," that's a red flag, you feel me? That's when you start to think like, "Okay, what do she got waiting for me?"

I observed wanted men try to reduce the chance of their intimates informing by cultivating secrecy and unpredictability. Chuck and Reggie referred to this strategy as "dipping and dodging" or "ducking in and out." Chuck, age 20, remarked:

> The night is really, like, the best time to do whatever you got to do. If I want to go see my

mizz [mother], see my girl, come through the block and holla at [say hello to] my boys I can't be out in broad day. I got to move like a shadow, you know, duck in and out, you thought you saw me, then bam, I'm out before you even could see what I was wearing or where I was going.

When Steve, age 19, had a bench warrant out for failure to appear in court, he was determined, he said, never to go back to jail. He slept in a number of houses, not staying more than a few nights in any one place. On the phone, he would lie to his family members, girlfriend, and fellow block members about where he was staying and where he planned to go next. If he got a ride to where he was sleeping, he requested to be dropped off a few blocks away, and then waited until the car was out of sight before walking inside. For six months, nobody on the block seemed to know where Steve was sleeping.

Cultivating unpredictability helps wanted men reduce the risk of friends and family informing on them. In fact, maintaining a secret and unpredictable routine decreases the chance of arrest by many of the other paths discussed previously. It is easier for the police to find a person through his last known address if he comes home at around the same time to the same house every day. Finding a person at work is easier if he works a regular shift in the same place every day. Cultivating secrecy and unpredictability, then, serve as a general strategy to avoid confinement.

◆ Being Wanted as a Means of Accounting

Once a man is wanted, maintaining a stable routine, being with his partner and family, going to ork, and using the police may link him to the authorities and lead to his confinement. Yet when wanted men (or social analysts) imply that being wanted is the root cause of their inability to lead "respectable" lives, they are stretching: long before the rise in imprisonment, urban ethnographers described the distrust that Black people felt toward the police and one another, and the difficulties poor Black men faced in finding work and participating in the lives of their families (Anderson 1999; Cayton and Drake [1945] 1993; DuBois [1899] 1996; Duneier 1999; Edin and Lein 1997; Liebow 1967; Newman 1999; Stack 1974). While legal entanglements may exacerbate these difficulties, being wanted also serves as a way to save face and to explain inadequacies.

Liebow (1967:116) wrote that the unemployed men he spent time with accounted for their failures with "the theory of manly flaws." For example, instead of admitting that their marriages failed because they could not support their spouses, they explained that they were *too manly* to be good husbands—they could not stop cheating, or drinking, or staying out late. For the young men of 6th Street, being "on the run" takes the place of, or at least works in concert with, the "manly flaws" described by Liebow as a means to retain self respect in the face of failure.

Mike, age 21, had a bench warrant out because he did not show up to court for a hearing in a drug possession case. During this time, he was not making what he considered to be decent money selling drugs, and he had been unable to pay his son's Catholic school fees for more than a month. Parents' Day at his son's school that year was a Thanksgiving fair, and Mike had been talking about the day for weeks.

The night before the fair, Mike agreed to pick up his children's mother, Marie, and go to the school around 10:00 the next morning. The next morning, Marie began calling Mike's cell phone at 8:30. She called around 13 times between 8:30 and 9:30. I asked Mike why he did not pick up and he said that it was not safe to go, considering the warrant. At noon, he finally answered her call. By then the fair was almost over and Marie had caught the bus back and forth herself. She was yelling so loudly that Steve, Chuck, and I could hear her voice through the phone:

What the fuck good are you on the streets if you can't even come to your son's fair? Why I got to do everything myself—take him to school, pick him up from school, take him to the doctor. . . . And you on some "I'm falling

back. I'm laying low. I can't be up at no school. I can't do this I can't do that." What the fuck I'm supposed to tell your son: "Michael, Daddy can't come to the fair today because the cops is looking for him and we don't want him to get booked." Is that what you want me to say?

Mike called her some names and hung up. Before going back to sleep, he mentioned what a "dumb-ass" she was:

Do she want me to get locked up? How I'm going to be there for my kids if I'm locked up? She don't be thinking, like, she don't have to look over her shoulder, you know what I'm saying. She be forgetting I can't just do whatever I want, go wherever I want.

Mike seemed convinced that going to the fair would put him at risk, and at the time I believed this to be the reason he stayed home. But a few months later, although he was still wanted for the same bench warrant, he attended a parent–teacher conference.

Alice: I thought you didn't want to go up there. Remember Marie was mad as shit the other time you didn't go.

Mike: I'm cool now because I just paid the school fees. I ain't want dude to come at my neck [get angry], like, "Where the money at? Why you ain't pay?" I wasn't trying [didn't want] to hear that bullshit.

From this, I gathered that Mike had not gone to Parents' Day earlier in the year at least in part because he had not paid the school fees and did not want to confront the school's administration. Once he paid the bill, he proudly attended the next event, a parent–teacher conference. The warrant provided him with a way to avoid going to Parents' Day without admitting that he did not want to go because he could not pay the school fees.

Warrants also serve as an important explanation for not having a job. Steve had a warrant out for a few weeks when he was 21, and repeatedly mentioned how he could not get work because of this warrant:

> If I had a whip [car] I'd go get me a job up King of Prussia [a mall in a neighboring county] or whatever. But I can't work nowhere in Philly. That's where niggas be fucking up. You remember when Jason was at McDonald's? He was like, "No, they [the police] ain't going to see me, I'm working in the back." But you can't always be back there, like sometimes they put you at the counter, like if somebody don't show up, you know what I mean? How long he worked there before they [the police] came and got him? Like a week. They was like, "Um, can I get a large fry and your hands on the counter because your Black ass is booked!" And he tried to run like shit, too, but they was outside the jawn [the restaurant] four deep [four police officers were outside] just waiting for him to try that shit.

Although Steve now and then invoked his warrant as an explanation for his unemployment, the fact was that Steve did not secure a job during the six years I knew him, including the times when he did not have a warrant.

James, age 18, moved with his aunt to 6th Street, and after a while became Reggie's "young-boy." Like the other guys, he talked about his court cases or mentioned that he had to go see his probation officer.

Steve, Mike, Chuck, and I were sitting on Chuck's back-porch steps one afternoon when Reggie drove up the alley way and announced: "Yo, the boy James he clean, dog! He ain't got no warrant, no detainer, nothing. He don't even got like a parking ticket in his name."

Reggie told us he had just been to James's mother's house across town, and she had complained to him that James had not yet found a job. James's mother informed Reggie that James had no pending cases, no warrants or detainers or anything "in the system that would hold him" and so should have no problem finding employment. When Reggie finished explaining this to us, Mike continued the conversation:

Mike: What happened to that case he caught? Damn that was a little minute ago [a while ago].

Chuck: I think he spanked that jawn [the case was dropped].

Reggie: I wish I would get my shit [warrant] lifted. I'd be bam, on my J-O [job], bam, on my A-P [apartment], bam, go right to the bank, like, "Yeah, motherfucker, check my shit, man. Run that shit. My shit is clean, dog. Let me get that account." I be done got my elbow [driver's license] and everything.

Reggie explained how his wanted status blocks him from getting jobs, using banks, obtaining a driver's license, and renting an apartment. Yet the things that Reggie thought a "clean" person should do were not things that Reggie himself did when he was in good standing with the authorities over the course of the years that I knew him. Nor were they things that most of the other men on the block did. Alex, Mike, and Chuck looked for jobs when they did not have warrants out for their arrest, but others, like Reggie and Steve, did not. None of them obtained a valid driver's license during the six years I knew them.[9] Only Mike secured his own apartment during this time, and he kept it for only three months. To my knowledge, none of the men established a bank account.

Being wanted serves as an excuse for a wide variety of unfulfilled obligations and expectations. At the same time, it is perhaps only because being wanted is in fact a constraining condition that it works so well as a means of accounting for failure. Having a warrant may not be the reason why Steve, for example, did not look for work, but it was a fact that police officers did go to a man's place of work to arrest him, and that some of the men experienced this first-hand. In the context of their ongoing struggles, what they said amounted to reasonable "half-truths" (Liebow 1967) that could account for their failures, both in their own minds and in the minds of others who had come to see their own lives in similar terms.

◈ Discussion

The presence of the criminal justice system in the lives of the poor cannot simply be measured by the number of people sent to prison or the number who return home with felony convictions. Systems of policing and supervision that accompanied the rise in imprisonment have fostered a climate of fear and suspicion in poor communities—a climate in which family members and friends are pressured to inform on one another and young men live as suspects and fugitives, with the daily fear of confinement.

Young men who are wanted by the police find that activities, relations, and localities that others rely on to maintain a decent and respectable identity are transformed into a system that the authorities make use of to arrest and confine them. The police and the courts become dangerous to interact with, as does showing up to work or going to places like hospitals. Instead of a safe place to sleep, eat, and find acceptance and support, mothers' homes are transformed into a "last known address," one of the first places the police will look for them. Close relatives, friends, and neighbors become potential informants.

One strategy for coping with these risks is to avoid dangerous places, people, and interactions entirely. A young man thus does not attend the birth of his child, nor seek medical help when he is badly beaten. He avoids the police and the courts, even if it means using violence when he is injured or becoming the target of others who are looking for someone to rob. A second strategy is to cultivate unpredictability—to remain secretive and to "dip and dodge." To ensure that those close to him will not inform on him, a young man comes and goes in irregular and unpredictable ways, remaining elusive and untrusting, sleeping in different beds, and deceiving those close to him about his whereabouts and plans. If a man exhausts these possibilities and gets taken into custody, he may try to avoid jail time by informing on the people he knows.

Whatever the strategy, a man finds that as long as he is at risk of confinement, staying out of prison and participating in institutions like family, work, and friendship become contradictory goals; doing one reduces his chance of achieving the other. Staying out of jail becomes aligned not with upstanding, respectable action, but with being an even shadier character.

Family members and romantic partners experience considerable hardship because of their association with men who are being sought or supervised by the state. Specifically, I found that family members living with a relative or boyfriend with a warrant out for his arrest are caught between three difficult lines of action: allowing him to stay in their homes and placing their own safety and security in jeopardy, casting him out, or betraying him by turning him in to the police.

It is possible that issuing warrants to a large group of young men for minor probation violations or delinquencies with court fees, while straining family life and making it difficult for men to find and keep a job, also serves to discourage them from committing crime. Although this article notes some instances of warrants potentially encouraging crime (e.g., by keeping men from participating in the formal labor market or by leading men with warrants to become the target of robbers), I cannot speculate as to the net effect of such policies on crime or violence. The data presented here merely suggest that current policies in Philadelphia grant a sizable group of people—before they are convicted of crimes and after they have served a sentence—an illegal or semilegal status, and that this status makes it difficult for them to interact with legitimate institutions without being arrested and sent to jail.

More surprisingly, the system of low-level warrants and court supervision has the unintended consequence of becoming a resource for women and relatives who, possessing more legal legitimacy, can use it to control their partners and kin. Girlfriends, neighbors, and family members threaten to call the police on young men to "keep them in line," and occasionally they call the police or get a man arrested as payback for some perceived wrong. Young men also turn their wanted status into a resource by using it to account for shortcomings or failures that may have occurred anyway. Because being wanted is understood by 6th Street residents to be deeply constraining, young men with little income, education, or job prospects can call on their wanted status to save face and to assuage the guilt of failing as a father, romantic partner, or employed person.

Contemporary theories of social stratification and political sociology argue that the criminal justice system has become a vehicle for passing on disadvantage (Western 2006) and "an instrument for the management of dispossessed and dishonored groups" (Wacquant 2001:95). The findings presented here confirm these important theses, but my fieldwork also suggests that those so managed are hardly hapless victims, immobilized in webs of control. Instead, men and women on 6th Street evade and resist the authorities, at times calling on the state for their own purposes, to make claims for themselves as honorable people, and to exercise power over one another.

◇ Conclusions and Theoretical Implications

Young men on the run in Philadelphia can tell us something about how power operates in contemporary society. Indeed, the policing of the modern ghetto may be usefully juxtaposed to the influential theory of power Foucault outlines in *Discipline and Punish* (for discussions of Foucault's dominant position in the sociology of punishment see Cohen 1985; Garland 1990).

Foucault's (1979) theory of power begins with the prison and extends to work houses, almshouses, military barracks, cities under tight regulation during cholera epidemics, and finally to modern society. He argues that popular illegalities were widespread in early modern society, and sovereigns made no systematic attempts to stamp them out. Instead, sovereigns intervened sporadically, making gruesome public examples of a small number of cases. Taking the prison as an example, Foucault suggests that modern punishment is organized not on the principle of occasional fear-inspiring public brutality, but on a panoptic system of inspection, surveillance, and graded rewards and punishments. The law is enforced systematically: individuals are carefully monitored and examined and files are kept on them. The age of popular illegality is replaced by the age of rational discipline.

At first glance, the Philadelphia neighborhood I studied, with its video cameras on street lamps, frequent police stops and searches, and monitoring of residents through probation, parole, and house arrest, seems to resemble the panoptic fortress town Foucault envisioned in *Discipline and Punish* (1979). Yet the ghetto cannot be placed under the general umbrella of the panopticon. A different form of power exists there, and with different results for the people involved.

Foucault suggests that in prisons, army camps, and other such panoptic places, authorities accomplish cooperation through "constant, uninterrupted supervision" and a system of graded punishments and rewards. People are coaxed into compliance through careful training, examining, and monitoring, through minute attention to the movements and gestures of the body. Eventually, subjects come to internally monitor themselves (Garland 2001).

In comparison to places like prisons, monasteries, or army camps, the monitoring and supervision of ghetto residents is incomplete. Enclosed spaces make near perfect surveillance and enforcement possible: people can live unlawfully only if they do not get caught or if the authorities look the other way (Sykes [1958] 2007). In spaces like the 6th street neighborhood, however, many people break the law without the authorities knowing; many others are known to be in violation but the authorities do not have the resources or the ability (or, to be more cynical, the desire) to locate them all and bring them to justice. This opens up the possibility of people existing in the spaces between identification, discovery, and apprehension.

Surveillance and supervision in the ghetto are incomplete not only because people are widely able to break the rules and to evade the authorities, but also because the forms of supervision do not strive to be all-encompassing in the first place. Residents of the neighborhood I studied do not find that their movements are tightly controlled and regimented, as they would be in a prison or convent; they do not eat, sleep, and live together under the watchful gaze of one central authority, nor is their privacy and personal property permanently denied them (Foucault 1979; Goffman 1961; Sykes [1958] 2007). Supervision around 6th street is not based on constant observation and disciplining, but on a kind of checkpoint or flashpoint system, whereby certain people are only occasionally (if not randomly) monitored, searched, observed, or dispossessed.

These occasional examinations (the urine test during a probation meeting, the stop and frisk on a street corner, the raid of a house, or the running of a driver's name in the police database to see if any warrants come up) are put to use not—as Foucault envisioned—to dole out a range of small punishments and rewards in the interest of correction and training, but to identify people who may qualify for prison and to bring those people into the hands of the state.

This form of power—occasional, incomplete, and for the purpose of identifying candidates for extreme sanction—does not seem to produce orderly subjects. Self-discipline and the internalization of norms makes little sense in a context in which following the rules (e.g., appearing in court, showing up to probation meetings, or turning oneself in when accused) may *hasten* one's removal to prison.

A final point of comparison: Foucault argues that power based on fear (the public hangings) was replaced in the modern era by power based on observation, examination, and discipline. In the 6th street neighborhood, one indeed finds monitoring and supervision, but this monitoring does not put an end to fear. In fact, the lives of residents are organized precisely around fear, that is, the fear of being sent to jail.

Garland (1990:168) argues that a significant failing of *Discipline and Punish* is that it describes "the control *potential* possessed by modern power-knowledge technologies as if it were the reality of their present-day *operation*." By studying the ghetto ethnographically, we can see how the forms of power Foucault envisioned operating in a panopticon actually pan out when applied to a neighborhood. People in the modern policed ghetto do not live as tightly controlled and disciplined subjects. Rather, they are living as semilegal or illegal people, coping with the daily threat of capture and confinement. The life of a suspect or a fugitive is quite different from the life of a captive, even though broadly speaking, the same forms of power—observation, examination, the keeping of files—may sustain them both.

One can of course argue that wanted people, poised to perpetuate their own criminality, have indeed internalized the norms that disciplining powers sought to instill. In this sense, a status group of fugitives fits nicely into Foucault's functionalist ideas about the production of delinquency and its political uses (Foucault 1979:272). But to argue this is, I believe, a stretch. Fugitives are, in point of fact, resisting the will of the authorities, and whether or not this resistance is in the end liberatory, their daily lives and the forms of power governing them are clearly distinct from those of inmates subject to panoptic power.

Rather than placing the ghetto, along with the rest of society, under a "generalized panopticism" (Garland 1990:146), the 6th street situation suggests an alternative form of power. In cases where a state (or some other power) is in the business of severely sanctioning a group of people (e.g., by killing them, deporting them, forcibly sending them to war, or placing them in institutions like prisons, concentration camps, or plantations) we will see one group of people who are charged with administering the sanction and another group who are receiving it. If the sanction is confinement in a prison, workhouse, or mental asylum, we may see a group of people living as inmates or subjects as described by Foucault's panopticon (or in the way that Sykes [1958] (2007) described people living in prisons or Goffman [1961] described people living in total institutions). But we will also see, outside of these institutions, an apparatus charged with identifying, catching, and judging likely candidates, and a group of people living with the risk of sanction and trying to avoid it, as fugitives.

Instead of thinking of residents of the modern ghetto as inmates of prisons or other panoptic places, we might compare ghetto residents to other semilegal or illegal people who qualify for some sanction and who are trying to avoid it: undocumented immigrants who are at risk of being deported, Jews living in Nazi Germany who may be sent to concentration camps, draftdodgers or deserters from the army who may be imprisoned or shot, escaped slaves who may be found and sent back to the plantations, or communists in the United States and Europe when the party was illegal. It is with these groups that residents of the modern ghetto may find some common experience. It is this kind of social situation that should be taken into account if we are to fully grasp the effects of policies like mass incarceration.

◈ Notes

1. Although this body of research points overwhelmingly to the detrimental effects of ncarceration and its aftermath, this picture is complicated by close-up accounts of prisoners and their families. Comfort (2008) shows how women visiting incarcerated spouses find that the prison's egulations in some ways enhance their relationships. As romantic partners, inmates contrast favorably to "free men."

2. Ethnographies of ghetto life published more recently rely on fieldwork conducted in the 1980s and early 1990s, before the change in policing practices and crime laws took their full effect (see, e.g., Anderson 1999; Bourgois 1995; Venkatesh 2006; Wacquant 2004; for exceptions, see Jacobs 1999; LeBlanc 2003).

3. Data on the number of police off icers in Philadelphia is taken from the Federal Bureau of Investigation, Uniform Crime Reports (1960 through 2000). Population estimates of Philadelphia are taken from the U.S. Bureau of the Census.

4. I use quotes when I wrote down what people said as they spoke (by typing it directly onto a laptop or by using a cell phone text message). I omit the quotes when I noted what people said after an event or conversation, and I paraphrase when I wrote down what people said at the end of the day in my field notes. Since I did not use a tape recorder, even the speech in quotes should be taken only as a close approximation.

5. I counted men who lived in a house for three days a week or more (by their own estimates and in some cases, my knowledge) as members of the household. I included men who were absent because they were in the military, at job training programs (like JobCorp), or away in jail, prison, drug rehab centers, or halfway houses, if they expected to return to the house and had been living in the house before they went away.

6. These violations are not the same as the "disorderly conduct" that became the focus of "quality of life" policing in places like New York during the 1990s. "Quality of life" policing arrests people for minor offenses like urinating in public, jumping turnstyles, or public drinking (Duneier 1999). The young men in this study were initially arrested for more serious offenses such as drug offenses, and then were served warrants when they failed to show up for court dates during the pretrial and trial, to pay court fees at the end of the cases, or to follow the dictates of probation and parole sentences they were issued after or instead of completing time in jail or prison.

7. In Philadelphia, the courts can issue an arrest warrant if a person fails to pay fines for traffic violations or misses a court date in regard to these violations. A person can also be imprisoned for failing to pay moving violation fines (Philadelphia County, 33 Pa.B. Doc. No. 2745 and Pa.B. Doc. No. 03–1110).

8. This is a fairly common thing to do. Some people get others arrested simply to extort money from them, which they request in exchange for not showing up as a witness at the ensuing trial.

9. Obtaining a driver's license requires a birth certificate or passport, a Social Security card, and two proofs of residence. Obtaining these items, in turn, requires identification and processing fees. One must undergo a physical exam by a doctor, pay for and pass a written permit test, and locate an insured and registered car with which to take the driving test. Because men drove without proper documentation, they got tickets, which had to be paid before they could begin the application process.

◈ References

Anderson, Elijah. 1978. *A Place on the Corner.* Chicago, IL: University of Chicago Press.

———. 1999. *Code of the Street.* New York: W. W. Norton.

Becker, Howard. 1963. *Outsiders.* New York: Free Press.

Beckett, Katherine. 1997. *Making Crime Pay.* New York: Oxford University Press.

Black, Donald. 1983. "Crime as Social Control." *American Sociological Review* 48(1):32–45.

Bourgois, Philippe. 1995. *In Search of Respect.* New York: Cambridge University Press.

Cayton, Horace and St. Clair Drake. [1945] 1993. *Black Metropolis.* Chicago, IL: University of Chicago Press.

Cohen, Stanley. 1985. *Visions of Social Control.* Cambridge, MA: Cambridge University Press.

Comfort, Megan. 2007. "Punishment Beyond the Legal Offender." *Annual Review of Law and Social Science* 3:271–96.

———. 2008. *Doing Time Together.* Chicago, IL: University of Chicago Press.

DuBois, W. E. B. [1899] 1996. *The Philadelphia Negro.* Philadelphia, PA: University of Pennsylvania Press.

Duneier, Mitchell. 1999. *Sidewalk.* New York: Farrar, Straus and Giroux.

Edin, Kathryn and Laura Lein. 1997. *Making Ends Meet.* New York: Russell Sage Foundation.

Foucault, Michel. 1979. *Discipline and Punish. New* York: Vintage.

Garland, David. 1990. *Punishment and Modern Society.* Chicago, IL: University of Chicago Press.

———. 2001. "Introduction: The Meaning of Mass Imprisonment." Pp. 1–3 in M*ass Imprisonment: Social Causes and Consequences,* edited by D. Garland. London, UK: Sage.

Glaze, Lauren and Thomas Bonzcar. 2006. "Probation and Parole in the United States, 2005." *Bureau of Justice Statistics Bulletin.* U.S.

Department of Justice, NCJ 215091. Retrieved March 2009 (http://www.ojp.usdoj.gov/bjs/pub/pdf/ppus05.pdf).

Goffman, Erving. 1961. *Asylums.* New York: Anchor Books.

Hagan, John and Ronit Dinovitzer. 1999. "Collateral Consequences of Imprisonment for Children, Communities, and Prisoners." *Crime and Justice* 26:121–62.

Hammett, Theodore M., Mary P. Harmon, and William Rhodes. 2002. "The Burden of Infectious Disease among Inmates of and Releases from U.S. Correctional Facilities, 1997." *American Journal of Public Health* 92(11):1789–94.

Jacobs, Bruce. 1999. *Dealing Crack.* Boston, MA: Northeastern University Press.

LeBlanc, Adrian Nicole. 2003. *Random Family.* New York: Scribner.

Liebow, Elliot. 1967. *Tally's Corner.* Boston, MA: Little, Brown.

Newman, Katherine. 1999. *No Shame in My Game.* New York: Vintage and Russell Sage.

Nurse, Anne. 2002. *Fatherhood Arrested. Nashville,* TN: Vanderbilt University Press.

Pager, Devah. 2007. *Marked: Race, Crime, and Finding Work in an Era of Mass Incarceration.* Chicago, IL: University of Chicago Press.

Pettit, Becky and Bruce Western. 2004. "Mass Imprisonment and the Life-Course: Race and Class Inequality in U.S. Incarceration." *American Sociological Review* 69:151–69.

Philadelphia Adult Probation and Parole Department. 2007. *2006 Annual Report.* Retrieved March 2009 (http://fjd.phila.gov/pdf/report/2006appd.pdf).

Reiss, Albert J. 1992. "Police Organization in the 20th Century." *Crime and Justice* 15:51–97.

Rubenstein, Gwen and Debbie Mukamal. 2002. "Welfare and Housing-Denial of Benefits to Drug Offenders." Pp. 37–49 in *Invisible Punishment: The Collateral Consequences of Mass Imprisonment,* edited by M. Mauer and M. Chesney-Lind. New York: New Press.

Simon, Jonathan. 2007. *Governing through Crime.* New York: Oxford University Press.

Stack, Carol. 1974. *All Our Kin.* New York: Harper Colophon Books.

Sykes, Gresham. [1958] 2007. *Society of Captives.* Princeton, NJ: Princeton University Press.

Uggen, Chris and Jeff Manza. 2002. "Democratic Contradiction? Political Consequences of Felon Disenfranchisement in the United States." *American Sociological Review* 67(6):777–803.

United States Department of Justice, Federal Bureau of Investigation. September 2007. *Crime in the United States, 2006.* Retrieved March 2, 2009 (http://www.fbi.gov/ucr/cius2006/arrests/).

Venkatesh, Sudhir. 2006. *Off the Books.* Cambridge, MA: Harvard University Press.

———. 2008. *Gang Leader for a Day.* New York: Penguin Press.

Wacquant, Loïc. 2001. "Deadly Symbiosis: When Ghetto and Prison Meet and Mesh." *Punishment & Society* 3(1):95–133.

———. 2004. *Body and Soul.* New York: Oxford University Press.

Western, Bruce. 2006. *Punishment and Inequality in America.* New York: Russell Sage Foundation.

Western, Bruce, Leonard Lopoo, and Sara McLanahan. 2004. "Incarceration and the Bonds between Parents in Fragile Families." Pp. 21–45 in *Imprisoning America,* edited by M. Patillo, D. Weiman, and B. Western. New York: Russell Sage Foundation.

Wildeman, Christopher. 2009. "Parental Imprisonment, the Prison Boom, and the Concentration of Childhood Disadvantage." *Demography* 46: 265–80.

Williams, Terry. 1992. *Crackhouse.* Reading, MA: Addison Wesley.

READING 34

This article takes readers inside a cottage for violent offenders in one state's end-of-the-line juvenile correctional facility. Inderbitzin spent hundreds of hours in the cottage interacting with both the adolescent inmates and the staff members charged with their supervision and care. The goal of the article is to contrast the lessons the institution intended to impart to its "residents" with the life lessons the young men actually learned during their incarceration. She begins by using her observations and interviews to help the reader understand what it is like to be a juvenile behind bars identifying the "pains of imprisonment," discussed largely in the adult corrections literature but less often a major concern in the juvenile justice literature. Pains of incarceration are many, and much of it focuses on the loss of autonomy and poor living environments. She makes the very interesting point that because these youth were basically raising themselves prior to their arrest and

Source: Inderbitzin, Michelle. 2006. "Lessons From a Juvenile Training School: Survival and Growth." *Journal of Adolescent Research* 21(1):7–26.

incarceration and had held a great deal autonomy, the period of incarceration literally stunts the transition to adulthood. Clearly, the institution intended to promote education, basic work proficiencies, "life-skills, anger management, victim empathy and cultural literacy." Indeed, many of the staff worked hard in these areas despite the low quality of the resources and unique backgrounds of the youth that presented many challenges to their stated intentions. The youth did learn some important things from the staff, and there was evidence that the boys trusted some staff more than others and garnered various lessons and emotional support from them. Alternatively, by many accounts, it was too little and too late. The boys also learned from the other youth in the cottage, including keeping quiet and staying in their place until they earned the right to speak out. There were also elements of a "crime school" so commonly perceived of prisons for youth and adults. The picture painted is bleak but not insurmountable. As you read it, think about whether you believe "training schools" or juvenile prisons are an effective way for society to respond to serious delinquents. Are there other viable options?

Lessons From a Juvenile Training School

Survival and Growth

Michelle Inderbitzin

There are those who believe that the idea of a separate justice system for juveniles, after more than a century in existence, has outgrown its usefulness. They argue that as long as young offenders commit serious crimes, they should be prepared to face the consequences; indeed, it seems that "recent reforms in juvenile justice have placed the notion of youth itself on trial" (Grisso & Schwartz, 2000, p. 5). In spite of such arguments, however, the juvenile justice system continues its mission, and those who speak on its behalf espouse the ideals of rehabilitation and the malleability of youth.

The central question in this article concerns the function and utility of juvenile training schools as institutions of social control and as agents of change for adolescent inmates. More specifically, I examine one such institution in light of the rhetoric surrounding reform schools and the reality of daily life within the institution's walls and then evaluate its effectiveness based on the lessons learned by young offenders who serve a portion of their adolescence there. After spending a significant percentage of their lives confined to a juvenile correctional facility, what do young offenders think they have learned? What will they take away from their time in the institution? How will they have changed?

More than two decades ago, apparently the best that could be said for juvenile institutions was that "at least some training schools do not have as damaging an effect on juveniles as do prisons" (Haskell & Yablonsky, 1982, p. 446). In the 1970s, Massachusetts, under the helm of Jerome Miller, took a bold step and attempted to deinstitutionalize virtually all of the juvenile offenders in the state. At that time, reform schools ("an old-fashioned but honest name," according to Miller, 1998, p. xvii) were thought to do more harm than good, and Miller managed to close down all such institutions and replace them with alternative programs and placements in the community. Proponents of deinstitutionalization argued that the negative lessons learned and the stigma associated with incarceration far outweighed any benefit for individuals in the system (Miller, 1998). In addition, studies from that era report conditions in state training schools that today would certainly be viewed as unacceptable: Cottage "parents" frequently used physical means to punish the boys in their care—striking, shaking, and shoving them(Weber, 1961); boys were housed in the "tombs," an extreme form of isolation and were not allowed to speak while in their cottage living unit (Feld, 1999; Miller, 1998); and younger and weaker boys were regularly victimized by their tougher counterparts (Bartollas, Miller, & Dinitz, 1976; Feld, 1977; Polsky, 1962).

During the past two decades, the United States has made a clear movement to get tough on juvenile crime, and the sentencing of juvenile offenders has become increasingly punitive (Feld, 1999). As such, the categories of comparison have drastically changed. In the 1960s and 1970s, when compared to deinstitutionalization and community alternatives, juvenile correctional facilities were often viewed as the strictest of punishments for juvenile offenders—the last resort for the state's most incorrigible youth. These days, the possibilities for punishment have shifted to the point that reform schools now seem to be the kinder, gentler option—the two alternatives facing serious juvenile offenders are now generally confinement in juvenile correctional facilities or confinement in adult prisons.

The past two decades have also witnessed a relative dearth of ethnographic studies on training schools. The heyday of studies of the inmate culture and the inner workings of training schools seemed to be in the 1960s and 1970s (Bartollas et al., 1976; Feld, 1977; Polsky, 1962; Weber, 1961; Wooden, 1976). In fact, some researchers have suggested that

interest in the conditions of training schools in the United States has fallen to such a degree that it is hard to make meaningful comparisons (Chesney-Lind & Shelden, 2004, p. 224). The findings from the earlier works were overwhelmingly negative, and the authors painted dark pictures of juvenile institutions. Feld (1998), in reviewing the evidence some 20 years after his own sociological study of state training schools, concludes: "Evaluations of training schools, the most common form of institutional treatment for the largest numbers of serious and chronic delinquents, report consistently negative findings.... They constitute the one extensively evaluated and clearly ineffective method to treat delinquents" (Feld, 1998, p. 237).

Bortner and Williams (1997) conducted one of the more recent, in-depth studies of a model program operating in two juvenile prisons. The model program they describe was created in response to a class-action lawsuit against Arizona's system of juvenile corrections. In much the same way earlier research condemned practices in state training schools as damaging to young inmates, the lawsuit suggested that Arizona's juvenile correctional facilities were punitive, coercive, and inhumane (Bortner & Williams, 1997, p. x). The model treatment program sought to provide youths the skills necessary to succeed in society, emphasizing accountability, responsibility, mutual respect, and personal efficacy. It offered a new goal and vision for society's treatment of delinquent youth. The innovative program was never fully implemented and ultimately came to be viewed as a failure. Although the changes did not last, Arizona's experiment with new programming in juvenile correctional facilities provides at least one example of thinking outside of the prison box in treating young offenders.

Interestingly, some recent studies (Forst, Fagan, & Vivona, 1989; Lane, Lanza-Kaduce, Frazier, & Bishop, 2002) suggest that the juvenile offenders themselves found their time in the "deep end" of juvenile corrections to be their most helpful or productive placement. Lane et al. (2002) describe deep end juvenile programs as residential commitment facilities that are the most restrictive in the state, with more physical security, closer supervision, and longer periods of confinement than other programs and facilities (p. 433). In interviews, the youths cited a combination of available programming, caring staff members, and smaller populations as making their time in juvenile correctional facilities a better experience in their perception than the more punitive jails and prisons where they were incarcerated alongside generally older, stronger, more criminal adults. In addition, sanctions earlier in the more "shallow end" of the juvenile system, including probation, day programs, and short-term placements in low-risk, least restrictive residential programs, proved to have little effect on the young offenders; the shorter sentences did not give them enough time away from their lives to become fully immersed in the programming.

Developmental psychologists argue that:

> adolescence in modern society is an inherently transitional time during which there are rapid and dramatic changes in physical, intellectual, emotional, and social capabilities . . . other than infancy, there is probably no period of human development characterized by more rapid or pervasive transformations in individual competencies. (Steinberg & Schwartz, 2000, p. 23)

Because they work primarily with adolescents, juvenile justice agencies have the potential to exert enormous influence over the rapidly changing lives of their captive populations. As such, it seems we should pay particular attention to the treatment of adolescent offenders.

Although little research is being conducted inside training schools and juvenile institutions, there is now a great deal of attention being paid to issues of prisoner reentry (Altschuler & Brash, 2004) as increasing numbers of inmates are released from correctional facilities to return to their communities. This is an especially interesting dilemma for juvenile offenders who are literally becoming men behind bars; most will leave the juvenile prisons and training schools where they served their sentences as legal adults with virtually no safety nets in place (Furstenberg, Rumbaut, & Settersten, 2005).

Arnett (1998) makes the point that "the transition to adulthood is characterized not by a single event but by an extended process of preparation for the challenges and responsibilities of adult life" (p. 311). Young Americans identify three main criteria for the transition to adulthood: accepting responsibility for one's self, making independent decisions, and becoming financially independent (p. 295). One question of interest is whether this transition to adulthood is stunted or accelerated by incarceration in a juvenile correctional facility. Because many young offenders were largely living on their own and supporting themselves while still teenagers in the community, I would argue that the transition to adulthood was accelerated for them prior to their confinement. During their incarceration, however, when adolescent inmates' responsibilities and ability to make decisions are severely limited, the transition to adulthood is likely stunted.

For most American young people, "Emerging adulthood is a time of looking forward and imagining what adult life will be like, and what emerging adults imagine is generally bright and promising. . . . Whatever the future may actually hold, during emerging adulthood, hope prevails" (Arnett, 2004, p. 206). This point brings up a second question of particular interest for adolescent inmates: Does hope manage to prevail for a particularly troubled population of emerging adults, incarcerated young men, most of whom are minority males who grew up poor, living with troubled families in disadvantaged neighborhoods? Going inside juvenile institutions and listening to the young inmates as they pass through different stages of their confinement is an important step in answering such questions.

Evaluating the current state of juvenile justice, Van Vleet (1999) argued that "get-tough measures . . . have returned much of the youth corrections system to the training school mentality that was largely abandoned during the decades of deinstitutionalization" (p. 204).

He goes on to describe incarceration in a juvenile correctional facility as "punishment with treatment components added on" (pp. 209–210). The availability of and the quality of treatment components is one important difference between juvenile and adult institutions; given their younger, developing populations, juvenile correctional facilities tend to be more focused on rehabilitation than are adult prisons (Altschuler & Brash, 2004) and are better able to utilize approaches grounded in developmental knowledge (Scott, 2000).

In the current study, I sought to find out—from the ground level—what is happening in juvenile correctional facilities, to discover how serious juvenile offenders experience incarceration in a state training school. To do so, I focused on the following questions: What lessons does the institution attempt to teach its population of adolescents and emerging adults? What lessons are the inmates actually learning? What, ultimately, will these young offenders take with them back into the community? Are training schools still a viable response for violent juvenile offenders?

◈ Method

The training school in this study houses the state's most serious problem children still held under the jurisdiction of the juvenile justice system. The population of chronic and violent male offenders in this juvenile prison ranges in age from 15 to 20. Most of them have done time and served sentences in other juvenile institutions, and this facility was often their last stop in the juvenile system. If they committed further crimes, they would face adult consequences.

The maximum-security institution in this study is very much a juvenile prison. As Bortner and Williams (1997) point out in their own study of a juvenile prison in Arizona: "The special language of juvenile justice denies the realities of prison conditions. . . . It is impossible to ignore the level of control, the razor wire, electronic gates, and the harsh and punitive nature of these institutions, historically and currently" (pp. xvi–xvii). Likewise, the institution in this study has a razor wire fence surrounding the perimeter, a full-time security staff, and locked rooms within locked living units. At the time of this study, there were about 200 boys sentenced to this training school. Based on his offense type, each was assigned to a cottage living unit that would be his home during his incarceration. The boys would attend school, work in the institution, go to recreation at the gym, and eat their meals in the institution's cafeteria, but each night they would return to their cottage. In attempting to see long-term interactions and deeper layers of meaning, I chose to focus on the "Blue" cottage, a cottage housing a population of 18 to 26 violent offenders at any given time and widely regarded as home to the toughest offenders in the toughest training school in the state.

The ethnographic data for this study were gathered through observations during a period of approximately 15 months. During the course of the study, I averaged approximately one visit per week, generally staying for 7 or 8 hours at a time. I often chose to visit and observe on Saturdays and afternoons or evenings when the boys would be out of school and spending time in the cottage. Most of the time, I simply hung out in the cottage, watching, listening, and interacting with the *residents* (the school's preferred term for its inmates) and the staff members.

In response to the boys' initial cynicism about talking to an outsider, I chose not to do formal interviews, preferring instead to gather information through less intrusive means—conversing informally, listening to the residents and the staff members, asking questions, and paying attention to the interactions in the cottage. In my role as a researcher, I went from being an outsider to being a welcome diversion; within a few months, many of the boys looked forward to my visits as they helped to break the monotony of their daily lives. This gave me an opportunity to have ongoing discussions with the boys and the staff members; I was able to ask the same question in different ways and at various times, and I was able to follow up questions and conversations weeks and months later as circumstances changed and the boys went through different phases of their sentences. After each visit, I took extensive field notes detailing events, conversations, and my own thoughts; the field notes were then the data for analysis.

This case study of a single cottage of violent offenders may not have been representative of the larger institution, let alone representative of juvenile corrections more generally. Yet, the body of research on training schools—and, to some extent, adult prisons—largely fit the reality of life in this cottage. It rang true enough that I came away convinced that inmate cultures share at least some universal issues. The present study is offered, then, as a supplement to the classic pieces on prison culture (Goffman, 1961; Irwin, 1970; Sykes, 1958) and as a glimpse into life inside a modern day training school. Ultimately, I wanted to find out how serious young offenders experienced punishment in the state's end-of-the-line juvenile institution. This article is one part of the answer; it is a recounting of lessons I learned in spending time attempting to delve beneath the rhetoric while witnessing the patterns of daily life in the Blue cottage. To protect the identity of young men who hope to have better futures, all names have been changed.

◈ Results

One of the primary goals of this study was to understand the effect of time inside the institution on the individuals, to closely examine the experiences, the adaptations, and the survival strategies of residents in the Blue cottage. The focus of this article is on the lessons that the boys learned during their incarceration. Some of the lessons were abstract, some were concrete, some physical, some mental. Some the institution tried to teach, others were the inescapable result of the experience of incarceration. I will begin by discussing the pains of imprisonment and how the young offenders learned to deal with them. I will then move to lessons in conformity the institution intended, informal lessons learned from cottage staff members and other inmates, lessons learned in relation to family and friends, and lessons learned over time. Finally, I will discuss the lessons that the

broader society can learn about training schools and their effect on young offenders.

Learning to Deal With the Pains of Imprisonment

The first lesson all of the boys had to learn is one with which inmates have been dealing for generations: learning to survive the daily frustrations and challenges inherent in the structure of the institution. A defining aspect of the residents' lives in the juvenile prison was their indignation over losing liberties, what Sykes (1958) calls "pains of imprisonment." TJ, a 20-year-old African American, expressed how much he hated doing time in the institution and how the loss of liberty grated on him. He explained that he hated the fact that he had to pound on his locked door to get out to go to the bathroom, how everyone else controls your life when you are locked up. His feelings fit perfectly with Sykes and Messinger's (1960) discussion of the deprivation of autonomy:

> Rejected, impoverished, and figuratively castrated, the prisoner must face still further indignity in the extensive social control exercised by the custodians. The many details of the inmate's life, ranging from the hours of sleeping to the route to work and the job itself, are subject to a vast number of regulations made by prison officials. The inmate is stripped of his autonomy; hence, to the other pains of imprisonment we must add the pressure to define himself as weak, helpless, and dependent. (Sykes & Messinger, 1960, pp. 14—15)

The young inmates had to ask permission to shave, to shower, to make phone calls, to get paper and a pencil, to send letters. In discussing the deprivation of liberty, Sykes (1958) makes the point that treating inmates like helpless children poses a severe threat to their self-image. This becomes an interesting question when dealing with juvenile inmates who have never experienced full acceptance into the adult world. The oldest inmates—those who had reached the age of 19 or 20—felt the threat most acutely, but many of the boys in the cottage had basically been independent and on their own for some time before being incarcerated, so the restrictions still stung. It may be that when dealing with a population of juvenile offenders, the deprivation of autonomy is less severe than it is for adults, but such treatment may pose more damage in the long term to self-concepts that are not yet fully formed.

In addition to the loss of many small privileges and most of their autonomy, the residents also chafed at the loss of privacy. Because few of them were assigned to rooms by themselves, they often had to deal with irritating roommates. I heard many complaints about roommates—some were told to me in conversation, others were taken to the staff in the hopes of changing the situation. Sometimes the issue was about race or age—African American residents did not want to room with White residents; older residents did not want to room with immature boys (although by state law, children younger than 18 could not be placed in a room with those older than 18). The complaints of the residents were wide ranging: Some were disgusted by the "funky" smells generated by their roommates, and at least one unpopular roommate was known for wetting his bed. Others complained about having to "play counselor" for their roommates and having to listen to their problems at all hours. And some roommates, they said, were just plain annoying—talking all the time or asking too many questions. The real issue, it seemed, was the lack of privacy.

As Sykes (1958) points out in discussing the pains of imprisonment and particularly the deprivation of goods and services: "There are admittedly many problems in attempting to compare the standard of living existing in the free community and the standard of living which is supposed to be the lot of the inmate in prison" (p. 67). Although times have changed enough that these inmates did not have to go through all of the degradation and mortification ceremonies that Sykes (1958) and Goffman (1961) describe, they were, on their entrance, stripped of most of their own possessions and given state-issue replacements of basic necessities.

The boys frequently expressed their annoyance at having to live with what they deemed inferior products. When Tony, a 20-year-old Latino, was about to be transferred out of the institution to a group home, one small privilege that he was excited about was the opportunity he would have to choose and to purchase nice soap. The residents were even skeptical about some of the treats that the institution provided. For example, cottages often ordered pizzas from a local restaurant on Friday nights. Tony said that the pizza was often "skunky;" he believed that the restaurant, knowing that the institution would likely order pizza on Fridays, probably saved all of their old, unused crusts for the institution's order. Although he had no proof that the restaurant did this, his belief was strong. The residents' complaints about the quality of the products provided by the institution generally fell on deaf ears.

The food at the institution was described by both staff members and residents as "all starch," filling but also fattening and not as healthy as it could be. The Latino boys particularly complained that the food was bland and never had enough spices, seeming to agree with Sykes' (1958) point that "a standard of living can be hopelessly inadequate, from the individual's perspective, because it bores him to death" (p. 68). Even the staff regularly made fun of the food, one of them warning me not to eat there unless I was "starving to death." Perhaps because the food offered subsistence and little else, the boys often begged staff members to give them their desserts or to share with them whatever snacks or treats they might have brought in from the outside. Individuals would ask the staff members who served as their counselors to bring them in something "eatable" for their birthdays, graduations, or other special occasions. When they were lucky enough to get candy or food from their families, the boys were often generous in sharing their stashes with friends and others in the cottage.

Along with different and better food, the residents were very eager for something, anything different to do to relieve the monotony of their days and nights in the institution. They would often try to convince the staff to rent movies or video games for them. One night, I witnessed an interaction where a resident, Alex, and the cottage supervisor played a game of pool with the stakes being that the supervisor would rent Alex a video game if he won. With such motivation, Alex played a great game of pool, and the supervisor was compelled to rent him a game during the next week. The boys were also eager for magazines, catalogues, or different books to read, particularly because, as one young man expressed to me, "The library here doesn't have shit." On occasions when I would bring my laptop computer to the cottage, the boys would beg me to bring it out and then would line up to play card games or checkers on the computer and would stand back and offer advice to the person currently playing. They always treated the computer with the utmost respect, encouraging me to bring it in on my next visit.

Lessons the Institution Intended: School, Life Skills, Work

Among the lessons that the institution hoped to transmit to its residents were basic life skills and conforming attitudes. Boys younger than 18 were required to attend school in the institution, working toward the completion of their high school diploma or a GED. Most of the inmates of the training school were severely behind academically; their time inside essentially forced them to at least go through the motions of attending school. Once they earned a diploma or GED, their opportunities for formal education essentially ended. The only way that a motivated student could take college courses was if he or his family could afford to finance correspondence or distance learning courses. For most of the boys in this study, this was not a realistic possibility. Although they could not further their education while in the institution, the cottage staff members did encourage young men who would be getting out soon to consider attending community college. They spent a good deal of time with interested individuals showing them how to fill out applications for financial aid, advising them on courses, and helping them get their paperwork in order.

As part of their programming, each cottage was responsible for conducting classes on topics such as life skills, anger-management, victim empathy, and cultural literacy. Although they had virtually no training to do so, cottage staff members were expected to lead the classes and attempt to impart knowledge the young men would need when returning to the community. The institution provided photocopied notebooks of ideas for lessons, but the quality of the classes varied widely, largely dependent on the skill, commitment, and creativity of the staff member in charge. The connection of some of the materials to the reality of the boys' lives was highly questionable.

Several meetings were centered around videotaped programs: The drug and alcohol group viewed a fairly generic video on a White female's addiction, and the cultural literacy group was shown a tabloid-style video that advanced a conspiracy theory about the death of Jesus. The staff member in charge gave an awkward introduction to the video, saying, "Don't get mad; it's just a viewpoint. Be open-minded," but he failed to make it relevant to the topic of the class or the boys' lives.

The life skills class was a better example of tailoring the curriculum to the population. In it, the staff member, Luke, led frank discussions about sex and birth control and about paying bills and managing money. He tried to teach the residents how to plan their finances and arranged for them each to have a "checking account" for the money in their institutional accounts. It turned out to be more challenging than the staff had predicted, however, because the boys kept lending each other checks and messing up their accounts.

Along with a high school education and the competencies learned in their treatment groups, the boys also learned basic work skills and what would be expected of them as employees. Nearly all of the boys performed some sort of work in the institution. Some worked in the kitchen, some in the laundry, some in maintenance. Two jobs that were particularly sought after were helping out the staff in the gym for recreation and driving staff members and guests around the campus in a small golf cart or tram. All of the jobs paid the same minimal amount ($1 an hour at the end of the study), but the work itself was considered an important part of the learning experience for inmates. It taught them characteristics that would be expected in a job in the community: to show up on time, to perform their assigned duties, and to cooperate with authority figures.

Lessons Learned From Cottage Staff Members

In their daily interactions with the juvenile offenders, the Blue cottage staff members strove to model prosocial behaviors in the hopes that the boys would learn conforming attitudes and behaviors. They hoped to offer them a glimpse of another set of values, another lifestyle they could choose. In addition, they worked to be consistent in their dealings with the young men in the cottage so that none of the individuals would feel singled out for unjust treatment.

The boys learned about consequences both big and small during their time in the cottage and the larger institution. They saw the long-term consequences of their crimes as the days of their confinement added up to months and years. They learned about short-term consequences for their behavior in their dealings with the cottage staff who sanctioned them for their bad behavior and rewarded them for positive steps. For many of the boys, it was the first time they had ever been so closely monitored and held accountable for their actions. It was often the first time an adult had taken a real interest in what they were doing and what they were thinking.

Although they did the best they could with limited resources and difficult circumstances, staff members feared their intervention might come too late for many of the young men in the cottage. For example, one night after spending nearly 2 hours individually counseling a boy named Andre, a staff member, Luke, told me that he wished he could do a lot more to give these kids a chance. He explained that Andre "did not get much socialization" from his mother; he remembered sleeping on the yard as a very small child, waiting for his mother to come home. Luke said that when he asked Andre how he will raise his own children, "he knew how it should be" and he spoke of how he would "consequent" his own children to teach them responsibility

for their actions. Although Andre knew how things "should" be, he never really learned how to behave himself. Luke said that Andre understood all of this, but he was learning to behave while incarcerated, which Luke believed was "fucked up." As Andre's counselor, Luke put a great deal of time and effort into trying to help him and teach him before he returned to the community.

Along with the prosocial skills that were modeled, the boys learned other skills from the staff members who essentially served as their surrogate parents, coaches, big brothers, and counselors during their time in the cottage. Staff members taught them to play chess and cribbage, showed them how to improve their athletic skills, and encouraged them in their artistic endeavors. They spent a lot of time talking to the boys about their friends and their families, helping them to make concrete plans for their return to the community.

Two examples illustrate the range of the lessons imparted by the cottage staff. In the first, a young man was involved in an assault within the institution. With new criminal charges being filed, he could no longer stay in the juvenile justice system, and he was to be transferred to an adult institution. Before his transfer, the cottage supervisor went over to the lockdown unit where he was being temporarily held to spend some time talking to him, advising him "how not to get killed in prison." On an entirely different level, cottage staff members were reminded of the youth of some of their charges as they watched them grow, their bodies filling out and maturing during their incarceration. Without family members around to guide them into manhood, many of the boys sought help and advice from the more trusted staff members. Such guidance was poignantly illustrated when I witnessed Luke patiently teach a young man how to shave his face for the first time.

Lessons Learned From Other Inmates

At least as important as the lessons learned from the staff members and from the programming provided by the institution were the lessons the young offenders learned from their fellow inmates. Peer pressure and one's peer group standing are at least as important for institutionalized juveniles as they are for children in other populations (Preveaux, Ray, LoBello, & Mehta, 2004); in fact, the influence of peers is likely magnified in a total institution (Goffman, 1961) where your peers are your only public.

One of the first things new boys learned was to keep their mouths shut until they had proven themselves to the other members of the Blue cottage. This was clearly illustrated at dinner one night when I sat with a group of boys, and they told me that a particularly quiet individual was "too young to have any say yet" and he had to "sit and take it and be quiet." The boys who had "big mouths" and did not learn this quickly enough found that there was often a physical price to be paid as tougher inmates with longer tenure in the cottage taught them a lesson they would not soon forget. There were several instances throughout this study where I would notice fresh bruises or black eyes on one of the inmates, and I was told that individual had been "taken down a notch." The consensus in the cottage was generally that the boy had deserved the beating he got, if not more.

Along with learning how and when to keep their mouths shut, the boys in the cottage also had to learn to get along with others. They were virtually never alone, and so they had to find a way to compromise and to live in relative peace. They learned to be a little more tolerant. Rival gang members had to share the same space in the Blue cottage and learn to put their vendettas on hold. They learned who, if anyone, to trust.

The institution did have some elements of the "crime school" that correctional facilities are feared to be. The young inmates grew tougher as they grew older, and some became more criminally sophisticated; they spent a great deal of their time and energy trying to think of ways to be better criminals. Many of the boys in Blue had a history of selling drugs, and they thought if they were smarter in their actions and slow to turn to violence, they could return successfully to the drug market to make their money. Those individuals were quick to point out that they had not been caught and punished for selling drugs; most were in the institution for robbery or assault or some other act of violence.

As one example, Marco, a 19-year-old Latino, was incarcerated for being the "trigger man" on a drive-by shooting. As he neared the end of his sentence, Marco vowed that he was finished with gang violence, telling me: "I'm not putting in anymore work, though . . . no more drive-bys." He did intend to sell drugs when he was back in the community, but he had thought carefully about how to reduce the risk. He said that he would not take a lot of risks and would not be a visible dealer out on the street corner. Instead, he planned to make his deals with a pager; with a pager, he said, "you know who is calling you, and you can arrange to meet in a safe place." He also said that he would not carry the drugs in plastic baggies, because "baggies are used to prove intent to sell/deliver," which would carry a longer, more severe sentence.

In addition to thinking about ways to earn money while staying out of prison, Marco spent some of his time in the institution trying to figure out ways to beat the system; although he enjoyed writing for the training school's student newspaper, he also went to considerable effort forging a GED certificate. It was clear that he was smart and skilled enough to earn his GED legitimately, but he chose instead to try to forge it. Although it was a very good effort, the forgery was ultimately detected.

The residents of Blue also learned lessons from their day-to-day interactions. They learned to negotiate with each other and with staff members for small privileges. They learned how to fight verbal battles and to take or deflect teasing when it was aimed at them. In their attempts to stave off boredom, they improved their skills at video games, card games, pool, cribbage, and chess. After being soundly beaten at the cottage's two video games, one of the boys called Alex a "video game addict." Alex responded simply: "What else is there to do but play video games and watch TV?" A few of the boys exercised their creativity by writing poetry and raps and drawing pictures. Some took on leadership roles and learned how to teach their own hardwon conforming skills to others. Ultimately, from each other, the inmates learned how to survive their time in the institution.

Lessons Learned in Relation to Family and Friends

An important and sometimes painful lesson for the young men in this study was learning how to manage long distance relationships with friends and families, including their own children. Throughout their sentences, they learned who would be there for them and what loyalty really means in tough times. In combating their loneliness and frustration, it was important for the residents to feel that their friends in the community remembered them and cared what happened to them. A couple of the boys expressed their contempt for fair-weather friends. They made the point that people who they had not heard from the whole time they were locked up suddenly started calling them again as they were about to get out. They said that they were suddenly acting like their best friends, acting like nothing had changed after basically ignoring them for most of the time they were incarcerated. The residents prized loyalty and no longer valued such inconsistent friends.

In maintaining relationships throughout their sentences, the telephone and the mail served as important lifelines for the residents (Sykes, 1958). Phone calls and visits provided the boys a chance to keep in contact with the outside world. Yet, even that contact was severely restricted as mail was scanned and sometimes censored by staff members as they checked it both coming in and going out of the institution. Letters with gang references or veiled threats were confiscated. The number of telephone calls made by each of the boys was also carefully monitored and regulated by cottage staff members. Although there was more flexibility with incoming calls, the institution was far from most of their hometowns, and the boys' long distance calls out were generally limited to 5 minutes.

The phone and the mail were particularly important for communicating with girls. Many of the boys had met their current girlfriends while locked up. Friends shared their pictures of girls with each other, they shared their phone calls from girls with each other, and they sometimes even shared girls with each other, passing numbers and addresses to their friends, "like a pen pal," one of the young men suggested with a knowing laugh. The boys were well aware of who was receiving how many phone calls from girls, and they often teased each other about juggling girls or about how they hadn't been getting many phone calls at all lately.

Some of the boys had more serious, long-term relationships with girls "on the outs." Many of the young men (perhaps a third of the boys in the cottage at any given time) were already fathers. Although there were differing levels of involvement with their children and "my baby's mom," they all seemed to take a certain amount of pride in their paternity, and most said that they hoped to be good fathers and be there for their kids as they grew up. TJ and Marco, particularly, spoke often of their young daughters and proudly showed off Polaroid pictures and tattoos of their daughters' names and images. Many of their plans for the future centered around doing whatever was necessary to provide better lives for their little girls.

The residents' relationships with their girlfriends went through many ups and downs during their time in the institution. On one of my visits, the cottage supervisor told me that it had been a pretty quiet week and that a lot of the boys were having "girl problems" and were fighting with their girlfriends. He mentioned a few of the residents by name and said that he had heard them "crying on the phone" to their girls. Especially acute was the frustration that these boys felt on hearing rumors about their girlfriends seeing other men and not being able to confront them face-to-face. When I asked Alex one day, "What's up with your girl?" his response illustrated the general frustration and lack of efficacy the young inmates often felt when he said: "What's up with her? You know as much as I do. Nothing I can do about it while I am in here." The residents sometimes came to me for a female perspective, something clearly lacking in the male institution, but the seeds of doubt were easily planted and difficult to remove. Troubled teenagers to begin with, the young men in the Blue cottage faced a formidable challenge in dealing with and maintaining relationships from inside the institution.

Lessons Learned Over Time

Some lessons were simply the result of being locked up for months and years in a juvenile correctional institution. Whether they liked it or not, the young men in the Blue cottage were forced to learn patience. Much of their time was spent waiting. Their daily lives were filled with waiting to be let out of their rooms, waiting to be allowed to shower, waiting to go to meals or recreation, waiting to be escorted to school or their jobs, waiting to use the phone, waiting for their next visit. Even watching television was a lesson in waiting. They would see advertisements for a new movie and would express their excitement over seeing the film, but the reality was that many of them would not be able to see that movie for years. They would see beautiful women on television and know that it would be months or years before sex with their girlfriends was a possibility. Ultimately, one thing their sentences taught all of the boys in the cottage was to find a way to endure the waiting and to survive their own impatience.

Finally, their time in the institution offered these young men a chance to reflect on their lives and their place in the world. It gave them the opportunity to really think about who they were before their incarceration, who they were turning into during their time in confinement, and who they wanted to be when they got out and grew up. Even in the confines of a juvenile correctional facility, "Emerging adulthood is arguably the period of the life course when the possibility for dramatic change is greatest" (Arnett, 2004, p. 190). Although not all of the boys took full advantage of the opportunity for such introspection, some clearly did. TJ, for example, made the comment that his 22-year-old unemployed brother should rob a bank and get locked up for 2 to 3 years; he thought it would give him a chance to get his life together because "prison gives you perspective."

◆ Discussion: Lessons Learned About Training Schools

Bartollas et al. (1976) concluded their study on a juvenile training school nearly 30 years ago with this dire message:

This is certainly not the first, nor is it likely to be the last, in a long series of books, monographs, and articles which indict the juvenile correctional system as anti-therapeutic, anti-rehabilitative, and as exploitative and demeaning of keepers and kept alike. The juvenile correctional institution, not unlike any other total institution, is or can be more cruel and inhumane than most outsiders ever imagine. . . . The juvenile institution is a culmination of the worst features of a free society. (p. 259)

Juvenile institutions are clearly not a panacea for the problems of juvenile delinquency, but as I argued earlier, they look better or worse depending on what we compare them to. Currently, violent adolescents who are considered a danger to the community are generally sentenced to one of two options: training schools or adult prisons. With prison as the alternative, training schools appear to do less harm to the young offenders in their midst (Austin & Irwin, 2001), or as Feld (1998) suggests: "Despite extensive judicial findings of deplorable conditions of confinement, juvenile correctional facilities probably remain less harsh or abusive than most adult prisons" (p. 234).

Conditions of confinement were not, in fact, deplorable in the training school in this study, but incarceration and the pains of imprisonment would leave significant marks on all of the young males, regardless. Although incarceration appears to be a turning point for some offenders who desist from crime, for nearly all who pass through a correctional facility, it adds to the cumulative disadvantage and the obstacles they will face on their release. Incarceration may weaken community bonds, contribute to school failure and unemployment, and ultimately increase the likelihood for adult crime (Laub & Sampson, 2003).

The rationale for a separate system for juveniles is the belief that there is something qualitatively different about adolescents and that they should not be intermingled with adult offenders. Although those youths who have committed serious and violent crimes are often viewed as beyond rehabilitation (Lipsey, 1999), those working in the juvenile justice system continue to profess hope for the rehabilitation and resocialization of the young offenders in their care (Caeti, Hemmens, Cullen, & Burton, 2003). Following the developmental perspective, they recognize that damage done by the criminal justice system carries long-term consequences that are nearly impossible to reverse (Steinberg & Schwartz, 2000). As such, allowing even serious delinquents to remain in the juvenile justice system helps to diminish those long term consequences and reaffirms the belief that young offenders have a chance to be resocialized and pointed toward more conforming futures, that they are capable of learning valuable life lessons during their time in the juvenile system.

Most of the boys in the Blue cottage would serve relatively long sentences for their violent offenses. If resocialization was to occur while they were under the jurisdiction of the juvenile justice system, the end-of-the-line training school was generally their most stable placement, the place where they endured a state mandated time out from their lives and were encouraged to consider what they wanted their futures to hold.

In spending time with the adolescent inmates in this study, it was impossible to ignore the very fact of their youth. They were, for the most part, still boys literally growing up and maturing behind bars. There was still an air of invincibility and enthusiasm in many of the boys and young men in the Blue cottage; most had not yet fully committed to the convict world. They held on to at least some of their vulnerability and some hope for a better future. The juvenile system allowed them to make bad choices without necessarily throwing their lives away. As Feld (1996) explains: "One premise of juvenile justice is that youths should survive the mistakes of adolescence with their life chances intact" (pp. 425—426).

Compared to adult prisons, training schools such as the one in this study offer such young offenders a reprieve. They offer troubled adolescents one last opportunity to grow up a little, learn important lessons, and emerge from the institution with a chance to start their lives over. Many of them will cross the legal boundary into adulthood during their confinement; they enter the institution as boys and leave it as young men with new rights and responsibilities, facing their futures with both fear and hope. Emerging adulthood may hold particular promise for young men who are also emerging from juvenile prisons, for as Arnett (2004) has argued, "There is something about reaching emerging adulthood that opens up new possibilities for transformation for people who have had more than their share of adversity during their early years" (p. 205).

I heard again and again from individuals in this study, that "the system" cannot force anyone to change, that individuals have to want to change, they have to want to get out of "the life." The desire to change happened for some of the young men during their time in the Blue cottage as they matured and made strides toward becoming conforming adults. They are the success stories of the institution. In their efforts to overcome disadvantaged backgrounds and their own criminal histories, they provide an important lesson to the larger community by offering a compelling reason to strengthen the programming and opportunities in our juvenile correctional facilities and to continue giving adolescent offenders one last chance in the juvenile system.

◈ References

Altschuler, D. M., & Brash, R. (2004). Adolescent and teenage offenders confronting the challenges and opportunities of reentry. *Youth Violence and Juvenile Justice, 2,* 72–87.

Arnett, J. J. (1998). Learning to stand alone: The contemporary American transition to adulthood in cultural and historical context. *Human Development, 41,* 295–315.

Arnett, J. J. (2004). *Emerging adulthood: The winding road from the late teens through the twenties.* New York: Oxford University Press.

Austin, J., & Irwin, J. (2001). *It's about time: America's imprisonment binge* (3rd ed.). Belmont, CA: Wadsworth.

Bartollas, C., Miller, S. J., & Dinitz, S. (1976). *Juvenile victimization: The institutional paradox.* New York: John Wiley.

Bortner, M. A., & Williams, L. M. (1997). *Youth in prison.* New York: Routledge.

Caeti, T. J., Hemmens, C., Cullen, F. T., & Burton, V. S., Jr. (2003). Management of juvenile correctional facilities. *The Prison Journal, 83,* 383–405.

Chesney-Lind, M., & Shelden, R. G. (2004). *Girls, delinquency, and juvenile justice* (3rd ed.). Belmont, CA: Wadsworth.

Feld, B. C. (1977). *Neutralizing inmate violence: Juvenile offenders in institutions.* Cambridge, MA: Ballinger.

Feld, B. C. (1996). Juvenile (in)justice and the criminal court alternative. In J. G. Weis, R. D. Crutchfield, & G. S. Bridges (Eds.), *Juvenile delinquency* (pp. 418–427). Thousand Oaks, CA: Pine Forge Press.

Feld, B. C. (1998). Juvenile and criminal justice systems' responses to youth violence. In M. Tonry & M. H. Moore (Eds.), *Youth violence* (pp. 189–261). Chicago: University of Chicago Press.

Feld, B. C. (Ed.). (1999). *Readings in juvenile justice administration.* New York: Oxford University Press.

Forst, M., Fagan, J., & Vivona, T. S. (1989). Youth in prisons and training schools: Perceptions and consequences of the treatment-custody dichotomy. *Juvenile and Family Court Journal, 40,* 1–14.

Furstenberg, F. F., Jr., Rumbaut, R. G., & Settersten, R. A., Jr. (2005). On the frontier of adulthood: Emerging themes and new directions. In R. A. Settersten Jr., F. F. Furstenberg Jr., & R. G. Rumbaut (Eds.), *On the frontier of adulthood: Theory, research, and public policy* (pp. 3–28). Chicago: University of Chicago Press.

Goffman, E. (1961). *Asylums.* New York: Anchor.

Grisso, T., & Schwartz, R. G. (2000). Introduction. In T. Grisso & R. G. Schwartz (Eds.), *Youth on trial: A developmental perspective on juvenile justice* (pp. 1–5). Chicago: University of Chicago Press.

Haskell, M. R., & Yablonsky, L. (1982). *Juvenile delinquency* (3rd ed.). Boston: Houghton Mifflin.

Irwin, J. (1970). *The felon.* Berkeley: University of California Press.

Lane, J., Lanza-Kaduce, L., Frazier, C. E., & Bishop, D. M. (2002). Adult versus juvenile sanctions: Voices of incarcerated youths. *Crime & Delinquency, 48,* 431–455.

Laub, J. H., & Sampson, R. J. (2003). *Shared beginnings, divergent lives: Delinquent boys to age 70.* Cambridge, MA: Harvard University Press.

Lipsey, M. W. (1999). Can intervention rehabilitate serious delinquents? *The Annals of the American Academy of Political and Social Science, 564,* 142–166.

Miller, J. G. (1998). *Last one over the wall: The Massachusetts experiment in closing reform schools* (2nd ed.). Columbus: Ohio State University Press.

Polsky, H. W. (1962). *Cottage six—The social system of delinquent boys in residential treatment.* New York: Russell Sage.

Preveaux, N. E., Ray, G. E., LoBello, S. G., & Mehta, S. (2004). Peer relationships among institutionalized juvenile boys. *Journal of Adolescent Research, 19,* 284–302.

Scott, E. S. (2000). Criminal responsibility in adolescence: Lessons from developmental psychology. In T. Grisso & R. G. Schwartx (Eds.), *Youth on trial: A developmental perspective on juvenile justice* (pp. 291–324). Chicago: University of Chicago Press.

Steinberg, L., & Schwartz, R. G. (2000). Developmental psychology goes to court. In T. Grisso & R. G. Schwartz (Eds.), *Youth on trial: A developmental perspective on juvenile justice* (pp. 9–31). Chicago: University of Chicago Press.

Sykes, G. M. (1958). *The society of captives: A study of a maximum security prison.* Princeton, NJ: Princeton University Press.

Sykes, G. M., & Messinger, S. (1960). The inmate social system. In R. A. Cloward (Ed.), *Theoretical studies in social organization of the prison* (pp. 5–19). New York: Social Science Research Council.

Van Vleet, R. K. (1999). The attack on juvenile justice. *The Annals of the American Academy of Political and Social Science, 564,* 203–214.

Weber, G. H. (1961). Emotional and defensive reactions of cottage parents. In D. R. Cressey (Ed.), *The prison: Studies in institutional organization and change* (pp. 189–228). New York: Holt, Rinehart & Winston.

Wooden, K. (1976). *Weeping in the playtime of others: America's incarcerated children.* New York: McGraw-Hill.

READING 35

In reviewing the literature of the link between prejudice (attitudes or opinions about a group) and discrimination (unfavorable behavior directed toward individuals of a group), Pager and Quillian found that sociologists largely stopped studying the link by the mid-1970s while psychologists have continued to focus on the link between the two. Although psychologists made important inroads in this area, the authors felt there were holes only the sociological approach could fill. They were particularly interested in the link between prejudice and discrimination as it relates to hiring practices and created an experimental study to test whether employers would be willing to hire ex-offenders and how race factored into that decision, if at all. They used four "matched testers" with similar attributes and stated backgrounds except that two were white and two were black (one each with a criminal record and one

Source: Pager, Devah, and Lincoln Quillian. 2005. "Walking the Talk? What Employers Say Versus What They Do." *American Sociological Review* 70:355–380. Reprinted with permission.

without). They compare the hiring success rate of black and white ex-offenders, finding that only 5% of employers called back black ex-offenders while 17% of whites with criminal records received a callback. Pager and colleagues have continued this line of research, finding in a 2009 employment study that black and Latino applicants with clean backgrounds fared no better than white applicants just released from prison. If you wish to learn more on this topic, you can read the 2009 study by Pager, Bonikowski, and Western on the supplemental website.

Walking the Talk?

What Employers Say Versus What They Do

Devah Pager and Lincoln Quillian

In 1930, Richard LaPiere, a Stanford professor, traveled twice across the country by car with a young Chinese student and his wife. The purpose of the trip, unbeknown to his travel companions, was to assess the reactions of hotel and restaurant proprietors to the presence of Chinese customers. During the course of 251 visits to hotels, auto camps, restaurants, and cafes, only once were they refused service. Six months later, LaPiere mailed a survey to each of the proprietors in which one of the questions asked, "Will you accept members of the Chinese race as guests in your establishment?" More than 90 percent of the respondents indicated unequivocal refusal. The discrepancy between these proprietors' responses to the surveys and their actual behavior is indeed striking: Although nearly none of the proprietors expressed a willingness to accept the patronage of Chinese customers, virtually all of them did so when confronted with the situation (LaPiere 1934). If we were to make generalizations based on either the survey results or the field study alone, we would develop radically different views on the level of racial hostility toward the Chinese at that time in history.

LaPiere's study provides a much needed reality check for researchers who rely on expressed attitudes for insight into the nature and causes of discriminatory behavior. Unfortunately, there have been very few efforts to provide the kind of comparison offered in LaPiere's study. Measures from surveys often are accepted as an adequate proxy for behaviors, with little effort to validate this assumption.

The current article seeks to make headway in this discussion, following up on the insights provided by LaPiere more than 70 years ago. In this discussion, we compare the self-reported attitudes exhibited by a sample of Milwaukee employers with their actual behavior in real-life employment situations. By placing our analysis within the context of research on discrimination in contemporary labor markets we hope to underscore the degree to which method matters in our interrogation of the social world.

◈ Racial Attitudes, Discrimination, and Contemporary Labor Market Inequality

In the years since LaPiere's study, much has changed about race relations in the contemporary United States. In present times, it would be extremely rare to find respondents willing to state racial objections as candidly as those reported in LaPiere's survey. Indeed, trends in racial attitudes demonstrate steady movement toward the endorsement of equal treatment by race and the repudiation of direct discrimination. According to surveys conducted in the 1940s and 1950s, for example, fewer than half of whites believed that white students should go to school with black students or that black and white job applicants should have an equal chance at getting a job. In contrast, by the 1990s, more than 90 percent of white survey respondents endorsed the principle that white and black students and job applicants should be treated equally by schools and employers (Schuman et al. 2001).

Consistent with these trends, many indicators of social and economic status show that African-Americans have made great strides in approaching parity with whites. Blacks, for example, are now nearly equal to whites in rates of high school completion, and have become increasingly well-represented in occupational sectors previously dominated by whites (Farley 1997; Mare 1995; Wilson 1978). Likewise, in the decade after the Civil Rights Movement, and again during the 1990s, the wage gap between black and white workers was substantially reduced (Couch and Daly 2002; Harrison and Bennett 1995; but see Western and Pettit forthcoming). The rapid social mobility among blacks in the United States provides support for the notion that the progressive trends apparent in measures of racial attitudes reflect a real shift in the opportunities now available to African-Americans. In fact, these positive indicators have led some prominent academics to proclaim the problem of discrimination solved. Economist James Heckman, for example, has asserted that "most of the disparity in earnings between blacks and whites in the labor market of the 1990s is due to the differences in skills they bring to the market, and not to discrimination within the labor market." He went on to refer to labor market discrimination as "the problem of an earlier era" (Heckman 1998:101–102). Indeed, for many observers of contemporary race relations, the barrier of discrimination appears to have withered away, leaving blacks the opportunity to pursue unfettered upward mobility.

And yet, despite the many signs of progress, there remain important forms of social and economic inequality that continue to differentiate the experiences of black and white Americans. According to many indicators, blacks, and black men in particular, continue to lag far behind their white counterparts. Some indicators show black men doing steadily worse. African-Americans, for example, experience roughly double the rate of unemployment experienced by whites, with very little sign of change over time. Likewise, rates of joblessness among young black men have been rising over time (Holzer, Offner, and Sorensen 2005).

As a further troubling indicator, many of these young black men, instead of making their way through school and into jobs, are instead increasingly finding themselves housed in an expanding number of correctional facilities. Approximately 1 in 3 black men will spend some time in prison over his lifetime, as compared with only 1 in 17 white men (Bonczar 2003). Among young black high school dropouts, this figure rises to nearly 60 percent. Rivaling other conventional social institutions—such as military service, employment, and marriage, incarceration has now become a typical event in the life course of young disadvantaged men (Pettit and Western 2004).

How can we explain the discrepancies between these varied measures? On the one hand, the progressive trends in racial attitudes may reflect a genuine openness among white Americans to racial integration and equality. In this case, the continuing difficulties facing segments of the black population may simply reflect the "bumpy road" on an otherwise steady trajectory toward racial parity (Gans 1992). Further, white racial attitudes are not the only barrier to black mobility. Changes in the economic structure, family composition, and crime policy, among other factors, may each exert an exogenous influence on the black population in ways that inhibit mobility, independent of the racial openness of contemporary institutions. From this perspective, continuing black disadvantage could be explained by a reasonable lag between changing attitudes and outcomes, as well as by the multiple influences that shape patterns of racial inequality.

On the other hand, traditional survey measures of racial attitudes may not accurately reflect the degree to which race continues to shape the opportunities available to African-Americans. Indeed, a great deal of evidence suggests that racial stereotypes remain firmly embedded in the American consciousness, affecting perceptions of and interactions with racial minorities even among respondents who overtly endorse the principle of equal treatment (Devine and Elliot 1995). Substantial levels of discrimination have likewise been detected by experimental field studies, which find consistent evidence of racial bias against black applicants in housing, credit, and employment markets (Bertrand and Mullainathan 2004; Turner, Fix, and Struyk 1991; Yinger 1995). As a further reflection of lived experience, the large majority of blacks continue to perceive discrimination as routine in matters of jobs, income, and housing (Feagin and Sikes 1994).

Given the available information, it is difficult to evaluate the extent to which direct discrimination plays a role in shaping the opportunities available to blacks in contemporary society. Surveys of racial attitudes portray one optimistic picture, whereas indicators of economic and social inequality present more mixed results. It is only through direct comparisons of these differing measures that we can assess how and why they may project such divergent conclusions.

In this article, we focus on the specific issue of employment discrimination. Substantively, we are interested in assessing the degree to which employer preferences or biases influence the opportunities available to stigmatized workers. Methodologically, we seek to assess the degree to which choice of measurement strategy affects our understanding of these processes. In our analysis of survey data and behavioral outcomes, we engage with LaPiere's central concern about the correspondence between measured attitudes and behaviors.

We begin with a review of the literature on the attitude-behavior relationship since LaPiere's study, focusing specifically on the case of attitudes toward and treatment of stigmatized groups. We then turn to concerns regarding the use of survey measures as proxies for measures of discrimination. Finally, we discuss the results from a matched field experiment and telephone survey that are the basis of our empirical results. Throughout this discussion, we seek to emphasize that investigations of important substantive concerns cannot be separated from a discussion of the methods by which these investigations take place.

 Attitudes and Behaviors

Understandings of the Attitude-Behavior Relationship

Attitude questions are frequently asked because they are believed to be illuminating about one or more behaviors of interest. One of the most common uses of attitude research is to assess prejudices, stereotypes, and other measures of social distance with the goal of gaining insight about the nature of discriminatory behavior (National Research Council 2004). Attitude questions have been widely used as tools to assist in understanding the basis of behaviors such as discrimination in employment (Bobo, Johnson, and Suh 2000), residential mobility related to white flight (Farley et al. 1994; Krysan 2002), and the influence of race on voting patterns (Sniderman and Piazza 1993).

Because of the difficulty of gathering data on discrimination in natural settings, many substantive sociological studies of discrimination rely on easier-to-gather survey or interview data in the place of behavioral measures. Some studies focus on attitudinal indicators alone, leaving the connection to behavior implicit. Others ask respondents about past behavior or anticipated behavior in response to hypothetical situations. A wide range of survey scales and specific survey techniques have been developed to measure specific forms of prejudice and discrimination (National Research Council, 2004, chapter 8).

As one important example, a survey technique that has become increasingly popular for assessing situational discrimination involves use of the vignette question, which elicits reactions from respondents about fairly detailed hypothetical scenarios (Sniderman and Grob 1996). An influential early example of the vignette method was developed by Reynolds Farley and colleagues for a better understanding of the attitudinal sources of racial segregation (Farley, Bianchi, and Colosanto 1979; Farley et al. 1978; Farley et al. 1994). With Farley's approach, respondents are asked to express the level of discomfort they would experience living in hypothetical neighborhoods of varying racial compositions, and to estimate the likelihood that they would move out of such neighborhoods. Farley's innovative technique has become widely used in subsequent research, in part because it is easily combined with experimental survey techniques (discussed in the next section) (Emerson, Yancey, and Chai 2001; Krysan 2002).

A key assumption of vignette studies is that reported hypothetical behavior is an accurate proxy for the behavior that would be observed if the respondent actually encountered the situation. In the case of vignette studies that attempt to illuminate the process of white flight, for example, the assumption is that respondents who say they would feel discomfort or would move is highly related to the behavior of moving out (or not moving in) that would occur if the respondent actually lived in the hypothetical neighborhood. Although a perfect attitude-behavior correspondence is not required, these studies make the assumption that the two are related. An almost complete separation between attitudes and corresponding behaviors would undermine the rationale behind most attitudinal studies.

The expectation of attitude-behavior correspondence results naturally from the view that human action is the product of conscious mental states. Several psychologists, most notably Fishbein and Ajzen (1975), have formally modeled the relationship between these components to describe the formation of attitudes and their subsequent influence on behavior. In their model, feelings or beliefs about an object give rise to positive or negative evaluations of the object. These evaluations then influence behavioral intentions, which ultimately influence behavior (Ajzen 2001; Fishbein and Ajzen 1975). If attitudes can be measured successfully by survey questions or interviews, then these should have at least some power to predict overall patterns of behavior toward the attitude object.

Despite the clarity and intuitive appeal of this model, what is most striking about past investigations of the attitude-behavior relationship is the wide range of correlations reported across different studies. Both Deutscher (1966) and Wicker (1969), for example, review a number of studies that find virtually no relationship between attitudes and behaviors. Schuman

and Johnson (1976) also discuss a number of notable studies in which a zero or negative correlation between attitudes and behaviors was found. In their review, however, they conclude that a majority of research on the attitude-behavior relationship finds a moderate positive relationship. With examples for each extreme, their article reports correlations close to zero among attitude-behavior assessments of racial bias and transient economic transactions, while demonstrating correlations exceeding .85 among studies of voting behavior. Most others are shown to fall somewhere in between (Schuman and Johnson 1976).

This literature supports the conclusion that no simple formula can describe the attitude-behavior relationship. Rather, tremendous variation exists in the measurement of attitudes and their associated behaviors, and assumptions about their correspondence should be reviewed with caution.

Attitudes and Behavior Toward Stigmatized Groups

Despite the appeal of using attitudinal measures as proxies for behavior, particularly for hard-to-measure behaviors such as discrimination, a number of factors complicate the relationship between verbal expressions on surveys and actual behaviors directed toward members of stigmatized groups. First, social surveys have long been plagued by the problem of social desirability, or the phenomenon that respondents seek to give socially appropriate answers to questions, even if this involves distorting the truth (Bradburn 1983). In the contemporary United States, the norms of racial equality are so strong that survey respondents are unlikely to feel comfortable expressing negative opinions about members of other racial groups (Crandall 1994). When asked questions about race or other sensitive issues, respondents may be led by these pressures to shift their opinions subtly (or in some cases not so subtly) in the direction of answers they perceive to be the most socially acceptable. To the extent that real-world discrimination continues, this has the effect of biasing survey results in the direction of politically correct, nonprejudicial responses, and of weakening the relationship between measured attitudes and behavior.

Researchers have adopted creative techniques to minimize the problem of social desirability bias, using experimental survey designs to avoid direct group comparisons. These methods build on the split-ballot survey design, in which randomly chosen subsamples of a survey are primed with one of several variants of a survey question to assess responses to a particular group or condition (Sniderman and Grob 1996).[1] For instance, Schuman and Bobo (1988) used a split-ballot design in which half the sample was asked about objections to a Japanese family moving into their neighborhood, while the other half was asked about objections to a black family moving into their neighborhood. Had each respondent been asked about both a black and a Japanese family on the same survey, they may have biased their responses toward similar evaluations of the two groups, consistent with norms of equal treatment. Through statistical comparisons across the two groups, split-ballot studies are thought to produce valid population-level estimates of the importance of race for the question of interest while reducing concerns about social desirability bias that arise from direct racial comparisons. Experimental survey designs have clear advantages for the measurement of sensitive topics, and their results have indeed shown a greater incidence of prejudice than those from traditional survey designs (Schuman 1995; Schuman and Bobo 1988).

We view social desirability bias, then, as a problem that has received substantial attention in the research literature, with some promising developments. Nevertheless, to our knowledge, no research has provided a behavioral validation of experimental survey results. We have little concrete evidence, therefore, with which to evaluate when and to what degree experimental survey measures are in fact accurate proxies for behavior.

A second problem in using attitudinal measures as proxy assessments for discriminatory behavior concerns the emphasis of this method on consciously held beliefs or feelings. With the use of such measures, subjects are typically prompted for their attitudes in ways that allow for some degree of conscious deliberation. However, a growing literature in psychology has documented the existence and influence of implicit attitudes toward stigmatized groups that may influence judgments and actions without conscious awareness (Devine 1989). The intrapsychic processes that promote discrimination are likely to be more strongly activated in the context of a live interaction than in the abstract context of a survey question (Fiske 2004). Discrimination resulting from these interaction-triggered implicit stereotypes would necessarily remain undetected in survey responses, even those using an experimental design.

Creating a similar problem, some measured forms of discrimination may be perceptible only in the context of direct interaction. Social psychological evidence suggests that whites commonly experience heightened levels of social discomfort in the presence of blacks, at times leading to behaviors that are in effect discriminatory despite (accurately reported) nonprejudicial attitudes (Poskocil 1977). For instance, Word, Zanna, and Cooper (1974) show that white subjects conducting mock interviews with trained black applicants make more speech errors, ask fewer questions, and terminate interviews more quickly than with similar white applicants (see also Dovidio, Kawakami, and Gaertner 2002). Again, because these forms of discomfort are activated only by direct social contact—not by questions about hypothetical situations or prejudicial attitudes—these alternate psychological sources of discriminatory behaviors are unlikely to be captured by questions on survey instruments.

Finally, discriminatory action often is strongly influenced by situational factors, further reducing the extent of attitude-behavior correspondence. Complex decisions about where discrimination may be expressed are influenced by a combination of prevailing social norms as well as context-specific considerations (Merton 1949). In hiring, for instance, employers must balance their need for employees, the applicant pool, and other situational contingencies together with their taste for applicants along several dimensions. These situational factors can sometimes overwhelm the influence of prejudice in discriminatory action, resulting in a low correspondence between the two.

Indeed, it is notable, for example, that LaPiere's (1934) study found higher levels of racial bias apparent in the survey responses than in the field situation. Similar studies by Kutner, Wilkins, and Yarrow (1952) and Saenger and Gilbert (1950)—but focused on discrimination against blacks rather than the Chinese—report similarly counterintuitive results. These findings are especially remarkable in light of the contemporary literature on social desirability bias, which overwhelmingly assumes that survey reports will tend to underestimate the amount of discrimination that will occur. We believe the direction of the discrepancy between self-reports and behavior in these three studies most likely results from the importance of situational factors (Ajzen 1991). In the context of these studies, open discrimination likely would have involved some direct interpersonal confrontation. Unlike the decision not to call someone back for a job interview (a relatively passive form of discrimination), the refusal of service, or other more active forms of discriminatory treatment, can impose significant social costs.[2] In LaPiere's investigation, for example, the discriminator risked creating an uncomfortable interpersonal situation, possibly resulting in a scene. In certain cases, then, behaviors may be constrained in ways that verbal expressions are not, again leading to a lower correspondence between the two.

The historical evolution of strong norms against openly racist statements makes it less likely that contemporary field studies would find nearly as high a level of openly expressed prejudice as found in the aforementioned three studies (Schuman et al. 2001). And more recent, if indirect, comparisons of attitudes and behaviors usually have found stronger signs of racial discrimination in behaviors than in self-reports of behavioral intentions (Crosby, Bromley, and Saxe 1980). At the same time, it remains plausible that situational factors could still result in higher levels of stated than actual discrimination in certain cases, depending on the context and the attitudinal instrument.

The complexities involved in the relationship between attitudes and behaviors toward stigmatized groups emphasize the need for careful assessments of our measurement tools. The links between these measured attitudes and observed behaviors require systematic evaluation. Unfortunately, despite the frequent use of verbal expressions to draw conclusions about behaviors, very few studies directly calibrate survey responses with corresponding behavioral assessments.

Explicit Studies of Prejudice-Discrimination Correspondence

Whereas the sociological literature on the attitude-behavior relationship is small, the recent literature on the specific attitude-behavior case of prejudice and discrimination (in sociology) is virtually nonexistent.[3] Indeed, we turned instead to research in psychology for guidance in these matters. Social psychologist Susan Fiske (2004), in a recent, comprehensive meta-analysis, examine 54 studies containing empirical investigations of prejudice-discrimination correspondence. Consistent with the findings from the attitude-behavior literature more generally, Fiske finds wide variation in the relationship between prejudice and discrimination across studies, with correlations ranging from −.38 to .69, with a mean of .26. Her results thus support a general association between prejudice and discrimination, albeit at low average levels and with great variability across situations (see also Schutz and Six 1996).

The Fiske (2004) review, primarily featuring the work of psychologists, shows that sociologists have largely abandoned the study of prejudice-discrimination correspondence since the mid-1970s. Of the 10 articles in sociology journals included in the Fiske review, the most recent was published in 1973. This is not because sociologists have stopped using attitudinal measures and survey items to study discrimination against marginalized groups, as demonstrated by reviews such as those of Krysan (1999) and Schuman et al. (2001). Rather, sociologists have done little recent work to validate the assumption that these attitudinal measures are associated with discrimination. Krysan's (1999) review, for instance, notes the issue of attitude-behavior correspondence, but does not cite any recent studies on the topic. Instead, Krysan points to the similar trend directions for racial attitude items and corresponding behavioral indicators from unrelated samples and studies (Krysan 1999:139). Evidence of this sort does support a correspondence of attitude and behavior toward stigmatized groups, but only weakly so because a similar trend direction of indicators over time provides only very general evidence of meaningful correspondence.

In contrast to sociologists, among psychologists, the correspondence of attitudes and behavior toward stigmatized groups continues to be the subject of considerable research. Psychological research of this type has provided several important insights into the correspondence between different types of attitudes and behaviors, pointing to, for example, varying relationships between explicit/conscious attitudes, implicit/unconscious attitudes, and various forms of behavior (Dovidio et al. 2002). From a sociological standpoint, however, these studies have some important limitations, most notably those arising from a reliance on behavioral measures obtained in laboratory settings. For instance, the studies Fiske (2004) reviews use outcome behaviors such as ratings of perceived friendliness in interaction with a mock interviewer, subtle behavioral measures such as the number of blinks and the length of eye contact, or the results of role-playing situations. These outcomes often are far removed from the actual decisions made in their social contexts—to hire, to rent, or to move, to name a few—that are most relevant to understanding the behavioral processes that produce disadvantage among members of stigmatized groups.

For our purposes, the most relevant studies comparing prejudice and discrimination are those that assess these factors in realistic social settings, focusing on forms of discrimination that produce meaningful social disparities. Unfortunately, the three studies that fit this description each were conducted more than 50 years ago (Kutner et al. 1952; LaPiere 1934; Saenger and Gilbert 1950). We have very few means by which to assess the correspondence between contemporary racial attitudes and the incidence of discrimination.

Employer Attitudes and Hiring Decisions

The current study provides an opportunity to investigate these processes in a contemporary context. Bringing together a unique combination of data, we present a direct comparison of self-reported attitudes and corresponding behavior in the context of a real-world setting with important implications for inequality. The substantive focus of this study is on employers' willingness to hire blacks and/or ex-offenders for an entry-level position in their company. In both cases, the sensitive topics under investigation lead us to question the use of employer reports alone. By calibrating the estimates we received from surveys with behavioral measures from an experimental audit study, we are able to gain insight into the consistency between these two important indicators of group preference.

Measures of attitudes come in many forms, ranging from abstract statements of feelings (e.g., "I don't like members of group X") to more concrete statements of intended action (e.g., "I would not hire members of group X"). The latter, referred to as behavioral intentions, are considered the form of attitude that should most closely correspond to observed behavior, because of their conceptualization in terms of specific measurable action (Fishbein 1967; Fishbein and Ajzen 1975; Schuman and Johnson 1976). Thus a weak relation between behavioral intentions and behavior suggests an even weaker relation between the behavior and more general attitudinal measures. In the current study, we rely on the behavioral intentions expressed by employers as an indicator of their attitudes about blacks and ex-offenders. Comparing what employers said they would do in a hypothetical hiring situation with what we observed them doing in a real hiring situation forms the basis of our current investigation.

◈ Methods

In the first stage of the study, employers' responses to job applicants were measured in real employment settings using an experimental audit methodology. Between June and December of 2001, matched pairs of young men (testers) were sent to apply for a total of

350 entry-level job openings in the Milwaukee metropolitan area.[4] The two white testers (one with a fictional criminal record and one without) applied for one set of randomly selected jobs ($n = 150$), and the two black testers (using profiles identical to those of the white pair) applied for a second set of jobs ($n = 200$).[5] The preferences of employers were measured based on the number of call-backs to each of the applicants, as registered by four independent voice mail boxes. Additional voice mail boxes were set up for calls to references listed on the testers' resumes. For a more detailed discussion of the research design, see Pager (2003).

The findings of the audit showed large and significant effects of both race and criminal record on employment opportunities. Call-backs were received by 34 percent of whites with no criminal record, 17 percent of whites with criminal records, 14 percent of blacks without criminal records, and 5 percent of blacks with criminal records (Pager 2003). Thus, overall, blacks and ex-offenders were one-half to one-third as likely to be considered by employers, with black ex-offenders suffering the greatest disadvantage.

The second stage of the study provided employers with the opportunity to express their hiring preferences verbally in the context of a telephone survey. Several months after completion of the audit study, each of the 350 employers was called by interviewers from the Michigan State Survey Research Center and asked to participate in a telephone survey about employers' hiring preferences and practices (see Pager [2002] for more detailed discussion of the survey instrument and results). Calls were directed to the person in charge of hiring for each establishment. The final survey sample included 199 respondents, representing a 58 percent response rate (Appendix A).

During the course of this survey, employers were read a vignette describing a job applicant with characteristics designed to match closely the profile of the testers in the audit study. Employers who had been audited by white testers were read a vignette in which the hypothetical applicant was white, and employers who had been audited by black testers were read a vignette in which the applicant was black. In this way, the survey design mirrored the split-ballot procedures

used by Sniderman and Piazza (1993) and Schuman and Bobo (1988), avoiding direct racial comparisons within the same survey.

The wording of the vignette was as follows:

> Chad is a 23-year-old [black/white] male. He finished high school and has steady work experience in entry-level jobs. He has good references and interacts well with people. About a year ago, Chad was convicted of a drug felony and served 12 months in prison. Chad was released last month and is now looking for a job. How likely would you be to hire Chad for an entry-level opening in your company?

Employers were asked to rate their likelihood of hiring this applicant with the following range of responses: very likely, somewhat likely, somewhat unlikely, and very unlikely.

The vignette presented in the survey was designed to correspond closely to the profile of the testers in the audit study. Chad, the hypothetical applicant, was presented with levels of education, experience, and personal qualifications similar to those on the resumes presented by the testers. The type of crime was identical, although the prison sentence in the vignette (12 months) was shorter than that reported in the audit study (18 months).[6] Thus the vignette aimed to measure employers' self-reports concerning how they would respond to such an applicant, whereas the audit measured how they actually did respond to an applicant with almost identical characteristics. The parallel scenarios of the vignette and audit should maximize the correspondence between the two measures (Schuman and Johnson 1976).

In the current study, the primary outcome of interest represents the employers' willingness to hire an applicant depending on his race and criminal background. As described earlier, in the survey, employers were asked to report how likely they would be to hire the applicant described in the vignette. In the actual employment situations, by contrast, we measured the number of employers who responded positively to testers after they had submitted their application. In most cases, this simply involved the employer inviting the tester to come in for an interview, although in a few cases, the applicant was offered the job on the spot. As we later discuss, the behavioral indicator should thus provide a highly inclusive measure of "willingness to hire," given that a call-back represents only an initial step in the hiring process.

◈ Results

In the following section, we examine the relationship between the survey results and the audit study. Initially, we compare the *level* of willingness to hire blacks and ex-offenders indicated by the audit results and the survey. We then examine the *association* between the two measures, considering whether employers who indicated high willingness to hire ex-offenders in the survey called back testers in the criminal record condition at higher rates than those who indicated low willingness to hire in the survey. In each of these comparisons, we seek to assess the degree to which what employers say is accurately reflected in what they do.

Figure 1 presents the key results from both data sources. The first two columns represent the percentage of employers who reported that they would be "very likely" or "somewhat likely" to hire the hypothetical applicant, depending on whether he was presented as white or black. We include the "somewhat likely" group here to correspond to our behavioral measure, which is a call-back rather than an actual hire (see discussion below).

The second two columns represent results from the audit study, illustrating the percentage of call-backs received by each group. In the audit study, call-backs also can be considered a measure of "willingness to hire," given that this represents a first cut in the hiring process. Although a call-back is by no means a guarantee of employment, given that employers typically call back several applicants before selecting their preferred hire, it does indicate a favorable initial review.

The results of the two outcomes, however, are anything but comparable. As Figure 1 shows, employers reported a far greater willingness to hire drug offenders in the survey than was found in the audit. In the survey, more than 60 percent of the employers said they were somewhat or very likely to hire a drug offender irrespective of the applicant's race. In the audit, by contrast, only 17 percent of white and 5 percent of black applicants with drug felonies actually received a call-back.[7]

The disparities apparent in these results are extremely consequential for our understanding of the social world. In the survey data, employers' responses present a view of openness to blacks or applicants with drug felonies that is far greater than the reality measured in actual hiring situations. Accepting the survey results as an accurate indicator of the opportunities available to blacks and ex-offenders would grossly understate the barriers to employment they face.

Although the results of this initial comparison are compelling, there remain several possible objections to equating the findings from our survey measure with those from the audit study. First, collapsing the categories of "very" and "somewhat" into one category may artificially exaggerate the distance between survey and audit results. Indeed, if we look only at the "very likely" category, the discrepancy is far less striking. There is a literature on the meaning of vague quantifiers that attempts to offer greater precision to our understanding of these terms (Pace and Friedlander, 1982; Schaeffer, 1991). Lichtenstein and Newman (1967), for example, report that respondents assigned a mean probability of .87 to the phrase "very likely" and a mean probability of .59 to the phrase "somewhat likely." Whatever the exact probabilities to which these terms correspond, this literature indicates that such phrases imply a greater likelihood of hire than not. Remember that employers with greater reservations about the applicant also had the option of "somewhat unlikely" to indicate their ambivalence.

Whereas the survey asked employers to rate their likelihood of *hiring* the applicant, the audit merely measured whether the applicant was invited back for an interview or not. Although a call-back may represent a necessary condition to the decision to hire, it is by no means sufficient. In fact, according to the survey results, employers reported interviewing an average of eight

Figure 1   Expressed Willingness to Hire a Drug Offender According to Employer Survey and Audit

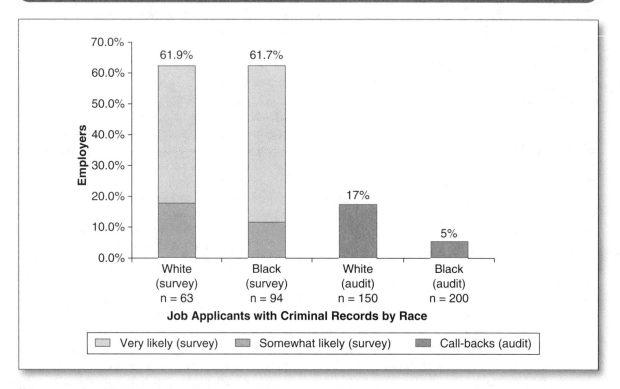

Note: Survey results include employers who said they were "very likely" or "somewhat likely" to hire the hypothetical applicant (with "very" at bottom of columns). Audit results represent the percentage of call-backs for each group. Differences between within-race comparisons of survey and audit results are significant on the basis of a two-sample test proportions ($p < .05$).

applicants for the last noncollege job they had filled. Furthermore, employers on average reported interviewing 55 percent of the applicants that applied (Pager, 2002). Although these self-reported estimates may be inflated, they provide some evidence that the interview stage is far from synonymous with a hire. Rather, a call-back may in fact represent a fairly low bar of approval.

Thus, despite the different metrics on which our measures are based, we believe they provide roughly comparable indications of interest in the applicant, corresponding to a moderately favorable review. In the results presented later, we provide an analysis of individual-level correlations that should be unaffected by these concerns.

A second possible objection to this comparison is that the very framing of the vignette item may artificially exaggerate the difference between survey and audit results. When considering a hypothetical applicant, employers do not have to take into account alternative possibilities among the applicant pool. Thus the hypothetical applicant may exceed the minimum threshold for acceptability even if in actuality there tend to be other applicants who are better qualified. By contrast, the tester in the audit study is competing with a pool of real applicants of varying quality. To the extent that real applicants provide better qualifications than does the tester's profile, the tester will receive few call-backs for reasons unrelated to race or criminal record.

An alternative way of presenting the information that addresses this concern is to calculate the likelihood that a tester with a criminal record will receive a call-back *relative to* a white tester without a criminal record. White testers without criminal records in this case represent a kind of baseline, presenting a given set of qualifications common among all testers, but without the handicaps of minority status or a criminal record. Employers who made callbacks to white testers without criminal records signaled that this level of education and experience was sufficiently desirable to make the first cut. Relative to this baseline, we can assess the proportion of blacks and whites with criminal records who received call-backs, thereby reducing the effect of employer nonresponses attributable to extraneous factors.[8]

Figure 2 displays the results of this procedure, comparing the likelihood of hire based on the survey and audit results with audit results recalculated as a ratio of the percentage of testers in the offender condition who received call-backs to the percentage of white testers with identical qualifications but no criminal background who received call-backs. Overall, 34 percent of white applicants with no criminal records, and with the given set of human capital characteristics presented by all testers, received call-backs. This group serves as our baseline (denominator) for calculating the relative call-back rates for the other groups. Only 17 percent of white testers with identical characteristics plus a criminal record received call-backs, indicating that white testers with a criminal record were 50 percent as likely to receive call-backs as those without

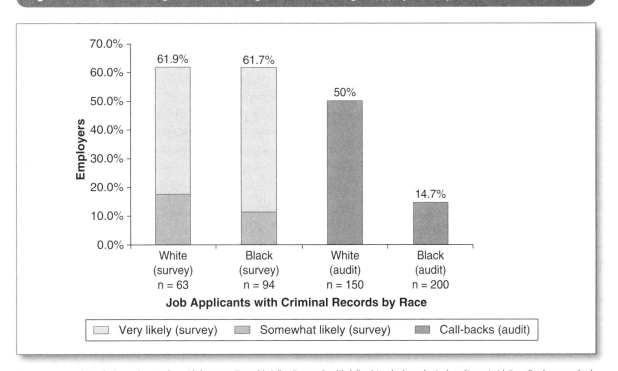

Figure 2   Expressed Willingness to Hire a Drug Offender According to Employer Survey and Recalibrated Audit

Note: Survey results include employers who said they were "very likely" or "somewhat likely" to hire the hypothetical applicant (with "very" at bottom of columns). Audit results represent the ratio of the percentage of call-backs for each group to the percentage of call-backs for white nonoffenders. Differences in within-race comparisons of survey and audit results are marginally significant for white applicants ($p < .06$) and significant for black applicants ($p < .05$) on the basis of a two-sample test of proportions.

a criminal record (Figure 2). Black ex-offenders were the least likely to continue in the employment process—only 5 percent received call-backs—indicating that they were just less than 15 percent as likely to receive a call-back as a similar white tester without a criminal record.

The differences between self-reports and behaviors in this comparison, although smaller, remain consistent when call-back frequency is judged relative to that for white nonoffenders. In the case of white ex-offenders, the distance between the survey and audit results has narrowed substantially, although it remains marginally significant statistically. The case for black applicants, on the other hand, maintains a clear and dramatic difference. Even relative to contemporaneous call-back rates for white testers, the call-back rate for black ex-offenders (14.7) remains far short of the survey estimates of hiring likelihoods (61.7). For black ex-offenders, the survey and audit measures provide dramatically different indications of willingness to hire.

Whatever measure is used, two main findings remain clear: First, whereas the survey responses present a rather benign view of the employment barriers facing ex-offenders, the audit results tell a very different story. Employers indicate a high level of willingness to hire drug offenders, but in actual employment situations, they are less than half as likely even to call back such applicants relative to those without criminal records. This result underscores the importance of using great caution in relying on employers' self-reports as an accurate reflection of behavior.

Second, the degree to which race is a factor in hiring decisions is virtually undetectable in the survey results, in sharp contrast to what we find in the audit study. Table 1 shows the relative risk of receiving a call-back for white and black applicants in the survey and audit. In the survey, although separate employers were asked the vignette in which the hypothetical applicant was white or black, the estimates of hiring likelihoods for both applicants were virtually identical.[9] By contrast, actual behavioral measures in the audit show that white ex-offenders are more than three times as likely to receive consideration from employers as black

ex-offenders.[10] These results suggest that employer surveys, even those with split-ballot designs, do not always provide an effective way to gauge the degree to which sensitive characteristics such as race affect actual employment opportunities. Later, we discuss the methodological and theoretical processes that might account for these differences.

Finally, we turn to the issue of individual-level consistency between survey reports and audit results. Even if the levels of openness to hiring ex-offenders are inconsistent between survey and audit, it remains possible that a *correlation* exists between the two: Employers who indicate willingness to hire ex-offenders may be more likely to hire an ex-offender than employers who do not indicate such willingness, even if the overall openness to hiring ex-offenders is strongly overstated in the survey results. This final analysis allows us to compare the survey responses with the audit outcomes at an individual rather than an aggregate level. The results of this cross-tabulation are presented in Table 2.[11] Consistent with the results reported earlier, we find that the survey responses have very little connection to the actual behaviors exhibited by these employers.

Among those who reported a favorable likelihood of hiring an applicant with a prior drug conviction in the survey, 7.3 percent made calls to the tester with the criminal record in the audit study, relative to 6.7 percent of those expressing an unfavorable likelihood. This difference is in the expected direction, but is only slightly greater than zero (0.6 percent), and far too small to reach statistical significance. Likewise, correlational measures for ordinal data, such as Kendall's Tau-b, show nearly zero association between survey and audit.[12] Considering the possibility that our relatively small sample size limits the reliability of these estimates, we calculate confidence intervals allowing us to assess the potential relationship that would obtain if we had used a larger sample. A 95 percent confidence interval for the difference in percentages includes a range from −8.6 to 8.8 percent, indicating that we are 95 percent confident that employers who indicate "yes" are no more than 8.8 percentage points more likely to make a call-back than employers who indicate "no."[13] A difference of 8.8 percentage points for making a

---

Table 1	Comparison of the Influence of Race on Hiring: Audit Versus Survey

Relative Willingness to Hire	Survey	Audit
White vs. Black (White/Black)	1.00	3.33
95% CI	(.78, 1.29)	(1.65, 6.73)

Note: The difference in white/black ratios between the survey and audit is statistically significant at $p < .001$ (Mantel-Haenszel test, $\chi^2 = 12.01$, 1 df).

Table 2	Individual-level Consistency Between Employers' Self-Reports and Behavioral Outcomes

Survey Results	Audit Results (for Testers Presenting Drug Felony)	
	No Call-Back	Call-Back
Likely to Hire Drug Offender		
No	56	4
	(93.3%)	(6.7%)
Yes	89	7
	(92.7%)	(7.3%)
Difference of Percentages		0.6%
(95% CI)		(−8.6%, 8.8%)
Correlation (Kendall's Tau-b)		.012
(95% CI)		(−.143, .167)

Note: This table includes all employers who responded to the survey. Call-backs in the right column above represent calls to the tester in the criminal record condition only.

call-back still is a fairly low level of correlational consistency.[14] We can thus be fairly confident that, given this pattern of results, even a much larger sample would be unlikely to produce a substantial relationship between survey and audit results.

These results cast strong doubt on the accuracy of survey data for indicating relative likelihoods of hiring. Individuals who report a higher likelihood of hiring an ex-offender are only trivially more likely to do so.

Confirming the aggregate findings described earlier, the individual-level associations presented here appear to be no better at establishing a relationship between attitudes and behaviors.

Nevertheless, several limitations of this analysis must temper its conclusions. In the following discussion, we consider possible threats to the validity of our findings caused by measurement error or study design. In the first case, we consider the possibility for error in the survey or audit results, either of which could lead to a weakened correlation between the two.

In the case of the survey, the most plausible source of measurement error arises from those cases in which the survey respondent was different from the individual who reviewed the testers' applications. To the extent that hiring practices vary within firms depending on the individual manager or human resource officer, the consistency between survey and audit results will be attenuated. Although recent evidence suggests that labor market discrimination typically operates at the level of the firm rather than the level of individual discriminatory actors,[15] this possibility remains a potential source of measurement error. Nevertheless, although within-firm heterogeneity may indeed affect the individual-level consistency in measures of attitudes and behavior, there should be no effect on the average level of support for hiring ex-offenders in the aggregate (as presented in Figures 1 and 2). In cases wherein respondents differ, there is little reason to believe that the hiring agent would be systematically more or less likely to consider hiring ex-offenders than would the survey respondent.[16]

In the audit study, measurement error also may pose a problem. Because each employer was visited only once, we have only one data point with which to assess their hiring tendencies. Given the many factors at play in any given hiring situation (e.g., the urgency with which the position must be filled, the number and quality of other applicants), any single data point representing an employer's treatment of an ex-offender may be subject to the measurement error of circumstance.[17] Nevertheless, the almost complete absence of association between survey and audit measures leads us to question random error as a sufficient explanation. If the hiring process tends to be so complex as to defy any straightforward relationship between the abstract intentions of employers and their ultimate decisions, this would imply more than a simple problem of measurement. Indeed, we later discuss the complexity of hiring decisions as one of our hypothesized explanations for the discrepancy between outcomes.

More systematic forms of error can creep into an audit design if the experimental procedures are somehow compromised. Of primary concern are the potential biases that can be caused by the performance of testers, either because of poor matching or because of testers' self-fulfilling expectations (Heckman and Seligman 1993). Fortunately, a rather direct test of this hypothesis is possible. One would expect that if differences in testers' personalities or behavior shaped the outcomes (above and beyond any effects of race or criminal condition), we should see stronger results among those cases in which the testers had the opportunity to interact with employers. Applications submitted with little or no personal contact should be far less affected by such concerns. Analyzing the outcomes for these two kinds of tests, we find no evidence of tester bias. In fact, the main effects of both race and criminal background are substantially attenuated among those who did have personal contact with the employer (Pager 2003). This suggests that instead of exaggerating negative stereotypes, the appealing characteristics of these testers actually worked to reduce the measured effects, thus biasing the results in a direction consistent with the survey responses. It is unlikely then that these various sources of error can account for the significant disconnect between the survey and audit results.

A final limitation of the comparison provided earlier is its reliance on a single survey item. Flaws in the survey design or peculiarities of the question wording could lead to anomalous patterns of responses. Fortunately, an additional item was included in the survey that allows for similar comparisons to be drawn. Whereas the vignette most strongly paralleled the audit situation—including a match of the applicant's race—the second item also probed employers' willingness to consider hiring ex-offenders, in this case focusing on a generic applicant with a criminal record. The exact wording of this item was "Next, I am going to list several types of applicants. Please tell me if you would accept each type for the [most recent noncollege] position . . . an applicant who has a criminal record?" As described earlier, we compare those who answered that they "definitely" or "probably" will hire with those who answered "definitely" or "probably" not in relation to the audit outcomes.[18] The correlation between this measure and the audit results is again very small. The correlation coefficient from Kendall's

Tau-b is .0003 (95 percent confidence interval, −.154 to .155). Again, our tests for significance in this case cannot reject the hypothesis of no relationship.

The various aforementioned limitations must certainly temper our conclusions. Nevertheless, the almost total lack of correlation between the survey and audit results is troubling. If these findings are an accurate assessment of the level of consistency for these and related measures, then studies that use similar survey items to draw conclusions about characteristics or circumstances associated with discrimination may come to strongly misleading conclusions.

On the basis of several methods for assessing the attitude-behavior relationship, all comparisons tell a similar story: it is difficult to get an accurate picture of actual hiring outcomes based on responses to the employer survey used in this study. Employers generally express a greater likelihood of hiring applicants with criminal records, and a far greater likelihood in the case of black applicants, than we see in actuality. Furthermore, employers who indicate greater willingness to hire an ex-offender in response to a survey question seem to be only slightly more likely actually to offer an interview to such an applicant. Both in terms of making aggregate- and individual-level predictions, our evidence points to weak correspondence between survey results and actual hiring outcomes.

◈ Attitudes and Behaviors: Why Do They Differ?

Why might employers' survey responses present results so discrepant from their actual behavior? Several theoretical explanations could be used to account for this incongruity. In this section, we provide a discussion of these explanations, considering the range of underlying processes that may give rise to differing outcomes.

Social Desirability and Compensatory Estimation

As discussed earlier, efforts to measure attitudes about sensitive topics are complicated by the problems of social desirability bias. According to this perspective,

respondents may conceal their true feelings about blacks or ex-offenders in answering survey questions. If this is the case, the discrepancy between self-reports and behaviors should be viewed as the difference between false and true measures of a respondent's attitudes. Although social desirability pressures certainly result in some distortion of survey results, we do not believe that this can account fully for the differences between expressed willingness to hire ex-offenders and the actual employment outcomes based on applicants' criminal record. In fact, at other points in the survey, respondents expressed strong opposition to considering applicants with criminal records other than drug felonies: nearly 70 percent of employers expressed an unwillingness to hire an applicant who had been convicted of a property crime, and more than 75 percent were self-described as unwilling to hire an applicant who had been convicted of a violent crime (Pager, 2002; see also Holzer, Raphael, and Stoll 2003).[19] It therefore seems unlikely that social (or legal) pressures to accept ex-offenders whitewashed employer responses. High levels of acceptance were reported only for the applicant described as a drug felon.

Social desirability bias may be a greater concern in the measurement of racial preferences from the survey results, which is where we find the largest disparities between expressed attitudes and observed behaviors. To preempt this concern in the current study, we used a split-ballot format in which each employer responded to only one hypothetical (black or white) candidate. It remains possible, however, that social desirability bias is a problem if, even in the absence of direct comparisons by race, employers are aware that the race of the hypothetical applicant has been specified and therefore make conscious or unconscious efforts to compensate verbally for any negative reactions they may have to a black applicant. If respondents do in fact suppress negative reactions to race-specific targets, even when no racial comparison is provided, this calls into question the effectiveness of split-ballot survey designs as a strategy for measuring underlying racial prejudice. Any self-reported attitude toward a black target may in fact be distorted by the respondent's own compensatory estimation procedure.

Abstract Versus Specific Considerations

A second possible explanation for the discrepancy between measured attitudes and behaviors in this study relates to differences in the criteria used to evaluate a hypothetical versus an actual job candidate. It is plausible that the affirmative responses of employers considering the acceptability of a hypothetical applicant indicate their genuine willingness to consider hiring an applicant with a criminal record *in the abstract*. In these general terms, apart from the minority of employers who categorically reject all applicants with criminal records, a prior conviction is not typically grounds for immediate disqualification. Rather, if the applicant's overall characteristics exceed a minimum threshold of employability, the respondent is likely to indicate a willingness to hire.

By contrast, in actual employment situations, the applicant's characteristics are judged not only according to some minimum threshold, but also relative to the pool of available applicants, and to the specific requirements of a job. In this case, many more contingencies are at play, and the presence of a criminal record may become a salient criterion by which to weed out less-qualified applicants.[20] Even if the employer genuinely believes that she or he would hire the applicant described in the abstract vignette, when confronted with the situation in real life, the contingencies of the hiring process may render hypothetical scenarios irrelevant.

Recognizing this potential disconnect, we made efforts to calibrate the behavioral responses to a concrete indicator of employability at that place and time. In this case, the white nonoffender, our baseline in Figure 2, serves this function by providing assurance that this level of qualification was sufficient to elicit a callback during that particular hiring process. Despite this adjustment, the willingness to hire expressed in the survey appears to be much higher than in the audit. Even if differences between the exact vignette and the audit situations can explain some of the discrepancies between survey and audit measures of overall willingness to hire, this explanation cannot account for the considerable difference in race effects detected by these comparisons. In the survey, black and white applicants appear equally likely to receive offers, whereas in the audit, there is a large gap in favor of white applicants. An investigator using these survey data alone would be strongly misled about the role of race in shaping actual hiring decisions.

The Intensity of Priming

A third perspective on the discrepancy between self-reports and behaviors proposes that the priming of characteristics during a phone interview may not elicit the same intensity of response as the in-person presentation of the same characteristics. Hearing a description of a hypothetical black ex-offender is quite different from seeing a young black man approach one's business in search of employment. The live interaction may trigger feelings of fear, anxiety, or threat in ways that a recited vignette does not (Poskocil 1977). These feelings may then influence employment decisions in ways that cannot be fully replicated in hypothetical scenarios in surveys.

Similarly, social psychological evidence suggests that racial stereotypes exert many of their effects indirectly, by coloring the evaluation of ambiguous information (Darley and Gross 1983). When employers are evaluating applicants, for example, an energetic, outgoing, young white applicant may be viewed as motivated and eager to work, whereas a similarly energetic, outgoing, young black male may be seen as a hustler or a "player." Even relatively straightforward cues can be interpreted in vastly different ways, depending on the context of the situation or the characteristics of the actor (Sagar and Schofield 1980). Again, these sorts of distortions would most likely operate during in-person evaluations. The vignette, by contrast, leaves less room for distorted interpretations, because according to the explicit description, the hypothetical candidate "has good references and interacts well with people." This class of explanations suggests that discriminatory behavior in the employment of ex-offenders, especially African-Americans, may have a basis in sources other than consciously believed attitudes toward these groups.

In the article discussed earlier, LaPiere (1934) reinforces the view that surveys may elicit a different set of considerations than do concrete experiences. According to LaPiere, survey responses constitute "verbalized reaction[s] to a symbolic situation," or reactions to a highly abstracted representation of reality (p. 231). According to this viewpoint, survey responses do tell us something meaningful about the attitudes of respondents, but we have no way of anticipating the degree to which these expressed attitudes will be reflected in any particular set of behaviors. Certainly, it is difficult to anticipate how any individual, including oneself, may react to a situation previously encountered only in hypothetical terms. In the case of hiring decisions about individuals with stigmatizing characteristics, our results suggest that very little can be implied from these self-reports of employers for the accurate prediction of employment outcomes.

It is not possible using the current data to demonstrate conclusively which underlying process may have generated the observed discrepancies. In fact, it is highly plausible that more than one process may have been at work simultaneously. What these results do demonstrate, however, is that employers' expressed willingness in the survey taps into a set of processes very different from those measured through our behavioral study. Although these processes may be related to a common underlying disposition, the correspondence between the two can be quite weak. It is important that researchers recognize these limitations before drawing inferences about behavior from the self-reports of survey respondents.

Rethinking the Role of Attitudes

What can we conclude from these results regarding the usefulness of data on attitudes? Should we disregard all employers' self-reports? Certainly, it would be premature to advise such a radical stance. In fact, despite the large discrepancies between the self-reports and behaviors measured in the current study, we believe that survey results remain useful, even if they cannot be viewed as an alternative procedure to the measurement of actual discrimination.

Even in cases in which expressed attitudes have little relationship to measured discrimination, survey data can nevertheless tell us something useful about how employers *think* about important hiring issues. Responses to the survey suggest, for instance, that many employers who discriminate against blacks do not necessarily do so because of a principled belief that black employees should not be hired. In fact, we think it likely that many employers genuinely believe their own responses to surveys, professing the value of equal opportunity, while simultaneously justifying their behavior in hiring situations on grounds other than race (e.g., assumptions about the family/social/educational backgrounds of black applicants; see Kirschenman and Neckerman 1991). In this case, the difference between employers' self-reports and their actual behavior represents a meaningful discrepancy between two legitimate realities. The resolution of these differences represents an important focus of sociological investigation in its own right. Although low correlations between attitudes and associated behaviors often are viewed as a purely methodological test of survey questions, in many cases, these discrepancies actually may provide clues toward a better substantive understanding of the cognitive-emotional basis for action.

Furthermore, it remains possible that survey research may provide a better proxy for behavior in situations that are less complex and subject to fewer contextual influences than hiring. Action in any real social situation is the result of many factors other than the actor's attitude toward the object, including norms, perceived consequences of the action, and implicit or unconscious attitudes toward the object. The many complex influences on hiring decisions make these situations exactly the sort for which survey measures are least likely to be an effective substitute. Indeed, the three "classic" studies that found very weak associations between expressed behavioral intentions and behaviors all were studies of discrimination in social situations (Kutner et al. 1952; LaPiere 1934; Saenger and Gilbert 1950). We believe it possible that survey responses may provide a much more effective proxy for behavior in other contexts, such as those that involve voting (Traugott and Katosh 1979), signing of a petition (Brannon et al. 1973), or patterns of consumer behavior (Day et al. 1991), in which the link between behavioral intentions and actual behavior is less subject to contextual influences apart from the respondent's attitude or intention.

Finally, we have focused on only a few of the many survey techniques that have been developed to measure prejudice and discrimination. Though our measure of behavioral intentions was designed to offer the closest match to the audit context, it remains possible that other more abstracted measures of racial bias may in fact correlate more closely with measures of discrimination. There is an extensive literature that attempts to investigate modern or subtle forms of racial attitudes using survey questions (National Research Council 2004, chapter 8), and certain of these alternative approaches could prove more effective at capturing behavioral outcomes than what we found in this study.

Three sociological approaches that we believe to be especially promising place their respective emphasis on stereotype measurement, past behavior, and in-depth interviews. The first of these, group stereotype measurement, has a long history in the social sciences, with research demonstrating a persistence of racialized attributions across numerous dimensions (Devine and Elliot 1995). As a recent example, researchers have developed a series of scales measuring respondents' images of different racial groups along a wide range of social and psychological characteristics (Bobo and Kluegel 1997; Smith 1991). Survey techniques such as these have shown respondents to rate blacks as worse or inferior relative to other groups on dimensions such as criminality and intelligence, suggesting that traditional measures of racial attitudes may be missing a great deal of underlying racial bias.

A second approach, used extensively by Harry Holzer and colleagues, asks employers to focus on the last worker hired, thereby grounding responses in a concrete recent experience (Holzer 1996; Holzer, Raphael, and Stoll 2003). By focusing on a completed action, Holzer is able to avoid the ambiguities of hypotheticals or general statements; and by focusing on actual outcomes, he is able to document "revealed preferences" rather than expressed ones. Likewise, Holzer's format calls for race to be assessed only as one incidental characteristic in a larger series of questions concerning the recent employee, thereby reducing the social desirability bias often triggered when the subject of race is highlighted. Whereas recall or motivational biases emerge as concerns in the reporting of prior experiences (Bradburn, Rips, and Shevell 1987), this particular approach focuses on a well-defined event that leaves less room for error-prone estimation.

Finally, some data suggest that in-depth in-person interviews may be more effective in eliciting candid discussions about sensitive hiring issues than other modes of interviews (Kirschenman and Neckerman 1991; Moss and Tilly 2003; Wilson 1996). In-depth interviews offer the opportunity for respondents to discuss the complexities and, at times, the inconsistencies in their views of various groups, thereby going beyond the more generalized assessments expressed in traditional survey items. Likewise, the opportunity for rapport-building in the in-person interview context may reduce social desirability pressures, making respondents feel at greater ease in expressing counter-normative beliefs.[21]

Although each of these represents a promising approach, our results caution against the unreflective assumption that the results of any method are necessarily good proxies for behavior. None of these techniques has yet been subjected to direct assessments by comparison of their responses with corresponding behavioral measures, a step we view as necessary for understanding the relation of these measures to behavioral outcomes. LaPiere's (1934) warning, that hypothetical scenarios often cannot convey the experience of concrete situations, deserves to be taken more seriously by current generations of survey and interview researchers.

◈ Conclusion

LaPiere (1934) showed a striking inconsistency in the way hotel and restaurant proprietors reacted to Chinese customers in person, as compared with how they responded in surveys. The current study notes a similar discrepancy between employers' self-reported likelihood of hiring a particular applicant and their actual hiring behaviors when faced with a nearly identical candidate. We found an especially large and robust disparity between the reported likelihood of employers hiring black ex-offenders and actual rates of hiring. The low correlation between expressed and observed hiring outcomes presents an epistemological worry: our assessments of the degree of disadvantage faced by black ex-offenders would be substantially underestimated on the basis of the survey results alone. Moreover, we found little correlation between greater expressed likelihood of hiring ex-offenders in the survey and actual increased rates of call-backs for ex-offenders in real hiring situations. Given that most research on hiring preferences and practices comes from the self-reports of employers themselves (Downing 1984; Holzer 1996; Husley 1990; Jensen and Giegold 1976; Waldinger and Lichter 2003; Wilson 1996), these results indeed have serious implications.

In terms of the methods used to measure discrimination, these findings suggest that sociologists may need to reevaluate what is learned from studies that use vignettes of hypothetical situations to study behaviors toward stigmatized groups. Although we believe that these vignette studies often do tell us about respondents' abstract beliefs, in some cases these beliefs may have relatively little influence on the behavior of interest. Feelings and evaluations in a concrete social situation may be very different from those in the abstracted situation of the survey, but the two often are treated as nearly identical. An important next step in evaluating the contribution of survey measures for understanding behaviors of interest is to relate these items to actual behavior.

More broadly, these results suggest the limits of survey questions alone for understanding the changing nature of racial inequality. Survey questions indicating a liberalizing of racial attitudes among white Americans have been cited widely as evidence supporting the declining significance of race in American society. But if the items analyzed in this study have any bearing on survey responses more generally, we have reason to

question that changing public opinion on matters of race has any necessary correspondence to the incidence of discrimination. Rather, our results support the perspective that there has been a growing gap between the principled statements and beliefs of white Americans in favor of racial equality and their concrete actions.[22] Survey questions provide one important perspective on American race relations, but they must be combined with other information for a complete picture.

Fortunately, methods to improve our understanding of the prejudice–discrimination relationship are readily available and feasible for even small groups of researchers. The comparison of survey measures and behavioral indicators does not require an unprecedented level of resources. Even for pedagogical purposes, sociology teachers could readily incorporate the dual design within a two-semester timetable. Whereas audit studies of labor markets can be quite involved, numerous other everyday social settings provide countless opportunities for implementing small-scale experiments: searching for an apartment, shopping, hailing a taxi, passing security checkpoints, and the like (for an example of a classroom application of the audit methodology, see Massey and Lundy 2001). Moreover, the investigation of prejudice and discrimination could be usefully applied to many other groups: Asians, Latinos, Muslims, women with criminal records, gays and lesbians, to name just a few.

For creative sociology teachers, then, a single class could readily achieve a paired audit study and telephone survey with sufficient sample sizes for meaningful comparisons. Both substantively and methodologically, the pairing of survey and audit research can yield important insights for the study of contemporary discrimination.

It is not the case that employers' thoughts and beliefs can tell us nothing about important employment issues. In fact, in many cases, surveys and other methods of eliciting employer opinions can provide useful information about attitudes and beliefs. In other cases, surveys may provide a very close reflection of actual employer behaviors. What this research emphasizes, however, is the importance of testing one's assumptions and providing external validation of key results. In the case of employers' behavior with respect to hiring black ex-offenders, the survey results presented here are far off base. The correspondence between self-reports and behaviors with respect to other important hiring outcomes has yet to be established.

◈ Appendix A

Survey Design and Implementation

The baseline survey instrument was developed by Harry Holzer and his colleagues.[23] It includes questions about the company such as size, industry, employee turnover, and racial composition; questions about hiring procedures such as the use of interviews, personality or aptitude tests, and background checks; questions about the last worker hired for a position not requiring a college degree including age, race, and sex of the worker, recruitment method, wage, and promotion opportunities; and questions concerning the employer's attitudes about various kinds of applicants including welfare recipients, applicants with long spells out of the labor market, unstable work histories, or criminal records. In addition, several survey items were added to mirror the audit study more closely (as described earlier).

The survey was administered by the Michigan State Survey Center. The final survey sample included 199 respondents, representing a 58 percent response rate. Response rates were calculated according to the basic formula $(I + P)/(I + P + R)$, where I equals the number of completed interviews, P equals the number of partial interviews, and R represents the number of refused eligible numbers (Groves and Lyberg, 1988). Between the time of the audit and that of the survey, two companies had declared bankruptcy, and an additional two had nonfunctioning numbers. These firms were dropped from the survey sample and excluded from the denominator for calculations of response rates.

Typical response rates for academic telephone surveys range from 50 to 80 percent. The current survey falls toward the lower end of the range of acceptable response rates as the result of several possible factors. Response rates for surveys of top management and organizational representatives typically lag behind those of employees or the general population (Baruch 1999).

Likewise, there has been increasing resistance of businesses to participation in surveys, given the proliferation of market research firms and academics seeking employer participation for the growing number of studies involving businesses (Remington 1992). There has been a notable downward trajectory in the response rates from business surveys over the past 25 years (Baruch 1999; Cox et al. 1995), with increasing numbers of refusals citing that participation was against company policy (Fenton-O'Creevy 1996, cited in Baruch 1999). Even among the general population, Curtin, Presser, and Singer (2000) reported that the number of calls required to complete an average interview and the proportion of interviews requiring refusal conversion doubled between 1979 and 1996. The inundation of telemarketers (and, to a lesser extent, survey research) matched by the technological advances of caller-ID and privacy managers has made it increasingly difficult to recruit survey respondents for academic research (Remington 1992).

To assess the possible bias that may result from selective participation, two comparison tests were made. The first test compared basic characteristics of employers who responded to the survey with the characteristics of those eligible for participation but refused. On the basis of industry, location, and call-back rates, the two groups were very similar, although some differences in occupational distribution were apparent: employers for restaurant jobs were the most likely to respond to the survey, whereas employers for laborer or service positions were the least likely. This difference probably has to do with the accessibility of employers in locally run restaurants, as compared with those in decentralized factories, warehouses, or companies. In an effort to account for this overrepresentation, key outcomes are recalculated using weights to achieve the sample distribution of the audit study (available upon request). A reweighting of the survey sample to match the distribution of the audit sample produced only a slight change in the mean likelihood (from .62 to .60). It is unlikely, therefore, that differential response rates of employers across industries have any effect on the survey outcomes or on the differences between survey responses and observed behavior.

Even without these adjustments, however, the distribution of responses on key attitude items closely matches that for a previous sample of Milwaukee employers. In a second test of sample bias, basic employer characteristics from the current sample were compared with an identical set of questions asked of a more representative sample of Milwaukee employers in 1999 (Holzer and Stoll 2001). Although the earlier Milwaukee survey included a broader geographic area and oversampled large firms, the general attitudes expressed by employers in both samples were strikingly similar (Table A1). The consistency of these findings provides some reassurance that the current sample can serve as a useful gauge for the priorities and concerns of employers in the broader Milwaukee metropolitan area.

Table A1 Comparison of Employer Attitudes and Characteristics Across Two Milwaukee Surveys

Variable	Pager 2002	Holzer and Stoll 2001
Employees (n)	66.95	180.47
Vacancies (n)	4.48	7.79
Minority-owned Companies (%)	8.40	8.41
Unionized Employees (%)	9.30	15.19
Industry		
Manufacturing (%)	12.43	20.00
Retail trade (%)	49.72	21.00
Services (%)	21.47	39.00
Other industry (%)	16.38	20.00
Hire Welfare Recipient		
Definitely/probably would (%)	97.40	96.62
Definitely/probably not (%)	2.60	3.37
Hire Applicant with GED		
Definitely/probably would (%)	98.80	97.23
Definitely/probably not (%)	1.20	2.77
Hire Applicant with Criminal Record		
Definitely/probably would (%)	49.20	49.20
Definitely/probably not (%)	50.80	50.80

(Continued)

Table A1 (Continued)

Variable	Pager 2002	Holzer and Stoll 2001
Hire Applicant Unemployed ? 1 year		
Definitely/probably would (%)	70.90	80.15
Definitely/probably not (%)	29.00	19.86
Hire Applicant with Unstable Work History		
Definitely/probably would (%)	60.50	67.49
Definitely/probably not (%)	39.50	32.51

Note: GED = General Education Diploma.

◈ Appendix B

Table B1 Comparison of Employers' Self-Reports and Behavioral Outcomes for Overlapping Sample

Survey Results	Audit Results	
	No Call-Back	Call-Back
Likely to Hire Drug Offender		
Very Unlikely	31	1
	(96.9%)	(3.1%)
Somewhat Unlikely	25	3
	(88.3%)	(10.7%)
Somewhat Likely	69	5
	(93.2)	(6.8)
Very Likely	20	2
	(90.9 %)	(9.1 %)

Note: N = 99 respondents. Data shown as number of respondents with percent in parentheses.

◈ Notes

1. As the name implies, split-ballot designs commonly use two experimental groups. More recent work has taken advantage of computer-assisted telephone interviewing to extend this design to include many more variations in survey questions, including variation across multiple dimensions (see Sniderman and Grob 1996 for a review).

2. Laboratory studies have found that whites behave more aggressively toward blacks than toward other whites, but only when the consequences to the aggressor are low, such as when acting under conditions of anonymity, or in situations with limited possibility of retaliation or punishment (Crosby et al. 1980).

3. Prejudice refers to negative judgments or opinions about a group (attitudes). Discrimination refers to unfavorable treatment directed toward members of a group (behavior).

4. Jobs were randomly selected from ads placed in the Sunday classified section of the *Milwaukee Journal Sentinel* and on Jobnet, a state-sponsored Internet job site. Entry-levels jobs are defined as those requiring no more than a high school degree and limited work experience. Testers were 23-year-old college students from Milwaukee chosen for their effective styles of self-presentation and for their comparability in terms of physical and interpersonal attributes.

5. The tester pair rotated which member presented himself as the ex-offender for each successive week of employment searches, such that each tester served in the criminal record condition for an equal number of cases. By varying which member of the pair presented himself as having a criminal record, unobserved differences within the pairs of applicants were effectively controlled. The criminal record used in all cases was a felony drug conviction. Although the more general term "ex-offenders" is used in reference to this group, it is important to note that the relationship between attitudes and behaviors may differ for individuals convicted of different crimes.

6. The length of sentence was varied moderately between survey and audit to avoid arousing suspicion.

7. Call-back rates include all the employers from the audit study, even those who did not complete the survey. Including only respondents captured in both samples produces even more disparate results. Call-back rates for white and black ex-offenders in the overlapping sample are 14 and 3 percent, respectively, demonstrating an even greater distance from the survey results.

8. Similarly, we can consider the proportion of employers who reported that they were likely to hire an ex-offender (61.9 or 61.7 percent) as relative to an implicit baseline of 100 percent for a hypothetical applicant similar to the one described in the vignette, but without a criminal record. To the extent that some employers would report it not likely that they would hire such an applicant (if, for example, they hire only applicants with college experience), the

ratio of the self-reported likelihoods of hiring an ex-offender relative to a nonoffender would be even larger, thus rendering the contrast between the self-reports and behavioral outcomes even greater.

9. Even if we were to restrict our attention to the "very likely" category, the black–white ratio (1.5) still would vastly understate the degree of racial disparity apparent in the audit.

10. This result is calculated as a ratio of the call-back rate for white drug offenders (25/150) relative to the call-back rate for black drug offenders (10/200).

11. The percentage of call-backs is lower than for the aggregate comparisons because of survey nonresponse. A full breakdown of survey responses (including all four survey response categories) by audit results is presented in Appendix B. Given the small sample sizes in this final comparison, a further breakdown by race of the tester would be impossible. Analyses, therefore, include all call-backs to testers in the criminal record condition regardless of race.

12. The individual-level comparison further allows us to reconsider the practice of combining "very" and "somewhat" likely responses into a single category. To investigate this question, we recalculated Kendall's Tau-b between the audit call-backs and the vignette question using the four survey answers, with separate "very" and "somewhat" categories. Instead of producing stronger results, this coefficient is not statistically significant, and the negative sign is opposite that expected (Tau-b = −.0391).

13. This confidence interval is calculated using the "plus 4" method of Agresti and Caffo (2000). The Agresti and Caffo method has the advantage of providing accurate (and slightly conservative) intervals even when the count of successes or failures is very small. By contrast, the methods in standard introductory statistics books usually require at least five successes and failures for each group.

14. Similarly, the upper limit of the 95 percent confidence interval for Kendall's Tau-b suggests that the degree of correlational consistency in a large sample probably would be quite low (below .167). The confidence interval for Kendall's Tau-b is asymptotic, and thus should be regarded with more caution than the confidence interval for the proportion, which is computed by a method with good small-sample properties.

15. Recent studies have found that firm-level variables such as the presence of a human resource apparatus, the use of applicant tests, and affirmative action policies have far more influence on the racial composition of a company than the individual characteristics of hiring managers or owners (Holzer 1996; Holzer and Neumark 2000).

16. One might also question whether possible changes in the economic climate at the time of each measurement may be responsible for some of the disparity. The unemployment rate in Milwaukee averaged 4.8 percent during the time of the audit, whereas in the 2 months during which the survey was administered, it had risen to nearly 6 percent (Bureau of Labor Statistics 2002). Given that employers' openness to less desirable workers increases in the context of tight

labor markets (Freeman and Rodgers 1999), we would rather expect more favorable responses from employers during the period of the audit study relative to the period of survey data collection.

17. As in the case of the survey, measurement error in the audit results will attenuate individual-level associations, as presented in Table 2, but should not affect the aggregate comparisons presented in Figures 1 and 2.

18. In the original survey, 25 percent of the respondents gave the response "it depends." As a conservative estimate, these respondents were treated as "willing to hire," producing a stronger correlation than when they are excluded from the analysis. In fact, the association of survey and audit becomes slightly negative when this category is excluded. (By contrast, the correlation coefficient from Kendall's Tau-b for this survey item and the original vignette item was .55).

19. Questions about specific crime types followed the presentation of the initial vignette described earlier. Employers were asked to report the likelihood of hiring Chad if, instead of a drug crime, he had been convicted of a property crime, such as burglary, or of a violent crime, such as assault. Response categories for property/violent offenders were "very likely" (10/7 percent), "somewhat likely" (21/17 percent), "somewhat unlikely" (32/29 percent), and "very unlikely" (37/47 percent).

20. Indeed, in response to the second more general survey question discussed earlier, when employers were asked about their willingness to hire a generic applicant with a criminal record (with no additional information provided), a large fraction of employers refused the forced-choice response categories, insisting instead that "it depends"—on the crime, on the length of time since the conviction, on the type of job, and numerous other considerations. In this case, then, the employers themselves acknowledged that any estimation given in the abstract would have very little bearing on how they might respond in making an actual hiring decision.

21. For a critique, see National Research Council (2004), p. 175.

22. This perspective has also found support from certain well-designed surveys that manage to capture respondents' contradictory or competing beliefs (Bobo, Kluegel, and Smith 1997; Kinder and Sears 1981).

23. The first version of this survey was developed for the Multi-City Study of Urban Inequality Employer Survey (Holzer 1996). Holzer, Stoll, and Raphael (2002) later modified the initial instrument to focus more closely on applicants with criminal records. The instrument used for the current study was further modified to reflect the priorities of this research project.

◈ References

Agresti, Alan and Brian Caffo. 2000. "Simple and Effective Confidence Intervals for Proportions and Differences of Proportions Result from Adding Two Successes and Two Failures." *American Statistician* 54:280–88.

Ajzen, Icek. 1991. "The Theory of Planned Behavior." *Organizational Behavior and Human Decision Processes* 50:179–211.

——. 2001. "The Nature and Operation of Attitudes." *Annual Review of Psychology* 52:27–58.

Baruch, Yehuda. 1999. "Response Rate in Academic Studies—A Comparative Analysis." *Human Relations* 52:421–38.

Bertrand, Marianne and Sendhil Mullainathan. 2004. "Are Emily and Greg More Employable than Lakisha and Jamal? A Field Experiment on Labor Market Discrimination." *American Economic Review* 94:991–1013.

Bobo, Lawrence, Devon Johnson, and Susan A. Suh. 2000. "Racial Attitudes and Power in the Workplace: Do the Haves Differ from the Have-Nots?" Pp. 491–522 in *Prismatic Metropolis: Inequality in Los Angeles*, edited by Lawrence Bobo, Melvin Oliver, James Johnson Jr., and Abel Valenzuela Jr. New York: Russell Sage Foundation.

Bobo, Lawrence and James Kluegel. 1997. "Status, Ideology, and Dimensions of Whites' Racial Beliefs and Attitudes: Progress and Stagnation." Pp. 93–120 in *Racial Attitudes in the 1990s: Continuity and Change*, edited by Steven A. Tuch and Jack K. Martin. Westport, CT: Praeger.

Bobo, L., J. R. Kluegel, and R. A. Smith. 1997. "Laissez Faire Racism: The Crystallization of a 'Kinder, Gentler' Anti-Black Ideology." Pp. 15–42 in *Racial Attitudes in the 1990s: Continuity and Change*, edited by S. Tuch and J. Martin. Westport, CT: Praeger.

Bonczar, Thomas P. 2003. "Prevalence of Imprisonment in the U.S. Population, 1974–2001." *Bureau of Justice Statistics Special Report.* Washington, DC: U.S. Department of Justice, NCJ 1976.

Bradburn, N. M. 1983. "Response Effects." Pp. 289–328 in *Handbook of Survey Research,* edited by P. Rossi, J. Wright, and A. Anderson. New York: Academic Press.

Bradburn, Norman M., Lance J. Rips, and Steven K. Shevell. 1987. "Answering Autobiographical Questions: The Impact of Memory and Inference on Surveys." *Science* 236:157–61.

Brannon, Robert, Gary Cyphers, Sharlene Hesse, Susan Hesselbart, Roberta Keane, Howard Schuman, Tomas Viccaro, and Diana Wright. 1973. "Attitude and Action: A Field Experiment Jointed to a General Population Survey." *American Sociological Review* 38:625–36.

Bureau of Labor Statistics. 2002. Local Area Unemployment Statistics. (Online Public Data Query). Retrieved March 1, 2003 (http://www .blr.gov/lan/home.htm).

Couch, Kenneth and Mary C. Daly. 2002. "Black-White Wage Inequality in the 1990s: A Decade of Progress." *Economic Inquiry* 40:31–41.

Cox, Brenda G., David A. Binder, B. Nanjamma Chinnappa, Anders Christianson, Michael J. Colledge, and Phillip S. Kott. 1995. *Business Survey Methods.* New York: John Wiley & Sons.

Crandall, C. S. 1994. "Prejudice against Fat People: Ideology and Self-Interest." *Journal of Personality and Social Psychology* 66:882–94.

Crosby, Faye, Stephanie Bromley, and Leonard Saxe. 1980. "Recent Unobtrusive Studies of Black and White Discrimination and Prejudice: A Literature Review." *Psychological Bulletin* 87:546–63.

Curtin, Richard, Stanley Presser, and Eleanor Singer. 2000. "The Effects of Response Rate Changes on the Index of Consumer Sentiment." *Public Opinion Quarterly* 64:413–28.

Darley, J. M. and P. H. Gross. 1983. "A Hypothesis-Confirming Bias in Labeling Effects." *Journal of Personality and Social Psychology* 44:20–33.

Day, Dianne, Boon Gan, Philip Gendall, and Don Esslemont. 1991. "Predicting Purchase Behaviour." *Marketing Bulletin* 2:18–30.

Deutscher, Irwin. 1966. "Words and Deeds: Social Science and Social Policy." *Social Problems* 13:235–54.

Devine, Patricia. 1989. "Stereotypes and Prejudice: Their Automatic and Controlled Components." *Journal of Personality and Social Psychology* 56:5–18.

Devine, P. G. and A. J. Elliot. 1995. "Are Racial Stereotypes Really Fading? The Princeton Trilogy Revisited." *Personality and Social Psychology Bulletin* 21: 1139–50.

Dovidio, John, Kerry Kawakami, and Samuel Gaertner. 2002. "Implicit and Explicit Prejudice and Interracial Interaction." *Journal of Personality and Social Psychology* 82:62–68.

Downing, David. 1984. "Employer Bias toward the Hiring and Placement of Male Ex-Offenders." Ph.D. dissertation, Department of Education, Southern Illinois University, Carbondale, IL.

Emerson, Michael, George Yancey, and Karen Chai. 2001. "Does Race Matter in Residential Segregation? Exploring the Preferences of White Americans." *American Sociological Review* 66:922–35.

Farley, Reynolds. 1997. "Racial Trends and Differences in the United States 30 Years After the Civil Rights Decade." *Social Science Research* 26:235–62.

Farley, Reynolds, Suzanne Bianchi, and Diane Colasanto. 1979. "Barriers to the Racial Integration of Neighborhoods: The Detroit Case." *Annals of the American Association of Political and Social Sciences* 441:97–113.

Farley, Reynolds, Howard Schuman, Suzanne Bianchi, Diane Colasanto, and Shirley Hatchett. 1978. "Chocolate City, Vanilla Suburbs: Will the Trend toward Racially Separate Communities Continue?" *Social Science Research* 7:319–44.

Farley, Reynolds, Charlotte Steeh, Maria Krysan, Tara Jackson, and Keith Reeves. 1994. "Stereotypes and Segregation: Neighborhoods in the Detroit Area." *American Journal of Sociology* 100:750–80.

Feagin, J. and M. Sykes. 1994. *Living with Racism, the Black Middle Class Experience.* Boston, MA: Beacon Press.

Fishbein, M. 1967. "Attitude and the Prediction of Behavior." Pp. 477–492 in *Readings in Attitude Theory and Measurement,* edited by M. Fishbein. New York: Wiley.

Fishbein, M. and I. Ajzen. 1975. *Belief, Attitude, Intention, and Behavior.* Reading, MA: Addison-Wesley.

Fiske, Susan. 2004. "Predicting Discrimination: A Meta-Analysis of the Racial Attitude-Behavior Literature." Working Paper. Department of Psychology, Princeton University.

Freeman, Richard B., and William M. Rodgers III. 1999. "Area Economic Conditions and the Labor Market Outcomes of Young Men in the 1990s Expansion." Working Paper No. 7073, Cambridge, MA: NBER.

Gans, Herbert. 1992. "Second-Generation Decline: Scenarios for the Economic and Ethnic Futures of the Post-1965 American Immigrants." *Ethnic and Racial Studies* 15:173–192.

Groves, Robert M. and Lars E. Lyberg. 1988. "An Overview of Nonresponse Issues in Telephone Surveys." Pp. 191–212 in *Telephone Survey Methodology,* edited by Robert M. Groves, Paul P. Biemer, Lars E. Lyberg, James T. Massey, William L. Nicholls II, and Joseph Waksberg. New York: Wiley.

Harrison, R. and C. Bennett. 1995. "Racial and Ethnic Diversity." Pp. 141–210 in *State of the Union, America in the 1990s,* vol. 2, *Social Trends 1990 Monograph Series,* edited by R. Farley. New York: Russell Sage Foundation.

Heckman, James. 1998. "Detecting Discrimination." *The Journal of Economic Perspectives* 12:101–116.

Heckman, James and Peter Seligman. 1993. "The Urban Institute Audit Studies: Their Methods and Findings." Pp. 187–258 in *Clear and Convincing Evidence: Measurement of Discrimination in America,* edited by Michael Fix and Raymond J. Struyk. Washington, DC: Urban Institute Press.

Holzer, Harry. 1996. *What Employers Want: Job Prospects for Less-Educated Workers.* New York: Russell Sage Foundation.

Holzer, Harry and David Neumark. 2000. "What Does Affirmative Action Do?" *Industrial and Labor Relations Review* 53:240–71.

Holzer, Harry, Steven Raphael, and Michael Stoll. 2003. "Employer Demand for Ex-Offenders: Recent Evidence from Los Angeles." Discussion Paper No. 1268–03, Institute for Research on Poverty, University of Wisconsin, Madison, WI.

Holzer, Harry, Paul Offner and Elaine Sorensen. 2005. "What Explains the Continuing Decline in Labor Force Activity among Young Black Men?" *Labor History* 46:37–55.

Holzer, Harry and Michael Stoll. 2001. *Employers and Welfare Recipients: The Effects of Welfare Reform in the Workplace.* San Francisco, CA: Public Policy Institute of California.

Husley, Lonnie Freeman. 1990. "Attitudes of Employers with Respect to Hiring Released Prisoners." Ph.D. dissertation, Department of Industrial Education, Texas A&M University, TX.

Jensen, W. and W. C. Giegold. 1976. "Finding Jobs for Ex-Offenders: A Study of Employers' Attitudes." *American Business Law Journal* 14:195–225.

Kinder, D. and D. O. Sears. 1981. "Prejudice and Politics: Symbolic Racism Versus Racial Threats to the Good Life." *Journal of Personality and Social Psychology* 40:414–31.

Kirschenman, Joleen and Katherine Neckerman. 1991. "'We'd Love to Hire Them, but . . .': The Meaning of Race for Employers." Pp. 203–232 in *The Urban Underclass,* edited by Christopher Jencks and P. Peterson. Washington, DC: Brookings Institute.

Krysan, Maria. 1999. "Prejudice, Politics, and Public Opinion: Understanding the Sources of Racial Policy Attitudes." *Annual Review of Sociology* 26:135–68.

——. 2002. "Whites Who Say They'd Flee: Who Are They, and Why Would They Leave?" *Demography* 39:675–96.

Kutner, Bernard, Carol Wilkins, and Penny Rechtman Yarrow. 1952. "Verbal Attitudes and Overt Behavior Involving Racial Prejudice." *Journal of Abnormal Social Psychology* 47:649–52.

LaPiere, Richard T. 1934. "Attitudes vs Actions." *Social Forces* 13:230–37.

Lichtenstein, Sarah and J. Robert Newman. 1967. "Empirical Scaling of Common Verbal Phrases Associated with Numerical Probabilities." *Psychonomic Science* 9:563–64.

Mare, R. D. 1995. "Changes in Educational Attainment and School Enrollment." Pp. 155–213 in *State of the Union: America in the 1990s*, vol. I, *Economic Trends*, edited by R. Farley. New York: Russell Sage Foundation.

Massey, Douglas and Garvey Lundy. 2001. "Use of Black English and Racial Discrimination in Urban Housing Markets: New Methods and Findings." *Urban Affairs Review* 36:452–69.

Merton, Robert K. 1949. "Discrimination and the American Creed." Pp. 99–126 in *Discrimination and the National Welfare*, edited by Robert M. MacIver. New York: Harper and Row.

Moss, Philip and Chris Tilly. 2003. *Stories Employers Tell: Race, Skill, and Hiring in America*. New York: Russell Sage Foundation.

National Research Council. 2004. *Measuring Racial Discrimination*. Panel on Methods for Assessing Discrimination, Committee on National Statistics, Division of Behavior and Social Sciences and Education, edited by Rebecca M. Blank, Marilyn Dabady, and Constance F. Citro. Washington, DC: The National Academies Press.

Pace, C. Robert and Jack Friedlander. 1982. "The Meaning of Response Categories: How Often Is 'Occasionally,' 'Often,' and 'Very Often'"? *Research in Higher Education* 17:267–81.

Pager, Devah. 2003. "The Mark of a Criminal Record." *American Journal of Sociology* 108:937–75.

——. 2002. "The Mark of a Criminal Record." Doctoral dissertation. Department of Sociology, University of Wisconsin–Madison.

Pettit, Becky and Bruce Western. 2004. "Mass Imprisonment and the Life Course: Race and Class Inequality in U.S. Incarceration." *American Sociological Review* 69:151–69.

Poskocil, A. 1977. "Encounters Between Blacks and White Liberals: The Collision of Stereotypes." *Social Forces* 55:715–27.

Remington, Todd D. 1992. "Telemarketing and Declining Survey Response Rates." *Journal of Advertising Research* 32:6–7.

Saenger, Gerhart and Emily Gilbert. 1950. "Custom Reactions to the Integration of Negro Sales Personnel." *International Journal of Opinion and Attitude Research* 4:57–76.

Sagar, H. and J. W. Schofield. 1980. "Racial and Behavioral Cues in Black and White Children's Perception of Ambiguously Aggressive Acts." *Journal of Personality and Social Psychology* 39:590–8.

Schaeffer, Nora Cate. 1991. "Hardly Ever or Constantly? Group Comparisons Using Vague Quantifiers." *Public Opinion Quarterly* 55:395–423.

Schuman, Howard. 1995. "Attitudes." Pp. 68–89 in *Sociological Perspectives on Social Psychology*, edited by Karen Cook, Gary Fine, and James House. Boston, MA: Allyn & Bacon.

Schuman, Howard and Lawrence Bobo. 1988. "Survey-Based Experiments on White Racial Attitudes toward Residential Integration." *American Journal of Sociology* 94:273–99.

Schuman, Howard and Michael P. Johnson. 1976. "Attitudes and Behaviors." *Annual Review of Sociology* 2:161–207.

Schuman, Howard, Charlottee Steeh, Lawrence Bobo, and Maria Krysan. 2001. *Racial Attitudes in America: Trends and Interpretations*. Rev. ed. Cambridge, MA: Harvard University Press.

Schutz, Heidi and Bernd Six. 1996. "How Strong is the Relationship Between Prejudice and Discrimination? A Meta-Analytic Answer." *International Journal of Intercultural Relations* 20:441–62.

Smith, Tom W. 1991. *Ethnic Images: General Social Survey Technical Report, 19*. Chicago, IL: National Opinion Research Center, University of Chicago.

Sniderman, Paul M. and Douglas B. Grob. 1996. "Innovation in Experimental Design in Attitude Surveys." *Annual Review of Sociology* 22:377–99.

Sniderman, Paul M. and Thomas Piazza. 1993. *The Scar of Race*. Cambridge, MA: The Belknap Press of Harvard University Press.

Traugott, Michael W. and John P. Katosh. 1979. "Response Validity in Surveys of Voting Behavior." *Public Opinion Quarterly* 43:359–77.

Turner, Margery, Michael Fix, and Raymond Struyk. 1991. *Opportunities Denied, Opportunities Diminished: Racial Discrimination in Hiring*. Washington, DC: Urban Institute Press.

Waldinger, Roger and Michael Lichter. 2003. *How the Other Half Works: Immigration and the Social Organization of Labor*. Berkeley, CA: The University of California Press.

Western, Bruce and Becky Pettit. Forthcoming. "Black-White Wage Inequality, Employment Rates, and Incarceration." *American Journal of Sociology*.

Wicker, A. W. 1969. "Attitudes versus Actions: The Relationship of Verbal and Overt Behavioral Responses to Attitude Objects." *Journal of Social Issues* 25:41–78.

Wilson, William Julius. 1978. *The Declining Significance of Race*. Chicago, IL: University of Chicago Press.

——. 1996. *When Work Disappears: The World of the New Urban Poor*. New York: Vintage Books.

Word, C. O., M. P. Zanna, and J. Cooper. 1974. "The Nonverbal Mediation of Self-Fulfilling Prophecies in Interracial Interactions." *Journal of Experimental Social Psychology* 10:109–20.

Yinger, John. 1995. *Closed Doors, Opportunities Lost*. New York: Russell Sage Foundation.

CHAPTER 12

Deviant Careers and Career Deviance

I felt a little inferior at first, because I had no knowledge myself of nudist camps . . . I started to enjoy myself, but I couldn't quite feel comfortable. In the nude. In front of a lot of people. A lack of confidence. By not having complete knowledge. I really didn't know what to expect.

—A soon-to-be nudist's first experience at
a nudist camp. (From Weinberg, 1966, p. 20)

A really bad work day is, nobody's calling, [you're] stressed trying to pick from people that you kind of don't want to have over because you don't know them, they might be—they're probably not cops but it's not clear, because they either won't give their work number or they won't do something [else that is part of her screening process]—and trying to [decide] to see them or not to see them, since it's already pledged as a work day and not [a day off]. . . . Just sitting around and waiting is really one of the higher-level bad days, I think.

—A really bad day for an "*elite prostitute.*"
(From Lucas, 2005, p. 524)

I can if somebody says something to me that I don't like you know it doesn't bother me any more . . . it meant (after being saved) that I could literally get ease with myself and not jump up and beat the crap out of somebody or if somebody comes and gets something from me and didn't bring it back you know at a certain time I'd go and beat the crap out of them.

—An ex-offender previously incarcerated in a state facility describing how being
"saved" helped keep him from violence in situations that would have provoked
him earlier. (From Giordano, Longmore, Schroeder, & Seffrin, 2008, p. 117)

◈ Introduction

The three stories above seem quite different. The first discusses a novice nudist's first experience at a nudist camp and how she felt as she entered a new deviant context and form of deviant behavior. The second is an "elite prostitute" whose worst "working day" is where she is ambivalent about what work (i.e., clients) she will take. The final quote is from ex-offender who believes that his spirituality helps prevent him from violence when he normally would have "beaten the crap out of someone." What links these very different quotes is that they are quotes from persons deemed deviant by much of society, but they are each at different stages of a deviant life course. The first is entering a deviant lifestyle, the second presumably is actively involved in a deviant career, and the last one is desisting from a violent history. These are the themes of this chapter, how deviance changes over time and often has a beginning, a middle, and an end.

As the title of this chapter implies, a distinction can be made between deviant careers and career deviance. The term *deviant careers* implies an actual career: a job, room for possible advancement (or dismissal), "regular" pay, and possibly even taxes. But there is clearly the idea that there is work for money, a beginning and an end (retirement, change in jobs, or death). The careers, however, are ones that are formally or informally sanctioned (socially, morally, or legally) or are typically disrespected by society, or at least certain segments of society. For simplicity, examples might include dancers in strip clubs, sex workers in pornography and certain prostitutes, drug dealers and smugglers, and professional thieves, among others.

The notion of "career deviance" brings a different connotation. Our view of a career deviant is one who becomes involved in crime or other deviance, not so much as a career, per se, but a sequence of deviant events occurs over time with a beginning and an end. The career can be very short such as a rebellious youth who has a few run-ins with the law, or it could be a long-term pattern of sexual encounters with same-sex strangers in public restrooms. The major commonality about deviant careers and career deviance is time. Many of the theories we have discussed are static in nature and attempt to distinguish deviants from conformists with any number of variables (e.g., social bonds, self-control, strains, association with deviant peers). Thinking about deviance in terms of careers forces us to think longitudinally (over time) and brings up some very interesting questions that are not necessarily intuitive. Thinking longitudinally, we start to recognize that different factors may influence (1) the onset of deviance, (2) continuation or escalation of deviance, (3) and desistance from deviance (be it almost immediate or gradually over time). We also start thinking about whether deviants specialize in particular forms of deviance or are generalists, engaging in many forms of deviance given the opportunities available and whether specialization or diversification changes over time.

◈ Criminal Careers and Career Criminals

We raise this distinction between deviant careers and career deviance, in part, because of a very large debate in criminology, referred to by some as the "great debate" (Soothill, Fitzpatrick, & Brian, 2009, p. 14) escalating in the 1980s and continuing today. The debate is largely between those who believe that longitudinal research is too expensive and not necessary for a thorough understanding of criminal behavior and those who believe longitudinal designs are crucial. The former typically believe that the factors that affect criminal behavior are relatively static, and cross-sectional designs are perfectly appropriate to test theories and develop appropriate programs and policies. The latter believe that different factors may affect the **onset/initiation** of criminal behavior, its continuation, and possible escalation and the factors that may affect **desistance** or moving out of a criminal career. This is not a trivial debate, and both sides have made important points. For example, it may seem "obvious" to many that knowing when different types of criminal behaviors begin, how long they persist across the life course, and when different types of offenders age out of crime is useful information. Indeed, several statistical analyses and reviews seemed to support the conclusion that groups of offenders who consistently offend over time could be incapacitated, significantly lowering rates of crime (see Blumstein & Cohen, 1979; Farrington, Gallagher, Morley, Ledger, & West, 1985; Greenberg, 1985). Alternatively, others disagree and argue that similar factors affect criminal behavior whether it is early or late in the game. They seriously challenge these notions, both theoretically and statistically, showing that offenders age out of crime fairly early in the life course and that the "career criminal" paradigm is basically without merit (Gottfredson & Hirschi, 1986).

We bring this debate regarding career criminals and criminal careers to your attention because we feel that it is important that students have at least heard of the debate. For the student of the sociology of deviance for which this book was written (as opposed to criminal behavior), this is just one small tree in a huge forest. First, there are many forms of deviance that we have no interest in trying to stop, particularly through incarceration. Second, the chronological age that people typically begin to engage in deviance may not be terribly interesting in itself. Alternatively, why some people become interested in a particular form of deviance or the circumstances of why they initiate the behavior is fascinating to most all of us. Why do people begin to use or sell drugs, turn tricks, enter a nudist colony, begin a career in pornography or become a compulsive consumer of porn, or any number of other deviant behaviors? Similarly, estimating the length of a deviant career may be somewhat interesting but probably not as interesting as how people live a deviant lifestyle, the challenges they face with conventional society, or the dangers inherent in many deviant careers. Finally and related, what pushes or pulls people out of careers of deviance? Indeed, the process of desistance, getting out of the business or "out of the life," is one of the most interesting aspects of the sociological study of deviance.

DEVIANCE IN POPULAR CULTURE

The subject of deviant careers and career deviance has gained momentum in recent years as more and more scholars have focused on issues of desistance and community reentry. As you learned in the last chapter, labeling is often an important factor in deviant careers; once labeled, it can be extremely difficult to get a job, rent an apartment, or lead a conforming lifestyle. Here we offer several examples of films that address this issue:

The Released—This PBS Frontline documentary (available to watch online) is about mentally ill inmates being released back into the community with no care or safety net. The filmmakers follow several men over an extended period of time to show their struggles trying to manage their mental illness and survive in the community.

Tequila Sunrise—a popular fictional film from the 1980s starring Mel Gibson as a successful drug dealer trying to leave his illegitimate business and start a conforming one. In one memorable scene, he tries to explain how difficult it can be to leave the drug dealing scene, detailing a list of people that don't want him to quit, each for his or her own reasons.

(Continued)

(Continued)

The Woodsman—In this dark film starring Kevin Bacon, a convicted sex offender is released after 12 years in prison. The film follows his attempts to build a conforming and quiet life in the community.

Sherrybaby—After 3 years in prison, a drug addict with a troubled history struggles to reconnect with her young daughter. The strong performance by Maggie Gyllenhaal showcases the difficulty of trying to rebuild relationships and become a good mother.

◈ Getting Into Deviance: Onset of a Deviant Career

At a very general level, it doesn't take much to initiate many deviant acts. Sneaking a drink from the parent's liquor cabinet, stealing a cigarette from an unguarded purse, breaking into an unlocked home, or cheating on a spouse or partner after too much drinking is fairly easy given the opportunity, a little interest or motivation, or especially some encouragement. Becoming a serious underage drinker or smoker, a burglar, or a career cheater will likely take more effort. The entrances to deviant careers will vary considerably depending on the behavior of interest, so in this section of the book, we discuss several different forms of deviance to provide the reader with some idea of the complexities and tremendous variation in ways individuals get into a career of deviance.

Quite some time ago, Howard Becker (1953) developed a series of socially interactive stages that he argued one needed to go through to become a user of marijuana. He contended that to become a "marijuana smoker," one must (1) learn to smoke the drug properly, (2) feel the intoxicating "high" associated with smoking marijuana, and (3) come to understand the feeling of intoxication as pleasurable. That is, one needs to learn to take in the smoke and hold the smoke for some time to get enough THC (the active chemical in marijuana) to actually get intoxicated. He argues that even if enough THC is ingested, individu-

als don't always feel the high of the drug, and even when they do, they may not find it terribly enjoyable. More recent research supports Becker's theory but suggests that times too have changed, at least to some extent. For example, most of Becker's research subjects did not get high their first time, but perhaps that was because of the quality of the marijuana in the 1950s versus the 1980s and 1990s. More recent research (Hallstone, 2002; Hirsch, Conforti, & Graney, 1990) shows that most first timers do feel the effects of smoking pot the first time, and some recall their very first experience as pleasant. However, the first experience need not be pleasurable and may in fact be quite negative physically (dry mouth, coughing, etc.) and emotionally. As one of Hallstone's (2002) respondents reported when asked if he enjoyed getting high the first time,

> Umm. . . . (emphatically) nooo! I was scared. I was very scared because not only could I not tell anybody, but um . . . I did not know if I was going to come down, how long it was going to last, and is my mom going to know. (p. 839)

▲ **Photo 12.1**   Marijuana can be experienced in very different ways, especially among novice users.

Marijuana is clearly the most popular and widespread illegal drug in this country. A 2010 survey of 8th, 10th, and 12th graders conducted by the Monitoring the Future showed lifetime prevalence of marijuana use at 17%, 33%, and 44%, respectively. When asked about the availability of marijuana, 41% of 8th graders, 69% of 10th graders, and 83% of 12th graders said that it would be fairly or very easy to obtain. That is, nearly a majority of 8th graders, a clear majority of 10th graders, and the vast majority of 12th graders reported that they could get marijuana fairly or very easily. Given the innocuous or even positive representation of marijuana in the media, few would be surprised that even "good kids" have experimented with the substance. Alternatively, consider what might be required for the initiation of harder, less "popular" drugs such as heroin, which has been tried by around 1% of people. Or, in line with a true deviant career, what is involved in becoming a drug dealer?

P. A. Adler and Adler (1983) studied a group of upper-level drug dealers and smugglers (mostly marijuana and cocaine in a "southwest county" in California). They found three routes to becoming upper-level drug dealers and smugglers: low-level entry, middle-level entry, and smuggling, which was considered the highest level. People who started at the bottom, as it were, were largely heavy drug users who basically had to deal to support their own habits. Most low-level dealers stay low-level dealers, not having the motivation and/or never developing the skills or the resources to make it into the middle level. The Adlers found that only about 20% of their upper-level dealer sample began as low-level dealers, and most of these dealers came from other parts of the country after they had moved into mid-level dealing before moving into the lucrative California market.

Middle-level entry was more common (about 75%) among their sample of upper-level dealers, and these dealers often came from other professions, some conventional and others on the seedier side. For example, one of the mid-level dealers was involved in a conventional real estate business but was laundering money through the business. Mid-level dealers had money and went in big, but they still had to learn the drug trafficking trade, including "how to establish business connections, organize profitable transactions, avoid arrest, transport illegal goods, and coordinate participants and equipment" (P. A. Adler & Adler, 1983, pp. 198–199). These were largely entrepreneurs who wanted to make it to the top and found the social networks needed in the drug subculture to make that happen.

Only a small proportion of the smugglers (about 10%) got into smuggling on their own; even upper-level drug dealers didn't have the knowledge, skills, connections, equipment, and other resources to embark on their own smuggling operation. Rather, "most novice smugglers were recruited and trained by a sponsor with whom they forged an apprentice-mentor relationship" (P. A. Adler & Adler, 1983, p. 199). Through this relationship, the recruits learned the techniques, acquired resources, and, most important, made contacts, and they eventually branched out or, in some cases, took over the operation when someone retired from the business. This is clearly consistent with differential association and social learning theories discussed in Chapter 6. It also brings up the notion of stratification within deviant careers. Just as there are hierarchies in conventional business (workers, supervisors and managers, upper administration, presidents and owners), so too is there stratification in the world of deviant careers. Just as in conventional organizations, upward mobility is possible but not always easy.

Other research on entering the business of drug dealing, including crack and meth, shows that it actually looks somewhat similar to that of upper-level dealers (see Dunlap, Johnson, & Manwar, 1994; Murphy, Waldorf, & Reinarman, 1990; VanNostrand & Tewksbury, 1997). Most research suggests that the motivations, techniques, and contacts need to be learned over the course of time for a full career to develop.

Truly getting into deviance often requires the acquisition of a deviant identity. As people come to define themselves as drinkers and smokers, they drink and smoke; it is part of their identity. Socially, drinkers are offered alcoholic beverages, and it is understood that when smokers walk outside, they are probably going for a cigarette. But how do deviant identities emerge? Penelope McLorg and Diane Taub (1987) provide an excellent example of how anorexics and bulimics move through a process from very conforming behavior, to primary deviance, to secondary deviance. Specifically, through participant observations of a self-help group BANISH (Bulimics/Anorexics in Self-Help), they conducted qualitative interviews with 15 participants and found that the women and men they studied started out quite conventionally. They had strong attachments to their families, did well in school, and internalized the cultural norms that slim is beautiful. They were rewarded when they lost weight, but like most dieters, they often were unable to maintain lowered weights, resulting in seemingly extreme behaviors to maintain desired weights. Here the anorexics and bulimics moved into a stage of primary deviance where they did not consider themselves anorexic or bulimic, the deviance was largely unknown to others, and the outcome of their behaviors was both psychologically and socially rewarding—they were slim and therefore more beautiful. At some point, however, friends and family came to recognize compulsive behaviors surrounding food and exercise among anorexics and evidence of binging and purging among bulimics. As with many other forms of deviance, friends and families were resistant to labeling the behaviors problematic, and among anorexics, there was a great deal of denial when called out on their compulsive behaviors. In contrast, bulimics tended to know that binging and purging was abnormal and unhealthy and, when confronted, were more likely to admit that they were bulimic.

By the nature of McLorg and Taub's (1987) study design, all of the anorexics and bulimics were part of a self-help group designed to help those stigmatized as deviant regain a sense of normality. Their disorder, then, became a master status, something that provided a new identity that dramatically affected their lives.

What should be clear from this section is that getting into deviance takes many forms, and various stages of development are required in almost any career in deviance.

◈ Risk and Protective Factors for Onset

Over the past several decades, great concerns have arisen over the onset of certain forms of deviant behavior, including drug and alcohol use, violence, teen pregnancy, high-risk sexual behavior, and other problematic behaviors. Because of societal concern over these issues, a tremendous amount of literature has emerged attempting to find factors that are positively related to deviant involvement (risk factors). Intricately related is a line of research that attempts to find factors that minimize the deleterious effects of risk factors (protective factors). An overview of **risk and protective factors** for adolescent problem behaviors, developed by the Social Development Group at the University of Washington, is provided in Figure 12.1. Risk factors have been categorized under several domains, including (1) individual and peer factors (e.g., rebelliousness of the child and deviant peers), (2) school (e.g., lack of commitment to school), (3) family (e.g., family conflict and management problems), and (4) the community (e.g., availability of alcohol and drugs and economic deprivation). Protective factors that mitigate the risk factors are also listed by domain. Protective factors are particularly important because they provide insights for developing effective policy and programs based on research evidence. So at the community level, we might encourage programs that provide opportunities for conventional involvement and rewards for doing good things in the neighborhood. High-risk families might be targeted and offered parent training courses or social supports that help them manage daily life. There are obviously a number of school-based programs that encourage students to feel that they are a part of the institution and structured activities to make them committed to doing well in school. Similarly, we might encourage individual counseling or other programs (be they school or family based) to help young persons become attached to prosocial individuals (e.g., mentors) and institutions (the family or the school).

Figure 12.1   Risk and Protective Factor Framework

The following graph supports a public health model using a theoretical framework of risk reduction and protection enhancement. Developments in prevention and intervention science have shown that there are characteristics of individuals and their families and their environment (i.e., community neighborhood, school) that affect the likelihood of negative outcomes including substance abuse, delinquency, violence, and school dropout. Other characteristics serve to protect or provide a buffer to moderate the influence of the negative characteristics. These characteristics are identified as risk factors and protective factors. (Arthur, Hawkins, et al., 1994, Hawkins, Catalano, Miller, 1992).

Domains	Risk Factors	Adolescent Problem Behaviors						Protective Factors	Social Development Model (SDM)
		Substance Abuse	Depression & Anxiety	Delinquency	Teen Pregnancy	School Drop-Out	Violence		
	Risk factors are characteristics of individuals, their family, school, and community environments that are associated with increases in alcohol and other drug use, delinquency, teen pregnancy, school dropout, and violence. The following factors have been identified that increase the likelihood that children and youth may develop such problem behaviors.							*Factors associated with reduced potential for drug use are called protective factors. Protective factors encompass family, social, psychological, and behavioral characteristics that can provide a buffer for the children and youth. These factors mitigate the effects of risk factors that are present in the child or youth's environment.*	*SDM is a synthesis of three existing theories of criminology (control, social learning, and differential association). It incorporates the results of research on risk and protective factors for problem behaviors and a developmental perspective of age, specific problem, and prosocial behavior. It is based on the assumption that children learn behaviors.*
Community	Availability of alcohol/other drugs	✓					✓	Opportunities for prosocial involvement in community	
	Availability of Firearms			✓			✓	Recognition for prosocial involvement	
	Community laws and norms favorable to drug use, firearms, and crime	✓		✓			✓		
	Transitions and mobility	✓	✓	✓		✓			
	Low neighborhood attachment and community disorganization	✓		✓			✓		
	Media Portrayals of Violence						✓		
	Extreme economic deprivation	✓		✓	✓	✓	✓		
Family	Family history of the problem behavior	✓	✓	✓	✓	✓	✓	Bonding to family with healthy beliefs and clear standards.	
	Family management problems	✓	✓	✓	✓	✓	✓	Attachment to family with healthy beliefs & clear standards	
	Family conflict	✓	✓	✓	✓	✓	✓	Opportunities for prosocial involvement	
	Favorable parental attitudes and involvement in problem behaviors	✓		✓			✓	Recognition for prosocial involvement	
School	Academic failure beginning in late elementary school	✓	✓	✓	✓	✓	✓	Bonding and Attachment to School	
	Lack of commitment to school	✓		✓	✓	✓	✓	Opportunities for prosocial involvement Recognition for prosocial involvement	
Individual / Peer	Early and persistent antisocial behavior	✓	✓	✓	✓	✓	✓	Bonding to peers with healthy beliefs and clear standards.	
	Rebelliousness	✓		✓		✓		Attachment to peers with healthy beliefs & clear standards	
	Friends who engage in the problem behavior	✓		✓	✓	✓	✓	Opportunities for prosocial involvement	
	Favorable attitudes toward the problem behavior (including low perceived risk of harm)	✓		✓	✓	✓		Increase in Social skills	
	Early initiation of the problem behavior	✓		✓	✓	✓	✓		
	Gang Involvement	✓		✓			✓		
	Constitutional factors	✓	✓	✓			✓		

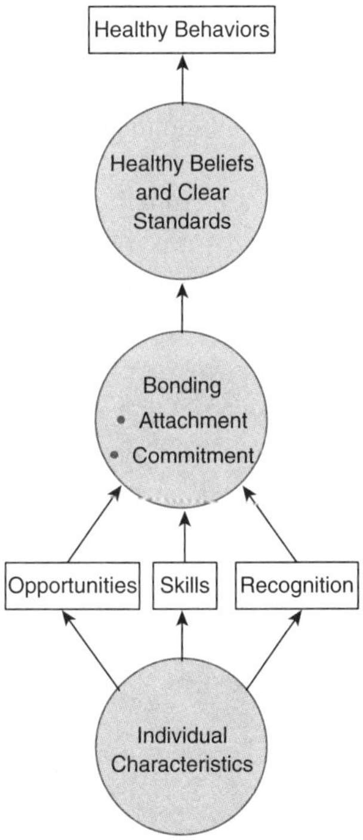

Source: The Substance Abuse and Medical Services Administration, U.S. Department of Health and Human Services (http://sde.state.ok.us/Schools/SafeHealthy/pdf/RiskProtectFactor.pdf).

◈ Maintaining a Deviant Career: Living the Life

Living the life of a deviant can be exciting, challenging, difficult, taxing, demoralizing, frightening, upsetting, and a host of other adjectives depending on the type of deviance and where in the deviant career we look. Consider the upper-level drug dealers discussed by P. A. Adler and Adler (1983) earlier. On one side, many dealers were drawn to the business because of the fun and excitement of the party and druggy lifestyle and the potential to make large sums of money. On the other side, dealing and smuggling was real work with many risks, including the dangers of associating with other criminals (some not to be trusted) and getting busted by law enforcement. In this section, we describe two studies concerning the lives of very different types of sex workers: women who exchange sex for drugs and money in the streets and elite prostitutes who also exchange sex for larges sums of money and expensive material goods. The comparison sheds light on how class and power differentiate the deviant careers of those involved in different levels of prostitution.

The daily living with deviance can be physically and emotionally draining. A large body of research has developed describing the lives of street prostitutes and the stigma, social rejection, and abuses they face on a day-to-day basis (see Farley and Barkan, 1998; Hunter, 1993; Nixon, Tutty, Downe, Gorkoff, & Ursel, 2002). Recently, Jolanda Sallman (2010) reported on her interviews with 14 women recruited from a program that provided social services ("prostitution-specific services") to women in need. Because these women did not necessarily consider themselves to be "prostitutes" or "sex workers," she began each interview with the following:

> I'm interested in learning as much as possible about what it's like to be a woman who has sex for material goods, such as money, drugs, shelter, or clothing. I'm particularly interested in hearing about your experience. It would be helpful for me if you would begin by describing a situation that stands out for you. (p. 149)

From these interviews, she derived five themes that provide insights into the daily lives of these women. First was living with the labeling and stigma by members of society (including the conventional citizen, pimps, and the police) who viewed them as nothing more than "whores," "dispensable," "garbage," and "less than human." Such devaluation led directly to the second theme that involved comments concerning the day-to-day living with violence. The prostitutes reported being kidnapped, raped, gang raped, beaten, and pimps who cut them with knifes. Responses to these victimizations showed clear evidence of their stigmatized and devalued status. One pimp immediately put a prostitute back on the street after she had been kidnapped and raped at knifepoint by a "john." The police response to rapes was equally demoralizing as law enforcement officers seemed either not to believe a prostitute could be raped or to think that it was a good thing. The third theme involved living with discrimination, especially by the criminal justice system, which often denied the women's victimization or blamed them for it. The fourth theme involved how their experiences had altered their perceptions of themselves even after they had given up prostitution. That is, their own devalued sense of self (self-stigma) remained even after they stopped engaging in sex in exchange for drugs and money. A final and almost positive theme that Sallman (2010) unearthed in her interviews had to do with "resistance." Here she describes how some of the women refused to accept societal stigma, often lashing out at those who judged them negatively.

▲ **Photo 12.2** Sociological research shows the very different lives of elite sex workers and street prostitutes.

The research is clear that violence is prevalent in the working lives of both indoor and street prostitutes (Raphael & Shapiro, 2004), but compare the prior descriptions with the following analysis of the lives of 30 elite prostitutes interviewed by Ann Lucas (2005). The women she interviewed unanimously voiced positive sentiments regarding their profession. They found it lucrative, empowering in terms of interpersonal skills and boundary setting, and often as having less exposure to sexual harassment. These women felt very in control of their environments:

I think that they think, a lot of times, that they've rented me for an hour so I should have to do anything they want to. I think, maybe, it takes them by surprise that I walk in and take charge of the situation, and I'm like, "OK, let's do this" and they can make suggestions but if I don't want to do something I'm not gonna do it. (p. 520)

For some of these women, prostitution was clearly a means to an end in terms of finance and lifestyle. Some "stressed their ability to be independent, to have control over their work and non-work lives, to be able to afford some indulgences, and to vary how much they worked each month" (Lucas, 2004, p. 526). Others stressed the nonsexual nature of their work, providing conversation and company to lonely men, some of them regulars. This is in contrast to other work that describes prostitutes as "exploitative, man-hating con artists; whether friendly or strictly professional, these women largely appreciated and respected their clients" (Lucas, 2004, p. 536).

The point of this comparison between drug-using street prostitutes and elite sex workers is not to generate debate about the morality and politics of prostitution, although there is plenty there to discuss. Rather, the point is to highlight massive differences in two seemingly similar deviant careers and how social class and power affect the lives of "deviant women" who exchange sex for material goods. This reiterates an emerging theme in this chapter—that just like social stratification in conventional careers, there is also important stratification in deviant careers. In a conventional organization, there are usually clear levels related to pay, power, flexibility, and other benefits. So it is true in many deviant careers.

STUDIES IN DEVIANCE

Leaving the Streets: Transformation of Prostitute Identity Within the Prostitution Rehabilitation Program

By Sharon S. Oselin (2009), in *Deviant Behavior, 30,* 379–406

While most research in the area of deviant careers examines how individuals assume deviant identities, Oselin (2009) examines the process by which someone with a deviant identity (or label) sheds that label for a nondeviant identity. Specifically, Oselin examines the role that the Prostitution Rehabilitation Program (PRP) plays in the new identity of women exiting prostitution.

The PRP is considered initially to be a "total institution," meaning that the participants in the program are heavily restricted in their freedoms and behaviors. However, as the participants move through the program, it becomes a "quasi–total institution" in that they are allowed more freedoms. For example, at the beginning of the program, participants are not allowed to make unsupervised phone calls,

(Continued)

(Continued)

leave the premises without a chaperone, or have contact with anyone from their past. Later in the program, some of these restrictions are lifted.

Oselin spent 6 months collecting data at the PRP, volunteering for approximately 140 hours and interviewing eight ex-prostitutes and three staff members (which were all the residents and staff in the program during those 6 months). She examined both how the women talked about themselves and how they behaved during this time period.

Oselin (2009) found that the participants moved through three distinct stages as they transformed their identities. She called these stages rookie, in-between, and expert and found that as the participants got better at talking the PRP talk and mastering the behavior required of them (to attend school, attend life skills classes, and remain celibate while in the program, for example), they successively moved through the stages until they no longer considered "prostitute" to be part of their identity. Oselin suggests that the organizational structure of the PRP is important to this change because it promotes both the language and behavior of change.

◈ Getting Out of the Game: Desistance From Career Deviance

If you think about most traditional theories of deviance, they have typically focused on two questions: (1) Why do people begin to engage in deviance, and (2) why does deviance persist (Paternoster & Bushway, 2009)? For example, Hirschi's (1969) early social control theory, which we covered in Chapter 7, would say that deviance is fun, easy, and rewarding and people are drawn toward it. Deviance is initiated because of a lack of social controls (attachment, commitment, involvement, and beliefs) that usually prevent people from initiating deviance. Unless there is a significant change in social bonds (e.g., a good job, investment in school or marriage), deviance persists because bonds remain weak. His later theory with Gottfredson (Gottfredson & Hirschi, 1990), which focused on self-control, shares a similar perspective and furthermore insists that self-control is stable and that is why deviance persists. Strain theorists (especially Agnew's individual-level version), introduced in Chapter 4, suggest that initial deviance is a reaction to frustration and anger, and deviance persists because the structure of society means certain people remain in stressful conditions (Agnew, 2006). Finally, differential association and social learning theories, covered in Chapter 6, suggest that deviance emerges when definitions favorable to deviance outweigh definitions unfavorable to deviance. To the extent people are, for example, immersed in a subculture conducive to deviance, the deviance is likely to continue. This is the way these theories have typically been used. However, with the emergence of the **criminal career paradigm** or the **life course perspective** introduced earlier in Chapter 7, people started to be much more concerned with the tail end of the deviant career and how and why criminals and other deviants desist.

Surely, the theories above might be used to explain desistance. Social controls or bonds can emerge by entering a solid relationship such as marriage or obtaining stable employment (Sampson & Laub, 1993). Or, one might escape situations that produce strain or develop skills to help deal with frustrating conditions (Agnew, 1997). Finally, people sometimes do change their social networks and therefore the definitions they are exposed to, enabling them to exit a deviant career (Akers, 1998). Indeed, social control, strain, and differential association theories have all been placed within a life course perspective and can be used to help explain the desistance process (Agnew, 2006; Sampson & Laub, 1995; Warr, 2002). Importantly, the theories have also been used to identify key concepts associated with several theories and relate those ideas to desistance. For example, Peggy Giordano and her colleagues (Giordano, Longmore, Schroeder, & Seffrin, 2008) argue that "spirituality," a key component of many self-help and formal treatment programs as well as prison-based support groups, can be linked to desistance through each of these theories. Spirituality can be linked to social control theory through the bond of "belief" as well as informal agents of social control that deviants may associate with because of newfound spiritual beliefs. Similarly, because of newfound spirituality, deviants may begin to disassociate with nonbelievers and begin to associate with believers who reinforce nondeviant definitions. Finally, spirituality and association with other believers may provide a source of social support that reduces frustrations and strains that earlier may have led to deviant involvement.

They interviewed incarcerated adolescents (half male and half female) in 1995 and again in 2003. Quantitative analyses of these data lend no support to the idea that spirituality (closeness to God and church attendance) was related to desistance. However, the sample size was fairly small and therefore difficult to detect statistical significance. Indeed, few variables in their model were statistically significant.

Alternatively, in-depth qualitative interviews with 41 of the incarcerated youth seemed to suggest that spirituality was a strong "hook" for some offenders to change their lives and desist from criminal involvement. These qualitative comments were related to the theories discussed earlier. For example, spirituality often brought couples or parents and children together, increasing attachment and social control. Said one respondent, "Without Christ and the church we would never be together, and I mean we already know that. We prayed a lot and we know it's through prayer that we're together and our family's together" (Giordano et al., 2008, p. 119). Another references the bond

▲ **Photo 12.3** Can religion "save" people from a career in deviance?

of involvement: "If you would have told me ten years ago or say the last time I seen you, seven years ago that I would be singing in the choir regularly, going to church regularly I probably would have thought you were crazy" (p. 114). In terms of differential association and social learning, another said, "The things that preacher say from out of the Bible. I love that. He's just teaching you the ways to live. To live like the way God wants you to live right" (p. 114). Finally, referencing social support and ability to reduce strain, one stated, "I don't worry like I used to before. I know all things are in the Lord's hands and I know he takes care of me" (p. 117).

Spirituality can be seen as a "hook," something that some involved in career deviance can grab hold of to help them use their own **human agency** to open doors out of the lifestyle they wish to exit. Spirituality is clearly something that will garner more theoretical and empirical attention as federal money is invested into faith-based approaches to reforming criminals and other deviants. Other "hooks" such as new relationships, occupations, and geographic moves away from "bad influences" are also likely to be carefully studied both quantitatively and qualitatively in the future.

Exiting a deviant career can be difficult. P. A. Adler and Adler's (1983, p. 202) upper-level drug dealers and smugglers had a hard time "phasing out" of their careers because they had become accustomed to the "hedonistic and materialistic satisfactions the drug world provided" and, in fact, had a hard time finding legitimate jobs because they had been out of the lawful labor market for so long they had few legal opportunities. The drug-using lifestyles of alcoholics and drug addicts are also difficult to leave. Recovery requires motivation, social support, and often treatment; still, the process is often plagued by back-and-forth periods of abstinence and use (Brownell, Marlatt, Lichteustein, & Wilson, 1986).

Recently, Lynda Baker and her colleagues reviewed several general and prostitution-specific models of change, as well as the empirical literature on the specific barriers women face when exiting prostitution (Baker, Dalla, & Williamson, 2010, pp. 588–590). Barriers included

1. Individual factors
   a. Self-destructive behavior and substance abuse
   b. Mental health problems
   c. Effects of trauma from adverse childhood
   d. Psychological trauma/injury from violence
   e. Chronic psychological stress
   f. Self-esteem/shame and guilt
   g. Physical health problems
   h. Lack of knowledge regarding services

2. Relational factors
   a. Limited conventional formal and informal support
   b. Strained family relations
   c. Pimps
   d. Drug dealers
   e. Social isolation

3. Structural factors
   a. Employment, job skills, limited employment options
   b. Basic needs (e.g., housing homelessness, poverty, economic self-sufficiency)
   c. Education
   d. Criminal record
   e. Inadequate services

4. Societal factors
   a. Discrimination and stigma

Through an analysis of previous models and the barriers that women face when exiting prostitution, the authors developed an integrated model described in Figure 12.2. The integrated model focuses on prostitution but could also be used to understand exiting other deviant careers (drug dealing, drug and alcohol addiction, anorexia/bulimia, etc.). The first stage is immersion, and technically, this stage is not about change at all but precedes an inkling of leaving the business—that is, the woman is immersed in a lifestyle of prostitution. In the second stage, the woman becomes aware that things are not as they should be. Of course, at either part of this stage, there are the barriers listed above to leaving, and the woman could (and often does) return to the immersion stage. If the woman makes it past this stage, she enters the stage of deliberate planning and preparation. At this stage, attempts are made to contact informal social support (e.g., family and friends) as well as formal agents of social support such as drug and alcohol treatment centers and homeless shelters. The initial exit period begins when the woman actively and behaviorally works to get out of the lifestyle. She may use informal contacts such as family and friends or she may invoke formal measures such as counseling or drug treatment. Breaking through the barriers is critical at this stage, and human agency becomes especially important. At this point,

> Some women may enter a drug treatment program, actively engaged and ready to change; they may rely on their support system (e.g., sponsors), internalize knowledge gained, and then apply newly acquired skills to their own lives. Others may begin a treatment program, fail to utilize available support or internalize knowledge and, therefore, be unable to make behavioral changes. These women will likely abandon the program prior to completion and eventually return to the sex industry. It is at this stage of the model that a woman's internal desire and motivation to exit are severely tested. (Baker et al., 2010, p. 592)

In the former case, the woman may enter the final exit stage or she may not—she may reenter the business. In the latter case, the woman will almost always go back to prostitution, and in either case, there may be what Sanders (2007) termed the "yo-yoing," where multiple attempts are made to exit the business and lifestyle. Baker and colleagues (2010) conclude that very often the final exiting stage comes after many attempts to exit a career in prostitution.

Figure 12.2 Baker, Dalla, and Williamson's (2010) Integrated Model of Exiting Prostitution

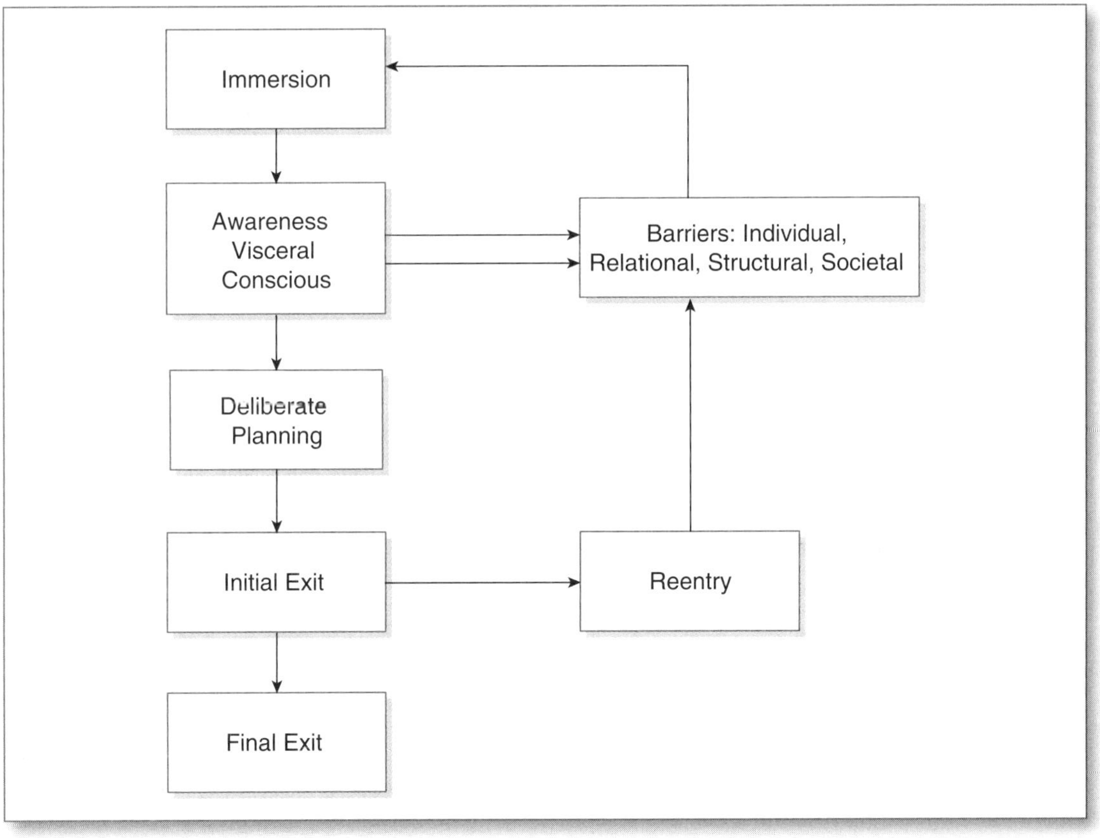

Source: Adapted from Baker et al. (2010).

NOW YOU . . . THINK ABOUT DEVIANT CAREERS

Those labeled as sex offenders are often assumed to be some of the most likely to become career offenders. For this reason, Megan's Law has mandated that sex offenders register—making their status of sex offender public information. Government registry websites list these men and women by name and oftentimes address. However, over the years, the label of sex offender has been applied to a wide array of behaviors beyond those of rapist and child molester. These behaviors include urinating in public, streaking, engaging in a consensual relationship with someone younger than age 18, and having consensual sex in a public place.

A report conducted by Robert Barnoski (2005) of the Washington State Institute for Public Policy tracked the recidivism rate of sex offenders released from Washington state prisons. Below are the recidivism rates (by year). In addition, Barnoski found that compared to all felony offenders, felony sex offenders had the lowest recidivism rates.

Year	5-Year Rate	Year	5-Year Rate
1986	6%	1993	8%
1987	7.5%	1994	6%
1988	7.5%	1995	4.4%
1989	6%	1996	3%
1990	7%	1997	2%
1991	8%	1998	3%
1992	6%	1999	3.7%

First using the figures above, describe the recidivism rate of sex offenders. How do you think it compares to other offenders (or actually do the research)? Now, using your understanding from this chapter of deviant careers, discuss the expected and actual recidivism rates for sex offenders. What does this mean for understanding sex offending as a deviant career? How might the broad set of behaviors defined as sex offenses and the public treatment of sex offenders affect our beliefs about their deviant careers?

◈ Conclusion

In this chapter, we have discussed deviant careers, meaning one's work is deviant, and career deviance, meaning a period of deviant behavior that has a beginning, a middle that might include **escalation** or **specialization,** and an end, which we view as a process. In fact, each stage of many deviant careers or career deviances can be viewed as a process. The obvious exception might be a quick, untimely death before one even considers exiting the career. We should note that in this chapter, we have focused on deviant behaviors that are criminal or at least unhealthy (e.g., smoking, excessive drinking, and eating disorders), cases where we felt most students would expect or hope to see an end to the behaviors. Many forms of deviance do not fit this model. Homosexuality is still considered deviance by many in our society, but most of us recognize that one's sexual orientation may not and should not change over time. As well, various mental and physical disorders and the behaviors that accompany them may not change greatly over the life course.

Still, the career paradigm does offer some useful insights into the initiation process, a better understanding of how people manage their deviant careers or career deviance, and the process of desistance for many forms of deviance. A prestigious sociologist, Francis Cullen (2011), in his Sutherland Award Address, lamented how the study of deviant careers became less popular with the rise of survey research so easily used in schools to study "delinquency." He described how static, cross-sectional research is now falling to the wayside (or at least that it should) and that we need to take a life course perspective, including longitudinal data collection, if we are to advance the study of crime and deviance. We agree that cross-sectional designs are limited, especially when it comes to studying career deviance and deviant careers, and we hope more longitudinal designs will emerge focused on noncriminal forms of deviance. However, it is the reemergence and popularity of the study of life course deviance that excites us, no matter what research design is needed to address the issues in question.

EXERCISES AND DISCUSSION QUESTIONS

1. How might different factors influence people to initiate, persist, and exit a deviant career?

2. Consider any deviant behavior that you might have been involved in. What factors motivated you to initiate them? If you persisted, what factors led you to do this and, if you didn't, what factors motivated you to stop?

3. What deviant behaviors might best be explained from a life course perspective, and which ones probably can be explained from a static perspective?

4. Choose a theory from the list below and describe how it might be particularly useful to employ from a life course perspective. Would any of the theories not work well in a life course perspective? Why?

   a. Differential association/social learning

   b. Social control or bonding

   c. Self-control

   d. Labeling

   e. Conflict

   f. Critical theories (feminist, peacemaking, critical race theory)

5. If you had to study just one aspect of deviance in the life course (e.g., onset/initiation, persistence/escalation/specialization, desistance), what would you study and why?

KEY TERMS

Criminal career paradigm

Desistance

Escalation

Human agency

Life course perspective

Onset/initiation

Risk and protective factors

Specialization

READING 36

Anorexia is obviously not a career in the sense that one makes a living through an eating disorder, although eating disorders are often associated with certain careers. In addition, it is like a "drug-using career" in that different factors may affect onset, escalation, and desistence. While the focus of the article is social class, the author also argues for "approaching anorexia as a deviant career of conversion" using class as an organizing factor. The research is based on in-depth interviews with anorexic patients ($n = 14$) and observations in two hospitals in France (1997–2001). The author describes stages in career conversion: (1) commencement, where the anorexic moves from simply dieting and commits to transforming herself; (2) going on, which involves keeping up the conversion, using new techniques of weight loss and developing new ways of measuring success at weight loss; (3) still going on but dealing with concerned others; and (4) the final stage (at least for these young women)—the hospital phase, which has to do with the desistance process.

The Fifth Element

Social Class and the Sociology of Anorexia

Muriel Darmon

A great deal has been written about the socio-cultural basis of anorexia nervosa. Indeed, perhaps too much for the preferences of scholars in the field: in an appraisal of a recent book, one described herself as 'someone in feminist theory, women's studies, and medical discourse analysis who had hoped she would go to her grave without ever having to read another word about anorexia nervosa' (Treichler, in Gremillion, 2003). Yet, despite an abundance of sociological writing on the subject of anorexia, gaps remain in this literature. Surprisingly enough, sociologists researching anorexia have shied away from the one element that is traditionally theirs to study: social class. Instead, social scientists have geared their focus towards four alternative elements: a gender bias rendering women more at risk than men; the most affected age group (adolescent girls); historical time periods (especially from the 19th century onwards, and especially since the 1960s); and cultural-geographical boundaries (western countries and Japan). Compared to the abundance of research on the above four themes, and considering the relevance and specificity of class analysis in sociological thought, the class position of anorexic individuals has been understudied, causing social class to have a limited role in theorizing about eating disorders.

This article provides an analysis of anorexia that highlights this 'Fifth Element' while elaborating a sociological analysis of anorexia. It also illustrates the usefulness of approaching anorexia as a deviant career of conversion while reconstructing the 'social space' of class culture, class dispositions and class practices in which this career develops. This will be done by identifying anorexic food practices and body uses as those of the upper and middle classes, revealing the anorexic conversion as a particularly class-oriented one, and also by deciphering diagnostic stereotypes and acts of non-compliance during the hospital phase. This article proposes an analysis of anorexia in which social class is not limited to a set of

Source: Darmon, Muriel. "The Fifth Element: Social Class and the Sociology of Anorexia." *Sociology* 43: 717–733, 2009. Reprinted with permission.

values or representations, as is often done in social scientific studies of anorexia. It instead regards class practices, class dispositions and class habitus not as causes, but, rather, as *social conditions of possibility* (or social conditions of likelihood) of the anorexic career.

Methods

This article draws from research conducted in France from 1997 to 2001, based on repeated in-depth interviews with anorexic patients from two different hospitals (six patients in Hospital H, eight in Clinic C) and five months of observations of the everyday life and talk therapy sessions in the units in which they were hospitalized. The research included interviews with some of their teachers (11 interviews), snowball interviews with formerly diagnosed anorexics (3) and comparative interviews on body and food practices with high-school girls (11 interviews).

The persons interviewed as anorexic patients were all adolescent girls, and were all from the upper and middle classes. Class membership was defined based on both parents' and grandparents' occupations and diplomas, which were obtained through a short questionnaire filled in by patients after each first interview. Data on parents were also accessible through medical records. The class membership in the sample ranged from Anne, whose father has a diploma from the French elite school system of 'grandes écoles' and is the head of a company (and his father is CEO of a major car company), and whose mother is an engineer, again with a diploma from a 'grande école'. Anne was coded as 'upperclass, with both cultural and economic capital'. At the other end of the spectrum, Sidonie's father has a high school diploma, owns a restaurant, and had parents who were skilled workers in the railway industry. Sidonie's mother did not finish high school, helps her father at the restaurant, and comes from a family of sewers. Sidonie was thus coded as 'middle-class from working-class background, with more economic than cultural capital'.[1]

Interviews began with a general question on the subjects' experience with anorexia and were conducted to allow a detailed description of the practices that constitute the anorexic career. In the course of observation, I paid close attention to the words that were used to classify, label and discuss pathologies and patients. Therefore, and somewhat untraditionally, practices have been gathered mainly through interviews, and categories and representations through observation.

◈ Looking for the Fifth Element

As has been stated previously, the elusiveness of the Fifth Element (class) is merely relative to the intensive study of the other four elements. Social class is far from being altogether neglected in social scientific studies of anorexia, but it has been mainly confined to three modes of appearance.

First, social class is often present as a factor in the quantitative epidemiology and etiology of anorexia. Epidemiologically speaking, from the 1960s to the 1980s there was a strong consensus that anorexic patients came from upper- and middle-class families. Since the 1980s, this assumption has been questioned (for a review see Gremillion, 2003). Nonetheless, there are still convincing studies that illustrate a positive correlation between anorexia nervosa and high socio-economic status. For example, a recent retrospective survey of a 33-year period in the UK, based on an unusually large sample size (692) and using univariate analyses and logistic regression, confirms that 'social class distribution was consistently weighted toward social classes 1/2' from which came the majority of patients (67.5%) (McClelland and Crisp, 2001).

There has been much discussion about the potential bias towards the upper and middle classes as conveyed by medical recruitment, modes of registration, diagnosis procedures and stereotyping from as early as the 19th century (Brumberg, 1988) or more recently (Gremillion, 2003). Second to none in the identification of a specific class recruitment of anorexic patients, such analyses nevertheless leave open the question of the *mechanisms* through which membership in a class group plays a part in anorexia as a *process* and not only as a statistical datapoint. This process is precisely the issue that this article tries to tackle.

Social class is secondly mentioned when a social trajectory, namely an upwardly mobile one, is thought to foster anorexia or eating disorders (Bordo, 1993; Gremillion, 2003). To the best of my knowledge, this claim has not been proven, since it may be very difficult to be sure about the upward mobility of young girls who have not yet achieved their final class status or who have higher diplomas than their mothers, but in a context of growing education for women.

Finally, social class has been analysed as shaping a set of values and attitudes that cause or facilitate anorexia. This has been approached in three ways:

1. By equating thinness and frailty with high social status and differentiation from lower classes, as early as the 19th century (Brumberg, 1988) as well as more recently (Gremillion, 2003).

2. Upper and middle classes enjoy higher education and educational achievement, which contradicts traditional female gender socialization and can therefore foster anorexia (Lawrence, 1987).

3. A 'middle class context'—i.e. an emphasis on success at school or in the public domain or specific definitions of individuality and independence—by itself, or through conflict with other social norms, creates a pathway to anorexia (Evans et al., 2004; Turner, 1996).

This article shares with these studies the claim that what constitutes anorexia can be related to a class position and context, while adding two contributions which endeavour to be more specific. First, a primary task of this article is to specify 'what constitutes anorexia', and to locate it within a sociological framework as a 'deviant conversion career'. Second, while the primary focus on class has been on class representations and values, this article takes them into account only as one element deriving from a class

position, among other important factors such as class practices and class dispositions or class habitus. Following Bourdieu (1979), class position is thus defined as a location in a 'social space' of class practices and judgments on practices—that is to say a location both in social hierarchies and in perceptions of social hierarchies.

 ## Anorexia as a Deviant Conversion Career

The idea of anorexia as a 'deviant career' (Becker, 1963) emerged from fieldwork analysis as a way of understanding the objective and subjective modifications that took place during subjects' experience of anorexia as it was described in interviews. It was useful to depart from 'conventions' on the subject, coming both from medical and psychological professionals and from 'experts by group membership' (anorexics) (Becker, 1998: 7; Darmon, 2008).

Previous studies have considered the concept of an 'anorexic career'. McLorg and Taub (1994[1987]) distinguish between three phases: 'Conforming behaviour', 'Primary Deviance', and 'Secondary Deviance', but focus primarily on the labelling process and its effects, rather than on the anorexic activity itself. Peters (1995) also distinguishes three phases in the anorexic career: the 'Diet Phase', the 'Ascetic Phase', and the 'Starvation Neurosis Phase'. In Peters' phases the anorexic activity is more obvious (as their names show) but is tied to underlying, unconscious or mainly biological 'causes' ('a Pavlovian stimulus/ response' or a 'starvation neurosis') that depart from the sociological imagination. In these two studies, what is left behind is precisely what this article focuses on: the anorexic activity itself, which can be seen as a self-conversion work.[2] To paraphrase Ekins (1997) on 'male femaling', the anorexic conversion work similarly 'emerged as the single major social process being researched. It was pervasive and fundamental. It was patterned'. From early on, it was necessary (and illuminating) to recognize anorexics as girls who strenuously work *on* themselves *at* converting themselves in various domains, 'in various ways, in various contexts, at various times, with various stagings and with various consequences' (Ekins, 1997: 2). I identify four phases in the anorexic career, briefly defined as follows:[3]

Phase One is 'Commencement: the beginning of the commitment to transforming oneself'. The 'simple diet', which is commonly seen as the first step to anorexia, is but one element of this process. The process can include a wide range of transformation practices concerning the body (e.g. diet, haircut, change of style in clothing, change of sport or pace in the exercise regimen) and also concerns culture at large (e.g. intensification of schoolwork—noticeable by teachers and which grade sheets bear witness to—self-motivated reading programs or 'cultural' work-out sessions). One subject, Yasmine, describes 'what happened at the beginning', in such a way that epitomizes this multifaceted process of 'taking charge' of oneself:

> I thought to myself: you've got to grow muscle, you know, but I'm kind of lazy [she smiles] so at first I chose to lose weight, 'you lose this huge bottom you have and nobody will see you're not fit' (. . .) and there was school, too. Even school subjects I used to hate, I was into them, I got into them, 'nothing will stand in my way' (. . .). I threw myself into everything . . . Even sports, I used to hate sports since I was a kid, I hate that! But then, I tried hard, I threw myself into it, I became a straight-As sport student! (. . .) Also, I began reading. I mean real reading. Quite a lot of books, you know. I wanted to have an ironclad culture; I wanted to make one for myself. Before that, I used to read, but only what I liked and when I liked it. There I wanted to MAKE myself an ironclad culture (. . .) What else . . . Oh, clothes . . . I came to choose better outfits, more chic. Black slacks, tight tops, jackets, formal shoes . . . Quite classy . . . Hair well-done, make-up. (Yasmine)

Phase Two is 'Going on: keeping up the conversion'. A new type of work is engaged in, based on new techniques—first and foremost weight-loss techniques, but also techniques for measuring the effectiveness of the *previous* techniques—and on a rationalization of everyday life around this commitment and its different fields, corporal and/or cultural. It culminates with a new 'diet' in the original meaning of the word, a 'general conduct and organization of life, including form of dress, behaviour and attitudes' (Turner, 1996: 176). This work makes it possible to remain 'in' the anorexic career. Habits are actually moulded to meet this goal, and part of this new work is directly aimed at building and incorporating individual dispositions to make it possible *and* likely to continue, as described in these two excerpts:

> I didn't go directly from 'eating normally' to 'almost stopping eating' because it was not possible. What I did for a time was to eat a snack at five; when I came back from school, I ate OK, I drank milk, I ate cookies, so that I was not hungry at dinner and I could prevent myself from eating at dinner. And after that, snack was only every other day, and then every three days (. . .). There was food I ate a lot of, to be sick, so that I could be so disgusted by it that I would never eat it again. Just to make sure I was disgusted, and would never put them in my mouth again. That's how I came to like less and less kinds of food (. . .) I voluntarily disgusted myself, so that I wouldn't eat, so that I wouldn't have any appetite for this kind of food. (Nadège)

> You realize you can get used to whatever you want to get used to (. . .) [Before anorexia] I used to enjoy candies, but I did manage to convince myself I was disgusted by it. I managed to say to myself: 'You don't like that, you're disgusted by that, this is going to make you sick'. Maybe there is some kind of pleasure, saying to yourself you can get used to everything. (Annabelle)

Here, incorporation is therefore the explicit aim of systematic work on body malleability and on deeply rooted somatic sensations such as tastes and disgust. Furthermore, the interviewees describe a step-by-step process of learning to recognize and to enjoy the sensation of an 'empty stomach', and to loath 'feeling full'. This is why we can say they work and count *on* time, since the work they perform aims at enabling the body to go on 'by itself' and the person to stay on the anorexic path over time. During this second phase, however, it slowly becomes a work *of* time on the person herself. Time is working on *them* because anorexic 'dispositions' are actually incorporated as a result of these repeated practices (Bourdieu, 1997; Lahire, 2003). New likes and dislikes, reflexes, representations ('it was beyond my control'; 'When I looked at food, I didn't see food any more, I saw calories! And when I ate food, I just felt the calories on my tongue!') merge into a new set of dispositions which then become 'second nature' (Bourdieu, 1979; Wacquant, 1989). The existence of this new habitus is made obvious by *exits* from the anorexic career. Exits at the end of the first phase are easy; all of the high-school interviewees who tried to lose weight just 'gave up'. Leaving the anorexic career at the end of the second phase, as some snowball interviewees who were never hospitalized did, is different from just 'giving up' because it involved a whole new, and reversed, work on oneself—a new conversion back to previous dispositions. This illustrates that an anorexic set of dispositions has been incorporated and must be fought and overcome.

Phase Three is still about 'Going on', but the commitment has now to be sustained in spite of whistleblowers and the surveillance network that has gradually woven around the young girls. More and more people (family, friends, teachers, doctors) are watching more and more aspects of their lives (diet practices, but also physical exercise, use of bathroom scales, or school work, which is, at some point, interpreted through medical categories as 'hyperactivity'). A new and specific work emerges in response to this surveillance: a 'discretion work', designed to make problematic actions less perceptible, followed by 'illusion work', which aims at making them invisible.

Phase Four is the Hospital phase: in this phase, the hospital has to deal with the anorexic habitus as it has been constructed throughout the first three phases. The hospital work is about reversing the anorexic commitment by redefining it as pathological, negotiating the acknowledgment of its pathological nature with the patient, and obtaining her participation in a new—and now collective—conversion work. The conversion is initiated this time by the medical institution itself, defined as a way 'back to normality'—which can have various meanings depending on the therapeutic orientation of the medical unit.

◈ The Social Space of the Anorexic Conversion

As an analytical tool, the notion of career can be used to 'turn people into activity' (Becker, 1998), and to shift from a definition of 'identity' to one of action: one is not born an anorexic, one must become one, and to 'be' (labelled) anorexic, one has to 'do' the things detailed above. Drifting away from the traditional use of the notion of career in sociology, this article purports to show that to 'do' those things, you have to 'be' somebody specific. This article demonstrates that the characteristics of the anorexic career echo those of its recruitment groups, age, gender, and especially, in this article, social class. This deviant conversion career can therefore be related to the 'social space of social classes' it develops in, and the behaviours seen as resulting from, or typical of, the pathology are interpreted as social practices located in such a space.

A Class-Situated Set of Practices, Attitudes and Values

First, if we analyse what constitutes the anorexic career as a set of practices like any other set of practices, we see that they are located in a specific place within the social space: anorexic food practices, body practices and school practices are those of the upper and middle classes, and more specifically those who have more cultural than economic capital.

One key example of this is found in food consumption. The idea here is to compare what seem to be 'anorexic' food practices, that is to say behaviours that seem specific to anorexia, with their 'normal' counterparts, and to locate them within the social space of food consumption. The data Bourdieu used to draw the social space of food consumption in *La Distinction* are dated, but recent statistical studies show that food consumption is still strongly class based today in France.[4] Therefore, the notion of class tastes and food dispositions still stands. It is possible to compare the description of food consumption in the interviews with statistics available on food consumption in France around the 1990s (to eliminate evolutions and differences linked with national specificities and historical changes). In particular, what the interviewees eat and what they don't eat is not chosen randomly, or only according to the calorie intake of each food. They mentioned, for example, 'living on' green apples, grapefruits, greens and vegetables, non-fat yoghurts, lean meats, fish and seafood—'simple' food but also sometimes exotic ones such as 'curry gambas'. These selections reveal 'dominant tastes' (Bourdieu, 1979) for they single out foods that are consumed in greater amounts by the upper classes in France today, such as fish, fruits and vegetables, light dairy products or exotic food (Cavaillet et al., 2004; Grignon and Grignon, 1999; Herpin and Manon, 1997). 'Restrictive' anorexia is therefore not only about 'restricting' food: it is about choosing a certain *type* of food, with certain properties, both calorific *and* social, at the expense of another. Foods that are refused are those that are strongly associated with working-class tastes, such as bread, *charcuterie,* or *plats en sauces.* As Grignon and Grignon (1999: 168) say about 'regular' food practices, 'among foods reputedly fattening, one more often avoids reputedly "common" foods, that is to say foods over consumed by farmers and blue-collar workers, which act as a foil and become scapegoats'. In some cases, social properties of foods can even be isolated from calorific properties, despite the fact that 'dominant taste' is often a taste for light foods. For example, the interviewees repeatedly described using large amounts of hot liquid as a stomach-filling zero-calorie snack, but they always

mentioned tea, and not coffee. Tea and coffee seem technically identical, but one of them—tea—is very specific to French upper classes today, while the other is not (Cavaillet et al., 2004).[5] The way food is chosen is also very telling:

> I selected food based on what it looked like … It had to be things that were pretty to look at, that weren't gross. (Nadège)

> My aunt and my uncle, when they saw me like that, they tried to take me out to very fancy restaurants. They knew me quite well … And in fact, it worked! I was actually eating in those places, even if it meant not eating three days before and three days after! (Véronique)

Aestheticizing food and meals as described above (rather than eating them), throwing away food or leaving it on a half-finished plate, displaying self-restraint and 'substance relegation' (Bourdieu, 1979) by 'forgetting' to eat or 'not being hungry'; all these dispositions are stereotypical habits of the upper and middle class and are clearly in opposition with working-class ones (Boltanski, 1969; Grignon and Grignon, 1980; Schwartz, 1990).[6] A similar connection can be shown to exist between anorexic sport and school practices and those of the upper and middle class in these fields (Darmon, 2003). Therefore, seemingly 'typically anorexic' practices, however pathological they may appear, clearly echo their 'normal' and class-biased counterparts.

A Class-Based Ethos

Furthermore, if we now turn to the 'anorexic ethos', it also reveals close allegiance with specific upper- and middle-class attitudes and values. For example, the corporeal asceticism anorexics display is also a corporeal elitism that distinguishes lower-class body configurations and manners as both crude and loose. It constructs corporeal capital as a 'total capital', which can, so to speak, incorporate and express *cultural* capital:

> I knew I was skinny, I knew it. But it was not enough for me. I knew that for other people,

it wasn't nice, but to my eye it was ... my eye was different and I felt happy to cultivate this difference (...) I remember I felt the utter despise for people who thought food meant congeniality (...): the very image of a lack of control and letting oneself go (...) There was one part of my family where there were ... three sisters who were ... fat ... crude ... ugly ... silly! [She laughs] It went together. And to me, the appearance went together with the intellect, the thinner I was, the smarter I was [the word fine she uses means both 'thin' and 'smart' in French] (...) When I was anorexic, this is very strange, but I felt ... I felt really at ease speaking, thinking ... I felt gifted ... And now, it's funny but I don't feel that way any longer, as if giving up anorexia had also meant giving up on the intellectual ground. (Véronique)

Such a resemblance between the anorexic world view and the upper- and middle-class one can also be found in the constant display of an ethos of control over corporeal destiny that contrasts with a more fatalist body acceptance in the working classes (Featherstone, 1987; Schwartz, 1990). This ethos is all the more salient among the interviewees that they are young and female, and therefore belong to two other groups who share this conception of the body and of the self as linked together and as structurally 'unfinished' businesses (Darmon, 2003).[7] The interviewees' discourse additionally bears witness to the existence of a more general ethos of control over social destiny which is clearly that of the middle and upper classes. This ethos might be opposed to the working class 'taste for chance', seen in how the anorexics' favourite game, described below by Camille, can be opposed to working-class preferences for lottery and games of chance (Hoggart, 1957; Weber, 1989):

This is very difficult for me to accept what I can't control, what I don't know, what comes by chance, what is 'like that', (...) what comes around even if I didn't look for it. (Christine)

At the hospital, we [anorexics] were playing checkers. It was not your usual checkers, it was much more complex, we were going very fast, the idea was to make one's way very fast so that the opponent could not see it and could do nothing about it, we were real checkers champs at X [a unit specialized in the treatment of anorexia]! (Camille)

Such an urge for control is usually analysed through psychological or psychiatric diagnoses, but it arrives at a new meaning when tied to class position and habitus. The social space in which the anorexic career develops is therefore made perceptible by taking into consideration the *location* both of the practices that constitute the anorexic career and of the ethos it displays. It moreover appears in the *orientation* of it as self-transformation work—but a transformation into what?

A Class-Oriented Conversion

This section demonstrates that the self-conversion at issue is one oriented towards the upper regions of social space by focusing again on body and food practices (for a similar analysis on sport, school and cultural practices, see Darmon, 2003).

First and foremost, losing weight is understood as a step up on the feminine social ladder, since the higher one's social origin and occupation, the lower one's weight—this being true in France for women (Bodier, 1995) and adolescent girls (De Peretti and Castetbon, 2004), with a strengthening of these social patterns since the 1980s (De Saint-Pol, 2007).

Second, the result of the self-transformation that takes place during the first phases of the anorexic career is the acquisition of dominant habits and practices: a dominant taste for foods, as when Priscille or Emily describes a 'before [anorexia]' liking of McDonald's, fries, sausages, and an 'after' [during anorexia] liking for fish, seafood, or oysters; or when Yasmine or Louise refer to a makeover involving the dominant clothing style (more slacks, formal shoes, skirts and dresses, but fewer jeans, tee-shirts and sneakers). Somatic sensations themselves are the object of such 'upwardly work'. We recall that the interviewees had to learn (or teach themselves), step-by-step, to be disgusted by greasy or sugary food, to enjoy the sensation of an 'empty stomach', or to loathe 'feeling full'. This can be seen as incorporating a dominant *somatic* culture involving dislike or even nausea for feelings of repletion, contrary to the satisfaction expressed about these sensations by members of the working classes (Boltanski, 1971). What is produced through the first phases of the career is therefore a new and dominant 'body use' [*usage due corps*] that goes down deeply to somatic sensations themselves. It is shaped through a more and more extreme repression of the working-class tastes or body uses that were present before. The anorexic career might therefore be described as an upward trajectory in the 'universe of class bodies' (Featherstone, 1987: 125) and even in the universe of deep-down class sensations. Moreover, the very existence of this work is *downplayed* by the interviewees, which bears witness to their adherence to the dominant model of a thin body obtained by 'miracle' rather than through crude 'hard work' (Bourdieu, 1979):

> I was trying to give the impression I ate normally, because I wanted to pretend I was thin while eating. That was the message I was trying to send: I was thin but I ate normally, or even I ate more than people usually do, I wasn't thin because I did not eat . . . (Louise)

The first three phases of the anorexic career and their self-transformation process are, thus, deeply shaped by the social space in which they develop. Yet, once in the hospital, will this social space of social classes give way to solely medical dimensions?

 ## The Social Space of the Hospital Phase

Medical institutions, in which the last phase occurs, are actually far from neutral spaces in regards social class.

Anorexia and Bulimia as Social-Class Stereotypes

It can first be argued that diagnoses of eating disorders involve social-class stereotypes, by which anorexia nervosa is implicitly associated by physicians with upper classes and bulimia nervosa with lower classes.[8]

Such an underlying social space appears in classical clinical texts on eating disorders, such as the following excerpt by Hilde Bruch in which true social 'prestige' is attributed to anorexics while bulimics are almost explicitly associated with financial need and even delinquency:

> [Bulimics] make an exhibitionistic display of their lack of control or discipline, in contrast to the adherence to discipline of the true anorexics . . . The modern bulimic is impressive by what looks like a deficit in the sense of responsibility (. . .). Though relatively uninvolved, they expect to share in the prestige of anorexia nervosa. Some complain about the expense of their consumption and will take food without paying for it. (Bruch, quoted in Gordon, 1990: 135)

This social distribution also comes into play in the everyday medical discourse within the therapeutic units, such as when 'typical' anorexic patients are described with attributes that are those of the upper and middle classes:

> At coffee break, a psychologist comes to me and says: 'Oh, I had to tell you, today I saw a very typical anorexic girl! She spoke to me about school, of course! I asked her: what else, than school? Well, she spoke to me about

playing the piano! What else? Well, ballet of course! School, the piano, ballet: a nice young lady like they used to make them in the good old days!' (Fieldnotes)

'Sense of repartee', 'very subtle in the interaction', 'articulate', 'sharp'. (Medical records, on anorexic patients)

Furthermore, 'typical anorexic families' are commonly described as composed of a 'feminine' father—that is to say, one closer to upper- and middle-class definitions of masculinity—and an 'often professional over-ambitious mother'. These families are strongly distinguished from 'typical bulimic families' as counterparts to one another in a way that suggests social-class stereotypes and oppositions:

Typically, anorexics' families are families where people don't show off their feelings and don't go into open conflicts, they have nothing to do with bulimics' families, which are over-fighting, very unstable, no organization, no stability, lots of shouting . . . it's a picture and its negative. In the family interview with Alexandra [a bulimic patient] and her family, they were shouting, they were ripping their heads off . . . (Staff meeting, Fieldnotes)

Finally, this opposition between anorexics and bulimics (and, indeed, their families) and its social connotations make their way into the patients' discourse, where anorexia is attributed greater social prestige than bulimia, and therefore becomes an almost *likeable,* or at least *preferred,* stigma in comparison, even for a young girl who didn't accept the anorexic label at first:

I would not acknowledge I was anorexic . . . But this friend asked me: 'but are you bulimic or anorexic?', and I said 'no!', 'no!, I'm not bulimic, I'm anorexic, OK?' The idea I was purging was unbearable . . . It was dirty and sick, whereas anorexia . . . anorexia, it's like being a delicate flower, isn't it? and that's it. (Anne)

This hierarchy between anorexia and bulimia could explain some of the aforementioned biases towards upper and middle classes conveyed by diagnosis procedures, but may also be interpreted as a medical perception of the social attributes linked with the social class status of their patients. The latter becomes more obvious in a close-up on a particularly difficult patient, described below.

A Class-Based Resistance to Medical Control

Anorexic patients are well known for their 'resistance' to the hospital's actions and point of view. They are generally defined as 'difficult', 'non-compliant' and 'resisting' patients, and were depicted as such at the fieldwork sites of this research. This resistance is generally interpreted as psychological and, importantly, is linked to mental pathology. It can, however, be illuminating to look at such resistance as a social will and way of acting, made possible by distinctive class resources. This is not to say that *only* upper- and middle-class patients can display a resistance to medical power. But the specific ways in which anorexic patients resist medical power is not absent of social class dispositions and attitudes.

This can be illustrated by focusing on a single case, informed both by the two interviews with the young girl and through observation of her stay at the hospital. During the five months of observation, three anorexic patients were deemed as 'particularly non-compliant' with Camille, a 17-year-old patient from Clinic C, as the one recognized as the most difficult. Camille is the daughter of a communication consultant and a medical doctor, both with high-level diplomas, placing Camille at the first tier of the sample in terms of class.[9] Since she turned 14 years old, Camille has been in and out of hospitals under the diagnosis of restrictive anorexia nervosa. Her medical trajectory (its length and variety) has obviously provided her with a deep insider's knowledge of the medical institution. She employed this professionalization as a patient (Barrett, 1996: 162), as a strategic weapon in the 'serious game' (Goffman, 1961) of resisting medical intervention and point of view. But it might be argued that her relation to the hospital is also shaped by her cultural and symbolic capital. For example, she speaks with irony of Clinic C as the 'hotel-restaurant-school' she is living in, while insisting that the services offered by this institution do not deserve her patronage. In contrast with difficult patients studied by Barrett (1996), Camille is not so much 'using the place as a motel' (1996: 162) than as an overrated deluxe hotel!

> When I first came here, into this room, I had my blanket changed, it was a lousy purple one, I had it changed to this green one (...) I told him [the well-known specialist of anorexia who used to treat her in his high-profile hospital], your hospital is a lousy place, it is very depressing for me to go to such a lousy place. (Camille)
>
> 17:09 Camille is very unhappy about her room, she thinks it's too small.
>
> 10:11 Clinical interview: Camille is very provocative and aggressive towards [the head psychiatrist]. She threatens to leave the hospital if she is not given a better room. (Medical and nurses records)

Additionally, Camille constantly voices contempt for the members of the treatment team who are not doctors:

> Camille had an appointment at 1:15 with Carole [a nurse]. She just forgot! I reminded her of it, she was nearly arrogant. (Nurse record)
>
> Camille is interacting only with the medical team and she gives the silent treatment to the nurse team—why? (Nurse record)
>
> When asked 'why', she replied that her grandmother—who used to be a journalist in a famous newspaper—taught her to 'rather talk to God than to His saints' [a French saying]. (Staff meeting record)

This contempt for both the 'lousy' hospital and the 'subordinate' nurses may be explained by her class position, as may be her attitudes towards doctors, with whom she combines a daring fighting spirit with a form of class solidarity and connivance (both of which she may well be exaggerating during the interview, though doctors acknowledged she had 'stood up to Y' and thrown him off balance):

> I told Y [her previous therapist, a well-known specialist of anorexia]: 'you stopped saying anything interesting during sessions long ago, you don't understand anything any longer, your theater stuff [the psychiatrist is using psychodrama as a therapeutic method] is so silly, I'm so fed up of humoring you' ... I stood up to leave the room, he tried to prevent me from doing it, so I said: 'Oh this is what your idea of freedom of speech boils down to! You will never see me again', it lasted two months, he was writing to me every week, I finally accepted to sit with him, and we talked, but I did not accept to go on therapy with him (...) I never spoke to him since. (Camille)
>
> I finally met with Mr. X. [Dr. X, a head psychiatrist at Clinic C], and he seemed OK, quite nice. And he told me: 'you come whenever you want, there will be a place for you', and usually you wait one or two years before hoping for a vacancy here, and only three days after was I accepted! Actually, there must have been a phone call from Y that may have eased things a bit ... (Camille)

Camille is the one who makes decisions about the beginning, the end and the particular techniques used in her treatment. She is the one who decides what is 'interesting' and what is not. She is the one giving the 'silent treatment' to the nurses while enjoying 'special treatment' for herself. This radical overturn of the doctor—patient power relation is all the more striking because it originates from a young girl (some of the stories she describes happened when she was 14 or 15 years old), confronting senior male doctors. It might therefore be seen that social class dispositions (such as self-assurance, a sense of entitlement, familiarity with the medical world which her mother belongs to, or a relation to 'speech' and discourse that comes with a high level of cultural capital) can account for Camille's challenges to medical authority, as well as the specific forms her challenges take.

◈ Conclusion

Epidemiological research has identified a significant association between upper- or middle-class membership and a woman's probability of becoming anorexic, but the extant literature has yet to address the social processes underlying this association. In order to fill this gap this article has proposed understanding anorexia as a deviant career—a career that is a conversion into an anorexic set of practices and orientations that can be understood as a distinctive type of Bourdieuian habitus. This article has argued that this set of practices and orientations reflects strong resonances with practices and orientations clearly identified with middle- and upper-class status.

Such an argument should not be interpreted to mean that anorexia cannot, or does not, exist among members of the working classes. On the contrary, this approach provides a structure from which to analyse such cases as 'atypical' in terms of social class, or, alternatively, as signs of diffusion of representations or practices from one social location to another. The inscription of the anorexic career in a social space is also not to be equated with the explanation of eating disorders as related to family socialization; it nevertheless defines a 'locus' where the very practices of anorexic conversion find facilitating dispositions. This is not understood as causes *per se* but, rather, as social conditions of possibility or of likelihood.

The model offered has been constructed by combining two sociological traditions—a symbolic interactionist approach and a Bourdieuian approach—that are usually deemed incompatible. The symbolic interactionist approach to deviant careers is seen as powerful in highlighting the processual dimension of social life, the meaning people give to their activity, and the way such activity is seen and labelled by others. Yet it is also said to evade questions of the structural determinations of practice. Conversely, the Bourdieuian approach to practice is seen as paramount in revealing hidden and underlying social influences, *par excellence* those of social class, but it is often said to lack an analysis of the activity itself. The theoretical articulation used in this article (career *and* habitus, process *and* structure, label *and* class) is offered as a way to take the best of two worlds.

◈ Notes

1. The criteria regarding economic and cultural capital provided by (Pinçon and Pinçon-Charlot, 2000) and deriving from their research on French bourgeoisie were used to differentiate upper classes from middle classes.

2. For an inventory of existing literature on religious conversion careers, see Gooren, 2005, and for a sociology of conversion processes in other settings than religious ones, and a stress on their variations, see Greil and Rudy, 1983. What is meant here by 'conversion' is an actual transformation of the individual, and not only a change in his/her conceptions, world views or self-identity (Darmon, 2006: 113–21).

3. For a detailed analysis of the anorexic career, see Darmon, 2003: 77–245.

4. For a review of the existing literature on the subject and a demonstration of the persistence of class variations, see Régnier et al., 2006.

5. This is probably one instance of a specificity deriving from a social and national space of eating practices, since the opposition between coffee and tea could be reversed elsewhere—or replaced by other alternatives involving diet sodas, low-fat lattes or fancy mineral waters.

6. More recent research on this kind of class-oriented French attitude towards food is not available, but the persistence of class variations in food consumption (Régnier et al., 2006) and the strengthening of class variations as far as body sizes are concerned (De Saint Pol, 2007) strongly suggest it still exists.

7. For a general theory of the contemporary construction of the body as 'a project which should be worked at and accomplished as part of an individual's self identity', see Schilling, 1993: 5, and for a theory of body modification see Featherstone, 1999. For an analysis of the relation between anorexia and social injunctions of transformation on female bodies, see also MacSween, 1993: 174.

8. For a study of diagnosis as a social category in an American context, where race comes into play as much as class, see Gremillion, 2003: 157–92 on the social class stereotypes underlying the diagnosis opposition between anorexic and borderline patients.

9. The two other anorexic patients who were deemed as 'particularly non-compliant' during my fieldwork at the hospital were significantly also located at the top of the sample in terms of class.

◇ References

Barrett, R. (1996) *The Psychiatric Team and the Social Definition of Schizophrenia*. Cambridge: Cambridge University Press.

Becker, H. S. (1963) *Outsiders*. New York: The Free Press of Glencoe.

Becker, H. S. (1998) *Tricks of the Trade. How to Think about your Research while You're Doing it*. Chicago, IL: University of Chicago Press.

Bodier, M. (1995) 'Le corps change, son image aussi', INSEE *Première* 356: 1–4.

Boltanski, L. (1969) *Prime éducation et morale de classe*. Paris: EHESS.

Boltanski, L. (1971) 'Les usages sociaux du corps', *Annales* E.S.C. 26(1): 205–33.

Bourdieu, P. (1979) *La Distinction. Critique sociale du jugement*. Paris: Minuit.

Bourdieu, P. (1997) *Méditations pascaliennes*. Paris: Seuil.

Bordo, S. (1993) *Unbearable Weight. Feminism, Western Culture, and the Body*. Berkeley, CA: University of California Press.

Brumberg, J. J. (1988) *Fasting Girls. The History of Anorexia Nervosa*. Cambridge, MA: Harvard University Press.

Cavaillet, F., N. Darmon, A. Lhuissier and F. Régnier (2004) *L'alimentation des populations défavorisées en France*. Document de travail 2004–9. Ivry sur Seine: INRA-Corela.

Darmon, M. (2003) *Devenir anorexique: une approche sociologique*. Paris: La Decouverte.

Darmon, M. (2006) *La socialisation*. Paris: Armand Colin.

Darmon, M. (2008) 'La Notion de carrière: un instrument interactionniste d'objectivation', *Politix* 82(21): 149–67.

De Peretti, C. and K. Castetbon (2004) 'Surpoids et obésité chez les adolescents scolarisés en classe de troisième', *Etudes et résultats* DREES 283.

De Saint-Pol, T. (2007) 'L'obésité en France: les écarts entre catégories socials s'accroissent', *Insee Première* 1123.

Ekins, R. (1997) *Male Femaling. A Grounded Theory Approach to Cross-dressing and Sex-changing*. London: Routledge.

Evans, J., E. Rich and R. Holroyd (2004) 'Disordered Eating and Disordered Schooling: What Schools Do to Middle Class Girls', *British Journal of Sociology of Education* 25(2): 123–42.

Featherstone, M. (1987) 'Leisure, Symbolic Power and the Life Course', in J. Horne, D. Jary and A. Tomlinson (eds) *Sport, Leisure and Social Relations*, pp. 113–38. London: Routledge.

Featherstone, M. (1999) 'Body Modification: An Introduction', *Body and Society* 5(2–3): 1–13.

Goffman, E. (1961) *Asylums. Essays on the Social Situation of Mental Patients and Other Inmates*. Garden City, NY: Doubleday.

Gooren, H. (2005) 'Towards a New Model of Conversion Careers: The Impact of Personality and Contingency Factors', *Exchange* 34(2): 149–66.

Gordon, R. A. (1990) *Anorexia and Bulimia: Anatomy of a Social Epidemic*. Cambridge: Blackwell.

Greil, A. L. and D. L. Rudy (1983) 'Conversion to the World View of Alcoholics Anonymous: A Refinement of Conversion Theory', *Qualitative Sociology* 6(1): 5–28.

Gremillion, H. (2003) *Feeding Anorexia: Gender and Power at a Treatment Center*. Durham, NC: Duke University Press.

Grignon, C. and C. Grignon (1980) 'Styles d'alimentation et goûts populaires', *Revue française de sociologie* 21(4): 531–69.

Grignon, C. and C. Grignon (1999) 'Long-term Trends in Food Consumption: A French Portrait', *Food and Foodways* 8(3): 151–74.

Herpin, N. and N. Manon (1997) 'Approvisionnement, menus et obésité dans les foyers les plus pauvres', in S. Lollivier and D. Verger 'Pauvreté d'existence, monétaire ou subjective sont distinctes', *Economie et Statistique* 308–309–310: 117–18.

Hoggart, R. (1957) *The Uses of Literacy. Aspects of Working-class Life with Special Reference to Publications and Entertainments*. London: Chatto & Windus.

Lahire, B. (2003) 'From the Habitus to an Individual Heritage of Dispositions. Towards a Sociology at the Level of the Individual', *Poetics, Journal of Empirical Research on Culture, the Media and the Arts* 31: 329–55.

Lawrence, M. (1987) 'Education and Identity: The Social Origins of Anorexia', in M. Lawrence (ed.) *Fed up and Hungry: Women, Oppression and Food*, pp. 207–25. London: Women's Press.

McClelland, L. and A. Crisp (2001) 'Anorexia and Social Class', *International Journal of Eating Disorders* 29(2): 150–6.

McLorg, P. A. and D. E. Taub (1994[1987]) 'Anorexia Nervosa and Bulimia: The Development of Deviant Identities', *Deviant Behavior* 8, republished in P. A. Adler and P. Adler *Constructions of Deviance: Social Power, Context, and Interaction*, pp. 249–61. New York: Wadsworth.

MacSween, M. (1993) *Anorexic Bodies. A Feminist and Sociological Perspective on Anorexia Nervosa*. London: Routledge.

Peters, N. (1995) 'The Ascetic Anorexic', *Social Analysis* 37: 44–66.

Pinçon, M. and M. Pinçon-Charlot (2000) *Sociologie de la bourgeoisie*. Paris: La Découverte.

Régnier, F., A. Lhuissier and S. Gojard (2006) *Sociologie de l'alimentation*. Paris: La Découverte.

Schwartz, O. (1990) *Le monde privé des ouvriers. Hommes et femmes du Nord*. Paris: Presses Universitaires de France.

Shilling, C. (1993) *The Body and Social Theory*. London: Sage.

Turner, B. S. (1996) *The Body and Society. Explorations in Social Theory*. London: Sage.

Wacquant, L. (1989) 'Corps et âme. Notes ethnographiques d'un apprenti-boxeur', *Actes de la recherche en sciences sociales* 80: 33–67.

Weber, F. (1989) *Le Travail à-côté*. Paris: Editions de l'EHESS-Inra.

READING 37

In the early 1990s, David Brown (1991) published an interesting article focusing on how deviant people often exit their careers by helping those "like themselves." Alcoholics, drug addicts, offenders released from prison, those with eating disorders, and other deviants become committed to changing their deviant ways, are transformed, and, in turn, have a calling to help others and even gain the education requirement to become counselors. In this article, Sharpe and Hope argue that at least some deviants may exit the particular deviant career but still be involved in deviant activities. Borrowing ideas from symbolic interactionist and self-control theories, they describe the scandals in the drug and alcohol treatment industry in Texas to show that other deviant behaviors may be picked up following a conversion to a nondeviant status as the actors gain access to different illegitimate opportunities.

The Professional Ex- Revisited

Cessation or Continuation of a Deviant Career?

Susan F. Sharp and Trina L. Hope

The process of exiting a deviant career has been the focus of a number of studies (cf. Meisenhelder 1977; Anspach 1979; Luckenbill and Best 1981). Brown (1991) used this perspective in his study of *professional ex-s,* "persons who have exited their deviant careers by replacing them with occupations in professional counseling" (p. 219). The individual is thus transformed, abandoning a deviant lifestyle for a more conventional one that is grounded in the former deviant status. The former prisoner, eating disorder victim, addict, or alcoholic deliberately embraces the deviant status to qualify as a counselor for others similarly afflicted. Indeed, the abandoned deviant lifestyle ultimately provides both legitimacy and income. The individual now shares his or her personal recovery process, seen as almost sacred, having undergone "a transforming therapeutic resocialization" (Brown 1991,

223). In the current study, we focus on one type of professional ex-: the former substance abuser who becomes a substance abuse counselor.

The current study offers an alternate view of the professional ex-. It suggests that becoming a professional ex- may not always signify "salvation" (Brown 1991, 228). Instead, at times it may provide a facade of legitimacy, behind which deviant behavior continues. The distinction between a deviant role and a deviant career is relevant to this approach.

While Brown's (1991) description is linked to a particular type of deviance, we suggest that the professional ex- may continue to engage in deviant behavior, having merely exited one type of deviant *role.* The alcohol and drug treatment industry scandals that occurred in Texas during the mid-1990s are presented in support of our contention.

Source: Sharpe, Susan F., and Trina L. Hope. 2001. "The Professional Ex- Revisited: Cessation or Continuation of a Deviant Career?" *Journal of Contemporary Ethnography* 30:678–703. Reprinted with permission.

◆ Propensity Toward Deviance: Fluidity Versus Stability

Sociological approaches suggest two widely divergent views of deviant careers. On one hand, we find those who explore the processes of entering and abandoning deviant careers and lifestyles. In this approach, deviance is seen as fluid, with individuals moving into and out of deviant careers. The professional ex-'s transformation to legitimacy exemplifies this approach.

However, other experts suggest that the propensity to engage in deviance is virtually immutable. If this is the case, one might expect the professional ex- to continue to engage in deviant behaviors. This perspective is exemplified in Gottfredson and Hirschi's (1990) general theory of crime, also known as self-control theory. A brief examination of these opposing perspectives may help clarify the issue.

Deviant Careers: Symbolic Interactionist Theory and Fluidity

Symbolic interactionist theory supports the idea of fluidity, suggesting that individuals move into and out of deviant careers. This perspective focuses on ways in which identity is continuously renegotiated through interaction with the social environment (Cooley 1902; Mead 1934; Goffman 1959; Blumer 1969). "Here the self is constructed through adjustment. The issue is for the actor to fit his/her self into the dominant character of the situation or structure: adjusting to an obdurate reality" (Fine 1993, 78). From this viewpoint, the self is constantly in flux, and identity is continuously emerging. This ties in well with the concept of exiting a deviant career. Fine (1993) suggested that, in a different situation, the individual will adjust his or her self-concept of fit the new reality. Thus, a former alcoholic who has become a professional ex- develops a new definition of self to fit the new situation. He or she could then be expected to discard characteristics that no longer apply.

Abandonment of a deviant career may occur due to either internal forces or external ones. For examples, Briathwaite (1989) argued that "shame" can be a constructive force, coercing the deviant back into compliance with group norms. Others suggested that deviants are pushed or pulled into conventionality. Adler (1992) applied this approach to drug dealers. Significantly, she noted that the movement away from deviance and toward conformity was characterized by inconsistency. Cessation of drug dealing was often followed by lapses back into the behavior. Over time, the periods between lapses became longer, ultimately resulting in transition into a new nondeviant lifestyle. Still others suggest that the deviant may go through a process of withdrawal in preparation for return to the larger society, as in the case of prisoners (Irwin 1970; Schmid and Jones 1991) and female street criminals (Sommers, Baskin, and Fagan 1994).

According to this approach, the deviant individual may go to great lengths to avoid detection or to control the information the information others obtain about them (Goffman 1963; Herman 1993). Alternately, he or she may attempt to redefine the behavior or condition as nondeviant (Horowitz and Liebowitz 1968; Meisenhelder 1977; Anspach 1979; Stall and Biernacki 1989). Still others may extend the old deviant roe into a new "conventional" one (Brown 1991; Rice, 1992; see also Ebaugh 1988). Indeed, the individual may even rely on former experience to develop an entirely new field of endeavor, as in the case of emergence of codependency treatment professionals (Rice 1992).

Deviant Careers: Self-Control Theory and Stability

The current study proposes a different approach to the idea of the deviant career, within the framework of Gottfredson and Hirschi's (1990) self-control theory. Self-control theory provides a unique perspective on the professional ex-. First, in contrast to the notion of deviance as fluid, Gottfredson and Hirschi not only emphasized the *stability* of deviance over the life course, they critiqued the use of the term *career* to refer to crime and deviance over time. Second, the specific case studied here provides a nice example of Gottfredson and Hirschi's discussion of white-collar crime and offenders. Before applying their theory to the issue of the professional ex-, however, a discussion of their distinction between crime and self-control is necessary, along with the importance of stability and versatility.

In 1983, Hirschi and Gottfredson suggested that age has a direct effect on crime—one that is invariant across time, culture, sex, race, and various criminal acts. In a follow-up piece (Hirschi and Gottfredson 1986), they introduced the distinction between crime and criminality as a way of solving some of the problems introduced by their age-crime argument. Here, they noted that the *tendency* to engage in crime remains stable, even though criminal *behavior* follows the age-crime curve. This distinction between crime (behavior) and criminality (tendency) is important in understanding the questions of stability versus fluidity, especially with regard to the professional ex-.

Gottfredson and Hirschi (1990) defined *criminality* as the stable differences across individuals in the propensity to commit criminal acts: "Criminality may be defined as the tendency of the actor to seek short-term, immediate pleasure without regard for long-term consequences" (Hirschi and Gottfredson 1986, 58). Gottfredson and Hirschi (1990) later defined criminality by *self-control,* the differential tendency of people to avoid criminal acts regardless of the circumstances in which they find themselves. They began their discussion of the concept of self-control by describing six elements of criminal acts and the corresponding characteristics of those engaging in such acts. According to the authors, crime and analogous behaviors provide immediate gratification of desires; easy or simple gratification of desires; excitement, thrill, and risk; few or meager long-term benefits; little skill or planning; and pain or discomfort for the victims (p. 89). Correspondingly, those lacking in self-control will "tend to be impulsive, insensitive, physical (as opposed to mental), risk-taking, shortsighted, and nonverbal, and they will tend therefore to engage in criminal and analogous acts" (p. 90). Furthermore, they suggested that deviance, criminality, and recklessness are parts of a single larger category that is characterized by a focus on the attainment of immediate pleasure coupled with lack of concern about future harmful consequences. The low self-control individual is thus one who is likely to choose, when the opportunity is presented, immediate

gratification, despite the potential of long-term negative consequences.

Gottfredson and Hirschi (1990) asserted that their concept of self-control is unique because it explicitly addresses stability as well as versatility. The former suggests that the tendency to engage in criminal or deviant acts emerges early in life and persists over time (Caspi, Bem, and Elder 1989; Sampson and Laub 1993; White et al. 1990; Wright et al. 1999). Versatility suggests that low self-control manifests itself in a variety of criminal and analogous acts (Britt 1994; LeBlanc and Girard 1997). When discussing versatility, Gottfredson and Hirschi asserted, "In our view, the common element in crime, deviant behavior, sin and accidents is so overriding that the tendency to treat them as distinct phenomena subject to distinct causes is one of the major intellectual errors of positive thought" (p. 10).

Gottfredson and Hirschi's (1990) theory of self-control provided a clear distinction between criminality and crime, suggesting that those with low self-control will be more likely to engage in crime and behavior analogous to crime. The theory has been empirically tested by a variety of researchers, and the overall results have been favorable (Pratt and Cullen 2000). It has not, however, been used to explore the phenomenon of the professional ex-.

When using the concept of self-control to further our understanding of the professional ex-, one of the first critiques that Gottfredson and Hirschi (1990) applied to the fluidity argument is the use of the word *career* in reference to crime. They said,

> What is the meaning of the idea of a career? Whether applied to dentistry, college teaching, or crime, the concept of a career implies several things. It suggests a beginning, as in "When did you become a teacher?" and end, as in "When did you quit teaching?" Give a beginning and an end, the career concept also implies variable duration or length, as in "How long did you (or how much longer do you plan to) teach?" (p. 266)

Central to the career paradigm are the assumptions that offenders should engage in more serious or specialized crime as they age and that the concepts of "onset, dura-tion, and desistance might lead to a better understand-ing of the crime problem" (p. 266). Gottfredson and Hirschi pointed out that offenders do not specialize and do not engage in more serious crime over time, and those who are deviant at one age are more likely to be deviant at another age. They concluded,

> If offenders do not specialize in particular types of crime, if they do not become progres-sively more criminal or more skilled in crime as the years pass, and if they do not make enough money from crime to live, then how do we account for the continued interest in career criminals? (p. 267)

Thus, low self-control is not a career choice. Instead, it is a propensity toward crime and analogous behaviors that is established early, persists over time, and manifests itself in a variety of behaviors. It does not necessarily involve and embracement of the role of deviant or a transformed self-image—it is simply an "individual characteristic relevant to the commission of criminal acts" (Gottfredson and Hirschi 1990, 88).

From the perspective of self-control theory, then, we would expect the professional ex- (someone who has exhibited low self-control behavior in the past) to continue to participate in deviant behaviors. This is not because of limited choices or poor self-concept, as sug-gested by the labeling approach (Lemert 1951; Becker 1963; Erikson 1966; Schur 1971). Instead, he or she is attracted to behaviors that result in immediate gratifica-tion given the right opportunity. Cessation of drinking or drug use, as in the case of the "recovering" substance abuse counselor, may be the result of "natural sanc-tions" rather than improved self-control, "governed more by its physiological effects than by its social con-sequences" (Hirschi and Gottfredson 1994, 4). However, compared to others of the same age, low-self-control individuals remain more likely to engage in a variety of criminal, analogous, or reckless behaviors. The profes-sional ex- who has stopped using alcohol or drugs should thus still be likely to engage in other behaviors that provide short-term gratification.

Although Gottfredson and Hirschi (1990) asserted that low self-control is a major predictor of criminal behavior, they also recognized that it is the intersection of low self-control with criminal opportunity that pro-duces crime. Routine activity theory (Cohen and Felson 1979) reminds us crime occurs when a victim, an offender, and opportunity come together in the legiti-mate and illegitimate routines of daily life. Working as a counselor in a drug treatment center provides the professional ex- with ample opportunities for a variety of deviant behaviors.

The Professional Ex- as a White-Collar Offender

Gottfredson and Hirschi (1990) have always maintained theirs to be a general theory of crime and deviance—explaining all types of crimes, including white-collar crimes and white-collar offenders. They said,

> In fact, we would suggest that any theory of crime making claim to generality would apply without difficulty to the crimes of the rich and powerful, crimes *committed in the course of an occupation,* and crimes in which a position of power, influence, or trust is used for the pur-pose of individual or organizational gain. (p. 183, emphasis added)

Contrary to the assumptions held by both academ-ics and laypeople, Gottfredson and Hirschi (1990) chal-lenged the image of white-collar crimes as complicated, well-planned acts and the image of white-collar offend-ers as intelligent people of high status and influence. The problem with most research, they contended, is that it compares high-status white-collar offenders to low-status "street" offenders—ignoring high-status, white-collar, *nonoffenders,* as well as low-status white-collar offenders. They reminded us that white-collar crime is relatively rare and that "when opportunity is taken into account, demographic differences in white-collar crime are the same as demographic differences in ordinary crime" (p. 196). In other words, when opportunity is taken into account, embezzlement is more often committed by those of lower status (i.e., the young, nonwhites) than those of higher status.

Overall, Gottfredson and Hirschi (1990) reminded us that because occupations generally require traits like dependability, punctuality, and self-control, people with jobs will tend to be less criminal overall than people without jobs. They argued that if the typical street offender were given the opportunity to commit white-collar crime, he would certainly take it, even without extended exposure to a crime-producing "business culture" (p. 198). By hiring the professional ex- (a person with a history of deviance), treatment programs are essentially providing us with an experimental test of Gottfredson and Hirschi's assertions.

One reason white-collar offending is relatively rare is because the opportunity to engage in such behavior depends on an occupation, and generally employers try to avoid hiring employees with deviant histories. The professional ex-, however, is hired *because* of his or her deviant history. From the perspective of self-control theory, the fact that professional ex-s engaged in enough occupational deviance to cause the treatment industry scandals in Texas is certainly not surprising.

The Professional Ex-: Implications of the Two Approaches

To explore the utility of low self-control as an explanation of continued deviance among professional ex-s, the current study focuses on individuals involved in the field of alcohol and drug abuse treatment. Events that occurred in the state of Texas during the early 1990s will be offered as evidence. In particular, we present a case study of an agency that was embroiled in the funding scandals.

Brown (1991) has presented an image of the professional ex- making a transition from deviant to conforming behavior, using past deviance as the foundation for the new legitimacy. In contrast, we argue that the role of professional ex- may also represent a continuation of deviant behaviors. This approach is important in extending our knowledge of career deviance, as research has concentrated on the "exit" from a particular type of deviance (cf. Irwin 1970; Shover 1983;

Adler 1992). Scant attention has been paid to whether the individual is engaging in other types of deviance. A distinction between deviant *career* and deviant *role* is germane to the argument. If the concepts of the generality and stability of deviance are accurate, cessation of a particular form of deviance would not necessarily indicate cessation of all forms of deviant behavior. Instead, it may only indicate cessation of one deviant behavior in favor of another.

One final issue must be addressed: the conceptualization of deviance. Perhaps no other issue is more controversial in the field sociology, with conceptualizations of deviance ranging from moral or absolute stances to social constructionist approaches. However, the debates about what acts should be considered deviant fall outside of the scope of this work, and we use a definition of deviance that is in keeping with the theoretical basis of the study. Following Hirschi and Gottfredson (1994), deviance is conceptualized as "acts of self-interest" that "provide immediate benefit at the risk of long-term cost to actors who find opportunities for such acts appealing" (p. 10). In other words, for the purposes of the analyses that follow, an act is deviant if the goal is short-term pleasure or gain, the act has a high potential for negative consequences, and the actor engages in it despite the consequences. Thus, financially lucrative crime, smoking, illicit sex, and gambling all meet the criteria of the definition.

Method

The analyses center on a case study of one nonprofit substance abuse treatment agency (hereafter referred to as ARC). This organization became the focus of a scandal that occurred in Texas during the early 1990s. A large nonprofit organization, ARC administered substance abuse treatment programs for medically indigent individuals. The programs operated by ARC included a detoxification program, two outpatient programs for adults, inpatient treatment for adults, inpatient treatment for adolescents, a halfway house for recovering individuals, a halfway house for criminal justice referrals, a program for offenders under the supervision of the federal criminal justice system, and a long-term residential facility for adults. At times, ARC also operated an adolescent outpatient program, a female adolescent program, a women's program, and a satellite program in a neighboring county.

During the 1990s, Texas was rocked by a series of scandals in the alcohol and drug abuse treatment field. Eventually, criminal proceedings against a number of individuals resulted, as well as the investigation and restructuring of the Texas Commission on Alcohol and Drug Abuse (TCADA). TCADA funded and supervised substance abuse treatment throughout the state. The case study of one organization is imbedded in the larger context of the investigations that began with this agency.

The case study method is suitable for two reasons. First, it provides a richness of detail not as readily available through survey data (Feagin, Orum, and Sjoberg 1991; Geis 1991; Orum, Feagin, and Sjoberg 1991). Although limited in generalizability, the data derived in a case study can provide insights into human interaction not accessible through questionnaires (Sjoberg et al. 1991, 32). Equally important, case studies may bring into question a current theory by uncovering new information. "Although they cannot establish a generalization, they can invalidate one and suggest new research directions" (Reinharz 1992, 69). In the current study, this is our primary objective. Our focus is to suggest that cessation of a deviant career may not be an accurate description.

Instead, we offer an alternative view—that individuals may cease one type of deviance due to natural sanctions but continue to engage in other forms.

The data came from four sources: newspaper accounts, official records of investigations conducted by TCADA, direct observation, and in-depth interviews. By using this variety of sources, a detailed picture emerges.

First, we obtained copies of all currently available articles documenting the treatment scandals from the archives of the primary newspaper in the city where ARC was located. In addition, we obtained articles on investigations in two other Texas cities. Attempts to locate articles in the archives of three other cities were unsuccessful. A total of thirty-two newspaper articles from March 1994 through June 1997 were examined.

We also obtained reports of official investigations of ARC from TCADA. These were used to substantiate the veracity and accuracy of the newspaper accounts (see Wolcott 1990, 27). The official documents included the original complaint, the summary report of the complaint, summaries of findings, the agreed administrative order between TCADA and ARC, and correspondence between TCADA and ARC related to the investigations.

The third source of data was direct observation. Like Brown (1991), one of the authors worked in the field of substance abuse treatment. Furthermore, from 1989 through late 1991, she directed a program for ARC. These personal observations allowed insider's access to events as well as familiarity with the agency and the individuals involved (Reinharz 1992; Lofland and Lofland 1995). In late 1989, she began keeping a journal of questionable events that occurred in the day-to-day operation of the agency. The journal was kept due to concerns about possible illegalities and self-protection. Other journal entries followed conversations with the two top administrators of the organization as well as with employees. Copies of invoices for questionable purchase and internal memorandums were also kept. These records became a postfacto source of data, as the original purpose was not research.

The final source of data consisted of relevant observations by other "insiders." During 1995, the same author conducted in-depth interviews with fifteen treatment professionals employed by the agency. Participants were obtained using a modified snowball sampling strategy, beginning with five former employees and coworkers. All participants were counselors or supervisors who had worked for ARC during the early 1990s, and all but one claimed professional ex- status. Interviews were semistructured. Participants were asked open-ended questions about illegal behavior or deviant behavior they had observed as well as about behaviors in which they had personally participated. The interviews were conducted under strict assurances of anonymity. Thus, to protect these participants, audiotapes were destroyed, and pseudonyms were used. Eight interviews were taped; in the others, extensive notes were taken. Behaviors were deemed deviant if they met the criteria used by Gottfredson and Hirschi (1990) as acts of self-interest engaged in without consideration of the potentially negative consequences. (See the Appendix for summary descriptions of the interview participants.)

◈ Findings

Professional Ex-s in the Drug Treatment Industry

In the state of Texas, all substance abuse counselors must be licensed by TCADA, which also acts as a watchdog over counselor behaviors. In addition, TCADA licenses all substance abuse treatment programs in the state and is a major funding source. In mid-1999, there were 5,271 licensed chemical dependency counselors in Texas. There is, however, no may to determine the percentage claiming professional ex- status since alcoholism is covered by the Americans with Disabilities Act. This makes it illegal to inquire whether an applicant is an alcoholic. It is noteworthy, however, that TCADA requires two years of abstinence from alcohol and drugs prior to licensure, suggesting that the agency has reason to believe that many applicants have substance abuse histories (Hernandez 1999).

Personal experience suggested that the majority of those working in the substance abuse treatment field were former substance abusers. For example, during the two years that one of the authors ran a program for ARC, twenty-seven direct service employees self-identified as professional ex-s. Only one employee during that period (a cook) did not claim to be in recovery from substance abuse. This pattern was consistent throughout ARC. Indeed, many employees were former clients, as was the case with ten of the fifteen interview participants. At the time of hiring, the author was the only program director out of nine that was not a former client. Furthermore, the executive director, the director, and the chairman of the board also claimed professional ex-status.

ARC and the Texas Treatment Scandal

On March 29, 1994, the general public in the state of Texas became aware of scandal brewing in the substance abuse treatment industry. The *American-Statesman* headline asserted, "Center's Audit Uncovers Gifts, Lavish Bonuses" (Elliott 1994d). The story, based on an audit resulting from an anonymous tip (TCADA 1993, 1994d), detailed allegation of financial impropriety, including excessive bonuses, expensive gifts, and overbilling. ARC was a private nonprofit agency funded by state and federal grants. In less than three years, top officials were alleged to have paid themselves and other employees bonuses totaling more than three hundred thousand dollars. In addition, government funds were allegedly used to buy rare books, sapphire cufflinks, and expensive cigars for the two administrators (Elliott 1994d).

Within days, additional allegations were made. Mileage reimbursement to one administrator totaled more than twenty thousand dollars in a two-year period. At state reimbursement rates, this was equivalent to about sixty-seven thousand miles of travel (or two and a half times around the equator). In addition, state funds were used to pay air travel for family members, lease payments on a personal luxury vehicle, expensive meals, and personal interest-free loans (The allegations keep piling up 1994). It was also reported that the chairman of the board of directors received payment for services. This was in direct violation of the contract with the TCADA. Other board members had received fees for services rendered, also in violation of the contract (White and Elliott 1994). Within days, further information was disclosed. During the time the administrators were receiving excessively high bonuses (one received more than three times his annual salary in bonuses in less than three years), counselors providing direct services were significantly underpaid, resulting in high employee turnover (Elliott 1994e). At the same time, official state data indicated that more than half of the intended clients of the center were unable to obtain services (Copelin 1994).

These revelations were even more startling in light of further allegations. One of the administrators, with the knowledge and consent of the another, was accused of setting up a dummy corporation that received an additional $187,500 in payments during 1993. Furthermore, the chairman of the board of directors knew about these additional payments but did not inform other board members (Copelin 1994).

The above scenarios would only hint at the existence of deviant behavior if no further action had occurred. However, actions taken by ARC and the criminal justice system indicated that many of the allegations had merit (Elliott 1997a, 1994b, 1994c, 1994f, 1995a; White 1994a, 1994b). First, ARC agreed to refund more than $1 million to the funding agency (TCADA 1994a; Elizondo 1996). Furthermore, current board members were not to be reappointed or employed by the agency in the future (Elliott 1994a, 1995a; TCADA 1994a).

Allegations against the top administrators were substantiated. For example, the TCADA investigation provided detailed information about the use of ARC funds to purchase rare books, with receipts altered to hide the nature of the purchases (TCADA 1994b, 1994c, 1994e, 1996a, 1996b; Austin Rehabilitation Center 1996). Review of petty cash records indicated frequent withdrawals with little or no documentation, large bonuses, and conflicts of interest (TCADA 1996a, 1996b). Two years after the scandal broke, one of the administrators pled guilty to charges of conspiracy to commit money laundering whereas the other plead guilty to making false statements (Herrera 1996b). In 1997, the former was sentenced to five years in federal prison and fined two hundred thousand dollars. In late 1996, the latter was placed on probation and fined five thousand dollars (Herrera 1997).

These events were not isolated. Indeed, the events divulged to the public were similar to those observed by one of the authors. The first observation of self-serving deviant behavior occurred only three weeks after employment began. This event was the catalyst that prompted careful documentation. A call from ARC administrative offices indicated that several new televisions had been donated to the program. A staff member was sent to pick these up and deliver them to the treatment site. Hours later, some

very used televisions arrived. The staff member relayed the following story:

> I don't know what's happenin'—it was too— you know—I had to—[the chairman] told me to put TVs in the van and follow him. We went out to his house and he said it would be just a minute. This kid came out and carried them inside. [The chairman] told me to help and then to take these old TVs and put them on the van.

The used televisions were delivered to the program, while the new ones remained at the chairman's home. When approached about the televisions, one of the executives later charged with misappropriation of funds advised the author to ignore what had happened: "Just forget about it—we've got lots of money to spend. Go down to [a local appliance store] and buy four televisions. Do any of your staff need a TV?"

The next concern involved the costs of furnishings for the program, which were purchased from a store whose top executive was also a member of the ARC board. The prices reflected in the invoices appeared excessive, particularly in light of the fact that ARC was mandated to provide services to an indigent population. Apparently, TCADA eventually agreed. Subsequent purchases of $153,195 from the same store were disallowed because they were "considered unnecessary and no prior TCADA approval [was] obtained" (TCADA 1996b, 4).

Another incident involved the potential of a TCADA commissioner's earning a very large fee. ARC was considering expansion of one program and began looking for suitable properties. One property under consideration was selling for almost 1 million dollars, and the realtor trying to arrange the sale was a TCADA commissioner. Essentially, if the sale had transpired, the TCADA commissioner would have received a substantial fee, paid out of the funds that he was involved in providing to the agency. Shortly after this incident, the paycheck of the author began including five hundred dollars per month as a bonus. When the executives were approached about this, she was told that this was a way to get around pay limitations. Furthermore, one of them expressed belief that employees should get extra perks since the company had no retirement plan. It was at this point that the author resigned.

Six interview participants worked as program directors for ARC, five of whom self-identified as professional ex-s. Several reported similar experiences. For example, Val relayed an interesting experience. She received instructions to purchase a grandfather clock from a business operated by one of the board members. The invoice for the clock was for more than nine thousand dollars. In addition, gold-plated faucets were installed in her center. She said, "What was going on? A $10,000 clock? For these kids? Please—give *me* that money and I'll make sure my staff have a good Christmas." She was told by one of the executives to not worry about "things that don't concern you." She also expressed concern about inadequate nutrition for the clients, claiming that her budget did not allow the purchase of much meat or fresh produce. Instead, the clients were fed government commodities. She became concerned about the integrity of the agency and quit shortly thereafter.

That facility was then taken over by Diane, the only interview participant not claiming to be a professional ex-. Initially, she had faith in the two top executives, and after six months, she moved to a larger program as director. It was at the latter facility that she began having concerns. She discovered falsification in the billing procedures and resigned. "Something just smelled bad. At first, I thought it was just a mistake. [The director] got angry and told me the billing was just fine and to quit tilting at windmills."

Similarly, Andrea claimed that she was instructed to falsify dates on client discharges, allowing ARC to bill the state for clients that had already left. She also relayed a story that provides additional insight into the behavior of professional ex-s. One of her roommates, Joe, was ARC's accountant as well as coordinator of the aftercare program. Joe was asked to resign after the discovery that he had embezzled almost twenty thousand dollars to cover gambling debts. No criminal charges were filed, Joe received severance pay, and he claimed he was not required to repay the stolen funds.

At first, Andrea thought it was compassionate, but in light of later issues, she decided it was a cover-up: "I mean, $20,000? And no consequences? I thought, man, I should be an accountant. You know—I mean, I could do a lot with $20,000. But then, I started thinking, '[The director] never does anything without a motive,' you know." Joe's case is interesting for two reasons. First, he was a professional ex-, and the embezzlement and gambling were indicative of both versatility and stability of deviance. In addition, the lack of consequences for his behavior suggests that he may have been aware of questionable financial transactions and able to use his knowledge as leverage.

Not all of the program directors described agency wrongdoing. Lizette staunchly supported the agency and its executives, and she argued that the investigation was a "witch hunt" designed to discredit the two executives. She commented that the two executives "deserved" more pay and that the bonuses and dummy corporation allowed them to receive fair pay. "People don't know how hard he works—he's always up there on the weekend. He hasn't had a vacation in years. So, this is—I mean it's only fair." However, it is noteworthy that Lizette herself benefited substantially from her employment at the agency. She was one of the "others" who had received bonuses equal to almost double her salary during 1993. After the scandals broke, Lizette left the agency. According to Paula, who took over Lizette's duties, the paperwork was in disarray at the time that she left, and client charts were discovered hidden: "You wouldn't believe the mess—there were charts that hadn't had entries in months. We found them in drawers, in closets—it was fucking unbelievable."

Lizette moved to another agency, where she supervised Belinda, another participant. Belinda reported that Lizette appeared to be misappropriating funds. She had documented numerous instances of checks drawn for cash with no documentation. She eventually reported here observations to TCADA, and Lizette resigned. Currently, Lizette is awaiting sentencing for a number of offenses including forgery and forged prescriptions. "Mmm-hmm. She learned from the best—sitting there nodding out like a junkie. She just come around to get money, her and that no-good [another professional ex-]. They be flying high."

While the above events are disturbing, alone they provide little evidence of widespread ongoing deviance by professional ex-s. However, they led to widespread investigations throughout Texas. By late 1994, allegations against treatment centers across the state were emerging (Herrera 1996a; Robbins 1996e, 1996d, 1996a). There were reports of expenditures for large bonuses, personal gifts, a professional weight trainer for the executive director, weekend resort trips, mariachi bands, and acrylic fingernails (Ann Richards joins 1995; Herman 1995; Herrera 1996a).

The scandal added to earlier concerns about TCADA's management (Elliott 1994b, 1995b, 1995c; TCADA: A chronology 1995; Phenix 1995; Oberwetter 1996). In 1995, a state senate committee was appointed to investigate TCADA, followed by the Texas Rangers. Ultimately, TCADA was placed under conservatorship (TCADA: A chronology 1995; Ann Richards joins 1995; Elliott 1995a; Robbins 1996c, 1996b, 1996e; Burton 1997).

Self-Reported Deviance

The interviews also provided evidence of ongoing deviance by the participants, both white-collar and non-white-collar. Lizette was not the only participant engaging in deviant behaviors. Andrea described a scam to obtain money from local restaurants. She would eat at a local restaurant, then she would return claiming a waitress had spilled a beverage on her suede coat. She would present a receipt from a dry-cleaning establishment and demand reimbursement. Andrea obtained reimbursement from seven restaurants in a two-week period. She also reported violation of counselor ethics by engaging in sexual liaisons with two clients during the time she was employed by the agency, including an adolescent:

> It was terrible—how low can I go, you know what I mean? I mean, I'm sleeping with [the client] and then going to family group and telling his mother how to have a better relationship with him. I mean, that's fucked up.

Lizette also reported a sexual liaison with a client. And, at Val's facility, a female counselor was discovered partially clothed and in bed with an adolescent female client. Lisa became an unwed mother after becoming a professional ex-. It is noteworthy that in all but the last example, these behaviors could have resulted in loss of jobs and/or counseling licenses, as well as arrest and prosecution (TCADA 1998a, 1998b, 1999).

Other activities met the self-control definition of deviance. Theft was commonplace. For example, one morning the lock and the seals on the freezer at the facility run by one of the authors were discovered broken. Interviews with several staff provided no insight, but eventually the clients admitted that one of the staff had used a knife to pry the freezer open to get ice cream. This behavior was not unusual. The general consensus seemed to be that staff members were underpaid and that taking home food and supplies was a way to supplement their income. Furthermore, staff members were aware of questionable activities by those at higher levels in the organization, and they argued that if the "bigshots" could steal, so could they, that it was expected and justified. Greg, the staff member who pried open the freezer, said that he did not believe that his actions were wrong since "everyone" stole from the program.

Lester agreed, stating that the level of theft by "frontline" employees was "minor in comparison" to that of the "biggies."

A few participants admitted using their professional ex- status to operate as drug dealers. Mark, who worked in a halfway house for parolees, stated that job provided a low-profile way to sell drugs. Essentially, his argument was that many of the clients had no intention of remaining drug free anyway, so it was not wrong to sell them drugs: "Somebody was gonna make some cash—might as well be me. I never sold to anybody who wasn't already using, so I don't feel guilty. Why should I? They don't pay me enough to do that!" Likewise, Frank argued that he only sold marijuana to clients, not the more "dangerous" drugs such as heroin or crack. Thus, he capitalized on his status as a professional ex-, but he did not consider it to be in conflict with his role in helping addicts to recover from drug use.

Finally, two participants reported engaging in aggressive behavior. Kevin was arrested while at work for threatening his estranged wife with a gun. He was also charged with assault due to a domestic violence episode, whereas Lloyd physically attacked a coworker who called him a "tight-ass."

◈ Discussion

This study calls into question the assumption that individuals exit a deviant career when they cease a particular from of deviant behavior (Brown 1991). Indeed, our examination of the professional ex- calls into question the concept of deviant "careers" in general. It appears that the professional ex- may abandon substance abuse because of natural sanctions such as health issues or legal sanctions. By conceptualizing deviance as general rather than specific (substance abuse, for example), a more detailed picture of deviance among professional ex-s emerges.

We have attempted to present a different perspective. Our data clearly suggest that cessation of substance abuse may be only part of the story. Brown (1991) argued that the professional ex- was a member of "a redemptive community" that "provides a reference group whose moral and social standards are internalized" (p. 228). However, many of our participants continued to engage in a wide variety of deviant behaviors, lending support to self-control theory in several ways.

First, the behaviors are indicative of versatility, including fraud, gambling, drug dealing, theft, illicit sex, and assaults. Furthermore, many of the behaviors identified at ARC meet the criteria of "acts of force or fraud undertaken in pursuit of self-interest." Clearly, there is a link between the propensity to commit crime and to engage in analogous behaviors (i.e., substance abuse).

Second, our findings indicate that deviance has an element of stability. Individuals who appear to transition out of a deviant career may instead continue to engage in deviance. Participants other than Diane, who was not a professional ex-, claimed to be abstinent from alcohol and drugs. However, the agency executives as well as the majority of interview participants reported ongoing deviance. Consistent with Gottfredson and Hirschi's (1990) predictions, low-self-control individuals, when presented with opportunities for deviance, are likely to take them. Rather than providing a chance at redemption, the new occupations held by professional ex-s provided ample opportunity for a variety of criminal acts. And, considering the seemingly cavalier way deviance was viewed by the agency, the costs of such behavior (at least in the short term) seemed minimal.

Third, these findings call into question interactionist explanations of deviance such as labeling theory (Lemert, 1951; Becker 1963; Goffman 1963; Erikson 1966; Schur 1971; Thoits 1985). This approach assumes that the detection of and reaction to deviant behavior result in stigma, which in turn contributes to the development of a deviant identity and blocked opportunities. However, professional ex- status not only results in new career opportunities and a new positive "identity" but provides new opportunities for deviance as well. Indeed, out findings support Gottfredson and Hirschi's (1990) assertion that white-collar crime differs little from other forms of crime—all it requires is the intersection of a low-self-control individual with the right set of circumstances.

The two top executives at ARC used their status as professional ex-s to commit fraud. Indeed, their professional ex- statuses created the opportunity for fraud and embezzlement. Given the opportunity through positions of authority, these administrators did exactly what self-control theory would predict (Gottfredson and Hirschi 1990, 183). The white-collar crime of other ARC employees and the widespread reported fraud throughout the Texas treatment industry suggest that these men were not unique.

While our findings suggest support for self-control theory, they are not, of course, generalizable. First, we do not have a random sample of professional ex-s. Therefore, it is impossible to conclude that professional ex-s as a whole are likely to continue in other forms of deviance on cessation of substance abuse. More important, we have no comparison group. Thus, we cannot say with any confidence that the professional ex-s in our study differ from individuals in similar careers. This suggests the need for further research. Ideally, we need a comparison group similar to professional ex-s in terms of licensing requirements. Nurses would be a potentially good choice. First, like professional ex-s, nursing jobs range from hands-on direct care providers all the way up to program administrators. In addition, at some levels of both nursing and substance abuse counseling, a college education is not required.

Because of their established history of low self-control, we would predict that compared to those in occupations with similar licensing criteria, professional ex-s should be more deviant. Overall, the professional ex-s we describe in this study fit the image of the low-self-control offender described by Gottfredson and Hirschi (1990), as well as their description of the typical white-collar offender: "The central elements of our theory of criminality are, however, easily identifiable among white-collar criminals. They too are people with low self-control, people inclined to follow momentary impulse without consideration of the long-term costs of such behavior" (p. 191). In contrast to those who critique the general theory as being unable to explain white-collar crime (Reed and Yeager 1996), our findings concerning the behaviors of the professional ex-suggest just the opposite.

◈ Appendix

Interview Participants[a]

Diane	Director of two programs for ARC during 1994 and 1995, not a former substance abuser, white female, midthirties.
Andrea	Director of three programs for ARC from 1984 to 1993, professional ex-, white female, early forties.
Lizette	Director of two programs for ARC from 1985 to 1996, professional ex-, white female, midforties.
Belinda	Counselor for ARC from 1990 until 1992, professional ex-, black female, early thirties.
Lloyd	Counselor for ARC from 1988 until 1995, professional ex-, white male, late forties.
Paula	Counselor for ARC, later director of a program, 1993 to 1996 and 1998 to present, professional ex-, white female, early fifties.
Lisa	counselor for ARC, 1988 to present, professional ex-, white female, early forties.
Lester	Counselor for ARC 1990 to 1992, professional ex-, white male, late twenties.
Greg	Counselor for ARC 1990 to 1992, program director 1992 to 1993, professional ex-, white male, midforties.
Mark	Counselor for ARC 1993, professional ex-, white male, early thirties.
Vince	Counselor for ARC, 1989 to 1995, professional ex-, black male, late twenties.
Frank	Counselor for ARC, 1989 to present, professional ex-, black male, early thirties.
Pam	Counselor for ARC, 1989 to 1994, professional ex-, white female, early thirties.
Val	Counselor for ARC, 1989 to 1990, program director 1990, professional ex-, white female, midtwenties.
Kevin	Counselor for ARC, 1989 to 1992, professional ex-, white male, early forties.

a. Information concerning these individuals is deliberately sketchy to avoid possible identification.

◈ References

Adler, Patricia A. 1992. The "post" phase of deviant careers: Reintegrating drug traffickers. *Deviant Behavior* 13 (2): 101–22.

The allegations keep piling up. 1994. *American-Statesman,* March 31.

Ann Richards joins Washington-based law firm as adviser. 1995. *American-Statesman,* February 14.

Anspach, Renee R. 1979. From stigma to identity politics: Political activism among the physically disabled and former mental patients. *Social Science and Medicine* 13:765–73.

Austin Rehabilitation Center. 1996. Letter to TCADA, re: task force audit findings, July 25.

Becker, Howard S. 1963. *Outsiders: Studies in the sociology of deviance.* New York: Free Press.

Blumer, Herbert. 1969. *Symbolic interactionism.* Englewood Cliffs, NJ: Prentice Hall.

Braithwaite, John. 1989. *Crime, shame and reintegration.* New York: Cambridge University Press.

Britt, Chester. 1994. Versatility. In *The generality of deviance,* edited by Travis Hirschi and Michael Gottfredson, 173–92. New Brunswick, NJ: Transaction.

Brown, J. David. 1991. The professional ex-: An alternative for exiting the deviant career. *Sociological Quarterly* 32:219–30.

Burton, Michael C. 1997. Bill tightens state's grip on TCADA. *Lubbock Avalanche-Journal,* March 7.

Caspi, Avshalom, D. Bem, and Glen H. Elder Jr. 1989. Continuities and consequences of interactional styles across the life course. *Journal of Personality* 57:375–406.

Cohen, Lawrence E., and Marcus Felson. 1979. Social change and crime rate trends: A routine activity approach. *American Sociological Review* 44:488–608.

Cooley, Charles Horton. 1902. *Human nature and the social order.* New York: Scribner.

Copelin, Laylan. 1994. Center fires Whittington: $187,500 more in payments led to action. *American-Statesman,* April 19.

Ebaugh, Helen Rose Fuchs. 1988. *Becoming an ex: The process of role exit.* Chicago: University of Chicago Press.

Elizondo, Juan B., Jr. 1996. State could recover portion of misspent anti-drug dollars. *American-Statesman,* March 26.

Elliott, David. 1994a. ARC agrees to refund $1 million to the state: Rehab center reaches settlement after audit showed fiscal impropriety. *American-Statesman,* September 7.

———. 1994b. Audit of commission shows improvement. *American-Statesman,* April 20.

———. 1994c. Board relieves administrators of fiscal duties: Austin Rehabilitation Center's finances to be handled by interim committee. *American-Statesman,* April 1.

———. 1994d. Center's audit uncovers gifts, lavish bonuses. *American-Statesman,* March 29.

———. 1994e. Salaries of center counselors below par: Meanwhile, top administrators got six-figure incomes. *American-Statesman,* April 2.

———. 1994f. State gives rehab center grant despite misspending. *American-Statesman,* July 12.

———. 1995b. Legislators urge dissolving TCADA board: Conservatorship likely for alcohol and drug abuse agency amid evidence of mismanagement. *American-Statesman,* April 13.

———. 1995c. State substance abuse agency has its proposed budget slashed; cut of $16 million would affect treatment for nonviolent convicts. *American-Statesman,* March 10.

Erikson, Kai T. 1966. *Wayward puritans.* New York: John Wiley.

Feagin, Joe R., Anthony M. Orum, and Gideon Sjoberg. 1991. Conclusion: The present crisis in U.S. sociology. In *A case for the case study,* edited by Joe R. Feagin, Anthony M. Orum, and Gideon Sjoberg, 269–78. Chapel Hill: University of North Carolina Press.

Fine, Gary Alan. 1993. The sad demise, mysterious disappearance, glorious triumph of symbolic interactions. *Annual Review of Sociology* 19:61–87.

Geis, Gilbert. 1991. The case study method in sociological criminology. In *A case for the case study,* edited by Joe R. Feagin, Anthony M. Orum, and Gideon Sjoberg, 200–23. Chapel Hill: University of North Carolina Press.

Goffman, Erving. 1959. *The presentation of self in everyday life.* New York: Doubleday Anchor.

———. 1963. *Stigma.* Englewood Cliffs, NJ: Prentice Hall.

Gottfredson, Michael, and Travis Hirschi. 1990. *A general theory crime.* Palo Alto, CA: Stanford University Press.

Herman, Ken. 1995. Audit of drug programs finds millions spent on trips, gifts, fingernails. *American-Statesman,* August 5.

Herman, Nancy J. 1993. Return to sender: Reintegrate stigma management strategies of ex-psychiatric patients. *Journal of Contemporary Ethnography* 22:295–330.

Hernanadz, Lisa. 1999. Telephone conversation between the author and Lisa Hernanadz, attorney, Sanctions Division, Texas Commission on Alcohol and Drug Abuse, June 14.

Herrera, Clara G. 1996a. Drug programs face "questioned costs"; after audits, 12 area entities among those to answer questions about TCADA money. *American-Statesman,* May 21.

———. 1996b. Former drug program director pleads guilty to stealing money. *American-Statesman,* September 5.

———. 1997. Ex program director gets five-year term: Man, whose scandalous doings led to reform of state agency, also fined $200,000. *American-Statesman,* March 21.

Hirschi, Travis, and Michael R. Gottfredson. 1983. Age and the explanation of crime. *American Journal of Sociology* 89:552–84.

———. 1986. The distinctions between crime and criminality. In *Critique and explanation: Essays in honor of Gwynne Nettler,* edited by T. F. Hartnagel and R. Silverman, 55–69. New Brunswick, NJ: Transaction

———. 1994. The generality of deviance. In *The generality of deviance,* edited by Travis Hirschi and Michael R. Gottfredson, 1–22. New Brunswick, NJ: Transaction.

Horowitz, I., and M. Liebowitz. 1968. Social deviance and political marginality. *Social Problems* 16:281–96.

Irwin, John. 1970. *The felon.* Englewood Cliffs, NJ: Prentice Hall.

LeBlanc, Mark, and Stephanie Girard. 1997. The generality of deviance: Replication over 2 decades with a Canadian sample of adjudicated boys. *Canadian Journal of Criminology* 39:171–83.

Lemert, Edwin M. 1951. *Social pathology.* New York: McGraw-Hill.

Lofland, John, and Lynn H. Lofland. 1995. *Analyzing social settings.* 3d ed. Belmont, CA: Wadsworth.

Luckenbill, David F., and Joel Best. 1981. Careers in deviance and respectability: The analogy's limitation. *Social Problems* 29:197–206.

Mead, George Herbert. 1934. *Mind, self, and society*. Chicago: University of Chicago Press.

Meisenhelder, Thomas. 1977. An exploratory study of exiting from criminal careers. *Criminology* 15:319–34.

Oberwetter, James C. 1996. State alcohol, drug agency deserves second chance. *American-Statesman,* December 17.

Orum, Anthony M., Joe R. Feagin, and Gideon Sjoberg. 1991. Introduction: The nature of the case study. In *A case for the case study,* edited by Joe R. Feagin, Anthony M. Orum, and Gideon Sjoberg, 1–26. Chapel Hill: University of North Carolina Press.

Phenix, Jann. 1995. TCADA's woes rooted in denial. *American-Statesman,* September 25.

Pratt, Travis C., and Francis T. Cullen. 2000. The empirical status of Gottfredson and Hirschi's general theory of crime: A meta-analysis. *Criminology* 38:931–64.

Reed, Gary E. and Peter Cleary Yeager. 1996. Organizational offending and neoclassical criminology: Challenging the reach of a general theory of crime. *Criminology* 34:357–82.

Reinharz, Shulamit. 1992. *Feminist methods in social research*. New York: Oxford University Press.

Rice, John Steadman. 1992. Discursive formation, life stories, and the emergence of codependency: "Power/knowledge" and the search for identity. *Sociological Quarterly* 33 (3): 337–64.

Robbins, Mary Alice. 1996a. Agency denies wrongdoing, agrees to pay settlement. *Amarillo Globe,* December 10.

———. 1996b. Commission votes to continue TCADA role. *Lubbock Avalanche-Journal,* December 18.

———. 1996c. Review panel recommends continuation of TCADA. *Lubbock Avalanche-Journal,* October 22.

———. 1996d. State resolves questions over substance abuse funds. *Lubbock Avalanche-Journal,* November 23.

———. 1996e. Two area treatment centers get clearance after review by state. *Lubbock Avalanche-Journal,* November 16.

Sampson, Robert J., and John H. Laub. 1993. *Crime in the making: Pathways and turning points through life*. Cambridge, MA: Harvard University Press.

Schmid, Thomas J., and Richard S. Jones. 1991. Suspended identity: Identity transformation in a maximum security prison. *Symbolic Interaction* 14:415–32.

Schur, Edwin M. 1971. *Labeling deviant behavior*. New York: Harper and Row.

Shover, Neil. 1983. The later stages of ordinary property offenders' careers. *Social Problems* 31:208–18.

Sjoberg, Gideon, Norma Williams, Ted R. Vaughan, and Andrea F. Sjoberg. 1991. The case study approach in social research: Basic methodological issues. In *A case for the case study,* edited by Joe R. Feagin, Anthony M. Orum, and Gideon Sjonberg, 27–79. Chapel Hill: University of North Carolina Press.

Sommers, Ira, Deborah R. Baskin, and Jeffrey Fagan. 1994. Getting out of the life: Crime resistance by female street offenders. *Deviant Behavior* 15:125–49.

Stall, Ron, and Patrick Biernacki. 1986. Spontaneous remission from the problematic use of substances: An inductive model derived from a comparative analysis of the alcohol, opiate, tobacco and food/obesity literatures. *International Journal of the Addictions* 2:1–23.

TCADA: A chronology. 1995. *American-Statesman,* April 18.

Texas Commission on Alcohol and Drug Abuse. 1993. Report of complaint, December 21.

———. 1994a. Agreed administrative order between Texas Commission on Alcohol and Drug Abuse and Austin Rehabilitation Center, Inc.

———. 1994b. Confidential report of investigations, Mr. Ron Whittington, LCDC, no. C-0194-124.

———. 1994c. Letter, notice of intent to take disciplinary action, February 24.

———. 1994d. Memorandum, counselor-related complaint initiation/closure notice, February 16.

———. 1994e. Memorandum, supplement to report of investigation no. C-0194-124.

———. 1996a. Letter to Austin Rehabilitation Center, re: ARC task force questioned costs, August 7.

———. 1996b. Letter to Austin Rehabilitation Center, re: task force audit findings, November 16.

———. 1998a. *Rules and statutes.* Chapter 142: Investigations and hearings.

———. 1998b. *Rules and statutes.* Chapter 150, section 61: Ethical standards.

———. 1999. Sanctions—Disciplinary actions: Licensed counselors. Available online: www.tcada. State.tx.us/sanctions/counselor .html.

Thoits, Peggy A. 1985. Self-labeling processes in mental illness: The role of emotional deviance. *American Journal of Sociology* 91:221–49.

White, Jerry. 1994a. Center's contract may allow purchases. *American-Statesman,* May 7.

———. 1994b. Grand jury subpoenas treatment center's files, top officials. *American-Statesman,* April 6.

White, Jerry, and David Elliott. 1994. Audit finds conflict of interest at center: The rehabilitation center's Board Chairman McCabe also was paid to act as chaplain. *American-Statesman,* March 31.

White, Jennifer L., Terrie E. Moffitt, Felton Earls, Lee Robins, and Phil A. Silva. 1990. How early can we tell? Predictors of childhood conduct disorder and adolescent delinquency. *Criminology* 28:507–28.

Wolcott, Harvey F. 1990. *Writing up qualitative research*. Newbury Park, CA: Sage.

Wright, Bradley R. Entner, Avshalom Caspi, Terrie E. Moffitt, and Phil A. Silva. 1999. Low self-control, social bonds and crime: Social causation, social selection, or both? *Criminology* 37:479–514.

Glossary

Age-crime curve: an observed relationship between the likelihood to engage in crime and age. The relationship is low in the early childhood/adolescent years, peaks in late adolescence, and then declines as individuals age out of adolescence.

Anomie: a state of normlessness where society fails to effectively regulate the expectations or behaviors of its members.

Attachment: "emotional" component of the social bond that says individuals care about what others think.

Belief: component of the bond in social control theory that suggests the stronger the awareness, understanding, and agreement with the rules and norms of society, the less likely one will be to deviate.

Body modification: includes piercings, scarification, extreme tattooing, and reconstructive and cosmetic surgery.

Broken windows theory: basically the notion that social and physical disorder lead to greater disorder and other forms of crime and deviance.

Central business district: the commercial area of a city where most of the business activity occurs.

Civil commitment: a process whereby offenders, particularly sex offenders, who are perceived to be a risk to the community can be held indefinitely after completing the sentences handed down by the criminal justice system.

Collateral consequences of imprisonment: damages, losses, or hardships to individuals, families, and communities due to incarceration of some members.

Collective efficacy: conditions of some neighborhoods where there is trust, cohesion, and a willingness to act for the common good.

Commitment: "rational" component of the social bond that says individuals weigh the costs and benefits of their behavior.

Concentric zones: a model of urban cities, generally consisting of and moving out from the central business district, the zone in transition, zone of the working class, residential zone, and commuter zone.

Conflict: a theoretical perspective that considers how society is held together by power and coercion for the benefit of those in power (based on social class, gender, race, or ethnicity).

Conflict subculture: from Cloward and Ohlin's theory—conflict subcultures develop in disorganized neighborhoods where young people are deprived of both conventional and illegitimate opportunities; frustration and violence are defining characteristics.

Covert observation: refers to public observation where the researcher does not let the human subjects under study know that they are researchers and they are being studied.

Criminal career paradigm: a view that there are some criminals who offend at high rates across the life course.

Criminal subculture: from Cloward and Ohlin's theory—criminal subcultures develop in poor neighborhoods where there is some level of organized crime and illegitimate opportunity for young people growing up in the area.

Critical race theory: a theoretical perspective that examines the use of law, the legal order, and institutions in maintaining white privilege and supremacy.

Cultural deviance theory: a theory emphasizing the values, beliefs, rituals, and practices of societies that promote certain deviant behaviors. Related, subcultural explanations emphasize the values, beliefs, rituals, and practices of subgroups in society that distinguish them from the larger society.

Definitions: attitudes, values, orientations, rationalizations, and beliefs related to legal and moral codes of society.

Deinstitutionalization: encourages keeping offenders or the mentally ill in the community, to the extent that doing so is a reasonable option. The idea is that there is less disruption, labeling, and stigma if the individuals can be treated outside of prisons, mental hospitals, juvenile facilities, and so on.

Demedicalization: when behaviors are no longer assigned or retain medical definitions. As one example, homosexuality was once defined as a form of mental illness, but it has been demedicalized and is no longer considered a medical issue.

Desistance: the process of ending a deviant career or career in deviance. This can be abrupt (e.g., "quitting cold turkey") or a gradual process (e.g., a self help recovery process where individual go between periods of use and abstinence)

Dialectical materialism: the belief that nature (the material world) is full of contradictions (conflict) and that through a process of negotiating those contradictions, we can arrive at a new reality.

Differential association: social interactions with deviant as opposed to conventional others.

Differential location in the social structure: social and demographic characteristics of individuals that define or influence their position or role in the larger social structure (e.g., age, sex, socioeconomic status).

Differential reinforcement: the balance of rewards and punishments (anticipated and/or actual) that follow from deviant behaviors.

Differential social location in groups: social and demographic characteristics of individuals that define or influence one's position or role in the larger social structure, such as social class, age, gender, or race/ethnicity.

Differential social organization: conditions of social units based on social and demographic characteristics that define communities or larger social/geographic units (e.g., sex ratio, % living under poverty).

Elite deviance: criminal and deviant acts committed by large corporations, powerful political organizations, and individuals with prestige and influence; may result in physical harm, financial harm, or moral harm.

Escalation: some deviant behaviors accelerate or intensify over time, such as persistent drug use that may increase in frequency or quantity.

Ethics in research: much effort has gone into the ethical implications of researching human subjects, which can be quite complex when studying deviant behavior. Generally, the subject should be asked for consent to participate and his or her confidentiality protected.

Experiments and quasi-experimental designs: generally, experimental designs require random assignment to a treatment or control condition. Quasi-experiments usually relax this requirement.

External control: formal controls that society places on an individual to keep him or her from engaging in crime or deviance.

False consciousness: laborers' lack of awareness of the exploitation they are experiencing at the hands of the owners of the means of production and capitalism.

Felon disenfranchisement: the loss of the right to vote in local and national elections after conviction for a felony offense; laws vary by state.

Feminist criminology: a theoretical perspective that defines gender (and sometimes race and social class) as a source of social inequality, group conflict, and social problems.

Field research: generally involves getting out into the environment and studying human behavior as it exists in the "real world."

Folkways: everyday norms that do not generate much uproar if they are violated.

General strain theory (GST): Robert Agnew's version of strain theory; suggests that strain at the individual level may result from the failure to achieve valued goals and also result from negative relations/stimuli.

Human agency: that people can and do make choices that have implications for themselves and others.

Human subjects: living persons being observed for research purposes.

Imitation: observing behavior and reenacting modeled behavior in actuality or in play.

Indirect controls: controls placed on an individual from an outside source, such as the disapproval of parents.

Institutional review boards: independent groups who review research to protect human subjects from potential harms of the research.

Institutional anomie theory: from Messner and Rosenfeld—argues that the major institutions in the United States, including the family, school, and political system, are all dominated by economic institutions; the exaggerated emphasis on monetary success leads to crime and deviance.

Institutionalization/prisonization: when individuals who have been confined to a prison, mental hospital, or other total institution become so used to the structure and routine of the facility that they lose the confidence and capability to exist independently in the outside world.

Instrumental Marxism: the theory that the state (for example, politicians or the police) is an *instrument* of the capitalists.

Internal control: rules and norms exercised through our conscience.

Involvement: component of the social bond that suggests the more time spent engaged in conforming activities, the less time available to deviate.

Laws: the strongest norm because it is backed by official sanctions (or a formal response).

Liberal feminism: focuses on gender role socialization and the roles that women are socialized into.

Life course perspective: a theoretical perspective that considers the entire course of human life (from childhood, adolescence, and adulthood to old age) as social constructions that reflect the broader structural conditions of society.

Low self-control: the inability of an individual to refrain from impulsive behavior designed to increase immediate gratification.

Master status: a status that proves to be more important than most others.

Medicalization of deviance: a process by which nonmedical problems and behaviors become defined and treated as medical conditions; examples might include medical illness, hyperactivity, alcoholism, and compulsive gambling.

Mores: "moral" norms that may generate more outrage if broken.

Nonintervention: the policy of avoiding intervention and action for as long as possible. For example, labeling theorists often suggest we should tolerate some level of minor deviance and misbehavior before taking official action and labeling individuals deviant.

Normative: assumes that there is a general set of norms of behavior, conduct, and conditions for which we can agree.

Norms: rules of behavior that guide people's actions.

Observational research: generally research involving pure observation such as watching children interact in the playground or bartenders checking licenses in a "college bar."

Onset/initiation: the beginning of a career in deviance, which can be short- or long-lived.

Overt observation: refers to studies where the researcher makes human subjects aware that they are being observed.

Pains of imprisonment: as described by Gresham Sykes, the pains of imprisonment include deprivation of liberty, deprivation of goods and services, deprivation of heterosexual relationships, deprivation of autonomy, and deprivation of security.

Participant observation: research activity where the researcher is actively involved in the behaviors being studied. For example, a recovering alcoholic researcher might study the behaviors of others in AA meetings.

Peacemaking criminology: a theoretical perspective focused on the belief that there must be a new way of seeing and organizing the world around compassion, sympathy, and understanding.

Persistence: subsequent to onset or initiation, some deviant behaviors continue for some length of time.

Physical deviance: generally thought to be of two types: (1) violating norms of what people are expected to look like and (2) physical incapacity or disability.

Physical disorder: condition of some neighborhoods with high levels of, for example, litter, graffiti, vandalism, and "broken windows."

Polygamy: a subculture in which men are allowed and encouraged to take multiple wives.

Positive deviance: a concept that is still under debate but generally understood as intentional behaviors that depart from community norms in honorable ways.

Postmodern feminism: questions the idea of a single "truth" or way of knowing and understanding.

Poverty: a lack of resources or financial well-being.

Primary deviance: common instances where individuals violate norms without viewing themselves as being involved in a deviant social role.

Protective factors: factors that reduce the impact of risk factors. That is, protective factors are not simply the opposite of risk factors.

Radical feminism: focuses on the sexual control of women, seeing their oppression emerging from a social order dominated by men.

Reintegrative shaming: a reaction to deviant behavior that views the offender as a good person who has done a bad deed; this process encourages repair work and forgiveness rather than simply labeling the individual as a bad person.

Relative deprivation: judging oneself or one's situation as lacking in comparison to a key reference group.

Relativist: assumes that the definition of deviance is constructed based on the interactions of those in society.

Residual rule breaking: deviance for which there exists no clear category—acts that are not crimes yet draw attention and make the societal audience uncomfortable.

Restorative justice: typically involves bringing the victims, offenders, and community members together in a mediated conference where the offenders take responsibility for their actions and work to restore the harm they have caused, often through restitution to the victim and service to the community.

Retreatist subculture: from Cloward and Ohlin's theory—similar to Merton's adaptation of retreatism, a subculture based around drug use, drug culture, and relative isolation from the larger society.

Risk factors: factors that place certain individuals at greater risk for engaging in deviant (often unhealthy) behaviors.

Scientific method: analysis and implementation of the best way to complete a task.

Secondary data: data collected by other researchers that will presumably be reanalyzed by another researcher.

Secondary deviance: when an individual engages in deviant behavior as a means of defense, attack, or adjustment to the problems created by reactions to him or her.

Self-fulfilling prophesy: once labeled, individuals' self-conceptions may be altered, causing them to deviate and live up to the negative label.

Self-injury: harming oneself by cutting, burning, branding, scratching, picking at skin or reopening wounds, biting, hair pulling, and/or bone breaking.

Sexual deviance: largely determined by community, culture, and context, sexual deviance may include exotic dancers, strippers, sex tourism, anonymous sex in public restrooms, bisexuality, online sexual predators, prostitutes, premarital chastity, and many others.

Social bond: bonds to conformity that keep us from engaging in socially unacceptable activities.

Social cohesion: neighborhoods characterized by positive social interaction, trust, and a sense of community.

Social consensus: general agreement by the group.

Social construction: subjective definition or perception of conditions.

Social contract: the process by which individuals give up some personal freedoms and abide by general rules of conduct to live in a community and enjoy the protection and companionship of the group.

Social disorder: conditions of some neighborhoods with high levels of, for example, unmonitored youth misbehaving, drug dealers, people openly and illegally using alcohol or other drugs, and fighting.

Social disorganization: neighborhoods that lack the ability to control delinquent youth and other potentially problem populations.

Social structure: organization of society, often hierarchical, that affects how and people interact and the outcomes of those interactions.

Socialist feminism: focuses on structural differences, especially those we find in the capitalist modes of production.

Sociological imagination: link between our personal lives and experiences and our social world.

Specialization: a primary interest and focus on one form of deviant behavior (e.g., marijuana use), to be contrasted with "generality of deviance" (e.g., drug use, theft, and violent behaviors).

Stigma: a mark of deviance or disgrace; a negative label or perceived deviance often leads to stigma that may then reduce an individual's life chances.

Strain: lack of opportunities for conventional success may lead to strain, which can manifest in anger, frustration, and deviance.

Structural characteristics (of social disorganization): include poverty, residential mobility, and racial/ethnic heterogeneity.

Structural impediments: obstacles on the road to conforming success, for example, lack of education, poor access to legitimate careers, and so on.

Structural Marxism: a theory that law is less about maintaining power and benefits for the ruling class and more about maintaining the interests of the *capitalist system.*

Subcultures: a distinct group within the larger culture that has its own subset of norms, values, behaviors, or characteristics.

Symbolic interactionism: a micro-level, relativist sociological perspective that is focused on individuals and the meanings they attach to objects, people, and interactions around them.

Theoretically defined structural variables: measures based on social theories of deviance such as anomie/strain, social disorganization, or patriarchy, among others.

Theory: a set of assumptions and propositions used for explanation, prediction, and understanding.

Total institutions: institutions such as prisons, jails, and mental hospitals in which all aspects of life are conducted in the same place, in the company of a group of others, with tightly scheduled activities that are closely supervised and monitored.

Trajectory: classification of individuals according to their pattern of offending over time.

Transition: short-term changes in social roles within long-term trajectories, such as dropping out of school, divorce, and desistance from delinquency.

Zone in transition: an area of a city that usually borders the central business district. The name comes from the notion that the poorest groups (often recent immigrants) are forced to live there, and as they secure financial stability, they move out, so it is an area in transition of different populations.

References

Abel, R. (1982). The contradictions of informal justice. In R. Abel (Ed.), *The politics of informal justice: Vol. 1. The American experience* (pp. 267–320). New York: Academic Press.

Adams, M. S., Robertson, C. T., Gray-Ray, P., & Ray, M. C. (2003). Labeling and delinquency. *Adolescence, 38*(149), 171–186.

Adler, F. (1975). *Sisters in crime: The rise of the new female criminal.* New York: McGraw-Hill.

Adler, P. A. (1993). *Wheeling and dealing: An ethnography of an upper-level drug dealing and smuggling community* (2nd ed.). New York: Columbia University Press.

Adler, P. A., & Adler, P. (1983). Shifts and oscillations in deviant careers: The case of upper-level drug dealers and smugglers. *Social Problems, 31*(2), 195–207.

Adler, P. A., & Adler, P. (2007). The demedicalization of self-injury: From psychopathology to sociological deviance. *Journal of Contemporary Ethnography, 36*(5), 537–570.

Agnew, R. (1985). Social control theory and delinquency. *Criminology, 23,* 47–61.

Agnew, R. (1992). Foundation for a general strain theory of crime and delinquency. *Criminology, 30*(1), 47–87.

Agnew, R. (1997). Stability and change in crime over the life course: A strain theory explanation. In T. P. Thornberry (Ed.), *Developmental theories of crime and delinquency, advances in criminological theory* (Vol. 7, pp. 101–132). New Brunswick, NJ: Transaction.

Agnew, R. (2006). *Pressured into crime: An overview of general strain theory.* Los Angeles: Roxbury.

Aguirre, A., Jr. (2000). Academic storytelling: A critical race theory story of affirmative action. *Sociological Perspectives, 43*(2), 319–339.

Akers, R. L. (1985). *Deviant behavior: A social learning approach* (3rd ed.). Belmont, CA: Wadsworth.

Akers, R. L. (1996). Is differential association/social learning cultural deviance theory? *Criminology, 34*(2), 229–247.

Akers, R. L. (1998). *Social learning and social structure: A general theory of crime and deviance.* Boston: Northeastern University Press.

Akers, R. L., & Cochran, J. K. (1985). Adolescent marijuana use: A test of three theories of deviant behavior. *Deviant Behavior, 6*(4), 323–346.

Akers, R. L., & Sellers, C. (2004). *Criminological theories: Introduction, evaluation, and application* (4th ed.). Los Angeles: Roxbury.

American Civil Liberties Union (ACLU). 2007. *Firestorm: Treatment of vulnerable populations during the San Diego fires.* San Diego, CA: Author.

Andersen, C. (1999). Governing aboriginal justice in Canada: Constructing responsible individuals and communities through "tradition." *Crime, Law & Social Change, 31,* 303–326.

Anderson, E. (1999). *Code of the street: Decency, violence & the moral life of the inner city.* New York: W. W. Norton.

Anderson, L., Snow, D. A., & Cress, D. M. (1994). Negotiating the public realm: Stigma management and collective action among the homeless. *Research in Community Sociology, 1,* 121–143.

Arter, M. L. (2008). Stress and deviance in policing. *Deviant Behavior, 29,* 43–69.

Ashworth, A. (1993). Some doubts about restorative justice. *Criminal Law Forum, 4,* 277–299.

Atkinson, M. (2011). Male athletes and the cult(ure) of thinness in sport. *Deviant Behavior, 32*(3), 224–256.

Atkinson, M., & Young, K. (2008). *Deviance and social control in sport.* Champaign, IL: Human Kinetics.

Bader, C. D. (2008). Alien attraction: The subculture of UFO contactees and abductees. In E. Goode & D. A. Vail (Eds.), *Extreme deviance* (pp. 37–65). Thousand Oaks, CA: Pine Forge Press.

Baker, L. M., Dalla, R. L., & Williamson, C. (2010). Exiting prostitution: An integrated model. *Violence Against Women, 16*(5), 579–600.

Barak, G. (1991). Homelessness and the case for community-based initiatives: The emergence of a model shelter as a short-term response to the deepening crisis in housing. In H. E. Pepinsky & R. Quinney (Eds.), *Criminology as peacemaking* (pp. 47–68). Bloomington: Indiana University Press.

Barnoski, R. (2005). *Sex offender sentencing in Washington state: Does community notification influence recidivism rates?* (Document No. 05–08–1202). Olympia: Washington State Institute for Public Policy.

Bartollas, C., Miller, S. J., & Dinitz, S. (1976). *Juvenile victimization: The institutional paradox.* New York: John Wiley.

Becker, H. S. (1953). Becoming a marihuana user. *American Journal of Sociology, 59*(3), 235–242.

Becker, H. S. (1973). *Outsiders.* New York: Free Press. (Original work published 1963)

Beckett, K., & Herbert, S. (2010). *Banished: The new social control in urban America.* Oxford, UK: Oxford University Press.

Beirne, P. (1979). Empiricism and the critique of Marxism on law and crime. *Social Problems, 26,* 373–385.

Bendle, M. F. (1999). The death of the sociology of deviance? *Journal of Sociology, 35,* 42–59.

Benson, M. L., Wooldredge, J., & Thistlethwaite, A. B. (2004). The correlation between race and domestic violence is confounded with community context. *Social Problems, 51*(3), 326–342.

Bentham, J. (1970). *An introduction to the principles of morals and legislation* (J. H. Burns & H. L. A. Hart, Eds.). London: Athlone Press. (Original work published 1789)

Bernard, T., Snipes, J., & Gerould, A. (2009). *Vold's theoretical criminology.* Oxford, UK: Oxford University Press.

Bernasco, W., & Block, R. (2009). Where offenders choose to attack: A discrete choice model of robberies in Chicago. *Criminology, 47*(1), 93–130.

Blalock, H. M., Jr. (1967). *Toward a theory of minority group relations.* New York: John Wiley.

Blevins, K. R., & Holt, T. J. (2009). Examining the virtual subculture of johns. *Journal of Contemporary Ethnography, 38*(5), 619–648.

Blumstein, A. (1995). Youth violence, guns, and the illicit-drug industry. *Journal of Criminal Law and Criminology, 86,* 10–36.

Blumstein, A., & Cohen, J. (1979). Estimation of individual crime rates from arrest records. *Journal of Criminal Law and Criminology, 70,* 561–585.

Boeringer, S., Shehan, C. L., & Akers, R. L. (1991). Social context and social learning in sexual coercion and aggression: Assessing the contribution of fraternity membership. *Family Relations, 40,* 558–564.

Bohm, R. M. (1982). Radical criminology: An explication. *Criminology, 19,* 565–589.

Bohm, R. M. (1997). *A primer on crime and delinquency.* Belmont, CA: Wadsworth.

Braithwaite, J. (1989). *Crime, shame and reintegration.* Melbourne, Australia: Cambridge University Press.

Braithwaite, J. (2000). Shame and criminal justice. *Canadian Journal of Criminology, 42*(3), 281–298.

Braithwaite, J. (2002). Setting standards for restorative justice. *British Journal of Criminology, 42,* 563–577.

Braithwaite, J., & Mugford, S. (1994). Conditions of successful reintegration ceremonies: Dealing with juvenile offenders. *British Journal of Criminology, 34*(2), 140–171.

Braswell, M. C., Fuller, J., & Lozoff, B. (2001). *Corrections, peacemaking, and restorative justice: Transforming individuals and institutions.* Cincinnati, OH: Anderson.

Bridges, G., & Crutchfield, R. (1988). Law, social standing, and racial disparities in imprisonment. *Social Forces, 66,* 699–724.

Broidy, L. (1995). Direct supervision and delinquency: Assessing the adequacy of structural proxies. *Journal of Criminal Justice, 23,* 541–554.

Brown, J. D. (1991). The professional ex-: An alternative for exiting the deviant career. *Sociological Quarterly, 32*(2), 219–230.

Brownell, K. D., Marlatt, G., Lichteustein, E., & Wilson, G. (1986). Understanding and preventing relapse. *American Psychologist, 41*(7), 765–782.

Browning, C. R. (2002). The span of collective efficacy: Extending social disorganization theory to partner violence. *Journal of Marriage and Family, 64*(4), 833–850.

Burgess, R. L., & Akers, R. L. (1966). A differential association reinforcement theory of criminal behavior. *Social Problems, 14,* 128–147.

Burgess-Proctor, A. (2006). Intersections of race, class, gender, and crime: Future directions for feminist criminology. *Feminist Criminology, 1*(1), 27–47.

Bursik, R. J., Jr. (1988). Social disorganization and theories of crime and delinquency: Problems and prospects. *Criminology, 26*(4), 519–551.

Cain, M. (1974). The main theme of Marx' and Engels' sociology of law. *British Journal of Law and Society, 1*(2), 136–148.

Campbell, D. T., & Stanley, J. C. (1963). *Experimental and quasi-experimental designs for research.* Chicago: Rand McNally College.

Capaldi, D. M., Kim, H. K., & Owen, L. D. (2008). Romantic partners' influence on men's likelihood of arrest in early adulthood. *Criminology, 46*(2), 267–299.

Cancino, J. M. (2005). The utility of social capital and collective efficacy: Social control policy in nonmetropolitan settings. *Criminal Justice Policy Review, 16*(3), 287–318.

Castle, T., & Hensley, C. (2002). Serial killers with military experience: Applying learning theory to serial murder. *International Journal of Offender Therapy and Comparative Criminology, 46*(4), 453–465.

Cernkovich, S. A., & Giordano, P. C. (1987). Family relationships and delinquency. *Criminology, 20,* 149–167.

Cernkovich, S. A., Giordano, P. C., & Rudolph, J. L. (2000). Race, crime, and the American Dream. *Journal of Research in Crime and Delinquency, 37*(3), 131–170.

Chambliss, W. J. (1964). A Sociological analysis of the law of vagrancy. *Social Problems, 12*(1), 67–77.

Chambliss, W. J. (1973, November/December). The Roughnecks and the Saints. *Society,* pp. 24–31.

Chambliss, W. J. (1975). Toward a political economy of crime. *Theory and Society, 2,* 149–170.

Chambliss, W. J. (1978). *On the take: From petty crooks to presidents.* Bloomington: Indiana University Press.

Chambliss, W. J. (1999). *Power, politics, and crime.* Boulder, CO: Westview.

Chambliss, W. J., & Seidman, R. B. (1971). *Law, order and power.* Reading, MA: Addison-Wesley.

Chamlin, M. B. (2009). Threat to whom? Conflict, consensus, and social control. *Deviant Behavior, 30,* 539–559.

Chesney-Lind, M., & Shelden, R. (2003). *Girls, delinquency and juvenile justice.* Belmont, CA: Wadsworth.

Clear, T. R. (2007). *Imprisoning communities: How mass incarceration makes disadvantaged neighborhoods worse.* New York: Oxford University Press.

Clemmer, D. (1958). *The prison community.* New York: Holt, Rinehart & Winston. (Original work published 1940)

Clinard, M. B., & Meier, R. F. (2010). *Sociology of deviant behavior.* Belmont, CA: Wadsworth.

Cloward, R. (1959). Illegitimate means, anomie, and deviant behavior. *American Sociological Review, 24*(2), 164–176.

Cloward, R., & Ohlin, L. (1960). *Delinquency and opportunity: A theory of delinquent gangs.* New York: Free Press.

Coker, D. (2006). Restorative justice, Navajo peacemaking, and domestic violence. *Theoretical Criminology, 10,* 67–85.

Cole, D. (1998). *No equal justice: Race and class in the American criminal justice system.* New York: New Press.

Comfort, M. L. (2002). "Papa's house": The prison as domestic and social satellite. *Ethnography, 3*(4), 467–499.

Comfort, M. L. (2003). In the tube at San Quentin: The "secondary prisonization" of women visiting inmates. *Journal of Contemporary Ethnography, 32*(1), 77–107.

Comfort, M. L. (2008). *Doing time together: Love and family in the shadow of the prison.* Chicago: University of Chicago Press.

Conrad, P. (1992). Medicalization and social control. *Annual Review of Sociology, 18,* 209–232.

Cragg, W. (1992). *The practice of punishment: Towards a theory of restorative justice.* London: Routledge.

Crenshaw, K., Gotanda, N., Peller, G., & Thomas, K. (1995). Introduction. In K. Crenshaw, N. Gotanda, G. Peller, & K. Thomas (Eds.), *Critical race theory: The key writings that formed the movement* (pp. xiii–xxii). New York: New Press.

Cullen, F. T. (2011). Beyond adolescent-limited criminology: Choosing our future—The American Society of Criminology 2010 Sutherland Address. *Criminology, 49*(2), 287–330.

Cullen, F. T., & Agnew, R. (2006). *Criminological theory past to present: Essential readings* (3rd ed.). New York: Oxford University Press.

Cullen, F. T., & Messner, S. F. (2007). The making of criminology revisited: An oral history of Merton's anomie paradigm. *Theoretical Criminology, 11*(5), 5–37.

Daly, K., & Chesney-Lind, M. (1988). Feminism and criminology. *Justice Quarterly, 5,* 497–538.

Daniel, M. (2006, April 17). Suspect had three guns on bus. *Boston Globe.* http://www.boston.com/news/local/massachusetts/articles/2006/04/17/suspect_had_three_guns_on_bus/

Davies, S., & Tanner, J. (2003). The long arm of the law: Effects of labeling on employment. *The Sociological Quarterly, 44*(3), 385–404.

De Li, S. (2004). The impacts of self-control and social bonds on juvenile delinquency in a national sample of midadolescents. *Deviant Behavior, 25*(4), 351–373.

DeKeserdy, W., Ellis, D., & Alvi, S. (2005). *Deviance and crime: Theory, research and policy.* Cincinnati, OH: Anderson.

Downing, S. (2009). Attitudinal and behavioral pathways of deviance in online gaming. *Deviant Behavior, 30*(3), 293–320.

Dunlap, E., Johnson, B., & Manwar, A. (1994). A successful female crack dealer: Case study of a deviant career. *Deviant Behavior, 15,* 1–25.

Durkheim, E. (1951). *Suicide.* New York: Free Press. (Original work published 1897)

Edwards, M. L. (2010). Gender, social disorganization theory, and the locations of sexually oriented businesses. *Deviant Behavior, 31*(2), 135–158.

Einstadter, W., & Henry, S. (1995). *Criminological theory: An analysis of underlying assumptions.* Fort Worth, TX: Harcourt Brace College Publishers.

Einwohner, R. L. (2003). Opportunity, honor, and action in the Warsaw ghetto uprising of 1943. *American Journal of Sociology, 109*(3), 650–675.

Elliot, D. S., & Menard, S. (1996). Delinquent friends and delinquent behavior: Temporal and developmental patterns. In J. D. Hawkins (Ed.), *Delinquency and crime: Current theories* (pp. 28–67). New York: Cambridge University Press.

Environmental Protection Agency. (2011). Climate change, basic info. Retrieved June 30, 2011, from http://www.epa.gov/climatechange/basicinfo.html

Erikson, K. T. (1966). *Wayward puritans: A study in the sociology of deviance.* New York: Macmillan.

Fan, S. (1997). Immigration law and the promise of critical race theory: Opening the academy to the voices of aliens and immigrants. *Columbia Law Review, 97*(4), 1202–1240.

Faris, R. E. L., & Dunham, H. W. (1939). *Mental disease in urban areas.* Chicago: University of Chicago Press.

Farley, M., & Barkan, H. (1998). Prostitution, violence, and posttraumatic stress disorder. *Women and Health, 27*(3), 37–49.

Farrington, D. (1986). Age and crime. *Crime and Justice, 7,* 189–250.

Farrington, D., Gallagher, B., Morley, L., Ledger, R., & West, D. J. (1985). *Cambridge study in delinquent development: Long term follow-up, first annual report to the Home Office.* Cambridge, UK: Cambridge University Press.

Feld, B. C. (1977). *Neutralizing inmate violence: Juvenile offenders in institutions.* Cambridge, MA: Ballinger.

Ferrell, F., & Hamm, M. S. (1998). *Ethnography at the edge: Crime, deviance, and field research.* Boston: Northeastern University Press.

Fleisher, M. S. (1995). *Beggars and thieves: Lives of urban street criminals.* Madison: University of Wisconsin Press.

Frailing, K., & Harper, J. (2010). The social construction of deviance, conflict and the criminalization of midwives, New Orleans: 1940s and 1950s. *Deviant Behavior, 31*(8), 729–755.

Fremont Arts Council. (2010). Fremont Solstice Parade. Retrieved October 14, 2010, from http://fremontartscouncil.org/events/summer-solstice-parade/

Fremont Fair. (2010). Fremont Fair homepage. Retrieved October 14, 2010, from http://www.fremontfair.org/

Fuller, J., & Wozniak, J. F. (2006). Peacemaking criminology: Past, present, and future. In F. T. Cullen, J. P. Wright, & K. R. Blevins (Eds.), *Taking stock: The status of criminological theory* (pp. 251–276). New Brunswick, NJ: Transaction.

Gastil, R. D. (1978). Comments. *Criminology, 16*(1), 60–64.

Gauthier, D. K., & Chaudoir, N. K. (2004). Tranny boyz: Cyber community support in negotiating sex and gender mobility among female to male transsexuals. *Deviant Behavior, 25*(4), 375–398.

Giordano, P. C., Longmore, M. A., Schroeder, R. D., & Seffrin, P. M. (2008). A life-course perspective on spirituality and desistance from crime. *Criminology, 46*(1), 99–132.

Glueck, S., & Glueck, E. (1950). *Unraveling juvenile delinquency.* Cambridge, MA: Harvard University Press.

Goffman, A. (2009). On the run: Wanted men in a Philadelphia ghetto. *American Sociological Review, 74,* 339–357.

Goffman, E. (1961). *Asylums.* Garden City, NY: Anchor Books.

Goffman, E. (1963). *Stigma: Notes on the management of spoiled identity.* Englewood Cliffs, NJ: Prentice Hall.

Goode, E. (1991). Positive deviance: A viable concept? *Deviant Behavior, 12*(3), 289–309.

Goode, E. (2005). *Deviant behavior* (7th ed.). Upper Saddle River, NJ: Pearson Education.

Goode, E. (2008a). *Deviant behavior* (8th ed.). Upper Saddle River, NJ: Pearson Prentice Hall.

Goode, E. (2008b). The fat admirer. In E. Goode & D. A. Vail (Eds.), *Extreme deviance* (pp. 80–90). Thousand Oaks, CA: Pine Forge Press.

Gottfredson, M., & Hirschi, T. (1986). The true value of lambda would appear to be zero: An essay on career criminals, criminal careers, selective incapacitation, cohort studies and related topics. *Criminology, 24,* 213–234.

Gottfredson, M. R., & Hirschi, T. (1990). *A general theory of crime.* Stanford, CA: Stanford University Press.

Gourley, M. (2004). A subcultural study of recreational ecstasy use. *Journal of Sociology, 40*(1), 59–74.

Gove, W. R. (1975). The labeling theory of mental illness: A reply to Scheff. *American Sociological Review, 40,* 242–248.

Greenberg, D. (1985). Age, crime, and social explanation. *American Journal of Sociology, 91,* 1–21.

Greenberg, D. F., Kessler, R. C., & Loftin, C. (1985). Social inequality and crime control. *Journal of Criminal Law and Criminology, 76,* 684–704.

Greenwood, P. W. (1992). Substance abuse problems among high-risk youth and potential interventions. *Crime & Delinquency, 38,* 444–458.

Grinberg, E. (2010). No longer a registered sex offender, but the stigma remains. CNN.com. Retrieved February 15, 2010, at http://www.cnn.com/2010/CRIME/02/11/oklahoma.teen.sex.offender/index.html

Gusfield, J. (1967). Moral passage: The symbolic process of public designations of deviance. *Social Problems, 15*(2), 1785–1788.

Gusfield, J. (1968). On legislating morals: The symbolic process of designating deviance. *California Law Review, 56*(1), 54–73.

Haas, H., Farrington, D. P., Killias, M., & Sattar, G. (2004). The impact of different family configurations on delinquency. *British Journal of Criminology, 44*(4), 520–532.

Hackney, S. (1969). Southern violence. *American Historical Review, 74,* 906–925.

Hagan, J. (1985). *Modern criminology: Crime, criminal behavior, and its control.* New York: McGraw-Hill.

Hagan, J. (1989). *Structural criminology.* New Brunswick, NJ: Rutgers University Press.

Hagan, J., Gillis, A. R., & Simpson, J. (1985). The class structure of gender and delinquency: Toward a power-control theory of common delinquent behavior. *American Journal of Sociology, 90,* 1151–1178.

Hagan, J., Gillis, A. R., & Simpson, J. (1990). Clarifying and extending power-control theory. *American Journal of Sociology, 95*(4), 1024–1037.

Hagan, J., Shedd, C., & Payne, M. R. (2005). Race, ethnicity, and youth perceptions of criminal injustice. *American Sociological Review, 70,* 381–407.

Hagan, J., Simpson, S., & Gillis, A. R. (1987). Class in the household: A power-control theory of gender and delinquency. *American Journal of Sociology, 92*(4), 788–816.

Hallstone, M. (2002). Updating Howard Becker's theory of using marijuana for pleasure. *Contemporary Drug Problems, 29,* 821–845.

Hamm, M. S. (2004). Apocalyptic violence: The seduction of terrorist subcultures. *Theoretical Criminology, 8*(3), 323–339.

Haney, L. A. (2010). *Offending women: Power, punishment, and the regulation of desire.* Berkeley: University of California Press.

Harcourt, B. (2001). *The illusion of order.* Cambridge, MA: Harvard University Press.

Harris, A. J., & Lurigio, A. J. (2010). Introduction to special issue on sex offenses and offenders: Toward evidence-based public policy. *Criminal Justice and Behavior, 37*(5), 477–481.

Hayes, T. A. (2010). Labeling and the adoption of a deviant status. *Deviant Behavior, 31,* 274–302.

Haynie, D. L. (2002). Friendship networks and delinquency: The relative nature of peer delinquency. *Journal of Quantitative Criminology, 18*(2), 99–134.

Heimer, K., & Matsueda, R. L. (1994). Role-taking, role commitment, and delinquency: A theory of differential social control. *American Sociological Review, 59*(3), 365–390.

Higgins, G. E., Tewksbury, R., & Mustaine, E. E. (2007). Sports fan binge drinking: An examination using low self-control and peer association. *Sociological Spectrum, 27*(4), 389–404.

Hinton, S. E. (1967). *The outsiders.* New York: Penguin.

Hirsch, M. L., Conforti, R. W., & Graney, C. J. (1990). The use of marijuana for pleasure: A replication of Howard Becker's study of marijuana use. *Journal of Social Behavior and Personality, 5,* 497–510.

Hirschfield, P. (2008). The declining significance of delinquent labels in disadvantaged urban communities. *Sociological Forum, 23*(3), 575–601.

Hirschi, T. (1969). *Causes of delinquency.* Berkeley: University of California Press.

Hirschi, T., & Gottfredson, M. R. (1995). Control theory and life-course perspective. *Studies on Crime Prevention, 4*(2), 131–142.

Hochstetler, A., Copes, H., & DeLisi, M. (2002). Differential association in group and solo offending. *Journal of Criminal Justice, 30*(6), 559–566.

Holt, T. J., & Copes, H. (2010). Transferring subcultural knowledge on-line: Practices and beliefs of persistent digital pirates. *Deviant Behavior, 31*(7), 625–654.

Hudson, B. (1998). Restorative justice: The challenge of sexual and racial violence. *Journal of Law and Society, 25*(2), 237–256.

Huiras, J., Uggen, C., & McMorris, B. (2000). Career jobs, survival jobs, and employee deviance: A social investment model of workplace misconduct. *The Sociological Quarterly, 41*(2), 245–263.

Humphreys, L. (1970). *Tearoom trade: Impersonal sex in public places.* Chicago: Aldine.

Hunt, P. M. (2010). Are you kynd? Conformity and deviance within the Jamband subculture. *Deviant Behavior, 31*(6), 521–551.

Hunter, S. K. (1993). Prostitution is cruelty and abuse to women and children. *Michigan Journal of Gender & Law, 1,* 91–104.

Inderbitzin, M. (2006). Lessons from a juvenile training school: Survival and growth. *Journal of Adolescent Research , 21,* 7–26.

Inderbitzin, M. (2007). Inside a maximum-security juvenile training school: Institutional attempts to redefine the American dream and normalize incarcerated youth. *Punishment & Society, 9*(3), 235–251.

Inderbitzin, M., & Boyd, H. (2010). William J. Chambliss. In K. Hayward, S. Maruna, & J. Mooney (Eds.), *Fifty key thinkers in criminology* (pp. 203–208). New York: Routledge.

Irvine, C. (2008, October 27). Tattooed leopard man leaves hermit lifestyle behind. Telegraph.co.uk. http://www.telegraph.co.uk/news/newstopics/howaboutthat/3265474/Tattooed-Leopard-Man-leaves-hermit-lifestyle-behind.html

Jackson, P., & Carroll, L. (1981). Race and the war on crime: The sociopolitical determinants of municipal police expenditures in 90 non-southern cities. *American Sociological Review, 46.* 390–405.

Jacobells v. Ohio, 378 U.S. 184, 197 (1964).

Jang, S. J., & Smith, C. A. (1997). A test of reciprocal causal relationships among parental supervision, affective ties, and delinquency. *Journal of Research in Crime and Delinquency, 34,* 307–337.

Jensen, G. F. (2007). The sociology of deviance. In C. D. Bryant & D. L. Peck (Eds.), *The handbook of 21st century sociology* (pp. 370–379). Thousand Oaks, CA: Sage.

Jobes, P. C., Barclay, E., & Weinand, H. (2004). A structural analysis of social disorganisation and crime in rural communities in Australia. *Australian and New Zealand Journal of Criminology, 37*(1), 114–140.

Johnson, R. E. (1986). Family structure and delinquency: General patterns and gender differences. *Criminology, 24,* 65–84.

Jones, A. L. (1998). Random acts of kindness: A teaching tool for positive deviance. *Teaching Sociology, 26*(3), 179–189.

Junger, M., & Marshall, I. H. (1997). The interethnic generalizability of social control theory: An empirical test. *Journal of Research in Crime and Delinquency, 34,* 79–112.

KFMB-News 8. (2010). Man flashes undercover cop during sting operation at Lake Murray. Retrieved October 14, 2010, from http://www.cbs8.com/global/story.asp?s=12842252

Kitsuse, J., & Spector, M. (1973). Toward a sociology of social problems: Social conditions, value-judgments, and social problems. *Social Problems, 20*(4), 407–419.

Kitsuse, J., & Spector, M. (1975). Social problems: A reformulation. *Social Problems, 21*(2), 145–159.

Klein, H., & Shiffman, K. S. (2008). What animated cartoons tell viewers about assault. *Journal of Aggression, Maltreatment & Trauma, 16*(2), 181–201.

Klein, J. D., & St. Clair, S. (2000). Do candy cigarettes encourage young people to smoke? *British Medical Journal, 321,* 362.

Kornhauser, R. R. (1978). *Social sources of delinquency: An appraisal of analytic models.* Chicago: University of Chicago Press.

Kotlowitz, A. (1988). *There are no children here: The story of two boys growing up in other America.* New York: Anchor.

Kovandzic, T. V., Vieraitis, L. M., & Boots, D. P. (2009). Does the death penalty save lives? New evidence from state panel data, 1979 to 2006. *Criminology and Public Policy, 8,* 803–844.

Krakauer, J. (1996). *Into the wild.* New York: Anchor.

Krohn, M. D. (1999). On Ronald L. Akers' Social learning and social structure: A general theory of crime and deviance. *Theoretical Criminology, 3*(4), 437–493.

Krohn, M. D., & Akers, R. L. (1977). An alternative view of the labeling versus psychiatric perspectives on societal reaction to mental illness. *Social Forces, 56*(2), 341–361.

Krohn, M. D., & Massey, J. (1980). Social control and delinquent behavior. *Sociological Quarterly, 21,* 529–543.

Kubrin, C. E., Stucky, T. D., & Krohn, M. D. (2009). *Researching theories of crime and deviance.* New York: Oxford University Press.

Laforgia, M. (2011, May 21). Huge doses of potent antipsychotics flow into state jails for troubled kids. *The Palm Beach Post.*

Lankenau, S. E. (1999). Panhandling repertoires and routines for overcoming the nonperson treatment. *Deviant Behavior, 20*(2), 183–206.

LaPrairie, C. (1998). The "new" justice: Some implications for aboriginal communities. *Canadian Journal of Criminology, 40*(1), 61–79.

Laub, J. H., & Sampson, R. J. (1988). Unraveling families and delinquency: A reanalysis of the Gluecks' data. *Criminology, 26,* 355–379.

Lefkowitz, B. (1997). *Our guys: The Glen Ridge rape and the secret life of the perfect suburb.* Berkeley: University of California Press.

Leiber, M. J., & Stairs, J. M. (1999). Race, contexts, and the use of intake diversion. *Journal of Research in Crime and Delinquency, 36*(1), 56–86.

Lemert, E. (1951). *Social pathology.* New York: McGraw-Hill.

Levit, N. (1999). Critical of race theory: Race, reason, merit, and civility. *Georgetown Law Journal, 87,* 795.

Liazos, A. (1972). The poverty of the sociology of deviance: Nuts, sluts, and preverts. *Social Problems, 20,* 103–120.

Link, B. G., Phelan, J. C., Bresnahan, M., Stueve, A., & Pescosolido, B. A. (1999). Public conceptions of mental illness: Labels, causes, dangerousness, and social distance. *American Journal of Public Health, 89*(9), 1328–1333.

Liska, A. E., & Messner, S. F. (1999). *Perspectives on crime and deviance* (3rd ed.). Englewood Cliffs, NJ: Prentice Hall.

Lowenkamp, C. T., Cullen, F. T., & Pratt, T. C. (2003). "Replicating Sampson and Groves's test of social disorganization theory. *Journal of Research in Crime and Delinquency, 40*(4), 351–373.

Lucas, A. M. (2005). The work of sex work: Elite prostitutes' vocational orientations and experiences. *Deviant Behavior, 26*(6), 513–546.

Luhman, R. (2002). *Race and ethnicity in the United States: Our differences and our roots.* Fort Worth, FL: Harcourt College.

Lukács, G. (1971). *History and class consciousness: Studies in Marxist dialectics.* Cambridge, MA: MIT Press. (Original work published 1920)

Maass, A., Cadinu, M., Guarnieri, G., & Grasselli, A. (2003). Sexual harassment under social identity threat: The computer harassment paradigm. *Journal of Personality and Social Psychology, 85*(5), 853–870.

Madden, M., & Lenhart, A. (2009). *Teens and distracted driving: Texting, talking and other uses of the cell phone behind the wheel.* Washington, DC: Pew Internet and American Life Project. Retrieved January 20, 2011, from http://pewinternet.org/Reports/2009/Teens-and-Distracted-Driving.aspx

Maier, S. L., & Monahan, B. A. (2010). How close is too close? Balancing closeness and detachment in qualitative research. *Deviant Behavior, 31*(1), 1–32.

Mannheim, K. (1959). *Ideology and utopia: an introduction to the sociology of knowledge, A harvest book; HB 3.* New York: Harcourt Brace. (Original work published 1936)

Mantsios, G. (2010). Making class invisible. In D. Newman & J. O'Brien (Eds.), *Sociology: Exploring the architecture of everyday life readings* (8th ed., pp. 236–241). Thousand Oaks, CA: Pine Forge Press.

Manza, J., & Uggen, C. (2006). *Locked out: Felon disenfranchisement and American democracy.* New York: Oxford University Press.

Martin, D. (2002). Spatial patterns in residential burglary: Assessing the effect of neighborhood social capital. *Journal of Contemporary Criminal Justice, 18*(2), 132–146.

Martin, J., & O'Hagan, M. (2005, August 30). Killings of 2 Bellingham sex offenders may have been by vigilante, police say. *Seattle Times.* http://community.seattletimes.nwsource.com/archive/?date=20050830&slug=sexoffender30m

Maruna, S. (2011). Reentry as a rite of passage. *Punishment & Society, 13*(1), 3–28.

Marx, K. (1992). *Capital: Volume 1: A critique of political economy.* London: Penguin. (Original work published 1867)

Marx, K. (1993). *Capital: Volume 2: A critique of political economy.* London: Penguin. (Original work published 1885)

Marx, K., & Engels, F. (1957). *The holy family.* London: Lawrence and Wishart.

Marx, K., & Engels, F. (1961). *The communist manifesto.* In A. P. Mendel (Ed.), *Essential works of Marxism* (pp. 13–44). Toronto: Bantam. (Original work published 1848)

Matsueda, R. L. (1992). Reflected appraisals, parental labeling, and delinquency: Specifying a symbolic interactionist theory. *American Journal of Sociology, 97*(6), 1577–1611.

Mauer, M. (2005). Thinking about prison and its impact in the twenty-first century: Walter C. Reckless Memorial Lecture. *Ohio State Journal of Criminal Law, 2,* 607–618.

Mayo, H. B. (1960). *Introduction to Marxist theory.* New York: Oxford University Press.

McCarthy, B., Hagan, J., & Woodward, T. S. (1999). In the company of women: Structure and agency in a revised power-control theory of gender and delinquency. *Criminology, 37,* 761–788.

McCleary, R., & Tewksbury, R. (2010). Female patrons of porn. *Deviant Behavior, 31*(2), 208–223.

McLorg, P. A., & Taub, D. E. (1987). Anorexia nervosa and bulimia: The development of deviant identities. *Deviant Behavior, 8*(2), 177–189.

Merry, S. E. (1989). Myth and practice in the mediation process. In M. Wright & B. Galaway (Eds.), *Mediation and criminal justice: Victims, offenders, and community* (pp. 239–250). London: Sage.

Merton, R. K. (1938). Social structure and anomie. *American Sociological Review, 3*(5), 672–682.

Merton, R. K. (1957). *Social theory and social structure* (Rev. and enlarged ed.). Glencoe, IL: Free Press.

Merton, R. K. (1964). Anomie, anomia, and social interaction: Contexts of deviant behavior. In M. B. Clinard (Ed.), *Anomie and deviant behavior* (pp. 213–242). New York: Free Press.

Messmer, H., & Otto, H.-U. (Eds.). (1992). *Restorative justice on trial: Pitfalls and potentials of victim-offender mediation: International research perspectives.* Amsterdam: Kluwer.

Messner, S. F., & Rosenfeld, R. (2007). *Crime and the American Dream* (4th ed.). Belmont, CA: Wadsworth.

Mestrovic, S. G., & Lorenzo, R. (2008). Durkheim's concept of anomie and the abuse at Abu Ghraib. *Journal of Classical Sociology, 8*(2), 179–207.

Meyer, A. G. (1963). *Marxism: The unity of theory and practice.* Ann Arbor: University of Michigan Press.

Miller, J. G. (1998). *Last one over the wall* (2nd ed.). Columbus: Ohio State University Press.

Mills, C. W. (2000). *The sociological imagination.* Oxford, UK: Oxford University Press. (Original work published 1959)

Minor, K., & Morrison, J. T. (1996). A theoretical study and critique of restorative justice. In B. Galaway & J. Hudson (Eds.), *Restorative justice: International perspectives* (pp. 117–133). Monsey, NY: Criminal Justice Press.

Moffitt, T. E. (1993). "Life-course-persistent" and "adolescence-limited" antisocial behavior: A developmental taxonomy. *Psychological Review, 100,* 674–701.

Moffitt, T. E. (2003). Life-course-persistent and adolescence-limited antisocial behavior: A 10-year research review and a research agenda. In B. B. Lahey, T. E. Moffitt, & A. Caspi (Eds.), *Causes of conduct disorder and juvenile delinquency* (pp. 49–75). New York: Guilford.

Moffitt, T. E. (2006). Life-course-persistent versus adolescence-limited antisocial behavior. In D. Cicchetti & D. Cohen (Eds.), *Developmental psychopathology* (2nd ed., pp. 570–598). New York: John Wiley.

Monk-Turner, E., Edwards, D., Broadstone, J., Hummel, R., Lewis, S., & Wilson, D. (2005). Another look at handwashing behavior. *Social Behavior and Personality: An International Journal, 33*(7), 629–634.

Monroe, J. (2004). Getting a puff: A social learning test of adolescents smoking. *Journal of Child & Adolescent Substance Abuse, 13*(3), 71–83.

Morash, M. (1999). On Ronald L. Akers' social learning and social structure: A general theory of crime and deviance. *Theoretical Criminology, 3*(4), 437–493.

Moyer, I. L. (2001). *Criminological theories: Traditional and nontraditional voices and themes.* Thousand Oaks, CA: Sage.

Muftic, L. R. (2006). Advancing institutional anomie theory: A microlevel examination connecting culture, institutions, and deviance. *International Journal of Offender Therapy and Comparative Criminology, 50*(6), 630–653.

Mumola, C. J. (2000). *Incarcerated parents and their children* (Bureau of Justice Statistics Special Report, NCJ 182335). Washington, DC: Bureau of Justice Statistics.

Murphy, S., Waldorf, D., & Reinarman, C. (1990). Drifting into dealing: Becoming a cocaine seller. *Qualitative Sociology, 13,* 321–343.

Neff, J. L., & Waite, D. E. (2007). Male versus female substance abuse patterns among incarcerated juvenile offenders: Comparing strain and social learning variables. *Justice Quarterly, 24*(1), 106–132.

Netter, S. (2010, September 16). Student's body modification religion questioned after nose piercing controversy. abcnews.com. http://abcnews .go.com/US/students-body-modification-religion-questioned-nose-piercing- controversy/story?id=11645847&page=1

Neve, L., & Pate, K. (2005). Challenging the criminalization of women who resist. In J. Sudbury (Ed.), *Global lockdown: Race, gender, and the prison-industrial complex* (pp. 19–34). London: Routledge.

Nixon, K., Tutty, L., Downe, P., Gorkoff, K., & Ursel, J. (2002). The everyday occurrence: Violence in the lives of girls exploited through prostitution. *Violence Against Women, 8,* 1016–1043.

Nye, F. I. (1958). *Family relationships and delinquent behavior.* New York: John Wiley.

Ogden, S. (2005). The prison-industrial complex in indigenous California. In J. Sudbury (Ed.), *Global lockdown: Race, gender, and the prison-industrial complex* (pp. 57–66). London: Routledge.

O'Hagan, M., & Brooks, D. (2005, September 7). Man says he'll plead guilty to killing sex offenders. *Seattle Times.* http://community.seattletimes .nwsource.com/archive/?date=20050907&slug=sexoffender07m

O'Malley, P. M., & Johnston, L. D. (2007). Drugs and driving by American high school seniors, 2001–2006. *Journal of Studies on Alcohol & Drugs, 68*(6), 834–842.

Orcutt, J. D. (1983). *Analyzing deviance.* Chicago: Dorsey.

Oselin, S. S. (2009). Leaving the streets: Transformation of prostitute identity within the prostitution rehabilitation program. *Deviant Behavior, 30,* 379–406.

Osgood, D. W., & Chambers, J. M. (2000). Social disorganization outside the metropolis: An analysis of rural youth violence. *Criminology, 38*(1), 81–115.

Pager, D. (2007). *Marked: Race, crime, and finding work in an era of mass incarceration.* Chicago: University of Chicago Press.

Pager, D., & Quillian, L. (2005). Walking the talk? What employers say versus what they do. *American Sociological Review, 70,* 355–380.

Park, K. (2002). Stigma management among the voluntarily childless. *Sociological Perspectives, 45*(1), 21–45.

Paternoster, R., & Bushway, S. (2009). Desistance and the "feared self": Toward an identity theory of criminal desistance. *Journal of Criminal Law and Criminology, 99*(4), 1103–1156.

Patterson, G. R., & Dishion, T. J. (1985). Contributions of families and peers to delinquency. *Criminology, 23,* 553–573.

Payne, A., & Welch, K. (2010). Modeling the effects of racial threat on punitive and restorative school discipline practices. *Criminology, 48,* 1019–1062.

Pepinsky, H., & Quinney, R. (1991). *Criminology as peacemaking.* Bloomington: Indiana University Press.

Percival, G. L. (2010). Ideology, diversity, and imprisonment: Considering the influence of local politics on racial and ethnic minority incarceration rates. *Social Science Quarterly, 91,* 1063–1082.

Petts, R. J. (2009). Family and religious characteristics' influence on delinquency trajectories from adolescence to young adulthood. *American Sociological Review, 74*(3), 465–483.

Piquero, A. R., Daigle, L. E, Gibson, C., Piquero, N. E., & Tibbetts, S. G. (2007). Research note: Are life-course-persistent offenders at risk for adverse health outcomes? *Journal of Research in Crime and Delinquency, 44,* 185.

Ploeger, M. (1997). Youth employment and delinquency: Reconsidering a problematic relationship. *Criminology, 35*(4), 659–675.

Porter, B. E., & England, K. J. (2000). Predicting red-light running behavior: A traffic safety study in three urban settings. *Journal of Safety Research, 31,* 1–8.

Pruitt, M. V. (2008). Deviant research: Deception, male Internet escorts, and response rates. *Deviant Behavior, 29*(1), 70–82.

Pruitt, M. V., & Krull, A. C. (2011). Escort advertisements and male patronage of prostitutes. *Deviant Behavior, 32*(1), 38–63.

Quinney, R. (1963). Occupational structure and criminal behavior: Prescription violation by retail pharmacists. *Social Problems, 11,* 179–185.

Quinney, R. (1970). *The social reality of crime.* Boston: Little, Brown.

Quinney, R. (1995). Socialist humanism and the problem of crime: Thinking about Erich Fromm in the development of critical/peacemaking criminology. *Crime, Law, and Social Change, 23,* 147–156.

Rampona, J. (2004, November 28). What happens to the homeless? Criminalizing the necessary and life-sustaining actions of homeless people adds to the burden of living in constant exposure to the elements. *Arkansas Democrat-Gazette.*

Rankin, B. H., & Quane, J. M. (2002). Social contexts and urban adolescent outcomes: The interrelated effects of neighborhoods, families, and peers on African-American youth. *Social Problems, 49*(1), 79.

Rankin, J. H. & Kern, R. M. (1994). Parental attachments and delinquency. *Criminology, 32,* 495–515.

Rankin, J. H., & Wells, L. E. (1990). The effect of parental attachments and direct controls on delinquency. *Journal of Research in Crime and Delinquency, 27,* 140–165.

Raphael, J., & Shapiro, D. L. (2004). Violence in indoor and outdoor prostitution venues. *Violence Against Women, 10*(2), 126–139.

Reed, M. D., & Rountree, P. W. (1997). Peer pressure and adolescent substance use. *Journal of Quantitative Criminology, 13*(2), 143–180.

Reiman, J., & Leighton, P. (2009). *The rich get richer and the poor get prison: Ideology, class, and criminal justice* (9th ed.). Englewood Cliffs, NJ: Prentice Hall.

Robinson, M. M., & Murphy, D. (2009). *Greed is good: Maximization and elite deviance in America.* Lanham, MD: Rowman & Littlefield.

Ronai, C. R., & Ellis, C. (1989). Turn-ons for money. Interactional strategies of the table dancer. *Journal of Contemporary Ethnography, 18,* 271–298.

Rosenfield, S. (1997). Labeling mental illness: The effects of received services and perceived stigma on life satisfaction. *American Sociological Review, 62*(4), 660–672.

Rosenhan, D. L. (1973). On being sane in insane places. *Science, 179,* 250–258.

Rowe, D. C. (2002). *Biology and crime.* Los Angeles: Roxbury.

Rubington, E. S., & Weinberg, M. S. (2008). *Deviance: The interactionist perspective.* Englewood Cliffs, NJ: Prentice Hall.

Rutter, M., & Giller, H. (1984). *Juvenile delinquency: Trends and perspectives.* London: Guilford.

Sallman, J. (2010). Living with stigma: Women's experiences of prostitution and substance use. *Affilia, 25,* 146–159.

Sampson, R. (1999). On Ronald L. Akers' social learning and social structure: A general theory of crime and deviance. *Theoretical Criminology, 3*(4), 437–493.

Sampson, R. J., & Groves, W. B. (1989). Community structure and crime: Testing social-disorganization theory. *American Journal of Sociology, 94*(4), 774–802.

Sampson, R. J., & Laub, J. H. (1993). *Crime in the making: Pathways and turning points through life.* Cambridge, MA: Harvard University Press.

Sampson, R. J., & Laub, J. H. (1994). Urban poverty and the family context of delinquency: A new look at structure and process in a classic study. *Child Development, 65,* 523–541.

Sampson, R. J., & Laub, J. H. (1995). Understanding variability in lives through time: Contributions of life-course criminology. *Studies on Crime and Crime Prevention, 4*(2), 143–158.

Sampson, R. J., & Raudenbush, S. W. (2004). Seeing disorder: Neighborhood stigma and the social construction of "broken windows." *Social Psychology Quarterly, 67,* 319–342.

Sampson, R. J., Raudenbush, S. W., & Earls, F. (1997). Neighborhoods and violent crime: A multilevel study of collective efficacy. *Science, 277,* 918–924.

Sanders, T. (2007). Becoming an ex-sex worker. *Feminist Criminology, 2*(1), 74–95.

Scarce, R. (2008). Earth first! Deviance inside and out. In E. Goode & D. A. Vail (Eds.), *Extreme deviance* (pp. 177–188). Thousand Oaks, CA: Pine Forge Press.

Scheff, T. J. (1966). *Being mentally ill: A sociological theory.* Chicago: Aldine.

Scholinski, D. (with Adams, J. M.). (1997). *The last time I wore a dress: A memoir.* New York: Riverhead Books.

Schur, E. M. (1973). *Radical non-intervention: Rethinking the delinquency problem.* Englewood Cliffs, NJ: Prentice Hall.

Schur, E. M. (1983). *Labeling women deviant: Gender, stigma and social control.* Philadelphia: Temple University Press.

Sharp, S. (1998). Relationships with children and AIDS—Risk behaviors among female IDUs. *Deviant Behavior, 19,* 3–28.

Shaw, C. A., & McKay, H. (1969). *Juvenile delinquency in urban areas.* Chicago: University of Chicago Press. (Original work published 1942)

Simmons, J. L. (1965). Public stereotypes of deviants. *Social Problems, 13*(2), 223–232.

Simon, D. R. (2008). *Elite deviance* (9th ed.). New York: Pearson Education, Inc.

Simon, R. J. (1975). *The contemporary woman and crime.* Rockville, MD: National Institute of Mental Health.

Simons, R. L., Simons, L., Burt, C., Brody, G. H., & Cutrona, C. (2005). Collective efficacy, authoritative parenting, and delinquency: A longitudinal test of a model integrating community and family level processes. *Criminology, 43*(4), 989–1029.

Skipp, C. (2009, July 25). A bridge too far. *Newsweek.* http://www.newsweek.com/2009/07/24/a-bridge-too-far.html

Skogan, W. (1990). *Disorder and decline: Crime and the spiral of decay in American neighborhoods.* New York: Free Press.

Smart, C. (1977). Criminological theory: Its ideology and implications concerning women. *British Journal of Sociology, 28,* 89–100.

Smith, C., & Krohn, M. D. (1995). Delinquency and family life among male adolescents: The role of ethnicity. *Journal of Youth & Adolescence, 24*(1), 69.

Sokol-Katz, J., Dunham, R. & Zimmerman, R. (1997). Family structure versus parental attachment in controlling adolescent deviant behavior: a social control model. *Adolescence, 32,* 199–216.

Soothill, K., Fitzpatrick, C., & Brian, F. (2009). *Understanding criminal careers.* Cullompton, UK: Willan.

Spitzer, R. L. (1976). More on pseudoscience in science and the case for psychiatric diagnosis: A critique of D. L. Rosenhan's 'On being sane in insane places' and 'The contextual nature of psychiatric diagnosis.'" *Archives of General Psychiatry, 33*(4), 459–470.

Spitzer, S. (1975). Towards a Marxian theory of deviance. *Social Problems, 22,* 638–651.

Spitzer, S. (1983). Marxist perspectives in the sociology of law. *Annual Review of Sociology, 9,* 103–124.

Spreitzer, G. M., & Sonenshein, S. (2004). Toward the construct definition of positive deviance. *American Behavioral Scientist, 47*(6), 828–847.

Stark, R. (1987). Deviant places: A theory of the ecology of crime. *Criminology, 25*(4), 893–909.

Steffensmeier, D. J., Allan, E. A., Harer, M. D., & Streifel, C. (1989). Age and the distribution of crime. *American Journal of Sociology, 94*(4), 803–831.

Stiles, B. L., & Clark, R. E. (2011). BDSM: A subcultural analysis of sacrifices and delights. *Deviant Behavior, 32*(2), 158–189.

Strang, H., & Braithwaite, J. (2001). *Restorative justice and civil society.* Cambridge, UK: Cambridge University Press.

Sudbury, J. (Ed.). (2005). *The global lockdown: Race, gender, and the prison-industrial complex.* London: Routledge.

Sullivan, L. (2010, October 28). Prison economics help drive Arizona immigration bill. NPR online. Retrieved February 3, 2011, from http://www.npr.org/templates/transcript/transcript.php?storyId=130833741

Sullivan, M. L. (1989). *"Getting paid": Youth crime and work in the inner city.* Ithaca, NY: Cornell University Press.

Sumner, W. G. (1906). *Folkways: A study of the sociological importance of usages, manners, customs, mores, and morals.* Boston: Ginn & Company.

Sutherland, E. H. (1934). *Principles of criminology.* Philadelphia: Lippincott.

Sutherland, E. H. (1947). *Principles of criminology* (4th ed.). Philadelphia: Lippincott.

Sutherland, E. H. (1949). *White collar crime.* New York: Holt, Rinehart & Winston.

Sykes, G. M. (1958). *The society of captives.* Princeton, NJ: Princeton University Press.

Sykes, G. M., & Matza, D. (1957). Techniques of neutralization: A theory of delinquency. *American Sociological Review, 22*(6), 664–670.

Tannenbaum, F. (1938). *Crime and the community.* Boston: Ginn.

Taylor, E. (1998). A primer on critical race theory. *Journal of Blacks in Higher Education, 19,* 122–124.

Thio, A. (2009). *Deviant behavior.* New York: Allyn & Bacon.

Thompson, W. E., Harred, J. L., & Burks, B. E. (2003). Managing the stigma of topless dancing: A decade later. *Deviant Behavior, 24*(6), 551–570.

Thornberry, T. P., Lizotte, A. J., Krohn, M. D., Farnworth, M., & Sung Joon, J. (1994). Delinquent peers, beliefs, and delinquent behavior: A longitudinal test of interactional theory. *Criminology, 32*(1), 47–83.

Tong, R. P. (1998). *Feminist thought: A more comprehensive introduction.* Boulder, CO: Westview.

Tonry, M. (2011). *Punishing race: A continuing American dilemma.* New York: Oxford University Press.

Trammell, R. (2009). Values, rules, and keeping the peace: How men describe order and the inmate code in California prisons. *Deviant Behavior, 30,* 746–771.

Traub, S. H., & Little, C. B. (1985). *Theories of deviance* (3rd ed.). Itasca, IL: F. E. Peacock.

Tuggle, J., & Holmes, M. (1997). Blowing smoke: Status politics and the Shasta County smoking ban. *Deviant Behavior, 18*(1), 77–93.

Turk, A. T. (1969). *Criminality and legal order.* Chicago: Rand McNally.

Turk, A. T. (1976). Law as a weapon in social conflict. *Social Problems, 23,* 276–291.

Turk, A. T. (2002). Crime causation: Political theories. In J. Dressler (Ed.), *Encyclopedia of crime and justice* (2nd ed.). New York: Macmillan References USA.

Uggen, C., & Inderbitzin, M. (2010). The price and the promise of citizenship: Extending the vote to non-incarcerated felons. In N. A. Frost, J. D. Freilich, & T. R. Clear (Eds.), *Contemporary issues in criminal justice policy: Policy proposals from the American Society of Criminology Conference* (pp. 61–68). Belmont, CA: Cengage/Wadsworth.

Uggen, C., Manza, J., & Thompson, M. (2006). Citizen, democracy, and the civic reintegration of criminal offenders. *Annals of the American Academy of Political and Social Science, 605,* 281–310.

Umbreit, M. (1994). *Victim meets offender: The impact of restorative justice and mediation.* Monsey, NY: Criminal Justice Press.

Van Voorhis, P., Cullen, F. T., Mathers, R. A., & Garner, C. C. (1988). The impact of family structure and quality on delinquency: A comparative assessment of structural and functional factors. *Criminology, 26,* 235–261.

VanNostrand, L., & Tewksbury, R. (1997). The motives and mechanics of operating an illegal drug enterprise. *Deviant Behavior, 20,* 57–83.

Vazsonyi, A. T., & Klanjsek, R. (2008). A test of self-control theory across different socioeconomic strata. *Justice Quarterly, 25*(1), 101–131.

Veysey, B. M., & Messner, S. F. (1999). Further testing of social disorganization theory: An elaboration of Sampson and Groves's 'community structure and crime.' *Journal of Research in Crime and Delinquency, 36*(2), 156–174.

Vold, G. B. (1958). *Theoretical criminology.* New York: Oxford University Press.

Wacquant, L. (2000). The new "peculiar institution": On the prison as surrogate ghetto. *Theoretical Criminology, 4,* 377–389.

Walsh, A. (2000). Behavior genetics and anomie/strain theory. *Criminology, 38*(4), 1075–1107.

Warner, B. D., & Pierce, G. L. (1993). Reexamining social disorganization theory using calls to the police as a measure of crime. *Criminology, 31*(4), 493–517.

Warr, M. (1993). Parents, peers, and delinquency. *Social Forces, 72,* 247–265.

Warr, M. (2002). *Companions in crime: The social aspects of criminal conduct.* Cambridge, UK: Cambridge University Press.

Weinberg, M. S. (1966). Becoming a nudist. *Psychiatry: Journal for the Study of Interpersonal Processes, 29,* 15–24.

Weinberg, M. S., Williams, C. J., & Pryor, D. W. (2001). Bisexuals at midlife: Commitment, salience, and identity. *Journal of Contemporary Ethnography, 30*(2), 180–208.

Wells, L. E., & Rankin, J. H. (1988). Direct parental controls and delinquency. *Criminology, 26,* 263–285.

West, C. (1995). Forward. In K. Crenshaw, N. Gotanda, G. Peller, & K. Thomas (Eds.), *Critical race theory: The key writings that formed the movement* (pp. xi–xii). New York: New Press.

Western, B. (2006). *Punishment and Inequality in America.* New York: Russell Sage Foundation.

Wilson, J. Q., & Kelling, G. (1982). Broken windows: The police and neighborhood safety. *Atlantic Monthly, 249,* 29–38.

Wolfgang, M. E., & Ferrcuti, F. (1967). *The subculture of violence: Towards an integrated theory in criminology.* Beverly Hills, CA: Sage

Wright, E. R., Gronfein, W. P., & Owens, T. J. (2000). Deinstitutionalization, social rejection, and the self-esteem of former mental patients. *Journal of Health and Social Behavior, 41*(1), 68–90.

Wright, J., & Cullen, F. T. (2001). Parental efficacy and delinquent behavior: Do control and support matter? *Criminology, 39*(3), 677–705.

Yacoubian, G. S., Jr., & Peters, R. J. (2005). Identifying the prevalence and correlates of ecstasy use among high school seniors surveyed through 2002 Monitoring the Future. *Journal of Alcohol & Drug Education, 49*(1), 55–72.

Yip, A. K. T. (1996). Gay Christians and their participation in the gay subculture. *Deviant Behavior, 17*(3): 297–318.

Zehr, H. (1990). *Changing lenses: A new focus for crime and justice.* Scottsdale, PA: Herald Press.

Photo Credits

Chapter 1

Photo 1.1, p. 3: Photodisc/ThinkStock

Photo 1.2, p. 3: ©JMW Scout/iStockphoto

Photo 1.3, p. 7: Comstock/Thinkstock

Chapter 2

Photo 2.1, p. 47: © Murdo McLeod/The Guardian

Photo 2.2, p. 53: © Deseret Morning News/ Getty Images

Photo 2.3, p. 58: http://www.flickr.com/photos/ eelssej_/

Chapter 3

Photo 3.1, p. 89: © alexey_ds/istockphoto

Photo 3.2, p. 98: © Brand X Pictures/ Thinkstock

Chapter 4

Photo 4.1, p. 150: © Steve Cole/iStockphoto

Photo 4.2, p. 155: ©H-Gall/iStockphoto

Photo 4.3, p. 156: ©Associated Press

Chapter 5

Photo 5.1, p. 204: ©Photos.com/Thinkstock

Photo 5.2, p. 215: ©Thomas Nast/Library of Congress

Photo 5.3, p.210 : ©rusm/istockphoto

Chapter 6

Photo 6.1, p. 238: © Associated Press

Chapter 7

Photo 7.1, p. 287: ©Dylan Ellis/Thinkstock

Photo 7.2, p. 296: © Jack Hollingsworth/ Thinkstock

Chapter 8

Photo 8.1, p.340: http://karlgoestocoimbra .files.wordpress.com/2011/05/025192046186_ bluray_ws_2d_clr.jpg

Photo 8.2, p. 345: ©thepixelchef/iStockphoto

Photo 8.3, p. 346: ©Stockbyte/Thinkstock

Chapter 9

Photo 9.1, p. 376: ©BananaStock/Thinkstock

Photo 9.2, p. 380: ©eyeidea/iStockphoto

Photo 9.3, p.380: ©Stephen Strathdee (sharply_done)/istockphoto

Chapter 10

Photo 10.1, p. 428: ©Rubberball/istockphoto

Photo 10.2, p. 429: ©Brand X Pictures/Thinkstock

Photo 10.3, p. 429: ©Filo/istockphoto

Photo 10.4, p. 435: © Stockbyte/Thinkstock

Chapter 11

Photo 11.1, p. 488: ©Comstock/Thinkstock

Photo 11.2, p. 489: © Can Stock Photo Inc. / oscar-cwilliams

Photo 11.3, p. 491: © Getty Images/Thinkstock

Photo 11.4, p. 492: ©Louoates/iStockphoto

Chapter 12

Photo 12.1, p. 562: ©Doug Menuez/Thinkstock

Photo 12.2, p. 566: ©RapidEye/iStock

Photo 12.3, p. 569: ©Stockbyte/Thinkstock

Index

Figures, notes, and tables are indicated by f, n, and t following the page number.

Absolutist perspective, 19, 21–22
Abu Ghraib, 155–156, 168–188
    approved vs. abusive activities, 180
    cultural insensitivity and, 184–185, 186n7
    insufficient training, 180–181
    intelligence gathering and, 182
    norms and, 182
    self-correcting mechanisms, failure of, 183
    social integration of military units, 181–182
    socio-cultural analysis, 178–179
Abuse. *See* Domestic violence; Substance abuse; Violence
Adler, F., 431
Adler, Patricia A., 50–51, 70, 95, 563, 566, 569
Adler, Peter, 50–51, 70, 563, 566, 569
Adolescents, 300–308, 309–322. *See also* Juvenile delinquency
Advantageous comparison, 80, 81, 85t
African Americans. *See* Racial/ethnic considerations
Age-crime curves, 294, 294f, 600
Aggression
    bullying and, 108, 109, 111, 114
    domestic violence and, 246–249
    moral indignation and, 22
    as sensitive topic, 140
    social disorganization theory and, 228
    social learning theory and, 241, 246–249
    substance abuse and, 457–458
    whites toward blacks, 555n2
Agnew, Robert, 153, 155, 158
Agresti and Caffo method, 555n13
Akers, Ronald, 234, 237–239, 240–241, 270, 437
Alcohol abuse. *See* Substance abuse
Alden, Helena, 271
Allan, E. A., 294
American Dream, 154–157, 188–201
Amish subculture, 55, 60–69
Anderson, E., 244

Anomie and strain theories, 146–201
    in Abu Ghraib, 155–156, 168–188
    crime and, 154–155, 158, 190–193, 199, 568, 569
    critiques of, 157
    cultural insensitivity and, 184–185
    defined, 147, 600, 603
    differential opportunity theory and, 151–152, 188, 190–191, 193–195, 199
    Durkheim on, 147–148, 168–188
    general strain theory (GST), 153, 158, 190, 601
    institutional anomie theory, 154–155, 156–157, 190, 192, 199, 601
    literature review, 155–157
    Merton's adaptations to, 148–150, 160, 188–201
    overview, 13, 146–147
    relative deprivation and, 158, 602
    social structure and, 160–168
Anorexia, 574–585
    beauty ideals and, 50
    class-based resistance to medical control, 582–584
    as deviant conversion career, 576–578
    as social-class stereotype, 581–582
    social space and, 578–584
Arrest warrants for traffic violations, 518n7
Arter, Michael L., 154
Attachment, 287, 296–297, 302, 600
Ayella, Marybeth, 122, 123

Baker, Lynda, 570, 571
Bandura, Albert, 55, 80
Barak, Gregg, 429
Barclay, E., 208
Barker, E., 131n2
Battered women. *See* Domestic violence
Beccaria, Cesare, 285
Becker, Howard S., 341, 342, 343, 350, 562

Beckett, K., 488
Beirne, Piers, 379
Beliefs, 287, 302, 600
The Bell Curve (Herrnstein & Murray), 482*n*3
Bendle, M. F., 11
Benson, M. L., 209
Bernasco, W., 212
Berzoff, Joan, 70
Bhopal industrial disaster (1984), 82–83, 85*t*
Blacks. *See* Racial/ethnic considerations
Blalock, H. M., Jr., 390
Blaming, 449–468
    contexts of violence, 452–453
    corporate deviance and, 80, 82, 85*t*
    culture of, 453–464
    research methodology, 450–452
Blevins, Kristi R., 54
Block, R., 212
Body modification, 51, 600
Boeringer, S., 241
Boots, D. P., 91
Boruch, R. F., 142*n*1
Bossuet, Jacques, 186*n*2
Braithwaite, John, 347, 350
Branch, Kathryn A., 246
Bristol Victims Support Scheme (Britain), 464*n*1
Brody, G. H., 212
Broken windows theory, 210, 217–224, 227, 600
Brown, David, 586
Browning, C. R., 212
Bullying, 108–122
    aggression and, 108, 109, 111, 114
    cellular phones and, 113
    cyberbullying, 111–115, 120*n*4
    defined, 109–110
    future research needs, 118–119
    traditional, 109–111
Burgess, Robert L., 237
Bursik, R. J., Jr., 206, 207
Burt, C., 212
Business ethics, 86

Cadinu, M., 89
Cancino, J. M., 212
Capece, Michael, 271
Capitalism, 377–381, 387–388, 432
Caprara, Gian-Vittorio, 55, 80
Career deviance. *See* Deviant careers and career deviance
Cecil, J. S., 142*n*1
Central business districts (CBDs), 205, 600

Chambers, J. M., 208
Chambliss, William, 345–346, 353, 354, 387–388
Chamlin, Mitchell B., 91, 386–387
Chandler Redevelopment Initiative (Arizona), 482*n*5
Chandler Roundup (Arizona), 468–484
Chaudoir, N. K., 98
Children and adolescents, 300–308, 309–322. *See also* Juvenile
    delinquency
Civil commitment, 495, 600
Clear, Todd, 489, 497
Clinard, M. B., 4
Cloward, Richard A., 151–152, 188
Cochran, John K., 241, 246
Cohen, Ben-Zion, 300
Coker, Donna, 433
Collateral consequences of imprisonment, 494, 600
Collective consciousness, 175–176
Collective efficacy, 210–212, 600
Collectivist societies, 64
College students
    computer crime and, 253–270
    substance abuse and, 270–283
Collins, P., 465*n*3
Colonial model, 406–407
Comfort, Meagan, 497
Commitment to social bonds, 287, 302, 600
Communism, 391–398
Community investments, 445–446, 448*n*1
Computer crime, 253–270, 322–338
    extent of, 261–264
    literature review, 254–255
    neutralization techniques, 326–327, 328–334
    online consumer misbehavior, 324–326
    research methodology, 258–261, 259*t*, 268–269*nn*2–7, 327–328
    social learning theory and, 255–258, 264–266
Concentric zones, 205, 218, 600
Confidentiality, 142*n*1, 370*n*8
Conflict subcultures, 152, 600
Conflict theory, 375–426
    Chambliss and, 387–388
    crime and, 31, 385–388
    critiques of, 388–389
    defined, 600
    discrimination and, 390
    groups and, 383–385
    Gusfield and, 382
    Kitsuse and Spector and, 382–383
    laws and, 379–380, 382, 384–385
    literature review, 390
    Marxist theory and, 377–381

overview, 376–377, 382
police brutality and, 415, 416
power and, 384–386, 406, 415
Quinney and, 385–386
racial profiling and, 404–414
revolution and, 378–379
Turk and, 384–385
Vold and, 383–384
Conformity, 148, 160, 193–196
Conrad, P., 488
Consent forms, 106
Content analyses, 97–99
Convict-lease system, 398–403
Copes, H., 241
Corporate deviance. *See* Elite deviance
Correctional facilities, 438–449, 491, 492–494, 494*f*, 519–532.
　　　See also Incarceration
Covert observations, 96, 124, 600
Crenshaw, K., 434
Crime. *See also* Juvenile delinquency
　age and, 294, 294*f*, 600
　anomie and strain theory and, 154–155, 158, 190–193, 199,
　　　568, 569
　computers and, 253–270, 322–338
　conflict theory and, 31, 385–388
　control theory and, 31–32, 291–292, 568, 569
　data sources on, 99–100
　deviance and, 26–34
　differential opportunity theory and, 151–152, 188, 190–191,
　　　193–195, 199
　domestic violence, 225–232, 246–252, 449–468, 465*n*14
　labeling theory and, 27–28, 345–347, 349–350, 508
　macrosociological developments, 31–32
　microsociology of, 33
　poverty and, 166–167, 205–206
　sanctions and, 28, 32
　social disorganization theory and, 205–206, 207, 210
　social learning theory and, 253–270, 568, 569
　stigma and, 347
　theoretical perspectives on, 26–29
　violent, 99, 100*f*
Criminals. *See also* Deviant careers and career deviance
　career paradigm, 560–561, 568, 573, 588–589, 600
　disenfranchisement of, 495, 601
　employment and, 495, 532–558
　sex offenders, 495–496
　stigma and, 494
　subcultures, 151–152, 600
Critical race theory, 434–435, 437, 468–484, 600
Critical theories, 427–484
　blame and responsibility, 449–468

critiques of, 437
feminist perspective, 431–433, 437, 601
overview, 5, 427–428
peacemaking perspective, 428–430, 437, 438–449, 602
race theory, 434–435, 437, 468–484, 600
Cullen, Francis T., 148, 208, 212, 573
Cults, 122–132, 138
　access maintenance for studies, 126–129
　research contingencies, 123–126
Cultural deviance theories, 207, 244, 600
Cultural insensitivity, 184–185
Cutrona, C., 212
Cyberbullying, 111–115, 120*n*4
Cyberdeviance, 54, 108–122

Darmon, Muriel, 574
Davies, S., 348
DAWN (Drug Abuse Warning Network), 101, 102
Deductive closure, 142*n*1
Definitional process of deviance, 382–383
Definitions of behaviors, 235–236, 237, 247, 256, 600
Dehumanization, 80, 82, 85*t*
Deinstitutionalization
　defined, 600
　juvenile delinquency and, 350, 521
　mental illness and, 215, 350
De Li, S., 103
Delinquency. *See* Juvenile delinquency
DeLisi, M., 241
Demedicalization, 488, 600
Department of Health and Human Services (HHS), 101
Depersonalization, 368–369
Desistance, 560–561, 568–571, 571*f*, 586–599, 600
Deviance. *See also* Deviant careers and career deviance;
　　　Researching deviance; Social control theories
　conceptions of, 4–5
　crime and, 26–34
　cultural theories of, 207, 244, 600
　cyberdeviance, 54, 108–122
　diversity of, 47–59
　forms of, 48–57, 49*t. See also* Elite deviance
　mystification of, 18–25
　normative perspective, 4, 5, 28, 385, 602
　physical, 50–51, 70, 602
　positive, 56–57, 602
　power and, 20–21, 352, 382, 384
　primary, 342, 344, 602
　relativist perspective, 4–5, 14, 18, 19–20, 377, 602
　secondary, 342, 343, 348, 508, 602
　sexual, 52–53, 242, 602
　social construction of, 4, 5, 13, 376–377, 603

sociological imagination and, 5–7, 177, 603
subcultures and, 52–53, 54–55, 244
theory and, 8–11, 13, 603. *See also specific theories*
in workplace, 56, 56*t*
Deviant careers and career deviance, 559–599
anorexia as, 574–585
criminal career paradigm and, 560–561, 568, 573, 588–589, 600
desistance and, 560–561, 568–571, 571*f*, 586–599, 600
escalation of, 572, 601
maintenance of lifestyle, 566–567
onset/initiation of, 560–561, 562–564, 602
overview, 560
persistence of, 568, 602
risk and protective factors, 564, 565*f*, 602
self-control theory and, 586–599
Dialectical materialism, 378, 601
Differential association, 601. *See also* Social learning theory and differential association
Differential location in social structure, 239, 601
Differential opportunity theory, 151–152, 188, 190–191, 193–195, 199
Differential reinforcement, 238, 248, 256, 601
Differential social location in groups, 239, 601
Differential social organization, 239, 601
Diffusion of responsibility, 80, 82
Direct social controls, 286, 302
Discrimination. *See* Racial/ethnic considerations
Displacement of responsibility, 80, 81, 85*t*
Dissent, 21–22
Diversity of deviance, 47–59
corporate deviance, 55–56
in cyberspace, 54
elite deviance, 55–56
pathology of, 21–22
physical deviance and appearance, 50–51
positive deviance, 56–58, 602
in relationships, 52–53
in subcultures, 54–55
workplace misconduct, 55–56
Domestic violence, 225–232, 246–252, 449–468, 465*n*14
Drug abuse. *See* Substance abuse
Drug Abuse Warning Network (DAWN), 101, 102
Du Bois, W. E. B., 398–399
Dumas, Alexia, 322
Dunham, H. W., 214
Durkheim, Emile, 147–148, 168–188

Edwards, Michelle, 209
Elite deviance
defined, 601
maximization and, 196–199, 200

moral disengagement mechanisms and, 80–86, 85*t*
overview, 55–56
self-control theory and, 589–590
Elliot, D. S., 243
Employment
attitude-behavior relationship, 535–536, 547–550
call-back rates, 533, 541–547, 555*n*7, 555*n*11
criminals and, 495, 532–558
economic climate and, 555–556*n*16
labeling theory and, 348
racial attitudes, 533–535, 541–547, 542*f*, 543*f*, 545*t*
stigmatized groups, 536–538
testers, 532, 539–541, 555*nn*4–5
workplace deviance and, 56, 56*t*
Engels, Frederick, 377, 379, 391–392
Escalation of deviance, 572, 601
Ethical considerations, 86, 105–106, 135, 137–138, 140–141, 601
Ethnic considerations. *See* Racial/ethnic considerations
Euphemistic labeling, 80, 81, 85*t*
Experimental designs, 89–92, 601
External constraint, 21
External social controls, 285–286, 288, 302, 601
External validity, 90, 91

False consciousness, 378–379, 601
Family
ghetto life and, 509–512
juvenile delinquency and, 290–291, 293, 296–297
violence. *See* Domestic violence
Faris, R. E. L., 214
Feagin, Joe R., 415
Federal Bureau of Investigation (FBI), 99
Felon disenfranchisement, 495, 601
Feminist theory, 270–283, 431–433, 437, 601
Ferracuti, F., 244
Field research
cults and, 123–132, 138
defined, 601
gender considerations in, 139
types of, 93–96
Fleisher, Mark, 95–96
Folkways, 4, 601
Ford Pinto case, 83–84, 85*t*
Foucault, M., 465*n*15
Frailing, K., 98
Fream, Anne M., 253

Gabbidon, Shaun, 404
Gauthier, D. K., 98
Gemeinschaft societies, 64
Gender considerations. *See also* Women

control theory and, 290–291
feminist perspective and, 270–283, 431–433, 437, 601
in field research, 139
social learning theory and, 270–283
General strain theory (GST), 153, 158, 190, 601
Gillis, A. R., 290
Giordano, Peggy, 569
Glossary, 600–603
Goffman, Alice, 488–489, 499
Goffman, Erving, 50, 348, 490
Goode, Erich, 52, 56, 242
Gottfredson, M., 96, 103, 291–292, 297, 568
Gracia, Enrique, 225
Grasselli, A., 89
Group conflict theory, 383–385
Groves, W. B., 207–208, 208*f*
GST. *See* General strain theory
Guarnieri, G., 89
Gusfield, J., 382

Hagan, J., 290, 390, 491
Hallstone, M., 562
Hamm, M. S., 55
Harcourt, B., 210
Harer, M. D., 294
Harper, J., 98
Harris, Lloyd C., 322
Hate groups, 104, 104*f*
Hayes, Terrell A., 349
Haynie, Dana, 241
Health and Human Services (HHS), 101
Heimer, K., 348
Herbert, S., 488
Hermeneutics, 465*n*4
Herrero, Juan, 225
Herrnstein, R. J., 482*n*3
Hierarchies of credibility, 24
Higgins, G., 241
High-status deviants, 42–45
Hills, Stuart L., 18
Hinduja, Sameer, 108
Hirschfield, P., 346
Hirschi, Travis, 96, 103, 286–287, 291–293, 297, 568
Hispanics. *See* Racial/ethnic considerations
Hochstetler, A., 241
Holmes, M., 97
Holt, Thomas J., 54
Holzer, H., 556*n*23
Homelessness, 429–430, 432–433, 435
Hope, Trina L., 586

Human agency, 569, 601
Human subjects, 105–106, 601
Humphreys, Laud, 105
Hunt, Pamela M., 239–240
Hypotheses, 9

ICPSR (Inter-University Consortium for Political and Social
Science Research), 103–104
Illegitimate opportunities, 151–152, 188–190, 193, 194–197, 199–200
Imitation, 238, 247, 256, 601
Immediate gratification, 291
Immigration law enforcement, 468–484
citizenship policing and, 476–477
critical race theory and, 470–472
domestic function of policy, 469–470
Incarceration. *See also* Correctional facilities
collateral consequences of, 494, 600
of mothers, 444–447
pains of, 491–492, 519, 524–525, 602
power and, 516–517
reentry into society, 494–495
social control and, 488–489, 499–519
of women, 438–449
Inderbitzin, Michelle, 519, 520
Indirect social controls, 286, 302, 601
Individualism, 6–7, 155
Informed consent, 106, 464–465*n*2
Initiation of deviance. *See* Onset/initiation of deviance
Innovation, 149, 193–196
Institutional anomie theory, 154–155, 156–157, 190, 192, 199, 601
Institutionalization/prisonization, 490, 601
Institutional Review Boards (IRBs), 87–88, 89, 105, 601
Instrumental Marxism, 379, 380, 601
Interactionist theories, 27–28, 341, 343, 347. *See also* Labeling
theory
Intergenerational transmission theory, 246–247, 248, 250–251
Internal coercion, 21
Internal colonialism, 406–407
Internal social controls, 285–286, 288, 302, 601
Internal validity, 90, 91
Internet crime, 322–338
Inter-University Consortium for Political and Social Science
Research (ICPSR), 103–104
Intimate partner violence. *See* Domestic violence
Investment in local communities, 445–446, 448*n*1
Involvement, 287, 302, 601
IRBs. *See* Institutional Review Boards

Jails. *See* Correctional facilities
JJDP (Juvenile Justice Delinquency Prevention) Act (1974), 350

Jobes, P. C., 208
Jobs. *See* Employment
Johnson, N. B., 139
Johnston, L. D., 102
Jones, A. L., 56
Juvenile delinquency
   correctional facilities and, 492–493, 519–532
   deinstitutionalization and, 350, 521
   family and, 290–291, 293, 296–297
   labeling theory and, 345–347, 349–350, 353–362
   social control and, 492–493, 519–532
   social disorganization theory and, 205–206, 207
Juvenile Justice Delinquency Prevention (JJDP) Act (1974), 350

Kelling, G., 210, 217–218
Kibbutz society, 300–308
Kilbourne, Brock K., 131*n*3
Kinsey, Alfred, 92, 132
Kitsuse, J., 382–383
Klein, H., 99
Kokaliari, Efrosini, 70
Kornhauser, Ruth, 207
Kotlowitz, A., 202
Kovandzic, T. V., 91
Krull, A. C., 97

Labeling theory, 340–374
   crime and, 27–28, 345–347, 349–350, 508
   employment and, 348
   impact of, 349–351, 369
   juvenile delinquency and, 345–347, 349–350, 353–362
   literature review, 347–348
   mental illness and, 344–345, 348, 363–370
   overview, 341–342
   power and, 341, 345–346, 352, 370–374
   process of, 342–343
   racial profiling and, 405–406, 411
   reintegrative shaming and, 347, 602
   theoretical background of, 342
Lanza-Kaduce, Lonn, 271
Latinos. *See* Racial/ethnic considerations
Laub, J. H., 293, 297
Law enforcement
   ghetto life and, 501, 503–509
   immigration law enforcement, 476–477
   police violence, 415–426
Laws
   conflict theory and, 382, 384–385
   criminology and, 31
   defined, 601

   Marxism and, 379–380
   as norms, 4
Lee, Raymond M., 132, 133
Lefkowitz, Bernard, 346, 370, 371
Legitimate opportunities, 151–152, 188–190, 193, 195–197, 199–200
Lemert, Edwin, 342
Lenhart, Amanda, 243
Lersch, Kim M., 415
Liazos, Alexander, 10, 11
Liberal critics of criminal justice policies, 448*n*1
Liberal feminism, 432, 601
Life course theory, 292–295, 297, 568, 601
Lindenberg, Siegwart, 309
Littré, Émile, 186*n*2
Lorenzo, Ronald, 156, 168
Loseke, D., 465*n*11
Lowenkamp, C. T., 208
Low self-control, 291–292, 601
Lucas, Ann, 567

Maass, A., 89
Macrosociology, 26, 30, 31–32
Madden, Mary, 243
Maier, Shana L., 96–97
Male peer support theory, 246–247, 248, 250–251
Mama, A., 465*n*14
Mantsios, G., 55
Manza, Jeff, 495
Marijuana, 101*f*, 102, 241, 562–563
Martin, D., 212
Maruna, S., 494, 496
Marx, Karl, 377, 378–380, 391–392. *See also* Conflict theory
Mason, J., 465*n*3
Master status, 343, 347, 601
Matsueda, Ross, 341, 347–348
Matza, D., 288–289, 322
Mauer, Marc, 494
Maximization, 188–201
Mayo, H. B., 378
McCarthy, B., 291
McCleary, R., 94
McKay, Henry, 205–206, 207
McLorg, Penelope, 563, 564
Medicalization, 487–488, 601
Meier, Robert F., 4, 26
Menard, S., 243
Mental illness
   data sources on, 101–102
   deinstitutionalization and, 215, 350

labeling theory and, 344–345, 348, 363–370
social disorganization theory and, 214–217
stigma and, 345, 348, 366
violence and, 214–217
Merton, Robert K., 148–150, 160
Messner, Steven, 148, 154–155, 188, 208
Mestrovic, Stjepan G., 156, 168
Microsociology, 26, 30–31, 33
Miller, Jerome, 349–350
Mills, C. Wright, 5–6
Miner, Horace, 14
Minorities. *See* Racial/ethnic considerations
Moffitt, T. E., 293
Monahan, Bryan A., 96–97
Monitoring the Future (MTF), 102–103
Monroe, J., 240
Monto, Martin, 103
Moral disengagement mechanisms, 80–86, 85*t*
Moral indignation, 22–23
Moral justification, 80, 81, 85*t*
Mores, 4, 602
Morgan, Karen J., 449
Mothers in prison, 444–447
Moyer, I. L., 437
MTF (Monitoring the Future), 102–103
Muftic, L. R., 157
Mugford, S., 347
Multi-City Study of Urban Inequality Employer Survey, 556*n*23
Murphy, Daniel S., 188
Murray, C., 482*n*3
Mystification, 24, 25

Nacirema tribe study, 14–17
National Association of Victim Support Schemes (Britain), 464*n*1
National Institute of Justice (NIJ), 103
National Survey on Drug Use and Health, 101
Neighborhood social disorganization. *See* Social disorganization theory
Nestle infant formula case, 84, 85*t*
Neutralization techniques, 288–289, 322–338
Nonintervention, 350, 602
Normative perspective, 4, 5, 28, 385, 602
Norms
   categories of, 4
   defined, 4, 39, 602
   physical deviance and, 50–51
   sanctions and, 37, 40, 41
   sexual deviance and, 52–53
   status and, 37–38, 39, 40–41, 43–44
Nye, F. I., 286

Objectification, 72–73
Observational research, 94–96, 123–132, 602
Offenders. *See* Criminals
Ohlin, Lloyd. E., 151–152, 188
O'Malley, P. M., 102
Online crime, 322–338
   appeals to higher loyalties, 332–333
   denial of injury, 329–330
   denial of responsibility, 333–334
   denial of victim, 329
   justification by comparison, 331–332
   neutralization techniques and, 326–327, 329–334
   normalcy claims, 330–331
   relative acceptability claims, 331–332
   research methodology, 327–328
Onset/initiation of deviance, 560–561, 562–564, 602
Orcutt, J. D., 351
Ormel, Johan, 309
Oselin, Sharon S., 567–568
Osgood, D. W., 208
O'Shea, Timothy C., 217, 218
Overt observations, 96, 602

Pager, Devah, 495, 532, 533
Pains of imprisonment, 491–492, 519, 524–525, 602
Participant observations, 94, 95–96, 123–132, 602
Partner violence. *See* Domestic violence
Patchin, Justin W., 108
Payne, A., 390
Peacemaking perspective, 428–430, 437, 438–449, 602
Pepinsky, Hal, 428
Persistence of deviance, 568, 602
Peters, R. J., 102
Physical deviance, 50–51, 70, 602
Physical disorder, 210, 217–224, 602
Pierce, G. L., 209
Ploeger, M., 241
Police violence, 415–426
   penalties for, 418–419, 422–423
   power-conflict theory and, 416
   racial differences in, 416–418, 421–422
   research methodology, 419–421
   situational aspects of, 418, 422
Polygamy, 53, 602
Poole, Mary Jo, 437
Positive deviance, 56–58, 602
Positivist perspective. *See* Normative perspective
Postmodern feminism, 432, 602
Poverty, 166–167, 205–206, 602

Power
    conflict theory and, 384–386, 406, 415
    control theory and, 290–291, 352
    deviance and, 20–21, 352, 382, 384
    incarceration and, 516–517
    labeling theory and, 341, 345–346, 352, 370–374
    laws and, 384–385
    police brutality and, 415, 416
    premodern vs. modern, 465n15
    racial profiling and, 406, 411, 412
Powerlessness, 368–369
Pratt, T. C., 208
Prejudice. *See* Racial/ethnic considerations
Primary deviance, 342, 344, 602
Priming, intensity of response, 548–549
Prisons. *See* Correctional facilities; Incarceration
Protective factors against deviant careers, 564, 565f, 602
Pruitt, M. V., 97
Pseudopatients, 364–366, 370n7
Punishment, 72, 176. *See also* Sanctions; Social control theories
Pure observations, 94–95

"Quality of life" policing arrests, 518n6
Quane, J. M., 212
Quasi-experimental designs, 90–92, 601
Quillian, Lincoln, 495, 532, 533
Quinney, Richard, 385–386, 428, 438

Racial/ethnic considerations
    conflict theory and, 390
    criminals and, 495, 532–558
    critical race theory, 434–435, 437, 468–484, 600
    domestic violence context, 465n10
    employment and, 495, 532–558
    hate groups and, 104, 104f
    heterogeneity, 205–206
    incarceration and, 499–519
    law enforcement's descriptors for, 482n1
    in police violence, 416–418, 421–422
    prejudice distinguished from discrimination,
        532, 538–539, 555n3
    racial profiling, 404–414, 468–484
    slavery and, 398–403
    white supremacy, 104, 434–435
Radical feminism, 432, 602
Radosh, Polly F., 438, 439
Random sampling, 93, 125
Rankin, B. H., 212
Raphael, S., 556n23
Raudenbush, S. W., 210, 224n1

Reactionist perspective. *See* Relativist perspective
Rebellion, 149, 160, 193–194
Reed, M. D., 241
Reiling, Denise, 55, 60
Reintegrative shaming, 347, 602
Relative deprivation, 158, 602
Relativist perspective, 4–5, 14, 18, 19–20, 377, 602
Renzetti, Claire M., 132, 133
Researching deviance, 87–144
    content analyses, 97–99
    ethical considerations, 105–106, 135, 137–138, 140–141, 601
    experimental designs, 89–92, 601
    field research, 93–96, 123–132, 138, 139, 601
    Institutional Review Boards (IRBs) and, 87–88, 89, 105, 601
    methodological approaches to, 89–97
    overview, 88–89
    scientific method and, 9, 9f, 602
    secondary data sources, 99–104, 602
    sensitive topics and, 132–144
    surveys, 92–93
    theory and, 8–11, 13, 603
Residual rule breaking, 344, 602
Restorative justice, 350, 429, 602
Retreatist subcultures, 149, 152, 193–194, 602
Ricoeur, P., 465n4
Riesman, David, 186n4
Risk factors for deviant careers, 564, 565f, 602
Ritualism, 149, 193–194
Robinson, Mathew B., 188
Romero, Mary, 468, 469
Rosenfeld, Richard, 154–155, 188
Rosenfield, S., 348
Rosenhan, David, 344–345, 363–370
Rountree, P. W., 241
Rubington, E. S., 4

Sallman, Jolanda, 566
SAMHSA (Substance Abuse and Mental Health Services
        Administration), 101–102
Sampling, 92–93, 125–126, 136–137
Sampson, Robert, 207–208, 208f, 210–211, 224n1, 293, 297
Sanctions
    crime and, 28, 32
    defined, 4
    norms and, 37, 40, 41
    status and, 37, 38–39, 41–45
    types of, 81
Sanders, T., 571
Scapegoating, 185–186
Scheff, T. J., 344

Schlesinger, James, 186n6

Scholinski, Daphne, 487

Schur, Edwin, 350, 352

Scientific method, 9, 9f, 24–25, 602

Secondary data sources, 99–104, 602

Secondary deviance, 342, 343, 348, 508, 602

Self-concept, 32–33, 343, 345

Self-control theory

    in children and adolescents, 309–322

    critiques of, 297

    deviant careers and, 586–599

    elite deviance and, 589–590

    low self-control and, 291–292, 601

    overview, 291–292

    truancy and, 309–322

Self-fulfilling prophecies, 341–342, 368, 370n12, 602

Self-injury

    defined, 50–51, 602

    as social control method, 77

    by women, 70–79

Self-sanctions, 81

Sellers, Christine S., 238, 246

Sensitive topics in research, 132–144

    confidentiality, 142n1

    defining, 133–134

    issues and problems in, 135–142

    research process and, 134–135

Sexual deviance, 52–53, 242, 495–496, 602

Shame, 347, 602

Shaming, 347, 602

Sharp, Susan F., 295, 586

Sharpe, Elaine, 103

Shaw, Clifford, 205–206, 207

Shehan, C. L., 241

Shiffman, K. S., 99

Shopping While Black, 404–414

    literature review, 407–409

    research methodology, 409–410

Short, James F., Jr., 26

Silver, Eric, 215

Simon, D. R., 55

Simon, R. J., 431

Simons, L., 212

Simons, R. L., 212

Simpson, J., 290

Skinner, William F., 253

Skogan, W., 210

Slavery, 398–403

Small, Albion W., 203

Smart, C., 431

Social bonds

    children and, 309–322

    commitment to, 287, 302, 600

    components of, 286–287

    defined, 602

    life course theory and, 292–293

    truancy and, 309–322

Social cognitive theories, 81–82

Social cohesion, 211, 603

Social consensus, 388, 603

Social construction of deviance, 4, 5, 13, 376–377, 603

Social contracts, 486, 603

Social control theories, 284–338, 486–558. *See also* Sanctions;
    Self-control theory

    children and adolescents and, 300–308, 309–322

    classical theory, 285–287

    computer crime and, 322–338

    conformity and, 31–32

    correctional facilities, 438–449, 491, 492–493, 494, 494f,
        519–532

    crime and, 31–32, 291–292, 568, 569

    critiques of, 297

    direct, 286, 302

    effects of, 496–497

    external, 285–286, 288, 302, 601

    gender considerations and, 290–291

    indirect, 286, 302, 601

    internal, 285–286, 288, 302, 601

    juvenile delinquency and, 492–493, 519–532

    in kibbutz society, 300–308

    life course theory, 292–295, 297, 568, 601

    literature review, 296–297

    medicalization and, 487–488, 601

    neutralization techniques and, 288–289, 322–338

    overview, 285, 486–487

    pains of imprisonment, 491–492, 519, 524–525, 602

    policing and incarceration, 488–489, 499–519

    power-control theory, 290–291, 352

    purpose of, 491

    reentry into society and, 494–495

    self-injury and, 77

    sexual deviance and, 495–496

    spirituality and, 569

    total institutions, 490–491, 603

    truancy and, 309–322

Social disorder, 210, 217–224, 225–232, 603

Social disorganization theory, 202–232

    broken windows theory and, 210, 217–224, 227, 600

    collective efficacy and, 210–212, 600

    crime and, 205–206, 207, 210

defined, 603
history and early work on, 203–204
juvenile delinquency and, 205–206, 207
mental illness and, 214–217
overview, 13, 202–203
physical disorder and, 210, 217–224, 602
rebirth of, 207–209, 208*f*
social disorder and, 210, 217–224, 225–232, 603
structural characteristics of, 206, 603
violence and, 214–217, 225–232
Social facts, 280
Socialist feminism, 432, 603
Socialization
family and, 290–291, 293, 296
Merton on, 148
Social learning theory and differential association, 233–283
Akers and, 234, 237–239, 240–241, 270
crime and, 253–270, 568, 569
cultural deviance theories and, 244
domestic violence and, 246–252
feminist perspective and, 270–283
limitations of, 242–243
literature review, 240–242
overview, 233–234
social structure and, 238–239, 238*t*, 270–283
substance abuse and, 241, 270–283
Sutherland and, 233, 234–236, 235*t*
violence and, 246–252
Social sanctions, 81
Social structure
anomie and, 160–168
defined, 603
social learning theory and, 238–239, 238*t*, 270–283
Sociological imagination, 5–7, 177, 603
Sonenshein, S., 57
Specialization, 572, 603
Spector, M., 382–383
Spirituality, 569
Spitzer, Robert, 363
Spitzer, Steven, 380, 382
Spreitzer, G. M., 57
Stark, Rodney, 203, 207
Status
master, 343, 347, 601
norms and, 37–38, 39, 40–41, 43–44
sanctions and, 37, 38–39, 41–45
Steffensmeier, D. J., 294
Stigma
crime and, 347
criminals and, 494

cults and, 130–131
defined, 603
mental illness and, 345, 348, 366
physical deviance and, 50, 51
Stoll, M., 556*n*23
Strain, 147, 603. *See also* Anomie and strain theories
Streifel, C., 294
Structural characteristics of social disorganization, 206, 603
Structural impediments, 148, 603
Structural Marxism, 379–380, 603
Structured/unstructured interviews, 465*n*3
Subcultures
Amish settlements, 55, 60–69
conflict, 152, 600
criminal, 151–152, 600
cults, 122–132, 138
defined, 603
deviance and, 52–53, 54–55, 244
kibbutz society, 300–308
retreatist, 149, 152, 193–194, 602
Substance abuse
aggression and, 457–458
by college students, 270–283
data sources on, 101–103
employer's willingness to hire drug offender, 541–544, 542–543*f*, 545*t*
gender differences, 272–273
marijuana and, 101*f*, 102, 241, 562–563
research methodology, 274–276
social learning theory and, 241, 270–283, 282*n*1
Substance Abuse and Mental Health Services Administration (SAMHSA), 101–102
Suicide, 101, 147
Sumner, W. G., 4
Supervision in families, 297
Survey research, 92–93
Sutherland, Donald, 151
Sutherland, Edwin, 233, 234–236, 235*t*
Sykes, Gresham M., 288–289, 322, 491–492
Symbolic interactionism, 341, 603

Taguba, Antonio, 186*n*6
Taibbi, Matt, 186*n*1
Tannenbaum, Franklin, 342
Tanner, J., 348
Target populations, 92–93
Taub, Diane, 563, 564
Terror Management Theory (TMT), 61, 67
Tewksbury, R., 94
Thapar-Björkert, Suruchi, 449

Theoretically defined structural variables, 239, 603
Theory, 8–11, 13, 603. *See also specific theories*
Thio, A., 4
Thistlethwaite, A. B., 209
Thompson, M., 495
Thornberry, T. P., 243
Three Mile Island disaster (1979), 84–85, 85*t*
Tinga, Frank, 309
TMT (Terror Management Theory), 61, 67
Total institutions, 490–491, 603
Trajectories, 293, 603
Trammell, Rebecca, 493
Transitions in life course, 293, 603
Truancy, 309–322
    bullying and, 111
    predictors of, 315
    prevalence and development of, 314–315
    study method, 311–313
Tuggle, J., 97
Turk, A. T., 377, 384–385

Uggen, Christopher, 495
Uniform Crime Reports (FBI), 99–100
Union Carbide India Limited (UCIL), 82–83, 85*t*

Validity, 90, 91
Value-conflicts, 382–383
Veenstra, René, 309
Veysey, B. M., 208
Victimization, 449–468
    contexts of violence, 452–453
    culture of blaming and responsibility, 453–464
    research methodology, 450–452
Victim's Charter (Britain), 465*n*6
Vieraitis, L. M., 91
Violence
    criminality of, 99, 100*f*
    domestic, 225–232, 246–252, 449–468, 465*n*14
    mental illness and, 214–217
    police brutality, 415–426. *See also* Police violence

    social disorganization theory and, 214–217
    social learning theory and, 246–252
    women and, 225–232, 449–468
Vold, George, 383–384

Wahrman, Ralph, 37
Wanted Men, 499–519
    ethnographies of, 518*n*2
    family and friends, 509–512
    policing and, 500–501, 503–509
Warner, B. D., 209
Warr, M., 243, 245
Weinand, H., 208
Weinberg, M. S., 4
Welch, K., 390
West, Cornell, 434
White-collar crime. *See* Elite deviance
White supremacy, 104, 434–435
Wilson, J. Q., 210, 217–218
Wolfgang, M. E., 244
Women. *See also* Feminist theory
    bullying and, 120*n*3
    in correctional facilities, 438–449
    domestic violence and, 225–232, 246–252, 449–468, 465*n*14
    homelessness and, 432–433
    objectification and, 72–73
    peacemaking perspective and, 438–449
    self-injury and, 70–79
    victimization and, 449–468
Wooldredge, J., 209
Workplace. *See* Employment
Wright, J., 212

Yacoubian, G. S., Jr., 102

Zeira, Ruth, 300
Zimbardo, Philip, 90
Zones in transition, 205, 603
Zsolnai, Laszlo, 55, 80

About the Editors

Michelle Inderbitzin primarily studies prison culture, juvenile justice, and transformative education. She has published papers in *Punishment & Society, Journal of Adolescent Research, The Prison Journal, Journal of Offender Rehabilitation, International Journal of Offender Therapy and Comparative Criminology,* and *Criminology & Public Policy,* and is currently working on research about prison education, broadly defined. Dr. Inderbitzin earned her PhD in Sociology from the University of Washington and has been a faculty member at Oregon State University since 2001. Along with her on campus classes on crime and deviance, she regularly teaches classes and volunteers in Oregon's maximum-security prison for men and its juvenile correctional facility for girls.

Kristin Bates is a professor of criminology and justice studies in the Department of Sociology at California State University San Marcos. Her research focuses on racial, ethnic, and gender inequality in criminal justice policies. She is currently involved in a study examining the community impact of civil gang injunctions. Her most recent work is a co-edited book: *Through the Eye of Katrina: Social Justice in the United States,* now in its second edition.

Randy Gainey is professor and Chair of the Department of Sociology and Criminal Justice at Old Dominion University. His research focuses on racial and ethnic disparities in sentencing decisions, alternatives to incarceration, neighborhood characteristics and crime, and quantitative methodologies. He is co-author of two other books: *Family Violence and Criminal Justice: A Life-Course Approach,* now in its third edition and *Drugs and Policing.* His articles have recently appeared in *Criminology, Justice Quarterly, Theoretical Criminology, The Prison Journal, The Journal of Criminal Justice* and *The Journal of Crime and Justice.*

®SAGE research**methods**
The Essential Online Tool for Researchers

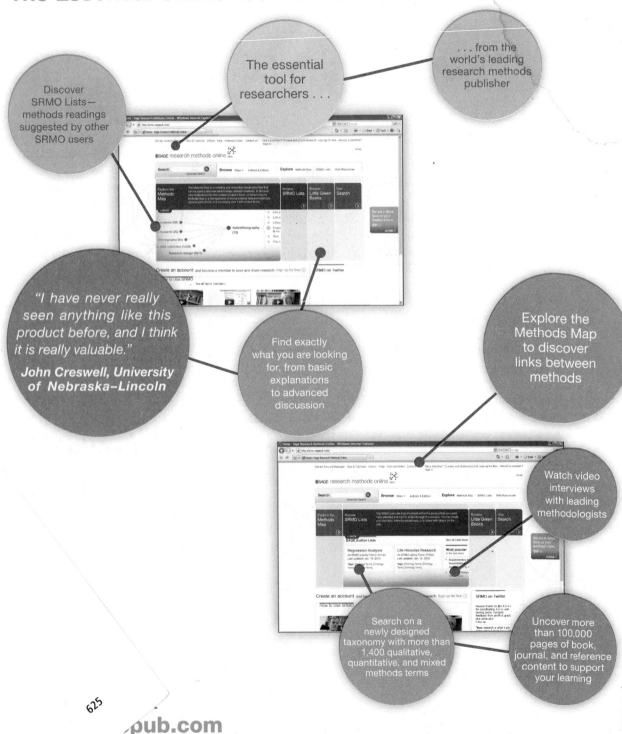

Discover SRMO Lists— methods readings suggested by other SRMO users

The essential tool for researchers . . .

. . . from the world's leading research methods publisher

"I have never really seen anything like this product before, and I think it is really valuable."

John Creswell, University of Nebraska–Lincoln

Find exactly what you are looking for, from basic explanations to advanced discussion

Explore the Methods Map to discover links between methods

Watch video interviews with leading methodologists

Search on a newly designed taxonomy with more than 1,400 qualitative, quantitative, and mixed methods terms

Uncover more than 100,000 pages of book, journal, and reference content to support your learning

pub.com